CHAPMAN
PILOTING
SEAMANSHIP & SMALL BOAT HANDLING

61ST EDITION

CHAPMAN PILOTING

SEAMANSHIP & SMALL BOAT HANDLING

HEARST MARINE BOOKS

NEW YORK

ISBN 0-688-11683-3 Standard
ISBN 0-688-11684-1 Presentation

Printed in the United States of America

1 2 3 4 5 6 7 8 9 10

The 61st Edition of Chapman Piloting: Seamanship & Small Boat Handling was produced for Hearst Marine Books by

ST. REMY PRESS

PUBLISHER	Kenneth Winchester
PRESIDENT	Pierre Léveillé
Senior Editor	Dianne Stine Thomas
Art Director	Chantal Bilodeau
Researcher	Jennifer Meltzer
Contributing Editors	Robyn Bryant
	Elizabeth Cameron
	Marc Cassini
	Alfred LeMaitre
	Daniel McBain
	John Turnbull
Contributing Art Director	Odette Sévigny
Picture Editor	Christopher Jackson
Studio Photographer	Robert Chartier
Designers	Hélène Dion
	Sara Grynspan
Illustrators	Maryse Doray
	Robert Paquet
Proofreader	Judy Yelon
Indexer	Shirley J. Manley
Managing Editor	Carolyn Jackson
Managing Art Director	Diane Denoncourt
Administrator	Natalie Watanabe
Administrative Assistant	Dominique Gagné
Production Manager	Michelle Turbide
System Coordinator	Jean-Luc Roy

Contributing Writers
Alston Colihan
Phil Friedman
Gene Hamilton
Katie Hamilton
Wayne Lilley
André Mele
Mike Milne
Marianne Tefft

61st Edition

The Consultants

Max W. Edelstein is a certified consulting meteorologist with more than forty years of experience in the field. As a member of the U.S. Power Squadrons (USPS), he headed the National Weather Committee for three years and taught the weather course in the Santa Barbara Power Squadron for seventeen years. He is currently National Educational Course Coordinator for the USPS.

Dan Fales, executive editor of *Motor Boating & Sailing* magazine since 1980, started in the magazine business in 1968 as the boating and outdoor editor of *Popular Mechanics*. Thereafter, he was executive editor of *Rod & Gun*, executive editor of *Motor Boating*, managing editor of *Popular Mechanics,* and editor of *Eastern Sea.* Mr. Fales is also a former president of Boating Writers International and has served as a member of the board of the Pioneer School at South Street Seaport. He and his wife own and cruise a 36-foot custom-built lobster yacht.

Erich Frey is a cartographer with the Coast and Geodetic Survey of the National Oceanic and Atmospheric Administration (NOAA) and has been involved in the production and maintenance of nautical charts for twenty-four years. As a member of the External and Cooperative Affairs Group in the mapping and charting branch, he is responsible for communicating with other government and private agencies and with hydrographic offices of other countries. His primary involvement is in the area of standards, procedures, and general policies of nautical charting.

Maurice Gagnon is a professional boatbuilder and boat repair expert, based in Montréal, Québec, with more than twenty years experience. A technical consultant and marine surveyor, he is also a cruising sailor.

Budd Gonder is a writer specializing in U.S. Coast Guard licensing. He holds a full certificate in the USPS, and is active with the organization on a national basis as well as with his own Santa Barbara, Calif., Power Squadron. He taught in public school for twenty-eight years before turning to full-time writing. He lives with his wife in the beachside community of Summerland, Calif., and sails his Columbia 28 for recreation.

Sid Stapleton is the author of *Stapleton's Powerboat Bible, Stapleton's Power Cruising Bible,* and *Emergencies at Sea.* He has been a contributing editor of *Motor Boating & Sailing* magazine and author of its monthly Seamanship column since 1983. In researching material for his books and magazine articles, he has voyaged through most of the world's primary cruising grounds. In 1993, he and his wife embarked on a 15-month, 15,000-mile cruise from Maine to Glacier Bay, Alaska, by way of the Caribbean and the Panama Canal aboard their 50-foot trawler *America's Odyssey.*

Ed Homonylo is a free-lance photojournalist based in Toronto, Ontario. He has documented the plight of that city's homeless and has photographed throughout Southeast Asia.

TABLE OF CONTENTS

A MESSAGE FROM THE COMMANDANT OF THE COAST GUARD

The two most important items a boater can have are skill and judgement. In fact, it's been said that a superior boater is one who uses his superior judgement to stay out of situations requiring the use of his superior skills. That is why this book is so important to every boater. Being in a boat on the water is a wonderful experience, but it's also a challenging one.

For those of you who are opening this book for the first time, I urge you to open it again and again. There's a very simple and direct correlation: The more knowledge and information you have, the safer you are as a boater.

In recent years, not only has the number of boats on our waterways increased, but so has their speed. Because of this, every one of us has an increased responsibility to actively promote safe boating. I urge each of you to make a commitment to learn the skills of effective navigation, practice good seamanship, follow the rules of the road, and be aware of what safety equipment you should never be without. I also encourage you to take advantage of the excellent safe boating courses offered by the U.S. Coast Guard Auxiliary and the U.S. Power Squadrons. By doing these things, I know you'll enjoy many years of safe and enjoyable boating. Good luck!

Sincerely,

J. W. KIME
Admiral, U. S. Coast Guard

FOREWORD

I first met Charles F. Chapman at a United States Power Squadrons meeting on marine radio communications; it was New York, in early 1959. As is all too often the situation with me, I disagreed with the speaker on some topics, and stood up to say so—a lively discussion ensued. After the meeting, Mr. Chapman, who had also been at the meeting, introduced himself—hardly necessary, since everyone, including me, knew of "Chap," a Past Chief Commander and holder of membership certificate No. A1.

We had a short but pleasant conversation, and soon thereafter he asked me to write a series of feature articles on marine electronics for *Motor Boating* magazine, of which he was the editor. As it turned out, I was to write for the magazine for a number of years.

My relationship with Chap continued even when I retired from the U.S. Marine Corps in May of 1964, bought a boat and went cruising—no home berth, just cruising from the Florida Keys up to Canada, and back when the weather got too cold up North. During this time, I wrote, at Chap's request, a chapter on marine electronics for *Piloting, Seamanship and Small Boat Handling;* the chapter was based on my articles in the magazine.

In September of 1965, a message caught up to me: Chap wanted me to come to New York. He wanted me to take his job as publisher so that he could retire; he was then 84 years of age. I couldn't help but wonder if he knew that my wife was beginning to pressure me to stop cruising and go back to work! Although the offer was attractive, I was reluctant to take an office job in New York City. To make a long story short, I eventually agreed to take over the writing, reorganizing and updating of his book.

Piloting, Seamanship & Small Boat Handling is now many years and many editions older. This new 61st edition not only has been updated with the help of numerous organizations and professionals in various fields, but also takes advantage of the latest technologies. The transition in design, and from black-and-white to color, seems to have happened as quickly and remarkably as did the world's transition from typewriter to computer.

Still actively involved in keeping *Chapman Piloting* up to date, Mack Maloney lives with his wife, Florine, in Pompano Beach, Florida. They cruise in local waters much of the year, and in the Bahamas most summers .

Whether you have been boating as long as I have, or you are experiencing your first thrill on the water, I join the *Chapman* editorial team in offering you "The Bible of Boating" for the '90s, for powerboaters and sailors, men and women, young and not-so-young alike. Following in the true *Chapman* tradition, it remains clear, thorough and always comradely—a manual designed to help you and everyone aboard your boat stay safe, have fun and become as skilled a boater as you aspire to be. Above all, I wish you as much joy from your boating years as I have had from mine.

Elbert S. Maloney

Elbert S. Maloney

THE TRADITION OF *CHAPMAN PILOTING*

With this, the 61st edition, *Piloting: Seamanship & Small Boat Handling* continues the tradition of excellence established 76 years ago with the first edition. As always, every word in the book has been reviewed to assure that the information is as current, comprehensive and authoritative as each previous edition has been. These standards have earned this book the reputation as the most famous reference on boating operations in the world.

The story of how this book became so famous and has endured so long has many parts. It begins with a dynamic personality, parallels the extraordinary growth of boating as one of America's favorite leisure activities, reflects the continuing need for boating safety, testifies to the talent and dedication of hundreds of people who have been directly involved with the contents of the 61 editions, and consistently benefits from the unqualified support of one of this country's great communications corporations.

As Chief Commander of the United States Power Squadrons, Charles F. Chapman is seen reviewing the fleet at a Squadron summer activity.

Charles F. Chapman

No history of this book can be told without first telling the history of the man whose name has become synonymous with boating, and who has influenced so many generations of boating enthusiasts. Charles Frederic Chapman was born in Norwich, Connecticut, in 1881. With easy access to the nearby Thames River, Chap, as he was affectionately known throughout his life, became interested in boats, and quickly decided that his life's interests lay afloat. At Cornell University he studied naval architecture and mechanical engineering, but after graduation in 1905 his nautical career seemed beached when he took a job at the New York Telephone Company.

Although landbound, Chap refused to give up on his boyhood dreams. He soon joined the New York Motor Boat Club and bought his first motorboat. She was the *Megohm*, a trim 16-footer powered by a pint-sized, one-lung Detroit engine that produced all of two horsepower.

Chap was a true pioneer. He ventured forth on the waters of the East Coast at a time when only a relative handful of adventurers owned boats. He launched himself into his club's activities full speed ahead. As chairman of

the Motor Boat Club's race committee he organized what became one of the most popular competitions in the sport—a 235-mile round trip on the Hudson River between New York City and Albany. With the temperamental engines and round-bottomed displacement hulls of the time, the race was more a matter of endurance than speed, as the early finishers took some 30 hours to complete the course. The success of this race opened the door for Chap to organize a number of other competitions among small and moderately priced boats—classes the racing rules had previously overlooked.

But Chap was not content with only the role of organizer. He began racing himself, and soon was declared a rising star among motorboat pilots. In 1909 the boat Chap was skippering in an ocean race from New York to Marblehead, Massachusetts, caught fire and sank. While three men balanced in a tiny dinghy, three others clung to life by hanging on to its gunwales. Eventually, the entire crew was rescued by a passing schooner. No doubt the incident played a large part in Chap's lifelong dedication to the instruction of boating safety.

By 1912 he was brought to the attention of a man busy building his own reputation—William Randolph Hearst. Hearst owned the magazine *Motor Boating* and was looking for an editor. "It's yours, Chap. Take it and run it as you wish," was the assignment. And that is exactly what Chap did—for the next 56 years!

The year Chap took over the helm of the magazine it sold for 10 cents a copy and reached a few thousand readers a month. Chap set his sights high, declaring, "The boating business is a sleeping giant and I'm trying to wake it." *Motor Boating* soon began to grow in both stature and circulation. In 1987, now called *Motor Boating & Sailing*, the magazine celebrated its 80th anniversary and a circulation of some 142,000 subscribers. Chap watched his "sleeping giant" of an industry grow at such a pace that today there are over 15 million boats on U.S. waterways.

As boating grew, so, unfortunately, did boating accidents and fatalities. In an effort to increase safe practices on the water and create a more informed group of participants, Chap used the pages of *Motor Boating* to start what he called "The Correspondence Course." Each month an article on a particular subject would appear, and would end with a series of questions. Readers from all over the country sent in answers, and those who passed were given a certificate. This was to become the first formal boating safety course in the nation and it led in 1914 to a forerunner of the book you now hold in your hands.

But Chap also used his knowledge elsewhere to further the cause of boating education. In 1913 and 1914 he was one of ten men who met first at the Boston Yacht Club and later at the New York Yacht Club to form the United States Power Squadrons. Over the years, many stories have evolved as to why this group was founded, but probably the most interesting is Chap's own recollection. When interviewed in 1972 by *The Ensign* magazine, the official publication of the USPS, Chap remembered:

"At the turn of the century, practically all boats, both pleasure and commercial, were powered by steam... Navigation [laws] applied only to steam vessels and they were governed by a board of steamboat inspectors, who were very old seagoing men. These inspectors had no use whatsoever for small internal combustion-powered craft and it was their idea and fondest hope to gain control of these boats. A small group of us felt that the internal combustion powerboats should be protected from these steamboat men, and we formed this group to impress them with the fact that we would instruct the members on rudiments of boat-handling and thus remove one of the objections which they had to small craft. That was really why USPS was formed."

1917: The First Piloting

And so the stage was set for Charles F. Chapman to begin the project that now serves as perhaps his most fitting monument—the publication of *Piloting: Seamanship & Small Boat Handling*. As a prime mover in the establishment of motorboat racing as a national sport, as the editor of *Motor Boating*, as a founder of the U.S. Power Squadrons, and as a dedicated instructor of boating safety, Chap was associated with all aspects of the burgeoning recreational activity.

But it was not recreation that Chap had in mind during the early days of World War I, when assistant Secretary of the Navy Franklin D. Roosevelt requested that he prepare an instructional manual for the Naval Reserve Forces. He did so in an incredible three days, and in 1917 the first edition of *Practical Motor Boat Handling, Seamanship & Piloting* was published. The book contained 144 pages in a 5-inch by 7-inch format and was a combination of articles that

Chap had run in his "Correspondence Course" and new material appropriate for the military boatman. The subtitle tells all:

"A handbook containing information which every motor boatman should know. Especially prepared for the man who takes pride in handling his own boat and getting the greatest enjoyment out of cruising. Adapted for the yachtsman interested in fitting himself to be of service to his Government in time of war."

In addition to preparing the manual, Chap offered the Navy the use of the Power Squadrons' "machinery ready to put into instant operation the training of great numbers of men required for the Naval Reserve Forces." Roosevelt accepted this offer with gratitude, and within a year more than 5,000 men who attended Squadrons' classes and used the instruction manual entered the armed services.

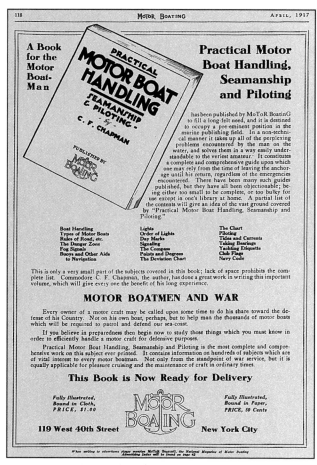

This is how it all began! Chap assembled material that had been published in *Motor Boating* magazine, and created a handbook for instruction of volunteer boatmen assisting the U.S. Navy in World War I. This slim volume, which would evolve into the "Chapman's" that we know today, was listed in this April 1917 advertisement at a paper-bound price of 50 cents.

11

After the War Chap's energy showed no signs of slowing. He formed the National Outboard Racing Commission in 1927. He served for 25 years as chairman of the American Power Boat Association (APBA) Racing Commission, which sanctions such famous events as the President's Cup and the Gold Cup Regatta. In 1921 he teamed up with Gar Wood, the legendary designer/helmsman of fast powerboats, to race offshore from Miami to New York. Their record 47-hour and 15-minute run stood unbroken for three decades.

By the 1920s *Motor Boating*'s circulation and advertising linage had grown dramatically. By 1922 Chap's book had undergone six revisions and in that year was retitled *Piloting: Seamanship & Small Boat Handling.*

By now, the emphasis of the book was clearly recreational boating, instruction and safety. Still mostly a compilation of articles from the magazine, the book took on the appearance of a scrapbook of the sea and a home instruction course in boat operation. It was used as the major reference by the USPS in the free courses it offered to the public (still a practice today), and was constantly revised to keep up with advances in the boating industry and always-changing government regulations.

Through time, *Piloting: Seamanship & Small Boat Handling* has acquired numerous nicknames, including: "the Bible of Boating," "the Blue Book," and just plain "Piloting" or "Chapman's." Today, its readers probably refer to it most often as "Chapman's," even though the original author was not directly involved with the book after his retirement in 1968, at the age of 86.

Help from many quarters

While Chap directed each new edition for almost 50 years, he counted on help from many assistants, and indeed, from the book's readers. With each new edition came suggestions from staff members, professional boat captains, airplane pilots, amateur sailors, cruising boaters and others who love the sea. He also relied on the cooperation of the U.S. Power Squadrons, the U.S. Coast Guard Auxiliary, the Army Engineers, the Coast & Geodetic Survey (now a part of NOS, the National Ocean Service), the U.S. Navy, and most of all the U.S. Coast Guard. Scores of manufacturers of equipment, boats, instruments and other nautical gear have always aided the staff in checking technical information and providing illustrations.

But through all those years, a handful of individuals have made contributions that may be almost as responsible as Chap himself for keeping the first 60 editions of this book the most popular, authoritative and current book on boating published. Their names include William H. Koelbel, who worked closely with Chap for more than 20

Seen here is the clubhouse of the New York Yacht Club, where many of the early organizational meetings of the United States Power Squadrons were held.

years and wrote a number of chapters during that time; Morris Rosenfeld, the famed marine photographer; Morris's son Stanley, who continued the tradition; Peter Barlow, Gardner Emmons, Dr. John Wilde, Robert Danforth Ogg, co-inventor of the Danforth anchor, and Gale Foster of the Cordage Institute.

Also to be mentioned as contributors are the readers, the unofficial helpers. The members and instructors of the U.S. Power Squadrons make suggestions, catch the minor typographical mistakes, sometimes argue with the editors about flag etiquette or fine points of navigational techniques and, perhaps most importantly, ask hundreds of meaningful questions.

Beginning in 1966, a new program of modernization was instituted for "Chapman's." Indeed, it was initiated by Chap himself, who at the age of 84 was still an active publisher and also still serving on the Flag and Etiquette Committee of the U.S. Power Squadrons. First E.S. Maloney (Col. U.S. Marine Corps, Ret.) was assigned to the work of completely rewriting the book, several chapters a year, with updates in every chapter as a flood of governmental and technical changes swept over recreational boating. Then, when Chap retired in 1968, John Whiting succeeded him as editorial director of *Piloting: Seamanship & Small Boat Handling* and as publisher of *Motor Boating* (soon thereafter renamed *Motor Boating & Sailing*).

Tom Bottomley joined the crew working on the book in 1968. It was indeed a crew. There was an exceptional degree of cooperation and dedication between Bill Koelbel and Tom, between the various outside contributors and the staff at the office, and among the notable support people, particularly Ruth Smith, who had been Mr. Chapman's famous assistant for four decades. It was as though this book were a 12-meter racing yacht, going for the America's Cup. Both Koelbel and Bottomley were winch grinders, sail handlers, mastmen, bowmen. Mack Maloney was navigator and tactician rolled into one.

Mack Maloney, in sheer volume of work as well as its excellence, deserves special singling out. He had spent his boyhood in Virginia Beach, Virginia, where his front yard was the Atlantic Ocean. Since then he has never been far from salt water, even during his 28 years in the Marine Corps. By the time Chap was preparing to retire, Mack had already written a number of chapters in the book and was recognized as an authority on many boating subjects. It was Chap's personal request that Mack step in for him and take over the principal authorship of the book.

Ever since 1966, Mack has been the man in constant touch with the appropriate agencies in Washington, DC, and the man behind the typewriter and computer—adding chapters, rewriting specialists' contributions where necessary, making the book work as a textbook, keeping track of the necessary changes, and working with the editors in the planning and execution of each new edition. Through the 60th Edition, Mack was indeed the author of "Chapman's." Now, with this extensively revised 61st edition, he has moved on to become the "Editor Emeritus,"

Chap was an avid and highly competent motorboat racer. Over the years, he won many trophys, including the Gold Cup shown above.

the reviewing authority for all material prepared by other authors and editors.

Maloney is deeply involved in that bridge between high technology and age-old seamanship. He is a member of the Institute of Navigation and was on its governing council. He is a member of the United States Naval Institute, and author of the finest book that organization publishes, *Dutton's Navigation & Piloting*. He is a member and Vice-Chairman of the U.S. Coast Guard's Navigation Safety Advisory Council. He was a member of the national educational staff of the United States Power Squadrons for many years, serving with distinction as Director of Education from 1971 to 1976. He is also an active member of the Education Department. His skill as a writer and editor has helped the book continue as the major text used in one of the largest adult education programs in the U.S.

Tom Bottomley, like Bill Koelbel, had first been on the editorial staff of *Motor Boating* magazine. Beginning in 1968 Bottomley was involved with "Chapman's," serving as the book's managing editor for a dozen years. His familiarity with every law and regulation passed over the years, and his technical acumen and book-production expertise were called upon countless times. This book could not have reached its state of excellence without Tom Bottomley's work.

Although *Piloting: Seamanship & Small Boat Handling* is now in its 77th year, and has passed its three millionth copy, it is somewhat astounding to realize that the book has had only three publishers and just one publishing company in all those years. From the days when William Randolph Hearst used to visit Chap's office regularly to look at pictures of new boats and quiz the editor on new developments, to the present in which more than 100 companies make up this vast communications empire, the Hearst Corporation has always fully supported the continuing work which has enabled this famous book to remain in its rightful place as "the Bible of Boating."

BOATING BASICS

1 THE LANGUAGE OF BOATING

Nautical words form such a large part of English that few readers will find the language of boating completely new. Everyone knows that "A 1" means "highly rated" and that "headway" is progress. It hardly matters that words such as these had a nautical origin. It hardly matters, that is, until we step aboard.

In this chapter you will be acquainted with words grouped into general areas of basic boating knowledge. To emphasize their significance as boating terms, these words have been italicized.

You will also encounter new words throughout the following chapters; these are not italicized, so as to avoid interfering with your reading. Usually new terms will be explained within their context, but you may also refer to the Glossary of Nautical Terms in Section 8.

LEARNING THE BASICS

Whatever your style of recreational boating—sail or power, 60-footer or small boat, racing, cruising or just "getting out on the water"—learning and using proper nautical terms will expand your interest in boating. While you needn't be excessively "salty" in your speech, there are important reasons for knowing and using the right terms for objects and activities around boats.

Your enjoyment of boating will be far greater when you can communicate easily with the whole *crew* and other boaters with whom you cruise and perhaps even compete. In times of emergency, many seconds of valuable time may be saved when correct, precise terms are used for needed tools or actions.

With a little practice you will soon be in the habit of thinking directly in nautical terms, rather than "shore" terms with mental translation. You will find nautical language more natural and have the satisfaction that your boating language is helping to hone your boating skills.

Although one chapter cannot include all of the nautical words in common use, and no two experts would agree on a complete list, we can prepare you in this chapter for the various topics covered in *Chapman*. Later chapters will often provide refined definitions and introduce more new words.

What is a boat?

The division between *boat* and *ship* is not precise, though most would place it at about 65 feet of length. Navigation Rules (*Chapter 6*) make a distinction at 20 meters, or about 65.6 feet. *Craft* and *small craft* often carry the same meaning as boat, while the term *vessel* is used particularly in legal and reg-

An auxiliary sailboat uses sails for propulsion except in calms and for close-quarter maneuvering where power may be used.

A yacht is a power or sail vessel used for recreation and pleasure, as opposed to work. The term is usually reserved for boats approximately 40 feet (12.2 m) or more in length, and is also applied to prestigious government craft.

ulatory contexts without reference to size. *Yacht* connotes luxurious accommodation whether the boat is sailed or powered with an engine. This usually implies a boat more than about 40 feet (12.2 m) in length, though there are many smaller boats which seem to deserve the term. It is also widely used when referring to prestigious government craft used by officials and dignitaries, such as a presidential yacht or a state governor's yacht.

A boat's basic means of propulsion will place it in the *powerboat* and *motorboat* category or the *sailboat* category. However, a sailboat operating under the power of its *auxiliary engine* (with or without the help of its sails) is legally a powerboat. Most sailboats more than about 18 feet (5.5 m) in length carry an auxiliary engine of some type and those with larger engines permanently installed in the *hull* are often known as *auxiliaries*. Small open sailboats are called *daysailers* and those used primarily for racing can be known as *racing dinghies*, though the word *dinghy* also refers to a very small boat used to ferry crew and supplies.

A hybrid category exists between powerboats and sailboats—*motorsailers* have powerful engines and modest sails. Though they share the benefits of both sailing and powerboating, they are relatively inefficient in either mode.

A sailboat with a large engine takes advantage of sails and power, but sacrifices efficiency in both modes of propulsion.

Cruisers carry some form of overnight accommodation and if they are powerboats are also known by their engine type. They might be *outboard cruisers, inboard cruisers* or even *inboard/outboard (I/O) cruisers.* Powerboats too small to offer overnight accommodation can be *daycruisers, runabouts* or *sportboats.* Some boats of this size are *utility boats*—for general service applications.

A dinghy can be propelled by *oars,* by sail or by a very small motor. If such a dinghy is squared-off at both ends, it is called a *pram.* As mentioned previously, dinghies may be used to ferry crew and supplies. In that case, the dinghy would be a *tender,* though tenders can also be much larger. Small tenders are sometimes suspended from their main vessels in *davits.* The *launch* is similar to the tender, but it suggests elegance and a length of at least 20 feet (6.1 m).

Houseboats are much more houselike than boatlike, and today the term should be reserved for *barges* with living accommodation. *Housecruisers* are a step closer in their evolution toward boats—their hulls are generally better suited to higher speed and small waves.

A *hydroplane* is a racing-style powerboat that travels so quickly that much of the force supporting its weight is created by air pressure, rather than water pressure or buoyancy.

Hydrofoil boats, on the other hand, have hydrofoils ("water wings") that create lift while immersed, supporting a hull above the water. Until very recently, the horsepower requirements of hydrofoil boats made engines necessary, but now sail-powered boats are also using hydrofoils.

A more common form of high-speed travel under sail is the *sailboard,* whose main distinction from other boats

is that it is steered mainly by alternating the position of its wishbone-rigged sail. Today, board sailing is a popular and well-established water sport.

Multihulls

Boats with more than one hull are known collectively as *multihulls.* Among multihulls, there are *catamarans,* which have two hulls that are either the same or mirror images of each other, and *trimarans,* which have three hulls, a central hull and two smaller outer hulls. Although most multihulls are sailing craft, specialized powerboats are often built with more than one hull.

Inflatables

Although *inflatable* boats are usually associated with tenders of less than 10 feet (3 m), for years, inflatables have been built in very large sizes—often up to 25 feet (7.6 m) in length

Today, board sailing is a popular water sport, a particular favorite of the young and the physically fit.

Rigid-bottom inflatable boats, often referred to as RIBs, are built both as small tenders and as larger sportboats. Even larger RIBs, often powered by diesel engines, are used as rescue craft.

and longer. Small inflatables are most often used as tenders where their major advantage is that they can be deflated and stowed in a small space. In this mode they often double as *life rafts* though they lack many of the protective features that one would associate with a proper life raft (*Chapter 4*).

The primary consideration with inflatables is the quality of the fabric and the gluing process used in their construction. High-quality fabrics that resist abrasion and sunlight, and high-strength glued seams, are expensive to manufacture, making useful inflatables more expensive than ordinary boats of similar length. However, they can provide greater capacity and more stability for the same length—both factors crucial in the choice of a tender. Inflatables are also favored for their soft contour, which spares the finish of the main hull when the tender is alongside.

Inflatables can be difficult to row, if not impossible in a chop, so they are often powered with a very small outboard motor. A recent development has seen the combination of inflatable and conventional boats in what is called a *rigid inflatable* boat, or *RIB*, as shown opposite. RIBs are built with a two-part hull; the lower part closely resembles the bottom of a high-speed powerboat while the upper part consists of an inflated tube. This allows RIBs both the efficient, high-speed performance of a conventional powerboat and the enormous stability of an inflatable. As for disadvantages, RIBs are more difficult to stow than the non-rigid variety.

BASIC HULL TERMS AND DIRECTIONS

Since directions aboard a well-piloted boat are expressed differently than on land, there are some basic terms that must be mastered before communications between boaters can be made absolutely clear. *Forward* is easy enough, but its opposite is *aft*, not backward. The right-hand side of a boat, when you are facing forward, is the *starboard* side—the left-hand side is the *port*. A position aft of another is *abaft* it, as a *bearing* (a direction to a landmark, for example) might be abaft the boat's beam (width). Anything running across the boat is *athwartships* as is a swim platform or the *thwart*, or bench seat, of a rowboat. Along the centerline is *fore-and-aft*. *Amidships* means "in the middle," whether fore-and-aft, or athwartships. *Inboard* is toward the center, *outboard* away from it. If you were climbing a sailboat's *rigging* (the gear used to support and adjust the mast), you would be *aloft*, while anyone *abovedecks* is merely on the deck, not actually above it.

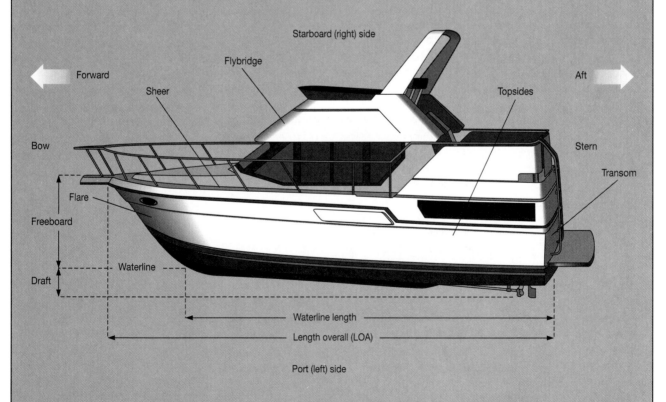

Starboard (right) side
Flybridge
Forward
Sheer
Bow
Flare
Freeboard
Draft
Waterline
Aft
Topsides
Stern
Transom
Waterline length
Length overall (LOA)
Port (left) side

These terms relate to the hull, and directions aboard a boat. Note that port and starboard sides remain the same, no matter which way one is facing, and that LOA is figured differently for sailboats. Refer to Chapter 10 for terms specific to sailboats.

DESCRIBING BOAT TYPES

Yacht designers, or *naval architects*, will tell you that when they begin the design of a cruising boat—power or sail—they often begin at the inside and work out. Apart from the fundamental assumptions of safe operation, a cruising boat's main function is to accommodate its owner and crew in as much comfort as they can afford, if not more.

Though we often describe a boat primarily by its *length overall (LOA)*, what is often more important is how much living space is actually available—and while living space usually increases with length, the relationship is anything but straightforward. Aboard most cruising sailboats in the range of 25 to 35 feet (7.6 to 10.7 m), very important compromises are struck between living space, aesthetics and performance. Below about 25 (7.6 m) feet, compromises become sacrifices.

Powerboats, unlike sailboats, are well-suited to the kind of interior accommodation most of us are accustomed to: rooms with basically rectangular shapes. This happy coincidence between the needs of interior layout and the hull shapes that work best under power is due to the availability of large engines. Cruising powerboats, with some exceptions, are not faced with the need to slide through the water gently with low horsepower, but can ride up and over it on large, almost flat surfaces. Their shape perfectly suits spacious interiors that are, more or less, rectangular.

The ruling dimension for a cruising boat designer is, of course, the height of the average boat buyer: 6 feet. To allow the owner to stand, the length of a boat must be at least four times this average person's height. For both powerboats and sailboats, it would be no less than 24 feet (7.3 m).

Since one question novice boat buyers ask is "How many does it sleep?", builders are anxious to furnish the maximum number of *berths*, even knowing that most crews seldom use them all. However, when they do, a measure of privacy must be provided. One set of berths is segregated from another by transverse walls called *bulkheads*, usually forming a *forward cabin* or *forecastle* with a *V-berth*, which is actually two berths joined at the toe to fit into the bow of the boat.

Powerboat types

Powerboat builders use numerous terms to distinguish various configurations, and they are not always consistent. However, a few basic terms survive the changes in style. A runabout usually seats four, though a *bowrider* style has additional seating in the bow accessed via the *walk-through windshield*. Although the runabout provides no formal sleeping accommodation, many boaters camp under a cloth covering called a *camper top*.

With a slight increase in overall length, to about 20 feet, the volume of the bow forward of the control station becomes just large enough to enclose a *cuddy cabin*. While not luxurious, the cuddy does offer shelter in wet weather and can also enclose a portable toilet. Traditionally called a *head*, in recent legal parlance this might be a *marine sanitation device*, sometimes shortened to *MSD*. The head may be connected to a *holding tank*, where sewage is temporarily held for discharge—or *pump out*—at specifically equipped marinas.

Center-consoles, sportboats and daycruisers

The *center-console* boat has become very popular in the last few years because it provides the maximum area of usable deck space for a boat's overall length. By reducing seating to one or two bench or swivel seats and opening up the deck,

The walk-around style borrows elements of the center-console and the cuddy cabin. A narrow bridge allows access to a low foredeck with bulwarks, while basic accommodation and storage space is included in the cabin. This configuration is well suited to fishing and patrol or rescue work.

the center-console allows fishing enthusiasts room to maneuver in front of, behind and around the steering position and makes most activities other than cruising far easier. Center-consoles range in size from less than 15 feet to about 35 feet (less than 4.6 to about 10.7 m).

In the range of 20 to 25 feet (6.1 to 7.6 m), *sportboats* differ from *daycruisers* mainly in engine size and styling. However, the basic elements of their layout are very similar. At this length, sufficient height can be gained to allow a very small cabin with sitting headroom in the bow. The daycruiser cabin will probably have a V-berth, a portable head under the V-berth, and a small *galley*, or kitchen, consisting of a countertop stove and a basin, as well as a folding table.

Express and sedan cruisers

Above about 25 feet (7.6 m), powerboat styles begin to diverge as the differences in their accommodation layout are reflected in sharp differences in their hull shapes; *express cruisers* form one branch and *sedan cruisers*, usually called *convertibles*, form the other.

The express yacht is the sportier version of the sedan—with generally less cabin space and more room for both the engine and bridge.

An express cruiser, sometimes called a *sunbridge*, takes the basic sportboat configuration and enlarges it—right up to 40 feet (12.2 m) or more, while the sedan/convertible cruiser puts the main interior space (and lower control station) on the same level as the *cockpit.*

While a large express cruiser might have complete accommodation and only somewhat less cabin area than a convertible, the interior is almost entirely within the hull. The *foredeck* is long and unobstructed, broken only by *hatches*—openings providing access to space below—and, on its more vertical surfaces, windows. The control station, or *bridge*, of an express cruiser is set well aft and a step above the floor of the cockpit (which is called the *sole*). A raked *radar arch* provides an excellent mounting position for both communication and navigation equipment including radar sets, but

A power cruiser's flybridge, also called a flying bridge, is a high steering position, originally intended as a platform from which to spot game fish.

it will be a few years before many of them support small, inexpensive radar sets. Stylish and often high-powered, the express cruiser is also a simpler boat to build than a sedan or *flybridge* style of comparable size.

Sedans and convertibles divide their interior space into two parts; a main *salon* is at the level of the cockpit and the forward cabin is below the foredeck. The bridge is at the forward end of the main cabin and is often duplicated as a flybridge on a second level above the main cabin. A small canopy called a *bimini* shades the flybridge. Sedans and convertibles in the lower range of sizes usually place their galleys within the main cabin. This is known as "galley-up."

Aft cabin and double cabin cruisers

As length increases, it becomes possible to open up sleeping accommodation below the level of the deck at the stern. This configuration is called an *aft cabin*, as shown on page 22. Usually, the engines are moved forward to the middle area of the hull and the style is called a *double cabin*. At this size, the galley can be joined to the *forecabin* below deck level ("galley-down"). Also, there may be room at deck level for a middle cabin called the *main salon*. This configuration is called a *tri-cabin*.

Sportfishermen

Though primarily designed for offshore fishing, *sportfish* styles also appear in what are essentially cruising boats. These have a much longer foredeck, a short main salon, a larger cockpit, sometimes lowered closer to the water and, in purpose-designed game-fishing boats, a very high *tuna tower* supporting a control station at a maximum elevation for the best possible visibility.

Trawlers

Within the commercial fishing community, the word *trawler* has a specific meaning, but in the recreational boating community the word is used more loosely. In general, among

The trawler was originally designed as a low-speed fishing vessel. As a recreational type, trawlers are fuel-efficient and offer better handling in rough weather.

Sailboat styles

Sailboat builders are less inclined to identify their boats as types according to their cabin layouts—probably because less variety is possible. Instead, sailboats are usually known by their *sail plans*, the number and position of their sails, as described on pages 38 and 39. Sailboats almost always have a *cockpit* placed near or at the *transom*, the back of the hull *(page 19)*, and the interior accommodation ahead of the cockpit. The exception is the *center-cockpit*, which roughly corresponds to the aft cabin style in powerboats.

With sufficient width at the stern, it becomes possible to build a compact cabin behind or partially under the cockpit. As this aft cabin grows in size with increasing hull length, the cockpit itself can be moved forward to a more central position. However, to maintain useful space below, it is necessary to raise the cockpit *sole* to the level of the deck. The result is ungainly in center-cockpit boats of less than about 40 feet (12.2 m).

While the interior space receives the most attention from new boat buyers, it is actually the cockpit where most sailors' and powerboaters' time is spent.

Sailboat cockpits

Aboard a sailboat the cockpit is both patio and control center—its layout is a set of compromises between access to control lines and *winches* (devices used to haul on lines), and space to stretch out. The cockpit consists of bench seats that should be close enough to each other that crew members can brace themselves as the boat tilts—or, in nautical language, *heels*. Cockpit seats sometimes lift open to reveal

boaters, any boat more than about 25 feet (7.6 m) in length that does not carry sufficient horsepower to lift itself out of the water and *plane* at or near the surface is called a trawler, shown above. Since the trawler hull rides through and not over the water, it is considered a *displacement* hull design—described in detail on page 26.

The trawler's shape is usually narrower and rounder, offering somewhat less interior space for the same overall length. To prevent rolling, trawlers sometimes carry a very small sail called a *steadying sail*. These boats are popular for traveling at a reduced speed—7 to 8 knots, and ideal for waterways where speeds are limited, as well as long passages when fuel weight becomes critical.

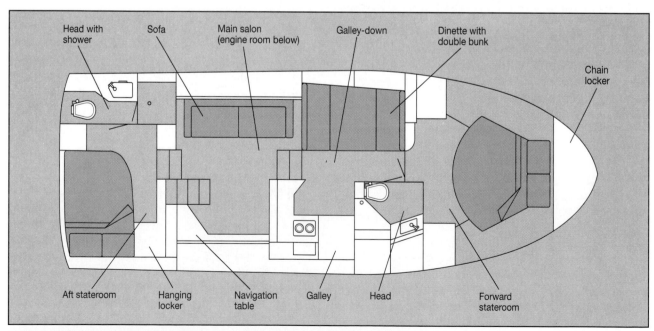

Head with shower | Sofa | Main salon (engine room below) | Galley-down | Dinette with double bunk | Chain locker

Aft stateroom | Hanging locker | Navigation table | Galley | Head | Forward stateroom

At about 35 feet in length, powerboat hulls can have enough freeboard and beam to allow for spacious accommodation with standing headroom in the quarters. On this boat, the main salon is raised above the engine installation amidships. and the galley is "galley-down."

stowage for sailbags, an inflatable life raft, *mooring* lines (for anchoring), sheets, an outboard motor, winch handles and the accumulated etcetera of life afloat.

A *pedestal* may stand in the aft end of the cockpit, topped by a *binnacle*, a case that houses a *compass (Chapter 17)*. The pedestal may also support the *wheel*, the steering controls for the *rudder*. The rudder is an underwater blade used to steer the boat and, depending on the boat, is adjusted by either a wheel or a *tiller* (a handle fixed directly to the top of the *rudder post*, the through-hull shaft on which the rudder pivots). Regardless of whether a boat uses a wheel or tiller, the steering controls are called the *helm* and the person (man or woman) handling those controls is traditionally known

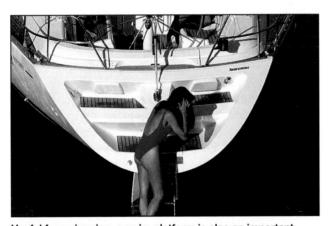

Useful for swimming, a swim platform is also an important safety feature, sometimes allowing an overboard crew member to be brought aboard.

as the *helmsman*. While very large wheels restrict movement in the boat's cockpit, they do allow the helmsman to see what he or she must see—the *luff* (forward edge) of the *headsail*, for example—by sitting to one side or the other of the cockpit, or by perching on the *coaming*, the raised edge that surrounds all but the leanest and meanest racing cockpits.

Leading from the sailboat cockpit to the main cabin or salon "below" is a *companionway*, consisting of a steep set of ladder-like steps, *grab rails* and a *sliding hatch*. The part of the cockpit that you step over at the top of the companionway is the *bridge*. This may be a grand name for what is essentially a barrier, but it is a very important barrier. If the cockpit were to fill with water from a large wave, this barrier would keep several hundred pounds of water out of the *bilge*, the interior hull space under the cabin. With a bridge, the cockpit is *self-draining* through at least two *scuppers* (drain holes) leading from the lowest point on the cockpit sole (the floor of the cockpit) through the hull. Of course, the cockpit sole must be above the *load waterline (LWL)* of the hull.

Aft of the cockpit there is often stowage space called a *lazarette,* accessed through a hatch in the deck. The lazarette, in more recent designs, is giving way to two or three steps from the level of the cockpit sole to a small platform near the water; this is called a *swim platform*. Useful for swimming, this "back porch" is also an important safety feature as it allows a crew member to be brought back on board during a rescue. Powerboats have had swim platforms for years and are now using gates through the transom, the back of the hull, to permit easier access. You will read more about crew overboard in Chapter 4.

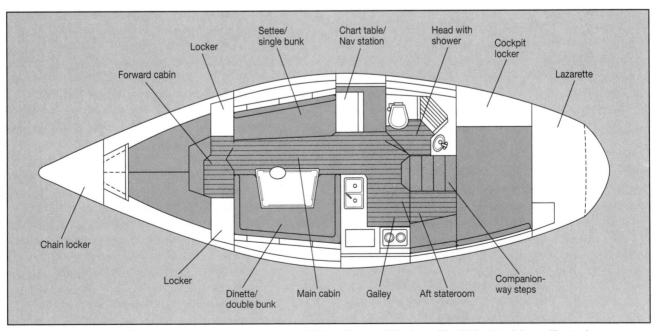

Below-deck accommodation varies widely, depending on the LOA and beam of the boat. The 34-foot cruising sailboat shown above offers generous cruising accommodations: a double V-berth, a double aft cabin, a U-shaped settee with a dining table that can be lowered to form another double berth, and another settee across from the dinette that provides a single berth.

Powerboat cockpits and bridges

The central element of the small powerboat cockpit is the control console. The designer must place the controls as well as the instruments and radios within easy reach and yet ensure that sight lines are adequate and instruments are easily legible. As the length of a powerboat is increased, it becomes possible to raise the control position above the level of the cockpit sole—where it can more easily be given its traditional name, bridge.

While there may now be somewhat more area available, it is still a challenge to arrange all of the electronics and radio equipment in a practical fashion. One common, and sometimes overlooked, problem is placing the compass in a position that is conspicuous but which leaves the compass as free as possible of the magnetic influences of radios—particularly their speakers—and other electronic, electrical and metal elements.

At about 30 feet (9.1 m) of LOA it becomes possible to provide a flying bridge, usually abbreviated to the term "flybridge." The flybridge has become a popular configuration because it allows more confident control of the boat. The flybridge is often protected from sunlight by a *bimini*—a rectangular canopy on a light framework. Various controls, instruments and radios are sometimes duplicated, with one set on the flybridge and another set at the main bridge at the forward end of the main salon. Called a *dual station* arrangement, this design allows for a comfortable steering position in any weather.

The main cabin

Aboard both sail and powerboat cruisers, the *main cabin* usually serves triple-duty as sleeping accommodation, living area and galley. It may also accommodate a *chart table* or *nav station*. Lighter and wider shapes for sailboat hulls have allowed designers to develop the *quarter berth*, once a simple fore-and-aft sleeping space for a crew member on standby, into the *aft stateroom (page 23)*, previously the hallmark of a luxurious powerboat. Somewhere in this layout a bathroom, or head, must be placed with its marine toilet (also named a head) and washbasin.

Stowage and lockers

While these basic elements of boat interiors accommodate the crew members themselves, space must be found for the gear and *stores* (supplies) that each brings aboard. Sometimes, scant attention is paid to the need for *stowage* and *lockers*. Usually at least one *hanging locker* is provided, designed to hold carefully pressed going ashore clothes or soggy *foulweather gear*—too often, it must hold both.

Stores for the galley are ranged throughout the boat's interior, wherever space can be found. Aboard a sailboat, the bilge (the lowest part of a hull's interior) is ideal for careful stowing of heavy cans and bottles, provided the labels are stripped (to avoid clogging the *limber holes* that ensure

Aboard both sailboats, as shown above, and powerboats, the main cabin often consists of a galley and living area with settees that convert into berths for sleeping.

drainage to the lowest part of the bilge) and provided that there is sufficient depth. To get access to the bilge, you would lift a section of the cabin sole, the floor of the cabin.

Floor, as a nautical word, has more to do with construction as you will read later in this chapter. *Ceiling* also has a nautical meaning—it refers to the covering, often very light wooden planking or slats, that hides the inside surface of the hull. The surface that corresponds to the ceiling of an ordinary room is known as the *deckhead* and is often covered, or even upholstered, with a *headliner*.

In addition to matters of convenience, properly planned stowage aboard a boat can affect the handling of your boat and your ability to respond to emergencies. The following points are worth considering:

■ To keep the center of gravity as low as possible, plan your stowage carefully: Heavy items generally should be stowed low and light items, high.

■ Heavy gear is usually best stowed midships, freeing the ends for light gear and stores. This will help avoid changing the handling characteristics of the boat.

■ Light items that must be kept dry are best stowed high, carefully wrapped.

■ Especially for long cruises, storage of food is practically a science. Perishables are stowed in the icebox which, on boats with sufficient power, is often equipped with refrigeration. Refer to Chapter 23 for more information on refrigeration and batteries.

■ In some boats a stowage plan is necessary for safety reasons—for quick access to emergency equipment or tools and parts, for example.

DESCRIBING HULLS

A vessel floats because water exerts a buoyant force that exactly equals the weight of the water that the vessel displaces. Successful floaters weigh less than the weight of the water their hulls could displace. (Floating in salt water is different from floating in fresh water because salt water is heavier. A hull of the same weight needs to displace a smaller volume of salt water than of fresh.) As a boat is settled into the water—imagine it being lowered in *slings* by a crane—it reaches a level of equilibrium where the weight of the displaced water exactly equals the weight of the boat. That level is the *waterline* and is often marked by a *boot-top*, a contrasting band painted all along the hull just above the waterline. The paint on the hull below the waterline is often *anti-fouling* paint, applied to deter marine growth.

If vessels were required merely to float, they might all look the same depending only on their size and the material we used to build them. But once we begin to push a boat through the water, we meet the complex laws of physics that inspire the extraordinary diversity of the hull shapes that are built today. Over the years, that diversity has fostered a vocabulary of hull-shape words as well as words that indicate locations.

Parts of the hull

We have already learned that the bow is the beginning of the hull and the stern is the end. Both words can be used to indicate areas of the hull without distinct limits. In between is the *midships*. The transom, shown on page 19, is the back surface of the hull. Powerboats usually have wide transoms, and sailboats, small—in some cases the transom disappears completely and we have a *canoe stern*. Such a hull is *double ended*. If the transom is above the water, this is a *counter stern*, and a transom angled forward is a *reverse transom*.

The extreme forward part of the bow is the *stem*, a word left over from a time when there was actually a structural wooden piece in that position. If the profile of the bow curves outward, as most powerboat bows do, it is said to have *flare*. If it is convex, as many sailboat bows are, it used to be called a *spoon bow*. A bow that is straight and nearly vertical is a *plumb bow*, one that leans forward is *raked*. It was once the

fashion to shape a slight inward curve at the stern and midships, described as *tumblehome*, but molded construction now makes this shape problematic.

Yacht designers pay a lot of attention to the curve of the *gunwale* (pronounced "gun'l"), both in profile and from more natural angles. The gunwale is the structural element at the upper edge of the hull, and its shape strongly affects the boat's appearance. The often subtle curve of the gunwale is the *sheer*. Sometimes a *reverse sheer* is used, especially to increase a powerboat's interior space or to emphasize the pointiness of a sport boat's bow.

If you were to remark that a boat had a "nice" sheer you would actually be using a word that, at one time, had a more specific meaning—a *nice* curve was one that was not irregular or distorted. Today we would say it was a *fair* curve. The traditional assumption has been that fair curves (or *lines*) make fast hulls. But this is not necessarily so according to recent science; unfortunately it is possible to have a fast hull that is awkward looking.

A hull that is *fine* is narrow, as opposed to *beamy*. A beamy boat will usually have a *bluff* bow, while a fine one will have a fine bow, or *entry*, the place where water flow comes under the influence of the hull shape. The water flow leaves the hull as it flows under the *aft run*, which, in general, would be wide and flat for fast hulls, and narrow and curved for slow ones.

Freeboard, illustrated on page 19, is the vertical distance from the waterline to the gunwale. Freeboard is higher at the bow than at the stern, at least in North American and European boats. The surface of the hull from the waterline to the gunwale, with the exception of the transom, is the *topsides* and not even the popular shoe bearing that name will allow you to walk on it.

From the waterline to the bottom of the hull is known as the *bottom*, but boats have acquired distinct appendages like the fins on a fish, and these are usually described separately from the hull shape. The distance from the waterline to the lowest part of the boat is called the *draft*. On a sailboat, the lowest part of the boat usually is the toe of the keel, the deep appendage or fin under the hull. On a powerboat, the lowest

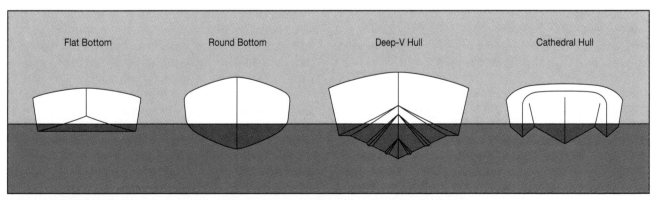

A flat bottom boat is inexpensive to build; a round bottom provides a soft ride. The deep-V hull is used on high-speed offshore craft; cathedral hulls have good stability.

point is usually the propeller tip. Draft also refers to the minimum amount of water in which a boat will float; a boat is said to "draw" a certain amount of water.

On sailboats, the main fin is the keel, though the word also refers to the place in the bottom of any hull where, at one time, you would have found a distinct structural piece.

When reading about hull shapes, you will often see the word *section*, which has almost the same meaning to boaters as it does to engineers: Boaters normally mean "cross section," the two-dimensional shape you would see from the bow or stern if you were to cut the hull crosswise.

Planing and displacement hulls

Early in this century, most boaters became familiar with the experience of planing—achieving dynamic lift in addition to buoyancy. Today, a boat's ability to lift itself out of the water and ride along on top of it is almost taken for granted by powerboaters and crews of small, racing sailboats. But boats

Hydrodynamic forces lift a planing hull partially out of the water to reduce drag and wave-making resistance. This makes high speeds possible without excessive power.

such as larger sailboats and trawler powerboats with less horsepower at their disposal require subtler solutions. These hulls are known as displacement hulls because they are expected to achieve lift only by displacing water.

In addition to planing and displacement hulls there are two small but increasingly important categories: hulls that achieve lift through air pressure (such as *tunnel hull* hydroplanes) and hydrofoil boats that "fly" on small, immersed wings.

Displacement powerboat hulls

Large, low-speed powerboats with displacement hulls *(page 22)* are sometimes known as trawlers. While low horsepower limits speed, trawlers may have clear advantages in conditions where high speed is impossible due to sea conditions, or is simply unnecessary. Fuel consumption can be sufficiently low that longer ranges become possible—ranges in hundreds of *nautical miles* are not uncommon, especially for a trawler-style boat with a single diesel engine. Greater displacement

is also possible with little penalty in overall performance. High speeds of some displacement hulls create additional lift which, in fact, makes them semi-displacement hulls.

Trawler hulls are usually rounded and would be described as *round bottom* hulls. A round bottom powerboat hull will normally have no discontinuity in the curve of its section between the gunwale and the keel. To put it another way, the *turn of the bilge* is slack.

Occasionally, a displacement hull will be *flat bottomed*, but this is for ease of construction rather than efficiency. Flat bottomed hulls, and other types too, will have *chines*, which are the "corners" where the side of the hull becomes the bottom. A *single chine* hull has one chine on each side.

The V-hull

So much horsepower is available in contemporary boats that the planing hull has become the standard type. If a hull is expected to spend most of its time on top of the water in planing mode, its characteristics in displacement mode are almost irrelevant. This explains why so many powerboats are difficult to manage at low speed. Instead of creating smooth water flow at low speeds, emphasis is placed on the presentation of large flat planing surfaces. Where no rough water is encountered, these surfaces can be perfectly flat, but in most cases a planing hull must negotiate waves.

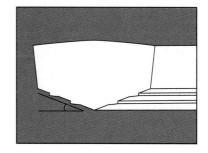

Hulls with deadrise angles of 16° to 19°, such as the one shown at left, are considered to be modified-V types, while steeper angles, as high as 23°, are deep-V types.

The compromise between planing and *sea-keeping* qualities has led to almost universal acceptance of the *V-hull* developed in the mid-1950s. A steep *deadrise*, the angle formed at the transom by the V, provides acceptable wave-riding qualities along with sufficient planing ability to achieve high speed. Many variations have since been tried, but almost all fall within the *modified-V* type, typically considered to include boats with about 16 to 19 degrees of deadrise at the transom. Other variations involve the number and placement of *lifting strakes* according to water conditions they are expected to handle. An old word, *strake* now refers to a lengthwise strip with a triangular section, molded into the hull to provide a narrow horizontal surface and an edge to grip against sideways forces. Similarly shaped edges above the waterline are *spray rails*. Deep-V and modified-V hulls are very sensitive to small changes in the angle of propeller thrust and to adjustments in *trim tabs*, rectangular control flaps that project along the water's surface at the transom when the hull is planing.

SAILBOAT HULLS

A sailboat hull is different from any other hull in its need for a large lateral resistance surface. For the boat to move ahead, the wind forces pushing the boat sideways must be thwarted and converted to forces that move the boat forward. On a small boat this can be done by simply extending a board down into the water and securing it there. There are several methods: A *centerboard (right)* is a relatively thin plate that can be swung down through the keel for greater lateral area, but which can be raised to lessen the boat's draft. On some sailboats, a *daggerboard* is forced down vertically in lieu of a pivoted centerboard. Some boats may have a pair of *leeboards*, which look like external "centerboards," attached to the outside of the hull, port and starboard; only one is lowered at a time.

As boats get larger, they require the additional righting force provided by ballast—usually in the form of a lead or iron keel attached to the lowest part of the boat's hull. A full keel *(right)*, usually found on cruising boats, evolved from wooden construction methods. It has been replaced, in recent designs, by the *fin keel*, which offers better handling, both for racing and cruising, and less resistance. Any deep keel, fin or full, prevents a sailboat from entering shallow water. However, shallow ballast keels can be combined with centerboards to permit efficient lateral resistance and shallow water access. A small keel-like projection just ahead of the rudder, on a fin keel boat, is called a *skeg*. It offers little or no performance advantage, but it may protect the rudder shaft.

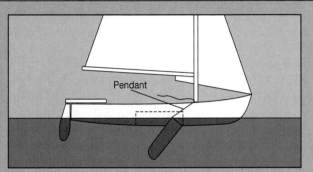

A centerboard is raised or lowered in its *trunk* by a *pendant* (or *pennant*) to permit adjustment according to the point of sail, or for shallow water.

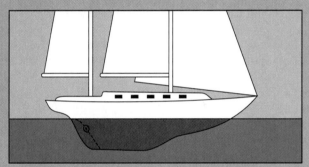

A full keel is usually found on larger boats. It may have poured-in ballast, or bolted-on outside ballast that acts as a grounding shoe.

Ballasted hulls

Since sailboats must be able to support the *heeling force* created above the deck by sails, most hull shapes are designed to provide the buoyancy that is important in resisting forces that can cause a boat to tip—*heeling* or *listing*. (Heeling is leaning over from the force of sails, in contrast to listing, which is leaning over due to weight distribution.) A flat bottom hull resists strongly and immediately, but may ultimately give up with a sudden *capsize*, turning bottom side up. At the other extreme, round bottomed hulls—such as a narrow canoe—may offer no resistance. When the shape of the hull cannot be relied upon for ultimate stability, *ballast* is added.

Ballast once was accomplished by heavy material carried inside the hull. Then late in the last century builders began adding additional weight to the keel to improve stability. This first consisted of cast iron, then lead castings bolted to the outside of the keel. Where larger or ocean-going yachts were concerned, these ballast keels were faired into the shape of the hull, but the ballast keel gradually became a separate fin even for ocean-going sailboats. Because ballast does not provide any beneficial effect until the boat is actually heeled, ballasted sailboats are designed to operate at an angle of heel.

The force exerted by the wind on the sails creates a heeling (leaning over) effect, which is to be expected on all sailboats.

BOAT CONSTRUCTION

Pleasure boat building underwent a revolution about 35 years ago. The principal material in boat building was wood until the late 1950s, when polyester resins and glass fiber became accepted as durable and economical materials. Within only three or four years, almost the entire pleasure boat industry converted to molded plastic construction.

While wooden boat construction had placed severe limits on the designer, it had allowed the *boatwright*, the craftsman boat builder, wide latitude to express his taste and expertise through his skill in manipulating the material. *Fiberglass* (fiber-reinforced plastic) molding created exactly the opposite effect: It took yacht designers only a little time to realize that molding allowed unprecedented freedom for their ideas in both structure and style. But the leveling effect on the craft of boat building was soon apparent.

This effect is also apparent in the losses to our boatbuilding vocabulary. Words such as "carlin" and "plank rabbet," for example, no longer have meaning in the context of boat construction except among wooden boat aficionados. However, there are enough wooden boat enthusiasts and enough wooden boats that many novice boaters may someday find themselves experiencing the unique pleasures of replacing a rotted plank or varnishing a vast expanse of *brightwork*—a boat's wooden trim. For that reason alone, the language of wooden boat construction is worth preserving along with a thorough understanding of the more recent vocabulary of fiberglass construction.

Wooden-boat terms

Most wooden yachts built in North America before the Second World War were built in *carvel* construction. Each separate plank was fitted to the *frames,* or ribs, of the boat and butted flush with its neighbor to form a fairly smooth outer surface. The slight gap between each plank was sealed by *caulking*, forcing a fiber and tar compound, called *oakum*, into the gap with a metal tool. After the boat was launched, the planks would swell, tightening the seal.

At the same time, a very small number of boats were produced using a Scandinavian method of overlapping each plank against the other and riveting or bolting through both. This method was called *lapstrake* construction. (A strake, used in the context of wooden boats, is a continuous line of planking.)

Smaller yachts, especially those produced in series, were often built on a *jig*, a dimensionally correct framework that held the frames in position until the hull was stable and could be removed and turned upright for finishing.

Many boat builders in the pre-war era used extremely well-defined series production methods to turn out a sound and

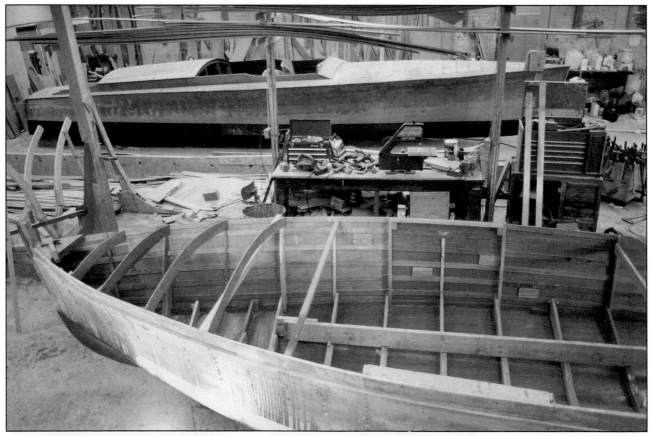

On wooden boats, frames (also called ribs) are set into the keel at a right angle, then covered with planking. Each continuous line of planking along the hull from bow to stern is called a strake.

consistent, cost-controlled product for a large market. Larger yachts, particularly those built as a one-off contract, would be built by the older method of first laying a keel, then erecting frames on it to be covered from the bottom, where the *garboard* strake was attached, to the gunwale, where the sheer strake completed the topsides. Each plank might have been *rabbeted*, given a shoulder along both edges to allow a more secure fit and a wide enough gap for easy caulking.

Where the frame met the keel, the boat was reinforced with heavy floors, roughly triangular pieces that joined the frame to the keel and, in a ballasted sailboat, carried the long bolts that attach the exterior ballast to the hull.

Wherever wooden members were joined at near right angles, *knees*, triangular braces of wood and, later, metal, could be added to stiffen the joint. A very substantial and carefully fitted member at the bow, the stem, accepted the plank ends and tied them together. The stem was usually reinforced where it met the keel by a *breast hook*; the transom carried the plank ends in a graceful curve. The deck was formed, usually with a slight convexity, a *camber*, by carefully shaped deck beams, covered with *cover boards,* which were then caulked, and sealed with canvas, stretched, nailed tight and painted until waterproof. *Carlins* provided fore-and-aft stiffness to the deck beams and accepted the bolts holding important deck fittings such as the *deck bit* or *samsonpost.*

In addition to these fairly universal names were numerous other peculiar and local words for the myriad of parts, most of them hand-shaped, that went into the construction of even a simple wooden boat.

From planking to plywood

In the late 1920s wooden boat building began to see some influence from aircraft construction, which was also executed largely in wood. Glues were improved and, as a result, plywood received some respect as a secondary material. But it was not until after World War II that plywood molding was recognized as a sophisticated technique.

Molded plywood construction, usually called *cold molding*, means the use of a convex mold onto which strips of supple ply are stapled and glued, gradually building up a light but very strong *stressed skin* that has very little need of interior framing.

Hard-chined hulls

Preformed plywood also assumed huge importance in small boat building. Though plywood offered limited scope in shaping a hull, it proved advantageous: It was inexpensive, easy to use and very strong for its weight. Fortunately, its shaping limitation coincided with the availability of cheap, powerful engines that were a perfect match for the boxlike *hard-chined* hulls that resulted. Various methods were devised to disguise the essential box character of plywood hulls. These included softer, rounded chines of planked material, double chines, as well as forced or *tortured ply* shapes that deviated slightly from the basic simple and conic curves that were available in any sheet material.

Despite these restrictions, the waterways quickly filled with amateur-built boats brought to life from the pages of *Rudder, Popular Mechanics* and other do-it-yourself magazines of the late 1940s and 1950s.

The term hard-chined hull also applies to steel and aluminum construction, still popular today because of the evolution of special epoxy coatings that enable the steel and aluminum to be encapsulated to prevent electrolysis or corrosion, while keeping the strength needed for work or pleasure boats. These materials are generally for the serious enthusiast, who shuns the production line look and prefers the character of a custom-built craft.

The shift to plastic

Then came the chemists. With several drums of *thermosetting* resin, a few cans of *catalyst* (a curing agent), some bolts of white glass-fiber cloth and a mold, just about anybody

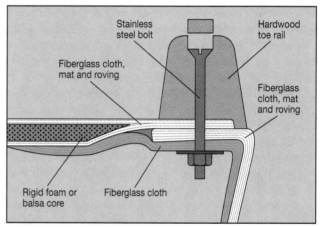

The full name for fiberglass, "fiber-reinforced plastic," properly describes the material as glass fibers embedded in a thermosetting plastic. High performance hulls are often reinforced using fibers made of carbon fiber or Kevlar.

could get into the boatbuilding business. Early molded boats were fairly timid imitations of carvel planked wooden yachts. Since no one was really sure how strong fiberglass was and how long it would last, most erred on the side of safety. The result, as we know today, was heavy and almost indestructible hulls. More recently built fiberglass hulls are much lighter, much less likely to deteriorate cosmetically, and are as indestructible as their predecessors.

The principal advances in molded construction, at least for boats on long production runs, involve the use of rigid foams and *balsawood* cores. Since fiberglass is a strong but heavy and not very stiff material, sufficient panel stiffness can be achieved by separating two layers of glass with a light but compression-resistant core. *Cored construction*—also called *composite construction*—is now almost universally used in

There are many advantages to fiberglass construction: Surfaces can be of any desired compound curvature. Multiple identical hulls, super-structures and lesser components can be made economically from reusable molds. In addition, plastic hulls resist attack by marine organisms, although they do require anti-fouling paint.

many areas of series-produced hulls and decks. The structure might also be stiffened by the use of box sections called *high-hat* sections forming a grid or running longitudinally inside the hull or deck.

Other advances have been made in *gel coat* formulation to provide a glossier and more color-retentive surface. Gel coats and barriers have also been formulated to prevent *osmosis*, the insinuation of water through the gel coat that produces blisters.

A typical *mold schedule*, or list of layers, consists of gel coat; possibly an osmosis barrier; alternating layers of mat (cloth that is made of irregular short fibers), regular fiberglass cloth and *roving* (the stiff, coarse woven cloth); and occasionally chopped strand sprayed onto the surface with a pneumatic gun. This series might be followed by the core material and further interior layers. Each layer is *laid up*, or hand-rolled into place against the highly polished surface of a concave mold, or *tool*.

Other secondary parts of the boat are also molded in fiberglass, usually with a simpler schedule than is used for the hull. The major parts are lifted from their molds to receive various fittings and equipment such as *cleats*, winches, hatches, rails, *windlasses*, tanks, etc. and electrical harnesses before they are assembled into a boat.

The hull-deck joint

The chief engineering problem, once the molding is complete, is how best to attach the deck to the hull. Theories abound, but, in general, the best *hull-deck joints* offer large surfaces for *bedding compound* and other sealers and adhesives, thick wood or metal bearing plates for through-bolt attachment

and a box-shaped section for stiffness. Add to this the provision of *rubbing strakes* and *stanchion bases*, and you have a proper marriage of deck to hull. At this point, the boat is almost complete. In fact, many smaller powerboats are actually shipped without engines. The design of modern inboard/outboard engines, commonly called I/Os, has made it possible for engines to be installed at the dealer level to suit the particular buyer.

Molded construction is also used for one-off, high-performance racing yachts, both power and sail. While the methods are very similar, one-off projects make more use of better materials such as *unidirectional* and other more specialized glass cloths, *epoxy* resins and reinforcing material other than glass fiber, such as *Kevlar* and *carbon fiber*.

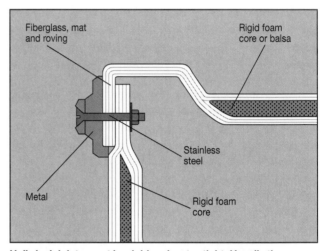

Hull-deck joints must be rigid and water-tight. Usually they are formed from a molded box-section and are liberally caulked with elastic and adhesive fillers, then through-bolted with stainless steel bolts. The hull-deck joint shown above is appropriate for a small powerboat.

Carbon fiber is also used in the construction of very sophisticated and expensive racing masts, but modern sailboat *spars* are, for the most part, extruded in aluminum alloy. While most masts and *booms* (the horizontal spar at the base of what is usually the *mainsail*) are simple tubes, more efficient shapes can be fabricated by cutting and rewelding basic extrusions. Aluminum is strong and easily worked and mast failures are rare except aboard hard-pressed racing boats. Its main advantage, however, is the material's light weight, which helps keep the boat's center of gravity low. Many replicas of older ships now carry aluminum spars that are dressed to look like either steel or wood.

In terms of industrial design, today's molded boat can be considered a great success. An extremely durable, strong and safe product, it costs far less than the equivalent vessel built in wood and has brought boating to a much larger group of owners than was ever contemplated in the days of the boatyard craftsman.

COMMUNICATING DIRECTION UNDERWAY

When you are *underway, grounding* a boat is just what it sounds like—making contact with the bottom. If you were *aground* you would not make any *headway, leeway* (away from the direction of the wind, or with the wind), or *sternway*—you would not have any way on at all. But according to the Rules of the Road, you would be "underway with no way on."

Once your anchor is *aweigh* (when you have *weighed* anchor), your anchor is broken out of the bottom and lifted clear. As your boat begins to make *steerageway* again—with enough speed through the water for the rudder to be effective—it would create a *wake.* Your wake would be *dead astern* and your destination, with any luck, *dead ahead.* Your wake would become a *wash* if you were careless about your speed and it threatened to erode or damage the shoreline.

Underway in a sea, the hull might begin to *pitch* (rock fore-and-aft), *roll* or *yaw*— swinging its centerline off course, usually as the stern is pushed around by a *following sea.* When a yaw gets out of hand, the boat may *broach to*, with the hull broadside. In sailboats, this may be dangerously exacerbated by a *spinnaker*, the balloonlike sail flown forward of the mast.

If the wind were to increase to Beaufort 8 or 9—measurements of wind strength according to the *Beaufort Wind Scale*

(Chapter 14)—you might decide to *heave-to* (retain a slight forward motion, just enough to allow control). In a sailboat you would have the steadying effect of your sail area, though you would certainly take at least one *reef* (sail reduction) if the wind were a "Force 8 or 9." A powerboat, in this situation, might be headed into the wind and speed reduced to a level that steerage against the waves could be maintained.

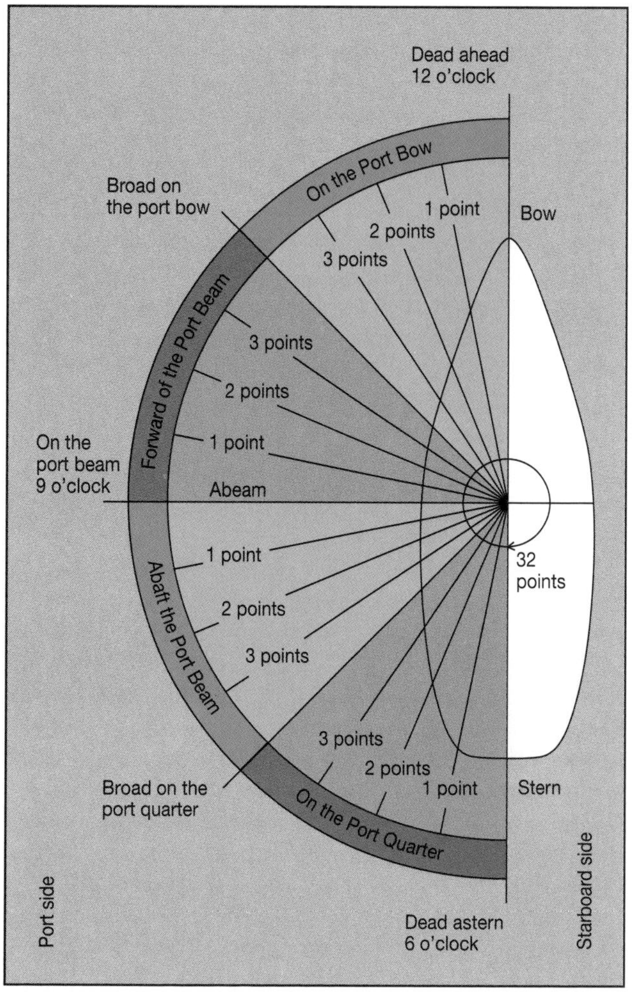

A *sea anchor* or *drogue* could be set to slow the boat by dragging through the water. A sea anchor, described in Chapter 11, is a cone of heavy canvas that acts somewhat like a parachute. In this situation you might begin to wonder about the quality of your *piloting*, and to ask yourself this question: Are you certain of your last *fix*, your last *position determination* from landmarks, or *aids to navigation*? Perhaps you have only a "DR track" (*dead reckoning* track) for the last several hours. That means you have been estimating your position, or dead reckoning, according to your speed and compass course. If you were on a *leeshore*, being carried toward land by the wind and unable to make headway, your attention would be fixed on the *depth sounder* and you would be wondering if you were in danger of running aground. You would be far more secure if you were under a *weather shore*, being protected from the gale and carried into deeper water.

If any charted landmarks or aids to navigation were visible, you would take a bearing. The sighted object might be *abeam* if it were 90 or 270 degrees from your course, or *broad on the bow* if it were midway between dead ahead and abeam. If it were between abeam and dead astern, it would be *broad on the quarter*. In each case, you would specify either the port or starboard side.

All of these *relative bearings* (that is related to your own course, rather than to true or magnetic north) can be made more precise by the use of a traditional 32 point system, shown at left. Using the point subdivisions, each point represents 11.25 degrees: A bearing might be "3 points abaft the port beam," which, for the practiced crew, is more useful than "over there, that way." However, an easier system relies on everyone's familiarity with a (non-digital) clock face. The same bearing might be expressed somewhat less precisely as "about 8 o'clock."

If you finally decided to call for help, you would probably call on Channel 16 on your *VHF* (very high frequency). Once in contact you would provide an accurate description of your position. Chapter 19 describes how to report a *relative position*, one in relation to a charted aid to navigation or landmark, or a *geographic position*, one related to the geographic coordinates of *longitude* and *latitude (page 40).*

Diagram labels: Dead ahead / 12 o'clock; Broad on the port bow; On the Port Bow; Bow; 1 point; 2 points; 3 points; Forward of the Port Beam; 3 points; 2 points; 1 point; On the port beam / 9 o'clock; Abeam; 1 point; 2 points; 3 points; Abaft the Port Beam; 3 points; 2 points; 1 point; On the Port Quarter; Broad on the port quarter; Stern; Starboard side; Port side; Dead astern / 6 o'clock; 32 points

In a traditional 32 point system, the circle on which your boat is centered is divided up into eighths, like a pie; each eighth is subdivided by 3 points. Each pie section has a name in the following pattern; on the (port or starboard) bow, forward of the (port or starboard) beam, abaft the (port or starboard) beam, on the (port or starboard) quarter.

DECKS, FITTINGS AND LINES

Deck styles have become fairly standardized. While you may see older sailboats with a slightly raised section at the aft end of the cabin, called a *doghouse*, most boats have a *trunk cabin* style— with no raised section. Some racing boats raise the level of the gunwale (or raise the freeboard) high enough that the deck can be uninterrupted by any *cabinhouse*, or *superstructure*, at all. These are called *flushdeck* designs. The deck might also be raised at the bow to provide more space below. This would be called a *raised deck* style.

Because the deck is an important structural part of the boat, its design is partly dictated by its strength. This is particularly the case when the mast is supported by the deck.

Fittings and equipment

The range of fittings and equipment that the novice boater must learn is perfectly illustrated by two modern boat types: on one hand, the high-powered sport runabout, and on the other, the high-powered racing sailboat.

The sport runabout is almost bereft of anything we might call nautical hardware. Its deck is a gleaming sweep of plastic with hardly any indication that it might ever be tied to a pier. If we look closely we can probably find a couple of cleats that would accept a mooring line or the loop of a *fender lanyard* to tie protective *fenders* (pneumatic cylindrical cushions) over the boat's side while waiting for a trailer ramp.

The high-powered sailboat, on the other hand, seems to have no other purpose than to carry hardware. Like the fittings section in a well-stocked *chandlery*—a marine supplies store— the racing dinghy (even boats of this sophistication are called by this diminutive) has an example of every variety of *block* and *camcleat*. Blocks are pulleys, and camcleats are toothed line pinchers.

The difference between the two is that, in the case of the sport boat, the engine is self-contained and normally hidden from view. The racing dinghy, by contrast, is a kind of wind engine entirely open to view. In both cases, the hardware is appropriate to the means of propulsion.

Making fast

Making fast, or securing, a rowboat to a wharf can be as simple as taking a *painter* ashore and looping it over a *bit*. A painter is a light line usually permanently fixed to a ring bolt near the bow of a tender and a bit is a wooden or metal fitting near the edge of a pier. A tender is a utility boat used for going ashore from a larger boat that has been *moored*, or kept at anchor. (A mooring refers to an anchorage with permanent ground tackle, with a pennant and buoy to which the boat is secured.) While the painter is adequate for making fast a tender, a boat only slightly larger and heavier begins to present a challenge even if you're only coming ashore for lunch or tying up for a few minutes.

Even a small *auxiliary* sailboat (one with a light engine, perhaps an outboard), or an outboard runabout, needs some well-made and well-placed hardware to secure it to a pier.

First, a substantial *deck cleat* must be *through-bolted*, with a *backing plate* under the deck. While a good quality casting, well installed, is adequate for making fast in a dock, you should not invest your confidence in a deck cleat when it becomes necessary to tow your boat. Larger and heavier boats are often fitted with a forward bit or samsonpost, a stout wooden or metal post with a horizontal *normanpin* around which a line can be hitched. The best of these are actually built through the deck and are *stepped*, or attached, directly to the keel, becoming an integral part of the boat's structure. If you think this is just tugboat talk, imagine the forces created when even a moderately heavy boat is jerked through steep waves under tow. You will read about towing in Chapter 11.

Rather than placing one cleat in the center at the stern, most builders place a cleat near each side. Space is often more restricted here and care must be taken to ensure that such a *sterncleat* has enough space around it to be useful. Additional cleats are often placed at the gunwale, about a third of the boat's length from the bow. These cleats are extremely useful for setting *spring lines* (also called "springs"), additional mooring lines that run from the forward part of the boat aft to a point on the pier or from the stern area (the quarter), forward. On a sailboat, in the absence of such deck cleats, springs can be made fast to the *chainplates*, the attachment points where *shrouds* (side wires holding up the mast) meet the deck or a stanchion base, though a cleat is always preferable. A winch can serve a similar purpose as a bit for making fast an aft spring.

Staying on deck

The deck cleat or bit is most useful when you can easily reach it; you must have something to hold onto and a *non-slip* surface to stand on. At the very least there should be a protective *toe rail* or a grab rail. (These also serve as two possible

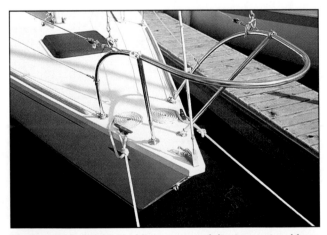

The foredeck should provide a secure pulpit, strong stanchions and lifelines, and a toe rail to brace against. Cleats or samsonpost must be strong enough for anchoring and for towing when necessary. The fittings on this racing sailboat have been chosen for their light weight, not their strength.

Used for pulling up the anchor rode, the windlass is available in manual, electric and hydraulic models in either a vertical or a horizontal design. The model shown is a vertical electric type.

attachment points for safety harnesses as discussed in Chapter 3.) A barrier at the edge of the deck aboard larger boats is a *bulwark* and it is usually topped by a *rail*. At the stern, the rail would be a *taffrail*.

If a deck is wider than your arm span, usually the case with boats more than about 25 feet (7.6 m) in length, *lifelines* should be fitted. Lifelines are wire ropes (often coated in white plastic) that run bow to stern, discussed in Chapter 3. Vertical posts that support the lifelines are *stanchions*, which are used as braces. Since occasionally a crew member is thrown against a stanchion, there is little point in making them of light tubular metal and screwing them into the deck. Instead, they should be heavy, bolted and braced, and capable of withstanding a forceful blow. Welded at the bow and stern of most sailboats and some powerboats are two types of stainless steel fence, called the *bow pulpit* and *stern rail*. These provide secure attachment points for lifelines, and are essential to crew safety when anchoring and making fast.

Making up lines

Wherever a mooring line runs over the edge of a deck, it should be protected by a *chock*. A chock provides a smooth surface for the line to rub against and a suitable *lead* to the cleat. On larger boats, chocks evolve into *hawse holes* through which you would lead a *hawser*, a very heavy mooring line or *anchor rode*. *Rodes*—anchor lines—are *stowed* in a *chain locker* and, when needed, are *broken out*. Anchoring is discussed in Chapter 12.

Chafe is a serious problem for mooring and anchor lines since boats are usually in motion, even made fast to a pier. Protective *chafing gear* is often fitted to mooring lines where they pass through a chock or over any obstruction. Chafing gear might consist of plastic hose split and bound to the line, or even heavy canvas wrapped around it. On traditional boats

with a great deal of rigging (gear used to support and adjust sails), *baggywrinkles*, looking like brushes made of flayed rope, might be fitted to the rigging to avoid chafing the sails.

A boat more than 30 or 35 feet (9.1 to 10.7 m) long, especially if frequently at anchor, is generally fitted with a special type of rotating-drum winch called a windlass to handle the heavy work of retrieving an anchor and long rode. A windlass is powered by an electric motor, hydraulically or by hand with a lever.

Essential to securing a boat is protection against damage from the pier or from other boats that might be *rafted*, or tied up, alongside. Fenders are rigged from the gunwale or lifelines on lanyards. Setting fenders properly is a skill well worth

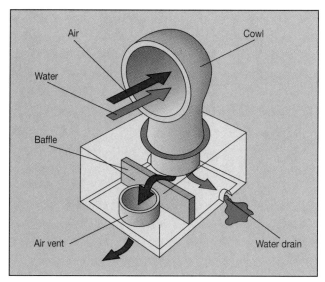

A Dorade vent is particularly useful for allowing air below to the main cabin and head, while blocking incoming spray.

acquiring, even where your boat is equipped with a *rubbing guard*, a vinyl and aluminum or wood and metal strip along the gunwale. Though they are bulky and difficult to stow, you always seem to need one more fender than you have aboard.

Other deck fittings

In addition to deck fittings used for making fast and for controlling the rigging on a sailboat, you will also encounter nautical ventilators and windows. Ventilation is a particular problem on a boat with small space and dampness. Air has to be let in and water kept out, and one of the best solutions is the *Dorade vent*. A Dorade has a cowl atop a two-part box— a box with a barrier in the middle. Air flows over the barrier and through the deck, but water is trapped and allowed to drain back out onto the deck. In rough weather, the cowl should be turned aft (away from the wind), or shut down.

Nautical windows are called *deadlights* when they cannot be opened, and *portlights* when they can. Larger portlights are just too much like windows to be called portlights—so we simply call them *windows*.

PROPULSION AND CONTROL

A propeller blade is curved and acts very much like other *foils* (curved surfaces, such as sails, keels, rudders and, of course, hydrofoils, that create forces by moving through fluids). Propeller blades divide a stream of water to create both lift and drag.

In order to create a useful force, or thrust, a propeller must have a slip angle. The blade's tip, traveling a larger circle, is moving through the water at a much higher relative speed than the blade's root—at the propeller hub—so a much smaller angle is needed to achieve the same forward motion. That's why a blade is twisted from its root, at the propeller *hub*, to its tip, creating the angle.

Propellers, often called simply "props," are usually classed by the number of blades, the direction of rotation, the diameter and the pitch. For example, a three-blade R 13" x 19" would turn clockwise (facing forward), would be 13 inches in diameter and would travel 19 inches forward in one rotation. Therefore, the pitch of the propeller is 19 inches. Of course, some of this distance is actually lost to slip.

Propeller efficiency

Just as sails have to be *trimmed* constantly because the *boat speed* and wind speed constantly change, a propeller would do a more efficient job if it could be trimmed for each speed that it is expected to travel—and for each level of horsepower it is expected to transmit to the water. In fact, variable-pitch propellers, such as the one shown opposite, will soon become widely available for use on standard inboard/outboard boats.

In general, where more horsepower is available per pound of boat, a propeller with more blade area and higher pitch will be appropriate. Since the blade tips, if driven too fast, will begin to *cavitate*, or create tiny, low-pressure bubbles in the water, there is a limit to the speed at which most props can be turned. Usually, if more horsepower needs to be applied, the diameter and blade area are increased and the *shaft speed* is reduced.

The *propeller shaft* is like a drive shaft in a car. This is where *reduction gears* are used to reduce the speed of the propeller shaft without reducing engine speed. Very light, fast boats with powerful engines may increase blade area and decrease diameter until the propeller actually lifts the transom of the boat. These are called *cleaver props*. A more extreme propeller type is designed to act at the surface of the water and is call a *surface piercing prop*.

Propwalk

Propellers must turn either *right-* or *left-handed*. The difference would be unimportant except that propeller blades act unevenly as they swing through a full turn. The blade at the bottom of the circle moves through deeper water at a higher pressure and creates more thrust and more transverse force than the blade at the top of the circle. The imbalance in transverse forces pushes the shaft slightly sideways producing *propwalk*—the tendency to move sideways, especially at low speeds and when maneuvering in reverse (when the propeller blades' curve is "backward" and is extremely inefficient).

Propwalk can be canceled out when two propellers are used on separate shafts and driven by two separate engines. Such *twin screw* installations are arranged so that the port prop turns counterclockwise and the starboard propeller turns clockwise. Twin screws are much easier to handle at low speed partly because they don't walk, but mainly because each prop's thrust can be varied independently to produce a push or pull on one side or the other. (Engines are also left-

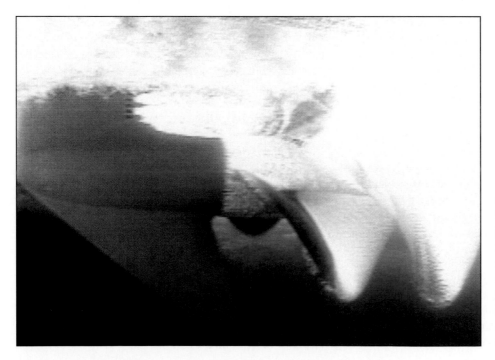

Propellers move through the water using much the same principle that a sail uses to move a sailboat—curved "foils" (the blades) create a pressure difference; a low pressure on the forward surface and a high pressure on the aft surface. As a result, propellers are less efficient in reverse.

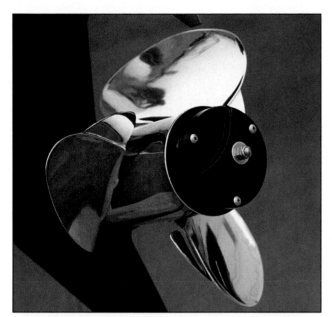

The recently introduced variable-pitch propeller answers the need for greater efficiency through a wide range of speeds.

and right-handed but the convention in naming them is opposite to the propeller convention. With engines, you assume that you are facing aft, not forward, when describing them as left or right.)

A more recent method of increasing the efficiency of fixed blade propellers is to mount two counter-rotating props one behind the other (with one shaft rotating inside the other). The props can be tuned to each other so that the aft one takes advantage of the flows created by the forward one, and the two balance each other so as to run in a straight line. This type of arrangement is shown on page 36.

At higher speeds, both the rudder and the propeller blades are acting with maximum efficiency; the forward thrust is much greater than the transverse thrust so the effect of prop-walk is not important. At low speeds, however, propwalk can be quite substantial.

Engine and drive types

Engines that are attached to the transom are *outboards*. These generally produce higher horsepower for their weight and are somewhat more convenient to fit and service, especially in the smaller range of horsepower. They present the propeller axis parallel to the surface (unlike props on inboard installations that angle the prop slightly downward), and allow easy adjustment of this *trim angle*.

Most medium-sized powerboats built today are equipped with an inboard/outboard engine. I/Os, as they are more commonly called, provide the dual advantage of an outboard propeller and an inboard engine. The outboard drive allows for an articulated, or steerable, propeller (just like an outboard), greatly simplifying steering control and mechanical installation, and allowing easy adjustment of the angle of propeller

thrust. The inboard engine can be larger. Since it is based on an automotive block, it also can be less expensive to produce than an outboard of similar horsepower.

An engine installed entirely inboard must drive its propeller through a *stuffing box* (or *shaft log*) that keeps the water out where the propeller shaft passes through the hull. A fresh-water boat would have its engine cooling water supplied from the lake through a *sea cock*, a heavy metal or plastic through-hull fitting of a type that is also used for other water supply and discharge. Sea cocks and their associated piping must be treated with respect as they can be all that stands between floating and sinking.

An inboard-outboard's "outdrive" or "lower unit" allows the use of a powerful inboard engine and a steerable and trimmable propeller shaft. Production efficiencies have made this configuration the standard for boats from 18 to 28 feet (5.5 to 17.7 m).

The layout planned for a boat's accommodation may require that an inboard be located in the extreme aft end of the hull rather than the more conventional position amidships. If this is the case, the power can be transmitted through *V-drives*—with the engines facing "backward." This adds a level of mechanical complexity.

The lift and drag of sails

Sails extract power from the wind by dividing a stream of air into two paths, shaping both paths into a curve, then allowing them to rejoin smoothly. The path that flows across the concave, or *windward*, side of the sail reaches a higher pressure than the flow on the opposite, convex, or *leeward* (cor-

The Duoprop makes practical use of an old concept—two props, on the same shaft, are better than one. Since each prop rotates in a different direction, each tuned to the other, horsepower can be transmitted to the water more efficiently. Greater speed and better steering control can result.

rectly pronounced "loow'rd") side. This variation in pressure can be used to propel the hull; this concept is explained in Chapter 10.

As sailcloth, rigging wire and metal masts have improved in strength, it has become possible to extend the height of sailboat *rigs* (spars, standing rigging—the gear used to support the sails— and sails) without increasing weight. Greater height allows either more sail area or the same area presented with a more efficient shape. Reduction in rigging weight, more stable hulls and better deck equipment have gradually made possible simpler sail plans.

The standard racing and cruising boat configuration now comprises two sails—a mainsail, attached to the mast, and a *headsail*, or *jib*. The area of the headsail is usually smaller than the area of the mainsail, though it is inherently more efficient, being free of the disturbing effect of the mast. This standard *sloop* configuration, shown on page 38, not only presents lots of sail area in relation to a fairly small amount of rigging; it also takes advantage of the extra power produced by an accelerated passage of air between the headsail and the main. This is called the *slot*, and racing sailors pay a good deal of attention to its adjustment.

Under the surface

While the sails present an airfoil to the wind, the keel of a sailboat performs a similar task as it moves through the water. Today's fin keel is also a lifting foil. When presented at a slight angle of attack, the fin develops lift, as well as drag.

Direction is controlled by a third foil, the rudder. A powerboat rudder (or rudders on a twin-engine boat) is placed in the stream of water pushed aft by the propellers. At speed, the powerboat rudder can easily produce a substantial side force so the area of the rudder can be quite small. The same rudder, operating at low speed, might be barely effective; operating in reverse, with no propeller thrust to divert, it may have no apparent effect at all. This is one of the reasons that maneuvering a powerboat at low speed, especially one with a single screw, is an art. Chapter 9 tells you more about what to expect and the techniques involved.

Sailboats have larger rudders than powerboats for two reasons: They operate at low speeds without the accelerated thrust of a propeller, and also carry some of the responsibility for *lateral resistance*—the tendency not to slide sideways.

Both sailboat and powerboat rudders may be *balanced*—they may have some of their area placed forward of their turning axis so that they can be adjusted with less pressure on the helm. Turned to present an angle of attack to the oncoming stream of water, the rudder creates lift that pulls the stern off course and spins the boat around an imaginary point called the *center of lateral resistance* located somewhere near the forward edge of the keel, or, on a powerboat hull, about one-third of the waterline length aft of the entry, in forward motion. Since every use of the rudder produces drag, racing sailors take care to *tune* their boats in such a way that less rudder is required.

Controlling the sails

The shape and position of the sails is controlled by *sheets*, lines attached to the aft, lower corners (*clews*) of each sail. The mainsheet is generally rigged as a *block and tackle*, providing a mechanical advantage to match the force of the sail. Headsail sheets are led from the sail to a block, or pulley, on deck and then to either of two sheet winches near the cockpit. *Halyards*, the lines that pull the sails up and hold them there, and other control lines are also led to winches, but they usually share a winch. While one line is being adjusted with the winch, the others are held fast by *linestoppers*, sometimes called *line clutches*, that use a cam-action pincher that can be opened with a lever. Some of the linestoppers can release a line a fraction of an inch at a time, enabling fine adjustment. Winches might be *self-tailing* winches, such as the one shown opposite, which self-secure their lines, and can be easily operated by one person.

Sheets primarily control the angle of the sail from the centerline of the boat, so further sail shape controls are needed. These include a *boomvang* to control tension on the trailing edge (the *leech*) of the mainsail by pulling down on the boom (which supports the foot of the mainsail), especially when the mainsail is away from the centerline of the boat. A line called a *cunningham*—named for its inventor—moves the "belly" or draft of the sail farther forward or aft according to the speed of the wind. Halyards, the lines that pull the sails up, can also be adjusted to control sail shape. A very light halyard might also be used to raise flags, small flags called *pennants* and *burgees*—then it would be a *signal halyard*. (A burgee is a triangular, rectangular or swallowtailed flag denoting club or squadron membership.) Refer to Chapter 26 for more information on flags, pennants and burgees.

When the top, or *head*, of the mainsail is at the top of the mast, it is at the *truck*, the collection of *sheaves* (pulleys) that carry the halyards.

More sophisticated racing sailboats also control the bend of their masts and the tension on their rigging wires while underway. Mast bend, induced by pulling on the *backstay* (the

A winch revolves in one direction and, with a few turns of the sheet on it, helps to trim the sails. A self-tailing winch, such as the one shown above, is useful in reducing the labor of dealing with sheets, enabling one person to do the work of two.

wire that runs from the top of the mast to the transom) flattens the mainsail shape. A tight backstay also flattens the shape of the headsail by pulling the *forestay* into a straighter line. Somewhat less control is exerted over the shrouds or sidestays, though these too can be adjusted underway on some boats.

Almost all shrouds can be easily adjusted when not underway. This is done with *turnbuckles*, which are tubular screws. Turnbuckles are attached to the chainplates with heavy, peg-like *clevis pins* and *cotter pins* that hold the clevis pins in place. Racing sailors make adjustments to the shrouds by changing the *fore-and-aft* angle of the *spreaders*, the near-horizontal struts over which the shrouds are led. Mast bend can also be changed on some boats by tensioning the *jumper stays*. These are intermediate stays that run from a point in the mid-height of the mast to the top over a set of smaller spreaders, called *diamond spreaders*. Finally, mast bend can be controlled by running backstays. Refer to Chapter 10 for detailed information on sail shape and how to adjust it.

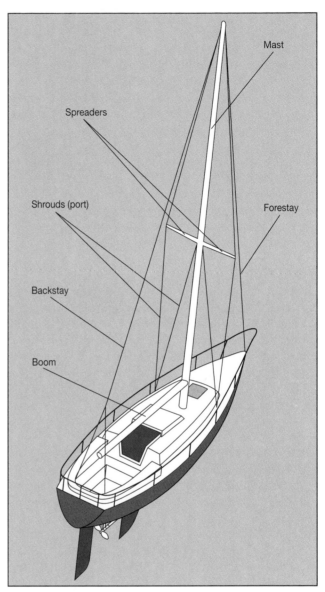

Standing rigging components support the mast under the tremendous strains placed on it by the sails. The sailboat pictured above has a split backstay, a common technique that allows adjustment with a simple bridle.

Additional sails

When the wind is behind, most sloops, cutters, ketches and yawls will fly additional *downwind* or *reaching* sails. The most familiar of these, because it is so large and colorful, is the spinnaker. A spinnaker is flown free of the mast and stays—it is attached at three points and is *set* out, ahead of the boat.

Spinnakers require a considerable amount of rigging and skill to fly. In addition to the halyard, two lines from the bottom corners of the spinnaker to the stern of the boat are called spinnaker sheets. These are actually both the same, but the one on the windward side of the boat is called the guy. Each time the boat is *jibed* (turned so as to change *tack*, or direction), the line that was the sheet becomes the guy and vice versa. The guy is rigged over the end of a horizontal spar called a spinnaker pole, which needs both a pole *uphaul* and a pole *downhaul* to control its position. Each time the boat is jibed, the spinnaker pole must be detached from the former guy and reattached to the new one. If all of this seems complicated to you, you're not alone. In fact this is the simplest of spinnaker rigs—there are many other complications as spinnakers increase in size.

There have been many successful methods for simplifying this kind of *offwind* sailing. Variations of near-spinnaker, usually with names like *Gennaker* or *DRS* (for drifter/reacher/spinnaker) are two of the most common. These are also large, rounded and flown free of the standing rigging, but they are shaped much more like a jib and are controlled with only one sheet at a time.

Shortening sail

When less sail area is required, the skipper will shorten sail first by changing to a smaller headsail—perhaps from a larger genoa to a smaller one, or from a genoa to a jib. Headsails are often numbered, with a "number one" being the largest and a "number three" the smallest working headsail. There might be a still smaller jib called a *storm jib*, made of very strong cloth and designed to provide balance more than drive.

If sail must be further reduced, the mainsail can be reefed (this is quite different from *furling*, which is a way of wrapping it up for storage). Most sloops have *jiffy reefing*—one or two horizontal rows of ties that allow the crew to lower the main halyard and gather in an area at the bottom of the sail. Some sloops have a convenient roller reefing arrangement.

Recently, sailmakers have been making *fully battened* mainsails. These have *battens* (stiffening slats) that extend the width of the sail rather than just a couple of feet from the leech.

While the sloop sail plan seems to have won the evolutionary contest to date for the general-purpose sailboat, there are other old and new sail plans that have specific strengths and appeals.

When the wind blows too strongly for comfort or safety, it is time to take a reef in your mainsail by tying the reef points (shown above) under the foot of the sail, as described in Chapter 10.

The sloop

The most popular sail plan is the *sloop*, which has one mast and two sails. The forward one is the *jib* or *headsail* and the aft one is the *mainsail*, also called the *main*. The jib is attached along its leading edge, or *luff*; the after edge is the *leech* and the bottom edge is the *foot*. The jib is attached to the *stay* with *hanks*, strong hooks that have spring-loaded closures. An alternative design uses a semi-flexible track or *foil* on the stay that accepts a *bolt rope* that is sewn along the sail's luff. Such tracks offer better air flow over the luff; they also make more efficient sailing possible.

When a sloop's jib is hoisted from the top of the mast, it is a *masthead sloop*. If it's hoisted from any lower point, it is a *fractional rig* (spanning a fraction of the mast), typically a *three-quarter* or a *seven-eighths rig*. Fractional rigs, with the forestay attached lower than the *backstay*, allow the bend of the mast to be easily controlled by altering the tension on the backstay—desirable on high-performance boats. Headsails can have many names, depending on their size, weight and shape. The smallest is a *storm jib*, followed by a *heavy weather jib* and a *working jib*. Genoas, reaching very far aft with a greater surface area than the main, also come in a number of sizes.

Sometimes the jib is small enough that it can be *tacked* (turning the boat so that the wind blows on the other side) without releasing one sheet and gathering the other. This rig arrangement, called *self-tending*, makes the boat much easier for one person to handle. Some self-tending jibs, called *club-footed jibs*, have a small boom attached to the foot.

The cutter

Similar to the sloop, the *cutter* has its mast closer to midships, leaving room for a larger foretriangle. Two headsails fill it. The forward sail is a *yankee*; the smaller one is called a *staysail*. In light airs the yankee can be replaced by a genoa.

The purpose of a cutter rig is twofold. The total sail area is divided into smaller sails that are more easily handled. When the going gets rough, the reduced canvas is closer to the mast, giving added safety in a seaway. This rig has been a longtime favorite of cruising sailors who prefer a one-mast rig.

The ketch and yawl

The *ketch* and *yawl* look alike. Both have a tall mainmast forward and a short *mizzen mast* aft that flies a *mizzen sail*. The distinction between a ketch and yawl is a common topic of debate among sailers. Traditionally, the governing rule is the location of the mizzen mast: If it is ahead of the rudder post, the boat is a ketch; however, if it's behind the rudder post, the boat is a yawl.

Both the ketch and the yawl may have either a masthead or a fractional rig forward of the main mast. Both may fly a large jiblike sail between the masts, called a *mizzen staysail*. Both are divided rigs, meaning the total sail area is divided into manageable sizes that can be easily handled by a small crew.

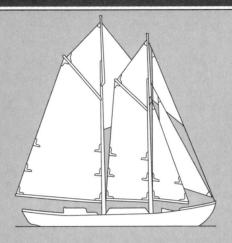

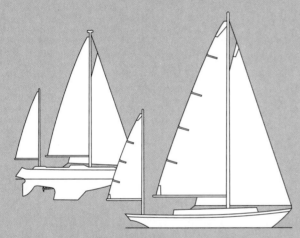

Because of the extra rigging and mast surface area exposed to the wind, or *windage*, these rigs are less effective on smaller yachts, where windage is relatively more important. The ketch and yawl rigs are popular among cruising sailors for long distances, and their mizzen masts are a practical location for mounting electronics.

The schooner

A *schooner* is a vessel with at least two masts (in the last century, some carried up to seven). The mainmast is aft and generally taller. The forward mast is called the mizzen and can have multiple headsails. The most common headsail combination includes—from the bow aft—the flying jib, the *yankee* and the *staysail*, although other names have been used for them at various times.

Schooners were originally workboats, mainly fishing vessels. Equipped with tall powerful rigs, they raced back home from the Grand Banks to get top dollar for their catch—the beginning of sailing races in the U.S. Schooners were originally gaff-rigged, with main and mizzen rectangular sails supported by a spar at their top edge. Often, above those sails, there flew a triangular sail or *topsail*. For extra power, a sail

called a *fisherman*, was set between the masts. These complex rigs required more deck hands than are standard today; the modern schooner rig is variable and may carry a *marconi* rig with triangular sails, a *loose footed* or boomless mizzen and sometimes only one headsail.

Schooners are most comfortable in steady tradewinds on long ocean passages. Although they don't go to windward as well as other rigs, they make up for it when the wind is on the beam, or aft of it.

The catboat

A boat with only one mast set forward and one sail is a *catboat*. Traditionally these were small, inshore boats (the lack of redundancy in the rig was an issue when rigs were less reliable). The catboat was a useful design for coastal fishermen because the hull was more accessible for catch or cargo and the single sail was easy to single-hand. However, the traditional catboat might not be as close-winded (able to sail close to the wind direction). Today's catboats have been developed on larger hulls that have more sophisticated controls.

Recent cat-rigged designs use *unstayed* masts (masts that have no standing rigging to hold them up, but are supported by the deck). With less windage and high, narrow profiles, they perform as well as sloop rigs and are used on all sorts of racing and cruising boats. These boats include fast, experimental types with sails very similar to those used on sailboards, with very bendy masts and wishbone booms. Some record-breaking boats even use two cat sails side-by-side. As to what these might be called—some future edition of *Chapman Piloting* will have to be consulted.

Knowing where you are, where you want to go and how to do it safely are the three fundamentals of navigation. Whether traveling at high speed on a small lake and avoiding underwater hazards, or crossing an ocean, you have a moral and legal responsibility to know how to navigate. Part of navigation is the technique of basic piloting and position determination. Much of this book, particularly Section 5, is devoted to those subjects.

While this responsibility weighs on every owner, it also brings great rewards: No doubt you will recognize the tremendous pleasure that can be taken from successfully piloting a small craft. Piloting and chartwork offer an intellectual challenge both in terms of rational calculation and the intuition of a practiced eye.

The basic elements of piloting are the *chart* (your nautical map), the compass and a *log* to measure speed. Usually you would also carry a depth sounder or its traditional predecessor, the *lead line*, from which Mark Twain took his name. ("Mark twain" was a measurement on the lead line used to navigate riverboats over Mississippi River sand bars.) A lead is dropped, or swung and dropped, on a light line marked with colored and textured ribbons. Sometimes tallow is applied to a cavity in the bottom of the cylindrical lead so that a bottom sample can be brought to the surface to determine how well an anchor might hold.

A *barometer* is a more familiar element and common aboard small yachts. The measure of atmospheric pressure, or the change in pressure, that it provides is a reliable indicator of changing weather. *Binoculars* have a special place

Although some boaters might describe a lead line as "old-fashioned," it is a handy backup to an electronic depth sounder, for an emergency such as checking depths all around a boat that is aground, and for determining the nature of the bottom.

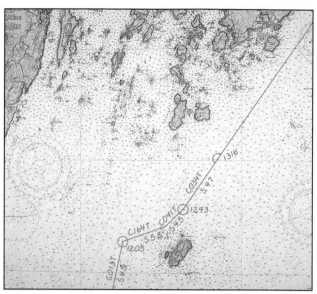

A careful skipper plots courses on a chart, and notes the time of significant events, especially course changes. Chapter 20 covers important procedures for determining position.

aboard a boat, of course, especially because they improve vision at night. By the way, "a pair of binoculars" is incorrect—"a binocular" refers to a pair of monoculars.

Charts and chartwork

The chart offers a wealth of information, all of it ready for interpretation by a skilled reader. Every chart is a representation of a water mass overlaid with a grid system. The lines of the grid are, of course, latitude and longitude. Lines of latitude are *parallels* because they are parallel to the equator. Lines of longitude are *meridians*—they cut across the parallels at 90°. The type of chart most often used for navigation shows latitude and longitude lines meeting at right angles, though there are charts that represent this grid in other ways. A position's latitude can be anywhere from 0° at the equator to 90° at the poles, either North or South. A position's longitude would be from 0° at the *prime meridian* (Greenwich, England) to 180°, either east or west.

A *mile* is assumed to be a nautical mile if you are at sea, while distances on inland waterways, including the Great Lakes, are commonly given in *statute miles*. The difference between the two is about 15 percent, the nautical mile being longer. This is not an arbitrary measure—a nautical mile is the distance between two points on the surface of the earth that, if connected to the center, would form an angle of one *minute*, or one-sixtieth of a degree. Another, and sufficiently accurate way to state this is that 60 nautical miles equals one degree of latitude. This means that the scale on the east and west sides of most charts, the latitude scale, can be used to measure nautical miles.

In waters where distances are measured in nautical miles, the measure of speed is the *knot*—one nautical mile per hour.

Keep in mind that you cannot travel "knots per hour" because a knot measures speed, not distance. Speeds on inland waters are often measured in (statute) miles per hour. Depths are measured in both feet and *fathoms* (1 fathom=6 feet) so it is important to confirm from the chart which unit the numbers represent. The metric system is also making its way into charts, as is explained in Chapter 18. Kilometers and meters are used to measure distance, and meters to measure depth.

True and magnetic bearings

A *course* is the direction a boat travels, and a *true course* is one that is referred to *true north*, or geographic north. *Magnetic north* is the direction a compass would point if it were not subject to any local interference and a *magnetic course* refers

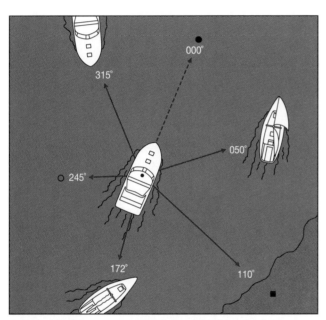

Relative bearings are measured as angles from dead ahead clockwise around the boat. Directions are always shown as three digits, using zeroes if necessary (050, not 50).

to magnetic north. *Variation* refers to the angular difference between magnetic north and true north at any particular point on the earth. It's important to know that variation is well named—it changes so much and so inconsistently that it must be checked on every chart and factored in to any calculation of direction that relies on a compass reading. *Deviation* is the error in a magnetic reading due to local influences such as the magnetic properties of metals in and around the boat, particularly within 2 or 3 feet of the compass. Deviation is devious—it changes with the boat's orientation and might even change from one season to another. The combination of variation and deviation is *compass error*.

Bearings are *plotted* on a chart to determine a position (called a fix) and a pilot begins to estimate the boat's present position—based on his most recent *fix*. Chapters 19 and 20 explain several ways to obtain a fix.

Aids to navigation are established by various government authorities to indicate safe and unsafe waters. *Buoys*, for example, are floating objects that mark a channel or any significant location; they may be lighted and may carry audible signals such as gongs and whistles. Buoys are painted according to a particular scheme *(Chapter 22)*. *Daybeacons* are fixed aids with a distinctive sign, mounted on pilings and following a color scheme similar to that used for buoys. *Lights* consist of lights mounted on fixed (not floating) objects and have characteristic color and on-off patterns. Lights range in size from tiny (a two-foot light on a *breakwater*) to huge (the familiar towering lighthouse). But they are all known as *lights*.

While this text deals with piloting, you might also become interested in *celestial navigation*, the determination of position by reference to the sun, moon, planets and stars. A *sextant* (a precision navigating instrument to measure angles) would be essential, as well as a *nautical almanac* and a set of *sight reduction tables*, along with an accurate *chronometer*.

Piloting and navigation are going through some revolutionary changes as you will read in Chapter 25. Electronic radio receivers and computers are making it possible to find positions very accurately by receiving signals from orbiting satellites and making automatic calculations based on the information in the signal. *Satnav*, an earlier version of this technology, is being replaced by a new system known as the *Global Positioning System (GPS)*. GPS receivers have readouts like the one shown below.

Such units—designed for boat owners—are convenient, accurate and, now, inexpensive. Like every technological development in navigation they will bring better information to more boaters more quickly—and they occasionally will fail unexpectedly. Careful study of the navigation chapters in this book will help you be aware when it happens.

The Global Positioning System has virtually replaced the older Transit satellites. GPS is now available in compact units, as shown above, which track several satellites. This instrument combines a GPS antenna, receiver and processor.

THE BOATING ENVIRONMENT

In the Pacific it's a *typhoon*, in the Atlantic, a *hurricane*, and in the Indian Ocean we call it a *cyclone*. Whether or not we feel the immediate effects of tropical storms *(Chapter 14)*, they affect our boating environment almost everywhere.

Water movement and sea states

Large undulations, generated by distant storms and unrelated to any local causes, are called *swells*. The surface of an ocean swell may be perfectly calm as it rolls almost undiminished across thousands of miles. It might also be textured as the wind creates pressure on the backs of tiny ripples in a *catspaw*, then gradually builds the ripples into *waves*. Each *crest* reaches higher above its *trough* as the wave travels faster and faster over a longer *fetch*, the distance the wave travels free of obstructions. As the wind increases, it tears at the wave tops, revealing *whitecaps* and throwing off *spume*. When this heavy *sea* encounters shallow water the energy it contains can no longer be absorbed by the circular water movement in each wave; the crests rise and *break*, while *surf* crashes ashore.

The same sea, meeting a *current*, explained in detail in Chapter 15, will rear up, creating a *rip*, sometimes amplified by the long funnel of an *inlet*. Over long fetches of shallow water strong winds may create waves of only moderate height, a chop, but viciously steep and short—even more dangerous than ocean waves of greater size.

Currents range from huge, persistent ocean currents, like the Gulf Stream and the California, to the strong but short-lived *undertow*, or *rip current*, of a beach where spent surf finds its way back into the ocean. The largest currents are part of the world's five *gyres*—giant circular oceanic currents. There are two gyres in the northern hemisphere. They both

Current is the horizontal flow of water, and a buoy's leaning often is an indication of the speed at which the water is moving. In coastal areas, currents result from changes in tidal levels.

travel in a clockwise direction, one circling the North Atlantic, the other the North Pacific. Three gyres in the southern hemisphere circle the South Atlantic, the South Pacific and the Indian Ocean in a counterclockwise direction.

Currents respond to the push of *prevailing winds*, to variations in density that are due to different levels of salinity, and to differences in temperature. While the gyres are surface currents, there are other equally important countervailing, deep currents.

Regular, intermittent currents that respond to the movement of the sun and the moon are called *tidal currents*. *Tides*, discussed in Chapter 15, are the actual rises and falls in local water level as tidal currents force masses of water against and away from the shore. Incoming tidal currents *flood*, then *ebb* as they retreat—more strongly as *spring tides* when the

Waves result from local wind action on the water surface, but may travel great distances as swells. They crest over and become breakers as they move into shallower waters. Dangerous waves form over bars such as this one off a Pacific Coast inlet.

Marinas provide a sheltered harbor for yachts and small boats. Piers extend into the water and finger piers project from them. Each boat's space is called a slip, or a well. A *Travel Lift (center)* is a self-propelled sling lift and a *gin* is a light crane, especially one used for unstepping masts. Powerboats less than about 25 feet are often stacked in dry storage *(background)* with a large forklift truck. In some marinas, they are retrieved and launched in time for each outing, then re-stacked.

moon and the sun are in *conjunction* and pulling in parallel directions, and more gently as *neap tides* that occur at the quarter moon.

Every current has a *set* by which we convey its direction, and a *drift*, meaning its speed. Since the speed of the tidal current and the level of the tide are so important to coastal navigation, governments publish *tide tables* and *tidal current tables*. These allow predictions based on measurements at reference stations.

When there is no tidal current drift we have a period of *slack*; when there is no rise or fall in the tide we have a *stand*. You may be surprised to learn that a stand seldom occurs during slack; Chapter 15 explains why.

Shaping the coast and shoreline

As currents flood and ebb, they sculpt the river and lake beds and the coastal shallows of the world's oceans. *Hazards to navigation* are created and made more hazardous as they shift. *Bars* form across river mouths despite our efforts to *dredge* clear channels. In an attempt to control the coastal environment near important harbors, we build breakwaters parallel to the shore to absorb the energy of incoming seas, and rigid-structure *groins*, built perpendicularly to the beach to limit erosion as sand is carried away by near-shore currents. *Riprap—large* chunks of concrete, for example—is sometimes laid down to limit the erosion of river banks and artificial as well as natural islands on which aids to navigation may be mounted.

Harbors and docks

Though most of us would say we have "stood on a dock," it's unlikely—the *dock* is the area of water in which a vessel lies when made fast. We were probably on a *wharf*, or a *quay* if parallel to the shore, a *pier* or *jetty* if not. (By the way "kay" is a good pronunciation of quay, though in salty company "key" is safer.) Away from a commercial harbor, in a yacht basin, or small craft harbor, you might make fast to a *finger pier*, leaving your boat in a *berth* or *slip*. In parts of Canada and the midwestern U. S., that slip would be a *well*. Any of these structures might be supported by heavy wooden or steel *piles* or *pilings* driven vertically into the harbor bottom. Two or three of these bound together become a *dolphin*. The layout of slips, quays and piers in a harbor defines a *fairway* leading to a channel and possibly to a *roadstead*, where vessels can safely anchor while waiting to make fast at a wharf.

If a yacht is *hauled out* for maintenance or winter storage, it might be hauled up the *ways* on a *marine railway*. These days it is more likely to be hauled from a slip by a *Travel Lift* (a brand name) and wheeled in its slings to a place in the boatyard where it will be supported by a cradle or blocked. Powerboats less than 25 feet (7.6 m) in length are often stacked, by a forklift truck, in *dry storage*. Any mast or other spar removed from the boat might be hauled with the help of a *gin*, a light crane or derrick. A crane might also be used for boats stored onshore, or *drysailed*—one of boating's most confusing misnomers as such boats are anything but dry when they are actually sailing.

2 OWNING A BOAT

Becoming a boat owner can be a complicated and exciting process. Often the search for the right boat is an enjoyable exercise in planning and daydreaming. But keeping the process on course takes some know-how and frequently the services of knowledgeable professionals.

This chapter will tell you the legal and financial details of boat purchase and ownership as well as the various ways that boaters organize and enjoy their own style of boating.

BOATING: A LIFELONG ACTIVITY

Boating is a sport, a pastime, a family activity, an obsession and a way of life. For some it is all of these at once; others spend their entire boating "career" following a single course.

Perhaps the luckiest boaters are those who have never had to introduce themselves as novices—those who grew up by the water, knocking around a boatyard, marina or yacht club. For them, the language of boating is learned unconsciously, the etiquette of boating is learned like table manners and the skills are just picked up along the way. *Chapman Piloting* can correct their few bad habits and offer a reliable reference.

For the rest of us, boating is learned through careful study and supervised practice. Classes in boating are offered by various organizations in North America, principally the U.S. Power Squadrons and the Canadian Power and Sail Squadrons. Other organizations, such as the United States Coast Guard, its Auxiliary and the American Red Cross, teach skills specific to sailing or to powerboating; often these are offered at minimal cost to both children and adults. You will find information on boating classes and other organizations later in this chapter and in Chapter 27.

Like any community of enthusiasts, boaters respect skills and experience—regardless of whether they are evident

Still actively involved in the creation of *Chapman Piloting*, Elbert S. (Mack) Maloney, shown here at age 73 with his wife, Florine, continues to enjoy blue-water cruising on his trawler.

among dinghy sailors or owners of megayachts. In fact, some avid boaters do not actually own a boat, but are still involved in organizing, teaching courses, crewing on race boats and promoting the sport.

Boating as a family, or later in life

There are few activities that offer as much variety as boating, or that are as well suited to both children and adults. Even sailboat racing, for example—at least at club levels—can be enjoyed by children of only nine or ten years of age.

Since boat ownership is often expensive, the decision to purchase a boat is usually one made by both partners of a couple, and is intended to include the children. In fact, the involvement of families has effected changes in boat design—resulting in boats with more useful living space that are safer to operate. The participation of women in particular has created women's competitions in sailing and powerboat racing, though both sports are among the few sports in which women also compete against men.

However, competition is far from the minds of most boaters. By and large, boating is a social activity that encourages a mixture of ages and skill levels. Most boating is a weekend pursuit consisting of day cruising or a short hop to a familiar anchorage. Holiday cruises reach farther afield, but even when several days are available, owners of larger boats tend to cruise within less than a hundred miles of home port.

As boat owners get older, many still get plenty of time on the water. The quality of today's equipment and rigs makes sailboats less of a physical challenge and generally easier to handle. As for powerboating, it can be enjoyed as long as the skipper remains alert. The skipper of the winning 1992 America's Cup Yacht, Buddy Melges, was 62 years old at the time of the race.

Those who learn boating skills in childhood will be competent, confident boaters by their teenage years.

BUYING A BOAT

J.P. Morgan's immortal advice on boat buying is always worth noting: If you have to ask "How much?", you can't afford it. Architect of a vast American financial and industrial empire, Morgan built *Columbia*, which defeated *Shamrock* in the America's Cup in 1899 and 1901. His memorable words hold a hard kernel of truth. Quite apart from an individual's credit worthiness, many boat owners will confess that if the boat is to be truly a "pleasure boat" it should not add to the owner's day-to-day financial burden. They can argue convincingly that the best boat to own is the one that you can afford from ready cash—an unlikely scenario for many people.

It should also be pointed out that boats almost never appreciate in value. The mistaken notion that boat ownership could be an inflation hedge, or that by trading in and "buying up" one could make real gains in value, has led to a number of retail and manufacturing business failures in the U.S. and Canada. Occasionally these failures place a number of boats on the used market at extremely low prices.

Remember, however, that while these prices may be apparent bargains in relation to the price of a new boat, they may not be so attractive when future sales values are considered.

Shopping for the right boat

Evaluating a craft at a boat show is not easy—certain qualities are apparent, others may be concealed. Nevertheless, boat shows provide most buyers with the best opportunities to make comparative decisions. Even if you are convinced that you will be buying a used boat, take advantage of boat shows, and go with a plan.

If your schedule permits, choose a day when attendance is low so that you have time to examine a number of boats in detail. Take along a notebook. While you will spend most of your time looking at boats, don't forget that much of your experience with a particular boat will depend on the quality of the engines and equipment it carries. Those manufacturers may also be represented at the show, so visit them too. If you

BOAT BUYER'S CHECKLIST

The questions that follow are general and apply mainly to cruising boats with inboard engines. As you plan your first trip to the boatyard or showroom, use these considerations to develop a more complete list that serves your particular boating needs.

✓ Is the boat suitable? It seems obvious, but maybe not. Have you decided how many people will usually be aboard, and for how long? Will you be preparing meals for them? How often? Are you looking at more boat than you need, or have time to maintain or the finances to properly equip?

✓ Even if you feel comfortable about the reputation of the builder and the quality of the boat you are buying at a particular price, will the next buyer feel the same way? The real cost of your purchase is the cost of the capital you borrow to cover the gap between buying and selling prices. Are you buying a boat with a predictable resale value, or are you prepared to pay for an unusual boat?

✓ Do all the crew members feel secure on the foredeck—even in dark, rough conditions? Is the cockpit comfortable? On a sailboat, would the cockpit be comfortable at an extreme angle of heel, or would you slide off the seats? Could someone fall against the lifelines and stay on board?

✓ If you suddenly needed five fenders and 60 feet of towing line, where would they be stowed? Could you put on life jackets without going below? Is there a second exit from the cabin in case the companionway is blocked? Would you have access to fire extinguishers if the engine or the galley were burning?

✓ Is the hull fair, or are there distortions or hard spots that indicate stress? Are there any indications that bulkheads, keel or deck are not rigid and rigidly attached to the hull?

✓ Are the rudder stock and the propeller shafts straight? Remember that any boat more than a season old has probably grounded. Consider the area in which the boat has been used; could it have hit rocks?

✓ Has the boat been used in salt water or fresh water? What effect has any salt water exposure had on cooling and engine parts, particularly on an outboard drive? Are "stainless steel" fittings of a high-quality alloy, or will they rust?

✓ Are there "plastered over" repairs to gel-coat damage? Was the damage caused by stress crazing (tiny, hairline cracks resulting from stress at corners and edges) above the waterline, or by osmosis blistering below the waterline?

✓ On a wooden hull, are there any soft spots? Prod with an awl or a knife wherever planks join the stem, keel, sternpost or frames—wherever ventilation or drainage might not be good. Look for rust spots made by fastenings.

✓ Can the builder demonstrate that fuel and electrical systems, ventilation and mechanical installations (including the head) meet Coast Guard recommendations and state or provincial laws? Does a surveyor agree?

✓ How does the cabin smell? (New boats will smell of styrene and vinyl.) Can you smell any mildew?

come away from the boat show overwhelmed with specifications and feeling a strong, irrational attachment to a particular boat, don't worry; you're not alone. Remember that your opinions may change quickly as you gain some experience on the water, so don't plan to make a purchase decision based solely on a boat show encounter. Many manufacturers are willing to set up various forms of "test drive." Sailboat dealers, in particular, make use of sailing school settings as a way to offer some on-the-water experience, and many simply keep a boat in the water for that purpose.

Think seriously about what kind of boating you will actually want to do. For example, if you live in a cold climate, you should make a hard-nosed assessment of the number of weekends you expect to be able to spend on the water. Will your teenage children really want to spend all those weekends with you, and will the whole family really want to stay on board overnight? Is it more likely that you will do a good long day cruise once every weekend?

Although younger children can be more manageable on board (with some important cautions that are dealt with in Chapter 3), typically they are not interested in more than an hour of one activity. If the favorite beach or ice cream stand is more than an hour's cruising time away, you may be looking at the wrong boat.

Will your family enjoy some casual sailboat racing at a yacht club or a marina? If everyone is enthusiastic, choose a boat that offers a manageable challenge. This is where the apparent complexity and high labor content of sailing is actually the point: Everyone has an important role.

On the other hand, if you're never certain how many hands will be on deck, you may want to look seriously at a boat that can be operated single-handed. In a powerboat this might mean a boat that has twin engines and easy access fore and aft so that docking is predictable and leisurely, even with no one else aboard. In sailing boats, this could mean a cat-rigged cruising boat that would allow you to enjoy both single- and

✓ Are routine engine chores going to be easy or awkward? Try reaching the filler caps, intakes and filters. Can fuel tanks be opened up for cleaning? Is there any evidence that fuel or oil has leaked into the bilge? If you are considering a used boat, could you have a fuel sample analyzed?

✓ Are maintenance logs, manuals and warranty cards available for major items of equipment?

✓ Are sea cocks used for through-hull inlets and outlets rather than plumber's gate valves? Are hoses wire-reinforced? Are connections made with two stainless steel hose clamps? Are these and other through-hull installations, such as the log and depth sounder, protected with emergency plugs?

✓ Has wiring (and/or rewiring) been neatly done? Is the insulation at connections supple, or brittle from overheating?

✓ Is the boat properly grounded in case of a lightning strike (Chapter 23)? Are major metallic masses (engine, keel, etc.) connected to a common ground plate with a high-current connector?

✓ Has electrolysis protection (Chapter 23) been installed— sacrificial zincs and polarity indicators for shore power?

✓ Does the safety equipment meet legal requirements, as defined in Chapter 3? Do all fire extinguishers aboard have up-to-date inspections?

✓ Is the seller willing to have every piece of electronic equipment checked for failures?

✓ Check the boat's compass for damage: Do you spot any bubbles or scratches?

✓ Keep in mind that all boats leak. Is the bilge water stagnant (suggesting a slow leak) or fresh (suggesting a fast leak)? Is the electrical pump protected with filters and a reliable float? What equipment is available for bailing the bilge if there were an electrical failure?

✓ Do the decks or windows leak? Can you spray a hose at them and still have dry bedding below?

✓ Are you sufficiently interested in a used boat to pay a marine surveyor for a "survey of condition"? Can you or the seller afford to act on the surveyor's recommendations? If you are interested in a new boat, is the builder willing to permit a survey?

✓ Have you spoken to owners of similar boats at local clubs and marinas? (Remember, however, that owners of the same make of boat may not be inclined to criticize.)

✓ Have you checked into the availability of storage at marinas and boatyards, and do you know the associated costs?

✓ Have you prepared a budget? This may help you resist the temptation to buy a larger boat than you need or can afford.

✓ Have you taken advantage of the United States Coast Guard's free boat information service? Call 1-800-368-5647. Deficiencies for many boat makes and models have been recorded and are available to prospective buyers.

short-handed cruising, and even to entertain a group of non-sailing friends in comfort and safety.

Boaters who will be using their boats primarily for overnight cruising will place much greater demands on the interior living space. It's important to recognize that the addition of a six-foot berth does not mean the capacity to go cruising with one more person. Berths are easy and inexpensive to build and they look convincing at boat shows, so there tend to be more berths than the number of people the boat can comfortably support on a longer cruise. Remember that accommodating one additional person for more than an overnight trip requires more capacity for stowage of clothing and bedding, more capacity for galley stores, more water capacity and washing facility. All of this implies greater hull displacement and horsepower (or sail area) and probably much more cost per foot of boat length. In the extreme case, sailboats designed for offshore cruising (out of the sight of land) or powerboats built for long-range voyages are much different boats than boats for weekend use.

Your boating budget

In general, new boaters tend to overestimate their needs and their budget. In fact, it is not uncommon to find boaters of long experience who have sold boats and replaced them with smaller ones. It is also true that when many people recount their fondest boating memories there's often a strong element of "making do." The gradual climb from small to large yachts is not inevitable or even necessarily desirable; in some cases it is simply not affordable.

Estimating your boat purchasing power is too complex and personal an issue to deal with here, though information about boat financing can be found on page 49. However, you should know that the overall purchase cost or monthly carrying cost of the boat itself should not consume your boating budget all on its own. You will incur many costs as "overhead"—fixed expenses such as moorage and storage fees, insurance and fuel are fairly obvious. But other costs are contingent and significant. For example, few new boats are sufficiently well equipped with ground tackle, fenders, mooring lines and safety equipment. These are not extras; they are fundamental to safe operation and many are legal requirements, as explained in Chapter 3.

This, for some people, is a strong argument for the choice of a used boat rather than a new one. As a rule, you may be happier in the long run with a boat that is a notch below your size limit, but can be equipped and maintained—and extensively used—without continual second thoughts about your financial liability. It will also require less maintenance, less attention and will provide, for most families, a lot more fun.

Buying used

Boats experience fundamental deterioration at a very slow rate. In fact, strongly built fiberglass hulls may never completely disintegrate, although engines and other equipment experience various rates of corrosion that lower the worth of a used boat. In general—with cautious choice and a willingness to re-equip—an owner can realize tremendous value in a used boat. A 25-year-old boat in active use is not at all uncommon and, among well-cared-for wooden yachts, there are many examples of 50-year-old models still being cruised, raced and enjoyed.

Properly surveyed—examined by a professional prior to a purchase—a used boat is a known quantity with predictable performance and predictable maintenance costs. Very often it is better equipped than a new boat—not only in terms of the amount of equipment but also in terms of the reliability of the items that actually figure into the price. In some circumstances, the seller can provide a valuable

Used boats are often listed in boating magazines, newspapers, at some new-boat sales offices and with boat brokers. Before deciding to buy a used craft, become familiar with the model that you are considering.

service to the new owner by passing on important information and advice about his former boat. Beware of boats that were used for racing; these can be severely stressed beyond feasible reconstruction.

Competitive classes

Anyone who is interested in boating as a sport may find that the choice of boat is very simple—you buy the boat that is locally accepted as a class racing boat.

In sailing, this may mean that a racing class is the popular choice and, even though it might not completely meet your other requirements as a boat, the competitive and social aspects of membership in its class are far more important. Such sailboat classes often involve whole families and even generations, and offer tremendous opportunities for recreation and friendship.

Similarly, powerboat racing is organized so as to allow participation at all financial levels and also to ensure a high degree of professionalism and safety in competition. But racing is not the only form of competition. Powerboat owners also test their piloting skills in challenging "predicted log" contests that are designed on somewhat the same principle as automobile rallies.

Financing the purchase

Since the majority of us will have to seek financing when we buy a boat, it is wise to consider boats from our banker's point of view. In recent years, banks have become eager to lend money for boat purchases in a similar fashion to automobile loans despite some difficulties peculiar to boating. Although banks are usually confident of the value of any particular automobile, they sometimes can find the valuation of a boat to be problematic.

First, the used boat market does not have the size and stability of the used car market, or the consistent separation of wholesale from retail pricing. Second, it is usually more difficult to establish who really owns a boat and whether he has paid all of his bills.

As is true of the automotive market, there are regularly published pricing reports. One of the most widely used, and more reliable, is the *BUC Used Boat Price Guide*. The "BUC Book" is actually three volumes covering a range of years from the early part of the century to the current year. BUC publishes the used boat guide three times each year and also publishes a *New Boat Price Guide* annually.

Using pricing data in the BUC guides, and in other pricing guides, requires careful interpretation. Typically it would be dealers, brokers, banks, surveyors and tax assessors who would use the data, but the "BUC Books" are available to anyone from the publisher *(Appendices)*, or in many libraries.

Though, for obvious practical reasons, the data is not based on all boat sales, many years of collection and analysis have produced a reliable pricing guide, especially for boats

Before seeking the expertise of a boat broker, check the broker's reputation by consulting a marine insurance agency, a well-known marine surveyor or the Yacht Architect and Broker's Association.

in the larger sizes. As is the case with all such statistical data, interpretation must be made for regional variation and for boat condition and the "BUC Books" offer specific advice in the preface as to how this interpretation should be made.

BUC also provides a valuation service used by individuals selling or buying a particular boat. Once "market value" has been established, the lender and borrower can negotiate their down payment and interest rates as well as the appropriate collateral because the lender is confident that he knows how much the boat is worth.

The next obstacle is the establishment of clear title and non-encumbrances—liens, mortgages, etc. In most cases this too is more difficult in the boat market than in the automobile market. The exception is in transactions involving boats which are federally documented (in Canada, "Registered"), but this is by far the minority *(page 54)*.

The net result of this is that boat loans require a greater down payment on the borrower's part and often additional collateral in the form of a home mortgage. The bank may require a valuation survey (which may differ in extent and quality from a "condition survey" conducted solely for the benefit of the prospective buyer). Typically, a marine mortgage carries with it the whole range of rights and obligations that accompany any property mortgage including provisions for power of sale and priority of claims.

Using a broker

In such a climate of legal complexity, many buyers and sellers seek the help of a broker. The brokerage business is not a profession in the legal sense. While there are brokerage associations that endorse brokers and mediate claims, brokers tend to do business according to local custom. Their fees vary, and the range of service that they provide can vary a great deal.

Usually a broker will make an agreement with a seller. The agreement will specify several aspects of the relationship, such as those listed below.

- The time period during which the broker works on the seller's behalf to the exclusion of other brokers. (There are also non-exclusive agreements, described on page 50.)
- A time period following the "exclusive" period during which the seller might be liable for commission payment if a deal is struck with a party who was introduced by the broker.
- The percentage of the sale price that will be charged as the broker's fee—commonly 10 percent, but it varies.
- Evidence and warrant that the seller really does own the boat and that there is no other financial or material interest claimed by other parties.
- A description of what the boat is and what equipment it will carry when it is sold.
- A warranty that the boat is insured for the purpose of showing it to a buyer.
- Assurance that the broker and buyer will have access to the property on which the boat is stored.

Once this agreement is signed, the seller and the broker have entered into a contract and the broker begins to advertise and show the boat. When the buyer and seller arrive at an agreeable price and terms, with the salesmanlike intervention of the broker, then an agreement to purchase is drawn up based on a fairly standardized document.

An important aspect of this agreement to purchase is that a future closing date is specified. In the intervening time, the buyer can investigate title, search for state-registered (or provincially registered) bills of sale or chattel mortgages or any other claims that may exist on the boat. The buyer must be assured that no sales taxes are owed on previous transactions and that, if the boat was built outside of the country, customs and excise taxes have been paid in full. If any of these taxes or duties has not been paid, the naive buyer can suddenly find that he or she is the "owner" of a repossessed or seized boat.

Some brokers will agree to list a boat non-exclusively. This may be an appropriate choice where a boat will be advertised on a broker's network and where cooperating brokers have specific agreements between themselves as to who is paid commission fees and under what circumstances. However, an agreement to list non-exclusively with two or more competing brokers can become problematic.

In a local market, where buyers will consult anyone who claims to represent a specific boat, it becomes very difficult to determine who contributed commissionable service to the sale. The seller may end up paying for the confusion.

Verification of title

With regard to such searches of title, there is an important difference between a boat that is registered by state (or licensed by province) and one that is documented or registered. In the latter case, bills of sale, mortgages and other "instruments of title" are registered with the federal government and are easily accessible. In the case of a licensed boat, such a search might have to be conducted state to state and may be expensive and inconclusive.

Using a surveyor

There are usually very persuasive reasons for commissioning a marine survey. As much as a buyer may feel confident in assessing a boat's condition, he or she seldom has the experience that a yacht, or marine, surveyor can accumulate in a few years of practice. Like brokers, surveyors work outside of the legal definition of a profession, but do maintain associations that limit membership to qualified peers.

A good marine surveyor will point out that there is only one type of survey that is ultimately valuable to the prospective buyer—a complete condition survey. It can be expensive and, since the purchase may not go through, it can be speculative. Typically, the surveyor will earn his fee simply by reporting repairs that should be undertaken at the seller's expense. In that case, the surveyor works on the buyer's behalf and

Generally a survey is conducted when the boat is out of the water. The marine surveyor gives the person who commissions the survey an extensive report on all structural elements of the boat, including suggestions regarding needed repairs.

reports to him or her. Although the seller may also commission a condition survey (or an "insurance survey"), this is the seller's survey and its value to a buyer might be questioned.

Insurance companies and banks are also eager to have a surveyor comment on the boat that they may be insuring or claiming as loan collateral. The surveyor's ability to determine value for insurance or lending purposes is widely accepted in the business, albeit sometimes naively.

In any case, the report the surveyor makes to an insurance company or bank is of limited value to a buyer and should not be relied upon as a condition survey. Obviously the value of a survey report deteriorates rapidly with time and the phrase "recent survey available" may carry an element of wishful thinking.

Buying new

The purchase of a new boat is often less complicated with regard to transference of title and, in general, more assurance can be given as to warranties and obligations.

However, some interesting complications can arise. For example, a new boat is often purchased during the winter and held on the dealer's property for commissioning in the spring. Should the business fail in the meantime, does the buyer have a clear and enforceable claim to a boat which may have become entangled in the claims of various lenders to the failed business? Are all component parts, such as engines hauled out for service, clearly part of the purchase? If a custom boat is being built and has been partially paid for, who owns it if the business declares bankruptcy?

Each of these questions may have slightly different answers depending on the state or provincial jurisdiction. A buyer need not be alarmed about such slight possibilities, but he or she should be aware of them.

THE PAPERWORK OF BOAT OWNERSHIP

Since paperwork always has its own national characteristics, we will treat American owners separately from Canadian owners, looking first at the procedures required in the U.S.

The Federal Boat Safety Act of 1971 (often referred to as FBSA/71) is the principal legislation affecting pleasure boat owners. It establishes safety standards for boats and equipment, provides for state numbering systems and allows financial assistance to states for boating safety programs.

There are some basic definitions required to understand the act. For example, "vessel" means any watercraft excluding seaplanes, while "boat" means non-commercial, leased, rented and chartered boats and small passenger vessels carrying fewer than six people. Some parts of the act pertain only to boats; others, such as numbering, pertain to a broader category—in this case, any boat or vessel that is not documented by the federal government. (Documentation is covered in more detail on page 54.)

While boat numbers are usually administered by the states, the system is nationally uniform. (Alaska, for example, continues to have its boats registered by the Coast Guard.)

All vessels must be numbered whether they are used on waters subject to federal jurisdiction or on the high seas—if they are owned in the United States and are equipped with any propulsion machinery, regardless of horsepower. Some exceptions apply, notably documented vessels, but even here, some states require registration and may collect fees such as sales tax and user fees. Some states may exempt racing craft and some may include non-powered boats.

The state that numbers the boat is the one in which the boat is most used—not necessarily the one in which the owner lives or the one where it is stored or which it visits.

Certificate of number

The paper issued is known as a Certificate of Number and must be on board whenever the boat is in use, ready for presentation. Three years is the maximum period of issue, but states may choose to set shorter periods. Each number has two parts: a two-letter identification of the state and a further combination of letters and numbers to identify the boat. (The state symbol does not necessarily match the two-letter symbol used by the Postal Service.)

Even if a dinghy or tender has its own propulsion, a state may exempt it from numbering if it is "used as a tender for direct transportation between that vessel and the shore, and no other purpose." Even then, it must carry the parent boat's number, followed by a space or hyphen and the number 1.

A dinghy used with a vessel not having a number, such as a documented boat, must be registered and have its own number, as for any other boat, if it is propelled by a motor of any horsepower. The act also provides for the style and legibility of the numbers: not less than 3 inches high, not outlined, no script or obliques, and one contrasting color.

The number must be displayed at the forward half of the boat on both sides. (In some states, a validation sticker is required to confirm payment of current fees in that state.) Boats with a heavy flare may show the numbers best if they are placed aft of the bow.

Inflatables can be marked with flexible rubber numbers. Specifications for display are designed to ensure legibility.

A common misconception is that numbers must be right at the bow of a boat. The legal requirement is that they must be on the forward half of a vessel, and actually they should be far enough aft from the stem to ensure ease of readability.

When a boat is transferred to another state, the old number must be removed, and a new one obtained.

Refer to the Appendices for addresses of authorities to whom application must be made for a Certificate of Number. When a boat remains in the state after a sale, the same number is reassigned to the new owner. The act also allows states to deny a number if state and local taxes have not been paid. Although a period of grace is recognized for boats that are changing states of principal use, boats can also visit other states and, according to state rules, have their number recognized "temporarily."

When a boat is sold, destroyed or abandoned or is in a new state of principal use for more than 60 to 90 days, depending on the state, a report must be made to the issuing office within 15 days. The Certificate of Number is considered invalid and must be surrendered. Theft and recovery of a boat must also be reported. If the owner changes address, that too must be reported within 15 days.

The FBSA/71 also provides for Operator's Safety Certificates for the operators of numbered vessels, but since

Correct	Incorrect
ME 456 R **ME-456-R**	**ME456R** *ME 456 R* *ME 456 R*

Correct style and relative spacing of registration numbers is shown at left. Letters and numbers without spacing, and use of italics or script characters (*right*), is incorrect.

the Coast Guard has not issued pertinent regulations, little use has been made of the provision, except by some states to regulate young operators.

Accident reports

When an accident occurs, a report must be made if there is more than $500 in damages or if there has been serious personal injury or loss of life. The reporting time is one day in the case of death, two days in the case of an injury or disappearance of the vessel; otherwise, it is 10 days. Most states require that the report be made to state authorities. If the state has no such requirement, the report must be made to the USCG. Most states pattern their report form after the USCG form (CG-3865). Commercial vessels must use a different form.

While information relating to boat numbering is part of the public record, accident reports are not, and their content cannot be used in a civil suit.

Federal recreational vessel fees

In late 1992, the U.S. Department of Transportation announced changes to the Recreational Vessel Fee (RVF) law requiring the purchase of RVF decals for certain boats. Plans include repealing the RVF program on October 1, 1994, using the following phase-out schedule:

■ Retroactive to Oct. 1, 1992, the threshold for recreational vessels required to pay the Recreational Vessel Fee is raised to vessels more than 21 feet in length. "A" decals, which were required for vessels 21 feet or less, are no longer required.
■ Effective Oct. 1, 1993, the threshold is raised to recreational vessels that are at least 37 feet in length. As of that date, "B" decals, currently required for vessels over 21 feet but less than 37 feet, will no longer be required.
■ Effective Oct. 1, 1994, the RVF program is terminated. "C" decals, previously required on vessels at least 37 feet but less than 40 feet in length, and "D" decals applicable to recreational vessels 40 feet and over, will no longer be required.

No changes have been proposed for recreational vessels already exempt from RVF requirements, or to the waters where RVF requirements apply. Fees for RVF decals ($35.00 for "B" decals, etc.) remain unchanged. Boaters who purchased RVF decals on or after Oct. 1, 1992, and are no longer required to display them, will receive a refund for the full decal value upon application to the USCG. For more information, call the USCG Boating Safety Hotline toll-free number (1-800-368-5647).

Regatta regulation

The USCG usually regulates regattas, but in some cases passes responsibility to the states. Where the USCG is the authority, you must submit an application to the District Commander at least 30 days in advance. Approval is often followed by special local regulations and issued with the *Notice to Mariners* series *(Appendices)*. There may be penalties for violations.

PAPERWORK FOR THE CANADIAN OWNER

Vessels owned by Canadian citizens (which can also mean a Canadian corporation) must be registered. But pleasure boats under 20 register tons (a fairly complex measure of a vessel's cargo-carrying capacity) are exempt, as are ships under 15 register tons that are used only on the lakes, rivers or coasts of Canada. Vessels that are not registered, the vast majority of small pleasure craft, may be licensed. Registration is, therefore, an option for pleasure yachts.

If a vessel is foreign-built, it may be registered only by consent of the Minister of Transport, but consent is normally granted on application for vessels less than 20 tons.

The chief officer of customs at any approved port is a "registrar of British ships," who keeps a register book containing identity particulars of ships registered in that "port of registry."

Before being registered, a Canadian vessel must be surveyed by a surveyor approved by the Minister of Transport. The surveyor measures the vessel's tonnage and describes the vessel then submits the survey to the registrar. Every registered vessel must be named and the name approved to ensure that each name is unique. The vessel's name is marked on each side of the bow and the name and port of registry are marked on the stern. In addition, the ship's official number and a number denoting the register tonnage are carved on its main deck

beam. The Minister of Transport normally exempts small pleasure vessels from the requirement to have a scale of feet indicating draft marked on each the stem and sternpost.

An application for registration is made along with a declaration of ownership giving information regarding the citizenship of the owner, the time and place the vessel was built, the name of the master, the number of shares in the vessel, etc. A builder's certificate and a bill of sale must also be presented to the registrar. The registrar then presents a Certificate of Registry which must be carried on the vessel.

Licensed boats

Small craft, those less than 20 register tons, are usually licensed instead of registered. Every boat with more than 10 hp must be licensed. While the license is evidence of ownership, it should not be relied upon as proof of ownership.

When ownership is transferred, the seller is required to sign and deliver the transfer form that is printed on the reverse of the license. He must also advise the customs house from which the license was issued as to the new owner's name and address. The buyer then sends the transfer form or a separate application to the issuing customs house, which then issues the new owner a license with the original vessel number.

COMMERCIAL OPERATION, CHARTERING AND CUSTOMS

While the federal government will allow an unlicensed operator to carry freight commercially on a vessel less than 65 feet, to carry passengers for hire, a license is required for an operator of any boat.

The amateur boater may assume that his activities are in no sense commercial and that the guests aboard his boat are not passengers. But there are some common circumstances in which authorities would disagree.

Who is a passenger?

First, we might look at who is *not* a passenger. The owner or his or her representative is not, nor are the operator of the boat, paid members of the crew who have not paid or contributed for their passage and, as you might expect, any guest on a boat being used for pleasure who has not contributed any consideration for his or her passage.

But this last category—guests—is troublesome. A boat owner should have a clear understanding of the circumstances under which his guests might legally be passengers. Some are clearer than others.

The controversy for recreational boaters has centered on whether food and drinks or sharing gas expenses for an outing constitute "consideration," i.e. payment in exchange for the trip. Generally, any skipper receiving payment is required to have a USCG operator's license to ensure proper training and public safety. (The lowest level USCG license allows up to six passengers, the so-called "six-pack" license.)

Since the current law never defined the term "consideration," the USCG has been left to struggle with interpreting each situation on a case-by-case basis. Enforcement has been sporadic and often inconsistent. As a result, boat owners have been confused. The vague wording in federal law has made it difficult for the Coast Guard to know when an outing is an unlicensed charter disguised as a trip by "friends," or when a trip is a recreational outing with no commercial purpose. When guests are deemed passengers, the owner must be a licensed operator under USCG regulation. This matter is currently under study, and the rules may soon change. The focus is on simplification and easing the situation regarding guests who contribute minor items of food and drink.

License for six or fewer passengers

According to the present legislation, vessels of any size, while carrying not more than six passengers must be under the charge of a licensed operator. This license is now called "Operator of Uninspected Passenger Vessel" (OUPV). These are issued for inland, Great Lakes and near-coast waters.

Licenses are issued by the Officer in Charge, Marine Inspection, U.S. Coast Guard at Regional Examination Centers. Traveling Examination Teams may visit other ports to administer examinations for groups of applicants. Much of the processing of applications and renewals can be handled by mail.

An applicant for an OUPV must be 18 and fluent in English (Spanish may be substituted in Puerto Rico), and must be free of drug-law convictions. Each applicant is fingerprinted and must be a citizen (exceptions can be made for applicants to operate non-documented vessels). There are some limited licenses, but in general an applicant must have 12 months' experience, three months of which must be within the last three years. At least three months of his or her experience must be coastal if the application is for coastal operation. Three other people must recommend the applicant, and he must show evidence of first-aid training plus a currently valid certificate in cardiopulmonary resuscitation (CPR).

Physical fitness must be in evidence and a USCG physical examination form must be signed. Visual acuity and color vision are checked, but waivers can be requested.

Applying for an OUPV license

Each applicant must pass a written examination. The subject will be related to the waters concerned and may include chart reading and piloting, magnetic compass principles and use, tide and tidal current calculations, vessel handling, fire fighting and other emergencies, first aid, rules and regulations, pollution rules and sanitation laws, radio communications and "any other subject considered necessary to establish the applicant's proficiency." There are specific rules regarding re-examination on failure.

The OUPV license is valid for five years. As of the press date of this edition, the U.S. Coast Guard is in the process of establishing fees for these and other licenses. Information on OUPV license fees may be obtained by contacting any USCG Regional Examination Center.

Boat operators at camps, yacht clubs, marinas and educational organizations may have a Limited Operator or Uninspected Passenger Vessel license. They would require three months' experience and evidence of completion of an approved course such as those offered by the U.S. Power Squadrons or Coast Guard Auxiliary. A limited exam, appropriate to the local waters, is administered.

Licenses for more than six passengers

Operators of small passenger vessels, carrying more than six passengers, require a license as a "Master of Steam or Motor Vessel of Not More Than 100 Gross Tons." Licenses are issued for specific types of waters, such as inland, Great Lakes or near-coastal. Two years' experience is required. The terms of this and other licenses, and the requirements and procedures for renewal can be obtained from the USCG.

Drug testing

The USCG has established mandatory drug testing programs. All licensed crew members are subject to the program if they are required to be on board. Unlicensed crew members are subject to testing if involved in the vessel's operation.

The actual test may be required under any one of the following conditions: pre-employment, reasonable cause, after a serious marine accident, whenever a physical examination is requested (a renewal for example) or randomly. While the program focuses on commercial mariners, it does include self-employed mariners and recreational boaters who hold a license, even if they do not use it for employment.

Chartering

Many boaters choose to charter, rather than own a boat. This often makes good economic sense, especially if your boating time is limited to vacation weeks. Also, you may have thoroughly explored the cruising grounds accessible in your own boat and want to venture farther.

Your charter can be either "crewed" or bareboat. In a crewed charter, the owner furnishes a captain and often a mate and cook, who retain all responsibility for the operation of the boat. Bareboat charters, on the other hand, appeal to those who want to handle the boat themselves, without paid crew. Such charters may or may not include provisions and stores. Before the voyage, a charter agreement is signed and usually a deposit made.

Chartering your own boat

Some owners choose to have their boats "earn their keep" as charter boats. Although this can be done directly by the owner, most charter through an agent or broker.

If you charter directly, your charter agreement should be examined by your lawyer. (And your tax situation should be examined by your accountant.) Using an agent or broker means that you are freed of much of the paperwork and liability. Your relationship to the broker need not be exclusive.

Before making even the first move toward chartering, check your marine insurance policy. Most likely, it prohibits chartering, but the restriction might be removed with a higher premium. You may also want to increase your liability insurance. If you are going to offer crewed charters, you will be carrying passengers for hire. In U.S. and Canadian waters this will require the appropriate license, as described on page 53. Keep in mind that bareboats with more than 12 passengers must pass an inspection and that a U.S. documented vessel must be operated by a U.S. citizen.

Although these guidelines are up to date as this edition goes to press, keep in mind that the federal statute governing chartering may soon be amended. Before making plans to charter your boat, check with federal officials.

International voyages

Whenever boats cross international boundaries, certain customs regulations must be obeyed. The procedure has been simplified for recreational boats so as not to interfere with a pleasure cruise, but severe penalties still apply when the rules are not observed.

The terms "clearing" and "entering" are commonly used in connection with a vessel's voyage between ports of two nations. Clearing means obtaining permission to sail by presenting the ship's papers to a customs official. Entering is when an owner "enters" his vessel by having the ship's papers accepted by an authority. A vessel might be required to clear from a home port and enter on arrival at a foreign port. Travelers should check with their local Health Department or travel agency for inoculations or vaccinations required before visiting specific countries.

A U.S.-licensed yacht or a documented yacht used solely for pleasure boating can leave the United States without clearing. Similarly, such a boat is not required to make formal entry (unless it is engaged in trade, or is violating customs or navigation laws or has visited any other vessel more than 3 miles off the coast). However, the craft must make a report to the proper authority to cover such matters as the importation of items purchased out of the country.

Reporting your arrival in the U.S.

There are four separate legal aspects of entering the United States and each involves its own government agency. Offices of Customs, Immigration, Public Health Service, and Animal and Plant Quarantine must all be reported to if they exist in the port of entry.

Every vessel coming into the United States must choose a port where these regulations can be met. The "Q" signal flag

DOCUMENTED VESSELS

Boats that are not numbered may be documented at the federal level. Documentation is only possible for boats of at least 5 net tons. (Net tonnage is a measure of a vessel's cargo-carrying capacity—its gross tonnage, or entire enclosed volume, less the total of non-cargo-carrying volumes such as engine compartments. A yacht of 5 net tons is typically about 30 feet in length.) Documented boats must also be owned by a citizen of the United States or a partnership, all of whose members are U.S. citizens, or by a corporation which meets specific requirements as to the nationality of its ownership. The captain and officers, but not the crew, of a documented vessel must be U.S. citizens.

A Certificate of Documentation (form CG-1270) is issued for all types of vessels. This basic form is then endorsed for the authorized use of the vessel—yachts receiving the "Pleasure Vessel License." Such a license has two advantages. First, it allows the legal authority to fly the national ensign (national flag); second, it permits the recording of bills of sale, mortgages and other instruments of title with the federal officials. This gives additional security to the buyer or mortgagee and facilitates financing and transfer of title. Documentation is particularly useful when cruising foreign waters.

A simplified method of measurement is allowed for boats used exclusively for pleasure. Three dimensions—the length, breadth and depth of the hull (not of the keel)—are multiplied and divided by 100. Net tonnage is assumed to be 0.9 times the (plain yellow, rectangular) should be hoisted 12 miles off-shore, and only one person—the captain—may go ashore for the sole purpose of telephoning or notifying the authorities. The crew and guests must remain on board until permission has been granted to land. Nothing should be removed from the boat until the authorities have given their approval.

All boats must report to Immigration on return to a U.S. port. Alien passengers must be reported; a heavy penalty or fine may be imposed for failure to detain passengers or crew.

In many U.S. ports a simplified service has been established where a single official will represent all the authorities and bring all the necessary forms. In some areas, all that is needed is a telephone call to a local or toll-free telephone number. Whatever the requirements, they must be obeyed.

The United States Customs Service now levies an annual "Processing Fee" on boats of 30 feet or more. Most boaters pay the $25 fee in advance and get a numbered sticker to be placed on their boat.

Entering Canada

U.S. boats cruising to Canada may secure a Cruising Permit with the right of free entry and clearance from May 1 until October 31. This permit is issued at no charge by the Canadian Customs authority at the Canadian port where the vessel first enters the country. It must be surrendered to United States Customs when leaving Canadian waters. If the boat does not leave Canadian waters, it is free to visit other Canadian ports until the permit is surrendered or expires. Even if you have a cruising permit, you must report at any port where a customs official is located.

A Canadian boater with a craft of less than 5 tons is allowed to enter the border waters of the United States for a one-day outing without applying for admission at a U.S. port of entry. A Canadian Border Landing Card is available without advance application; this is good for repeated day-long visits until the end of the boating season. It is only good for border waters, however; trips farther south require normal official entry procedures.

Environmental regulations

Increasingly extensive regulations dealing with waste, garbage and oil-contaminated bilge water apply to pleasure boats in both the United States and Canada. In general, cruising boats must respect the regulations in each other's waters. Specific information on meeting these requirements is contained in Chapter 16.

---

gross for sailboats and 0.8 times the gross for powerboats. Owners of unusual boats can submit explanatory sketches with their applications.

Applications for Optional Simplified Measurement must be directed to the Commandant (G-MVI-5/SM) at United States Coast Guard Headquarters, 2100 Second Street S.W., Washington, DC 20593-0001. The applications must state the owner's name and address; the vessel's name and rig, overall length, and breadth and depth, as well as the builder's name, and the vessel's model, serial number and official number if previously documented. If the vessel is new, information about its construction must be submitted on a Builder's Certification (form CG-1261).

Owners of pleasure boats have the option of submitting a formal measurement made by the American Bureau of Shipping. For commercial vessels, this more detailed measurement is required. Once the boat is measured, the owner must submit an Application for Documentation (form CG-1258). When the application is received, an "official number" will be assigned to the vessel and the owner will be notified. The owner must then have the vessel properly marked, with the number, as prescribed by law, and then must submit evidence of this action on form CG-1322.

Special requirements for evidence of a chain of ownership may apply to a vessel that was documented at one time and whose documentation has been dropped. The fee for initial documentation is $100. However, smaller fees apply for surrender or replacement when, for example, the vessel's owners change.

Marking a documented boat

The USCG prescribes how a documented recreational vessel must be marked. The Official Number must be marked in a permanent manner on a structural part of the hull. The name and hailing port, along with the state, must be clearly marked together on some exterior part of the hull, usually the transom.

Every year, the Certificate of Documentation must be renewed. Form CG-1280 is submitted at the home port before the last day of the month in which the certificate expires. There is no fee. A renewal sticker form (CG-1280-A) is mailed back to the owner for placement on the certificate.

Surrender of documentation

Certain circumstances require the surrender of the Certificate of Documentation. These include a change in ownership, a change in the tonnage, a change in name or home port and several other changes that affect the vessel's identification or ownership.

Vessels which engage in activities not authorized by their documentation, for example pleasure boats that engage in business by direct or indirect charging of fees, may be forfeited and the owner severely penalized. Documentation does not exempt a vessel from compliance with other state laws or regulations.

JOINING THE BOATING COMMUNITY

Volunteer organizations are active in almost every aspect of boating. They range in size and influence—from local sailboat racing committees to the national organization of the United States Power Squadrons (USPS) in the U.S. and its corresponding organization, the Canadian Power and Sail Squadrons (CPSS) in Canada.

The United States Power Squadrons is a non-government organization, self-supporting and dedicated to boating safety through education. Many sailboat owners are members, though the Squadrons were originally powerboat-oriented.

The USPS has been in operation since 1912 when it originated in the Boston Yacht Club in response to the new popularity of powerboating and the need for formal education. In 1914, Charles F. Chapman, after whom this book is named, attended a meeting at the New York Yacht Club that resulted in the formation of the "United States Power Squadrons."

Both the USPS and the CPSS have conducted thousands of courses in boating and piloting. Such courses are available in almost every major city in North America. More information about the USPS and the CPSS is found in Chapter 27.

Boating clubs

Many boat owners are members of clubs that provide varying degrees of moorage and storage services and other recreational services. They range from ultra-exclusive to small and friendly, with the vast majority in the latter category.

Clubs are often organized around a program of sailboat racing and cruising, though most have large powerboat memberships as well. Given the volunteer and sporting character of clubs, new members are usually welcomed whenever they show a strong interest in boating as a sport. In addition, many clubs conduct inexpensive learn-to-sail programs for the children of members and non-members as well as summer evening courses for adults. Most clubs eagerly recruit members from these sailing classes. Within most regions of North America, clubs have formed umbrella racing associations for the conduct of amateur sailing regattas for various classes and types of boats. To promote traveling, many clubs allow for guest privilege exchange with other clubs.

Class racing association

Operating along with such regional associations are sailboat class associations. These are volunteer groups that administer racing for a particular "class" sailboat. Class or "one-design" racing is based on the principle that boats should be limited in their differences so as to provide competition in which the skills of their crews, rather than the designs (and therefore the cost) of the boats is the deciding factor. Some one-design classes, such as Star and Dragon, for example, have long, colorful histories that go as far back as the early 1920s. Today, they are institutions on the North American racing scene.

Among these sailing class associations are those whose boats have been chosen by the International Olympic Committee for Olympic competition. These have a particular responsibility and work closely with the United States Sailing Association and the United States Olympic Team.

In addition, the United States Sailing Association administers racing rules, protests and appeals and takes every opportunity to bring sailing to a wider population. In Canada,

Regattas at the regional level are usually conducted with a high degree of professionalism, though the competition is generally sociable and welcoming of new sailing enthusiasts.

The American Power Boat Association grants a seal of approval each year to nearly 400 events run by member clubs, service groups and some local tourism bureaus. To help ensure high standards for the running of a regatta, only approved APBA officials handle refereeing, scoring, timing and inspection duties.

similar functions are performed at the national level by the Canadian Yachting Association, and more locally by provincial sailing and sports organizations.

Powerboat racing

Powerboat racing in the United States is organized on a professional and semiprofessional basis by the American Power Boat Association (APBA) in addition to many other associations that have responsibilities for particular types and sizes of powerboat. The APBA administers safety standards for competitors and racers.

Cruising associations

Even solitary long-distance cruising sailors and powerboaters are often members of associations. By and large these are devoted to providing cruising information and additional charts and to preserving cruising grounds from urban and industrial incursion. They also provide information and encouragement to would-be voyagers by publishing accounts of their members' experiences. They can also provide sources for material, repairs and insurance policies at a group rate.

Rescue teams

There has been a long tradition in North America of volunteer maritime rescue organizations. Often these are very small groups that maintain a rescue boat in one specific port and offer their abilities without regard to payment, and with little regard to danger to themselves. They may also conduct local safety demonstrations and cooperate with the Coast Guard in search and rescue efforts.

Both the U.S. and Canadian Coast Guards maintain Auxiliaries made up of volunteers who contribute time and expertise aboard small Coast Guard patrol and rescue boats. Chapter 27 gives more information on these organizations.

WRITING AN OPERATOR'S MANUAL

During your years as a boat owner, there will be many times when having the correct information immediately at hand will offer one or more advantages: It may save money on repair bills, or save a weekend of good weather for boating rather than repairs. It may even save a life.

As a new owner, be diligent about collecting and compiling manuals for every major piece of equipment aboard the boat. Make sure, too, that you have addresses and phone numbers for all of the suppliers and service companies that you might have to contact while cruising away from your home port.

In addition to various published owner's manuals, start writing and compiling your own. Not only is the information valuable, but the process of writing will force you to investigate and think through each system and potential problem related to your boat. Make sure that the information is accessible in your absence so that your crew or service people will not have to waste time wondering how to proceed.

Trace each system and draw neat, simple diagrams that will be useful in dark, wet and worrisome conditions. Consider placing numbered tags on some connections and switches, and be sure to make clear reference to them in your manual.

Diagram the correct position of lifting slings or boatyard blocks. Make notes on the size and specifications of your boat's halyards, other running rigging or high-wear parts so that replacements can be ordered easily by phone before a cruise or regatta. Also make sure you know your propeller specifications before leaving your home waters. (At one time or another, you may be forced to order one before you can lift the boat to remove the damaged propeller.)

Note the locations of spare parts, such as cotter pins, that may be needed in a hurry.

Racing skippers often keep notes on ideal settings for sail trim and other controls. You may not need to go quite that far, but some information about performance—both under power and sail—is useful on long cruises for speed prediction and control of fuel usage. (This information is also recorded in a navigation log.)

Keep all notes on durable paper and protect them from water; use pens with non-soluble (or indelible) ink. Note that photographs are often useful documents (especially a photograph of the mast truck when halyards are tangled or lost, or pictures of valuables, which simplify insurance claims for theft or damage).

When it is time to sell your boat, use your operator's manual as a sales tool. No buyer can fail to be impressed with a clear and complete document.

SAFETY FIRST

3 THE SAFE BOAT

Practically anyone who can start an engine or hoist a sail can climb aboard a boat and head out onto the water. For the well-being of everyone aboard, however, there is more to boating than that. Boating begins with safety.

Although every chapter in this book covers some aspect of safe boating, this chapter gives you the basics—how to meet legal requirements and other safety needs, and guidelines for choosing and maintaining equipment. Refer to page 74 for safety tips that even experienced boaters should review periodically. You will also be directed to other parts of the book for further reading.

For skippers and crew members alike, a safe boating course is essential. Such courses are offered in most areas, as discussed in Chapter 27.

SAFETY AWARENESS ON BOARD

Defining the roles aboard

As the skipper of a boat, you are responsible for the vessel, for the safety of those aboard and for others in boats nearby—swimmers, water-skiers and anyone else who may be affected by your boat's course or its wake. This applies to all sizes of boats, on all waters and at all times. One of the challenges is accepting the responsibility without letting it detract from your enjoyment of boating.

To be an effective skipper, you must know yourself, your abilities and your limitations. You must know your job so well that you perform all tasks confidently, without having to think about the details involved. Equally important is a knowledge of your crew and your boat, and what you can reasonably expect of them in an emergency.

Good communication is key to a safe and enjoyable outing on the water, and it is essential to ensure that everyone aboard agrees to the safety rules you define for your boat. Before you leave the dock, make sure that other members of the crew know what is expected of them; they should also be acquainted with the location and proper use of all essential equipment aboard.

Remember that a boat traveling through the water can cause injury just as easily as a car moving on the highway. As skipper, you must be able to concentrate; distractions such as loud music or rowdy behavior by passengers can easily divert you from your important tasks. Maintain a safety consciousness at all times: If you establish your authority as the leader and delegate with tact, each outing or voyage is likely to be safe and fun.

Even the most experienced skipper will admit to being fooled at times by unexpected events such as changing wind or current. "Plan ahead" is one of the best pieces of advice in boating. When guests aboard have little or no boating experience, take them on a tour of the boat, pointing out danger areas such as the boom or a sheet under load. On the water,

Apart from the skipper, one other crew member should be fully capable of recovering a person who falls overboard, or of returning to port should the skipper be incapacitated.

dangerous situations can develop with amazing speed, so vigilance and foresight are important—both outside and inside the boat. Devote your full attention to your boating tasks; have an answer to every threat, and a plan to take you out of every danger. Spend time assessing the types of crises with which you might have to deal, assemble the appropriate tools and equipment, and practice the procedures best suited to solving the crisis before it becomes a disaster.

Safety in the water

For many people, the boating experience includes swimming. You can best ensure that water activities are as safe as possible by enrolling in a water safety training class, and by following the safety guidelines below.

- Swim at supervised swimming areas, and only in daylight.
- Know your personal limits; avoid overextending yourself.
- Always swim with at least two other people, never alone.
- Before diving, make sure the water is deep enough and hazard-free. Enter the water the first time with your feet first.
- When tired or overheated, stay out of the water.
- Rely on your swimming ability for support, not on inflatable plastic toys or air mattresses.
- At all times, non-swimmers should wear personal flotation devices (PFDs, available in various types, *pages 64 and 65*).
- Prohibit dunking and pushing, which may be dangerous.

While on board the boat, if a crew member inadvertently falls into the water, don't jump in. Use a reaching, throwing or floating assist such as a paddle, cushion, life ring (preferably a Type IV PFD) or a rescue line with a float attached. Crew overboard procedures are covered in Chapter 4.

Respecting U.S. federal requirements

Your primary safety system is your boat itself—in good repair and operable condition, and outfitted with the proper safety equipment. Although needs depend on the type of boat you use and the nature of the boating that you do, the regulations on operation and U.S. Coast Guard-approved safety equipment are mandatory for daysailers, powerboats and bluewater cruisers alike. It is your legal responsibility to carry the required equipment listed on page 62, to keep that equipment in proper working order and to operate your boat in a safe manner. In addition, boats longer than 39 feet are obliged by law to carry a copy of the *Navigation Rules (Chapter 6)* when operating in inland waters.

Satisfying Canadian requirements

In Canada, minimum required safety equipment is approved by the Canadian Department of Transport (DOT), and varies with the length of the boat. As of the print date of the 61st edition of *Chapman Piloting*, proposed revisions to the Canadian regulations were not yet approved. For the most recent Canadian Coast Guard (CCG) information on safe boating and required safety equipment in Canada, call the CCG toll-free number: 1-800-267-6687.

U.S. COAST GUARD MINIMUM REQUIRED SAFETY EQUIPMENT

Equipment	Class A Less than 16 feet (4.9 m)	Class 1 16 feet to less than 26 feet (4.9-7.9 m)	Class 2 26 feet to less than 40 feet (7.9-12.2 m)	Class 3 40 feet to not more than 65 feet (12.2-19.8 m)
Personal flotation devices* (see also pages 61, 63 and 64)	One Type I, II, III, IV or V** device for each person (also applies to canoes and kayaks of any length).	One Type I, II, III or V** PFD for each person on board or being towed on water skis, etc., plus one Type IV*** PFD available to be thrown.	One Type I, II, III or V** PFD for each person on board or being towed on water skis, etc. plus one Type IV available to be thrown.	
Fire extinguishers* (see also pages 69-90) **When no fixed fire extinguishing system is installed in machinery space(s)**	At least one B-I type approved hand-portable fire extinguisher. Not required on outboard motorboats less than 26 feet (7.9 m) in length and not carrying passengers for hire if the construction of such motorboats will not permit the entrapment of flammable gases or vapors.		At least two B-I type approved hand-portable fire extinguishers, or at least one B-II type approved hand-portable fire extinguisher.	At least three B-I type approved hand-portable extinguishers, or at least one B-I type plus one B-II type approved hand-portable extinguisher.
When fixed fire extinguishing system is installed in machinery space(s)	None		At least one B-I type approved hand-portable fire extinguisher.	At least two B-I type approved hand-portable fire extinguishers, or at least one B-II approved unit.
Ventilation (see also pages 76-79)	Boat operator is responsible for keeping the ventilation systems in operating condition, making sure openings are free of obstructions, ducts are not blocked or torn, blowers are operating properly and worn out components are replaced with equivalent equipment.			
Whistle or other sound signaling device (see also page 71)	Boats up to 39.4 feet (12 m): any device capable of making an "efficient sound signal."			Boats 39.4 to 65.7 feet (12-20 m): device meeting technical specifications of Inland Rules Annex III, audible ½ mile.
Bell	None required if boat equipped with device capable of making an "efficient sound signal at intervals of not more than 2 minutes."			Boats 39.4 to 65.7 feet (12-20 m): bell producing a sound pressure level not less than 110 dB at one meter.
Backfire flame arrester (also called flame arrester, see also page 73)	Every gasoline engine installed in a motorboat after April 25, 1940, except outboard motors, must be equipped with an acceptable means of backfire flame control.			
Visual distress signals (see also page 71)	All vessels used on coastal waters, the Great Lakes, territorial seas and those waters connected directly to them, up to a point where a body of water is less than two miles wide, must be equipped with visual distress signals. Vessels owned in the U.S. operating on the high seas must be equipped with visual distress signals. The following vessels are not required to carry day signals, but must carry night signals when operating from sunset to sunrise: ■ Recreational boats less than 16 feet (4.9 m) in length. ■ Boats participating in organized events such as races, regattas or marine parades. ■ Open sailboats less than 26 feet (7.9 m) in length not equipped with propulsion machinery. ■ Manually propelled boats.			
Navigation lights	Must comply with International or Inland Navigation Rules (Chapter 6).			

* Must be USCG-approved
** Type V must be worn to qualify as required safety equipment
*** Type IV not required for canoes or kayaks greater than 16 feet in length

In addition to the federal equipment carriage requirements for recreational vessels (*above*), the owner/operator may also be required to comply with additional regulations specific to the state in which the vessel is operated.

LIFESAVING EQUIPMENT

Any time anyone goes boating, there's a chance of falling overboard. A personal flotation device—a lifesaving device commonly called a PFD, or life jacket—is designed to help keep your head above water and assist you in maintaining a position that permits proper breathing.

PFDs are among the most essential safety equipment that any boater can own. Most importantly, the PFDs aboard your boat must be used. The fact is, 90 percent of deaths in boating result from drowning, and 80 percent of those drowning victims were not wearing a personal flotation device. (In fact, four of every five people killed in boating accidents in general were not wearing PFDs.) Many of these deaths were avoidable. An average adult needs additional buoyancy (the force,

Horseshoe buoys, popular particularly on ocean cruising and racing sailboats, are approved throwable PFDs in the U.S., but not in Canada.

in pounds, that keeps you afloat) of 10 to 12 pounds in order to remain afloat. All United States Coast Guard- and Canadian Department of Transport-approved PFDs provide this amount of buoyancy. Personal flotation devices also offer protection against another cause of boating accident casualties—hypothermia (*Chapter 5*).

When shopping for a PFD, get the facts you need. Check the labels for U.S. Coast Guard or Canadian Department of Transport approval. Do not skimp on quality; the more easily worn life preservers and buoyant vests provide much greater protection. They are worn, rather than grasped, and so will keep an injured or exhausted person afloat.

PFDs are classified in "types," as shown on pages 64 and 65. Choose a model that fits the person who will be wearing it most often, and one that suits the type of boating you will be doing. Many models are comfortable and attractive; this increases the chances that someone will be wearing it before an emergency arises.

The most popular PFDs are fabric-covered Type II nearshore buoyant vests and Type III flotation aids. The fabric covering most often used is one of several types of nylon or polyester. These synthetic fabrics have a number of advantages for use in PFD construction. They are economical, durable and resistant to rot caused by microbes. They can be dyed in a wide range of colors, increasing the chances of a rescuer spotting them. They are easy for PFD manufacturers to work with. They "drape" reasonably well, and therefore are good for constructing wearable articles. The nylon fabrics used are similar to those often used in constructing jackets and camping gear.

Nylon and polyester are plastics, however, and like many plastics they can start to break down after extended expo-

Children do not float well in a face-up position and tend to panic easily. Type II PFDs are best for small children; an infant vest should have built-in rollover and head-support features.

A water-skier being towed is considered on board the vessel for compliance with PFD carriage requirements. Ski belts are not USCG approved for safety. Although not required by federal law, it is advisable for a skier to wear a PFD designed to withstand the impact of hitting water at high speed. Some state laws require skiers to wear a PFD.

sure to the ultraviolet (UV) light in sunlight. Fabric manufacturers can include UV inhibitors to slow the degradation process, and dyes used to color the devices may also provide some protection. Generally, darker dyes provide more protection than light or bright dyes, such as "neon" (fluorescent) shades, but this is not always the case. Fabric-covered PFDs should ordinarily last at least several boating seasons in normal use (vacations, weekends and evenings, for example). PFDs used every day in direct sunlight will probably have to be replaced more often.

Another type of personal flotation device is the inflatable, which relies on a carbon dioxide cartridge that inflates the vest in order to provide the required buoyancy. Inflatable models are either manual (a ripcord is pulled to activate the CO_2 cartridge) or automatic, with a water-sensitive mechanism that automatically activates the CO_2 cartridge upon contact with the water.

Remember that small outboard boats as well as sailing dinghies are more likely to capsize than are larger inboard-engine boats; consequently there is a greater possibility that the occupants will find themselves in the water. Regardless of the type of boat you operate, however, think of personal flotation devices as necessary operating equipment. Insist on an absolute "rule of the boat": Adult non-swimmers, all children, anyone boating alone or anyone who must do a job that could result in being swept overboard must wear a PFD whenever the boat is underway. This also applies for a dinghy outing—even if only a quick row to shore. When PFDs are not being

CHOOSING PERSONAL FLOTATION DEVICES

To meet U.S. Coast Guard boating requirements, you must have the proper type and number of PFDs aboard. Wearable devices must be "readily accessible," and throwable devices "immediately available." Be sure to choose this lifesaving equipment carefully. When buying PFDs, shop for a proper fit for each person aboard. Also make sure flotation devices are approved by the U.S. Coast Guard in the U.S. or, for Canadian vessels, the Department of Transport in Canada.

Try on your new personal flotation device to see if it fits comfortably snug. Then test it in shallow water or in a swimming pool to see how it performs. To check the buoyancy of your PFD in the water, relax your body and let your head tilt back. Make sure that your PFD keeps your chin above water and that you can breathe easily.

Remember, your PFD may not perform the same in swift or rough water as in calm water. The clothes you wear and items in your pockets may also change the way a PFD performs. The USCG recommends that boat owners test their PFDs at least once a year. If your mouth is not well above the water when you test it, get a new PFD or one with more buoyancy.

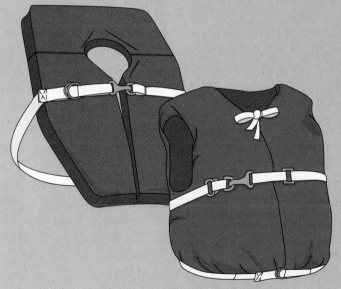

TYPE I
Also called an off-shore life jacket, a Type I PFD is the easiest to pull on in an emergency. It provides the most buoyancy, and is effective for all waters, especially open, rough or remote waters requiring extended survival. It is designed to turn most unconscious wearers to a face-up position. Type I is available in jacket or bib models, as shown. The adult size provides at least 22 pounds buoyancy, the child size, 11 pounds minimum.

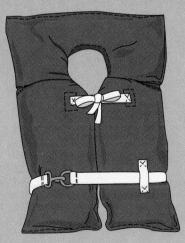

TYPE II
A Type II PFD, or near-shore buoyant vest, is intended for calm, inland water or wherever there is a good chance of quick rescue. This type will turn some unconscious wearers to a face-up position in the water. However, the turning action is not as pronounced or as effective for as many people as a Type I. An adult size provides at least 15½ pounds buoyancy; a medium child size provides 11 pounds. Infant and small child sizes each provide at least 7 pounds buoyancy.

worn, they should at least be out and readily available. For those who take pets aboard their boats, pet vests are available at most marine supply stores.

Maintaining your PFDs

PFDs aboard your boat are only useful if they are kept in operable condition. Be sure to maintain this essential equipment by following the guidelines below. It is important to remember that, like any other item of equipment on your boat, a PFD eventually gets old and worn, and therefore must be replaced.

■ Check each personal flotation device's buoyancy with regular trials in shallow water. Each should hold its owner so that he or she can breathe easily.

■ After use, always air-dry each flotation device thoroughly, away from any direct heat source. Then store it in a dry, well-ventilated, easily accessible place on board the boat.

■ Check twice a year for mildew, leaks, insecure straps, frayed webbing, broken zippers or hardened stuffing; replace as necessary. Clean with a mild soap and running water; avoid using strong detergents or gasoline, and do not dry clean.

■ Avoid kneeling on PFDs, or using them as fenders.

■ Avoid contact with oil or grease, which in some cases causes kapok materials to deteriorate and lose buoyancy.

■ Check PFDs that use kapok-filled bags for flotation: Make sure the kapok has not hardened and that there are no holes in the bags. Squeeze the bag and listen for an air leak. If water has entered the bag, the kapok will eventually rot. Destroy

TYPE III
Also known as a flotation aid, a Type III PFD is good for calm, inland water, or where there is a good chance of quick rescue. It is designed so wearers can place themselves in a face-up position in the water. The wearer may have to tilt the head back to avoid turning face-down in the water. The Type III has the same minimum buoyancy as a Type II. Available in many styles, colors and sizes, it is generally the most comfortable type for continuous wear. Float coats and fishing vests are examples of this type of PFD.

TYPE V
A Type V hybrid inflatable PFD is the least bulky of all PFD types. It contains a small amount of inherent buoyancy and an inflatable chamber. When it is inflated, its performance is equal to a Type I, II or III PFD, as noted on the PFD label. U.S. regulations also recognize certain Type V special-purpose devices, including wet suit, deck suit and whitewater types. Most Type V PFDs must be worn underway (by someone above-decks) to be acceptable.

TYPE IV
A Type IV PFD, or throwable device, is intended for calm, inland water with heavy boat traffic, where help is always present. It is not designed to be worn, but rather to be thrown to a person in the water, then grasped and held by the user until the rescue occurs. Type IV devices include horseshoe buoys (approved for U.S. use), ring buoys (approved for Canadian use) and buoyant cushions.

and replace the PFD in any of the following cases: if the kapok filling is hard, if you feel a large quantity of air coming from the bag, if the kapok is waterlogged or if the PFD smells of mildew.
■ Check PFD covers periodically. A cover that has torn due to weakened fabric is obviously unserviceable; a weak cover could split open and allow the flotation material inside to be lost. Badly faded bright colors can also be a clue that deterioration has taken place. Compare fabric color where it is protected—under a body strap, for example—to where the fabric is exposed. A PFD with a UV-damaged fabric cover should be replaced. Another simple test is to pinch the fabric between thumb and forefinger of each hand and try to tear it. If the fabric cover can be torn this way, the PFD should definitely be destroyed and discarded.

Lifelines, safety nets and harnesses

Make sure that everyone on board follows the traditional mariner's advice: "One hand for yourself and one for the boat." No matter how seasoned your sea legs, when the weather is rough, keep your center of gravity low whenever you move about the boat. (Further ensure stability by grasping handholds, for example.)

On sailboats, lifelines serve as boundaries for the deck, particularly when children or pets are aboard. Many people reinforce those boundaries by rigging nylon netting along the lifelines, or between the hulls of catamarans or trimarans. When small children are adventurous, however, or when the boat is pitching, rolling or heeling, safety harnesses provide additional safety insurance.

Netting rigged along lifelines of a sailboat is an excellent safeguard against children falling overboard.

In addition to ensuring that you know a child's whereabouts at all times, a safety harness is essential in other conditions for boaters of all ages. It will keep you aboard even if you fall, and should be worn anytime you are sailing alone, whenever any crew member is on deck in heavy weather, when going on deck alone at night while underway, when going aloft or whenever you feel there is a danger that you might lose your footing.

Put on the safety harness before going on deck, and keep in mind that a safety harness is only as strong as its attachment point. The best attachment point is a jackline, or jackwire—a bow-to-stern trolleylike wire on a sailboat deck, onto which safety harness tethers are securely clipped. In the absence of a jackline, a harness should be hooked to the windward side of the boat—only onto a sturdy through-bolted fitting (a cleat, winch or stay, for example); the mast; or stainless steel eyes of a toe rail or a grab rail. Keep in mind that lifelines and stanchions cannot be relied upon to withstand a great deal of force; therefore, they are unsuitable attachment points.

When shopping for safety harnesses, choose only models designed for use aboard a boat, with reinforced nylon webbing, stainless steel hardware and a tested strength of at least 3,000 pounds. The harness should fasten at the chest, with a catch that responds only to firm, positive action for release; the USCG recommends quick-release-under-load catches and buckles. A harness should have a stainless steel snap hook at the end of a tether no longer than 6 feet. If you attach a sailing knife to the harness, in a sheath and with a lanyard, you will always have a tool handy.

Each safety harness aboard your boat should be adjusted to fit the person who will wear it, then labeled to ensure quick identification when needed in an emergency. Stow your harnesses in dry places and inspect them regularly for wear and tear, along with your other safety equipment.

A safety harness ensures that you know where your children are at all times aboard a boat.

SAFETY AFLOAT

Fueling the boat safely

Fueling a boat properly is an essential element of good seamanship. Whether you are planning a day's outing or an extended cruise, before starting out make sure you have enough fuel on board, and if any is needed, fill the tank safely. Practice the "one-third rule": Use one-third of your fuel going out, one-third to get back and keep one-third in reserve. Remember that although diesel fuel is non-explosive, it will burn nonetheless. Whether you use gasoline or diesel fuel, follow the step-by-step procedures below—carefully and completely—every time you fuel a boat.

Of primary importance is the condition of your fuel tanks. If you have portable fuel tanks, make sure that they are constructed of sturdy material and in good condition, that they are free of excessive corrosion and do not leak. The vents on portable tanks must be operable; the tanks themselves should have a vapor-tight, leak-proof cap. Avoid excessive movement of portable tanks. Permanent fuel tanks and lines should also be free of corrosion and must not leak. Tanks must be vented to the outside of the hull. The fill pipe and plate must be located outside of closed compartments and outboard of the cockpit, and must fit tightly.

Before fueling

- Fuel before dark whenever possible, and secure your boat to the fueling dock.
- Stop engines, motors, fans and other devices that can produce a spark. If the electrical system has a master switch, turn it off. Turn off all galley fires and open flames.
- Close all ports, windows, doors and hatches so that fumes cannot blow aboard and below.
- Disembark all passengers and any crew members not needed for the fueling operation.
- Prohibit all smoking on board and near the boat.
- Make sure that an approved, well-maintained fire extinguisher is close at hand.
- When refueling an outboard, remove portable tanks from the boat and fill them on shore. Refer to Chapter 8 for more information on fueling portable tanks.

While fueling

- Guard against static sparks by keeping the nozzle or can spout in contact with the fill opening.
- Avoid spilling any gasoline.
- Avoid overfilling: Filling a tank until fuel flows from the vents is dangerous.

After fueling

- Close fill openings.
- Wipe up any spilled gasoline; dispose of wipe-up rags safely on shore.
- Open all ports, windows, doors and hatches, then turn on the bilge blower. Be sure to ventilate the boat for a minimum of four minutes.

PRE-DEPARTURE FLOAT PLAN

1 NAME AND PHONE NUMBER OF PERSON REPORTING

2 DESCRIPTION OF BOAT
Type of boat; color of hull, deck and cabin; trim; registration number; length; name of boat; make; any other distinguishing features.

3 PERSONS ABOARD
Name, age, address, telephone number of skipper and each crew member.

4 MEDICAL PROBLEMS OF ANY PERSON ABOARD

5 ENGINE TYPE
Horsepower, number of engines, fuel capacity.

6 SAFETY AND SURVIVAL EQUIPMENT
Personal flotation devices, flares, mirror, visual distress signals, flashlight, food, paddles, water supply, anchor, life raft, dinghy and EPIRB *(Chapter 24)*, any other safety or emergency equipment.

7 MARINE RADIO
Type, frequencies.

8 TRIP EXPECTATIONS
Departure points, route, destination, expected date and time of arrival. Expected date of return.

9 ANY OTHER PERTINENT INFORMATION

10 VEHICLE LICENSES
Color, make and license number of automobile and trailer, and where they are parked.

11 SUGGESTED DATE AND TIME TO CALL COAST GUARD OR LOCAL AUTHORITY FOR SEARCH

12 TELEPHONE NUMBERS TO CALL FOR FURTHER INFORMATION OR IN CASE OF EMERGENCY

13 COMPETENCY OF PEOPLE ABOARD
Boating skills and emergency first-aid training.

Before departing on your trip, give a responsible relative or friend the information suggested in the float plan above. (Do not attempt to file your float plan with the Coast Guard, which does not have the staff to keep track of boats.) Notify the person holding the float plan of any changes in your plans—especially in the case of a late arrival.

- Sniff low down in tank and engine compartments or, if you have a detector (*page 70*), make sure it is working properly. If you detect any odor of gasoline, do not start the engine; continue ventilation actions until the odor can no longer be detected. Check for any drips and liquid fuel.
- Be prepared to cast off lines as soon as the engine starts; get clear of the pier quickly.

Loading and capacity for U.S. boats

The terms loading and capacity relate to the weight of people, fuel and gear that can be safely carried. The safe load of a boat in terms of people depends on a number of characteristics, including hull volume and dimension, the weight of the engine and, if an outboard, how it is mounted. The number of seats in a boat is not an indication of the number of people it can safely carry.

The U.S. Coast Guard safety standard covering Display of Capacity Information applies to manufacturers of monohull boats less than 20 feet in length, except sailboats, canoes, kayaks and inflatables. The standard became effective for applicable boats manufactured after November 1, 1972. The standards originally required the following:
- Boats powered by outboards: the maximum persons capacity in pounds, maximum weight capacity (persons, motor and gear) in pounds and maximum horsepower capacity.
- Boats powered by inboards and stern drives: the maximum persons capacity in pounds and maximum weight capacity (persons and gear). (The Coast Guard Safe Powering Standard does not apply to inboards, stern drives, etc.)
- Manually propelled boats: the maximum persons capacity in pounds and maximum weight capacity (persons and gear).

The Display of Capacity Information Standard was amended in August 1980 to require display of the persons capacity in terms of the number of people, in addition to the number of pounds. There are also voluntary industry standards covering capacity labels for boats to which the Coast Guard reg-

ulations do not apply, e.g. some boats 20 feet or longer in length, pontoon boats, inflatables, etc. The labels are substantially the same; however, they cannot display the words "U.S. Coast Guard" because such displays would suggest compliance with the Coast Guard standard when, in fact, the standard does not apply to such boats.

Most boats give satisfactory and more economical service with motors of less horsepower. In fact, overpowering in relation to the maximum horsepower capacity reduces the "level flotation" capabilities of the boat, as defined by the USCG Flotation Standard.

It is worth noting that, although it is not a violation of any federal law for a boat operator to exceed the values displayed on the U.S. Coast Guard Maximum Capacities label, there may be local consequences. Some states, for example, consider overloading or overpowering a boat beyond the values displayed on the capacity label a violation, and may cite an operator who exceeds posted limits. In addition, some insurance companies will not insure a boat that is powered with a larger motor than the Maximum Horsepower Capacity displayed on the label, and some boat manufacturers will void any applicable warranties for the same reason.

Also keep in mind that the limits defined on capacity plates apply in good to moderate weather conditions. In rough waters, keep the weight well below the limit. People represent a "live" load; moving about affects a boat quite differently than static loads like the engine or fuel tank. If your boat's capacity is fully used, or if the weather becomes rough, distribute the load evenly; keep the weight low, and avoid abrupt changes in distribution. Shift human or other weight only after stopping or slowing.

Canadian capacity plates

In Canada, vessels not over 5 meters (16.4 ft.) long, (to be increased to 6 meters in 1993), powered by outboard motor(s) of 7.5 kW (10 horsepower) or more, must have a Transport

Overloading is a major cause of boating accidents and can worsen the outcome of any mishap while underway. Be sure to check the boat's capacity plate before loading.

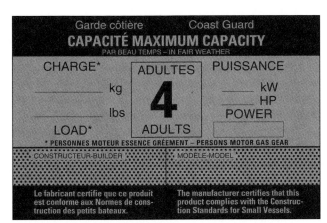

The Transport Canada Capacity Plate must be permanently attached in a prominent position, clearly visible by the operator. Where there is no console, the preferable location is the inboard side of the boat's transom. Even if the vessel is not equipped with engines of 7.5 kW (10 hp)—but could be—it is required by small vessel regulations to carry this plate.

Canada Capacity Plate (issued by the Canadian Coast Guard) affixed in a prominent place on the boat's console or on the inboard side of the transom if there is no console. The plate shown above gives the boat's recommended maximum gross load capacity (all-inclusive weight carried, including people, motor, gas and equipment) as well as the maximum kilowatts of engine power. Without exception, the owner of a boat that carries one or more engines with a capacity in excess of the recommended kilowatt power could be liable for prosecution should a mishap occur.

Before buying a boat, call the Canadian Coast Guard for guidance—at toll-free number 1-800-267-6687. Remember that it is the manufacturer who should supply the plate with all details completed. In the case of a home-built boat, the builder must make the application directly to the Coast Guard.

Boarding a boat

Stepping aboard a small boat, whether an outboard or dinghy, is an important basic boating skill. If you are boarding from a pier, step into the boat as close to the center as possible, keeping your body weight low. Keep lines tight or have someone steady the boat while you board. If boarding from a beach, come in over the bow.

Never jump into a small boat or step on the gunwale. If you must take a motor or any other gear aboard, place it on the edge of the pier where you can easily reach it from the center of the boat. Better yet, after you have boarded the boat, have someone on the pier hand it to you, as shown in the photograph at right.

If stepping into a light dinghy on a beach, don't forget that the unsupported sections of a boat out of the water are quite vulnerable. By stepping in the boat when it is on a beach, a rock could be driven through the hull by your weight all on one foot.

Using a pre-departure checklist

Another measure of good seamanship is the procedure you follow before actual departure. Whether you are in home waters or far away, make a final weather check (*Chapter 14*) close to departure time each day. Prepare your own pre-departure checklist for use each time you depart, and revise it as your boating experience grows and your needs change. Use the following guidelines to help you design a checklist suited to your specific needs. Before you depart, ensure the following:
- All safety equipment is aboard, accessible and in good working condition.
- The bilge has no fuel fumes and little or no water. (On an inboard-engine boat, "sniff" the bilges for fumes, and operate the blower for at least four minutes.)
- All loose gear is stowed securely. Dock lines and fenders should be stowed immediately after getting underway.
- All guests have been properly instructed in the dos and don'ts of safety and operational matters aboard.
- Engine oil levels are adequate; water level is sufficient in closed cooling systems. After starting engines, check overboard flow of cooling water.
- Fuel tanks are as full as you need. There is enough fuel aboard for your anticipated cruising, plus an adequate reserve if you must change your plans.
- A second person on board is capable of taking over for you, and operating the radio, in case you become disabled.

Hand gear to a person seated in a small boat; do not attempt to step aboard carrying heavy or bulky items.

In addition to common use aboard boats, some of the safety equipment listed below (identified with an *) is also legally required by the USCG.

Bilge pump or bailer

Although federal regulations do not require dewatering devices— a bucket or other bailer on unpowered boats or electric bilge pumps on boats with engines—they are required by some state laws. Required or not, these items are recommended for safe boating. In Canada, even the smallest boat must have at least a bailer on hand.

Boathook

A hook on a pole is invaluable for fending off, placing lines over piles, picking up pennants of mooring buoys and recovering articles dropped over the side. When marked with rings at one-foot intervals—a mark in a different color or size should be added for the boat's draft—a boathook is useful for probing around a stranded boat in search of deeper water.

Charts and navigation publications

Essential for planning your course and navigating safely, charts and navigation publications, such as those covered in Chapter 18, should be up to date.

Compass

Desirable on almost any boat, for both emergency and regular use, a compass and piloting instruments (Section 5) are recommended for piloting purposes.

Detectors and alarms

A well-thought-out alarm system can alert you to a wide variety of dangers, from burglars on deck to explosive vapors trapped below.

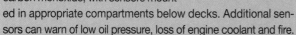

A float switch mounted above the normal bilge-water level, for example, can signal flooding in the bilge. Other detectors indicate dangerous levels of gasoline, propane, hydrogen fumes or carbon monoxide, with sensors mounted in appropriate compartments below decks. Additional sensors can warn of low oil pressure, loss of engine coolant and fire.

For detecting burglars coming aboard, neither home nor automobile alarms are practical aboard an occupied boat; install only an alarm that is specifically designed for marine use.

Electronic equipment

VHF radio is the basic piece of electronic safety equipment used in receiving weather reports and Coast Guard warnings as well as transmitting requests for assistance. Other operational safety items include electronic depth sounders; fuel vapor detectors; radio direction finders (RDFs) and navigation equipment such as Loran, GPS and radar.

EPIRB (emergency position-indicating radio beacon)

This automatic radio transmitter, described in Chapter 24, should be carried on any boat operating offshore.

Fenders

Carried in appropriate sizes and numbers, fenders are useful for normal berthing, and when two boats must make fast to each other while underway or at anchor.

First-aid kit

An essential item of safety equipment, the kit (Chapter 5), should be accompanied by a first-aid manual and supplemented by one or more first-aid courses.

Flame arrester*

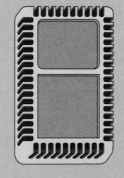

With some minor and technical exceptions, every inboard gasoline engine must be equipped with an acceptable means of backfire flame control—or "flame arrester." Flame arresters no longer require Coast Guard approval; the USCG now accepts flame arresters complying with Underwriters Laboratories (UL) Standard 1111 or Society of Automotive Engineers (SAE) J1928. When in use flame arresters must be secured to the air intake of the carburetor with an airtight connection. Elements must be clean, and grids must be tight enough to prevent flames passing through.

Flashlight or searchlight

A searchlight—installed on larger craft, hand-held on smaller boats—serves both as a night piloting aid and as an emergency signaling device. A multicell flashlight or electric lantern can serve these functions, although sometimes less effectively.

Ground tackle

Ground tackle (Chapter 12) includes anchors, anchor rode (line or chain) and all the shackles and other gear used in anchoring. All ground tackle must be in good repair and operational condition and, after use, should be carefully re-stowed so that the main anchor is ready for use and auxiliary and storm anchors are readily accessible.

Lead line

A hand-held lead line is useful as a backup to the electronic depth sounder, and is particularly handy when necessary to probe around a stranded boat in search of deeper water. A dollop of wax is affixed to the bottom of the lead to obtain a sample of bottom consistency.

Life rafts

For everyone who cruises or fishes offshore, a rigid or inflatable life raft should be considered mandatory. Standards for life rafts—size, capacity ratings, seaworthiness, sturdiness—are set by Safety of Life at Sea (SOLAS) international conventions, and are adapted for use in the U.S. by the USCG. Life rafts are discussed in Chapter 4.

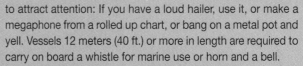

Lightning protection

Although lightning strikes very few North American boats per year, lightning protection aboard your boat *(Chapter 23)* could help avoid considerable damage to your boat and may save the lives of those aboard. Two types of lightning protection should be installed—one to guide the charge of a main strike safely down into the water, the other to protect electronic equipment from a damaging power surge.

Sails for heavy weather and sail rig modifications

The average set of sails is designed for moderate wind and stress, and not for quick-action adjustment in heavy weather.

Jiffy (or slab) reefing uses a set of lines and blocks for quick and secure sail reduction; it is particularly useful for a single-handed sailor. A roller reefing system, often found on headsails, rotates around an axis, pulling the sail down and around like an upside-down window shade. Although reefing by either of these methods is a compromise—convenience weighed against efficient sail shape—the loss of sailing efficiency is made up by the gain in sailing safety.

Storm sails, made of heavier cloth and strongly reinforced at stress points with extra-sturdy edge bindings, are designed especially to handle the extra pressure of high winds. Chapter 10 offers a detailed description of sails.

Sound signaling devices*

The *Navigation Rules (Chapter 6)* require sound signals to be made under certain circumstances, including the meeting, crossing and overtaking situations that are described in the *Rules*. All vessels, including recreational vessels, are required to sound fog signals during periods of reduced visibility; therefore, you must have some means of making an efficient sound signal. In an emergency, for example, you can use any loud noise

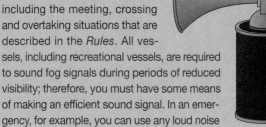

to attract attention: If you have a loud hailer, use it, or make a megaphone from a rolled up chart, or bang on a metal pot and yell. Vessels 12 meters (40 ft.) or more in length are required to carry on board a whistle for marine use or horn and a bell.

In Canada, vessels less than 12 meters (40 ft.) must have aboard a means of making an efficient sound signal; longer vessels require a whistle for marine use and a bell.

Spare parts and tools

The list of tools and spare parts to be carried aboard is best developed by skippers for their own boats. Depending on the type of boat, how it is normally used, and the capabilities of the crew, the list may include items such as simple tools, plugs, cloth, screws, nails, wire, tape and other objects for making emergency repairs at sea; spare bulbs for the navigation lights and various mechanical and electrical spare parts.

Visual distress signals*

Most boats—and all boats operating in open waters (offshore and the Great Lakes)—must be equipped with visual distress signals, classified by the USCG for day use only (D), night use only (N) or combined day-and-night use (D/N). Each device must be in serviceable condition, readily accessible and certified by the manufacturer as complying with USCG requirements. (Launchers manufactured before January 1, 1981, intended for use with approved signals, are not required to be Coast Guard approved.) Distress flares, smoke flares and meteor rockets have expiration dates—42 months after the date of manufacture.

Remember that USCG regulations prohibit any display of visual distress signals on the water, except when assistance is required. Use emergency signals only when in distress *(Chapter 4)*, and only when help is close enough to see the signal.

In Canada, vessels over 55 meters must carry CCG-approved flares according to the length of the vessel. USCG flares are not acceptable. In Canada, the CCG-approved flares show the date of manufacture rather than expiry. Flares are considered effective for 48 months from the date of manufacture.

Windshield wipers

Although windshield wipers may seem like minor equipment, they are invaluable in rainy or misty conditions. Wipers may be operated by hand or electric motor. The best choice of wiper is a sturdy commercial version used by commercial fishermen and tugboats. A "clear view" screen is an effective, but somewhat expensive, solution consisting of a circular piece of glass, motor-driven at high speed to spin the water away by centrifugal force. Some boaters use a product designed for racing-car drivers; this substance coats the windshield, forcing water and salt to bead and quickly fall off the glass.

* Legally required by U.S. Coast Guard *(page 62)*

FIREFIGHTING EQUIPMENT

USCG-approved fire extinguishers

On board a boat, fire extinguishers are required if any one or more of the following conditions exist:

■ Inboard engines.

■ Closed compartments under thwarts and seats where portable fuel tanks may be stored.

■ Double bottoms not sealed to the hull or which are not completely filled with flotation materials.

■ Closed living spaces.

■ Closed stowage compartments in which combustible or flammable materials are stored.

■ Permanently installed fuel tanks. A portable tank can be removed from the boat for refilling without the use of tools.

Approved extinguishers are classified by a letter and number symbol. The letter indicates the type fire the unit is designed to extinguish. (Type B, commonly used on boats,

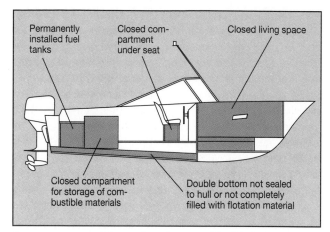

Any one or more of the enclosed spaces identified above makes carrying a fire extinguisher a legal requirement.

FIRE EXTINGUISHER CONTENTS

Class	Foam in gals.	CO_2 in lbs.	Dry Chemical in lbs.	Halon in lbs.
B-I	1.25	4	2	2.5
B-II	2.5	15	10	10

Units approved for use on boats are hand-portable, B-I or B-II classification, and have the characteristics shown above.

is designed to extinguish fires involving flammable liquids such as gasoline, oil and grease.) The number indicates the relative size of the extinguisher (minimum extinguishing agent weight). U.S. Coast Guard-approved hand-portable and semiportable fire extinguishers bear a metal nameplate that provides the manufacturer's name and the unit's type, capacity and operating instructions.

For marine use, all required hand-portable fire extinguishers and semiportable and fixed fire extinguishing systems must be approved by the USCG or, in Canada, one of four organizations: Board of Steamship Inspection (Transport Canada), Underwriters Laboratories of Canada, British Board of Trade for marine use, or the USCG. Check each unit regu-

larly to ensure that gauges, if any, are free and nozzles are clear. Extinguishers may contain any of the following extinguishing agents listed below. (See Chapter 4 for information on use of extinguishers.)

■ Dry Chemical is an agent widely used because of its convenience and relative low cost. The cylinder contains a dry chemical in powdered form, along with a propellant gas under pressure. These extinguishers tend to "pack" or "cake"; shake them periodically, and store where there is least engine vibration. Dry chemical extinguishers without gauges or indicating devices must be inspected every six months.

■ Foam is a combination of water and a chemical foaming agent, and is most effective for fires involving flammable liquids—gasoline, solvents, grease, oil and some paints. Although foam will work on fires involving wood, cloth, paper, rubber and many plastics, it leaves a messy residue. It should not be used for electrical fires.

■ Carbon Dioxide units consist of a cylinder containing CO_2 under high pressure, a valve and a discharge nozzle at the end of a short hose or pipe on a swivel connection. This type of extinguisher is advantageous because it leaves no messy residue to clean up after use and causes no harm to the interior of engines as some other types may do. A disadvantage,

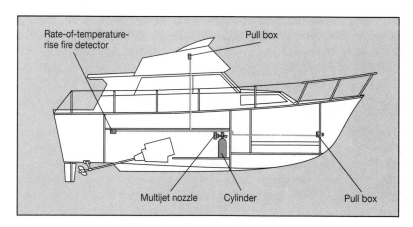

Boats powered by inboard engines, particularly those fueled by gasoline such as the one shown at left, often are fitted with a built-in CO_2- or Halon-type fire extinguishing system. It may be activated manually, or automatically by temperature-rise sensors. A discharge indicator must be mounted at the helm station.

however, is that the state of charge can be checked only by weighing the cylinder and comparing this figure with a stamped figure on or near the valve. Weigh a CO_2 unit annually; if the gross weight is reduced by more than 10 percent of the net weight, the unit is not acceptable and must be recharged. CO_2 units may be used where a fixed system installed in an engine compartment is operated either manually or automatically by heat-sensitive detectors.

■ Other liquefied gas systems include Halon 1301, a colorless, odorless gas that stops fire instantly. It is heavier than air and sinks to lower parts of the bilge. Humans can tolerate a 7 percent concentration, which is more than enough to fight fire for several minutes. Although effective, Halon is currently being phased out for environmental reasons. According to a 1987 international treaty to eliminate ozone-destroying chemicals, the use of Halon will be banned in developed countries by the year 2000.

Until the year 2000, Halon 1301 may still be used in built-in systems activated manually or automatically; for restoring protection after use, additional tanks can be carried. Halon 1211, a closely related chemical, is used in hand-portable extinguishers. Manufacturers recommend that Halon extinguishers be weighed at least once a year to meet the standards stated on the label.

SAFETY ASPECTS OF APPLIANCES

Several items generally found on boats are not safety equipment per se, but have definite aspects of safety about their design, installation or operation that must be considered.

Galley stoves

Stoves should be designed, manufactured and approved for marine use, and most commonly use alcohol, kerosene, electricity, liquefied petroleum gas (LPG) or compressed natural gas (CNG) fuel. Electricity is probably the safest source of heat for cooking aboard a boat, but shore power or an auxiliary generating plant is required to produce the large amounts of AC power required. Because of their inexpensive and simple nature, alcohol stoves are widely used on boats; with precautions, such installations can be quite safe. Although plain water will extinguish alcohol fires remember that alcohol floats, so the fire could be spread by water.

LPG stoves are excellent for cooking, but can present a serious safety hazard unless installed and operated in accordance with strict rules (American Boat and Yacht Council Standard A-22 and National Fire Protection Association Standard 302). Pressure kerosene provides a high temperature source of heat, but is sometimes difficult to control. Gasoline is unsafe as stove fuel, and should never be used for cooking on a boat. The use or storage of portable stoves with attached LPG or CNG bottles is prohibited inside a boat with accommodation areas.

Fuel for alcohol and kerosene stoves may be supplied to the burners either by a gravity or a pressure system—provided fuel tanks cannot be filled while the burners are in operation, except where the supply tank is remote from burners and the filling operation will not introduce a fire hazard. A removable or accessible liquid-tight metal drop pan at least ¾ inch (1.9 cm) deep should be provided under all burners. Pressure tanks should have suitable gauges and/or relief valves.

Stoves should be permanently and securely fastened in place and adequately ventilated when in operation. All woodwork or other combustible material around a stove, including smoke stacks, must be effectively protected with non-combustible sheathing. Portable stoves must be secured while in use.

Refrigeration

On some boats, refrigeration is simply a matter of ice to keep food fresh and to cool beverages. Although this method of refrigeration offers no safety hazards, freshwater drip tends to promote dry rot and/or odor. Water from melting ice should be piped overboard—not into the bilge. A collection sump, with pump, helps make the task easier.

Many boat owners, however, opt for the convenience of mechanical refrigeration—usually an electric-motor-driven compressor. These marine units use a non-toxic and non-flammable refrigerant, non-sparking motors, safety valves on high-pressure portions of the system and construction designed to survive the rigors of marine service.

Heaters

Cabin heaters, sometimes used on boats in northern waters, include built-in electrical heaters, which are safe. Portable electrical heaters should be used only if secured in place while in operation and with proper ventilation. Gasoline is unsafe for fueling a boat's heaters. Likewise, portable kerosene or alcohol heaters are not recommended for two reasons: they produce carbon monoxide, and because of the fire potential of spilled fuel. Any heater that consumes oxygen from the cabin presents a danger of asphyxiation.

Any heater discharging combustion products must be vented through a stovepipe and a Charlie Noble, a stovepipe fitting in a cabin top or deck. Many sailors favor coal-, charcoal- or wood-burning heaters for the even, dry heat they deliver, despite the mess they create and the problems of storing fuel. LPG heaters should have an automatic device to shut off fuel supply if the flame is extinguished; pilot lights should not be used.

Every heater aboard a boat must be designed specifically for marine use, and must be securely fastened whether in use or in storage. The area in which it is installed must comply with ventilation requirements. Finally, remember that any burner system that may adversely affect safety in reaction to the normal motion of the boat is not an acceptable appliance.

BOATING SAFETY CHECKLIST

Is your boat as safe as it can possibly be? If you can answer "Yes" to the following questions, chances are that the vessel is safely equipped and that you operate it safely.

✓ Do you carry legally required and other safety equipment aboard—and do you know how to use it?

✓ Before getting underway, do you review, with everyone aboard, emergency procedures and identify all safety equipment and exits (where appropriate)?

✓ If you carry a life raft aboard your boat, have you included its proper deployment as part of your routine safety training? At least one crew member should know, for example, where the raft is located, how to inflate it quickly and to inflate it on deck rather than belowdecks or in the cockpit.

✓ Are you aware that it is illegal to operate a vessel while intoxicated? When alcohol or drugs are mixed with boating, the results can be fatal. (At least 50 percent of all boating accidents are alcohol-related.)

✓ Do you check local weather reports before departure, and keep a weather eye open during your voyage (Chapter 14)?

✓ Are your lifesaving equipment and fire extinguishers readily accessible at all times?

✓ Do you avoid overloading your boat with people or gear?

✓ Do you make sure you have good non-skid surfaces on deck and on the soles of shoes of everyone aboard?

✓ Do you keep bilges clean and electrical contacts tight?

✓ Do you guard rigidly against any fuel system leakage?

✓ Have you recently requested a Coast Guard Auxiliary Courtesy Marine Examination (page 75)?

✓ Have you taken any safe boating courses (Chapter 27) or first-aid courses (Chapter 5)?

✓ Before departing, do you leave a Float Plan (page 67) so someone knows where you are boating and when you are expected to return? Do you notify the holder if plans change?

✓ Are you familiar with the waters that you will be using: tides, currents, sand bars and any other hazards you may encounter (Sections 4 and 5)?

✓ Do you know your personal limitations and responsibilities? Remember that exposure to sun, wind and cold water affect your ability to react.

✓ Are you aware that a sailboat mast touching a power line could electrocute you? Check your clearances while underway.

✓ If you are a non-swimmer, are you planning to learn to swim? It could save your life, or someone else's.

✓ Are you and your crew prepared for any emergencies that could occur (Chapter 4)?

✓ Do you know and obey the Rules of the Road (Chapter 6)?

✓ Do you watch, and heed, posted speeds; do you slow down in anchorages?

✓ When towing a water-skier, do you remember that two people are required in the boat: one to operate the boat and one to watch the skier?

✓ Do you know your fuel tank capacity and fuel consumption at various RPMs, and the cruising radius this gives?

✓ Do you take maximum precautions when taking on fuel (page 67)? Do you practice the "one-third rule" by using one-third of the fuel going out and one-third to get back, keeping one-third in reserve?

✓ When anchoring, do you allow adequate scope (Chapter 12)? Are you far enough away from neighboring boats?

✓ If someone falls into the water, do you know what to do? Avoid jumping in; use a reaching, throwing or floating assist such as a paddle, a cushion, a Type IV PFD life ring or a rescue line with a float attached.

✓ Do you avoid relieving yourself over the side of the boat in a standing position? This is a common cause of accidents resulting in drowning.

✓ Whenever possible, do you, and those aboard your boat, remain seated while underway?

✓ Do you know that standing in a small boat raises the center of gravity, often to the point of capsizing? Standing for any reason or even changing position in a small boat can be dangerous, as is sitting on the gunwales or seat backs or in a pedestal seat while underway.

USCG AUXILIARY SAFETY REQUIREMENTS

Federal and state requirements provide for the bare necessities of boating safety equipment, and should be considered only the beginning of equipping a boat for safety. Expanding the boater's safety checklist is one important role of the U.S. Coast Guard Auxiliary, which, in most areas, offers a Courtesy Marine Examination (CME) for boats. The examination is free of charge, and a decal is awarded to each boat that meets federal safety requirements and additional safety items established by the Auxiliary. These requirements, listed below, are in addition to, and generally more demanding than, legal requirements; they serve as an excellent safety guide for all boat owners.

Requirements for USCG Auxiliary decal

- **Personal flotation devices** *(pages 63-66)*. Boats 16 feet or longer must have at least two wearable and one throwable personal flotation device; boats less than 16 feet in length, a minimum of two PFDs.
- **Fire extinguishers** *(pages 72-73)*. Boats under 26 feet long, of open construction or which have a built-in fire extinguisher system, must carry an additional hand-portable extinguisher. All hand-held fire extinguishers must be mounted in a readily accessible location.

    Sailboats 16 feet or more in length, even without any auxiliary power source or fuel tanks, must have at least one B-I type extinguisher.
- **Navigation lights** *(Chapter 7)* must be fitted and in good working order. A sailboat with an auxiliary engine must be capable of separately showing the lights of either a sailboat or a powerboat; the lights must be wired so that the display can be changed from one to the other.
- **Visual distress signals** *(page 71)*. Every boat must have acceptable visual distress signals even if not legally required by the USCG. On inland rivers and lakes, any device suitable for attracting attention and getting assistance may be carried to serve the purpose.
- **Ground tackle** *(Chapter 12)*. An anchor of suitable type and weight for the particular boat, along with line of appropriate size and length, is a valuable safety item should the engine fail and the boat be in danger of drifting or being blown into hazardous waters.
- **Bilge pump and bailer**. All boats must have a bilge pump or bailer of a suitable size, and in proper operating condition. Most common are an installed electrical pump for boats longer than about 18 feet, and a hand scoop-type bailer on smaller craft. A manual bailer is required for the Courtesy Marine Examination in addition to mechanical pumps, in case the power fails.
- **Propulsion.** All Class A boats must carry a second means of propulsion, for example a paddle, oars or an alternate mechanical means that may require a separate battery and fuel source.
- **Fuel systems.** Because, according to Courtesy Marine Examination requirements, there is no such thing as a portable

In most boating areas, skippers can obtain a USCG Auxiliary Courtesy Marine Examination of their boats. A boat that meets the requirements receives a decal for the current year; the color of the decal changes each year. Failure to pass the CME is not reported to any authorities, nor does it carry any penalty to the owner.

fuel tank larger than 7 gallons, any fuel tank larger than 7 gallons must meet all requirements for permanent tanks. Portable fuel tanks (7 gallon capacity or less) must be constructed of sturdy, non-breakable material in safe condition. Tanks must be free of excessive corrosion and must not leak. Any vents must be capable of being closed; the tank must have a vapor-tight, leak-proof cap.

All tanks must be properly secured in the boat to prevent excessive movement. Permanent fuel tanks (over 7 gallons capacity) and fuel lines must be free of excessive corrosion and must not leak. Permanent fuel tanks must be grounded. The fuel fill pipe must be securely fitted to the fuel fill plate and located outside of a closed compartment where any spilled fuel will be directed overboard. A vent terminating outboard of the hull and compartments must lead to each permanent fuel tank.

- **Seaworthiness.** The boat must be free from fire hazards, in good overall condition, with the bilges reasonably clean and the visible hull and structures generally sound. The maximum persons capacity and maximum horsepower capacity must not be exceeded.
- **Appliances**—galley stoves or heaters, for example—and their fuel tanks must be of a marine type, and installation must present no hazard to the craft and its occupants. Appliances must be properly secured and the system must not leak. (No odor of fuel must be detected when the system is turned on.) There must be no flammable material in the vicinity of stoves or heaters.

    Adequate ventilation must be provided for appliances as well as their fuel supplies. Appliance shut-off valves must be readily accessible. Only common appliance fuels must be used. Due to their volatile nature, gasoline, naphtha and benzene are prohibited for use as appliance fuels if a boat is to pass a Courtesy Marine Examination.

■ **Electrical wiring** must be in good condition and properly installed. No exposed areas or deteriorated insulation is permitted. The electrical system must be protected by fuses or manually reset circuit breakers. Switches and fuse panels must be protected from rain or spray. Batteries must be secured to prevent movement, and the terminals covered to prevent accidental arcing.

■ **Registration/documentation papers.** CME requirements are the same as the federal requirements: The owner/operator of a vessel must carry a valid Certificate of Number *(Chapter 2)* whenever the vessel is in use. The person in command of a documented vessel must have the Certificate of Documentation *(Chapter 2)* issued to that vessel on board the boat unless the Certificate is being submitted to a documentation officer.

■ **State requirements.** The owner/operator may be required to comply with additional regulations specific to the state in which the vessel is registered or operated. Therefore, the boat will be checked against the requirements of the state in which the CME is conducted.

■ **Inflatable boats.** A Courtesy Marine Examination decal is awarded to an inflatable boat that meets all requirements for a craft of its size plus some additional specifications. For example, the boat

must have a minimum of three separate non-interconnected air chambers and an installed rigid transom; a strap-on outboard motor mount is not acceptable.

CME requirements for sailboats

Sailboats without mechanical power, either installed or detachable, are required to have personal flotation devices for each person on board the boat; the type of PFD varies with the size of the boat. Sailboats longer than 16 feet are eligible to become Coast Guard Auxiliary Facilities if they meet certain prescribed standards. These requirements can serve as a general guide to all owners of sailing craft as to desirable safety equipment.

Sailing craft under 26 feet in length are required to carry one B-I hand fire extinguisher, and larger boats must have on board two such units. These sailboats must meet the Courtesy Marine Examination standard of one approved lifesaving device on board for each berth, with a minimum of two such devices. In addition, such craft must meet all standards for motorboats other than those relating to propulsion machinery, fuel systems and ventilation of related compartments. This leaves in the requirements such items as an anchor with line, distress flares, and standards for galley stove installation and general electrical wiring—all matters that affect safe operation of the boat.

THE CANADIAN COAST GUARD AUXILIARY EXAMINATION

Canada has a similar Coast Guard Auxiliary examination program, administered by the Canadian Coast Guard and the Canadian Coast Guard Auxiliary. Requirements are similar to those in the U.S., although the vessel must meet CCG standards regarding the boat's mandatory safety equipment.

Of particular note are some of the ways in which the Canadian examination differs from its U.S. counterpart.

■ For vessels in Canada to complete the Courtesy Examination (CE) inspection, the owner must have on board the vessel's license or registration papers.

■ If the boat is equipped with a radio, a radio station license is required, and the operator must have a "Restricted Radio Operator's Certificate."

■ In Canada most small vessels are "licensed" and issued a number *(Chapter 2)*. A vessel referred to as "documented" in the U.S. is referred to in Canada as a "registered" vessel. No external number appears on a registered Canadian vessel— only the name of the vessel and the port where it is registered.

According to regulations, the Courtesy Examination decal "shall be issued only if the vessel and its equipment completely

comply with all applicable regulations. The boater/fisherman must repair or rectify minor faults or deficiencies 'on the spot,' before the decal may be issued." The decal attests simply that, at the time of examination, the required equipment was on board and appeared to be in good working order.

In Canada, the Courtesy Examination (CE) is conducted by both the CCG and its Auxiliary organization. The decal awarded to boats passing inspection is a different color each year, and should be affixed to the boat's starboard side window or housing.

There are many public and private organizations devoted to the promotion of boating safety. Those that are perhaps best known by boaters as sources of boating safety courses and information include the U.S. Power Squadrons, Canadian Power and Sail Squadrons, U.S. Coast Guard Auxiliary and Canadian Coast Guard Auxiliary—described in detail in Chapter 27—and the American National Red Cross, described in Chapter 5. Others, including those listed below, promote safety by establishing standards for boats and equipment, for their installation and use.

The American Boat & Yacht Council, Inc.

The ABYC is a non-profit public-service organization founded to "improve and promote the design, construction, equipage, and maintenance of small craft with reference to safety." Membership is open to both companies and individuals. The ABYC develops and publishes "Safety Standards"—recommended specifications and practices for making small boats as free from dangerous defects or deficiencies as possible. Standards are stated in terms of desired performance. They are prepared by Project Technical Committees formed as broadly based groups of recognized authorities. All technical reports and safety standards are advisory; the Council has no powers of enforcement.

The ABYC does not "approve" boats, equipment, materials or services. Some standards refer to other standards or to testing laboratories. Standards are reviewed and revised periodically, then published as supplements to the complete looseleaf format *Safety Standards for Small Craft*. This publication—a handy reference—is available from the ABYC at Suite 3, 405 Headquarters Drive, Millersville, MD 21108.

The Marine Department of Underwriters Laboratories, Inc.

A not-for-profit corporation in existence since 1894, this organization has testing facilities in North Carolina. Commonly called UL, it serves industry and the boating public by conducting safety investigations and tests of marine products, by developing Marine Safety Standards and by preparing special Marine Supplements to UL Electrical Safety Standards.

The principal activity of the Marine Department is testing boating equipment for safety, a process that begins with manufacturers voluntarily submitting product samples. These are then tested for compliance with appropriate safety requirements, and evaluated for overall design and construction in relation to their use. After a product has successfully completed the evaluation and complied with all of the UL requirements, the Marine Department conducts a follow-up investigation at the factory to confirm that the manufacturer's production controls comply with UL requirements.

A device that passes all its tests is "listed" by UL and may carry both on the product and in its advertising the UL "listing mark," consisting of the Laboratories' name or symbol, as shown

Only products commercially available are eligible for UL listing. The presence of a UL or UL-Marine label on any device means simply that a production sample has been successfully evaluated relative to safety requirements.

above, the product name, a control number and the word "Listed." The name of the device is included, with the name of the manufacturer, in the annual UL Marine Product Directory. Listing is an expression of UL's good-faith opinion that the item meets minimum applicable safety standards; listed products are re-tested periodically to ensure that they continue to meet the UL safety requirements. Keep in mind that, while UL listing is desirable in a product, it is not a guarantee of quality or performance, nor are all listed products of the same class necessarily equivalent in quality, performance or merit.

The label may, however, be the basis on which "authorities having jurisdiction" grant approval for use. Such authorities include individuals making judgments for their own purposes, industry people making judgments for components of original equipment installations, marine surveyors for insurance purposes and administrators of regulations making judgments required by law.

The National Fire Protection Association

Called the NFPA, the organization issues codes, standards and recommended practices for minimizing losses of life and property by fire. Activities include all aspects of the science and methods of fire protection. NFPA does not approve, inspect or certify any installations, procedures, equipment or materials, nor does it approve or evaluate testing laboratories. It does prepare, by coordinated action of committees of experts, codes and standards for the guidance of all persons in the matter of fire protection. Frequently, NFPA codes and standards are written into law or regulations by various governmental units. A good reference for boaters, the NFPA's booklet *Fire Protection Standard No. 302 for Motor Craft (Pleasure and Commercial)* is available from the NFPA, 470 Atlantic Ave., Boston, MA 02110.

Miscellaneous organizations

Other organizations that prepare design, safety and construction standards for boats and motors include the National Marine Manufacturers Association (NMMA); the American Bureau of Shipping (ABS); Society of Automotive Engineers (SAE); Lloyds of London; North German Lloyds and Veritas. Boats manufactured in any country may be built to conform to standards of any of these organizations.

SAFE VENTILATION

Good ventilation serves several important purposes aboard a boat. Proper ventilation is required by U.S. Coast Guard regulations because it is essential for removing explosive vapors prior to starting a boat's engine, particularly after fueling. Ventilation of enclosed passenger carrying areas such as the wheelhouse or accommodation spaces is also important in preventing the accumulation of carbon monoxide—one potential cause of boating fatalities. (Regardless of whether your craft is a sailboat or powerboat, if it has a permanently installed gasoline engine, refer to Chapter 9 for information on the prevention of carbon monoxide poisoning.) Finally, from a comfort point of view, good ventilation keeps fresh air flowing through a boat's living spaces and helps control mildew in bedding and upholstery.

The USCG ventilation regulations apply to all gasoline powered boats, including most outboards. Vessels for hire that carry more than six passengers are subject to special regulations (consult a USCG Marine Safety Office for details). Since diesel fuel does not conform to the Coast Guard definition of "volatile" fuel, legal requirements for "natural" or "powered" ventilation systems do not apply. Remember, however, that although diesel fuel does not explode, it does burn; a broken fuel line can cause a fire. Installing a ventilation system in a diesel-powered boat is a sensible step toward safety.

The U.S. Coast Guard regulations described below apply to gasoline-powered boats. The particular regulations which apply to a boat depend upon its date of manufacture. Historically, the regulations covering ventilation began as an operator requirement. Like the early regulations which required all boat operators to carry life preservers, operators of most gasoline-powered motorboats (except open boats) built after April 25, 1940, were required to equip every engine and fuel tank compartment with a natural ventilation system. Boat builders and operators could supplement a boat's ventilation system by installing a bilge blower; however, a bilge blower is part of a powered ventilation system. Powered ventilation was not required by regulation until 1980 when it became part of the Coast Guard safety standard applicable to the boat builder. An "open boat" was one which met each of the following conditions:

■ Engine and fuel tank compartments shall have as a minimum 15 square inches of open area directly exposed to the atmosphere for each cubic foot of net compartment volume.

■ There must be no long or narrow unventilated spaces that are accessible from such compartments in which a flame front could propagate.

■ Long, narrow compartments (such as side panels), if joining engine or fuel compartments and not serving as ducts thereto, shall have at least 15 square inches of open area per cubic foot provided by frequent openings along the full length of the compartment formed.

In 1979, the United States Coast Guard revised the ventilation regulations by requiring "powered" ventilation systems on gasoline powered inboard and inboard/outdrive boats.

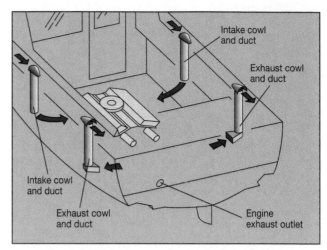

A natural ventilation system is an arrangement of supply openings or ducts from the atmosphere (located on the exterior surface of the boat) or from a ventilated compartment or from a compartment that is open to the atmosphere.

The change was intended to lessen the possibility of fire and explosions, which were the primary cause of property damage and the second most common cause of personal injury from boating accidents.

A natural ventilation system is effective only when a boat is moving fast enough to force air through the ventilation ducts, or when the wind is at sufficient velocity and direction to blow through the ducts. It had become obvious that there was a definite need for some type of forced ventilation on boats to remove explosive and flammable gases before the engine was started. In fact, boating accident statistics indicated that most fires and explosions occurred while the boat was "dead" in the water after fueling.

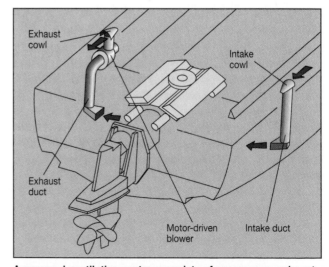

A powered ventilation system consists of one or more exhaust blowers. Each intake duct for an exhaust blower must be in the lower one-third of the compartment and above the normal accumulation of bilge water.

VENTILATION REQUIREMENTS FOR SMALL POWERBOATS					VENTILATION REQUIREMENTS FOR LARGE POWERBOATS		
		Minimum Inside Diameter for Each Duct (Inches)			Two-Intake and Two-Exhaust System		
Net Volume (Cu. Ft.)	Total Cowl Area (Sq. In.)	One-Intake and One-Exhaust System	Two-Intake and Two-Exhaust System		Vessel Beam (Ft.)	Minimum Inside Diameter for Each Duct	Cowl Area (Sq. In.)
Up to 8	3	2	—		7	3	7.0
10	4	2¼	—		8	3¼	8.0
12	5	2½	—		9	3½	9.6
14	6	2¾	—		10	3½	9.6
17	7	3	—		11	3¾	11.0
20	8	3¼	2½		12	4	12.5
23	10	3½	2½		13	4¼	14.2
27	11	3¾	3		14	4¼	14.2
30	13	4	3		15	4½	15.9
35	14	4¼	3		16	4½	15.9
39	16	4½	3		17	4½	17.7
43	19	4¾	3		18	5	19.6
48	20	5	3		19	5	19.6

Note: 1 cu. ft. = 0.028 cu. m; 1 inch = 2.54 cm; 1 cu. in. = 16.39 cu. cm

Note: 1 foot = 0.305 m; 1 inch = 2.54 cm; 1 sq. in. = 6.45 sq. cm

Ventilation must be adequate for the size and design of the boat—with no constriction in the ducting system that is smaller than the minimum cross-sectional area required for efficiency. Where a stated size duct is not available, the next larger size should be used. To determine the minimum cross-sectional area of cowls and ducts of powerboats with small engine and/or fuel tank compartments, refer to the chart above, left—based on net compartment volume (the difference between total volume and the volume occupied by the engine, tanks and other accessories). For most cruisers and other large powerboats, use the chart above, right—based on the craft's beam.

The existing regulations require both powered and natural ventilation systems to be used in compartments that have a permanently installed gasoline engine. Only natural ventilation systems are required for fuel tank compartments. Ventilation is not required for fuel tank compartments where the fuel tank vents to the outside of the boat, since the accumulation of fuel vapors in the compartment is improbable. However, regulations require ignition protection of any electrical component in a compartment containing a fuel tank in order to limit the probability of an explosion if gasoline leaks.

The USCG Ventilation Standard applies to manufacturers of all boats that have gasoline engines for electrical generation, mechanical power or propulsion. The standard applied to all boats built after July 31, 1980—except manufacturers were given the option of electing to comply with the standard any time after July 31, 1978.

While the Ventilation Standard is a manufacturer requirement, operators are legally responsible for maintenance of

their boats' natural and/or powered ventilation systems. This means boat owners must ensure that, when replacing any components in the ventilation system of a boat built after July 31, 1978, replaced components are similar to those that were originally installed by the boat manufacturer.

Ventilation system requirements

All vessels that were built after April 25, 1940, and that use gasoline for purposes of electrical generation, mechanical power or propulsion are required to be equipped with a ventilation system.

A natural ventilation system consists of at least two ventilator ducts, fitted with cowls or their equivalent:
- A minimum of one intake duct that is installed to extend from the open atmosphere to the lower portion of the bilge.
- A minimum of one exhaust duct installed so as to extend to a point at least midway to the bilge or at least below the level of the carburetor air intake.

A powered ventilation system consists of one or more exhaust blowers. Each intake duct for an exhaust blower should be in the lower one-third of the compartment and above the normal accumulation of bilge water.

Between April 25, 1940 and July 31, 1978, the regulations covering ventilation systems applied to the owner/operator. ■ **If your boat was built between April 25, 1940 and July 31, 1978**, a natural ventilation system is required for all engine and fuel tank compartments, and other spaces to which explosive or flammable gases and vapors from these compartments may flow, except compartments which are open to the atmosphere. There was no requirement for a powered ventilation system; however, some boats were equipped with a blower.

The United States Coast Guard Ventilation Standard, a manufacturer requirement, applies to all boats built on or after August 1, 1980. Some builders, however, began manufacturing boats in compliance with the Ventilation Standard as early as August 1978.

> **WARNING!**
> GASOLINE VAPORS CAN EXPLODE.
> BEFORE STARTING ENGINE OPERATE BLOWER FOR
> 4 MINUTES AND CHECK ENGINE COMPARTMENT
> BILGE FOR GASOLINE VAPORS

> **WARNING!**
> FUEL VAPORS ARE A FIRE AND
> EXPLOSION HAZARD. DO NOT STORE FUEL OR
> FLAMMABLE LIQUIDS HERE. VENTILATION
> HAS NOT BEEN PROVIDED

Help prevent disaster by posting a warning label, such as the one shown at top, in any unventilated space into which a crew member might attempt to put a gasoline or cleaning solvent container. The warning label shown at bottom is required near each ignition switch on a boat in compliance with powered ventilation requirements in the USCG Ventilation Standard.

THIRTEEN STEPS TO SAFETY MAINTENANCE

Most marine safety equipment needs some sort of maintenance—ranging from regular, ongoing attention to periodic checks at weekly, monthly or annual intervals. Following the guidelines below, custom design a checklist for your particular boat, adding to it as you install or modify equipment. Make an entry in the boat's log of all inspections, tests and servicing of fire extinguishers. Not only will this record essential checks; it may prove valuable for insurance surveys or claims. Remember, just as important as periodic checks is follow-up repair. Never delay maintenance related to safety, and avoid operating a boat that has any safety defect.

1 **Keep your bilge absolutely free of dirt and trash.**
Check frequently and clean out as often as needed. Accumulations of dirt, sawdust, wood chips and trash in the bilge will soak up oil and fuel drippings. In addition to creating a fire hazard, this may also clog limber holes—drainage holes—and bilge pumps.

2 **Inspect lifesaving equipment.**
At the beginning and mid-point of each boating season, check the condition of lifesaving equipment (pages 63-66). Replace below-par lifesaving devices immediately. Attempt repairs only where full effectiveness can be restored; if in doubt, ask for U.S. Coast Guard advice.

3 **Check installed fire-extinguishing systems at the beginning and mid-point of each boating season, or as recommended by the manufacturer. Check portable extinguishers at least monthly.**
Refer to pages 72-73 for details about maintenance.

4 **Discharge a fire extinguisher periodically, even though it is not needed for fighting a fire.**
In addition to good maintenance, this provides valuable practice. Discharge one of the portable units each year on a regular rotation basis—preferably in the form of a drill with all crew members participating. Away from the boat, put out an actual small fire in a metal pan or tub. When discharging a CO_2 extinguisher, always hold the nozzle by the plastic handle; never unscrew the hose from the cylinder to discharge it openly.

After a fire extinguisher has been removed for testing or practice discharge, have it serviced by a competent shop and reinstalled as soon as possible. Make sure that there are always enough extinguishers aboard to serve your boat's safety needs.

5 **Check the engine and fuel system frequently for cleanliness and leaks. If you find any leaks, take immediate action.**
Wipe up any oil or grease drippings and stop leaks as soon as possible. Do not use the boat, and—with all loads turned off so that no sparks will jump—disconnect the leads from the battery so the engine cannot be started.

6 **Check the entire fuel system annually, inch by inch, including fuel lines in areas not normally visible.**
When replacing fuel system components, use equivalent replacement parts—never automotive parts. If any joints or lengths of tubing or hose are worn or damaged, call a qualified mechanic without delay.

7 **Maintain your boat's bilge ventilation system in top operating condition.**

- **If your boat was built on or after August 1, 1978**, it might have either (1) a natural ventilation system or (2) both a natural ventilation system and a powered ventilation system. If your boat bears a label containing the words, "This boat complies with U.S. Coast Guard safety standards," etc., you can assume that the design of your boat's ventilation system meets applicable regulations.
- **Boats built after August 1, 1980**, which comply with the United States Coast Guard Ventilation Standard, display at each ignition switch a label which contains the information shown opposite.

Requirements for boat operators

All boat owners are responsible for keeping their boats' ventilation systems in good operating condition (regardless of the boat's date of manufacture). This means making sure that system openings are free of obstructions, that ducts are free from any blockage or damage and that all blowers are operating properly. In addition, any damaged or worn out components are replaced with equivalent equipment designed for marine use.

Elements of ventilation

Ducts, which are legally required and essential to the system, are designed for safety and long life. They should be made of non-ferrous, galvanized ferrous or of sturdy high-temperature-resistant materials. Ducts should be routed clear of, and protected from contact with, any hot engine surfaces.

Although not legally required in new boats, intake cowls normally face forward in an area of free airflow underway; exhaust cowls face aft creating a suction effect. Openings (or sets of openings) should be located with respect to each other—horizontally and vertically—in order to prevent the recirculation of fumes exhausted from a ventilated compartment. In addition, intake openings should be positioned to avoid picking up vapors from fueling operations.

8 Have a qualified professional inspect your boat's electrical system thoroughly every year, including all wiring in areas not normally visible.

Search for any cut or chafed insulation, corrosion at connections, excessive sag or strain on conductors and other visible signs of deterioration. Test leakage by opening each circuit at the main distribution panel, with all loads turned off, measuring current flow. Ideally, there should be no current flow; current of more than a few milliamperes indicates electrical leakage that should be identified and corrected without delay.

Keep in mind that connections at the boat's storage batteries need special attention. Disconnect them and, using a wire brush, remove all corrosion. Next, replace and tighten the connections, then apply a light coat of grease or other protective substance.

9 If all through-hull fittings, struts, shafts, etc. are connected electrically by an internal bonding system *(Chapter 23)*, have this wiring checked annually.

Although the skipper can make a visual check of the bonding system, an electrical expert with specialized equipment is needed for a thorough evaluation. Make especially careful checks where connections are made to the protected fitting or other metal part; connections in the bilge are subject to corrosion and development of poor contacts with high electrical resistance. If there are any signs of corrosion at points of connection between bonding wires and through-hull fittings, ask for a complete electrical test.

Remember that, in terms of possible electrolysis (stray current corrosion) damage, a bonding system with one or more poor connections may be worse than no system at all.

Electrolysis causes weakening of through-hull fittings—bolts or struts and rudder posts, for example—that could result in serious safety hazards.

10 Perform an annual safety inspection of the hull and fittings below the waterline.

On wooden boats, check hull planking for physical damage and for any general deterioration from age. Check fiberglass hulls for any cracks, especially at points of high stress. Call in an expert if you find any suspicious areas.

11 If the boat is normally kept in the water, haul it out periodically for bottom cleaning and repainting.

After the boat has been hauled out, check to make sure that all through-hull fittings and their sea cocks are in good condition and operating freely; disassemble and lubricate if necessary. Include fastenings that are susceptible to damage from electrolytic action.

12 Check underwater fittings annually.

This includes shafts, propellers, rudders, struts, stuffing boxes and metal skegs. Repack stuffing boxes as often as necessary to keep them from leaking excessively, while also checking shafting for alignment and excessive wear at strut bearings. Examine propellers to see if they need truing up.

13 Choose replacement parts carefully.

Whatever parts you replace—for fuel, electrical or ventilation systems; navigation light bulbs; or anything aboard your boat—make sure you use equivalent components that are designed specifically for marine use.

4 EMERGENCIES UNDERWAY

Whether caused by rough weather, medical reasons, overconfidence or just plain carelessness, emergencies aboard a boat are the greatest test of a skipper's abilities. How quickly he or she can react to—and minimize the effects of—an accident, a fire or other crisis on board a boat can often make the difference between mishap and disaster, or even life and death.

This chapter deals with preparing for potentially serious situations, from running aground and assisting other vessels to flood control aboard. It explains how to be equipped and ready—both mentally and physically—and how to call for help when you need it. Also refer to Chapter 11 for the special seamanship techniques required for adverse weather conditions and Chapter 5 for information on dealing with medical emergencies.

PREPARING FOR EMERGENCIES

Experienced skippers prepare themselves for dealing with emergencies as a matter of routine. They also prepare their crew. Whether their crew members are part of a proficient, competitive team, family and friends, or guests out for a casual afternoon cruise, the seasoned skipper is already aware of, and prepared for, the dangers that may present a threat to the safety of everyone aboard. The location of emergency equipment—fire extinguishers, personal flotation devices, radio, visual distress signals, etc.—should be shown to everyone aboard.

The emergencies that most often result in accidents, listed in the box at right, can all be prevented by the steps described in Chapter 3, which explains safety guidelines for your boat, and in the chapters of Section 3, all of which will help you improve your seamanship skills.

The foremost cause of accident is collision. In the end, the prevention of collisions falls on the fitness and judgment of the skipper—the person in control of the vessel's direction and speed. Preparation for emergencies must begin there, with the skipper's knowledge of the Navigation Rules *(Chapter 6)*, and his awareness of alert and careful behavior in every situation he may encounter. A lookout, in addition to the helmsman, can also be a major factor in preventing collisions.

Of course, emergencies are unplanned, and they occur aboard even the most prudently managed vessel. But strategies to cope with almost every emergency can be rehearsed. A well-practiced routine will protect the boat and its crew from most threats and, in many cases, prevention is only a matter of clear information and simple skills.

As a fundamental precaution against emergency, every boat should be well maintained. All systems and equipment, such as the battery above, should be checked frequently, and kept in top operating condition.

BOATING ACCIDENTS

According to USCG statistics on 34,759 reported boating accidents during a recent five-year period, the following thirteen causes are cited, in order of frequency of occurrence. The consequences were serious: more than 4,800 fatalities, 18,400 injuries and nearly $120 million in property damage. Although each type of accident resulted in some fatalities, those indicated with an asterisk were responsible for approximately 90 percent of total fatalities.

▪ Collision with other vessel.*

▪ Collision with a fixed object.*

▪ Capsizing.*

▪ Other casualty; unknown.*

▪ Falls overboard.*

▪ Grounding.*

▪ Fire or explosion of fuel.

▪ Collision with floating object.

▪ Swamping/Flooding.

▪ Sinking.

▪ Struck by boat or propeller.

▪ Falls within boat.

▪ Non-fuel-related fire or explosion.

The importance of emergency drills

Even the best plans are valuable only if they have been tried out and evaluated, then practiced periodically. Rehearse the procedures discussed in this chapter until they become second nature. Practice each operation with the entire crew at the beginning of each boating season, then once again on a staggered schedule later in the season. Make every effort to keep the drills enjoyable without reducing their serious nature.

When you invite guests aboard, think of them as "temporary crew." You may not be able to train them in drills, but they should certainly be shown where the PFDs are, and how to use them. Inform them in a casual, relaxed manner rather than an air of alarm. If the guests will be aboard for an extended cruise, expand their knowledge to such items as the location and operation of fire extinguishers and bilge pumps.

SUMMONING ASSISTANCE

The marine environment can be unforgiving, and what may initially be a minor problem can rapidly develop into a situation beyond your control. For this reason, let someone know when you are experiencing even relatively minor difficulties—before your situation turns into an emergency.

The USCG serves as Search And Rescue (SAR) coordinator for all maritime emergencies and is the appropriate point of contact concerning safety. If you are in "distress"—if you and/or your boat are threatened by grave or imminent danger requiring immediate assistance—the USCG will take immediate action. Increasingly, help will be provided by commercial assistance operators for a fee, but there will be instances where speed of response or lack of commercial towing craft will result in the use of USCG or USCG Auxiliary craft.

TRANSMITTING A MAYDAY DISTRESS CALL AND MESSAGE

Only when grave and imminent danger threatens life or property and immediate help is required should you use the distress procedure—radiotelephone alarm signal (if available)—and MAYDAY. Transmitted on Channel 16 or 2182 kHz (SSB), it should be heard by boats, USCG stations and other shore stations within range. Speaking slowly, clearly and calmly, use your marine radio *(Chapter 24)* to communicate the following information:

1 "MAYDAY...MAYDAY...MAYDAY."

2 "THIS IS (boat name)...(boat name)...(boat name)... (your call sign)."

3 "MAYDAY (boat name) POSITION IS (vessel position in degrees and minutes of latitude NORTH or SOUTH and longitude EAST or WEST, or as a distance and magnetic or true bearing from a well-known navigation landmark)."

4 "WE (state nature of your emergency)."

5 "WE REQUIRE (state type of assistance required)."

6 "ABOARD ARE (number of adults and children on board) AND (safety equipment aboard). (State conditions of any injured.)"

7 "(Boat name) IS A (boat length in feet)-FOOT (type: sloop, sportfisherman, etc.) WITH A (hull color) HULL AND (trim color) TRIM."

8 "I WILL BE LISTENING ON CHANNEL (16 or 2182)."

9 "THIS IS (boat name, call sign). OVER."

TRANSMITTING A PAN-PAN URGENCY CALL AND MESSAGE

Transmit a Pan-Pan urgency signal and message only to communicate that the safety of a vessel or person is in jeopardy, but the danger is not life-threatening. This call may be preceded by the radiotelephone alarm in only one type of emergency—if someone falls overboard from your boat and you require the assistance of other vessels to retrieve him.

1 "PAN-PAN...PAN-PAN...PAN-PAN" (properly pronounced "pahn-pahn").

2 "ALL STATIONS (or the name of a particular vessel)."

3 "THIS IS (boat name)...(boat name)...(boat name)... (your call sign)."

4 "WE (state nature of your emergency)."

5 "WE REQUIRE (state type of assistance required or give other useful information such as your position, a description of your vessel, and/or the number of people on board)."

6 "(Boat name) (your call sign)."

7 "OVER."

CANCELLING A MAYDAY OR PAN-PAN

If you have transmitted a Mayday or Pan-Pan call, then find that you no longer require assistance, cancel the message using the format described below.

1 "MAYDAY" or "PAN-PAN."

2 "HELLO ALL STATIONS, HELLO ALL STATIONS, HELLO ALL STATIONS."

3 "THIS IS (boat name) (your call sign)."

4 "THE TIME IS (state the time of transmission by 24-hour clock)."

5 "SEELONCE FEENEE" (to cancel Mayday) or "CANCEL PAN-PAN."

6 "OUT."

How to signal distress and urgency

Aboard most boats, the radio is the primary means for getting assistance. (Refer to Chapter 24 for information on radio operation and operators' permits.) Channel 16 VHF/FM and 2182 kHz MF/SSB are dedicated distress and calling frequencies that are monitored by the Coast Guard at all times. Citizen's Band (CB) is no longer monitored at most USCG stations.

On the high seas far offshore, farther than about 20 miles (37 km), you should call the Coast Guard directly on one of their 4 or 6 MHz (4000 or 6000 kHz) or higher working frequencies. A more effective procedure, however, would be to call a "High Seas Marine Operator" on one of the calling or working frequencies selected for the distance and time of day; these operators are constantly alert for calls of all kinds. You will be patched through (connected) to the Rescue Coordination Center at no charge; you may then be directed by the Coast Guard to shift to one of their working frequencies for continued communications.

The USCG's primary SAR role is to assist mariners in distress. If you are in distress, first use, if possible, the international radiotelephone alarm signal—two audio tones of different pitch, 1300 and 2200 Hz, transmitted alternately ¼ second of each tone. (Some sets have automated Channel 16 selection and transmission.) The purpose of this signal is to attract the attention of people on watch and, at some stations, to activate automatic devices giving an alarm. It must be used only to announce that a distress call or message is about to follow. Next, immediately transmit a Mayday call on the radio. Speaking slowly, clearly and calmly, use the format for transmission suggested opposite.

If you require the assistance of other vessels, but the danger is not life-threatening—in the case of a crew overboard, for example—the situation is one of urgency. Broadcast the Pan-Pan urgency signal, shown opposite. The Pan-Pan signal has priority over all transmissions except the Mayday distress call and message. Once the Mayday or Pan-Pan emergency is over, the signal broadcast "to all ships" must be canceled, using the format shown opposite.

Radio silence

The signal "Seelonce (the French pronunciation of "silence") Mayday" has been adopted internationally to control transmissions on the distress frequency, telling all other stations to leave the air and maintain radio silence. This signal is to be used *only* by the unit in distress or the station controlling the distress traffic. Any other station that considers it necessary to advise one or more other stations of the need to keep off the air should use the signal "Seelonce Distress" followed by its identification.

The signal to indicate the end of radio silence and permission to resume normal operation is "Seelonce Feenee" (French for "silence ended") or "pru-donce" (French for prudence). This signal may be transmitted only by the station that has controlled the distress traffic.

Flames in a bucket

Code flags November and Charlie

Smoke

Gun fired at one-minute intervals

Parachute red flare

Square flag and ball

"Mayday" by radio or radio-telephone alarm

Radio-telegraph alarm

Morse code SOS

Fog horn sounded continuously

Dye marker (any color)

Person waving arms

Red meteor flares

Position indicating radio beacon

Black square and ball on orange background

These distress signals are contained in both the Inland and International Rules; refer also to Chapter 6. Although these are the ones that are officially recognized, in an emergency you may use any means possible to summon help, including flying the national ensign upside down. A strobe is permissible in some areas; the Inland Rules recognize a high intensity white light flashing at regular intervals from 50 to 70 times per minute.

If you hear a Mayday call

If you are not in distress but you hear a Mayday call, listen carefully—do not transmit. As you listen, try to determine if your boat is in the best position to take the necessary action, or if some other vessel is better located or better equipped to deal with the situation.

If yours is the logical boat to render assistance, reply with a call to the distressed vessel as follows: "Name of boat in distress)...(name of boat in distress)...(name of boat in distress). This is (your boat name)...(your boat name)...(your boat name and call sign). Received Mayday." When the other vessel has acknowledged your call, continue with your offer of assistance by giving your position, your speed toward the scene of distress and the estimated time to get there. But be sure before you transmit that you will not be interfering with the signal of another vessel better situated to render immediate assistance. Keep in mind that the "Good Samaritan" Provision *(Chapter 6)* protects you from liability.

REPORTING BOATING ACCIDENTS

Boating Accident Reports are intended to assist the Coast Guard in determining the cause of accidents and making recommendations for their prevention, and in compiling appropriate statistics. In case of collision, accident or other casualty involving a vessel subject to the Federal Boat Safety Act of 1971, the operator must make a formal report within 48 hours if the incident results in any of the following circumstances:

■ Death.

■ An injury requiring medical treatment beyond first aid.

■ The disappearance of a person from a vessel under circumstances that indicate death or injury.

The report must be filed within 10 days if the incident results in either property damage totaling more than $500 or in complete loss of a vessel. Most state boating laws require that reports of boating accidents be made to a designated state office or official. If, however, there is no state provision for reporting such incidents, a report must be made to the Coast Guard Officer in Charge, Marine Inspection, nearest the site of the accident.

Coast Guard regulations on accident reporting list the information that must be furnished. The Boating Accident Report—CG-3865—may be used in recreational boat reports to the Coast Guard; states normally use this form or one of their own patterned after it. (Note that reporting requirements and forms are different for boats in commercial operation.)

If yours is not the logical boat to take action, maintain radio silence but monitor the frequency closely for any further development. Start making notes so that you can record the events in your boat's log. When another station transmits a distress message, the words "Mayday Relay" must be spoken three times before station identification.

Making a non-distress call

If your situation is not a distress, simply call "Coast Guard." If alternate sources of assistance are available, the Coast Guard will normally coordinate the efforts to assist you. If you have a friend, marina or commercial firm that you want contacted, for example, the Coast Guard will attempt to do so. You may also contact them directly on Channel 16 VHF/FM or through the marine operator. If this is unsuccessful, the Coast Guard will make a Marine Assistance Request Broadcast (MARB) on your behalf. This announces that you need help, gives your location and invites others to come to your aid.

Thereafter, if you do not accept services offered in response to the first MARB, you have two options. The USCG will supply information about commercial firms, if available, so you may contact them directly. Or, if you request, the USCG will make a second MARB to see if other help is available.

If you do not have a marine radio, attempt to signal a fellow boater who can either assist or call the Coast Guard for you. In a distress situation, use flares or any other distress signaling device to catch the attention of people aboard other boats in the vicinity. Refer to the officially recognized signals shown on page 85.

Keep in contact with the Coast Guard at regular intervals, and tell them when help arrives. If someone offers help but cannot get to you within a reasonable time, usually not to exceed one hour, contact the Coast Guard to arrange other assistance. In addition, inform the Coast Guard if conditions change sufficiently to cause alarm—for example, if a medical emergency develops, a storm approaches, your boat begins taking on water or your last reported position changes.

If the Coast Guard or Coast Guard Auxiliary arrives to assist you and you require a tow, they normally will tow you to the nearest location where you can either arrange for repairs or a tow back to your home port. However, if a commercial firm is available to help you safely in a reasonable time, the Coast Guard will not provide direct on-scene assistance. Since you will have to pay for the commercial firm's services, inquire about fees before accepting that service. Remember that if you agree to the assistance of a commercial firm and then refuse this service when it arrives, you still may be legally obligated to pay a fee.

In addition to Coast Guard, Coast Guard Auxiliary and commercial firms, others that may be available to assist you include a fellow boater, local fire or police department or another public agency. Keep in mind that a Good Samaritan, although well-meaning, may not have the equipment or skills needed to help you safely and effectively.

DEALING WITH FIRE AND EXPLOSION

Preventing fires aboard

Fire safety is something that everyone who owns or operates a boat should practice. Each year, boating fires and explosions injure hundreds of boaters and cause millions of dollars in property damage. While there is a greater chance of a fire or explosion on a boat than on land, many of these accidents can be prevented.

Fuel and fuel vapors are two of the leading ingredients in all boating accidents involving fires and explosions. Follow the guidelines for safe fueling *(pages 65-66)*, as well as the following reminders provided by the United States Coast Guard and the National Fire Protection Association.

General and seasonal checks

■ Be alert for damage to your boat's fuel system. Over a period of time, fuel fittings and fuel hoses wear out. Inspect these fittings and hoses regularly, especially near the engine where engine heat can accelerate deterioration.

■ Inspect fuel tanks annually. Pay particular attention to bottom surfaces, which may have been in contact with bilge water, and any part of the tank that touches the boat structure. The tank could have rusted or been damaged due to rubbing and abrasion. A suitable vent pipe for each tank should lead outside the hull; vents should never terminate in closed spaces such as the engine compartment or under the deck.

■ Be sure the fuel fill pipe is tightly fitted to the fill plate and located outside closed compartments. The fill pipe should also be located where any spilled fuel will be directed overboard. Look for fuel fill hoses that are dry and cracked or soft and mushy. Such hoses should be replaced with marine fuel hoses immediately.

■ If a hose or fuel tank leaks, replace before using your boat.

■ On a boat with portable fuel tanks, make sure the vents can be closed and that the tanks have vapor-tight, leak-proof caps. The vent on a portable tank should be open when the motor is running, but when the tank is not in use, the vent and the cap should be tightly closed.

■ Never leave motor fuel or other flammable liquids in open buckets. Choose non-volatile cleaning fluids.

■ If the boat has powered ventilation (a bilge blower), make sure the blower operates.

■ If your engine is equipped with a backfire flame arrester, keep the flame arrester screen on the carburetor clean.

■ Be sure heating and cooking appliances on board are secured and operate properly. Refer to the owner's manual for the appliance for guidance on inspecting for leaks in valves and connections; never use a match.

■ In the galley, fit splashproof covers to appliances and controls. Keep the galley clean, especially the sides of pans and any grease filters. Never leave the galley unattended when power or fuel is switched on.

■ Make sure that flammable items are stowed safely and cannot come into contact with cooking or heating appliances or hot engine parts.

Pull out the extinguisher lock pin and squeeze the two handle levers together. Aim at the base of the flame with a sweeping motion; hold the stream steadily on the base of the flames until you are certain the fire is out. Dry chemical extinguishers are effective for 5 to 15 feet from the nozzle, Halon 1211 for 9 to 15 feet, Halon 1301 up to 6 feet and CO_2 up to 3 feet.

■ Install a sniffer-type alarm if your galley stove uses a heavier-than-air fuel such as propane, or if the boat has a gasoline engine. Otherwise, fumes from these fuels may settle in the bilge, undetected by crew members; an open flame or spark could ignite the fumes.

■ Make sure that Coast Guard-approved fire extinguishers *(page 60)* on board are in working order—that gauges register and that nozzles are clear. Take a boating safety course that teaches the correct use of a fire extinguisher aboard a boat. The time to learn is *before* a fire occurs.

■ Look for bare wires or loose electrical connections; these might cause a short in your boat's electrical system, which could start a fire.

■ Do not store small disposable propane cylinders or charcoal lighting fluid on board.

■ Discourage or minimize drinking of alcohol while the boat is underway.

■ Do not smoke when in bed, refueling or changing gas bottles. Never leave a lighted cigarette unattended; put it out when finished, and use an ashtray that will not slide off a table and overturn should the boat rock or heel over.

■ Dispose of paper and packing material as soon as stores are broken out.

■ Keep light bulbs clean; make sure that wattage is proper for each fitting.

■ Never store oily cloths or combustible material in lockers.

■ If working with wood chips, sawdust and shavings, sweep up and dispose of the scraps as soon as possible.

■ When hauled out, if your boat does not have a metal hull, install an earth lightning conductor.

■ Conduct a bow-to-stern inspection, checking for loose fuel, gas fumes and any malfunctioning instruments.

ASSESSING FIRE EXTINGUISHER CONTENTS

Contents	Use (type of fire)*	Advantages	Disadvantages	Precautions
CO_2	A, B, C	Smothers a fire and does not conduct electricity, so can be used on any fire.	Less effective in open areas where winds or drafts exist. If ignition source has not been removed, fire can re-flash. Will stop a running engine. Can smother fire-fighter in a closed space.	Do not touch discharge horn when in operation. Use caution in unventilated areas.
Dry Chemicals	A, B, C or B, C	Inhibit chemical process of combustion.	Can stop an engine. Can leave a residue that can damage electronic equipment or machinery.	Should never be partially discharged. If discharged even briefly, the nozzle may later leak. Discharge completely and recharge.
Foam	A, B	Most effective with Class B fires; will work on Class A fires.	Leaves a messy residue. Should not be used on Class C fires.	
Halon	Commonly available in portable units and fixed systems for fighting Type A, B and C fires, but is currently being phased out for environmental reasons. According to a 1987 international treaty to eliminate ozone-destroying chemicals, the use of Halon will be banned in developed countries by the year 2000 *(Chapter 16)*.			Gauges may be unreliable; have weight tagged annually.
Pyrene and Carbon Tetrachloride	Commonly used in past; still found in older extinguishers. GENERATE TOXIC GAS THAT CAN BE FATAL. DO NOT USE.			DO NOT USE.

*A=Ordinary combustibles: wood, cloth, rubber, paper, many plastics
B=Flammable liquids: gasoline, solvents, grease, oil, some paints
C=Electrical equipment: wiring, fuse boxes, energized electrical equipment

Equip your boat with fire extinguishers that are USCG- or Canadian DOT-approved *(page 72)*. **Such extinguishers are available with various contents, as described above.**

Before casting off

- "Sniff" your bilges. Usually your nose is the best fuel/vapor detector. This will mean getting down on your hands and knees; however, it is the best way to check.
- Operate the bilge blower for at least four minutes before starting an inboard engine. If you still smell fumes after four minutes, try to find what is causing them and make repairs before starting the engine.
- Make sure the location of your fire extinguishers is known to all persons on board.
- When refueling, close all hatches, ports and other openings; shut off all engines and motors; and refrain from smoking. Fill all portable tanks on the pier.
- After refueling, wipe up or wash off any excess or spilled fuel; open all hatches and ports, and let the boat air out. "Sniff" your bilges. Operate the bilge blower for at least four minutes before starting an inboard engine.

Taking quick action

Unfortunately, sometimes fires do occur despite a skipper's best efforts. Chances are, however, that this will result in a less severe emergency if the required firefighting gear *(pages 70-71)* is on board, in good working condition and readily accessible, and if those aboard respond with speed.

A fire may start with a dramatic explosion or on a much smaller scale. The skipper of a vessel, even a small one, should have in mind the action to be taken if fire strikes. The first consideration must be for the passengers, and the skipper should have a plan for abandoning ship if need be *(page 99)*. If you have a gasoline explosion, there usually is little you can do except reach for a personal flotation device and go over the side. When clear of the danger, account for all crew members. Give whatever assistance you can to anyone in need or in the water without a buoyant device. Keep everyone together in a group.

If abandoning ship is not immediately indicated, take the following steps as quickly as possible:
- Head the boat, if possible, so the flames blow outboard, not inboard.
- Make a radio distress call *(page 84)*, if time permits, giving the boat's location.
- Make sure the passengers move to the safest areas of the boat, such as the bow, with their life preservers on.
- Reach for the appropriate fire extinguisher *(pages 70-71 and chart above)*, and fight the fire as described opposite. Remember that a typical small marine fire extinguisher has a discharge time of only 8 to 20 seconds. From the start of the discharge, aim at the base of the fire, not the smoke.

Fighting fires of various types

■ **Galley fires.** Fires in the galley are most likely to be fueled by flammable liquids such as grease, propane or alcohol, or by combustible solid materials such as paper, wood or fabric. A U.S. Coast Guard-approved Type A/B extinguisher will be effective against both kinds of fires. If no extinguisher is available, use materials at hand such as baking soda or a water-soaked towel. If using baking soda, pour some in your hand, then throw it at the base of the flames. Do not use water on grease fires; the grease will float on top of the water and can carry flames to other parts of the vessel. The same is true of alcohol stove fuel.

If your stove uses propane for cooking, turn off the fuel supply from the tank. (The shut-off valve should be near the stove but neither behind it nor in a location that will require reaching through flames.) Once the fuel supply is cut off, let the fire burn itself out. If necessary, soak nearby wooden or fabric surfaces with water to keep the fire from spreading.

■ **Gasoline, diesel oil or grease fires.** Use a Type B foam, CO_2 or dry chemical extinguisher. Do not use water, which will only spread the flames. A common source of deck fires aboard boats is the gasoline used to fuel the dinghy's outboard motor. Although Coast Guard regulations do not require that a fire extinguisher be carried in most dinghies, you should keep a Type B extinguisher aboard and make certain it is nearby whenever you are handling gasoline.

■ **Fires belowdecks.** Fires in a vessel's cabins or lockers will most often be fueled by combustible material such as wood, paper or fabric. You should have a Type A extinguisher mounted below where you and your crew can get to it easily, even in the dark. If no Type A extinguisher is available, flood the fire's base with water and/or rob the fire of oxygen by closing a door or hatch to snuff it out.

If you must open a door or hatch behind which fire may be burning, feel its exterior first. If it is too hot for you to touch, the fire is probably still burning. If you must open the door or hatch, have a portable Type A extinguisher ready, open the door slowly, stay as low as possible, and keep the door or hatch between yourself and the possible fire.

■ **Engine fires.** Shut off all engines, generators and fans sharing the engine space involved with the fire, then close any engine-room doors or hatches. If the engine-room fire extinguisher system has not discharged automatically, activate it manually. Order a trained crew member to stand by the life raft and prepare to launch it; order the crew into life jackets. Transmit a Mayday distress call and message or Pan-Pan urgency call and message *(page 84)*. If the engine-room fire extinguisher has discharged, keep all engine-room doors and hatches closed for 15 minutes before opening.

Use a portable fire extinguisher appropriate to the type of material that is burning *(chart, opposite)*. Aim the extinguisher at the base of the flames, through the smallest access hole to the engine compartment; this avoids spreading the flame into the rest of the boat.

■ **Electrical fires.** Use an approved Type C fire extinguisher designed specifically for this purpose; never use water, which conducts electricity. Fires in electrical-wiring insulation cannot sustain themselves without a great deal of oxygen; if your circuit panels are encased in a heavy metal box, in many cases closing the box will be sufficient to extinguish a fire.

Fire aboard a boat is a serious matter. If the fire starts with an explosion, there usually is little you can do except grab a life preserver and go over the side immediately.

CONTROLLING LEAKS

At the first sign of water entering your boat, quickly try to identify where the water is coming in and the nature of the leak. If your boat is damaged by collision with another boat or if you hit a submerged object, especially at high speed, the location of the leak will probably be obvious.

However, a more likely cause of leaks is failure of through-hull fittings and related parts such as hoses, keel bolts, underwater exhausts, stuffing boxes and rudder posts; check these locations first. This is where a thorough knowledge of your boat is essential. If you have taken the time to diagram the location of every through-hull fitting on your boat, you will be well prepared to find the problem more quickly, and to deal with the situation in a calm, logical way.

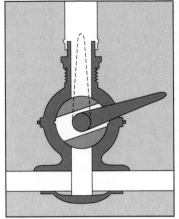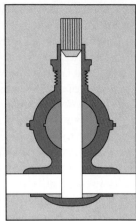

If the cause of the leak is a damaged hose, closing the sea cock *(above, left)* should solve the problem. However, if a through-hull fitting fails and its sea cock or gate valve cannot be closed, hammer in a plug to stem the inflow of water *(above, right)*.

Preparing in advance for leak control

Even if you can't prevent a leak, you can be well prepared to repair it with speed and confidence. The following precautions may help when your boat begins taking on water:
- Install the largest possible manually operated diaphragm pump; such units are available with a capacity of one gallon per stroke. Mount the pump so that you can operate it continuously without excessive fatigue.
- Have on board softwood plugs—one of appropriate diameter for each size of through-hull fitting in your boat, tapered so they can be driven into place from the inside.
- To prepare for the possibility of hull damage, stock a small, strong tarpaulin with corner grommets. When dock lines are attached, the tarpaulin can be maneuvered to cover a damaged hull area from the outside, then secured. Alternatively, there is a commercially available product that operates as a "leak umbrella," which is inserted from the inside of the boat through a large opening in the hull, then opened up in umbrella-like fashion to cover the hole and secured with the handle. Although this may not stop all leaking, it can significantly reduce the water inflow.
- Be prepared to take advantage of the engine to gain full pumping capacity, as shown at right. The alternative system shown can also be used to admit a small, controlled amount of water into the bilge for testing the operation of automatic bilge pump controls, and for cleaning.

Taking immediate action

As soon as you suspect damage that might cause a threatening leak, switch on all electric bilge pumps. (Even if you discover no leak, the pumps will not be damaged by a brief run while dry.) Assign someone the task of calling for emergency assistance *(page 84)*—even before you are sure that you will need help. Activate a manual pump if you have an extra person on board. Then investigate for possible damage.

Caution for boats connected to shore power, or when an on-board 120-volt AC genset is running: If your boat has suffered hull damage as the result of a collision with another boat or an object, consider the possibility that the collision might also have damaged the vessel's electrical system. If a live electrical wire has been knocked loose and is discharging current into bilge water, anyone stepping or reaching into that bilge water could suffer a serious, possibly fatal, shock. If any electrical wires have been pulled loose and come into contact with bilge water, or you notice any electrical sparking, shut down the main breakers in your AC and DC electrical panels before exposing yourself to the water in the bilge.

Remember that a boat floats as long as water is pumped out faster than it leaks in. Assign someone to investigate the extent of the damage by checking the bilge. If conditions permit, make this investigation yourself. If leaking is rapid, plug the leak and do everything possible to remove the water. Do whatever works fastest with the materials at hand, from the emergency pumping procedure shown below to forming a bucket brigade. If your leak occurs offshore, keep in mind that USCG aircraft carry pumps that can be dropped in floating containers to boats that need them. Emergency operating instructions are on and in the containers.

Stopping the inflow of water

The action that you take to stem the flow of water into your boat will depend on the nature of the leak itself. Almost anything soft can be stuffed into a hole in the hull—from cushions and pillows to bedding and spare sails (never PFDs; you might need them). As quickly as possible, reinforce soft plug materials with something flat and solid, such as a hatch cover, battens or bed slats. Assign a crew member to hold the plug in place. The plug should be monitored at all times by one crew member, while other members continue pumping the water that has entered the boat. In the meantime, head the boat to a nearby destination where necessary repairs can be made.

If the material is applied from the outside—the most effective method, since water pressure will help to hold it in place—the boat must be stopped while the temporary patch or plug is positioned and secured. If you are going to try to reach shore with such a rig in place, make certain its top edge is well above your vessel's waterline.

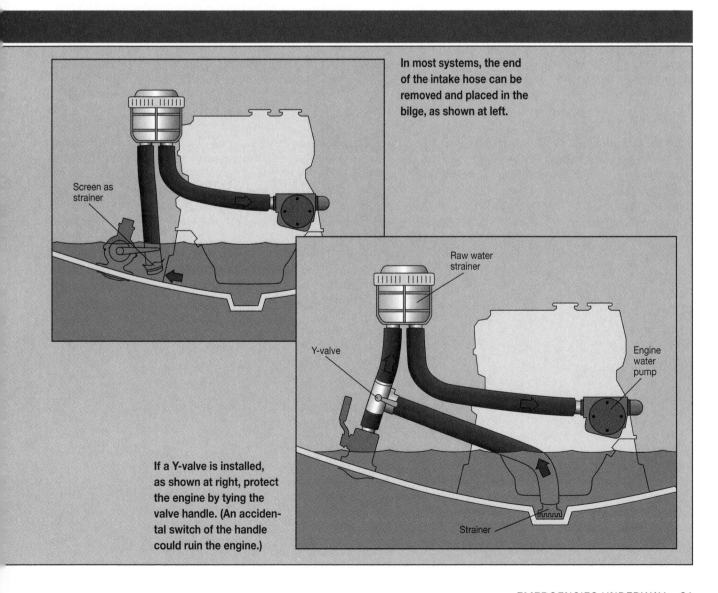

In most systems, the end of the intake hose can be removed and placed in the bilge, as shown at left.

Screen as strainer

Raw water strainer

Y-valve

Engine water pump

If a Y-valve is installed, as shown at right, protect the engine by tying the valve handle. (An accidental switch of the handle could ruin the engine.)

Strainer

CREW OVERBOARD

One of the most frightening emergencies that can occur aboard a boat is a crew member falling overboard. Traditionally called "Man Overboard," this life-threatening crisis is being called, with increasing frequency, "Crew Overboard" (COB). Although man-overboard drills have been a routine part of boating courses for decades, they have been largely overlooked by many powerboat and sailboat operators.

During the last decade, on-the-water research on sailboats and powerboats alike has led to some dramatic changes in recommended crew-overboard techniques. Testing by the Naval Academy Sailing Squadron in Annapolis and the Sailing Foundation of Seattle, Washington, has shown that the priority is getting the boat near the victim as soon as possible so that he or she stays in sight of those on deck. Once the person in the water disappears, the odds of a successful rescue are low.

Crew-overboard victims face a number of dangers, including panic, injury during the fall and hypothermia. For those aboard the boat, quick thinking and coordinated action are essential to an effective rescue. Control of the situation is most likely to be maintained by those who have prepared themselves with regular drills. For such boaters, the retrieval of the crew overboard will be automatic and effective without many shouted orders, and the trip or outing will continue without undue stress.

The simplest and most efficient procedure is to follow the four steps listed below:

1. Shout "CREW OVERBOARD" and keep eyes on the victim. When someone has fallen overboard, immediate action is vital. Any crew member who sees a person go overboard should immediately and loudly shout, "CREW OVERBOARD STARBOARD" or "CREW OVERBOARD PORT," while keeping his or her eyes on the victim, pointing emphatically to the person in the water. This crew member should not accept any other duties.

Every second counts; this is an all-hands-on-deck procedure. The crew members on board should put on approved personal flotation devices and harnesses. (The last thing you want is another crew overboard to recover.) All crew members should come on deck to assist in the maneuvers. Some crew will be assigned exact duties while others will automatically add eyes on the victim.

2. Simultaneously, jettison a crew-overboard rig. One crew member will jettison the rig—depending on the equipment aboard. This might range from a personal flotation device to

Constant vigilance is essential in a crew-overboard rescue. Anyone who sees the crew member fall should shout loudly, "Crew overboard, starboard (or port) side," then point toward the victim. Make sure that one or several crew members keep the victim in sight at all times.

PREVENTING COB ACCIDENTS

■ **Slipping and falling.**
Even in calm, dry weather, decks can be slippery—salt incrustations attract moisture. Plastic decks can be especially dangerous because they are smooth and do not absorb moisture; the molded anti-skid pattern traps evaporated salt in the indentations. In contrast, unfinished teak absorbs moisture and presents one of the best non-skid surfaces, wet or dry. A number of aggressive non-skid patterns and coatings are available. Though some people complain that these coatings are uncomfortable for bare feet, remember one rule of thumb of the careful boater: Wear deck shoes at all times, especially when underway.

■ **Safety equipment failure.**
When equipment is undersized, old or worn, it can be worse than no equipment at all: It provides a false sense of security. Lifelines, harness tethers, fittings and snaps should be inspected regularly for wear and corrosion, as well as proof-tested for 3,000 pounds—the shock load of a crew member projected in the lifelines, falling overboard and dragging in the water.

■ **Relieving over the side.**
One of the most common causes of COB and subsequent drowning is a crew member relieving himself over the side of the boat in a standing position. Avoid this disaster; go below and use the head.

■ **The importance of COB drills.**
Unfortunately, despite all preventive efforts, accidents can still occur. *The need for crew-overboard drills cannot be emphasized enough.* Your entire crew should practice the maneuver until recovery is second nature. Practice often, first with a floating cushion, then with a swimmer and another boat standing by. These drills can often make the difference between a tragedy and a mishap on the water.

a sophisticated COB module containing a single-person life raft with a drogue to slow down its drift, a life vest, an 8-foot pole, a strobe light, a radio beacon, survival food, etc.

For most boats, however, a practical and effective system is a buoyant weighted pole at least 8 feet long, with its top marked by a large international orange flag and a water-activated strobe light. Such a rig usually includes a horseshoe life ring, a whistle and a small drogue. It is highly visible, and serves a double purpose: It focuses the action so that both the skipper of the boat and the COB will try to aim for the lighted pole.

The rig must be launched quickly—in a matter of seconds. If you do not have such a crew-overboard rig, throw the buoyant device that can be deployed the fastest—for example, a United States Coast Guard-approved cockpit cushion (ideally, high-visibility red or orange) or a quick-release life ring. Throw the device upwind of the victim so that it can blow toward him. (Other boats use a Lifesling or other patented recovery device, which should be used according to the manufacturer's specific instructions.)

In addition, three other tasks should be assigned: One crew member should note compass heading, wind speed, wind direction and time. Another crew member should be issuing a Pan-Pan radio call *(page 84)* to alert both the Coast Guard and other boats in the vicinity of the emergency. Finally, throwing a constant line of floating debris will aid in tracking the COB.

3. Also simultaneously, the helmsman should stop the boat's forward progress as soon as possible and then quickly reverse course.

■ On a powerboat, go in reverse gear to slow down, and proceed to turn toward the victim in a simple circle.

In a study conducted by the Seattle Sailing Foundation's Safety at Sea Committee, 300 actual live-victim recoveries were made. After testing four different maneuvers for boats under power, the Committee found that this simple turn—involving an immediate reduced-speed return—meets every criteria for small craft crew-overboard rescue. It keeps the boat close to the victim, and is the safest, most reliable and quickest of all the methods tried—regardless of the experience of the operator.

■ On a sailboat, it is always best to head into the wind immediately, using the Quick-Stop method shown above, right. (Even if you opt to start your engine, continue, at least initially, under sail. Dropping the sails costs precious time and sacrifices some control of the boat.)

If a spinnaker is set, lead the guy forward to the forestay, round up into the wind and haul the sheet tight. Drop the halyard (or cut it, if need be) and collect the spinnaker under the boom and into the hatch. Do not worry about neatness; only the speed of the recovery is important.

In the case where the COB signal has clearly been given some time after the person has fallen overboard, it may be best to jibe as this maneuver has a greater likelihood of revers-

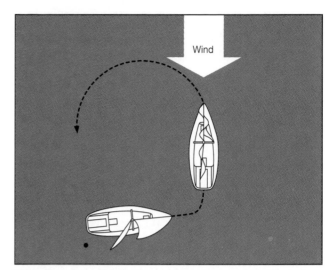

The Quick-Stop method of rescue stops a sailboat's forward progress by immediately heading into the wind and tacking back to the person in the water.

ing course with the fastest speed, moving the boat nearer the person in the water. (Remember that the victim may drift downwind, especially in large waves.)

At night or in reduced visibility, and when you are not sure when the person fell overboard, the Williamson Turn *(below)* might be your best way of reversing course: Put the helm hard over, turning toward the side (if known) over which the person fell overboard—until your heading has changed 60 degrees. Then quickly reverse the rudder and come around 240 degrees. You should then be heading back on the exact reciprocal course.

4. Getting closer to the victim. Under power, you can motor slowly alongside the victim, aiming just to windward or lee-

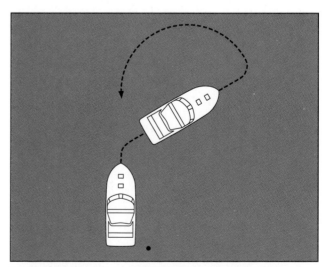

The Williamson Turn, a traditional rescue technique, is usually the rescue method of choice when the location of the crew overboard is questionable. This maneuver is also used in compass compensation, as described in Chapter 17.

WINDWARD VS. LEEWARD APPROACH		
	Advantages	*Disadvantages*
Windward	▪ Creates a lee for the crew overboard. ▪ Ease of throwing a line or horseshoe ring. ▪ Best position from which a swimmer can retrieve victim.	▪ Wave action can suddenly throw a smaller boat on victim with disastrous results. ▪ A fast-drifting boat can push a COB under.
Leeward	▪ Victim is protected from the boat going over or pounding on top of him. ▪ Close enough to pick up victim.	▪ Wave action can throw victim against the boat. ▪ Difficulty of staying to leeward. ▪ Boat may drift away faster than victim. ▪ Difficulty of throwing line or horseshoe ring against wind to victim. ▪ If COB is unconscious or injured, a swimmer might have to fight heavy waves to reach victim.

The direction of approach used by the rescue boat is controversial. Practice crew-overboard drills often; make sure you consider various wave and wind conditions, and vary the approach accordingly.

ward according to your judgment. The direction is controversial: If coming from windward in high winds and wave action, you may drift over the victim. Otherwise, in general, recovery is easier if you come from windward.

Plan to get no closer than 10 feet, and to reach a dead slow speed as you draw alongside. Remember that a boat traveling at more than one knot is impossible to either hang onto or stay with, even if a line is thrown from the deck.

If you are sailing to the victim, you may choose one of the two options described below; both methods also help to steady the deck for the actual recovery. (If you are unfamiliar with any of the sailing terms used here, refer to Chapter 10 and/or the Glossary.)

▪ The Rod-Stop Method. If you are on a close reach, use the "Rod-Stop Method," named for the well-known sailor and yacht designer Rod Stephens. As you approach the COB, dowse, roll up or luff the jib. Cast off the main sheet and tie a preventer to the boom, bringing the boom all the way out to leeward. Hold the boom down and flatten the sail, using the boomvang, cunningham and outhaul. The sail will fill at one moment on one side, at another moment on the other side, moving the boat ever so lightly forward. To get underway again just let go of the preventer and trim the sails.

▪ Heaving-to. Another option—if the boat is either close-hauled or on a close reach—is to "heave to" until you reach the crew overboard. (Heaving-to, described in Chapter 10,

involves setting the sails so that a boat makes little headway.) Then you can either tack, leaving the jib backed, or stay on the same tack and haul the jib sheet to back it. The boat will then stop and keep going forward slightly.

5. Recovering the crew overboard. One way to quickly recover your victim is to use the increasingly popular COB retrieval system called the Lifesling. This patented product features a padded sling at the end of a long line that you tow behind your boat, moving around in a circle until the victim can grab it in order to place under his arms for hoisting and retrieval, as shown below.

Whether you use a Lifesling or another method of retrieval, getting an exhausted, heavy victim on deck can be quite a challenge. In most cases, the person in the water will not be able to climb aboard due to extreme fatigue and waterlogged clothing. This stage can have tragic consequences if not acted upon efficiently and immediately. You must make a quick decision as to whether the recovery will be active or passive, as described below.

▪ In an active recovery, the swimmer is able to assist in getting on deck. You can use a sturdy ladder amidships. (Beware of using the transom; the COB could be pulled under the stern.) You can also rig two or three different lengths of line between a stanchion and another stanchion or a cleat, forming a makeshift ladder. Another alternative is to rig a line from a fixed point amidships, so that it reaches below water level, then lead it back around a stanchion to the windlass. Use this

The Lifesling is a system that dramatically improves the chances of rescuing a conscious victim. In order to recover an unconscious victim, another crew member must enter the water to position the sling on the victim for hoisting aboard.

line as a lift to help the victim aboard. (Watch toes and limbs so as not to be caught against the hull.)

- In a passive recovery, however, the victim may be hypothermic, exhausted or injured. (When falling overboard, a person often hits the lifelines and grabs on, dislocating a shoulder.) Or, even worse, the crew overboard may be unconscious. If the victim is a child or an elderly person, two or three strong adults may be able to lift him on board. But if the victim is an adult with waterlogged clothes, you will need a mechanical advantage.

On a powerboat the anchor windlass may help; otherwise, you can try a block and tackle. Unless you are certain of being able to come back on board, do not go over the side, even wearing a PFD. If you do enter the water, you must wear a PFD—for additional buoyancy and to keep both hands free and ready to use. In a small boat, there is also a danger of capsizing while recovering, so take special care.

On a sailboat, recovery can be easier because of the opportunities of using the boom with a block and tackle (the boom-vang); be careful to prevent the boom from flogging back and forth while winching up. Another way is to lift the victim in the belly of the jib. (Although some people recovered this way have experienced claustrophobia, they were brought aboard nonetheless.) A third alternative is to use the main halyard, if the mainsail is down, or any other halyard that can be a lead to a sturdy winch.

WHAT TO DO IF YOU FALL OVERBOARD: SURVIVAL FLOATING

Just as important as acquiring the skills necessary for rescuing a crew overboard is a knowledge of how to help yourself if you are the person overboard. The following tips can help you stay afloat until you are recovered.

- Keep your clothes on. If your shoes are light enough for you to swim comfortably, leave them on. If they weigh you down, however, remove them. Remove any heavy objects from any pockets in your clothing.

- If you can float on your back fairly easily, save energy by doing so. Kick only when necessary.

- While signaling for help or waiting for rescue, tread water to stay in an upright position, moving your hands back and forth and using a kick that requires little energy. Remember, the more you move around in cold water, the quicker your body temperature can drop, and the faster hypothermia can set in.

- In warm water, conserve your energy by using the facedown floating technique shown below, called survival floating. Each move you make should be slow and easy.

- Every second counts. As soon as a heaved line reaches you, quickly tie a bowline (Chapter 13) around your chest. If a Lifesling reaches you, slip it on immediately.

- As the rescue boat approaches, stay away from both the stern and the bow of the boat.

- When trying to board the boat, don't rush; it is important to make effective use of your remaining energy.

With your mouth above the water's surface, hold your breath, put your face in the water, and let your arms and legs dangle for several seconds. Then tilt your head back to raise your face above the surface, only high enough for your mouth to clear the water. As you raise your face, exhale. As your mouth clears the water, gently press down with your arms and bring your legs together. This will help keep your mouth above water. Take another breath and repeat the cycle.

DEALING WITH OTHER EMERGENCIES

Collision

The USCG advises that vessels operating at average speeds in excess of about 50 knots are increasingly common today. With greater congestion on many U.S. waterways, it is more important than ever before to be alert and to maintain a constant lookout. In fact, according to recent USCG statistics, collision with another vessel is the most common type of accident *(page 83)*. In 1991, for example, the most frequent "causes" of boating accidents were "improper lookout," "other vessel at fault" and "operator carelessness."

If your course appears to be converging with another vessel's, take careful compass or relative bearings every few min-

Many boating areas are relatively open expanses of water without specific channels. Boats may approach from one or more directions, often several at a time. Every skipper must know who has the right of way and what signal to give in each situation.

utes; increase their frequency as the gap narrows. If the bearings move forward, the other boat will cross ahead of you; if the bearings move aft, the boat will cross behind you. But if the bearings remain constant, you are on a collision course, and must take immediate action. Do not wait until the last moment. Slow down or speed up; continue to take bearings. Or turn radically toward the other boat's wake, letting that boat pass ahead, then turn back on your original course.

Although a converging course is difficult to judge with any boat, large commercial vessels offer a particular challenge. As soon as you spot a freighter, tanker or ferry, assign a crew member to lookout duty. Nothing should distract this person from looking at and taking bearings on the vessel until it's clearly ahead. Unless you are certain that you will cross its bow at least one mile ahead, alter your course so the vessel

crosses your bow. If your boat is on a bow-to-bow reciprocal course with another vessel, alter course to starboard by at least 20 degrees.

Even if you have the right of way, the *Navigation Rules (Chapter 6)* require you to do everything you can to avoid collision—even if it means reversing. If a collision seems imminent, and the other vessel's crew obviously doesn't see you, do everything you can to make your boat visible. Attract attention by shining a bright hand-held light on your sails, by firing flares or turning on a strobe light to attract the other crew's attention.

Deadheads

A deadhead is a log or piece of timber which has become so waterlogged that little buoyancy remains. It usually floats with one end down, showing only a few inches of the other end; it barely rises and falls and is extremely difficult to spot, particularly from a fast boat. Deadheads are more dangerous than rocks or reefs because they are uncharted and may appear almost anywhere. The only action a boater can take is precautionary; maintain a sharp lookout while underway.

Dismasting

A broken mast can result from improper tension on the standing rigging, a broken fitting or—as in the case of ocean racing—pushing the boat past its performance limits. In any case, this emergency demands immediate attention. Make

Make sure that an incoming tide will meet your boat's keel first, instead of the cockpit coaming, and that through-hull fittings are closed. Otherwise the hull might flood before it has a chance to float.

sure that all crew members are wearing PFDs, then direct them to take quick action to clear and secure all stray lines, rigging, sails and other loose gear—anything that could foul the propeller. That done, now it is safe to turn on the engine.

One great danger of dismasting is severe damage to your hull. In this case you must decide immediately to cut the mast loose and get free of it, or to try to save it. In the latter case, it is essential to secure the mast tightly against the hull and cushion it with a mattress or pillows. Some resourceful sailors can jury rig a new spar—from the mast stump or a whisker pole, for example—in order to catch at least some wind.

Grounding

A vessel "grounds" when it touches bottom, and if stuck there it is "aground," or "stranded." Running aground is more often an inconvenience than a danger; however, it can be a traumatic experience, particularly if the grounding is unexpected and your vessel has significant way on when it strikes the bottom. Grounding can also cause significant damage. Whatever the circumstances it is important to follow certain steps: Keep calm, check for crew injuries, check for damage to the hull, steering and propulsion system. Check for any water coming in; if there is any, stopping the leak takes precedence over getting off. Determine which way deep water lies, if tide is rising or falling and if wind and current are carrying the vessel harder aground. On a powerboat, check your raw water intake strainer to be sure it is not clogged.

In many cases, a little know-how and some fast work can minimize the period of stranding. For many skippers, the first instinctive act is to gun the engine into reverse in an effort to pull off; often, this will compound your problems. Techniques for getting off include careful backing off with sails and/or engine and kedging—using an anchor to move the boat by pulling on the anchor rode. The techniques for freeing your boat—described in detail in Chapter 11—depend on the type of boat, the type of bottom, the state of the tide and the wind direction and force.

If extrication is impossible until tide change, protect the hull with any materials at hand. Call for help *(page 84)* and/or set off distress signals *(page 85)*. Make ready the dinghy; make sure all crew members are wearing life jackets and make other preparations for abandoning ship *(page 99)*. If another vessel arrives, it is usually most practical for the assisting vessel to pass a tow line to you. The assisting craft has the ability to maneuver, making the passing procedure safer and more effective. Once the line has been thrown or floated over, follow the procedure given in Chapter 11.

Heavy weather

The ability to read weather signs *(Chapter 14)* and to make decisions that will affect your boating safety are among the most important skills you can acquire. In anticipation of high winds and rough seas, a prudent skipper takes certain precautions. Depending on the type of boat you operate and the weather conditions, your heavy weather checklist will include many of the procedures listed below:

- Secure all hatches; close all ports and windows.
- Remember that "free" water in bilges adversely affects a boat's stability. Pump bilges dry, and repeat as required.
- Secure all loose gear; put away small items and lash down the larger ones.
- At the first sign of weather worsening, make sure that everyone on board is wearing a PFD.
- Break out any emergency gear that you might need—hand pumps or bailers, sea anchor or drogue, for example.
- Check your position, if possible, and update the plot on your chart.
- Plan to alter course to sheltered waters, if necessary.
- Reassure your crew and guests; instruct them what to do and what not to do, then assign them a task to take their minds off the situation.

Swamping, foundering and capsizing

A boat is "swamped" when it fills with water from over the side. The causes can vary, from large waves coming over the gunwales or the transom to reduced freeboard because the boat is overloaded. Or swamping may result from a sudden squall, a heavy wash from a larger vessel or, in the case of small sailboats, sudden changes in the wind. Most small wooden boats have enough buoyancy to remain afloat, and will not founder—sink—when swamped; most small fiberglass boats have buoyancy built into them in the form of plastic foam flotation material. Use anything at hand to bail out the water; otherwise, hand-paddle to the nearest shore.

A boat is "capsized" when it is knocked down so it lies on its side in the water or turns over—a frequent occurrence among small sailboats that are especially sensitive to sudden changes in the wind. Most small boats will remain in that position, unless righted, and will float enough to support you.

Having capsized or swamped, it is important to remain calm and conserve energy. The general rule is to ensure that all crew members are wearing PFDs and that they stay with the boat; there may be possibilities of righting it, and rescuers will be able to find you more easily. Leave the boat only if there is a fire or if the boat is headed toward a dam, waterfall or other hazard. If the capsized boat is a small centerboard sailboat, improve your chances of recovery by trying to keep it from turning over. Get into the water immediately and stand on the centerboard, providing lever action; this is a technique taught in most basic sailing courses. If possible, have a crew member attach a life jacket or other flotation device to the end of the mast.

Take precautions against swamping and capsizing: Watch that loaded items do not shift from side to side; guard against too much power or speed on turns, and the wash of large boats. Take waves head on, or fine on the bow, at low speeds, giving the hull a chance to ride over rather than dive into them. Do not broach.

HELICOPTER RESCUE

The U.S. Coast Guard uses helicopters as well as surface craft for rescue and assistance work. Recently, the USCG has provided fixed wing aircraft with VHF/FM droppable radios. This equipment may be delivered to the distressed vessel if the Coast Guard is unable to establish communication.

When Coast Guard assistance is provided by helicopter rather than surface craft, the boat's skipper must know how to participate in the assist. Such a rescue is most effective with the advance preparations described below.

Prior to helicopter arrival

■ If possible, listen continuously to VHF Channel 16 (156.8 MHz) or 2182 kHz (SSB), or other specified frequency.

■ Select and clear the most suitable hoist area. For sailboats and powerboats, this often means clearing a dinghy or raft from the deck, and towing rather than stowing it.

■ If the hoist is performed in the dark, light the pickup areas as well as possible. Avoid shining any lights on the helicopter, however; this could blind the pilot. If there are obstructions in the vicinity, focus a light on them, making the pilot aware of their positions.

■ To facilitate the helicopter pilot's approach, make sure that he or she knows the pickup area location before the helicopter arrives.

■ Remember that there will be a high noise level and significant rotor downwash under the helicopter, so conversation between the deck crew will be almost impossible. Arrange a set of hand signals between those who will be assisting.

Assisting the hoist

■ Change the boat's course, permitting the craft to ride as easily as possible with the wind on the bow, preferably on the port bow. (The helicopter pilot rides on the starboard side of the helicopter, which helps to give him or her the best view of the boat.)

■ Reduce speed if necessary to ease the boat's motion, but continue to maintain steerageway.

■ On a small craft, there is not enough deck space to permit hoisting directly from the boat. In that case, you must assist the victim into the dinghy for hoisting from there.

■ If you do not have radio contact with the helicopter, give a "thumbs up" signal when you are in all respects ready for the hoist; use a flashlight at night.

■ Avoid static shock by allowing the basket or litter to touch down on the deck prior to handling.

■ If a trail line is dropped by the helicopter, guide the basket or litter to the deck with the line.

■ Place the injured person in the basket, sitting with hands clear of the sides, or strap the victim in the litter. If possible, the person should be wearing a life jacket. Signal the helicopter hoist operator when ready for hoist; ask the victim to nod his head if he is able, and deck personnel to give a "thumbs up" signal.

■ If necessary to take a litter away from the hoist point, unhook the hoist cable, keeping it free for the helicopter to haul in. Do not secure the cable to the vessel or attempt to move a litter without unhooking it.

■ When the victim is strapped in the litter, signal the helicopter to lower the cable. Hook up the cable and signal the hoist operator when ready to hoist. Steady the litter to keep it from swinging or turning.

■ If a trail line is attached to the litter, use it to steady the litter, while maintaining moderate tension. Make sure that crew members' feet are clear of the line.

LIFE RAFTS

Any boat that operates more than several miles offshore should be equipped with a life raft with the following features: stowage on deck, gas cylinder inflation, water ballast pockets or bladders, insulated floor, a canopy, boarding ladder and lifelines, a painter, locator lights, a survival and first-aid kit, a rainwater collector, a drogue or sea anchor and an Emergency Position Indicating Radio Beacon (EPIRB) and other signaling devices. The raft should accommodate the largest number of people likely to be aboard while the boat is offshore.

Even with today's search and location techniques, your position and predicament will not necessarily be known by rescue authorities. Even EPIRB signals present many difficulties to the Coast Guard for receipt and verification, let alone location of the source. Weather may prohibit search and rescue for many hours. In other words, if you get into a life raft, you should expect to spend an indeterminate length of time there.

A four-person life raft is one rated to support four people while it is half-inflated. It does not mean comfortable space for four people during an extended period. On the other hand, a raft loaded to capacity may be more stable and will be warmer.

The use of life rafts aboard yachts had a severe test in 1979 during the Fastnet Race. The experience of most crews who abandoned their yachts in favor of their life raft was sobering. In general, life rafts are harder to spot from an aircraft or other vessel than a yacht, may offer less shelter than a yacht (even a disabled one), and can be less stable. The main lesson learned from the Fastnet was that "you should never step *down* into a life raft"—if your boat is still afloat, even in very bad condition, you are most likely safer on board it than in a raft. The life raft is for survival when no other option is available.

Life rafts are cumbersome, expensive to purchase—and they require expensive annual inspections. But if you operate your boat in any circumstances where a collision, fire or sudden uncontrollable leak might place you and your crew in the water, away from other boats that might offer help, and drifting farther offshore, you must have one.

ABANDONING SHIP

The act of abandoning ship is filled with potential hazards, and should be undertaken only if your vessel is fully on fire or is in imminent danger of sinking. Abandon ship only as a last resort: In many cases, even vessels that have been seriously damaged will remain afloat for hours, even days, due to their natural buoyancy or to air trapped inside their hulls or superstructures.

At the first indication that a fire or a breach of your hull's integrity may become grave enough to require abandoning ship, mentally run through the procedure, as discussed below, and alert your crew that you are considering that extreme course of action. Give the abandon-ship order only when you are sure that no other option is viable.

■ As soon as you even wonder if you might have to abandon ship, make certain that all crew members are warmly dressed and wearing personal flotation devices. In waters below 60°F (15°C), crew members should also put on immersion suits. Remember that exposure to hypothermia (extreme loss of body heat) is one of the greatest dangers. Long pants, long-sleeved shirts, sweaters and jackets—even if they are soaked—can help preserve valuable body heat. If you have to order your crew into the raft, they could very well wind up in the water, and warm clothing and a PFD could prove to be the difference between life and death.

In offshore situations, all the PFDs aboard your vessel should be Type I and, at a minimum, should be fitted with reflective patches and a whistle. Even better, they should also be equipped with strobe-type personal rescue lights and mini-B or Class S EPIRBs *(Chapter 24)*.

■ Instruct a trained crew member to stand by the life raft and prepare to launch it. If you carry your life raft belowdecks

Consider a life raft as part of your offshore "survival kit." Shop carefully; sacrificing quality for a lower price could one day make the difference between mishap and disaster.

and/or it must be manually inflated, the crew member should know where it is located as well as how to inflate it quickly, and that it must be inflated on deck rather than belowdecks or in the cockpit.

■ The moment you decide to abandon ship, transmit a Mayday distress call and message *(page 84)*. After transmitting the distress message, wait 30 seconds for any vessel receiving it to respond. Then, if there is no response, transmit the distress call and message (preceded by a radiotelephone alarm signal, if possible) a second time over that same channel. If there is still no answer, retransmit the distress call and message on any channel frequently used in the area. A good second choice of VHF would be Channel 22A (157.1 MHz), which is the primary USCG liaison channel. Good second choices of SSB frequencies would be 2670 kHz, a primary USCG working channel, and ITU Channel 424 (ship's transmit carrier 4134 kHz; ship's receive carrier, 4426 kHz), which is continuously monitored by the Coast Guard as part of its Contact and Long Range Liaison (CALL) system.

■ Gather emergency supplies. If you are boating offshore, you should have an abandon-ship bag accessible at all times, stowed where you can grab it quickly on your way to the life raft. Such a bag should include signaling equipment; medical supplies; provisions, including at least a half-gallon of fresh water per person or a hand-operated reverse osmosis watermaker or solar still; clothing and fishing supplies. Also make sure that your vessel's EPIRB *(Chapter 24)* gets into your life raft.

■ Make certain that your life raft is tethered to the boat, and launch it. In heavy seas, launch to leeward amidships—the boat's most stable point. Once you have launched the raft, one crew member should steady it while a second crew member boards.

■ Load the rest of your crew into the life raft and have them fend it off from your vessel while you load your emergency gear, to avoid snagging the life raft on anything that might puncture it. If at all possible, the crew should step or jump directly from your vessel into the life raft rather than jumping into the water and then trying to crawl up into it. This not only lessens the danger of crew members being swept away from the raft, but in cold waters, it also reduces the danger of hypothermia.

■ Make sure your EPIRB is securely attached to your life raft. Activate it as soon as you enter the raft, and leave it activated. If you have reason to believe that someone is within visual range, fire a red meteor or parachute flare as soon as you depart your vessel.

■ If your boat is afire or about to sink, cut the lines tethering the life raft to it. But if it is merely awash, remember that an awash vessel is a larger target to spot than a lone life raft. Keep the life raft tethered to the boat as long as possible. (In heavy seas, free the heaving line and pay out the full length of the raft's tether—keeping the raft away from the boat to avoid a puncture or being trapped beneath the boat.)

5 FIRST AID AFLOAT

This chapter provides first-aid basics, and is based on the premise that medical help will be quickly available. It is intended as a reference, to be used in conjunction with first-aid and cardiopulmonary resuscitation (CPR) courses offered by the American Red Cross, the American Heart Association, Canada's St. John Ambulance, or local health and emergency associations. These courses teach you lifesaving skills that help you stay calm during medical emergencies, help you make educated decisions and, in some cases, aid you in keeping a victim alive until you reach shore or until emergency medical help arrives.

Whatever type of boating you do, invest in a good quality first-aid kit and have on hand at least one comprehensive first-aid manual written for boaters.

RESPONDING QUICKLY TO MEDICAL EMERGENCIES

On land, emergency medical assistance is usually just moments away. But on the water, you are on your own—at least for a longer period of time. As skipper of a boat, you are responsible for dealing with medical emergencies aboard, an obligation that relies on formal first-aid training and stocking the necessary supplies. It also means knowing the physical condition, and any medical problems, of everyone aboard your boat.

Your confidence and competence in handling medical emergencies should be on a par with your seamanship skills. That level of confidence comes from knowledge and practice; both can be acquired and honed by basic and advanced first-aid courses. Enrolling in these classes shows your concern for those aboard your boat, and a commitment to preparing for emergencies. Perhaps most important, you learn to stay calm

When taking quick action in a medical emergency, check the victim for a medical identification bracelet or pendant. This may provide lifesaving information about a diagnosed medical condition, allergy, sensitivity or prescribed medication.

in emergencies because you know what to do. You can then make decisions and take the appropriate steps to keep a victim alive or to keep injuries stabilized until you can obtain emergency medical service.

Your legal responsibility

Legally, a victim must give consent before a person trained in first aid begins to help him or her. The law assumes that an unconscious person would give consent. If a victim is conscious, make sure you ask permission before administering first aid. If you are helping a victim previously unknown to you, ask a simple question: "My name is . . . I know first aid and I can help you until emergency help arrives; is that all right?"

The recommendations for CPR and breathing emergencies in this chapter assume that the victim is an adult or a child no younger than eight years old. For infants and younger children, the care is similar; however, some of the techniques vary because infants and children vary in size. If you are likely to have infants or children under eight aboard your boat frequently, enroll in a first-aid course that specializes in first-aid techniques for that age group.

Calling for emergency help

In a medical emergency, it is essential to make sure that help is on the way—soon rather than too late. Even when in doubt about the severity of the victim's condition, save precious

BASIC FIRST-AID KIT

In addition to at least one comprehensive first-aid manual, your boat should be equipped with a first-aid kit designed specifically for your needs, according to the length of your voyages and the areas in which you cruise. Day and weekend boaters, for example, need at least a kit stocked with basics, such as a thermometer, tweezers, alcohol, sunscreen, bandages of various sizes, scissors, an eye-washing cup and a hot-water bottle/ice bag. Use of more specific items requires proper training.

Depending on the cruising waters and the crew members aboard, it may also be wise to stock items such as remedies for seasickness and jellyfish stings. On the other hand, long-range offshore cruisers require more extensive first-aid supplies and lifesaving equipment, as well as a wide range of prescription medications. In order to reduce the care-giver's risk of infection, every first-aid kit should also include a waterless antiseptic hand cleaner and disposable gloves.

When assembling your first-aid kit, consult more than one source to assess your needs. There are a number of books available on the subject of first aid for boaters and medical emergencies at sea. Also discuss your needs with the instructors of any first-aid or safe-boating courses in which you enroll. Finally, get your doctor's advice; if you stock prescription medications, make sure the expiry dates are clearly marked, and that each prescription is replaced when necessary. Once your supplies are assembled, store them in a watertight container in a dry, secure compartment. Review your kit periodically, making sure that it continues to suit your needs and that each item is in good working order.

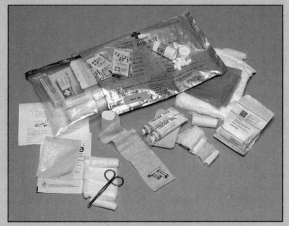

A number of companies offer kits designed for various boating needs—ranging from basic kits for day outings (above) to more extensive offshore cruising kits. Be sure to add any necessary supplies not included in the kit.

seconds by sending a distress signal or a "Pan-Pan" call *(Chapter 4)*. Remember the old adage that it's better to be safe than sorry; you can always cancel the call if you get the situation under control.

Chances are the help will come from boats in the immediate vicinity. Until help arrives, take whatever first-aid measures you are qualified to perform. You usually can make contact with a doctor through the Coast Guard on VHF Channel 16 or SSB frequency 2182 kHz. The Coast Guard has access to military and U.S. Public Health physicians and, through its AMVER (Automated Mutual-Assistance Vessel Rescue) system, keeps track of ships at sea that have medical staff aboard. If you cannot reach the USCG, try to contact Medical Advisory Systems, Inc., on SSB frequency 2182 kHz or 16590 kHz. This private company operates the Medical Telecommunications Response Center in Owings, Maryland, staffed around the clock by its own physicians. It serves primarily commercial marine vessels and remote industrial locations that subscribe to its services, but will provide assistance to non-subscribers in a life-threatening emergency.

Monitoring vital life signs

A primary survey can help you check for life-threatening conditions and give urgent first-aid care. While another crew member is calling for help, check quickly for the following danger signs: unconsciousness, loss of breathing, loss of heartbeat (pulse) and severe bleeding. If you are alone on the boat and you find the victim is unconscious, call for help immediately, then return and complete your check of the victim's vital signs. If there is no other crew member aboard, and the victim is a child, don't delay: Immediately give any necessary rescue breathing or CPR—for one minute—then go and call for emergency medical help.

If the respiratory or the circulatory system fails to function properly, the supply of oxygen to the body is decreased. In such cases the victim needs rescue breathing or CPR to stay alive until emergency help arrives. Otherwise, keep the victim comfortable and wait for emergency assistance; continue to monitor the victim's breathing and pulse rate.

If the victim vomits, or you must leave an unconscious person, roll him or her onto his or her side and clear the mouth and throat. Stabilize the person by bending his or her upper leg at the hip and knee. Raise the victim's head slightly, extend the lower arm straight out under it, and gently lower the head until it is supported by the extended arm.

Rescue breathing or artificial respiration *(Step 5)* is a way of breathing air into someone's lungs when natural breathing has stopped or when a person cannot breathe properly on his or her own. The air that you breathe into the victim contains more than enough oxygen to keep that person alive.

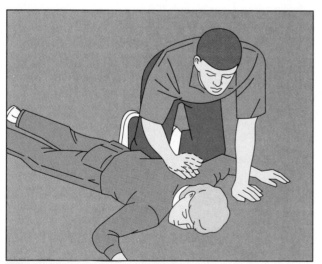

1 Check for responsiveness. Determine whether or not the victim is conscious. Tap or gently shake the victim, and ask, "Are you all right?" If the person responds, he is conscious and breathing, and has a pulse. If the victim could be injured, do not move him; most injured people will find the most comfortable position for themselves. Caution: If you suspect that the victim has suffered a spinal injury, move him or her only if absolutely necessary, keeping the head and back in a straight line. If there is no response, and if no one has yet called for emergency help, send or have someone send a distress signal, as described in Chapter 4.

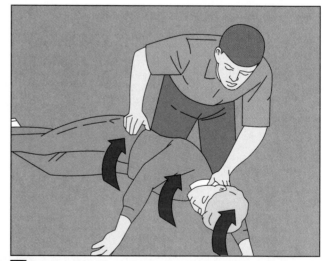

2 Roll the victim onto his back if necessary to check for breathing. Remember that unconsciousness can indicate a life-threatening condition. The tongue may have relaxed and fallen to the back of the throat, blocking the airway. This can cause breathing to stop, then the heart to stop beating. Therefore, the next step is to open the victim's airway.

If it is necessary to move the victim into a face-up position, kneel facing the person. Place one hand on his shoulder and the other on his hip. Then roll him toward you as a single unit, moving your hand from the person's shoulder to support the back of his head or neck.

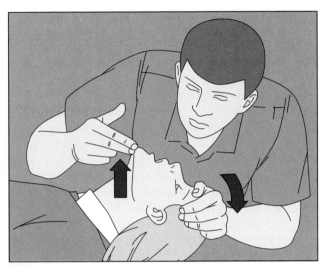

3 Open the airway. Opening the passage that allows the victim to breathe is the most important action for successful resuscitation. If the victim is unconscious, open the airway with a gentle head-tilt/chin-lift action, as shown by the arrows above.

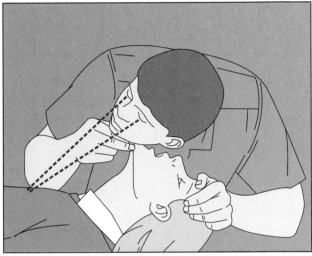

4 Check for breathing. For 3 to 5 seconds, watch the chest to see if it rises and falls, listen for breathing and feel for air coming out of the victim's nose and mouth. (Chest movement alone does not mean that the victim is breathing.)

If the victim is not breathing, act immediately, giving two full, slow breaths *(Step 5)* to get air into the lungs. If the person is breathing, keep the airway open and monitor breathing. Check for severe bleeding and control it, if necessary *(page 106)*.

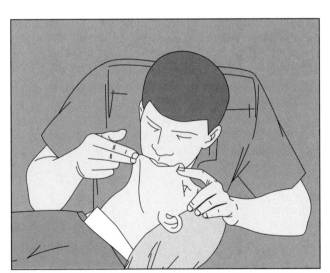

5 Rescue breathing: Give two full, slow breaths. Keeping the victim's head tilted back and the chin lifted, pinch the nose shut. Seal your lips tightly around the person's mouth. Give two full, slow breaths, each lasting 1½ to 2 seconds. Watch for the chest to rise, indicating that your breath is going in.

If the chest rises, check for pulse *(Step 6)*. If you do not see the victim's chest rise and fall as you give breaths, you may not have the head tilted far enough back to open the airway adequately. Retilt the victim's head and try again to give breaths. If your breaths still do not go in, the airway could be obstructed: While a crew member calls for emergency medical service, give first aid for an airway obstruction *(page 105)*.

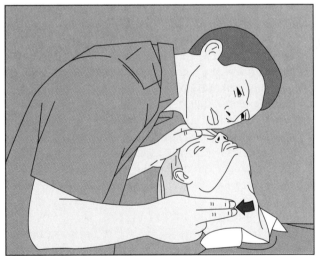

6 Check for pulse. Locate the victim's Adam's apple, then slide your fingers into the groove on the side of the neck. Applying moderate pressure, feel for the pulse, as shown above, for 5 to 10 seconds.

If the person does not have a pulse, check for and control severe bleeding *(page 106)*. Then begin CPR *(page 104)*. If there is a pulse, check for, and control, any severe bleeding, then continue to monitor breathing. If breathing stops, repeat rescue breathing: Give one breath every 5 seconds, as shown in Step 5; recheck pulse and breathing approximately every minute, or after 10 to 12 slow breaths. Continue rescue breathing until emergency medical help arrives.

TECHNIQUES FOR FIRST AID

Recognizing the signs of a heart attack

Heart attacks occur when one or more vessels feeding blood to the heart become clogged, cutting off its blood supply. As a result, the heart may stop pumping blood, causing the victim to stop breathing—a condition known as cardiac arrest.

A heart attack victim whose heart is still pumping has a much better chance of surviving than someone whose heart has stopped. Although any heart attack can lead to cardiac arrest, nearly half of all heart attack victims wait two or more hours before going to the hospital. You can improve a heart attack victim's chances of survival significantly by taking quick action that keeps the heart from stopping.

The key to a prompt response to a heart attack lies in detecting its signs. A heart attack can be difficult to identify; it is often mistaken for indigestion or heartburn. The victim may not appear to be ill, or may deny that he or she is having a heart attack. However, you should be alert to the following early warning signs of a possible heart attack:

- Pain in the chest area, which the victim may describe as tight or crushing pressure, squeezing, fullness or aching. The discomfort is usually centered across the chest behind the breastbone, but it may radiate to the shoulders, arms, neck, jaw or back.
- Sweating.
- Nausea.
- Shortness of breath or labored breathing.

Treating a heart attack victim

Place the victim in a comfortable sitting position. Loosen any restrictive clothing at the neck, chest and waist. Since the victim's survival and recovery can depend on how quickly professional care is administered, immediately have someone call for emergency medical help. You may be asked to provide the following information, if available:

- The victim's name and age.
- Any previous medical problems.
- The location and duration of the pain.
- The type of pain (for example: is it dull, sharp or heavy?).

Treating a cardiac arrest victim

If the victim's heart stops beating, the victim does not have a pulse. You must administer CPR (cardiopulmonary resuscitation) immediately. CPR combines chest compressions and rescue breathing in an effort to restore breathing and heart function. Courses in CPR are offered by the American Red Cross and the American Heart Association; such a course should be taken by every boater. However, you can and should provide this lifesaving technique to a person whose heart has stopped even if you have not taken a course. Basic CPR steps are illustrated at right.

CPR has two objectives. First, by providing rescue breathing, you supply the lungs with oxygen. And second, by compressing the victim's chest, you circulate blood and oxygen to the brain, and other parts of the body.

Treating a choking victim

Being able to recognize when someone is choking is key to saving the victim. There are two types of obstructions that you need to know about—partial airway obstruction and complete airway obstruction. It is important to be able to recognize the differences between them.

When a person has a partial airway obstruction, he can cough forcefully in an attempt to dislodge the object, and may be able to speak. He may also wheeze between breaths. If the victim is able to cough forcefully or is wheezing, do not interfere with attempts to cough up the object. Stay with the person and encourage continued coughing. If coughing persists, call for emergency medical help.

ADMINISTERING CPR

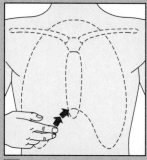
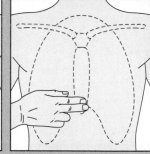

1 Monitor vital life signs *(page 102)*; if the victim does not have a pulse, begin CPR. Kneel facing the victim's chest, and locate the compression point on his chest. Slide the index and middle fingers of one of your hands along the bottom of the victim's rib cage until you reach the notch at the lower end of the breastbone. Place your middle finger on the notch and place your index finger next to it on the breastbone, as shown above.

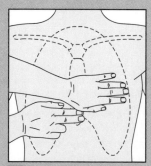
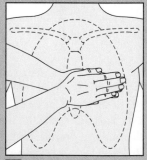

2 Place the heel of your other hand next to the index finger already in position.

3 Place the heel of the hand you used to locate the breastbone notch directly atop the heel of your other hand. Keep your fingers off the victim's chest.

A choking victim can communicate distress by using the universally recognized signal—clutching the throat with one or both hands, as shown.

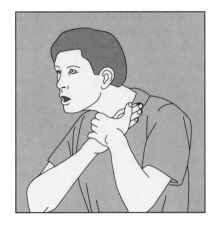

Someone with a completely blocked airway, however, is unable to speak, breathe or cough. Sometimes the victim may cough weakly and ineffectively or make high-pitched noises. All of these signals tell you the victim is not getting enough air to sustain life. Act immediately: Ask another crew member to call for emergency help.

Airway obstruction (unconscious victim)

1. Give 6 to 10 abdominal thrusts. Place the heel of one hand against the middle of the victim's abdomen, and the other hand directly on top of the first hand, as shown in Step 1 at the top of page 106. Press into the victim's abdomen with upward thrusts, as shown.

4 Position yourself to compress the victim's chest by aligning your shoulders directly above your hands and locking your elbows. Keep your arms straight.

5 Compress the victim's chest 15 times. Compress the breastbone 1½ to 2 inches at a rate of 80 to 100 compressions per minute. (Fifteen compressions should take 9 to 11 seconds.) To help to pace yourself, count aloud: "One and two and three and four..." Push down as you say the number and come up as you say *and*.) Push down and come up smoothly, keeping your hands on the victim's chest at all times.

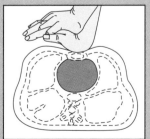

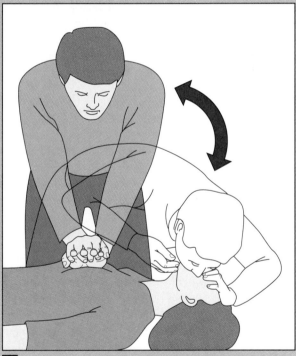

6 Open the victim's airway and give two full, slow breaths *(page 103, step 5)*. This cycle of compressions and breaths should take about 15 seconds. For each new cycle of compressions and breaths, use the correct hand position by first finding the notch at the lower end of the sternum. Perform four more cycles of 15 compressions and two breaths, then check for a pulse every few minutes. If necessary, continue administering compressions and breaths until the victim's pulse and breathing are restored or emergency medical help arrives.

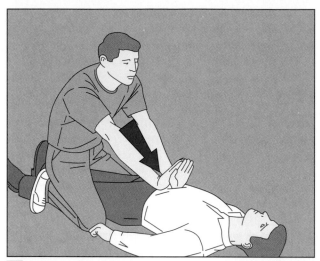

1 When giving abdominal thrusts to an unconscious victim, straddle the victim's thighs and give quick, upward thrusts.

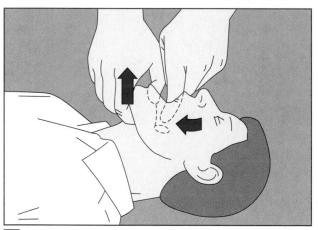

2 Lift the lower jaw and use a hooking action to sweep the object out of the airway.

2. Finger-sweep for the obstruction. As shown above, Step 2, grasp both the tongue and the lower jaw between your thumb and fingers, and lift the jaw. Then slide your finger down the inside of the cheek, as shown above, to the base of the tongue, attempting to sweep the object out.

3. Open the airway *(page 103, Step 3)* and give two full, slow breaths, as shown on page 103, Step 5. Tilt the victim's head back, and pinch the nose shut. Then seal your lips tightly around the person's mouth, giving two slow breaths, each lasting 1½ to 2 seconds. Watch the chest during the procedure to see if your breaths go in.

If the breaths go in, check pulse and breathing. If there is a pulse, but no breathing, continue rescue breathing until help arrives. If there is neither pulse nor breathing, administer CPR *(page 104)*. Also check for, and control, severe bleeding.

If the breaths do not go in, repeat Steps 1 through 3 until the obstruction is removed or the victim starts to breathe or cough, or until medical help arrives.

Airway obstruction (conscious victim)

1. Give abdominal thrusts. Wrap your arms around the person's waist. Then make a fist, placing the thumb side of the fist against the middle of the person's abdomen just above the navel and well below the lower tip of the breastbone. Grasp the fist with your other hand. Press your fist into the victim's abdomen with a quick upward thrust, as shown below, Step 1.

2. Repeat abdominal thrusts. Repeat *(below, Step 2)* until the object is coughed up, until the victim starts to breathe or cough forcefully, or until medical help arrives. If the person becomes unconscious, treat the victim for a complete airway obstruction *(page 105)*.

Controlling bleeding

Loss of blood from arteries, veins and capillaries may be internal or external. External bleeding is easy to identify; you may not be able to identify internal bleeding. In either case, uncontrolled bleeding can be life-threatening.

To control external bleeding, follow the guidelines below:
- Place direct pressure on the wound with a dressing such as a sterile gauze pad or any clean cloth. Place a hand over the pad and press firmly. If a pad or cloth is not available, have the

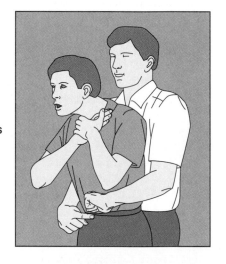

1 In the case of an airway obstruction, the objective of abdominal thrusts to a conscious victim is to simulate a cough, which can help to release the obstruction.

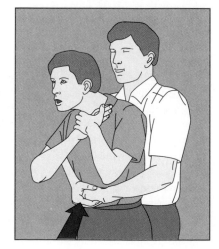

2 Each abdominal thrust should be a separate and distinct attempt to dislodge the object.

injured person apply pressure with his or her hand. As a last resort, use your own bare hand. (Take precautions, as suggested in the box, below right.)

- Elevate the injured part above the level of the heart if you do not suspect a broken bone.
- Apply a pressure bandage to hold the gauze pad or cloth in place. Wrap the bandage snugly over the dressing to keep pressure on the wound.
- If blood soaks through the bandage, add more pads. Do not remove any blood-soaked pads; leave them in place and put clean pads on top of them. If bleeding continues, make sure that emergency medical personnel have been called.
- Continue to monitor the vital signs. Watch the victim closely for signals that his or her condition is getting worse. Care for shock if necessary *(page 113)*. If bleeding is not severe, provide additional care as needed.

If you suspect internal injury, the best help you can provide is to call for emergency help immediately. While you are waiting, follow the guidelines below:

- Monitor the vital signs *(page 102)*.
- Help the victim rest in the most comfortable position.
- Maintain normal body temperature.
- Reassure the victim.
- Care for other injuries or conditions.

Handling heat and cold exposure

For boaters, four factors can have a major effect on how well the body maintains its temperature: air temperature, water temperature, humidity and wind. Humidity and wind intensify the effects of heat or cold.

Illnesses caused by exposure to temperature extremes can become life-threatening, and require immediate attention, as described below. When boating conditions pose a risk of heat or cold exposure, the following precautions can help your body manage these extremes.

- Wear appropriate clothing, including a hat.
- Take frequent breaks from extreme temperatures and exposure to strong sunshine.
- Ask yourself the following questions: Am I drinking enough water, frequently enough? Is my activity too strenuous?

Treating heat illnesses

When you suspect that a crew member has suffered an overexposure to heat, take the following action immediately: Move the victim out of the sun, to a cooler location, if possible. Encourage him or her to drink cool water slowly—about 4 ounces every 15 minutes. Loosen any tight clothing, and remove any clothing soaked with perspiration. Apply cool, wet cloths to the skin and fan the victim to increase evaporation. Let the victim rest comfortably, and discourage him or her from resuming activities the same day. Watch carefully for any changes in condition; If the victim refuses water or vomits, or you detect a change in consciousness, call for emergency help immediately.

- **Heat cramps** are painful muscle spasms. The symptoms are severe muscle contractions, usually in the legs and abdomen, but sometimes in other voluntary muscles. Although the body temperature is usually normal, and the skin is moist, these cramps may indicate that the victim is in the early stages of a more severe heat-related emergency.

To treat heat cramps, have the victim rest comfortably in a cool place, and provide cool water or a commercially available sports drink. (The victim should not take salt tablets or salt water.) Lightly stretch the muscle and gently massage the area. Thereafter, watch carefully for signals of heat-related illness, and encourage the victim to continue drinking fluids during and after activity.

- **Heat exhaustion**, an early stage, and the most common form, of heat-related illness, results in a form of mild shock when fluid loss causes decreased blood flow in the vital organs. The condition may be preceded by heat cramps, and is signaled by any of the following symptoms: cool, moist, pale or red skin; headache; nausea; or dizziness and weakness. The body temperature may be normal or below normal.

Unless treated immediately, heat exhaustion can quickly develop into heat stroke, the most severe heat emergency. Make sure the victim rests in a cool place and drinks cool water. Meanwhile, if the body temperature rises, the victim vomits or the condition otherwise worsens, call for emergency help immediately and treat for heat stroke. Position a vomiting victim on his or her side, and stop giving fluids until help arrives.

REDUCING THE RISK OF INFECTION

One of the easiest steps you can take to prevent infection while giving first aid is to maintain good personal hygiene practices such as hand-washing before and immediately after giving care. In addition, since germs can enter the body through breaks in the skin, you should always try to take precautions to prevent direct contact with a person's body fluids, including blood, when giving first aid.

You can reduce the risk of infection while giving care by following the guidelines below:

- Place an effective barrier between you and the victim's body fluids—for example, disposable gloves or plastic wrap. When controlling bleeding, ask the victim to help you by applying direct pressure, or place a dressing or other clean dry cloth between your hand and the wound.

- Wash your hands thoroughly with soap and water after providing care, even if you have worn gloves.

- Avoid eating, drinking and touching your face while providing care or before washing your hands.

Although a deep suntan was at one time considered healthy, today's medical recommendations warn about the dangers of chronic overexposure to the sun. Medical research shows that too much ultraviolet radiation not only causes your skin to age prematurely; more importantly, the sun's harmful rays may cause skin cancer to develop.

Since boating involves hours on end in the sun, you can minimize the risk by taking the precautions below. Remember that even on cloudy days, sand, water and other surfaces reflect light that can burn severely.

■ Protect your skin with a good quality commercial sunscreen that protects against both ultraviolet beta (UVB) rays and ultraviolet alpha (UVA) rays. Commercial sunscreens come in various strengths. The American Academy of Dermatology recommends year-round sun protection including use of a high Sun Protection Factor (SPF) sunscreen for everyone, but particularly for people who are fair-skinned and sunburn easily.

The Food and Drug Administration (FDA) has evaluated SPF readings and recognizes values between 2 and 15. It has not been determined whether sunscreens with ratings over 15 offer additional protection.

Apply sunscreen 15 to 30 minutes before exposure to the sun and reapply it often (every 60 to 90 minutes). Swimmers should use sunscreens labeled as water-resistant and reapply them as described on the label.

■ Wear sunglasses, which protect your eyes from UV rays. According to the American Red Cross, ophthalmologists recommend sunglasses that have a UV absorption ability of at least 90 percent.

■ Remember that exposure to the sun between 10:00 a.m. and 2:00 p.m. is the most harmful. Select clothing that minimizes your exposure: a hat with a wide brim or visor, shirts with long sleeves, and long pants.

■ **Heat stroke** occurs when the body's temperature-control system, which produces perspiration to cool the body, stops working. The body temperature can rise so high that brain damage and even death may result unless the body is cooled down quickly.

If you detect heat stroke symptoms—high body temperature, up to 106°F; red, hot, dry skin; progressive loss of consciousness; rapid and weak pulse; or rapid, shallow breathing—take immediate action. Heat stroke is life-threatening. Have someone call for medical help immediately, and cool the victim fast. Wrap wet sheets around the body and fan it, and treat for shock (page 113) while waiting for emergency help to arrive. If the victim is conscious, offer cool water to drink slowly—about 4 ounces every 15 minutes.

If the victim's condition worsens—if you observe a change in consciousness, for example—take further steps to cool the body. If you have cold packs aboard, place them on areas with large blood vessels—the wrists and ankles, on the groin, in the armpits and on the neck. Avoid applying rubbing alcohol, which closes the skin's pores. Monitor the vital signs, and maintain an open airway. Be prepared to administer rescue breathing or CPR. Give nothing by mouth.

Treating hypothermia

Hypothermia is a general body cooling that occurs when the body can no longer generate sufficient heat to maintain normal body temperature. The condition is signaled by symptoms including shivering; dizziness; slow, irregular pulse; numbness; confusion; weakness; impaired judgment or glassy stare; drowsiness and apathy. As the victim's condition worsens, the pulse rate and breathing rate decrease, and the level of consciousness decreases. If hypothermia is not treated quickly, death could result.

If you suspect hypothermia, call for emergency medical service immediately. Get the victim out of the cold and into dry clothing. Move him or her to a warmer place, if possible; wrap the victim in blankets, and warm up his or her body slowly. (Avoid rapid rewarming, which can cause dangerous heart rhythms.) If the victim is fully conscious, give warm liquids to drink. Monitor the vital signs: If necessary, be prepared to give rescue breathing and CPR. Continue to warm the victim until emergency help arrives.

Hypothermia victims whose core temperature has fallen low enough to weaken their respiration or pulse or trigger irrational behavior or unconsciousness can experience severe cardiac arrhythmia as their core body temperature returns to normal; they must be transported as rapidly as possible to professional medical assistance. If medical help is more than 15 minutes away, attempt to arrange helicopter evacuation.

Treating frostbite

Prolonged cold temperatures may freeze parts of the body. The affected areas will be cold, hard and numb. Immediately transport the victim to shelter. Warm the affected area in tepid water, gradually increasing the water temperature to between 102 and 105°F. If warm water is not available, wrap the affected area in clothing or blankets. Do not rub the affected area or expose it to excessive heat. Discontinue warming efforts as soon as the skin color returns. If normal color does not return to the affected area and the skin continues to exhibit a whitish color, transport the victim to medical assistance as quickly as possible.

ACTING QUICKLY IN MEDICAL EMERGENCIES

Listed below are some medical emergencies that can occur while you are boating. Although some are life-threatening and others pose an annoyance, it is important in each case to monitor the vital signs *(page 102)*, and to call for help right away. Remember, you may need medical service quickly; if the victim recovers or the situation becomes less urgent, you can always cancel the emergency call.

Anaphylaxis

Many victims of certain types of ingested poisons, foods, or stings or bites from insects or hazardous marine life, suffer a severe allergic reaction called anaphylaxis. This is a type of shock and requires specific treatment.

Anaphylaxis is often marked by a flushing, itching or burning of the victim's skin, especially in the face and upper chest; swollen welts spreading over the body; swelling of the face, tongue and/or lips; and a bluish coloring to the lips. The victim may also experience a tightness or constriction in the chest; wheezing and/or coughing; and difficulty in exhaling.

Many people who are subject to such severe allergic reactions carry with them a small kit containing injectable epinephrine and an oral antihistamine. If such a kit is available, inject the epinephrine; if the victim is conscious, administer the kit's oral antihistamine. Watch the victim closely. The injection of epinephrine may relieve the symptoms momentarily, but they may recur and the victim may require more injections of epinephrine or additional oral antihistamines.

If epinephrine and antihistamines are not available, the victim of anaphylaxis may experience severe difficulties in breathing and cardiac arrest. If the victim stops breathing, open and maintain the airway *(page 103)* and administer rescue breathing *(page 103)*. If there is no pulse, administer CPR *(page 104)*. Continue these steps until medical help arrives.

Burns

Burns are often classified by depth; the deeper the burn, the more severe it is. Generally, there are three depth classifications, described below. The most important action you can take is to decide whether or not a burn requires emergency medical help; refer to the box at right.

- **Superficial (first degree) burns**. If the victim's skin is red but not blistered or weeping, the injury is a first-degree burn, a burn that has injured only the top layer of the skin. Immerse the affected area in cool (not ice) water or cover it with a cloth soaked in cool water for a short period. If necessary, apply a dry dressing; cover it with a bandage.
- **Partial-thickness (second degree) burns.** If the victim's skin is blistered or weeping, the injury is a deeper, second-degree burn. Immerse the affected area in cold (not ice) water or cover it with a cloth soaked in cold water. Do not break any blisters that may be present; do not attempt to remove burned tissue; and do not apply any kind of antiseptic sprays or ointments. Apply only a dry dressing and a bandage. If possible, keep the affected areas above the level of the victim's

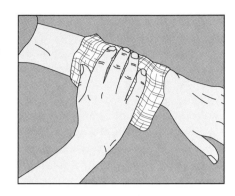

After immersing a burned area in cold water, cover gently with a dry, sterile dressing.

heart. If the affected area is extensive, it may be necessary to treat the victim for shock *(page 113)*. Call for emergency medical help before initiating treatment.
- **Full-thickness (third degree) burns.** If the victim's skin exhibits a white, gray or black charring, he or she is suffering from a still deeper, third-degree burn. Call for medical help.

Do not attempt to remove any burned tissue or adherent clothing. Shock may accompany third-degree burns. If the affected area is limited, immerse in cold water, or apply cold compresses or wet sheets or towels. Do not apply any sprays or ointments. Apply only a dry, sterile dressing and a bandage. If the affected area is the head or an extremity, elevate it above the level of the victim's heart. If the burned area is large or deep, treat the victim for shock *(page 113)*. If you suspect shock, do *not* give the victim fluids, even though thirst is likely, and do *not* give the victim alcohol.

IDENTIFYING CRITICAL BURNS

A critical burn is one that requires the attention of medical professionals. Knowing whether you should call for emergency medical help is often difficult. It is not always easy or possible to assess the severity of a burn immediately after injury. Even superficial burns to large areas of the body or to certain body parts can be critical. You cannot judge severity by the pain the victim feels because nerve endings may be destroyed. Call for emergency help in any of the following circumstances.

- A burn victim experiences breathing difficulty.

- A burn covers more than one body part.

- A burn affects the head, neck, hands, feet or genitals.

- A partial-thickness or full-thickness burn affects a child or an elderly person.

- A burn results from fire, hot grease, chemicals, explosion or electricity.

Chest pain

A victim who complains of tightness or a severe pain in the chest may be suffering from a lack of oxygen to the heart muscle. If the tightness or pain follows a period of exertion, emotional stress, or even a big meal, it may be angina, which is due to a constriction of the vessels that deliver blood to the heart. The pain of angina most commonly begins under the breastbone and may spread to the left arm, the jaw and the upper region of the abdomen. An attack of angina in itself is not life-threatening and does not result in permanent damage to the heart. If it is the result of exertion or stress, it can often be relieved simply by allowing the victim a rest period in a cool, calm location, during which the supply of oxygen gradually equals the heart muscle's oxygen requirement.

Many individuals who suffer occasional attacks of angina carry nitroglycerin tablets, which rapidly dilate blood vessels, thus dramatically increasing the flow of oxygenated blood. Medication should be given as prescribed.

Tightness or severe pain in the chest that lasts more than 10 to 15 minutes may be the result of a far more serious situation—a blood clot blocking the main artery that delivers blood to the heart muscle—a heart attack, described on page 104. If the blockage is complete, the heart can immediately develop an irregular beat or cease to beat at all, and death can be virtually instantaneous. If the blockage is not complete but is substantial, death or serious damage to the heart muscle may result within minutes of the onset of the attack.

If an individual aboard your vessel complains of tightness in the chest or severe chest pain that meets the above description, your response may literally be the difference between the person's life and death:

■ Remain calm and reassure the victim.

■ Have the victim rest comfortably. If the chest pain is severe, or if chest discomfort does not go away within 10 minutes, call for emergency help *(Chapter 4)*. If you will not be able to transport the victim to professional medical assistance within 30 minutes, request emergency helicopter evacuation.

■ If a person experiences difficulty in breathing, or stops breathing, loses his or her pulse, his eyes roll back in the head, or a seizure occurs, that person may well be experiencing serious and life-threatening cardiac arrest. As quickly as possible, lay the victim on his back on a hard surface, and take the following actions, described on page 103. Make certain the airway is clear; check for breathing; if necessary, assist in breathing with two slow breaths; and check his pulse. If you do not detect a pulse, administer CPR *(page 104)*.

Convulsions and seizures

Protect someone having a convulsion or seizure from injury but do not attempt to restrain the person. Loosen any clothing. Move objects that might cause injury. Protect the victim's head by placing a thin cushion beneath it. If there are fluids in the victim's mouth, place him or her on one side. Do *not* attempt to thrust an object between the teeth.

Most convulsions and seizures last only a few moments; the best course of action is to prevent the victim from getting injured. Most victims will experience respiration difficulties during the attack. Maintain an open airway *(page 103)*; if the victim stops breathing, administer rescue breathing, as shown on page 103, with one exception: If you cannot get air through the victim's mouth, cover the victim's nose with your mouth and give breaths through the nose.

Once the convulsion or seizure has passed, the victim is likely to be exhausted and may be dazed or semi-conscious. Allow the person to rest quietly and do not attempt to give any fluids until he or she is fully conscious.

If the victim has suffered convulsions or seizures in the past, the incident probably is not serious and requires no further intervention on your part. If the victim has forgotten to take anti-convulsant medication prescribed for seizures, he or she should take it upon wakening. If this is the person's first convulsion or seizure, transport the victim to medical assistance quickly or call for emergency help.

Drowning accidents

Enter the water to rescue a drowning victim only as a last resort, since by doing so you risk becoming a drowning victim yourself. The rule is, "THROW, TOW, ROW, and only then, GO." First, throw the victim a floating object, such as a PFD, a life ring or a buoyant cushion. If that is impractical, throw or push an object such as a rope or dinghy oar out to the victim and tow him to safety. If the distance is too great, attempt to row out to the victim in a dinghy or any other object that will float. Only if all these methods are impractical should you enter the water and attempt a rescue yourself. Even then, wear a PFD, and be alert to the probability that the person will be panicky and may attempt to grab hold of you and could pull you down. If at all possible, approach from behind and try to get the person to calm down, then wrap your arm over his shoulder and grasp with your hand below the armpit to tow the person to safety on his back.

Remove the victim from the water, open the airway *(page 103)* and check for breathing. Give rescue breathing if necessary. If your breaths will not go into the victim, prepare to administer abdominal thrusts. If you do *not* suspect injury to the head or spine, turn the victim's head to the side.

Check the victim's pulse for one minute, keeping in mind that pulse may be difficult to detect in a victim of near-drowning. If you do not detect a pulse, administer CPR. Continue rescue breathing or CPR until medical arrives. All victims of near-drowning should receive follow-up medical care.

Fainting spells

An impending fainting spell may be signaled by one or more of the following symptoms: extreme pallor and/or perspiration, cold or clammy skin, shallow or uneven breathing, dizziness, numbness or tingling of the hands or feet, nausea and distorted vision.

Move the victim to a well-ventilated area—on deck if possible. Have the person sit, with the head between the knees. Loosen clothing at the neck, chest and waist. Place a fainted victim on his or her back on a flat surface with the head lower than the feet; elevate the legs and feet with a pillow or blanket. Monitor the vital life signs and call for medical help.

Foreign particle in eye

Small foreign bodies such as sand or grit lying in the lower half of the eye or any chemical entering the eye can often be removed by blinking. Otherwise, tilt the head back and to the side (in the direction of the injured eye) and try gently flushing the eye with clean water or a mild saline solution. If the object remains or pain or discomfort continues, flush until help arrives.

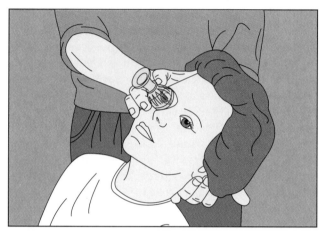

When chemicals or foreign particles enter the eye, flush it continuously with water.

Fractures and dislocations

Do not attempt to set a fracture or force a dislocated bone back into its socket. Immobilize the affected area with a splint constructed of any material that is close at hand, such as a dinghy oar, a rolled newspaper or magazine, or even a pillow. Control any bleeding *(page 106)*, and treat the victim for shock *(page 113)*.

If you suspect a spinal injury, do not move the victim; refer to the guidelines for spinal injuries *(below)*, and call for medical assistance immediately.

Head and spinal injuries

If you suspect injury to the head or spine, call immediately for emergency medical help. While waiting for help to arrive, provide the following care:

■ Minimize movement of the head and spine, using a technique that the American Red Cross calls "in-line stabilization": Place your hands on both sides of the victim's head, position it gently, if necessary, in line with the body; support it in that position until medical help arrives. (However, do *not* use this technique in any of the following circumstances:

if the victim's head is severely angled to one side; if the victim complains of pain, pressure or muscle spasms on initial movement of the head; or if you feel resistance when attempting to move the head. In these circumstances, support the victim's head in the position in which it was found.)

■ Maintain an open airway *(page 103)*.
■ Monitor consciousness and breathing.
■ Control any external bleeding.
■ Maintain normal body temperature.

Insect bites and stings

Although most insect bites are minor—resulting in a bump on the skin, itching for a few hours, and subsequent skin irritation—the effects can be more serious. If the venom is potent, as is the case with some spiders and scorpions, the entire body may be affected. About one of every ten people stung by a bee, wasp, hornet, fire ant or, most commonly, a yellow jacket may experience an allergic reaction.

To treat a mild insect bite, remove the stinger and venom sac, if any, immediately. Avoid using tweezers, which can squeeze additional venom from the sac into the victim. Instead, scrape the stinger and sac off the skin. (A credit card works well for scraping.) For reactions such as severe swelling, keep the affected area below the level of the victim's heart. Apply ice or cold cloths to the site of the bite.

Symptoms of an allergic reaction may include hives, itchy eyes, swelling around the eyes, mouth, tongue or throat; difficulty in breathing; numbness or cramps; mental confusion; nausea; vomiting and even loss of consciousness. Severe reactions to insect stings may indicate anaphylaxis *(page 109)*, and can occur within 20 minutes or may be delayed as long as several hours or days. At the first sign of an allergic reaction, call for emergency medical help.

Internal bleeding

An individual who suffers a major blow to the abdomen which injures the spleen, a victim who suffers a fracture of the ribs or a large bone, or a person who suffers from a bleeding ulcer, can lose a life-threatening amount of blood with little or no external signs of the bleeding. Bleeding, however slight, from the rectum, non-menstrual bleeding from the vagina, blood in the victim's urine or stool, or the coughing or spitting up of blood can be signals of internal bleeding. Bleeding from the nose, mouth or ears can also indicate internal bleeding, especially if it is not obviously the result of a cut inside the mouth or recent scuba-diving activity.

If the victim is suffering from severe internal bleeding, these signs often will be accompanied by symptoms of shock, such as a weak, rapid pulse; cold, moist skin; discoloration of skin (bruising) in the injured area; dull eyes with pupils that are slow to respond to light; excessive thirst; nausea; vomiting; anxiety and a feeling of depression. The stomach of a person suffering from a lacerated spleen may become tender and swollen.

Aside from treating the victim for shock *(page 113)*, there is virtually nothing you can do to treat severe internal bleeding without advanced medical training and sophisticated equipment. The victim's condition may well be life-threatening. You should call for help and, if you cannot transport the victim to medical assistance within half an hour, request helicopter evacuation.

Poisoning

The most important thing is to recognize that a poisoning may have occurred. If you then have even a slight suspicion that the victim has been poisoned, call for medical assistance immediately, giving any clues about the cause and victim's condition. Monitor the vital life signs *(page 102)*. The victim of poisoning generally looks ill and displays signals common to other sudden illnesses. The signals of poisoning include nausea, vomiting, diarrhea, chest or abdominal pain, breathing difficulty, sweating, loss of consciousness and seizures. Other signals of poisoning are burn injuries around the lips or tongue or on the skin. You may also suspect a poisoning based on any information you have from or about the victim.

In a marine environment, poisoning may occur in one of the following four ways:

■ Inhalation, most commonly of gases such as carbon monoxide from an engine *(Chapter 9)* or other combustion, or fumes from toxic products such as paint.

■ Absorption, through contact with skin, of substances from poisonous plants found ashore (including poison ivy, poison oak and poison sumac) and poisonous products aboard some boats, such as insecticide.

■ Injection, through bites or stings of insects, spiders, ticks, snakes and other animals, or as drugs or medication injected with a hypodermic needle.

■ Ingestion, from swallowing cleaning products, medications and any toxic materials found aboard a boat.

The severity of the poisoning depends on the type and amount of the substance, how it entered the body, and the victim's size, weight and age. Some poisons act fast; others slowly. Some have characteristic signals; others do not.

As for first aid, follow these general principles for any poisoning emergency:

■ Survey the scene to make sure it is safe to approach and to gather clues about what happened.

■ If you can remove the victim from the source of the poison, without endangering your own life, do so if necessary.

■ Assess the victim's airway, breathing and circulation. A victim of inhaled poison needs oxygen as soon as possible. Get a conscious victim to fresh air immediately. Remove an unconscious victim from the environment, maintain an open airway, and give rescue breathing *(page 103)* if necessary.

■ Follow all instructions of the emergency medical service dispatcher or other medical professional.

■ Do not give the victim anything to drink or eat unless advised by medical professionals. If the poison is unknown

and the victim vomits, save some of the vomitus, which the hospital may analyze to identify the poison.

■ If a poison plant contacts the skin, immediately wash the affected area thoroughly with soap and water. If a rash or weeping lesion has begun to develop, apply a paste of baking soda and water to the area several times a day to alleviate some of the discomfort. Lotions such as Calamine or Caladryl may help soothe the area. Antihistamines such as Benadryl may also help dry up the lesions. If the condition worsens and large areas of the body or the face are affected, the person should see a doctor.

If other poisons, such as chemicals, contact the skin, flush the affected area continuously with large amounts of water. Continue to flush until emergency help arrives.

■ See page 111 for first aid when insect bites and stings occur.

■ Some marine life (sting rays, sea anemones, certain fish and jellyfish and other marine animals) give painful stings that may cause serious problems such as allergic reaction, paralysis, and cardiac and respiratory difficulties. Immediately soak the area in sea water, and carefully remove any visible pieces of fingers or tentacles. Do not handle tentacles with bare hands. If it is available, apply a baking soda paste. Ice or even a paste of meat tenderizer will reduce swelling.

Call for emergency help in any of the following cases: if you do not know what caused the sing, if the victim has a history of allergic reactions to marine life stings, if the sting is on the face or neck or if the victim develops any severe problems such as breathing difficulties.

Seasickness

While seasickness itself is hardly a life-threatening emergency, extreme cases can lead to severe dehydration, which can have serious consequences. The malady results from a disruption of the balance mechanism in the inner ear, which can be triggered by the motion of the vessel on the sea and/or by such visual signs as a tossing foredeck or rolling waves.

The best approach for individuals who are prone to seasickness is to prevent its onset. Many find the most effective preventative to be a patch affixed to the mastoid bone just behind the ear. Others find they are best helped by over-the-counter oral motion-sickness compounds. Either of these preventatives should be used according to directions. Either can cause extreme drowsiness and a dry mouth. Still others have reported success from wristbands that purport to work by exerting force on an accupressure point.

Once at sea, anyone who begins to feel queasy should refrain from eating heavy foods or drinking alcoholic beverages. Some people do, however, find that nibbling on a soda cracker and sipping a carbonated beverage helps to settle their stomachs.

Individuals who experience severe seasickness to the point of actually vomiting often react in one of two ways: After the initial attack, some people "get their sea legs" and have no further problems; others find themselves caught up in a cycle of violent vomiting. If this continues for more than 12 hours, it can lead to serious consequences from dehydration. The most dependable treatment is simply to return to shore. After a few hours on dry land, a victim will generally be able to take liquid nourishment and will recover without medical attention. If returning to land is impossible or does not relieve the symptoms, the most effective treatment is over-the-counter motion-sickness suppositories. Once on shore, such a victim should seek professional medical help.

Shock

Shock is a collapse of the cardiovascular system in which the flow of blood, which carries oxygen to the body's vital organs, slows and can eventually cease, resulting in death. After even a few minutes without an adequate flow of oxygenated blood, the cells of certain organs, primarily the brain and the heart, die and cannot be regenerated.

Shock can be brought on by a number of causes, such as severe blood or fluid loss due to a large open wound, burn or internal bleeding; damage to the spinal cord that disrupts its control of the nervous system; the dilation of blood vessels in reaction to excessive heat; and failure of the heart to pump effectively.

The signs of shock may include cold, clammy skin; profuse sweating; a pale skin color and, in the advanced stages of shock, a bluish color to the lips; shallow, labored gasping or rapid breathing; a weak, rapid pulse; extreme thirst; nausea; or vomiting.

To treat for shock, clear and maintain the victim's airway *(pages 105-106)*. Lay the victim on his or her back and cover with blankets or clothing to keep warm. If the victim exhibits no signs of head, neck or back injuries or is not experiencing convulsions, seizures or respiratory distress, elevate the feet 8 to 12 inches higher than the head. Reassure the victim, and control any external bleeding as soon as possible to minimize blood loss. Do not give the victim anything to eat or drink, even though he or she is likely to be thirsty. Never give a victim of shock any type of alcohol. Keep the victim comfortable until help arrives.

Sprain or strain

To relieve pain and swelling of a sprained joint or strained muscle, rest it as much as possible and administer cold treatments for 72 hours, then heat treatments. For a cold treatment, apply an ice pack or plastic bag of ice cubes wrapped in a towel for 15 to 20 minutes. For heat treatment, apply a hot-water bottle for the same time interval. For additional relief to a sprained ankle, use an ankle bandage; for a sprain or strain to the arm, use an arm sling.

Stroke

Stroke is the result of an insufficient supply of oxygenated blood to the brain. If the flow of oxygenated blood to the brain is interrupted for more than six minutes, irreversible

An ice pack, often useful for treating sprains, is a worthwhile addition to your first-aid kit.

damage is likely to occur in that portion of the brain that has lost its supply of oxygen.

Stroke can be caused by a gradual narrowing of the arteries that supply blood to the brain; by the blockage of these arteries by a blood clot that forms elsewhere in the body, such as in the heart; or by the rupture of an artery. The first two causes of stroke normally are associated with the elderly or with those who suffer from heart disease. The rupture of an artery serving the brain, however, can be the result of an inherent weakness in the artery and can occur suddenly and unexpectedly in young and otherwise healthy people.

The signs of stroke include partial or complete paralysis of the face muscles and/or the extremities on one side of the body; varying levels of consciousness, ranging from confusion or dizziness to a total loss of consciousness; difficulties with speech, vision or swallowing; convulsions and headache.

Stroke victims often suffer paralysis of the airway following the incident. If you suspect stroke, immediately check and, if necessary, open and maintain the victim's airway *(page 103)*. A stroke victim is likely to be extremely frightened. Calm and reassure the victim as much as possible. If there is any paralysis, lay the victim with the paralyzed side down and pad all extremities carefully to avoid further injury.

There is nothing you can do aboard the boat to relieve the symptoms of stroke or to determine its likely consequences, which can range from mild and temporary disability to severe disability and death. Any victim who you suspect has suffered stroke should be evacuated for medical treatment as quickly as possible.

Vomiting and diarrhea

Vomiting and diarrhea are common digestive upsets caused by infection, food poisoning, a food allergy or overeating. Treat episodes of diarrhea and vomiting in the same way: Stop all eating and drink only water—occasional sips for vomiting, as much as can be tolerated for diarrhea. If symptoms persist, consult a physician. Once the vomiting or diarrhea has passed, replace lost fluids for about 6 hours before reintroducing solid food.

THE ART OF SEAMANSHIP

6 RULES OF THE ROAD

Except for marked channels, there are no clearly defined paths for boats to follow. Skippers have open expanses of water on which to navigate, and their courses often cross the tracks of other vessels in the same waters. The caution needed on water, even though traffic is much less than on land, is just as important as on sidewalks, streets and highways.

For every boater, knowledge of the basic rules of navigation is a must. This chapter introduces those rules. It gives you the information you need to avoid collision in a variety of circumstances—what actions to take, what signals to give, the sound signals required in "thick" weather, and guidelines for other special situations you are likely to encounter.

INTRODUCTION TO THE RULES

Imagine yourself underway, on a clear day with calm weather and less than one-foot seas, moving at about 20 knots across a large, open bay. There is a vessel in sight on your port side, more than four miles distant. A few minutes later, you can gauge the boat's speed; it seems to be traveling faster than yours.

Your attention is occupied for a minute while you search for a familiar landmark. When you look around and notice the other boat again, something has changed. Now it looks as if your courses may converge; the other skipper seems to have reduced his speed as well. There's no danger, you think—he must have seen you; surely you both know that you have the right of way.

A couple of minutes later, he doesn't seem to be altering his course. In the next moment you decide that he does not, in fact, know that you have the right of way. Now you're close enough to make him out at the helm, and he is not even looking at you.

Impulsively, you reach for the throttle and cut the engines back—just as he suddenly alters course to starboard. Your boat drops off a plane, and he is heading right for you. There's nothing else you can do but curse the skipper. You watch his open mouth as he swings back onto his original course and continues on his way.

The two of you were nearly involved in one of the more than 3,000 collisions reported to the United States Coast Guard each year. Many of these are fatal; this one would have injured at least one of the two skippers involved.

Boaters suffer collision accidents more than any other accident type. (The next largest category is running into fixed objects—which often goes unreported.) The biggest reported cause for collisions is "improper lookout"; the next is "other vessel or operator at fault."

Generally, you will have an open expanse of water on which to navigate, and your course often will cross the paths of other vessels. Safety-conscious skippers know that it's even more

In addition to knowing who has the right of way, every skipper must have enough experience to anticipate other skippers' reactions and judge how best to avoid situations in which right of way is contested.

important to practice "defensive driving" on the water than on the neighborhood streets. On the water, each situation is much less predictable, visibility is usually worse and, unlike most cars, even the most responsive boat cannot "stop on a dime" to avoid another vessel.

For that reason, boaters must know the navigational rules that apply to their own boating areas and how to follow them to avoid collisions. When it comes to safe vessel operation, the rules concerning, for example, what type of lights to carry or what signals to use, may vary. But the fundamental "rules of the road"—a boater's right-of-way blueprint—apply to every vessel. (Vessel is defined as "every description of water craft, including non-displacement craft and seaplanes, used or capable of being used as transportation on water.")

Under the laws of the U.S., Canada, Great Britain and at least 30 other maritime nations, a skipper is responsible for knowing and following the relevant navigational rules. That means, whether you command an oil tanker or ride the waves clinging to a sailboard, you are legally compelled to know the rules that apply in the location in which you operate.

Remember that skippers have been found liable for substantial sums when they have ignored or violated the right-of-way rules. And most likely, your marine insurance company also will ask you to document your ability to operate your vessel competently—according to the time-tested habits of good seamanship and with regard to applicable legislation. In the event of a collision, your ability to prove that you operated your vessel correctly (that you knew and applied the rules appropriately in the circumstances) could make a big difference to the financial settlement of a law suit. Most importantly, knowing and obeying the rules can save your life.

Who makes the rules

Since the 1840s, seafaring nations have worked to codify the rules and regulations governing the duties of a skipper of any vessel encountering another vessel in international or domestic waters. The following general classes of rules may affect boaters in North America:

■ **The International Regulations for Preventing Collisions at Sea, 1972.** Adopted in 1977 and amended by the International Maritime Organization in 1981 and 1989, the International Rules (commonly called 72 COLREGS) apply to "all vessels on the high seas and in all waters connected therewith navigable by seagoing vessels" outside of established navigational lines of demarcation.

These 38 rules are divided into five sections of subsets (General, Steering and Sailing Rules, Lights and Shapes, Sound and Light Signals, and Exemptions), with the rules governing conduct and collision avoidance preceding those concerning mandatory equipment.

There also are four Annexes to the Rules, providing technical details to assist mariners in complying with the rules.

■ **The 1980 U.S. Inland Navigation Rules.** The Inland Rules apply to "all vessels upon the inland waters of the United

States, and to vessels of the United States on the Canadian Waters of the Great Lakes to the extent that there is no conflict with Canadian law" *(Rule 1 Application)*. They replace the former Inland Rules, the Western Rivers Rules, the Great Lakes Rules, their respective pilot and interpretive rules, and part of the 1940 Motorboat Act.

■ **Regulations issued periodically by federal departments and agencies.** In the United States, the five Annexes to the Inland Rules (four of which closely parallel those of the 72 COLREGS) comprise these regulations. Generally, they are promulgated by "the Secretary of the Department in which the Coast Guard is operating" or by authority delegated to the Coast Guard commandant.

■ **Local regulations.** These rules may be issued by state or other local authorities. Generally, these regulations conform to the Inland Rules and Coast Guard regulations, but they elaborate on minor details of limited scope. This category of rules and regulations is too diverse to be outlined in full in this volume; however, you should be familiar with all regulations that apply to the waters you use.

■ **The federal rules in Canada.** Canadian regulations may be found in the 1991 Canadian Coast Guard publication, *Collision Regulations: International Regulations for Preventing Collisions at Sea, 1972 with Canadian Modifications.*

Sequence of consideration

Because the Inland Rules apply on waters inside demarcation lines at the entrances to most (but not all) harbors, bays, rivers and inlets, they apply to most U.S. recreational boaters.

In content and language, the Inland Rules parallel the 72 COLREGS. Many rules and provisions are identical. However, there are some distinct differences that reflect the varying conditions on inland rivers and waterways, as well as traditional practices.

To provide information of greatest benefit to most boaters, this chapter describes the Inland Rules. This information is intended as a guide to understanding these complex rules. It is to be used as a supplementary reference, *not* as a replacement for the rules. Throughout the chapter, specific rule references are provided in parentheses.

The International and Canadian Rules are discussed in detail only where their specific provisions differ materially from those of the Inland Rules.

Application of the rules

■ **The Inland Rules** apply to all vessels operating on the navigable waters of the United States seaward until the international lines of demarcation (clearly marked with a purple dashed line on nautical charts) and to U.S. vessel operators on the Great Lakes, to the extent that there is no conflict with Canadian law. This generally includes rivers, lakes, harbors and some bays such as Chesapeake Bay. However, in Alaskan waters, Puget Sound and most Hawaiian waters, the International Rules apply throughout.

Each operator of a self-propelled vessel 12 meters or more in length is required to carry on board and maintain for ready reference a copy of the Inland Navigation Rules. The latest edition of the *Navigation Rules* contains the International Regulations for Preventing Collisions at Sea, commonly called the 72 COLREGS, and the Inland Navigation Rules, which supersede the old Inland Rules, Western Rivers Rules, the Great Lakes Rules and other Pilot Rules, plus their respective pilot and interpretive rules. The book also includes sections on COLREGS demarcation lines, penalty provisions, alternative compliance, the vessel bridge-to-bridge radiotelephone regulations and a table for conversion between metric and customary units. Changes to the *Navigation Rules* are published, as they occur, in the *Notice to Mariners* publications.

How to order
Navigation Rules, International and Inland, stock number 050-012-00287-8, is available by telephone order at (202) 783-3238, or by mail (Superintendent of Documents, U.S. Government Printing Office, Washington, DC 20402). The price of the *Navigation Rules* is $8 ($10 outside the U.S.) Some credit cards are accepted.

The Rules in Canada
For further information about operating your vessel in Canadian waters, contact Navigation Safety, Canada Building, Tower 2, 1200-344 Slater St., Ottawa, Ontario K1A 0N7; or call (613) 991-3136 or (613) 991-3137.

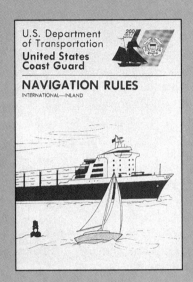

The operator of each self-propelled vessel 12 meters or more in length is required to carry on board, and maintain for ready reference, a copy of the Inland Navigation Rules contained in this publication.

■ **The Canadian Rules (or Collision Regulations)** apply to every vessel licensed or registered in Canada or Canadian ocean data acquisition system (ODAS) located within any waters, any other vessel or ODAS in Canadian waters or fishing zones, or any exploration or exploitation vessel pursuant to a Canadian license. If the Collision Regulations conflict with those of any jurisdiction in which a Canadian vessel or ODAS operates, then the vessel must comply with the rules of that jurisdiction.

General definitions
Before discussing the specific steering and sailing rules of the road, you should be familiar with a few key definitions used throughout the Inland Rules. Each of them is identical to those of the 72 COLREGS:

As described earlier, a vessel may be any type of water craft, from a non-displacement vessel to a seaplane (any aircraft designed to maneuver on water). A *power-driven vessel* is any vessel propelled by machinery; a *sailing vessel* is any water craft under sail. (A sailboat under power alone, or under sail and power, is considered a power-driven vessel.) A *vessel engaged in fishing* includes any vessel fishing with nets, lines, trawls or other apparatus that restricts maneuverability. (Vessels fishing with trolling lines or other apparatus that does not restrict maneuverability are not considered to be "engaged in fishing" for the purposes of these rules. This means that, generally, sport fishing boats are *not* "engaged in fishing" according to the Rules. Consequently, a sport fishing boat should be considered a power-driven vessel for determining lighting and right of way.)

A vessel is *underway* when it is not at anchor, made fast to the shore, or aground. A *vessel not under command* is a vessel that, through some exceptional circumstances, is unable to maneuver to keep out of the way of another vessel, such as one with an inoperative engine or malfunctioning steering. A *vessel restricted in its ability to maneuver* is a vessel whose work restricts its range of motion. Such vessels may be engaged in laying, servicing or collecting a navigation mark, submarine cable or pipeline; dredging, surveying or underwater operations; replenishing or transferring people, provisions or cargo while underway; launching or recovering aircraft; clearing mines; or towing another vessel if severely restricted in its ability to deviate from its course.

Vessels are deemed to be *in sight* of one another only when one can be observed visually from the other. *Restricted visibility* means a condition where visibility is restricted due to fog, mist, snow, rainstorms, sandstorms or similar causes.

In Canada
The *Great Lakes Basin* includes Lakes Ontario, Erie, Huron (including Georgian Bay), Michigan and Superior; their connecting and tributary waters; and the Ottawa and St. Lawrence rivers and their tributaries as far east as the lower exit of St. Lambert Lock near Montreal.

STEERING AND SAILING RULES

The Steering and Sailing Rules (*Part B of the Inland Rules*) are aimed at collision prevention under any conditions. Certain rules map out the conduct of vessels when in sight of each other in any visibility, while others specifically govern vessel conduct in restricted visibility.

Rule 2[a] of the Inland Rules is known as "the rule of good seamanship." Simply, it obliges you legally to do whatever you can do to avoid collision.

General prudence

As described in the section "Avoiding Collision," Rule 2[b] calls on boaters to give "due regard" to all possible navigational hazards, boat limitations and special circumstances that could prompt a departure from the rules to avoid immediate danger. As a result, this rule is known as "the rule of general prudence."

Lookouts

For example, every vessel must always post a lookout who, by means of sight, hearing and other available and appropriate means, will keep the skipper and crew apprised of the ongoing situation and any risk of collision (*Rule 5*).

Often, recreational boaters and short-handed crews fail to take seriously the need for a lookout. Typically, the helmsman plays this role—and a dozen others; however, according to the rules, the lookout must be qualified, alert and have no other responsibilities.

When you are using an automatic steering device or autopilot, you still need a lookout. And using radar at night or in fog does not justify the failure to post a lookout, usually forward of the bridge or on the bow, where he or she can see and hear well. (In the case of power-driven vessels, the noise of most motors renders the helmsman virtually useless as a listening lookout.)

If you usually operate your vessel solo or with a short-handed crew, the rules don't mean that you necessarily must change your style. In the event of a collision, however, you'll bear the burden of proof to establish that a proper lookout could not have prevented the accident.

Determining safe speed

Clearly, the safe speed for, say, a powerboat operated on a little-traveled waterway in off-season may be drastically different than that for the same boat maneuvering in a crowded harbor on Fourth of July weekend.

Every vessel "shall at all times proceed at a safe speed" such that it can take proper, effective action to avoid collision and stop within a distance appropriate to the prevailing circumstances and conditions.

Although many states and municipalities post speed limits or no-wake zones, among the factors that will determine "safe speed" are the following:

- Visibility.
- Traffic density, including fishing boats and other vessels.
- Your boat's maneuverability, especially its stopping and turning ability in the prevailing conditions.
- At night, the presence of confusing shore lights or back scatter from your own vessel.
- Prevailing wind, sea and current conditions.
- The proximity of navigational hazards.
- Your boat's draft in relation to water depth.

If your vessel is fitted with operational radar, the rules outline additional factors to consider when determining a safe speed (*Rule 6*).

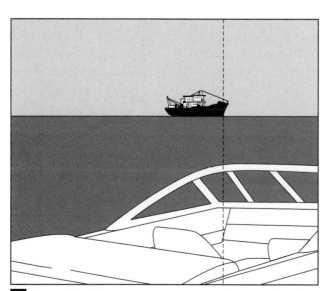

1 Even without the use of a compass, another vessel can be "eyeballed." On first sighting this freighter gives no clue as to its speed. The small-boat skipper lines it up with the windshield and the corner of the companionway.

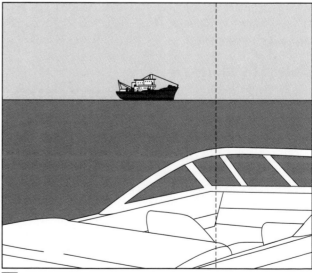

2 When the freighter seems to fall behind, whose course or speed has changed? Has the small boat kept a constant heading and speed since the first sighting? If so, it will pass ahead of the freighter.

Determining the risk of collision

When does the risk of collision exist? The rule of thumb is this: If you are not sure, then assume that the risk exists. Here is what the Inland Rules say: "Every vessel shall use all available means appropriate to the prevailing conditions to determine if risk of collision exists. If there is any doubt, such risk shall be deemed to exist" *(Rule 7[a]).*

Actions to avoid collision

When you have plenty of sea room, take early and substantial action. Simply altering course is probably your best bet for avoiding a close-quarters situation. In any case, your action should result in passing the other vessel at a safe distance. Continue to check the effectiveness of your action until the other vessel is past and clear. If necessary "to avoid collision or allow more time to assess the situation," reduce speed or take all way off (stop your vessel) by stopping or reversing your means of propulsion *(Rule 8 [c], [d] and [e]).*

Tracking the other vessel's relative position

The prescribed method of determining whether you're on a collision course is to track the relative bearing from your boat to the approaching boat. If the compass bearing to the approaching vessel does not change appreciably, either forward or astern, then a risk of collision exists *(Rule 7[d][i]).* That's when the navigational rules begin to apply, and you should take the appropriate action for the circumstances.

Still, even when an appreciable bearing change is evident, the risk of collision may exist. At short range, an appreciable change of bearing may mean a dangerously close passing distance. At long range, an appreciable change of bearing may mask smaller, undetectable changes.

Consequently, you should evaluate both ranges and bearings when gauging the risk of collision, and be sure to confirm your conclusions by sight and sound. Thereafter, any course change that you make in the presence of another vessel should be so pronounced, definite and early enough so that the skipper of that vessel cannot mistake your intentions visually or by radar *(Rule 8).* Slight changes may fail to make your intentions clear.

What is "immediate danger"?

In rendering decisions in the event of collision, courts assess the question of "immediate danger" under the given circumstances in detail.

Rules 8 and 16 govern the duty of the give-way vessel (the vessel that must maneuver). Rule 17 discusses the responsibilities of the stand-on vessel *(page 124).* The best way to think about this responsibility is as a three-tiered response. Consider, for example, the following situation: You are at the helm of a sailboat under sail, and a powerboat is approaching at a distance.

- **Tier one:** Although the powerboat is on a collision course, it is still a distance away; here you *must* maintain your course and speed to allow the powerboat to avoid you *(Rule 17[a][i]).*
- **Tier two:** The powerboat keeps approaching, and is getting uncomfortably close, or appears to have not seen your vessel. You *may* at this point maneuver to avoid collision *(Rule 17 [a][ii]).*
- **Tier three:** You decided not to maneuver, and now the powerboat is so close that a collision is imminent unless you take action. Now you *must* take action to avoid the collision *(Rule 19[b]).*

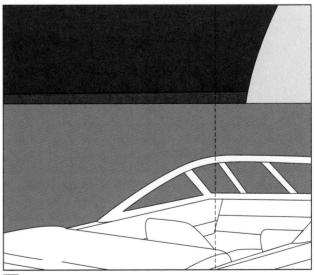

3 In the third stage, danger has reappeared. The small boat may actually have the right of way, but a skipper who forced his claim in such a situation would be extremely discourteous and foolish.

4 The small boat skipper should alter his course or speed in stage three so that stage four never occurs. Survivors of collisions between freighters and small boats are, in most cases, aboard the freighter.

Maneuvering in a narrow channel

If you are traveling by power-driven vessel or sailboat along a narrow channel or fairway, you must stay as close as safely possible to the starboard side and the outer limit of the channel *(Rule 9[a][i])*.

Traffic separation schemes

According to Rule 10, "each vessel required by regulation to participate in a vessel traffic service shall comply with the applicable regulations." A vessel traffic service (VTS) may be established at selected ports to control heavy congestion. Normally, the VTS provides traffic advisories to large vessels and may, at times, control their movements.

Although recreational boaters are not usually subject to VTS regulation, you should know the restrictions placed on the movements of larger vessels in the area in which you operate and plan your route accordingly.

Right-of-way definitions

Two key definitions are used to differentiate between the two vessels encountering each other: The "burdened" or "give-way" vessel is the one that does not have the right of way, that is, the one that must take any necessary action to keep out of the way of the other. The "stand-on" vessel (formerly called the "privileged" vessel) is the one that has the right of way, that is, the one that is allowed to proceed unhindered in a meeting situation.

Technically, the right-of-way rules take effect only when the possibility of collision exists. The status of the stand-on or give-way vessel is established at that moment, not necessarily when the vessels first sight each other. If every skipper obeys the rules, however, it is virtually impossible for a nautical collision to take place.

General right-of-way provisions

Except for certain designated vessels—such as vessels in narrow channels, participants in a vessel traffic service, or overtaking vessels—all vessels may be ranked in a kind of right-of-way "pecking order."

Any vessel listed is the give-way vessel when encountering higher-listed vessels, and is the stand-on vessel when encountering lower-listed vessels:

- Vessel not under command.
- Vessel restricted in its ability to maneuver.
- Vessel engaged in fishing.
- Sailing vessel.
- Power-driven vessel.

For example, a commercial fishing boat would have right of way over a powerboat; that same fishing boat would be required to cede right of way to a vessel restricted in its ability to maneuver. *(Refer to Rule 18, Responsibilities Between Vessels. and Rules 9, 10 and 13 for exceptions.)*

Remember, even if you are certain of your right of way, be aware that other skippers may not know the rules. Always be prepared to take necessary steps to avoid collision.

Action by the give-way vessel

Whenever you are required to give the right of way to another vessel, your job is straightforward: "So far as possible, take early and substantial action to keep well clear" *(Rule 16)*.

MAKING YOURSELF EASY TO SEE

The speed of a large ship, even when first seen at a distance, can be deceptive, particularly viewed head-on. Oceangoing vessels often travel at four, five or six times the speed of a sailboat or trawler-type yachts. In poor visibility the time from first sighting to collision can be less than a minute. You may have little time to make yourself conspicuous and to decide what alteration of course may be needed.

At night, a large vessel viewed against the city lights of shoreline may reveal itself as a ship only by its relative speed. If courses converge, an easily perceived relative speed may mean the ship is already too close for safe maneuvering. Keep an alert lookout forward and astern at all times.

While the ship is probably using radar, there is no guarantee that your non-metallic boat is easily visible on the screen. The ship's radar viewer could be set to view a range more appropriate to some other large vessel of which you are unaware. Put your boat on the radar screen by carrying a radar reflector (in the "catch rain" orientation) to send a clear and unambiguous signal *(Chapter 25)*.

While you must be equipped with legal lighting *(Chapter 7)*, you must also make sure that lights aboard your boat are not obscured by flags, sails, canvas covers or anything else.

If you feel there is any chance that you have not been noticed, make your own boat visible by casting a steady light on your sails or even on your topsides at irregular intervals. Use your VHF to communicate with the bridge of the cargo ship on Channel 13, and monitor Channel 16.

Examine the approaching vessel's lights carefully. If you see only one sidelight (red or green), you can be fairly sure that you are not in the direct path of the ship. If you see both red and green lights and if there is any doubt about the other vessel's distance or speed, alter your course or speed immediately. If you are under sail, consider starting your engine.

In Canadian waters

A vessel less than 20 meters (65.4 feet) long must carry a radar reflector (when essential for its safety) within radar navigation areas, unless not feasible to install.

TRAFFIC SEPARATION SCHEMES

The International Maritime Organization (IMO) has adopted several routing measures, including traffic separation schemes (TSSs), to improve the safety of navigation in areas of converging traffic, congested areas or areas where the freedom of movement of shipping is constrained in some way.

The rule governing TSSs is based on principles and definitions drawn from the IMO publication, *General Provisions on Ships' Routeing* (sic). TSS locations are charted using symbols described in that publication. Consequently, it is important to keep your charts up to date with information available periodically in *Notices to Mariners* and other publications.

A TSS is a routing system that separates opposing traffic streams by appropriate means and by the establishment of traffic lanes. A traffic lane is reserved for one-way traffic. Natural obstacles may define a traffic lane.

Like a highway median, a separation zone or line separates the traffic lanes of vessels traveling in opposite or nearly opposite directions. It may divide traffic lanes from adjacent open waters, or it may separate traffic lanes designated for particular classes of vessels heading in the same direction. A related routing measure is an inshore traffic zone that comprises a defined area between the landward boundary of a TSS and adjacent coast.

Provisions

When you are using a traffic separation scheme, proceed in the appropriate traffic lane for your vessel and "go with the flow" of traffic in that lane. Keep clear of the TSS or line by as wide a margin as possible.

Normally, enter or leave a traffic lane at its termination point. When joining or leaving a traffic lane, proceed at as small an angle as practicable to the general flow of traffic.

If possible, avoid crossing traffic lanes. But if you must cross lanes, attempt to cross on a heading at right angles to the general traffic flow *(Rule 10[b] and [c])*. Normally, you must not enter or cross a separation zone or line except to avoid immediate danger or to fish in the zone.

Vessels of less than 20 meters (65.6 feet), sailboats and fishing vessels are free to use an inshore traffic zone at any time. Normally, however, you should operate within the appropriate traffic lane of the adjacent TSS whenever it's safe to do so *(Rule 10[d])*. Vessels of less than 20 meters and sailboats also must not impede the safe passage of a powerboat following a traffic lane *(Rule 10[j])*.

Safe use of routing systems

As explained in Cockroft & Lameijer, *A Guide to the Collision Avoidance Rules*, the IMO *General Provisions on Ships' Routeing* (sic) has established the following principles on the use of routing systems:

- Routing systems are intended for 24-hour use in all weather conditions, in ice-free waters or under light ice conditions where ice-breaking assistance is not required.
- Unless otherwise stated, all ships should use routing systems. Before using a routing system, consider your vessel's draft, the charted water depth, the possibility of changes in the seabed since the last survey and possible meteorological or tidal effects on water depths.
- At junctions where traffic meets from various directions, a true separation of traffic is impossible. Remember that a vessel proceeding along a through-going route does not necessarily have right of way.
- If your vessel's draft does not require you to operate in a deep-water route, then avoid using that route.
- As much as possible, keep to the starboard side in any two-way route or deep-water route.
- Arrows printed on charts in connection with routing systems indicate the direction of travel within the system.

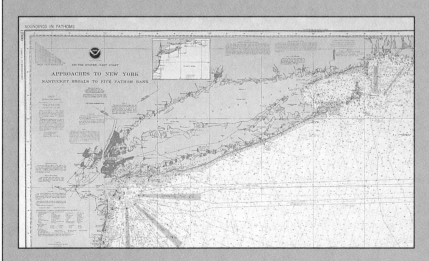

Traffic separation schemes are indicated on NOS charts. The example at left shows the approaches to New York harbor.

Action by the stand-on vessel

Whenever you have the right of way, your first job is to maintain your course and speed. If it is apparent that the other skipper is doing nothing—or taking insufficient action—to keep out of your way, then you may take your own action to avoid or aid in avoiding collision. Of course, your action does not relieve the give-way vessel of its obligation to keep out of the way *(Rule 17[b] and [d]).*

Port/starboard tacks

When two sailboats under the propulsion of their sails (that is, neither one using an auxiliary engine) are approaching each other and a risk of collision exists, one of them must keep clear of the other. If they are on opposite tacks (each boat having the wind on a different side), the port/starboard rule is the first to be applied *(Rule 13[a]).*

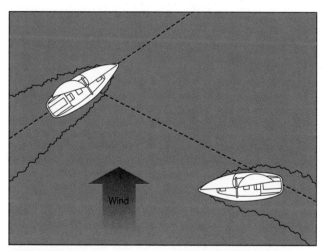

PORT/STARBOARD. Sailboats meeting each other may be on opposite tacks (one with the wind on the starboard side, the other with the wind on the port side). The boat with the wind on the starboard side is on a starboard tack, and starboard tack has right of way. Starboard tack skippers, especially if they are racing, may call "starboard" to make clear to the other vessel that they intend to stand on. If in doubt, the skipper should assume that his boat has no right of way.

When each boat has the wind on a different side, the one with the wind on the port side is on a port tack and is the give-way vessel. Port tack keeps clear of starboard tack. The boat with the wind on its port side will have its sails set on the starboard side.

Windward/leeward

When two sailboats under the propulsion of their sails (that is, neither one using an auxiliary engine) are approaching each other and a risk of collision exists, one of them must keep clear of the other *(Rule 13[a]).* The windward/leeward rule applies. When both boats have the wind on the same side, the windward vessel (the one nearest the direction from

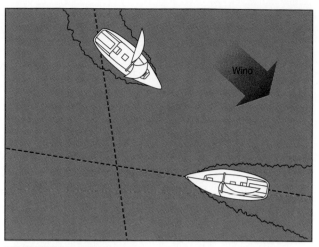

WINDWARD/LEEWARD. When sailboats approach on the same tack (both with the wind coming over the same side), one will be to windward of the other—farther in the direction from which the wind is blowing. That is the windward boat, and it must keep clear of the leeward boat. The logic of this rule is that a leeward boat may have its wind blocked and would be restricted in its ability to maneuver.

which the wind is blowing) is the give-way vessel and keeps clear of the leeward vessel (the vessel farthest from the direction from which the wind is blowing).

The windward side is the side opposite that on which the mainsail is carried. If a vessel with the wind on the port side sees a vessel to windward and cannot determine with certainty whether the other vessel has the wind on the port or starboard side, it must keep out of the way of the other.

Sail's right of way over power

Generally, a sailboat has the right of way over a powerboat, including another sailboat operating under auxiliary power—which, as far as the rules are concerned, is, at that time, a powerboat. The powerboat or auxiliary-powered vessel must keep out of the way of the sailing vessel *(Rule 18[a]).*

However, there are exceptions. Take, for example, the situation described on page 128—a sailboat overtaking a powerboat. Here, the overtaking rule prevails over the usual right of way of sail. Thus, the sailboat (give-way vessel) must keep out of the way of the powerboat (stand-on vessel).

A sailboat may also be the give-way boat, vis-à-vis a powerboat if the powerboat is a commercial fishing vessel (but not a trolling vessel), a vessel not under command, or a vessel restricted in its ability to maneuver *(Rule 18[b]).*

Overtaking

If you are closing in on another vessel from more than 22.5 degrees abaft that vessel's beam, then you're overtaking it. An overtaking vessel must always keep clear of a vessel being overtaken. The overtaking vessel is the give-way vessel; the overtaken vessel is the stand-on vessel *(Rule 13[a]).*

SOUND AND LIGHT SIGNALS

In addition to maneuvering safely and appropriately in line with the navigational rules and avoiding collision, the U.S. Inland and International Rules require you to make specific, identifiable sound and light signals.

Under the U.S. Inland Rules, sound and light signals are given to communicate your intentions and to gain the other skipper's agreement. Under the International Rules, however, the signals do not communicate intent but are sounded upon the actual act of altering course. (For this reason, the latter's signals often are called rudder signals. They don't require a reply; however, the other skipper may decide to take similar action and, if so, is obliged to sound the same signal.) There is an exception in the International Rules: "Intent requiring response is communicated when sounding signals in an overtaking situation" (Rule 34[c]). Each set of rules establishes the appropriate signals and their correct use in their respective Parts D—Sound and Light Signals.

In this section, the appropriate sound and light signals required in given navigational situations under each set of rules are discussed in detail. Signals required in restricted visibility are described on pages 131 to 133.

Sound signal definitions

A whistle is a sound-signaling device that can produce the prescribed blasts and that meets specifications. A short blast on the whistle means a blast of about one second—or the time it takes to say "one thousand one." A prolonged blast means a blast of about 4 to 6 seconds (Rule 32). Remember, "whistle" is a technical term for what is usually a horn; it is not a referee's whistle.

The necessary equipment

If your power- or sailboat is less than 12 meters (39.4 ft.) long, you must carry a whistle (horn); you may carry a bell, or "some other means of making an efficient sound signal." There are no specific regulations for small boats in terms of the range or source of signal power.

If your vessel is at least 12 meters (39.4 ft.) long, however, you must carry a whistle and a bell. If you don't have a bell aboard, you must carry some other manually operable device capable of producing a similar sound. (Rule 33 [a]).

What the U.S. Inland Rules require

Annex III contains detailed specifications for sounding equipment, including different whistle tones and audibility ranges.

- A pushing or towing vessel will sound a whistle whose characteristics are those of the combined composite length of the vessel and its tow. International Rules have no provisions for a pushing or towing vessel.

- Bells and gongs shall be made of corrosion-resistant material and shall be designed to give a clear tone.

- Sailboats under sail need not sound signals.

According to Rule 1(b)(ii), any sound-signaling equipment that is acceptable under the International Rules may also be used on inland waters.

Light signals

To ensure that another vessel can decipher your intentions, you may complement your whistle signals with light flashes. Regardless of your vessel's size, a fitted maneuvering light must be one all-round white or yellow light, visible at a minimum range of 2 miles and synchronized with the whistle.

If, like most boats, your vessel has only one masthead light, you may carry your maneuvering light wherever it may best be seen—but not less than one-half meter (19.7 inches) above or below the masthead light. Remember, a maneuvering light is an all-directional light and should not be obscured in any direction (Rules Annex I, ss. 84.23).

To signal your intentions when meeting or crossing another vessel, make the following signals for at least one second per flash:

- One flash means "I intend to leave you on my port side."

- Two flashes mean "I intend to leave you on my starboard side."

- Three flashes mean "I'm operating astern propulsion" (Rule 34[b][i], [ii] and [iii]).

Unlike the U.S. Inland Rules, a maneuvering light used with whistle signals must be white only—yellow is unacceptable. The light must be visible for at least 5 miles. Under the International Rules, when maneuvering and not overtaking, light signals have the following meanings:

- One flash means "I'm altering my course to starboard."

- Two flashes mean "I'm altering my course to port."

- Three flashes mean "I'm operating astern propulsion."

Your light signal need not be synchronized with the whistle signals; however, the same number of flashes and blasts should be emitted. Each light signal must last about one second, and there must be at least 10 seconds between successive signals (Rule 34[b]).

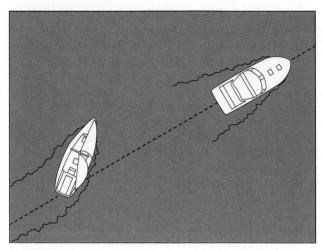

OVERTAKING. If you are closing in on another vessel from a direction more than 22.5 degrees abaft that vessel's beam, then you are overtaking the slower vessel. Your boat is the give-way vessel; the overtaken vessel is the stand-on vessel. You must keep clear. This rule applies even to a sailboat overtaking a motorboat, for the duration of the encounter.

By day, it can be difficult to ascertain your position relative to the other vessel's beam. When in doubt, assume that yours is the overtaking vessel and maneuver accordingly. At night, in an ideal situation, you will easily know that you're the overtaking vessel if you can't see either of the sidelights of a vessel ahead *(Rule 13[b] and [c])*. (Practically speaking, the arc of visibility of sidelights on many small craft leaves much to be desired.) Under Canadian Rules, you are deemed to be overtaking when you can see the other vessel's sternlight or all-around white light.

An overtaking vessel remains an overtaking vessel for the duration of any encounter with another vessel. "Any subsequent alteration of the bearing between the two vessels shall not make the overtaking vessel a crossing vessel, or relieve it of the duty of keeping clear of the overtaken vessel until it is finally past and clear" *(Rule 13[d])*.

Even if the overtaking vessel comes up on the starboard side of the overtaken vessel and moves into its danger zone *(page 131)*, the overtaking vessel does not become the stand-on vessel with the right of way. There is, however, one important exception to this rule: In a narrow channel, fairway or traffic separation scheme, a vessel of less than 20 meters in length, a fishing vessel or a sailing vessel traveling slowly cannot impede the passage of a larger vessel that can only navigate within the narrow channel or that is itself following a traffic separation scheme.

Under Inland Rules, if your powerboat is in sight of, and is overtaking, a powerboat, you must sound the following:
■ One short blast means "I intend to overtake you on your starboard side."
■ Two short blasts means "I intend to overtake you on your port side" *(Rule 33[a])*.

If the overtaken vessel's skipper is in agreement, he must reply by sounding a similar signal. If he is in doubt, he should sound a staccato, five-blast signal.

The International Rules state that the overtaking vessel must indicate its intention to overtake by sounding one of the following signals:
■ Two prolonged blasts on the whistle immediately followed by one short blast means "I intend to overtake you on your starboard side."
■ Two prolonged blasts followed by two short blasts means "I intend to overtake you on your port side."

The overtaken vessel agrees to the overtaking vessel's signal with one of the following:
■ One prolonged blast, one short blast, one prolonged blast and one short blast in that order *(Rule 34[c][ii])*; or, if in doubt, the vessel will sound:
■ Five short and rapid blasts, possibly followed by a fire-flash light signal *(Rule 34[d])*.

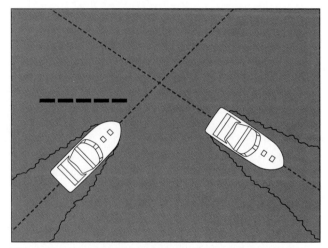

The danger signal is five short blasts. It is used when danger is evident, often because the other boat's intentions have not been made clear. Here the boat at right is backing into danger.

The danger signal

You can always sound the danger signal if you're unsure of the situation. If you disagree with or are confused about the other vessel's intentions, or if you're not sure that sufficient action is being taken to avoid collision, give at least five short, rapid blasts on the whistle.

You also can blow five or more staccato blasts to tell another skipper that you consider his or her actions to be dangerous to either vessel. For example, you may see another vessel backing into an obstacle or other danger. Use the five-blast signal to alert the other skipper.

Listen for the other vessel's signal and re-send your reply. Meanwhile, take precautions to avoid collision until you have agreed with the other vessel about passing safely *(Rule 34[a][ii] and [d])*. In most cases, it makes sense to slow or stop your vessel until all parties understand the situation.

Using radio communication

In most instances, you may wish to make a safe-passage agreement with another vessel using your VHF radio: Vessels over 20 meters, and certain other vessels as specified in the Rules, must use Channel 13 in areas other than the Lower Mississippi River, where Channel 67 is designated. (If a small craft has VHF aboard, it must monitor Channel 16 when not communicating.) If you reach agreement with another vessel in a meeting, crossing or overtaking situation by radiotelephone, you may—although it is not required—sound the appropriate whistle signals. If you are unable to reach agreement by radio telephone, you and the other vessel must exchange timely whistle signals, and these shall prevail *(Rule 34)*.

The International Rules do not specifically discuss the use of VHF radio communication in place of whistle signals. (However the Vessel Bridge-to-Bridge Radiotelephone Act is applicable on navigable waters of the U.S. inside the boundary lines, the 3-mile limit. This applies to every power-driven vessel of 20 meters or over in length.)

In some cases, employing whistle signals with VHF radio backup may be the best way to ensure safe passage.

Meeting head-on

When two boats under power approach each other head-on or nearly head-on, they're in a meeting situation. This is exactly the same as, say, passing another car on a narrow road.

The rule of thumb is "pass port to port." This means that, unless otherwise agreed, each vessel should pass on the port side of the other. Neither vessel has the right of way, and both vessels must alter course to starboard, if necessary, to provide clearance for safe passage *(Rule 14[a])*.

How can you be sure that two vessels are approaching on reciprocal or nearly reciprocal courses? By day, the situation exists when you see the other vessel ahead or nearly ahead; by night, either you see its masthead lights in a line or nearly in a line, or you see both sidelights *(Rule 14[b])*. Although there is no hard-and-fast mathematical definition for "head-on," however, the courts have generally held that a point 11¼ degrees on either side of the bow is the boundary within which vessels are considered to be meeting head-on. Note the following important points:

■ The rule doesn't apply to two vessels that will pass clear of each other if each maintains its existing course and speed.
■ If you're still unsure, assume that the risk of collision exists and take appropriate action to avoid it *(Rule 14[c])*.

A powerboat operating on the Great Lakes, Western Rivers, or other waters designated by the Secretary and proceeding downbound with the current has the right of way over an upbound vessel *(Rule 14[d])*.
■ This does not apply to sailboats, but remember if the engine is in use, it is a power-driven vessel.
■ The downbound vessel—on the Great Lakes, Western Rivers, etc.—proposes the manner of passing and initiates the appropriate maneuvering signals *(Rule 14[d])*.

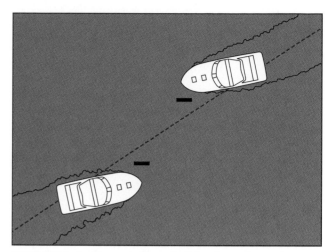

HEAD-ON. In head-on meetings, both boats must sound one short blast. Next, "show your port side," then make a single, distinctive alteration of course to starboard so that there can be no doubt that you have recognized the potential danger and are following the normal course of action. If there is any uncertainty about whether your courses converge, assume they do.

According to the International Rules, in case of meeting another vessel, neither the upbound nor the downbound vessel has the right of way, and no specific maneuvering signals are mandated.

Crossing

When two boats under power are crossing and there is risk of collision, the vessel with the other on its own starboard side is the give-way vessel and must keep out of the way *(Rule 15[a])*. If there is risk of collision, the give-way vessel must avoid crossing ahead of the stand-on vessel.

Beware of any boat approaching yours in the area from dead ahead to a point 22.5 degrees abaft or behind your beam to starboard. Any approaching boat in this "danger zone" has the right of way *(page 131)*.

In a crossing situation where there is risk of collision, you must avoid crossing ahead of a power-driven vessel on your own starboard side.

Usually, altering your course to starboard is the best method of keeping out of the way of a vessel on your starboard bow. If another boat is approaching from near your starboard beam, however, reducing speed or making a major course change to port are probably your best bets for avoiding collision.

On the Great Lakes, Western Rivers or other waters designated by the Secretary, a vessel (even a sailboat) crossing a river must keep clear of a power-driven vessel proceeding up- or downriver *(Rule 15[b])*. This is comparable to the situation on land in which a side street has a stop sign to prevent cars from interfering with traffic on the main artery.

Fishing boats must not block (or anchor in) a channel or fairway to other traffic *(Rule 9[b], [c] and [g])*.

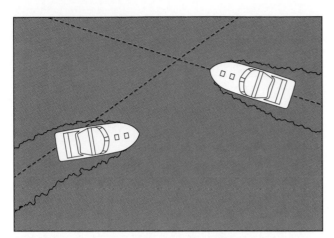

CROSSING. When two boats approach each other, one is on the starboard side of the other. The boat that is on the starboard side of the other has the right of way. The starboard side extends from the bow to a point 22.5 degrees abaft of abeam; boats within this sector are considered to be crossing. If a boat were aft of this sector, it would be overtaking. (Refer to "The Danger Zone" on page 131.)

If your vessel can navigate safely only within a channel or fairway, no other vessel is permitted to cross the channel. If you are unsure about the other vessel's crossing intentions, sound the danger signal *(Rule 34[d] and Rule 9[d]).*

Maneuvering and warning sound signals

Under Inland Rules, when two powerboats are in sight of each other and meeting or crossing within a half-mile of each other—and there is risk of collision—both skippers must indicate their intentions with the following sound signals:

■ One short blast means "I intend to leave your boat on my port side."

■ Two short blasts mean "I intend to leave you on my starboard side."

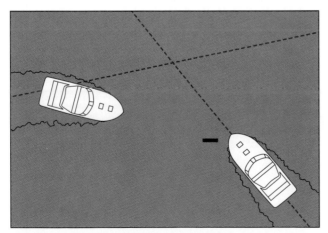

One blast means "I intend to leave you on my port." Two blasts mean "I intend to leave you on my starboard." The vessel signaling has the right of way.

■ Three short blasts mean "I'm operating astern propulsion" *(Rule 34[a][i]).*

If you hear a one- or two-blast whistle signal and you agree with the other vessel's intentions, simply sound the same whistle signal and make your safe-passage maneuver. Avoid cross signals such as answering one blast with two blasts, or vice versa.

In short, in a meeting situation, both vessels must sound one blast, give way to starboard, and pass port-to-port. Either vessel may signal first; however, the vessel that is (or whose skipper believes it to be) the stand-on vessel customarily signals first.

Remember, these signals should be used only when two vessels see and are within a half-mile of each other. Never use these signals in fog or other reduced-visibility conditions; for the appropriate signals to be used under reduced visibility, refer to pages 131-133.

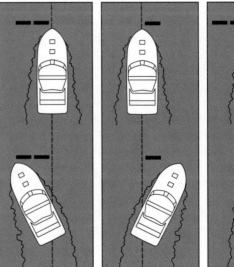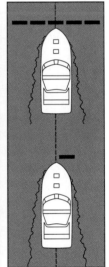

The overtaking boat signals first: One blast for "I intend to leave you on my port," two blasts for "I intend to leave you on my starboard." If the way is safe, the overtaken boat replies with the same signal. If not, it issues the danger signal, five short blasts.

If it appears that two vessels will meet or cross free and clear of each other, there is no need for whistle signals. In case of doubt, however, the safest procedure is to assume the risk of collision and signal for clarification of the other skipper's intentions.

Under International Rules

In a meeting and crossing situation, power-driven vessels in sight of each other must indicate their maneuvers with the following signals:

■ One blast means "I'm altering my course to starboard."

■ Two blasts means "I'm altering my course to port."

■ Three blasts means "I'm operating astern propulsion."

Unlike the U.S. Inland Rules, the International Rules do not include the condition that vessels must signal when visible within one-half mile of each other. And, as noted in the introduction to this section, these rudder signals do not require a reply—unless your vessel is overtaking another vessel or rounding a bend—but they do require you to signal every course change.

The U.S. Inland Rules establish conduct for vessels in all waters and in all overtaking situations; however, the International Rules come into play only in a narrow channel or fairway and only if the overtaken vessel must take action to permit safe passage. These rules are discussed in Rule 9[a][i], "Maneuvering in a Narrow Channel."

Rounding a bend

If you are nearing a bend in a narrow channel or fairway or approaching an obstruction that may obscure an oncoming vessel, be sure to "navigate with particular alertness and caution." There is also a special signal to use: To check for approaching vessels, sound one prolonged blast. This signal must be answered with one prolonged blast by any approaching vessel within earshot (Rules 9[f], 34[e]).

If you hear your signal returned, then you and the other vessel must exchange the usual sound signals when you come into sight of each other. If you don't hear your signal returned, you may consider the channel ahead to be "all clear." But be sure to proceed with care.

Although radio communication is not "officially" a part of the rules in this situation, skippers will often make a "security" call on VHF Channel 13 or 16 if, for example, their vessel has limited maneuverability or is particularly wide. If you should hear a "security" radio call while you are negotiating a narrow channel, you should answer it as you approach the area.

Leaving a dock or berth

When you're powering your boat away from a dock or berth, you must sound one prolonged blast (Rule 34[g]). Remember, if you're pulling away from a dock or berth while another vessel is passing in the channel or nearby open water, you won't have the right of way—even if you're in the other vessel's "danger zone." You have stand-on status in a crossing situation established only when you're "fully in sight."

Although the International Rules do not call for a particular signal in this situation, they don't prohibit one either. Therefore, it is probably a good idea to sound one prolonged blast whenever you leave a dock or berth.

Encountering a ferry

Neither set of rules gives special privileges to ferries, but the courts have held that these unwieldy craft are entitled to a reasonable degree of freedom to enter and leave their slips. As a result, it's good sense to avoid passing unnecessarily close to piers, wharves or piles where you might have limited options in reacting to the movements of other vessels.

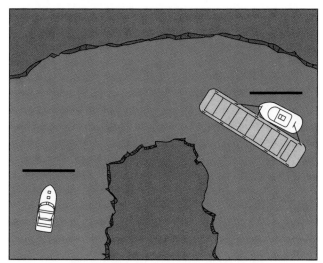

When a boat is approaching a bend in a river, where a boat approaching from the other direction could not be seen at a distance of half a mile, it should sound a special signal of one prolonged (4- to 6-second) blast. If no reply is heard the channel ahead should be safe.

Attracting attention

To attract the attention of another vessel, you may make sound and/or light signals that cannot be mistaken for any authorized signal (or, under the International Rules, any aid to navigation). You also may direct your searchlight beam toward a danger, in such a way as not to embarrass any vessel. (Under the International Rules, high-intensity intermittent or revolving lights, such as strobe lights, must not be used; refer to Rule 36. However, strobes are permitted under Inland Rules [Rule 37]).

Signals for drawbridges and locks

The distinctive signal to have a drawbridge opened for your passage is one prolonged blast, followed within 3 seconds by one short blast. If necessary you can make this signal with a bell, a horn or any clearly hard-sounding device—even shouting. Just be sure to remain well clear of the bridge until the bridge tender acknowledges your signal.

If the bridge can be opened immediately, the tender will sound: one prolonged, one short blast signal. If he cannot, he will sound five short blasts. You are then prohibited from attempting to pass through the closed draw.

When the drawbridge is to be closed, the tender will sound five short blasts. You must reply with five short blasts, or he will keep signaling until that is done.

In hours of heavy road traffic, some bridges may have restricted hours of operation. During such periods, only privileged vessels (government craft or tugs with tows, for example) may request an opening with five short blasts instead of the usual signal.

This sequence is valid also for many bridges in succession. If more than one vessel approaches the bridge, each vessel must signal independently; however, the tender is not required to reply to each signal. Should the bridge be open, you must give the opening signal and, if there is no response within about 3 seconds, you are free to proceed with caution through the draw.

In the event of poor weather or equipment malfunction, you may use visual signals or a combination of sound and visual. You may signal a bridge using a white flag that is readily visible for half a mile by day and a bright white light visible at the same distance by night. Raise and lower your signal vertically in full sight of the bridge tender until acknowledged. If the bridge will open immediately, the tender will repeat the signal. If the bridge cannot be opened—or if it is to close immediately—the tender will wave a red flag horizontally by day and a bright light horizontally by night. Some bridges use mechanical devices and/or flashing lights to communicate the same message.

Signals for locks are often the same as those for bridges—but not always. Before approaching any lock, consult the appropriate *Coast Pilot, Navigation Regulations*, or cruising guide for the proper signals and maneuvers. By VHF radio, you may request a bridge opening or get information about the bridge's status and appropriate actions, usually over Channel 13. (Generally, radio-equipped bridges are identifiable by signs or symbols located near your approach.)

If agreement is reached by radio communication, you are not required to make sound or visual signals. However, both you and the bridge tender must continue to monitor the selected channel—often Channel 13, occasionally Channel 12 or 16—until your vessel has cleared the draw. If you cannot maintain radio contact, you must return to sound and/or visual signals.

Unnecessary openings

Before you attempt to pass through a bridge, know the vertical clearance required for your vessel. Clearance gauges are maintained on many bridges.

Coast Guard regulations provide criminal and civil penalties for boat owners and operators who cause unnecessary openings because of "any non-structural vessel appurtenance not essential to navigation or easily lowered." If you think it's "easier" to request an opening than to reorganize your deck equipment, think again—that decision could be expensive. On the other hand, the same regulations also provide penalties for any bridge tender who "unnecessarily delays the opening of a draw after the required signal has been given."

THE RULES AND DISTRESS SIGNALS

When you, your crew or your vessel are in distress, anything goes. In an emergency, you can and should blast, flash, beat, ring or shout anything possible to summon help. Rule 37 and Annex IV apply for both the International Rules and the U.S. Inland Rules as follows:

- A gun or other explosive signal fired at intervals of approximately one minute.

- A continuous sounding with any fog-signaling apparatus.

- Rockets or shells, throwing red stars fired one at a time at short intervals.

- A signal made by radiotelegraphy or by any other signaling method consisting of the group ...---... (SOS) in Morse Code.

- A signal sent by radiotelephone consisting of the spoken word "Mayday" (*Chapter 4*).

- The International Code Signal of distress indicated by N.C.

- A signal consisting of a square flag having above or below it a ball or anything resembling a ball.

- A rocket parachute flare or a hand flare showing a red light.

- Flames on the vessel (as from a burning tar barrel or oil barrel, for example).

- A smoke signal giving off orange-colored smoke.

- Slowly and repeatedly raising and lowering arms outstretched to each side.

- The radiotelegraph alarm signal.

- The radiotelephone alarm signal.

- Signals that are transmitted by emergency position-indicating radio beacons.

- Approved signals that are transmitted by using radiocommunication systems.

Finally, one signal is approved by the U.S. Inland Rules alone:

- A high-intensity white light flashing at regular intervals from 50 to 70 times per minute.

In Canadian waters
You may also use a square shape or anything resembling a square shape.

RESTRICTED VISIBILITY

Rule 19 of the U.S. Inland and International Rules applies to vessels not in sight of each other when navigating in—or near—an area of restricted visibility. Thus, the provisions of Rule 19 apply when, say, you're traveling in fog or even when you simply see fog ahead. Always proceed at a "safe speed," appropriate to the circumstances and visibility conditions. Safe speed depends on your vessel's initial speed, its stopping power, local traffic and other factors.

Engine availability
Whenever visibility is restricted, a power-driven vessel must have its engines ready for immediate maneuver. The same advice also makes sense for sailboats with auxiliary power *(Rule 19[b]).*

Using radar information
If your radar alone detects the presence of another vessel, you must determine whether your two craft are at close quarters and whether a risk of collision exists. If there is risk of collision, you must alter your course "in ample time"—but you must *not* do the following:
- Do not alter your course to port for a vessel forward of your beam, except when overtaking.
- Do not alter your course toward a vessel on your beam or abaft your beam *(Rule 19[d]).*

Whenever you act to avoid risk of collision in restricted visibility, be sure to monitor the effectiveness of your action to ensure that a new risk of collision does not develop. Post a visual lookout, and monitor your radar closely.

Fog signals
When you hear a fog signal apparently forward of your beam—or if you can't avoid a close-quarters situation with a vessel forward of your beam—and a risk of collision exists, you must immediately reduce your speed to the minimum at which you can stay on course. Take all way off by putting your engines in reverse, if necessary *(Rule 19[e]).*

How close is "close quarters"? The Rules are not specific; however, in restricted visibility in open ocean, a close-quarters situation generally is considered to begin when another vessel is as near as two miles in any direction forward of the beam. This is the typical audible range of the whistle of a large vessel in still conditions *(Rules Annex III, ss. 1[c]).*

Remember, the apparent direction of sound signals can be extremely misleading in fog. Keep a good lookout by sight and sound and continue to monitor your radar. Make sure you know the position and the movement of another vessel before altering your course. Navigate with extreme caution until the danger of collision is past.

Never forget that the danger signal is not a substitute for a fog signal. However, if a vessel detects an immediate danger by radar or other means, it could—under the rule of good seamanship *(Rule 2)*—sound the danger signal to alert the other vessel.

THE DANGER ZONE

Not mentioned specifically in the Rules of the Road, but implicit in them, is the notion of a danger zone: Imagine an arc of a circle centered on your boat that starts at dead ahead and sweeps around the starboard side to a point 22.5 degrees aft of your beam. Any boat that approaches yours from a point within this arc is very likely to have right of way over your boat.

There may be situations in which it does not have right of way (such as river-crossing and overtaking), but assuming that you have the freedom to maneuver safely, you will never increase the danger of collision by giving way to a boat in this zone.

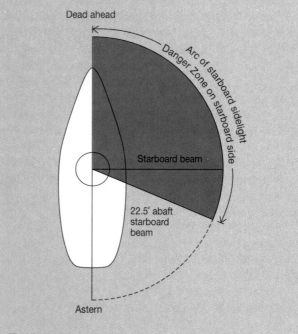

The danger zone is a concept implicit in the Rules of the Road, and should be firmly understood by every boater.

Taking all way off
The following is taken from Cockcroft & Lameijer's *A Guide to the Collision Avoidance Rules.*

If you're navigating without radar and you hear a fog signal forward of your beam, what should you do? The courts have held that you should reverse your engines in the following instances:
- You hear the signal for the first time in close proximity.
- You hear the signal dead ahead.
- The signals are narrowing the beam that is moving toward your bow.
- You see another vessel looming out of the fog, but you can't tell its course.
- You hear a sailboat's fog signal forward of your beam.

■ You hear the signal of a vessel at anchor and the tide is setting toward it. If you put your engines astern—especially full astern—be sure that engine noise will not obliterate further sound signals.

If collision is unavoidable

It's not a happy thought, but the rule of thumb is this: Stop as quickly as possible and face the danger. If there's any doubt on which side a vessel approaching directly and at relatively high speed may attempt to pass, you should present as small a target as possible. The effects of collision will be much less if you take the impact end-on rather than broadside.

Sound signals

When there is little chance of identifying an approaching vessel visually, you must be certain that you can identify the type of vessel, its position, and its movements by sound alone.

Do not signal too often

Keep in mind that the U.S. Inland and International Rules state that signals in restricted visibility should sound at intervals of "not more than two minutes" (one minute for bell and gong signals). Soundings should be automatically timed or measured to reasonable accuracy; use the second hand of your watch or ship's clock.

Two minutes is a relatively brief signaling interval; even if you're concerned about collision, you should not signal more often. Use the intervals between your blasts to listen for other vessel's signals—as valuable for safety as blowing your own whistle or horn.

If your signals are sounded automatically, interrupt them from time to time to make sure you aren't signaling in time with another vessel.

What the U.S. Inland Rules require

Distinctive sound signals must be given by different types of vessels in various conditions when in or near an area of restricted visibility. Known as fog signals, these are used just as often when visibility is limited for other reasons—day or night. You can use the same equipment for fog signals and maneuvering and warning signals.

The courts have ruled that fog signals should be sounded whenever visibility is reduced to the distance at which side-lights are required. Sound signals may serve two purposes: They alert nearby vessels to the presence and approximate position of the signaling vessel, and they may indicate its status (such as whether the boat is underway or at anchor) or limitations on maneuverability (such as whether it's towing or being towed, sailing or fishing, etc.).

Power-driven vessels underway

A power-driven vessel making way through the water must sound one prolonged blast. This signal must be repeated at intervals of not more than two minutes (Rule 35[a]).

If that vessel is underway but stopped and making no way through the water, it must sound two prolonged blasts two seconds apart (one prolonged blast followed by another two seconds later). The signal must be repeated at intervals of not more than two minutes (Rule 35[b]).

If a vessel is towing or pushing another vessel ahead, is not under command, is restricted in its ability to maneuver (underway or at anchor), or is a fishing boat (underway or at anchor), it must sound one prolonged blast followed by two short blasts. This signal must be repeated every (but not more than) two minutes (Rule 35[c]).

Sailing vessels underway

In restricted visibility, a sailboat must make one prolonged blast followed by two short blasts. The signal must be repeated at intervals of not more than two minutes (Rule 35[c]).

Vessels towing and being towed

A vessel engaged in towing or pushing another must sound one prolonged blast followed by two short blasts at intervals not greater than two minutes.

If manned, a vessel being towed, or the last vessel towed in a line, must sound one prolonged blast followed by three short blasts. This signal should be repeated at intervals of not more than two minutes. When possible, this signal should be sounded immediately after the towing vessel's signal (Rule 35[e]). Unmanned tows do not sound fog signals.

Vessels at anchor

If your vessel is at anchor in restricted visibility, you must ring a bell rapidly for about five seconds at intervals of not more than one minute.

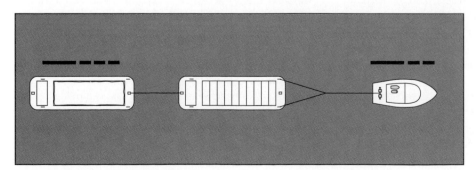

A manned vessel being towed astern (or the last vessel if more than one is being towed) sounds a signal of one prolonged blast followed by three short blasts at intervals of not more than two minutes, immediately after the towing vessel sounds its own signal.

If the vessel is 100 meters (328.1 ft.) long or more, the bell must be sounded in the forepart of the vessel; immediately thereafter, the gong must be sounded rapidly for about five seconds in the after part of the vessel *(Rule 35[f])*. In addition, an anchored vessel may sound a three-blast signal—one short, one prolonged, one short—to warn other vessels of its position and the possibility of collision *(Rule 35[f])*.

Under the U.S. Inland Rules, if your vessel is less than 20 meters (65.6 ft.) long, or if it is a barge, canal boat, scow, or "other nondescript craft," you can forego fog signals if you are anchored in a "special anchorage" area designated by the Secretary *(Rule 35[j])*. The International Rules do not provide for such special anchorage areas.

Vessels aground

If your boat is aground, you must sound the same bell signal (and the gong signal, if applicable) as a vessel at anchor. Additionally, you must give three separate and distinct bell strokes immediately before and after the rapid bell-ringing *(Rule 35[g])*. You must repeat this complete signal every minute. When you're aground, your signal sequence is:

- Three separate and distinct bell strokes.
- Rapid bell-ringing for five seconds.
- Three more separate and distinct bell strokes.

You may also sound a whistle signal, especially if you detect an approaching vessel and there is risk of collision. Although the appropriate signal is not specified, you might sound one of the following:

- One short blast, followed by one prolonged blast, followed by one short blast.
- Two short blasts, followed by one prolonged blast, meaning "You are running into danger" (the letter "U" of the International Code).

Exception for small craft

In U.S. waters, if your boat is less than 12 meters (39.4 ft.) long, you do not need to sound the above fog signals. But if you don't, you must make "some other efficient sound signal" every two minutes *(Rule 35[h])*.

In Canadian waters, this exception does not apply.

Pilot vessels

When engaged in pilotage duties in restricted visibility, a pilot vessel may sound an "identity" signal of four short blasts. Naturally, a pilot vessel also would be obliged to make the normal signals of a vessel underway, underway with no way on, or at anchor *(Rule 35[i])*.

Other vessels

A fishing vessel or a vessel otherwise restricted in its ability to maneuver must sound a prolonged blast followed by two short blasts at intervals of not more than two minutes.

Under the International Rules only, a vessel constrained by its draft sounds this same signal. Take note that this category of vessel is not included in the Inland Rules *(Rule 35 [c])*.

PENALTIES—VIOLATION OF INTERNATIONAL RULES

The International Navigational Rules Act of 1977 provides stiff penalties for violations of the International Rules.

These penalties are the same as those for the violation of the 1980 U.S. Inland Rules: The Inland Navigational Rules Act of 1980 provides that any person "who operates a vessel" in violation of that Act or any regulation issued thereunder—and this includes the various Annexes—is liable for a civil penalty of not more than $5,000 for each violation.

The Act also provides for withholding customs clearance for any vessel whose owner or operator has unpaid penalties. This is important for foreign vessels in U.S. waters; if penalty proceedings are not complete before the vessel's sailing date, clearance is normally granted after the posting of a bond.

Penalties for negligent operations can be issued to any person operating a vessel in a negligent manner; anyone whose negligence endangers the life, limb or property of a person is liable to the U.S. Government for a civil penalty of not more than $1,000. In the case of gross negligence, the penalty can be as high as $5,000. Your vessel may also be liable.

Should you be involved in a marine casualty situation, you are responsible for providing assistance and information. Failure to do this could cost you a fine of not more than $1,000 or imprisonment for not more than two years. Do not forget that your vessel may also be liable.

Obligation to render assistance

You must also provide assistance to any individual found at sea who is in danger of being lost—as long as you can do so without danger to your vessel or those aboard your boat. Failure to do this could make you liable for a fine of not more than $1,000 or two years in prison, or both.

The "Good Samaritan" Provision

Any person who complies with the specified assistance duties described above, or any other person who gratuitously and in good faith renders assistance at the scene of an accident or other boating casualty without the objection of any person being assisted, cannot be held liable for any civil damages as a result of rendering assistance, or of any act or omission in providing or arranging salvage, towage, medical treatment, or other assistance where he acts as an ordinary, reasonable prudent person would have done under the same or similar circumstances.

7 NAVIGATION LIGHTS AND DAY SHAPES

If you have ever navigated at night, you have observed passing vessels or perhaps even the passing shoreline and wondered, "What's that boat up to now?" At dusk, at night, in inclement weather, or in an unfamiliar harbor, you know just how confusing "that light over there" can be.

This chapter is designed to acquaint you with the identifiable navigational lights and day shapes that must be displayed by various types of vessels. These lights and shapes will help you to recognize sailboats and power-driven vessels, and to distinguish them from aids to navigation or even objects ashore. They may also tell you something about the status or activities of other vessels. Proper interpretation of what you see can help ensure safe navigation.

THE IMPORTANCE OF LIGHTS AND SHAPES

Basically, you must be able to identify lights and shapes for the same reason that you need to know the Rules of the Road on the water: to prevent collision. According to the Rules, every vessel must carry navigation lights of a specified color; that is, white, red, green or yellow. The Rules also prescribe the arc, range of visibility and location of the navigation lights. (Conversationally, navigation lights displayed while a vessel is underway are called "running lights," while those displayed at anchor or while moored are called "riding lights.")

Navigation lights are important for two major reasons: First, they help you identify the position of another vessel relative to your boat. As outlined in Chapter 6, you must be able to determine another vessel's orientation with respect to

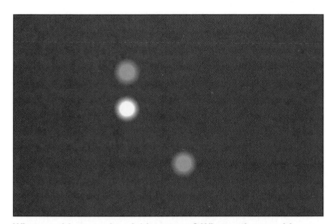

What would you make of this pattern? What action would you take? It's a fishing trawler underway, and you're looking at its starboard side. You would have to alter course to avoid both the vessel and its nets.

your boat to ascertain who has the right of way. Second, they provide clues about the size of that other vessel, its characteristics and what it is doing.

During the day, day shapes serve similar purposes as navigation lights. Always black in color, day shapes are objects of specified shape, size and placement on a vessel. During normal operation day shapes are not required to help boaters determine the relative position and motion of another vessel. However, they are useful to indicate special situations, such as being anchored or engaged in fishing, or where visual information alone may be misleading—for example, when a sailboat with sails raised also is operating under power.

Defining your responsibility
When you're operating at night, you will need to be able to count on your knowledge of navigation lights to guarantee your vessel's safety. Often, the only information available about another vessel and its movement will come from its navigation lights. Especially when you're operating in busy traffic, or in a near-shore area where city lights may confuse your vision, you must be confident in your ability to identify and interpret navigation lights.

Even in daylight and with good visibility, it is important to recognize day shapes. Often, the day shapes carried by another vessel will give you important information—indicating that vessel's activities, or limitations that you wouldn't know otherwise.

According to the Rules, your responsibility also includes ensuring that your vessel displays lights of the appropriate color, intensity and visibility, and in their proper location. Don't assume that the people who built your boat have done your compliance work; check it yourself.

You should be aware that, during factory and boat show inspections, USCG standards personnel frequently observe that many manufacturers of recreational boats do not have a good understanding of the Rules governing proper installation of navigation lights. Some manufacturers are installing navigation lights that do not meet the requirements of the International or the Inland Rules. Deficient, improperly installed equipment can seriously endanger lives.

Once you have ensured that your boat's lights are the appropriate ones, and properly located, make absolutely sure that you know which lights to turn on (and which not to turn on), and when.

Who makes the rules
As discussed in Chapter 6, the 1980 U.S. Inland Navigational Rules, the 1972 International Rules of the Road (known as 72 COLREGS), and the Canadian Collision Regulations (International Regulations for Preventing Collisions at Sea, 1972 with Canadian Modifications) also govern the type, size, placement and use of lights and shapes—always with the goal of promoting safe navigation.

In each case, the rules governing lights and shapes are contained in Part C, "Lights and Shapes" *(Rules 20 to 31)*. Technical information concerning positioning and other details and specific information for fishing vessels is found in Annexes I and II. *(Annex V contains U.S. pilot rules for lights, and certain other rules also apply.)*

Generally, the rules governing lights and shapes apply to boats of any size; however, there are some differences in the rules as they apply to small and large vessels. There also are some differences in the rules for U.S. inland, international and Canadian waters.

Sequence of consideration
Because most North American boaters operate on the waters of rivers, lakes, bays and sounds governed by the U.S. Inland Navigational Rules, those Rules concerning lights and shapes will be presented in this chapter in detail. The 72 COLREGS and the Canadian rules will be presented in terms of how they differ from the U.S. Inland Rules.

If you should wish to look up a particular rule in any appropriate Coast Guard publication, bracketed references to specific rules, paragraphs and subparagraphs are provided throughout this chapter.

THE U.S. INLAND RULES

The U.S. Inland Rules apply inside the demarcation lines separating inland and international waters at entrances to bays, sounds, rivers, inlets and other bodies of water. Generally, they apply to all vessels, regardless of nationality, on such waters. They also apply to U.S. vessels on the Canadian waters of the Great Lakes, providing these Rules don't conflict with Canadian laws or regulations *(Rule 1[a])*.

The International Rules apply to all vessels once they clear the jetties or headlands at a harbor entrance. In some areas of coastal New England, the lower Florida Keys, Puget Sound, Washington, and offshore land masses, such as Catalina Island, California, and Block Island, Massachusetts, however, the International Rules apply even in harbors, bays, inlets and rivers. Always be sure to check your coastal charts to determine the location of demarcation lines, which are distinguished by dashed magenta lines.

General regulations

You must display the appropriate lights in all weathers from sunset to sunrise. At night, you may display only those lights that are unmistakably in keeping with the Rules. Any other lights displayed must not "impair the visibility or distinctive character" of your required lights or "interfere with the keeping of a proper lookout" *(Rule 20[a] and [b])*.

When visibility is restricted, you also must display the appropriate lights even between sunrise and sunset. During the day, you also may display lights "in all other circumstances when it is deemed necessary" *(Rule 20[c])*.

During the day, you must comply with the rules concerning shapes *(Rule 20[d])*. Because each type of navigation light must cover a standard arc of visibility, some lights are visible only from ahead, along part of a vessel's side, from astern, or all around. Various vessel lights are described at right *(Rule 21[a] to [g])*. In addition to those definitions, it is important to understand terms that apply to positioning signals and complying with the technical details.

For this purpose, the Rules also provide the following definitions *(Annex I, § 84.01)*: "Height above the hull" means the height above the vessel's uppermost continuous deck; for a recreational boater, this is usually measured as the gunwale or the sheer line. This height is measured from the position vertically beneath the light's location. For vessels at least 20 meters (65.6 ft.) long, the term "practical cut-off" means 12.5 percent of the minimum luminous intensity corresponding

DEFINING NAVIGATION LIGHTS

Masthead light
A white light placed over a vessel's fore-and-aft center line, showing an unbroken light over a 225-degree arc, from right ahead ("dead ahead") to 22.5 degrees abaft the beam on either side of the vessel. Power-driven vessels 50 meters (164 feet) or more in length require a second masthead light.

On boats less than 12 meters (39.4 feet) long, the masthead light may be off the center line but should be placed "as nearly as practicable" to it. You might look for a masthead light at the top of a mast, but you won't always find it there. For example, powerboats do not have masts, but they do have masthead lights. On these vessels, the masthead light often is located on a short staff on the cabin top. On sailboats, the masthead light usually is partway up the mast; the anchor light actually is at the masthead.

Sidelights
Colored lights, green on the starboard side and red on the port side, showing an unbroken light over a 112.5-degree arc, from right ahead to 22.5 degrees abaft the beam on their respective sides. (The sum of the arcs of the green and red sidelights is the same as that of the white masthead light.)

If your vessel is less than 20 meters (65.6 feet) long, the sidelights may be combined in one lantern carried on the boat's fore-and-aft center line. If your vessel is less than 12 meters (39.4 feet) long, you should carry that combination light "as nearly as practicable" to the fore-and-aft center line.

Stern light
A white light, placed as nearly as practicable at the stern, showing an unbroken light over a 135-degree arc, from 67.5 degrees from right aft ("dead astern") on each side of the vessel.

Towing light
Means a yellow light having the same characteristics as the stern light defined above.

All-round light
Shows an unbroken light over a 360-degree arc. Depending on what its function is, an all-round light may be white, red, green or yellow.

Flashing light
Flashes regularly at least 120 times a minute. This extremely rapid flashing rate is used to lessen any possible confusion with a quick-flashing buoy or other aid to navigation.

Special flashing light
A yellow light flashing regularly at 50 to 70 times a minute. This light is placed as far forward and "as nearly as practicable" on the fore-and-after center line of a tow and shows an unbroken light over an arc of 180 to 225 degrees, from right ahead to abeam and no more than 22.5 degrees abaft the beam on either side of the vessel. This will also be seen on a hovercraft in the non-displacement mode (hovering).

112.5° 135 225° 360°

Each type of navigation light covers a specific arc of visibility. When these types and their arcs are understood, the orientation of the vessel becomes clear.

to the greatest range of visibility for which Annex I requirements are met *(Table 84.15[b])*.

Visibility of lights

Depending on your vessel's size, your lights must be sufficiently intense *(Annex I)* to be visible over the following distances *(Rule 22[a] to [d])*:

- **Vessels at least 50 meters (164 ft.) long.** Masthead lights: 6 miles. Sidelight, stern light, towing light and all-round light (all colors): 3 miles. Special flashing light: 2 miles.
- **Vessels at least 12 meters (39.4 ft.) but less than 50 meters (164 ft.) long.** Masthead light: 5 miles; if the vessel is less than 20 meters (65.6 ft.) long: 3 miles. Sidelight, stern light, towing light, all-round light (all colors) and special flashing light: 2 miles.
- **Vessels less than 12 meters (39.4 ft.) long.** Masthead light: 2 miles. Sidelight: 1 mile. Stern light, towing light, all-round light (all colors) and special flashing light: 2 miles.
- **Inconspicuous, partly submerged vessels or objects being towed.** White all-round light: 3 miles.

Lights for power-driven vessels underway

Generally, power-driven vessels must exhibit (1) a masthead light forward, (2) a second masthead light higher than and abaft of the other, (3) sidelights and (4) a stern light. Note, however, that this rule of thumb may change if the power-driven vessel is engaged—in towing or in pushing another boat, for example.

Preferably, your masthead light should be positioned forward of amidships; however, if your vessel is less than 20 meters (65.6 ft.) long, you may position your masthead light "as far forward as is practicable" *(Rule 23[a][i])*.

If your vessel is less than 50 meters (164 ft.) long, however, you need not display a second masthead light aft, but may do so if you desire *(Rule 23 [a][ii])*. Other special cases are listed below.

- **Air-cushion vessels.** In addition to the lights specified for all power-driven vessels, an air-cushion vessel less than 50 meters (164 ft.) long, operating in the non-displacement mode, must exhibit an all-round flashing yellow light "where it can best be seen" *(Rule 23[b])*.

- **Smaller vessels (less than 12 meters).** If your power-driven boat is less than 12 meters (39.4 ft.) long, you may replace the individual masthead light(s) and stern light with a single, all-round white light. As is the case for larger vessels, however, sidelights also are required *(Rule 23[c])*.
- **Vessels operating on the Great Lakes.** If you are operating a power-driven vessel of any size on the Great Lakes, you may replace the second masthead light and stern light with an all-round white light, carried in the position of the second masthead light and visible at the same minimum range *(Rule 23[d])*.

Lights for towing and pushing vessels

Towing vessels may be less maneuverable, but they don't have any additional right of way granted them unless they show restricted ability to maneuver. The purpose of the tow-

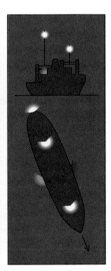

Vessels that carry both forward and aft masthead lights (more than 50 meters, or 164.1 feet) provide a range that indicates their orientation. The forward light is always lower than the aft light: Imagine a wedge indicating direction. If the two lights are in line, the wedge is pointing at you. Normally, these higher lights will be seen before the red and green sidelights.

ing lights is to alert you that it is a tug and tow, so you look for the tow astern, or tow wire. To bring this situation to attention at night or in conditions of restricted visibility, special navigation lights and shapes are prescribed, as described below. Inland Rules call for the display of yellow towing lights astern on some power-driven vessels. These changes also require side lights and, in some cases, flashing yellow lights on barges being pushed or towed alongside.

- **Towing astern.** When towing astern, a power-driven vessel must display (1) two masthead lights in a vertical line, (2) sidelights, (3) a stern light and (4) a yellow towing light in a vertical line above the stern light.

However, when the length of the tow measured from the stern of the towing vessel to the after end of the tow exceeds

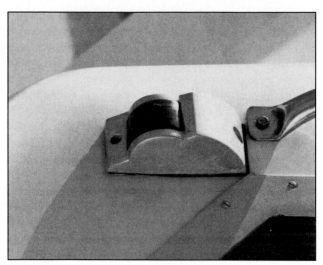

Sidelights (the red and green lights) must cover an arc of 112.5 degrees. This mounting prevents spill-over when seen from dead ahead.

200 meters (656.2 ft.), the towing vessel must display three masthead lights in a vertical line, or, by day, a diamond shape where it can best be seen *(Rule 24[a])*.

On the Western Rivers (except below the Huey P. Long Bridge on the Mississippi River), and on waters specified by the Secretary, however, a power-driven vessel pushing ahead or towing another vessel must display only sidelights and two towing lights in a vertical line *(Rule 24[i])*.

■ **Lights for towed vessels.** When a vessel or object is being towed, it must exhibit sidelights, a stern light and, when the length of the tow is more than 200 meters (656.2 ft.), or, by day, a diamond shape where it can best be seen *(Rule 24[e])*.

Vessels being towed alongside or pushed in a group may be lighted as one vessel. In that case, a pushed vessel that is not part of a composite unit must exhibit sidelights at the forward end and a special flashing yellow light. Similarly, a vessel being towed alongside must exhibit sidelights at the forward end and a stern light *(Rule 24[f])*.

If an inconspicuous, partly submerged vessel or object is being towed, it must exhibit a diamond shape at or near its aftermost extremity, and one or more all-round white lights, depending on its dimensions. The towing vessel also may direct a searchlight toward the tow to indicate its presence to an approaching vessel *(Rule 24[g])*.

If an inconspicuous, partly submerged vessel or object is being towed, it must exhibit, if it is less than 15 meters (49.2 ft.) in breadth, one all round white light at or near each end. If it is at least 25 meters (82 ft.) wide, it must display four all-round white lights to mark its length and breadth. If the tow is more than 100 meters (328.1 ft.) long, and the vessels or objects towed alongside—such as liquid-filled bags (dracones), log rafts or other nearly awash objects—are being lighted as one, it must display enough lights so that the distance between them is not more than 100 meters (328.1 ft.).

A diamond shape at or near the aftermost extremity of the last vessel or object being towed, should be attached *(Rule 24[g][i] to [v])*.

For safety's sake, you always must strive to light your tow. When it's impracticable to light the tow in the prescribed way, you must take "all possible measures" to light the towed vessel or object "or at least to indicate the presence of the unlighted vessel or object" *(Rule 24[h])*.

■ **Towing a distressed vessel.** If you help a vessel in distress or otherwise needing assistance and you don't normally engage in towing operations, you are not obliged to display the prescribed lights. The Rules specify, however, that "all possible measures shall be taken to indicate the nature of the relationship between the towing vessel and the vessel being assisted," such as shining a searchlight to illuminate the tow *(Rules 24[j] and 36)*.

■ **Pushing ahead or towing alongside.** When pushing ahead or towing another vessel alongside, a power-driven vessel

Boats less than 20 meters (65.6 ft.) can combine their sidelights into one unit. The total arc for sidelights is 225 degrees (112.5 x 2), the same as for the masthead light.

generally must display (1) two white masthead lights in a vertical line (in place of either the forward or after masthead light specified by Rule 23[a][i] and [ii]), (2) sidelights, and (3) two towing lights in a vertical line *(Rule 24[c])*. If the two vertical white lights are displayed aft, a forward masthead light must be carried *(Rule 24[d])*.

■ **Composite units.** When a pushing vessel and a vessel being pushed ahead are rigidly connected in a composite unit, they are considered a single power-driven vessel. These vessels should exhibit the lights appropriate for power-driven vessels of their given length *(Rules 23 and 24[b])*.

Lights for sailing vessels underway
All sailboats must carry the same sidelights and stern light as a power-driven vessel of the same size, but they should not display a white masthead light *(Rule 25[a])*.

If your sailboat is less than 20 meters (65.6 ft.) long, you can display separate sidelights and a stern light, or you can combine these lights in one lantern, carried at or near the top of the mast where it can best be seen. If your boat is a yawl, ketch or other multiple-masted vessel, you can presume (although the Rules don't specifically state) that "the mast" means the main mast *(Rule 25[b])*. (If you do combine these lights, however, then you must not display additional navigation lights.) You may display those lights and two additional all-round lights (the upper red and the lower green) at or near the top of your mast, where they can best be seen *(Rule 25[c])*. Such displays are rare because of the additional power drain and the required minimum one-meter separation above the uppermost sail.

You should note that a combination masthead light cannot be used when you're operating under power, since you won't be able to satisfy the rules for power-driven vessels (carrying a white forward light higher than the sidelights). You will need a set of standard lights for use when you're operating under power. (For details of appropriate day shapes when motoring, see also "Sailboats operating under power" below.)

■ **Sailboats less than 7 meters.** Ideally, sailboats less than 7 meters (23 ft.) long also should exhibit sidelights and a stern light when underway. If this is impracticable, however, these smaller boats must keep at hand an electric torch (flashlight), or lighted lantern with a white light, to exhibit in sufficient time to prevent collision *(Rule 25[d][i])*.

■ **Sailboats operating under power.** If you are motoring with your sails up, you must exhibit a conical shape (apex down) forward, where it may best be seen. This signal tells other skippers that you are not entitled to a sailboat's usual right-of-way privileges, even though your sails are set.

However, if your boat is less than 12 meters (39.4 ft.) long, you may (but you are not obliged to) exhibit this day shape *(Rule 25[e])*.

Lights for vessels under oars

A rowboat, dinghy or other craft being propelled by oars may (but is not obliged to) show the lights of a sailing vessel—sidelights and a stern light—when underway. Otherwise, an electric torch (flashlight) or lighted lantern with a white light must be kept at hand to prevent collision *(Rule 25[d][ii])*.

Vessels anchored or aground

Generally, when anchored, your vessel must exhibit (1) an all-round white light or, by day, one ball in the forepart where it can best be seen and (2) an all-round light at or near the stern and lower than the other signal *(Rule 30[a])*.

Depending on the size of your vessel, there may be a few additions or acceptable variations to the rule, as follows: (1) If your vessel is less than 50 meters (164 ft.) long, you may exhibit an all-round white light where it can best be seen instead of the otherwise-prescribed signals fore and aft *(Rule 30[b])*. (2) If your vessel is at least 100 meters (328.1 ft.) long,

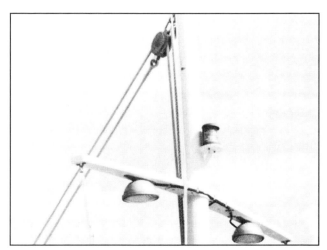
Masthead lights are misnamed as they are usually mounted below the masthead. They are white and cover an arc of 225 degrees.

you also must illuminate your decks with your available working or equivalent lights. (Smaller vessels may, but are not obliged to, do so.) *(Rule 30[c])* (3) If your vessel is less than 20 meters (65.6 ft.) long and you are anchored in a designated anchorage, you are not obliged to display the required anchor lights and shapes *(Rule 30[g])*. These special anchorage areas usually are found near yacht clubs and marinas, or in popular cruising areas. In these areas, you can leave your boat unattended on a mooring without displaying an anchor light continuously after sunset.

If your vessel is less than 7 meters (23 ft.) long and when you are not anchored in or near a narrow channel, fairway, anchorage or normal navigation area, you are not required to display the prescribed all-round white light(s) fore and aft *(Rule 30[e])*.

When a vessel is aground, it must display the appropriate lights for an anchored vessel of its length. In addition, if prac-

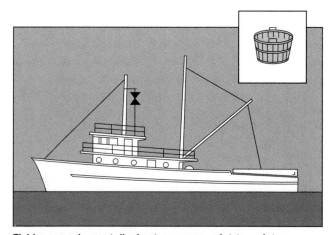
Fishing vessels must display two cones point-to-point as a day shape. A basket can be substituted for boats less than 20 meters (65.6 ft.).

ticable, a vessel aground must display two all-round red lights in a vertical line, or, by day, three balls in a vertical line. All signals should be displayed where they can best be seen *(Rule 30[d])*. If your grounded vessel is less than 12 meters (39.4 ft.) long, however, you are not obliged to exhibit the prescribed lights and shapes *(Rule 30[f])*.

Lights for commercial fishing vessels

When you are actively fishing, whether underway or at anchor, your boat must exhibit the lights and shapes prescribed in Rule 26; however, when your vessel is not actually engaged in commercial fishing, you must exhibit only the lights and shapes prescribed for a vessel of that length.

■ **Fishing boats.** Vessels engaged in fishing other than trawling must exhibit two all-round lights in a vertical line (the upper red and the lower white), or, by day, a shape consist-

A white stern light with a 135-degree arc shines from dead astern to a point 22.5 degrees abaft each beam, matching the area not covered by masthead and sidelights. On boats less than 12 meters (39.4 ft.) it may be combined with the masthead light as a single all-round white light.

ing of two cones with their apexes together in a vertical line one above the other. If your vessel is less than 20 meters (65.6 ft.) long, you may substitute a basket for these shapes.

When your outlying gear extends more than 150 meters (492.1 ft.) horizontally from the vessel, you also must display an all-round white light, or, by day, a cone (apex upward) in the direction of the gear. When underway, your vessel also must display sidelights and a stern light.

■ **Fishing in close proximity.** When you are fishing in close proximity to other vessels, you also may exhibit the following signals, as described in Annex II.

■ **Trawlers.** Generally, while engaged in the "dragging through the water of a dredge net or other apparatus used as a fishing appliance," you must exhibit the following: (1) Two all-round lights in a vertical line (the upper green and the lower

white), or, by day, a shape consisting of two cones with their apexes together in a vertical line, one above the other. (On a vessel less than 20 meters (65.6 ft.) long, you may substitute a basket for these shapes.) (2) A masthead light abaft of and higher than the all-round green light. This light is optional for vessels less than 50 meters (164 ft.) long. (3) Sidelights and a stern light, whenever your trawler is underway.

If you are engaged in trawling with demersal or pelagic gear, you may exhibit the following *(Annex II, § 85.3)*. When shooting nets: two white lights in a vertical line. When hauling nets: one white light over one red light in a vertical line. When the net has come fast upon an obstruction: two red lights in a vertical line.

If you are engaged in pair trawling, you may exhibit the following. By night: a searchlight directed forward and in the direction of the other vessel in your pair. When shooting or hauling nets, or when nets have come fast upon an obstruction, you may exhibit the same lights prescribed for trawlers using demersal or pelagic gear.

■ **Purse seiners.** If you are engaged in fishing with purse seine, you may exhibit two yellow lights in a vertical line, only when your vessel is hampered by its fishing gear. The lights must flash alternately every second, and with equal light and occultation duration *(Annex II, § 85.5)*.

Lights for sport fishing boats

Trolling is not "trawling," and sport fishing is not considered commercial fishing in the Rules. While trolling, sportfishermen are not nearly as restricted in ability to maneuver as a vessel engaged in trawling or fishing with heavy nets or gear; therefore, under the Rules, they are not considered to be fishing or trawling for the purposes of the Rules. Courtesy should be practiced by those who come upon a recreational fisherman with lines trolling astern.

Not under command or restricted

Rule 27 prescribes various light-and-shape configurations for different types of vessels restricted in their ability to maneu-

When a large vessel (20 meters, or 65.6 ft.) is not under command, it must display two black balls, one above the other.

ver; however, these lights and shapes should not be confused with distress signals *(Annex IV) (Rule 27[h]).*

Generally, vessels less than 12 meters (39.4 ft.) long are not obliged to follow this rule; however, dive boats of all sizes must do so *(Rule 27[e] and [g]).*

■ **Not under command.** If your vessel is not under command (that is, unable for some reason to maneuver according to the Rules of the Road and, therefore, unable to keep out of the way of another vessel), you must display the following signals: two all-round red lights in a vertical line where they can best be seen, or, by day, two balls or similar shapes in a vertical line where they can best be seen *(Rule 27[a][i] and [ii]).* If your not-under-command vessel is making way through the water, you also must display sidelights and a stern light *(Rule 27[a][iii]).*

■ **Restricted maneuvering.** If your vessel is restricted in its ability to maneuver (and it is not engaged in clearing mines), you must exhibit the following: three all-round lights in a vertical line (the upper and lower lights must be red and the middle one white) where they can best be seen, or, by day, three shapes in a vertical line (the upper and lower balls and the middle, a diamond) where they can best be seen *(Rule 27[b][i] and [ii]).*

If such a vessel is making way through the water, the usual masthead lights, sidelights and a stern light are required *(Rule 27[b][iii]).*

When your vessel is at anchor, you must display the three all-round lights and three shapes prescribed above and the appropriate light(s) or shapes prescribed for vessels at anchor. The latter signals are described in the section "Vessels anchored and aground" on page 139 *(Rules 27[b][iv] and 30).*

■ **Towing vessels.** If your towing activities severely limit the ability of your vessel and its tow to change course, your vessel must display the usual lights prescribed for a towing vessel of its size, or, by day, three all-round lights and three shapes, as described in the section "Restricted maneuvering" above *(Rules 24 and 27[c]).*

■ **Dredging or underwater operations.** When restricted in its ability to maneuver, a vessel engaged in dredging or underwater operations must display the appropriate signals for such vessels, as described in the section "Restricted maneuvering" above *(Rules 27[b][i], [ii], [iii] and [d]).* When an obstruction exists, you also must display additional lights or shapes to assist other vessels in negotiating their way around your vessel, as follows: (1) Two all-round red lights or two balls in a vertical line to indicate the side on which the obstruction exists, and (2) two all-round green lights or, by day, two diamonds in a vertical line to indicate the side on which another vessel may pass *(Rule 27[d][i] and [ii]).*

When at anchor, dredging and underwater operation vessels must exhibit the lights and shapes that have been described above—not those specified in Rule 30 for anchored vessels *(Rule 27[d][iii]).*

■ **Small dive boats.** Whenever the size of your dive boat makes it impracticable to display the lights and shapes otherwise specified for vessels engaged in underwater operations, you must exhibit the following: (1) three all-round lights (the upper and lower red and the middle white) in a vertical line where they can best be seen, and (2) rigid replica of the International Code flag "A" (white and blue and swallow tailed) not less than one meter (3.3 ft.) tall and visible all-round *(Rule 27[e]).*

Remember that the "A" signal indicates the status of your vessel; that is, that its maneuverability is limited—for example, if divers are connected to your vessel by lines or hoses. If your vessel's maneuverability is not limited, do not display the signal. Normally, you will need to erect at least two "A" flag replicas in a crisscross or square arrangement to ensure all-round visibility. Also note that flexible cloth "A" flags are not acceptable substitutes for the prescribed signal.

The Inland Rules do not recognize the use of the familiar red-with-white-stripe diver flag. The Code Alpha, or restricted in ability to maneuver flag, signals the other boater that a vessel is unable to maneuver (for example, due to underwater operations). However, the red/white diver flag is still very useful to mark that divers are in the water either on a vessel or on a float over the divers. In addition, many states prescribe that vessels must keep a minimum distance from a diver flag, usually 100 to 150 feet and/or must slow up in the vicinity of divers.

Lights for pilot vessels

An off-duty pilot vessel must exhibit the appropriate lights or shapes for a vessel of its length *(Rule 29[b]).* When on duty, a pilot vessel must display two all-round lights (the upper white and the lower red) in a vertical line, at or near the masthead. In addition, a pilot vessel underway also must display sidelights and a stern light *(Rule 29[a][i] and [ii]).*

When at anchor, a pilot vessel must display the two all-round lights and the appropriate anchor light, lights or shape prescribed for anchored vessels *(Rules 29[a][iii] and 30).*

Lights for seaplanes

If a seaplane cannot exhibit the appropriate lights and shapes, the Rules state that it must "exhibit lights and shapes as closely similar in characteristics and position as is possible" *(Rule 31).*

Pilot rules for lights

■ **Law-enforcement vessels.** A federal or state law-enforcement vessel, or other governmental vessel, may display a flashing blue light when engaged in direct law-enforcement activities. This light must not interfere with the visibility of the vessel's navigation lights *(Annex V, § 88.11[a] and [b]).*

■ **Public safety vessels.** A special identifying light for vessels engaged in special missions, such as Coast Guard Auxiliary or USPS vessels on government sanctioned "public safety activities," may display an alternately flashing red and yellow light. Public service activities include search and rescue, traffic or crowd control, medical assistance and assisting disabled vessels, as well as patrolling parades, regattas and other on-water celebrations. This light is not to be used for routine towing. The public safety light is in addition to the usual navigation lights and may not interfere with or replace any required lights. It does not grant the vessel towing it any special privileges.

■ **Floating or trestle-supported dredge pipelines.** These pipelines must display lights at night and in restricted visibility. Where the pipeline crosses a navigable channel, yellow lights must be equally spaced along the pipeline, no more than 10 meters (32.8 ft.) apart. Where the pipeline does not cross a navigable channel, the lights must be sufficient to show clearly the pipeline's length and course. Each light on the pipeline must be visible all-round for at least 2 miles on a clear, dark night; must flash 50 to 70 times a minute; and must be located one meter to 3.5 meters (3.3 to 11.5 ft.) above the water. There also must be two all-round, non-flashing red lights at each end of the pipeline, spaced one meter (3.3 ft.) apart vertically, with the lower red light at the same height above water as the flashing yellow lights *(Annex V, § 88.15).*

■ **A barge at bank or dock.** In this case, the vessel must be lit with white lights visible for one mile on a clear, dark night. *(Annex V, § 88.13 lists the circumstances requiring lights and light characteristics.)*

■ **Passing under a bridge.** Your vessel may lower its lights or day shapes as necessary. When clear of the bridge, you must reposition your lights and day shapes immediately *(Annex V, § 88.09).*

Other provisions

The navigation lights of the International Rules waters are permitted on U.S. Inland Rules waters, but not vice versa. This means that a boat lighted in compliance with the U.S. Inland Rules may be in violation of the International Rules when proceeding seaward of the demarcation line.

If your signals comply with those prescribed by the International Rules, you may use them in lieu of those prescribed by the U.S. Inland Rules, but you may not mix and match *(Rule 1[b]).* If you operate your boat outside the area demarcated by the U.S. Inland Rules, this option means you won't need to change signals when moving from one body of water to another.

Lights for government vessels

These lights-and-shapes rules, however, do not apply to Navy and Coast Guard vessels of the United States—submarines and aircraft carriers, for example— when the departmental Secretary certifies that their special construction makes compliance impossible. In such cases, however, their lights must comply as closely as is feasible *(Rule 1[e]).* Naval ships and vessels proceeding in convoy may use special station or signal lights that, as much as it is possible, cannot be mistaken for any of the navigation lights prescribed in the Inland Rules *(Rule 1[c]).*

Lights for submarines

Occasionally, a submarine's normal navigation lights—which are low and closely spaced—are mistaken for those of small boats. Under Rule 1(e), however, U.S. submarines must display a special, distinctive light.

The distinguishing light is an amber beacon with one flash per second for three seconds (three flashes) followed by three seconds of darkness. Rule 1(e) specifies that the beacon should be located where it will best be visible, as nearly as possible all-round, and not less than 2 feet above or below the masthead light.

A surfaced submarine shows its normal navigation lights as well as an amber beacon that flashes once per second three times then is off for three seconds.

Exemptions

To facilitate the change to the 1980 U.S. Inland Navigation Rules from the former Inland, Great Lakes and Western Rivers rules, the Rules provide for some exemptions to lighting requirements. Exemptions apply to "any vessel or class of vessels, the keel of which was laid, or which was at a corresponding stage of construction" before December 24, 1980. Newer vessels must comply fully with the Rules *(Rule 38).*

All vessels are exempted from repositioning lights to conform with metric rather than imperial measurements.

■ Vessels less than 150 meters (492.1 ft.) long are exempted from repositioning masthead lights horizontally, in compliance with the Rules.

■ Vessels less than 20 meters (65.6 ft.) long with lights that meet the specification of the Motor Boat Act of 1940 are exempted from meeting the visibility ranges and color specifications of the Rules.

■ Power-driven vessels at least 12 meters (39.4 ft.) but less than 20 meters (65.6 ft.) long are exempted from showing a masthead light forward and a stern light aft, provided they show an all-round white light aft.

POSITIONING AND TECHNICAL DETAILS

In addition to knowing what lights and shapes to display in various circumstances, you must know where to put them, and what kinds to choose in order to comply with the Rules. You should be familiar with the following specifications.

Masthead lights

- Always place masthead lights clear of all other lights or obstructions *(Annex I, § 84.03[f])*.
- Vessels more than 12 meters (39.4 ft.) long must carry a separate foward masthead light and a stern light. The forward light needn't actually be at the masthead, but it must meet Annex I placement requirements.
- On vessels more than 20 meters (65.6 ft.) long, the masthead light must be at least 5 meters (16.4 ft.) above the hull; if the vessel's beam is greater than 5 meters, however, the light's height must be at least that dimension but needn't exceed 8 meters (26.2 ft.) *(Annex I, § 84.03[a])*.
- On vessels at least 12 meters (39.4 ft.) but less than 20 meters (65.6 ft.) long, the masthead light must be at least 2.5 meters (8.2 ft.) above the gunwale *(Annex I, § 84.03[c])*.
- On vessels less than 12 meters (39.4 ft.) long, the masthead light (or the all-round light, if used) must be at least one meter (3.3 ft.) higher than the sidelights *(Annex I, § 84.03[d])*. It must be screened if necessary to prevent interference with your vision from the helm *(Annex I, § 84.09[b])*.

In a sailboat equipped with an auxiliary engine, the switch panel must include a separate circuit for the masthead light so it can be turned off when the vessel is under sail alone.

Note: The Coast Guard wants to encourage the use of two masthead lights on power-driven vessels less than 50 meters in length. Therefore, under a Coast Guard interpretation of the subparagraph 3[a] of Annex I, power-driven vessels less than 50 meters in length do not have to meet the minimum separation requirements of half the vessel length specified.

Anchor lights

An anchor light may be where it can best be seen. It is an all-round light and should follow directives of installation as

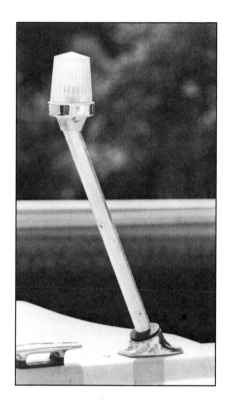

In International Rules waters, a white all-round stern light may be offset from the center line only on craft up to 12 meters (39.4 ft) in length.

seen in the next section. The U.S. Coast Guard advises owners of boats to make sure their running lights and anchor lights are not used in conjunction while navigating. The Coast Guard also advises boaters to refrain from displaying additional lights that might be confusing to other boaters who are navigating at night.

To use a strobe light as an anchor light or as an anti-collision light is improper and may result in civil penalties. A strobe light is a distress signal under Inland Rules only and doesn't meet the definition for an all-round light.

All-round lights

A boat's all-round (360-degree) white running light is the most important of a small boat's navigation lights because it can be seen from any direction. The most common problem associated with this light is that it is frequently mounted on a staff that is too short. As a result, the light is obscured when the vessel is underway because of the tendency of the bow to rise when the boat is moving, or the light is obscured by canvas tops or other equipment owners add after purchasing a boat.

The Rules allow for a maximum of 6 degrees of blockage by masts, topmasts or structures.

If the all-round light is obscured from any direction, while the vessel is at rest or underway, or by any part of the boat structure or its equipment, owners are strongly urged to buy a longer staff, even if it means purchasing a removable staff, rather than one that telescopes. Owners are also urged to remember to extend the staff fully when turning on their boats' running lights.

YOUR RESPONSIBILITY

It is the responsibility of the owner/operator of a vessel that the craft show the proper navigation lights for its size and the waters in which it is operating. It is not the responsibility of the manufacturer, importer or selling dealer. Many boats are delivered with lights that do not meet legal requirements with respect to technical characteristics or placement on the vessel. Remember also that the angles of visibility must be met when the boat is underway—if your boat rides at a significant bow-up angle, take that into consideration when installing and/or checking your navigation lights.

Sidelights

On all vessels, sidelights must be at least one meter (3.3 ft.) lower than the (forward) masthead light. Deck lights should not interfere with the sidelights *(Annex I, § 84.03[g])*.

On power-driven vessels at least 20 meters (65.6 ft.) long, sidelights must be placed at or near the sides of the vessel, not in front of the forward masthead lights. Sidelights must be provided with mat black inboard screens to cut off light at the prescribed "ahead" limit of each arc of visibility *(Annex I, § 84.05[c] and 84.09[a]).*

On vessels less than 20 meters (65.6 ft.) long, screens also must be used if needed to meet the cut-off requirements and to prevent excessive spillover from sidelights. A combination light using one vertical filament bulb and a very narrow division between sectors does not need a screen.

One common navigation light installation error that Coast Guard inspectors frequently find is the installation of flush-mounted sidelights in the forward part of the hull of a boat, usually below the rub rail. As a result, the lights are installed "cross-eyed" when they are mounted too far forward and when mounted too far aft. Because the lights cannot be seen from a position dead ahead, the operator of an approaching vessel may be confused about the relative direction in which the boats are traveling. This can lead to maneuvering errors.

Sidelights that are installed in the contour of the bow without providing a mounting surface tooled to be parallel with the fore and aft center line of the vessel are not in compliance with the Inland or International Navigation Rules. International Navigation Rules require that sidelights be installed above the uppermost continuous deck. Therefore this configuration is not in compliance with International Navigation Rules.

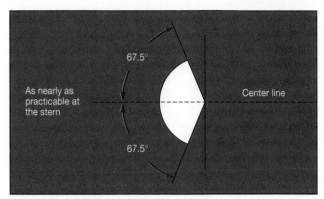

According to Navigation Rules, a power-driven vessel underway less than 12 meters (39.4 ft.) in length may exhibit either (1) a masthead light, sidelights and a stern light or (2) an all-round white light and sidelights. Most manufacturers of boats less than 20 feet in length install lights in the (2) configuration. Since the all-round light on these boats is usually installed near the stern, many people refer to them as stern lights.

Another factor in proper installation of sidelights on a power-driven vessel is that they must maintain their required minimum intensity in a vertical sector from 5 degrees above to 5 degrees below the horizontal. They must also maintain at least 60 percent of their minimum required intensity from 7.5 degrees above to 7.5 degrees below the horizontal.

For vessels under sail, sidelights must maintain their required minimum intensity in a vertical sector from 5 degrees above to 5 degrees below the horizontal and at least 50 percent of their minimum required intensity from 25 degrees above to 25 degrees below the horizontal to allow for heel. Installing flush-mounted sidelights, designed to be mounted to a vertical surface in the hull contour, without providing a mounting surface tooled to be vertical, shifts the vertical coverage sector. This also results in non-compliance with the Navigation Rules.

Stern lights

Neither the Rules nor Annex I specify vertical or horizontal placement of stern lights, but they should be as nearly as possible "at stern." Some owners install davits on the stern of their boats to allow them to raise and carry a dinghy. Others rest the dinghy on its side on a swim platform. While these owners no longer have to tow the dinghy, many such installations fail to account for the fact that, when the dinghy is aboard, it blocks visibility of the stern light to an overtaking vessel.

Day shapes

To prevent collision and enhance navigational safety during the day, the Rules call for use of black day shapes by certain vessels in particular situations.

The shapes must be of the following sizes: Balls must have a diameter of at least 0.6 meters (23.6 in.). Cones must have a base diameter of at least 0.6 meters (23.6 in.) and a height

DAY SHAPES	
Length	**Diameter of Sphere***
65.6 ft. (20 m)	23.6 in. (60 cm)
40 ft. (12.2 m)	14.5 in. (37 cm)
12 m (39.4 ft.)	14.2 in. (36 cm)
35 ft. (10.7 m)	13 in. (33 cm)
30 ft. (9.1 m)	12 in. (30 cm)
10 m (32.8 ft.)	11.8 in. (29.9 cm)
25 ft. (7.62 m)	9 in. (22.8 cm)
7 m (23 ft.)	8.3 in. (21 cm)
20 ft. (6.1 m)	7 in. (17.7 cm)

* The diameter of the base of the inverted cone should be the same as listed for a sphere. The length of the sphere should equal the diameter of the cone.

Shapes for recreational boats need not be as large as those for vessels longer than 20 meters (65.6 ft.), but they must meet the minimum sizes indicated at left and be constructed of black material.

equal to the diameter. Diamonds must consist of two cones with a common base. The vertical distance between shapes must be at least 1.5 meters (4.9 ft.).

If your vessel is less than 20 meters (65.6 ft.) long, you may use smaller shapes appropriate to the size of your vessel. The distance between shapes also may be reduced *(Annex 1, § 84.11)*.

The importance of range lights

When a vessel carries two masthead lights, it carries its own range—a valuable aid to assist onlookers in determining its relative heading at night. Since these white lights are brighter and higher than the sidelights, they normally will be seen well before colored lights can be read for their meaning.

You can use the range lights on a vessel just as you would use range lights at sea or on land. As usual, the relative location of the two range lights will be the key:
■ If you see the two white lights lined up one over the other, the other vessel is heading directly toward you. The danger of collision may exist.
■ If the lower (forward) range light is to the left of the higher (after) white light, the vessel is heading to your left as you face it. If the lower white light is to the right of the higher one, then the vessel is heading to your right as you face it.

You can gauge the angle of approach by looking for the red or green sidelights to confirm your reading of the range. As well, you can note the horizontal distance between the two white lights.

If the horizontal distance between the two white lights decreases, then the vessel is turning so that it will approach you more directly bow-on. If the horizontal distance between the two white lights increases, however, the other vessel is turning away from you.

The USCG urges owners replacing navigation lights, particularly in congested areas and waters frequented by high performance boats, to use larger, brighter navigation lights.

The ball-diamond-ball pattern in this day shape signals that this vessel is restricted in its ability to maneuver. It might be dredging, for example.

The main reasons why boat manufacturers use only the minimum size navigation light fixtures are probably because of esthetics and to reduce glare. Some manufacturers have begun offering retractable cleats. No violation exists between sunrise and sunset if a vessel has no lights or does not exhibit them. The U.S. Coast Guard believes it is also possible to design retractable navigation light fixtures. A large retractable fixture would be invisible during the day and could be fitted with screens that would prevent glare when a vessel is operated at night.

As the average speeds at which recreational boats are operated increases, there's no question that when selecting navigation lights, bigger is better.

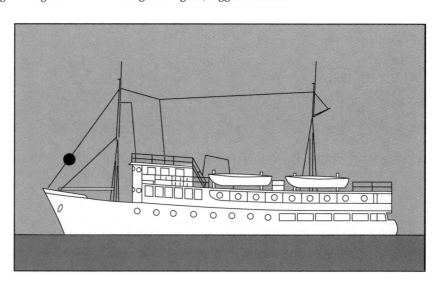

Vessels more than 20 meters (65.6 ft.) must show they are at anchor with a ball day shape, unless they are in a designated anchorage area.

INTERPRETING RUNNING LIGHTS

The following pages are designed to help sort out lights in the dark and guide you in identifying the boats associated with them. Refer to the legend at right; the colored text gives information on International Rules where they differ from the Inland Rules (otherwise they agree).

POWER-DRIVEN VESSEL 12 M BUT LESS THAN 20M IN LENGTH (AND VESSEL ENGAGED IN SPORT FISHING, TROLLING OR DRIFT FISHING).

White, 225°, vis. 3 mi. at least 2.5 m above gunwale.

Separate red and green, 112½°, or combination, vis. 2 mi. above hull at least 1m below masthead light.

White, 135° vis. 2 mi.

R After masthead light may be shown but not required. (Exception allowed on Great Lakes: fitted with inboard screens if necessary to prevent being seen across bow.) Same. No exception for Great Lakes.

POWER-DRIVEN VESSEL LESS THAN 12 M IN LENGTH (AND VESSEL ENGAGED IN SPORT FISHING, TROLLING OR DRIFT FISHING).

White, 225°, vis.2 mi. can be less than 2.5 m above gunwale, but at least 1 m above sidelights.

Separate red and green, 112½°, or combination, vis. 1 mi. above hull at least 1 m below masthead light.

White, 135°, vis. 2 mi.

R May be off center if necessary; may show only all-round white light, vis. 2 mi. and sidelights. Same. Less than 7 m and less than 7 kt max. speed, need have only all-round white light, and may have sidelights, if practical.

SAILING VESSEL UNDER 20 M IN LENGTH.

None

Separate red and green, 112½°, or combination, vis. 2 mi.

White, 135°, vis. 2 mi.

R Optional addition—two all-round lights at or near top of mast, red over green, separated at least 1 m, vis. 2 mi.

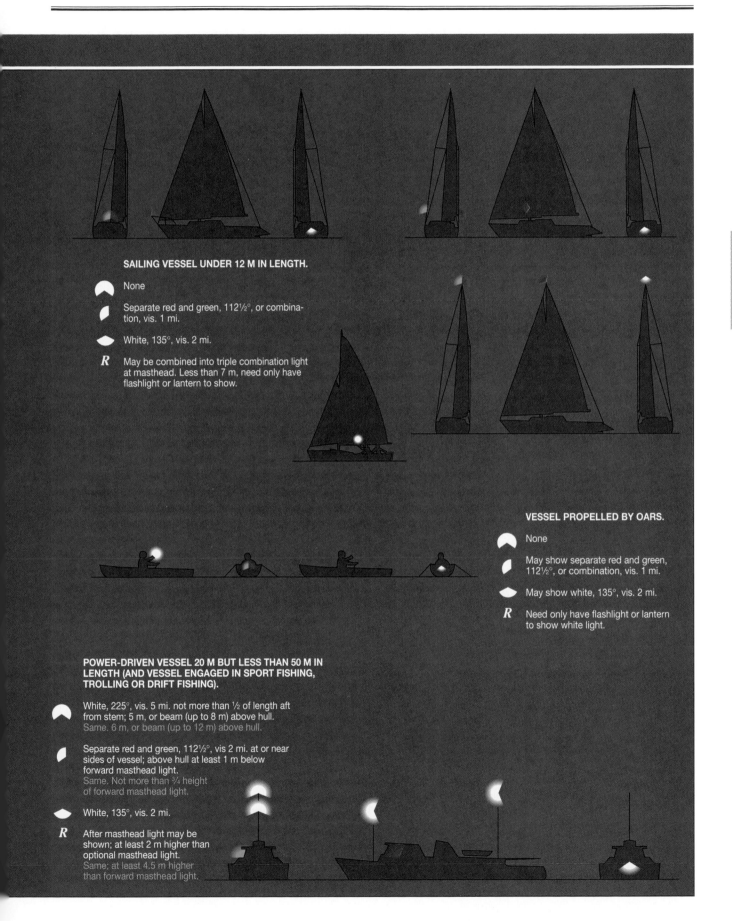

SAILING VESSEL UNDER 12 M IN LENGTH.

None

Separate red and green, 112½°, or combination, vis. 1 mi.

White, 135°, vis. 2 mi.

R May be combined into triple combination light at masthead. Less than 7 m, need only have flashlight or lantern to show.

VESSEL PROPELLED BY OARS.

None

May show separate red and green, 112½°, or combination, vis. 1 mi.

May show white, 135°, vis. 2 mi.

R Need only have flashlight or lantern to show white light.

POWER-DRIVEN VESSEL 20 M BUT LESS THAN 50 M IN LENGTH (AND VESSEL ENGAGED IN SPORT FISHING, TROLLING OR DRIFT FISHING).

White, 225°, vis. 5 mi. not more than ½ of length aft from stem; 5 m, or beam (up to 8 m) above hull.
Same. 6 m, or beam (up to 12 m) above hull.

Separate red and green, 112½°, vis 2 mi. at or near sides of vessel; above hull at least 1 m below forward masthead light.
Same. Not more than ¾ height of forward masthead light.

White, 135°, vis. 2 mi.

R After masthead light may be shown; at least 2 m higher than optional masthead light.
Same; at least 4.5 m higher than forward masthead light.

POWER-DRIVEN VESSEL 50 M OR MORE IN LENGTH.

White, 225°, vis. 6 mi. not more than ½ of length aft from stem; 5 m, or beam (up to 8 m) above hull. Same. Not more than ¼ of length aft from stem; 6 m, or beam (up to 12 m) above hull.

Separate red and green, 112½°, vis 3 mi. at or near sides of vessel; above hull at least 1 m below forward masthead light. Same. Not more than ¾ height of forward masthead light.

White, 135°, vis. 3 mi.

R After masthead light required; at least 2 m higher and spacing of at least ¼ vessel length, (up to 50 m) aft of forward masthead light. (Special provision for Great Lakes.) After masthead light required; at least 4.5 m higher and half of vessel length (up to 100 m) aft of forward masthead light.

VESSEL TOWING ASTERN; TOW LESS THAN 200 M OVERALL FROM STERN OF TOWING VESSEL.

Two white, arranged vertically, 225° vis. determined by length of vessel.

Normal for size of vessel, vis. determined by length of vessel.

Yellow towing light, 135°, over white, 135°, vis. determined by length of vessel.

VESSEL BEING TOWED ASTERN.

None.

Normal for size of vessel, vis. determined by length of vessel.

White, 135°, vis. determined by length of vessel.

R A group of vessels is lighted as a single vessel if length of tow exceeds 200 m, a diamond shape where can best be seen.

VESSEL 50 M OR LESS PUSHING AHEAD OR TOWING ALONGSIDE.

Two white, arranged vertically, 225°, vis. determined by length of vessel.

Normal for size of vessel, vis. determined by length of vessel.

Two yellow towing lights, 135°, vis. determined by length of vessel. White, 135°, vis. determined by length of vessel.

VESSEL BEING PUSHED AHEAD OR TOWED ALONGSIDE.

None

Normal for size of vessel; at forward end.

Normal for size of vessel (not used or pushed ahead) White, 135° vis. determined by length of vessel.

R Also special yellow flashing light at center of forward end if pushed ahead. A group of vessels is lighted as a single vessel. No special yellow flashing light provision in these rules; vessel pushing has white stern light.

VESSEL TOWING ASTERN; TOW 200 M OR MORE OVERALL FROM STERN OF TOWING VESSEL.

Three white, arranged vertically, 225°, vis. determined by length of vessel.

Normal for size of vessel, vis. determined by length of vessel.

Yellow towing light, 135°, over white, 135°, vis. determined by length of vessel.

VESSEL ENGAGED IN COMMERCIAL TRAWLING

(Not necessarily forward masthead lights).
Two green over white, arranged vertically, 360°, underway or at anchor, vertical spacing 1 m
Vertical spacing 2 m for vessels 20 m or more in length, 1 m for shorter vessels.

When making way through the water, normal for the size of vessel.

R Vessel less than 50 m may exhibit a masthead light abaft of and higher than the all-round green light.
Lower light above sidelights at least twice vertical spacing.
Lower light not less than 4 m (2 m if under 20 m in length) above hull.

VESSEL ENGAGED IN COMMERCIAL FISHING, OTHER THAN TRAWLING.

(Not necessarily forward masthead lights.)
Two red over white, 360°, underway or at anchor.

When making way through the water, normal for size of vessel.

R When not actually fishing, show normal masthead lights for vessel its size.

VESSEL AT ANCHOR; 50 M OR MORE IN LENGTH.

None.

None.

None.

R White all-round light in forepart of vessel not less than 6 m above hull. A second white, all-round in after part, not less than 4.5 m lower than forward anchor light, vis. 3 mi.

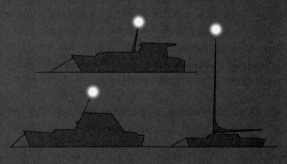

VESSEL AT ANCHOR LESS THAN 50 M IN LENGTH.

None.

None.

None.

R White, all-round light where can best be seen, vis. 2 mi. (not required if less than 7 m in length and not anchored in a narrow channel or where vessels normally navigate).

INTERPRETING RUNNING LIGHTS (continued)

VESSEL AGROUND.

None.

None.

None.

R Normal anchor light(s) plus two red all-round lights of same visibility range.
(Not required if less than 12 m in length for inland.)

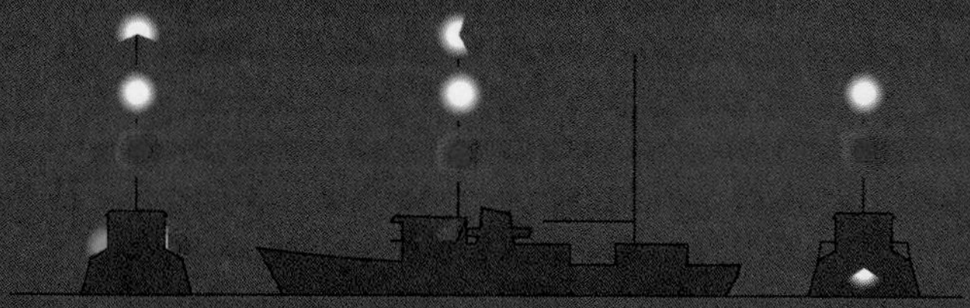

PILOT VESSEL.

Do not show if on pilot duty; normal if underway and not on pilot duty.

When underway, normal for size of vessel.

R Two all-round lights, white over red, at masthead. If at anchor, in addition to anchor lights.

VESSEL NOT UNDER COMMAND—NOT MAKING WAY.

None.

If making way through the water, normal for size of vessel.

R Two red all-round lights, vertically where can best be seen.

VESSEL RESTRICTED IN ABILITY TO MANEUVER.

When making way through the water, normal for size of vessel.

R Three all-round lights vertically, red-white-red, where can best be seen. If at anchor, normal anchor light(s).
(Not required if less than 12 m in length for inland.)

VESSEL CONSTRAINED BY ITS DRAFT.

Normal for size of vessel.

R Three all-round lights, arranged vertically, and equally spaced where best can be seen.

THE INTERNATIONAL RULES

The 1980 U.S. Inland Rules and the Canadian rules are derived from the 72 COLREGS and parallel them in format. Often, the language of like-numbered Rules is identical.

Because vessels on international waters generally are larger and distances they travel are greater, the 72 COLREGS tend to differ from the U.S. Inland Rules by prescribing fewer specific lights and shapes for smaller vessels. In this section, the review of the 72 COLREGS for lights and day shapes is limited only to the few substantial differences between the two sets of Rules.

Where the Rules apply
The 72 COLREGS apply to vessels in two situations:
- All U.S. vessels on the high seas not subject to another nation's geographic jurisdiction.
- All vessels in U.S. waters, outside the prescribed demarcation lines at entrances to bays, rivers, harbors, inlets, etc. In the absence of demarcation lines, they also are applied within those bodies of water, along specified coastlines, and up connecting rivers to their limits of continuous navigation.

Requirements for lights and day shapes
Unlike the U.S. Inland Rules, the 72 COLREGS do not include provision for use of a special flashing light, that is, the yellow light used at the bow of barges pushed ahead on inland waters. Similarly, the 72 COLREGS do not contain exceptions regarding the placement of masthead lights and sidelights for vessels less than 12 meters (39.4 ft.) long *(Rule 21)*.

Power-driven vessels underway
If your powerboat is less than 7 meters (23 ft.) long, with a maximum speed of no more than 7 knots, you may replace the required one or two masthead lights, stern light and sidelights with an all-round white light and, if practicable, sidelights *(Rule 23[c][ii])*.

If your powerboat is less than 12 meters (39.4 ft.) long, you may displace your masthead light or all-round white light off your vessel's fore-and-aft center line, provided that your sidelights are combined in one lantern aligned as nearly as possible with that light *(Rule 23[c][iii])*. Consider the following caution: If your boat's sidelights are flush-mounted in the hull below the gunwale, your vessel does not comply with the requirement that sidelights be above the "uppermost continuous deck."

Vessels constrained by their draft
A vessel in this class—specific to the 72 COLREGS—may (but is not obliged to) display three all-round red lights (aligned vertically where they can best be seen) or a cylindrical day shape, in addition to the lights prescribed for power-driven vessels *(Rule 28)*.

Reference to CAD vessels, as they are called, is not found in the Inland Rules and therefore such lights will not be seen in inland waters.

Sailboats underway
When operating under power with their sails up, sailboats of all sizes—including those less than 12 meters (39.4 feet long), which are exempt under Inland Rules—must exhibit a conical shape forward, point down, where it can best be seen *(Rule 25[e])*.

Towing vessels and tows
In addition to the two vertical masthead lights and sidelights, a vessel pushing a tow ahead or towing alongside must display a single white stern light (rather than two yellow towing lights aligned vertically, as required under the U.S. Inland Rules) *(Rule 24[c])*.

A vessel being pushed ahead (not part of a composite unit) will not carry a special flashing yellow light, as displayed in inland waters *(Rule 24[f][i])*. In the case of dracones being towed, these liquid-filled sacks do not need to exhibit a light forward *(Rule 24[g][i])*.

An inconspicuous, partly submerged vessel or object at least 25 meters (82 ft.) wide must exhibit two additional all-round white lights at or near the extremities of their breadth. If the vessel is at least 100 meters (328.1 ft.) long, the distance between them must not exceed 100 meters (328.1 ft.) *(Rule 24[g][ii] and [iii])*.

Other towed vessels or objects where the length of tow exceeds 200 meters (656.2 ft.) are required to display a single diamond shape where it can best be seen by other vessels. *(Rule 24[g][iv])*.

Anchored or aground
The 72 COLREGS make no provision for boats less than 20 meters in length anchored in special anchorage areas; however, all other provisions parallel those of the U.S. Inland Rules *(Rule 30)*.

Positioning and technical details of signals
Because vessels operating under the 72 COLREGS tend to be larger than those operating under the U.S. Inland Rules, the specifications concerning vertical and horizontal positioning and spacing of lights tend to be greater.

For example, when two masthead lights are carried, the after light must be at least two meters (6.6 ft.) vertically higher than the forward one under the U.S. Inland Rules. Under the 72 COLREGS, however, the after masthead light must be at least 4.5 meters (14.8 ft.) vertically higher than the forward one.

Day shapes
In addition to the day shapes prescribed under the U.S. Inland Rules, the 72 COLREGS authorizes use of a cylinder shape. This shape must have a diameter of at least 0.6 meters (23.6 in.) and a height which is twice its diameter. The use of this shape is authorized only aboard a vessel that is constrained by its draft.

8 TRAILERBOATING

The pleasures of recreational boating are not related in any way to the size of one's boat, although size has a very real bearing on the type of boating activities that can be accomplished safely. While there are some elements of seamanship that apply to every type of boat, there are nonetheless significant differences between the requirements for small, open outboard or stern-drive-powered vessels, and larger inboard-powered cruisers.

This chapter focuses on the smaller craft that can be trailered, and covers the selection, equipment and use of such boats, which represent the vast majority of all registered boats in North America.

THE BOAT

Trailerable boats come in a wide range of sizes, designs and construction materials, and prices vary accordingly. At the lower end are the 8-foot prams that can be car-topped or used as tenders; at the upper end are the high-performance racing-type speed boats that can take up to four motors of 300 or more horsepower each.

The use of the boat

The key to selecting the "right" boat for a particular skipper is the use, or uses, for which the craft is intended. Obviously, the boat for water-skiing is not the boat for trolling, and the boat for an afternoon outing may not be the perfect one for a week's cruise. Not all boating families will agree on just one or even two uses, and few families can afford a separate craft for each type of activity desired.

Compromise is inevitable, but if all possible factors are considered in advance the likelihood of disappointment is reduced. Be sure to take into consideration the type of waters on which the boat will be used—protected lakes and rivers, coastal bays or offshore.

Hull designs

There are two basic hull types—displacement and planing—and many variations of the latter. Although, in general, displacement boats cruise through the water and planing hulls lift and skim over the surface, often it is difficult to make a sharp distinction between types of hulls.

Planing hulls receive a large part of their support at normal speeds from the dynamic reaction of water against the bottom, and a lesser part of their support from buoyancy that diminishes with increased speed but never quite disappears at any speed. Generally, planing begins when the water breaks cleanly away at the chines and transom. With today's high horsepower, most cruisers have some planing action, and practically all runabouts are of the planing type.

Small boats designed to take outboard or stern-drive power can be classified into the following hull forms:

■ **Flat bottom** (displacement type). Usually rowboats or skiffs 14 to 18 feet (4.3 to 5.5 m); used for fishing or utility purposes on shallow streams and small protected lakes. Generally heavy and roomy for their length, and slow.
■ **Round bottom** (displacement type). Dinghies, tenders, car-top boats, occasionally runabouts 12 to 18 feet (3.7 to 5.5 m). At slow speeds these hulls are often more easily driven and maneuvered than the flat-bottom craft. (Many light, round-bottom boats will also plane.)
■ **Vee bottom.** The most popular type of hull design, the vee bottom, is used for runabouts, utilities and cruisers when speed is a factor. It is available in the following varieties:

The flat bottom, popular on the U.S. west coast, has a bottom that is either flat or a shallow V. The trihull (or cathedral) is a V bottom with two smaller V shapes on each side of the hull. The deep V uses the same degree of dead rise from bow to stern (10 to 26 degrees).

The modified V has a deep V in the front and tapers off to a shallow V in the stern, and has a hard or soft chine. This is the most popular competition ski boat construction type.
■ **Hydroplanes.** Generally used for racing. The bottom, which is flat, may be "stepped"—that is, divided into two levels, about amidships. The resultant notch reduces wetted surface, increasing speed.

Size and loading

Because overloading a small boat can be exceedingly dangerous, *the safe limits for a particular boat must be known*. Coast Guard rules require that U.S. boats under 20 feet (6.1 m) (except sailboats and some special types) manufactured after October 31, 1972, carry a "capacity plate" showing maximum allowable loads. Since August 1980, plates for outboard boats have shown a maximum horsepower for motor(s), maximum number of persons and maximum weights, both for persons only, and for motor, gear and persons. Plates for inboard, stern-drive and unpowered vessels omit the maximum power rating. Boats manufactured before this regulation may carry no capacity plate, or one based on a formula that is no longer used.

Added buoyancy

Boats less than 20 feet (6.1 m) in length, manufactured since July 31, 1973, carry built-in flotation installed in accordance with U.S. Coast Guard regulations (the exceptions being sailboats and some special types). It is possible to add positive flotation to older boats to ensure the safety of yourself and your passengers. This can be in the form of sealed air chambers, or masses of plastic foam.

The buoyancy units should be located as high as possible in the hull so that the boat, if swamped, will remain in an upright position and not capsize. This provides greater safety than a capsized hull; persons in the water will be able to hold on easily, and they may be able to recover some form of emergency signaling, bailing or other needed equipment.

An outboard motor clamps onto the transom; large, heavy ones are usually bolted in place; smaller motors, which are portable, may be removed when not in use. A self-bailing motor well is a safety item that lessens the chance of water entering the craft.

THE MOTOR AND ITS ACCESSORIES

Outboard vs. I/O

An outboard motor is a detachable power plant, complete with drive shaft and propeller, that operates on one to six cylinders. The fuel tank and operating controls are usually separate; on the smallest motors, they may be mounted on the powerhead itself. Although usually a gasoline-fueled motor (a two- or four-cycle design up to 45 hp, a two-cycle design for higher horsepowers), it may be diesel-powered—or electric for trolling or other low-power applications.

The outboard is either clamped or bolted to a cutout in the transom, or mounted on a separate bracket bolted to the transom. It can be tilted into or out of the water, either by hand for the smaller units or, on larger units, with the help of hydraulics. Smaller outboards are generally steered by a hand-held tiller. The medium range has wheel-controlled steering with push-pull cables, and larger units will be assisted hydraulically (power steering).

Around the 100 horsepower mark, the inboard-outboard (I/O, also called stern drive or outdrive) can be used. This combines the inboard, four-cycle gasoline or diesel engine mounted inside the hull, bolted through the transom to a drive unit that resembles the lower section of the outboard motor. This is intended to combine the greater power and efficiency of an inboard engine with the directed-thrust steering, tilt-up capability, and other advantages of outboard propulsion.

Boats of stern-drive design can be included with outboards, except for matters directly relating to the engine itself. They are usually in the size category of medium and larger outboard boats, handle similarly, are used for the same general purposes, and can be trailered.

Two-cycle outboards offer trailerboaters a great advantage by providing a much higher horsepower-to-weight ratio than four-cycle stern drives. Two-cycle outboard motors are built of lightweight cast aluminum, and also pull more horsepower out of smaller-displacement blocks. For example, a 115-hp stern drive (with an engine built of cast iron) which has 181-cubic-inch (3,000-cc) displacement weighs in at 625 pounds while a 115-hp outboard with 105-cubic-inch (1,721-cc) displacement, built by the same manufacturer, weighs in at 315 pounds, almost half the weight for the same power. Today's outboards, at least the larger ones, have eliminated the need to mix gasoline and oil through efficient oil-injection systems.

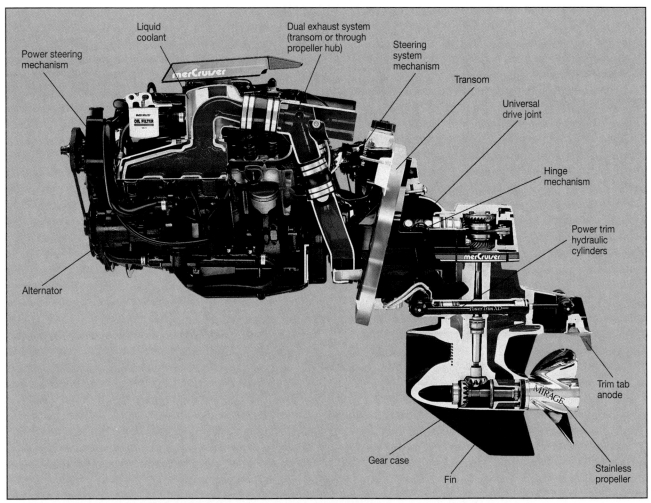

The inboard/outboard combines the inboard gasoline or diesel engine with the outboard-type drive.

The outboard provides a high horsepower-to-weight ratio, compromising on fuel economy and noise level.

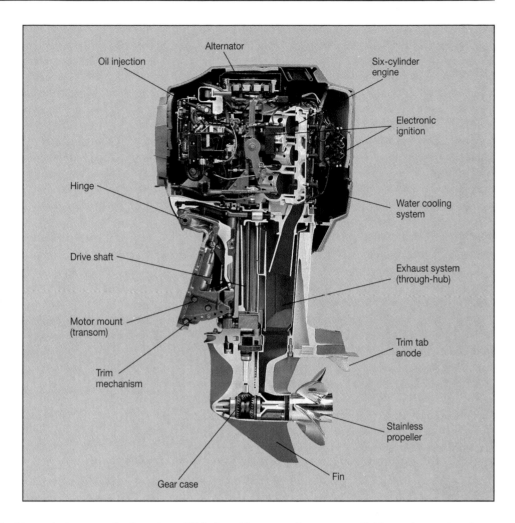

Oil injection

Alternator

Six-cylinder engine

Electronic ignition

Hinge

Water cooling system

Drive shaft

Exhaust system (through-hub)

Motor mount (transom)

Trim tab anode

Trim mechanism

Stainless propeller

Gear case

Fin

Outboard wells use up valuable cockpit space. Outboard "brackets," however, can be attached to the boat's full transom, leaving the motors outside the boat. Putting the motor a couple of feet aft of the transom places the propeller in "cleaner" water, away from any turbulence created by the hull, allowing the propeller a better "grip" on the water. Brackets are generally used with large outboards and boats in the 20- to 30-foot range. Brackets can prove particularly useful for twin-motor installations, and are most popular in 24- to 28-foot (7.3- to 8.5 m) offshore-style fishing boats, where increased cockpit space is appreciated, but twin engines are needed.

Stern-drive engines offer the greater fuel efficiency of four-stroke (four-cycle) engines and the convenience of inboard-engine maintenance. Stern drives are suitable for boat designs where the owner wants the convenience of an outboard (a drive leg that tilts out for servicing or prop maintenance and helps the boat reach optimum trim) and the appearance of an inboard, where the engine is hidden inside the boat.

Outboard motor selection

While horsepower always seems to be the first consideration in most people's motor selection, other factors, such as weight, starting method and price, may in fact be even more important.

With the wide range of motors available on the market, however, it is not very difficult to select a model suitable for almost any application.

The horsepower required for a boat will depend upon size and weight of the boat (loaded), and the desired speed. A displacement hull of 14 feet (4.3 m) or so will serve adequately for lake and river fishing with a 10-horsepower motor; any greater horsepower would be wasted in an attempt to drive the boat faster than hull speed.

For water-skiing behind a planing hull of 16 to 18 feet (4.9 to 5.5 m), motors of 40 to 75 horsepower are suitable. A larger outboard will make the boat go faster, provided the hull has the capacity for greater power, but speed does not increase in direct proportion to motor power.

Small (trolling) motors and electrics

Very small single-cylinder gasoline outboards, ranging from 2-hp models that weigh under 25 pounds to 4- and 5-hp motors 45 pounds or less, offer inexpensive, reliable power for dinghies, small inflatables, punts and small sailboats. Most of these outboards are simple, with integral gas tanks, 360-degree steering (allowing you to reverse by spinning the entire engine) and no transmission.

For an uncluttered cockpit, the OMC Sea Drive is a motor designed to be mounted on a bracket behind a full transom.

Even smaller 12-volt electric motors, with fractional horsepower ratings, are bow-mounted on small fishing boats as auxiliary motors to pull them along at trolling speeds. These motors are quiet and usually rigged for remote control, with the operator controlling the motor with his feet, while using his hands to continue fishing.

At least one electric-powered outboard designed to be the main motor is now on the market, available in 2.2-hp or 3.5-hp versions. The motor, however, requires about 400 pounds of batteries, limiting its use to fairly large displacement boats.

Electric starting

All small outboard motors, and some medium-power models, are started by pulling a rope that is wound around the top of the flywheel. This is not practical for the larger motors, so electric starting systems are provided. The electrical system, with its battery and alternator, has the added bonus of making possible the use of electronic gear on the boat.

Electric starting means added weight and cost, but this is offset by the greater convenience that this type of starting provides. In general, motors less than 10 horsepower will be manually started; those more than 40 horsepower will have electric starting; motors between these sizes may have either method of starting.

Single or twin installations

Many outboard hulls are designed to allow the fitting of either one or two motors on the transom. There are definite advantages and disadvantages to each arrangement, given the same total horsepower.

The most common reason for twin motors rather than a single one is the added safety the system provides. Properly maintained outboard motors are extremely reliable, but if one should fail, the other will bring the boat home. Disadvantages of the twin rig include the greater initial cost—about 1⅓ times the price of a single large motor, an additional battery (or larger single one), more complex control systems, greater weight in the boat (about 50 percent more), greater underwater drag, and greater fuel consumption (not doubled, but greater by ⅓ to ½). Twin motors, and their batteries and fuel tanks, take up greater space within the boat than that needed for a single-motor installation. Pairs of larger engines are now available with counter-rotating propellers; this is highly desirable to balance out strong torque effects.

A special case is the large outboard cruiser where use of two motors is required to meet horsepower needs, and the weight and space requirements are less important. In such an

This multi-purpose open-deck 25-foot trimaran-type-hull boat has twin, high-power, low-maintenance outboards. They provide high-speed day cruising and rough-water romping.

installation, twin motors will also allow the use of more efficient propellers with larger blade area.

If a boat is performing to certain standards with a single motor, what will result if a second motor of the same power is added (assuming that boat is rated to handle the double horsepower)? The added weight and drag, combined with hydrodynamic factors, will hold the speed increase to about 25 percent, although this will vary widely with specific installations. Fuel consumption, with both engines running at the same rpm, will be about 1½ times that of the single motor rig.

A combination to be considered is a single large motor adequate for all normal operation, plus a smaller motor of 4 to 10 horsepower. The smaller motor is used for trolling while fishing—large motors should not be run at slow speeds for extended periods—and for emergency back-up. A 6-horsepower motor will move a medium-size outboard hull at 3 to 4 knots and get it home or to assistance.

The best way to understand propellers is to know the basic parts, shown at right.

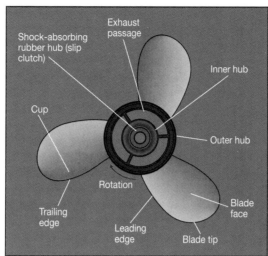

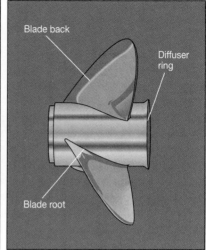

Propellers

Although most outboard motors are sold complete with a "stock" propeller, suitable for an average boat under average conditions, some motors, especially the larger ones, are offered with a choice of several propellers. Keep in mind that a stock propeller may not have the optimum diameter or pitch, or both, for a particular application.

Manufacturers publish tables of recommended propeller sizes for various applications, but these should be used only as initial guides. If you know another owner who has an identical boat and motor combination, whose style of boating matches yours, and who is getting the best performance from his rig, your decision may be easy.

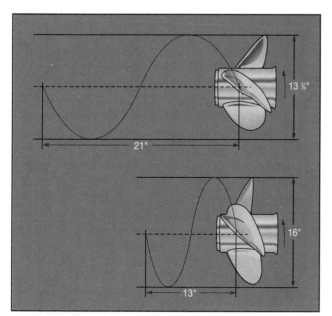

Pitch is the distance a propeller moves in one revolution just like a screw in wood. A 13¾ " x 21" propeller has a 13¾" (35 cm) diameter with 21" (53 cm) of pitch (*top*). A 16" x 13" propeller has a diameter of 16" and 13" of pitch (*bottom*).

Otherwise, the answer lies in experimentation. In any case, the "right" propeller for any boat in a specific application is the one that allows the motor to turn up to its full rated rpm (revolutions per minute), but no more. It is necessary for the motor to turn to full rated rpm in order to develop full rated power. However, if it will turn faster than that, the propeller is too small and full power is not being developed at the rated maximum rpm (which must never be exceeded, except for very brief bursts).

If the boat is used for more than one type of activity—cruising and fishing or water-skiing, for example—the same motor will require different propellers for the most efficient operation in each type of use. As a spare propeller is an excellent safety item, the purchase of a more efficient one is not all "added expense"—the stock propeller becomes the spare.

Diameter and pitch

Diameter is defined as the distance across the circle made by the blade tips as the propeller rotates. Its size is determined by the rpm at which the propeller will be turning, as well as the amount of power delivered through it. Note that diameter will need to be greater as horsepower increases and conversely as rpm decreases; diameter will tend also to be larger as propeller surface increases.

The pitch of a propeller determines its "bite" on the water, and thus the rpm which the motor can turn up (this is also affected by propeller diameter). Motor rpm is, of course, related to boat speed—a lighter, faster boat, for example, will use a propeller of greater pitch than a vessel that is heavy and designed for slower operation. Once again, experimentation is really the only way of selecting the best match of propeller to suit the craft.

If a single motor is "doubled up" with another similar to it, this will require a change of propeller on the original motor. The faster speed obtained with the additional horsepower will call for a greater pitch, probably one, but possibly two, inches more—but only actual trials will tell for sure.

Materials

Most stock propellers on inboards are bronze. On outboards and stern drives they are aluminum. These are well suited for a conventional purpose and easy to repair. Propellers of stainless steel and other high strength alloys are advantageous for special applications such as fishing, water-skiing and racing. They are more expensive both in purchase and repair. Plastic is used mainly for propellers of the smaller motors such as electric trolling or sailboat models.

Shear pins and slip clutches

Because outboard boats often operate in fairly shallow water, the drive shaft, gears and other internal parts of the motor are subject to damage should the propeller hit an underwater object. To prevent such damage, the motors are equipped with either a shear pin (smaller motors) or a slip clutch (larger motors) on the propeller shaft.

A shear pin is made of a relatively soft metal. It transmits the drive from the propeller shaft to the propeller, and is just strong enough for this. Upon impact with a rock or other hard object by a propeller blade, this pin is broken, sheared off near the end, and the impact is not transferred to the inner parts of the motor. To restore operation it is necessary to remove the propeller and install a new pin, so always be sure to carry spares.

To overcome the nuisance of having to replace sheared pins, manufacturers developed slip clutches in which a rubber inner hub is used to transmit the drive power. Under normal loads there is no slippage, but upon impact with a hard object (or even with the sudden load of a too-quick shift of gear or advance of the throttle), the rubber hub slips somewhat to absorb the strain from the propeller blade. Obviously there is no internal component to be replaced after impact, and it provides adequate protection for the motors.

PROPELLER TYPES

Propellers are classified according to their construction, material and design. Six types of propellers are generally available, four of which are shown below.

■ The basic aluminum or conventional propeller is designed to be run fully submerged and can be run slightly surfaced with light loads.

■ High reverse thrust is useful for workboats, large slower boats and auxiliary sail-power applications. The blades provide the same thrust in forward or reverse.

■ Basic stainless steel is similar to the basic aluminum and has slightly thinner blades. It has a higher strength and durability for a wide variety of medium- to high-horsepower applications. It also resists corrosion in salt water.

■ The cleaver-style surfacing propeller has its blades with the trailing edge cut on a straight line. This is a true high-rev racing performer designed for surface-piercing stern drives and outboard applications. The cleaver provides less bow lift than the chopper.

■ The chopper-style, another surfacing propeller, is for sport boaters for speeds higher than 50 mph. It has more bow-lifting capabilities and is known for the tenacious way in which it refuses to break loose on a plane, a much desired characteristic. It comes with weed-chopping fingers.

■ Stainless steel high-performance or racing propellers are of the cleaver type with higher-pitch range because of the combination of high horsepower and lightweight boats. Speeds are in the 90 mph range.

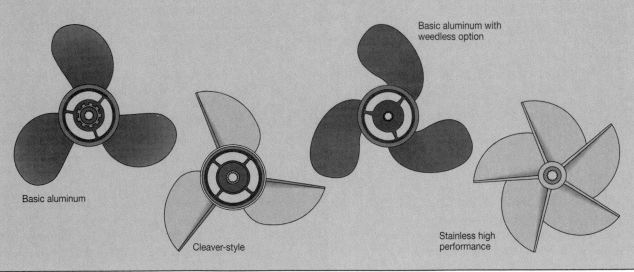

Basic aluminum

Cleaver-style

Basic aluminum with weedless option

Stainless high performance

TRAILERBOAT EQUIPMENT

From the moment it is launched, each trailerboat must meet all legal requirements for a craft of its size, plus any additional equipment required by state or local regulations. Boaters venturing into new waters subject to other regulations than "at home" should check with a marina operator, park ranger or other local authority to avoid inadvertent violations. The prudent traveler will be aware of, or will find out about, any local requirements such as anchoring limitations, special cruising permits, speed limitations, etc.

Operational equipment

Here are some basic items which you should have aboard your vessel—depending on its size and intended use, and considering the distance away from your base of operation.

- Compass *(Chapter 17)*.
- Charts and piloting instruments *(Chapter 18)*.
- Tools and spare parts.
- Safety chain for an outboard motor.
- Extra fuel tanks.
- Anchor and line *(Chapter 12)*.
- Tachometers (good for speed curve). A tachometer is important when running trials to select the optimum propeller; it often is used as a reference for operating at cruising or trolling speeds. In the absence of a speedometer, a series of timed runs at regular increments of engine speed can be used to establish a speed curve for the boat. This curve gives you boat speed through the water at any motor setting. (Refer to Chapter 19 for details on establishing a speed curve.) An electronic tachometer can be fitted to almost any outboard motor. The instrument, when properly calibrated, indicates engine revolutions per minute.
- Speedometer. As an alternative to developing a speed curve with a series of timed runs, a speedometer can be installed, and speed taken directly from it. This instrument also is quick and simple to install, and the more expensive models offer a reasonable degree of accuracy. Most all models can be calibrated by doing a series of timed runs, but even if a speedometer is not accurate in absolute terms, it can be used to determine the relative speeds obtained with various motor and propeller combinations. Calibration is necessary, however, when it is to be used in navigation.
- Electronic depth sounder. Many outboard boats can carry an electronic depth sounder and put it to good use. Special transom mounts are available for smaller boats on which through-hull mountings may not be practical.
- A radio—VHF/FM—is often installed when the outboard has a battery for electric starting motors and an alternator to keep the battery charged. VHF equipment, with its smaller antennas, is especially suitable for smaller boats. Small hand-held VHF sets *(Chapter 24)* are useful in outboard boats, especially if used with an installed antenna.
- Flashlight or lantern. Every outboard craft should be equipped with a flashlight or electric lantern, whether or not plans include using the boat after dark. The light should be

The trim angle has a distinct effect on the planing angle of the boat, which alters top speed and handling. Illustration A shows a drive that is trimmed too far "in," while the drive in illustration B is trimmed too far "out." The drive in illustration C is well trimmed.

waterproof, and it should float if accidentally dropped overboard. Extra batteries, stored in a waterproof container, will often prove valuable in an emergency. Batteries in the flashlight or lantern, and the spares, should be renewed at the start of each boating season, regardless of their apparent condition. The flashlight is also important while traveling on the roads in case of trailer or car trouble.

Boat covers

Covers keep out dirt and protect the interior during off-season storage. Usually of Dacron or similar synthetic fabric, covers may be available in a style that covers your boat, from stem to stern, plus the outboard motor; others may cover only the open parts of the boat. Covers are excellent for keeping out rain as well as the dirt and leaves that accumulate when the boat is on its trailer. Be sure that the cover provides adequate ventilation for the interior to prevent rot of interior woodwork, and other forms of fungus growth.

The cover must fit the boat, and must be capable of being adequately secured by means of snaps or a drawstring. (Snaps or other mechanical fasteners should be protected from corrosion by a non-staining lubricant; a silicone grease stick is excellent for this purpose.) A cover is of the greatest value when a boat is being trailered, but it must be fastened down adequately to prevent wind damage. In outdoor storage, a cover must also be adequately supported internally to prevent the formation of pools of rainwater that will stretch (and eventually tear) it, dumping the water into the boat.

For some outboards, tops are available to provide protection against rain, and shade in the hot sun, while the boat is in operation. Enclosure panels, with clear plastic inserts, also may be available, offering considerable protection against rain and spray, as well as allowing comfortable boating in cool weather. Such tops and panels should be removed before trailering the boat at highway speeds.

OUTBOARD MOTOR BASICS

An outboard motor or small inboard/outboard drive can be used for widely varied purposes, some of which include fishing, water-skiing, cruising and skin diving. In any application, greater safety and enjoyment will result if you understand and employ the following boating practices.

Adjusting the motor

Begin your outboarding by installing the motor properly in the boat, according to the manufacturer's diagrams. Seat the motor squarely on the center of the transom and securely tighten the bracket screws. Some motors come with a special mounting plate; with others you may want to use a rubber pad to reduce vibrations and to prevent the transom from being marred. Be sure to connect a safety chain or cable from the motor to the hull.

Twin motors are usually installed by a dealer, as are large single motors of the high-horsepower range. Twin motors should have the proper spacing; 22 inches (55.9 cm) is recommended by the ABYC for motors up to 75 horsepower, and 32 inches (81.3 cm) for larger motors. Standard motor position dimensions are furnished to the boat manufacturers.

If a combination of a large and small motor is used, the large one is mounted on the center line, with the small "kicker" off to one side, usually on a bracket designed for such use. (Such a bracket allows the motor to be raised entirely clear of the water when not in use, reducing drag.) The low horsepower of the small motor won't present any significant steering problems from its off-center position.

Motor height

Although there is a high degree of standardization in the design of transom cutouts for motor mounting, it is wise to check that the lower unit of the motor is correctly located with respect to the bottom of the hull. Standard shaft lengths are 15 and 20 inches (38 and 51 cm), and 25 inches (64 cm) for the high-horsepower engines. There are some variations, however, and a transom can be modified if necessary to ensure proper motor positioning. The "anti-cavitation plate" on the lower unit should line up with the transom chine, except for some installations on deep-V hulls.

If the motor is too high, a smooth flow of water will not reach the propeller and it will not be able to get a proper "grip" on the water. This may cause "ventilation," in which the propeller spins in aerated water with possible damage to the engine from excessive rpm. If the motor is too low, drag will be increased due to both the greater area of the lower unit in the water and a distorted flow over and under the anti-cavitation plate. Attention to this detail of installation will provide both increased speed and decreased fuel consumption.

Thrust-line adjustment

Most outboard motors are equipped with a tilt adjustment, allowing the boater to vary the angle of thrust of the propeller. For best performance, the drive of the propeller should

On small motors, all controls are on the powerhead, either on the side for shift, such as the one shown here, or on the tiller arm. This installation is on a small sailboat.

be in a line parallel to the flat surface of the water at the boat's most efficient operating angle, whether as a planing hull or in the displacement mode.

If the motor is in too close to the transom, the thrust line is upward from the horizontal, pushing the stern up and the bow down, making the boat "plow" through the water unnecessarily. On the other hand, if the motor is tilted too far out from the transom, the thrust line is below the horizontal, and the bow is forced up too high while the stern "squats," as shown on page 177, bottom, center.

Boats differ in design, and loading conditions vary widely with any specific boat, so manufacturers make the adjustment of the tilt angle as easy as possible. On stern-drive engines and some larger outboard motors, an electro-hydraulic adjustment is provided; just push the button for "up" or "down."

Be aware of the inefficiency of an improper thrust angle, and do not neglect to change the adjustment to current operating conditions. The best angle may vary with water conditions. On some boats, an adjustment with the motor tilted out (bow up) for smooth water may give more speed, and a better ride in rough water may be obtained with the motor trimmed in a bit. Remember that only actual trials will tell for sure.

Special applications of tilt

While underway, the tilt feature of outboard motor and stern-drive lower units can be used to advantage for several special situations. If the propeller becomes fouled with weeds, it is, for example, often a simple matter to stop the motor, tilt it up, clear off the vegetation, lower the motor, restart it, then continue on your way. If a smaller motor shears its pin, it is often possible to replace it with the motor tilted up, making it unnecessary to unmount the motor completely in order to work on it in the boat.

It is also possible to tilt the lower unit up far enough so the boat can clear shoal areas. (Take care not to tilt it so much that the cooling water intake comes above the surface, and watch out that the propeller does not strike rocks or other hard objects that might damage it.) Proceed slowly when using this technique.

With I/Os, many manufacturers recommend not to power with the drive unit partially or all the way up. Otherwise, you risk excessive wear on the flexible couplings.

Mixture controls

Many outboard motors have controls for adjusting the fuel-air ratio. This adjustment allows you to obtain optimum performance while cruising at low speeds, and, in the case of most smaller motors, for high speeds as well. Adjustment controls are located outside the motor cover so that they can be used easily while underway.

You can minimize the possibility of engine damage due to improper setting and help produce the best results by following the instructions in your owner's manual.

Changes in fuel, air temperature and altitude (such as going from mountain lakes to a lower elevation, or vice versa) may require changes in mixtures. Any adjustment should be made with the motor thoroughly warmed up, and the boat loaded to normal trim. Most motors also have a manual choke for starting.

Fuels and oils

The drive for a cleaner environment has resulted in the availability of "no lead" gasoline with other chemicals added to maintain octane ratings. In many cases these fuels have given the older motors a few problems. Recent models are designed for current gasolines.

Outboard motors are generally of low compression ratio and can use fuels of modest octane rating. Actually these engines now are designed for these fuels. Keep in mind that marine engines normally operate under a constant load, unlike autos and trucks that go uphill and downhill, with frequent changes of load. It is always best to follow the fuel recommendations in your owner's manual. Two-cycle outboard motors use a mixture of gasoline and lubricating oil. It is essential that both of these be of the correct type and that the mixture ratio be that specified by the manufacturer.

Many outboards are now oil injected, providing an optimum ratio for any speed. This is especially valuable for the larger power sizes, enabling them to be used at the lower end of their speed range without fouling the motor.

The typical outboard motor has its lubricating oil mixed into the gasoline fuel supply; there is no separate crankcase.

An oil injection system will automatically mix oil and fuel to the precise operating ratio from 100 to 1 to 50 to 1. It reduces oil consumption at idle speed to reduce smoke. The oil reservoir of the size of a battery box can treat at least 150 gallons (568 liters) of fuel.

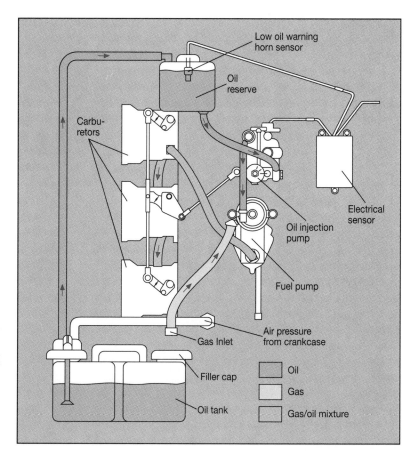

Consequently, special properties such as "low ash" are required, and many normal features such as detergents must be limited or avoided.

The best oil to use in a two-cycle motor is one specifically made and sold for that purpose by oil companies or outboard manufacturers. The oil will be certified as TC-W (two-cycle, water-cooled) and it will contain no harmful compounds. Take note that although the motor manufacturers do not *make* the oils that bear their names, presumably they set the specifications for them. Using oil from the motor's manufacturer will ensure greater compatibility between the oil and motor.

The TC-W specifications now include three categories:
- TC-W is the original standard.
- TC-W2 is the improved standard needed to compensate for lower fuel qualities. It provides a cleaner burn, has more detergent and is more efficient.
- TC-W3 addresses the higher horsepower engines. It meets even more demanding specifications in order to cope with the now-common use of low-grade "pipeline" gasolines. It can be used in any size motor.

Oil-fuel mixture ratios

Motor manufacturers specify the correct ratio of gasoline to oil for each of their models. Although for older motors the ratio was 24 to 1, for most of today's motors it is 50 to 1. Motors made outside of the United States may have different requirements. The amount of oil to be used is sometimes given as ounces or fractions of a pint, which should be added for each gallon of gasoline.

Many marinas now have a special pump installed that dispenses pre-mixed gas and oil. In some instances this mixture is fixed at an established blend, usually at a 50 to 1 ratio; however, at other pumps, controls can be set to any one of several standard gas/oil ratios.

As a safety measure, portable tanks should be removed from the boat and filled on the gas pier or wharf. Wipe the tanks clean and dry before putting them back aboard.

Fueling procedures

There are two aspects of fueling an outboard boat that must be given careful attention—safety and the proper mixing of the oil and gasoline. Fueling a boat safely is an essential element of good seamanship. Whether you are planning a day's outing or an extended cruise, before starting out make sure you have enough fuel on board, and if any is needed, fill any auxiliary tanks safely. Refer to Chapter 3 for information about the safety aspects of fueling.

With portable tanks, filling is now easy. The new oils are made to readily mix with the fuel. It is important to remember that for safe fueling, tanks smaller than 6 gallons should be removed from the boat. This simple procedure is common: Determine the amount of oil for the estimated amount of fuel needed, and pour the oil and fuel into the tank. Further mixing is not needed; it would only build up fumes and pressure inside the tank. Carefully wipe off the outside of the tank, and return it to the boat (if you have removed the tank for fueling) after any odor of fumes has disappeared.

For safety, portable tanks should be secured in the boat. A simple way is to provide wooden blocks on the hull or floorboards to prevent sideways or endways movement of the tank, with straps over the top of the tank to hold it down in rough going.

If your fuel tanks are larger than 6 gallons, they are best left in the boat for filling. These, and permanently installed tanks, are filled after all doors, hatches, windows, etc. are closed to keep any gasoline vapors from getting below. After fueling and cleaning up, open all hatches and ports, and allow time for ventilation to clear bilges and any enclosed spaces before starting the engine.

The mixing of gasoline and oil for larger tanks that cannot be shaken can be done in several ways—all of which are time-consuming but very important, even more so than getting the exact fuel-oil mixture ratio. Keep in mind that some higher-horsepower motors now have separate gasoline and oil tanks with provision for oil injection at a ratio that varies with engine speed.

Extra fuel tanks

It is often necessary to carry additional fuel to make long runs without stops. Select a spare tank or container carefully; it must be made for that specific use. The material of the tank and its design must be intended specifically for containing gasoline in a marine (often salt-water) environment. Homemade or converted tanks are hazardous. Tanks from the manufacturer of your motor, or a reputable manufacturer specializing in marine tanks, are best.

Fuel tanks should be stored in a well-ventilated area, and secured against unnecessary movement. They should be protected from spray or rain. Inspect at least once each season. Dents and scratches can damage the plating that protects underlying steel from rust. A tank that shows any signs of rust should be replaced.

THE TRAILER

The addition of a trailer to a boat provides considerable operational flexibility to the skipper. It allows traveling to distant boating areas that would be otherwise inaccessible, and storage of the boat at the owner's home—saving marina fees, and facilitating routine maintenance. Also, there is less of a chance for marine organisms to attach themselves to the hull. This reduces the need for periodic and costly applications of antifouling paint.

Selecting the right rig

Trailerboaters face the unique challenge of not only having to determine what type of boat and propulsion will meet their needs, but also to match up that boat with a trailer and a vehicle (together, called a rig) that can safely haul, launch and retrieve the boat. On the other hand, it limits the size and style of boat. Most trailerboats will fall into the 14- to 25-foot category and weigh 1,000 to 4,000 pounds. Although boats up to 40 feet or longer can be trailered legally without special permits, 8.5-foot width limitations in most states and provinces mean that only high-performance or specialty boats much over 25 feet fall into the trailerable category.

Trailerboaters are also limited in a practical sense by the expense of specialized tow vehicles that are needed to haul large heavy loads. The choice of tow vehicle, boat and trailer must be made carefully so the combination works well, while fitting the boater's needs. If you already own a boat, shop carefully for a suitable trailer and vehicle. But if you already own a vehicle suited and equipped for towing, you will be limited in your purchase of a boat and trailer by the vehicle's rated towing capacity.

Considering vehicles

Since the more a tow vehicle weighs, the more sway it can absorb, a tow vehicle should weigh at least as much as the rig it is pulling. In other words, weight determines whether the tow vehicle will be in firm control of the trailer or the trailer will be pushing the vehicle around. A heavier trailer can throw both vehicles into a violent swaying motion that could easily cause the driver to lose control.

Wheelbase is another important factor to consider when gauging the ideal fit between trailer and tow vehicle. Cars and small trucks with short wheelbases make poor tow vehicles. Alternatively, long-bed pickups, with their equally long wheelbases, perform marvelously. Just like a tow vehicle that is too light, one that is too short may be controlled by a trailer. Also note that vehicles with long wheelbases can be hard to maneuver in tight quarters.

Horsepower is another consideration when choosing the ideal tow vehicle. So how much is enough? One rule of thumb suggests adding the weight of the boat and trailer and then knocking off one of the zeros. The remainder gives an idea of how many cubic inches worth of engine you need to adequately haul the load. For example, a 3,000-pound rig would require a 302-cu. in. (5.0-liter) engine, while a 3,500-pound rig

requires a 351-cu. in. (5.8-liter) engine. Similarly a large 4,600-pound rig needs a 460-cu. in. (7.5-liter) big-block.

When looking at vehicles, there are other factors that should be added to the equation. Remember that four-wheel-drive vehicles work as well on slippery launch ramps as they do on ice and rain-soaked pavement. Also note that a manual transmission's clutch will wear out sooner than an automatic transmission when it is used for extensive towing. In addition, the automatic is much easier to use, giving you freedom from the constant up- and downshifting necessary to keep the engine in the torque curve.

Depending on the engine's horsepower rating and its rear axle ratio, a tow vehicle is assigned what is called a Gross Vehicle Weight Rating or GVWR. This figure specifies the maximum loaded weight in pounds of the tow vehicle, its boat and the trailer. In other words, the number tells you how large a trailered boat your car or truck can safely pull.

Because trailering a big boat imposes heavy loads on the engine, the drivetrain, suspension, electrical system, brakes and tires, any vehicle destined to pull a boat on weekends really needs the special factory towing package. This will greatly extend the life of your vehicle.

A car used with a trailer may need some modifications in the way of "beefing up" to give fully satisfactory performance. Rear springs and/or shock absorbers may require replacement by heavier duty units because of the added weight transferred from the trailer tongue. The turn-signal flasher unit may need replacement with one that can handle the additional load of the trailer signals.

Driving with a boat trailer behind the car is not as easy as ordinary driving, especially when the craft is high and wide. A second external rear-view mirror on the car's right side will make passing both safer and easier. If the boat is quite wide, it is best to install the external mirrors that project out far enough to give a clear view behind the boat; these are the mirrors often used on cars that pull house trailers.

If a heavy trailer is to be pulled, it may be desirable, or even necessary, to add a cooler for crankcase oil and transmission fluid. Vehicle manufacturers are becoming increasingly specific in the maximum loads that can be towed without modifications, and just what modifications are available. When in doubt, be sure to check your owner's manual, and *don't void your warranty*.

Selecting a trailer

Like boats and motors, trailers also come in many varieties. They range in price from economy to premium. A light-duty trailer may be adequate if all your boating is done locally; a heavy duty one may be needed if you plan long hauls.

In general, premium models use better construction techniques and materials, and they are often better designed. Economy-priced trailers tend to have fewer cross-members along their frames, which means they have fewer support rollers, with wider spaces between them. Many inexpensive models also use a lighter-gauge steel stock in their frames and are usually bolted together rather than welded—a good weld is a far stronger bond.

As a general rule, it is important to remember that the capacity of the trailer should exceed the combined gross weight of boat and trailer by about 20 percent. This surplus capacity is intended to handle the extra weight of any gear you will be carrying on board.

Trailer length is critical because the boat's stern area, particularly the transom, must have adequate support. The boat must be able to fit on the trailer bed so that the transom is directly over the aftermost supports; if there is any overhang, the hull will be distorted. This is also true for stern-drive craft, but it is particularly important for outboards, where the full weight of the motor(s) is on the transom. A "hook" (a downward bend) in the hull at the stern, caused by a too-short trailer, can affect both the boat's speed and its general handling characteristics.

In a boat's natural environment—the water—the hull is uniformly supported and there are no concentrations of pres-

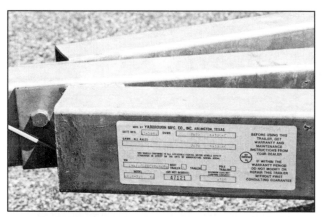

The capacity plate on this trailer tongue shows its load capacity, tire pressures to be maintained and other data.

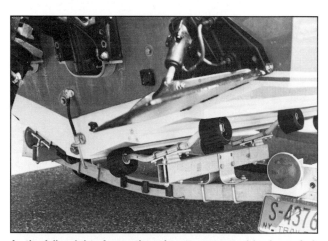

As the full weight of an outboard motor or stern drive is carried on the boat's transom, it is essential that there be adequate support under this portion of the hull.

sure on the hull. However, a trailer can provide support only in limited areas, so the trailer bed must fit the contours of the hull as closely as possible. Plenty of padding and bracing also may be needed.

Supports may take the form of rollers or of padded bars or stringers (bunks), or a combination of some of each. Some trailers, with multiple pairs of rollers on pivoted bars, are designed to conform to the hull shape automatically; these are the self-leveling models. Each type of support system has its advantages and disadvantages; the way the boat will normally be launched and loaded must be considered.

Rollers of hard rubber are widely used on trailers that tilt and allow the boat to move backward into the water by gravity. Their disadvantage is that each roller has very little area of contact with the hull with a consequence of high pressure in this area. The more rollers there are, the better, provided that the height of each is adjusted properly; the depth of the indentation into the roller by the keel is a rough guide as to the weight being carried at that point. Bunks provide the maximum area in contact with the hull, and thus the minimum of point contact pressure. These are excellent for boats that normally are lifted from the trailer, as by a crane's slings. They have considerable surface friction, however, and are generally less suitable for sliding the boat off the trailer into the water—unless special features are provided.

There also should be side supports to hold the boat firmly in position on the trailer bed, and a bow chock to keep the boat from moving farther forward. All of these supports must be adjustable and positioned so that they can carry out their functions. Location of the bow chock, for example, should be adjusted so that the transom will be directly over its supports. The boat's position on the trailer also affects the weight at the trailer tongue and coupling. Any unbalanced condition, once the hull is properly mated to the trailer bed, is properly corrected by shifting the location of the axle and wheels, not the bow chock.

Wheels and tires

When shopping for a trailer the first thing you will probably notice is that some trailer tires are smaller in diameter than automotive tires. Small wheels position the axle closer to the ground so that the trailer rides as low as possible. The low center of gravity optimizes stability during fast turns and in strong crosswinds.

But the downside is that smaller tires sink deeper into potholes and turn at a higher rpm than the automotive tires with which they are running. Those two factors translate into a shorter tire life. As a rule, small tires are the best choice for light boats over short hauls while larger and/or tandem tires are the better choice for heavier rigs and long hauls. The larger tires provide a smoother ride.

Many of the more expensive models come with tandem tires—four tires on two axles. Other trailers employ three axles and six tires, and there are both benefits and drawbacks

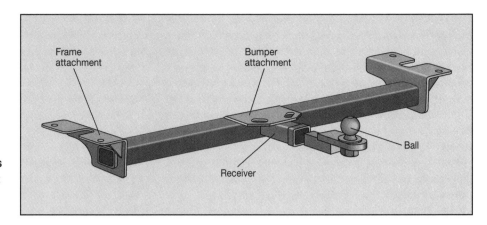

This Class II frame-mounting hitch features a removable ball mount for better appearance and convenience.

to this multi-axled arrangement. On one hand, they cost more to purchase and maintain. And because they resist sharp turns, maneuvering in close quarters is more difficult. On the other hand, four to six wheels track very straight—an immense help when backing a big rig down a launch ramp. As a good general rule, buy the best tires you can afford for both tow vehicle and trailer; they will last longer.

Hitches and couplers

The hitch is a very important option for a towing vehicle; it is the main link between it and the trailer. While hitch balls are mounted on fixed platforms or draw-bars that insert into receiver-type hitches, couplers mounted on the front of the trailer tongue are designed to fit neatly over the various balls, with a lever or screw on top that engages a latch that encloses the ball. Once the screw or lever is engaged, the coupler prevents the trailer tongue from bouncing off the ball, while still allowing the trailer to pivot from side to side and, to a certain extent, up and down.

Hitches are divided into four classes:

■ **Class I hitches** (standard fixed ball bumper hitches) are designed for light duty loads of up to 2,000 pounds with no more than 200 pounds of tongue weight (amount of trailer weight measured at the tongue). The utility bumper of a light truck or van fits in this category. Some may have frame attachment points.

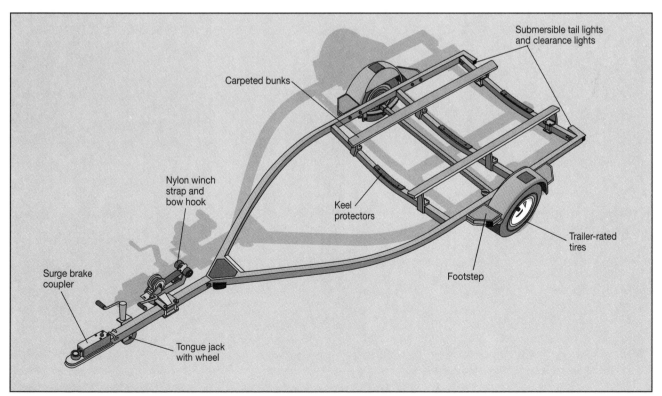

A well-designed light-duty trailer is often fitted for one size of boat and weight only, but still can offer reliable and affordable use over many years.

■ **Class II hitches** are weight-carrying hitches, fixed ball or receiver type, designed to tow up to 3,500 pounds (GTW) with no more than 300 pounds tongue weight. These are basically bumper hitches for the heavier-duty trucks and vans, or brackets installed on the car's frame and the bumper, since few car bumpers can now handle alone this kind of weight.

■ **Class III hitches** are weight-carrying or weight-distributing receiving hitches designed to tow up to 5,000-7,500 pounds (GTW), depending on the size and structure of the tow vehicle. These frame hitches distribute weight using spring bars, mounted between the trailer and the hitch, that transfer the tongue weight to the front wheels of the tow vehicle.

■ **Class IV hitches** are weight-carrying or weight-distributing hitches designed to tow up to 7,500-10,000 pounds (GTW), depending on the size and structure of the tow vehicle.

Hitch balls

Hitch balls on the towing vehicle must match the coupler on the trailer tongue and its GTW rating. Balls vary in diameter from 1 ⅞" to 2 ⁵⁄₁₆" and shanks vary from ¾" to 1 ⅜". For the same size ball, shanks may vary and have different GTW ratings. The diameter and GTW rating are normally stamped on each ball. *Never use a mismatched coupler and ball.*

Use safety chains. When hooking them to the hitch, cross them so they will catch and cradle the tongue should the coupler or ball fail. This simple step will keep the tongue off the pavement, preventing a potentially deadly accident from happening: It will stop the tongue from digging into the road and pole-vaulting the trailer and boat into oncoming traffic.

Keep in mind that the chains need to be long enough that they don't bind in the middle of a tight turn or when backing

TRAILER TERMINOLOGY

■ **Ball mount.** That part of the hitch that connects the hitch ball to the coupler on the trailer.

■ **Bearing Buddy.** Replaces the dust cover on the axle hub; as well, the Bearing Buddy allows the wheel bearings to be greased without disassembly.

■ **Bumper hitch.** Trailer hitch bolted to the rear bumper. Usually rated for Class I towing applications.

■ **Class I hitch.** A weight-carrying hitch whose capacity is rated at up to 2,000 pounds gross trailer weight, and up to 200 pounds tongue weight.

■ **Coupler.** That part of the trailer that connects the tongue to the hitch ball.

■ **Electric brakes.** An independent braking system for a trailer, actuated electrically from the tow vehicle.

■ **Frame-mounted hitch.** A hitch that is mounted or welded to the frame of the tow vehicle.

■ **Gross axle weight rating (GAW).** Specifies the maximum weight an axle is designed to carry. This figure includes the weight of the vehicle plus any load supported by the axle. Caution: Never exceed the GAW.

■ **Gross trailer weight rating (GTW).** Weight of the trailer with all of its cargo.

■ **Gross vehicle weight rating (GVW).** The maximum weight the vehicle is designed to carry, including the weight of the vehicle plus any load normally added.

■ **Hitch ball.** That part of the hitch that couples to the trailer—in essence, a ball joint. The ball allows the trailer to swivel freely when cornering.

■ **Hitch receiver.** The component part of a hitch that receives the shank. Also called a hitch box.

■ **Receiver hitch.** A hitch with a receiver, from which the hitch shank can be removed.

■ **Safety chains.** Required by law in most states, these connect the trailer to the hitch, providing an extra measure of safety.

■ **Spring bars.** Spring steel bars in a weight-distributing hitch that distribute weight throughout the tow vehicle and trailer.

■ **Step bumper hitch.** A hitch found on many utility vehicles.

■ **Surge brakes.** A hydraulic braking system that is activated by the inertia of the trailer pushing against the tow vehicle during deceleration.

■ **Tongue weight.** The amount of trailer weight that is measured at the tongue.

■ **Weight-carrying hitch.** A trailer hitch that accepts all of the tongue weight of a trailer.

■ **Weight-distributing hitch.** A frame-mounted hitch that consists of a shank, a ball mount and spring bars, as well as hookup brackets.

■ **Wiring harness.** Wiring connecting a trailer's lights to the two vehicles' electrical system.

The trailer hitch should be of a type that bolts or is welded to the car frame for safety. Do not use a hitch that is merely attached to the vehicle's bumper.

into the boatyard, yet not so long that they drag on the pavement. Note: Never hook the chains to the bumper.

On trailers equipped with surge brakes, there will also be a third chain. Attach it to the auxiliary brake handle mounted on the tongue. Should the trailer break free, the crisscrossed chains will keep the trailer from pole-vaulting, while the third chain activates the surge brake.

Distributing weight

Weight-distributing hitches spread the tongue weight among all trailer and vehicle wheels. Such hitches are generally used to handle heavy loads that would otherwise put too much weight in back of the vehicle, but must be approached with some caution. Trailer manufacturers warn that such hitches, if overloaded or improperly installed, can cause malfunctions or impairment in operation of hydraulic surge brakes.

Tongue weight should be between 5 and 10 percent of GTW. With a small rig, the tongue weight can be determined using a bathroom scale; on heavier rigs, use a shipper's scale.

Too much weight on the tongue pushes down the back of the tow vehicle, forcing it to "squat." As well as putting undue strain on the vehicle's suspension, this can take needed weight off the tow vehicle's front wheels, making the vehicle "hairy" and hard to steer.

Too little weight on the tongue makes the trailer "tippy" and gives it the tendency to pull up on the tow vehicle. That makes the trailer unstable and more likely to swing from side to side or "fishtail."

The best way to balance a trailer is to move the axle(s) until the desired ratio is obtained. In balancing the whole rig, another very important guideline to consider is the gross axle weight rating (GAW), which is the maximum weight an axle is designed to carry, and is closely related to the tires. This figure includes the weight of the vehicle (with full tank and passengers) plus any load supported by the axle.

It is important never to exceed the GAW. This can be achieved by reading the appropriate figures on each of your tires; they will have a maximum for single wheel and one for dual wheel. It cannot be stressed enough that these loads must never be exceeded per axle. To ensure safety, take your rig either to a transport company scale or the local highway trucker scale and ask them to give you a reading per axle.

Lighting system

In order to operate safely and legally on the public roads, trailers must be equipped with signal and safety lights that can be operated by the driver. Trailers less than 6 feet 8 inches wide (80 inches) need red reflector lights at the back, combining stop, tail and signal lights, along with a white license plate light. White marker lights on each side of the frame just ahead of the wheels are also required. Trailers larger than 6 feet 8 inches must add a group of three red identification lights in the middle of the trailer's back cross-frame, as well as an amber clearance light mounted on the front of each fender.

While many trailers being built today are equipped with fully waterproof lights, many still have lights that are simply "submersible." That means the lights can be submerged in water and will drain on their own. Such lights, however, must be disconnected from the automobile—and their power source—before boat-launching time. Even with waterproof lights, disconnecting is always a good idea in order to rule out the possibility of any leaks or shorts in the wiring that could blow bulbs or fuses.

The standard trailer wiring harness, best installed by professionals but easy to repair in a pinch, is a four-prong connector with the green wire going to the right turn signal, yellow to the left, brown to tail lights, rear markers and rear side lights, and white to ground. That means left gets a combination of yellow and brown wires, while right gets a green and brown combination. Seven-wire harnesses are also available with a blue wire for trailer brakes or other extra equipment, red for charging batteries in the trailer or boat, and light green for backup lights.

Trailer builders suggest that you check your wiring for corrosion, bare wires, cracked insulation or other potential shorts at least twice a year; replace and repair any worn or damaged parts and apply waterproof grease to plug contacts and bulb bases to prevent corrosion. Be sure to check that your lights are all working any time you head out onto the road.

Brakes

Generally, a lightly loaded trailer can be easily handled by the towing vehicle's brakes. Larger loads need an independent trailer braking system. Minimum trailer weights for brake requirement regulations vary from one state to the other. The same applies for Canada. Some trailer manufacturers suggest brakes for any load over 1,000 pounds.

Trailers can be equipped with electric brakes which are activated in tandem with the towing vehicle's hydraulic system, or manually via a dashboard or steering column control. This system can be adjusted according to the trailer load, works well on the road, permitting independent braking of the trailer to either slow down or even stop the whole rig. On the other hand, when backing up, the system tends to be less efficient. It's also prone to corrosion and component failures after being immersed in water.

A very popular choice is surge brakes. Hydraulically operated and independent from the tow vehicle, these are activated by a pressure-sensitive master cylinder in a special coupler mounted on the trailer tongue. These brakes are activated when the tow vehicle slows down: As the trailer surges forward, the trailer brakes come on, and the harder the load pushes, the harder the brakes are applied. The brakes come off as the trailer slows and the lead on the coupler is relieved. In this way, the surge brakes control themselves, according to the trailer's braking needs.

Trailer manufacturers warn trailerboaters not to shift into a lower gear, using the tow vehicle's engine as a brake constantly instead of intermittently. This could result in overheating the trailer's brakes and putting them out of commission. It is better to approach a hill slowly, then brake repeatedly while heading down the hill, giving the brakes time to cool between applications.

Surge brake couplers are now arranged to tolerate backing up without the need to deactivate them unless you are backing up a gradient or steep hill. Most states and provinces require that the brakes be equipped with a "breakaway" connection which activates the surge brakes if the trailer parts company with the tow vehicle.

Boaters are also warned to avoid getting the brakes wet whenever possible and, if they do get wet, to allow them to dry while the trailer is running. Test the brakes before each trip and after greasing the trailer wheels; inspect the brake linings regularly and replace them when worn.

Accessories

A variety of accessories designed to make trailerboating easier and more pleasurable is available. There are non-skid walkways that can be attached to the frame, allowing you to stay

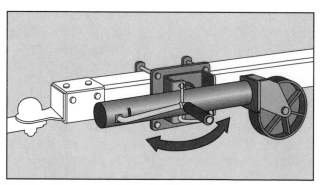

Using a dolly-style tongue jack is like having an extra person helping to move the trailer manually.

higher and drier during launching and recovery; guide posts, guide rollers and padded bunk guides that help keep the boat properly aligned on a still-submerged trailer; and even waterproof lights that will light up the frame of a submerged trailer, making it an easy target in the dark.

There are a number of accessories available to help line up your hitch ball and trailer couple single-handed, including "aerials"—with balls and "guides" that lead the coupler toward the ball. With practice you should be able to park your hitch very close to the trailer coupler with great regularity. One accessory, the dolly-style tongue jack, should be standard equipment for trailers. The jack, equipped with a wheel to allow the tongue and entire trailer to be moved by hand, is usually raised and lowered by a handle-operated worm gear, with a pivot and pin that allow it to be flipped up out of the way once the trailer is hitched to the tow vehicle. The dolly wheel and the jack allow you to raise the trailer tongue above the level of the hitch ball, back the vehicle into place, then easily maneuver the coupler right into place, and drop it effortlessly onto the ball. A great advantage of this method is that it prevents bruised knuckles and fingers.

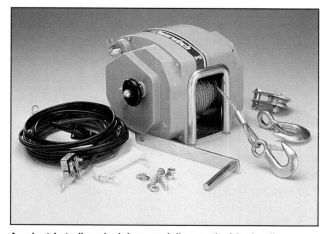

An electric trailer winch is especially practical for loading heavier boats often in less-than-perfect conditions.

Winches

A winch is needed to help ensure the orderly launching of the boat and easier effective retrieval. While a single-speed manual winch will work fine for small boats up to about 1,000 pounds, most trailers should be equipped with a two-speed manual winch. This allows you to pull the boat out of the water quickly during the initial stages of retrieval, while the boat still has some buoyancy, while keeping the increased purchase of the lower speed available when the boat has cleared the water and the winch is pulling its entire weight.

Electric winches are also available, making recovery of the boat a matter of hooking up and flipping a switch. Expensive high-quality electric models are especially desirable for heavy boats that are often launched under less than ideal conditions, for example, on too-steep ramps.

Whether manual or electric, the winch must be mounted so that the winch-line runs level with the boat's bow-eye. It should have an unimpeded run aft and, during recovery, should bring the bow snug against the bow-stop rollers, with the bow-eye between them. The manual winch needs to be cleaned and greased regularly, while the electric winch should be maintained according to the manufacturer's specifications.

Mast and other supports

Sailboat spars, as stated earlier, can be carried lashed to the boat's deck, on special brackets built onto sailboat trailers, or in custom-made cross-bar brackets mounted on the deck or cabin-top. However, if the spars protrude aft beyond the boat's transom and the end of the trailer, the end of the spar must be marked with a red signal flag for safety.

Tie-downs

Once your boat is loaded onto a trailer, with the bunks or rollers all making close contact with the hull, you must ensure that it is well-secured before heading out onto the highway. Most trailers are designed so that the boat can be secured with a safety chain or U-bolt at the bow and two nylon-web tie-downs on the transom. The winch line attached to the boat's bow-eye should be tight, but you cannot count on it alone to hold the boat.

When being transported, a boat must be held firmly on the trailer so that it cannot shift or bounce on the bed. In storage at rest, tie-downs should be slacked off a bit to reduce any distorting strains on the hull.

For a long highway trip, you may wish to secure the boat with additional tie-downs on each side of the boat, near the stern, where the engine—and most of the boat's weight—is located. These tie-downs must be padded when in contact with the boat. They act like sandpaper and actually can work their way through the gel coat and fiberglass; they also wear out the anodizing of the aluminum.

Powerboat drive legs, either outboard or inboard-outboard, are best trailered and stored in the full-down position. If this doesn't allow enough clearance off the road, the engine or drive can be tilted up, and a wooden block wedged into the gap to take some of the strain. Check your motor manual to determine optimum block placement. Also remember to remove the blocking before tilting the motor or stern drive back down.

A canvas or synthetic cover, fitted to cover the top of the boat neatly and fitted with a sort of drawstring to pull it tight under the gunnels, will help keep highway grime off the boat. Such a cover, however, must be well-secured to stay tied down on the road, and may require a web of extra covering ropes. Whether or not the boat is covered by a tarp, any gear left inside (especially if it is light enough to be blown away) should be either stored in a locker or belowdecks or removed. Carefully secure any loose gear.

A fixed-keel sailboat, with a high center of gravity, will naturally need to be well-secured by a network of tie-downs to the sides, front and back of the trailer. The mast and boom can be set on pads and secured to the boat's deck, if it is flat enough, or in specially built cross-member frames that hold the mast level, allowing it to be secured above the boat's superstructure. Such a rig must be lower than the 13'6" height limit set by most states and provinces.

Insurance

Know fully the status of your insurance coverage in regard to pulling a trailer with your car. Some automobile policies allow this, others do not, and some provide limitations on hauling a trailer. Check your policy carefully and, if necessary, consult your insurance agent. If an endorsement is needed don't delay or neglect to get it, even at the cost of a small additional premium. *Be protected, especially in your liability coverage.*

Regulations and licensing

All trailers must be registered with provincial or state transport departments and must bear an affixed license plate. As long as the boat and trailer combination does not exceed 8'6" in width, about 75 feet in length and 13'6" in height, no additional permits will be needed. If you're hauling a double or triple-axle trailer, though, remember that you will have to pay more to use toll roads. These are general guidelines, however; for specifics, check with local authorities.

If you're planning to haul a rig larger than maximum dimensions, arrange for special permits: Contact state and provincial highway authorities in areas you wish to transit. These permits might differ from one state to the other.

FOLLOWING A SAFE PRE-DEPARTURE PROCEDURE

Balance your boat

Check the weight at the trailer tongue; shift equipment and/or axle(s) as necessary. Try to store heavy items as low as you can, keeping the center of gravity as low as possible. All sharp objects should be padded and propped in such a way so they will not shift around should you have to jam on the brakes in an emergency, or inadvertently ride up a curb. Also avoid the unnecessary weight of a full fuel tank; empty water containers and holding tanks; you can easily fill up once you reach your destination.

Check the boat

■ Make sure that the outboard or stern drive has adequate clearance from the road. Check with the manufacturer for proper transport position: You may have to tilt the motor up as far as possible and block or tie it in order to relieve tilt mechanism strain.

Trailering clips are often available to protect stern-drive components on short or long hauls.

■ Check all container lids or caps on board. From the fuel, water and holding tank lids to two-cycle oil can lids, all should be secure. Make sure loose containers are protected from possible puncture by any object. Should spilling occur, it should be restricted to the immediate area.
■ Check that the battery is secure in its box and well lashed.
■ The boat's towing eye must be secure and free of play.
■ Remove all loose gear (antennas, flags, lines, cushions, etc.) from the deck and cockpit; store these items below.
■ For safety during transport, remove a fire extinguisher from the boat and put it in the towing vehicle. (This is especially recommended if the boat is covered, as a stray cigarette butt, from a passing car, could land on the cover and start a fire.)

Check the trailer

■ Ensure proper coupler function; a dab of oil or grease goes a long way in preventing rusting. Check the locking mechanism and have a security pin in place. A padlock can replace that pin to prevent theft.
■ Check for proper tire pressure. Grease wheels, using a grease gun if the trailer is equipped with Bearing Buddies. Check the sidewalls for cracks—if any are present, change the tires. Check the tightness of wheel lugs, and don't forget the spare wheel tire.

■ Check rollers and bunks, and adjust for proper support of the boat.
■ If the winch handle is removable, place it in the back of the car. If it is permanently mounted, check to see that the mounting nut is secure. Check the cable or strap in the winch drum— if frayed, it is unsafe. Make sure that the locking lever has a positive engagement; lubricate the mechanism.
■ Check the wiring harness for either bare wires or nicks, and repair as necessary.

Check the vehicle

■ Adjust tire pressure to manufacturer's recommendations. Check the spare tire at the same time.
■ Check hitch installation and tightness of the ball mount.
■ Check engine and transmission oil, and radiator coolant. (Remember, these will be working harder).
■ Are tool box and spares kit in trunk?

Tie everything down

■ Check your tie-downs; one nick in a strap or cable will greatly reduce its load-rating.
■ You need to take precautions against the boat shifting forward if you need to jam the brakes. The boat should be secure against the bow chock on the trailer. Should there be a possibility that the bow of the boat may ride up the bow chock, add one or two other tie-downs from the eye to a strong point on the trailer.
■ If you decide on extra side tie-downs, it is important that you prepare in three ways: First, use a piece of carpeting or custom sleeve fitted over the tie-down to protect the boat against gel coat damage.

Second, avoid routing the straps over anything like a cleat, windshield, cushions, the plastic hatch cover or a railing. Employ the ratchet mechanism on the tie-down to tighten it. Remember, the tension that can be generated by the ratchet often equals the weight of the boat and can permanently damage any part of it.

Third, do your best to position the ratchet mechanism on the driver's side of the road for ease of checking through his mirror. This way, if a tie-down goes slack, the driver will be able to spot it.

■ Avoid positioning a tie-down ratchet against or close to any part of the boat. The vibration generated by the wind pressure will cause knocking on the hull or part of the boat. This can result in a pitted patch of gel coat or aluminum. If you must, try padding the ratchet device.
■ Always tie the loose end of a tie-down securely to any object; if the tie-down is left hanging, it will fly in the wind and fray to shreds.
■ Make sure that all tie-downs are tight enough to prevent the boat from bouncing on the trailer, but not too tight so as to distort the hull. The boat should travel with the trailer as one, with the trailer's suspension absorbing the shocks of the road.

Cover the boat

Consider the following points when covering your boat:

■ Remove a folding canvas top; it is not designed to take the wind speeds of highway travel.

■ Be sure the cover is snug and well tied. If it has a chance to flap in the wind, it will destroy itself. Dust, dirt and rain must not be able to get under it.

■ If you travel on dirt roads, cover the winch in order to reduce the possibility of grit and debris getting into the mechanism and damaging it.

Hooking up

When hooking up your trailer to the tow vehicle, use the following as a checklist:

■ Coat the hitch ball with a light coat of grease in order to reduce friction.

■ After joining the coupler to the hitch ball, always make sure the coupler is tightened properly and locked according to its design; when in doubt, refer to the manufacturer's instruction manual.

■ Connect the safety chains immediately, so they won't be forgotten. If they have an "S" hook, make sure that the open end of the hook goes up through and not down through it; it will prevent it from bouncing off. A shackle is probably better. Cross your chains.

■ Raise the parking wheel to its "on the road" position.

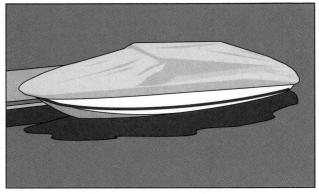

A well-fitted cover will prevent rain and falling debris from entering the boat either at the pier or while traveling.

■ If you have a weight-distributing hitch, be sure to set up the spring bars and adjust them so that the bars will level both the trailer and tow vehicle. The tow vehicle should never squat.

■ Systematically check that all lights on the trailer and tow vehicle, including the parking lights, turn signals, emergency flasher, brake lights and license plate lights are in good working order.

■ Finally, before leaving, make sure that you are carrying all necessary documentation, including your car, trailer and boat registrations and proof of insurance, as well as any necessary road permits.

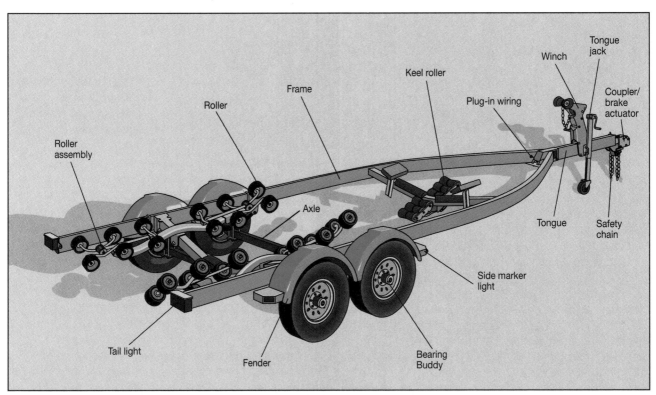

Some heavy-duty trailers are designed for a variety of boat lengths, weights and hull shapes. Double and triple axles are not uncommon, and trailer wheel brakes are a must.

STEERING WITH A TRAILER

Driving and steering a vehicle with a 20- to 30-foot articulated extension is neither easy nor intuitive. Although some drivers readily adjust, most need practical advice and practice. Perhaps the best and simplest advice is to slow everything down. Consider and plan your moves carefully, and remember that you cannot move as quickly in, for example, your van and boat-trailer combination as you would in your two-door sport coupe.

The guidelines below are intended to help hone your skills in negotiating a trailer. Along with practice, these will help you anticipate how both trailer and vehicle will behave, and to take the necessary actions required for safety.

Moving forward

■ Learn to accelerate, slow down and stop with smooth, steady motions.

■ When driving at highway speeds, allow more room between yourself and the vehicle in front than you normally would; that gives you plenty of time to slow down if the vehicle in front hits the brakes.

■ On multi-lane roads, signal well before you need to turn, and be sure drivers in the other lane—who may be moving faster—have slowed down and are expecting your move. Even though you are already keeping a sharp lookout on the rear-view mirrors (on big frame-mounted mirrors, if those are needed to see back past the boat and trailer), you will want to watch even more closely when changing lanes.

■ When passing, delay returning to your lane to allow space for the trailer; in fact, passing should be minimized.

■ When turning left at an intersection, the boat will tend to follow the path of the tow vehicle as you'll have lots of room to make a smooth arcing turn.

■ When turning right, into a right-hand lane, you may need to swing wide into the left-hand lane in order to keep the trailer clear of right-side curbs or the roadside.

■ With a turn in any direction, do not cut too closely; at worst, you could jack-knife the tow vehicle into the boat and trailer.

■ Be wary of parking lots or driveways that don't give you enough space to maneuver.

Moving backward

Driving a trailer backward is even trickier and takes even more practice. If you're just starting out, try to find a large deserted parking lot—an office or mall parking lot on Sunday, for example—where you can practice backing in peace, without hazardous obstacles or curious onlookers. That way, you'll have plenty of confidence when you first pull up to the launch ramp. Remember that in backing up, the vehicle is pushing rather than pulling the trailer. That means, if you want the trailer to back straight, you have to keep the tow vehicle running exactly straight.

■ Turning the steering wheel right will turn the back of the tow vehicle right and the back of the trailer left. However, if you just keep going, the rig will jack-knife.

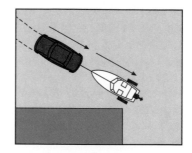

1 When positioning at a ramp, remember that the trailer always backs in the direction opposite to that of the car. As you approach in reverse, swing close to the ramp.

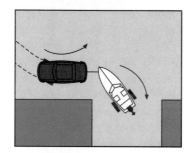

2 Then cut the car in toward the driveway.

3 Cut the car wheels to the left and back slowly into the ramp as the trailer moves to the right.

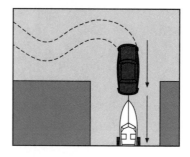

4 Finally, straighten the car wheels to follow the trailer as it backs straight down the ramp.

■ If you want the boat to keep backing up to the left, you have to follow the trailer and swing the car around in an arc behind it, which means steering back in the opposite direction.

■ Turning the steering wheel left swings the back of the tow vehicle left and moves the trailer sharply to the right.

■ If you want to keep moving the trailer to the right without jack-knifing you have to swing the steering wheel back to the right, bringing the tow vehicle roughly in a line with the arc of the trailer.

■ The trick with backing up is to maneuver the trailer into the direction in which you want to move it, then follow it, driving either in a wide arc or straight back.

■ When moving straight back, use a series of shallow S-shaped turns for "corrections," to keep the rig moving straight.

LAND STORAGE

Because most trailerable boats are stored on land between uses and during the offseason, such boats usually spend more time on a trailer bed than in the water. In addition to keeping both the trailer and boat in good repair, there are other guidelines for safe and careful storage of both, which are covered below.

■ **Protect against theft and damage.** You can create at least partial protection against the theft of your boat and its trailer by installing a special fitting that is secured to the trailer coupling with a keyed lock—remember, if they can't "hitch up," they can't haul it away.

When the car is not pulling the trailer, cover the hitch ball with an old, split-open tennis ball or a ball cover. This will

Locks for trailers can either be of the specialized type (*left*) or of the padlock style.

prevent any grease on the ball from rubbing off on clothing and will provide some protection against rust. Some owners unbolt the ball from the hitch and store it in the trunk or on another protected spot.

If your boat will be stored outside for an extended period of time, it is a wise decision to remove the battery, electrical components and even the motor—if possible—and store these items indoors for greater protection against both theft and corrosion.

■ **Keep water out.** Rainwater in the boat is undesirable for many reasons—mainly because water collection can rapidly increase weight on the trailer, often beyond its capacity. A cover is desirable, and should be supported so that pockets of rainwater cannot form, stretching the fabric and breaking through it. Cross-supports under the cover and frequent fastening points around the edge will keep the cover sag-free; allow some "give" in the cover if the fabric is subject to shrinking when wet.

■ **Drain accumulating water.** Whether your boat is protected with a cover or not, the best way to get rid of accumulated water is to raise the tongue of the trailer, allowing water to run aft and out the drain hole. Crank down the parking wheel to raise the tongue, or, alternatively, block it up securely. Make sure the drain is *open*.

■ **Ease strains on the hull.** If tie-downs remain taut after over-the-road travel, slack them off or remove them. This will eliminate any strains and possible distortions to the hull that might occur during long storage periods.

■ **Block up the trailer.** If you do not expect to use your rig for several weeks or months, the trailer frame should be jacked up and placed on blocks in order to reduce the strain on springs and tires. Be sure to use enough blocking to prevent distortion of the trailer frame—which in turn could distort the hull of your boat.

The blocks need be just high enough to take the greater part of the load, but if the trailer wheels are clear of the ground, reduce air pressure in the tires by 10 to 15 pounds. Remember that you must have means at hand to restore pressure when the blocks are later taken out for the next trip: Do not deflate tires unless you can pump them up again right on the spot.

■ **Check the rig frequently.** When your boat is stored and out of regular use, try to set up a schedule of weekly visits by yourself or someone else acting on your behalf. (Checking at the same time each week will help you remember to do so.) On each visit, thoroughly inspect the vessel for peeling paint and any other visible signs of physical deterioration. It is recommended that you take the necessary corrective action immediately, before any minor problems escalate into major ones.

MAINTENANCE, TOOLS AND SPARES

Boat trailers are often neglected, and of all their components their wheel bearings are the most critical. Trailers are driven for long periods of time on the highway, often loaded close to their limit, and after a short rest period, if any, are immersed in water during launching and retrieval.

The water seeps into their wheel hubs, emulsifying the grease, and destroying its lubricating capabilities. If left unattended for any length of time, the water will corrode the bearings' rollers, resulting in grit in the mixture. Of all the stranded trailers, wheel bearing failure is one of the main causes.

When traveling, keep some tools handy for any of the most common incidents; the usual screwdrivers, pliers, wire stripper and cutters, hammer and small sledge hammer, tire pressure gauge, small hydraulic jack, lug wrench and large wrench for the spindle nut, a grease gun loaded with axle grease, a good flashlight, a few rags, some 2-by-4s for blocking the wheels, and last but not least, some waterless hand cleaner.

Always keep a few spares on hand: a complete hub assembly (hub, pre-packed bearings, seals, lug nuts and cotter pins), a spare wheel with a mounted tire, a few feet of wire and some terminals, a spare of each type of light bulb for the trailer. Roadside flares or reflective warning triangle might come in handy and perhaps a 12-volt tire pump that connects to a battery, and a few spare fuses for the electrical system.

LAUNCHING AND RETRIEVING

Both launching a boat from its trailer, and its retrieval (loading), are important skills. In each instance, the steps to be taken must be carefully planned and executed to avoid damage to the boat or motor, as well as injuries to people.

Using a ramp

Although a ramp is not the best way to get a boat into the water, it is the method used most often. Ramps vary widely in their characteristics: Many are surfaced with concrete, while others are hard-packed dirt or sand—and sometimes reinforced with wood or steel planking. Some ramps are wide enough for only one launching operation at a time; others can accommodate many rigs simultaneously.

The quality of a ramp depends on its slope, how far it extends into the water, and the condition of its surface. The angle of slope is not critical, but it should be deep enough so the trailer need not be backed down so far into the water that the wheel bearings of the tow vehicle become submerged.

Make pre-launch preparations well away from the ramp to help avoid line-ups for ramp use.

Make sure you have inspected the ramp before you line up at the ramp and do any last minute checks.

Line up the car and trailer and back the rig down the ramp, as described in the text.

If the slope is too steep, however, you may need an excessive pull to get a loaded trailer up and off the ramp. The ramp should extend far enough into the water that trailers can be backed down without running off the lower end, even in low water conditions. (Many surfaced ramps develop a sharp drop-off at their lower end; if the trailer has rolled past this point, getting trailer wheels back up over this lip is a problem.) A dirt or sand ramp must be firm enough to support the trailer and car wheels. A surfaced ramp must not have a coating of slime that could make footing dangerous, and provide inadequate traction for the car.

Preparing for launching

While the trailer's wheel bearings are cooling down, remove the boat cover, fold it, and store it in the car or boat. Tie-downs can be removed and stored in a safe place, but leave the winch line taut. If the outboard motor or stern-drive lower unit has been in the down position during trailering, tilt it up. If the trailer's lights will be submerged, disconnect the plug to the vehicle's electrical system.

If you are launching a sailboat, now is the time to untie the mast and rigging and proceed to hoist the mast. On most trailerable sailboats, hoisting the mast is more easily done on land than when afloat.

Remove or relocate equipment stowed in the boat so that the boat will trim properly when launched. If the fuel or water tanks are empty, or only partially filled, it may be most convenient to top them up now.

Ensure adequate control of the boat by using two lines. Attach both a bow and a stern line. If you are planning to move the boat to a pier or seawall once it is in the water, put over the side any fenders that might be needed.

"Preview" the launching. Study the ramp and surrounding water area for any hazards, such as a slippery or too-short surface; estimate the wind and current effects. If in doubt, don't hesitate to ask another skipper who has just launched or retrieved a boat. If you have time, it is useful to watch the launching operations of others, noting any peculiarities of the ramp that may be new to you.

Now check the drain plug, if one is used. (Occasionally even an experienced skipper launching a boat suffers the embarrassment of water pouring in the drain.) Look about to make sure that no item of preparation has been forgotten, then *check the drain plug again*.

Launching the boat

Line up the car and trailer so that the backing process will be as straight and as short as possible. On a wide ramp, give due regard to others and don't take up more than your share of space.

Back the rig down, preferably to the point where the trailer's tires—but not the axle bearings—are in the water. Next, set the parking brake on the car; for added safety, block a wheel on each side of the car. Then have one person man the winch controls, while one or two other helpers take the bow and stern lines.

While a crew member disconnects the bow hitch line, one or two others control the boat with the bow and stern lines.

Release the trailer tilt latch, if it is of this type. Tighten the winch brake and release the anti-reverse lock. *Do not,* under any circumstances, disconnect the winch cable from the boat. At this stage, a craft should slide easily off the trailer, its speed controlled by the winch brake; in some instances, a push or two may be needed to get it started. Be sure the motor is tilted up so the propeller and skeg will not dig into the bottom as the boat slides down.

When the boat is floating free of the trailer, unhook the winch line. Move the boat aside and make it fast to a pier, beach it, or otherwise secure it temporarily. Return a tilted trailer bed to a horizontal position, and latch it in place. The winch line may be rewound on the drum if desired, or secured by catching the hook on a member of the trailer frame and taking up the slack.

Make sure one or two crew members take hold of the bow and stern lines before giving the boat a light push to float it.

Remove the blocks from the car's wheels, and drive the car to an authorized parking area—be sure to give consideration to others by clearing the ramp promptly, and selecting a parking spot that will neither take up unnecessary space nor block others from using the ramp. If it is possible, hose down with fresh water any parts of the trailer that got wet during the launch.

Use a padlock on the coupling or safety chain to prevent theft of the trailer. Place the chocks at the wheels of the trailer if it is detached from the car and if the parking area has any slope.

At the boat, lower the stern-drive unit to its operating position, and connect the fuel line if necessary. Complete any preparations needed for getting underway—transferring equipment to the boat from the car, for example. Then load up your crew, and clear away from the launching area as rapidly as can be done with safety.

Secure the boat temporarily while parking the trailer. In this example, the trailer is still in the water to illustrate how far the trailer needs to enter the water in order to launch the boat.

Reloading on the trailer

Beach the boat or make it fast to a pier, and get the car and trailer from the parking area. If the boat will not be used in the next day or so, it is a good idea to disconnect the fuel line of an outboard while the motor is running at a fast idle. Let it run until all the fuel in the motor is used up; this will help prevent the formation of gum and deposits in the carburetor and fuel lines.

Back the trailer to the water's edge, make sure that the electrical plug at the vehicle is disconnected. Set the car brakes and block the wheels. If the trailer bed tilts, release the latch and push the frame into the "up" position. Then tilt up the boat's motor or stern-drive unit, and work the boat into position to move onto the first rollers, with the keel of the boat in line with the trailer.

As with launching, both a stern and bow line help in boat maneuvering during reloading. It may be possible for one of the crew to wade into the water to guide the boat into position. (You can keep your feet dry by using a walkway installed on the trailer frame.) Run out enough winch cable to engage the hook in the boat's stem eye; be careful to watch out for kinks in the cable and remember never to handle a steel line except with gloves.

Crank in the winch line and the boat should come onto the trailer bed; a tilted frame will come down to the horizontal position by itself when the boat moves up it. Often a winch has a lower-geared speed that is useful for the initial pull to get the boat started, and a higher-speed mode to use once the pull gets easier.

Do not allow anyone to be in line with the winch cable. A cable under load may snap like a rubber band when it breaks, and can throw a hook or fitting great distances, so *keep clear.*

When the boat is fully positioned on the trailer, latch down the tilt mechanism (if it is of this type), remove the wheel

Except for dealing with the mast, launching and retrieving a sailboat is identical to the process for a powerboat. Always be sure to check carefully for overhead power lines and use great caution if there are any located nearby.

Raising a sailboat's mast can be trouble-free if properly set up. This trailer is galvanized with rear guide posts and built-in ladder at the bow hitch.

blocks, and move the rig clear of the ramp so that others can use it. Do not overlook the other preparations that must be made for road travel, but move away from the launching area to do them.

Launching by crane

The use of a crane or traveling lift with padded slings is the launching method that is probably the most easy on the boat. When it is exercised with care, this method of launching minimizes strains on the hull.

Although the slings are usually provided by the crane operator, check to make sure that these are of adequate strength before entrusting your boat to them. You also should be familiar with the proper placement of slings so as to ensure a safe balance of your boat—your dealer should be able to provide you with this information.

While the boat is in the slings, use both bow and stern lines to control any swinging motion between the trailer and the water.

SMALL BOAT HANDLING

Although boat handling on outboards and stern drives is covered in Chapter 9, there are some details that specifically relate to lighter, trailerable craft. We will deal with those concerns in this section.

Although the vast majority of trailerable boats have wheel steering, some are still equipped with outboard motors with tiller handles. The operator sits in the stern of the boat and pushes the tiller handle away from the direction of the intended turn. On the smallest outboards, reverse is achieved by turning a half circle with the engine.

The smaller the boat in relation to the size of the engine, the more you will feel the effect of the engine's torque. In proportion to the engine's force, the boat will tend to heel to one side as a reaction to the powerful spin of the propeller. A propeller with more pitch will tend to "walk" sideways as it achieves higher speeds in the water.

Trim

Remember that the number of seats in a boat is not an indication of the number of persons that it can carry safely. Overloading is a major cause of boating accidents, so stay within the true limits of your craft (check the official capacity plate). The factors affecting trim become increasingly critical as the load approaches the boat's capacity, and also as boat size decreases.

Before getting underway, trim your boat as well as possible, as shown in the illustrations below. In smaller craft it is dangerous for passengers to change places or to move about while the boat is scooting along briskly. If such movement becomes essential, slow or stop the boat first. (In rough weather remember to maintain sufficient momentum to retain steerage control, and to keep the boat headed into wind and waves.) Anyone moving must keep low and near the boat's center line.

Stability

Since outboards are often run at relatively high speeds, their stability becomes an important safety issue. Some hulls will run straight ahead quite steadily, but have a tendency to heel excessively, or even flip over, when turned sharply.

The underwater shape of the hull is a key factor in stability. Today, most outboard and stern-drive boats are of deep-V or modified-V form, or of the multiple-hull cathedral type. These designs provide a higher degree of stability in normal operation; however, they resist turning—attempts to make a sharp turn at high speed may cause broaching (uncontrolled turning broadside to the seas or to the wind). This is also the case with some older, flat-bottom hull forms that have keels to provide directional stability.

Conversely, a flat-bottom boat without a keel has little directional stability, and may skid out sideways when a turn is attempted at excessive speed. Initially the boat will point off in the new direction, but actually will continue to travel along what is essentially its old course.

In any case, the faster a boat goes, the more important it is to reduce speed to a safe level before starting a turn; never turn more sharply than necessary. Normal operation seldom requires a sudden, sharp, high-speed turn.

Reversing

Most outboard motors have a reverse gear that enables them to be backed down. Unless restrained, an outboard motor has the tendency to tilt itself up and out of the water when thrust is reversed. On many models, there is a manually operated reverse lock that must be latched into place to keep the motor down while engaged in backing maneuvers. For normal running, however, it is important that this latch be released so that the lower unit will be free to tilt up if it strikes an underwater obstruction.

 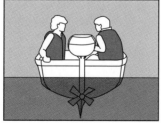

Proper lateral trim *(near left)* **is important for safety. If the load is concentrated to port** *(far left)*, **the boat might capsize in a tight left turn or if hit by a wave or wake.**

Overload forward causes boat to "plow." Running with the bow down may allow the boat to dig into an oncoming wave.

Overload aft causes boat to "squat," placing the transom dangerously low to the water.

Distribute passengers and gear so the boat is level; fore-and-aft trim is important for best performance and comfort.

Inflatable boats are constructed of air-filled tubes, with flexible or rigid floors. The transoms and seats are built of wood, metal or composites.

These highly stable platforms have found widespread acceptance as yacht tenders, dive boats, workboats and all-round pleasurecraft. The material used to build most inflatables is a high-strength woven polyester or nylon fabric that is impregnated with flexible but durable "plastomer" coatings. The inside layers of some inflatables is made of neoprene—a stretchy but airtight rubberlike material expanded with air.

Inflatables are stable, unsinkable when inflated and capable of carrying great weights; they also have the advantage of collapsing into small, portable packages. Although they are difficult to row, inflatables are easily driven by outboard motors. Because they are made of fabric that is subject to abrasion and wear, care should be taken during use and while being inflated and deflated.

Types

The traditional inflatable dinghy or tender was built with plywood floors and inflatable tube seats and controlled by a tiller-mounted outboard. The boats are now available with more sophisticated accommodations such as remote-control consoles with rigid seats and even "radar-arch" bars for mounting radio antennas and lights. The flat-bottom inflatable hull has given way to a wide variety of hull shapes, including inflated V-hulls and V-hulls with inflated "sponsons." Some very rigid inflatable floors are also available.

Rigid hull inflatable boats (RIBs) combine the stability and sea-keeping ability of regular inflatables with the speed and handling capabilities of regular V-hulls. Because of the hulls' added strength and stiffness they can carry more powerful outboards; rigid seats, consoles or storage areas can also be added. Most RIBs are in fact small fiberglass V-hulls surrounded by inflatable tubes. Strength can be built into the boat and the stability for which inflatables are known is available when needed—while the boat is operating at slow speeds or at rest—but the V-hull comes into play when the boat is on plane and running at speed. While traditional inflatables are usually deflated and disassembled for travel, rigid inflatables are normally left inflated and carried on a bunk-style trailer.

Inflatables need lower horsepower to perform the same work as heavier types of boats; overpowering an inflatable adversely affects maneuverability and balance. Be sure to check the height of the motor to reduce excessive spray around the engine while underway.

Inflatables towed behind larger boats should have loose equipment removed. The tow should be from "tow" rings—usually installed by the manufacturer—mounted on the forward underside of the inflatable's bow area. From these tow rings, a bridle should be created, centered foward of the bow.

A popular position for towing inflatables with sailboats and slower powerboats is snugged up against the transom of the tow vessel. With faster powerboats, a dinghy is nor-mally towed astern on a longer line; to reduce strain on the line, it should ride on the forward side of the stern waves. The use of three-strand nylon lines for towlines or trailer tie-downs is not recommended. This type of line, with exposure to sun and salt, can be quite abrasive, and constant rubbing against the inflatable can cause damage. Braided lines, either nylon, polyester or polypropylene are the best choice because they float. In fact, this is a good way to recycle old braided dock lines or jib sheets as the fuzz around these lines softens the outer layer.

Maintenance

Most manufacturers of inflatable boats recommend mild detergent cleaners. Mild abrasive scrubbers will help remove serious grime. Minor cuts and abrasions can be repaired using sandpaper, cleaner, glue and a patch. Extensive repairs should be done by a professional.

Like other boats, inflatables will grow barnacles or become coated with scum if left in the water unprotected. A special anti-fouling paint is available for them. A properly inflated boat will be rigid in the water and will not sag or flex with the waves; the operating pressure of a properly inflated boat varies among manufacturers.

Since wet wood will eventually warp and rot, wood components of any model need regular painting and varnishing. Also, metal components should be kept clean and free from corrosion. Valves should be cleaned once or twice a year, or monthly if the boat is regularly inflated and deflated. Valve cleaning should be done with mild soapy water and an old toothbrush. Check the O-rings; if cracked or pitted, they permit air leakage and should be replaced. Do not use petroleum jelly, silicones or petroleum distillates on the valves. Clean the boat fabric with mild soapy water at least twice a year with the floor system removed and the bilge well cleaned. As for fiberglass components, treat them as any other fiberglass item, with regular compounding and waxing.

An inflatable boat joins lightness of construction to a safe, wide platform and soft contours.

JET-DRIVE BOATS

Various boats, ranging from planing to displacement-type hulls, and from small "personal watercraft" to very large yachts, use water jet propulsion. Although handling characteristics can differ significantly depending on the boat, the major features of a jet boat include the following:

- Instant response in accelerating, stopping or making any sort of turn.
- Low drag because of the lack of appendages.
- Shallow draft.
- Safety around people in the water.
- Absence of hull vibration or torque effects, which eliminates high-speed cavitation.

The principle of operation is borrowed from aircraft jet propulsion. Rather than having a traditional propeller immersed below the hull, the water jet system draws water through an intake duct and debris screen, fitted flush to the bottom of the hull. A high-performance axial flow impeller pumps high vol-

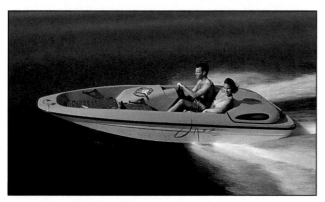

A popular use of the jet drive is for "fun" because of its increased safety and maneuverability in operation.

umes of water, discharging it via a nozzle projecting through a sealed transom opening. This results in a powerful forward thrust. Steering is provided by a single piece deflector mounted on the tailpipe, remotely controlled, and is self-centering (the boat tends to return, by itself, to a straight course).

Reverse is achieved by a deflector or "clam shell" that is lowered to divert the flow of water forward. If done suddenly on a small boat, it stops the boat in its own length—a maneuver that should not be done at high speed because of possible injuries to passengers and/or somersault of the light craft. Because there is no gearbox, shifting from forward to reverse at any speed does not overload the engine. Only the direction of the external water stream is altered in stopping or reversing. The pivot point of a light displacement jet boat can be as little as 2 feet forward of the jet nozzle. Without rudder or lower unit drag, sharp turns can be made; it is possible to reverse course in little more than the boat's length. Getting into a tight space at a pier can be accomplished by using short bursts of power alternately in forward and reverse.

Jet-drive boats with the best handling characteristics are those designed specifically for this means of propulsion. Their

hulls are designed to ensure that the aerated water from the bow wave does not enter the jet, thus avoiding the creation of slip and minimizing power loss.

Personal watercraft

A personal watercraft is a common introduction to boating for young people. Because such craft sometimes use the same waters as other powerboats, it is important that boaters be informed about their use and about how to avoid collision.

A personal watercraft is classified by the U.S. Coast Guard as a "Class A Inboard Boat" and is subject to the same laws and requirements as conventional boats. According to the Rules of the Road, there is no difference between operating a personal watercraft and any other craft. As skipper of a personal watercraft, you are operating the most maneuverable type of boat. Accordingly, you have the responsibility to protect yourself from collisions. With no navigation lights aboard, a personal watercraft may not be used after dark.

Remember that both the owner and the skipper are responsible for the safety of everyone aboard, as well as any damage that may occur from the watercraft's wake—an important consideration when lending or borrowing such a craft. Manufacturers recommend that no privately owned personal watercraft be operated by anyone below the age of 14 or rented to anyone below age 16. The actual minimum age requirement may vary from one state or province to the other.

Personal watercraft operation: do's and don'ts

- Do know how to swim, and even if you do, wear a PFD.
- Do always attach the tether cord to your vest before you start the engine.
- Do go slowly until you are in a clear area.
- Do make sure you can be seen at all times.
- Do have aboard an up-to-date chart of the waters where you are intending to go boating.
- Do check for, and obey, "no wake" signs.
- Do look behind you for traffic as you prepare for each turn.
- Do keep a substantial distance between your watercraft and every other person or craft in or on the water.
- Do avoid ship channels whenever possible; if absolutely necessary, cross them vigilantly and quickly.
- Do operate courteously. Showing respect to others on the water will help maintain a high public regard for your sport. Only a few irresponsible operators can bring about restrictive local regulations that may reduce your chances to fully enjoy your craft.
- Do slow down and be extra cautious on your way home. Numerous studies have shown that the fatigue caused by the glare, motion, noise and vibration during a day on the water will reduce your reactions to nearly the same level as if you were legally intoxicated.
- Do *not* speed in congested areas.
- Do *not* speed in fog or stormy conditions.
- Do *not* come too close to another vessel.

WATER-SKIING

Since every boater is likely to encounter water-skiers at one time or another while underway—or to participate in the sport—a mention of water-skiing is relevant in terms of safety. This brief coverage of the subject is intended to help the boater anticipate dangerous situations and to respond quickly and accordingly.

The boat

Water-skiing doesn't require a large boat with a high powered engine. Although tournament and show skiers use very sophisticated equipment, the average skier can use the family boat, whether outboard, inboard or stern drive. Although it is possible to ski behind a boat as small as a personal watercraft and even behind an inflatable with a 20-hp engine, the normal length is 14 to 20 feet (4.3 to 6.1 m). It is generally accepted, though, that 75 hp is approximately the minimum size for a tow motor. The most important factor is the size of the engine: It must be more powerful than the required minimum for the activity. Otherwise, the water-skiing can overexert the motor, reducing its useful lifespan.

When pulling skiers, it is important to maintain constant speed—ideally using a speedometer and/or a tachometer to ensure that the engine won't exceed its maximum rpm. To achieve maximum efficiency when towing skiers, using a smaller pitch propeller will help to keep the power to its maximum in the ranges of speed used. Top-end speed may be lower but acceleration will be better.

The towline for the skier must be mounted either on a high point inside the transom on a post called the "pylon" or on a bridle attached at two points through-bolted on the stern that are designed for this purpose. Never tie to one corner only, this could cause a small boat to upset and greatly hinder maneuverability on larger boats.

Since verbal communication between the skier and the boat's crew is difficult if not impossible, it is essential that a universally accepted group of signals be used. Using the observer as an intermediate to the driver, the skier is able to communicate his wishes by these gestures, shown below.

Safe water-skiing: do's and don'ts

- Do learn good swimming skills. This is important for the skier and for the boat's crew.
- Do wear a PFD that is secure, durable and is not too bulky or awkward.
- Do familiarize yourself with safe boating procedures (*Chapter 3*). Although most boating fatalities result from collision, capsizing or falls overboard, with personal watercraft and water-skiing, falling overboard is often considered part of the fun.
- Do learn about water-skiing from a qualified instructor.
- Do make yourself visible if you fall in waters where traffic exists. Hold a ski halfway up to alert boats nearby.
- Do insist on having a competent observer in addition to the driver—someone who is appointed to watch the skier at all times and report to the driver of the boat. That observer should be able to physically assist the skier in case of need. Above all, the lookout should remember that objects and other boats present the greatest danger. An observer is a legal requirement in most states.
- Do always look ahead if you are the driver. Plan your speed and turns according to the skier's ability.
- Do return quickly to a fallen skier.
- Do check equipment regularly, especially before skiing; skis with nicks could cut or scrape skin. Make sure ski lines are free of tangles, loops and knots.
- Do *not* ski in shallow water (water less than about 6.5 feet or 2 meters deep).

Speed up

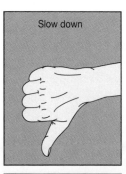
Slow down

Turn

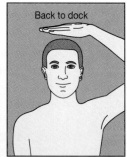
Back to dock

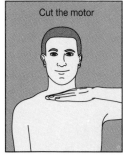
Cut the motor

OK after a fall

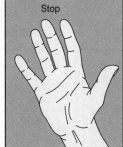
Stop

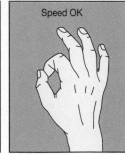
Speed OK

Since verbal communication between the skier and the boat crew is difficult if not impossible, it is essential that a universally accepted group of signals be used. Using an observer as an intermediate to the driver, the skier is able to communicate his wishes by these gestures.

- Do *not* ski near boats, docks or swimming, scuba diving, sailing and fishing areas. Also avoid close proximity to the shore, stationary objects, narrow channels and harbors, and busy areas.
- Do *not* put any part of your body through the bridle or place the handle behind the neck or knees. A fall in this position has the potential for serious injury.
- Do *not* ski at night (established as being from one hour after sunset until sunrise).
- Do *not* dry land at a dock or beach. Any error in judgment could result in an injury.
- Do *not* drive on any course that could jeopardize the ski-

er's safety—for example, when circling closely to follow a skier, a boat could inadvertently strike the skier if he or she should fall.

- Do *not* prevent people on shore, or other boaters, from enjoying the peacefulness of open waters and beaches. Noise carries farther on the water than on land, particularly when it is otherwise quiet. Remember that early morning and late afternoon are times when many boaters value quiet most. When water-skiing or operating personal watercraft at high speeds, stay away from anchorages, shoreline areas with homes, campgrounds and other places where people go for peace and quiet.

SAFE OPERATION OF SMALL CRAFT

A carefully matched boat, motor and propeller, operated in accordance with the law and with courtesy, will go a long way toward eliminating many accidents and worries. But some possibility for trouble always exists; the wise boater should be prepared to act in an emergency. Much of the information listed below is of particular interest to small boat and personal watercraft operators as well as water-skiers. Refer also to Chapters 3 and 4 for more extensive safety-on-the-water and emergency information.

Common causes of accidents involving small craft
- Overloading, overpowering and improper trim.
- High speed turns, especially in rough water.
- Failure to keep a lookout for obstructions and other boats.
- Going out in bad weather (or not starting for shelter soon enough when weather starts turning bad).
- Standing up in a moving boat.
- Having too much weight too high in the boat, as when someone sits on the deck of a small outboard.
- Leaks in the fuel system.
- Going too far offshore.

Safe operating procedures
- **Allow no one on the bow.** A crew member who slips off the boat may be run over by the boat before the skipper can take action.

- **Stand clear of hazards.** Strong river and tidal currents or mooring under large objects (mooring or moored vessel, barge, etc.) can pull a small boat beneath the surface. Give them a wide berth.

- **Slowing and stopping.** Watch your own stern wave; it could overtake you and swamp your boat.

- **Fuel consumption.** There is no excuse for running out of fuel. Keep tanks near full and know the fuel consumption on a

per-hour or per-mile basis. Always plan for a reserve of at least one-third of your total capacity.

- **Leave word behind.** If you are going offshore or for a long run on inland waters, or even just fishing some distance away from home, tell someone ashore what your plans are, giving as much detail as possible (Chapter 3).

- **Watch the weather.** The smaller the boat, the more vulnerable it is to approaching bad weather. Take early evasive action; head for safe waters while there is ample time. Always keep an eye on the weather.

- **Carry distress signals.** Even though the size of your craft might not warrant the need to carry emergency equipment and flares during the day, it is nevertheless good practice to carry some in case you are delayed or stranded. Learn the proper emergency procedures.

- **Watch for squalls and storms.** If you get caught in bad weather, the information included in Chapter 11 is good even for small craft. The basic safety rules apply: Everyone should wear a PFD. Go slow. Check your weight distribution. If the motor quits, keep the bow to the waves. Don't let water accumulate in the boat.

- **Know what to do if you capsize.** Unless your life is threatened, stay with the boat, which is easier to spot than a swimmer alone. All boats built after July 1973 must carry flotation to keep them upright.

- **Know what to do in case of accident.** If you are involved in a boating accident, you are required to stop and help without endangering your boat or passengers. You must identify yourself and your boat to any person injured or to the owner of the property damaged. See Chapter 4 for information on reporting accidents and recovery procedures.

9 SEAMANSHIP UNDER POWER

What boater does not envy the skipper of a well-kept yacht as it pulls up to a crowded dock, eases into reverse and magically settles into the berth?

In reality, there is no magic involved in maneuvering a boat; it responds to the laws of physics. However, discovering the relationship between the physical laws and boat behavior can be an exasperating experience.

In this chapter the handling characteristics of single-screw, twin-screw and outboard or stern-drive boats are explained in principle. With practice, you will be ready to meet the real test—maneuvering in and around docks and busy harbors.

BASIC PRINCIPLES OF BOAT HANDLING

The ability to steer well—called helmsmanship, when referring to either men or women—is a quality that cannot be learned from a book or in a classroom. However, understanding the basic principles of boat handling will make it easier for you to practice in a variety of situations.

The art of helmsmanship

It is important to realize that boats are nearly as individualistic as people, particularly in their steering characteristics. Deep-draft and shallow-draft vessels handle differently. Boats that steer by changing their thrust direction—outboards and stern drives—respond differently than boats steered by rudders; the response of heavy displacement hulls to helm changes is quite unlike that of light planing hulls.

The secret of good helmsmanship is to know your boat. If you skipper your own craft, this comes quickly as you gain experience with it. If you take the wheel or tiller of a friend's boat, however, take it easy at first with helm changes, until you get the "feel" of the craft's response.

Steering is often done by compass. The helmsman must keep the compass lubber's line on the mark of the card that indicates the course to be steered. If the course to be steered is 100 degrees, and the lubber's line is momentarily at 95 degrees, the helmsman must "swing the boat's head" with right rudder, 5 degrees to the right, to bring the lubber's line around to 100. Remember, the card stands still while the lubber's line swings around it. Any attempt to bring the desired course on the card up to the lubber's line will produce exactly the *opposite* result.

As a vessel swings with a change in course, the inexperienced helmsman tends to allow it to swing too far, from the momentum of the turn and the lag between the turn of the wheel and response of the craft. The experienced helmsman knows how to steady on the new course without over-swinging. In almost all power cruisers, this requires that the helmsman return the rudder to the neutral, midships, position *before* the craft reaches the intended new heading. The helmsman will often need to use a slight amount of opposite rudder to check the boat's swing.

A zigzag course also brands the helmsman as inexperienced. The goal is a straight course, which can be achieved, after the boat has steadied, by only slight movements of the wheel. The experienced boater at the helm anticipates the vessel's swing and, turning the wheel slowly and deliberately, makes corrections with little rudder instead of going well off course before correcting.

When holding a course it helps to pick out a distant landmark. But you must also drop your eye periodically to the compass to check your course, and look back periodically at the aids or landmarks you have passed, making sure that you remain on your proper track. Even though you may be steering quite precisely toward your objective, the wind or a cross-current may be setting you to one side. If in a narrow channel, you could soon be out of it and aground.

Basic boat terms

Certain basic boating terms apply specifically to boats equipped with one or more engines—whether inboard (mounted within the hull), outboard (mounted on the transom and detachable), or the combination inboard-outboard (I/O) type. Thrust for the movement of the boat through the water is achieved by the rotation of a propeller (or "screw"), which draws in water from ahead and pushes it out astern. A boat with one propeller is termed a single-screw type. Boats with two propellers are referred to as twin-screw craft. Sailboats fitted with an engine are called auxiliaries. The handling characteristics are similar to those of the single-screw powerboat.

Steering is accomplished in one of two ways. An inboard engine operates according to a "fixed screw": Turning a rudder or rudders diverts the thrust developed by the propeller(s), which in turn turns the boat. An outboard or I/O powered boat operates without a rudder. Moving the motor and propeller, or outdrive unit, directly turns the propeller thrust, changing the boat's direction.

Just as a person has a left and right side, a boat has a left or port side or a right or starboard side as you stand and look forward on it. Turning around while aboard and looking aft will not change the port and starboard sides of the boat.

A boat is said to be making headway when it is going forward in the water and sternway when it is backing up. A boat is turning to port when its bow is moving to the left when making headway. A boat is said to be going to port when making sternway if its stern is moving to port.

Right and left rudder refer to the direction the rudder must be turned to cause the bow to turn to the right or left as the boat makes headway. The same is true when making stern-

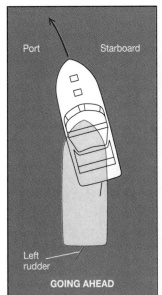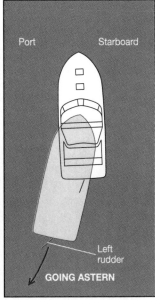

With left rudder in a boat going ahead *(above, left)*, the stern is thrown to starboard, bow to port. With left rudder when going astern *(above, right)*, the stern is thrown to port.

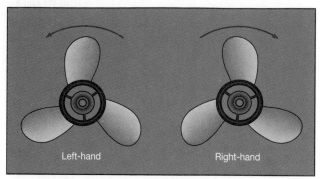

If you stand at the stern of a boat that is out of the water, and look at its propeller, you will be looking at the driving face of the propeller blades. If the propeller must turn to the right (clockwise) to push water toward you, the propeller is right-handed; if it turns in the opposite direction it is left-handed.

way. A boat with left rudder applied will turn its bow to port while making headway and swing its stern to port when making sternway.

Propellers are said to be right-handed or left-handed depending on the direction they turn. The difference is important because propeller rotation has a great bearing on how a boat maneuvers, especially when reversing. A propeller that turns clockwise when driving the boat ahead is right-handed, one that turns counterclockwise is considered left-handed. Most single propeller boats have right-handed propellers; dual propeller boats are likely to have a right-handed propeller on the starboard side and a left-handed propeller on their port.

It is not always easy to determine the hand of a propeller by looking at the rotation of the engine alone. The engine is bolted to a transmission that may change engine rotation depending on its reduction gearing. The rotation of the coupling connecting the transmission to the propeller shaft is,

This sport-fishing boat with its planing-type hull has only part of the hull in contact with the water when on a plane.

however, a true indication of the propeller shaft rotation. If, looking forward toward the transmission from aft of it, the shaft and coupling rotate clockwise when the transmission is in forward, then the shaft has a right-hand propeller.

Hull shape

In addition to propeller and rudder configuration, the hull shape of a boat has a strong influence on how it handles. Given the same wind and sea conditions, a trawler with its heavy displacement hull and deeper draft will behave differently than a lighter sport-fishing boat with its shallower draft, planing hull, flying bridge and, possibly, tuna tower.

Displacement-type hulls are heavily built and have a large load-carrying capacity, but are limited in the speed at which they can be driven through the water. Sailboats, trawlers and most large yachts fall into this category. Planing-type hulls are sometimes lighter in weight. They have less draft, and can be driven through the water fast enough to cause the hull to rise up out of the water and plane on top of it, keeping only a part of the hull in contact with the water. As a planing hull eventually slows down, it reaches a point where it reverts to the displacement mode.

Wind and current

A boat's handling characteristics are affected by wind and current, no matter what type of hull and power combination it has. Keeping a course or maneuvering in close quarters may be straightforward on a calm day during a slack tidal current, but the boat may become quite ill-mannered when coping with a stiff crosswind or crosscurrent. Since bows on many power-boats are higher than the sterns, they tend to fall off the wind when backing, despite anything that is done with the helm.

Hull type has the most effect on how a boat reacts to the current. Displacement-type hulls with considerable draft are affected by current to a greater extent than shallower-draft, lighter, planing-type hulls. Water is much denser than air, so a half-knot crosscurrent may have more effect on a displacement cruiser than a stiff 15- to 20-knot wind. On the other hand, given the same conditions, a planing-type hull with a high tuna tower could be more affected by wind than by current. Neither a displacement nor planing boat can ignore the wind or current. Skippers of both will find one of them a major factor affecting the boat's maneuverability. This becomes most apparent while running at low speed in close quarters.

Two boats of roughly the same size, one with a considerable hull draft forward but little aft, and another with relatively greater draft aft but more superstructure forward, have radical differences in their handling qualities. The governing factor is the relative area presented above the water to the wind, compared with the areas in the water, both fore and aft.

Finally, skippers sometimes refer to propellers as "wheels," especially when describing right- or left-handedness. Since most of the discussion in this chapter is about steering, we will use "propeller" exclusively.

UNDERSTANDING PROPELLERS AND RUDDERS

Powerboats are driven through the water by the action of their propellers, which act like pumps—drawing in a stream of water from forward (when going ahead), and throwing it out astern. Moving these streams of water aft creates an opposite forward thrust at the propellers, which is transmitted to the boat through the propeller shaft and its supporting structure. This drives the boat forward.

How propellers create thrust

The curved blades of the propeller are similar to other curved foils found on boats, for example a sailboat's sail, a fin keel or a rudder on any type of boat. When such a foil passes through a fluid, the flow is divided into two streams, one on either side

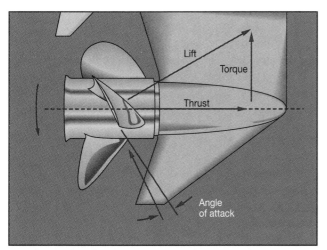

This illustration shows the relationship between lift, thrust and propeller torque.

of the foil. When a rudder is in a straight position, the water flows evenly on both sides. Turning the rudder causes an uneven flow, building pressure on one side and reducing it on the other. The rudder will then tend to move toward the low pressure, creating lift, and turning the boat in that direction.

A propeller blade creates force in a very similar way to the rudder. If the propeller were designed with blades that were flat rather than curved, and if the blades were simply spun around without any angle to their direction of travel, the propeller would turn through the water like a disk with equal flow on each side. However, this is not the case. The blades of the propeller are both curved and angled; as they pass through the water, they create lift. There is a low pressure area on the side of the blade facing forward and a high pressure area on the side facing aft.

Although the water drawn into the propeller does not actually flow from directly ahead like a thin column of water, for our purposes here it can be considered as coming in generally parallel to the keel. As the propeller ejects the water, it imparts a twist or spiral motion to that water. (The direction of rotation is dependent on the way the propeller turns.) This flow of water is called "screw current."

Regardless of whether the propeller is rotating to move the boat ahead or astern, the part of the current which flows into the propeller is called the "suction screw current." The part of the current ejected from the propeller is called the "discharge current." Discharge current, spiral in motion, is a compact stream of water that exerts greater pressure than the broader suction current.

Placing the rudder behind the propeller in the discharge current increases the steering effect because the rudder is acting in an accelerated flow. (Of course, there is a small rudder action from any flow of water past it even if the propeller is not turning.) A twin-screw cruiser has twin rudders, one behind each propeller, keeping the rudder blades directly in the propellers' discharge currents.

The pressure difference created by the propeller blade is called lift, and its force is roughly perpendicular to the blade itself. Lift can be divided into two components—a thrust component in the direction of travel and a torque component in the opposite direction of propeller rotation. You can easily see the effect of propeller torque when a runabout with a large engine accelerates; as the propeller begins to accelerate, the boat tends to dip on one side (generally on the port side with a right-hand propeller).

Unequal blade thrust

Turning propellers not only create forward or reverse thrust with their discharge current. They also produce forces that tend to push the propeller to one side or the other, depending on the direction of rotation. The effect of this unequal blade thrust is commonly referred to as propwalk.

This effect is most noticeable on inboard boats that have a propeller shaft set through the hull at an angle to the horizontal. Since the propeller is attached to the end of this shaft, it is positioned at the same angle and the water that flows into

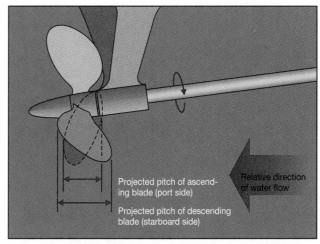

Angularity of the propeller shaft has the effect of increasing the pitch of the descending blade relative to that of the ascending blade, producing greater thrust to starboard. A left-hand wheel would produce greater thrust to port.

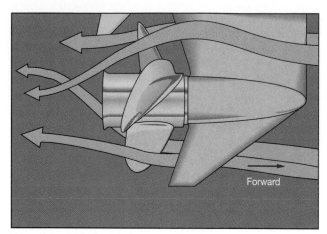

With the propeller turning ahead, suction screw current is drawn toward the propeller; the discharge current is driven out astern.

it meets the blades at different angles depending whether they are on the downward or upward part of their circle. The effective pitch of one blade is increased, the other reduced. For example, a forward-turning right-hand propeller would have the pitch of its starboard (descending) blade increased, while the pitch of the port (ascending) blade would be decreased. The relatively greater blade pitch on the starboard side creates a stronger thrust on that side. The stern of a single-screw boat with a right-hand propeller tends to go to starboard when the propeller is going ahead, with the bow turning to port; with reverse thrust, the effect that is created is just the opposite.

The importance of this factor is reduced as the shaft angle is decreased, so the effect of unequal blade thrust varies with each design. However, when the shaft angle is parallel to the flow of water into the propeller, the paddle wheel, or propwalk, effect may come into play: As an outboard is progressively raised, the propeller will eventually break the surface of the water. As this occurrence increases, a blade sweeping across the top, fanning through aerated water, will not pull as hard in a sideways or propeller torque direction as the fully submerged blade sweeping across the bottom of the propeller arc. This will cause a right-hand rotation propeller to "walk" to the right, much as a paddle wheel would do. This action in turn tries to pull the aft end of an outboard or stern drive to the right, causing the boat to go into a right-hand turn, if not resisted at the steering wheel.

Unequal blade thrust becomes more of a concern to lighter single-engine craft at higher speeds when the propeller is elevated closer to the water surface; the paddle wheel (propwalk) effect will eventually dominate any steering torque cause.

Ventilation and cavitation

Since all but a few high-speed, surface-piercing propellers rely on the smooth flow of water over their blades to create lift, a slight disturbance to this flow limits the overall efficiency of the propeller.

Ventilation occurs when air from the water's surface or exhaust gases from the exhaust are sucked into the screw current. The propeller then loses its grip on the water and over-revs, losing much of its thrust. Trying to turn an outboard too tightly at too high a speed often results in propeller ventilation.

Cavitation usually occurs at the tip of a propeller that is turning too fast. A spot on the tip of a propeller blade travels farther and faster during each revolution than does one near the hub. As the propeller rpms increase, the tip reaches a point where water simply can't flow past the tip without breaking down and forming small bubbles, much like boiling water. As these water vapor bubbles move along the surface of the metal, they eventually find an area of higher pressure where they collapse and cause damage. When collapsing, the bubbles release their stored energy onto the metal, acting like tiny jackhammers; the result is known as "cavitation burn."

Cavitation may result from a number of causes, including nicks in the leading edge, sharp leading edge corners (as shown below), improper polishing or poor blade design, severely bent propeller or broken blade tips, or ventilation.

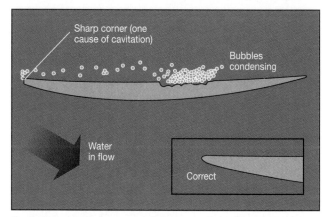

Cavitation results from a partial vacuum being formed by the blades of a propeller, with a consequent loss of thrust.

How a rudder acts

Most inboard boats have a vertical rudder blade located at the stern, attached to a rudder post that extends through a water-tight stuffing box into the boat. Movement of the steering wheel or tiller turns the rudder to port or starboard. The position of the rudder creates a higher pressure on one side of the rudder and a lower pressure on the other. As the rudder is pulled into its own lower pressure area, it takes the stern of the boat with it.

Steering wheels on motorboats are rigged in such a way that they turn with the rudder—turning the helm to port accordingly turns the rudder to port. Turning the helm to port thus gives left rudder; this then kicks the stern to starboard, so the bow in effect moves to port, starting a turn to the left. Conversely, turning the helm to starboard gives right rudder, throwing the stern to port so that the boat then turns to starboard (to the right).

The Arneson Drive is a high-performance system designed to reduce drag while enhancing positive-thrust steering. It uses surface-piercing propellers.

Small rudders are effective when there is considerable propeller current; but they develop little turning force at slow speeds or when the propeller is not turning. Sailboats and most single-prop heavy displacement powerboats have larger rudders and respond to the helm adequately at slow speeds.

At very slow propeller speeds, the boat's headway may not be sufficient to give control over the boat if wind or current are acting upon it. Take, for example, a strong wind on the port beam. Even with the rudder hard over to port, it may not be possible to make a turn into the wind until the propeller is speeded up—enough to exert a more powerful thrust against the rudder blade. As a vessel travels through the water, the minimum speed at which it can be controlled is called steerageway.

Turning circles

When any boat has headway and the rudder is put over to make a turn (to starboard, for example), the stern is first kicked to the opposite side (in this example, to port). The boat then tends to slide off obliquely, in a crablike fashion. Its momentum will carry it some distance along the original course before settling into a turn, in which the bow describes a smaller circle than the stern. The pivoting point may be aft from the bow between one-fourth and one-third of the boat's length, varying with different boats and changing for any given boat with its trim. While there is always a loss of speed in making a turn, the size of a boat's turning circle varies little with changes in speed, assuming a given rudder angle.

There is, however, a great difference in the size of turning circles for single-screw inboards as compared with outboards (or stern drive boats) because the shaft and propeller of the inboard are fixed on the center line and cannot be rotated. The twin-screw inboard, on the other hand, provides excellent maneuverability, as will be seen later.

It is important to consider the position of the rudder with respect to the pivot point of the hull when the boat is reversing. In this case, the pivot may be at one-fourth of the hull length from the transom. Therefore, the rudder is acting on a much shorter lever arm as it tries, sometimes in vain, to swing the hull off course.

When the boat has sternway (reversing) there is no powerful discharge current past the rudder, only the weaker, more diffuse suction screw current. The rudder normally would be turned to port (left rudder) to turn the stern of the boat to port; right rudder should normally turn the stern to starboard in backing. Under certain circumstances, the effect of the reversing propeller "walking" itself the other way may more than offset the steering effect of the rudder. The boat may actually continue to turn to the right, for example, despite left rudder angle.

Water depth also has an effect on a boat's steering. Even though the keel may be several inches above bottom, a boat's response to rudder action in shallow water is almost always very sluggish.

Steering with the propeller

In close quarters, a motorboat can often be turned within its own boat length by judicious use of rudder propeller power. Take, for example, a boat that has no headway: The throttle can be quickly opened and then closed, with the helm hard over. The stern then can be kicked around to port before the boat has a chance to gather headway. The exact technique of turning in limited space will be described in detail later in this chapter.

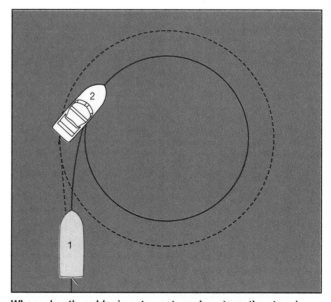

When a boat's rudder is put over to make a turn, the stern is kicked away from the direction in which the rudder moves. Then, after sliding obliquely along the course from 1 to 2, it settles into a turn in which the bow follows a smaller circle (red solid line) than the stern (red dotted line).

Outboard and inboard/outboard (I/O) boats do not have rudders. The boat is steered by directing the propeller thrust, by turning the outboard motor or stern-drive unit on which the propeller is mounted. Maneuvering an outboard or stern-drive boat is usually easier than a single-propeller inboard boat of the same type.

Directed propeller thrust makes slow speed maneuvering easier. The propeller discharge current is turned from side to side to create turning forces, unlike a boat with a rudder that must have water flowing by it to be effective. Outboard and stern-drive units are also designed to have very little or no shaft angle, so the propeller does not produce as much unequal blade thrust as does the propeller on an inboard boat. Larger, more powerful outboard motors and high-power stern-drive boats do, however, produce considerable propeller torque.

How an outboard or stern-drive boat reacts to the helm is difficult to predict exactly, but there are some general principles which apply in most typical situations. Some of these situations—basic maneuvers that any boater will likely have to complete during regular daily operation—are described below. This discussion assumes a typical boat with single outboard or stern-drive power.

Gathering headway

When an outboard or stern-drive boat is "dead in the water," that is, not moving forward or sternward, and the propeller is not turning, the boat will not respond to the helm. Since the propeller is not turning, it is not creating any discharge current, so no turning forces are created. Even though the boat may be moving over the bottom with a current, no water is passing by the lower unit of the outboard or stern-drive; therefore, it cannot act as a rudder.

As soon as the outboard or stern drive is shifted into forward gear, the propeller's action creates a discharge current and generates thrust. If the engine or stern drive is centered, the discharge current is directed straight back causing the boat to begin to move forward.

If you open the throttle quite quickly on a boat with a large outboard or stern drive, as you would when pulling a water-skier, for instance, the propeller will pull the stern of the boat to starboard like a single-screw inboard. Large outboards and some stern drives have small trim tabs located behind the propeller that help compensate for these forces, but a firm grip on the helm, before the throttle is opened, is also necessary.

As the boat gathers headway and the propeller begins to operate in the faster water flow for which it was designed, this unbalance usually lessens. If your boat wants to turn to port or starboard as soon as you let go of the helm, then the steering trim tab needs adjustment.

Turning

After the boat has gathered headway, with the helm amidships and the drive leg so that the boat is planing at a slight bow-up angle, the average boat tends to hold its course in a straight line fairly well. Once underway, the outboard or stern-drive boat is not affected to any significant degree by propwalk unless the drive leg is trimmed too far out or in.

If the helm is turned to the right or starboard, the outboard motor or stern drive is also turned in the same direction. The propeller's discharge current is directed to starboard, forcing the stern to port. Water flowing past the hull hits the lower unit on its starboard side, creating additional turning forces. The stern begins to move to port, causing the bow to turn to starboard.

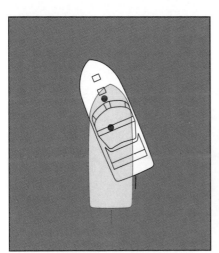

The boat in its gray position is dead in the water. When the forward gear is engaged, the stern is kicked to starboard; the amount of kick depends on the boat form and the amount of throttle given.

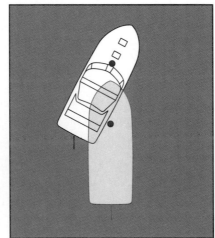

With forward motion when the helm is put over, the boat pivots around a point about one-third its length abaft the stem. Note that the stern swings through a wider arc than the bow.

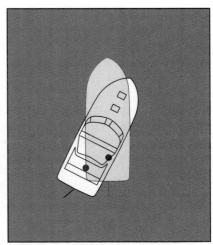

When backing down with the rudder to port, the pivot point is about one-quarter of the boat length forward of the stern. The bow, therefore, describes a wider arc than the stern.

STEP-BY-STEP DOCKING WITH AN OUTDRIVE

Outboard or inboard/outdrive powered boats are relatively easy to back up, but that may be scant comfort to the novice in a busy dock. The reversing propeller is turned in the direction you want to go, by using the wheel or motor handle or tiller. On some light displacement boats with shallow draft, the bow tends to be influenced by the wind.

When backing down in a crosswind, allow maneuvering room (to port in this example) and watch the bow carefully. If it begins to swing downwind you may have to stop backing, put the helm over to starboard (toward the wind) and go in forward to straighten the boat. A quick burst of power is all that is usually needed, but be careful that you don't knock your crew down with a sudden maneuver.

Set your speed to just overcome the effect of a crosswind. If it's not working, abort the maneuver early, reposition and wait for a lull in the wind.

1 Bring the boat to a stop by shifting into reverse. Put the helm over to port and begin backing in. Slow your speed by momentarily shifting into neutral.

2 Continue backing, with the helm over hard to port. Watch the bow, and begin to straighten the helm as the boat enters the slip.

3 Center the helm to align the boat parallel to the pier. If the stern is too close to the port side, shift to neutral, put the helm over to port and go forward for a second or two.

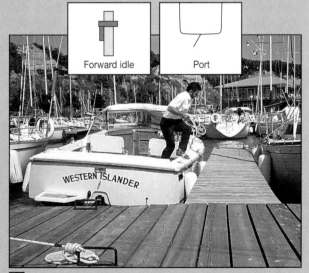

4 When fully into the slip, stop sternway by shifting into forward. Put the helm to port to kick the stern over close to the pier if necessary. Shift into neutral and secure the boat.

In order for the boat to begin its turn, the stern must be free to move to port. For example, the force of a water-skier tow line secured to the stern can make steering difficult, since it may prevent the stern from swinging to port. That is why competition ski boats secure the line to a towing post located well up into the boat, forward of the transom.

If the helm is turned to the left, the motor or stern drive turns to port; the stern of the boat moves starboard as the bow begins to turn to port.

At low speeds, there can be a considerable time lag between when the helm is put over and when the boat actually begins to turn. At high speeds, there is little lag in helm response. Small movements of the helm result in immediate action by the boat. The faster the boat moves through the water, the greater the forces generated by the water hitting the lower unit of the outboard or stern drive. Also, the discharge current increases in strength as the throttle is advanced and propeller rpm increases.

It is important to remember that the response of each boat depends on the maneuver and the speed at which it is undertaken. Actual experience at the helm at different speeds is the only way to become familiar with the handling characteristics of any boat.

Stopping

Unlike a car with brakes, your boat depends on reverse thrust in order to stop. Assume that the boat has headway, with the helm amidships and the propeller reversed. Now the propeller discharge current is directed backward, past the lower unit of the stern drive or outboard.

Depending on the throttle setting, the discharge current may not be strong enough to reverse the water flowing past the lower unit. As power is increased, the propeller discharge current becomes strong enough to stop the flow of water past the lower unit and, as the throttle is opened, more completely reverses its flow.

While water is flowing past the lower unit, there is some steering force generated, but when the discharge current stops the water flow, the boat will not respond to the helm. When the strong propeller discharge current is again flowing past the lower unit, steering is again restored. In addition to the force of the water hitting the lower unit, the propeller discharge current is directed by turning the outboard or stern drive, adding to the steering forces.

The propwalk of the reversing propeller tends to throw the stern to port, but to a lesser extent than a comparable inboard. This is why most experienced skippers make a portside landing when wind and current permit. They allow propwalk to walk the stern to port toward the wharf.

Backing down

If your boat is dead in the water with the motor or stern drive amidships, and you put it into reverse gear, the stern will be pushed slightly to port by the reversing propeller. The ten-

Having the tow line well forward of the transom will permit good maneuverability when towing a skier.

dency to back to port can easily be overcome by turning the engine or stern drive slightly to starboard.

Since outboards and stern-drive boats have the advantage of directing the propeller discharge current, and not relying on a rudder for steerage, you can also steer your boat by the judicious use of the throttle. The technique is to position the drive unit with the steering wheel while in gear or while at very low speed, then to give a short, sharp burst of throttle. The overall effect will be to push the stern in the desired direction while not adding an appreciable forward or sternward way to the boat.

As the boat begins to gather sternway, the water passing by the lower unit will begin to contribute to the steering force. Unlike most single-screw inboard boats, outboard and stern-drive boats back predictably. If the helm is put over to starboard, the motor or stern drive will turn to starboard, and will direct the propeller discharge current to port, moving the stern to starboard.

However, wind and current will affect how the boat backs. Outboard and stern-drive powered boats tend to be light displacement, shallow draft craft and, when backing down in a strong crosswind, the bow will tend to fall off downwind. This can cause steering difficulties. Remember that, in addition to the force of the wind on the forward topsides, the hull's pivot point has also moved aft, much closer to the drive unit. The steering forces are now acting on a much shorter lever as a result.

Usually, once sufficient headway is gathered in reverse, the force of the keel moving through the water is enough to keep the boat on track. Also remember that, when backing, the stern will lead as it moves to port or starboard, before the boat begins to turn.

SINGLE-SCREW INBOARD MANEUVERING

A single-screw inboard boat relies on water flowing past the rudder for maneuvering power. This is provided by the movement of the boat through the water and by the discharge current from the propeller. How well your boat responds to the helm in any given situation will depend largely on constant factors such as unequal blade thrust, propwalk and hull type. The variable factors are wind, current and the amount of rudder angle being used.

Every time you leave your slip or dock, certain basic maneuvers are necessary—getting underway, turning, stopping and backing down. Next is a description of how to perform these maneuvers in a single-engine inboard boat with a right-hand propeller—the most popular type. In addition, you will read about why your boat sometimes seems to have a mind of its own.

Gathering headway

Getting underway should be straightforward, but when you put the boat into forward gear with the rudder amidships it may not behave as you would expect. When you engage the forward gear and the propeller starts to turn ahead, the unequal blade thrust tends to move the stern to starboard. This can be frustrating when pulling away from a starboard-side dock. If you don't get your boat far enough away from the dock, the stern may swing in and hit it. Compensating by using right rudder may help, but it could also hamper the maneuver of getting away from the wharf or pier. The truly proper way to depart a wharf or pier is to back out—here the natural tendency of a boat will pull the stern out, and when the boat is clear of the dock, it can go forward, parallel to the wharf or pier face, at an adequate distance from it. If there is any tendency for wind or current to pin the boat against the wharf or pier face, go ahead on an after bow spring to get the stern out .

As the boat gathers headway, wake current (from the movement of the boat through the water) enters the picture, increasing pressure against the rudder. This tends to offset the effect of unequal blade thrust, and the average boat tends to hold course in a straight line fairly well.

From a purely theoretical standpoint, the unequal blade thrust, with a right-hand propeller, should tend to move the stern to starboard, and the bow to port. Once underway, the effect of unequal blade thrust is quite slight. Only in comparatively few cases will unequal blade thrust have a pronounced effect on steering, and in these it can be corrected by a small rudder tab.

Turning

Now that your boat has headway, assume the rudder is put to starboard. The water flowing past the hull hits the rudder on its starboard side, forcing the stern to port. The propeller's discharge current intensifies this effect by acting on the same side, and the boat's bow turns to starboard, the same side on which the rudder is set.

How fast a boat will react to the helm is dependent on the size of the rudder and hull shape, but the most influential factor is how fast the boat is moving through the water. At slow speeds, with the engine idling or turning slowly, a heavy boat will have a considerable lag between the time its helm is put over and the time the boat actually begins to turn. At idle speeds, there is less water flowing past the rudder, and the propeller discharge current is weak; so it may take a boat several seconds to begin a turn. You may also have to give the boat considerably more rudder to get the same response you achieved at higher speeds.

Of course, the opposite is also true. A boat traveling fast has a very powerful flow of water past the rudder; with a very strong propeller discharge current, it responds much more quickly to helm movement. At speed, a light fast-planing type inboard has a very positive feel to the helm, with no noticeable lag between helm movement and turning.

The boat's turning radius is determined by how much the helm is turned at both high and slow speeds. How quickly the boat responds to helm movement is basically a factor of how fast it is moving.

Stopping

Stopping a boat is achieved by reversing the propeller. Assume that your boat has headway, with the rudder amidships, and the propeller is reversed. The rudder has decreasing steering effect as the boat slows, and unequal blade thrust of the reversed propeller tends to throw the stern to port. At the same time, on some boats the propeller blades on the starboard side are throwing their discharge current in a powerful column forward against the starboard side of the keel and bottom of the boat, with little on the port side to offset this pressure. This also adds to the forces moving the stern to port.

If wind and current permit, an experienced boater will make a port-side approach to a pier with a single-engine boat that has a right-hand propeller. By reversing the propeller, the stern then is moved in toward the dock, instead of away from it.

Backing down

If the boat is lying dead in the water with no headway, rudder amidships, and the propeller is reversed, we again have the strong tendency of the stern to go to port as the discharge current strikes the starboard side of the hull. In each case where the discharge current of the reversing propeller is a factor, the strong current on the starboard side is directed generally toward the boat's bow but upward and inward in a spiral movement. The descending blade on the port side, on the other hand, tends to throw its stream downward at such an angle that its lesser force is largely spent below the keel. Therefore, the two forces are never of equal effect.

Until the boat gathers sternway from its backing propeller, it would not matter if the rudder were over to port or starboard. The discharge current against the starboard side is still the strong controlling factor and thus the stern will be moved to port.

Now visualize the boat gathering sternway as the propeller continues to reverse. Here arises one of the seemingly mystifying conditions that baffle many a new helmsman. The novice assumes that in order to back in a straight line the rudder must be amidships, just as it must be when going ahead on a straight course. But under certain conditions the boat may even respond to *right* rudder as the boater reverses by going to *port,* which is totally unexpected.

If the boater is learning by trial-and-error it is easy to come to the conclusion that it depends on the boat's fancy, while rudder position has nothing to do with control. Fortunately, something can be done about it.

■ **Backing with left rudder.** Consider a boat in reverse with left rudder. Here there are four factors all working together to throw the stern to port. Unequal blade thrust is pushing the stern to port; the discharge current of the propeller is adding its powerful effect; and now we add the steering effect of the rudder acting on the after side of the rudder blade, against which the suction current of the propeller is also working.

Remember this condition well, for it is the answer to why *practically every single-screw vessel with right-hand propeller easily backs to port,* although it may be obstinate about going to starboard when reversing.

■ **Backing with rudder amidships.** If, while backing to port, you bring the rudder amidships, you eliminate the effects of suction current and steering from the rudder. This leaves unequal blade thrust and the discharge current to continue forcing the stern to port.

■ **Backing with right rudder.** Assuming further that you have not yet gathered much sternway, you might expect that putting the rudder to starboard should make the boat back to starboard. The forces of unequal blade thrust and discharge current still tend to drive the stern to port, but the suction current of the propeller wants to offset this.

The effect of the discharge current is stronger than the suction so the overall tendency is still to port. With sternway, the steering effect of the right rudder is to starboard, but as yet you haven't way enough to make this offset the stronger factors.

■ **Steering while backing.** Opening the throttle to gain more sternway finally has the desired effect; with full right rudder you will find that the steering effect at considerable backing speed is enough (probably) to turn the stern to starboard against all the opposing forces. How well the boat will back to starboard—in fact, whether it will or not—depends on the design of the craft.

All of this means that if the boat will back to starboard with full right rudder, it may also be made to go in a straight line—but not with the rudder amidships. There's no use trying. The boat will need a certain amount of right rudder depending both on its design and on speed. While some boats

always back to port much better than to starboard, a boater can learn to control a particular boat with a reasonable degree of precision.

In some cases, boats may even be steered backwards out of crooked slips or channels—not, however, without a lot of backing and filling if there is much wind to complicate the situation. Generally, the trick is to keep the boat under control, making the turns no greater than necessary to keep the boat from swinging too much.

In backing situations, set the rudder first and *then* add maneuvering power by speeding up the propeller.

■ **Killing sternway.** There is one other situation to be considered, where you want to kill sternway by engaging the propeller to turn ahead. Regardless of the rudder position, unequal blade thrust with the propeller going ahead now tends to throw the stern to starboard, while the suction current is of little or no consequence. In this situation, unequal blade thrust may or may not be offset by the steering effect and the discharge current.

With rudder amidships, there is no steering effect and the discharge current does not enter into calculations. Therefore the stern will go to starboard. Now if you throw the rudder to port the discharge current of the propeller hits the rudder and drives the stern to starboard—even though the normal steering effect of left rudder sends the stern to port, with sternway. The powerful discharge current from the propeller going ahead is the determining factor.

If the rudder is put to starboard, the steering effect works with the unequal blade thrust, tending to move the stern to starboard, but the discharge current strikes the starboard side of the rudder and acts to kick the stern to port. Be sure to apply enough power so that the force of the discharge current outweighs the other factors, and the stern will indeed go to port.

Propeller action governs

From the above analysis it is clear that in a single-screw inboard boat you must be constantly aware of what the propeller is doing, in order to know how best to use the rudder. What the propeller is doing is even more important than whether the boat has headway or sternway.

Left-handed propellers

Maine lobstermen prefer a left-handed propeller because it allows them to back down quickly on a lobster pot while standing at the starboard helm station, near the gunnerhole, ready to lift the lobster pot aboard. Many commercial boats also operate a left-handed propeller, but for a different reason: It helps them leave a starboard pier and back up against it with more control.

If your boat is equipped with a left-handed propeller, you can generally reverse "port" and "starboard" in the foregoing discussions. But to be absolutely sure, make tests for all possible situations.

STEP-BY-STEP DOCKING WITH A SINGLE-SCREW BOAT

With a right-hand propeller, back to port when entering a slip. How fast you can turn your boat determines when to stop and when you should begin backing. A high freeboard and flybridge may respond to crosswind, so choose your moment so as to avoid sudden gusts.

Propeller action will help most single-screw boats turn to port when backing. With the helm hard to port, the boat should begin a turn into the slip.

Usually the boat will need some help kicking its stern farther to port to align itself with the slip. Going ahead with a short burst of power, with helm over to starboard, will accomplish this. Some right rudder will probably be needed to make the boat back in a straight line into the slip, but remember that the torque of the propeller to port (in reverse) often has more influence than the position of the rudder. If a short burst of power is needed, position the rudder first, then apply the power.

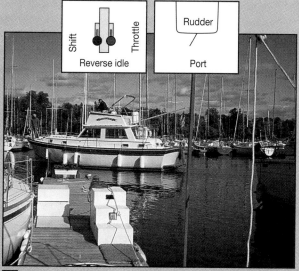

1 Shift into reverse to stop the boat, then put the helm over hard to port to start the turn into the slip. A slight increase in power will cause the boat to turn a bit quicker.

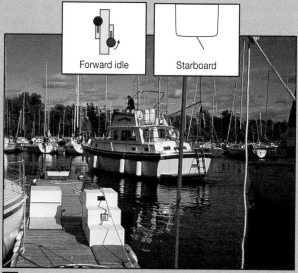

2 Shift into forward as you enter, put the helm over to starboard and open the throttle for a short burst of power. This kicks the stern to port, aligning the boat with the slip.

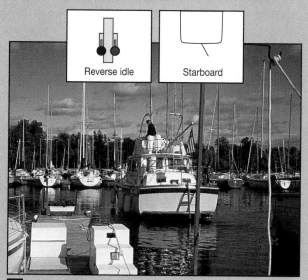

3 Shift into reverse and keep the helm to starboard in order to overcome the propeller walk to port and back straight into the slip.

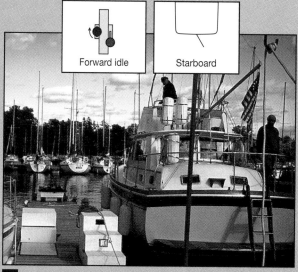

4 When fully in the slip, put the gear in forward to stop sternway. Keep the helm to starboard in order to kick the stern closer to the dock—or to port if it is too close.

TWIN-SCREW MANEUVERING

Twin-screw craft have two rudders, one directly behind each propeller. The propellers are counter-rotating, which balances any steering pull, and will generally rotate "out"—the right-hand rotation on the right side and the left-hand rotation on the left side.

Going ahead with the starboard wheel for a turn to port, the offset of the propeller from the center line adds greatly its effect of throwing the stern to starboard. Similarly, offset of the port wheel going ahead helps the steering effect when the port propeller is going ahead for a turn to starboard.

When reversing, the starboard wheel throws its discharge current against the starboard side of the hull to help the turn of the stern to port. Likewise, the port propeller reversing throws its stream against the port side of the hull to help the swing of the stern to starboard.

The important factors in turning and steering are thus combined by the outward-turning wheels. The steering effect is exerted in the same direction as the turning movement caused by the off-center location of the propellers.

Gathering headway

Unlike a boat with a single propeller, if the transmission gears of a twin-screw boat are put in forward together, the boat will begin to make headway without any tendency to pull to starboard or to port.

Turning

Clearly, having two propellers gives you the means of shifting one propeller or the other ahead or astern, independent of rudder control. In fact, much of a twin-screw boat's slow-speed maneuvering is done without touching the steering wheel; working the clutches and throttles is the key to controlling the boat's movements.

A boat's stern may be put to one side or the other by going ahead or backing down one propeller, without turning the other. Some headway or sternway in these cases accompanies the turn. The maximum turning effect is, of course, obtained when one propeller is turning ahead and the other is in reverse—the two effects are additive.

With practice, you can easily turn a twin-screw boat in a circle only a little larger than the boat's length. For example, to turn to starboard, the rudders can be set amidships while the port engine goes ahead and the starboard engine reverses; on most boats, turning the rudder will tighten the turn.

Start this type of turn with the engines at idle or turning slowly at the same speed. To turn to starboard, put the port gear in forward and the starboard gear in reverse. As the boat begins to turn, it may start to make some headway. (This is not surprising, since the boat drives forward more easily than it goes astern, and the propeller develops more thrust at a given rpm while turning ahead than astern because the propeller blades are curved so as to produce lift on the forward side.) To compensate, you will probably have to open the starboard throttle slightly to increase the rpm of the revers-ing starboard propeller. For both engines, a rate of rpm can be found that will turn the boat in its own length.

When the port engine is speeded up a little, the circle is larger and the boat makes some headway. If the port engine is slowed down, the circle is also larger, but the boat makes some sternway as the reversing starboard wheel pulls it around, stern to port.

Steering with the throttles

If your boat happens to sustain some damage to the steering gear, it can still make port by steering with the throttles (provided that the rudders are not jammed hard over to one side). One engine can be allowed to turn at a constant speed—the starboard one, for example. Then open the throttle of the port engine to speed up the port propeller and cause a turn to starboard. Closing the throttle of the port engine slows down the port propeller and allows the starboard propeller to push ahead, causing a turn to port; keep your speed moderate when doing this, as steering is not as positive as with rudders. Since most slow-speed maneuvering is done with the propellers, when you get back to port you will be able to maneuver into your berth.

Stopping

A twin-screw boat is stopped by reversing its propellers, but unlike a single-screw vessel, this will usually not throw the stern to one side.

When docking, the experienced helmsman of a single-screw boat usually tries to make a port-side approach so that, when the vessel is stopped, the reversing propeller will swing the stern toward the dock. The skipper of a twin-screw boat can use this technique on both port and starboard approaches. By reversing the outboard engine to check headway when coming up parallel to the dock, the stern will move in. On a port-side approach the reversing starboard right-hand propeller will move the stern to port. When approaching to put the craft's starboard side to the pier, the reversing port propeller will conveniently move the stern to starboard.

Backing down

The helmsman of a twin-screw vessel has a great advantage over the operator of a single-screw type because the boat will most likely answer the helm as expected. Not considering wind and current, most twin-screw boats can be steered with the rudder when backing down. Rudder action, however, will be less than when going ahead, since the propellers' discharge currents are directed away from the rudder rather than onto them.

In addition to rudders, the twin-screw vessel offers the possibility of using its throttles to slow down one engine or the other as an aid to steering while maintaining sternway. Alternatively, you can stop one propeller or go ahead on it for maximum control in reverse.

STEP-BY-STEP DOCKING WITH A TWIN-SCREW BOAT

Most twin-screw boats are maneuvered in close quarters by using the propellers. Depending on wind or current conditions, stop the boat in front of the slip, or slightly to windward or up current. (The rudder may be used if needed.)

The sequence below is intended as an example. Depending on the circumstances, this will sometimes be done in the opposite manner, swapping "starboard" for"port," and vice versa. In this example, both throttles are in idle and you begin backing.

As the boat gathers way, it will begin to back to port. By going forward with the port engine, the boat can be made to pivot and to align with the slip. When alignment is satisfactory, the port engine is also put in reverse to continue backing into the slip. Slight adjustment in direction can be made by putting either gear momentarily in forward. Going forward on the port engine kicks the stern to port; the starboard engine going forward kicks the stern to starboard.

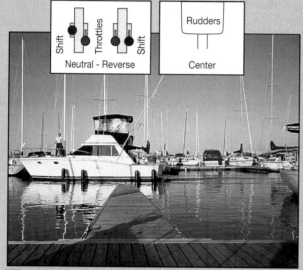

1 Stop headway with the starboard engine in reverse; the stern will begin to move to port. Then continue backing, with the starboard and port engines at idle.

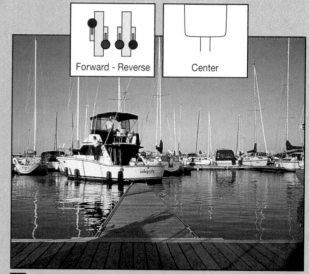

2 As sternway builds and you enter the slip, go ahead with the port engine to align the boat with the slip.

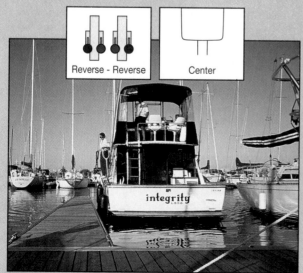

3 With the boat aligned with the slip, put both engines in reverse; continue backing into the slip. If either engine is put in forward, the stern will move in the same direction.

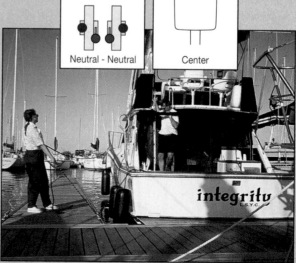

4 When fully into the slip put both engines in forward momentarily to kill all sternway. Secure the boat.

MANEUVERING IN TIGHT QUARTERS

Since most harbors and anchorages are congested places, handling a boat in these confined spaces can be a real test of your skills. In fact, in some harbors, leaving and returning to your berth can be the most harrowing part of a cruise. Most of the basic maneuvers that you will need to get underway from, and return to, your slip or mooring safely are covered below.

Getting underway

As skipper, you are responsible for the safe operation of your boat. Before you leave the slip, be sure that all your getting-underway procedures are completed. Make sure that all electrical cords and hoses are disconnected, and take off all but the last-minute dock lines. Avoid spending too much time at the dock or mooring warming up the motor; long periods of idling are not good for the motor or the transmission. The engine will warm up faster under the light load of a propeller.

Checking headway

The only way to stop a boat's headway is by reversing the propeller. Experiment with stopping the boat from different speeds. This will give you an idea about the propeller's ability to check the boat's headway. Consider the following:

■ Generally speaking, a larger diameter propeller, acting on a large volume of water, will exert a greater effect. Small propellers, especially those on outboards, may do a lot of churning before they can overcome the boat's momentum.

■ You can stop a fast boat in a short distance by cutting the throttles. Then, as the boat comes off of plane, shift into reverse and apply power.

■ When practicing these maneuvers, take the following precaution: When you need to go from forward into reverse or vice versa, slow the engine down while going through neutral. If you make a practice of shifting from full ahead into full astern, you will sooner or later tear up the gears. Warn crew members and passengers of your intentions so that they will not be unexpectedly thrown off balance, possibly injuring themselves.

■ Always remember to approach piers as well as other craft at a very slow speed. Failure of the transmission, or an unexpected stopping of the engine, can result in embarrassment or damage.

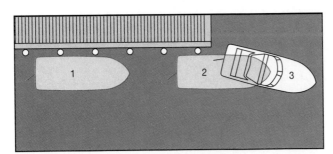

With right rudder, as the boat moves from 1 to 2 to 3, the stern is driven against the piles, with risk of damage. The rudder should be amidships until the boat is clear (or the craft should first be backed away from the face of the pier).

Turning in close quarters

Although turning a boat in a narrow channel or other confined waterway not much wider than the boat itself may seem impossible to the novice, it is really no more difficult than turning a car around on a narrow road.

Suppose, for example, that you have reached the head of a dead-end canal and must turn around. Assuming you have a single-screw boat with a right-hand propeller, steer to the left side of the channel and make all forward maneuvers to starboard and backing maneuvers to port, to take advantage of the boat's natural tendencies. Now, running at slow speed, put the rudder hard over to starboard and, as the boat begins to turn, check headway by reversing. Leave the wheel hard over to starboard (right rudder). Very little is gained by applying right rudder while going ahead and left rudder while going astern, since the boat will make little way through the water. As the reversing propeller stops the boat, open the throttle for an instant; the stern will be kicked farther to port. Then put the gear in forward and open the throttle for a short burst

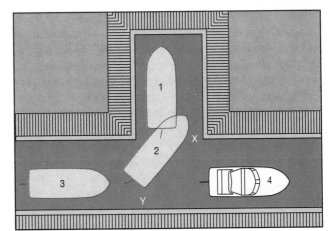

To back out from a slip, the boat should be able to make a short turn to port from 1 to 2, when reversing with left rudder, but if the bow swings wide it may hit at X and Y.

of power, to check any sternway and keep the stern swinging to port. As soon as the boat gathers headway, shift into reverse and back down to kick the stern to port; then shift into forward again.

Most single-screw inboard boats can be maneuvered in very tight quarters by using this technique. Unequal propeller thrust in combination with rudder action turns the boat. However, remember that this technique will only work with starboard turns on a right-hand propeller.

A twin-screw boat can reverse one engine and run ahead on the other in order to make the same turn. Although outboards and stern-drive boats can use this technique, they are usually able to make a turn like this with a single forward-reverse cycle. It will be necessary to turn the wheel from one side to the other when going from forward to reverse and vice versa.

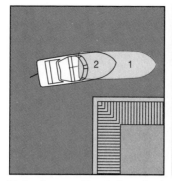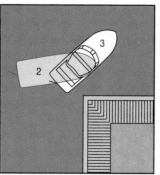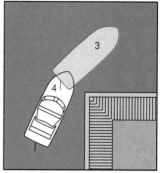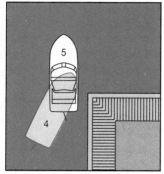

To back around to starboard, where space is limited, the boat starts *(left)* at 1 with right rudder and backs to 2, as it cannot turn short to starboard. At 2, the rudder is shifted to port, and the stern is kicked to starboard to position 3 by going ahead strong for a few seconds. From 3, the boat is backed to 4 with full right rudder. Here the rudder is put to port, and the boat moves ahead to 5. Backing down from 5, it will need a certain amount of right rudder to maintain straight course.

Backing to port from a slip

When leaving a slip, an experienced skipper will back a single-screw boat with a right-hand propeller to port. Suppose the boat is lying in a slip and you intend to back out into the channel. With left rudder, it will likely turn fast enough as it gathers sternway, aligning with the channel in one maneuver.

Before putting the boat in reverse, pull the boat to the port side of the slip, ensuring as much clearance as possible on the starboard side. Although some room is necessary on the port side because the stern immediately starts to move to port, more room is required on the starboard side because the bow will swing this way as the boat backs.

The starboard bow and port stern are the places to watch in executing this maneuver. If the boat turns sharper than expected, the starboard bow is in danger of touching the adjacent pier *(page 196, right)* or a boat in the adjacent slip. This could be corrected by going ahead with the propeller a few revolutions while backing out of the slip. Once the bow is clear of the slip, right rudder followed by a short burst of power in forward will help kick the stern over to port if it is not turning fast enough while making sternway.

Backing to starboard from a slip

In a different scenario, suppose you want to back out of the same situation outlined above or from a slip into a narrow canal that would require a sharp turn to starboard.

Reversing with full right rudder, you will not be able to turn short enough to steer around the 90-degree angle before you would come up on the opposite canal bank. Most likely, you will back to a position somewhere in the middle of the canal with the stern slightly to starboard. Now, by going ahead with left rudder, the stern is kicked further over to starboard.

Reversing once more, with full right rudder, the boat backs to starboard and, just as it begins to make sternway, you go ahead once more with left rudder. This checks the sternway and kicks the stern to starboard in alignment with the channel.

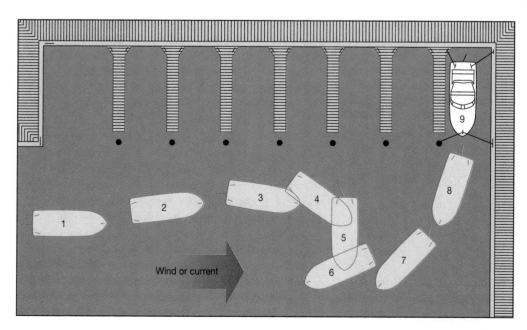

Backing into a berth between piles in a basin, where space allows a turn ahead under power to maneuver the bow partly into the wind before backing down: Note the right rudder from 5 through 8 keeps the stern from swinging to port.

Wind or current

Backing into a berth between piles

Many marinas and yacht clubs provide slips in which boats are berthed at right angles to a pier or wharf and made fast to piles. Normally, a short secondary pier, often called a finger pier or catwalk, extends out between each pair of slips. In this situation, it is much easier to board the boat if it is moored with the stern toward the dock. This arrangement makes for an easy departure, but requires backing into the slip upon return. There are many variables that come into play as you back into the slip: Wind, current and the location of other boats are just a few. At times some of these factors may be so disconcerting that you may decide not to back into the slip, but instead to dock bow first until conditions improve. A wise man who said "Discretion is the better part of valor" must have been thinking of this situation.

Now let's consider another situation: You have spent a nice day on the water, and are returning to your slip—one of hundreds located on a pier in a large marina; you want to back in. As you turn into the channel, the slip is to port and you are moving with a light wind and current. The channel is only a couple of boat lengths wide, so there is not much room for maneuvering. In this situation, the port side of the channel should be favored to allow for wind and current. Begin your turn before the slip, in order to position the boat upwind and/or up-current of it.

Depending on how quickly the boat can be turned, put the helm over to starboard well before you reach the slip. Because the channel is narrow, the boat will not be able to turn more than 90 degrees, almost into the wind, in a single maneuver *(page 197, top)*. As the bow approaches the other side of the channel, shift into reverse and open the throttle to stop headway and kick the stern to port. As soon as the boat gathers sternway, shift to forward and open the throttle to kick the stern farther to port; position the boat at about a 45-degree angle to the slip.

The turn should be timed so that the final position of the boat is slightly upwind from the slip, with the wind and current off the starboard quarter. If you are not upwind of the slip, complete the turn and run upwind until you are. If you are too far upwind, wait for the current to push you down closer to the slip.

Begin backing with right rudder. As soon as you start backing, the current and wind will push the bow to port so that, by the time the stern is entering the slip, the boat will be nearly parallel with the slip. Remember, when backing a boat with a right-hand propeller, use left rudder in combination with a short burst of forward power to move the stern to starboard. Left rudder with the propeller reversing should move the stern to port.

Getting clear of a pile

In maneuvering around slips and piles, you may be caught in a position where the wind and/or current hold the boat against the pile, preventing any maneuver. The solution is to rig a for-

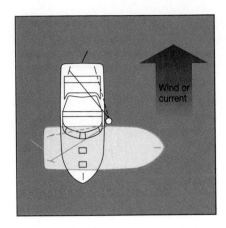

If pinned against a piling, use a forward spring line from a stern cleat to swing the boat into the wind or current.

ward spring line from the pile to an aft cleat, preferably on the side of the boat away from the pile. Then, by reversing with left rudder, pivot the boat around the pile and bring the bow into the wind or against the current. You can then clear the pile by going ahead with power as the spring is cast off.

In getting clear from this point, you may need a little left rudder to keep the stern clear of the pile, but don't use enough to throw the stern so far over that the starboard quarter is in danger of hitting an adjacent pile.

Plan maneuvers in advance

Obviously the number of possible situations—considering the differences in boats and the strength, direction and effect of wind and current—is almost infinite. Usually, however, applying one of the principles above, modified as needed, will permit a seamanlike handling of the problem.

Even though you know the principles, however, it pays to think ahead about the steps you will take. With a clear plan of action, you can take each step slowly and easily, and have time to keep the boat under perfect control. To avoid confusion, tell your crew the steps you plan to follow, the actions that each crew member will have to take, and the orders you will give when these actions are required. Even on occasions that call for swift and decisive action, you'll need calm, ordered judgment.

If your plan of action requires complete abandonment because of unforeseen conditions, don't hesitate to act accordingly. For example, if your plan for a clean approach to a pier or wharf has been upset by a freak current you couldn't calculate, back off and square away for another attempt. That in itself is good seamanship regardless of how others may judge your apparent "miss" on the first try. Common sense, if you act with deliberation, will enable you to work out a solution for any combination of conditions.

When you are at the helm and you have people on deck handling lines, give orders to each so that all action is under your control, instead of having two or three acting independently to cross purposes. This is especially imperative when your crew is not familiar with boats or with your method of boat handling.

Leaving a mooring

Yacht club and marina anchorages often have mooring buoys chained to mushroom anchors or heavy concrete blocks on the bottom. Boats are secured by a pennant or mooring line to a forward cleat or bitt. These boats are accessible from shore by dinghy or by club launch.

Getting away from the mooring is among the simplest of maneuvers, yet there is a right and a wrong way to go about it. When done incorrectly, the greatest dangers are getting the mooring line or dinghy painter fouled in the propeller, or colliding with a boat moored nearby.

After running through your departure checklist, make sure that the boarding ladders and fenders are brought on board. Then send someone forward to let the pennant go; there is usually a small buoy to float the pennant, making it easy to pick up again when you return.

If your mooring is in a bay or the day is calm, there may be neither wind nor current to move the boat when the mooring line is let go. To go ahead under such conditions would almost certainly foul the mooring line in the propeller. To avoid this, back away a few boat lengths, far enough so you can have the buoy in sight and give it ample room when you go ahead. You can decide to back away straight or turn as you reverse— depending on the position of neighboring boats.

When your mooring is in a stream, or if a tidal current flows past it, the boat will be set back when the mooring line has been let go. This usually simplifies the problem of getting away, so reversing may not be necessary.

In a wind (assuming the current is not stronger), the boat will be lying head to the wind. As the boat drops back from the mooring—whether or not the reverse gear is used—the bow will pay off to one side and allow getting away without additional maneuvering.

Boats with considerable freeboard have a strong tendency to "tack" back and forth as they lie at anchor in a wind; the same is true to an extent at permanent moorings. If the bow is tacking in this manner, and you want to leave the mooring buoy on one particular side, wait until the boat reaches the limit of its swing in the desired direction, then let the pennant go.

Picking up a mooring

Returning to the anchorage, approach your mooring at a slow speed. Note how other boats are lying at their buoys. They are heading into the wind or current (whichever is stronger), and your course in approaching your mooring should be roughly parallel to their heading. Stay clear of other moorings, or you may cut or foul them.

If your mooring is the only mooring in the anchorage, you will have to gauge the effect of wind and current on your boat as best you can. Pass by the mooring so you can judge the current and then approach—upwind, or against the current, or directly against any combination of these factors.

Shift into neutral when you estimate that you have enough headway to carry you up to the buoy. Station a crew member well forward on the bow, with a boat hook to pick up the pennant float. If you see that you are about to overshoot the mark, reverse enough to check the headway as the bow comes up to the buoy. If you fall short, a few slight kicks ahead with the propeller will help. The helmsman will not be able to see the mooring buoy, so good communication is essential. The person on the bow must indicate the buoy's position and maneuvering required to bring the boat close enough to reach the pennant with the boat hook; previously agreed-upon hand signals are preferable to shouting.

Do not expect the person forward to do the engine's work in holding the boat in position. Until the signal is given that the pennant eye has been secured on the bitt, keep the engine ready in case the boat tends to drop astern. Also, take care that the buoy does not chafe against the hull. If you do overshoot or fall off and your crew forward cannot reach the pennant, get clear and try again calmly.

When picking up a mooring, approach slowly so that you come to a halt as you reach the buoy. The forward crew member should not have to hold the boat against the wind while picking up the pennant.

DOCK LINES AND THEIR USES

Dock or mooring lines play an important part in the handling of vessels at a dock. Obviously, as boat size increases, more and heavier lines are needed. A small, light outboard craft requires fewer lines for secure mooring than does a heavy 50-foot trawler. But both skippers should know and understand how lines are used, so that they can decide which lines are appropriate. In addition to securing a boat in its berth, the proper use of lines can aid maneuvering close to docks.

Dock line terminology

Although most skippers speak quite loosely of bow and stern lines, it generally matters little as long as the line is made fast forward or aft. However, there are several lines that can be secured to the bow or stern and, depending on their direction and use, these are given other names. (Note that forward and after relate to the direction in which a spring line runs from the vessel, and not to where it is made fast on board.)

■ **Bow and stern lines.** According to correct nautical terminology, there is only one bow line. This is made fast to the forward cleat and run forward along the dock to prevent the boat from moving astern. The stern line leads from an after cleat to a pile or cleat on the pier astern of the boat; this line checks

the boat from going ahead. For securing a small craft, these lines are often the only ones that are required. If they are given the proper slack, they can allow for considerable rise and fall of the tide.

■ **Breast lines.** These are lines, secured to the bow and stern, that lead athwartships nearly at right angles to the vessel and to the dock. They are used on larger vessels to keep the boat from moving away from the dock or to pull the craft in for boarding. Large craft may use bow or quarter breasts, depending on where they are secured. Naturally, breast lines on large vessels are more important than on small ones.

Smaller recreational boats frequently will have only one bitt or cleat forward, and one or two aft, for securing dock lines. Additional cleats along the sides, properly through-bolted, give good flexibility in using dock lines.

■ **Spring lines.** Although only two spring lines generally are used at any one time, there may be as many as four: the forward bow spring, the after bow spring, the forward quarter spring and the after quarter spring. Bow springs are made fast to the vessel near or at the bow; quarter springs are near or at the stern. Forward springs lead forward from the vessel to the pier or wharf, and control movement sternward. After

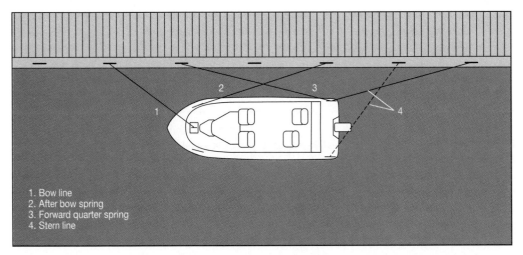

1. Bow line
2. After bow spring
3. Forward quarter spring
4. Stern line

As shown in this typical small boat mooring, crossing spring lines gains a greater length for them. This is particularly useful where tidal range is significant. The stern line is often run to the offshore stern cleat to gain better length while still holding the stern into the pier

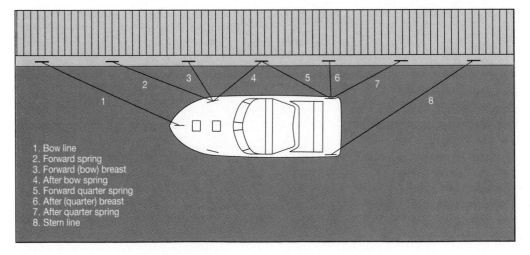

1. Bow line
2. Forward spring
3. Forward (bow) breast
4. After bow spring
5. Forward quarter spring
6. After (quarter) breast
7. After quarter spring
8. Stern line

Possible docking lines for a vessel include the eight types shown at left. A small boat will never need to use all of these. The stern line can be run to either stern cleat to gain better length and to hold the stern into the pier.

springs lead aft from the vessel, and check movement ahead. Spring lines are used to prevent movement in a berth, ahead or astern. They work with the bow and stern lines to keep a boat in position where there is a significant rise and fall of tide. This is particularly desirable where fenders must be kept in place against piles.

Sizing the line to the boat

On most recreational boats, dock lines are usually made from nylon, either of twisted rope or braided core and cover. Nylon is the preferred material because it stretches absorbing shock loads, is chafe-resistant for long life, and is easy on the hands.

The line's size varies with the boat. Typically, a 20- to 40-footer will use ½-inch diameter nylon lines, with larger yachts going up to ¾-inch lines. Smaller boats can use ⅜-inch nylon.

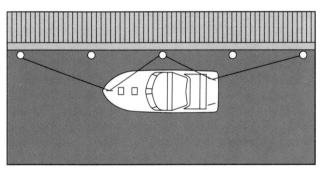

Separate spring lines may be placed on the same pile or onshore cleat, or a single line may be secured to bow, pile and stern.

Dock lines should be strong enough to hold the boat and have enough bulk to resist chafe, while not being so heavy as to lose their shock-absorbing characteristics. A light boat pulling against a ¾-inch line will come up hard against the line because the weight of the boat is not enough to cause the line to begin to stretch. On the other hand, a light ⅜-inch line holding a heavy boat will be very springy and probably strong enough for average conditions. However ⅜-inch line gives no margin for wear and chafe when under heavy strain.

Mooring a boat

Most average-sized boats can be made fast to a dock using four lines. The after bow spring is crossed with the forward quarter spring, and secured to separate dock cleats or piles. This arrangement provides longer springs, which can be drawn up rather snugly and still allow for a rise and fall of tide. If only one pile or cleat is available, position your boat so that this point is opposite amidships; then run both springs to it. The lines will be shorter, but still effective.

The bow and stern lines should make roughly a 45-degree angle with the dock. The stern line can be secured to the near-shore quarter cleat, but will work better if run to the offshore quarter cleat. The longer line will allow the boat to rise and fall with the tide with less tending.

When mooring your boat, fasten the lines securely at both ends. Often you will loop the eye splice of the dock line around a pile. If your boat has much freeboard, or the tide is high, the mooring line will lead down sharply from deck to dock. To prevent it from being pulled up off the pile, loop the eye splice around the pile twice. If the eye in your mooring line is too small to go around the pile twice, or even fit over the pile once, pull the line through the spliced eye to make a new loop.

If you must drop a line over a pile that already holds another boat's line, run the eye of your line up through the first eye from below. Then loop it over the pile. This will allow either line to be removed without disturbing the other. If you find that another line is dropped over yours on a pile or cleat, simply reverse the process: Get a little slack in the other line, then slip your eye up through its loop and over the top of the pile. Your line then can be dropped through the eye of the other.

When leaving a dock, or maneuvering against spring or other dock lines, it is convenient to be able to release the line from the pile or cleat—from aboard the boat—as soon as you get away from the dock. By looping a long line around the pile or cleat, and leading both ends on board, you can easily release it: Slip one end around the pile or cleat, then pull it back aboard. Be sure to release the end of the line without the eye splice, so it will run freely around the pile or cleat without hanging up at the splice.

To throw a line to someone on shore, coil the line in your weak hand (left if you are right-handed), making clockwise loops. Coil the line smoothly, avoiding figure-eights, then transfer about half the loops to your throwing hand and hurl them with a strong swinging motion while letting the loops pay out freely from your other hand. Hold tightly to the bitter end or, better yet, secure it to a cleat.

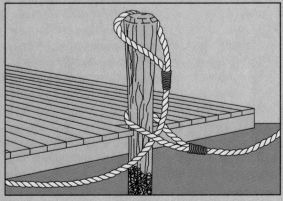

When two lines are on the same pile, the lower line can be removed without disturbing the upper line, by slipping it through the eye of the upper line.

If there is an offshore wind blowing, you may want to rig a slack line to the near-shore quarter cleat in order to pull the boat into the dock against the wind for easy boarding. However, you must always remember to loosen the line as the tide rises or falls, and to allow plenty of slack during the night, or when the boat is not tended.

Dock lines frequently have an eye splice in one end, but not the other. You must decide whether to use the end with a loop on shore or on the boat. If you are going to be on board, it is better to retain the plain end on board. This means that you can make adjustments without getting off the boat. If there will be no one on the boat, use the end with the eye on board; the plain end ashore will allow adjustment without the necessity of boarding.

If two lines are used with the idea of getting double the strength of one, they must be of equal length. Otherwise, the short one carries the full load until it breaks, leaving the single longer line to then carry the load.

Allowing for tidal range

Boaters on fresh-water streams and lakes have no tides to worry about when they tie up to a pier. But in tidal waters, failure to consider the tides can part lines, and may even sink the boat.

Long spring lines provide the most effective method for leaving a boat free to rise and fall. They also keep the boat from going ahead or astern, moving off fenders, or twisting in such a way as to get caught on dock projections. The longer a spring, bow or stern line can be, the greater the tidal range it can accommodate with a minimum of slack. Long lines allow each line to be adjusted, so that all do not come taut together at either extreme stage of the tide.

You should adjust the mooring lines to come up almost taut at either of the extreme tidal ranges; this adjustment may take some experimentation. Observe the boat at both high and low tide, and adjust the lines so they are snug, but not tight, at these stages.

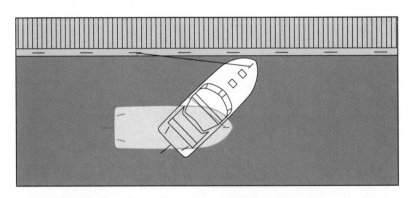

By going ahead on an after bow spring, the boat's bow is pulled into the pier, but the stern springs away.

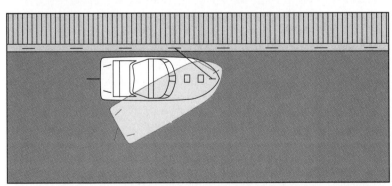

If the rudder is turned away from the pier, the stern will swing in as power is applied.

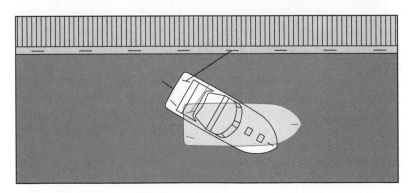

When backing on a forward quarter spring, the stern swings in, but the bow swings out away from the pier.

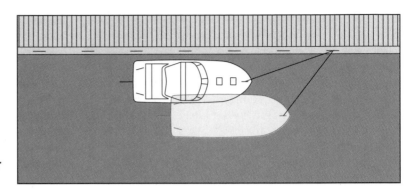

By reversing on a bow line, the boat can be sprung in nearly parallel to the pier or wharf face.

If you keep your boat in a slip, it is important to check the lines at the times of extreme high and low tides. Make sure that the lines are not so slack that the boat can move against a pile or finger pier. When mooring in a narrow slip with a large tidal range, it may be impossible to keep the boat from coming up against a pile or dock at mid-tide. The careful placement of fenders, either on the boat or secured to the dock or piling, may be the only way to protect your boat in this type of situation.

Maneuvering against dock lines

Depending on current or weather conditions, getting in and out of your slip or away from a pier can be challenging. Spring lines are the most useful dock lines since they can be used to assist maneuvering.

■ **Ahead on an after spring.** If it is possible to secure an after spring amidships or close to the boat's pivot point, the boat can be worked into a dock by running ahead slowly with the rudder turned away from the dock. Since the stern is free to swing as the discharge current acts on the rudder, the boat will move toward—and lie parallel to—the dock.

This technique is especially useful when short-handed; bringing the boat against the dock is simply a matter of passing a single line ashore. It is also helpful when maneuvering a large boat against a stiff offshore wind, where hauling in on bow and stern lines would require great effort. This is more theoretical than practical on many smaller boats, which have only the bow and stern (or quarter) cleats for securing spring lines to, while the pivot point is well aft of the bow; if possible, install an amidships cleat on each side of your boat.

■ **Reversing on a spring.** The stern is swung sharply toward the dock by the action of the forward quarter spring when reversing. Since stern movement is restricted, there is much less control. The bow is free to swing away from the dock with the wind or current. If you back on a forward bow spring, the stern is not as restricted, and the line has less effect on turning the boat. Unless there is a strong offshore wind or current, the boat will probably back parallel to the pier.

MAKING USE OF FENDERS

Fenders (they are NOT called "bumpers") are relatively soft objects of rubberlike plastic and filled with air under low pressure. They are used between boats and piles, pier sides and seawalls to protect topsides from scarring and to cushion any shock of the boat striking the fixed object. Some fenders can be inflated to different pressures with a hand pump. Most fenders are circular or square in cross section and of varying length.

Most fenders have eyes molded in each end for attaching a short length of light line that is used to suspend them along the side of a boat. Some models have a hole, through their center, through which a piece of line is run and knotted at each end.

Good quality fenders are not inexpensive but they are well worth the investment. Half a dozen substantial fenders are not too many for the average cruiser to carry.

Fenderboards

When fenders hang vertically from the boat's side, they give protection against the face of a solid pier or wharf as the boat moves fore and aft. If the boat lies against vertical piles, vertical fenders will not stay in place during the boat's forward and and aftward movement.

The solution to protecting the hull in many situations is with fenderboards—short lengths (approximately 4 to 6 feet) of heavy boards (2 inches by 6 inches is common), sometimes faced on one side with metal rub strips on rubber cushions. Holes are drilled, and lines attached, allowing the board to be hung horizontally, backed by two fenders.

The horizontal fenderboard rests against the pile bridging the two fenders. The boat can then move back and forth the length of the fenderboard, and still be protected from chafing against the pile.

Fenderboards also give excellent cushioning between two or more craft rafted together. One boat should put out the usual two fenders behind a fenderboard; the other puts over only its own two fenders. A second fenderboard should not be used, since one board could tangle with another.

Whenever you approach a pier or wharf, your close-quarters boat-handling skills will be tested. Although this maneuver is not difficult, wind, current and adjacent congestion can team up to present a challenging situation.

Approaching and pulling alongside a pier is not much different than picking up a mooring, except that you have little choice in the approach. This section covers the basic guidelines to consider when approaching a pier and docking a boat in the type of conditions you will likely encounter.

Approaching with caution

Since boats do not have brakes, and must rely on reversing the propeller thrust to stop, it is prudent to maneuver at slow speeds while in congested areas. Monitor your boat's wake as you make your way to your berth; it can affect your boat, and other boats nearby.

Depending on conditions, throttle down gradually to keep the boat under control. The goal is to proceed through the harbor or marina slowly, but with enough way on to maintain control. Approaching a pier too fast will require you to shift into neutral far from your berth. Even though the boat is moving through the water, the propeller is not turning and, consequently, there is no propeller discharge current acting on the rudder. Keep in mind that most boats have better slow-speed maneuverability if the propeller is turning: A slow approach allows you to keep the boat in forward until you are almost alongside the pier.

Have the dock lines ready to use fore and aft. Also have fenders in place to keep the boat from chafing against unprotected piles or dock edges. Lead all docking lines outboard of stanchions and shrouds, so that they will be clear when taken ashore.

The biggest mistake novice deckhands make is to secure a dock line before the boat has lost all headway. If you have a couple of hands aboard, assign one to the bow and one to the stern, with instructions not to make fast until headway is checked. Use reverse to stop the boat, cautioning your crew: Securing the bow or stern lines while the boat is still moving can cause the bow or stern to come crashing into the pier. The after bow spring line is the only dock line that should be used to stop the boat. If you are maneuvering into a tight berth, or against strong current or wind, this line will likely be the first one secured.

Calm conditions

Without wind or current to complicate landing, a skipper operating a boat with a single right-handed propeller will want to make a port-side approach to the pier. Time your approach speed so you will be several boat lengths from the dock when you shift into neutral. Since a reversing right-hand propeller will move the stern to port, approach the dock at a 10- to 20-degree angle. When alongside, shift into reverse to stop headway. Depending on your speed, a short burst of throttle may be necessary to stop the boat and to kick the stern to port, with the boat alongside and parallel to the pier.

Though a port-side approach is preferable, you can, with care, make a good landing with the dock on the starboard side. Approach the pier slowly at a much shallower angle, as nearly parallel as possible to the pier. Just before you have to reverse to check headway, turn the rudder to full left, swinging the stern in toward the pier. If the boat does not respond, give the propeller a kick ahead while the rudder is full left, in order to kick the stern to starboard. Then reverse to check your headway.

You can also bring the boat in parallel to the dock with an after bow spring line. Secure this line to a pile or cleat ashore, then put the gear in forward with the rudder still full left. The spring line prevents forward movement while the stern moves toward the pier.

Close quarters

Often you will find that the only empty berth in a crowded marina or yacht club lies between two docked boats. There may be little more than a boat length to squeeze into. Here again, the spring line comes into play.

A port side approach is preferable. Since boats are on both sides of the docking area, you will have to approach at a greater angle than if the pier were clear of other vessels. The aim is to place the bow as close to the pier as possible, without running up on the forward boat. Be sure you leave ample clearance

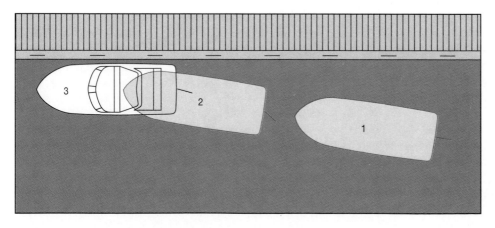

When it is necessary to make a landing starboard side to the pier, with a right-hand propeller, approach slowly at 1, nearly parallel to the pier or wharf face. The rudder is shifted to full left at 2, and the stern is swung to starboard with a short burst or power. Check the forward motion at position 3.

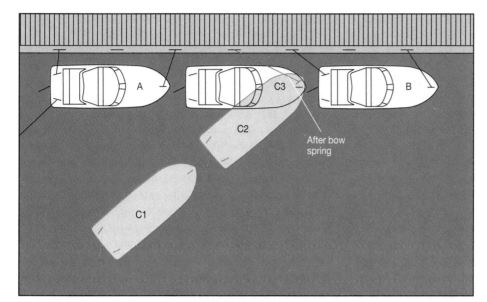

Landing between boats A and B, boat C approaches at a greater than normal angle. At position C2, a spring line is run aft to the pier or wharf from a forward cleat or bitt. Going ahead with propeller and right rudder, the boat swings into its berth at position C3.

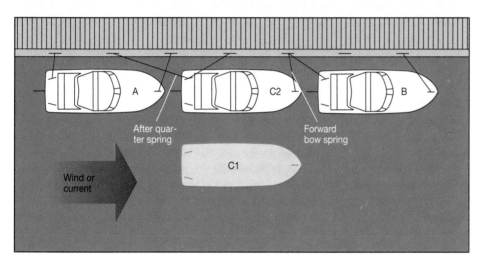

The boat can be worked into its berth, using the current, by setting the rudder to port and using just enough power to offset the drift to the current.

on your port side so that, when you back down to check headway, the stern does not hit the dock.

Have your crew stand by, ready to go ashore with the after bow spring line, or ready to throw the line ashore to someone on the pier who will tie you up. After the spring line is secured ashore, put the rudder over full right and go ahead slowly. While the propeller discharge current acting on the right rudder pushes the stern into the pier, make certain that the spring line is adjusted so that the boat cannot possibly move forward, into the boat ahead. Then, as the boat swings in, the spring line may be slacked off a little bit. Quite often you may find that a fender or two might be necessary at the point of contact.

Wind or current parallel to berth

Because water is many times denser than air, in most cases current should be considered first when planning an approach to a wharf. If the wharf happens to be on the shore of a river, or the bank of a tidal stream, the current will flow parallel to

it. In this case, the direction of the current should determine how you approach. Heading into the current will enable you to keep the propeller turning over slowly and water moving past the rudder.

If you were to approach the pier from the opposite direction, moving with a half-knot current, you would not only have to stop the boat dead in the water. You would also have to begin making half-knot sternway before your relative movement past the pier would stop.

The wind also must be reckoned with. Since propellers are not as efficient when reversing as when going forward, attempting to stop your boat in a strong following wind takes extra time. During this time, the rudder will be in the propeller's suction current, so it will be of little use in steering the boat. Stopping a boat going upwind is much easier and, if the wind is strong enough, the propeller can be kept turning ahead even as the boat comes dead in the water.

When approaching a pier with a current running or strong wind blowing parallel to it, stop your boat in the channel.

Assess the directions and relative strengths of the wind or current (at the time they may be opposing) before deciding on which approach is best:

■ If the wind or current is at your back, then pass downwind or downstream of the pier, turn around and proceed toward the dock upstream.

■ In coming up against wind or current, you can use that force to check your headway, instead of reverse. In the case of a strong current, your boat should respond to the helm when it has stopped next to the pier because there will still be a flow of water past the boat and its rudder.

Landings downwind or with current

If you can, avoid any landing in which wind or current are setting you down toward your berth. In this case, you are totally dependent on your reverse gear for stopping the boat. An error in judgment or a motor failure would put you in an embarrassing, if not dangerous, situation.

Sometimes, however, space will not permit you to turn before docking. Suppose, for example, you are coming into a canal lock with a strong wind astern. Proceed in, as slowly as possible while retaining control. With a single-screw right-hand-propeller boat, if possible, choose the port side of the lock, so that your stern will swing in against the lock face when you reverse. Once the boat's headway has been checked, get a line out from the stern or port quarter; the boat can lie temporarily on this line alone. If you get a bow line fast first, and miss making the stern line fast, you risk being turned end-for-end by the wind or current.

Landing on the leeward side

Since the wind can blow from any direction, it's not uncommon to find yourself approaching a pier with the wind blowing at right angles to the pier. If you have a choice as to which side of the pier you land, choose the leeward side. If the wind is strong, the windward side can be uncomfortable and your boat may pound against the piles. The rougher it is, the more important it becomes to dock on the leeward side. The wind will then hold the boat clear of the pier instead of pushing it against it.

Unless there is current to consider, make the leeward approach so the port side will rest against the pier. Depending on wind strength, you may have to point the bow into the wind a bit more than usual to keep it from falling away during your approach. Your biggest problem will be getting the stern to come into the pier against the wind.

Since you are going upwind, you can approach the pier a bit faster then normal, then reverse a bit harder, kicking the stern toward the dock. You may need to put the rudder hard right and go forward for a short burst to help get the stern in.

Have the crew take or pass the bow line ashore first. Then secure the stern line. If the stern begins to drift away from the pier before you can secure the stern line, run ahead on the bow line slowly with the rudder hard right. It will act as an after spring to help bring the stern into the pier. Be careful that neither the bow nor topside is damaged by the pier during this operation; have your fenders ready.

If you have a large, heavy boat, secure the after spring on a beam cleat first; then secure the stern line.

Holding with one spring

The use of a spring line also works well for temporary holding on the lee side of a pier or wharf. After coming alongside, rig the after spring line and go ahead easily until it takes a strain. Then put the rudder hard over, away from shore. Usually only idle speed is necessary to hold the stern up against the pier.

Close-quarters boat handling is one of the most important skills a boater can acquire. The key is practice—an opportunity that is ever-present (often under observation) in most yacht clubs and marinas.

CLEARING A BERTH

Getting safely away from alongside a pier or wharf can be either simple and easy, or complex and difficult, depending on wind direction, the set of any current and the proximity of other craft. Take advantage of any help you can get from the wind and current, and make good use of spring lines.

With wind or current ahead

When facing wind and current ahead, leaving a berth is not difficult. The biggest problem that skippers often create for themselves is to start forward without providing sufficient clearance between the pier and their boat. Remember that, for a boat to turn, the stern must be free to move. To pull away from a port-side pier, the stern must swing to port before the boat will begin to turn to starboard away from the dock. (It is not uncommon to see a boat rub its stern against the whole length of the pier as the skipper turns the wheel more and more to starboard in an effort to pull away.)

With smaller, lighter craft, all that may be needed to gain the necessary clearance from the dock is for someone to give the bow a push off. On the other hand, a larger boat will find it better to go ahead on the after bow spring, with the rudder turned in toward the pier. The natural propeller action plus rudder will swing the stern clear of the dock. You can then back down a short distance, and be clear of the pier to go ahead; remember that as you turn to starboard your stern will swing to port, back into toward the pier. With either procedure, don't try to cut away too sharply; your stern could come back in enough that your port quarter would strike the pier.

From a windward berth

Clearing a berth where the wind or current is pushing the boat against the pier does not necessarily have to be difficult, except in extreme conditions when it may be impossible to get the boat off the pier without working with the after bow spring.

Since the wind or current is holding the boat against the pier, cast off all dock lines—except the aft bow spring line. If the boat has only bow and stern lines, cast off the stern line, then transfer the bow line to an amidships position on the pier to convert it into a spring.

Go ahead easily on the spring with right rudder. The bow of the boat will come into the pier, and the stern will move away from the pier. If it does not respond with the rudder hard over, open the throttle to provide the kick necessary to work the stern around. Depending on the nature of the pier and the type of boat, you may need a fender or two at the critical spots between pier and boat.

Continue until the boat has turned enough: The stern should be far enough from the pier so it will not be blown back down on the pier when backing away. Get the spring line and fenders aboard, and back the boat away with rudder amidships. The stronger the wind or current, the more power is necessary to move the boat against it. If there are oth-

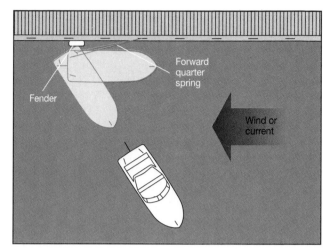

With wind or current ahead, back on a forward quarter spring to turn the stern in and the bow out, angling the boat to get clear by going ahead with the rudder amidships.

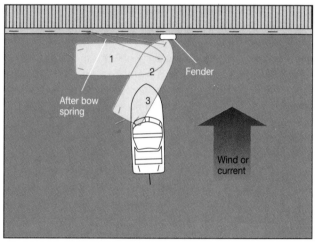

Here is how an after bow spring is used to leave the windward side of a pier or wharf. The boat goes ahead on the spring from 1 to 2, with the rudder set toward the pier. At 3 the line is cast off, and the boat backed into the wind.

er boats moored to the pier near you, back away with considerable power to gain sternway and some steerage as soon as possible. Continue backing away until well clear; a boat that is dead in the water will make much more leeway than one that is moving.

With wind or current astern

Instead of merely casting off all lines and going ahead, get the maneuverable stern out away from the pier and go astern before going ahead on the course.

Run ahead on the after bow spring. This allows the stern to go out into the current, or to be kicked out if necessary by power, going ahead with right rudder. If the current or wind is noticeable, often the stern swings out without aid from the engine. When the boat has swung out, anywhere

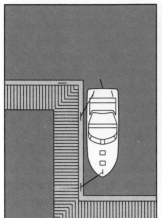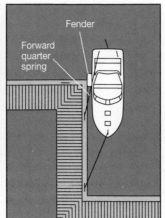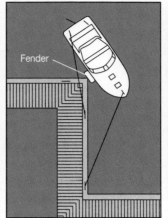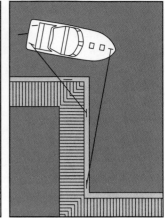

A forward quarter spring can be used to help the boat back out around the end of a pier. When the spring is taut, the boat reverses with full right rudder. Use a fender as necessary.

from 45 to 60 degrees depending on the particular situation, the spring is cast off. The boat backs off far enough to clear the structure before you go ahead with left rudder.

Backing around

We have already discussed backing out of a slip. But at times, it may be necessary to back out of the slip and make an almost-immediate sharp turn because of congestion, or to come up to the adjacent pier. In either case, the forward quarter spring line can be used in much the same way as described for using the after spring.

For example, let's say your boat is lying in its slip, starboard side to the land. The first step is to make the spring ready from a point near the corner of the slip to the after cleat—either amidships if there is only one, or the cleat on the starboard quarter, if there are two.

With the spring ready, but left slack and tended, cast off the bow line, or slack it away to be tended by someone on shore. Back the boat slowly with full right rudder. When the boat is about halfway out of the slip, take a strain on the spring to prevent backing farther. This will cause the boat to pivot as the stern is pulled around to starboard by the spring line. Be sure to protect the boat from the pier with a fender.

As you continue to back, the spring will pull the boat up to the pier. At this point, you should slack the spring as the boat comes parallel to the pier so you can back farther. If you plan to secure the boat to the pier, you can use the spring as a stern line, shifting it to the off-shore stern cleat.

This method is especially useful when there is a breeze off the structure that would tend to blow the boat away if maneuvering without lines. No human power is required, and it can be accomplished in a leisurely and seamanlike manner. But, as in any case where the stern is made fast to the shore with the bow free, take special care to keep the boat under control.

If the boat is to get underway after being backed around, no bow line is needed. When the boat has pivoted far enough,

with starboard quarter near the corner of the pier, idle the engine while casting off the shoreward end of the spring and bringing it aboard. To get underway from such a position, keep the rudder amidships until the stern of the boat is clear of the pier.

Turning in a berth

At times you may find it easier to turn your boat around at the pier than to attempt to leave the berth with adverse current conditions—particularly if the area surrounding the pier is congested.

To turn a boat with the starboard side against a pier, current coming from astern, first let all lines go except the after bow spring. Often the effect of the current will then be sufficient to throw the bow in toward the dock and the stern out into the current. If any factor, such as a beam wind, tends to keep the stern pinned against the dock, kick the stern out by going ahead easy with right rudder. Keep a fender handy as a protection to the starboard bow.

Take steps to prevent the bow from catching on the dock as it swings. A small boat will usually require a fender, but a large craft may have to reverse the engine just enough to keep the bow clear.

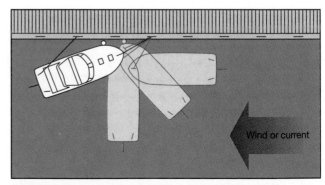

A boat can be turned end for end, using just the current and the spring lines.

As it swings in with the current, the fender should be made ready near the port bow. Also transfer the after bow spring from the starboard side to the port side. As the boat moves with the current, this line becomes the port forward bow spring. If the boat does not come alongside readily, even when helped by going ahead a little with right rudder, rig a forward quarter spring. Take a strain on the quarter spring and ease the bow spring. The current will push the boat back against this line and pull it parallel to the pier.

On a larger vessel, you will need to go ahead on a forward bow spring rigged on the port side. Going ahead easily with right rudder on this spring alone, the boat stays under control and eases in nicely. In turning a boat this way, make the turn with the bow to the dock, rather than the stern.

Turning with power

Consider a situation as described above, except there is neither wind nor current to assist in turning. Here the power of the engine can be used to swing the boat. Go ahead on an after bow spring with right rudder (starboard side toward the dock). This throws the stern out away from the dock; use a fender to protect the bow. Allow the stem to nose up against the dock, using another fender, if necessary, to cushion it.

As the boat swings toward a position at right angles to the dock, ease the spring. With the bow against the dock, the engine going ahead slowly, the rudder amidships, hold the boat in this position. Meanwhile, cast off the bow spring from on shore; re-rig it as an after bow spring on the port side (or use a second line for the port side). With right rudder again, the stern will swing all the way around; shift the fenders once more to protect the port bow.

In any maneuver involving the use of engine power against the spring, the strain on the line must be taken up slowly and easily. A surge of power puts a shock load on deck fittings that they were never designed to carry, and may even tear out the cleats. If the fastenings hold, the line may part.

Once the strain has been taken up easily, proper deck fittings and good line of adequate size will stand the application of plenty of power. Always bear this principle in mind when you are preparing to tow, or when you are passing a line to a stranded boat. Also remember that most docking lines are nylon, and can store considerable energy as they stretch. When the boat is put in neutral or the throttle is closed, the boat can be pulled back toward the dock. If nylon is stretched to the breaking point, it can snap back with lethal effect.

SAFEGUARDING AGAINST CARBON MONOXIDE

While most boaters are conscious of the potential dangers on the water, the risk of carbon monoxide poisoning is often forgotten. It is important to know the facts about this invisible killer, and to take the necessary steps to ensure safety on board.

Carbon monoxide gas (CO) is clear and odorless, and may be present even when exhaust smoke is not. Its initial toxic symptoms are deceptively similar to those of seasickness: headaches, dizziness and lack of coordination, as well as other symptoms—such as drowsiness. Moreover, the individual tends to lose any healthy fear that danger is imminent.

When carbon monoxide is inhaled, CO molecules attach to red blood cells like oxygen molecules in a person breathing clean air. The result is a lack of oxygen for the tissues with subsequent tissue death and, if prolonged, death of the individual.

Boaters whose craft are equipped with a permanently installed gasoline engine, gasoline powered generator, stoves, heaters or charcoal grills should be alert to the dangers of CO poisoning. They should ensure sufficient ventilation, be aware of the situations when danger is heightened, and inspect their exhaust systems frequently.

Cabin cruisers are particularly susceptible to problems involving carbon monoxide poisoning. The best way to prevent CO from migrating into passenger areas and accommodation spaces is to provide alternate sources of air. Leave a port in the windshield open and open a deck hatch. If you can feel a flow of air coming aft through the cabin and cockpit areas, you can reduce the chances carbon monoxide will be pulled forward and into the boat due to backdrafting.

Backdrafting is caused by air movement over or around a boat, creating a low pressure area at the stern that can increase CO levels on the boat. Dangerous concentrations of CO can also accumulate when a boat's engine or generator is operated while a boat is moored in a confined area such as a boathouse, next to a seawall or alongside other boats. Be aware of the effect your vessel's exhaust may have on other vessels and that another vessel's equipment may affect the CO levels on your boat.

The way to prevent CO problems due to leaks from exhaust systems is with regular inspections and maintenance. Look and listen for leaks in the exhaust systems of generators and propulsion engines. Look for discoloration around joints in the system. Make sure all hose clamps in the exhaust system are secured properly. Double clamping rubber hose connections at each end will help prevent the exhaust hose from vibrating loose. Make sure engine room bulkheads are completely sealed against leaks into accommodation areas. All holes or gaps in the engine room bulkhead for plumbing, wiring and controls should be sealed.

CO gas detectors have reached the point that their installation should be considered by all safety-conscious boaters.

If a passenger or crew member displays symptoms of CO poisoning, evacuate all accommodation spaces; give the affected person oxygen if available; contact medical help and, if the person is not breathing, perform CPR (Chapter 5).

10 SEAMANSHIP UNDER SAIL

Sailing is an old and complex art, and sailors can spend a lifetime at it and still find that there is more to learn. It is also a simple and a fairly safe activity. A beginning sailor can have a fine time in a sailboat on his or her first day out, provided a few precautions are observed regarding the weather and safety on the water.

Experienced powerboat people, as well as those new to watersports, are taking up sailing in increasing numbers. While most of the seamanship and piloting chapters in this book apply equally to both sailboats and powerboats, here are the terms used specifically on sailboats, and a description of the basic equipment used to accomplish certain sailing seamanship maneuvers.

HOW A BOAT SAILS

The art of sailing, one of the oldest studies in the world, has been joined by the science of sailing with its complex laws of physics and the lofty mathematics that describe them. Fortunately, along with the wind tunnels, sensing devices and computers that confront us with all of sailing's complexity has come technology that has broadened the methods and materials we use to build and to sail boats. The improvement in construction and safety of sailboats is palpable—and no less so the ability of modern sailors to take advantage of it—but both the art of sailing and the science of sailing are very much works in progress.

While sailors can take heart that the underlying physical phenomena can be used without being completely understood, it is not for nothing that sailing has been studied so assiduously for centuries. The interaction of the wind, water, hull, sails and keels—to say nothing of the involvement of sailors—is complex, often simultaneous, and indeed, at times invisible and even intuitive. But each progression in its understanding has led to easier and faster ways to sail.

Bear in mind that while the following discussion of how and why a boat sails is broken into sections so as to be intelligible, the elements that are discussed in isolation are in fact seldom isolated. On a sailboat, little happens that doesn't have an effect on everything else.

Bending the flow

Sails extract energy from the flow of air (the wind) by bending as it goes by. This is true of every kind of sail, ancient or new, and it is true whether the sail is moving across the wind, or being blown along with it. As they create a driving force from the wind, sails also create a small amount of drag—the smaller the better.

The underwater surfaces of a boat, whether they are the carefully shaped hulls and highly efficient fins of racing yachts, or old-fashioned cargo hulls, also act as foils bending the flow of water that passes around them. The interesting thing about sails ("airfoils") and keels ("hydrofoils") is that, while they are in one sense opposite, the principles that govern them are the same.

Push equals shove

A sailboat hull, driven by aerodynamic forces, accelerates until resistance from various forms of drag, both aero- and hydrodynamic, equal the driving forces. At that moment, the sailboat stops accelerating and travels at a constant speed—constant, that is, until something changes. This equalization of driving and dragging forces may be short-lived as the boat sails into a changing wind, is buffeted by waves, or when the delicate flow patterns are disturbed by its crew. Of course, if

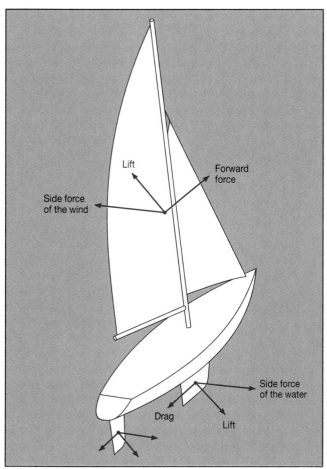

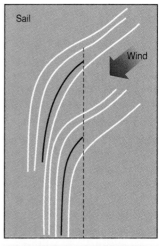

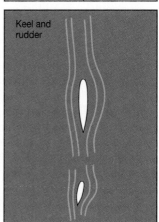

The sails and the underwater surfaces of a boat both act as foils. The sails bend the flow of air over their surfaces, converting some of it into forward and lateral motion ("lift"), and some into drag. At the same time, water flowing past the hull and its appendages produces lift to windward, as well as drag.

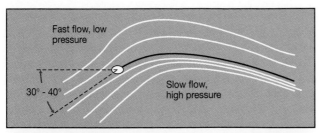

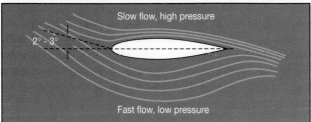

Thin foils, such as sails *(top)*, must be presented to the wind at an angle in order to create a low-pressure area across their leeward surface. The sails try to move into the low pressure area, producing forward and lateral movement. Thick foils, such as fin keels *(bottom)*, also must be presented to the water flow at an angle in order to create high- and low-pressure areas and "lift."

sailing carefully, the crew is trying to upset the equalization in favor of the driving forces—trying to make the boat accelerate. When the crew is successful, a larger drive is soon countered by a larger drag and, once again, the boat settles into a "steady state"—but at a higher speed.

Airfoils vs. hydrofoils

Sailboats and airplanes bear some kinship because both depend on a careful use of fluid motion over curved surfaces. But a sailboat operates between two fluid media—air and water, while a plane operates in only one. The airplane's airfoils (wings) both pull in one direction—upward.

The sailboat's foils pull in nearly opposed directions— the sails to leeward and the keel to windward. Each depends on the other to make the sailboat work—to make it move. Sails could not extract energy in any useful way without the work of the keel, and the keel could not do its work if the boat were not being pushed.

Historically, the airfoils on a sailboat (its sails) have received a lot more attention than the hydrofoils. Designers have developed complicated ways to make them more efficient over a range of wind speeds by changing their shape and their angle to the hull. On the other hand, hydrofoils have been left pretty much on their own while the boat is underway. But this is changing. Designers are now finding ways to modify the shape and orientation of fin keels too, as any America's Cup spectator knows.

Bernoulli's discovery

In the early 1700s, the Swiss scientist Daniel Bernoulli established that changing the velocity of air or water flow at a specific point brings about a consequent change in pressure at the same point. Bernoulli's theorem led to the principle of the venturi effect and the development of the curved foil. The most convincing demonstration of the venturi effect is easy to perform in the kitchen. First, run a stream of water from the faucet. Then, dangle a soup spoon by the tip of its handle and move its convex surface slowly toward the stream. Rather than being pushed away, as your intuition might suggest, it is pulled into the stream.

The most familiar practical application of the venturi effect is seen in the behavior of an airfoil such as an airplane wing. As the plane moves along a runway, the induced airflow (from the plane's motion) separates as it strikes the leading edge of the wing. The velocity of the airflow forced to travel over the airfoil's convex upper surface increases because it spans a greater distance than the air that travels beneath the wing.

Following Bernoulli's theorem, the increased velocity on the upper surface of the wing is accompanied by a decrease in pressure, relative to that on the under surface. Since a region of high pressure will try to push into one of low pressure, a force is produced. Aviators began calling this force "lift" and we use the same term when talking about boats. (The term "lift" also has another meaning, discussed later in this chapter.) Depending on the shape of the surface, the speed of the flow, the angle at which the foil meets the airflow and other factors, more or less lift is produced. The faster an aircraft's forward motion induces airflow across its wings, the greater the pressure differential and the greater the lift. Ultimately, the high pressure area beneath the wing, in attempting to displace the increasingly lower pressure area above it, lifts the wing—and the aircraft to which it is attached—upward and off the ground.

An asymmetrical airplane wing, curved on the upper surface and almost straight on the lower surface, can produce some of its lift even when it is pushed in a line parallel with the oncoming airflow—that is, with no "angle of attack." The sails on a sailboat, acting as a vertical wing or airfoil, ordinarily don't have thickness the way an airplane wing does. Without thickness and being symmetrical (because they have to produce lift alternately on both sides), sails must be presented to the flow of air at an angle. This is why sailboats lose their drive, or end up "in irons," when they are steered too close to the wind.

When sails are set at an efficient angle, air flows across their convex leeward surface and a low pressure area is created. The sail tries to move into it, impelled by the higher pressure on its windward side. This driving force created by the sails is transmitted to the hull through the mast, sheets and sail attachments. The boat begins to move, but not necessarily in the right direction—not yet.

At the same time that lift is being created, there is another force at work on the sails. This is the drag that results from friction and turbulence along the sail's surface and at its edges. Boats rely on the flow of the wind, relatively slow compared to the much faster airflow generated by an engine-powered aircraft. They are severely limited in the amount of energy they can exploit. When resources are scarce, skills are challenged even more. Being able to change the sail's shape and the angle at which air flows over it to suit varying wind strengths and directions is critical to extract the required lift from the available wind energy and to minimize the inevitable drag.

If there is no corresponding hydrofoil already at work, the result of this careful sail trimming is just unresisted sideways motion, resulting in slower airflow, resulting in less speed—in other words the boat slides aimlessly. You have probably seen this happen when a sailing dinghy leaves the wharf with its centerboard up.

The addition of underwater fins—a keel or centerboard and a rudder—vastly increases lateral resistance. Again, unlike most airplane wings, a sailboat's foils are symmetrical (because they have to work the same way on both sides). Hydrofoils, like sails, also have to meet the oncoming flow at an angle, called an angle of attack, before they develop any lift. Since most keels are rigidly attached to their hulls, the whole boat has to be aimed a couple of degrees to windward of the course it actually travels.

While this may seem inefficient, it really is the fastest way to sail. Skippers call this "sailing with a weather helm." ("Weather helm," it should be noted, is a measure not only of efficiency, but also of safety: In case of gear failure or lack of attention to the helm, the action of a boat with weather helm safely rounds up, rather than falling off—possibly into a dangerous jibe.) The angle required to produce lift from the keel and rudder (because the rudder too is a lifting surface) is only 2 or 3 degrees, but it does mean that the boat points in one direction while traveling in a slightly different one. The difference is called "leeway," and it is an issue in piloting because it affects the way that a navigator calculates his course and heading.

As the dinghy sailor lowers the centerboard, he or she might also allow the sail to aim its effort in a more forward direction by letting it out just a little. Now the airfoil and hydrofoil get down to work—against each other. As each begins to encounter faster flow (we are dealing in less than walking speed here, so "fast" is a relative term) each foil begins to produce lift. The centerboard produces lift to windward, as well as drag, while the sail produces lift to leeward, and slightly forward. It's the "slightly forward" that makes things happen.

Creating more lift (and causing less drag) is the Holy Grail of high-performance sail and keel design. (This also explains why there are now designers who specialize in "appendages," keels and rudders, and others who design hulls—both separate from the people who design the sails.) Of course, they have contrived a whole set of labels and rules to talk about it. Two important labels in this discussion are "center of effort" and "center of lateral resistance." These are really just two sides of the same coin because both centers involve

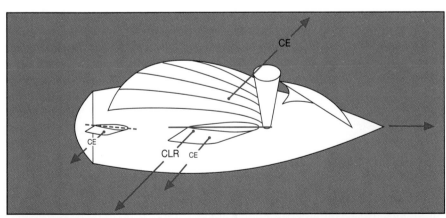

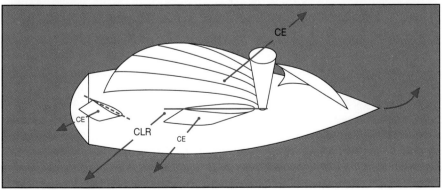

The center of effort (CE) is the position of the sum of all the lift and drag forces produced by the sails. The center of lateral resistance (CLR) is the equivalent position of all forces produced by the hull and its appendages. When the two centers are balanced against each other, the boat travels in a straight line *(top)*. When they are out of balance, the boat turns. Changing the rudder angle *(bottom)* shifts the position of the CLR aft so that the boat turns to leeward.

foils—"effort" for the sails, and "lateral resistance" for the keel and rudder.

Now that computers are able to analyze the contribution of every carefully shaped square inch of foil surface, the center of effort and its twin, the center of lateral resistance, are much easier to find. Both centers are simply the sum of all of the lift and drag forces at work anywhere on the foil. If you had to attach a string somewhere on the sail and another on the underwater surface, and pull the boat along by these two strings—creating the same force and balance as a particular strength and direction of wind—the center of effort is the place where you would attach the sail's string, and the center of lateral resistance is the place you would have to attach the underwater string. Yacht designers used to estimate the position of the center of effort by finding the geometric center of the triangles in a sail plan, connecting them, segmenting the connecting line in ratio to the areas of the triangle, then using their experience to estimate how far forward or aft the real balance point might be. The center of lateral resistance was found in a similar fashion. Today, designers still use experience, but it is supplemented by wind tunnel and tank testing of various shapes.

The balancing act

Both centers (called "CE" and "CLR") are constantly changing with boat motion and sail adjustment. Unfortunately, the net effect of lift and drag that the CE represents does not pull the boat straight ahead. Remember that we said the boat would start to move, but not in the desired direction. The force acting at the CE on the sails actually pulls mostly sideways, and the forces acting on the CLR on the hull, keel and rudder, act to windward and slightly aft. These forces are in balance when the boat is traveling in a straight line. When they are out of balance, the boat turns.

Keeping in mind that boats sail fastest when their keel and rudder are presented to the water flow at a slight angle, designers place the sails on the hull in such a way that, if no steering force were applied with the rudder, the boat would turn itself gently toward the direction of the wind (weather helm). When the boat is sailed, a straight-line course is achieved by the gentle application of 2 or 3 degrees of rudder angle. Balance between CE and CLR is achieved (the boat does not turn), and both underwater foils are presented to the oncoming flow of water at a slight angle of attack—so both foils, keel and rudder, develop a force that pulls the boat to windward. However, you can also have too much of a good thing. An excessive imbalance between CE and CLR, one that requires more than a slight rudder correction, causes the rudder to develop drag commensurate with the greater lift it is being forced to create. The boat decelerates—slower speed means less drive from the sails—and things settle back into the drive-drag equilibrium at a slower constant speed.

A "lee helm," the tendency to wander off to leeward, is even more costly. In this case, a straight-line course can only be achieved when the rudder is turned so as to create a force pulling to leeward (so that the bow is pushed to windward). This means that no windward lift is being created by the rudder, so all of it has to be created by the keel. The keel ends up at a more extreme angle of attack to produce this lift, and creates more drag as a result. Everything slows down.

It's worth pointing out here that these differences in balance are important to the cruising sailor as well as the racer. Though they are difficult to perceive—3 degrees is hard to see and often difficult to feel in the helm—they produce substantial differences on almost all points of sail. The racing sailor may lose a race, but the cruising sailor may make serious errors in navigation by failing to account for large leeway angles that result from excessive imbalance.

Incidentally, keels and rudders can be a lot smaller in area than sails because they operate in a denser medium. In addition, when they are pushed through the water at greater speeds, they can produce sufficient side forces with less area—that's why the crews of fast, planing catamarans often reduce drag by pulling their foils (usually daggerboards) a few inches up at high speeds, even though they are sailing upwind.

Conversely, if there is no speed at all, there is no flow and neither the keel nor the rudder can do its job. A boat that has no way on cannot be steered, which is why "steerageway" is so important. Skippers will often do whatever they can to get a boat settled down and underway so as to create some flow past the keel and rudder before they worry about what precise direction they're going.

Outsailing the wind

For most novice sailors, the idea that a boat can sail faster than the wind is questionable at best. Even the less ambitious claim—that a boat can receive more power from the wind as the boat picks up speed—seems contrary to common sense. After all, there is no source of power other than the wind.

But it's true, and an understanding of apparent wind, the stronger wind partly created by the boat's own speed, is crucial to sailing. Let's look at two extreme examples—a very slow boat and a very fast boat.

The slow boat is a Spanish galleon. It has no separate keel and, by recent standards, inefficient sails. It sails most effectively with the wind behind it, and even then, it doesn't sail very fast. If the galleon were just getting underway and if the wind were exactly on its stern and blowing at 10 knots, the wind felt by someone standing on deck would be 10 knots. As the galleon picked up speed, the wind felt on deck (the apparent wind) would decrease, because the ship would be moving along with it. The effect of the wind on the moving sails would also decrease. At somewhere around 2 knots of vessel speed through the water, the decreasing force created by the sails would exactly balance the increasing resistance of the hull (discussed later) and the galleon would stop accelerating and settle down for a long trip to Spain. Boat speed would be 2 knots, wind speed 10 knots, apparent wind speed 8 knots.

Now take the fast boat—an iceboat—in a similar situation. With almost no hull resistance to overcome, the iceboat picks up the same 10 knots of wind from directly astern and, within seconds, the skipper is aware of a rapidly decreasing apparent wind. His boat reaches a balance between the decreasing force of the wind and the increasing resistance of the iceboat at, for example, 9 knots (boat speed 9 knots, wind speed 10 knots, apparent wind speed 1 knot).

Now, 9 knots would be pretty exciting in a Spanish galleon, but in an iceboat, it's not worth chilly feet. So the iceboat skipper turns his boat so that it begins to travel on a line

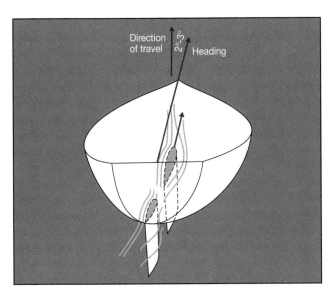

Since the keel and rudder must be presented to the water at a slight angle of attack (ideally 2° to 3°) in order to create maximum lift, the boat must be steered in one direction— its heading—to travel in a slightly different direction.

perpendicular to the wind. He does this without losing any speed, so his initial speed, after the turn, is still 9 knots. At that instant, the iceboat skipper feels the full force of the 10-knot wind, because he's no longer traveling away from it. He also feels the force of a 9-knot wind, just as if he were on a bicycle pedaling at 9 knots. These two vectors, at right angles to each other, can be added (vector addition is discussed in Chapter 20) with an apparent wind of about 13.5 knots flowing into the iceboat at an angle of about 47 degrees.

The Spanish galleon, still traveling at 2 knots, also turns so that it is sailing on a line perpendicular to the wind. The new wind across its decks is also a vector sum of the 10-knot wind and the 2-knot boat speed. The result is a less-than-impressive 10.3 knots at an angle of about 79 degrees. The galleon responds to this slightly stronger apparent wind (which is still hitting at an angle wide enough for its square sails to make use of) by accelerating. Again, the force on the

sails is balanced by the increasing resistance of the hull, and things settle down again—at 2.5 knots.

However, aboard the iceboat, things start to happen. Its highly efficient sail and almost-zero hull resistance respond to the new, stronger wind. It begins to accelerate again. The first one-knot increase in boat speed, to 10 knots, brings a new apparent wind; 14.1 knots, at a new angle of 45 degrees. This angle is still no problem for an iceboat sail so it responds to the new apparent wind strength by gaining another knot. Now the apparent wind is very close to 15 knots and the angle is still comfortable—producing more acceleration.

Where does it all end? Well, this is not perpetual motion (though, in an iceboat, it can often feel that way!). Things start to level off when the apparent wind goes so far forward that the sail begins to point too directly into the wind. It can no longer achieve a useful angle of attack and it luffs. At this point the iceboat is probably experiencing an apparent wind of almost 45 knots and is doing almost 40 knots of boat speed—pretty good for wind strength of 10 knots. In fact, with strong winter winds and cold, dense air, iceboats routinely travel at speeds of more than 50 knots. At that speed, their sails are strapped in tight regardless of what direction the "real" wind is blowing—their apparent wind is far more important, and it's blowing from almost straight ahead.

The effects of apparent wind on most sailboats are far more dramatic than aboard the galleon and far less than aboard the iceboat. Even a heavy racing sloop might increase its speed by 25 percent as a result of a stronger apparent wind. Sailboats that are less limited by their weight can easily double their speed with careful use of apparent wind.

There are some fundamental rules about apparent wind:
■ Except when sailing directly downwind, apparent wind will always come from "farther ahead" than the wind does.
■ Sailing on any angle ranging from perpendicular to the wind to an angle quite close to the wind, apparent wind will always be greater than the wind.
■ As wind strength increases, the angle of the apparent wind moves farther aft; conversely, as wind strength decreases, the apparent wind moves farther forward. A strong gust of wind is usually welcome because it provides more power applied from farther aft.

Heeling

For the most part, boats sail most efficiently in an upright position so that aerodynamic and hydrodynamic lift are converted into forward motion. But the same dynamic forces that pull the boat forward also try to push it over.

The sails, which have their CE at about 40 percent of the height of the mast, and the keel with its corresponding CLR well below the water, both act as levers with the hull in the middle as their fulcrum.

In general, there are two ways to counter these forces and prevent them from pushing the boat over and capsizing it. These are weight and width. Both have disadvantages.

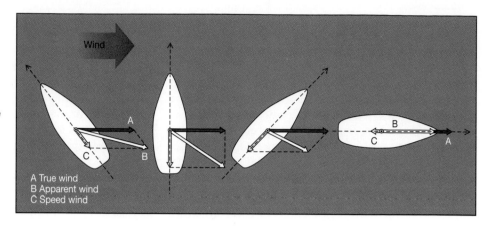

Apparent wind is the direction of the wind as it appears onboard. Both boat speed and the boat's angle to the true wind affect the direction and strength of the apparent wind. In this vector diagram, the narrow red arrow is true wind, the yellow arrow is wind speed, and the white arrow is apparent wind. Apparent wind is greatest when the boat is sailing perpendicular to, or at an angle close to, the wind.

A True wind
B Apparent wind
C Speed wind

Energy extracted from the wind is partly absorbed in the work of moving weight, especially if that weight begins to move up and down through waves, so any extra weight robs speed. Width makes a hull harder to push through the water (unless the boat is separated into two hulls, or three, that are spread apart).

Most sailboats use both weight and width to stay upright. The width of the hull is the first line of defense because it begins to provide substantial righting moment (it pushes back) as soon as the hull begins to heel. Fixed ballast gains in importance as the hull heels farther over.

Different sailboat designs rely more heavily on one or the other method. The classic heavy, narrow "meter boats," such as the 12-meter class formerly used in America's Cup competition, were intended to balance at a substantial angle of heel sailing close to the direction of the wind. Designers took advantage of this fact by shaping their hulls in such a way that they would have greater potential speed in their heeled underwater shape than in their upright underwater shape. The basic method is explained below in the discussion of form resistance.

Most recent racing designs such as the J-24 rely more on a wide, shallow hull. With this hull type, crew weight becomes even more important, especially because crew weight can begin to provide righting moment even before the hull begins to heel. That's why the best-sailed dinghies sail through gusts of wind without heeling—their crews move into position in perfect sympathy with the changing aerodynamic forces, converting every increase in power into forward acceleration, rather than heeling.

As the boat begins to heel, several factors work together to rob it of forward speed. The force created by the sails is now aimed partly downward instead of parallel to the water so that it is helping to immerse the hull rather than pulling it forward. Less sail area is exposed to the horizontal movement of the wind. A corresponding deterioration takes place underwater where flow across the keel and rudder are compromised. The part of the hull that is underwater becomes asymmetrical, creating turning forces that have to be counteracted.

A more subtle change also takes place. The forces creat-ed by sails and keel are no longer acting directly above and directly below the hull—they're both displaced sideways. The effect is similar to what would happen if you were pulling the hull with a towline. When the boat is upright, the towline pulls along the hull's center line. As the boat heels, the effect is as if the towline were uncleated and made fast again at the gunwale near the widest point of the beam. In this case, you would expect to fight the boat with its rudder to keep it on a straight course. When the boat heels, its propulsion forces operate away from the hull's center line. That's why boats that are allowed to heel too far under the pull of a spinnaker are so vulnerable to broaching. It also explains why, when a sailboarder leans back into the wind at high speed, he must also move to the tail of his board, holding the sail well aft of the point on which the board pivots when it changes direction.

It's no wonder that the Polynesian solution—separating the hull into two pieces (or three) and placing them far apart—is so attractive. With no penalty in weight, a catamaran or trimaran achieves huge righting moment at the slightest angle of heel.

However, that's not the whole story. When stability is achieved entirely by righting moment from hull width (or by spreading the hulls farther apart), righting moment is typically very high at small angles of heel—but decreases steadily to nothing as the boat heels farther over. In one sense, when you need it most, it's all gone.

The righting moment provided by fixed ballast is typically very small as the hull begins to heel, but steadily increases as the hull heels farther; in other words, the boat is initially "tender" and ultimately "stiff." In the extreme case, the mast is almost parallel with the surface of the water and the fixed ballast is held at a similar angle, almost sideways. At this radical stage, righting moment is at a maximum and heeling force at a minimum.

Keep in mind that these examples are highly simplified. Many other factors, such as the wave conditions present when such extreme heeling forces are at work, have to be considered by yacht designers. For example, even though the fixed-ballasted boat may not heel beyond this extreme angle, it may be filling itself with water. Even though the powerfully rigged, unballasted multihull may potentially capsize, it is less likely actually to founder (since it is generally lighter than water).

Boat speed

Few activities so inspire participants to seek the smallest improvement in speed that sailing does. Indeed, it is the potential for almost infinite improvement that is one of the joys—and at times the frustration—of sailing.

Most sailors are not particularly concerned with going faster than any other sailboat—they're more concerned with getting the most speed out of a sailboat that has been designed with speed-limiting rules. They want to maximize the potential of a boat that has been designed to sail within a class of boats that are all very much the same, if not actually identical in performance characteristics.

This historical limitation of sailboat design has led to a paradox: While sailors have developed the art of boat preparation, sail trim and steering to a high degree of refinement, and yacht designers have squeezed every last fraction of a knot from conventional hulls, keels and sails, the vast majority of sailboats have remained within a narrowly defined set of basic configurations. The imaginative application of pure science and engineering has not had much impact on the activities and experience of most sailors. Nevertheless, the principles that determine how fast a sailboat can go are eagerly studied and applied with an increasing degree of subtlety.

One of the chief enemies of speed for a sailboat, as for any vehicle traveling through the atmosphere, is drag. But sailboats encounter two kinds of drag whose relative importance varies with speed. The first and most obvious is the drag caused by the friction of air and water flowing over large surfaces that can never be perfectly smooth. For that reason, yacht designers take great pains to reduce the wetted surface of the hull. For any given volume, the shape with the least wetted surface is a sphere (that's why soap bubbles are spherical), but a sphere is not very useful for a hull.

The next best compromise might be a round tube. Many hulls are developed from that principle and have almost circular cross sections.

Drag is also caused by turbulent flow around the awkward shapes of deck fittings, rigging attachments, through-hull fittings and even the crew themselves. While attempts are made to streamline these, there are practical and rule-oriented limitations that most sailors happily accept.

Drag from friction and turbulence is most important at low speeds—not because it diminishes at higher speed (it doesn't) but because on the conventional sailboat another form of drag becomes even more difficult to control. This is "form drag," the process of energy loss through the formation of waves.

Imagine a sailboat moving through the water at less than a knot. Tiny wavelets stream from the hull at several points along its waterline. They don't seem to be connected. As speed increases, the wavelets grow into waves and seem to join, the trough of one running up into the crest of the next. At this point, you could measure the boat's speed by measuring the distance between one wave crest and the next: The speed of a surface wave is strictly related to its length. To measure the relationship, in knots, of waves in water, yacht designers use the square root of the wave length multiplied by 1.34.

Three crests along the side of the boat indicate that it is traveling at about half of its maximum speed. As speed increases, the bow wave grows in height and length, pushing the midships wave aft. As the last fraction of a knot is reached, the stern wave is almost falling behind the hull—but it can't. As the stern wave pulls aft, the stern settles down into it. Drag increases because the hull is actually inclined upward against the slope of the bow wave. The hull is trapped.

The implication is that you should always have enough horsepower to climb over the bow wave and convert from a floating or displacement mode of support to a planing mode. That option is available to very light boats that can carry

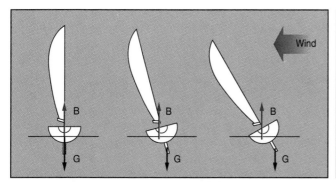 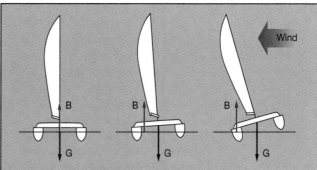

In the illustrations above, B is Center of Buoyancy and G is Center of Gravity. Boats use either weight *(left)*, or width *(right)*, to remain upright against the forces of the wind. Hulls stabilized primarily with weight have a very small righting moment as they begin to heel, but it increases steadily as the boat heels farther over. Such boats are initially tender and ultimately stiff. As the wind increases, the ballasted hull will lean over, increasing its righting moment, but the unbalasted hull has already achieved its maximum righting moment and will be very unstable.

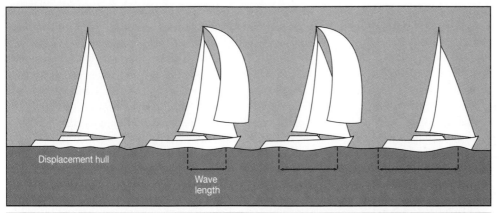

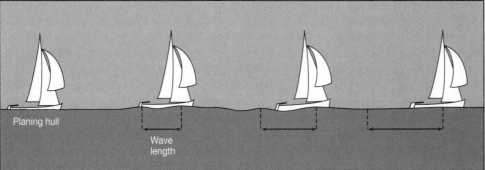

When a hull moves through the water, it produces waves that result in energy loss. The maximum speed of a conventional displacement hull *(top)* is a function of the longest wave it can make, which in turn is determined by hull length. No amount of sail can create enough power for it to climb over its own bow wave. On the other hand, the planing hull *(bottom),* like the racing dinghy and some multihulls, can carry enough sail to push it over its own bow wave and plane.

lots of sail (racing dinghies, multihulls, sailboards and even foil-supported boats), but it's not available within the realm of ballasted monohulls.

Therefore the implication for conventional boats is that, as long as a hull is trapped in its own wave, the vessel will never go faster than the longest wave it can make. That is the reason why longer boats are faster—and why, almost from the beginning of sailboat racing, length was heavily penalized by the rules.

The challenge, within the limitations of rules and economics, is to make a longer wave, so that the hull has a higher potential speed when the horsepower (wind) is available, but to do so without seriously compromising the hull's performance when horsepower is scarce.

One common strategy is to design a hull that has two "personalities"—a shape that is relatively narrow and fine at the ends of the waterline when upright (at low speed when form resistance is less important), and a heeled, or high-speed, shape that is full at the ends. An overhang at the stern is very useful in this regard; as the stern wave builds, the waterline becomes longer and fuller, delaying the point at which the stern begins to settle down into the wave.

Obviously, this dual-personality has limitations. In fact, if the designer has made the bow and stern of the boat especially fine so that they will be easier to push through the water, the waterline will actually seem short to the wave and the top speed will be lower. This leads to the paradox that hulls meant to travel at or near hull speed most of the time tend to be rather full in the bow and the stern, while hulls

expected to travel more slowly, while making more efficient use of lighter winds, might be finer fore and aft.

If heavy winds were always available on demand and if sailboats always traveled with large apparent winds, yacht design would of course be much simpler. However, maximum horsepower from a sailboat rig is rarely available and conventional hulls therefore have to be designed in order to strike the best compromises.

Some very light sailboats, such as racing dinghies, are able to provide lots of horsepower by having their crews hike out against the power of very large sails. Since they are short, these boats reach their wave-resistance limit at a very low speed (just over 5 knots). But they have lots of horsepower still to absorb. Without much fuss, they rise over their bow waves and plane, just like powerboats, often reaching a respectable 17 to 20 knots. Of course, it takes two heavy sailors and perhaps three straining sails to do it, but that's all part of the attraction.

Catamarans and trimarans, with their unique stability, also have physics on their side when it comes to making waves. Because their hulls can be so much narrower than a monohull, the waves they produce are consequently much smaller. While the relationship between wave length and speed still holds, the "hole in the water" that is created by the passage of a narrow hull is much smaller. The stern of a narrow hull doesn't have as far to settle, and drag does not increase as much or as suddenly. In one sense, the narrow hull of a catamaran or a trimaran doesn't have to plane because it has broken the hull-speed rule.

THE PARTS OF A SAILING RIG

Technology has contributed many innovations to the art of sail making, mainly in the area of sail material. The woven polyester fiber, usually referred to by the trade name Dacron, that replaced canvas and cotton, remains the most common of the new fibers. Nonetheless, in the constant quest for greater strength and less weight and stretch, Dacron has itself been surpassed by such wonder materials as Mylar, a non-woven polyester, as well as Kevlar and Spectra.

With few exceptions (such as the spinnaker, discussed separately later), a conventional triangular shape has emerged as the most popular sail configuration. The luff of a mainsail is attached to the mast while the foresail's luff is attached to a forestay. While some mainsails are "loose footed" and attached only at the fore and aft corners (the tack and clew), more often they are attached along the length of the boom either by a boltrope sewn into the sail or by slides. Most foresails are loose footed.

Sails are not flat like paper. They are very carefully cut and assembled so as to present a subtle shape, curving both along their horizontal lines and along their vertical lines. The quality of these curves and their ability to be slightly altered underway are what makes sailmaking such a competitive science. Not only must sailmakers design the right curves for each boat and for a variety of wind and wave conditions, they must also design a structure that will maintain its shape despite heavy stress and the effects of violent shaking and sunlight.

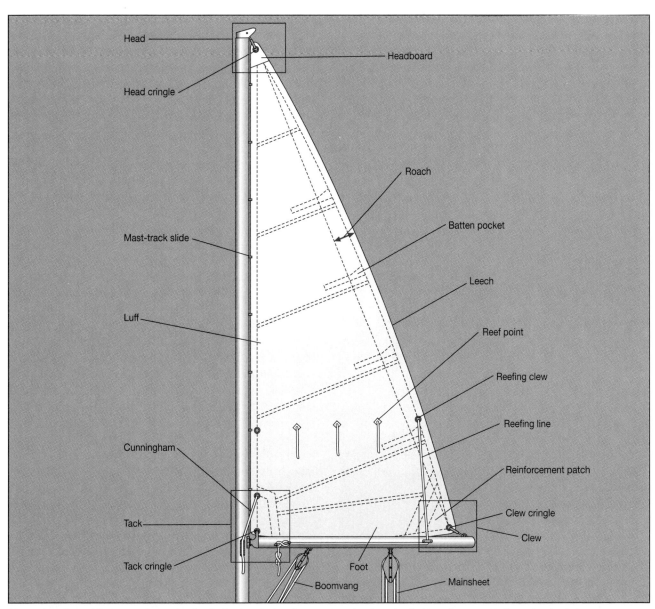

The mainsail would seem to be a simple cloth triangle, but its construction is actually based on a complex equation of curves that the sailmaker uses to create proper belly, or shape. Commonly made of Dacron, the sail is reinforced at the edges and corners with patches of extra material, and given extra stiffness in the roach by battens.

The largest stress on most sails, especially mainsails, is along the leech from the clew to the head. This unsupported edge has to accept the pull of the mainsheet and must also take the pressure of the wind flowing off its windward side. On almost all recent designs, the leech also carries a deep outward curve, a "roach." To counter these loads, most sailmakers lay out the sail material so that the low-stretch fibers of the weave run parallel to the leech. That design dictates panels of material that slope down from leech to luff.

But many other patterns are in use as well. Some place different materials at high-stress areas of the sail, even going so far as to stitch and weld strong fibers in elaborate elliptical curves that radiate out from the foot and luff. At the other extreme are cruising sails that can easily be rolled onto furlers and have very straight, soft leeches.

Battens provide additional support at the leech of a mainsail. Traditionally, they are flexible slats of wood or plastic that slide into long pockets. But that tradition is changing too. Catamaran sailors discovered that by extending battens from the leech all the way to the luff they could have a sail that would maintain a curve at very narrow angles to the oncoming airflow. Such sails have become popular even among cruising sailors who feel that, although they add extra weight, they are easier to manage and will last longer. Full-batten mains have led to a number of additional items of sail hardware to allow the forward end of the batten to be flexibly attached to the aft face of the mast, and so slide up and down freely despite the pressure.

Most sailors attach ribbon or pieces of wool to both sides of the sail; these telltales, or "ticklers," indicate the efficiency of airflow over the sail. Often sailmakers sew windows of plastic near the telltales to make the action of the leeward one more visible. Larger windows are sometimes sewn into dinghy mainsails and "deck sweeping" foresails for better leeward visibility when sailing or racing in confined conditions.

Spinnakers, in all their variations, are usually made of nylon. Since spinnakers can be allowed to stretch, a certain amount of shape deformation is traded for the ultimate strength and lightness nylon provides. However, the architecture of spinnakers is just as complicated as it is for other sails. The goal is to produce a very full camber, but one that still stands up to the flow of air from one edge to the other— spinnakers do not simply fill with air like a balloon. Lightness is a requirement to allow the sail to set high and away from the interference of the mainsail, and to present the largest possible area to the wind. The fact that spinnakers are usually colorful is a matter of tradition more than function, but it does mean they are easier to examine against a bright sky for fine-tuning the trim.

Standing rigging

Standing rigging is the structure designed to support the sails and to help transmit the power they develop to the hull. In most discussions the mast itself is considered the main component of the standing rigging. The idea that the standing rigging is set up permanently and should not move (hence "standing") has given way to high-performance engineering and tinkering. It is now fairly common to find standing rigging that is substantially altered while underway, and masts that are not only allowed, but forced, to bend. The distinction between standing and running rigging has begun to blur.

The evolution of mast making has focused on attempts to increase strength while reducing weight aloft. The challenge to make the structure lighter and stronger is complicated by the fact that for any given sail area, more power can be extracted with a tall narrow shape than with a short wide one. The "aspect ratio of sails" (the relation between height and width) is limited by the fact that they become harder to trim as they get taller; but in general, masts can never be too tall or too thin—and are often extremely expensive.

Traditional wooden masts and booms have given way to extruded aluminum tube and, more recently, to tubes made of composites of such materials as carbon fiber and epoxy. The simplest mast for a small, single-sailed dinghy (such as the Laser) is a round aluminum tube held in a simple socket

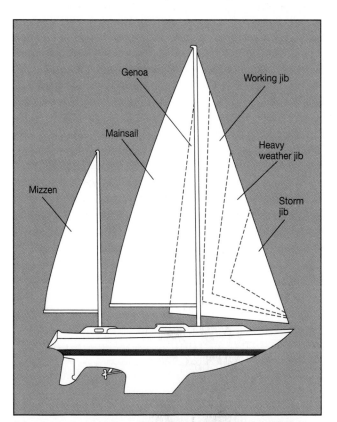

A boat may carry many sails of differing sizes and weights to suit different conditions of wind or point of sail. Shown here are the basic sails that a ketch might have aboard. Of the four jibs, only one would be used at a time. The genoa, for example, is the largest headsail, but is made of the lightest material to catch the slightest breezes. The storm jib is the smallest sail, and is made of the heaviest material to withstand storm winds.

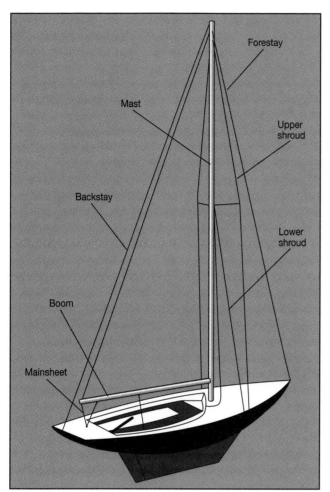

Standing rigging not only supports the sails; it also transmits the power they develop to the hull. The most common arrangement is a mast supported by stays and shrouds. Running rigging includes sheets for hoisting and trimming the sails.

in the deck. The sail is attached to the mast by means of a sleeve extending the full height of the luff.

Although free-standing masts are sometimes used on larger sailboats (some even have more than one free-standing mast and sail-sleeve attachment), a much more common arrangement uses traditional stays and shrouds as guy wires from the mast to the deck. The mast may pass through the deck to rest on a step at the keel ("keel-stepped") or fit into a step or tabernacle on deck ("deck-stepped").

There are almost infinite configurations for stays and shrouds, but at the forward side, there is always a forestay running from the bow (or near it) to the top of the mast (or near it). When the forestay is attached to a point just below the top of the mast (called a fractional rig), the top of the mast can be pulled backward to create a slight bow shape. (The reasons for doing this are described in the section on sail trim.) There might also be a secondary inner stay at the bow, either for more precise control of the mast bend or, as on a cutter rig, for carrying a second inner staysail.

On high-performance rigs there might also be a jumper stay running from the mast, over a strut (jumper strut or diamond strut) and back to the mast at the top. Tension on this stay holds the mast tip against the pull of the mainsail leech, especially in a fractional rig.

A backstay, running from the mast tip (or truck) to the stern, may be a single wire or be split into a bridle and attached to the aft deck at two points. Splitting the backstay makes it easy to adjust its tension because the bridle can be pulled together with a simple block and tackle. The configuration also allows easier access to the cockpit over the transom.

Additional backstays are sometimes used on high-performance rigs, and are considered part of the running rigging because they can be loosened completely when underway. In fact, one has to be loosened and the other tightened on each tack or jibe, the windward running backstay is tensioned to add to mast stability, while the leeward one is slackened to allow the mainsail to be trimmed out. Needless to say, the cockpit of such a boat is a noisy, crowded place on each tack.

In some smaller boats, the shrouds and stays run from tangs on the mast to chainplates at the deck. But to get adequate upper support for taller masts with this arrangement, the point of attachment at the deck would need to be outboard of the hull. Instead, struts called spreaders are fastened to the mast between the deck and hounds (the attachment point of the shrouds to the mast), pushing the shrouds outward to maintain supporting pressure on the upper mast.

Multiple spreader rigs are common, and these usually have multiple shrouds running from the chainplates over successive spreader tips to different levels of the mast. Some smaller rigs gain extra control over mast bend by using spreader roots that can vary the angle at which the spreaders are swept-back.

But the primary function remains much the same—to maintain stability of the mast and equalize the load on the mast so it will withstand the forces exerted on it by wind and sails, inertia as it swings, and by mechanical means, as when the mast is deliberately bent by means of a tackle or hydraulic pump to change sail shape.

Stays and shrouds on most modern boats are made of 1x19 stainless steel wire of appropriate diameter for the size of rig being supported. Stainless steel rod, though more expensive, has been growing in popularity because it has less stretch and more resistance to corrosion than wire. Rod diameter required to provide the same tensile strength is smaller than that of stranded wire, and so has less windage.

Integral to the strength of the standing rigging itself is the attachment point at the deck. Usually, shrouds and stays terminate in turnbuckles that are attached to the eyes of chainplates, which in turn are bolted directly to the hull.

Tuning the standing rigging involves careful tightening of the turnbuckles until the shrouds on both sides of the mast have the same tension and the mast remains in column vertically with no sideways bends.

Once the shrouds are tuned, the forestay and backstay(s) are tensioned by means of tackle or hydraulic pumps to induce mast bend or mast rake to accommodate different sailing conditions underway.

Running rigging

Running rigging includes all the gear used to raise and trim sails, and sometimes there is a bewildering amount of it. Many crews resort to color-coded line to distinguish one piece of running rigging from another. Perhaps the easiest way to understand running rigging is to go through the sequence that most crews would follow to get underway. We will assume that the boat is a 25-foot cruising and racing sloop with a centerboard—a fairly common type.

Many small cruisers adjust their backstay tension by pulling a choker downward over a Y-shaped bridle. Larger vessels often use hydraulic tensioning systems.

If it's not already attached to the boom, the first step is to pull the boltrope on the foot of the mainsail into the groove of the boom. The clew is pulled out to the end of the boom by hand, and attached to a short wire called an outhaul that will later be adjusted. The tack is attached to the gooseneck (the articulated fitting that couples boom to mast) by a short pin. Above the tack is another hole (a cringle) where another short adjusting line—the cunningham—may be attached.

Now, presuming the boat is ready to be cast off, or is already underway with the engine running, the mainsail can be pulled to the top of the mast. This requires that the main halyard be shackled to the headboard of the main and that the luff boltrope be slid into the groove of the mast (there might be sailslides instead). The halyard runs loosely up the truck of the mast, over a sheave (a wheel) and back down the mast to the deck. It may simply be cleated to the mast, or it may run through a block (pulley) to a cleat or linestopper near the cockpit. Part of the halyard's up-and-down journey may be inside the mast. Before the main is raised, a check is made to ensure that all of the lines attached to it are either free to run, or sufficiently loose so as not to restrict the main on its way up the mast.

When the skipper decides, the halyard is hauled, the head of the main rises to the top of the mast and the end of the halyard is cleated in place. Later, small adjustments may be made. With the main exposed to the wind, the sail flaps until the mainsheet is trimmed in. The mainsheet attaches near the end of the boom and controls the in-and-out position of the boom the way your arm controls the swing of a door. Now is also the time to make the initial adjustments of the outhaul and cunningham, which together control the position of the deepest part of the sail's curve by tensioning the cloth along the edges. After the tail of the main halyard is coiled and stowed, it might be necessary to ease the topping lift, a line or wire that supports the boom in a level position when the boat is at rest. Now the boomvang should be checked. This line, or telescoping pole, runs from the butt of the mast to the underside of the boom and resists the mainsail's tendency to lift up the aft end of boom. Of course, the mainsheet has a role here too.

Now it's time to raise the headsail. First, the skipper chooses which one to raise. It's common to have two or three, for different wind strengths, each a different size (smaller for more wind), with different curves and of different cloth weights.

The tack of the headsail is attached by a short pin or shackle to a point very close to the bottom of the forestay. Some boats are equipped with a foil on the forestay, which contains a groove to hold the boltrope sewn into the forestay's leech. Otherwise, the foresail is attached to the stay with a series of hanks—small spring-piston hooks. The headsail itself is loosely bundled on the foredeck; it may be necessary to tie it to the lifelines temporarily. The halyard is attached to the head and made ready to haul. But before the headsail is raised, sheets must be attached to the clew. Unlike the mainsheet, these are normally stowed when not in use. The headsail sheets are best tied through the clew cringle and led back, one on each side of the boat, through their sheet blocks (or fairleads) and draped over the coaming of the cockpit. It's important not to have them catch while the sail is being raised. (Sometimes, one long line is used for both sheets, attached to the clew at its midway point.)

When the word is given, the crew hauls the halyard and the headsail rises up the forestay. It luffs noisily for a few seconds while the halyard is cleated or stopped, then one of the sheets (depending on which tack the boat lays) is hauled in. Now, minor adjustments can be made to halyard tension, the position of the leads (which might run fore and aft on a track) and perhaps even headsail cunningham.

Now the boat is fully under sail. The engine is turned off. The centerboard, very likely, is lowered completely, perhaps using a light winch with a crank for a boat this size. Smaller boats employ a block and tackle called a centerboard tackle, and very small boats have a simple pendant.

From this point, most sail adjustments take place from the cockpit, using the mainsail and headsail sheets. The position of the traveler—a car that moves on a rail set crosswise on the boat to adjust the angle of pull on the mainsheet—also has to be set. Depending on many variables ("Basic Sail Trim," *page 225*), the traveler car is either pulled up to the windward side or let down to leeward. Once it is fixed in place, frequent small adjustments are made to the mainsheet to account for changes in apparent wind speed and angle. These adjustments both position the boom laterally and release or apply tension to the leech, depending on the traveler car's position. In some racing boats, the traveler tackle becomes the principal control for the main while sailing close to the wind.

Likewise, the headsails are frequently adjusted—some crews would say too frequently. Sail trim of the main and headsail are often coordinated in an effort to shape the layer of air that flows between them. Jib sheet adjustments are made with a winch. On boats larger than about 20 feet (6.1 m), even if the extra mechanical advantage of a winch crank is not necessary, the winch helps by snubbing the sheet until another hand grip is taken. When the wind increases, the headsail can hardly be moved without the mechanical advantage provided by the winch's gear ratio. (Set winch handles carefully; they're expensive and they sink.) Recently, most headsail winches are fitted with a self-tailer, a circular jaw that holds enough

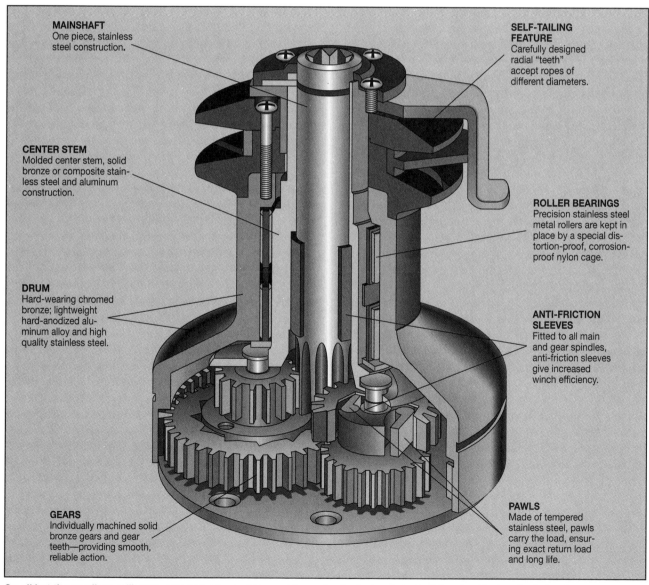

MAINSHAFT
One piece, stainless steel construction.

CENTER STEM
Molded center stem, solid bronze or composite stainless steel and aluminum construction.

DRUM
Hard-wearing chromed bronze; lightweight hard-anodized aluminum alloy and high quality stainless steel.

GEARS
Individually machined solid bronze gears and gear teeth—providing smooth, reliable action.

SELF-TAILING FEATURE
Carefully designed radial "teeth" accept ropes of different diameters.

ROLLER BEARINGS
Precision stainless steel metal rollers are kept in place by a special distortion-proof, corrosion-proof nylon cage.

ANTI-FRICTION SLEEVES
Fitted to all main and gear spindles, anti-friction sleeves give increased winch efficiency.

PAWLS
Made of tempered stainless steel, pawls carry the load, ensuring exact return load and long life.

On all but the smallest sailboats, winches are used to provide mechanical advantage for trimming the headsail sheets. Most modern winches are equipped with self-tailing devices, so that a single crew member can handle the winch.

tension on the sheet to prevent it from slipping against the surface of the winch drum. As the sheet is cranked in, the tail is peeled out of the jaw automatically. This means sail trim can be accomplished by one person, instead of two. For cruising, this is progress; for racing, it means less work for the crew.

The sails on a 25-foot boat are fairly easy to raise without the help of winches, but a larger boat might have a halyard winch, either mounted at the foot of the mast, or, more commonly, on the aft end of the roof of the cabin. Since winches are expensive, they are often shared among halyards and other adjusting lines. To hold one line in place while another is being winched, boats may now have linestoppers—simple levered clutches that clamp onto the line without damaging it. These are arranged, one per line, in front of the shared winch.

In place of linestoppers, lines may be held by camcleats with spring-loaded jaws that permit line in, but not out. Mainsheets, with their load-reducing block and tackle to provide mechanical advantage, are almost always held by large camcleats. Otherwise, camcleats are more common on small boats or for smaller, lightly loaded adjusting lines on large boats. Line is released by lifting up and out of the jaws.

Ordinary horned cleats are also useful for sheets, although they are less and less common for running rigging. Used properly, cleats can provide perfect holding power and quick release. (Refer to Chapter 13 for more information on cleating.)

So far we have explored all the line and hardware needed to get the sails up, adjust their shape, change their angle in relation to the apparent wind, and pull the centerboard up and down. We've pulled on the backstay, moved the traveler car, positioned the headsail leads. The next step—flying the spinnaker—perplexes and intimidates novices.

Flying the spinnaker

For this discussion, we will assume a conventional spinnaker because the others are simplifications of it. The spinnaker is attached at three points—the head and the clews. (Note that spinnakers have two clews although some sailors logically refer to the windward clew as the tack.) The head is attached to the mast by a halyard just like a headsail. The clews are attached to the deck with sheets, just like a headsail—except that there are always two separate sheets. The uniqueness of a spinnaker is that it is symmetrical, so that one sheet and one luff are on the windward side of the spinnaker on one tack, but on the leeward side on the other tack. As they change sides, they change names.

The leeward side of the spinnaker is the simplest. A sheet is attached to the clew; it runs aft to a block on the deck and is trimmed with a winch. When the spinnaker luffs, you pull the sheet in. The windward side is more complicated. Here, the clew also attaches to a sheet that runs aft to the deck at the stern. In this position, on the windward side, the sheet is now called the guy—though it's still the same piece of line. However, it is held away from the mast by a pole—a spinnaker pole—jut-

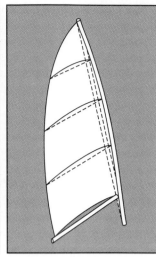

Using the backstay to tension the top of the mast aft will bow the middle of the mast forward and flatten the mainsail. The effect is to reduce draft and move it forward.

ting out at right angles and attached to the mast with an articulated coupling. The outboard end of the pole has a piston hook (or a similar device) that the guy runs through. The spinnaker itself is not actually attached to the pole.

That sounds simple, except that the pole has to be held both up and down. This is done with a pole uphaul and downhaul running from the pole (or a bridle on the pole) to the mast. Both up- and downhaul need their own blocks and, sometimes, winches. The loads created by the spinnaker can be heavy and variable.

For the cruising sailor, the chief advantage of the asymmetrical spinnaker is that so much of this spinnaker gear is eliminated. Asymmetry does away with the two clews and the sheets that change names. The cruising spinnaker is really a larger, lighter headsail that is tacked and jibed much the same way as a normal headsail, but is not attached along the forestay. Instead, it flies freely away from the forestay.

The racing approach to asymmetrical spinnakers is a little different. A pole is still used, but it has become a telescoping bowsprit. The spinnaker is typically not flown directly downwind (because these new, light boats sail fastest by tacking downwind), but is flown like a headsail, even though it is as big and almost as round as a conventional reaching spinnaker.

When measured against the relatively complex rigging of conventional sailboats, the popularity of wishbone cat-rigs is easy to understand. One sail does all the work and is controlled, for the most part, by one line—the mainsheet. The wishbone boom is suspended at its forward end by a choker line that attaches to a block on the mast and leads down to the foot of the mast and back to the cockpit. At its aft end, it is suspended, like a conventional boom, by the sail. The tightness or looseness of the choker line determines the depth or shallowness of the curve of the main in somewhat the same way that a conventional outhaul does.

BASIC SAIL TRIM

With practice, and by recording changes during trial and error experimentation, helmsman and crew will develop a feel for a boat's characteristics in different conditions and take appropriate measures to keep it "in the groove." Sail trim is a major component of achieving that goal, whether or not you are racing. The following are some elementary aspects of sail trim on each point of sail.

Sail shape

To some degree, the shape of a sail is restricted to the amount of "camber" or curve designed into it by the sailmaker. But the depth of the camber ("draft") can be controlled, and the position of the deepest part of the draft, with respect to the luff of the sail, can also be controlled. A more familiar, and eminently changeable, element of sail trim is the angle of incidence—the angle at which the leading edge meets the apparent wind.

As discussed in the preceding section on sailboat parts, a host of controls is available for trimming and shaping the sails for the conditions encountered. Be forewarned, however: There are no hard and fast rules for the order or degree with which each is used. Observation of the telltales on the sails and instruments in the cockpit, ability to hold a desired course, and the "feel" of the helm all measure the success of each action or combination of actions. Moreover, actions that produce a positive response on one boat may not on another. But if experimentation is the rule of sail trim, there are some fundamentals worth learning.

Mainsail shape

Changing the shape of the mainsail involves changing the depth of the draft to produce a flatter or fuller sail. Moving the mainsail's draft fore and aft is also a factor in improving the balance of the boat. Most of the time, the ideal position for maximum draft is one-third to one-half the way back from the mast. When sailing upwind, the object is to make the sail fuller at the leading edge, to direct total lift force forward and reduce side forces. When reaching, draft position is usually farther aft. Tensioning the clew outhaul to pull the clew aft reduces draft and moves it forward. The same effect is achieved by tensioning the backstay and boomvang to bend the top of the mast aft and bow the middle of the mast forward. As the mast bows forward, it pulls the middle of the mainsail and flattens it out. Increasing halyard tension and taking up the cunningham are also effective measures to move draft forward.

The mainsheet, combined with the boomvang and traveler, controls the tension on the leech of the mainsail. Leech tension is important for several reasons but the two principal considerations are twist and trailing edge shape.

In general, wind flows faster the higher it is from the water. That means that the top of a sail has to be trimmed to a different angle than the bottom, with the greater angle at the top—hence sail twist. To achieve a high degree of twist, you would usually ease the mainsheet, allowing the boom to rise. You might have to pull the traveler car to windward to prevent the boom from swinging too far from the boat's center line. The boomvang would be slack.

The opposite effect, removing twist, is achieved by trimming harder on the mainsheet, placing more tension up the leech, letting the traveler car down to position the boom somewhat away from the boat's center line, and using a tight boomvang. More pressure is carried high and aft by the mainsail and the leech "closes up"—begins to push airflow away to windward instead of just letting it flow easily aft.

While the basic decision to twist or close up the leech might be made according to the general wind strength and the point of sail, at the same time, gusts and lulls require adjustments to the mainsheet. Typically, the mainsheet is tensioned in lulls and eased (or even released) to open the leech and depower the sail in gusts. Upwind, the mainsheet usually provides most of the leech control. Off the wind or on a reach when the main is eased, the vang controls the leech. Many sails also have a "leechline" and a small cleat built into them to provide fine control as an adjunct to the coarse control of the mainsheet and vang. Care must be taken that the leechline is not so tight as to actually hook the leech to windward.

The traveler, of course, provides a means of balancing the mainsheet's vertical and horizontal pull on the boom. As the mainsheet is eased, and the boom moves to leeward, the angle of pull on the boom becomes more horizontal, removing tension from the leech. When the traveler car is eased to leeward, the pull of the mainsheet becomes more vertical, increasing leech tension.

The traveler car can also be pulled to windward in light air so that the mainsheet tension is more horizontal but the angle of the boom is still very close to, or right over, the center line of the boat. This allows sufficient twist, but a smaller angle of incidence to the flow of air at the luff. However, care must be taken not to overtrim the main. A rule of thumb is to keep the batten second from the top parallel to the boom; no battens—in fact, no part of the sail—should ever point to windward.

Headsail trim

The headsail, or jib, of many boats supplies as much drive as the main, or more. Not only are headsails often as large as the main, especially in masthead rigs with genoas, but the sail is presented to the airflow without the disturbing windage of the mast.

The tension on the forestay is the second most important control of headsail shape, after the position and tension on the sheet itself.

A loose forestay (created by loosening the backstay) creates sag, which in turn creates a full (deep draft) headsail. Sailmakers build a degree of allowance for forestay sag into the sail shape, but manipulating tension in the forestay has the

The relationship between the boat's heading and the direction of the wind has a traditional set of names. When there is the smallest practical angle between wind direction and heading, the boat is said to be "close-hauled," meaning that its sails (or yards on traditional vessels) are hauled in close to the hull. Another name for this is "beating."

When the angle between heading and wind direction is increased, the boat begins to "close reach," and when the angle is about 90 degrees, the wind is on the beam, so the boat is "beam reaching."

Further increases in angle bring the boat to a "broad reach"; with the wind almost directly aft, the boat is "running."

The term "running" sounds fast, and in traditional vessels, it may well have been. But the fastest point of sail for most modern boats is a close reach, and running today is actually very slow.

Remember that this pie-shaped diagram shows the relation between the boat and the wind, while the more important factor, especially for today's faster boats, is the relationship between the boat and its apparent wind—the wind that the sails feel. Very fast boats, like catamarans and racing dinghies, might seem to be swinging from a close reach right through to a broad reach in terms of the true wind, when they are in fact close reaching the apparent wind.

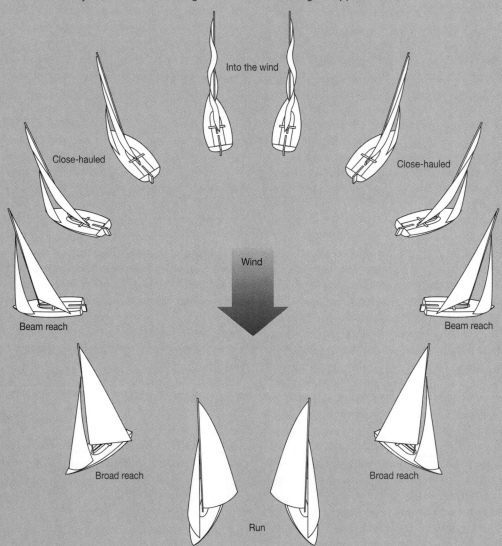

Into the wind

Close-hauled

Close-hauled

Wind

Beam reach

Beam reach

Broad reach

Broad reach

Run

A sailboat cannot sail directly into the eye of the wind, but modern sailboats usually can sail to within 45° of the wind, or closer, when close-hauled. A reach is the fastest point of sail, with the sails eased about halfway out. A run is aerodynamically simpler, but can be the most dangerous point of sail. The sails are extended as far out over the sides of the boat as possible, and can swing across with tremendous force.

same effect as straightening the mast: The sail is pulled tighter across the middle and becomes flatter.

Upwind, particularly in brisk winds, the jib halyard should be tensioned in order to keep the position of the deepest part of the draft as far forward as possible.

Key to trimming the jib, however, is the position of the clew. As the leeward sheet is eased, the clew will tend to move outboard and upward. The effect is a fuller sail. Tensioning the sheet pulls the clew aft, down and inboard, flattening the sail and decreasing the angle of incidence with the airflow.

Twist in the headsail is controlled by the position of the sheet lead (also known as the fairlead). As the lead is moved forward, the sheet pulls more on the leech—more downward. But as the lead is moved aft, the sheet pulls more on the foot—more backward.

In practice, it is often difficult to see the angle of the jib sheet accurately. But if the leech is fluttering, it indicates that the fairlead is too far aft, creating too much twist at the top of the sail; if the foot of the sail is fluttering or bellied out too far, the fairlead is too far forward, flattening the top of the sail too much.

Telltales

Proper sail trim is often elusive, even for experienced sailors. Yet while no one can actually see the wind, there remains a relatively simple solution: Place pieces of ribbon or yarn— about eight or nine inches long—at or near the luff on both sides of the headsail and mainsail. Their movement will reveal the action of the wind.

Jib telltales can serve to fine-tune sheet lead position and sheet tension. Although telltale positions will vary with preference, in general three telltales are placed on the jib about a foot behind the luff so that they divide the luff into four. (It's a good idea to avoid placing telltales too close to seams. It can be frustrating when they become caught on stitching in light air.) Some sailors also favor telltales at the point of maximum draft on their mainsail, and one at each batten pocket along the leech, in addition to three telltales at the luff positioned as for the jib.

In general, the object when trimming a sail is to have all the telltales streaming aft at the same time, indicating that the airflow across the two sides of the sail is even and smooth. When telltales lift and flutter, air is curling around the edge of the sail nearest the telltale instead of flowing strongly past it. When telltales droop, it's an indication that an "empty pocket" of air has been created and no energy is being extracted at that point.

If the leeward telltales are lifting or fluttering, they indicate that the boat can be steered on an angle closer to the apparent wind because the airflow is hitting the edge of the sail and tipping over it, resulting in a curl. If it is not necessary, or even desirable, to steer closer to the wind—if the boat is not sailing upwind, but reaching—the same correc-

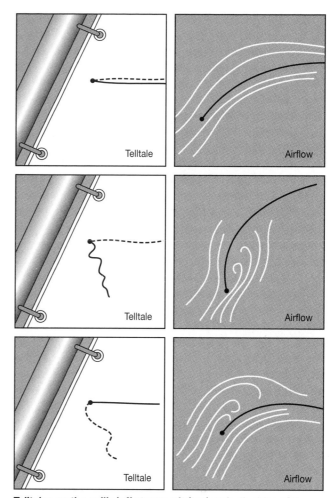

Telltales on the sail's luff stream aft *(top)* on both sides of the sail when airflow is even and smooth. A drooping telltale *(center)* indicates a dead pocket of air, with no force being extracted. Lifting and fluttering telltales on the leeward side *(bottom)* indicate that air is curling round the sail's edge.

tive effect can be achieved by letting the sail out. The leading edge of the sail thus meets the airflow more smoothly, and as a consequence the telltales stream aft.

Conversely, if a windward telltale lifts and flutters, the boat is too close to the apparent wind and must be "laid off," or steered at a wider angle to the apparent wind. If a course change is not desirable, the airflow can be corrected by pulling the sheet tighter and the sail closer to the boat's center line.

If the telltales nearer the foot of the sail (usually the headsail) are acting differently from the telltales nearer the head, then there is something wrong with the amount of twist. The sheet lead position should be changed until the telltales all react in a similar manner to changes in steering angle or sheet tension. For example, if the upper windward telltales are lifting while the lower ones are streaming, this is an indication that the sail has too much twist and the leads should be moved forward.

Fluttering or drooping telltales on the leech of the mainsail indicate that the air leaving the after edge is curling, creating drag; this is created by loosening of the leech tension, known as "opening up the leech."

The slot

The mainsail and the headsail work very closely together to shape the air that flows between them. This area between the sails is called the "slot." The headsail accelerates the air across the leeward surface of the main, helping it produce lift and substantially enhancing the low-pressure venturi effect.

If the jib sheet is eased, it permits the clew to rise and go too far outboard. The slot may become too open, so that there is no accelerated flow. If the jib is sheeted too tightly, the slot closes and the jib forces airflow to curl into the back of the main—"backwinding" the main and destroying the low pressure that is the whole object of the exercise. Sometimes this backwinding is acceptable if there is too much airflow and sufficient power is being taken from the headsail while the main acts to balance the pressures fore and aft to control steering.

The jib should generally be trimmed for course and conditions first, then the main trimmed so that the twist of the leech matches that of the jib, making the slot effective. On an upwind course, jib and main are usually trimmed as close to the center line as wind force will permit. On some boats, a second fairlead track or "barber-haul" system permits the headsail sheet lead to be positioned closer to or farther from the center line, as well as fore and aft, with much the same effect as adjusting the mainsheet traveler.

Upwind technique

The closer to the wind a boat sails, the less distance it must travel to reach a particular destination. But it also sails slower. Conversely, the farther off the wind it sails, the faster the boat moves. But it must sail a greater distance.

The objective of sailing upwind (variously called "pointing," "beating," or sailing "close-hauled" or "to weather") is to reach a specific point as quickly as possible by sailing a course that strikes the best compromise between higher speed and longer distance on the one hand, and lower speed but shorter distance on the other. The exact best compromise changes with wind speed and wave conditions.

In general, flatter sails are more efficient upwind than are full ones. They also should be sheeted as close to the center line as the wind strength will allow. The crew should be prepared to depower sails during gusts—either by easing the traveler car to leeward or by easing the mainsheet—so that excessive heeling doesn't contribute to leeway. Positioning crew to windward and even asking them to hike over the side will also help to counter heeling, thus allowing the keel to produce more lift and less leeway.

Constant adjustment of sails is called for in alternating gusts and lulls when close-hauled. Alternatively, the helmsman can "pinch" up in puffs and gusts, temporarily depowering the sails and keeping the boat "on its feet" (albeit at a temporary loss of speed), and bear off in lulls to accelerate.

Sailing close-hauled, the helmsman must determine how well the boat is balanced. If too much weather helm is required to keep the boat sailing a straight course, the center of effort has moved too far aft or the boat has heeled too much. To balance the boat, the sails can be depowered (flattened), the

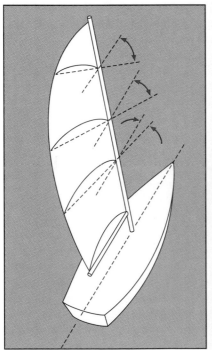 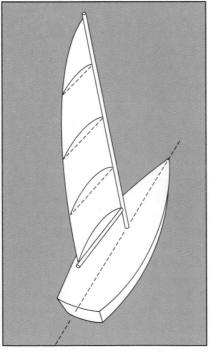

Because wind speed is faster higher above the water, sails need to be trimmed to a different angle at the top than at the bottom, with the greater angle at the top. Sail twist is achieved by easing the mainsheet, allowing the boom to rise *(far left)*. To remove twist *(near left)*, trim the mainsheet harder, and use the traveler to position the boom slightly farther off the boat's center line.

TACKING

Since a boat cannot set a direct course to a destination to windward, it must tack upwind. Each tack has a predeterminable compass heading, a factor of leeway and estimated speed; its length must be calculated to achieve the most efficient progress in tacking to windward.

A well-crewed boat should not fear tacking, a fundamental maneuver of sailing. In preparation, the helmsman announces, "Ready about," and bears off the wind a few degrees to add speed. The windward foresail sheet is prepared with a turn or two around the windward winch, while the leeward foresail is uncleated but kept on the winch ready to free. The winch handle should be at hand. If the traveler car is to windward, the crew member assigned to the mainsheet readies the car to be moved.

The helmsman should check the compass heading on the original tack. Once the boat and crew are readied, the helmsman announces, "Helm's a'lee" or "Coming about," and slowly luffs up into the wind, ensuring that the rudder is not cranked over so hard as to stall the boat.

As the headsail passes through the eye of the wind, the helmsman pushes the tiller or wheel over until the course is about 95 or 100 degrees from the original course. The original leeward sheet is cast off, and the new leeward sheet hauled in by hand until taut, then wrapped two more times around the winch. The winch handle is inserted for final foresail trimming. Simultaneously, the helmsman gradually lets the boat gather speed as the mainsheet trimmer moves the traveler and trims the main to complement the trim of the foresail. The objective bearing on the new tack will be about 90 degrees from the previous one, and 45 degrees to the true wind on the new windward bow. But the helmsman should allow the boat to accelerate slightly off the wind before sails are trimmed perfectly and the boat is steered up to the desired heading.

In the tacking diagram shown at right, the boat begins to turn at the bottom figure. Sails begin to luff as the bow heads into the wind. Momentum carries the boat onto the new tack (in this case the starboard tack) and the sails are then trimmed.

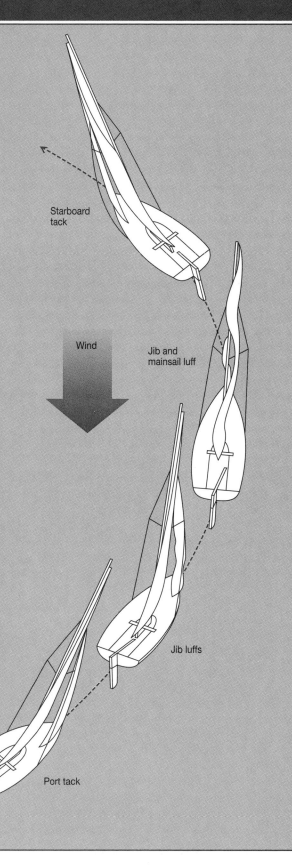

Starboard tack

Wind

Jib and mainsail luff

Jib luffs

Port tack

leech can be opened up, the boom can be eased out away from the center line, or all three.

To sail a windward course well, a crew must deal with several trade-offs in order to develop a strategy for reaching a windward mark. Factors such as wind strength, the possibility of a wind shift, sea conditions, strain on the boat, crew comfort (and perhaps how the competition is doing) must be weighed in order to set a course that efficiently and economically moves the boat toward the target.

Reaching technique

Bearing away from a close-hauled course onto a reach is a technique that puts most boats onto their fastest point of sail. But caution must be taken whenever this maneuver is put into practice: Continued care is required in order to maintain the boat's balance. Weather helm, as the boat tries to round up into the wind, is usually strongest on a close reach because an over-trimmed main will tend to keep the center of effort back and to twist the boat into the wind.

Moving the main traveler to leeward will change the angle of incidence of the leading edge of the sail to the apparent wind and ease heeling. But while main and jib should be trimmed for the course and wind strength, care must be taken that the main isn't eased so far that wind strikes its lee side too directly and stalls the boat. In centerboard boats, it helps to raise the board slightly to move the center of lateral resistance aft and more in line with the center of effort. A skilled crew might wish to cope with gusts by alternately easing and sheeting sails. But the helmsman should bear in mind that the rule that applied when close-hauled is now the opposite: When reaching, bear off in gusts and head up in lulls. It is essential to bear off because, as boat speed increases, the apparent wind moves forward. In a light boat, a quick jab to leeward will also help to "put the hull under the sails" and stabilize it momentarily.

In order to keep the rudder "biting" when reaching in heavy weather, crew weight should be aft and to windward. This is especially important in a following or quartering sea, because waves moving under the hull from behind can lift the stern and rudder out of the water, causing the boat to yaw with a momentary loss of steerage. But a helmsman who learns to "steer the waves" can often surf down them and exceed theoretical hull speed, one of the most exhilarating experiences in sailing. The boomvang should be used to adjust the curve of the leech and control the boom.

Reaching in very light conditions calls for different tactics. Moving crew weight forward and to leeward induces heel, making the sails "fall" to windward and giving them a better airfoil shape to utilize what little airflow exists.

Offwind technique

Sailing off the wind can be a pleasant respite after a long beat or reach. More sail may be carried because the apparent wind is not as strong. On the other hand, downwind sailing is not usually as fast as other points of sail, and unless caution is taken it can be the most dangerous point of sail.

Bearing off a reach onto a straight downwind course, ease the main as far out as possible. If possible, ease tension on the backstay (and leeward running backstay if so equipped) for fuller sail shape of the headsail. Sufficient tension on the upwind running backstay may be applied to give extra support to the mast. Most sailors prefer to broad reach downwind, jibing toward the target rather than sailing dead downwind. This is usually preferable for a light, fast boat. But even broad reaching, the narrowest angle toward the target may be best. And unless the wind comes slightly over one aft quarter, the foresail will become blanketed by the main's wind shadow. To put the foresail in clear air, it can be jibed across to the other tack so the boat is sailed "goosewinged" ("wing and wing"), with the leeside of both sails 180 degrees to the wind.

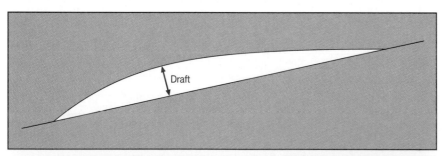

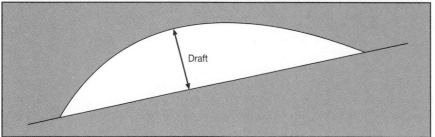

Changing the shape of the sails is accomplished by changing the depth of the draft to produce a flatter or fuller sail. The amount of draft required in different conditions varies with the point of sail. In general, flatter sails *(top)* are more efficient upwind than the fuller ones, as shown at bottom.

Uncontrolled jibes are to be avoided as they are hard on gear and a fast-moving boom is potentially dangerous. A controlled jibe, however, should be a normal part of sailing and is not something to be feared. When ready to jibe, the helmsman announces, "Prepare to jibe," and steers slightly off the wind. The mainsheet trimmer hauls the sheet in and cleats it as other crew releases the leeward headsail sheet and hauls in the windward sheet.

The helmsman then steers back toward the wind until the boom swings across the boat and is held by the cleated mainsheet. The mainsheet is then eased to the new windward side as the headsail is trimmed for the new course.

In the diagram at right, the boat is already sailing goosewinged (also called wing-and-wing), with the mainsail on the port side. The helmsman prepares to jibe the mainsail by turning the stern into the wind (bottom). **The wind then catches the mainsail and whips it across the boat, under control of the main sheet.**

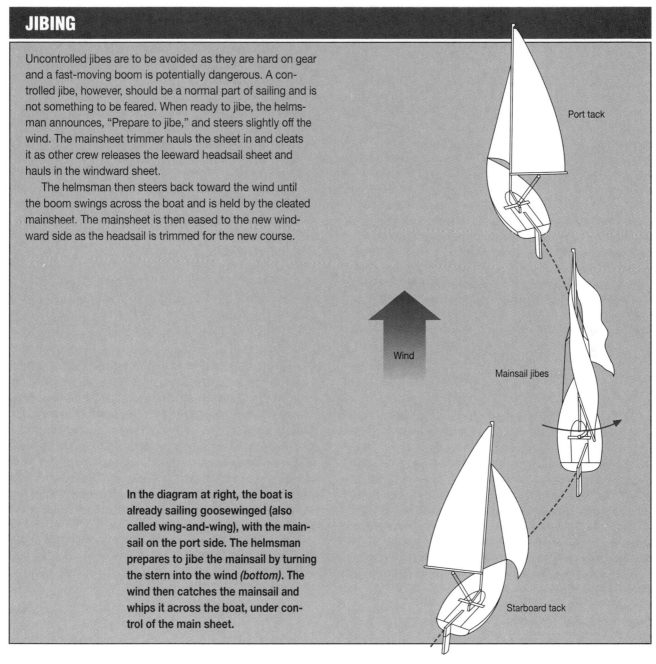

Port tack

Wind

Mainsail jibes

Starboard tack

Maintaining steady wind on a boomless foresail when goosewinged is often a problem. The remedy is a whisker pole extended from a fitting on the mast to the clew of the foresail—the precursor of the spinnaker pole. Some long-distance sailors, sure that the wind won't shift and reluctant to deal with the extra care a spinnaker requires, go so far as to fly two boomed foresails at once, one out each side, often with the main reefed or furled altogether.

Whenever the boom is outboard of the boat (sometimes when reaching and always when running), the mainsheet has less downward pull. In heavier weather downwind, waves may cause the boom to rise and fall as the boat rolls. Tightening the boomvang will help steady the boat. The mainsail may be at right angles to the center line of the boat, but if the boom is allowed to move too far forward, the boat will be "sailing by the lee."

If there is a danger that the wind might catch the front of the main and cause a "flying" or uncontrolled jibe, a "preventer" can be rigged. The mast attachment of a tackle type of boomvang can be moved farther outboard, toward the toerail. In heavy seas, however, care must be taken that the boom, which is held down by the vang, doesn't dip into the water as the boat rolls. Furthermore, too much tension on the vang may result in over-flattening the main sail. To maintain sail shape, the topping lift and vang can always be adjusted in concert.

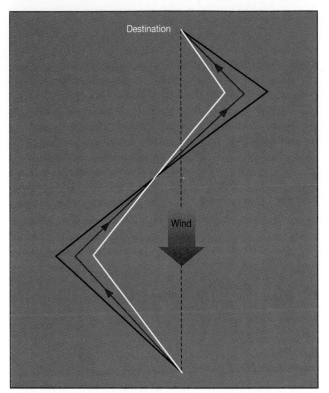

Sailing upwind requires consideration of several factors, including wind speed, wave conditions and level of comfort desired. In the example above, any of the three routes shown will lead to the same destination.

While a vang attached to the toerail will partially prevent the main from filling on its leeward side and jibing accidentally, it may also cause damage to the rigging if you do jibe uncontrollably. A better, perhaps safer, "preventer" can be rigged from the clew of the main to a block on the foredeck, and led to the cockpit where it can be eased if necessary.

In general, crew weight when sailing off the wind should be amidships fore and aft, and as far outboard as possible on both sides. In fresh conditions when a following sea is lifting the stern of the boat, moving weight aft is a measure that will help maintain steerage.

When sailing downwind, it is important to remember that wind strength is greater than it seems. Before "hardening up" to a reach, sails should be tended accordingly, perhaps even changed or reefed if the boat will be over-canvassed for the new point of sail.

Spinnakers and asymmetrical spinnakers

Sailors who wish to achieve maximum speed when sailing off the wind invariably turn to a spinnaker. Perhaps no sail has as many variations as the spinnaker (often called "chute" or "kite"). Sails that fall into the category are often called "flying sails" as they are attached to the boat only at their three corners, and do not have the stabilizing support at the luff that other foresails do.

The chute itself is constructed of lightweight material that fills easily, packs in a small launching bag or box, and is cut to billow with a full shape and curved luff and leech. Contrary to popular view, a spinnaker does not merely catch wind from behind and "push" the boat. Rather, air passing over its leeward side from luff to leech creates a mini low-pressure area into which the sail moves.

For the most part, spinnakers fall into one of two categories: conventional and asymmetrical. A conventional symmetrical spinnaker (luff and leech are of equal lengths and interchangeable) is more efficient directly downwind than asymmetrical models.

Before it is launched, care must be taken that the spinnaker has been properly packed with no twists, and that the head and two corners of the foot of the sail are accessible, preferably color-coded for port and starboard.

Assume that the spinnaker is being launched on the port side. Clip the inboard end of the spinnaker pole to the mast eye, with the pole sticking out the starboard (windward) side. Adjust the mast end to the height at which it is anticipated that the pole will be held when the sail is set.

The guy is run through the pole end (still on deck or lower than the pole end attached to the mast) and around the forestay, then clipped to the green-patched (starboard) spinnaker clew and led aft outside the shrouds. The sheet is attached to the red-patched port clew, then led outside the shrouds and aft to a turning block on the aft quarter. The halyard is attached to the head of the sail by means of a swiveling shackle. The spinnaker should be flown from a mast block that is above and ahead of the forestay.

Raise the spinnaker pole using the pole uphaul lift until it is at right angles to the mast. Take up the pole downhaul and cleat it, leaving just a little slack.

Before raising the sail, ensure that the pole is a few feet from the forestay and pay out some of the sail so that the tack is allowed to reach the end of the pole as the guy is tensioned and cleated. Finally, hoist and cleat the halyard. If the foresail is still flying it is now lowered and secured on deck or roller-furled. As the spinnaker fills, crew trim the sheet and guy, first positioning the guy (and the pole with it) according to the apparent wind angle. The pole should be (very roughly) 90 degrees to the apparent wind.

Sailing the chute

The primary rule of spinnaker sailing is to keep the luff from curling and the pole as square as possible to the wind. The closer the course is to dead downwind, the farther aft the pole is pulled and the more the sheet eased to add to sail fullness. In some cases, the halyard may be eased slightly as well to permit the spinnaker to move forward out of the disturbance from the main.

To reach, allow the pole to move forward, and trim the sheet. Care must be taken that the pole doesn't rest on the forestay; the power of a spinnaker is such that forestay damage is possible. A spinnaker is also capable of heeling the boat dramatically. The helmsman must bear off in gusts and "sail under the chute."

To jibe the chute, begin by swinging the main boom across the center line. Next, unclip the pole at the mast and, using the remote line to open the pole-end fitting, clip the former mast end over the sheet, which is to become the new guy. The final maneuver consists in attaching the former outboard pole end to the mast eye and trimming the former guy, which at this point becomes the sheet.

An alternative "dip-pole" jibe requires either a pole that fits inside the forestay, or one that can be retracted in such a way that allows it to do so. Throughout, the mast end remains attached to the mast. During the jibe, the guy is released by the remote trip line, the pole is retracted if necessary, and the pole topping lift is released in order to permit the pole to be dipped below and behind the forestay. Finally, the pole end is then clipped onto the former sheet, which now becomes the new guy, and the new sheet (which formerly was the guy) is hauled in and trimmed.

"Flying" a spinnaker off the wind can be a breathtaking experience. This powerful sail demands skill and constant attention.

Dousing the chute

The surest way of bringing down the spinnaker is first to depower by steering so that the spinnaker is blanketed by the main when the guy is eased forward. Foredeck crew unclips the guy from the pole using the remote trip line and the guy is eased. The sail, now held in the wind by the head and sheet, essentially becomes a large flag. Taking care not to let the sheet or guy fall into the water, one crew eases the halyard while another gathers the sail by the leech, under the main boom. With practice, it is possible to gather it directly into the storage "turtle," leaving the two lower corners and head exposed and ready for rehoisting.

Cruising spinnakers

From the foregoing, it isn't hard to see why conventional spinnakers are often eschewed by cruising sailors who sail short-handed. But all sailors seek to improve downwind performance, and the asymmetrical spinnaker, often called a "cruising chute," is viewed by many as the cruiser's answer. For reaching in particular, asymmetrical spinnakers, distinguished by a luff that is shorter than the leech, are also gaining favor with racers.

In the cruising form, a line at the tack is led through a block at the stemhead and run back to a cockpit cleat or stopper. The sheets are usually run outside the forestay. Sailing under cruising chute is much like reaching, though easing the sheets by easing the tack line, and perhaps the halyard, brings the sail forward and free of the main's shadow.

Jibing a cruising chute inside the forestay as one would a conventional foresail risks wrapping the halyard around the forestay, as well as damaging the large sail on foredeck fittings. Consequently, a cruising chute is usually jibed by letting the sheet go as the stern comes through the wind. The clew of the sail is allowed to fly free around the front of the headstay and the new sheet on the opposite side is taken up so that (unlike a conventional spinnaker) the reverse side of the chute is now the leeward side.

The asymmetrical chute's effectiveness decreases as the boat sails more downwind. Only in very light conditions should it be poled out like a genoa. However, it is often better than a symmetrical spinnaker for close reaching. A recent trend among larger racing yachts, including those in the America's Cup competition, has been adapted from racing dinghies such as the International 14 class. This system features a permanently mounted pole that can be extended forward through the hull at the bow to become a long sprit (like a bowsprit). Attaching the asymmetrical chute to the pole end means effective exposure to the wind when reaching.

Yet another variation on the spinnaker theme is the so-called gun-mount spinnaker system, which features a pole mounted at its middle on the fitting of a reinforced pulpit. The sail is tacked at both ends of the pole and the pole acts as a boom. Sheets to each end of the pole are used to trim the sail according to the course.

DOCKING UNDER SAIL

The wind that propels the sailboat can also be used to put on the brakes. That's why a skipper who wants to slow down, or stop, will begin by spilling wind from his or her sails (letting them out), then will point the bow of the boat into the direction of the wind. The whole rig, acting as windage, will slow the boat down, stop it and, eventually, force it backward.

This technique is useful for landing at a pier. Providing you can choose a "landing path" that heads the boat into the wind, you can sail across the wind, round up and, as the boat slows, carry it gently into position against the pier.

In stronger winds, everything is noisier and more exciting, but the braking force is also greater. It can be further strengthened if the crew pushes the boom outward against the wind as the boat is headed into the wind. This is called "backing the main."

Careful crew work and a little experience allow the skipper to judge how far the boat will carry on as the braking force of the wind is applied. Some skippers can even back down into a slip, but, in a busy dock, this maneuver should be reserved for emergencies.

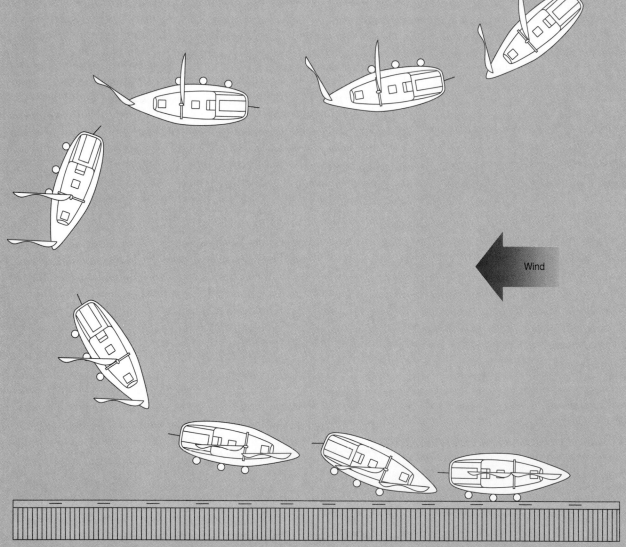

Wind

As the boat approaches the dock, the helmsman steers off the wind, and the main and jib sheets are loosened to spill the wind. Once the boat has depowered, the helmsman uses the remaining momentum to steer the boat across the wind, then round up into it alongside the dock. The distance that the boat will coast under such conditions must be determined by experience, but additional braking force can, if necessary, be supplied by backing the main against the wind.

SAIL HANDLING AND STOWAGE

Headsails

Roller furling for headsails is one of many innovations that promote simplified, convenient handling of sails; not surprisingly the system has been growing steadily in popularity. The mechanism typically consists of a headfoil that is fitted over the forestay. The foresail halyard is attached to a swivel that can both slide up and down the foil and swivel around on it. A reel-like drum at the base of, and fixed to, the foil has a furling line wound around it. The furling line finally leads back to the cockpit. Some models have a continuous line around the reel, led aft on blocks.

To raise the sail initially, the head is attached to the swivel and the boltrope fed into the groove of the foil. The tack is attached to the drum. The halyard on the swivel pulls up both the swivel and sail. When the furling line is hauled aft, the drum and foil turn around the forestay, rolling the sail around it as well. The furling line is cleated to store the sail furled on the forestay. To protect the sail from ultraviolet deterioration, a sacrificial protective strip is often sewn along the leech and foot. To set the sail, the furling line is released. Tension on a sheet unrolls the foresail, assisted by the wind once the aft part of the sail begins to fill.

In addition to saving storage space, foresail furling systems also permit the sail to be partially furled or reefed. To maintain proper angle of the sheets when the sail is reefed, jib fairleads must be moved forward on their tracks.

Mainsails

Roller furling systems exist in a number of variations for mainsails as well. Some feature an in-mast or behind-the-mast furler that begins by winding the luff of the sail, pulling

To store the lowered mainsail, pull the sail aft from the leech, flaking it on opposite sides of the boom as you go.

the clew forward. The disadvantage of such systems is that they preclude the use of battens, often require a loose-footed main, and add weight aloft.

In-boom furling systems that furl the foot of the sail on an internal roller are actually a refinement of older roller reefing systems that worked by wrapping the sail around the boom itself. In practice, the boom is supported by the topping lift while the halyard is released and a handle winds the roller in the boom. The customary difficulty of getting a proper sail set, which used to affect older systems, has been eliminated on many modern versions.

A more commonly employed (and distinctly less expensive) means of reefing is a "slab" or "jiffy" system that makes use of cringles at two or three reef points on each of the luff and leech. Reefing lines are fastened to the boom, led up through the cringles on the leech and down to a sheave at the boom end, and then forward to the gooseneck. To reef, the boat is taken head to wind, and the topping lift is tensioned in order to take the weight of the boom. The halyard and outhaul are then eased off and the reef cringle at the luff is hooked onto a tack hook. As the halyard is tensioned, the appropriate reefline is taken up to pull the new clew down and aft, and the topping lift is eased. The new foot of the sail is then secured, either by means of permanent lines on the sail or with sail ties led through cringles spaced between the leech and luff reefing points.

As unwieldy as all this sounds, with a certain amount of planning, a reef using a jiffy reefing system can usually be taken in or let out in less than a minute, and the resulting shortened sail can be set well.

Spinnakers

The lack of luff support makes spinnakers more unstable and more difficult to launch, jibe and "douse" or take down. Some new designs are equipped with a reinforced patch and a cringle in the center to which a "take down" or "retriever" line is attached to assist in dousing the sail, and sometimes for pulling the sail through a tubular launcher incorporated into the hull with a funnel-like outlet on deck. The retriever is then led through the tube to the cockpit. Now the doused sail, which is now stored in the tube, is ready to redeploy whenever it is needed.

Another technique for hoisting the spinnaker entails careful packing beforehand. The sail is pulled through a funnel-like device equipped with elastic bands stored on its narrow end. As the head of the sail is pulled out the narrow end, elastic bands are placed around it at intervals. The spinnaker is rigged and hoisted with the elastic bands in place. When the sheet and guy are trimmed, the bands break and permit the sail to fill.

A tubular sleeve with rings at each end (variously called a "sock," "sally," "chute scoop," etc.) may also be used. The spinnaker is stored inside the sleeve and attached to it. The sleeve is hoisted on the spinnaker halyard.

A line running the length of the sleeve is threaded through a block at the halyard end, and from there is attached to the ring at the bottom. The sock is hoisted fully with the sail inside, then the line is pulled in such a way that it will slip the sleeve upward. Wind filling the bottom of the sail usually helps to move the bottom ring and sock toward the halyard until the spinnaker billows and fills. The sleeve, meanwhile, remains at the head of the spinnaker while it is flying, and the line from the sleeve is cleated on deck. To douse the spinnaker, the sheet and guy are eased and the line attached to the sock's bottom ring is hauled in order to pull the sock down over the sail. In addition to being useful in dousing, a sock also can be used to control the sail to jibe whenever the boater is sailing shorthanded. The sock is merely pulled down over the sail, set up on the opposite tack and pulled up again to set the sail.

Storing sails

Foresails not stored on a roller system should be flaked—folded accordion-style—and dry before being bagged. Though not always the easiest thing to do in rough weather, the crew can control a hanked-on sail as it comes down on the side-deck by moving forward and pulling aft on the leech, securing the sail to the rail as they go. Ideally, another crew member, sitting back-to-bow in the bow pulpit, can control the luff to assist with flaking. If the flaked sail is to be bagged, the sheets are untied, and it is rolled neatly from the clew forward, ready to fit in the bag opening.

Hanks can be left on until the sail is stored. Sails that fit into a headfoil present a difficulty since they are controlled only by the halyard and tack when dropped. Care must always be taken to ensure that the sail does not fill on deck and then blow overboard.

An elongated bag—aptly referred to as a "sausage bag"—is often used in place of a conventional sail bag whenever using headsails constructed from new sail materials, such as Mylar or Kevlar, that can be damaged if they are folded too tightly. The zipper on the bag is opened lengthwise and clipped to the lifelines before the sail is dropped to the deck. Then, once the sail is dropped and flaked in the open bag, the full-length zipper is closed to enclose the sail.

A number of systems exist to help control the mainsail. Lazy jacks—ropes or wires running from mid-mast to the boom—keep the sail on the boom when it is dropped. Another system, called a Dutchman, features vertical lines running from the topping lift (or a similar line), through cringles on the sail and down to the boom. When the halyard is released, the vertical lines hold the sail in line with the boom.

To store the lowered mainsail on the boom, begin at the leech and pull the sail aft, flaking it on alternate sides of the boom. Sail ties can be used at intervals to lash the sail to the boom. As soon as possible, the sail should be covered to prevent ultraviolet degradation. Lazy jacks and the Dutchman may necessitate a special sail cover.

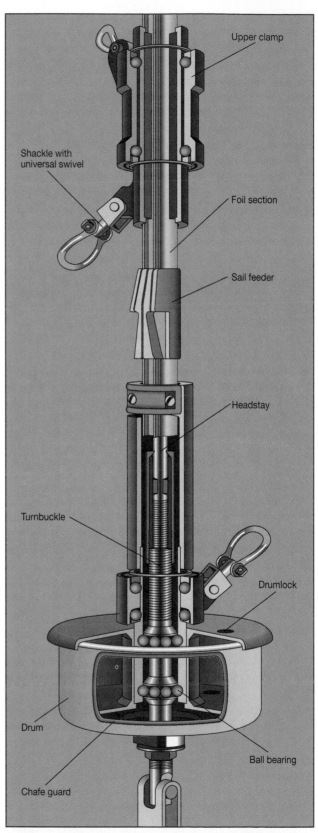

A sailboat's typical roller furling system uses a reel-like drum to contain the furling line. The furling line can be controlled from the cockpit.

NEW SAILBOAT TYPES

Sailing is undergoing another major step in its evolution. Techniques explored by sailboarders, multihull sailors and racing dinghy sailors for the last 20 years are now finding their way into the mainstream of sailing. In addition, techniques rooted in pure science and aircraft engineering—such as rigid wings and hydrofoils—are finding practical, if not popular, application.

Several factors are making sailing a faster and more exciting sport. One is the simple fact that most North Americans enjoy speed. Yet the cost of moving across the water at speed is very high. Many recreational boaters just can't afford to run a fast powerboat. For them, the thrill of a catamaran at high speed, not to mention the challenge of handling it, is an affordable choice.

Another factor is the availability of strong and light materials. In fact, many of the designs we consider recent and new have been around in slightly different forms for most of the century. For example, extremely light, flat-hulled racers with lots of sail area and asymmetrical spinnakers are very like the "sandbaggers" that were raced in New York Harbor late in the nineteenth century. What's different now is that such light, highly stressed designs can be built in strong materials, making ownership by mainstream sailors possible. Sandbagger sailing, on the other hand, was semi-professional and certainly not for the family man—just as America's Cup sailing today is very distant from family-oriented racing.

Multihulls

The most obvious "new" sailboat type is the catamaran or trimaran. In fact, the idea is ancient and was tried out as a racing design in the last century.

Multihulls first gained acceptance in the 1960s as light and fast recreational boats, but began to be seen as a practical (and even potentially safer) solution to long-distance cruising. Their high construction cost (at least in a production setting) and the general conservatism of the North American market kept them in the background through the '60s and '70s. However, in the '80s, European and some exceptional North American sailors successfully sailed multihulls in the open trans-ocean competition offered by such races as the Single-Handed Trans-Atlantic Race.

There are now several successful builders of production multihulls in Europe and North America and their general superiority, at least for racing, has been well demonstrated in various professional-level ocean races as well as Dennis Conner's famous defense of the America's Cup in 1988.

Along with the huge stability provided by two or three separate hulls, multihull designers have introduced such innovations as the rotating mast and the full-batten sail. By allowing the mast to rotate on a vertical peg at the foot, catamaran sailors are able to point the mast into the airflow and to induce the least amount of drag. By "over-rotating" they can more precisely control the shape of the full-batten sail. A rotating mast can also be built with a lighter and stronger section, because its wider surface can be regarded as sail area rather than parasitic drag.

Rigid wing sails

The wide rotating mast and very stiff, full-batten sails of catamaran competition eventually led to the rigid wing sail. First regarded as belonging exclusively to the radical realm of catamaran competition, and with no practical relevance to ordi-

North American sailors resisted multihulls for years, but designs such as this Jeanneau trimaran are winning them over.

nary recreational sailing (or conventional "yacht club" racing), the rigid wing is now proven as a feasible cruising rig. John Walker, British former aircraft designer, has created a cruising multihull powered by a three-part, rigid-wing sail. The trim of the sail is automatically controlled and electronically adjusted so that sailing the Planesail is more like driving a vehicle (or flying an aircraft). The skipper sits in a chair and manipulates switches and levers. There is no winch grinding, halyard hauling, or, in fact, any of the procedures described in the previous sections for sailing a conventional sailboat. Yet the Planesail has crossed the Atlantic under the power of the wind, sometimes in rough weather. This remarkable achievement owes almost nothing to the conservative traditions of racing-oriented yacht design.

Rigid wings have also been used in catamaran competition, where their somewhat higher weight can be compensated for with very widely spaced hulls that are able to yield much greater stability.

Planing hulls

Sailboats have been planing since the turn of the century, but it is only in that last 30 years that light, high-powered sailboats have become extremely popular. Boats with wide, light hulls are common, and many of these are equipped with trapezes that allow their crew (sometimes both skipper and forward hand) to suspend themselves horizontally over the surface of the water on the windward side.

The enormous increase in stability that trapezing allows is exploited by very large sail areas in relation to the weight of the boat and crew. Planing a boat of this type is possible even in winds of only 12 or 13 knots.

Trapezing is only practical on boats no longer than about 20 feet (6.1 m). At this size, the complexity of crew work and the number of trapeze artists required takes such boats out of the realm of recreation and into the realm of pure sport.

However, even without trapezes, there are many light, but ballasted, keel boats that are capable of planing in heavy winds. While such planing episodes can be brief (and are often assisted by a following sea that induces surfing), these light, flat-keel boats nevertheless achieve speeds well beyond the normal limit of the speed of a wave of a length equal to their displacement waterline.

Wing keels and bulbs

One of the refinements that has made it possible for a ballasted boat to sail beyond displacement hull speed is the use of very deep, and consequently lighter, fin keels.

A particular volume of lead ballast, if stretched downward, acts on the hull with a longer lever and can, therefore, provide more righting moment for the same weight. There are practical limits to the extent of draft that have to do with the mechanical stresses placed on a lifting surface like a fin keel, especially when it is swung violently by wave action at the surface (not to mention shallow water).

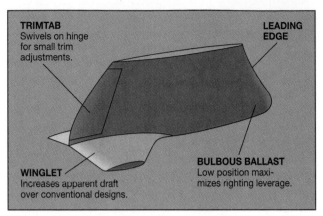

Wing keels are designed to position more ballast lower, without adding significantly to the boat's draft. Originally created for competition racing, they are now being used on cruising boats.

Recent design trends among America's Cup boats have suggested that the development of bulb keels will continue as a way to concentrate more ballast farther away from the hull.

Ironically, the wing keel, made famous by the first successful challenge of the America's Cup (by Australia, in 1983), was a successful design innovation that was very tightly tied to the design rules of the 12-meter class—which insisted on very high ratios of ballast to overall weight. Wing keels have found popular application outside of competition, in cruising boats that need both good windward performance and shallow draft. The volume of lead needed to provide righting moment can be formed into a shallower shape which, with winglets, need not be hydrodynamically inefficient.

The quest for greater righting moment without the penalty of weight has found yet another expression in the use of movable and expendable water ballast. There are two common approaches. In the most obvious method, water is taken on board, and held in tanks at the extreme beam of the hull. If the boat is working to windward on starboard tack, for example, its water ballast is pumped into the starboard tank where its weight provides the best righting moment. As or before the boat tacks, water is transferred, by pump or gravity, to the port tank, ready for the new tack. Of course, great care must be taken that the boat is not completely disabled should the ballast end up on the wrong side in heavy winds. The amount of water ballast carried, in relation to the boat's other stability, has to be carefully calculated by the designer. Of course, racing boats, especially single-handed ocean racers with the most to gain, take the greater calculated risks.

Another type of water ballast has nothing to do with racing or risk-taking. Several small, trailerable cruising sailboats have a different kind of water ballast which allows them to be light enough to tow behind a car but heavy enough to achieve good stability.

A long, low internal water tank is built into the hull at the lowest part of the bilge. A hole allows water to flow freely into and out of the tank. When the dry boat is launched, the tank fills up, adding, perhaps, a couple of hundred pounds at the lowest, and therefore, most advantageous, part of the hull. While this seems counter-intuitive to many sailors, it's easy to understand if you imagine, for a moment, that, instead of adding 100 pounds of water, you add 100 pounds of soft drink cans to the bilge. The effect is the same.

When it's time to go home, the (heavy) boat is pulled onto the trailer and, as soon as it begins to rise above its load waterline, the ballast tanks begin to empty. By the time the boat is at the top of the ramp, it's losing weight rapidly.

Sailboards

Currently, the second-fastest sailboat in the world is hardly a boat at all—it is a sailboard. Surprisingly, it doesn't look much different from the high-tech sailboards you see at any beach. As an exercise in motive efficiency, the sailboard is a very sophisticated device.

First, of course, its hull can hardly help but plane. But more important, it carries a huge amount of sail area in relation to its (and its crew's) overall weight. Since the mast is not stayed, the responsibility for holding it up does not fall on the hull. Rather, the weight of the crew is partly suspended against the very efficient lifting surface of the sail. Here, the aircraft notion of "lifting" has real merit; in fact, many sailboards are capable of short flights, given the right wave.

However, in setting a world speed record, the sailboard in question stayed very firmly on the water, finally reaching just over 44.66 knots.

Unfortunately, the sailboard may already have reached its maximum size. If it were any larger, it could not be controlled by one person.

The future of sailing

While thrill-seekers and speedsters may create another fad with boats like the Tri Foiler (a brand of boat with three rigid wingsails), the future of sailing, at least into the next century, probably rests with boats that would be more familiar to the average wharf-walker. The combination of high speed, long range, luxurious comfort and plenty of machinery and instruments has had an irresistible appeal to North American boat buyers for the last seventy years. That's why the majority of boats are powerboats.

But this powerboating domain may soon be raided by sailboats. A prototype that shows such promise is the Procyon. Developed as a demonstration of the sailing industry's capabilities, Procyon incorporates almost all of the innovations that have occurred in the design of displacement monohulls. At first sight, its most evident feature is an A-frame mast—two slender blades ascending from the gunwales to the head of the mainsail, supported by two track-mounted braces and very little else. The luff of the main, now free of the aerodynamic encumbrance of the mast, is mounted on a roller-furler, just like a headsail. At the same time, the boom is self-supported on a bracket.

Under the water are found more wondrous innovations. The ballasted fin keel, equipped with winglets, can be shifted sideways, allowing the skipper to place the fin's weight well over to the windward side. Water ballast can be moved from side to side electrically.

Naturally, Procyon's helm is elaborate and distinctive. While the boat's sail controls are in general fairly simple (the headsail, to cite just one example, is self-tacking with a single sheet), the electronic performance-monitoring and navigation devices are remarkably complex. Also complex are the controls for the hydraulic systems responsible for canting the keel, furling the sails and grinding the winches.

The very comfortably appointed Procyon will not suddenly be turned into a high-production luxury express cruiser, but each of the design team's innovations will find a niche at some level of the sailboat industry. And they will be joined by refinements and even further surprising innovations as more and more of the wind's immense power is converted into speed.

The Procyon demonstrates the advances made by the sailing industry. The prototype incorporates almost every design innovation yet developed for displacement monohulls, including a distinctive A-frame mast that eliminates the need for stays.

11 SPECIAL SEAMANSHIP TECHNIQUES

While most boaters would prefer to be out on the water in pleasant conditions, boating sometimes includes rough weather, running aground, or giving or requiring assistance. These situations are covered in this chapter, and how they are handled depends on two main factors: the boat's seaworthiness and the skipper's abilities.

Although seaworthiness depends largely on design and construction, it is important to remember that the average power cruiser or sailboat is seaworthy enough for normal conditions—*in the use for which it is intended*. Don't venture into waters or weather conditions beyond what your boat was designed to do, or beyond your own level of skill. An experienced skipper might bring a poor boat through a blow that a novice could not weather in a far more seaworthy craft.

BOAT HANDLING IN ADVERSE CONDITIONS

Knowing your boat in rough weather

"Rough weather" is a relative term. What seems a terrible storm to the fair-weather sailor may be nothing more than a good breeze to an experienced weather-wise mariner. On large, shallow bodies of water—for example, Lake Erie, Long Island's Great South Bay, Delaware Bay and Florida Bay—even a moderate wind will cause an uncomfortable steep sea with crumbling crests. Offshore or in deeper inland water, the same wind force might cause moderate seas, but the slow-rolling swells would be no menace to small craft.

Boat handling under adverse conditions is an individual matter for each skipper, since no two boats are exactly alike in the same sea conditions. When the going gets heavy, each hull design reacts differently; in fact, even individual boats of the same class may behave differently because of factors such as load and trim.

Each skipper must learn about his or her own boat, to determine how best to apply the general principles covered in the following sections. Reading books such as this and taking courses are important first steps. You can learn basic seamanship skills by absorbing facts and principles, but you'll have to pick up the rest by using that knowledge on the spot when the wind begins to blow.

Even when you're not practicing special seamanship techniques, work with theoretical situations. Ask yourself and your crew members on a regular basis about how to handle various difficulties. While cruising along on a calm day, for example, ask for suggestions about actions to take if the boat is suddenly grounded. This not only makes for interesting cockpit chatter, but also acts as a good basis for practicing the techniques.

Meeting head seas

The average well-designed power cruiser or larger sailboat should have little difficulty in meeting head seas. If the seas get too steep sided or if you start to pound, slow down by easing the throttle or by shortening sail. This gives the bow a chance to rise in meeting each wave instead of being driven hard into it. (A direct consequence of driving hard into a wave is that the

Reefed, with lee rail awash, the yawl is being driven hard in moderate seas.

This Coast Guard cutter is taking the waves at a 45° angle and, with judicious use of power and helm, will slowly gain way to deeper waters and longer swells.

force of the water hitting the superstructure can break ports or windows, or even lift a cabin top or coach roof.) In addition, use the following guidelines as they apply.

■ **Match your speed to sea conditions.** If conditions get really bad, slow down until you're making bare headway, holding your bow at an angle of about 45 degrees to the swells. The more you reduce headway in meeting heavy seas, the less strain will be exerted on the hull and superstructure.

■ **Avoid propeller racing.** If the seas lift the propeller clear of the water and it "races," this sounds dangerous—and it may be. First, there is a rapidly increasing crescendo of sound as the engine winds up, then excessive vibration as the screw bites the water again. You must reduce speed to avoid damaging the hull or engine. Don't panic—slow down and change your course until these effects are minimized. Keep enough headway so you can maneuver your boat readily. Experiment to find the speed best suited to the conditions.

■ **Adjust the trim.** You can swamp your boat if you drive it ahead too fast or if it is poorly trimmed. In a head sea, a vessel with too much weight forward may be too slow in rising under a bow wave, causing it to "plunge" into the next wave before rising from the first. Often, this can result in steering difficulty. Under the same conditions, too much weight aft will cause it to fall off.

Change the weight aboard, if necessary. On outboards, shift your tanks and other heavy gear. In any boat, direct your passengers and crew into position, and then tell them to remain in that position.

■ **Meet each wave as it comes.** You can make reasonable progress by nursing the wheel—by spotting the steep-sided combers coming in and varying your course accordingly; slow or even stop momentarily for the really big ones. Just as

PREPARATIONS FOR ROUGH WEATHER

In anticipation of high winds and rough seas, a prudent mariner takes certain precautions. Although no single list fits all boats or all weather conditions, some general guidelines are listed below. Storms can be a tremendous test of the knowledge, endurance, courage and cool judgment of skipper and crew alike. Remember, a well prepared boat and its crew members are much more likely to come through a storm with only minor mishaps.

■ Secure all hatches on the boat; close all ports and windows. Close off all ventilator openings, such as dorades and mushroom vents.

■ Since free water in bilges adversely affects a boat's stability, pump bilges dry; repeat as required.

■ Secure all loose gear; put away small items and lash down larger ones, including the anchors, anchor well lid, spinnaker pole and life raft.

■ Plug up the hawsepipe with a rag.

■ Charge your batteries, and avoid unnecessary drain on them until the blow is over.

■ Break out PFDs, and have everyone (including the skipper) on board wear one before the situation worsens; don't wait too long.

you adjust your speed when driving a car on a winding road, you must vary your boat speed to get through waves. If the person at the wheel can see clearly and act before dangerous conditions develop, the boat should weather moderate gales with little discomfort. Make sure the most experienced person aboard acts as helmsman, with an occasional break in order to stay sharp.

In and across the troughs

If your course requires you to run or turn broadside to the swells, bouncing from trough to crest and back up again, your boat may roll heavily, perhaps dangerously. In these conditions in a powerboat, it is best to run a series of tacks much like a sailboat.

Change course and take the wind and waves at a 45-degree angle, first broad on your bow and then broad on your quarter. You will make a zigzag course toward your destination, with your boat in the trough only briefly while turning. With the wind broad on the bow, the boat's behavior should be satisfactory; on the quarter the motion may be less comfortable but at least it will be better than running in the trough. Make each tack as long as possible to minimize how often you must pass through the trough.

To turn sharply, allow your powerboat to lose headway for a few seconds, throw the wheel hard over, then suddenly apply power. The boat will turn quickly as a powerful stream of water strikes the rudder, kicking you to port or to starboard, without making any considerable headway. You won't be broadside for more than a minimal length of time. This is particularly effective with single-screw boats. With a twin-screw powerboat, the engine on the side in the direction of the turn may be throttled back, or even briefly reversed.

Running before the sea

If the swells are coming from directly behind you, running before them is all right providing your boat's stern can be kept up to the seas without being thrown around off course. But in heavy seas a boat tends to rush down a slope from crest to trough, and, stern high, the propeller comes out of the water and races. The rudder also loses its grip, and the sea may take charge of the stern as the bow "digs in." At this stage, the boat may yaw so badly as to "broach"—to be thrown broadside

- Break out any emergency gear that you might require—hand pumps or bailers, sea anchors, drogues, etc.

- Seal off in a plastic bag provisions for each crew, including clothing, bedding, matches and food.

- Open cockpit lockers only if necessary; use caution if it becomes necessary to open them.

- Check your position, if possible, and update the plot on your chart; continue to update more often than usual.

- Make plans for altering course to sheltered waters, if necessary. Have the necessary charts ready, especially the ones for inlets and harbors. (Heading for an unknown harbor without a chart is pure folly.)

- Reassure your crew and guests. Instruct them in what to do, and what not to do, then assign them a task to take their minds off the situation.

- Make sure that navigation lights are working. Hoist the radar reflector. Check all flashlight batteries.

- Remember that being cold can affect your judgment. Have all crew members put on appropriate clothing: thermal underwear, thick socks, etc. Choose clothing that will remain warm when wet—for example, wool or polypropylene.

- Shut any sea cocks that will not be used, and then label them to avoid damage to running gear (for example, the engine if it is started).

- Wear your safety harness at all times in rough weather; it should fit snugly over your clothing.

- Bring the dinghy aboard, and lash it down securely.

- On a sailboat, prepare all reefing lines, set up the storm jib and trysail if it can be done independently from mainsail and foresails. Be ready to change to storm sails quickly. If you are running, rig a strong preventer that can be released from the cockpit.

- If you cook with gas, switch to a new tank now to avoid having to do so in rough seas. If you use kerosene for cooking or for lamps, now is the time to top up.

- Get out the motion sickness pills; it is better to take them before you get sick.

- Give your crew a good meal while you have the chance; it might be a while until the next one.

- Try to prepare some food in advance. Make a thermos of coffee or soup, and store something that can be eaten easily and quickly—sandwiches, perhaps—in a watertight container.

out of control—into the trough. Avoid broaching through every possible action. Unfortunately, today's powerboat designs emphasize beam at the stern so as to provide a large, comfortable cockpit or afterdeck—this width at the stern increases the tendency to yaw and possibly broach.

A sailboat will be more comfortable in a large sea with some sail up. Even a reefed mainsail or storm sail will help reduce the amount of roll and will help the boat to shoulder through some of the waves.

Reducing yawing

Slowing down to let the swells pass under your boat usually reduces the tendency to yaw, or at least reduces the extent of yawing. While it is seldom necessary, you can consider towing a heavy line or drogue (*page 246*) astern to help check your boat's speed and keep her running straight. Obviously the line must be carefully handled and not allowed to foul the propeller. Do not tow soft laid nylon lines which may unlay and cause "hockles" (strand kinks).

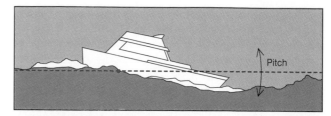

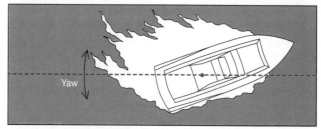

Pitching, rolling and yawing are normal motions of a boat. If they become excessive, or combine, they may be uncomfortable, even dangerous.

SEAMANSHIP FOR SAFETY IN "THICK" WEATHER

"Thick" weather refers to conditions of reduced visibility that are most severe and most often caused by fog, but may also be caused by heavy rain or snow, or by haze. Piloting and position determination, the legal requirements for sounding fog signals, and the meteorological aspects of fog are covered elsewhere in this book. Below we will consider only the aspects of boat handling and safety.

Avoid collisions.
You must see and be seen, hear and be heard. Take every possible action to see or otherwise detect other boats and hazards, and to make your presence known to others.

Reduce speed.
Both the Inland and the International Rules require reduced speed for vessels in low visibility—a safe speed "appropriate to the prevailing circumstances and conditions" (*Chapter 6*).

It is best to be able to stop short in time, rather than resort to violent evasive maneuvers to avoid a collision. The Navigation Rules require that, except where it has been determined that a risk of collision does not exist (by radar plot, perhaps), any vessel which hears a fog signal apparently forward of its beam must reduce speed to the minimum at which the boat can be kept on course. It shall, if necessary, take all way off, and, in any event, navigate with extreme caution until danger of collision is over (*Chapter 6*).

Post lookouts.
This is a requirement of the Navigation Rules, but it is also common sense. Most modern powerboat and sailboat designs place the helmsman aft or fairly far aft, where he or she is not an effective lookout, so you will probably need one or two additional people onboard as lookouts in thick weather.

Look and listen.
Despite the "look" in "lookout," such a person is as much for listening as for seeing. A person assigned as a lookout should have this duty as a sole responsibility while on watch. A skipper should post a lookout as far forward as possible when in fog and, if the helmsman is at inside controls, another lookout for the aft sector is desirable. Lookouts should be relieved as often as necessary to ensure their alertness; if the crew is small, an exchange of bow and stern duties will provide some change in position and relief from monotony. If there are enough people on board, a double lookout forward is not wasted manpower, but the two should not distract each other.

A bow lookout should keep alert for other vessels, listen for sound signals from aids to navigation and watch for hazards such as rocks and piles, breakers and buoys. Note that in thick weather, aids to navigation without audible signals can indeed become hazards. A lookout aft should watch primarily for overtaking vessels, but he may also hear fog signals missed by his counterpart on the bow.

Cutting down engine speed reduces strain on the motor caused by alternate stern-down laboring and stern-high racing.

Pitchpoling

The ordinary offshore swell is seldom troublesome when you are running before the seas, but the steep wind sea of some lakes and shallow bays makes steering difficult and reduced speed imperative. Excessive speed down a steep slope may cause a boat to "pitchpole"—to drive its head under in the trough, tripping the bow while the succeeding crest catches the stern and throws it end over end. When the going is bad enough that there is risk of the boat pitchpoling, keep the stern down and the bow light and buoyant, by shifting weight aft as necessary.

Shifting any considerable amount of weight aft will reduce a boat's tendency to yaw, but too much might cause it to be "pooped" by a following sea breaking into the cockpit. The secret is to do everything in moderation, not in excess. Adjust your boat's trim bit by bit rather than all at once, and see what makes it more stable.

How you respond to the challenge of piloting in fog is one of the greatest measures of seamanship skills.

The transmission of sound in fog is uncertain and tricky. Frequently the sound may seem to come from directions other than the true source, and it may not be heard at all at otherwise normal ranges.

Stop your engine.
When underway in fog in a boat under power, slow your engines to idle or shut them off entirely, at intervals, to listen for fog signals of other vessels and of aids to navigation. This is an excellent, practical action.

In these intervals keep silence on the boat so you can hear even the faintest signal. The listening periods should be at least 2 minutes to conform with the legally required maximum intervals between the sounding of fog signals. Don't forget to keep sounding your own signal during the listening period—you may get an answer from close by.

When proceeding in fog at a moderate speed, slow or stop your engines immediately any time your lookout indicates that he or she has heard something. The lookout can then have the most favorable conditions for verifying and identifying what he believes he has heard.

Use radar and radar reflectors.
Radar has its greatest value in conditions of reduced visibility. If your craft has radar, both the International and Inland Rules require that it be used. It must be on a long enough range scale as to give early warning of the possibility of collision, and all targets must be followed systematically. Use of radar, however, is not a substitute for adequate lookouts. Whether or not you have radar, you should carry a passive radar reflector; this is the time to open it and hoist it as high as possible. It increases your chance of being detected, and at a greater distance, by a radar-equipped vessel (your own radar in no way makes your own craft easier to detect).

Consider anchoring or laying-to.
If the weather, depth of water and other conditions are favorable, this may be safer than proceeding through conditions of low visibility. Do not anchor in a heavily traveled channel or traffic lane, of course.

If you cannot anchor, then perhaps laying-to—being underway with little or no way—may be safer than proceeding at even a much reduced speed. Remember that different fog signals are required when you are underway, with or without way on, and when you are at anchor (Chapter 6). By all means, sound the proper fog signal and keep your lookouts posted to look and listen for other craft and hazards.

Broadcast "SECURITE."
Some skippers of small fiberglass boats, not easily detected on radar even with a reflector deployed, make "SECURITE" calls on VHF Channel 16 to alert others to their presence.

Tacking before the seas

Use the tacking technique also when you want to avoid large swells directly astern. Try a zigzag track that puts the swells off your quarter, minimizing their effects—take the time to experiment with slightly different headings to find the most stable angle for your boat, but keep it under control to prevent a broach.

Running an inlet

One of the worst places to be in violent weather is an inlet or a narrow harbor entrance, where shoal water builds up treacherous surf that frequently cannot be seen from seaward. Inexperienced boaters, nevertheless, often run for shelter rather than remain safe (albeit uncomfortable) at sea, because they lack confidence in themselves and their boats.

When offshore swells run into shallower water along the beach, they build up steep waves because of resistance from the bottom. Natural inlets on sandy beaches, unprotected by breakwaters, usually build up a bar across the mouth. When the swells reach the bar, their form changes rapidly: They become short, steep-sided waves that tend to break where the water is shallowest.

Consider this when approaching from offshore: A few miles off, the sea may be relatively smooth while the inlet from seaward may not look as bad as it actually is. Breakers may run clear across the mouth, even in a buoyed channel.

If you must get through, the following suggestions may help. Radio the local Coast Guard station for recommendations. Do not attempt to run directly in. Wait outside the bar until you have had a chance to watch the action of waves as they pile up at the most critical (shallowest) spot in the channel. Usually the waves will come along in groups of three, sometimes more. The last sea will be bigger than the rest; by watching closely you should be able to pick it out of the successive groups.

■ Make sure your boat is ready. Close all hatches and ports, secure all loose gear, and get all crew members into PFDs; brief them about what to do and what not to do. When you are ready to enter, stand off until a big wave has broken or spent its force on the bar; then run through behind it. Watch the water both ahead and behind your boat; control your speed and match it to that of the waves.

An ebbing current builds up a worse sea on the bars than the flood because the rush of water outward works against and under the incoming swells. If the sea looks too bad on the ebb, it is better to keep off a few hours until the flood has had a chance to begin. As deeper water helps, the best time is just before the tidal current turns to ebb.

■ Departing through inlets is less hazardous then entering: The boat is on the safe side of the dangerous area, and usually has the option of staying there. If you do decide to go out, you can spot dangerous areas more easily. Remember, a boat heading into surf is sometimes more easily controlled than one running with the swells.

Heaving to

When conditions get so bad offshore that a boat cannot make headway, and begins to take too much punishment, it is time to "heave to," a maneuver whose execution varies with type of boat. Powerboats, both single- and twin-screw, will usually be most comfortable if brought around and kept to the seas, or a few points off, using just enough power to make bare steerageway while conserving fuel.

Sailboats traditionally heave to with the tiller lashed downwind (wheel lashed up), to keep the boat headed up. A small, very strong storm jib is sheeted to windward to hold the bow just off the wind, while a storm trysail replaces the mainsail and is sheeted flat. This is a small, strong triangular sail with a low clew and a single sheet. A loose-footed sail, it is not bent to the boom, which is secured in its crutch. The jib-trysail combination balances the tendency of trysail and rudder to head the craft into the wind against the effect of the jib to head it off. The result is, ideally, that the boat lies 45 degrees from the wind while making very slow headway.

"Lying ahull" is the next step down as the wind increases. All sail is dropped and secured; the helm is lashed to prevent damage to the rudder, and the boat is left to find its own way.

Using a sea anchor or drogue

In heavy to extreme weather, you may use either a sea anchor or a drogue to control the behavior of your boat.

A sea anchor looks and behaves like a parachute to be used in the water. It is designed to stop your boat in its tracks. A good size sea anchor may reduce your drift up to 90 percent; this is especially important when navigating on a lee shore. Especially when the crew is limited, it is practical for heaving to and leaving the boat to tend to itself. A sea anchor's diameter ranges from 5 to 40 feet, depending on the size and weight of the boat; the bigger the diameter, the more stable the sea anchor will be. Too small a sea anchor set off the bow will allow the boat to drift faster backwards, and while backing, it may damage the rudder. It may yaw and fall off into a broaching position.

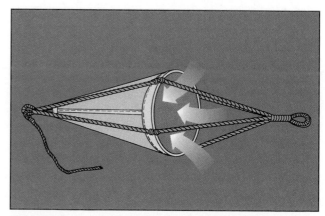

Shown above is a conventional drogue with the water moving through.

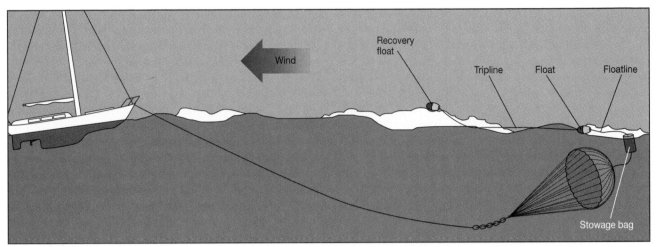

Pay out lots of rode. The parachute anchoring system relies very heavily on the stretch of the long nylon rode for yielding to the seas (and not standing up against them). Even in moderate conditions you should pay out at least 200 feet of rode, and 10 to 15 times the length of the boat in heavy weather conditions.

A drogue is towed astern and is to a boat what airbrakes are to an airplane. It is shaped like a cone, with a hoop to keep its mouth open. An opening at the apex lets the water stream through. The drogue is designed to slow down the boat while keeping it from broaching when running with the wind and waves. It will slow the boat down enough to reduce the strain of concentrating for hours or even days at keeping the boat at a slight angle before the waves. This means that, while running with the storm will give you those extra miles in the right direction if you have the sea room, you will also be with the storm that much longer. Though your boat will be easier to steer, the helmsman is still required, and may not let go of the helm to rest below.

The advantage of steerage when underway is obvious, and will be best when the drogue is on a bridle cleated ahead of the transom (like a ski boat). Different combinations of bridle or attachment points from the stern will be possible according to conditions.

A drogue has a smaller diameter opening than a sea anchor. A rule of thumb is that the mouth of a drogue may range at about 10 percent of the boat's waterline length. A low-pull drogue slows down the boat in order to keep steerage. A medium-pull (anti-capsize) type serves well when steerage capability is lost. A "series" drogue resembles a long warp with a multitude of very small drogues attached in line; although expensive, it is flexible in its use and easier to store.

Both the sea anchor and drogue will put tremendous strain on the boat's hardware and structure. Your boat must be strongly built to withstand waves that may pound on deck from either the stern or bow, depending on your position to the waves. The cockpit scuppers must be the fast-draining type to prevent pooping—swamping with water at the stern. Swivels must be used with the equipment to prevent the waves and the motion of the boat from twisting them shut, rendering them useless.

A modern parabolic drogue works on the flow of water rather than simply blocking it. It allows energy dissipation without creating a shock load during sudden acceleration.

You will also need a very long line to prevent either the sea anchor or drogue from being pulled out of a wave as the boat tends to pull harder while a steep wave goes under its bow or stern. Weighing them down will help keep them below the surface. Their efficiency will be proportionate to their size, and must be tried out in proper sea conditions. The boat's behavior will depend on factors like underwater profile, the windage of the rig, its riding sails and the length of the rode. A longer rode will give a smoother ride. In a pinch, a sea anchor or drogue can be made with available material on board, but will never be as efficient as a properly designed and tried out unit.

STRANDING: ASSISTING AND GETTING ASSISTANCE

It is a law of the sea that a boater must render assistance to a vessel in need of aid. Often, giving assistance means getting a tow line to another skipper to get him out of a temporary embarrassment or to haul him to a Coast Guard station or back to port; or else *you* may go aground, or a balky motor or gear failure may force you to ask a tow from a passing boat.

In either case, you should know what to do and why. Therefore, the problems of stranding, and their solutions, will be considered from both the viewpoint of needing assistance and of being the one who renders aid.

Stranding

Simple stranding, running aground, is often more inconvenient than dangerous. With a little know-how, the period of stranding may be mere minutes.

If grounding happens in a strange harbor, chances are you have been feeling your way along and have just touched bottom lightly. You should be off again with little difficulty if your immediate actions do not put you aground more firmly.

Right and wrong actions

When most skippers go aground, the first instinctive act is to gun the engine into reverse in an effort to pull off; this may be the one thing that you should *not* do, as it could damage your rudder and cause the raw water intakes of your engines to clog, resulting in engine damage. First check for any water coming in; if there is any, stopping the leak takes precedence over getting off. If there is no water coming in, or when it has been stopped and you are in tidal waters, immediately check the state of the tide. If the tide is rising, and the sea is quiet enough that the hull is not pounding, time is working for you; whatever you do to assist yourself will be much more effective with time. If you are grounded on a falling tide, you must, obviously, work quickly and precisely.

About the only thing you know offhand about the grounding is the shape of your boat's hull and its point of greatest draft, which is the part most likely to be touching. If the hull tends to swing to the action of wind or waves, the point about which it pivots is the part grounded.

Check the water depth around the boat: Deeper water may be to one side rather than astern. You can use a lead line, or a boathook or similar item. Check from your deck, all around; if you have a dinghy, check over a wider area. Examine also the points where the water meets your hull; if your normal waterline is well above the surface, you are more severely grounded than if there is no apparent change.

Cautions in getting off

Immediately consider the type of bottom. If it is sandy and you reverse hard, you may wash a quantity of sand from astern and throw it directly under the keel, bedding the boat down more firmly. If the bottom is rocky and you insist on reversing, you may drag the hull and do more damage than with the original grounding.

Also, if grounded forward, remember that reversing a single-screw boat with a right-hand propeller may swing the stern to port; this could swing the hull onto exposed pinnacles or to a greater contact with a soft bottom.

Using a kedge

The one *right* thing to do immediately after grounding is to take out an anchor and set it firmly; this is called a kedge, and the act of using it is kedging.

Unless your boat has really been driven on, the everyday working anchor will usually be heavy enough. Put the anchor and the line in the dinghy, make the bitter end fast to the boat's stern cleats, then go out as far as possible; let the line run from the stern of the dinghy as it uncoils. Taking the line out this way makes it much easier to row the dinghy or control it if an outboard motor is being used. With sailboats, it is often helpful to put out a "kedge" anchor with a line running to or near the top of the mast to heel the boat over, thus reducing draft.

If you have no dinghy, you may be able to swim out with an anchor, providing sea and weather conditions do not make it hazardous to go overboard. Use one or two life jackets or buoyant cushions to support the anchor out to where you intend to set it. Be sure to wear a PFD; it is essential to save your energy for the work.

When setting out the kedge, consider the sideways turning effects of a reversing single screw and, unless the boat has twin screws, set the kedge at a compensating angle from the stern. If the propeller is right-hand, set the anchor slightly to starboard of the stern. This will give two desirable effects: When pulling the kedge line while in reverse, the boat will tend to back in a straight line. When used alternately, first pulling on the line and then giving a short surge in reverse, the resulting wiggling action of stern and keel can help in starting the boat moving.

Increasing a kedge's pulling power

If you have a couple of double-sheave blocks and a length of suitable line on board, make up a "handy-billy" or "fall," and fasten it to the kedge line for more effective pulling. (A handy-billy should be part of a boat's regular equipment.)

During the entire period of grounding, keep the kedge line taut. The boat may yield suddenly to that continued pull, especially if a passing boat throws a wake that helps to break bottom suction and lift the keel off the bottom.

Two kedges set out at an acute angle from either side of the stern and pulled upon alternately may give the stern wiggle that will help you work clear. If the bottom is sandy, that same pull with the propeller going in reverse may wash some sand away from under the keel, with the desired result. If the kedge line is kept taut, try the maneuver with caution.

Move your crew and passengers quickly from side to side to roll the boat and make the keel work in the bottom. If you have spars, swing the boom outboard and put people on it to heave the boat down in order to raise the keel line. Shift heavy objects away from the grounded portion. If practical, remove internal weight by loading it into the dinghy or by taking it ashore; consider pumping overboard any excess water in your tanks. Unloading a boat is especially practical if the boat goes aground at high tide: While the tide is going down and coming back up, you have time to unload the heaviest items to create more buoyancy.

When to stay aground

The previous suggestions are based on the assumption that the boat is not holed. If it is holed, however, you may be better off where it lies than in deeper water. If the craft is badly stove, you might take an anchor ashore to hold it or pull it farther up until temporary repairs can be made. As the tide falls the damaged hull may be exposed far enough to allow some outside patching, provided you have some sort of patching material aboard. (Canvas, cushions and bedding can be used for temporary hull patches, as discussed in Chapter 4.)

What to do while waiting

While waiting for the tide to rise or for assistance to come, take soundings all around the boat. A swing of the stern to starboard or port may do more for you than any amount of straight backward pulling; soundings will locate any additional depth, or, conversely, shallow areas or rocks.

If another boat is present, it may be able to help you even if it cannot pull. Ask the assisting skipper to run the boat back and forth, making as much wake as is safely possible. That wake may lift your boat just enough to free it.

If your boat is going to be left high and dry with a falling tide, keep an eye on its layover condition. If there is anything to get a line to, even another kedge, you can make the boat lie over on whichever side you choose as it loses buoyancy. If the boat is deep and narrow, it may need some assistance in standing up again, particularly in soft mud; the suction of the mud and the boat's deadweight will work against it.

Assisting a stranded boat

The first rule of thumb when assisting another vessel is to *keep your boat from joining the other craft in its trouble.* Consider the draft of the stranded vessel relative to yours. Consider the size and weight of the grounded boat relative to the power of your engines. Also consider your level of skill. It is often better not to be a "hero"; but if you decide that you can safely and effectively assist, use the following guidelines. Otherwise, simply stand by until help arrives.

■ **Getting a line over.** Although it may seem easiest to bring a line to a stranded boat by coming in under engine power, bow on, then passing the line and backing out again, try this only if you are certain there is sufficient water. Make sure also that your boat backs well, without too much stern crabbing due to the reversed screw. Wind and current direction will greatly affect this maneuver. If your boat tends to broadside

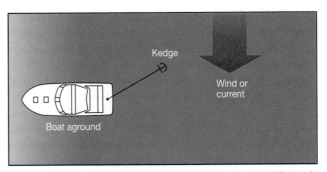

The first thing to do after going aground is to check hull integrity; next, to get out a kedge anchor to keep from being driven farther aground. It also may provide a means of pulling free as waves or the wake from another craft lifts your boat.

to the shallows as it backs, pass the line in some other manner. Using a monkcy fist *(Chapter 13)* can help.

Try backing in, with wind or current compensating for the reversed screw, keeping your boat straight and leaving the bow headed out. In any case, after the line is passed and made fast, do the actual pulling with your engines going ahead, to get full power. For greater maneuverability, make the line fast as far forward of the stern as practicable.

If a close approach seems unwise, consider dropping the kedge anchor or anchors for the stranded boat. Then send the line over in a dinghy or buoy it and float it over.

■ **Making the pull.** If wind and/or current are broadside to the direction of the pull, keep your boat anchored even while pulling. Keep a strain on your anchor line; otherwise, as soon as your boat takes the pulling strain (particularly if the line is fast to the stern), you will lose maneuverability. This means you gradually will make leeway, which could eventually put your boat aground broadside.

If you are pulling with your boat underway, secure the tow line well forward of your stern so that, while hauling, your boat can angle into the wind and current and still hold its position. This sort of action can impose tremendous strains, particularly on the stranded boat—even to the point of carrying away a fitting to which the towline is made fast. It must be remembered that ordinary recreational craft are not designed as tugboats. The cleats or bitts available for making the line fast may well not be strong enough for such a strain, nor are they likely to be located advantageously for such work. It is far better to run a bridle around the whole hull of the stranded boat and pull against this bridle rather than to risk damaging some part of the stern by such straining. If there is any doubt of your boat's ability to withstand such concentrated loads, use a bridle on your boat as well.

When operating in limited areas, the stranded craft should have a kedge out for control when it comes off. It should also have another anchor ready to be put over the side if necessary, to keep it from going back aground if without power. Keep all lines clear of the propeller, and make sure no sudden surge is put on a slack line.

In good weather with no sea running, towing another boat is fairly straightforward. It involves little more than maneuvering your boat into position forward of the other boat, and passing it a towline.

Generally speaking, the towing boat should pass its towline to the other craft. You may want to send over a light line first (plastic water-ski towline that floats is excellent), and use that to pull over the actual towing line.

When approaching a boat that is sitting dead in the water, in order to pass it a line, do not attempt to run in too close if there is any kind of sea running. Instead, just buoy a long line with one or more PFDs, tow it astern and take a turn about the stern of the disabled vessel; be careful that, in doing so, you do not foul the disabled vehicle's propeller. The crew of the assisted vessel can pick up the line with a boathook from the cockpit with far less fuss than by any heave-and-catch method, as long as you are to windward.

The most logical place to attach the line on the boat to be towed is that boat's forward bitt or cleats. Make sure that such fitting can take the load: The bitt or cleat should be fastened with through bolts of adequate diameter, washers and nuts—never with wood or self-tapping screws. If the fastening is to the deck, this must be reinforced on the underside with a backing plate of sufficient area. On a small sailboat with the mast going through the deck, wrap around the mast; if the mast is stepped on deck, do not tie to it—you will only pull it off. Remember, if an item of deck hardware pulls out under heavy load, the stretched towline can act as a slingshot, hurling the bitt or cleat with a force great enough to cause serious injury or death. A trailerable boat will have a bow eye that makes an excellent place for attaching a towline. On a runabout with a bow eye, be careful when towing at a sharp angle on a bow eye: If it is a cast-type bow eye, it may snap under improper alignment of tow.

Towing lines

■ Double-braided, or braid-on-braid, nylon is the preferred line for towing. It is stronger than three-strand twisted nylon of the same size and will not kink. Also, it has sufficient elasticity to cushion shock loads, but not so much as to create a snap-back hazard. Its disadvantage is that it does not float and must be watched to avoid entanglement in the towing vessel's propeller.

■ Three-strand twisted nylon has excessive stretch and dangerous snap-back action if broken under load, and it should not be used if it can be avoided.

■ Polypropylene line floats and is a highly visible bright yellow, but it has little elasticity and shock loads are heavily transferred to fittings on both the towed and towing craft. In addition, it has less strength (requiring larger sizes) and is stiff, making it difficult to stow and handle. It is also particularly subject to abrasion damage. With all these disadvantages, this line has therefore rather limited applications; it is suitable only for light towing loads in protected waters.

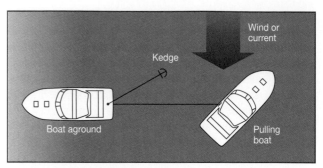

To aid in maneuverability if a bow anchor cannot be set, make the towline fast to a cleat forward of the stern on the upwind or up-current side of the pulling boat. Be sure the cleat is capable of taking the heavy strain.

Handling the towing boat

The watchwords here are extreme caution. The worst possible place to make the towline fast is to the stern of the towing boat, because the pull of the tow prevents the stern from swinging properly in response to rudder action; this limits the boat's maneuverability. The towline should be made fast as far forward as practicable, as in tug and towboat practice.

The deck hardware of the towing boat must be capable of carrying the load, the same as described above for the towed craft. If there is no suitable place forward, make a bridle from the forward bitts, running around the superstructure to a point in the forward part of the cockpit. Such a bridle must be wrapped with chafing gear wherever it bears on the superstructure or any corners, and even then it may cause some chafing of the finish.

Secure the towline so that it can be cast loose if necessary or, failing that, have a knife or hatchet ready to cut it. This line is a potential danger to anyone near if it should break and come whipping forward. Twisted nylon acts like a huge rubber band when it breaks, and has resulted in some serious accidents. Never stand near, or in line with, a highly strained towline, and keep a wary eye out at all times. Aboard the towed boat, have an anchor rigged and ready to drop in case the towline breaks or must be cast off.

If for any reason you must come near a burning vessel in order to tow it (for instance, to prevent it from endangering other boats or property), approach from windward so the flames are blowing away from you. Your light anchor, with its length of chain thrown into the cockpit or through a window of the burning boat, could act as a good grappling hook.

Often, if your small boat is trying to tow a larger one, it will encounter heavy resistance in the form of small waves hitting the larger boat; these waves can slow or even stop your progress. Also, crosswinds may make you drift faster than you want. One way to avoid these problems is to tie up alongside the towed boat. This will make your towing more efficient; on the lee of the boat, you will be protected from the towline. In this way, even a dinghy with an average outboard can usually tow a much larger craft.

In any towing situation, never allow anyone to fend off the other vessel with hands or feet. Remember that even the smallest boats coming together under these conditions can cause broken bones or severed fingers; with large vessels, the risk is the loss of a limb, or worse.

Likewise, never allow anyone to hold a towing line while towing another vessel, regardless of its size. This could result in badly torn tendons and muscles, the loss of a towline over the side or dragging the crew member overboard.

When not to tow

Towing can be a dangerous undertaking, as well as an expensive one, if it is not properly done. If you are not equipped for the job, stand by the disabled vessel. If your craft's engine is only barely adequate for your purpose, as in the case of a small sailboat with a small inboard or outboard engine, towing another boat in less than perfect conditions might be awkward. You may be able to put a line across and assist by keeping the other craft's bow at a proper angle to the sea until help comes.

In any case, do not try to be a hero. It is most often safest to call the Coast Guard or private salvage agency and turn the job over to them as soon as they arrive. We tend to forget that the most important concern of the skipper is the safety of people onboard, not the safety of the craft itself.

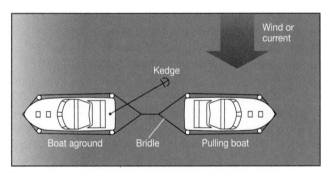

The best procedure is to put a bridle around the hull or superstructure of both boats in order to distribute strain over as wide an area as possible. Be sure to pad pressure points to guard against chafing or scarring.

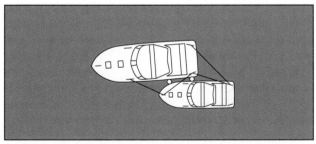

How springs are used when a boat takes a larger vessel in tow alongside: Fenders are rigged at points of contact, and springs are made up with no slack in them. Both boats respond as a unit to the towing boat's rudder action.

TOWING PRINCIPLES

Most importantly, start off the tow gently. A steady pull at a reasonable speed will get you to your destination with far less strain on boats, lines and crew members.

■ When towing, keep the boats "in step" by adjusting the towline length to keep both boats on the crest or in the trough of seas at the same time. Sometimes, as with a confused sea, this may not be possible. However, the idea is to prevent a situation where the boat being towed is shouldering up against the back of one sea, presenting maximum resistance, while the towing boat is trying to run down the forward slope of another sea. Then when this condition is reversed, the tow alternately runs ahead briefly, then surges back on the towline with a heavy strain. If there is any degree of uniformity to the waves, the strain on the towline will be minimized by adjusting it to the proper length.

■ As the tow gets into protected, quiet waters, shorten up on the line to allow better handling in close quarters. Swing as wide as possible around buoys and channel turns, so that the tow has room to follow.

■ A small boat in tow should be trimmed a little by the stern; trimming by the head causes it to yaw. In a seaway this condition is aggravated, and it is increasingly important to keep the bow relatively light.

■ It is easy for a larger boat to tow a smaller vessel too fast, causing it to yaw and capsize. Always tow at a moderate speed, something less than hull speed (1.34 times the square-root of the waterline length), and make full allowance for adverse conditions of wind and waves.

■ In smooth water, motorboats may borrow an idea from tugs, which often take their tow alongside in harbor or sheltered waters, for better maneuverability. The towing boat should make fast on the other craft's quarter, as shown at left.

■ In relatively calm waters, even a dinghy with a small outboard motor can tow a medium-size boat at slow speed, enough to get it into harbor or to a pier; tow astern or alongside as required for maneuverability.

■ Towing alongside is practical when the stranded boat has lost its steering capability, or when only one person is aboard the stranded boat and is using its dinghy to tow. Towing alongside is better in crowded areas where maneuvering is more critical.

12 ANCHORING

The essence of successful anchoring is to "stay put," without dragging, whenever the anchor is set.

In a quiet anchorage, in familiar surroundings, your ground tackle and methods of anchoring are seldom put to the test. Cruising into strange waters, however, finding inadequate shelter in an exposed anchorage during a blow, and unexpected variations in wind and current will surely test the capabilities of both tackle and technique.

The challenge of anchoring, then, breaks down into two parts: the equipment that every boat should carry and the knowledge of how to use it. On both counts, this chapter offers the information you need.

GROUND TACKLE: ANCHORS AND RODES

Anchors used by the first mariners, were stones used with crude rope—weights that might drag across the bottom. As anchor design and technology evolved, simple wooden hooks, then iron hooks, were added. A stock was installed perpendicular to the plane of the hooks to put them in a better position to "bite" the bottom. Holding power in softer bottoms was improved by adding broad flukes to the hooks. Today's anchors have highly specialized designs that enable them to quickly and deeply bury themselves in the bottom, thus achieving the greatest holding power for the least weight.

Choosing an anchor

If you scan a marine hardware catalog, without experience, you may be confused by the diversity of designs. What you should be buying, essentially, is holding power; sheer weight is no index of that. On the contrary, scientific design is the key to efficiency, and today's patented anchors, if properly manufactured, score high on a holding-power-to-weight basis.

■ **Lightweight type.** The lightweight, burying anchor developed by Richard Danforth in 1938 proved its mettle during World War II as a means of pulling off grounded landing craft during amphibious landings. The term Danforth, though a trade name belonging to one manufacturer, is often used generically to describe the design.

Although refinements by a number of manufacturers have led to subtle changes, including the use of aluminum rather than steel, Danforth's basic design remains the same as the original. The lightweight anchor's high holding-power-to-weight ratio (the ultimate measure of an anchor's efficiency) has made it a valued standard piece of equipment on thousands of recreational vessels.

Compared to other anchors, this popular type is easy to handle and stow. Its holding power is most effective in favorable bottoms such as clay, sand or mud. In rocky or weedy holding grounds, however, the flukes will tend to skip or sail across the bottom instead of digging in. The lightweight anchor's pivoting flukes also tend to collect mud, weeds and debris from the bottom.

In operation, the lightweight anchor at first rests flat on the bottom. Upward pressure on the shank turns its broad, pivoting flukes downward so their sharp points dig into the bottom. The rodlike stock at the crown end prevents the anchor from rolling and disengaging one or both flukes. Two rectangular surfaces of the crown, near the point where it connects to the shaft, are angled slightly inward, helping to maintain the flukes' downward attitude. As initial strain is placed on the shank, the flukes bury into the bottom. Subsequent pull on the shaft, initiated by the normal rode motion, continues to bury the anchor. Meanwhile, resistance offered by the flukes' broad base prevents the anchor from pulling in the direction of the stock to which the rode is attached.

A number of manufacturers produce anchors of the lightweight, burying type. In selecting an anchor, remember that all manufacturers have their own concepts of design, and "look-alikes" do not necessarily hold similarly. Be sure to check design and construction integrity. Variations between the angle of flukes to the shank on similar sized lightweight anchors (even from the same manufacturer) indicate suspect quality control.

When buying an anchor, also carefully inspect welds and overall construction. The lightweight anchor's most attractive feature—one of the highest holding-power-to-weight ratios

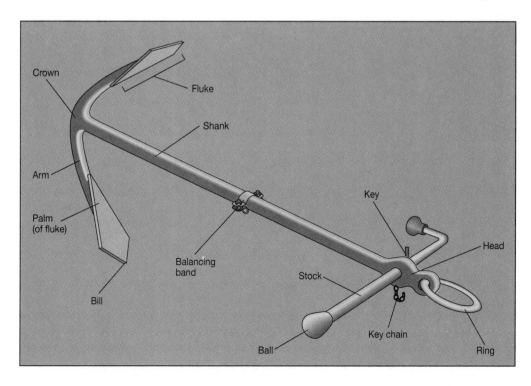

Anchor parts are identified on the traditional kedge anchor, but the terms are the same for most modern types.

■ **Anchor.** Designed to engage the bottom of a waterway and, through its resistance, to maintain a vessel within a given radius.

■ **Anchor chocks.** Fittings on the deck of a vessel used to stow an anchor when it is not in use.

■ **Anchor rode.** The line connecting an anchor to a vessel.

■ **Bow chocks.** Fittings on a vessel's rail, near its stem, having jaws that serve as fairleads for anchor rodes and other lines.

■ **Breaking out the anchor.** To unset it by pulling up on the rode when above it.

■ **Changing the nip on an anchor line.** To prevent the wear from occurring in the same place over an extended period by pulling the rode in or out.

■ **Ground tackle.** A general term for the anchor, anchor rodes, fittings, etc. used for securing a vessel at anchor.

■ **Hawsepipe.** A cylindrical or elliptical pipe or casting in a vessel's hull through which the anchor rode runs.

■ **Horizontal load.** The horizontal force that is placed on an anchoring device by the vessel to which it is connected.

■ **Mooring bitt.** A post or cleat through or on the deck of a vessel, which is used to secure an anchor rode or other line to the vessel.

■ **Scope.** The ratio of the length of the anchor rode to the vertical distance from the bow chocks to the bottom (depth plus height of bow chocks above water).

■ **Tripping an anchor.** A line attached to the crown or head of an anchor, used to pull out or "trip" an anchor that may otherwise be fouled below.

■ **Vertical load.** The lifting force placed on the bow of the vessel by its anchor rode.

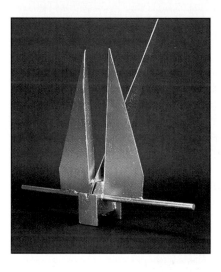

Lightweight-type anchors made of steel were originated by Danforth, but are now also manufactured by several other companies. Note the angled plates on the crown.

weeds. They also have a tendency to plane or fly off in the water as they are lowered.

■ **The plow anchor.** Unique in design, the plow anchor resembles none of the other anchor types. It was invented in England by Professor G.I. Taylor of Cambridge University; he called it the CQR. Its most distinctive feature is a shank that pivots longitudinally on a hinge, designed to reduce the tendency of the plowlike flukes to break loose when a swinging boat changes the direction of pull.

The plow has found wide acceptance because of its demonstrated efficiency in a variety of bottoms. Opinions vary as to its effectiveness in heavy grass or weed, which is not surprising since many weed growths resist penetration by any anchor. When the anchor is first lowered, it lies on its side

of all anchors—is negated if it breaks in use. However, refinements of the design have led to some clear improvements. Fortress lightweight anchors, for example, are made of an aluminum alloy and so are lighter for easier handling. A unique feature of these anchors is their ability to be assembled in either of two ways for different fluke angles in order to maximize holding power in normal or soft mud bottoms. Fortress anchors have shown even greater holding power than steel anchors of comparable size, plus increased ease in handling from their significantly lighter weight. Tests have verified the superior holding power in the types of bottoms described above, but they suffer the same handicaps of other lightweight-type anchors in bottoms covered by grass or

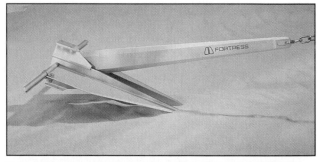

The Fortress anchor, made of aluminum alloy, has high holding power per pound of weight. It does better in softer bottoms and fares poorly in weeds. The shank angle can be adjusted to the type of bottom.

The plow anchor gets its name from the shape of its deep-burying fluke, pivoted at the end of the shank.

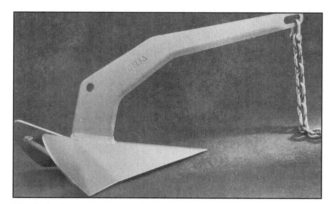

The Delta is similar to the CQR, except that it is one piece. Its holding power is slightly superior to other plow types.

on the bottom. Then, when a pull is exerted on the line, the plow rights itself after moving a short distance, driving the point of the plow into the bottom and finally burying the anchor completely if the bottom is soft. Suggested weights for CQR anchors may vary from 15 pounds (6.8 kg) for a 25-foot (7.6 m) boat to 60 pounds (27.2 kg) for 60-footers (18.3 m), with heavier sizes available for larger vessels. For best performance, the manufacturer recommends a minimum of 18 feet (5.5 m) of chain between the anchor and the rode.

Because of the pivoting feature of its shank, the plow anchor tends to remain buried over moderate changes in direction of pull on the line caused by wind or current shifts. There is no projecting fluke to foul the anchor line and the plow breaks out easily when the pull is vertical for raising the anchor. It is important to remember that a plow can lose its bite if an object jams in the hinge mechanism, keeping the plow at an extreme angle with the stock. Because plow anchors do not stow well on deck, they are usually hoisted to a bow roller fitting where they are secured.

Plow anchors are produced by a number of manufacturers and effectiveness may vary between different units; forged models are stronger than cast versions. Simpson-Lawrence has introduced a new plow-type anchor, the Delta, which has a solid, non-pivoting shank. It is weighted so that the pointed flukes are ready to dig in as soon as it reaches the bottom. Preliminary results in some tests have shown the Delta to have better holding power than the CQR and superior reset-

ting capability, notwithstanding its fixed shank. It is also somewhat easier to store on a bow roller since it does not have the bulky hinge.

■ **The Bruce anchor.** Another anchor from the United Kingdom is the Bruce. Originally developed for use with offshore oil and gas drilling rigs, it has been scaled down for use with small craft in sizes from 2.2 to 110 pounds (1 to 50 kg).

The Bruce anchor is designed to right itself no matter how it lands on the bottom, while digging in within two shank lengths. It is designed to reset itself immediately if it is pulled out by a change in direction of the anchor rode. Like the plow, it breaks out easily with a vertical pull.

■ **The Max anchor.** A new American-made contender called the Max closely resembles the Bruce in its fluke configuration and non-pivoting shank. Manufactured by Creative Marine, the Max's innovation is that its shank can be pinned

The Bruce anchor is shaped so that once it has been set, the direction of pull can change through 360° with lessened likelihood of breaking out. However, intentional breakout is easy on short scope. The anchor is said to work well in mud, sand and rocks.

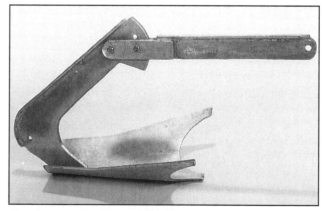

The Max anchor's greater holding power seems to come from the extra size flukes. The adjustability of the flukes means the angle can be increased when used in soft mud.

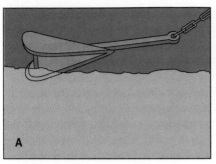
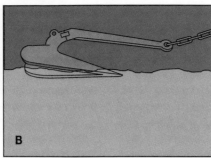
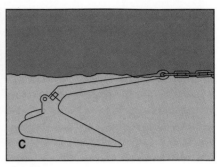

Illustrating how burying anchors work, a plow lands on the bottom on its side (A), gets a quick bite (B), and digs in deep as it rights itself (C).

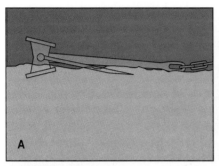
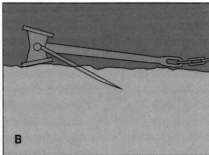
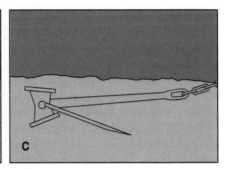

The lightweight type lands with its fluke flat (A), penetrates as the strain comes on the rode (B), and buries the flukes (C).

The kedge anchor must be heavier than a burying-type anchor of equivalent holding power. Its thin arms and flukes make it the best type to use in weeds or grass. The model shown above has thin, sharp flukes for better digging into hard bottoms.

in three different ways to adjust the angle between the shank and the flukes; it also comes in a rigid version. In a softer bottom, the angle can be increased to improve holding power, for example. Preliminary tests suggest that the Max's shovel-like flukes, which are broader than the Bruce's, also help it remain buried, thus giving it extra holding power. However, the Max anchor appears to take longer and travel farther on the bottom before setting.

■ **The kedge anchor.** In discussing kedge anchors it is important to distinguish between the more massive ancient types and the later versions designed for small boats. In glossaries, "kedge anchors" are often defined as light anchors (of any design) carried out from a vessel aground to free the vessel by winching in on the rode. Here, however, we refer to the kedge as an anchor with the more traditional type of arms, flukes and stock as distinguished from newer lightweight types. A few anchors that fall in this category are the Hereshoff, Fisherman and Yachtsman.

Although kedge anchors are not widely used on modern recreational boats, they do have their place in special applications. Some kedge anchors have relatively sharp bills and small flukes to bite better into hard sand bottoms. Others will have broader flukes on heavier arms for greater holding power in softer bottoms, and greater strength when hooking into rocks or coral heads. A kedge anchor is normally an excellent choice for bottoms with heavy growth of grass or weeds—one arm will penetrate the vegetation and dig into the bottom beneath.

Kedge anchors are not of the "burying" type; the shank lies on the bottom and one arm remains exposed. On the other hand, a kedge's "hook" design recommends it, probably above all other types, on rocky or coral bottoms where one fluke can find a crevice. Retrieval, with proper precautions, is not too difficult. Although today's kedge designs have a diamond-shaped fluke to lessen the risk of the anchor line fouling on the exposed arm, this possibility must be considered if a change in direction of pull of a half-circle or more occurs.

On nearly all designs where the stock is at the ring end, such as the various kedge anchors, the stock is loose and can be folded for better stowage. Frequently, a key is required to pin the stock of a kedge in its open position when set up ready for use. (The key is lashed in its slot to hold it in place.)

Other anchors

A variety of other anchor types exist. Some are less popular than the major types previously mentioned; others serve a more specific use. Five of these types are listed below.

■ **Navy type.** Some inexperienced boaters, seeing navy anchors on large ships, conclude that this type is best for all vessels, including small boats. This is simply not so. Ships use them because such stockless anchors can be hauled up into hawsepipes. Their ratio of holding-power-to-weight is so great that, if weight is held within reason for a small boat, holding power is far below safe limits.

■ **Grapnels.** Though used by some commercial fishermen, grapnels are not recommended for general anchoring service aboard recreational boats. These are also stockless models using, as a rule, five curved, sharp-billed, clawlike prongs symmetrically arranged around the crown end of the shank. Eyes may be cast in both ends of the shank—at the head in lieu of a ring for attachment of a rode (if used as an anchor) and at the crown end for a buoyed trip line. By dragging a small grapnel back and forth, a boater may grapple for a piece of equipment lost on the bottom.

■ **Folding types.** This highly specialized design allows all parts to fold against the shank into the smallest possible space for the most convenient stowage—at some sacrifice of holding power and strength. In one stockless type, there are two pairs of flukes at right angles to each other, almost in the manner of a grapnel. In rocky bottoms they hook readily and may be rigged to pull out easily, crown first. Such anchors are often excellent in bottoms with heavy growths of grass or weeds as one or two arms penetrate the vegetation to get a bite into the bottom. They frequently have less than desirable holding power in loose sand or soft mud due to small fluke area.

■ **The Northill.** This type is somewhat like a modified grapnel hook in appearance. At its crown end, two arms with sharpened flukes extend at right angles to the shank and two flukeless arms act as a stock. In some versions, such as the KB Ultralight, made from stainless steel, all four arms fold toward the shank for stowage.

■ **Mushroom type.** Used primarily in conjunction with permanent moorings, the mushroom anchor is discussed on page 274. Modified versions of the mushroom are manufactured for small craft such as canoes and rowboats, but their efficiency as anchors is at the lowest end of the scale.

The anchor line

All of the gear, taken collectively, that lies between a boat and its anchor is called the rode—whether it be synthetic fiber, chain or a combination of the two.

■ **Twisted nylon.** Nylon, in three-strand twist or double-braid form, is now by far the most widely used material for anchor lines. Other synthetics, such as Dacron, polypropylene and polyethylene, have less desirable characteristics. Chain makes a good anchor rode, but its weight, while desirable for anchoring, may necessitate having a winch or other mechanical assistance on board to hoist it. On a small boat, the weight of

A grapnel is shown as it might be used to recover a mooring chain. With a trip line rigged at the crown end, it can be used to anchor a boat on a rocky bottom.

an adequate length of chain, stowed in the bow, may be too great for proper trim.

For anchoring, perhaps nylon's greatest asset is its elasticity; nylon stretches a third or more under load. Its working elasticity is 15 to 25 percent, which is of particular value when a boat surges at anchor in steep seas. In such conditions there is a heavy shock load on fittings and ground tackle—unless provision is made to absorb it gradually. Nylon's elasticity does exactly that.

Some boaters unwittingly lose part or most of the advantage inherent in nylon by buying too large a line. Within the limits of safe working loads, the smaller the diameter the better the elasticity for given conditions. A practical limit is reached when small diameters (though rated high enough for breaking strength) are not convenient to handle. Some experienced boaters use nylon as light as ⅜-inch diameter on the working anchors of their 30- to 40-foot craft. As mentioned in Chapter 13, nylon line is highly resistant to rot, decay and mildew, but can be damaged by rust from iron fittings or a rusty chain. Nylon line should be stowed out of direct sunlight to prevent gradual deterioration from ultraviolet rays.

■ **Braided synthetic line.** Most nylon used for anchor lines is laid up by twisting three strands. Synthetics can, however, be laid up by "braiding." For anchoring (as well as for mooring or towing) a braided outer cover of nylon surrounds a braided inner synthetic core. This is commonly called "double-braided" or "braid-on-braid" line. The result is a line of exceptional stability with no inherent tendency to twist because of the nature of its lay. Consequently, it can be fed down into rope lockers without fear of kinking.

When braided nylon is handled on deck, it is advisable to "flake it down" in a figure-eight pattern, rather than the con-

A thimble made of bronze alloy (shown) or plastic should be used with synthetic rode to prevent the line from jumping out of the thimble when the eye splice stretches under load.

ventional clockwise coil used with twisted fibers. Because of the relatively smoother surface of braid, with more fibers to absorb the wear, chafe is less of a problem than it is with the twisted three-strand lay. Braided nylon retains an adequate degree of elasticity (14 percent at working leads, as opposed to 25 percent for twisted nylon).

■ **Chain.** As the size of the vessel increases, so does the required diameter of a nylon anchor line. For yachts 65 feet or more, nylon would run to diameters of up to ¾ inch or larger. This approaches a size that is difficult to handle; the alternative is chain.

From this it should not be inferred that chain is not also in use on smaller craft. Boats that cruise extensively and have occasion to anchor on sharp rock or coral often have chain; in some cases it is regarded as indispensable—it stands chafing where fiber lines won't.

In larger diameters, the weight of chain makes a sag in the rode that cushions shock loads due to surging. Once the slack has been taken up, however, the shock on both boat and

anchor is very much greater than with nylon. Consequently, pay particular attention to adequate scope with chain, as will be discussed below.

The three kinds of chain most used as anchor rode are "BBB," "Proof Coil" and "High Test." Chain is designated by the diameter of material in the link, but the links of the various types differ slightly in length. It is necessary to match the chain to the wildcat (a pulley designed for use with chain) of the anchor windlass; the differences in link length are slight, but enough to cause trouble if there is a mismatch. Although most windlasses have a capstan for either line or chain, or one for each, special models are available that can handle both if the line is spliced into the chain, rather than connected with a shackle.

Any type of chain may be used for anchoring—BBB is marginally stronger than Proof Coil; High Test is significantly stronger than either. The selection of specific chain type and size for your boat involves several factors, the first of which is adequate strength. A safe standard to use is a working load figured from the size of the boat and the conditions to be encountered—at 20 percent of the chain's breaking strength when new. But you must also consider weight. The chain must be heavy enough to provide a proper sag to cushion shock loads, but the length required for normal anchoring depths

A shackle and eye splice, with thimble, are commonly used to secure rodes to the anchor ring, or to a shackle in a short length of chain between the line and the anchor.

On this boat, the vertical windlass has a smooth drum for line over a gypsy for chain; they can be operated independently. The anchor chain passes around the gypsy and through a deck opening to the chain locker. The smooth drum can be used for a second anchor, or for warping the vessel into a berth.

must not be so heavy, when stored on board, that it affects the boat's handling characteristics or even its safety. The weight factor may dictate a combination of chain and line.

■ **Nylon-and-chain.** Today the ideal rode is a combination of nylon line and a short length of chain (6 to 8 feet or longer is desirable) between the line and the anchor.

One effect of chain in this combination rode is to lower the angle of pull, because chain tends to lie on the bottom. Of equal or even greater significance is the fact that today's lightweight anchors often bury completely, taking part of the rode with them. Chain stands the chafe, and sand has less chance to penetrate strands of the fiber line higher up. Sand doesn't stick to the chain, and mud is easily washed off. Without chain, nylon gets very dirty in mud.

Chain used in this manner may vary from ¼-inch diameter for 20-footers up to ⁷⁄₁₆-inch for 50 footers. It should be galvanized, of course, to protect against rust. Neoprene-coated chain is an added refinement, as it will not mar the boat, but such coating has a limited life in active use.

Securing the rode

The complete anchor system consists of the anchor and the rode, usually made up of a length of line plus a length of chain. Each element of the system must be connected to its neighbor in a strong and dependable manner.

Eye splice, thimble and shackle

There are various methods for securing the rode to the anchor ring. The preferred practice is to work an eye splice around a thimble and use a shackle to join the thimble and ring. With

nylon line you can use a galvanized metal thimble, or one of stainless steel; be sure to keep the thimble in the eye. A tight, snug splice will help; seizings around the line and the legs of the thimble (near the V) will keep the thimble in the eye splice when the line comes under loads that stretch the eye. Good quality thimbles—available in bronze alloy, or plastic for use with synthetic rope—are designed to hold and protect the line.

Where a shackle is used, put a bit of silicone spray or waterproof grease on the threads of the shackle pin to keep it from seizing up over a period of time. *Be sure to safety-wire the pin to prevent its working out accidentally;* stainless steel wire can be used, but a nylon "wire tie" is easier. Watch for corrosion if different metals are used in thimbles, shackles and rings. Also beware of rust stains on nylon; cut out and resplice in new thimbles if the line becomes rust-stained.

A thimble and shackle provide a ready means for backing up your line with a length of chain, if desired, shackling the chain in turn to the anchor ring. Shackles should be large enough so as not to bind against the ring.

Anchor bends and bowline

Some skippers would rather fasten their line directly to the ring using an anchor bend, seizing the free end to the rode. Others use a bowline with an extra round turn around the

This shackle, used to attach a short length of chain to the anchor, must now be secured by running a short length of noncorroding wire through the eye of the pin and around the side of the shackle.

An anchor bowline, above, with its extra turn around the ring, is a secure way to bend the rode to an anchor; for greater security, the loose end can be seized to the adjacent line.

ring. In either case, these procedures make it easy to turn the line end-for-end occasionally, or to remove the line from the anchor for easy handling when stowing.

Turning a line end-for-end greatly extends its useful life, as the lower end that has chafed on the bottom becomes the inboard end seldom used with normal scope. Eye splices may be used at both ends of the rode, or added as necessary when the rode is turned.

Even where the regular working anchor is kept made-up with a combination of line and chain, you should know how to bend a line directly to an anchor. This is often the handiest way to drop a light anchor for a brief stop, or to make up a second anchor when a bridle or stern anchor is needed.

Use shackles to secure chain cables to the anchor; stout swivels are often an added refinement. Since swivels are a weak point, they must be large; on an all-chain rode they are essential. Swivels, however, should not be used with twisted soft-laid synthetic lines; a hockle (kink) may be the result. Double-braided lines will not hockle, even though subjected to very heavy strains.

At the bitter end

To guard against accidental loss of the anchor, the bitter (inboard) end of the anchor rode should be made fast to some part of the boat. You may do this by leading the line below, perhaps through a deck pipe, and securing it to a strong point with an eye bolt or similar fastener.

On small boats where the entire length of rode is carried on deck, you can have an eye splice in the bitter end to fit a securely fastened ring or eye-bolt. In any case, make sure that the bitter end is fastened, but always have handy some means of cutting the anchor line in an emergency.

How many, how heavy?

The number of anchors you should carry depends upon several things—the size of your boat, whether it is used only in familiar sheltered waters or cruises to many harbors and, to some extent, the type of anchor.

Some small boats such as runabouts and utilities have only a single anchor, but this cannot be considered adequate. Even discounting the possibility of fouling one anchor so badly that it cannot be retrieved, there are occasions when it is desirable to lie to two. Consider the possibility that one anchor heavy enough for extreme conditions could be a nuisance in ordinary weather.

Many boats carry two anchors, proportioning the weight in the ratio of about 40 percent in one, 60 percent in the other. For cruising boats, three are undoubtedly better. This allows for two anchors to be carried on deck—a light lunch hook for brief stops while someone is aboard, and a working anchor for ordinary service, including anchorages at night in harbor.

Anchors are normally stowed in fitted chocks that are mounted on the foredecks of most cruising boats.

The third might be a big spare storm anchor possibly stowed below, selected for its holding no matter what else lets go, even under extreme conditions of wind and weather.

Anchor size and holding power

Down through the years there have been repeated attempts to reduce anchor weights to a simple formula or table based on boat length or tonnage. Recommendations have varied widely, gradually becoming lighter as more modern designs replaced old-fashioned kedge anchors. With the development of patented designs, however, came the problem of minor variations between manufacturers of anchors of the same general type. The result is that any table of anchor size vs. boat size can only be a broad recommendation, to be modified for individual craft and local situations.

Stowage

A boater's seamanship skills can be assessed by the attention given to stowing ground tackle. Exactly how each individual boater goes about it depends to some extent on the kind of boating, the size of the boat, and the way the boat is equipped. In any case, unless the deck is uncluttered—with gear ready for immediate use, yet secured so that it cannot shift—the boater will never rate high as a seaman.

Ordinarily a cruising boat will carry one, sometimes two, anchors on deck, made up and ready for use. On some small boats, where it is not feasible to leave anchors on deck at all times, or in cases where lines are stowed below at the home berth, at least one anchor and line should be prepared and made ready before getting under way from your slip or mooring. Engines do fail and, when they do, it's likely to be an embarrassing moment, with wind or current setting you down on a shoal or reef. Then it's too late to think about breaking out gear that should have been ready at hand.

An anchor lying loose on deck is a potential hazard. If the boat happens to roll, it may slide across the deck, leaving scars in its wake and damage to equipment. Conceivably it could go over the side, taking line with it that might foul a propeller. Every anchor on deck should be stowed in chocks that are available at marine supply stores to fit standard anchors. Lashings hold the anchors in the chocks. Hardwood blocks, properly notched, have often been used in lieu of metal chock fittings.

Rather than chocking to deck, anchors carried aboard sailboats may be lashed to bow rails or shrouds—off the deck, where there is no risk of their getting underfoot, and less risk of their fouling running rigging. Many boats with bowsprits or pulpits have a roller at the outboard end, to carry a "regular working" anchor in this outboard position. Some larger yachts have provision for hauling the anchor into a hawsepipe fitted into the topsides forward.

As the big spare storm anchor is used only on rare occasions, you can carry it in some convenient location below, or in a lazarette or in stowage space below a cockpit deck, accessible through a hatch. Chocks here should be arranged to carry the weight on floors or frames, never on hull planking. If the big anchor gets adrift, it could easily loosen a bottom plank on a wooden boat, or break through a fiberglass hull. (A large Fortress anchor can be stowed disassembled in its box as it takes less than five minutes to put it together with two ordinary wrenches.)

The big risk in stowing a spare anchor in an out-of-the-way corner is the possibility that other gear may be allowed to accumulate over and around it. Guard against that. The sole value of a storm anchor may some day depend upon your being able to get that big hook over quickly, bent to a long and strong spare rode that must be equally accessible.

Lunch hooks are small, and are seldom needed without warning, so there is justification for stowing them in some convenient locker. Keep them away from the compass, however, as they can be a potent cause of deviation (except, of course, for aluminum anchors).

Though small craft often carry their lines coiled on a forward deck or in an open cockpit, many cruising boats have a rope locker in the forepeak for such a purpose. Nylon dries quickly and can be fed down into lockers almost as soon as it comes aboard. Lockers must be well ventilated and arranged to assure good air circulation at all times. Dark, damp lockers are an invitation to dry rot and mildew; a vented hatch over the rope locker will permit exposure to a good flow of air.

The rode should always be ready to run without fouling. Line is often passed below through a deck pipe, slotted so that it can be capped even when the line is in use. Slots must face aft to prevent water on deck from finding its way below. Some cast mooring bitts are made with an opening on the after face, through which line can be passed below.

RECOMMENDED SIZES FOR WORKING AND STORM ANCHORS

Boat length ft (m)	Rode length ft (m)	Rode size in (mm)	Chain size* in (mm)	Danforth standard model	Fortress model no.	Plow lbs (kg)	Bruce lbs (kg)	Delta lbs (kg)
Up to 15 (4.6)	125 (38.1)	5/16 (8)	3/16 (5)	8-S	n/a	6 (2.4)	4.4 (2)	9 (3.6)
15 to 25 (4.6 to 7.6)	150 45.7)	3/8 (10)	1/4 (6)	13-S	FX-7	15 (6)	11 (5)	14 (5.7)
26 to 30 (7.9 to 9.1)	200 (61)	7/16 (11)	5/16 (8)	22-S	FX-11	25 (10.1)	16.5 (7.5)	22 (8.9)
31 to 35 (9.4 to 10.6)	300 (91.4)	1/2 (13)	3/8 (10)	40-S	FX-16	35 (14.1)	22 (10)	22 (8.9)
36 to 40 (10.9 to 12.1)	400 (121.9)	3/8 (16)	7/16 (11)	65-S	FX-23	45 (18.2)	33 (15)	35 (14.1)
41 to 50 (12.5 to 15.2)	500 (152.4)	5/8 (16)	7/16 (11)	130-S	FX-37	60 (24.2)	44 (20)	55 (22.2)
51 to 60 (15.5 to 18.3)	500 (152.4)	3/4 (18)	1/2 (12)	180-S	FX-55	75 (30.3)	66 (30)	55 (22.2)

* Recommended chain length: 1 foot of chain for each foot of yacht length. Larger vessels should use an all chain rode.

Recommended by various anchor manufacturers, these suggested anchor sizes are higher than the average fair weather needs. The sizes assume that in a blow you will have fair holding ground, a scope of seven to one and moderate shelter from heavy seas.

Chain won't soak up moisture, and is easy to stow in lockers. Where weight of chain in the bow of a small offshore cruising boat is objectionable, it can be overcome by splitting a long rode into two or three shorter lengths, stowed where convenient and shackled together as necessary. The chain portion of a combination nylon-and-chain rode is ordinarily shackled in place for regular use, but nylon, if left on deck, should be shaded as much as possible from the sun to protect surface fibers from damage by ultraviolet rays.

Scope

Once you have chosen an anchor of suitable design and size to provide adequate holding power, you must consider scope. It is a major factor that determines whether you will, in fact, hold or drag. Too short a scope can destroy the efficiency of the best anchor.

Although some books use the term "scope" to refer to the length of anchor rode in use, most often it is recognized as a ratio—the length of the anchor rode in relation to the height of the bow above the bottom of the body of water, as shown in the illustration below. Note two important factors: the height of the bow chocks above the surface and the range of the tide.

Let's assume you anchor in 10 feet of water with 60 feet of rode paid out. At first glance, this is a reasonable scope of 6:1. But if your bow chock is 5 feet above the surface, the ratio is immediately cut to 4:1 (60:15). Six hours later the tide has risen another 5 feet and now you have an actual scope of 3:1 (60:20), exactly half the original theoretical ratio, and much too slight for safety.

What is a proper scope? Under favorable conditions using nylon line, 5:1 might be considered a minimum; under average conditions, 7 or 8:1 is regarded as satisfactory. Tests show that proper scope ratios range between 5:1 and 10:1, the latter for heavy weather. Even in a very hard blow, in an exposed anchorage, you will probably never need a scope of more than 15:1 with an anchor of suitable holding power. Effective scope for given conditions varies with the type of anchor. With all-chain rodes, a scope of 3 to 5:1 is adequate for all normal conditions.

In our hypothetical example at left, the length of rode paid out should have been 140 feet (7:1) to 160 feet (8:1); 100 feet (5:1) might be regarded as a minimum.

For maximum efficiency, all anchors require a low angle of pull—preferably less than 8 degrees from the horizontal. With short scope, holding power is reduced because the angle of pull is too high, tending to break the anchor out. As the pull is brought down more nearly parallel with the bottom, flukes dig in deeper with heavier strains on the line. Surging, as a boat pitches in a sea, throws a great load on the anchor, particularly on short scope. With long scope, the angle of pull is not only more horizontal at the anchor, but the elasticity of a long nylon line cushions the shock loads materially.

Marking a line for scope

Granted that we know how much scope is required, how do we know when we have paid out enough? Keep in mind that estimates are risky. Plastic cable markers come in sets to mark various lengths (such as 25, 50, 75, 100, 125, 150 and 200 feet), and are attached by insertion under a strand or two of the line. In daylight such markers are fine; in the dark, however, the traditional markers (strips of leather, bits of cotton or flannel cloth, and pieces of marline with knots) have the advantage of being able to be "read" by feel.

For all practical purposes, five or six marks at intervals of 20 feet (say from 60 to 140 feet) should be adequate. One practical method is to paint wide and narrow bands of a red vinyl liquid called Whip-End Dip at significant points, calling wide bands 50 feet and the narrow ones 10. On chain rodes, as a measure of scope, some boaters have painted links white at intervals.

If you anchor frequently in the same depths, you may want to add a whipping *(Chapter 13)* to prevent chafe at two or three predetermined places along the line.

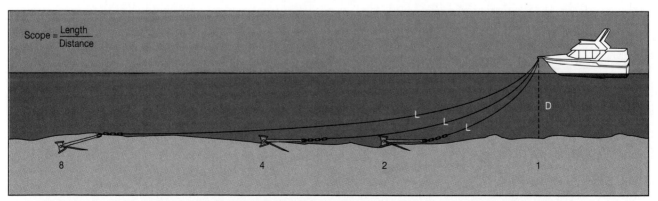

Scope, the ratio of rode length (L) to distance (D), from bow to the bottom (1), is critically important to safe anchoring. At (2) the rode length is twice distance (D), but the angle of pull tends to pull the anchor free. At (4), with L four times the distance D, the anchor can dig in, but there is still too much upward pull on the rode. At (8), scope 8:1, the short length of chain at the anchor lies flat on the bottom, and any pull helps to dig the anchor in deeper.

ANCHORING TECHNIQUES

So far we have discussed only equipment, or ground tackle. Let's now consider the technique—the art of anchoring. Before you can think about how to anchor, however, you must decide where you will anchor, and here, as in all phases of seamanship, a little foresight pays off handsomely.

Selecting an anchorage

There will be times, of course, when you will stop briefly in open water, coming to anchor for lunch, a swim, to fish, or perhaps to watch a race. But, for the most part, the real problem of finding an anchorage comes down to finding an anchorage where you can spend the night free from anxiety about the weather. Your safety in such a spot depends on three features—a good holding bottom, protection from the wind and water of suitable depth.

Types of bottoms vary widely, and there are good (though perhaps not "best") types of anchors for each bottom. Since it is impractical to carry the optimum anchor for every bottom type, it is necessary to select an area in which to anchor where the bottom best fits one of the anchors that you have.

Using the chart

The chart is the best guide in selecting a suitable location; anchorages are often described in "cruising guides" available for many boating areas. Sometimes you will be able to find a harbor protected on all sides, regardless of wind shifts. If not, the next best choice would be a cove, offering protection at least from the existing direction of the wind, or the quarter from which it is expected. As a last resort, anchorage may be found under a windward bank or shore—that is, where the wind blows from the bank toward the boat. In these latter two cases, watch for wind shifts, which could leave you in a dangerous berth on a lee shore.

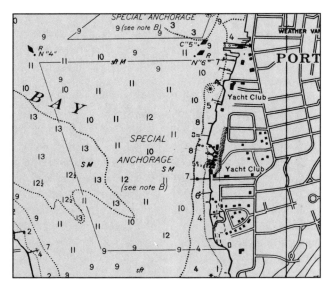

In charted special anchorage areas in U.S. inland waters, anchor lights are not required on boats less than 65.6 feet (20 m) in length.

BASIC CHARACTERISTICS:				
Cl. clay	M. mud	Oys oyster	stk. sticky	gn. green
Co. coral	Rk. rock	hrd. hard	bk. black	gy. gray
G. gravel	S. sand	rky. rocky	br. brown	wh. white
Grs. grass	Sh. shells	sft. soft	bu. blue	yl. yellow

Bottom characteristic abbreviations, as shown above.

Anchorages are sometimes designated on charts with an anchor symbol. Areas delineated on the chart by solid magenta lines, perhaps with the water area marked with yellow buoys, may be designated (U.S. internal waters) as special anchorage areas where lights are not required on vessels less than 65.6 feet (20 m) in length; refer to the chart below, left. Never anchor in cable or pipeline areas or in channels, both indicated on charts by broken lines in magenta.

Shallow depths are preferred for anchorage, because a given amount of rode will then provide a greater scope for better holding. Consider the range of tide, however, so that a falling level does not leave you aground or bottled up behind a shoal with not enough depth to get out at low water. You also must be alert to the special problems of reversing tidal currents if they occur where you are anchoring.

Characteristics of the bottom

The character of the bottom is of prime importance. While the type and design of anchor fluke have a direct bearing on its ability to penetrate, it may be stated broadly that mixtures of mud and clay, or sandy mud, make excellent holding bottom for most anchors. Firm sand is good if your anchor will bite deeply into it. Loose sand is undesirable. Soft mud should be avoided if possible. Rocks prevent an anchor from getting a bite except when a fluke is lodged in a crevice. Grassy bottoms, while they provide good holding for the anchor that can get through to firm bottom, often prevent a fluke from taking a good hold, except onto the grass, which then pulls out by its roots.

Sometimes bottoms that would otherwise provide reasonably good holding will be covered with a thick growth of vegetation that positively destroys the holding power of any anchor. Even if you happen to carry one of the fisherman's sand-anchor types, with its thin spidery arm and small flukes, expect it to pick up half a bushel of this growth. All you can do is clean it off and try elsewhere.

Characteristics of the bottom are generally shown on charts. By making a few casts with a lead line armed with a bit of hand grease, you can bring up samples of bottom as a further check. Chart abbreviations for some bottom characteristics are shown at the top.

How to anchor

Having selected a suitable place, and having the proper ground tackle on board, the next step is the actual process

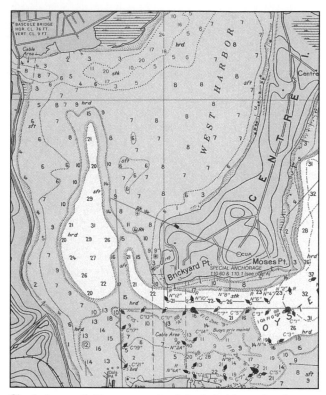

Charted range lights, or any pair of charted objects that form a range, are useful in selecting an anchorage spot, and as a means of checking to make sure the anchor is not dragging. The ideal anchorage is at the intersection of two ranges.

of anchoring: the approach, getting the anchor down, setting it, then making the anchor line fast. Each step must be done properly if a boat is to be secure. Never anchor a small boat by the stern—the freeboard is less, and swamping is much more likely to happen.

■ **Approaching the anchorage.** Having selected a suitable spot, run in slowly—preferably on some range ashore, selected from marks identified on the chart, or referring your position to visible buoys and landmarks to aid you in locating the chosen spot. Use of two ranges will give you the most precise positioning. (Later these aids will also be helpful in determining whether you are holding or dragging, especially if the marks are visible at night and it begins to blow after dark.)

If there are rocks, shoals, reefs or other boats to consider, give them all as wide a berth as possible, keeping in mind a possible swing of 360 degrees about the anchor with wind shifts or current changes.

Remember, too, that large yachts nearby may swing to a much longer scope than you allow—and, conversely, that you may swing much farther than a smaller boat nearby lying on a shorter rode. A vessel anchored by a chain will normally have a shorter scope and consequently a smaller swing circle; a boat on a permanent mooring will have the smallest movement of all. Observe how the boats that will be your

neighbors are anchored or moored. Visualize how you will swing with your intended scope, and avoid getting into a situation of overlapping swinging circles.

The risk of fouling a neighboring boat is aggravated when, in a current, the deep-draft vessel holds its position while a light-draft boat swings to a shift of wind not strong enough to influence the other. Keel sailboats may lie one way in a light current, powerboats in another way.

The boat that has already established its location in an anchorage has a prior claim to the spot. Do not expect its skipper to move if you later find yourself in an embarrassing position. Allow room enough so that you can pay out more scope if necessary in case of a blow, without being forced to change your anchorage, perhaps at night.

The way other boats lie, together with the set of nearby buoys, will help to determine how you should round up to the chosen spot. Begin by estimating the relative effects of the wind and current on your own boat and come up slowly, against the stronger of these two forces. In other words, head as you expect to lie after dropping back on the anchor. Running through the anchorage, take care that your speed is reduced to a point where the wake from your vessel cannot disturb other boats.

■ **Letting the anchor go**. Having taken a proper approach, you are ready to let the anchor go. Unless you must work single-handed, station one person on the forward deck. Enough line should be hauled out of the locker and coiled down so as to run freely without kinking or fouling. If previously detached, the line must be shackled to the ring, and the stock set up (if of the stock type) and keyed. Many an anchor has been lost for failure to attach the rode properly. Rodes, too, have gone with the anchor when not secured at the bitter end. Although lightweight anchors are always ready for use and do not have to be set up, always check to see that the shackle is properly fastened.

Although the practice is seen all too often, an anchor should not be lowered when your boat has any headway. The bow of a motorboat or a sailboat under power should be brought slowly up to the spot where the anchor is to lie, and headway checked with the reverse gear. Then, just as the boat begins to gather sternway slowly in reverse, the anchor is lowered easily over the side until it hits bottom, crown first.

Never stand in the coils of line on deck and do not attempt to "heave" the anchor by casting it as far as possible from the side of the boat. Occasionally, with judgment, a light anchor in a small boat can be carefully thrown a short distance if such action is required—taking care that it lands in its holding position—but the best all-round rule is to lower the anchor as described. That goal is to minimize the possibility of fouling.

■ **Setting the anchor**. An anchor must be "set" properly in order to yield its full holding power. The best techniques for setting an anchor will vary from type to type. Only general guidelines can be given here, and you should experiment to determine the best procedures for your boat, your anchors and your cruising waters.

With the anchor on the bottom and the boat backing down slowly, pay out line (this technique is sometimes called "veering"), preferably with a turn of line around the bitt. When the predetermined scope has been paid out, snub the line quickly, and the anchor will probably get a quick bite into the bottom.

Sometimes the anchor may become shod with a clump of mud or bottom grass adhering to the flukes; in these cases, it is best to lift the anchor, wash it off by dunking at the surface, and try again.

After the anchor is set, you can pay out or take in rode to the proper length for the anchorage, and for the prevailing and expected weather conditions. Scope must be adequate for holding, but in a crowded anchorage you must also consider the other boats.

When you must work single-handed, get your ground tackle ready to let go long before you arrive at the anchorage. Bring the boat up to the chosen spot and then lower the anchor as the boat settles back with wind and current, paying out line as it is accepted.

In some cases it is possible to set up a kedge anchor with its stock in place so the anchor can be let go quickly. Its chain rode leads outboard from the windlass, through a hawsepipe, up to the ring. The davit tackle can be hooked into the balancing band of the shank. A gypsy is provided for a fiber rode on the port side of the windlass.

Regardless of the type of anchor, after you have paid out full scope, reverse your engine to apply a back-down load in excess of any anticipated strains. This is particularly important if your boat is to be left unattended.

At this point, it is important to make a positive check that the anchor is holding, and not dragging. There are several ways to do this: If the water is clear enough that you can see bottom, you can detect any movement easily. If you cannot see bottom, select two objects on the beam that form a natural range, and watch for any change in their relationship; if none occurs, your anchor is holding. An even simpler method is possible if you are using a buoyed trip line from the crown of your anchor, described on page 268. When you are applying reverse power to test the anchor's holding, the float on this line should continue to bob up and down in one spot, unaffected by the pull on the anchor rode. If you see the float making a path through the water, however, you can be sure your anchor is dragging. In warm, clear tropical waters, it is an excellent practice to put on a mask and fins, and "swim the anchor," checking visually how well it is buried.

■ **Making fast.** Once the anchor has a good bite, with proper scope paid out, make the line fast and shut off the motor.

On boats with a forward bitt (samsonpost), an excellent way to secure the anchor line is to make two full turns around the bitt, and then finish off with a half-hitch around each end of the pin through the bitt. The bitt takes the load and the pin secures the line; this way, the line is more easily taken off the bitt than with a clove hitch or any other hitch.

Where a stout cleat is used to make fast, take a full turn around the base, one turn over each horn crossing diagonally over the center of the cleat, and finish with a half hitch around one horn, as shown in Chapter 13.

The fundamental idea in making fast is to secure the rode in such a manner that the line can neither slip nor jam. If the strain comes on top of a series of turns on a cleat, then you will find it nearly impossible to free if you want to change the scope, without first taking the strain off it.

If you must shorten scope, first clear the bitt or cleat of old turns or hitches. Do *not* throw new ones over the old.

A trick worth using when the sea is so rough that it is difficult to go forward on deck—especially if you are single-handed—is to set up the anchor in the aft cockpit, lead the line forward on deck through a closed chock and then back aft to the cockpit. (If there are stanchions for lifelines, the lead of the rode from chock to anchor must obviously be outside them.) When you're ready to let go, the anchor can be dropped on the weather side from the cockpit, with the line running through the bow chock and secured on a bitt or cleat aft.

Hand signals

Anchoring, like docking, involves good communication between the person on the foredeck and the helmsman. With noise from the engine and exhaust, and sometimes the wind, it is usually difficult for the helmsman to hear, even if crew members on deck can. A helmsman handling the boat from a flying bridge can usually hear better and, from this higher position, can see the trend of the anchor line.

In any case, it helps to have a pre-arranged set of hand signals. There is no need for standardization on this, as long as the helmsman clearly understands the crew's instructions. Keep the signals as simple as possible. Motion of the hands, calling for the helmsman to come ahead a little, or to back down, can take the most obvious form; pointing ahead or aft will do. Simply holding up a hand palm out—a "policeman's signal"—may be used to signal a "stop" to whatever action is then taking place.

When the anchor drags

Let's assume now that you have anchored with a scope of 7:1. You have inspected the rode and taken bearings, if possible, as a check on your position. Though the wind has picked up, you turn in, only to be awakened near midnight by the boat's roll. Before you reach the deck you know what has happened: The anchor is dragging and the bow no longer heads up into the wind.

This calls for instant action, not panic. A quick check on bearings confirms what the roll indicated: You're dragging, with wind abeam. Sizing up the situation swiftly, you note that danger is not imminent; there is still plenty of room to leeward, and there are no boats downwind to be fouled. Otherwise you would have to get underway, immediately, or be prepared to fend off.

The first step in trying to get the anchor to hold is to let out more scope. Don't just throw over several more fathoms of line; pay it out smoothly, with an occasional sharp pull to try to give it a new bite. If you're dragging badly and can't handle the rode with your hands, take a turn around the bitt and snub the line from time to time. If this doesn't work, start the engine and hold the bow up into the wind with just enough power to take the strain off the rode. This gives the anchor a chance to lie the throttle and lets the boat drift back slowly. If you haven't held when the scope is 10:1, get the anchor back aboard and try again with a larger storm anchor, or in another spot.

■ **Sentinel, buoy or sentinel and chain?** Suppose, now, that you have no spare storm anchor to fall back on. Can anything be done to increase your holding power? Here we enter an area of controversy about two different techniques. The objectives are quite different: You can choose to (1) lower the angle of pull on the anchor line or to (2) lessen the shock loads on the anchor or on the boat itself. We'll consider both procedures in turn.

For generations, cruising boaters have used a device known as a sentinel or kellet, shown below. In principle, the sentinel is nothing more than a weight sent more than half-way down the rode to lower the angle of pull on the anchor, putting a greater sag in the line that must be straightened out before a load is thrown on the anchor. Sometimes working with what they had readily at hand, boaters have shackled or snapped their light anchor to the main anchor line,

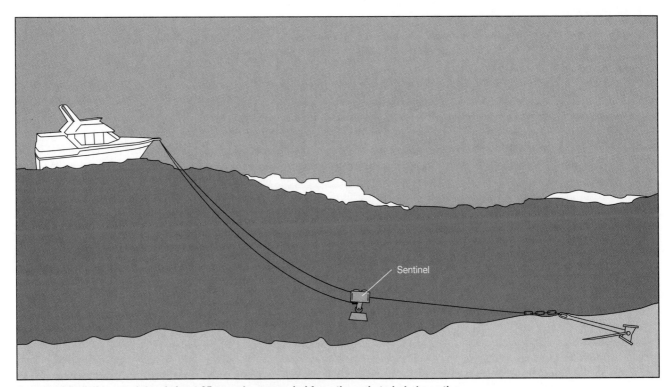

A sentinel (kellet) is a weight of about 25 pounds suspended from the rode to help keep the pull on the anchor as horizontal as possible to prevent dragging in rough weather.

A plastic foam buoy is designed to transmit the strain through a solid rod. Some models have the two connections at the same end of the buoy.

then sent it down the main rode with a line attached to its ring, to stop it at a suitable distance. A pig of ballast or other weight would do as well, provided it could be readily attached; commercially made devices are available that do this easily and neatly.

If a sentinel is used, it should be done with ample scope, and every precaution taken to avoid chafing the main rode.

The other school of thought uses a buoy rather than a weight, claiming that, properly used, the buoy can carry most of the vertical load in an anchoring or mooring system. This limits the basic load on the boat to the horizontal force required to maintain the boat's position. According to this argument, the buoy permits the boat's bow to ride up easily over wave crests, rather than being pulled down into them, with excessive loads on both rode and anchor.

If a buoy is used, the type found in a permanent mooring system, shown on page 274, is most effective. Its connection into the system should be as positive as it would be in a mooring buoy, with all strain carried directly by the rode. This ensures no "weak link." Provision should be made for carrying a proper buoy as part of the emergency equipment, rather than trusting to a makeshift device improvised under stress of weather.

In an alternate system, the chain and sentinel techniques can be combined. Carry a boat-length of substantial chain and a 25-pound pig of lead with a ring bolt cast in it. Stow these away in lieu of ballast. In threatening conditions, with breakers to leeward, shackle the chain to your biggest and best anchor, and the chain in turn to your best and longest nylon rode, with the ring of the pig lead shackled in where the chain and nylon join. This can only be an improvement over the same long scope of nylon without the benefit of the extra length of chain and added weight. In addition, it would seem to eliminate the problems of chafe at the sentinel and any tendency to hold the boat's bow down in the surge of pitching seas.

Getting underway

When you are ready to weigh anchor and get underway, run up to the anchor very slowly under power. You want to be able to take in the line easily without hauling the boat up to

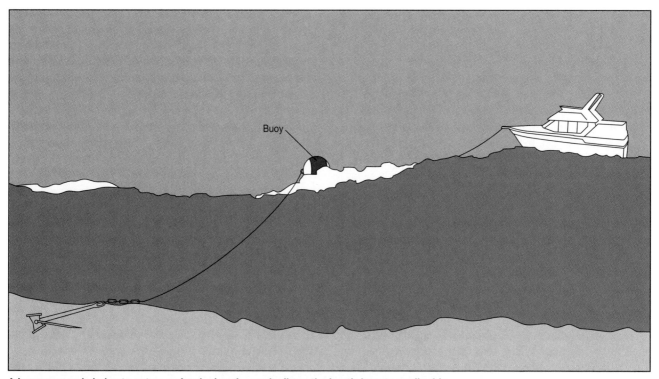

A buoy on a rode helps to act as a shock absorber as it allows the boat's bow to easily ride up wave crests without excessive strain being transmitted to the anchor itself.

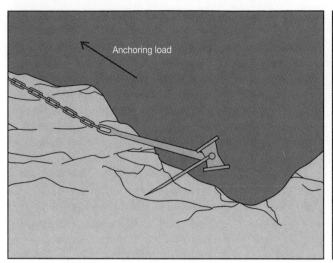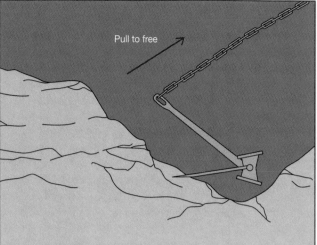

If an anchor fouls on a rocky bottom, the first attempt to clear it should be by reversing the original angle of pull *(left)* **with moderate scope, to draw it out** *(right)*.

it. In most cases the anchor will break out readily when the line stands vertically.

As the line comes in, you can whip it up and down, freeing it of any grass or weeds before it comes on deck. If the anchor is not too heavy, wash off mud by swinging it back and forth near the surface as it leaves the water. With care, the line can be snubbed around a bitt, and the anchor allowed to wash off as the boat gathers way, preferably sternway. Take the following precautions: Do not allow the flukes to hit the topsides, and be careful that water flowing past the anchor doesn't take hold of the anchor, pulling it out of your hands.

Although nylon anchor line will not be harmed by stowing without drying, it is undesirable to carry this additional moisture below decks. Coil the line loosely on deck and allow it to dry, but expose it to sunlight no longer than necessary.

In all anchor handling, avoid letting the anchor hit the hull at any time. Whether your boat is made of fiberglass, metal or wood, some gouges, dents or nicks may result. Guests are often eager to "help" get the anchor up, but unless they have some experience it's better to handle this part of the job yourself. Handle and stow lines carefully. If a bight or end of line slips over the side it is certain to run back under the bottom and get fouled in the propeller.

In a boat under sail alone, have your mainsail up before you break the anchor loose. The same procedure is used as stated above but there is no motor to help. However, it is possible to use your sails to assist.

Clearing a fouled anchor

If an anchor refuses to break out when you haul vertically on the line, snub it around the bitt and, under power, go ahead a few feet. If the anchor does not respond to this treatment, it may have fouled under some obstruction. To clear it, try making fast to the bitt and running slowly in a wide circle on a taut line. Changing the angle of pull may free it, or

a turn of line may foul an exposed fluke (if it's a kedge) and draw it out.

Probably the best way to break out of a fouled anchor is with a buoyed trip line—if you have been wise enough to rig one beforehand. Use a light line, but one that is strong enough to stand the pull of a snagged anchor—⅜-inch polypropylene, which floats, is a typical choice. Attach this line to the crown of the anchor—in some models an eye is provided for this. In a lightweight-type anchor, a hole can be drilled in one of the crown plates. The trip line should be just long enough to reach the surface in waters in which you normally anchor, with allowance for tidal changes. Pass the line through a wooden or foam float, or a plastic disposable bottle with a handle, and end the line in a small eye splice that can be caught with a boathook. If the anchor does not trip in a normal manner, pick up the trip line and haul the anchor up crown first.

If you haven't rigged a trip line, sometimes you can run a length of chain down the anchor line, rigged so that the power of another boat can be used to haul in a direction opposite to that in which the anchor line tends. This changes the angle of pull by 180 degrees. With a kedge, if one fluke is exposed, a chain handled between dinghies can usually be worked down the rode to catch the upper arm and draw the anchor out, crown first.

If the anchor is not fouled in something immovable, but merely set deeply in heavy clay, you can generally break it out by securing the line at low water and allowing a rising tide to exert a steady strain. Or, if there is a considerable ground swell, snub the line when the bow pitches low in a trough. There's some risk of parting the line this way, in case the fluke is fouled worse than you think.

In rocky bottoms, the first thing to try is reversing the direction of pull, opposite to that in which the anchor was originally set, using a moderate amount of scope.

There is a type of anchor in which the ring is free to slide the full length of the shank. Properly rigged, as shown on page 271, it is claimed to be virtually snag-proof.

If you have been anchored for a day or two in a brisk wind, the anchor may be dug in deep. Don't wait until you're ready to sail; 20 minutes before departure shorten the scope and keep a sharp watch. The boat's motion will tend to loosen the anchor's hold and save a lot of work when you finally go to break it out and raise it.

Using two anchors

For increased holding power in a blow, two anchors are sometimes set. If your working anchor drags, you can run out your spare storm anchor without picking up the working anchor. The important thing to remember is to lay them out at an angle, as shown at right—not in line—to reduce the risk of having one that drags cut a trough in the bottom for the other to follow.

When a boat has two anchors out and an extreme wind shift occurs (as with the passage of a squall line), special care is necessary. A change of pull on the anchor lines of 180 degrees, more or less, can bring the two rodes into contact with each other and neither anchor will hold or reset if pulled out. In some situations, one anchor is actually safer than two.

When setting two anchors, make fast the two rodes separately to two bitts or cleats; do not put one rode atop the other in case you have to make adjustments later.

Reducing yawing

Deep-draft sailboats usually lie well head to the wind, but powerboats often "tack" back and forth at anchor. Skiffs, with high freeboard and little draft forward, are among the worst offenders in this respect.

You can stop yawing by laying two anchors, lines leading out from either bow, making an angle of about 45 degrees between them. To do this, get one anchor down first and have a helper tend the line carefully as you maneuver the bow off to one side before letting the other go. Then you can settle back on both lines, adjusting scope as necessary.

With good handling, you can get two anchors down single-handed. The easiest way is to settle back on one anchor, making fast when the proper scope has been paid out. Then, go ahead with the propeller, rudder over enough to hold the line out taut so that you will be able to keep an eye on it at all times. When the line stands out abeam, stop your headway, go to the foredeck and let the other anchor go, then drop back, snub the line to set the anchor, and adjust the lines to equal scope.

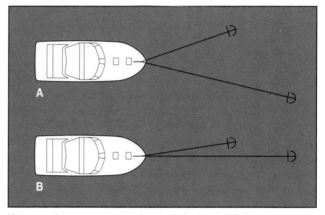

If two anchors are set out ahead of the boat, it is best to have the rodes at an angle, as at A, rather than in a straight line, as at B, to reduce the possibility of their fouling as the boat swings to wind or current.

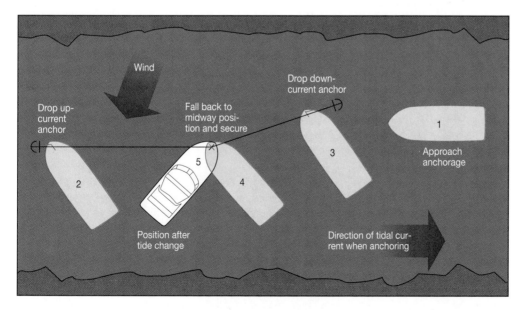

When anchoring in a narrow waterway with reversing tidal current, two anchors should be set from the bow as shown. Adequate scope should be used on each anchor, with the rodes adjusted so there is no slack in one when the other is taut.

Whenever a dinghy is available, the second anchor can be carried out in it; adjust the lines as required after both anchors are set.

Guarding against wind or current shifts

Sometimes you will need to anchor where the tidal current reverses, or wide wind shifts are likely. Here it is wise to set two anchors as security against an anchor breaking out and failing to set itself again.

The anchors are set 180 degrees apart with the bow of the boat at the midpoint between them, as shown on page 269. With both lines drawn up tight, the bow remains over essentially the same spot, and swinging is limited to the boat's length. This "Bahamian mooring" works best for a reversing tidal current with the wind blowing across the current so as to keep the boat always on one side of the line, between the two anchors.

When setting a second anchor for use as described above, set the up-current anchor in the conventional way, then back down until double the normal scope is out. After the down-current anchor is set, adjust the scope at the bow chocks until both are equal. When going ahead with a rode tending aft, take care not to foul the propeller.

If the two-anchor technique is used in a crowded anchorage to limit swinging radius, remember that other nearby boats may lie to one anchor only. That means the risk of the swinging circles overlapping is increased.

Stern anchors

In some anchorages, boats lie to anchors bow and stern. The easiest way to get these down is to let the bow anchor go first, then drop back with wind or current on an extra long scope (15 to 18 times the depth), drop the stern anchor, and then adjust the scope on both as necessary, taking a line for-ward. In tidal waters make allowance for increasing depth as the tide rises. The value of this arrangement is generally restricted to areas where permanent moorings are set explic-itly for this purpose, as in narrow streams or on occasions where there is no risk of getting a strong wind or current abeam. Under such conditions, the strain on a vessel's ground tackle could be tremendous.

Sometimes a stern anchor will be useful if you seek shel-ter under a windward bank. Let the stern anchor go from aft, carefully estimating scope as it is dropped, and pay out more scope as you run up toward the bank or beach. Bed a second anchor securely in the bank, or take a line ashore to a struc-ture or tree.

The stern anchor will keep the stern off and prevent the boat from ranging ahead. Remember to watch that stern line while the propeller is turning.

At piers and wharves

A berth on the weather side of a pier or wharf is a bad one, as considerable damage can be done to a boat pounding heavily against piles, even with fenders out. However, in cir-cumstances where such a berth is unavoidable, anchors can be used to help ease the situation. Keeping well up to wind-ward, angling into the wind as much as is practical, have a crew member let one anchor go on a long scope off the quar-ter (the port quarter if you will lie starboard side to the pier). As he or she pays out scope, run ahead and get another off the port bow, judging positions of both so you can drop down to leeward toward the pier on equal scope, with lines tend-ing off at a 45-degree angle. Properly executed, this maneu-ver will prevent your vessel from hitting the pier, and the lines you then carry ashore will be needed only to prevent the boat from moving ahead or astern. For more information, refer to Chapter 9.

In rafting, one boat only should be anchored. The other boat(s) are made fast to it, so that all will move as one in a wind shift. (The anchored boats shown at left also have a stern line to shore.) Raft only in light air and in calm water.

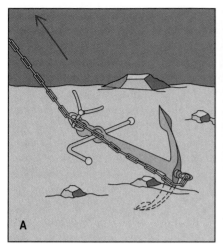
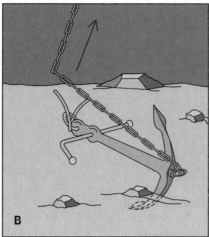
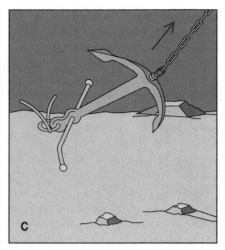

When scowing an anchor, the rode is attached to the anchor crown, led back along the shank and lashed at the ring. If the anchor is snagged (A), an upward pull (B) parts the lashing and the anchor can be drawn out crown first (C).

Rafting

At a rendezvous several boats frequently lie to a single anchor—this is a safe practice when there is little wind and a relatively smooth surface, and the skippers plan the process carefully. After one boat is anchored, the second vessel pulls alongside; take care that both boats are ready with plenty of fenders out. If you are the skipper of the second boat, stay about 6 to 10 feet (1.8 to 3 m) away from the anchored boat in order that you can heave bow and stern lines. If this cannot be done, run up to the anchored boat's bow at an angle of about 45 degrees, and pass a bow line first, then your stern line. Make sure you have no headway when lines are passed. As soon as the bow line is aboard the anchored boat, stop your engine so that there will be no chance of going ahead, breaking the anchor out.

If the boats involved are powerboats, allow your boat to drift astern until transoms align. On sailboats, however, you must consider the dangers of spreaders tangling in a rocking situation. Line up rafting sailboats so that the rigging is clear at all points aloft.

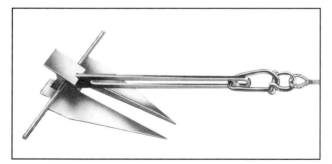

In some models of small-craft anchors, a line slides in a slot down the shank so the anchor can be drawn out backwards if it snags. For use when snagging is unlikely, the rode can be shackled directly to the eye at the end of the shank.

Once the boats are aligned, let the bow swing off and pull the sterns in close, for ease of stepping from one boat to another. To keep the boats in line and fenders in position, run a spring line from the stern of the arriving boat to a point well forward on the anchored boat.

If a third boat makes fast, the anchored boat should be in the middle; if more tie up always alternate them, port and starboard of the anchored boat. Each succeeding boat should use the same technique, always with a spring from the stern of the outboard boat forward to the one next inboard. Keels of all boats in the group should be nearly parallel. When at least four boats are tied together, it is a good precaution for the outboard boats to carry additional anchors out at a 45-degree angle. When it's time to turn in for the night, every boat should establish its own separate anchorage.

Anchoring at night

If you have no ranges with which to check your position when you are anchoring overnight (or if those you have are unlighted), you can rig a drift lead (the lead line will do). Lower it to the bottom, leave some slack for swinging, and make fast. If it comes taut, you've dragged. Don't forget to pick it up before getting underway.

In general, a vessel anchored at night must show an anchor light, two lights if over 164.0 feet (50 m) in length. Anchor lights are not required for vessels under 65.6 feet (20 m) in a "special anchorage area," however, or for craft less than 23.4 feet (7 m) when not in a channel, fairway or where other vessels normally navigate. Refer to Chapter 7 for further information.

Requirement for "anchor ball"

With the same exceptions as noted above for anchor lights, a vessel anchored during daylight hours must hoist a black ball shape where it can best be seen. This is not less than

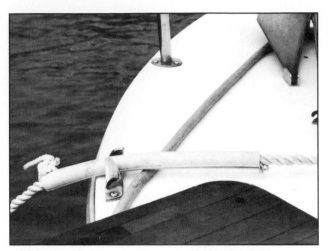

Split plastic tubing can be used to cover line where it passes through chocks to protect against abrasion.

The bulb cast into the shackle end of this mushroom mooring anchor adds to its weight and holding power.

23.6 inches (0.6 m) in diameter for ships, but it may be of lesser size for small craft. Refer to Chapter 7 for further information on anchor ball sizes.

On rocky bottoms

Avoid rocky bottoms or those with coral heads; these are hazardous at best, regardless of the type of anchor used. Before leaving a boat unattended, apply a test load to the anchor well in excess of any expected load.

If you normally anchor in rocky bottoms or suspect that the bottom is foul in the area where you must anchor, it is better to forestall trouble. One time-tested device is the buoyed trip line described on page 268.

An alternate scheme is to "scow" the anchor, as shown in the illustrations at the top of page 271, by bending the rode to the crown, leading it back along the shank, and stopping it to the ring with a light lashing of marline. With sufficient scope, the strain is on the ring, not on the lashing. When hove

up short, the strain is on the lashing. When this parts, the anchor comes up crown first.

There are anchors that have a slotted shank in which the ring can travel freely from end to end. If the anchor should snag, the theory is that when the boat is brought back over the anchor, the sliding ring can slip down the shank so the anchor will be drawn backward. There is, however, some risk: During a near-180-degree shift of wind or current, the anchor might pull out when you want it to hold. Some models have an eye at the end of the shank separate from the slot; if the anchor line is attached, the anchor functions in the normal manner.

Protecting the lines

Take extreme care to avoid chafe on the rode. Wherever the line comes in contact with chocks or rails, and rubs back and forth under continuous strain, outer strands may wear enough to seriously weaken the line. Mooring pennants are particularly susceptible to this, as are dock lines.

When lying at anchor, you can "freshen the nip" by paying out a little more scope from time to time, or you can protect the line at the point of chafe by wrapping strips of canvas around it. Today's chafing gear is available in the form of plastic or rubber sleeves, which can be slipped over the line, centered in a chock, and seized with thongs on either side to prevent shifting.

MAINTAINING GROUND TACKLE

Ground tackle

Ground tackle includes all the anchors, anchor rode (line or chain) and all the shackles and other gear that is used for anchoring. At least once a year, every set of ground tackle should be hosed clean and the chain rode should be inspected for deterioration (rusting, cracks or frayed or weakened fibers). Check any splices; all should have absolute integrity. (Note that, for complete safety, the only splice in an anchor rode should be the one that connects the rode to the thimble by which it is shackled to the chain or anchor.)

The anchor swivel, connecting shackle and pin, should be closely examined. The pin should be safety-wired to keep it from working loose, and the safety wire should be replaced during each annual inspection. The chain locker should also be hosed down. Ensure that the bitter end of the main anchor rode is connected to the boat (to prevent accidental loss of the anchor).

Lines

■ Keep lines free from sand and grit; dry them before stowing. Use a low-pressure hose to wash off grit, or slosh the line overboard, tied in a loose coil. Don't use a high-pressure nozzle—it may force grit deeper into the line.

A substantial, well-rounded samson-post is shown behind the drum of an electric anchor windlass. Take note of the horizontal normanpin that keeps the line from slipping off.

Chafing gear also comes in the form of lacing line or a white waterproof tape, to be applied around the line at bitts, chocks and other points of contact.

The increasing use of relatively light anchor rodes of small diameter (as small as ⅜ of an inch) points up the necessity of preventing chafe. The chafe that a ¾-inch line could tolerate might render a ⅜-inch line unsafe.

Using the proper fittings

Chafe is aggravated wherever a fitting has a rough surface to accelerate abrasion of the fiber. Even small nicks and scratches in a chock can damage a line by cutting fibers pro-

gressively, one at a time. Serious weakening of a line develops when it is forced to pass around any fitting with relatively sharp corners, such as a square bitt with only a minimum rounding of the edges—especially when the bitts are too small for their job.

Theoretically the ideal bitt is round and of generous diameter. The best chocks are those of special design with the largest possible radius at the arc at the point where the line will pass over it.

Mooring bitts especially must be fastened securely. The best bitt is the old-fashioned wooden bitt, long enough to have its heel fastened solidly to the boat's keel. If a cast fitting is used on deck, it must be through-bolted, and the deck below must be reinforced with a husky backing plate.

Guarding against damage from ultraviolet rays

The outer layers of all kinds of rope can be damaged by the sun's ultraviolet rays. Nylon line of relatively large diameter (upward of ¾ inch) receives negligible damage. As the diameter decreases, the problem becomes proportionally more serious. In ⅜-inch nylon, for instance, a great deal of the line is in the outer fibers. Take special care to shield such lines from unnecessary exposure to direct sunlight. Often the rode can be fed down into a locker. If it must be carried on deck, shade it, or, after a period of time, assign it to less critical uses and obtain a new anchor line.

■ Make sure lines are straight before any load is applied. Placing a strain on a kinked line can damage or break the fibers. Sharp bends are also harmful. Blocks should always have sheaves of adequate diameter, as described in Chapter 13.

■ Keeping in mind that most chafe and wear comes on the anchor end, periodically turn lines in regular use end-for-end. If you use one size for all anchor and mooring lines, you can put a new spare anchor line aboard each spring, put the former spare into regular use, and make the oldest anchor line into dock lines after cutting out any chafed sections.

■ Become familiar with the special techniques required for working with nylon line, as when making up eye splices, or even unreeling it from a coil. These techniques are described in Chapter 13.

Anchors and chain

■ Consider freshening up a galvanized anchor. Usually coated by the hot-dip process, which leaves a tough protective finish, galvanized anchors typically require no care except washing off mud. Occasionally they are freshened up in appearance by a coat of aluminum paint. You can also buy a spray coating

called "cold galvanize," which is heavy in zinc. This coating will temporarily improve the appearance of anchor and chain that are starting to rust, but it has poor wearing qualities when compared to hot-dip galvanizing.

■ If the chain comes up fouled with mud, give it a thorough cleaning. Some larger yachts have a faucet and hose connected to a fresh- or salt-water pressure system for this purpose.

Periodic inspection

■ Inspect all lines periodically, particularly anchor lines. Check the effect of abrasion, cuts, rust on nylon, broken or frayed yarns, variations in strand size or shape, and burns. Nylon line may fuzz on the surface although the yarns are not broken. This seems to act as a cushion, reducing further outside abrasion.

■ Compare the line to new rope. Untwist and examine the inside of strands; they should be clean and bright as in new rope. Nylon may be fused or melted, either inside or out, from overloads.

■ Join the yachting old-timers who know cordage. If in doubt, replace the line or get an expert opinion. Also see Chapter 13.

PERMANENT MOORINGS

Permanent moorings, as distinguished from ordinary ground tackle in daily use, consist of the gear used when boats are to be left unattended for long periods, as at yacht club anchorages. The traditional system often consists of a mushroom anchor, chain from the anchor to a buoy, and a pennant of stainless steel or nylon from the buoy to a light pick-up float at the pennant's end.

Mushroom anchors, especially the type with a heavy bulb cast in the shank can, through suction, develop great holding power under ideal conditions, if they have enough time to bury deeply into bottoms that permit such burying. Unfortunately, ideal bottom conditions are not always present. Often large cast concrete blocks, similar to those used by the Coast Guard to moor buoys, are put down in lieu of mushroom anchors.

Complicating the problem is the fact that anchorages are becoming increasingly crowded, so that boats cannot have adequate scope because of overlapping swinging circles. Add to this the threat of abnormally high hurricane tides that reduce scope to a less-than-safe ratio, and you have the explanation for the devastation wrought by several hurricanes along the Atlantic Coast.

Typical systems

The problem faced by the Manhasset Bay Yacht Club at Port Washington, New York, is typical. Here about 200 boats are moored in a limited space. If each boat could use a length of chain equal to five to seven times the depth of water (maximum 30 feet/9.1 meters), safety would be assured. However, this would require a swinging radius of several hundred feet for each boat, which is not possible. After exhaustive study the Manhasset boaters prepared a set of recommended standards. A generally similar system was adopted by the Lake Michigan Yachting Association, as shown below.

Guest moorings are often available at yacht clubs and some marinas. The launch operators will know which of those not in use for the night are heavy enough to hold your boat. As a rule, it's easier and safer to pick up such a mooring. In some places, a charge may be made.

A multiple-anchor system

One hurricane that ravaged the North Atlantic Coast swept through an anchorage in the New York area and tore almost every boat from its moorings. Only two survived. What these two had in common was an "unconventional" mooring sys-

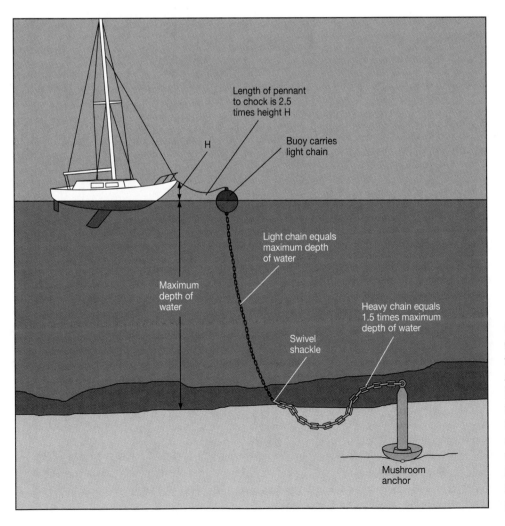

Length of pennant to chock is 2.5 times height H

Buoy carries light chain

H

Light chain equals maximum depth of water

Maximum depth of water

Heavy chain equals 1.5 times maximum depth of water

Swivel shackle

Mushroom anchor

In this diagram of mooring practice recommended by the Lake Michigan Yachting Association and approved by the U.S. Coast Guard, total scope is the length of heavy chain, length of light chain, and length of pennant. Minimum space between moorings should be 1.25 times total scope plus boat length.

	Overall boat length (feet)	Mushroom anchor minimum weight (pounds)	Heavy chain		Light chain		Pennant			Total minimum length of system, chocks to mushroom anchor (feet)
			Length (feet)	Diameter (inches)	Length (feet)	Diameter (inches)	Minimum length (feet)	Diameter nylon	Stainless steel (inches)	
Motorboats	25	225	50	7/8	20	3/8	20	7/8	9/32	70
	35	300	35	1	20	7/16	20	1	11/32	75
	45	400	40	1	20	1/2	20	1 1/4	3/8	80
	55	500	50	1	20	9/16	20	1 1/2	7/16	90
Racing sailboats	25	125	30	5/8	20	5/16	20	7/8	9/32	70
	35	200	30	3/4	20	3/8	20	1	11/32	70
	45	325	35	1	20	7/16	20	1 1/4	3/8	75
	55	450	45	1	20	9/16	20	1 1/2	7/16	85
Cruising sailboats	25	175	30	3/4	20	5/16	20	7/8	9/32	70
	35	250	30	1	20	3/8	20	1 1/2	11/32	70
	45	400	40	1	20	7/16	20	1 1/2	3/8	80
	55	550	55	1	20	9/16	20	2	1 1/2	95

MANHASSET BAY YACHT CLUB MOORING SYSTEM

System is based on maximum water depth of 20 feet; for greater depths, length of light chain should at least equal the expected maximum.

tem—multiple three anchors bridled to a common center, with chain and pennant leading from that center point to the boat.

The advantages of the multiple-anchor system are shown at right. Regardless of how the wind shifts, the boat swings through a small circle, despite the advantage of a relatively long total scope from boat to anchor. The short rode up from the three-way bridle minimizes any "tacking" tendency. Always there will be one or two anchors to windward, the strain tending in the same direction. With the use of today's lightweight anchors—rather than mushrooms—the greater the load, the deeper they bury. Mushrooms often need a relatively long period to bed in securely, but lightweight anchors will dig in almost immediately. Using a safety factor of 1.5, each anchor in the three-anchor system should have a holding power equal to the design holding power of a permanent mooring.

Mooring buoys

Buoys used in any mooring system should be of a type that transmits strain directly through the buoy, using chain or rod. Buoys perform a useful function in removing much of the vertical load; the pennant is under a more nearly horizontal load, and the boat's bow is freer to lift to heavy seas.

Making annual inspections

Because ordinary moorings often need a period of time for silting in before achieving their full holding power, annual inspection of chain, links, shackles and pins should be made early in the season—and never disturbed just about the time storm warnings are issued. On the other hand, it is also prudent to give the pennant from buoy to boat a double-check in mid-season, just before the August-September months when hurricanes most often strike.

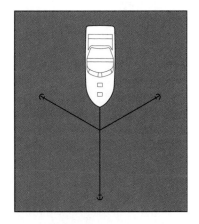

A permanent mooring system designed to be an improvement over the standard single mushroom anchor uses three lightweight anchors bridled 120° apart. A relatively short rode limits swing.

Split plastic tubing with ties at each end can be used, as shown on this auxiliary, to protect mooring lines from abrasion at the bobstay. It is lashed to the lines with thongs.

13 MARLINESPIKE SEAMANSHIP

From anchor rodes and dock lines to sheets, vangs and whippings, anyone helping with the work of a boat becomes involved with lines, knots and splices—and their proper use. The knowledge and the hand skills are as important to a powerboat skipper as to the owner of a sailboat. They comprise a subject recognized for its fascinating lore, for the beautiful artifacts that are a part of it, and for its sheer practicality. Working with cordage—the collective name for ropes, lines and "small stuff"—is an ancient skill that now takes in new technologies. This chapter helps you develop that skill.

HOW ROPE IS MADE

Rope is bought as rope. But once it is in use aboard a boat it is called line, or by the name of the rigging part it has become. Sailors will tell you that there aren't many ropes aboard a ship or boat. There is bolt rope, at the foot or luff of a sail, or a tiller rope, or a foot rope, or a few other rare ones. Everything else is a line.

Like a sailor's knife, rope goes back thousands of years. For centuries rope was made from natural fibers, especially flax, hemp and manila (from the wild banana plant). Most rope was "laid," usually three strands twisted together. Each strand is composed of three yarns, each of which is composed of multiple fibers as shown below. Sailors work with knots and splices that have been in use for centuries, based on the standard way rope was made by twisting fibers.

Since the mid-20th century, there have been more technological changes in rope than in the preceding thousand years. New synthetic fibers have altered the form of rope and even the way particular splices or knots are made and used. The new kinds of cordage are so superior that a boater has little reason to pay any attention to most of the old materials.

Probably more than half the rope now used in recreational boating in the U.S. is plaited, braided or double-braided (a core inside a cover), compared to the traditional three-strand laid rope. Small stuff, used for whippings and seizings, is also greatly changed. Shock cord and even monofilament line have special uses, all made possible by new materials.

Synthetic materials

The first important synthetic fiber to appear was polyamide (nylon). Nylon rope is very strong (more than twice as strong as the best yacht manila for the same size), has useful qualities of elasticity or controlled stretch, and has gone through successive technical improvements. The rope can be made according to need. It can be given various degrees of softness or hardness, and some variations in surface textures, to fit its intended uses. With its shock-absorbing elasticity it is well suited for dock lines and anchor lines.

High-intensity polyester fiber (Dacron, Terylene, Duron, Fortrel, A.C.E. and Kodel) is made into rope that is virtually

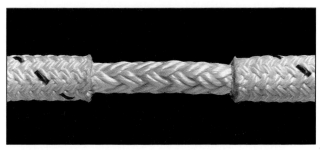

Braided line may be single-braid, or double-braid, as shown above. Single-braid in smaller sizes is used for flag halyards, sailbag ties and similar purposes.

as strong as nylon but has one important difference: The rope can be made to have very little stretch. This makes polyester fiber superior for special purposes like the running rigging on sailboats, where elasticity is undesirable. In manufacturing, polyester rope can be given varied finishes: woolly, smooth or textured to make it easy to grip, as required.

Aramid fiber (Kevlar), a newer material used for marine rope, combines strength and strong dimensional stability (near zero stretch). It is expensive and is used chiefly on competition sailboats.

Polypropylene rope is least expensive among the synthetics; it is about as strong as manila, but tends to deteriorate rapidly in sunlight. Its main advantage is that it floats, so it is suited to some commercial fishing applications as well as to water-ski tow ropes and dinghy painters. Using it as an economy measure may be unwise. It should be larger size than nylon and renewed frequently.

Three-strand rope

The construction of three-strand laid rope has changed little in thousands of years of nautical history except for varying surface textures. New materials and new machines have changed rope construction, giving us plaited and braided ropes. The various kinds of rope "geometry" are worth looking at in some detail, starting with the oldest. A basic knowledge of the anatomy of three-strand rope makes it easier to work, especially in splicing and in finishing off the ends, a subject discussed on pages 287-289.

Hold the rope so that the end is away from your body: The strands will be seen to have a twist that is clockwise—a "right-hand lay." Most rope is right-hand lay, and has been since the Pyramids were built. If you look at the twist in just one of the three strands, it is a left-hand twist. Finally, with all but the smallest ropes the fibers have an opposite twist within the strand. Because some tension is put on the rope in manufacturing, these opposite twists, of strand and rope, tend to keep the rope from unlaying, or untwisting.

The reason for noting the lay of the rope is this: When you splice you will be working with these twists, sometimes retwisting a short length of strand with your fingers, and splicing (interweaving) the strands back into the normal lay of

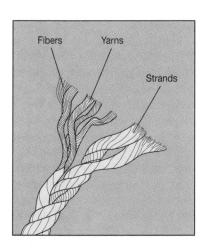

Three-strand rope is made up of three strands twisted clockwise in a right-hand lay. The individual strands have a left-hand lay, and the fibers will normally have a right-hand twist.

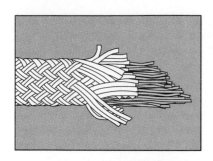

Shock cord is made up of rubber strands within a braided cover. It is generally used in short sections with loops and toggles at the ends.

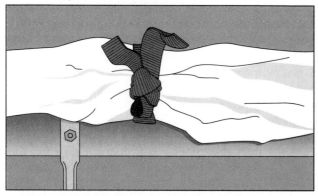

Nylon or polyester webbing is used for sail stops, for lashing a dinghy on deck, or as tie-downs to secure a boat on its trailer.

the rope. Since virtually all laid rope is right-handed, your fingers should learn to work with the twist, whether you are tying knots, splicing or coiling.

Laid rope comes in several degrees of hardness or stiffness. The technical terms are soft lay, medium lay and hard lay. For boating purposes you would use only medium lay. Sailmaker's lay is a variation, but unless you're making sails you won't need it. Very soft lay is sometimes on sale, and is superficially attractive—silky soft like milkweed seedpods. However, it is of little use on a boat because it kinks easily. Hard-laid rope, used commercially, may be too difficult to work with to be of any value on a boat.

You may read about, but seldom see, four-strand rope and left-hand lay rope; both are for special purposes. And there is one more twist: To make very large cables, such as those that tugboats or large ships use, three right-hand lay ropes can be twisted together, left-hand lay; this is called cable lay.

Most wire rope is made the same way: by twisting strands. However, the more intricate strandings, with 7 x 7 and 1 x 19 strands, are seen most often. In 7 x 7, seven strands, each in turn consisting of seven wires, are twisted together; in 1 x 19, 19 single strands make up the rope. This 1 x 19 wire rope is stronger but less flexible than the 7 x 7 type, and is used primarily for standing rigging.

Braided line

Small diameter single-braided or plaited line (¼-inch and smaller) is used for flag halyards, to tie the ends of sailbags, and for special purposes such as awnings. Most single-braid line can-

not be spliced unless it's a hollow braid. Plaited line, with eight parts, can be spliced.

Double-braided line is a widely used type. As its name suggests, this rope has a braided core inside a braided cover. For low-stretch applications the cover is polyester; the core is often a mixture of fibers with greater stretch. This construction has advantages for many purposes, but it requires special techniques for splicing. Double-braid is very flexible because both the cover and the core are composed of small strands. Its stretch depends on the materials used, and its resistance to abrasion is excellent because the wear is distributed over many strands. Braided line tends to coil evenly and unlike laid line is virtually kink-free.

On sail and power boats you will often see double-braid nylon used for dock lines because of its smooth running and easy-on-the-hands characteristics; occasionally it will be used for anchor lines. You'll see double-braid polyester used for sheets and halyards on racing sailboats.

Other types of rope

In addition to stranded and braided rope, several other forms of flexible materials have special uses aboard boats. These materials are not traditional cordage, but they do some of the same things rope or small lines will do.

■ **Shock cord**, which is multi-strand rubber with a synthetic cover, can stretch to at least twice its length. Its uses are endless: to hold topping lifts out of the way, to make lash-ups for furling sails, as gilguys to hold halyards away from the mast, and to hold a pair of oars on a cabin top or books in a rack.

Shock cord is not as strong as rope; its extreme elasticity makes it unsuitable for many purposes, and it cannot be spliced. Its ends are usually made up with plastic or metal clips to prevent fraying; eyes (actually looped ends in the shape of eye splices) are made the same way. A loop at one end of a short piece of shock cord and a toggle inset at the other end makes a good tie to keep a coil of line in place.

■ **Webbing**, woven of nylon or polyester, is used for sail stops (replacing the traditional sewn strips of doubled sailcloth) and for dinghy tie-downs as well as hold-downs for boats on trailers. Webbing is very strong, and when used for sail ties it holds well with a square knot or a slippery reef knot. Webbing is either single or hollow flat (double).

■ **Monofilament** is another kind of line found on boats. Its main use is for fishing lines and a heavier piece makes a good lanyard for a pocket stopwatch or small calculator. Monofilament fish line must be knotted only in certain specific ways or it will invariably come untied.

■ **"Small stuff"** is a term used by the typical old salt, sitting on a hatch cover making up whippings, servings and seizings. Waxed nylon line and flat braid (a plaited form also called parachute cord) is used for whippings to prevent chafe. Marline, a tan-colored two-strand string used for servings, is now scarce. Cod-line, a similar three-strand material, is useful if you can get it.

PURCHASING ROPE

In the course of boat ownership, you will need to make decisions about what size and type of rope to buy for new dock and anchor lines, or how to improve the rigging when replacing a sheet, vang or halyard. In addition to the factors already reviewed concerning elasticity and the form of rope, you need to consider other points, including size.

Strength and size

Experts advise that the working load for three-strand line should not exceed 11 percent of its tensile strength—the load, in pounds of "pull," at which the rope would break. Braided rope is normally specified for use at, or under, 20 percent of its tensile strength. As rope ages it inevitably suffers from abrasion and sunlight. Braided rope has the advantage that the core, providing a major part of the strength, is protected. All parts of laid rope will inevitably suffer from wear.

In practice, a common-sense approach is often the determinant. A small size of rope might be strong enough for a jib sheet, but a larger size will be easier to grasp with the hands.

The size of rope, in the United States, is customarily given as its diameter in inches, particularly in the recreational-boat sizes. But since most of the rest of the world measures rope by its circumference and in millimeters, you will see the "normal" sizes and metric comparison tables more and more frequently. In addition, manufacturers and sellers of rope know very well that a piece of braided rope, held loosely, is thicker than one that is stretched out. Because of this discrepancy, they market such rope only by its weight, which is a more accurate measure of the total amount of material. At some marine stores, however, you will find all types of rope sold by length, often in pre-packaged kits.

The retail availability of special kinds of rope can be a problem for boaters. An inland hardware store may stock several kinds and sizes of rope that are suitable mainly for farmers. Preferences and needs vary among commercial fishermen, powerboat owners and sailors.

Sometimes there are special solutions. If you can't find waxed flat braid for whippings at a marine dealer, talk to a

FIBER CORDAGE — TYPICAL WEIGHTS AND MINIMUM BREAKING STRENGTHS (POUNDS)*

Nominal Size (inches) Diameter	Nylon (High Tenacity—N.Y.)			Du Pont Dacron or H.T. Polyester			Polyolefins (H.T.) (Polypropylene and/or Polyethylene)			Double Nylon Braid			Polyester/Polyolefin Double Braid		
	Net Wt. 100'	Ft. per lb.	Breaking Strength	Net Wt. 100'	Ft. per lb.	Breaking Strength	Net Wt. 100'	Ft. per lb.	Breaking Strength	Net Wt. 100'	Ft. per lb.	Breaking Strength	Net Wt. 100'	Ft. per lb.	Breaking Strength
3/16	1.0	100.0	1 000	1.3	77.0	1 000	0.7	137.0	750	NA	NA	NA	0.8	133.0	900
1/4	1.5	66.6	1 700	2.1	47.5	1 700	1.2	80.0	1 250	1.7	60.3	2 100	1.7	60.2	1 700
5/16	2.5	40.0	2 650	3.3	30.0	2 550	1.9	53.0	1 850	2.8	36.0	3 500	2.6	38.4	2 600
3/8	3.6	28.0	3 650	4.7	21.3	3 500	2.9	34.5	2 600	3.3	30.0	4 200	3.5	28.5	3 500
7/16	5.0	20.0	5 100	6.3	15.9	4 800	3.9	25.5	3 400	5.0	20.0	6 000	5.1	20.0	5 100
1/2	6.6	15.0	6 650	8.2	12.2	6 100	4.9	20.4	4 150	6.7	14.9	7 500	6.8	15.0	6 800
9/16	8.4	11.9	8 500	10.2	9.8	7 700	6.2	16.0	4 900	8.3	12.0	9 500	NA	NA	NA
5/8	10.5	9.5	10 300	13.2	7.6	9 500	7.8	12.8	5 900	11.1	9.0	12 000	11.0	9.0	11 000
3/4	14.5	6.9	14 600	17.9	5.6	13 200	11.1	9.0	7 900	15.0	6.7	17 000	15.0	6.7	15 000
7/8	20.0	5.0	19 600	24.9	4.0	17 500	15.4	6.5	11 000	20.8	4.8	23 700	20.0	5.0	20 000
1	26.0	3.8	25 000	30.4	3.3	22 000	18.6	5.4	13 000	25.0	4.0	28 500	28.0	3.6	28 000

*These figures on synthetics are an average of those available from four large cordage manufacturers. Those for the rope you buy should be available from your dealer. Check them carefully.
Note: 1 inch = 2.54 cm. 1 foot = 0.3048 m. 1 pound = 0.4536 kg.

When buying rope, keep the following points in mind. A soft, sleazy rope may be stronger and easier to splice but it will not wear as well and is more apt to hockle or unlay than a firm, well "locked-up" rope. Blended ropes, part polyolefins and part other fibers, may be found. Multifilament (fine filament) polypropylene looks like nylon—don't expect it to be as strong. (It floats, nylon doesn't.) Spun, or stapled, nylon and Dacron are not as strong as ropes made from continuous filaments but are easier to grasp. These are sometimes used for sheets on sailing craft.

sailmaker. If all you need at the moment is a small size, waxed nylon dental floss is roughly similar. If you plan on making up a polypropylene dinghy painter that will float, and thus stay out of the way of propeller blades, try a source that supplies commercial fishing boats; and get the black rope—it's the most resistant to sunlight.

Selection

There are dozens of brands, configurations and combinations of materials, particularly in braided rope. Sometimes one characteristic, reduced stretch, for example, changes another, such as ease of splicing.

The surface textures of braided polyester ropes vary. Those made with continuous filaments are shiny, smooth and strong. Those made with spun yard (short filaments) are softer, fuzzier and not quite as strong. Select the shiny ones for halyards, and the fuzzier ones for sheets, where being easier on the hands and better gripping of the drums of winches are important qualities.

Some skippers who do a lot of night sailing use lines of different surface texture, with different feel for different purposes such as sheets and guys.

Color coding

The use of color coding for racing and cruising sailboats is common. The lines may be a solid color or have a colored "tracer." Some recommended uses are:

- Mainsail sheet and halyard—white
- Jib/genoa—blue
- Spinnaker—red and green for guys
- Vangs and travelers—black

Color coded line can also be useful on powerboats; for example, to identify dock lines of different lengths.

Blocks should be matched to the lines used. Otherwise, you run the risk of binding, jamming or chafing.

Choosing the size and strength

For most uses, the appropriate size of rope is one that is large enough to be comfortable in the hands under normal working situations. A flag halyard, which has very little strain on it, can be thin to reduce wind resistance.

Sail halyards must be strong enough to take the tremendous strain of the sail filled with wind, with minimum stretch, be resistant to abrasion at the sheaves, and still offer the least possible wind resistance.

The proper size of a line may be determined by still another factor: chafing. A dock line or anchor line, for instance, is used many times, sometimes chafes seriously and sometimes not at all, and yet should always be strong enough to hold under extreme storm conditions. A mooring pennant needs to be many times stronger than is required for the worst possible storm conditions, partly because the big fall storm may come at the end of the season, when the line has already been weakened by various small chafings. (Refer to Chapter 12 for more details on anchor and mooring lines.)

Matching rope size and blocks

If a line is a bit too large for a block, a fairlead or a chock, you run two risks: binding or jamming, and chafe. Sometimes the solution is not a smaller line but a larger block. Match the sheave with the proper size of wire or rope.

The diameter of the sheave in a block is important. The stress on a line making a 180-degree change of direction is obvious. To avoid premature wear and to reduce friction, use the largest possible block diameter. Recommended ratios for block diameter to the size of line are 8 to 1 for polyester and nylon lines, and 20 to 1 for competition lines like aramids. Sometimes naval architects use two small blocks at the top of the mast, each giving the halyard a 90-degree turn. Similarly, a fairlead that makes a change in direction in a line results in a certain amount of friction; if the line goes through the fairlead at an extreme angle, the friction is greater. In such a situation a block might well be better than the fairlead, to make line handling easier as well as to minimize abrasion.

Choosing quality rope

The problems of cheap rope may be hidden, but they are real. Some polypropylene rope, at the bottom of the cost scale, is made from large-diameter filaments. Rope with finer filaments costs more, but lasts twice as long and is much stronger. Hard-lay nylon, which may be old, is so difficult to work with that it may not be worth its low price.

As you work with the variety of lines aboard a boat, you will form the habit of constantly checking for chafe and other problems: a splice that is beginning to fray, a chock with a rough corner that will weaken a dock line by chafing, a block whose sheave tends to be stiff and needs cleaning and lubricating. Frequent inspection of gear and rigging, and replacement, lubrication or other suitable repair is an important part of good seamanship.

MARLINESPIKE TOOLS

For most everyday work with rope you need only your fingers and a good knife. But many marlinespike jobs need special tools, a few professional techniques, and some standard materials. Here is what you would find in an experienced sailor's "ditty bag" (a small bag for tools and personal items), and some of the extras that might be in the tool locker or on a home workbench—for most kinds of marlinespike work:

■ A good sharp knife, preferably the type called a rigging knife, with a built-in marlinespike and probably a hasp that is used for opening and closing shackles. A file from the engine tool locker will keep the blade sharp.

■ A large fid or marlinespike, for separating the strands of laid rope when splicing. You can usually splice small sizes of laid line, if it's fairly soft, using only your fingers. But a wooden fid or metal spike, used to separate the strands and to get

A typical ditty bag includes a number of marlinespike tools, from a sailmaker's palm to a hot knife. Keep all tools and materials well protected against moisture, which can render scissors and tools useless. A canvas ditty bag with plastic wraps for the metal tools will do, as will a tight-closing plastic box.

the strand you are working with through quickly and easily, makes any splicing easier, and is usually a necessity for larger sizes of rope. Special fids will be needed for splicing double-braided rope, with different sizes matched to the diameter of the rope. Several types of hollow fids and other special tools are on the market.

■ Sailmaker's needles (keep them in a small plastic bottle) for making whippings and repairing sail slide attachments and jib hank fastenings. Keep several sizes of needles on hand.

■ A sailmaker's palm to push the needles through the rope. Even if you don't expect to repair sails, a palm is a good hand-tool. Keep the leather soft: Apply neat's-foot oil twice a year.

■ Simple sharp-nosed pliers and a pair of scissors.

■ Waxed sail twine (tape and/or cord), and perhaps some old-fashioned brown marline for a traditional-looking project. As you will see on page 291, waxed nylon twine or lacing tape is used to make whippings on the ends of lines. Lacing tape, which is flat and plaited, is also used for sail fittings; even if you never sew a sail you'll need twine or tape for lashings. Many people also keep a piece of beeswax in their ditty bags for waxing twine.

■ Heat is the way to melt and seal ends of synthetic rope. A candle, matches or the flame of a galley stove will do it. To be safe, a reliable procedure is to heat up an old knife blade and apply it to the rope in order to melt it. On shore the hot-knife is still the best tool for the job.

■ An electric rope cutter. Not everyone needs the professional's tool, which plugs into an electrical outlet and uses a hot wire to melt the rope (quickly, smoothly, and sealing the ends). However, many amateur sailors who like to work with rope own one. Perhaps the handiest tool for the boat owner is an electric soldering gun, with a special cutting head obtainable from hardware stores. This knifelike head is also useful for melting and smoothing the fine strands of rope that are left after a splice is made. Electric rope cutters or hot knives require 120-volt AC power.

■ Plastic tape for temporary whippings. White tape with some stretch to it, black electrical tape, waterproof sail repair tape or first-aid tape will do. These are all adhesive tapes unlike the nylon lacing tapes referred to earlier.

■ Liquid, quick-drying plastic for dipping rope ends into as a substitute for a twine whipping or other end finish for a line. They are called Whip-It, Whip End Dip, or by similar names.

DEFINING MARLINESPIKE TERMS

Many marlinespike terms are best understood by handling line or by looking at illustrations. The *standing part* is the long end of a piece of line. If you loop the working part back on itself, you form a *bight*. If the bight is around an object or the rope itself, it is a *turn*. The extreme other end of the line is the *bitter end*. Bends, hitches, knots and even *splices* are all technically knots, but to the purist there are differences. A splice was only a form of interweaving of the strands—until braided rope came along with a new form.

A *whipping* is small twine or tape wrapped tightly around and through the end of a rope to keep it from unraveling. A *seizing* is a similar wrap-around, but for another purpose, such as *binding* two parts of a line together in a piece of rigging, or binding a sail hank to the sail. *Parcelling* is a more complex wrap-around, combining twine and tape, to take wear or prevent chafe. A new word is *locking*, which means sewing through the throat of a braided line eye splice to hold it in place.

When you handle lines aboard a boat, you soon learn some basic techniques; one of these is how to coil a line.

Coiling a line

Three-strand line, having its natural twist built in, should always be coiled clockwise so it won't kink, buckle and tangle. If you are working with a free dock line, either end can be used to start a coil. Otherwise, always start at the secured end—where the halyard or sheet is cleated, for example, and work toward the free end. Never start at the free end—you'll end up with a twisted, awkward coil that is anything but docile. If the line to be coiled is loose and untangled, it's easy. If it looks the least bit tangled, "overhaul" it by running it through your hands from one end to the other, preparing it to be coiled.

Now, start by holding the line in your left hand. With an easy sweeping motion, using your right hand, bring each coil to your left hand and take it in with your fingers. Remember the coils are always clockwise, and it takes practice. An even sweep of your arm, the same distance each time, will result in coils of the same size. Sometimes your thumb is used to add or control a twist. (Don't try to wind up the line over your elbow, unless you're a landlubber in the backyard doing clothesline.)

When working with braided line, which has no lay or twist to it, don't coil it! Simply hand a length from your right hand to your left hand and you will see a figure-eight develop. From this eight, the line will always pay out without kinking or fouling. But since coiling line is a frequent task aboard boats—sometimes with one kind of line and sometimes with another—get into the habit of making clockwise coils no matter what type of line you are handling.

Stowing a coiled line

What you do next with the coil or figure-eight depends on the circumstances. If the line is the end of a jib sheet that will be used again in a few minutes, or the unused part of a dock line that you need to keep in readiness, turn the coil so the free end is down and lay it on the deck, in the corner of the cockpit or in another convenient location.

If the coil is to be hung up, which is usually the case, there are several ways to do it. A completely free coil of line, such as a fairly heavy spare anchor line that is to be stowed for a while, can be tied up using shock cord or rope straps made up for the purpose, or small pieces of spare line. A newer, convenient method is to use cinch straps of Velcro self-adhering tape. If it is a very heavy and long line you would do best to lay it onto the deck in figure-eights—you couldn't hold the coil in your hand anyway. On a ship this is called faking down.

A free coil, such as an unused dock line that you may use again soon, is often handled as follows: Take a short arm's length of the end of the line and wrap the coil with three, four or five turns and then, using the last length of line, pass a loop through the entire end of the coil. Hang the coil up, on a cleat or hook, using this loop. By following this method, whenever you want to use the line, the loop will come out quickly and the whole coil will be readily available.

A halyard is handled similarly, with two exceptions:
- Don't wrap the coil. Leave it free, for quickest availability when the sail is to be dropped.
- Use the standing part of the line, not the free end, to make the pass-through loop, and to keep it from slipping loose give it a turn or two as you hang it on the cleat.

The flemish coil, the end of a line coiled nearly flat on deck or a dock, deals decoratively with the free end of a dock line or anchor line. It's easy to do and looks yachtlike, but if you leave it too long the coil will pick up dirt and moisture and leave a soiled mark on deck when it's taken up.

Of course an eye splice is most useful in one end of a dock line. A good practice is to make the eye at least three times larger in diameter than the size of any piling or bollard on which it is likely to be used.

When wrapping a coil, make a loop with the free end, pass it over the top and pull on the free end.

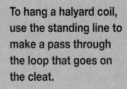

To hang a halyard coil, use the standing line to make a pass through the loop that goes on the cleat.

The term "faking a coil," or "flaking," means, simply, to lay the rope in the form of a figure eight.

KNOTS, BENDS AND HITCHES

The first principle in dealing with three-strand rope is that it has a twist, and you must work with it, not against it. This applies to splicing and knotting as well as to coiling.

You will also feel how a little friction of one part of the rope against another holds it fast. That's the second principle for any kind of rope: In knots, splices, bends or hitches, the pressure of the rope against itself, as it tightens, is what does the holding.

The third principle is a rule, a definition: A good knot is one that can be made almost automatically (your fingers learn to do it, just as they learn to write your name), that holds securely in the usage it is meant for, and that can be unfastened or untied readily. With practice you will be able to tie knots in the dark or in more than one position.

Some knots are adjustable; others are not. At times, the choice of which knot to use depends on the size or character of the line involved—there are variations in the way line works, as will be mentioned in this chapter.

Most of the following information about specific knots concerns their efficient use. The illustrations on pages 284 to 286 are for identification; the paragraphs below give additional information about tying or using each one.

Cleat hitches

One of the simplest knots, certainly the most used aboard a boat, involves nothing more than turns around a cleat. You may not have even thought of this as a knot—but it is. When fastening a line to a cleat, as with many things at sea, a small error at the start can cause problems later. Look closely at "cleating the line," illustrated on page 286; notice how the line bearing the load comes in at an angle to the base of the cleat. It then goes around the base of the cleat, passing under each horn once. This keeps the strain low on the cleat. The cleat should be mounted at an angle to the usual direction of strain.

Even half a turn, plus a firm hold on the line, usually creates enough friction to hold a boat at a dock until the whole turn can be completed. In fact, you should always take a half turn around a cleat when a load is coming on the line; this is an essential part of good line handling called snubbing. Never try to hold a load-bearing line in your bare hands—it can slip suddenly and burn your fingers and palms. Note that snubbing is nearly a whole turn, and also that the cross-over that will make the figure-eight should be made after the line goes around both horns of the cleat.

One and a half or two figure-eights are enough; more would add no security and would just take time to undo later.

There are two ways to complete the hitches on a cleat: You can leave the last turn free, perhaps keeping it under your eye if it is a jib sheet, for example. In this way the line can be instantly thrown off if necessary.

Secondly, for more security you can turn the last hitch over, so it is tightened to bind against itself. This might be best for a dock line or halyard, but is not safe for instant release

may be necessary. In a small sailboat, in puffy winds, you probably wouldn't cleat the main sheet all the way—you would take one turn and hold it tight in your hand. Similar figure-eight turns are sometimes used on mooring bitts.

Using the right knot

The knots described (most are shown in detail on pages 284 to 286) can be divided into two groups: basic knots used generally on boats, and a few specialized knots that come in handy at certain times.

You have seen that some knots are echoes of others, and that more than one knot is sometimes used for the same purpose. Here are some reasons: A knot may work well with rough-textured rope but may tend to slip when tied with new slippery synthetic line. One knot may work well with small line, while another works out better with heavier and stiffer line. The sheet bend can be tied in a hurry; it takes more time to make two bowlines when tying two long lines together, as for a tow. One bowline, with half the sheet bend tied into it (the becket hitch) has an advantage: It can be unfastened quickly.

Some of the potential problems are most easily solved by employing alternate methods. An anchor bend, for example, is customarily given some extra security with a short seizing or a constrictor knot made with sail twine. On other occasions, where the knot won't be in use as long as an anchor line might be, the free end can be passed through a strand of laid line; an extra half-hitch or two should be used with a clove hitch for extra security. The rolling hitch is the ideal knot for tying to another line under tension. It has the advantage of being adjustable, and it will hold better if doubled.

KNOTS AND STRENGTH OF LINE	
Type of knot, bend or hitch	Percentage of retained strength
Anchor bend	
Over 5/8" dia. ring	55-65%
Over 4" dia. post	80-90%
Two half-hitches	
Over 5/8" dia. ring	60-70% *
Over 4" dia. post	65-75% *
Square knot	43-47% **
Sheet bend	48-58% *
Carrick bend	55-60%
Bowline	67-75%

This table gives an indication as to how knots and splices reduce rope strength.

* Smaller sizes of nylon are liable to slip without breaking.
** Both nylon and combination ropes in smaller sizes are liable to slip.

MOST-USED KNOTS ABOARD RECREATIONAL BOATS

The recreational craft skipper does not need to have a large repertoire of knots, but the ones shown here are basic. Boaters should be familiar with them in detail, even to being able to tie them in the dark.

OVERHAND KNOT
Shown here chiefly because it's simple, and helps explain the figure-eight knot shown at left. Use it sparingly; it's almost impossible to untie after it is tightened. (It is useful to hold the end of a winch line on a trailer hitch.)

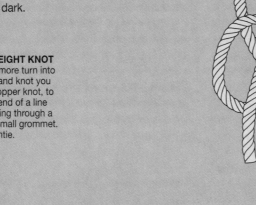

FIGURE-EIGHT KNOT
With one more turn into the overhand knot you have a stopper knot, to keep the end of a line from running through a block or small grommet. Easy to untie.

GRANNY
This is a knot that too many people tie automatically when they are trying to tie a square knot. They should teach their fingers to go the other way, because the granny is a useless knot. Sometimes it slips, sometimes it jams. It has no value at all on a boat.

BOWLINE
This is the most useful of all knots aboard a boat. Once learned (and practice is necessary) it is easy to make, never slips or jams, and can always be untied. Two bowlines, one on each line, are an excellent combination when you need to tie two lines together.

REEF KNOT OR SQUARE KNOT
If you are tying a bundle, this knot works; note that the two bitter ends are on the same side of the standing parts. If the line is under constant pressure, and if both ends are the same size, it can still be untied. If it is made with a strip of canvas or webbing, as in using gaskets to furl a sail, it is a useful knot and easily untied even when wet. If it is used to tie two lines together, to make a longer line, it is a mistake. Use the reef knot sparingly.

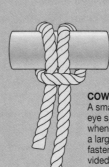

TWO HALF-HITCHES
For fastening a line to something else, such as a grommet in the corner of an awning. Quick and easy, but for many special purposes there are better knots you will prefer. A single half-hitch also has some special uses.

CLOVE HITCH
Commonly used to tie a line to a piling. This is often a mistake. Although very adjustable, it tends to slip, especially with slippery nylon line. It is best to take an extra half-hitch (or two half-hitches) to make it secure. If you use the same line from the bow to a piling, and then to the stern, the clove hitch is ideal. Both ends are taut and you have the adjustable feature.

COW HITCH OR LARK'S HEAD
A small existing loop (usually an eye splice) turned inside itself when you want to fasten a line to a large piling. It is also useful to fasten such a loop to a ring, provided the other end of the line is free. Many people use this hitch to fasten a jib sheet to the clew of a jib on a small sailboat.

SHEET BEND

This is an excellent way to tie two lines together, especially if they are of different sizes or textures. As you will realize when you practice tying knots, some are just variations on a theme. You can use part of a sheet bend to fasten onto a loop.

BECKET HITCH

This is really a sheet bend, in which one line has a loop, such as an eye splice or bowline. If an extra round turn is taken (near left), this is called a double becket hitch. This version is especially useful when the added-on line is smaller than the one with the loop.

SLIPPERY REEF KNOT

Half a square bow-knot. Good for furling a sail. This is always easier to untie than a square knot.

CARRICK BEND

This is one of the traditional ways to fasten two lines of the same size together. It looks beautiful in a drawing, but under strain it changes appearance. The carrick bend is probably best for fairly heavy, stiff lines of the same size.

BUNTLINE HITCH

This is excellent for fastening a halyard to a shackle. It is its own stopper knot and won't jam in a block as an eye splice might. Sometimes called the "inside clove hitch," or the "studding sail tack bend," this is easy to tie and untie. Another use is on a trailer winch snap shackle—a modern use for a hitch from square-rigger days.

ANCHOR BEND

Also called fisherman's bend. This is a standard way to fasten an anchor line to the ring of an anchor. It is excellent for making up a spare anchor, and it can be used in many other situations. The double loop reduces possible chafe and makes the half-hitches more secure. Of course there are other ways to make an anchor line fast, including a bowline or an eye splice over a thimble, plus a shackle. Seizing the free end of the standing end gives extra security.

ROLLING HITCH

To tie a small line to the standing part of a larger one, so it won't slip, use the rolling hitch. You can use this hitch to hold a jib sheet while riding turns are removed from a winch, to haul on any line, or to make an adjustable loop for an awning tie-down. The rolling hitch is also used to attach a line to a round wooden or metal object with the least possibility of slipping sideways. It will hold best when a second rolling hitch is made with the free end. It is also very useful for making a fender line fast to a lifeline or rail.

SURGEON'S KNOT
Tying the ordinary square or reef knot, even around a parcel, often requires a helper—someone to hold a finger on the half-formed knot until it is completed. If you take the extra turn of a surgeon's knot, the friction/tension holds it while you complete the knot. Surgeons, of course, call it a suture knot.

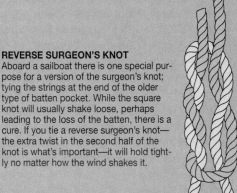

REVERSE SURGEON'S KNOT
Aboard a sailboat there is one special purpose for a version of the surgeon's knot; tying the strings at the end of the older type of batten pocket. While the square knot will usually shake loose, perhaps leading to the loss of the batten, there is a cure. If you tie a reverse surgeon's knot—the extra twist in the second half of the knot is what's important—it will hold tightly no matter how the wind shakes it.

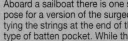

ASHLEY'S STOPPER KNOT
This makes a hefty stopper for the end of a line, looks seaman-like, and is easily undone. It takes a little longer to tie than the figure-eight, and should be drawn up with some care.

MARLINESPIKE HITCH
This is used to take up on a whipping or serving while it's being made—a good way to get it very tight. Withdraw the spike, and the hitch vanishes.

MONKEY FIST
Used to make a ball at the end of a heaving line. Make three loops around your hand, some 4 feet from the end of the line. Take the working end to make three more loops around, at right angles to the first three. The final set of loops is made around the inner group. Insert a pebble, if needed, and work turns to take up the slack.

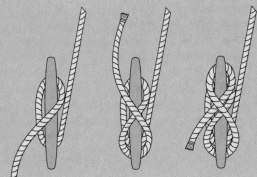

CLEATING A LINE
Start with a turn around the cleat, then go around the cleat so that the line passes under each horn once. Finish with a half-hitch over one horn. More wrappings and hitches are not needed, and they only slow the process of casting-off.

SPLICES AND SPLICING

Most stock sailboats come with all basic rigging supplied; it is usually not until something new is added or something old is replaced that a splice is even thought about. Power and sailing craft may have a made-up anchor line (usually not as long as it should be), but probably will not have enough dock lines. Marine dealers often sell dock lines of various lengths already made up, or you may want to make your own. A sailmaker will often be a good source for new jib sheets, other lines or small stuff. But in spite of the fact that many boat owners do not need to do much splicing, it is a good idea to know the basics. You can be a wise customer, and you can quickly make the occasional emergency repair if you know the rudiments of splicing.

Splicing, like knotting, is a finger art. In small to moderate sizes of three-strand line you can make splices without tools, although a knife and fid are extremely helpful. If you are splicing heavier line or braided line, simple tools are necessary—a fid or marlinespike for three-strand line, and a special fid for braided line.

As you can easily see in the illustrations, or by looking at a splice in three-strand line that is already made, the principle is simple: Three strands are tucked over and under so that they interweave with three other strands. If you are splicing the ends of two lines together in a short splice, the result

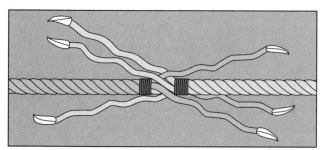

1 To start a short splice, unlay the strands of both rope ends for a short distance, about ten turns of the lay. Tape or fuse the six strands, or whip them, to prevent unlaying. A seizing is often made around each of the ropes, or each is wrapped with a piece of tape, to prevent strands from unlaying too far. These seizings or tape will be cut as the splice is completed.

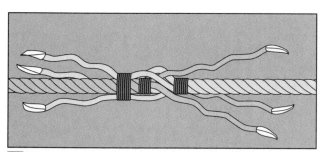

2 Next, "marry" the ends so that the strands of each rope lie alternately between strands of the other as shown. Now tie all three strands of one rope temporarily to the other—this is desirable, but not essential.

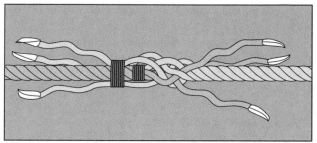

3 Working with the three free strands, remove temporary seizing from around the other rope and splice the strands into it by tucking the loose strands over and under successive strands from right to left against the lay of the rope. When first tucks have been made, snug down all three strands. Then tuck two or three more times on that side.

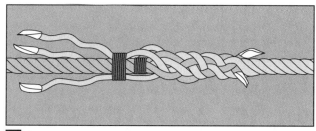

4 Next cut the temporary seizing of the other strands and the rope and repeat, splicing these three remaining strands into the opposite rope.

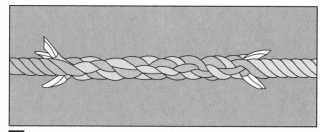

5 This shows how the short splice would appear if not tapered, after trimming off the ends of strands. Never cut the ends too close; otherwise when a heavy strain is put on the rope, the last tuck tends to work out.

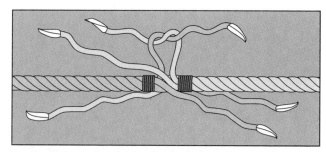

An alternative to the short splice technique shown in Steps 1 through 5, which some find easier, is to start as in Step 1, and tie pairs of strands from opposite ends in an overhand knot. This, in effect, makes the first tuck.

is obviously thicker. A short splice, therefore, won't go through a block of the correct size for the diameter of the line. A long splice is the solution—part of each strand is taken out and the tapered result makes a thin splice (with less strength). Most boat owners, however, will replace a broken line rather than splice it.

Making an eye splice

Although the short splice is the easiest to learn, an eye splice is much more often needed. The same principle—interweaving—applies, but there is one point where an error is easily made. Refer to the illustration below when following the instructions given here.

Start the eye splice by unlaying the strands of the free end six to ten turns of lay. Now tape or heat-seal the end of each strand to prevent it unlaying while being handled; whipping can be applied to the strand ends, but this action is rarely done as this is only a temporary intermediate action if the ends are to be tapered. It is sometimes helpful to place tape around the unlaid strands every four to six inches to help the "turn" in the strand.

Next form a loop in the rope by laying the end back along the standing part. Hold the standing part away from you in the left hand, loop toward you. The unlaid end can be worked with the right hand.

The size of loop is determined by the point x where the opened strands are first tucked under the standing part of the rope. If the splice is being made around a thimble, the rope is laid snugly in the thimble groove and point x will be at the tapered end of the thimble. The rope may be temporarily taped or tied to the thimble until the job is finished. Now lay the three opened strands across the standing part as shown in illustration A, so that the center strand "b" lies over and direct-ly along the standing part. Left-hand strand "a" leads off to the left, right-hand strand "c" to the right of the standing part.

Tucking of strand ends "a," "b" and "c" under the three strands of the standing part is the next step. Get this right and the rest is easy.

Always start with the center strand "b." Select the top-most strand (2) of the standing part near point x and tuck "b" under it. Haul it up snug but not so tight as to distort the natural lay of all strands. Note that the tuck is made from right to left, against the lay of the standing part.

Now take left-hand strand "a" and tuck under strand (1) which lies to the left of strand (2). Similarly, take strand "c" and tuck under strand (3), which lies to the right of strand (2). Be sure to tuck from right to left in every case.

The greatest risk of starting wrong is in the process of making the first tuck of strand "c." It should go under (3) from right to left and look like the drawing. The way you do it is to flop the whole thing over in your hands before making the tuck of strand "c." You'll notice that only one free strand "c" is untucked, and that only one of the original strands (3) in the standing part doesn't have a strand under it. Be certain that you make the third tuck in the right direction.

If the first tuck of each of strands "a," "b" and "c" has been correctly made, the splice at this point will look as shown in illustration B.

The splice is completed by making at least four full tucks in synthetic line with each of strands "a," "b" and "c." As each added tuck is made be sure it passes over one strand of the standing part, then under the strand next above it, and so on, the tucked strand running against the lay of the strands of the standing part. This is clearly shown in illustration D, the completed splice. Note c, c¹ and c², the same strand as it appears after successive tucks.

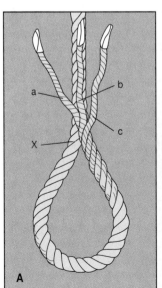 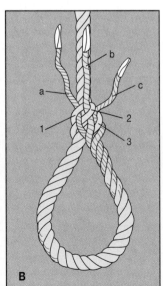 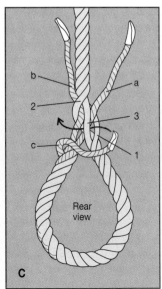 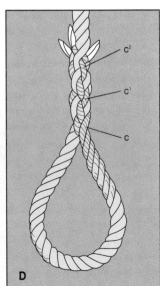

An eye splice forms a permanent loop in a line; it may be made around a thimble to guard against chafe (such as occurs on an anchor line), or around an eyelet as part of running rigging.

Tips for better eye splices

■ The splice can be made neater by tapering. This is done by cutting out part of the yarns from the tucking strands before the finishing tucks. In any case, the first three or four tucks are made with the full strands. After that, some prefer to cut out a third of the yarns, and make the last tuck. This produces an even taper. After the splice is finished, roll it on deck under foot to smooth it up. Then put a strain on it and finally cut off the projecting ends of the strands. Do not cut off the "tails" of synthetic rope too short.

The loose fibers may be fused with a hot knife (the blade heated over a flame) or a rope-cutting tool such as a soldering gun, but be careful *not* to melt the rope. Using an open flame around synthetic line is not recommended; in addition to preventing a fire hazard, this could melt the outer fibers, ruining that part of the rope.

■ The eye splice is often made on a metal or plastic thimble. When used this way it is necessary to work the splice very tightly and it is almost always desirable to add a whipping, using a needle and waxed nylon twine or tape. Refer to instructions for whipping on page 291.

■ Another way to make a synthetic rope splice tight is to place it in warm water so that the rope shrinks a bit.

■ In all splicing, careful re-laying of the rope—so that every strand is under the same even tension—is important.

■ Remember to insert the captive fitting in your splice before finalizing it. This is often forgotten during splicing steps, even by the experts.

Back splice

One other splice is seen occasionally on boats: the back splice at the end of a line. This makes a good, neat finish to a line, but it has a major disadvantage: If you want to unreeve the line at the end of the season, or to replace it, the back splice won't go through the blocks. Refer to the illustration above, right. A well-made whipping, shown on page 291, makes an equally neat finish. You can tie a figure-eight or Ashley stopper knot to keep the end from going through the block when you don't want it to.

Double-braided

An eye splice in double-braid looks difficult—but is relatively simple to learn. The technique has almost nothing to do with other kinds of splicing—it is just a logical way to use the cover and core of the braided line, since both are hollow. A thimble can be inserted during the splicing process.

Wire rope

Splices in wire rope, best left to professionals, and wire-to-rope, surely left to professionals, use techniques somewhat similar to three-strand splices, but differing in details. There is an equivalent to the long splice in the three-strand line but it isn't worth doing unless you are stuck and, perhaps most importantly, very adept at splicing wire rope.

The back splice is started by bringing each strand over the one to its left, and under the next one, as in A. The strands are then tucked as shown in B, for at least three strands, C. Longer strands can be used, and trimmed in thirds to provide a tapered finish.

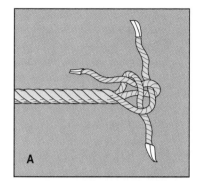

A

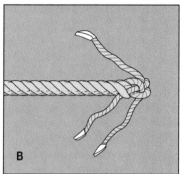

B

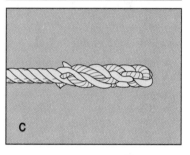

C

The way lines are handled, stored or dressed are an indication of the way the boat is generally cared for.

USE AND CARE OF ROPE

The proper way to coil a line, to flake it down in figure-eights, and to fasten to a cleat have already been discussed. Here are some additional pointers on using and caring for rope.

■ **Keep rope clean**. Dirt, sand, oil and acids are destructive to both natural and synthetic rope. Wash rope in a mesh bag or pillow case—that way it won't foul up your washing machine. Mild washing powder won't hurt either kind of rope. Dunking the end of a line when casting off from a pier will help to wash off any sand and dirt.

■ **Don't let it kink**. Kinking is annoying and can lead to breakage. Rope, even braided rope, should be taken off its original spool in a direct unwinding pull—not looped off over the top of the spool. Sometimes coiling new three-strand rope first against the lay, and then with the lay (clockwise), helps it to coil and run smoothly. As mentioned earlier, larger, stiffer ropes may need different handling from small, flexible lines. Double-braid can develop a twist when taken off and on winches. This can lead to kinking. Overhaul the line and take out the twist, as needed.

■ **Make small repairs promptly**. If an eye splice is coming undone or a whipping breaks, fix it with care before relying on the line again. An incomplete eye splice can be dangerous, and an unwhipped line end will keep right on coming apart unless it is fixed.

■ **Guard against chafe and abrasion**. You should "change the nip" on an anchor line every few hours, instead of letting the wear come on the same place over an extended period. You can use a leather or plastic chafe guard, which is best, or, if your line is small enough, one made from split garden hose. You can whip or serve a place in a dock line that goes over a gunwale or through a chock. Using small braided tape or cord is good for such a whipping because if it wears through it breaks and you can readily see it. Special chafing tape is also available. Some boat owners pre-whip dock lines and anchor lines at a number of convenient places and then adjust the lines so the whippings will be in the chocks. Pay particular attention to the metal gunwale molding. The fastening screws, when visible, may be protruding slightly or may have sharp edges. Often, scratches on these moldings will tend to leave sharp edges that will abrade any line or skin that is rubbed against it.

■ **Avoid friction damage**. Slipping, on a power winch, can result in friction heat that will damage a line.

■ **Use the right size line in a proper manner**. A line that jams in a block can tear itself apart. Heavy strains that do not break a rope can nevertheless weaken it. Both continual stretching and sudden shocks are damaging.

■ **Inspect your lines and rigging**. Even with the improvements in synthetic three-strand line, it is worthwhile to open the lay and inspect the interior strands, to see if the fibers have started to break or powder. Checking eye splices, whipped ends and places where lines go through sheaves, blocks or fairleads is the best way to detect signs of fraying, chafe and other deterioration.

Inspecting rope

All lines should be thoroughly checked at regular intervals. Frayed strand, powdered fibers inside the rope and stiffness are the signs of serious deterioration. In addition, one should go over the entire length of line, looking for cuts and nicks, exterior signs of abrasion and burns.

A slight abrasion fuzz on synthetic line, three-strand or braided, acts as a protective cushion. Pulled or cut strands in braided line are most serious; they can affect 20 percent of the line strength for each strand involved.

Eye splices should be inspected, inside and out, for distortion of the thimbles as well as a tendency for the splice to come undone.

Whippings and servings, of course, should be inspected regularly for excessive wear, so they can be renewed. Several times a season halyards should get a special inspection where they run through the block at the masthead when in use, because here the small motion always in the same place around the block, plus sharp bends in the line, lead to breakdowns. Anyone who has seen this suddenly cause a sail to drop and the internal halyard to drop inside the mast during a strong wind knows the wisdom of checking halyards. Many sailors will switch a halyard, end for end, at least once to extend its useful life.

Any three-strand lines that have had severe kinks or hockles can be assumed to have lost 30 percent of their strength. Never use force to straighten a kink. Instead, turn the line in your hands or trail it astern.

An old-fashioned cure for wear on a line is still useful with synthetic rope: reversing the line end for end. In other cases a small repair, a whipping to take the chafing, or a slight shortening of the line to make a new eye splice, may be the cure.

The ideal angle of pull on a cleat is a slight angle. It may not always be possible to do so when docking. It is advisable to verify that cleats used are well secured and that chafe can be avoided.

WHIPPING

Cutting a line means that it starts to fray and unravel at the end. In order to protect the ends of your lines, you can use a hot knife to seal them. Ends can also be taped, wrapped with an adhesive tape or dipped in an air-drying liquid plastic. A sleeve of color-coded shrink tubing can even be heat formed around the end as a protective measure.

Whipping is the proper and traditional way to protect ends. This is done by tightly winding small stuff or lacing twine around the line. The width of the whipping should approximate the diameter of the rope. Two whippings, a short distance apart, would be best; one near the rope end, and the second one a few rope diameters farther up.

The plain whipping, shown at right, is more easily accomplished, but may undo itself over time. It can be easily done and does not require a needle. The sailmaker's whipping, illustrated below, is ultimately far better, but it requires a palm and a sailmaker's needle, in addition to the cord or lacing twine. This whipping will last longer, as well as look better, than the plain whipping.

Another way to make a good-looking end for a line—provided it doesn't have to go through a block—is the back splice. This splice, shown on page 289, can be created by using either three-strand or braided line.

Two fancier rope ends, from the many that are available, are illustrated below, without instructions. The boater can learn to make them—or many of the other ornamental and useful knots and rope work—in any of several advanced books on marlinespike seamanship.

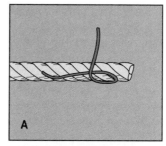

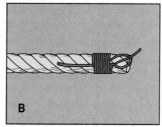

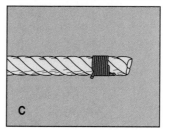

To make a plain whipping, begin at least an inch from the bitter end. Lay a loop of cord across the rope, leaving a tail of 5 or 6 inches on the bitter end (A). Then with the working piece of cord, wrap around the rope from the tail end toward the apex of the loop (B).

To finish off the whipping, insert the working end of the cord through the loop. Pull on the bitter end until the loop slides completely out of sight, and then clip the ends closely (C).

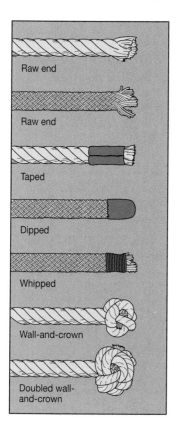

Ends of a three-strand or braided line can be taped, dipped in a sealer or whipped to prevent unlaying. Also shown is the wall-and-crown, a good-looking finish that combines two simple knots, and the manrope knot—a doubled wall-and-crown.

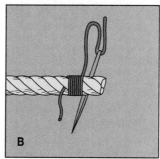

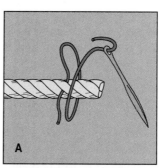

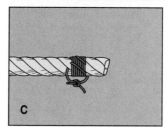

Sailmaker's whipping is started by stitching the cord through the line (A). Wind six or more turns around the line (B), and stitch back through it. Then bring the cord back over the turns along a groove between strands. Stitch through a strand to the next groove, and bring the cord back along this. Stitch through the next strand to the final groove (C), and finish with a square knot in the cord.

BLOCKS AND TACKLE

The use of a block and tackle (pronounced "tay-kle") or, to use a higher sounding name, mechanical appliances, on board a small boat is generally limited to sailboats. Any competent boater should have a basic knowledge of it, however, because its use enables one person to do the work of several.

Block and tackle is used when hoisting sails on a more traditional boat (a winch is used on a modern one), as well as setting sails and on boomvangs. With a block and tackle, one person provides the strength of two or three. No matter how small the sailboat, the sheets usually run through one or more blocks, using a mechanical advantage.

To see how this aids, go sailing in a 20-foot boat, in a moderate breeze, and bend a line to the boom. While underway, attempt to trim in the sail with your improvised sheet. It will come in, but it will be a struggle, so try it with the regular system of blocks and tackle and you will see with what ease the sail comes in. About the most common use of block and tackle on a motorboat is in hoisting the dinghy.

Terminology

A block consists of a frame of wood, metal or plastic, inside of which is fitted one or more sheaves (pulleys—the word is pronounced "shiv"), and is designated according to the number of sheaves it contains, such as single, double or triple. Block size is, of course, determined by the size of the rope that will run through it. Today, blocks are designed for a narrow range of line sizes. The diameter of the sheave should be a minimum of four times the diameter of the line going through it. Choosing the maximum diameter possible will reduce friction, thus reducing wear of lines and equipment.

Wire rope is also used, but usually only as halyard leads on sailboats and centerboard cables. This should be stainless steel, and sheaves should be as large as possible for long rope life. Make sure the rope cannot squeeze between the sheave and the cheeks of the block or your line may jam.

The term "tackle" is used to describe an assemblage of falls (ropes) and blocks. When you pass ropes through the

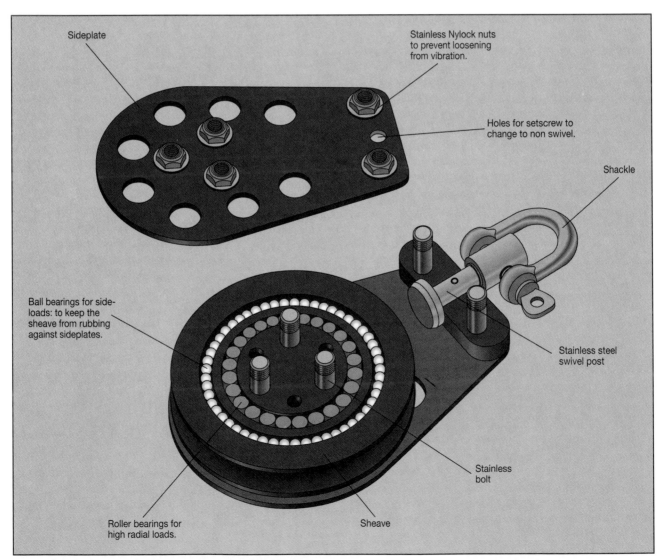

Shown above is an exploded view of a modern medium to high load capacity block used for cruising and racing purposes.

The mainsheet aboard a sailboat is an obvious tackle. It is expressed in ratios, from 2 to 1 on a small sailboat up to 20 to 1 on large racing machines.

blocks, you reeve them. The part of the fall made fast to one of the blocks, or the load, as the case may be, is known as the standing part, while the end upon which the force is to be applied is called the hauling part. To overhaul the falls means to separate the blocks; to round in means to bring them together; and the terms chock-a-block or two-blocked mean that the blocks are positioned tightly together.

Types of tackle

Tackles are named according to the number of sheaves in the blocks that are used (single, two-fold, three-fold purchase), according to the purpose for which the tackle is used, or from names handed down from the past (luff tackles, watch tackles, gun tackles, Spanish burtons, etc.). The tackles that may be found aboard cruising boats are now classified by ratio, as explained below:

■ **Ratio 1 to 1.** Traditionally called single whip, this is a single fixed block and fall. With a 1 to 1 ratio, there is no increase in power. The gain is therefore only in height of lift or in change in direction of pull.

■ **Ratio 2 to 1 or 3 to 1.** Traditionally called gun tackle, this ratio requires two single blocks. If the lower block is movable, double force is gained from the combination. If the upper block is movable, triple force is gained.

■ **Ratio 3 to 1 or 4 to 1.** Traditionally called luff tackle, these ratios require a double hook-block and single hook-block. The force gained is three times if single block is movable, and four if double block is movable.

■ **Ratio 4 to 1 or 5 to 1.** Traditionally called two-fold or double tackle, ratios of 4 to 1 or 5 to 1 require two double sheave hook-blocks. The force gained from this combination is four or five, depending upon block movement.

The force gained in all tackle combinations is theoretical only, as the friction of the blocks is ignored. The usual method of compensating for this friction, and calculating the actual force required, is to add 2 percent to the weight of the object for each sheave in the tackle before dividing by the number of falls. The actual friction will vary with the type of bearings and pins, state of lubrication and sheave diameter.

Aboard a racing sailboat today, a mainsheet tackle arrangement may be set up to have two levels of purchase: one primary, coarse adjustment with a ratio of 5 to 1 for jibing or rounding a mark when pressures are light and speed of sheeting is important; and one secondary, fine adjustment with a ratio of 20 to 1 when sailing to windward, especially in gusty conditions.

BLOCK MAINTENANCE

Block maintenance relates closely to its construction. Older blocks needed grease to ease friction. Today's use of synthetics and precision machining provides a product that is almost maintenance-free. Maintenance is now reduced to the following: Inspect periodically for fatigue, in particular for cracked or elongated shackles. Rinse often with fresh water to keep clean, and if lubrication is needed, a dry lubricant will usually suffice. Avoid leaving heavy tools on blocks when not in use. This may slightly deform the bearings.

Sheaves are now designed to accommodate the following: wire only, wire-rope combination (halyards), Kevlar and Spectra line with a special configuration that allows the line to flatten to avoid stress concentration and ratchet sheaves with their many-sided design that grips sheets tenaciously but allows line to be eased smoothly.

Large boats' sheaves and blocks generally come in three types of bearing systems:

■ Ball bearing for the freest running system; they have the lowest load carrying ability.

■ Roller bearing can carry more load but they have more friction at low loads. Combinations of ball and roller bearing give a free rolling system for loads that are moderate to high.

■ Bushings, impregnated with Teflon, combined with side load talls are used for loads too high even for roller bearings. These produce more friction than balls or rollers at low loads. Good examples are: masthead sheaves, runner block sheaves, wire sheaves and steering cable sheaves. Most blocks had previously a friction load of approximately 5 percent per sheave. Today's technology has brought it down to 2 percent per sheave.

WAVES, WIND AND WEATHER

14 UNDERSTANDING WEATHER

Weather is an important element of your boating experience; it can add to or detract from your environment, and it can have a vital bearing on your safety. As the skipper of a boat you need two different kinds of weather information: what to expect in the next hour or so, and what weather two or three days hence will bring. In order to make those kinds of predictions, you need not be qualified as a weather forecaster. However, you must be able to understand and properly use forecasts prepared by experts, and you must be able to correctly interpret local weather signs—wind shifts, changes in cloud patterns or ocean swells. This chapter tells you the basics.

WHERE WEATHER BEGINS

Weather doesn't just happen; there are basic causes and effects. An appreciation of the major influences—discussed briefly below—will lead to a better understanding of weather systems and their movements, as covered in this chapter. This is the basis for weather forecasting.

The earth's atmosphere

A mixture of gases—mostly nitrogen and oxygen—envelops the earth. Known as the atmosphere, it extends upward with decreasing density for many miles. From a weather standpoint, only the lowest 20 miles of atmosphere concern us. In fact, half of the atmosphere is in the lower 3½ miles.

Of the atmosphere's four layers, only the lower two—the troposphere and the stratosphere, and the boundary area between them called the tropopause—will be of interest to us. The height of the troposphere varies with latitude, averaging 11 miles at the equator but only 5 miles above the poles. This is the area that contains our weather systems.

Heat from the sun

Although the sun is some 93 million miles away, and only a fraction of its energy falls on the earth, it is the source of light and life, and its radiant energy ultimately determines the state of the atmosphere. The atmosphere absorbs more than half the sun's energy that reaches the earth, but 43 percent does penetrate to the surface.

The energy that is not reflected by clouds is partially absorbed and partially reflected from the land or water. Much of the solar energy that reaches the earth's surface is re-radiated as heat rays of longer wavelength. These are trapped in the lower atmosphere much the way the air in a greenhouse is warmed to grow plants. Various surfaces absorb and reflect different percentages of the incoming solar rays; these differences result in climatic differences between geographic regions and between land and sea.

The atmosphere moderates the sun's effect, filtering out excess (and harmful) rays by day, and holding in heat at night. Without our atmosphere, we would have to cope with extremes like those on the moon. Cloud cover directly affects the cooling off of the air at night as clouds reflect back a portion of the heat rising from the earth's surface; on clear nights, more heat is lost.

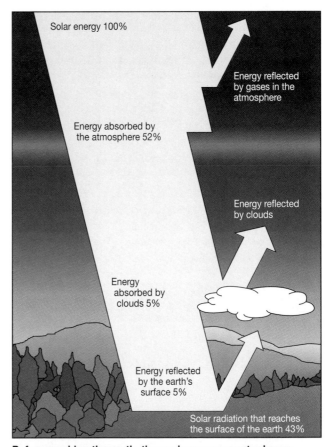

Before reaching the earth, the sun's rays encounter layers of gases, which either stop the rays, reflect them or let them through. Only about half of the sun's energy reaches the earth's surface, where it is absorbed or reflected.

READING THE CLOUDS

Clouds are the most visible manifestation of weather; winds and temperature can be felt, but not seen. In fact, not only are many cloud patterns beautiful and interesting to watch, but they can also be meaningful in interpreting weather conditions and trends.

How clouds form

There is more water in the air than you might think. Water evaporates from the oceans, lakes and rivers and can exist in the air in any of the following three physical states—vapor, liquid or solid.

A term you will often hear is relative humidity—the amount of water vapor present in the air as a percentage of the maximum possible amount for air at that temperature. This maximum amount decreases with a decrease in temperature. Consequently, the relative humidity of a mass of air increases as its temperature falls, even though the actual amount of moisture is unchanged. When the relative humidity reaches 100 percent and the air is further cooled, some moisture condenses into a visible form. The temperature at which this occurs is the dew point.

When warm moist air rises from the earth's surface, it expands and cools. The relative humidity increases, and, when it reaches 100 percent, clouds are formed; there may also be precipitation in the liquid form of rain or drizzle or the solid form of snow, sleet or hail. When moisture in the air condenses into a visible form at or very near the surface, this is fog. The various types of fog and the reasons for their formation are discussed in detail on pages 302-304.

Moist air is also sometimes cooled by horizontal movement—for example, by moving from warmer water surfaces to cooler land surfaces—or by movement up the slope of a hill or mountain range. A warm air mass may also be pushed up over a cold air mass, cooling to the point where clouds form and rain falls.

Identifying clouds

According to an international system of cloud classification, different cloud types have descriptive names that depend mainly upon appearance, but also sometimes upon the processes of formation as seen by an observer. Despite an almost infinite variety of shapes and forms, it is still possible to define the 10 basic types: Examples of these types are shown below and on the following pages.

High clouds

High clouds, found above about 18,000 to 20,000 feet, and described below, are composed of ice crystals.

Cirrus clouds are high and thin. They may have a fibrous (hairlike) appearance or a silky sheen, or both. They can move as fast as 200 miles per hour.

Cirrocumulus clouds are heavier and thicker than cirrus, but still without shading. Small elements may be more or less arranged in repeating patterns.

Cirrostratus is a high veil of ice crystal cloud through which the sun can be seen, along with a well-defined halo; it may herald an approaching storm system.

Cirrocumulus cloud puffs are smaller in apparent size than the sun or moon, which they would not obscure. This is sometimes called a "mackerel sky."

Cirrostratus covers the entire sky, with some thicker patches of altostratus below it. As cirrus clouds thicken, the lower portions become water droplets.

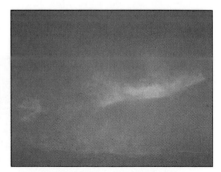

Ground haze, mixed with industrial smog, dissipates in morning sunlight which is not blocked by a thin layer of cirrostratus cloud.

- **Cirrus (Ci)**. Detached clouds in the form of white, delicate filaments, or white or mostly white patches or narrow bands. These clouds are often the first sign of a warm front.
- **Cirrocumulus (Cc)**. Thin, white globular cloud without shading, composed of very small elements in the form of grains or ripples, either merged or separate, and more or less regularly arranged. Most of the elements have an apparent width of less than one degree of arc.
- **Cirrostratus (Cs)**. Transparent, whitish cloud veil of fibrous (hairlike) or smooth appearance, totally or partly covering the sky, and generally producing halos around either the sun or the moon.

Middle clouds

Middle clouds, found from about 7,000 feet up to 20,000 feet and described below, are water droplet clouds.
- **Altocumulus (Ac)**. White or gray (or both white and gray) patch, sheet or layer of cloud, generally with shading, composed of layers, rounded masses, rolls, etc., which are sometimes partly fibrous or diffuse, and which may or may not be merged. Most of the regularly arranged small elements in these clouds usually have an apparent width of between one and five degrees of arc.
- **Altostratus (As)**. Grayish or bluish cloud sheet or layer of striated, fibrous or uniform appearance, totally or partly covering the sky, and having parts thin enough to reveal the sun at least vaguely, as through ground glass. Altostratus does not show halo phenomena.

Low clouds

Low clouds, described below, are found from near ground up to about 7,000 feet.
- **Nimbostratus (Ns).** Gray cloud layer, often very dark, the appearance of which is rendered diffuse by more or less continuously falling rain or snow, which in most cases reaches the ground. Nimbostratus clouds are generally thick enough throughout to blot out the sun. Low, ragged clouds frequently occur just below the main layer, with which they may or may not merge.

WEATHER PROVERB
Mackerel skies and mares' tails
Make tall ships carry low sails.
High-flying cirrus clouds, few in the sky, that resemble wisps in a mare's tail in the wind, signal fair weather. Only when the sky becomes heavy with cirrus, or mackerel, clouds—cirrocumulus resembling wave-rippled sand on a beach—can you expect a storm. There is an exception to this proverb, however. If cirrus clouds form as mares' tails with the hairs pointing upward or downward, the probability is for rain, even though the clouds may be scattered.

WEATHER PROVERBS
When boat horns sound hollow,
Rain will surely follow.
Anyone who has spent any time around boats knows the truth of this time-honored prophecy. Nor do you have to be sitting on a piling in a marina to notice the unusual sharpness of sounds on certain days—the more penetrating sound of a bell ringing or voices that carry longer distances are signs of the acoustical clarity when bad weather lowers the cloud ceiling toward earth. The tonal quality of sound is improved because the cloud layer bounces the sounds back, the way the walls of a canyon echo a cry. When the cloud barrier lifts, the same sounds dissipate in space.

Sound traveling far and wide
A stormy day does like betide.
This is another version of the first proverb, which suggests you can hear bad weather approaching—for example, if a train whistle is audible when normally it would be faint. The reason the sound carries farther is that the whistle was blown under a lowering cloud ceiling, whose extending barrier may not have reached your position yet.

Altocumulus—white or gray, or both—often appears in regular patterns across large areas of the sky. The pattern above is called a "mackerel sky."

Altostratus here is a thick, almost uniform cloud layer about 10,000 feet high. If this thickens and lowers, precipitation is on the way.

More altostratus that covers the entire sky, with widely scattered stratocumulus beneath it. This followed a day of warm, hazy sunshine in late May.

■ **Stratocumulus (Sc)**. Gray or whitish (or both) patch, sheet or layer of cloud. It almost always has dark parts, composed of tessellations (covering without gaps), rounded masses, or rolls. These are non-fibrous (except for "virga"—precipitation trails) and may or may not be merged. Most of the regularly arranged small elements in these clouds have an apparent width of more than five degrees of arc.

■ **Stratus (St)**. Generally gray cloud layer with a fairly uniform base, which may give drizzle, ice prisms or snow grains. When the sun is visible through the cloud, its outline is clearly discernible. Stratus does not produce halo phenomena (an ice crystal cloud phenomenon) except, possibly, at very low temperatures. Sometimes stratus clouds appear in the form of ragged patches.

Clouds of vertical development

Note that cloud groupings are not absolute or exclusive. Portions of cumulus and cumulonimbus become middle clouds, for example; at times altostratus and the tops of cumulonimbus may be at the heights of high clouds.

■ **Cumulus (Cu)**. Detached clouds, generally dense and with definite outlines, developing vertically in the form of rising mounds, domes or towers, of which the bulging upper part often resembles a cauliflower. The sunlit parts are mostly brilliant white; their bases are relatively dark and horizontal. Sometimes cumulus is ragged.

■ **Cumulonimbus (Cb)**. Heavy and dense cloud, with a considerable vertical extent in the form of a mountain or huge towers. At least part of its upper portion is usually smooth, or fibrous or striated, and it is nearly always flattened; this part often spreads out in the shape of an anvil or a vast plume. Under the base of this cloud, which is often very dark, there are frequently low ragged clouds that may be merged with it, as well as precipitation that sometimes appears in the form of virga—streaks of water drops falling from a cloud, which evaporate before they reach the ground.

Using clouds to predict the weather

Answers to the following series of questions are of particular use in predicting weather patterns:

■ What cloud form (or forms) do you observe?
■ Are the clouds increasing or decreasing in amount?
■ Are they lowering or lifting?
■ What was the sequence of cloud forms observed during the past few hours?

When viewed along with wind and pressure observations, as described on page 325, cloud observations can help to predict the weather effectively.

Nimbostratus, just prior to the onset of a steady rainfall. If the sun were in the picture, its image would be blurred, and there would be no halo.

Stratus has a thick, almost uniform look. This indicates stable air, and as there is little turbulence in this, any precipitation will be fine drizzle.

Stratocumulus is white with dark patches in thick portions of the clouds. This type may appear as rounded masses or rolls that may or may not be merged.

Cumulus of little development indicate continued fair weather; following the passage of a cold front, they may be accompanied by brisk winds.

More fair-weather cumulus. If they form in warm air ahead of a cold front, however, they can be accompanied by squalls and thunderstorms.

Cumulonimbus base as a line of heavy thunderstorms approaches. Squall winds reached 50 knots in gusts, and the accompanying rain was torrential.

WEATHER PROVERBS

The proverbs saying that a ring around the sun or moon is a sign of rain are frequently right, as explained below.

The moon with a circle brings water in her beak.

The familiar halo of the sun or moon is caused by the refraction of its light by ice crystals in cirrus clouds, which frequently appear when lowered air pressure and high clouds are present and rain is approaching.

A halo around the sun indicates the approach of a storm within three days, from the side which is most brilliant.
Halos predict a storm at no great distance; the open side of the halo tells from where it may be expected.

At first reading, these two sayings may seem contradictory. As cirrus and cirrostratus fronts push across the sky in the region of the moon or sun, the halo first appears, then becomes brightest in that part of the arc from which a low pressure system is approaching. Later, the halo becomes complete and the light is uniform throughout. As the storm advances, altostratus clouds arrive and obliterate the original and, for a time, the brightest part of the halo—the side nearest the oncoming storm. The sayings refer to different times in the life of the halo.

It is also true that when halos appear as double or triple, it signifies that cirrostratus clouds are relatively thick, such as would be the case in a deep, well-developed storm. Broken halos indicate a disturbed state in the upper atmosphere, with rain imminent.

Now, to put any confusion at rest about the forecast persistence of rain by the appearance of sun and moon halos, the U.S. National Weather Service has verified through repeated observations that sun halos will be followed by rain about 75 percent of the time. Halos around the moon have a rain forecasting accuracy of about 65 percent.

When a halo rings the moon or sun
The rain will come upon the run.

Halos are excellent atmospheric signs of rain, although they do not always foretell rain. Halos around the moon after a pale sun confirm the advent of rain, for you are viewing the moon through the ice crystals of high cirriform clouds. When the whole sky is covered with these cloud forms, a warm front may be approaching, bringing with it a long, soft rain.

Cumulus clouds normally are associated with fair weather, but local hot spots and extreme development can change them into storm cumulonimbus.

Cumulus may build in the afternoon, but later in the day will flatten as the surface cools and the supply of rising warm, moist air diminishes.

Stratocumulus is a thick, solid layer with a lumpy base. It is often formed by the spreading out of cumulus, and may be followed by clearing at night.

Cumulus development culminates in an anvil-topped cumulonimbus thunderhead that may tower 20,000 to 50,000 feet above the surface of the earth.

Cumulonimbus associated with summer showers results from local development of cumulus clouds. Rainfall is likely to be brief, but moderately heavy.

Altostratus represents warm air riding over cold air ahead of a warm front. The layer will grow thicker and lower, with continuous rain or snow.

FOG: CLOUDS AT GROUND LEVEL

Fog is merely a cloud whose base rests upon the earth's land or water. It occurs when the water vapor near the surface of the earth condenses. Condensation of water vapor in the low levels of the atmosphere may occur for one of two reasons: The air is cooled below its dew point, described in the box below, or the dew point is raised to air temperature through the addition of water vapor. The result is one of the six types of fog described as follows, of which only the first four frequently affect boaters:

■ **Radiation (ground) fog.** There are six requirements for the formation of radiation fog. It must be night. The air must be stable. And it must be colder than the air a short distance aloft. It must also be relatively moist. The sky must be clear so that the earth can readily lose heat by radiation to outer space. This enables the ground to become colder than the overlying air, which subsequently is cooled below its dew point both by contact with the ground (conduction of heat) and by the loss of heat to the ground. Finally, the wind must

Fog forms from the surface up. As successive layers of air are cooled enough to cause condensation, the depth of the fog increases and visibility is further restricted. Even with today's sophisticated electronic instruments, extreme caution is the watchword when a fog sets in.

DESCRIBING WATER VAPOR CONTENT

■ **Condensation**
A reduction to a denser form, as steam to water.

■ **Dew point**
The temperature at which the air would become saturated if cooled at constant pressure.

■ **Evaporation**
A process in which a liquid turns to a vapor without its temperature reaching the boiling point.

■ **Relative humidity**
The actual amount of water vapor in the air divided by the amount of water vapor that would be present if the air were saturated at the same temperature and pressure. It is expressed as a percentage.

Dew point indicates indirectly the amount of water vapor present, while relative humidity expresses the degree of saturation. Therefore, air that has a temperature and dew point of 75°F and 50°F respectively contains more water vapor than air with a temperature and dew point of 45°F and 45°F respectively, although the relative humidity is higher in the latter case.

■ **Saturation**
The point at which air would not absorb more moisture. The higher the temperature, the more water vapor the air can hold before it becomes saturated.

■ **Sublimation**
Conversion directly from a solid state to vapor.

be light to calm. If there is a dead calm, the lowest strata of air will not mix with the ones above, and the fog will form only to a height of 2 to 4 feet. If there is slight motion of the air—a wind of 3 to 5 knots— and consequently some turbulent mixing, the cooling is spread through a layer that may extend to a height of several hundred feet above ground. With stronger winds, the cooling effect is distributed through so deep a layer that temperature does not fall to the dew point and fog does not form.

Radiation fog is most prevalent in the middle and high latitudes, and can be predicted with considerable accuracy. It is local in character and occurs most frequently in valleys and lowlands, especially near inland lakes and rivers where you may be cruising. The cooled air drains into these terrain depressions; the lake or river then aids the process of fog formation by contributing water vapor. This raises the dew point of the air.

This type of fog may be patchy or uniformly dense. It bothers us chiefly in the late summer and early autumn. Shortly after sunrise in most areas, it will start to evaporate ("burn off") over the land, first at the lower layers. It is slow to clear over water, however, since the water warms less from night to day than does the land.

■ **Advection fog.** Since advection means "transport by horizontal motion," this type of fog is produced by winds carrying warm, moist air over a colder surface. It may form day or night, during any season of the year, especially over the sea.

For advection fog to form, the dew point of the air must be higher than the temperature of the surface over which the air is moving. That means the air can be cooled below its dew point by conduction and by radiation of heat to the colder surface. There are also two other requirements for the formation of advection fog: The air at a height of 100 feet or so must be warmer than the air just above the surface. In addition, the temperature of the surface—land or water—must become progressively colder in the direction toward which the air is moving.

For boaters, the most bothersome variety of advection fog is coastal fog. It forms when steady winds blow landward, carrying warm oceanic air across cold coastal water. The result is coastal fog, which may blanket a great length of coastline and, especially at night, may extend many miles inland, up bays and rivers.

Coastal fog can be seen on land as it blows past street lights. For example, consider the Pacific Coast, where the water close to land is often colder than the water well offshore. The prevailing winds in summer are onshore and the air (which frequently has come from mid-Pacific) is usually nearly saturated with water vapor. The same thing happens when southerly winds carry air across the Gulf Stream, then northward across the colder Atlantic coastal waters. Boaters on larger inland lakes may occasionally encounter this type of fog, especially when warm, moist air is carried over the colder lake surfaces.

Advection fog generally dissipates less easily than radiation fog. Unlike radiation fog, sunshine has no effect on advection fog over the water. Usually a change in wind direction is needed to bring colder air over a warmer surface.

■ **Precipitation (frontal) fog.** When rain, after descending though a layer of warm air aloft, falls into a shallow layer of colder air at the earth's surface, there will be some evaporation from the warm raindrops into the colder air. Under certain conditions this will raise the water vapor content of the cold air above the saturation point and precipitation fog—also called rain fog—will result. Because this type of fog is often found near frontal activity, it is sometimes known as frontal fog.

■ **Steam fog.** On the Mississippi and Ohio rivers, steam fog is a particular hazard to late evening or early morning boating in the autumn. When cold air passes over much warmer water, the lowest layer of air is rapidly supplied with heat and water vapor. Under certain conditions, mixing of this lowest layer with unmodified cold air above can produce a supersaturated (foggy) mixture. Because the water is much warmer than the air, vertical air currents are created and we observe the phenomenon of steaming, not unlike the steam that rises from a hot bath.

In winter, when cold air below about 10°F (-12°C) blows off the land and across the adjacent coastal waters, steam fog may be widespread and very dense. It is then called sea smoke. Along North American coastal waters, steam fog occurs most frequently off the coasts of Maine and Nova Scotia, and in the Gulf of St. Lawrence, where it can be a serious navigational hazard. However, its occurrence is not restricted to higher latitudes. Off the southeast coast of the U.S., steam fog has been observed as far south as Florida; it also occurs over the coastal waters of the Gulf of Mexico.

■ **Upslope fog.** When a low moving blanket of air is gradually elevated toward a cooler altitude by the slope of the land, upslope fog forms. Occurring frequently on the sides of mountains, this type of fog is common at New Hampshire's Mount Washington, for example, as well as in the Great Plains, where a southeast wind blows moist air from the Gulf of Mexico toward the Rocky Mountains. Where winds are strong, stratus or stratocumulus clouds will form instead.

■ **Ice fog.** At very low temperatures, the air may become full of ice crystals, which seriously restricts vision. In this case, the water vapor in the air has turned into ice. This process, in which a gas turns into a solid, is called sublimation.

The distribution of fog

In the United States, the coastal sections most frequently beset by fog range from the Strait of Juan de Fuca to Point Arguello, California, on the Pacific Coast, and from the Bay

Cold air passing over warm water picks up enough heat and moisture to form steam fog. Most prevalent during morning and evening of autumn months, it is found most often on inland rivers and small lakes and ponds.

Sea smoke in Great Harbor, Woods Hole, Massachusetts. Water temperature at the time of this photograph was +31.6°F (-0.2°C), and the air temperature, 30 feet above sea level, was +5°F (-15°C). The wind was from the northwest at about 20 knots.

of Fundy to Montauk Point, New York, on the Atlantic Coast. In these waters the average annual number of hours of fog exceeds 900—more than 10 percent of the year. In the foggiest areas, off the coast of northern California and the coast of Maine, fog is present about 20 percent of the year.

Going southward along both the Atlantic and Pacific coasts, the frequency of fog decreases, more rapidly on the Atlantic Coast than on the Pacific. The average annual fog frequency over the waters near Los Angeles and San Diego, for example, is about three times that in the same latitude along the Atlantic Coast.

Seasonal frequencies

The time of maximum occurrence of fog along the Pacific Coast varies both by year and locality. In general, however, over the stretch from Cape Flattery, Washington, to Point Arguello, the season of most frequent fogs runs from July through October, with more than 50 percent of the annual number of foggy days occurring during this period. However, along the lower coast of California from Los Angeles southward, the foggiest months are those from September through February, and the least foggy are from May through July.

On the Atlantic side, off the coast of New England, the foggiest months are usually June, July and August, with a maximum of fog generally occurring during July. In fact, during that month, some fog is normally encountered about 50 per-

cent of the time. Off the Middle Atlantic Coast, however, fog occurs mostly in the winter and spring months, with a tendency toward minimum frequency in summer and autumn. Along the South Atlantic Coast (from Cape Hatteras to the tip of Florida) and in the Gulf of Mexico, fog rarely creates a problem for boaters. It is virtually non-existent during the summer, and even in the winter and early spring season (December through March), when it has maximum frequency, the number of days with fog rarely exceeds 20 during this four-month period.

The Great Lakes as a whole tend to have fog in the warmer season. The explanation for this is to be found in the comparison of the lake temperatures with the air temperatures over the surrounding land area. From March or April to around the beginning of September the lakes tend to be colder than the air. Therefore, whenever the dew-point temperature is sufficiently high, conditions favor the formation of advection fog over the water.

The greatest fogginess occurs when and where the lakes are coldest in relation to the air blowing off the surrounding land. On Lake Superior, north-central Lake Michigan and northwestern Lake Huron, the time of maximum frequency is late May and June; elsewhere it is late April and May. Since the lake temperatures become colder from south to north and from the shores outward, the occurrence of fog increases northward and toward the lakes' centers.

THE WAYS OF WIND

Few elements have as powerful an impact on human life as the wind. This horizontal movement of air is alternately a force to be reckoned with, and enjoyed, by boaters everywhere.

Circulation patterns

The wind is explained by a fundamental law of physics: Heated air expands, becomes less dense, then tends to rise. Heated by the earth's surface, the air rises and is replaced by colder, heavier air, which in turn warms and rises. The process results in vertical currents over wide areas of the world.

The nearer the equator, the more surface heat there is to warm the air. Here the air rises and then flows toward the poles. Rising air is then replaced by a stream of colder air that flows from the poles toward the tropic regions. This simple pattern is modified by the earth's rotation.

In the northern hemisphere, the northward-flowing air at high altitudes is bent eastward and, by the time it reaches about 30° latitude, it has started to build up an area of higher pressure forcing some of the flow downward and back toward the equator. This steady flow, bent westward by the earth's rotation, becomes the reliable "northeast trade winds" of the northern sub-tropical zone. The portion that continues northward toward the pole eventually descends as the "prevailing westerlies" of the higher mid-latitudes. Between these regions exist the "horse latitudes," near 30°, where winds are weaker and less constant. Near the equator, where the warmed air rises and turns north or south, the region of weaker winds is called the "doldrums."

Local wind patterns

Temperature differences—heating and cooling air—cause localized breezes as well as global winds. Land heats up more quickly than water during hours of sunlight; air rising over land is replaced by air coming in from seaward. These winds (*below, top*) are the refreshing "sea breezes."

At night the land loses its heat more quickly, so the water's surface becomes the relatively warmer area, and the "land breezes" (*bottom*) flow toward the sea. In both cases, these breezes are felt close to the surface; a counterflow of air at higher elevation completes the local circulation pattern.

Wind on water

Every sailor is familiar with wind direction indicators that can be mounted at the masthead. Because a boat anchored or underway can head in any direction all around the compass, a few mental calculations are necessary before you can use this indicator, or any other—a yarn (telltale), flag or club burgee—to determine the true direction of the wind.

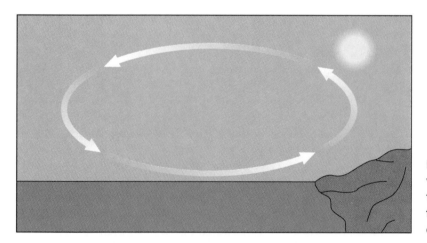

In daytime, when the land is warmer, air rises over the land, then is replaced by cooler air from seaward. This activity creates a sea breeze.

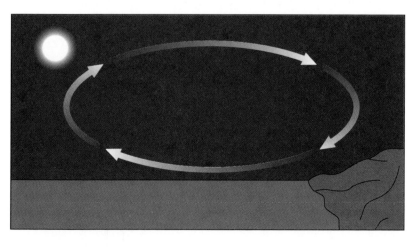

At night, the opposite occurs when the land temperature lowers the temperature of the sea. This creates a land breeze.

At anchor, the fly of the indicator will give you the bearing of the wind relative to the boat's bow; this must be converted to the true bearing of the wind itself. You can use your compass to obtain these values, provided you know its deviation on your heading as well as the variation for the anchorage. Also, remember that wind direction is always stated as the true direction from which—not toward which—the wind is blowing.

For measuring wind strength, an anemometer is needed. This is essentially a speedometer, consisting of a rotor with conical cups attached to the ends of spokes. It is designed for mounting at the masthead. Indications of the speed of the rotor are calculated and transmitted electrically to the wind indicator mounted in the cabin or elsewhere on the boat.

Another method of estimating the strength of the wind is the Beaufort Scale of Wind Force. To use it, boaters should obtain a State of Sea Card (M.O. 688A) published by the British Meteorological Office. This reference provides descriptions of 13 wind forces of the Beaufort Scale with a photograph to accompany each. This gives the observer a guide in esti-

mating wind strength in knots when making weather reports or in logging sea conditions. Other factors such as fetch, depth of water, swell, heavy rain, current and the lag effect between the wind getting up and the sea increasing may also affect the appearance of the sea. Range of wind speed and the mean wind speed are given for each force. By special permission, *Chapman Piloting* reproduces *(opposite)* six of these photographs (Forces 1, 3, 5, 8, 10, 12). Forces 0, 2, 4, 6, 7, 9 and 11, though not illustrated, may be estimated in relation to those above and below them in the scale.

True and apparent wind

So far we have been considering the determination of the direction and speed of the wind while at anchor. This is more difficult to do while underway. Using our true course and speed, we can determine, using a Maneuvering Board form *(Chapter 20)*, the approximate "true wind" direction and speed, provided we know the apparent direction and speed. Our wind indicator or owner's flag will give the apparent direction, and our anemometer will give us the apparent strength.

THE BEAUFORT WIND SCALE

Beaufort number	Miles per hour	Knots	International description	Effects observed on water
0	Less and 1	Less than 1	Calm	Sea like a mirror.
1	1-3	1-3	Light air	Ripples with appearance of scales; no foam crests.
2	4-7	4-6	Light breeze	Small wavelets; crests of glassy appearance, not breaking.
3	8-12	7-10	Gentle breeze	Large wavelets; crests begin to break, scattered whitecaps.
4	13-18	11-16	Moderate	Small waves 0.5-1.25 meters high, becoming longer; numerous whitecaps.
5	19-24	17-21	Fresh	Moderate waves of 1.25-2.5 meters taking longer form; many whitecaps; some spray.
6	25-31	22-27	Strong	Larger waves 2.5-4 meters forming; whitecaps everywhere; more spray.
7	32-38	28-33	Near gale	Sea heaps up, waves 4-6 meters; white foam from breaking waves begins to blow in streaks.
8	39-46	34-40	Gale	Moderately high (4-6 meters) waves of greater length; edge of crests begin to break into spindrift; foam is blown in well-marked streaks.
9	47-54	41-47	Strong gale	High waves (6 meters); sea begins to roll; dense streaks of foam; spray may reduce visibility.
10	55-63	48-55	Storm	Very high waves (6-9 meters) with overhanging crests; sea takes a white appearance as foam is blown in very dense streaks; rolling is heavy and visibility is reduced.
11	64-73	56-63	Violent storm	Exceptionally high (9-14 meters) waves; sea covered with white foam patches; visibility still more reduced.
12	74-82	64-71	Hurricane	Air filled with foam; waves over 14 meters; sea completely white with driving spray; visibility greatly reduced.

This table is based roughly on a scale for estimating wind speeds devised in 1805 by Admiral Sir Francis Beaufort of the British Royal Navy. The original Beaufort Scale was based on the effect of various wind speeds on the amount of canvas that a full-rigged frigate of the period could carry. The scale has since been modified and modernized.

Photographs from the British Meteorological Office show wind forces and their effects on the sea. Beaufort Force 1 (calm air) is shown in the photograph at upper left. Force 3 (gentle breeze) appears at center left. Force 5 (fresh breeze) appears at bottom left. Force 8 (gale) is shown at upper right. Force 10 (storm) is shown at center right. Finally, refer to bottom right for Force 12 (hurricane). Note how, in hurricane-force winds, the surface of the sea is completely obscured by driving foam.

OBSERVING PRESSURE CHANGES

Familiarity with atmospheric pressure is essential in the understanding of weather because the pressure distribution in the atmosphere controls the winds; to a considerable extent, it also affects the occurrence of clouds and precipitation. For the boater watching the weather, it is important to understand how the winds and weather relate to the pressure distribution as shown on a weather map.

Atmospheric pressure aboard is measured by two types of barometers. A mercurial barometer balances a column of mercury against the weight of the air. The pressure may be expressed in inches or millimeters of mercury, or in millibars (mb), a type of unit used in physics. Alternatively, an aneroid barometer, shown below right, operates according to the action of atmospheric pressure, which bends a metallic surface to move a pointer. The aneroid barometer indicates pressure in both inches of mercury and millibars.

The global circulation of the atmosphere takes place as a result of the unequal heating of the earth by the sun. This results in the building up of areas of above-average barometric pressure, with corresponding areas of below-average pressures. These are the Highs and Lows that are seen on weather maps, usually designated by the letters "H" and "L."

Highs, also known as "anti-cyclones," generally bring good weather, in the sense that there will be no precipitation and fewer clouds. However, approaching Highs often bring strong winds that may persist for quite a while. Lows, also called "cyclones" (but not to be confused with hurricanelike storms in the Pacific Ocean), generally bring bad or unsettled weather. Highs and Lows are rather large areas of "weather" and may measure many hundreds of miles in diameter. In the northern hemisphere, circulation around an area of high pressure is clockwise; around Lows, it is counterclockwise. In the southern hemisphere, circulation follows the opposite pattern. Winds are generally weaker in Highs than they are in low-pressure systems.

How Highs form

Areas of high pressure are formed by the descent of cold, dense air toward the surface of the earth in polar regions and in the horse latitudes (near 30° latitude). As air flows outward toward areas of low pressure, a clockwise circulation pattern is established due to the rotation of the earth. Highs form sequentially in the north polar region and move southward; as they reach the latitudes of the prevailing westerlies they are carried first southeastward, then eastward, and often finally northeastward.

The existence of the continents and the oceans distorts the theoretical picture of the formation of Highs and Lows; the actual process is quite complex. High-pressure "breeding zones" form in relatively specific geographical areas rather than in broad zones around the earth; these areas change between summer and winter.

How Lows form

The formation of low pressure cells is quite different from that of Highs. On the boundary between warmer air and cooler air, a horizontal, wavelike situation develops. This grows and becomes more and more distinct and may even "break" in the way that an ocean wave does on the beach. The boundary between the two areas of air of different temperature is termed a front, a major weather phenomenon discussed in detail on pages 311-314.

Small, local low-pressure cells may also develop over deserts or other intensely heated locations. Here, the air heated at the earth's surface expands, rises rapidly and creates an effect of low pressure; air rushes in from outside this area with a counterclockwise swirling motion. Lows can also form on the lee side of mountain ranges as strong winds blow across the peaks.

This barometer has scales in inches of mercury and millibars. Markings such as "Rain," "Change" and "Fair" are of little value.

THE BUYS-BALLOT LAW

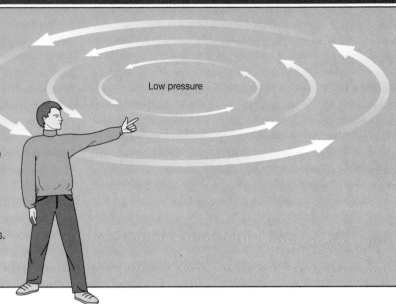

Buys-Ballot used the direction of the swirl to find the center of the storm. In 1858, he formulated a law stating that winds are perpendicular to the lines of barometric slope. Two years later, he put his observations into a paper entitled *Some Rules for Predicting Weather Changes in the Netherlands*. In that paper was his well-known rule, "with your back to the wind, low pressure is to the left." In the southern hemisphere, you face the wind to find the low pressure center with your left hand, as shown at right. The application of this law has enabled many sailors to head for calmer waters.

Low pressure

Using a barometer

A good barometer is a helpful instrument, provided you read it at regular intervals and keep a record of the readings, and provided you remember that there is much more to weather than just barometric pressure. The aneroid barometer is the type commonly seen on boats. The one shown opposite has several interesting features:

■ It has a pressure scale. You may be accustomed to thinking of barometric pressure in terms of inches of mercury, and the scale is graduated in these units. However, weather maps today are printed with barometric pressures shown in millibars. In addition, many radio weather reports specify this value, so the scale graduated in millibars, as well as in inches of mercury, eliminates any worries about conversions between units. The "standard atmospheric pressure" of 29.92 inches of mercury is equal to 1013.2 millibars, and 1 inch equals 33.86 millibars, or 1 millibar equals 0.03 inches of mercury.

SAMPLE BAROMETER READINGS		
Time	*Pressure (Inches)*	*Change*
0700	30.02	—
0800	30.00	-0.02
0900	29.97	-0.03
1000	29.93	-0.04
1100	29.88	-0.05
1200	29.82	-0.06

Logging pressure readings at regular intervals, as in the example shown at right, facilitates interpretation of the barometer.

■ It is a rugged instrument, with a high order of accuracy.
■ It has a reference hand, for use in keeping track of changes in pressure.
■ The words "Fair-Change-Rain," when they appear on the face of an aneroid barometer, are mainly decorative. It is not the actual barometric pressure that is important in forecasting; it is the direction and rate of change of pressure. However, it is important to remember that barometric changes for a moving vessel may be affected by three factors: diurnal pressure changes, movement of the pressure system and movement of the vessel. All of these must be considered before making any conclusions regarding the significance of any pressure changes.

Reading the barometer

An individual reading of the barometer tells you only the pressure being exerted by the atmosphere on the earth's surface at a particular point of observation at that time. However, suppose you have logged the pressure readings at regular intervals, as shown at left. In this example, the pressure is falling at a steady rate. Trouble is brewing. A fall of 0.02 inch per hour is a low rate of fall; consequently, this figure would not be particularly disturbing. But a fall of 0.05 inch per hour is a rather high rate.

Next, there is a normal diurnal change in pressure. The pressure is usually at its maximum value about 1000 and 2200 each day, at its minimum value about 0400 and 1600 local time each day. The variation between minimum and maximum may be as much as 0.05 inch change in these six-hour intervals (about 0.01 inch change per hour). Consequently, when the pressure normally would increase about 0.03 inch (0700 to 1000), our pressure actually fell 0.04 inch. Suppose, now, that at about 1200 you also observed that the wind was blowing from the NE with increasing force and that the barometer continued to fall at a high rate. A severe northeast gale is probably on its way. On the other hand, given the same barometer reading of about 29.82, rising rapidly with the wind going to west, you could expect improving weather—quite a difference.

Barometric changes and wind velocity

It is generally true that a rapidly falling barometer forecasts the development of strong winds. This is so because a falling barometer indicates the approach or development of a Low, and the pressure gradient is usually steep in the neighborhood of a low-pressure center. On the other hand, a rising barometer is associated with the prospect of lighter winds to come. This is true because a rising barometer indicates

GENERAL BAROMETER RULES

- Foul weather is usually forecast by a falling barometer with winds from the east quadrants.

- Clearing and fair weather is usually forecast by winds shifting to west quadrants from a rising barometer.

- When the wind sets in from points between south and southeast and the barometer falls steadily, a storm is approaching from the west of northwest, and its center will pass near or north of the observer within 12 to 24 hours, with the wind veering to northwest by way of south and southwest.

- When the wind sets in from points between east and northeast and the barometer starts to fall steadily, a storm is approaching from the south or southwest, and its center will pass near or to the south of the observer within 12 to 24 hours, with the wind backing to northwest by way of north.

- The rapidity of the storm's approach and its likely intensity will be indicated by the rate and the amount of fall in the barometer.

- A falling barometer and a rising thermometer often forecast rain.

- Barometer and thermometer rising together often forecast fine weather.

- A slowly rising barometer forecasts settled weather.

- A steady, slow fall of pressure indicates forthcoming unsettled or wet weather.

the approach or development of a High, and the pressure gradient is characteristically less steep in the neighborhood of a high-pressure center.

The barometer does not necessarily fall before or during a strong breeze. The wind often blows hard without any appreciable accompanying change in the barometer. This means that a steep pressure gradient exists (isobars close together, as seen on the weather map), but that the well-developed High or Low associated with the steep pressure gradient is practically stationary. In this case the wind may be expected to blow hard for some time; any slackening or change will take place gradually.

It sometimes happens that the barometer falls quite rapidly, yet the wind remains comparatively light. If you remember the relation between wind velocity and pressure gradient, you can conclude that the gradient must be comparatively small (isobars relatively far apart). The rapid fall of the barometer must be accounted for, then, in either one or two ways. Either a Low with a weak pressure gradient on its forward side is approaching rapidly, or there is a rapid decrease of pressure taking place right over your location, or both. In such a situation, the pressure gradient at the rear of the Low is often steep, and in that case strong winds will set in as soon as the barometer begins to rise. (It will rise rapidly under these circumstances.) The fact that the barometer is now rising, however, indicates that decreasing winds may be expected soon.

The barometer and wind shifts

Nearly all extra-tropical cyclones *(pages 318-319)* display an unsymmetrical distribution of pressure. The pressure gradients are seldom the same in the front as in the rear of an extra-tropical cyclone. During the approach of a Low the barometer alone gives no clue as to how much the wind will shift and what velocity it will have after the passage of the low-pressure system. This is particularly applicable to situations in which the wind blows from a southerly direction while the barometer is falling. The cessation of the fall of the barometer will coincide with a "veering" (a gradual or sudden change in wind direction in a clockwise sense—for example, SE to SW to NW) of the wind to a more westerly direction. Likewise, note that the wind will veer if the center of a Low passes to the north of the observer. However, if the low passes to the south of the observer, the winds will "back" (a change in wind direction in a counterclockwise direction—for example, SE to NE to NW). Unfortunately, if you have no information other than the variations in atmospheric pressure indicated by your barometer, you cannot foretell the exact features of the change.

In using barometric indications for local forecasting, remember that weather changes are influenced by the characteristics of the earth's surface in your locality. Check all rules against experience in your own cruising waters before you place full confidence in them.

AIR MASSES AND FRONTS

A general knowledge of air masses and fronts will make weather forecasts more understandable, as well as more useful.

Understanding air masses

Resulting from a stationary high-pressure region, an air mass is nothing more than a huge "blob" of air that descends from high-altitude global circulation. There is no corresponding feature or name for the low-pressure equivalent. By remaining over a homogeneous surface—continental or maritime, polar or tropical—for a sufficient period of time, it adopts the region's temperature and moisture content characteristics. Once developed, the mass tends to retain those characteristics, even while moving over different surfaces.

AIR MASS CHARACTERISTICS		
Observed weather	Stable air mass	Unstable air mass
Visibility	Poor	Good
Winds	Steady	Gusty
Clouds	Stratoform	Cumuloform
Precipitation	Steady	Showery

An air mass is a large body of air in which temperature and moisture conditions are essentially the same in all directions horizontally. It may be described as stable or unstable, as shown in the table above.

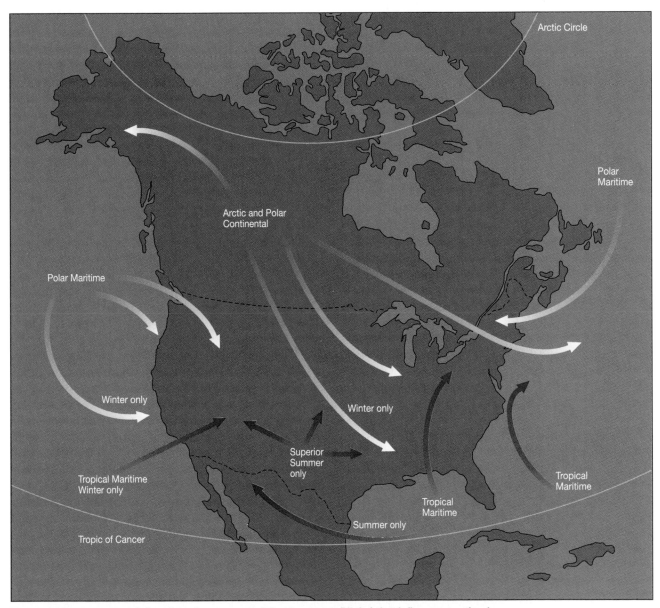

These are the sources and direction of movement of the air masses (Highs) that influence weather in North America. The properties of an air mass, and its conflicts with adjacent masses, are the causes of weather changes. Note that some are seasonal.

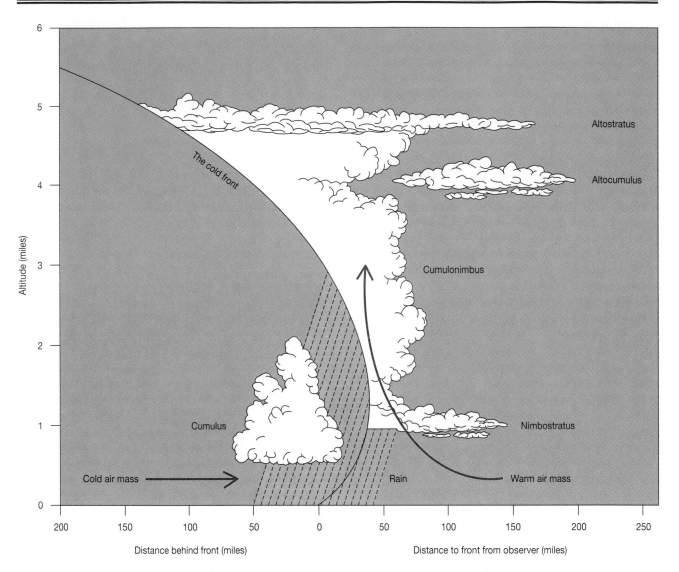

In this cross section of a cold front, a cold air mass is shown advancing, pushing aloft the warm air mass it displaces. Thunderstorms usually occur when temperature differences are great, and rapidly rising moist warm air ahead of the cold front forms towering cumulus clouds.

Those characteristics and their relationship with those of the surface over which the air mass is moving—warmer or cooler—define the air mass. It may cover an area as large as several hundred thousand square miles. The map on the previous page shows the principal air masses that affect North America and their general normal movement.

Because maritime and continental air masses differ significantly in their characteristics of temperature and humidity, they bring different kinds of weather. Oceans suffer less extreme variations of heat and cold than do continents, and maritime air masses change less with seasons. As a result, a maritime air mass moving over land tends to moderate any conditions of excess heat or cold.

Cold air masses are characterized by unstable internal conditions; the air next to the earth's surface warms and attempts to rise through the overlying layers of colder air.

On the other hand, a warm air mass remains relatively stable; air cooled by contact with the colder ground tends to sink and warm air above tends to stay there or rise. These conditions result in stronger, gusty winds within a cold air mass, but weaker, steadier winds in a warm air mass. Visibility is comparatively better in a cold air mass; rainfall often comes in the form of thundershowers from cumulonimbus clouds, rather than the drizzle from the stratus cloud formations that are typical of a warm air mass.

Weather fronts

A front is the boundary between two different air masses, one cold and one warm; the bodies of air do not tend to mix, but rather each moves with respect to the other. The passage of a front results in a change of weather conditions at that location, frequently for the worse (often violent).

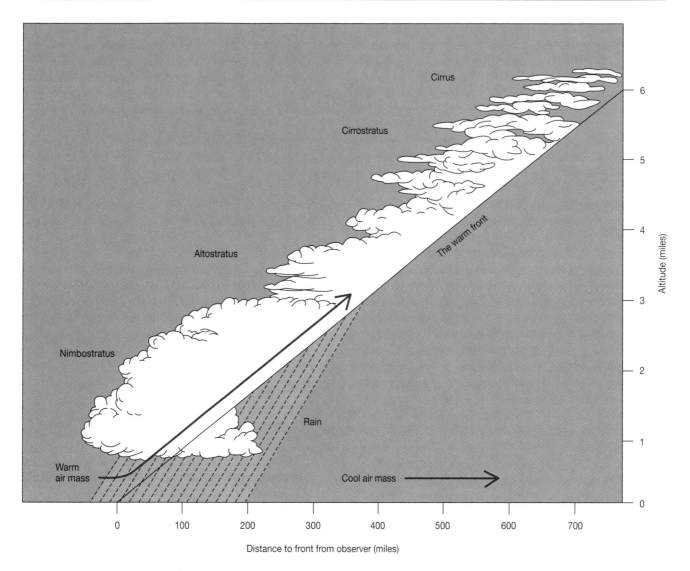

In this cross section of a warm front, the warm air is shown moving aloft on top of the underlying wedge of cold air, which retreats as the warm air advances. The cloud sequence as the front approaches is first cirrus, then cirrostratus, then altostratus, and finally, nimbostratus in the rain area.

■ **Cold fronts.** With a cold front, the oncoming cold air mass pushes under the warm air mass and forces it upward, as shown opposite. In the northern hemisphere, cold fronts generally lie along a NE-SW line and move eastward or southeastward. A cold front can travel 300 to 500 statute miles (500 to 800 km) per day, more in winter and less in summer.

A strong, rapidly moving cold front, such as often occurs in the spring when wide differences exist between adjacent air masses, will bring weather changes that may be quite intense but relatively brief in duration. These active cold fronts are often characterized by a line of strong thunderstorms. In late summer, when air mass differences are smaller, slower moving cold fronts may be accompanied by scattered clouds along the frontal boundary, but no precipitation.

A squall line is a line of thunderstorms ahead of an approaching cold front. Often these have the appearance of

WEATHER PROVERB
Winds that swing against the sun
And winds that bring the rain are one.
Winds that swing around the sun
Keep the rain storm on the run.

This traditional saying is based on the direction that a weather vane points, but observing a flag flapping in the breeze will serve just as well. The proverb means that a wind that changes its direction so that it moves from east to west, with the movement of the sun, almost always results in clear skies. But a wind that changes its direction against the movement of the sun, blowing first from the west, and then from the east, invariably brings dirty weather with it.

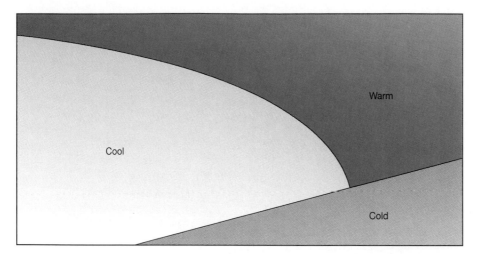

The cross section of a warm-type occlusion shows how the advancing cool air rides up on the colder air ahead, somewhat like a warm front does, and the warm air is then pushed aloft.

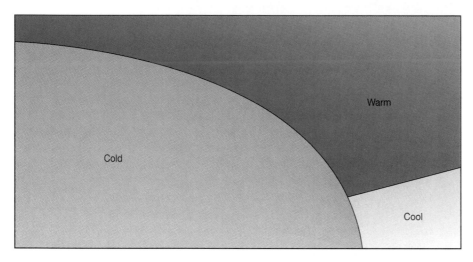

In this cross section of a cold-type occlusion, the advancing cold air moves under the cool air forcing the cool air aloft—acting like a cold front. Once again, the warm air is moved above the surface.

the cold front and may produce weather more severe than that of the front itself. The difference between these can be noted by watching the wind direction and humidity of the air behind the line. Winds may switch dramatically as the squall line passes, but they should soon return to a southerly or southeasterly direction. Also, since the squall line is embedded within the same air mass, the temperature and humidity values should return to those felt ahead of the squall line.

The approach of a cold front is indicated by a shift of the wind toward the south, then to the southwest. Barometric pressure readings fall. As the front approaches, clouds lower and build up; rain starts slowly but increases rapidly. As the front passes, the wind continues to veer westward, northwesterly, then sometimes northerly. After passage, the sky quickly clears, temperatures drop, pressure builds up, and the wind may continue to veer to the northeast. For a few days, the weather will have the characteristics of a cold (usually unstable) air mass.

■ **Warm fronts.** A warm front occurs when an advancing warm air mass reaches colder air and rides up over it, as shown above. Warm fronts are generally oriented in directions NS, NW-SE or EW and change their direction more often than cold fronts do. The rate of movement is slower, 150-200 miles (240-

320 km) per day, and thus warm fronts are eventually overtaken by the next following cold front.

Warm-front weather is generally milder than that of a cold front, and may extend several hundreds of miles in advance of the actual front. Clouds form at low levels and rainfall generally is more moderate but extended in time. The approach of a warm front is signaled by a falling barometer (but falling more slowly than for a cold front), a buildup of clouds and the onset of rain or drizzle. After the passage of the front there will be cumulus and/or stratocumulus clouds and temperatures will rise; the barometer will also slowly rise.

■ **Stationary fronts.** Occasionally a front slows down to the point of little or no forward movement. A stationary front brings conditions of clouds and rain, much like a warm front.

■ **Occluded fronts.** An occluded front involves warm air, cold air and cool air. It occurs after a cold front overtakes a warm front because of its faster movement, and lifts the warm air mass off the ground. The warm air and the cool air are pushed upward from the earth's surface, as shown above. The appearance on a weather map is that of a curled "tail" extending outward from the junction of the cold and warm fronts; this is a low-pressure area with counterclockwise winds.

STORMS

There are several thoughts that come to mind when the boater hears the word "storm." On one hand, it may refer to an individual cumulonimbus cloud. Or it might refer to a tropical or extra-tropical cyclone containing hundreds of thunderstorms. In any case, the word "storm" should cause the conscientious skipper to become very alert. The approach of a storm causes concern for the safety of crew, passengers and the boat itself.

Thunderstorms

A thunderstorm is the most powerful weather phenomenon on earth. Such storms can develop individually within a warm, moist air mass or above a high mountain, or collectively as part of a low pressure system or part of a squall line.

Thunderstorms occur most frequently, and with the greatest intensity, in the summers over all parts of the U.S. While they may strike at any hour, they are most common in the late afternoon and early evening over inland and coastal waters. The surrounding land has been a good "stove" for many hours, heating the air to produce strong upward currents. Over the ocean, well away from shore, thunderstorms more commonly occur between midnight and sunrise. Finally, thunderstorms are most frequent and most violent in subtropical latitudes. The southeastern part of the U.S. may average four thunderstorms per week in summer.

How thunderstorms happen

There are three requirements for the development of a thunderstorm. These are listed below:

■ There must be strong upward air currents, such as those caused by a warm front burrowing under and lifting warm air, or else by the heating of air in contact with the surface of the earth on a summer day.

■ The air parcels forming the storm must be buoyant relative to their neighbors outside the storm, and able to rise higher and higher until they pass the freezing level.

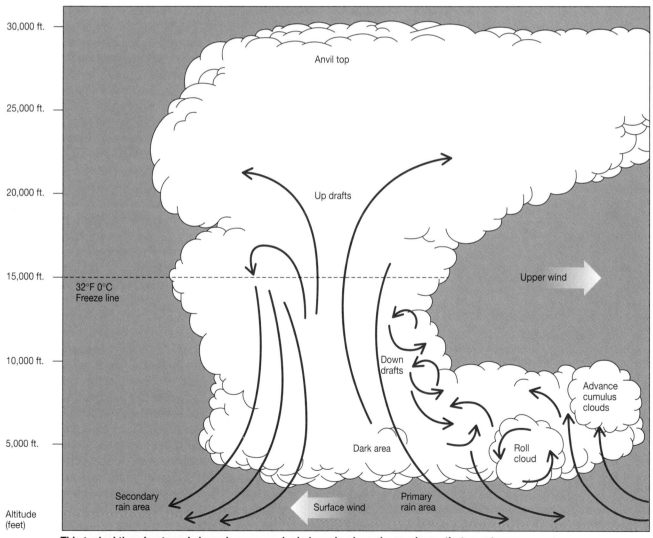

This typical thunderstorm is based on a cumulonimbus cloud, as shown above, that may tower from 25,000 to 50,000 feet high. The anvil top indicates the direction the wind is blowing.

■ The air must have a very large concentration of water vapor. The most promising thunderstorm air is of tropical maritime origin; you need to be particularly watchful whenever it appears in your cruising area, especially if there is a cold front approaching.

The life cycle of a thunderstorm usually lasts about an hour. However, subsequent thunderstorms will often develop near where another dissipates, feeding off moisture left by the earlier storm, making it seem as if the storm is longer-lived. As it begins, a cumulus cloud forms and grows vertically. Boaters should watch such growing storms very closely and be prepared to take evasive or protective actions. Vacuuming air from miles around its base, and feeding on moisture that may have been carried aloft by earlier clouds, the cloud continues growing. Eventually it develops into a cumulonimbus cloud.

Showing the growth of an anvil top, the top photograph was taken at noon, the middle photograph at 12h20, and the bottom photograph at 12h30.

LIGHTNING AND THUNDER

A buildup of dissimilar electrical charges occurs within a vertically developing cumulonimbus cloud, and between the cloud and the earth below. The earth normally has a negative charge. Portions of the cloud become charged electrically, both positive and negative. When the buildup of opposite charges becomes great enough, a lightning flash occurs within a cloud or between the cloud and ground. Actually what we think of as a flash is really a series of strikes back and forth over a period of roughly two-tenths of a second; a flash to the surface usually starts with a faint "leader" from the cloud followed instantly by a massive strike upward from the surface; about two-thirds of all lightning flashes are within clouds, however, and never reach the surface. A lightning flash is almost unbelievably powerful—up to 30,000,000 volts at 100,000 amperes. It happens so quickly that it is essentially explosive in nature.

The sudden, vast amount of heat energy released by a lightning flash causes the sound waves that are called thunder. This release of energy comes from the collapsing of the atmosphere around the lightning strike.

Lightning protection for boats is discussed in chapters 3 and 23.

Characteristics of a thunderstorm

Every thunderstorm cloud has four distinctive features, although you may not always be able to see all four as other clouds may intervene in your line of sight. The illustration of a cumulonimbus cloud, shown opposite, clearly shows these four features. At the top is a layer of cirrus clouds shaped like an anvil and consequently called an anvil top. This cloud layer leans in the direction toward which the upper wind is blowing, and tells us the direction in which the storm is moving. Cirrus clouds are composed of ice crystals rather than water droplets. The development of an anvil top is illustrated at left.

The next feature is the main body of the cloud—a large cumulus of great height with cauliflower sides. The cumulus must be very high as it must extend far above the freezing level if the cirrus anvil top is to form. The third feature is the roll cloud, formed by violent air currents along the leading edge of the base of the cumulus cloud. The fourth and most recognizable feature is the dark area within the storm, extending from the base of the cloud to the earth. At the center of the dark area is rain, at the edges a mixture of hail and rain.

Ahead of a thunderstorm, the wind may be steady or variable. As the roll cloud passes overhead, violent shifting winds accompanied by strong downdrafts may be expected. The wind velocity may reach 60 knots or more. Heavy rain, and sometimes hail, begins to fall just behind the roll cloud. After the storm, the weather quickly clears, bringing cooler temperatures and lower humidity.

If the cumulonimbus cloud is fully developed and towers to normal thunderstorm altitudes—35,000 feet (10.7 km) or more in summer—the storm will be violent. If the anvil top is low—only about 20,000 feet (6.1 km), as is usual in spring and autumn—the storm will be less severe. If the cumulonimbus cloud is not fully developed, particularly if it lacks an anvil top and the roll cloud is missing, only a shower (rain that starts and stops abruptly) may be expected.

The frictional stresses within the storm cloud, generated by the up and down drafts, trigger the lightning and thunder that give a thunderstorm its name. Individually, such storms can produce tornadoes, waterspouts or microbursts with winds measuring over 100 knots. They can spawn hailstones as large as grapefruits, and can generate lightning bolts of unbelievable power. The most violent thunderstorm—the hurricane—can wreak havoc over thousands of square miles.

The deadly tornado

When numerous thunderstorms are associated with a cold front, the storms are apt to be organized in a long, narrow band. The forward edge of this band is usually marked by a squall line, along which the cold downdrafts from a series of thunderstorms meet the warm air. Here the wind direction changes suddenly in vicious gusts, and a sharp drop in temperature occurs. The importance of squall lines is that they often spawn a most destructive type of storm, the tornado. According to the U.S. Department of Commerce (NOAA), "tornados occur in many parts of the world and all 50 states, but no area is more favorable to their formation than the continental plains of North America."

Tornadoes formed at squall lines often occur in families and move with the wind that prevails in the warm sector ahead of the cold front. This wind is usually from the southwest. The warm air typically consists of two layers, a very moist one (source: Gulf of Mexico) near the ground and a relatively dry layer above. The temperature decreases with altitude rather rapidly in each layer. When this combination of air layers is lifted along a squall line or cold front, excessive instability develops and violent updrafts are created.

A tornado is essentially an air whirlpool of small horizontal extent which extends downward from a cumulonimbus cloud and has a funnel-like appearance. The average diameter of the visible funnel cloud is about 250 yards (230 m) but the destructive effects of this system of whirling winds may extend outward from the tornado center as much as ½ mile (0.4 km) on each side. The wind speed near the core can only be estimated, but it undoubtedly is at least as high as 200 knots. Any thunderstorm can produce a tornado. However, the bigger the cumulonimbus cloud, the more likely it is that a thunderstorm will form.

Waterspouts

The marine counterpart of the tornado is the waterspout. The conditions favoring the formation of waterspouts at sea are similar to those conducive to the formation of tornadoes over land. Waterspouts are much more frequent in the trop-

MICROBURST: A DISASTROUS FORCE

There is potential danger lurking within the body of the thunderstorm in the form of a microburst. This is a concentrated column of sinking air that spreads out in all directions when it reaches the surface, generating winds of up to 120 knots. Microbursts often occur in a series of varying powers and dimensions. Although they last only a few minutes, they are known to have capsized and destroyed boats. The following three boating accidents, for example, occurred when thunderstorm activity was approaching the general area:

■ On 7 July 1984 the M/V *Scitanic* capsized on the Tennessee River near Huntsville, Alabama, and 11 passengers trapped inside the vessel were drowned.

■ On 9 June 1977 the charter fishing vessel *Dixie Lee II* capsized in the Chesapeake Bay with the loss of 13 lives in about 60- to 85-knot winds.

■ On 17 June 1978 the showboat *Whippoorwill* capsized on Lake Pomona, Kansas, with the loss of 15 lives in 50-knot winds.

Although microbursts are usually associated with seasonal thunderstorms, they can also occur during rainstorms that are not accompanied by thunder and lightning, such as along squall lines. The strongest winds are in or near the center of the storm where heavy rain, and frequently hail, is falling. Often the gust front precedes the microburst. This is a frontal zone of advancing cold air, characterized by a sudden increase in windspeed, and followed by gusty winds. The combination of these two strong wind systems can easily be fatal.

The best protection against microbursts is avoidance. Prepare for every boating trip by obtaining the latest marine weather forecasts. Listen to the NOAA weather radio channels. Continuous broadcasts of the latest marine weather information are provided on WX-1 (162.55 MHz), WX-2 (162.40 MHz) and WX-3 (162.475 MHz). Canada provides a similar service on Canadian Channel 21 (161.65 MHz). Remember that thunderstorms are dangerous weather systems that can have strong, gusty winds that vary in direction and speed. Be sure that your boat has adequate stability to help you cope with strong winds in the event of their unexpected occurrence.

A waterspout over St. Louis Bay, off Henderson Point, Mississippi. Note the cloud of spray just above the sea surface. This is the marine equivalent of a tornado.

ics than in middle altitudes. Although they are much less violent than tornadoes, waterspouts are nevertheless a very real danger to small craft.

A waterspout, like a tornado, forms under a cumulonimbus cloud. A funnel-shaped protuberance first appears at the base of the cumulonimbus and grows downward toward the sea. Beneath it the water becomes agitated and a cloud of spray forms above the surface. The funnel-shaped cloud descends until it merges with the spray; it then assumes the shape of a tube that stretches from the sea surface to the base of the cloud, as shown above.

The diameter of a waterspout may vary from 20 to 200 feet (6 to 60 m) or more. Its length from the sea to the base of the cloud is usually between 1,000 and 2,000 feet (300 to 600 m). It may last from 10 minutes to half an hour. Its upper part often travels at a different speed and in a different direction from its base, so that it becomes bent and stretched out. Finally, the tube breaks, usually at a point about one-third of the way up to the cloud base. When this happens, the "spout" at the sea surface quickly subsides.

The considerably reduced air pressure at the center of a waterspout is clearly indicated by the visible variations of the water level. A mound of water, a foot or so in height, sometimes appears at the core, because the atmospheric pressure inside the funnel is perhaps 30 to 40 millibars less than that on the surface of the water surrounding the spout. This difference in pressure causes the rise of water at the center.

Like the tornado, the visible part of a waterspout is composed mostly of tiny water droplets formed by the condensation of water vapor in the air. Considerable quantities of salt spray, however, picked up by the strong winds at the base of the spout, are sometimes carried far aloft. This has been verified by observations of a fall of salty rain following the passage of a waterspout.

Anticipating thunderstorms

The possibility of a thunderstorm may be first noticed from static crashes on an AM radio receiver. You can plot the approach, once the cumulonimbus cloud is visible, with a series of bearings. You can also estimate its distance from you. The thunder and lightning occur simultaneously at the point of lightning discharge, but we see the lightning discharge much sooner than we hear the thunder. Time this interval, in seconds. Multiply the number of seconds by 0.2 (or divide by 5); the result will be approximate distance off in statute miles (multiply by 0.34, or divide by 3, to get distance off in kilometers). Take care, however, that you are properly associating a particular flash with its thunder; this may be difficult if there is nearly continuous lightning.

Extra-tropical cyclones

The principal source of foul weather in the United States is the extra-tropical cyclone. Although other storms are more destructive, the extra-tropical cyclone is the ultimate cause of most of our weather troubles. Such a storm (in the northern hemisphere) is defined as a traveling system of winds rotating counterclockwise around a center of low barometric pressure and containing a warm front and a cold front.

How extra-tropical cyclones develop

The development of an extra-tropical cyclone is shown opposite. At A, there is a warm air mass, typically moist tropical air, flowing northeastward, and a cold air mass, typically polar continental, flowing southwestward. They are separated by a heavy line representing the front between them. At B, the cold air pushes down and under the warm air; the warm air rushes up over the cold air ahead of it. A cold front is born on the left, a warm front on the right. Where they are connected, the barometric pressure is lowered and the air starts circulating counterclockwise around this Low. At the rear of the cold front, a high-pressure area develops. At the same time, the whole system keeps moving in a general easterly direction; the dotted area represents rain. When warm, moist air is lifted, as it is when a cold air mass pushes under it or when it rushes up over cold air ahead, it cools by expansion. After its temperature has fallen to the dew point, excess water vapor condenses to form first clouds and then rain.

At C, the storm is steadily developing, with the low pressure area intensifying, the clouds and rain increasing and the winds becoming stronger. At D, the storm is fully mature; note how the gap has narrowed between the fronts.

By the time E is reached, the cold front has caught up with the warm front and an occluded front is formed; the storm is now at its height. When the situation at F is reached, the storm has begun to weaken. Soon the weather will clear, as a high behind the cold front reaches your area.

Extra-tropical cyclones often occur in families of two, three or four storms. It takes about one day (24 hours) for this disturbance to reach maturity with three or possibly four days more required for complete dissipation. In winter, these storms occur on the average of twice a week in the U.S.; in summer they occur somewhat less frequently and are less severe. Their movement is eastward to north of east at a speed in winter of about 700 miles (1,125 km) per day and in summer perhaps 500 miles (800 km). Such storms usually cover a large area; they can affect a given locality for two days or more.

Hurricane: the tropical cyclone

A "hurricane" is the popular term for a tropical cyclone in North America. Unlike the extra-tropical cyclone, it is not related to warm and cold fronts. A hurricane is defined as a storm of tropical origin with a counterclockwise circulation reaching 64 knots (75 mph) or more at the center. In its ear-lier stages with winds less than 33 knots, but with a closed circulatory pattern, the term is a "tropical depression." When the winds increase beyond 33 knots it is a tropical storm until it reaches hurricane strength. In the Western Pacific, the term used for tropical cyclones is "typhoon"; because of the greater expanse of ocean there, these storms often become larger and more intense than hurricanes.

The frequency of tropical cyclones varies around the world. In the Far East typhoons may occur in any month, although they are most common in late summer and early autumn. In North American waters, the period from early December through May is usually hurricane-free. August, September and October are the months of greatest frequency; during these months, hurricanes form over the tropical Atlantic, mostly between latitudes 8°N and 20°N. The infrequent hurricanes of June and November almost always originate in the southwestern part of the Caribbean Sea. (Interestingly, hurricanes do not occur in the South Atlantic.) Hurricanes also occur in the Eastern Pacific off the coast of Mexico, and infrequently the direct effect of these storms reaches well into the southwestern U.S. More frequently, the swells generated by these storms can cause much damage to coastal regions of southern California.

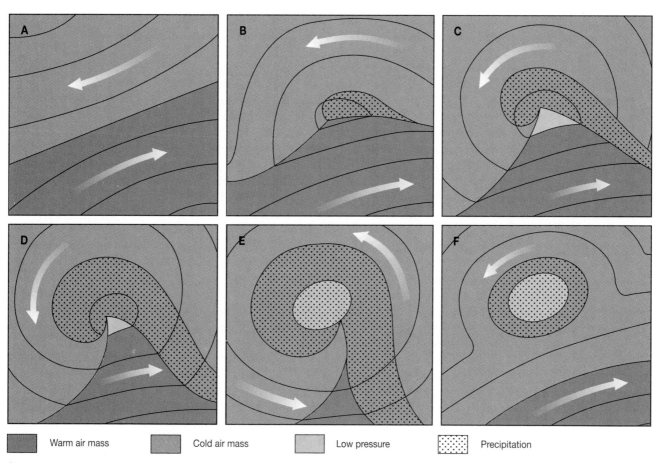

| ▨ Warm air mass | ▨ Cold air mass | ▨ Low pressure | ⬚ Precipitation |

Showing the development of an extra-tropical cyclone, as described in the text above, the thin lines are isobars that pass through points of equal barometric pressure. Arrows indicate wind.

The wall cloud around the eye of a hurricane, as seen from an aircraft within the eye. The upper edge of the cloud is at an altitude of nearly 40,000 feet.

How a hurricane develops

The birthplace of a hurricane typically lies within a diffuse and fairly large area of relatively low pressure situated somewhere in the 8°N to 20°N latitude belt. The winds around the low-pressure area are not particularly strong and, although cumulonimbus clouds and showers are more numerous than is usual in these latitudes, there is no clearly organized "weather system." This poorly defined condition may persist for several days before hurricane development commences. The development of weather satellites has greatly improved the ability of forecasters to watch vast ocean areas, where these storms originate, for any signs of hurricane development.

When development starts, however, it takes place suddenly. Within 12 hours or less the barometric pressure drops 15 millibars or more over a small, almost circular area. Winds of hurricane force spring up and form a ring around the area; the width of this ring is at first only 20 to 40 miles (32 to 64 km). The clouds and showers become well organized and show a spiral structure. At this stage the growing tropical cyclone acquires an eye. This is the inner area enclosed by the ring of hurricane-force winds. It expands to a width of 100 miles (160 km) or more by the time the cyclone reaches maturity. Within the eye we find the lowest barometric reading.

The eye averages about 15 miles (24 km) in diameter but may be as large as 25 miles (40 km). The wind velocities within the eye are seldom greater than 15 knots and often are less. Cloud conditions vary over a wide range. At times there are only scattered clouds, but usually there is more than 50 percent cloud cover. Through the openings the sky is visible overhead and, at a distance, the dense towering clouds of the hurricane ring can be seen extending to great heights, as shown above. This is the wall cloud. Seas within the eye are heavy and confused; the calm is only with respect to winds.

Tracking a hurricane

The usual track of an Atlantic hurricane is a parabola around the semipermanent Azores-Bermuda high-pressure area. Consequently, after forming, a hurricane will move westward on the southern side of this High, at the same time tending to work away from the equator. When the hurricane reaches the western side of the High, it begins to follow a more northerly track, and it advances progressively toward the right. The position where the westward movement changes to an eastward movement is known as the point of curvature.

Occasionally when a hurricane is in a position near the southeast Atlantic coast, the Azores-Bermuda High happens to have an abnormal northward extension. In this situation the hurricane may fail to execute a complete recurvature in the

Heading west from the Bahamas, Hurricane Andrew hit the coast of southeast Florida on August 24, 1992, as shown in this satellite image. The storm cut a swath of destruction across the state, before spinning over the Gulf of Mexico and then north into Louisiana and Mississippi.

vicinity of Cape Hatteras. It will skirt the western side of the High and come ashore along the southeast coast of the U.S., as occurred with Hurricane Andrew, a major storm of 1992.

The rate of movement of tropical cyclones while they are still in low latitudes and heading westward is about 15 knots, which is considerably slower than the usual rate of travel of extra-tropical cyclones. After recurving they begin to move faster, usually attaining a forward speed of at least 25 knots, sometimes 50 to 60 knots, as in the case of Hugo, a major hurricane of 1989. Other storms, particularly early in the season, form in the Caribbean Sea and move west and north into the Gulf of Mexico. Still other hurricanes follow quite erratic paths, even looping back on their tracks.

Hurricanes decrease in intensity after they reach middle and high latitudes and move over colder water. Many lose their identity by absorption into the wind circulation around the larger extra-tropical cyclones of the North Atlantic.

USING WEATHER FORECASTS

Although weather forecasting is a science that has improved in recent years, every skipper knows that it is far from infallible. Get your forecasts by any and all means possible, but keep an eye on present local conditions—and especially on changes in them. A forecast of good, safe conditions for your general area does not preclude temporary local differences that could be hazardous. Following a preliminary announcement on Channel 16, keep alert also for special warnings broadcast by the Coast Guard on VHF Channel 22A.

Weather maps

Information on weather maps is presented through symbols. The most frequently used symbols are described below; many others, used only by professionals, have been omitted.

■ **Station models.** A complete station model (*page 322*) for a reporting location typically includes information about wind direction and speed; temperature; visibility; cloud type, amount and height; current pressure at sea level and past change plus current tendency; precipitation in the past six hours; dew-point temperatures and current weather. Simplified station models will omit much of this information, and often simply show current weather and temperature, as well as wind direction and speed.

Cloud cover is indicated by the appearance of the circle in the center of the station model—open for clear, partially or totally solid for degrees of cloudiness. Current weather (rain, snow, drizzle, etc.) is shown by a symbol immediately to the left of the station circle. Wind direction is indicated by a

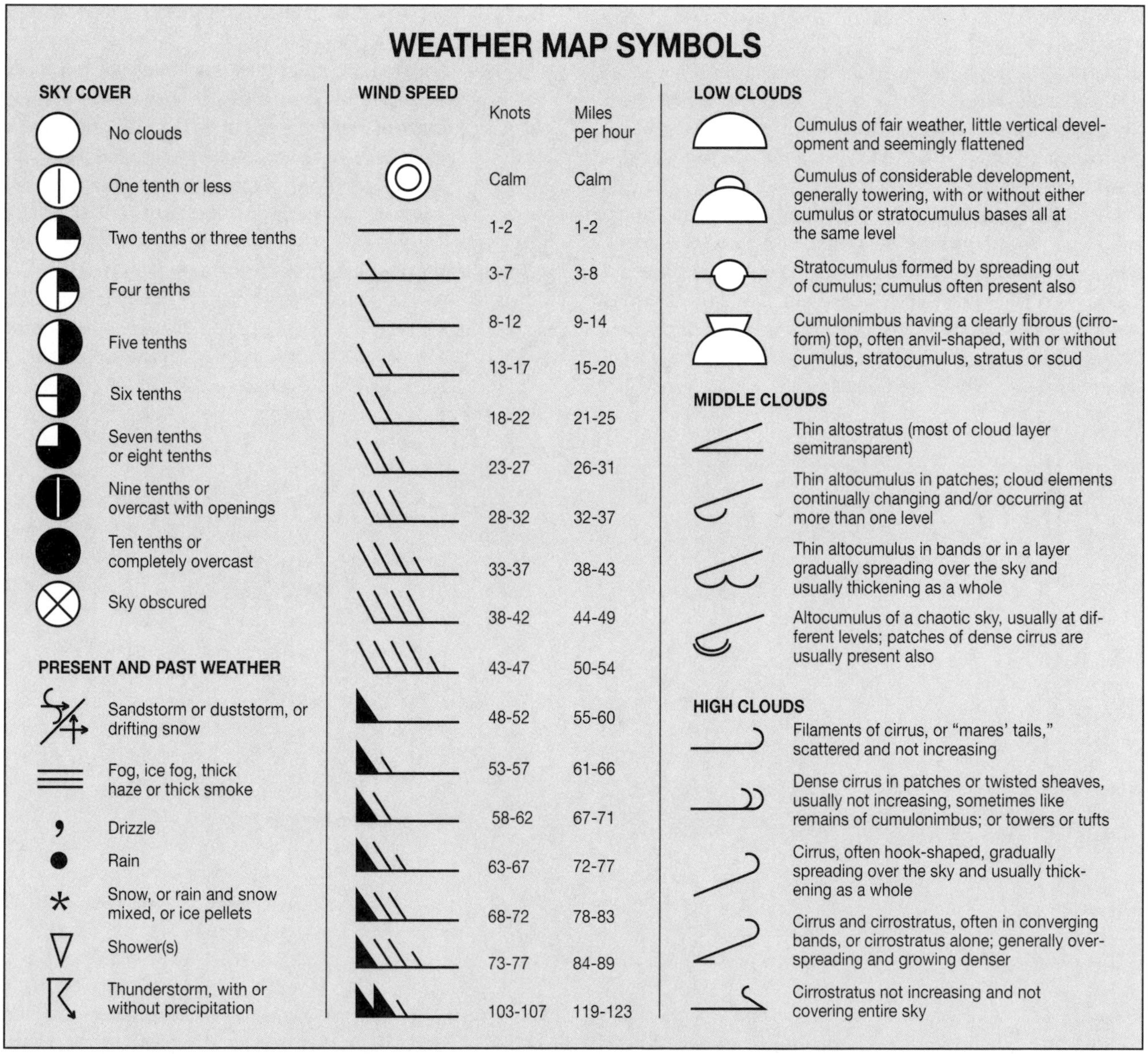

WEATHER MAP SYMBOLS

SKY COVER

- No clouds
- One tenth or less
- Two tenths or three tenths
- Four tenths
- Five tenths
- Six tenths
- Seven tenths or eight tenths
- Nine tenths or overcast with openings
- Ten tenths or completely overcast
- Sky obscured

PRESENT AND PAST WEATHER

- Sandstorm or duststorm, or drifting snow
- Fog, ice fog, thick haze or thick smoke
- Drizzle
- Rain
- Snow, or rain and snow mixed, or ice pellets
- Shower(s)
- Thunderstorm, with or without precipitation

WIND SPEED

	Knots	Miles per hour
	Calm	Calm
	1-2	1-2
	3-7	3-8
	8-12	9-14
	13-17	15-20
	18-22	21-25
	23-27	26-31
	28-32	32-37
	33-37	38-43
	38-42	44-49
	43-47	50-54
	48-52	55-60
	53-57	61-66
	58-62	67-71
	63-67	72-77
	68-72	78-83
	73-77	84-89
	103-107	119-123

LOW CLOUDS

- Cumulus of fair weather, little vertical development and seemingly flattened
- Cumulus of considerable development, generally towering, with or without either cumulus or stratocumulus bases all at the same level
- Stratocumulus formed by spreading out of cumulus; cumulus often present also
- Cumulonimbus having a clearly fibrous (cirroform) top, often anvil-shaped, with or without cumulus, stratocumulus, stratus or scud

MIDDLE CLOUDS

- Thin altostratus (most of cloud layer semitransparent)
- Thin altocumulus in patches; cloud elements continually changing and/or occurring at more than one level
- Thin altocumulus in bands or in a layer gradually spreading over the sky and usually thickening as a whole
- Altocumulus of a chaotic sky, usually at different levels; patches of dense cirrus are usually present also

HIGH CLOUDS

- Filaments of cirrus, or "mares' tails," scattered and not increasing
- Dense cirrus in patches or twisted sheaves, usually not increasing, sometimes like remains of cumulonimbus; or towers or tufts
- Cirrus, often hook-shaped, gradually spreading over the sky and usually thickening as a whole
- Cirrus and cirrostratus, often in converging bands, or cirrostratus alone; generally overspreading and growing denser
- Cirrostratus not increasing and not covering entire sky

The symbols shown above are those found on weather maps issued by the National Weather Service in the United States. The Specimen Station Model on page 328 shows how these symbols indicate weather conditions.

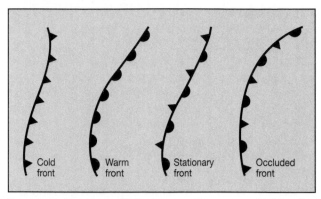

Fronts are shown as solid lines on weather maps, with triangles or half circles used singly or in combination to indicate the type of front. These symbols face the direction that the pressure system and its front are moving.

Cold front / Warm front / Stationary front / Occluded front

Fronts are shown as a heavy line. Cold fronts have a series of solid triangles on the line which point in the direction of movement, as shown at left. Warm fronts have solid half-circles on the line, again the side that they are on indicating the direction of movement of the front. An occluded front has alternating triangles and half-circles on the same side of the line. A stationary front has the same alternating symbols but with the triangles on one side of the line and the half-circles on the other, indicating no movement.

In some sketches, a cold front is shown by a solid heavy line while a warm front is two parallel fine lines; therefore, an occluded front is shown with alternating solid and open segments. On less detailed maps, a front may be shown as merely a heavy line labeled "Cold," "Warm" or "Stationary" Front. In TV color weather maps, a warm front is normally shown in red, with a cold front in blue and an occluded front in purple.

weather vane line radiating from the center, and wind speed by the number, size and shape of the "feathers" on the end of the weather vane. Temperature will normally be given in degrees Fahrenheit (degrees Celsius in Canada and other areas using the metric system).

■ **Air masses and fronts.** Air masses, if shown, are in large block letters, usually P for polar and T for tropical. Either of these may be further described as maritime (m) or continental (c). Consequently we have cP, mP and mT—the most common air masses— as well as cT. Since K indicates unstable, and W, stable, more precise labels would include cPk and mPw, for example. Highs are designated by a large block H, and Lows with an L.

■ **Isobars.** An isobar is a line connecting points of equal barometric pressure. Such lines are usually drawn on weather maps at intervals of four millibars of pressure—for example, 1020, 1024, 1028, etc.—and are labeled along the line or at each end. On some weather maps, isobars will be labeled for pressure in terms of inches of mercury—29.97, 30.00, 30.03, etc.

■ **Precipitation.** Any precipitation—rain, snow or hail—is shown by one of a series of symbols, as shown on page 321. On less detailed maps, areas of precipitation are often shown by shading or crosshatching, with a descriptive word nearby or different forms of shading used to distinguish rain, snow and other forms of precipitation.

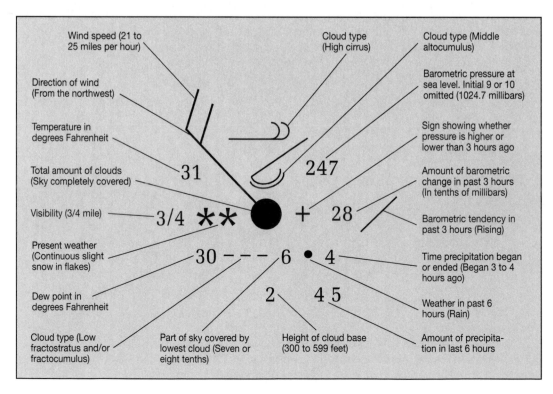

Wind speed (21 to 25 miles per hour)
Cloud type (High cirrus)
Cloud type (Middle altocumulus)
Direction of wind (From the northwest)
Barometric pressure at sea level. Initial 9 or 10 omitted (1024.7 millibars)
Temperature in degrees Fahrenheit
Sign showing whether pressure is higher or lower than 3 hours ago
Total amount of clouds (Sky completely covered)
Amount of barometric change in past 3 hours (In tenths of millibars)
Visibility (3/4 mile)
Barometric tendency in past 3 hours (Rising)
Present weather (Continuous slight snow in flakes)
Time precipitation began or ended (Began 3 to 4 hours ago)
Dew point in degrees Fahrenheit
Weather in past 6 hours (Rain)
Cloud type (Low fractostratus and/or fractocumulus)
Part of sky covered by lowest cloud (Seven or eight tenths)
Height of cloud base (300 to 599 feet)
Amount of precipitation in last 6 hours

31   247
3/4 ✳✳   + 28
30 – – – 6 • 4
2   4 5

The specimen station model at left shows how weather map symbols are used to indicate weather conditions.

Using weather maps

Unless you have a weather facsimile machine, it is quite unlikely that you would have a weather map, yet not have a printed or broadcast forecast. However, you might like to try your hand at making predictions from one or more weather maps.

Predictions from a single map are, of course, less accurate and less reliable than those based on a series of weather maps over regular intervals of time. Since there are many factors that can upset an orderly flow of events, a forecast from a single map can only be made for 6 to 12 hours ahead. (Make sure that you are using a map of actual conditions as of a specified recent time; many weather maps now printed in newspapers are for predicted conditions of the day of publication.) Assume that a front is advancing at roughly 20 miles an hour in the normal direction of movement. Sketch in the position of the front 12 hours after the date and time of the map—assuming that your map of actual conditions is recent enough that you still have time in which to make a usable 12-hour forecast. Then, with the knowledge of the conditions accompanying this front, you can make your own forecast.

If you have a series of maps of existing weather conditions at daily or half-daily intervals, you can make a much better forecast. Predict your frontal movement based on trends as well as actual events. If weather progressions tend to repeat themselves in your area, file sets of weather maps for typical frontal passages as additional guidance.

■ **Television weather maps.** Weather maps shown as part of local or network news programs also vary widely in level of detail. They do have advantages over newspaper maps in that they frequently show current conditions, and color is used for a more vivid presentation. Some TV weather reporters use animation to show predicted movement of fronts and weather patterns. Often satellite photographs, either still photos or time-lapse loops, are shown to explain conditions or trends. Current weather radar scans are also interesting and helpful in visualizing rain patterns out to a radius of about 125 miles (200 km).

Many local Cable TV systems carry "The Weather Channel"—a continuous live broadcast of weather conditions and forecasts. Information is highly detailed and several spe-

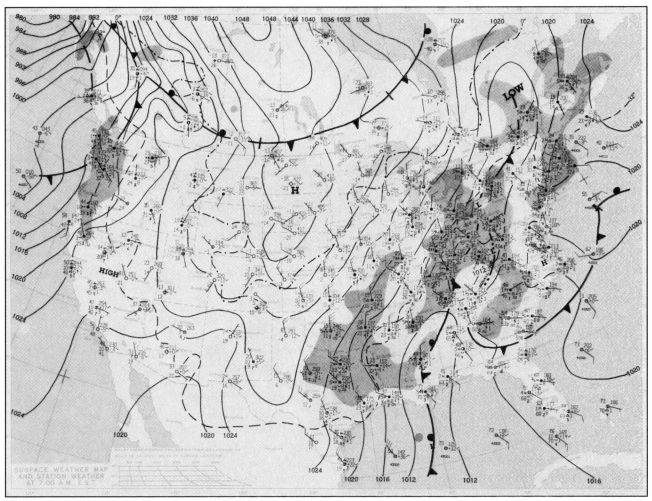

The daily weather map is mailed on a weekly basis from the National Weather Service to subscribers. The back of each Sunday map carries a full illustration and explanation of all symbols used.

WEATHER WARNING SIGNALS			
	Day Flags	**Night Lights**	**Explanations**
Small Craft			One red pennant displayed by day and a red light above a white light at night, to indicate that fairly strong winds up to 33 knots (38mph) and/or sea conditions dangerous to small-craft operations are forecast for the area.
Gale	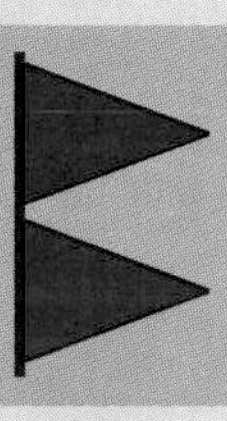		Two red pennants displayed by day and a white light above a red light at night, to indicate that winds ranging from 34 to 47 knots (39 to 54 mph) are forecast.
Storm			A single square red flag with black center displayed by day and two red lights at night, to indicate that winds 48 knots (55mph) and above (no matter how high the velocity) are forecast. Note: If winds are associated with a tropical cyclone (hurricane) the storm warning display indicates forecast winds of 48 to 63 knots (55 to 73 mph).
Hurricane			Two square red flags with black centers displayed by day and a white light between two red lights at night, to indicate that winds 64 knots (74 mph) and above are forecast. Hurricane warnings are displayed only for tropical cyclones. Hurricane warnings are not issued for the Great Lakes.

Although the National Weather Service has discontinued the official system of flags and lights shown at left, these may still be seen from some shore installations.

cialized services are included. Weather maps in a number of formats are shown, as well as satellite pictures and radar plots showing areas of significant weather activity. Periodically, the national information is interrupted for local weather reports and predictions.

■ **Other weather maps.** Other than the "surface analysis"-type map that is usually seen by the public, many other weather maps exist. These include upper-air maps for constant pressure levels, such as the 500-millibar map for an altitude of roughly 18,000 feet (5,500 m). These maps show how winds at these levels "steer" surface weather patterns; however, their use requires specialized training and experience.

Weather forecasts

The professional meteorologist takes great care in the preparation of forecasts. Your responsibility is to read or listen carefully for the facts.

Most times on a boat you will get your forecast by listening to a radio transmission. If it is a scheduled broadcast, get a pencil and paper ready and take notes; if you have to use an abbreviated format to keep up with the flow of information, expand your fragments into complete form as soon as possible while the data are still fresh in your mind. Using a small tape recorder can help. If it is a continuous broadcast, still take notes but listen a second time to expand your initial notes; lis-

ten as many times as necessary to get the details fully and accurately. Special severe weather warnings on NWS stations are preceded by a ten-second high-pitched tone—your cue to grab paper and pencil.

If you are watching a TV weather report and forecast, it is just as important to take notes, dividing your attention between the picture on the screen and your notepad.

In most instances, you will be able to get a forecast for your waters. If you can't, try to get a forecast for the region westward of you and apply your knowledge of weather movement to make a forecast for your own area.

Keep your weather-forecast notes and compare them with actual conditions later. You may be able to detect a pattern of error in the forecasts, such as weather frequently arriving 12 hours or so later than forecast. (Apparently, some forecasters would rather you be prepared a bit early for a storm arrival than to be caught short.)

Weather forecast advisories and warnings

The National Weather Service (NWS) has an ascending series of alerting messages—advisories, watches and warnings—for mariners. These are keyed to increasingly hazardous weather and sea conditions.

The Weather Service emphasizes that visual storm warnings that are displayed along the coast (*above*) are only supplementary to the written advisories and warnings given prompt and wide distribution by press, radio and television. Important details of the forecasts and warnings in regard to the time, intensity, duration and direction of storms cannot be given satisfactorily through visual signals alone.

Official information is issued by hurricane centers describing all tropical cyclone advisories, watches and warnings in effect. These bulletins include tropical cyclone locations, intensity and movement, and special precautions that should be taken. Advisories describe tropical cyclones and subtropical cyclones prior to issuance of watches and warnings. When a hurricane threatens, an NWS watch or warning may result. A hurricane watch is an announcement for specific areas that a hurricane or an incipient hurricane condition poses a possible threat to coastal areas—generally within 36 hours. A hurricane warning informs the public that sustained winds of 64 knots (74 mph) or higher associated with a hurricane are expected in a specified coastal area within 24 hours or less. This warning can remain in effect when dangerously high water or a combination of dangerously high water and exceptionally high waves continue, even though winds may be less than hurricane force.

The term "small craft advisory" needs some explanation. Small craft as defined by the Weather Service are "small boats, yachts, tugs, barges with little freeboard or any other low-

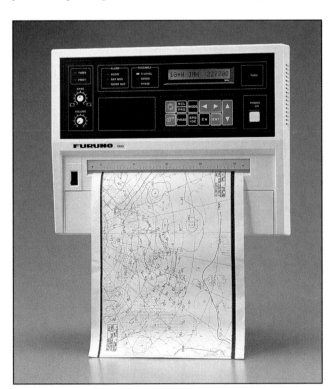

A weather fax, which prints out weather information on a chart, enables you to track (even from a distance) the center of a storm that may be heading in your direction. Such equipment, which requires a single sideband radio receiver, is usually found on seagoing boats.

READING LOCAL WEATHER SIGNS

While weather forecasts are helpful, and you should always take care to get them, they are not completely dependable and they are normally made for a relatively large area. To supplement the official forecast, look about your boat frequently. Notice both the current weather and changes over the last hour or so. Finally, you should know how to interpret the weather signs that you see in the clouds, winds, and pressure and temperature changes, as described in this chapter and summarized below. If you are not in home waters, local advice may assist you with forecasting, just as it does with navigation.

Watching the clouds *(pages 298-301)*

- Can you identify the cloud form(s)?

- Are they increasing or decreasing in amount?

- Are they lowering or lifting? In general, lowering and thickening cloud forms herald approaching wet weather. Holes in the clouds or fraying at the edges indicate that the weather may be improving.

- What has been the sequence of cloud forms during the last few hours? For example, cirrus clouds are often the advance agents of an extra-tropical cyclone.

Observing the wind *(pages 305-307)*

- What is the true wind direction? Remember that direction is determined with reference to the deviation of your compass and the variation for your particular anchorage, and that true direction is always stated as the direction from which—and not toward which—the wind is blowing.

- Can you measure or estimate the wind speed?

Pressure *(pages 308-310)* **and temperature**

- Is the barometric pressure rising? Is it falling?

- What is the rate of pressure change over a period of hours?

- What is the temperature reading? Although thermometer readings will not give as much information for weather predicting as data from other instruments, they are not without some value. For example, cold air carried down from a thunderstorm cloud with the rain may be felt as much as three miles in advance of the storm itself.

powered craft." A small-craft advisory does not distinguish between the expectation of a general, all-day blow of 25 knots or more and, for example, a forecast of isolated, late-afternoon thundersqualls in which winds dangerous to small craft will be localized and of short duration. It is up to you to deduce from your own observations, supplemented by any information you can obtain from radio broadcasts, which type of situation the advisory applies to, and how to plan your day's cruising accordingly.

Marine Weather Services charts

The National Weather Service publishes a series of 15 *Marine Weather Services Charts* that cover the coastal waters of the United States, the Great Lakes, the Hawaiian Islands, Puerto Rico and the Virgin Islands. These charts, of which the one below is an example, contain detailed information regarding the times of weather broadcasts from commercial stations, the locations of NWS continuous FM broadcasts and their frequencies, as well as other information useful to boaters. The day and night visual signals—no longer official, but continued from some locations—are illustrated and explained. These charts can be purchased from the Superintendent of Documents, Government Printing Office, Washington, DC 20402, from Regional GPO bookstores in many cities, and from some local sales agents for charts.

Boaters will also find interesting weather information on the various Pilot Charts of the North Atlantic and North Pacific Oceans issued by the DMA Hydrographic/Topographic Center. The Pilot Charts show average monthly wind and weather conditions over the oceans and contain a vast amount of data on subjects allied to weather. *Coast Pilot* volumes also contain information on weather broadcasts.

Weather maps at sea

Just because you are offshore and not receiving your daily newspaper, you need not be without a reliable and up-to-date weather map. Facsimile radio transmissions can be received by a high-frequency receiver and processed in a unit that prints a weather map line by line. These transmissions, often called radiofax, or weatherfax, are broadcast on regular schedules by a number of shore stations. The receiver can be your regular communications set, or it can be built into the printer; the latter is more convenient to use, but more costly. An onboard personal computer and printer can be fitted with special hardware and software. A number of different charts are transmitted: surface analysis, prognosis (forecasts for 12, 24, 36 or 48 hours), upper-air winds, wave analysis, sea water temperature, satellite photographs and others. Unlike radio broadcasts, these charts give "hard-copy" pictures of current or forecast conditions that you can study in detail.

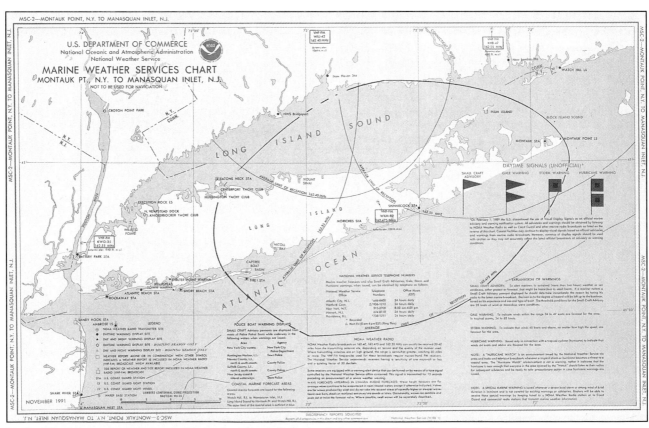

Marine Weather Services Charts provide the locations where visual signals may be displayed, and the locations, call signs and frequencies of the VHF-FM radio weather broadcast stations in the charted area.

BOAT WEATHER LOG
Yacht_____At/Passage_____ to _____
Day_____ Date_____ Time Zone_____ Skipper_____
1. Latest Weather Map: Date_____Time_____Summary of forecast and of
principal regional weather features: _____
_____
_____
_____
_____
2. Radio Weather Reports Received (state source and time): _____
_____
_____
_____
_____
3. Local Weather Observations
4. Remarks and Local Forecast for Next_____Hours (state time forecast
effective): _____

LOCAL WEATHER OBSERVATIONS
Time
Latitude—degrees, minutes
Longitude—degrees, minutes
Course—degrees mag.
—degrees true
Speed—Knots
Barometer—in. or mb.
—tendency
Clouds—form
—moving from
—amount
—changing to
Sea—condition
—swells
—moving from
Temperatures—air, dry bulb
—dewpoint
—water
Visibility
Wind—direction, true
—shifting to
—velocity, true
—force (Beaufort)
Weather—present

The weather log *(left)* is used to record information developed from weather maps, or received by radio, and the forecast based on this data. The reverse side of the page *(right)* is used for local weather observations. By recording this information and keeping the record, it is possible to develop considerable skill in making forecasts.

However, you don't need expensive equipment to receive this type of information. It is also broadcast in Morse code, from which you can sketch in your own weather map on the standard blank chart forms available at no charge from Port Meteorological officers at major ports. You don't need to know the code; all data are the figures 0 through 9, and these fit a simple pattern of five dots or dashes. Instructions on how to use the data are given in *Worldwide Marine Weather Broadcasts*, which also contains information on station frequencies and schedules. The speed of transmission is not fast, but accuracy in copying the figures, which are in groups of five, can be improved by using a tape recorder and replaying one or more times for double-checking or to fill any gaps. It is even better to have a two-speed recorder recording at the higher speed, then playing at the lower speed as you write down the figures.

Keeping a weather log

Although the latest Weather Service forecasts are readily available via radio, it is often helpful to record your own cloud and weather observations. You can then check the reliability of the latest prediction. Occasionally the professional forecaster misjudges the future rate of travel of the weather pattern, which may move faster or slower than anticipated. Or a new, unforeseen development in the pattern may occur.

The form of weather log shown above is suitable for use on recreational boats. The first weather items recorded are based on a reading of the latest weather map, if available, and a summary of any radio reports received. Then use the reverse side to jot down your local observations. Sufficient columns are available to permit the entry of these data six times during one 24-hour day, at four-hour intervals. Entries may be made using the standard weather code symbols or any other method you choose, provided you use the same system consistently.

From your own records and observations you can estimate how and to what extent the actual weather conditions during the next few hours might differ from those predicted in the official forecast.

WEATHER PROVERB
Lightning from the west or northwest will reach you,
Lightning from the south or southeast will pass you by.
This is a true saying, if you live in the north temperate zone. Lightning comes hand in hand with storm clouds, and thunderheads always loom over the horizon from the west or northwest, and usually move east. So lightning anywhere from the south to southeast will pass you by.

15 TIDES AND CURRENTS

An understanding of tides and currents is important to a skipper in coastal waters, as these can affect where he or she can travel or anchor safely, how long it will take to get there—or the speed needed to arrive at a given time—and the heading it is necessary to maintain in order to make good a given course over the bottom.

This chapter tells you how tides and currents are formed, and gives you the basics for applying that knowledge to your boating experience. It helps you determine the state of tide or tidal current flow in coastal waters; it also tells you how to allow for current and determine its strength. The tide level and *Tidal Current Table* exercises will help you hone your skills, so that you can make calculations quickly when you need to.

WHY WE HAVE TIDES AND CURRENTS

There are two terms that are often used incorrectly in connection with tides—the term "tide" itself and the term "tidal current." The material in this chapter will be more easily understood if these two terms are used in their formal sense.

Tide is the rise and fall of the ocean level as a result of changes in the gravitational attraction between the earth, moon and sun. It is a vertical motion only. Current is the horizontal motion of water from any cause. Tidal current is the horizontal flow of water from one point to another that results from a difference in tidal heights at those points. To say, "the tide certainly is running strongly today" is not correct, for tides may be high or low, but they do not "run." The correct expression would be, "the tidal current certainly is strong today." Remember—tide is vertical change in level while current is horizontal flow.

Tides originate in the open oceans and seas, but are only noticeable and significant close to shore. The effect of tides will be observed along coastal beaches, in bays and sounds and up rivers generally as far as the first rapids, waterfall or dam. Curiously, the effect of tides may be more noticeable a hundred miles up a river than it is at the river's mouth, because water piles up higher in its narrower stretches. Coastal regions in which the water levels are subject to tidal action are often referred to as "tidewater" areas.

Certain other terms used in connection with tidal action also must be understood. These are defined on page 330.

Earth, moon and sun

Tidal theory involves the interaction of gravitational and centrifugal forces. The inward attractions of the earth, on one hand, and the sun and the moon on the other, are balanced by the outward forces resulting from the revolutions of the earth and the moon in their respective orbits. The gravitational and centrifugal forces are in balance as a whole—otherwise the bodies would fly apart from each other or else crash together—but they are not quite in balance at most points on the earth's surface; this is what causes tides.

The effects of the sun and moon are best understood separately even though they act simultaneously.

Earth-sun effects

As the earth travels in its elliptical orbit around the sun it is affected by a centrifugal force that tries to pull it off into space. (Remember that we are talking about the centrifugal force related to the sun-earth system, and not that of the spinning of the earth on its own axis.) The earth is kept from flying off into space by the gravitational pull of the sun. These forces are in overall balance, but this balance is not exact at all points.

The centrifugal force is the same everywhere on the planet, always pulling away from the sun in a direction parallel to a line from the center of the earth to the center of the sun. Gravitational force does not act equally everywhere in a line

parallel to the line from the center of the earth to the sun. On the contrary, gravitational forces extend from each point on the earth's surface toward the center of the sun. Gravity is greater at points on the earth nearer the sun as a result of the lesser distance.

It's easier to visualize the action of these forces on tides by thinking of the earth as being a smooth sphere, without land masses, and uniformly covered with water. The gravitational and centrifugal forces cause the water to flow, respectively, toward the areas of the earth's surface that are nearest to, and the areas that are farthest from, the sun; these areas will have "high tides." The areas from which this water flows will have less water, and hence "low tides." (The tides on the side of the earth that is nearer the sun are slightly greater than those on the far side, but the difference is not great, amounting to only about 5 percent.)

As the earth rotates on its axis once every 24 hours, the point closest to or farthest from the sun constantly changes. Thus each point of the earth's surface would, in theory, have two high and two low tides each day. As a result of the tilt of the earth's axis, the pairs of highs, and of lows, will not normally be of exactly the same level.

Earth-moon effects

The moon is commonly thought of as revolving about the earth but, in fact, the two bodies revolve around a common point which is situated deep inside the earth. This point is located about 2,900 miles (4,667 km) from the center of the earth toward the moon, or about 1,100 miles (1,770 km) inside the earth.

Both the earth and the moon tend to fly away from this common point (centrifugal force), but the mutual gravitational attraction acts as a counterbalance and they remain roughly the same distance apart. However, the gravitational pull of the moon affects the waters of the earth in the same manner as the pull of the sun.

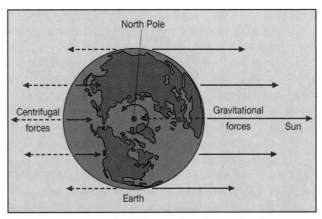

Tides result from the differences between centrifugal forces and gravitational forces. The forces illustrated here represent the interaction of the earth and sun; corresponding forces result from the relationship between the earth and the moon.

- **Diurnal tides.** Only a single high water and a single low water take place each day.

- **Semi-diurnal tides.** Two high water levels and two low water levels occur in each approximately 24-hour period.

- **High water** or **high tide.** The highest level reached by an ascending tide.

- **Low water** or **low tide.** The lowest level reached by a descending tide.

- **Range.** The difference between high water level and the following low water, or vice versa.

- **Mean low water (MLW).** The average height of all low waters at a place over a 19-year cycle.

- **Mean lower low water (MLLW).** The average height of the lower low waters over a 19-year cycle.

- **Mean high water.** The average height of all high waters over a 19-year cycle.

- **Mean higher high water.** The average height of the higher high waters over a 19-year cycle.

- **Tidal datum.** A reference level from which heights and depths are measured. On a chart this is known as a **chart datum**; this is the most important level of reference to the mariner. The level used as chart datum is normally low enough so that low waters don't go far below it. Tide heights are normally positive, but the height can be a small negative number, if the low water level falls below the datum. In the U.S., mean lower low water is used as tidal datum. Tidal data in the U.S. are determined relative to a 19-year period called a Tidal Datum Epoch. The most recent one was 1960-1978.

- **Height of tide** at any specified time is the vertical measurement between the surface of the water and tidal datum. Do not confuse height of tide with depth of water.

- **Mean sea level.** The average height of the surface of the sea for all stages of tide. It differs slightly from **mean tide level** (or half tide level), which is the plane midway between mean high water and mean low water. It is not used in navigation.

- **Stand.** The point when vertical movement ceases.

Combined effects

Now combine the earth-sun and earth-moon systems. Although the mass of the moon is only a tiny fraction of that of the sun, it is much closer to the earth (about 238,860 miles or 384,400 km) and its pull is about twice as powerful. As a result, the observed tide usually "follows the moon," although the action is modified by the sun's relative position. Tidal rhythm therefore is generally in tune with the apparent rotation of the moon around the earth. Since this "lunar day" is 24 hours and 50 minutes, the two high and two low waters each day occur about 50 minutes later than the corresponding tides of the previous day.

In the course of any one month, the sun, moon and earth are in conjunction—lined up. The moon is "new" when the line-up is in sun-moon-earth order and "full" when the order is sun-earth-moon, as shown on page 332. In both cases, the sun's tidal effect lines up with and reinforces the moon's tidal effect, resulting in greater-than-average tidal ranges (about 20 percent) called spring tides. (Note that this name has nothing to do with the season of the year.)

In the illustration on page 332, when the moon is at its first and third quarters, the tidal "bulge" caused by the sun is at right angles to that caused by the moon. (At this point,

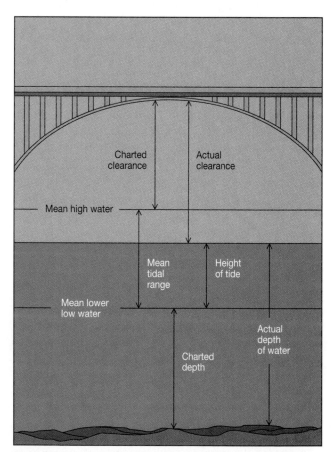

Mean lower low water is the reference datum for all **NOS** tide heights. Bridge clearances are measured from mean high water. Tidal range is the difference between these two levels.

they are said to be "in quadrature.") The two tidal effects are in conflict and partially cancel each other, resulting in smaller-than-average ranges (again about 20 percent)—these are called neap tides.

A separate monthly variation results from the fact that the earth is not at the center of the moon's orbit and the orbit is in the shape of an ellipse, not a circle. When the moon is closest to the earth (at perigee), the lunar influence is maximum and tides will have the greatest ranges. Conversely, when the moon is farthest from the earth (at apogee), its effect and tidal ranges are least.

The tidal range at any given point varies not only from month to month, but from year to year. Yearly variations in daily tidal ranges are caused by the changing gravitational effects

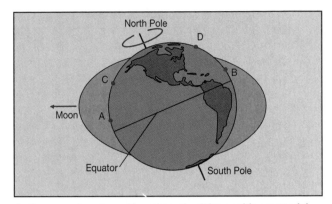

As the moon travels north and south of the earth's equatorial plane, it causes variations in the daily tidal cycle at any given location. Similar, but smaller, effects result from the sun's change in position with respect to the equator.

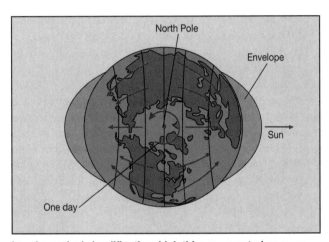

In a theoretical simplification, high tides are created on opposite sides of the earth at the same time. The gravitational attraction of the moon (or sun) pulls one way and the centrifugal force of the earth's orbit pulls the other way.

of the sun as that body's distance from the earth becomes greater or less—perihelion and aphelion. Tidal predictions repeat only in a cycle of roughly 19 years.

Types of tides

A tide that each day has two high waters approximately equal in height, and two low waters also about equal, is known as a semi-diurnal tide. This is the most common type, and, in the United States, occurs along the East Coast. Refer to the illustration on page 332, top.

In a monthly cycle, the moon travels north and south of the equator. The illustration above, right, shows the importance of this action on tides in certain areas. At a given time, for example, Point A is under the bulge in the envelope created by the moon's pull. Twelve hours later Point B is under the bulge, but as it is closer to the edge of the envelope, the height of water is not as high. This situation tends to give rise to a "twice daily" tide with unequal high and/or low waters, known as a mixed tide—the type experienced at San Francisco. In mixed tide areas, the more pronounced

of the two low waters is termed lower low water. Mean lower low water (MLLW) is the level used as the tidal datum. Likewise, the more significant of the higher tides is termed higher high water.

Now consider Point C in the illustration. This place is still under the bulge of the envelope. However, one-half day later, at Point D, it is above the envelope. Hence the tidal forces tend to cause only one high and one low water each day (actually, approximately each 24 hours and 50 minutes. This is a diurnal tide, typified by that at Pensacola, Florida.

Diurnal or mixed-type tides are more likely to occur when the moon is farthest north or south in its orbit. When the moon lies over the equator, the tendency toward tidal inequality is at a minimum, and the tides are semi-diurnal.

Actual tides

Tidal theory is modified in practice by many factors. The major one is the general configuration of the coastline, which interrupts, restricts and deflects tidal movements, but other factors include the following:

■ Water is actually somewhat viscous, rather than free-flowing, which produces a lag in reaction to tidal forces.

■ Friction is created as the ocean waters "rub" against the ocean bottom.

■ The depth to the bottom of the sea varies widely, influencing the speed of the horizontal tidal motion.

■ The depths of the ocean areas and the restrictions of the continents often result in "basins" that have their own way of responding to tidal forces.

Although these factors account for great differences between theoretical tidal forces and actual observed tides, there remain nevertheless definite, constant relationships between the two at any particular location. By observing the tide and relating these observations with the movements of the sun, moon and earth these constant relationships can be determined. With this information, tides can be predicted for any future date at a given place.

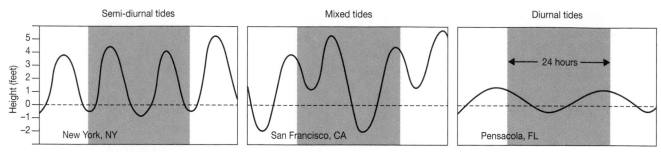

Semi-diurnal tides · Mixed tides · Diurnal tides

New York, NY · San Francisco, CA · Pensacola, FL

The daily cycle of tides (blue—a 24-hour period) varies widely from place to place. There are three basic types—semi-diurnal *(left)*, mixed *(center)* and diurnal *(right)*.

Special tidal situations

Peculiarities in the tide can be found almost everywhere, but none compare with those in the Bay of Fundy. Twice each day, the waters surge in and out of the Bay producing, at Burntcoat Head, the highest tidal range in the world—a typical rise and fall of nearly 44 feet (13.4 m). At normal spring tides, the water rises 51½ feet (16.9 m) and on perigee springs, as much as 53 feet (16.1 m).

The great range is often attributed to the funnel-like shape of the Bay, but the main cause is tidal water's tendency to oscillate in bays in cycles of 12 hours and 25 minutes (half a lunar day), just as the water in a washbasin will slosh when you move your hand back and forth at just the right frequency, depending upon the depth of the water and the shape of the basin. It would be a coincidence indeed if a bay were of such a shape and depth as to have a complete oscillation with a period of exactly 12 hours and 25 minutes. However, a bay can easily have a part of such an oscillation; such is the case in the Bay of Fundy.

A further factor in the large tidal ranges in the Bay of Fundy is that Fundy tides are controlled by the Gulf of Maine tides which, in turn, are controlled by the open ocean tides. The relationships between these tides are such as to exaggerate their ranges.

Another special tidal situation frequently encountered by the mariner is in various tidal inlets and estuary entrances. In many instances, the tidal conditions on the outside of an entrance may be quite different from those just inside, with complicated tidal height and current patterns in the inlets. For some shallow bays with constricted entrances, the tide may become negligible inside the inlets, and weather patterns may affect the water level variations more than the tide-producing forces.

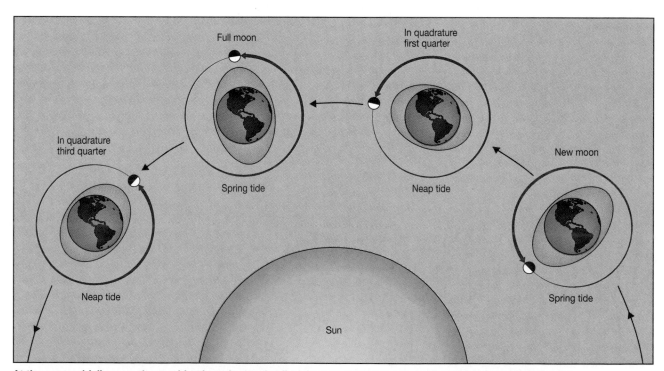

At the new and full moon, the combined gravitational pull of the sun and the moon produce the largest tidal variation. These tides, which occur twice a month, are called spring tides. At the first and third quarters of the moon, the two gravitational forces partially offset each other and the net tidal effect is minimal; these tides are called neap tides.

READING THE *TIDE TABLES*

The predicted heights of the tides used in U.S. tide prediction tables and nautical charts are reckoned from a specific reference plane. This reference plane, which up until 1987 was different for various coasts, is now Mean Lower Low Water (MLLW) for all areas.

The basic source of information on the time of high and low water, and their heights above (or below) the datum, is the *Tide Tables* published by the National Ocean Service (NOS). Any predictions appearing in newspapers or broadcast over radio and TV stations will have been extracted from these tables (and converted to daylight time, if in effect). Small-craft charts include tidal information in their margins or on the cover jacket.

Be sure to consider also seeking "local knowledge." Never hesitate to ask experienced local watermen when you are in unfamiliar waters and need information of any kind. The best tables prepared by electronic computers sometimes cannot compare with a knowledge of what to expect that is based on years of local experience.

Tide Tables

The NOS *Tide Tables* are of great value in determining the predicted height of water at any place at a given time. They are calculated in advance and published annually.

The *Tables* can be bought at any authorized sales agent for NOS charts, or by mail from the Superintendent of Documents, Government Printing Office, Washington, DC 20402, or from GPO Regional Bookstores in many cities. Tide/current tables and charts can also be ordered by calling (301) 436-6990 or by writing: NOAA, Distribution Branch, 6501 Lafayette Avenue, Riverdale, MD 20737. The official titles of the Tide and Current Tables are listed below:

- *Tide Tables, East Coast of North and South America including Greenland.*
- *Tide Tables, West Coast of North and South America including the Hawaiian Islands.*
- *Tide Tables, Europe and West Coast of Africa, including the Mediterranean Sea.*
- *Tide Tables, Central and Western Pacific Ocean and Indian Ocean.*
- *Tide Tables, Alaskan Supplement.*

The *Tide Tables* give the predicted times and heights of high and low waters for each day of the year at important points known as Reference Stations. Portland, Boston, Sandy Hook and Key West are examples of points for which detailed information is given in the East Coast *Tables*. Reference stations in the West Coast *Tables* include San Diego, the Golden Gate at San Francisco and Aberdeen, Washington.

Additional tables show the difference in times and heights between these reference stations and thousands of other points termed Subordinate Stations. From these tables, the tide at virtually any point of significance along the coasts can be computed. The West Coast *Tide Tables*, for example, contain predictions for 41 reference stations and about 1,100 subordinate stations in North and South America. The tables also contain clear instructions for their interpretation. Other nations have similar sets of tables for their waters.

Cautions

All factors that can be determined in advance are taken into account in tide predictions, but remember when using them that other factors can greatly influence the height of tides. Such influences include barometric pressure and wind. In many areas the effect of a prolonged gale from a certain quarter can offset all other factors. Tidal rivers may be affected by the volume of water flowing down from the watershed. Normal seasonal variations of flow are allowed for in the predictions, but unexpected prolonged wet or dry spells may cause significant changes to tidal height predictions. Intense rainfall upriver may change both heights and times of tides and the effects may not appear downstream for several days. You should therefore be careful whenever using the *Tide Tables*, especially since low waters can go considerably lower than the level predicted.

Explanation of the *Tables*

Table 1 of the *Tide Tables* provides the predicted times and heights of high and low water at the reference stations and is self-explanatory; note that heights are given in both feet and centimeters. Where no sign is given before the predicted height, the quantity is positive and is to be added to the depths as given on the chart. When the value is preceded by a minus sign (–), the "heights" are to be subtracted from charted depths.

Times are given in a four-digit system from 0000 to 2359, using the 24-hour clock *(Chapter 19)*. In many areas you must be careful regarding daylight saving time; the *Tide Tables* are published in local standard time, and you must add one hour if you are on daylight time.

Where there are normally two high and two low tides each date, they are roughly a little less than an hour later each succeeding day. Consequently, a high or low tide may skip a calendar day, as indicated by a blank space in the *Tide Tables, (table, page 334)*. If it is a high tide that is skipped, for example, you will note that the previous corresponding high occurred late in the foregoing day, and the next one early in the following day—see the sequence for late nighttime high tides on the extract of Table 1, for January 2 and 3.

A review of the *Tide Tables* will quickly show that at some places there will be only one high and one low tide on some days, with the usual four tides on other days. These tides are being affected by the position of the moon either north or south of the equator.

There are four tides when the moon is near the equator, and two tides a day when the moon is near maximum north or south declination. An example of this type of tide occurs at St. Petersburg, Florida. The daily inequality in the heights

Anchorage, Alaska, 1993

Times and Heights of High and Low Waters

January

Day	h m	ft	cm	Day	h m	ft	cm
1 F	0005	22.9	698	16 Sa	0115	25.3	771
	0631	6.1	186		0732	5.4	165
	1244	26.0	792		1332	28.3	863
	1927	3.9	119		2036	1.1	34
2 Sa	0123	21.9	668	17 Su	0255	24.6	750
	0728	8.3	253		0852	7.3	223
	1349	25.3	771		1446	27.1	826
	2045	3.4	104		2202	0.8	24
3 Su	0254	22.0	671	18 M	0417	25.5	777
	0903	9.4	287		1018	7.6	232
	1452	25.3	771		1556	26.8	817
	2155	2.2	67		2315	-0.4	-12
4 M	0421	23.3	710	19 Tu	0523	26.7	814
	1014	8.9	271		1129	6.5	198
	1548	26.0	792		1655	27.1	826
	2254	0.8	24				
5 Tu	0515	25.0	762	20 W	0011	-1.5	-46
	1108	7.9	241		0612	27.6	841
	1641	26.7	832		1222	5.2	158
	2350	-0.7	-21		1744	27.8	847
6 W	0558	26.5	808	21 Th	0056	-1.9	-58
	1159	6.5	198		0651	28.0	853
	1727	28.8	878		1306	4.3	131
					1827	28.5	869

February

Day	h m	ft	cm	Day	h m	ft	cm
1 M	0158	21.8	664	16 Tu	0359	25.0	762
	0739	10.1	308		1007	8.4	256
	1347	24.2	738		1537	24.9	759
	2101	3.1	94		2254	1.5	46
2 Tu	0335	22.6	689	17 W	0503	26.3	802
	0919	10.3	314		1113	6.4	195
	1503	24.8	756		1642	25.7	783
	2214	1.9	58		2349	0.1	3
3 W	0444	24.4	744	18 Th	0552	27.3	832
	1033	8.6	262		1203	4.6	140
	1609	26.4	805		1731	26.8	817
	2321	0.1	3				
4 Th	0533	26.3	802	19 F	0032	-0.7	-21
	1131	6.4	195		0628	27.9	850
	1706	28.5	869		1247	3.2	98
					1811	28.0	853
5 F	0016	-1.7	-52	20 Sa	0109	-0.9	-27
	0615	28.1	856		0657	28.3	863
	1229	4.0	122		1324	2.4	73
	1755	30.5	930		1848	28.8	878
6 Sa	0106	-3.4	-104	21 Su	0141	-0.8	-24
	0654	29.5	899		0721	28.8	878
	1319	1.8	55		1358	1.8	55
○	1845	32.0	975	●	1924	29.4	896

March

Day	h m	ft	cm	Day	h m	ft	cm
1 M	0603	8.1	247	16 Tu	0153	24.7	753
	1140	25.3	771		0813	9.6	293
	1901	2.6	79		1350	23.6	719
◐					2039	4.3	131
2 Tu	0113	22.7	692	17 W	0323	24.8	756
	0703	9.8	299		0942	8.4	256
	1252	24.2	738		1514	23.5	716
	2010	3.3	101		2217	3.8	116
3 W	0246	23.1	704	18 Th	0431	25.9	789
	0829	10.1	308		1049	6.1	186
	1417	24.5	747		1622	24.6	750
	2132	2.5	76		2315	2.3	70
4 Th	0405	24.8	756	19 F	0518	27.0	823
	0959	8.0	244		1139	3.8	116
	1537	26.2	799		1715	26.1	796
	2244	0.9	27		2359	1.3	40
5 F	0500	26.9	820	20 Sa	0555	27.8	847
	1109	5.2	158		1221	2.2	67
	1644	28.6	872		1753	27.4	835
	2347	-1.0	-30				
6 Sa	0544	28.8	878	21 Su	0035	0.7	21
	1208	2.4	73		0623	28.4	866
	1739	30.7	936		1259	1.1	34
					1829	28.5	869

Each reference station is given four pages in Table 1 and each page represents three months. Tide levels are shown in feet and centimeters.

of successive tides increases until the lower high tide and the higher low tide merge into each other and disappear, leaving only one high and one low tide in a day. These are not unusual in the tropics and are called "tropic tides."

Tides at subordinate stations

Table 2, "Tidal Differences and Other Constants" (page 338) gives the information necessary to find the time and height of tide for thousands of subordinate stations by applying simple corrections to the data given for the main reference stations. The name of the applicable reference station appears at the head of the particular section in which the subordinate station is listed. The following information is given in the columns of Table 2:

■ The number of the subordinate station (from the index at the end of the Tide Tables).

■ The name of the subordinate station.

■ The subordinate station's latitude and longitude.

■ The differences between time and height of high water at the subordinate station, and high water at the designated reference station as well as corresponding differences for low waters.

■ Mean and spring (or diurnal) tidal ranges.

■ Mean tide level.

To determine the time of high or low water at any station in Table 2, use the column marked "Differences, Time." This gives the hours and minutes to be added to or subtracted from the time of the respective high or low water at the reference station shown in boldface type in the fourth column above a group of subordinate stations. Be careful in making calculations near midnight. Applying the time difference may cause you to cross the line from one day to another. Simply add or subtract 24 hours as necessary.

The height of the tide at a station in Table 2 is determined by applying the height difference, or in some cases the ratio. A plus sign (+) indicates that the difference increases the height given for the designated reference station; a minus sign (-) indicates that it decreases the Table 1 value. (Remember that, on occasion, these calculations will produce a "minus tide" figure, meaning that actual depths of water will be less than those indicated on the chart.) Differences are not given in metric values. If they are needed, conversions from feet can be made using Table 7 in the Tide Tables.

In some cases, ratios are used. Ratios are identified by an asterisk, and are given as a decimal fraction by which the height at the reference station is to be multiplied to determine the height at the subordinate station.

In the column headed "Ranges," the mean range is the difference in height between mean high water and mean low water. This figure is useful for calculating mean high water, the datum commonly used for measuring vertical heights above water for bridge and other vertical clearances. The spring range is the average semi-diurnal range occurring twice monthly when the moon is new or full. Spring range is larger than the mean range for semi-diurnal or mixed tides, but is of no practical significance where the tide is of the diurnal type. In the latter case, the tables give diurnal range, which is the difference in height between mean higher high water and mean lower low water.

Special conditions at certain subordinate stations are covered by "endnotes" following Table 2.

Finding tides between high and low

Table 3 *(page 339)* provides detailed factors for calculating the height of the tide at any desired moment between the times of high and low waters. It can be used for either the reference stations in Table 1 or the subordinate stations of Table 2. Note that Table 3 is not a complete set of variations from one low to one high. Since the rise and fall are assumed to be symmetrical, only a half-table need be printed. Calculations are made from a high or low water, whichever is nearer to the specified time. The nearest tabular values are used; interpolation is not necessary.

If the degree of precision produced by using Table 3 is not required (it seldom is in practical piloting situations), a much simpler and quicker estimation can be made using the following 1-2-3-3-2-1 rule of thumb. The tide may be assumed to rise or fall 1/12 of the full range during the first and sixth hours after high and low water stands, 2/12 during the second and fifth hours, and 3/12 during each of the third and fourth hours. The results obtained by this rule will suffice for essentially all situations and locations, but should be compared with Table 3 calculations as a check when entering new areas.

Other tables

The *Tide Tables* also include four other minor tables which, although not directly related to tidal calculations, are often useful. Table 4 provides sunrise and sunset data at five-day intervals for various latitudes. Table 5 lists corrections for converting the local mean times of Table 4 to standard zone time. Table 6 tabulates times of moonrise and moonset for selected locations. Table 7 allows direct conversion of feet to meters. The inside back cover of the publication lists other useful data, such as the phases of the moon, solar equinoxes and solstices, for the year covered by the *Tables*.

Tables 1 through 6 are each preceded by informative material that should be read carefully prior to using the table concerned. The index of reference and subordinate stations is at the back of the volume.

Tidal effects on vertical clearances

The tide's rise and fall changes the vertical clearance under fixed structures such as bridges or overhead power cables. These clearances are stated on charts and in *Coast Pilots* as heights measured from a datum that is not the same plane as used for depths and tidal predictions. Normally, height datum is mean high water, the average of all high water levels. The use of this datum ensures that clearances and heights are normally greater than charted values.

It will thus be necessary to determine the height of MHW above the tidal datum. All charts now use mean lower low water as the reference plane; the plane of mean high water is above MLLW by an amount equal to the sum of the "mean tide level" plus one-half of the "mean range"; both of these values are listed in Table 2 of the *Tide Tables* for all stations.

If the tide level at any given moment is below MHW, then vertical clearance under a bridge or other fixed structure is greater than the figures shown on the chart; but if the tide height is above the level of MHW, then the clearance is less. Calculate the vertical clearance in advance if you anticipate a tight situation, but also observe the clearance gauges usually found at bridges. Clearances will normally be greater than the charted MHW values, but occasionally will be less.

Tide level exercises

The instructions in the *Tide Tables* should be fully adequate for solving any problem. However, examples are worked out here for various situations as guides to the use of the various tables. Comments and cautions relating to the solution of practical problems involving the *Tide Tables* are also given. The necessary extracts from the *Tide Tables* are given on pages 338 and 339.

EXAMPLE 1

Determining the time and height of a high or low tide at a reference station.

Problem: What is the predicted time and height of the evening low tide at Seattle, Washington on Monday 13 December?

Solution: Refer to Table 1. The excerpt in this chapter, shown on page 338, is taken from page 99 of the 1993 *Tide Tables*. Note that the entry for 13 December shows that the evening low water is predicted to occur at 2246 Pacific Standard Time (PST) and that the height will be -2.9 feet, or 2.9 feet below the tidal datum of mean lower low water. Actual depths will then be lower than the charted depths.

On the same date, morning low tide is 7.3 feet above the tidal datum of mean lower low water.

Note that on Wednesday 15 December, there is no evening low because the progression of the tides on a 24 hour and 50 minute cycle has moved the evening low tide past midnight into the next day. As a result, the table shows only three entries for Wednesday 15 December rather than the usual four.

EXAMPLE 2

Determining the time and height of a high or low tide at a subordinate station.

Problem: What is the predicted time and height of the morning low water at Yokeko Point, Deception Pass, on Saturday 13 November?

Solution: The Index to Table 2 in the back of the *Tide Tables* shows Yokeko Point as Subordinate Station number 1147. Locate Yokeko Point in Table 2 and note the time and height differences for low waters; be sure to use the correct columns. Apply the differences to the time and height of low tide at the reference station as follows:

Time		Height
09 53	at Seattle	5.9
+0:38	difference	-0.2
10 31	at Yokeko Point	5.7

Thus at Yokeko Point, on 13 November, the predicted morning low will occur at 1031 PST with a height of 5.7 feet above tidal datum.

Note: If the example had been November 30, the morning low water at Seattle for that date is at 1140. Adding the time difference of 0h 38m would have resulted in a time prediction at Yokeko Point of 1218, which is not a morning tide. In such cases, use the reference station low water that occurs before midnight the preceding day.

EXAMPLE 3

Determining the level of the tide at a reference station at a given time between high and low waters.

Problem: What is the predicted height of the tide at Seattle at 1700 on Sunday 28 November?

Solution: From Table 1, note that the given time of 1700 falls between a high tide at 1505 and a low tide at 2223. We compute the duration of fall and range as follows:

Time	Height
15 05	10.5
22 23	–1.1
7:18 time difference	11.6 feet range

The desired time is nearer to the time of high water, so calculations will be made using this starting point.

17 00 desired time
15 05 time of nearest high or low water
1:55 difference

The given time is 1h 55m after the nearest high water. Turn to Table 3, which is used to the nearest tabulated value; do not interpolate. Enter the upper part of the Table on the line for Duration of rise or fall of 7h 20m (nearest value to 7h 18m) and read across to the entry nearest 1h 55m—in this case 1h 57m in the 8th column from the left. Follow down this column into the lower part of Table 3 to the line for Range of tide of 11.5 feet (nearest value to 11.6). At the intersection of this line and column is found the correction to the height of the tide: 1.9 feet.

Since, as we have noted, the tide is falling, and we are calculating from high water, the correction is subtracted from the height of high water: 10.5 - 1.9 = 8.6 feet.

Thus, the predicted height of the tide at Seattle at 1700 PST on Sunday 28 November is 8.6 feet above the tidal datum.

Make sure that calculations are made for the right pair of high and low tides—and that the calculations are made to the nearest high or low water. Also, be careful to apply the final correction to the nearest high or low water as used in its computation. Do not apply it to the range. Apply it in the right direction: down from a high or up from a low.

EXAMPLE 4

Determining the predicted height of tide at a subordinate station at a given time.

Problem: What is the predicted height of the tide at Shelton, Oakland Bay, Puget Sound, at 2000 on Saturday 30 October?

Solution: First, use the steps from Example 2—find Shelton in the index, locate its number on Table 2 and note the time and height differences. Now, the times of the high and low waters on either side of the stated time must be calculated for the Subordinate Station using Tables 1 and 2. This is done as follows:

High water time		Height
15 51	at Seattle	10.4 feet
+1:26	difference	.26 ratio
17 17	at Shelton	13.1 feet

Low water time		Height
22 48	at Seattle	-0.4
+2:05	difference	0.92 ratio
00 53	at Shelton	0.37 (0.4)

Next we calculate the time difference and range:

Time		Range
00 53	low water	-0.4

EXAMPLE 5

Determining the time of the tide reaching a given height at a reference station.

Problem: At what time on the morning of Tuesday 30 November will the height of the rising tide at Seattle reach 3 feet?

Solution: This is essentially Example 3 in reverse. First determine the range and duration of rise (or fall) as follows:

Time		Height
22 56	(29th) low water	1.4 feet
06 25	high water	12.0 feet
7:29	duration/range	13.4 feet range

It is noted that the desired difference in height of tide is from the low water -1.4 - 3 = -4.4 or 4.4 feet. Enter the lower part of Table 3 on the line for a range of 13.5 feet (nearest to actual 13.4 feet) and find the column in which the correction nearest 4.4 is tabulated; in this case, the nearest value (4.7) is found on the 12th column to the right.

Proceed up this column to the line in the upper part of the table for a duration of 7h 20m (nearest to actual 7h 29 m). The time from the nearest high or low found on this line is 2h 56m. Since our desired level is nearer to low water than high, this time difference is added to the time of low water: 2256 + 2:56 = 0200.

Thus the desired tidal height of 3 feet above datum is predicted to occur at 0200 PST on 30 November.

Note that a similar calculation can be made for a Subordinate Station by first determining the applicable high and low water times and heights at that station.

EXAMPLE 6

Determination of predicted vertical clearance.

Problem: What will be the predicted vertical clearance under the fixed bridge across the canal near Ala Spit, Whidbey Island, at the time of morning high tide on 30 November?

Solution: Chart 18445 states the clearance to be 35 feet. The datum for heights is mean high water.

From Tables 1 and 2, we determine the predicted height of the tide at the specified time as follows:

At Seattle	12.7 feet
Ratio	0.92
At Ala Spit	11.68 (11.7)

From Table 2 we calculate the height of mean high water for Ala Spit.

Mean tide level	6.1 feet
½ mean range	3.5
Mean high water	9.6 feet above tidal datum

The difference between predicted high water at the specified time and mean high water is 11.7 - 9.6 = 2.1. This is above MHW and the bridge clearance is reduced; 35 - 2.1 = 33 feet, to the nearest whole foot.

On the morning of 30 November, the clearance at high tide under the fixed bridge across the canal near Ala Spit, Whidbey Island, is predicted to be 33 feet. This is less than the clearance printed on the chart.

17 17	high water	13.1
7:36	time difference	13.5 feet range

The time from the nearest high or low is calculated:

17 17	high water at Shelton
20 00	desired time
2:43	time from nearest high

With the data from the above calculations, enter Table 3 for a duration of rise or fall of 7h 40m (nearest to 7h 36m), a time from nearest high or low of 2h 49m (nearest to 2h 43m), and a range of 13.5 feet.

From these data, we find a correction to height of tide of 4.0 feet. We know that the tide is falling and therefore the height at

2000 will be less than the height at the closest high water at 1717. Therefore, the correction is to be subtracted from the Shelton high water height: 13.1 - 4.0 = 9.1 feet.

The height of the tide at Shelton, Oakland Bay, Puget Sound, at 2000 PST on Saturday 30 October is predicted to be 9.1 feet above datum.

Note that you must be sure to use the high and low tides occurring at the subordinate station on either side of the given time. In some instances, you may find that when you have corrected the times for the subordinate station, the desired time no longer falls between the corrected times of high and low tides. In this case, select another high or low tide so that the pair used at the Subordinate Station will bracket the given time.

Seattle, Washington, 1993

Times and Heights of High and Low Waters

	October					November					December			
11 M	0000 0635 1331 1948	8.5 1.6 11.2 4.0	259 49 341 122	**26** Tu	0219 0751 1415 2049	8.8 3.8 10.8 2.3	268 116 329 70	**11** Th	0239 0801 1348 2050	10.1 4.8 12.0 −0.9	308 146 366 −27	**26** F	0401 0854 1405 2120	10.3 6.7 10.5 −0.1	314 204 320 −3
11 Sa	0353 0845 1353 2118	11.4 7.2 12.0 −2.5	347 219 366 −76	**26** Su	0435 0918 1354 2124	11.1 8.0 10.5 −0.8	338 244 320 −24										
12 Tu	0119 0734 1407 2031	9.1 2.0 11.4 2.4	277 61 347 73	**27** W	0315 0840 1442 2121	9.4 4.3 10.6 1.4	287 131 323 43	**12** F	0341 0900 1428 2134	11.1 5.4 12.1 −2.0	338 165 369 −61	**27** Sa	0443 0940 1436 2148	10.9 7.0 10.5 −0.7	332 213 320 −21
12 Su	0445 0944 1441 2203	12.2 7.4 11.9 −2.9	372 226 363 −88	**27** M	0507 1003 1433 2200	11.6 7.9 10.5 −1.3	354 241 320 −40										
13 W	0228 0830 1439 2114	9.9 2.5 11.7 0.9	302 76 357 27	**28** Th	0400 0923 1505 2146	10.0 4.8 10.5 0.7	305 146 320 21	**13** Sa ●	0437 0953 1510 2216	11.9 5.9 12.0 −2.8	363 180 366 −85	**28** Su ○	0518 1019 1505 2223	11.4 7.2 10.5 −1.1	347 219 320 −34
13 M ●	0532 1037 1530 2246	12.7 7.3 11.6 −2.9	387 223 354 −88	**28** Tu ○	0540 1043 1515 2235	12.0 7.7 10.6 −1.6	366 235 323 −49										
14 Th	0329 0919 1515 2156	10.8 3.1 11.9 −0.5	329 94 363 −15	**29** F	0442 1001 1526 2218	10.5 5.3 10.4 0.1	320 162 317 3	**14** Su	0532 1044 1552 2301	12.4 6.3 11.8 −3.1	378 192 360 −94	**29** M	0551 1100 1537 2256	11.7 7.3 10.5 −1.4	357 223 320 −43
14 Tu	0616 1130 1616 2328	13.0 7.1 11.2 −2.5	396 216 341 −76	**29** W	0607 1122 1557 2313	12.4 7.4 10.6 −1.7	378 226 323 −52										
15 F ●	0428 1011 1550 2238	11.5 3.7 12.0 −1.6	351 113 366 −49	**30** Sa ○	0517 1037 1551 2248	10.9 5.7 10.4 −0.4	332 174 317 −12	**15** M	0621 1137 1635 2346	12.7 6.6 11.5 −2.9	387 201 351 −88	**30** Tu	0625 1140 1613 2332	12.0 7.3 10.4 −1.6	366 223 317 −49
15 W	0657 1219 1704	13.0 6.9 10.6	396 210 323	**30** Th	0636 1204 1642 2349	12.7 6.9 10.4 −1.4	387 210 317 −43										
				31 Su	0556 1115 1616 2320	11.2 6.1 10.3 −0.8	341 186 314 −24											**31** F	0705 1249 1734	12.9 6.2 10.1	393 189 308

TABLE 1. This is an excerpt of Table 1 from the 1993 *Tide Tables*.

TABLE 2 – TIDAL DIFFERENCES AND OTHER CONSTANTS

No.	PLACE	POSITION		DIFFERENCES				RANGES		Mean Tide Level
		Latitude	Longitude	Time High Water	Time Low Water	Height High Water	Height Low Water	Mean	Diurnal	
		North	**West**	**h m**	**h m**	**ft**	**ft**	**ft**	**ft**	**ft**
	WASHINGTON–cont. Saratoga Passage and Skagit Bay Time meridian, 120° W					on Seattle, p.96				
1133	Sandy Point, Whidbey Island	48° 02.1'	122° 22.6'	+0 03	−0 01	*0.99	*1.00	7.56	11.25	6.60
1135	Holly Farms Harbor, Holmes Harbor, Whidbey I.	48° 01.6'	122° 32.1'	+0 01	−0 04	*1.01	*0.99	7.76	11.44	6.67
1137	Greenbank, Whidbey Island	48° 06.3'	122° 34.2'	−0 03	−0 06	*0.99	*0.99	7.6	11.3	6.6
1139	Crescent Harbor, N. Whidbey Island	48° 17'	122° 37'	+0 04	−0 04	*1.03	*0.99	8.0	11.6	6.8
1141	Coupeville, Penn Cove, Whidbey Island	48° 13.4'	122° 41.4'	+0 15	+0 09	*1.01	*0.99	7.8	11.5	6.7
1143	La Conner, Swinomish Channel	48° 23.5'	122° 29.8'	+0 21	+0 39	*0.90	*0.95	6.74	10.34	6.06
1145	Ala Spit, Whidbey Island	48° 23.8'	122° 35.2'	+0 12	+0 26	*0.92	*0.95	6.9	10.5	6.1
1147	Yokeko Point, Deception Pass	48° 24.8'	122° 36.9'	+0 26	+0 38	−1.0	−0.2	6.9	10.5	6.1
1149	Cornet Bay, Deception Pass	48° 24.1'	122° 37.4'	+0 15	+0 26	*0.89	*0.95	6.6	10.2	6.0

TABLE 2. This portion of Table 2 appears in the 1993 *Tide Tables*. The time and height differences for subordinate station Yokeko Point must be applied to tidal information for its reference station, Seattle, noted in bold in the fourth column. Asterisks indicate ratios.

TABLE 2 – TIDAL DIFFERENCES AND OTHER CONSTANTS

1093	Dupont Wharf, Nisqually Reach	47° 04.1'	122° 40.0'	+0 41	+0 49	*1.20	*1.04	9.63	13.51	7.77
1095	Longbranch, Filucy Bay	47° 12.6'	122° 45.2'	+0 38	+0 47	*1.20	*1.02	9.7	13.5	7.7
1097	Devils Head, Drayton Passage	47° 10.0'	122° 45.8'	+0 40	+0 50	*1.25	*1.10	9.98	14.18	8.09
1099	Henderson Inlet	47° 09.3'	122° 50.3'	+0 47	+0 58	*1.24	*1.06	10.0	14.0	8.0
1101	McMicken Island, Case Inlet	47° 14.8'	122° 51.7'	+0 40	+0 52	*1.24	*1.06	10.00	13.96	8.01
1103	Vaughn, Case Inlet	47° 20.5'	122° 46.5'	+0 51	+0 57	*1.26	*1.06	10.2	14.1	8.1
1105	Allyn, Case Inlet	47° 14.8'	122° 49.4'	+0 48	+0 59	*1.26	*1.07	10.20	14.16	8.13
1107	Walkers Landing, Pickering Passage	47° 16.9'	122° 55.4'	+0 44	+0 55	*1.26	*1.07	10.20	14.15	8.12
1109	Shelton, Oakland Bay	47° 12.9'	123° 05.0'	+1 26	+2 05	*1.26	*0.92	10.6	14.2	7.9
1111	Arcadia, Totten Inlet	47° 11.8'	122° 56.3'	+0 49	+1 05	*1.28	*1.06	10.4	14.4	8.2
1113	Burns Point, Totten Inlet	47° 07.3'	123° 03.4'	+0 54	+1 07	*1.33	*1.06	11.0	15.0	8.5

TABLE 2. Another portion of Table 2 in the 1993 *Tide Tables* serves as a reference for Example 4, page 336.

TABLE 3.—HEIGHT OF TIDE AT ANY TIME

Time from the nearest high water or low water

Duration of rise or fall, see footnote (h.m.)	h.m.	h.m.	h.m.	h.m.	h.m.	h.m.	h.m.	h.m.	h.m.	h.m.	h.m.	h.m.	h.m.	h.m.	h.m.
4 00	0 08	0 16	0 24	0 32	0 40	0 48	0 56	1 04	1 12	1 20	1 28	1 36	1 44	1 52	2 00
4 20	0 09	0 17	0 26	0 35	0 43	0 52	1 01	1 09	1 18	1 27	1 35	1 44	1 53	2 01	2 10
4 40	0 09	0 19	0 28	0 37	0 47	0 56	1 05	1 15	1 24	1 33	1 43	1 52	2 01	2 11	2 20
5 00	0 10	0 20	0 30	0 40	0 50	1 00	1 10	1 20	1 30	1 40	1 50	2 00	2 10	2 20	2 30
5 20	0 11	0 21	0 32	0 43	0 53	1 04	1 15	1 25	1 36	1 47	1 57	2 08	2 19	2 29	2 40
5 40	0 11	0 23	0 34	0 45	0,57	1 08	1 19	1 31	1 42	1 53	2 05	2 16	2 27	2 39	2 50
6 00	0 12	0 24	0 36	0 48	1 00	1 12	1 24	1 36	1 48	2 00	2 12	2 24	2 36	2 48	3 00
6 20	0 13	0 25	0 38	0 51	1 03	1 16	1 29	1 41	1 54	2 07	2 19	2 32	2 45	2 57	3 10
6 40	0 13	0 27	0 40	0 53	1 07	1 20	1 33	1 47	2 00	2 13	2 27	2 40	2 53	3 07	3 20
7 00	0 14	0 28	0 42	0 56	1 10	1 24	1 38	1 52	2 06	2 20	2 34	2 48	3 02	3 16	3 30
7 20	0 15	0 29	0 44	0 59	1 13	1 28	1 43	1 57	2 12	2 27	2 41	2 56	3 11	3 25	3 40
7 40	0 15	0 31	0 46	1 01	1 17	1 32	1 47	2 03	2 18	2 33	2 49	3 04	3 19	3 35	3 50
8 00	0 16	0 32	0 48	1 04	1 20	1 36	1 52	2 08	2 24	2 40	2 56	3 12	3 28	3 44	4 00
8 20	0 17	0 33	0 50	1 07	1 23	1 40	1 57	2 13	2 30	2 47	3 03	3 20	3 37	3 53	4 10
8 40	0 17	0 35	0 52	1 09	1 27	1 44	2 01	2 19	2 36	2 53	3 11	3 28	3 45	4 03	4 20
9 00	0 18	0 36	0 54	1 12	1 30	1 48	2 06	2 24	2 42	3 00	3 18	3 36	3 54	4 12	4 30
9 20	0 19	0 37	0 56	1 15	1 33	1 52	2 11	2 29	2 48	3 07	3 25	3 44	4 03	4 21	4 40
9 40	0 19	0 39	0 58	1 17	1 37	1 56	2 15	2 35	2 54	3 13	3 33	3 52	4 11	4 31	4 50
10 00	0 20	0 40	1 00	1 20	1 40	2 00	2 20	2 40	3 00	3 20	3 40	4 00	4 20	4 40	5 00
10 20	0 21	0 41	1 02	1 23	1 43	2 04	2 25	2 45	3 06	3 27	3 47	4 08	4 29	4 49	5 10
10 40	0 21	0 43	1 04	1 25	1 47	2 08	2 29	2 51	3 12	3 33	3 55	4 16	4 37	4 59	5 20

Correction to height

Range of tide, see footnote (Ft.)	Ft.	Ft.	Ft.	Ft.	Ft.	Ft.	Ft.	Ft.	Ft.	Ft.	Ft.	Ft.	Ft.	Ft.	Ft.
0.5	0.0	0.0	0.0	0.0	0.0	0.0	0.1	0.1	0.1	0.1	0.1	0.2	0.2	0.2	0.2
1.0	0.0	0.0	0.0	0.0	0.1	0.1	0.1	0.2	0.2	0.2	0.3	0.3	0.4	0.4	0.5
1.5	0.0	0.0	0.0	0.1	0.1	0.1	0.2	0.2	0.3	0.4	0.4	0.5	0.6	0.7	0.8
2.0	0.0	0.0	0.0	0.1	0.1	0.2	0.3	0.3	0.4	0.5	0.6	0.7	0.8	0.9	1.0
2.5	0.0	0.0	0.1	0.1	0.2	0.2	0.3	0.4	0.5	0.6	0.7	0.9	1.0	1.1	1.2
3.0	0.0.	0.0	0.1	0.1	0.2	0.3	0.4	0.5	0.6	0.8	0.9	1.0	1.2	1.3	1.5
3.5	0.0	0.0	0.1	0.2	0.2	0.3	0.4	0.6	0.7	0.9	1.0	1.2	1.4	1.6	1.8
4.0	0.0	0.0	0.1	0.2	0.3	0.4	0.5	0.7	0.8	1.0	1.2	1.4	1.6	1.8	2.0
4.5	0.0	0.0	0.1	0.2	0.3	0.4	0.6	0.7	0.9	1.1	1.3	1.6	1.8	2.0	2.2
5.0	0.0	0.1	0.1	0.2	0.3	0.5	0.6	0.8	1.0	1.2	1.5	1.7	2.0	2.2	2.5
5.5	0.0	0.1	0.1	0.2	0.4	0.5	0.7	0.9	1.1	1.4	1.6	1.9	2.2	2.5	2.8
6.0	0.0	0.1	0.1	0.3	0.4	0.6	0.8	1.0	1.2	1.5	1.8	2.1	2.4	2.7	3.0
6.5	0.0	0.1	0.2	0.3	0.4	0.6	0.8	1.1	1.3	1.6	1.9	2.2	2.6	2.9	3.2
7.0	0.0	0.1	0.2	0.3	0.5	0.7	0.9	1.2	1.4	1.8	2.1	2.4	2.8	3.1	3.5
7.5	0.0	0.1	0.2	0.3	0.5	0.7	1.0	1.2	1.5	1.9	2.2	2.6	3.0	3.4	3.8
8.0	0.0	0.1	0.2	0.3	0.5	0.8	1.0	1.3	1.6	2.0	2.4	2.8	3.2	3.6	4.0
8.5	0.0	0.1	0.2	0.4	0.6	0.8	1.1	1.4	1.8	2.1	2.5	2.9	3.4	3.8	4.2
9.0	0.0	0.1	0.2	0.4	0.6	0.9	1.2	1.5	1.9	2.2	2.7	3.1	3.6	4.0	4.5
9.5	0.0	0.1	0.2	0.4	0.6	0.9	1.2	1.6	2.0	2.4	2.8	3.3	3.8	4.3	4.8
10.0	0.0	0.1	0.2	0.4	0.7	1.0	1.3	1.7	2.1	2.5	3.0	3.5	4.0	4.5	5.0
10.5	0.0	0.1	0.3	0.5	0.7	1.0	1.3	1.7	2.2	2.6	3.1	3.6	4.2	4.7	5.2
11.0	0.0	0.1	0.3	0.5	0.7	1.1	1.4	1.8	2.3	2.8	3.3	3.8	4.4	4.9	5.5
11.5	0.0	0.1	0.3	0.5	0.8	1.1	1.5	1.9	2.4	2.9	3.4	4.0	4.6	5.1	5.8
12.0	0.0	0.1	0.3	0.5	0.8	1.1	1.5	2.0	2.5	3.0	3.6	4.1	4.8	5.4	6.0
12.5	0.0	0.1	0.3	0.5	0.8	1.2	1.6	2.1	2.6	3.1	3.7	4.3	5.0	5.6	6.2
13.0	0.0	0.1	0.3	0.6	0.9	1.2	1.7	2.2	2.7	3.2	3.9	4.5	5.1	5.8	6.5
13.5	0.0	0.1	0.3	0.6	0.9	1.3	1.7	2.2	2.8	3.4	4.0	4.7	5.3	6.0	6.8
14.0	0.0	0.2	0.3	0.6	0.9	1.3	1.8	2.3	2.9	3.5	4.2	4.8	5.5	6.3	7.0
14.5	0.0	0.2	0.4	0.6	1.0	1.4	1.9	2.4	3.0	3.6	4.3	5.0	5.7	6.5	7.2
15.0	0.0	0.2	0.4	0.6	1.0	1.4	1.9	2.5	3.1	3.8	4.4	5.2	5.9	6.7	7.5
15.5	0.0	0.2	0.4	0.7	1.0	1.5	2.0	2.6	3.2	3.9	4.6	5.4	6.1	6.9	7.8
16.0	0.0	0.2	0.4	0.7	1.1	1.5	2.1	2.6	3.3	4.0	4.7	5.5	6.3	7.2	8.0
16.5	0.0	0.2	0.4	0.7	1.1	1.6	2.1	2.7	3.4	4.1	4.9	5.7	6.5	7.4	8.2
17.0	0.0	0.2	0.4	0.7	1.1	1.6	2.2	2.8	3.5	4.2	5.0	5.9	6.7	7.6	8.5
17.5	0.0	0.2	0.4	0.8	1.2	1.7	2.2	2.9	3.6	4.4	5.2	6.0	6.9	7.8	8.8
18.0	0.0	0.2	0.4	0.8	1.2	1.7	2.3	3.0	3.7	4.5	5.3	6.2	7.1	8.1	9.0
18.5	0.1	0.2	0.5	0.8	1.2	1.8	2.4	3.1	3.8	4.6	5.5	6.4	7.3	8.3	9.2
19.0	0.1	0.2	0.5	0.8	1.3	1.8	2.4	3.1	3.9	4.8	5.6	6.6	7.5	8.5	9.5
19.5	0.1	0.2	0.5	0.8	1.3	1.9	2.5	3.2	4.0	4.9	5.8	6.7	7.7	8.7	9.8

TABLE 3. When height of tide is plotted on a graph against time, the curve is very close to a cosine curve. Table 3, shown in part above, is another way of looking at the same data. It allows a quick and very close estimate of tidal heights between high and low. To use the table we must know three things—how many hours and minutes from high to low (or low to high), how many minutes are we into that rise or fall and, finally, what is the size of the rise or fall. The answer produced by the table is a correction factor that can be applied to a height value from the other tables.

CURRENTS

Current is the horizontal motion of water. It may result from any one of several factors, or from a combination of two or three. Although certain of these are more important than others, you should have a general understanding of all of them.

Tidal currents

Boaters in coastal areas will be affected most by tidal currents. The rise and fall of tidal levels is a result of the flow of water to and from a given locality.

The normal type of tidal current in bays and rivers is a reversing current, which flows alternately in one direction and then the opposite. Offshore, tidal currents may be of the rotary type, flowing with little change in strength, but slowly and steadily changing direction.

A special form of tidal current is the hydraulic type, which occurs when water flows from a higher to a lower level, as in some canals and at certain passes. Differences in the time and height of the high waters of two bays or sounds can cause a flow from one to the other and back again. A typical example of hydraulic current is the flow through the Cape Cod Canal between Massachusetts Bay and Buzzards Bay.

Remember to use the terms correctly—tide is the vertical rise and fall of water levels; current is the horizontal flow of water.

River currents

Boaters on rivers above the head of tidal action must still take into account river currents. (Where tidal influences are felt,

river currents are merged into tidal currents and are not considered separately.) River currents vary considerably with the width and depth of the stream and the season, as well as the recent rainfall.

Ocean currents

Offshore piloting frequently will require knowledge and consideration of ocean currents that result from relatively constant winds such as the trade winds and prevailing westerlies. The rotation of the earth and variations in water density are also factors in the patterns of ocean currents.

The ocean currents of greatest interest to North American boaters are the Gulf Stream and the California Current. The warm waters of the Gulf Stream flow in a northeasterly direction along the Atlantic Coast of the U. S. It is close to shore along southern Florida, but moves progressively farther to sea as it flows northward, where it both broadens and slows.

The California Current flows generally southward and a bit eastward along the Pacific Coast of Canada and the United States, turning sharply westward off Baja California, in Mexico. It is a flow of colder water and, in general, is slower and less sharply defined than the Gulf Stream.

Wind-driven currents

In addition to the consistent ocean currents caused by sustained wind patterns, temporary conditions may create local wind-driven currents. Wind blowing across the sea causes the

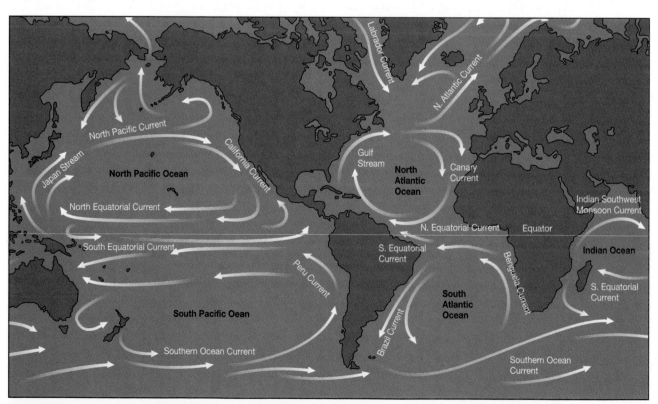

These are the major ocean currents of the world. The Gulf Stream off the East Coast and the California Current off the West Coast are those of most interest to North American boaters. Other currents exist at lower depths.

surface water to move. The extent of this effect varies, but generally a steady wind for 12 hours or longer will result in a discernible current.

The strength of a wind-driven current can be taken as 2 percent of the wind's velocity. The direction of the current will not be the same as that of the wind—a result of the earth's rotation. In the northern hemisphere, the current will be deflected to the right to a degree determined by the latitude and the depth of the water. The deflection may be only 15 degrees in coastal areas, or as great as 45 degrees on the high seas. It is greater in the higher latitudes.

Slack vs. stand

As tidal currents reverse, there are brief periods of no discernible flow, called "slack" or "slack water." The time of occurrence of slack is not the same as the time of stand, when vertical rise or fall of the tide has stopped.

Tidal currents do not automatically slack and reverse direction when tide levels stand at high or low water. High water at a given point simply means that the level there will not get any higher. Farther up the bay or river, the tide will not have reached its maximum height and water must therefore continue to flow in so that it can continue to rise. The current can still be flooding after stand has been passed at a given point and the level has started to fall.

As an example, consider the tides and the currents on Chesapeake Bay. High tide occurs at Baltimore some seven hours after it does at Smith Point, 140 miles from Cape Henry at the entrance to the Chesapeake. On a particular day, high water at Smith Point occurs at 1126, but slack water does not occur until 1304. The flooding current has continued for 1h 38m after high water was reached. Corresponding time intervals occur in the case of low water stand and the slack between ebb and flood currents.

In some passages, tidal currents are so strong that all but the fastest boats must avoid running against the strongest flood and ebb, planning their course, instead, for slack water. In the right direction, strong currents can double the over-the-bottom speed of a displacement hull.

The rise and fall of tides causes a flow into and out of coastal bodies of water and into rivers—sometimes for a surprising distance upstream. Tidal currents are often strong enough to become an important factor in your choice of both course and schedule.

In many places, the time lag between a low or high water stand and slack water is not a matter of minutes but of hours. At the Narrows in New York Harbor, flood current continues for about six hours after high water is reached and the tide begins to fall, and continues to ebb for roughly two and a half hours after low water stand. After slack, the current increases until mid-flood or mid-ebb, then gradually decreases. Where ebb and flood last for about six hours—as along the Atlantic seaboard—current will be strongest about three hours after slack. Thus, the skipper who figures his passage out through the Narrows from the time of high water, rather than slack, will start about two and a half hours too soon and will run into a current at nearly its maximum strength.

Current effects

A current of any type can have a significant effect on the travel of a boat with respect to the bottom. Speed can be increased or decreased. The course made good—its actual motion over the bottom—can be markedly different from that steered. For safe and efficient navigation, a boater must know how to determine and apply current effects.

Effect on course and speed made good

A current directly in line with a boat's motion through the water will have a maximum effect on the speed made good, but no off-course influence. The effect on speed, however, can be of significance in figuring your time of arrival at your destination. It can even affect the safety of your boat and its crew if you have calculated your fuel usage too closely and run into a bow-on current.

A current that is nearly at a right angle to your course through the water will have a maximum effect on the course made good and a lesser effect on the distance you must travel to reach your destination.

To assist your cruising, select departure times to take advantage of favorable currents, or at least to minimize adverse effects. A 12-knot boat speed and a 2-knot current, a typical situation, can combine to result in either a 10-knot or a 14-knot speed made good—the 40 percent gain of a favorable current over an opposing one is significant in terms of both time and fuel. For slower craft, the gains are even greater—50 percent for a 10-knot boat, 67 percent for an 8-knot craft, and 100 percent for one making only 6 knots.

Even lesser currents have some significance. A half-knot current can hinder a swimmer and make rowing a boat noticeably more difficult. A one-knot current can seriously affect a sailboat in light breezes.

Difficult locations

In many boating areas, there are locations where current conditions can be critical. Numerous ocean inlets are difficult or dangerous in certain combinations of current and onshore surf. In general, difficult surf conditions will be made more hazardous by an outward-flowing (ebbing) current. Refer to Chapter 21 for more information on inlet seamanship.

In many narrow bodies of water, the maximum current velocity is so high that passage is impossible for boats of limited power and substantially slowed for boats of greater engine power. Such narrow passages are particularly characteristic of Pacific Northwest boating areas, but do occur elsewhere. Currents in New York City's East River reach 4.6 knots and they are more than 5 knots at the Golden Gate of San Francisco. Velocities of 3½ to 4 knots are common in much-traveled passages like Woods Hole, Massachusetts, and Plum Gut, at the eastern end of Long Island, New York.

Tidal current predictions

Without experience or official information, local current prediction is always risky. For example, east of Badgers Island in Portsmouth Harbor (New Hampshire) the maximum ebb current is predicted at less than a half knot. Yet just southwest of the same island, the tabular maximum is 3.7 knots.

One rule is fairly safe for most locations—the ebb is stronger and lasts longer than the flood. Eighty percent of all reference stations located on the Atlantic, Gulf and Pacific coasts of the United States report currents stronger at the ebb. This is normal because river flow adds to the ebb, but hinders the flood.

On the Atlantic Coast, expect to find two approximately equal flood currents and two similar ebb currents in a cycle of roughly 25 hours. However, on the Pacific Coast two floods and ebbs differ markedly. On the Gulf Coast, there may be just one flood and one ebb in 25 hours. These patterns are similar to tidal action in their respective areas.

Don't try to predict current velocity from the time that it takes a high tide to reach a given point from the sea's entrance. Dividing the distance from Cape Henry to Baltimore by the time that it takes high water to work its way up Chesapeake Bay gives a speed of 13 knots. True maximum flood current strength is only about one knot.

Another important fact about tidal currents is that tidal currents at different places cannot be forecast from their tidal ranges. You would expect strong currents at Eastport, Maine, where the difference between successive high and low waters reaches as much as 20 feet. And you would be right—there are 3-knot currents there. But Galveston, Texas, with only a 2-foot range of tides, has currents up to more than 2 knots. So has Miami with a 3-foot range, and Charleston, South Carolina, with a 6-foot range. Both have stronger currents than Boston, where the range is often more than 10 feet, and as strong as at Anchorage, Alaska, where it's as much as 35 feet from some highs to the next low.

A good forecasting rule for all oceans is to expect strong tidal currents where two bays meet. The reason is that tidal ranges and high water times in the two bodies of water are likely to be different.

For the coasting skipper, here is another tidal current fact that may be useful near the beach—flood and ebb don't usually set to and from shore, but rather parallel with it. This is as true off New Jersey and Florida as it is off California and Oregon. However, a few miles offshore and in some very large bays the currents behave quite differently— the rotary current mentioned previously in this chapter is an example.

Tidal Current Tables

At any given place, current strength varies with the phase of the moon and its distance from the earth. Currents will be strongest when tidal ranges are greatest—near new and full moon—and weakest when tidal ranges are least—near first and last quarters. Current speed may vary as much as 40 percent above or below its average value.

The relationship between currents and tides enables us to predict tidal currents. The National Ocean Service publishes annually the following volumes of predictions:

- *Tidal Current Tables, Atlantic Coast of North America.*
- *Tidal Current Tables, Pacific Coast of North America and Asia.*
- *Regional Tide and Tidal Current Tables, New York Harbor to Chesapeake Bay.*

Each volume includes predictions of tidal currents in bays, sounds and rivers, plus ocean currents such as the Gulf Stream. General information on wind-driven currents is also included, although these of course result from temporary, local conditions and so cannot be predicted a year or more ahead. Your own past experience and local knowledge are the best sources of information about how storm winds affect local waters.

Tidal Current Tables are available at authorized National Ocean Service sales agents, and from the Superintendent of Documents, Government Printing Office, Washington, DC 20402.

Description of tables

The format and layout of the *Tidal Current Tables* is much the same as for the *Tide Tables* discussed earlier in this chapter. A system of reference stations, plus constants and differences for subordinate stations, is used to calculate predictions of current strength and time.

There are 22 reference stations in the Atlantic Coast volume (which covers the Gulf of Mexico as well), and 36 in the

TABLE 3.—SPEED OF CURRENT AT ANY TIME

TABLE A

Interval between slack and desired time (h. m.)	Interval between slack and maximum current													
	h. m. 1 20	h. m. 1 40	h. m. 2 00	h. m. 2 20	h. m. 2 40	h. m. 3 00	h. m. 3 20	h. m. 3 40	h. m. 4 00	h. m. 4 20	h. m. 4 40	h. m. 5 00	h. m. 5 20	h. m. 5 40
	f.	f.	f.	f.	f.	f.	f.	f.	f.	f.	f.	f.	f.	f.
0 20	0.4	0.3	0.3	0.2	0.2	0.2	0.2	0.1	0.1	0.1	0.1	0.1	0.1	0.1
0 40	0.7	0.6	0.5	0.4	0.4	0.3	0.3	0.3	0.3	0.2	0.2	0.2	0.2	0.2
1 00	0.9	0.8	0.7	0.6	0.6	0.5	0.5	0.4	0.4	0.4	0.3	0.3	0.3	0.3
1 20	1.0	1.0	0.9	0.8	0.7	0.6	0.6	0.5	0.5	0.5	0.4	0.4	0.4	0.4
1 40	------	1.0	1.0	0.9	0.8	0.8	0.8	0.7	0.7	0.6	0.6	0.5	0.5	0.4
2 00	------	------	1.0	1.0	0.9	0.9	0.8	0.8	0.7	0.7	0.6	0.6	0.6	0.5
2 20	------	------	------	1.0	1.0	0.9	0.9	0.8	0.8	0.7	0.7	0.7	0.6	0.6
2 40	------	------	------	------	1.0	1.0	1.0	0.9	0.9	0.8	0.8	0.7	0.7	0.7
3 00	------	------	------	------	------	1.0	1.0	1.0	0.9	0.9	0.8	0.8	0.8	0.7
3 20	------	------	------	------	------	------	1.0	1.0	1.0	0.9	0.9	0.9	0.8	0.8
3 40	------	------	------	------	------	------	------	1.0	1.0	1.0	0.9	0.9	0.9	0.9
4 00	------	------	------	------	------	------	------	------	1.0	1.0	1.0	1.0	0.9	0.9
4 20	------	------	------	------	------	------	------	------	------	1.0	1.0	1.0	1.0	0.9
4 40	------	------	------	------	------	------	------	------	------	------	1.0	1.0	1.0	1.0
5 00	------	------	------	------	------	------	------	------	------	------	------	1.0	1.0	1.0
5 20	------	------	------	------	------	------	------	------	------	------	------	------	1.0	1.0
5 40	------	------	------	------	------	------	------	------	------	------	------	------	------	1.0

TABLE 3A. Table 3 is in two parts: A and B. Table A is for all locations, except for a few unique locations, which are covered in Table B. It allows you to predict current at a particular desired time between the time of slack and the time of maximum flow.

TABLE 4: DURATION OF SLACK	**TABLE A**				
Maximum current	*Period with a speed not more than -*				
	0.1 knot	*0.2 knot*	*0.3 knot*	*0.4 knot*	*0.5 knot*
Knots	*Minutes*	*Minutes*	*Minutes*	*Minutes*	*Minutes*
1.0	23	46	70	94	120
1.5	15	31	46	62	78
2.0	11	23	35	46	58
3.0	8	15	23	31	38
4.0	6	11	17	23	29
5.0	5	9	14	18	23
6.0	4	8	11	15	19
7.0	3	7	10	13	16
8.0	3	6	9	11	14

TABLE 4A. Slack is a period during which the current flow slows down and reverses. The length of slack is a question of how slow is slow enough. Table 4, "Duration of Slack," is in two parts: Part A covers all locations except for a few that are covered in Part B. This table helps find the duration of a flow that is less than, or equal to, a desired value.

Pacific Coast volume. The predicted times and strengths of maximum flood and ebb currents, plus the times of slack water are given in table form for each reference station. The directions of the flood and ebb currents are also listed.

Table 2 lists time differences and speed ratios for hundreds of subordinate stations. Following the station number and descriptive location are latitude and longitude; for many stations the depth at which the current was measured is given in the column "Meter Depth." Time differences are given for maximum flood and ebb, and for minimum current (usually slack) before flood and before ebb. Speed ratios are tabulated for maximum current in both directions (given in degrees true for direction toward which current flows). Also listed are average speeds and directions, including speed at "slack," as currents do not always decrease fully to zero velocity. A few stations have only the entry "current weak and variable." A number of notes explaining special conditions at various stations are found at the end of Table 2.

Table 3 is presented in two sections, one of which applies to normal reversing currents and the other to hydraulic currents at specified locations. It provides a convenient means for determining the current's strength at times between slack and maximum velocity. Use the nearest tabulated values without interpolation.

Table 4 gives the duration of slack or weak currents for various maximum currents. Although slack water is only a momentary event, there is a period of time on either side of slack during which the current is so weak as to be negligible for practical piloting purposes. This period varies with the maximum strength of the current, being longer for weak currents. Two sub-tables give the duration of currents from 0.1 to 0.5 knots for normal reversing currents and for the hydraulic currents found at certain specified locations.

Table 5 applies only to the Atlantic Coast. It presents information on rotary tidal currents at various offshore points of navigational interest. These points are described in terms of their general location and specific geographic coordinates. Predictions of speed and direction are referred to the times after maximum flood at designated reference stations.

The inside back cover of the *Tidal Current Tables* has the same astronomical data as is found in the *Tide Tables*.

Current diagrams

For a number of major tidal waterways of the United States, *Tidal Current Tables* give current diagrams, such as the one shown on page 349. These diagrams provide a graphical means for selecting a favorable time for traveling in either direction along these routes. Unfortunately, these may be withdrawn from publication after 1993.

Time

The *Tidal Current Tables* list all predictions in local standard time in the four-digit pattern. Be sure to make an appropriate conversion to daylight time if this is in effect. Subtract an hour from your watch time before using the tables, and add an hour to the results of your calculations.

Cautions

As with tidal predictions, the data in the *Tidal Current Tables* may be upset by abnormal local conditions such as wind and rainfall. Use the current predictions with caution during and immediately after such weather abnormalities.

Note also that tidal current predictions are generally for a spot location only—the set and drift may be quite different only a mile or less away. This is at variance from predictions of high and low tides, which can usually be used over fairly wide areas around the reference station.

Tidal Current Table exercises

The *Tidal Current Tables* contain all information needed for determining such predicted conditions as the time of maximum current and its strength, the time of slack water, and the duration of slack (actually, the duration of the very weak current conditions).

Examples and solutions for typical total current problems follow, along with comments and cautions.

EXAMPLE 1

Determining the predicted time and strength of maximum current, and the time of slack, at a reference station.

Problem: What is the predicted time and strength of the maximum ebb current at Chesapeake Bay Entrance during the afternoon of 16 October?

Solution: As Chesapeake Bay Entrance is a reference station the answer is available by direct inspection of Table 1.

The table shown on page 346 is a typical page from the *Tidal Current Tables*. We can see that the maximum ebb current on the specified afternoon is 1.9 knots and that it occurs at 1454 EST (1554 EDT). An entry at the top of the page tells us that ebbs at this station have a set of 129 degrees true.

Problem: What is the predicted time of the first slack before flood at this station on 21 October?

Solution: Table 1 does not directly identify the slacks as being "slack before ebb" or "slack before flood"; this must be determined by comparing the slack time with the nature of the next maximum current that occurs.

From the table, we can see that the earliest slack that will be followed by a flooding current at Chesapeake Bay Entrance on 21 October is predicted to occur at 1000 EST (1100 EDT).

Notes

1. The times obtained from the *Tidal Current Tables* are standard; add one hour for daylight saving time if it is in effect.
2. The set of the current for a reference station is found at the top of the page in Table 1. It is also given in Table 2, which lists further information such as the geographic coordinates of the station.
3. The normal day at Chesapeake Bay Entrance, where the tide is of the semi-diurnal type, will have four slacks and four maximums. The tidal cycle of 24h and 50m will result in the occasional omission of a slack or maximum. You can see that a slack occurs very late on 20 October; the flood which follows it occurs on the following date.

EXAMPLE 2

Determining the time and strength of maximum current, and the time of slack, at a Subordinate Station.

Problem: What is the predicted time and strength of the morning flood current in Lynnhaven Inlet at the bridge on 16 December?

Solution: Table 2 *(page 347)* gives time differences and velocity ratios to be applied to the predictions at the appropriate reference station. There is an Index to Table 2 at the back of the *Tidal Current Tables* if it is needed to locate the given subordinate station.

For Lynnhaven Inlet bridge, the time difference and speed ratio are applied as follows:

Time		Velocity
09 50	Chesapeake Bay Entrance	1.2
-1:10	Lynnhaven factor	0.7
08 40	morning flood at Lynnhaven	0.8

The set (direction) of the current is also noted from the appropriate column of Table 2; in this case, it is 180° true.

Thus the predictions are for a maximum current of 0.8 knot setting 180° true at Lynnhaven Inlet bridge at 0840 EST on December 16.

Problem: What is the predicted time of the first afternoon slack water at Lynnhaven Inlet bridge on October 17?

Solution: Table 1 shows the first afternoon slack for this date as a slack before flood begins; but the time difference of -1.18 (from Table 2) would make it a morning slack at the subordinate station. So we must use the next slack, which is before ebb at 1858.

18 58 Chesapeake Bay entrance
-1:43 difference for subordinate station
17 15 at Lynnhaven Inlet bridge

Notes

1. Observe that Table 2 shows separate time differences for the four events of a tidal current cycle; always carefully check the column headings and select the proper time difference. Note also that the speed ratios for maximum flood and ebb currents are normally different.
2. The direction of the current at a subordinate station nearly always differs from that of the reference station; it must be taken from Table 2. No statement of current is complete without giving direction as well as strength.
3. Locations in Table 2 are often a point some distance and direction from a landmark or navigation aid. Several subordinate stations may be referred to the same base point.

Chesapeake Bay Entrance, Virginia, 1993

F—Flood, Dir. 300° True   E—Ebb, Dir. 129° True

October

Day	Slack h m	Maximum h m	knots
1 F		0220	1.2E
	0529	0810	0.8F
	1123	1456	1.2E
	1811	2037	0.7F
	2322		
2 Sa		0249	1.2E
	0603	0846	0.9F
	1201	1527	1.2E
	1851	2114	0.7F
	2357		
3 Su		0320	1.2E
	0640	0921	0.8F
	1239	1600	1.1E
	1932	2151	0.6F
4 M	0032	0356	1.2E
	0719	0956	0.8F
	1317	1640	1.0E
	2015	2230	0.5F
5 Tu	0107	0437	1.1E
	0800	1034	0.7F
	1356	1729	0.9E
	2059	2314	0.5F
6 W	0141	0527	1.0E
	0843	1119	0.7F
	1438	1824	0.9E
	2149		
7 Th		0001	0.4F
	0218	0622	1.0E
	0933	1209	0.6F
	1531	1915	0.8E
	2244		
8 F ○		0050	0.5F
	0307	0715	1.0E
	1030	1301	0.6F
	1638	2008	0.9E
	2339		
9 Sa		0143	0.4F
	0421	0813	1.0E
	1132	1400	0.6F
	1739	2108	0.9E
10 Su	0030	0246	0.5F
	0537	0918	1.1E
	1233	1508	0.7F
	1832	2206	1.1E
11 M	0118	0350	0.7F
	0644	1022	1.3E
	1335	1611	0.8F
	1922	2257	1.3E
12 Tu	0204	0442	0.9F
	0747	1120	1.4E
	1432	1703	1.0F
	2012	2346	1.4E
13 W	0250	0528	1.2F
	0846	1216	1.6E
	1527	1751	1.1F
	2101		
14 Th		0035	1.6E
	0336	0614	1.4F
	0941	1311	1.8E
	1619	1841	1.1F
	2150		
15 F ●		0125	1.7E
	0421	0705	1.5F
	1034	1405	1.9E
	1709	1934	1.2F
	2240		
16 Sa		0215	1.8E
	0510	0757	1.6F
	1126	1454	1.9E
	1802	2028	1.2F
	2330		
17 Su		0304	1.8E
	0601	0848	1.5F
	1218	1544	1.8E
	1858	2120	1.1F
18 M	0023	0353	1.7E
	0656	0939	1.4F
	1311	1638	1.7E
	1952	2212	1.0F
19 Tu	0117	0448	1.5E
	0753	1033	1.2F
	1405	1739	1.5E
	2050	2310	0.9F
20 W	0212	0552	1.3E
	0854	1132	1.0F
	1502	1842	1.3E
	2151		
21 Th		0011	0.7F
	0311	0657	1.2E
	1000	1235	0.8F
	1606	1943	1.2E
	2258		
22 F ◐		0112	0.6F
	0421	0801	1.1E
	1111	1339	0.7F
	1713	2047	1.1E
23 Sa	0001	0220	0.5F
	0532	0911	1.0E
	1222	1458	0.6F
	1813	2151	1.0E
24 Su	0101	0345	0.5F
	0636	1019	1.0E
	1330	1617	0.6F
	1904	2246	1.0E
25 M	0154	0443	0.6F
	0733	1115	1.1E
	1430	1703	0.6F
	1947	2329	1.0E
26 Tu	0239	0520	0.7F
	0825	1203	1.1E
	1519	1736	0.6F
	2025		
27 W		0006	1.0E
	0316	0552	0.8F
	0909	1246	1.1E
	1559	1811	0.6F
	2100		
28 Th		0038	1.1E
	0349	0625	0.8F
	0949	1326	1.2E
	1637	1848	0.6F
	2135		
29 F		0109	1.1E
	0420	0700	0.9F
	1026	1401	1.2E
	1711	1928	0.6F
	2209		
30 Sa ○		0142	1.2E
	0452	0738	0.9F
	1102	1434	1.2E
	1749	2009	0.6F
	2246		
31 Su		0217	1.2E
	0528	0815	0.9F
	1139	1506	1.2E
	1828	2048	0.6F
	2323		

November

Day	Slack h m	Maximum h m	knots
1 M		0253	1.2E
	0604	0851	0.9F
	1217	1539	1.2E
	1909	2125	0.6F
2 Tu	0001	0330	1.2E
	0644	0926	0.9F
	1255	1617	1.1E
	1951	2203	0.5F
3 W	0039	0411	1.2E
	0728	1004	0.8F
	1334	1704	1.0E
	2035	2244	0.5F
4 Th	0118	0501	1.1E
	0811	1047	0.8F
	1414	1757	1.0E
	2121	2333	0.5F
5 F	0201	0557	1.0E
	0902	1137	0.7F
	1458	1850	1.0E
	2212		
6 Sa		0025	0.5F
	0257	0655	1.0E
	1001	1233	0.7F
	1552	1941	1.0E
	2304		
7 Su ◐		0119	0.5F
	0416	0754	1.0E
	1108	1330	0.7F
	1653	2035	1.1E
	2355		
8 M		0218	0.6F
	0533	0900	1.1E
	1214	1435	0.7F
	1750	2133	1.2E
9 Tu	0044	0323	0.8F
	0639	1004	1.2E
	1319	1545	0.7F
	1844	2229	1.3E
10 W	0132	0420	1.0F
	0740	1108	1.4E
	1420	1643	0.6F
	1937	2320	1.4E
11 Th	0222	0508	1.3F
	0837	1204	1.6E
	1517	1733	0.9F
	2032		
12 F	0311	0011	1.6E
	0930	0555	1.4F
	1608	1258	1.7E
	2126	1823	1.0F
13 Sa ●	0400	0104	1.6E
	1021	0644	1.5F
	1658	1351	1.8E
	2218	1916	1.0F
14 Su	0449	0156	1.7E
	1110	0736	1.5F
	1748	1441	1.8E
	2310	2010	1.1F
15 M	0541	0246	1.7E
	1201	0829	1.5F
	1840	1529	1.8E
		2102	1.0F
16 Tu	0002	0334	1.6E
	0636	0919	1.4F
	1251	1618	1.6E
	1933	2152	0.9F
17 W	0056	0426	1.5E
	0731	1011	1.2F
	1341	1714	1.5E
	2028	2246	0.8F
18 Th	0149	0525	1.3E
	0830	1107	1.0F
	1431	1814	1.3E
	2124	2344	0.7F
19 F	0244	0629	1.2E
	0931	1205	0.8F
	1524	1909	1.2E
	2223		
20 Sa ☽		0043	0.6F
	0348	0731	1.0E
	1040	1304	0.7F
	1619	2003	1.0E
	2322		
21 Su		0142	0.6F
	0500	0836	0.9E
	1150	1406	0.5F
	1714	2059	1.0E
22 M	0019	0253	0.5F
	0607	0946	0.9E
	1300	1520	0.4F
	1802	2155	0.9E
23 Tu	0110	0406	0.6F
	0705	1047	0.9E
	1403	1623	0.4F
	1845	2240	0.9E
24 W	0156	0450	0.7F
	0757	1136	1.0E
	1457	1704	0.4F
	1927	2317	1.0E
25 Th	0236	0524	0.8F
	0844	1218	1.0E
	1539	1741	0.5F
	2009	2351	1.0E
26 F	0311	0556	0.8F
	0925	1258	1.1E
	1614	1818	0.5F
	2052		
27 Sa		0026	1.1E
	0348	0630	0.9F
	1003	1335	1.1E
	1649	1857	0.6F
	2134		
28 Su		0107	1.2E
	0421	0707	0.9F
	1040	1409	1.2E
	1724	1940	0.6F
	2215		
29 M ☽		0148	1.3E
	0457	0746	1.0F
	1117	1443	1.2E
	1802	2021	0.6F
	2255		
30 Tu		0229	1.3E
	0535	0825	1.0F
	1156	1518	1.3E
	1842	2100	0.6F
	2336		

December

Day	Slack h m	Maximum h m	knots
1 W		0309	1.3E
	0617	0903	1.0F
	1235	1556	1.2E
	1924	2138	0.6F
2 Th	0019	0351	1.3E
	0700	0942	1.0F
	1313	1639	1.2E
	2007	2220	0.6F
3 F	0105	0439	1.2E
	0749	1025	0.9F
	1351	1730	1.2E
	2051	2308	0.6F
4 Sa	0155	0537	1.1E
	0840	1114	0.8F
	1430	1822	1.2E
	2138		
5 Su		0000	0.6F
	0255	0638	1.1E
	0940	1209	0.8F
	1514	1913	1.2E
	2229		
6 M ○		0055	0.7F
	0409	0738	1.1E
	1048	1305	0.7F
	1609	2005	1.2E
	2320		
7 Tu		0151	0.8F
	0524	0844	1.1E
	1159	1408	0.6F
	1711	2103	1.2E
8 W	0013	0254	0.9F
	0630	0955	1.2E
	1308	1521	0.6F
	1813	2204	1.3E
9 Th	0108	0358	1.1F
	0730	1058	1.4E
	1410	1626	0.7F
	1912	2301	1.4E
10 F	0201	0452	1.2F
	0828	1154	1.5E
	1508	1719	0.8F
	2012	2355	1.5E
11 Sa	0255	0540	1.3F
	0921	1248	1.6E
	1558	1809	0.9F
	2110		
12 Su	0347	0049	1.5E
	1010	0629	1.4F
	1646	1341	1.7E
	2204	1901	0.9F
13 M ●	0437	0143	1.6E
	1059	0721	1.4F
	1733	1429	1.7E
	2255	1954	1.0F
14 Tu	0527	0232	1.6E
	1147	0813	1.4F
	1822	1514	1.7E
	2345	2045	1.0F
15 W	0619	0319	1.6E
	1232	0902	1.3F
	1912	1559	1.6E
		2132	0.9F
16 Th	0035	0406	1.4E
	0712	0950	1.2F
	1317	1645	1.4E
	2001	2221	0.8F
17 F	0125	0457	1.3E
	0807	1039	1.0F
	1358	1736	1.3E
	2051	2312	0.8F
18 Sa	0215	0556	1.1E
	0902	1132	0.8F
	1438	1825	1.1E
	2141		
19 Su	0310	0006	0.7F
	1003	0655	1.0E
	1517	1226	0.6F
	2232	1910	1.0E
20 M ○	0416	0059	0.6F
	1111	0752	0.9E
	1600	1318	0.5F
	2326	1952	0.9E
21 Tu	0525	0155	0.6F
	1221	0858	0.8E
	1649	1418	0.3F
		2038	0.9E
22 W	0018	0302	0.6F
	0626	1008	0.8E
	1329	1530	0.3F
	1739	2131	0.9E
23 Th	0107	0409	0.6F
	0721	1102	0.8E
	1428	1629	0.3F
	1830	2223	0.9E
24 F	0153	0453	0.7F
	0811	1145	0.9E
	1511	1711	0.4F
	1921	2307	1.0E
25 Sa	0237	0527	0.8F
	0856	1225	1.0E
	1549	1749	0.5F
	2012	2350	1.1E
26 Su	0317	0602	0.9F
	0937	1304	1.1E
	1622	1828	0.5F
	2102		
27 M		0035	1.2E
	0353	0638	0.9F
	1016	1342	1.2E
	1657	1910	0.6F
	2148		
28 Tu ○		0122	1.3E
	0430	0719	1.0F
	1054	1419	1.3E
	1732	1953	0.7F
	2233		
29 W		0207	1.4E
	0510	0800	1.1F
	1132	1455	1.4E
	1811	2035	0.7F
	2318		
30 Th		0250	1.4E
	0553	0841	1.1F
	1211	1533	1.4E
	1852	2115	0.8F
31 F	0006	0334	1.4E
	0640	0922	1.1F
	1249	1614	1.4E
	1933	2157	0.8F

TABLE 1. References to Table 1 in the tidal current exercises all refer to this excerpt from the *Tidal Current Tables*.

TABLE 2 – CURRENT DIFFERENCES AND OTHER CONSTANTS

No.	PLACE	Meter Depth (ft)	POSITION Latitude (North)	POSITION Longitude (West)	TIME DIFF. Min. before Flood	TIME DIFF. Flood	TIME DIFF. Min. before Ebb	TIME DIFF. Ebb	SPEED RATIOS Flood	SPEED RATIOS Ebb	Min. before Flood (knots)	Dir.	Max. Flood (knots)	Dir.	Min. before Ebb (knots)	Dir.	Max. Ebb (knots)	Dir.
	DELAWARE BAY and RIVER–cont. Time meridian, 75° W				on Delaware Bay Entrance, p.40													
4281	Riverview Beach, 0.75 n.mi. west of	15d	39° 39.40'	75° 32.38'	+3 52	+3 22	+3 31	+4 28	1.4	1.5	0.0	––	2.0	038°	0.0	––	1.9	225°
4431	Smith Island Shoal, southeast of	7	37° 05.3'	75° 43.5'	-1 36	-1 17	-1 35	-1 34	0.4	0.3	––	––	0.3	298°	––	––	0.4	068°
4436	Cape Henry Light, 2.2 miles southeast of		36° 53.9'	75° 58.7'	-1 16	-0 23	-0 10	-1 10	1.2	0.7	––	––	1.0	346°	––	––	0.9	165°
	CHESAPEAKE BAY																	
4441	Cape Henry Light, 1.1 n.mi. NNE of	15d	36° 56.33'	75° 59.98'	+0 26	+0 03	-0 04	+0 10	1.3	1.3	––	––	1.0	298°	––	––	1.7	113°
	. . . do . . .	38d	36° 56.33'	75° 59.98'	-1 42	-1 41	-1 36	-1 52	1.4	1.0	0.2	003°	1.1	275°	0.2	189°	1.2	106°
4446	Cape Henry Light, 2.0 n.mi. north of	15d	36° 57.53'	76° 00.63'	+0 12	+0 25	+1 00	+0 20	1.5	0.9	0.1	210°	1.2	289°	––	––	1.1	110°
	. . . do . . .	39d	36° 57.53'	76° 00.63'	-0 23	+0 10	+0 55	-0 17	1.5	0.5	0.1	012°	1.2	277°	0.1	190°	0.7	110°
	. . . do . . .	54d	36° 57.53'	76° 00.63'	-1 03	+0 07	+0 34	-1 05	1.1	0.4	0.1	002°	0.9	263°	0.2	177°	0.5	111°
4451	CHESAPEAKE BAY ENTRANCE	15d	36° 58.80'	75° 59.88'	Daily predictions						0.0	––	0.8	300°	0.0	––	1.2	129°
4456	Cape Henry Light, 4.6 miles north of		37° 00.1'	75° 59.3'	-0 27	+0 09	+0 19	+0 23	1.6	1.0	––	––	1.3	294°	––	––	1.3	104°
4461	Cape Henry Light, 5.9 n.mi. north of	14d	37° 01.40'	75° 59.55'	-0 59	-0 09	-0 26	-0 36	0.8	0.5	0.1	228°	0.6	307°	––	––	0.7	140°
4466	Lynnhaven Roads		36° 55.1'	76° 04.9'	-0 20	+0 18	+0 15	-0 10	1.0	0.7	––	––	0.8	280°	––	––	0.9	070°
4471	Lynnhaven Inlet bridge		36° 54.4'	76° 05.6'	-1 18	-1 10	-1 43	-2 30	0.7	1.1	––	––	0.6	180°	––	––	1.4	000°
	Chesapeake Bay Bridge Tunnel																	
4476	Chesapeake Beach, 1.5 miles north of		36° 56.69'	76° 07.33'	+0 29	+0 48	+0 06	+0 00	1.0	0.7	––	––	0.8	305°	––	––	0.9	190°
4481	Thimble Shoal Channel (Buoy "10")	15d	36° 58.73'	76° 07.57'	-0 04	+0 30	+0 45	+0 16	1.4	0.6	0.1	228°	1.1	302°	––	––	0.7	122°
4566	Cape Charles City, 3.3 n.mi. west of	15d	37° 15.87'	76° 05.62'	+0 38	+1 18	+1 03	+1 01	1.2	0.8	0.2	280°	1.0	355°	0.1	094°	1.0	187°
	. . . do . . .	40d	37° 15.87'	76° 05.62'	+0 16	+0 43	+1 10	+0 30	1.1	0.7	––	––	0.9	356°	0.1	284°	0.8	182°
	. . . do . . .	95d	37° 15.87'	76° 05.62'	+0 29	+1 00	+1 37	+1 24	1.2	0.7	0.1	223°	1.0	322°	––	––	0.8	138°
4571	New Point Comfort, 4.1 n.mi. ESE of	15d	37° 17.40'	76° 11.45'	+1 07	+1 22	+0 46	+0 46	1.0	0.8	0.3	296°	0.8	018°	0.3	098°	1.0	202°
4576	Wolf Trap Light, 0.5 mile west of		37° 23.4'	76° 11.9'	+1 43	+2 00	+1 34	+1 36	1.2	1.0	––	––	1.0	015°	––	––	1.2	190°
4581	Wolf Trap Light, 5.8 miles east of		37° 23.1'	76° 04.3'	+2 23	+2 40	+2 14	+2 16	1.1	1.0	––	––	0.9	015°	––	––	1.3	175°
4586	Church Neck Point, 1.9 n.mi. W of	15d	37° 24.20'	76° 00.78'	+0 46	+1 37	+1 36	+0 50	0.6	0.3	––	––	0.4	003°	––	––	0.4	177°
4591	Wolf Trap Light, 6.1 n.mi. ENE of	14d	37° 24.50'	76° 03.83'	+1 40	+1 58	+2 28	+2 11	1.6	0.9	0.2	275°	1.3	006°	0.2	098°	1.1	191°
	. . . do . . .	29d	37° 24.50'	76° 03.83'	+0 26	+0 55	+1 27	+1 07	0.8	0.5	0.2	099°	0.7	012°	0.2	279°	0.7	173°
4596	Wolf Trap Light, 5.2 n.mi. ENE of	15d	37° 24.50'	76° 05.00'	+1 43	+2 34	+2 41	+2 09	1.6	0.9	0.2	283°	1.3	010°	0.2	098°	1.1	187°
	. . . do . . .	40d	37° 24.50'	76° 05.00'	+1 07	+2 24	+2 43	+1 19	1.3	0.5	0.2	089°	1.0	352°	0.2	266°	0.7	183°
	. . . do . . .	63d	37° 24.50'	76° 05.00'	+0 24	+1 22	+2 05	+1 11	1.0	0.5	––	––	0.8	343°	––	––	0.6	158°
4601	Wolf Trap Light, 1.4 n.mi. NNE of	15d	37° 24.67'	76° 10.57'	+1 38	+2 16	+1 52	+1 19	1.4	0.9	––	––	1.1	005°	0.2	088°	1.2	175°
4606	Wolf Trap Light, 2.0 n.mi. NW of	14d	37° 25.00'	76° 12.90'	+0 03	+0 33	+1 05	+0 08	0.7	0.4	––	––	0.6	345°	––	––	0.6	166°
4611	Nassawadox Point, 1.9 n.mi. NW of	13d	37° 29.97'	76° 59.37'	+1 16	+1 43	+1 56	+1 36	0.8	0.5	––	––	0.6	352°	0.1	270°	0.6	178°
4616	Gwynn Island, 8.0 n.mi. east of	14d	37° 29.70'	76° 06.50'	+2 03	+3 03	+2 48	+2 33	1.2	0.9	0.2	267°	1.0	357°	0.2	090°	1.1	175°
	. . . do . . .	28d	37° 29.70'	76° 06.50'	+0 33	+1 07	+1 46	+0 23	0.7	0.4	0.2	102°	0.6	013°	0.3	281°	0.5	209°
4621	Gwynn Island, 1.5 n.mi. east of	16d	37° 30.03'	76° 14.70'	+0 59	+0 54	+0 54	+0 22	0.6	0.4	––	––	0.5	331°	0.1	227°	0.5	159°
4626	Stingray Point, 5.5 miles east of		37° 35.0'	76° 10.4'	+2 28	+3 36	+3 21	+2 32	1.2	0.7	––	––	1.0	343°	––	––	0.9	179°
4631	Stingray Point, 12.5 miles east of		37° 33.8'	76° 02.3'	+2 18	+3 00	+2 09	+2 36	1.2	0.6	––	––	1.0	030°	––	––	0.8	175°
4636	Powells Bluff, 2.2 n.mi. NW of	17d	37° 35.45'	76° 58.10'	+1 21	+1 29	+1 54	+1 23	0.8	0.5	0.1	101°	0.6	015°	0.1	284°	0.6	201°
4641	Windmill Point Light, 8.3 n.mi. ESE of	14d	37° 34.60'	76° 03.80'	+2 18	+2 57	+3 04	+2 46	1.1	0.7	0.1	270°	0.9	359°	0.1	095°	0.8	182°
	. . . do . . .	33d	37° 34.60'	76° 03.80'	+1 06	+1 22	+3 07	+2 14	0.6	0.3	0.2	099°	0.5	017°	0.2	255°	0.4	172°
4646	Windmill Point Light, 2.2 n.mi. ESE of	14d	37° 35.30'	76° 11.50'	+2 49	+2 38	+2 21	+2 29	0.8	0.7	0.1	079°	0.6	001°	0.1	081°	0.9	169°
	. . . do . . .	35d	37° 35.30'	76° 11.50'	+1 08	+1 35	+2 01	+1 44	0.8	0.3	––	––	0.6	342°	0.1	246°	0.4	175°
4651	Milby Point, 5.3 n.mi. WNW of	13d	37° 39.85'	76° 00.52'	+2 13	+2 30	+2 28	+2 32	0.7	0.5	––	––	0.6	016°	0.2	297°	0.7	210°
	. . . do . . .	38d	37° 39.85'	76° 00.52'	+0 32	+0 12	+1 12	+0 40	0.6	0.3	0.1	120°	0.5	043°	––	––	0.4	197°
4656	Bluff Point, 4.6 n.mi. east of	13d	37° 40.70'	76° 12.25'	+3 10	+3 25	+2 25	+2 46	0.4	0.6	––	––	0.4	003°	––	––	0.7	178°

References to Table 2 in the exercises all refer to pages 118 and 119 from the *Tables*—extracted here.

EXAMPLE 3

Determining the strength and set of a current at an intermediate time at a reference station.

Problem: What is the predicted strength and set of the current at Chesapeake Bay Entrance at 1620 EDT on 1 October?

Solution: Before entering the table, daylight time is first converted to standard time; 1620 EDT becomes 1520 EST. The times of slack and maximum current (ebb or flood) which bracket the desired time are found from Table 1. The interval between these times is determined, as is the interval between the desired time and the slack.

```
 18 11   time of slack
-14 56   time of maximum ebb current
  3:15   interval, slack—maximum current

 18 11   time of slack
-15 20   desired time
  2:51   interval, slack—desired time
```

Once you have established these time intervals, Table 3A is used to determine the ratio of the strength of the current at the desired time to its maximum strength. The nearest tabulated values are used—with no interpolation. In this example, the ratio at the intersection of the line for 3h 00m (closest to 2h 51m) and the column for 3h 20m (closest to 3h 15m) is found to be 1.0. Multiply the maximum current by this decimal factor, 1.2 x 1.0 = 1.2 (in this case, no difference).

From the times used, we note that the current is ebbing. From the top of Table 2, we determine that the direction is 129° true. So on 1 October, at 1620 EDT, the current at Chesapeake Bay Entrance will be 1.2 knots, setting 129° true.

Notes

1. Except as specially indicated, use Table 3A, the upper portion of Table 3. The lower portion (B) is intended for use in designated waterways only.

2. Be sure that the interval is calculated between the desired time and the time of slack, whether or not this time is nearer to the given time than the time of maximum current.

3. Note that calculations of current strength are rounded to the nearest tenth of a knot.

EXAMPLE 4

Determining the current at an intermediate time at a subordinate station.

Problem: What is the predicted strength and set of the current at a point 5½ miles east of Stingray Point (the subordinate station) at 0935 EDT on 16 October?

Solution: First, the predictions for time of slack and maximum current must be found for the subordinate station. Before entering the tables, our desired time of 0935 EDT must be converted to 0835 EST.

Slack		Maximum	Max velocity
0510	at Chesapeake Bay Entrance	07 57 flood	1.6 knots
+2:28	difference ratio	+3:36	-1.2
0738	at subordinate station	11 33	1.9 knots

With the information developed above, and the desired time, further calculations are made as follows:

```
  11 33  time of maximum at subordinate station
 -07 38  time of slack at subordinate station
   3 55  interval between slack and maximum current

  08 35  desired time when strength is needed
 -07 38  time of slack at subordinate station
   0 57  interval between slack and desired time
```

Using Table 3A, the intersection between the line of interval to desired time 1h 00m (closest to 0h 57m) and the column for 4h 00m (closest to 3h 55m), the speed ratio is found to be 0.4. Next, multiply 0.4 x 1.9 (the maximum speed of current at the subordinate station) = 0.8.

Table 2 indicates that the direction of maximum flood current at Stingray Point is 343° true.

The current at 0935 EDT at a point 5½ miles east of Stingray Point on 16 October is predicted to be 0.8 knot setting 343° true.

EXAMPLE 5

Determining the duration of slack (weak current) at a designated point.

Problem: For how long is it predicted that the current be not more than 0.4 knots around the time of first slack before flood 17 November at Chesapeake Bay Entrance?

Solution: Table 1 for this date shows the maximum currents on either side of this slack (0731) as 1.5 knots ebb (0426) and 1.2 knots flood (1011).

Use Table 4A to find the duration of current less than 0.4 knot for each maximum. One-half of each such duration is used for the period from 0.4 to 0 knots and then 0 to 0.4 knots.

The value for the ending ebb current is one-half of 62, or 31 minutes; for the beginning flood current, it is one-half of 94, or 47 minutes. The duration will be 31 + 47 = 78m.

EXAMPLE 6

Use of a current diagram.

Problem: For an afternoon run up Chesapeake Bay from Smith Point to Sandy Point Light at 10 knots on 21 October, what time should you depart from Smith Point for the most favorable current conditions?

Solution: Use the current diagram for Chesapeake Bay (shown on page 349) found near the end of the *Tidal Current Tables*. Draw a line on the diagram parallel to the 10-knot northbound speed line so that it fits generally in the center of the shaded area marked "Flood." (You might use parallel rules to walk the line across.) Find the point where this 10-knot line intersects with the horizontal line marked "Smith Point Light." Project downward from this point to the scale at the bottom of the diagram. The mark here is "0^h after ebb begins at the entrance." Referring to Table 1, it will be seen that on the given date, the afternoon slack before ebb occurs at 1606.

For a run up Chesapeake Bay to Sandy Point Light at 10 knots on the afternoon of 21 October, it is predicted that the most favorable current will be available if you leave Smith Point Light at about 1606 EST (1706 EDT).

Notes

1. Similar solutions can be worked out for southbound trips, but on longer runs you will probably be faced with favorable and unfavorable current conditions. Choose a starting time to minimize adverse conditions.

2. Conditions shown on *Tidal Current Diagrams* are averages and for typical conditions—small variations should be expected in specific situations.

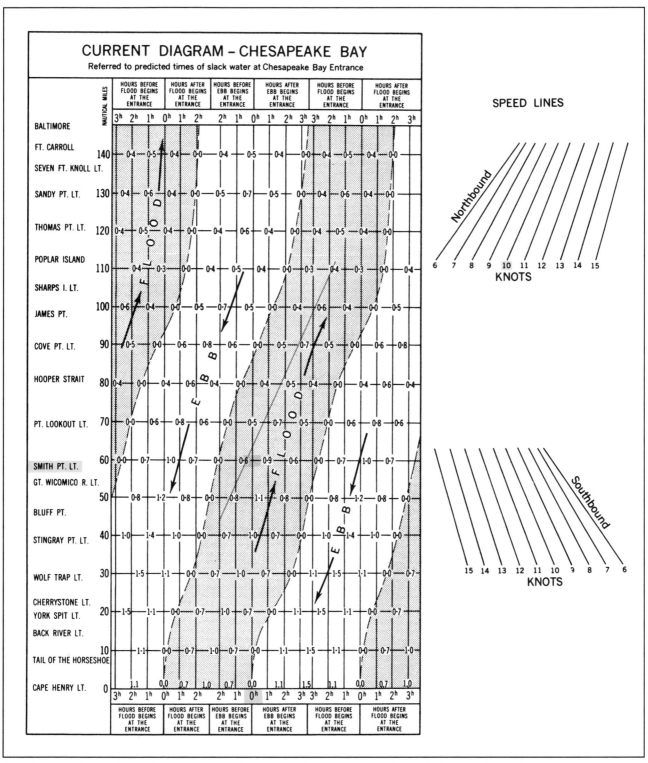

CURRENT DIAGRAM – CHESAPEAKE BAY
Referred to predicted times of slack water at Chesapeake Bay Entrance

A tidal current diagram helps choose the most advantageous time for a course of a particular speed up or down stream. A speed arrow is chosen from the right side, one representing the speed your vessel will travel, and it is walked across to the appropriate position on the diagram (with parallel rules or a plotting protractor) so that it lies, if possible, entirely within an area of advantageous current flow. The list of locations on the left side helps determine the length of the course line— the one shown here represents a trip from Smith Point Light to Sandy Point Light at 10 knots. By reading downward from the Smith Point intersection to the bottom scale, we can estimate that the best time to make such a trip, as far as current advantage is concerned, is at the slack before ebb at Chesapeake Bay Entrance. Table 1 tells what time that is.

16 BOATING AND THE ENVIRONMENT

While we consider ourselves stewards of most other wilderness areas of the planet, we have neglected the greatest wilderness of all: the seas. As users of this spectacular resource, our collective actions in and around the water are the lowest common denominator of the pollution problem.

The problem begins with each individual polluting act, whether willful or accidental. The good news is that this is also where the solution begins, with individual choices *not* to pollute. This chapter—the first of its kind ever to appear in *Chapman*—offers information intended to brighten the future of the boating environment for us and our children.

FUEL EFFICIENCY

The environment is increasingly a factor in the selection of a vessel. In coming years, the importance of this concern will grow in proportion to mounting awareness of the global crisis (to say nothing of rising fuel costs).

At the forefront of concerns to today's boater is fuel efficiency. Recreational craft are statistically the least efficient means of transportation in general use. Because recreational vessels use more fuel to do less work than any car, truck, bus, airplane or ship, boatowners should be aware of ways to maximize their boats' fuel efficiency.

Choosing a fuel-efficient boat

If you think only in terms of fuel efficiency, sailing craft are the obvious choice—what could possibly beat wind power? However, since powerboaters vastly outnumber sailors, and because sailboats are often motored more than they are sailed,

Although today's recreational craft are not yet equipped with exhaust aftertreatment, this is likely to change within the next few years. The United States Environmental Protection Agency (EPA) is gathering data on marine engine emissions.

efficiency under power must be examined for all boats—sail and power alike.

No boats currently in use or being manufactured must conform to any fuel mileage standards, nor are they required to have exhaust-emission control devices such as catalytic converters. Consequently, for many boat buyers, decision-making involves optimizing what is available. The objective should be to identify a vessel that offers the desired features and speeds, and yet which keeps power to a minimum (resulting in the lowest emissions).

In terms of efficiency, it is important to consider that all boats exhibit the lowest levels of resistance at hull speeds below the critical velocity of 1.3 times the square root of the waterline length. Various hull types are described below:

■ **Displacement hulls**, such as trawlers and sailboats, move more tonnage a greater distance for less fuel, and so are the most efficient. All oceangoing ships, tugboats and most military vessels are displacement hulls by reason of economy.

■ **Semi-planing or semi-displacement hulls** are found next on the efficiency scale. They are generally capable of doubling boat speed with a trebling of horsepower. The majority of the fastest military small craft fall into this category, where the value of speed overlaps the value of economy.

■ **Planing hulls** are the least efficient, but most popular, hull form. A typical large runabout that needs 250 horsepower to go 40 knots could go 5 knots with 5 horsepower: a fifty-fold increase in power for only an eight-fold increase in speed.

■ **Multihulls** offer the best potential for efficiency under power. Just as a sailing catamaran outstrips a monohull, a power catamaran achieves any given speed with far less power than a single hull.

Reducing environmental impact

Any vessel can be reengineered to have a less adverse impact on the environment. This can be undertaken after a thorough assessment of the boat's propulsion, generating and electric

POWERBOAT EFFICIENCY FORMULA

The following simple formula gives a thumbnail picture of the relative efficiency of any boat under power, where:

V = the boat's top speed

GPH = gallons per hour consumed by all engines at top speed. If no data are available, or if data seem unrealistic, use the following equations for average specific fuel consumption for similar engines:

diesel = .4 lbs. of fuel per horsepower-hour (hph)

gasoline = .5 lbs. per hph

outboard motors = .6+ lbs. per hph

(Example: 300 rated hp x .5 lbs = 150 lbs. One gallon of gasoline weighs 6.2 pounds, thus the engine will consume 150 / 6.2 = 24.2 gph.)

$\triangle$ = the boat's weight in pounds or kilograms (all comparisons must be based on the same unit of measure).

$$\frac{\left(\frac{\triangle}{GPH}\right) \times V}{10^4}$$

Long, thin power launches rate around 10 (in pounds); trawler yachts, 4 to 5; auxiliary sailboats, 4 to 5; power catamarans, 2 to 4; semi-planing cruisers, 2-3; planing cruisers cluster around 1; and muscleboats and runabouts average .8.

storage, electric appliances, septic system, potable water storage and heating, refrigeration, bilge and dinghy. These topics are covered in this chapter.

The condition of the boat's bottom is also a factor. A rough bottom increases drag, which decreases efficiency.

Propulsion

Emissions and fuel consumption can be reduced by scrupulous maintenance. Worn rings and cylinders allow 25 percent more unburned fuel and oil to escape with exhaust gases. Leaking seals and lines drip oil and fuel into the bilge, from which the fumes permeate the entire vessel. Once it is pumped overboard, oily bilge discharge becomes everyone's problem, with consequences ranging from a neighbor's irritation to endangered fish and waterfowl—as well as thousands of dollars in fines. Dirty injectors in diesel engines spray fuel into the cylinders in an uneven pattern so that much of it is not fully burnt and exits as sooty, acrid exhaust.

One or two new models of fuel-injected gasoline engines are now offered on the market. These—in conjunction with parallel developments in electronic engine management systems and combustion optimization for engines of all types—reduce emissions.

Turbocharged diesel engines are the most fuel-efficient engines available for marine use. (When low-sulfur diesel fuel becomes available, these may one day be the cleanest as well.) Most marine diesels have been developed for use in trucks, without exhaust aftertreatment, where they are under scrutiny by the enforcers of clean air legislation. Turbocharged gasoline engines with exhaust recycling would be the best option, offering the most power for the lightest weight, lowest fuel consumption, and lowest emissions, but such engines are not yet available for boats. To date, the recreational boat market remains dominated by engines with a low short-term—albeit high long-term—cost.

It is feasible to design and install exhaust aftertreatment in most inboard boats, but the expense and logistics of retrofitting such equipment can be discouraging. Such a modification requires dry exhaust, and thus an additional through-hull fitting for cooling water discharge. Design of the exhaust run will have to feature a somewhat larger pathway than is usual, incorporating space for pipe insulation, catalytic converter, and an exit configuration that will not allow any seawater into the system.

Although there are converter manufacturers who will help match a product to the application, any changeover must be designed and supervised by a naval architect and performed by reliable mechanics. Once boats are designed and built to accommodate such systems, the costs will be minimal, as they are for automobiles.

Apart from internal combustion, there is an emerging interest in electric propulsion. Horsepower for horsepower, electric energy is statistically (factoring all types of power plants, including coal) more than 100 times cleaner to produce than that from internal combustion. Electric propulsion is smooth, silent, clean and, with today's power technology, surprisingly strong.

Many boats in use today could easily be converted to electric propulsion with good results. Harbor craft, for example, quite frequently make short runs with many stops, for

THE NURSERY ZONE

Along the edges of many waterways lie shallows and plant-choked cul-de-sacs known to scientists as the wetlands—interface areas between well-drained and poorly drained soils. Because many of these areas are wet, boggy and sometimes have an odor of rotten eggs (hyrdogen sulfide), they are avoided by people and often used as trash dumps. They seem to be the most useless places on earth, but nothing could be farther from the truth.

While under overwhelming stress from shore development projects, pollution and erosion, marshes and wetlands are intensely involved with an important task. They nurture new life—species that are disturbed by wakes of speeding boats.

Ninety percent of the mid-Atlantic Ocean's fish species depend on southern mangrove marshes for the survival of their juvenile populations, and 80 percent of northern Atlantic species develop in the coastal wetlands of Chesapeake Bay, Delaware Bay, Jersey shore, Hudson River and the New England shoreline. When boating in these areas like these, remember to slow down.

Salt marshes, such as this one on the Assateague National Seashore, are exceedingly vulnerable to shoreline erosion. Boat wake, which results in turbidity and contributes to the eventual destruction of marshes, threatens important nursery areas for scores of species of fish and invertebrates.

which they could be quick-charged. Electric water taxis are economically feasible, as are electric rental fleets. Yacht club launches, in many instances, also could be converted to electric power.

When the duty profile of a boat is too stringent for the range and speed limitations of pure electric propulsion, some people may find hybrid power appropriate. Hybrid is similar to electric in that it features a battery bank, a motor controller, power control and an electric motor; however, it adds an internal combustion generator to the system. Generators, because they run at steady speeds, emit 30 percent fewer pollutants and—when used intermittently as a range extender or power boost for the batteries—can allow an owner to enjoy all of the best features of an electric boat with far fewer disadvantages.

In addition to challenging a sailor's skills, boating under sail saves fuel. This skipper has enjoyed a day on the water without having started his engine.

Fuel

It is difficult to control the quality of fuel coming aboard a vessel without chemical analysis, and even with analysis it is often impractical or futile to leave one gas dock in search of another that may or may not have a higher-quality product. Water, dirt, algae, sludge and other contaminants sometimes found in marine fuel will all interfere with efficient combustion. Change fuel filters often, and consider using ester-based fuel additives to reduce emissions.

Oxygenated fuel, which is going to be found at more and more marine gas pumps, provides more complete combustion, fewer emissions, and by virtue of a leaner mix, less carbon dioxide, a greenhouse gas that has been increasing dramatically over the last three decades. Try not to get upset by slightly higher prices. If, however, the price increases more than 12 to 15 cents per gallon, be wary of gouging, which has been occurring in some cities where oxygenated fuel is required by law.

Propeller

Most of a boat's inefficiency occurs at the propeller. A sailing yacht trying to power into a stiff headwind and chop with a small two-blade folding propeller may suffer inefficiency as great as 100 percent, whereas a tug with no load, turning an enormous multiblade propeller at slow rpm's, may be only 10 percent inefficient. Most recreational craft are subject to slip and cavitation losses in a range from 30 to 50 percent of total engine power.

Not surprisingly, propeller efficiency rises according to three factors: (1) as boat speed diminishes, (2) as a function of propeller diameter and (3) with lower operating propeller rpm's. With no changes in engine or exhaust technology at all, gains in efficiency on the order of 20 to 50 percent can be realized with an acceptance of lower speeds, different hull forms and deeper draft from larger propellers.

Batteries

If batteries are allowed to deteriorate into poor condition, they are hopelessly inefficient, and are the principal cause of non-propulsion energy waste. Power from shore outlets or ship-board generators pours into them, but very little becomes available to be used.

Batteries can be tested in a cursory way with a hydrometer, but a much more accurate test is cell-by-cell with a voltmeter. Stress-testing is another good way to get the truth out of a battery, as is the measurement and comparison of power-in to power-out. The best way to monitor and evaluate the power flow of a system is with an amp-hour counter.

Some battery companies will take their product back at little or no cost for a "gassing charge"—a carefully controlled process that can bring a dead battery back to life, giving it 90 percent of its capacity when new. *Never discard a dead battery*. The lead in its plates is highly toxic, and will leach steadily into the environment for years. Batteries are 95 percent

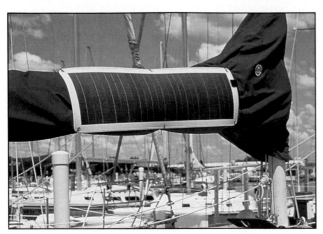

Flexible solar panels can be used in areas aboard a boat that are both convenient and out of the way.

recyclable; even the plastic casings are shredded and recycled. Save dead batteries to turn in when buying new ones—you will get money back.

Electrical system

Green and corroded contacts or wires are a sure indication that power is being lost. Voltage drop can be measured with a voltmeter. Any wire put into a boat must be of braided and tinned copper, and terminals should be the heat-shrunk and sealed type. A common fault, especially in aftermarket modifications, is the use of undersize wire.

Fluorescent lights can frequently be used to conserve power. For an equivalent amount of light, fluorescent bulbs will use one-third the power, and last much longer. (They do interfere with the functioning of Loran receivers, though.)

Underway, electric appliances such as refrigeration systems are less efficient than engine-driven ones; however engine-driven equipment requires running the boat's engine at anchor. Microwaves, while more efficient than electric ranges, consume excessive power by nautical standards; try to use them when plugged into shore power.

Alternate energy sources

The true cost of a gallon of gasoline or diesel fuel would be close to $5 if external oil-related problems were paid for "up front." These would include billions of dollars in health liabilities, treatment of contaminated ground water, cleanups like the Exxon Valdez incident, enforcement of clean air legislation and many, many other expenses.

But if a boat's systems are designed for efficiency and are maintained in good condition, great rewards—both personal *and* economic—can be gained from tapping the energy of the sun and wind. With managed power usage and favorable generating conditions, alternate energy can supplement a cruising boat's on-board power at no cost to the environment.

Efficiency in solar panels is an expression of how much of the solar energy striking the panel is converted to elec-

tricity, and the rule-of-thumb cost is $10 per watt. (The high initial cost of solar panels is offset by the fact that they require no maintenance other than occasional cleaning.) Solar panels come in three configurations, described below:

- Amorphous solar panels are flexible and cost the least, but are also the least efficient—on the order of 6 percent.
- Polycrystalline panels are rigid, and more expensive. They can achieve efficiencies of 10 percent.
- Monocrystalline cells are the cells that power solar racing cars and satellites. They can reach efficiencies of 30 percent, but must be assembled by hand, and are often made of highly toxic materials. Unless money is absolutely no object, these are best forgotten.

Solar panels are rated for the most favorable conditions: cloudless skies, perfect angle of incidence, sun overhead, the right ambient temperature and clean panel surface. Thus a 30-watt polycrystalline panel may produce only 10 to 15 watts much of the time, with surges up to 20, instead of the 30 you were expecting.

Wind generators, like solar panels, have proven themselves countless times aboard cruising yachts in all parts of the world.

Though noisier than solar panels, the wind generator, with its high output in windy and less-than-perfect conditions, has become a symbol of electrical self-sufficiency among bluewater sailors.

The whirling blades annoy some people, but the location—up on the backstay or on a pole off the transom—is out of the way. They are rated in amps instead of watts, but simple math can equate the two:

Amps x volts = watts

Watts / volts = amps

A wind generator producing 10 amps of 12-volt power produces 120 watts, theoretically comparable to four 30-watt panels in parallel also producing 12 volts. More complicated than solar panels, they have blades, bearings, stators and rotors that need attention and occasional replacement.

Another type of generator is a towed hydro-generator. Energy is created by the revolving of a rotor that turns in the water as the boat moves forward.

OTHER BOAT FEATURES

Waste systems

It is no longer acceptable to pump untreated sewage overboard anywhere but in the open ocean. In fact, it is illegal in all lakes, rivers, harbors, bays and sounds—anywhere a government agency has jurisdiction. Without a doubt, the days of installing a vestigial holding tank and a hefty diverter valve are over.

The appropriate system today features no overboard discharge, a large holding tank, and a pumpout fitting on deck. There are, however, a number of waste treatment devices for boats that chew, electrocute, and even incinerate your waste before it goes into the tank. Such treatment was designed to serve overboard discharge purposes, and makes little difference in the performance of a vessel's holding tank or the design of its plumbing.

Although manufacturers claim that their devices meet Coast Guard approval for overboard discharge, buyers must be aware that increasing numbers of communities and regional governing bodies are passing laws against any form of sewage discharge, in which case Coast Guard approval will not be protection against stiff fines.

In most areas, there is some leeway where "gray water" is concerned, allowing overboard discharge from a sump receiving shower and sink drains, and relieving stress on a boat's holding capacity. Before setting out, it is best to consult the local authorities in areas where you will be cruising, whether home waters or areas along the route of a passage—and definitely before buying a new boat or updating an existing one.

Lakes generally have the most stringent regulations, and for obvious reasons. Lake George, in upstate New York, requires all visiting boats to submit to an inspection, and any overboard head and gray-water discharge fittings are plugged with a tapered wooden dowel which is sawed off and sealed. Unless you voluntarily comply, a local official will be forced to plug the fittings for you, so you are wise to carry your own plugs, carefully fit and tried beforehand, in order to protect your gel coat.

Potable water

Finding good drinking water has always been a problem in boats. Even if the water coming aboard can be presumed safe, there are other considerations—the plastic taste from the dockside hoses and the condition of the fresh-water tank (is it still clean, free of algae, bacteria and contamination by the last filling?) Many boat owners decide to stock bottled water to get around the problem: They cook, clean and shower in tank water, but drink from bottles or plastic jugs.

Bottled water, however, must be packaged and transported, often over long distances, and behind each gallon of water lurks a gallon of oil that had to be consumed making the container, shipping and handling it, heating and lighting the store where it was sold, and so on.

More and more, boaters are agreeing that filtration is a far better solution to the water problem. There are reasonably priced units that mount under the sink and operate with no electricity, and hand-held units for less permanent applications. The best filter is one that removes small toxic molecules such as those from pesticides, herbicides, metals and petrochemicals, as well as the larger organisms that cause intestinal diseases. The boater is advised to consult consumer reports on filter efficiency, and to change filters at recommended intervals.

The bilge

One of the most common sources of oil in seawater is bilge discharge. Big ships discharge bilge water, and so do most small craft, whether we like to admit it or not. Oil and fuel leak into a vessel's bilges from sloppy oil changes, damaged con-

A pump out is a simple, no-mess and almost odor-free operation when proper equipment and facilities are at hand.

tainers, leaking fuel lines, the inevitable cleaning or fuel line bleeding project, leaking engine fittings, gaskets or seals, crankcase vent fumes, and from cleanup after other boat maintenance has been performed. *This material must not be pumped overboard.*

When performing maintenance on the engine, disconnect or switch off the bilge pumps. Practice the best hygiene possible under the circumstances. Carry a number of supplies that will aid in general maintenance, particularly maintaining clean bilges, as suggested below:

■ Rubber gloves for a good grip and to protect hands.
■ Cloth rags (not paper towels or disposable wipes).
■ A separate container for used rags.
■ Mirrors for best visibility and reduced chance of botching a connection and causing leaks, and for inspection of inaccessible areas of bilge.
■ Pans for positioning beneath the engine.
■ Used tin cans with string or wire hooks to hang beneath fittings being worked on.
■ Oil-absorbent pads for spills in work areas.
■ Sponges, biodegradable oil cleaners and rags dedicated to oil cleanup, stored in their own containers—recycled plastic milk jugs serve the purpose.
■ Oil-absorbent bilge "socks," which can be wrung out once they're dirty and then reused.
■ A sponge fastened to the end of a broom handle for cleaning inaccessible areas of bilge after contamination.
■ Coveralls dedicated to dirty work to keep oil residue from regular clothes out of washing machines and their drain water.
■ An organized file of shop manuals with which to research procedures beforehand, and to minimize hit-or-miss maintenance, one of the chief causes of bilge contamination.

The dinghy

Of the hydrocarbon pollution that is attributable to recreational boats, an overwhelming percentage is caused by two-cycle outboard motors. An average afternoon outing in a family runabout will spill two gallons of toxic petroleum hydrocarbons into the water and air (about 35 to 65 percent respectively). As soon as you are able, sell or recycle such an engine. Replace it with a four-stroke engine, if possible, or with a couple of 30-pound batteries (these are the heaviest that can be conveniently hoisted aboard) and an electric trolling motor.

Better still, get reacquainted with the pleasures and physical benefits of rowing. Any hard dinghy with a good pair of oars and oarlocks that allow you to feather the oars on the backstroke will, with a little practice, become an excellent workhorse. Not only does rowing provide the rower with some exercise, which is so notably lacking on long cruises, it also allows the exploration of little guts and marshes that are not accessible under power. In fact, many people, once indoctrinated to the cult of rowing, make it a point of honor.

A new generation of boating products

Whether because of legislative and public pressure, or a sense of conscience, manufacturers are offering increasingly more boating products made from recycled and recyclable materials. When shopping for provisions and boating parts and supplies, shop from an environmentally friendly perspective.

The fuel/air separator shown at left prevents overboard spillage during fueling, reducing fuel costs as it protects against water pollution.

Hazardous waste trapped in used oil filters contains acid, heavy metal, oil and sludge. In some states strict legislation is being passed regarding the disposal of these filters. Recyclable models, such as the one shown at right, are now available.

LITTER, SOLID WASTE AND RECYCLING

Litter that floats on the water and washes ashore on the scenic coastlines of the world continues to occur despite laws that prohibit dumping trash in all lakes, rivers, streams and navigable waterways in the United States.

Every year, thousands of volunteers participate in beach cleanups around the world. In 1989, for example, the Center for Marine Conservation reported that 65,000 people cleaned 3,000 miles of coast in 25 states and parts of Canada and Mexico. They picked up 861 tons of trash, more than 60 percent of which was plastic. In 1991 there were 130,000 volunteers and 1,500 tons of trash.

The plastic problem can be countered by recycling aboard your boat. In its simplest form, recycling involves a container for plastic, which can be shredded or compressed to take up less space, a container for glass, a container for metal, and a container for other trash.

Most marinas are now recycling, so boaters who day-trip frequently or stop dockside during their cruises should feel no burden. The long-term cruiser of remote areas has a different problem, but that person has typically developed a system of reusable containers and minimal trash because of space limitations.

Larger vessels can be outfitted with trash compactors so that solid waste takes up less space, but even small craft can benefit by subjecting trash to the human compactor—crumpling everything that is thrown out, and a few good stomps on whatever's in the trash can every now and then.

Metal containers should be washed out in spent dishwater before it is dumped, and with both ends removed, flattened. They take up very little space. Small plastic baskets or mesh bags are convenient recycling containers, and can be located under the sink, under furniture, or under the sole.

Buying habits have a great influence on the amount of solid waste you generate. If you buy small units of material, which are typically dressed up with lots of packaging to enhance visibility in the store, you will find yourself awash in trash. If you buy in bulk and pack food in reusable containers there will be much less waste material to contend with. You can also edit your solid waste while provisioning the boat. Much packaging material can be stripped off your food and supplies before embarking. Packaging that is made from several different materials, called "composite," should be avoided in favor of recyclable packaging.

Garbage, normally produced in relatively small amounts, can be isolated from general trash, which will not, then, smell bad. Garbage can be taken ashore for composting at home, or contributed to the gardens of people in the places your vessel is visiting.

Sailmakers at North Sails, Milford, Connecticut, employed centuries-old mariners' techniques to ensure historic authenticity of sails for the tall ship HMS *Rose,* yet worked on a 1992 fabric produced through Du Pont plastics recycling technology. Du Pont used conventional methods to recycle 126,000 plastic soda bottles and an advanced proprietary process to recycle plastic car fenders into pellets and resin from which yarn was spun and woven into sailcloth.

USCG REGULATIONS: DISPOSAL OF GARBAGE FROM VESSELS

Dumping of garbage into the sea is a worldwide problem—a problem documented by a Center for Marine Conservation project, during which volunteers collected 1,000 tons of garbage from U.S. seashores in just three hours. Sixty percent of this was plastic refuse, which can kill fish and marine wildlife and foul vessel propellers and cooling water intakes. Other forms of waterborne garbage can litter beaches and make people sick. Consequently, U.S. Coast Guard regulations prohibit dumping of plastic refuse, and garbage mixed with plastic, into any waters, and restrict dumping of other forms of garbage.

ILLEGAL DUMPING

INSIDE 3 MILES
(and in U.S. lakes, rivers, bays and sounds)
Plastic, dunnage, lining and packing materials that float
Any garbage except dishwater/graywater/fresh fish parts

3 to 12 MILES
Plastic, dunnage, lining and packing materials that float
Any garbage not ground to less than one square inch

12 to 25 MILES
Plastic, dunnage, lining and packing materials that float

OUTSIDE 25 MILES
Plastic

The USCG has issued these regulations to implement Annex V of the International Convention for the Prevention of Pollution from Ships, 1973, commonly known as Annex V of MARPOL (Marine Pollution) 73/78. They apply to all U.S. vessels wherever they operate (except waters under the exclusive jurisdiction of a state), and foreign vessels operating in U.S. waters out to and including the Exclusive Economic Zone (200 miles).

Equivalent information about regulations on garbage disposal in Canadian waters can be obtained from the Coast Guard: Canadian Coast Guard, Ship Safety, 344 Slater St., Ottawa, Ont. K1A 0N7. Tel: (613) 990-2309.

The terminology of garbage
■ Plastic includes but is not limited to: plastic bags, styrofoam cups and lids, six-pack holders, stirrers, straws, milk jugs, egg cartons, synthetic fishing nets, ropes, lines and bio- or photo-degradable plastics.

■ Garbage means paper, rags, glass, metal, crockery (generated in living spaces aboard the vessel—what we normally call trash), and all kinds of food, maintenance and cargo-associated waste. "Garbage" does not include fresh fish or fish parts, dishwater or gray water.

■ Dunnage is material used to block and brace cargo, and is considered a cargo-associated waste.

■ Dishwater means the liquid residue from the manual or automatic washing of dishes and utensils that have been pre-cleaned to the extent that any remaining food particles will not impede the operation of automatic dishwashers.

■ Graywater means drainage from a dishwasher, shower, laundry, bath and washbasin; it does not include drainage from toilets, urinals, hospitals and cargo spaces.

Vessel operator obligations
Observe the prohibition of disposal of plastics in any waters. Learn and conform to the regulations regarding disposal of other garbage. For example, the rules, in effect, make it illegal within 3 nautical miles to operate a garbage disposal in a galley sink if it discharges garbage overboard—even ground-up garbage. To make it easier to comply with the regulations, vessel operators may want to separate garbage according to the disposal limitations.

Placards
The regulations require U.S. recreational boaters and other U.S. vessel operators, if their vessel is 26 feet or more in length, to affix one or more placards to their vessel. Placards may be of any design as long as they conform to the following basic size, information and placard requirements. The placards warn against the discharge of plastic and other forms of garbage within the navigable waters of the United States, and specify discharge restrictions beyond the territorial sea (the territorial sea generally ends 3 nautical miles from the seashore), as outlined above. In addition, the placard must contain the warning that a person who violates these requirements is liable to civil and criminal penalties, as outlined under Enforcement. The placard must also note that state and local regulations may further restrict the disposal of garbage.

Placards for exclusive Great Lakes use
Commercial and recreational vessels used *exclusively* in the Great Lakes may use the Annex V placards described above or affix a placard that reads "The discharge of ALL garbage into the Great Lakes or their connecting or tributary waters is prohibited." (In the Great Lakes, it is illegal to dump anything except fresh fish, fish parts, dishwater or gray water anywhere, regardless of distance from shore.)

■ **Placard size and placement.** Operators shall ensure that one or more placards are displayed in prominent locations and in sufficient numbers so that they can be observed and read by the crew and passengers. These locations might include embarkation points, food service areas, galleys, garbage handling spaces, and common deck spaces frequented by passengers and crew. Each placard must be at least 9 inches wide and 4 inches high, made of durable material and lettered with letters at least ⅛ inch high. Placards may be purchased from local marinas, boat dealers and marine equipment suppliers.

■ **Waste management plans.** The regulations require U.S. recreational boaters and other U.S. vessel operators, if their vessels are 40 feet or more in length and engaged in commerce or equipped with a galley and berthing, to carry a Waste Management Plan if the vessel operates, or is certified to operate, beyond 3 nautical miles from shore.

The Waste Management Plan must be in writing and describe procedures for collecting, processing, storing and properly disposing of garbage in a way that will not violate the requirements displayed above. It must also designate the person who is in charge of carrying out the plan.

Boaters and other vessel operators who have specific questions about the form or content of a Waste Management Plan should contact the closest Coast Guard Captain of the Port.

Marina obligations

Ports and terminals that conduct business with a commercial vessel must be capable of receiving garbage from the vessel when it docks. Recreational boating facilities (such as marinas, yacht clubs and attending launching ramps), capable of providing wharfage or other services for 10 or more recreational vessels, must also provide adequate garbage reception facilities for any vessel that routinely calls. Marinas that receive garbage from boats returning from international voyages have special requirements—check with the closest Coast Guard Captain of the Port or Marine Safety Office *(Appendices)*. If a marina or terminal does not want to be directly involved in garbage collection and disposal, local firms may be retained to provide the service at the marina or terminal. Vessels must be conducting business with the facility or marina in order to qualify for the service. Terminals and marinas would not be expected to provide reception services to a vessel whose sole reason for docking was to offload its garbage; the operator may thus be charged a reasonable fee.

Enforcement

The United States Coast Guard enforces Annex V.

A person found to have violated these regulations may be liable for a civil penalty not to exceed $25,000 for each violation. In addition, criminal penalties not to exceed $50,000 and/or imprisonment up to five years may be imposed.

The Coast Guard may deny vessels entry to marinas and terminals not in compliance.

Reporting violations

Vessels denied access to offload garbage wastes at marinas or other terminals should contact the closest U.S. Coast Guard Captain of the Port or Marine Safety Office *(Appendices)*. Observation of boats and vessels in violation of Annex V may also be reported to the same offices.

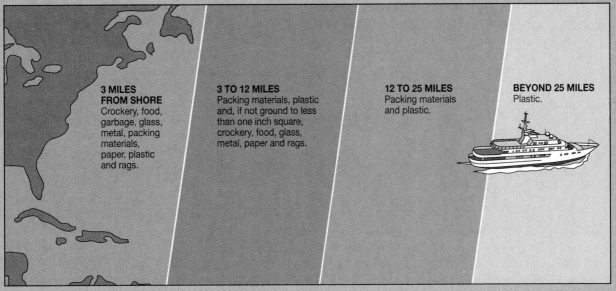

3 MILES FROM SHORE
Crockery, food, garbage, glass, metal, packing materials, paper, plastic and rags.

3 TO 12 MILES
Packing materials, plastic and, if not ground to less than one inch square, crockery, food, glass, metal, paper and rags.

12 TO 25 MILES
Packing materials and plastic.

BEYOND 25 MILES
Plastic.

United States Coast Guard regulations specifically prohibit dumping in the international zones as illustrated above.

TOXINS AND OTHER HARMFUL SUBSTANCES

Pesticides

Most insect sprays and strips are highly poisonous materials, with fumes that linger in the confined atmosphere of a boat interior far longer than in the typical homes for which they were developed. There may be long-term health effects attributable to these toxins.

- Avoid insect sprays and hanging strips.
- Fit your boat with easily handled small mesh screens.
- Carry a fly swatter for each area in the boat.
- Non-toxic bug repellents are available. Some don't work, but others do; do a little research.
- Much of the work an insect poison is required to do can be done with a vacuum cleaner and a frequent, regular regimen of housecleaning.

Cleaning supplies

In the small spaces typical of most boats, many common household cleaning agents can be a real health hazard, causing eye and lung irritation, dizziness, and other short-term problems in addition to probable long-term consequences. Often the fumes from cleansers last for hours after their use, and the combination of common cleaning materials can result in unexpected chemical reactions that are physically dangerous. There are also, of course, well-documented harmful environmental effects associated with many of the chemicals in detergents and cleansers.

- Avoid chlorinated products.

Aquatic weeds such as these in Lake Champlain, Vermont, are a nuisance to people, wildlife and the environment in general. The most obnoxious plants are often not indigenous to the area, spreading rampantly with few natural predators. Boaters are thus responsible for removing fragments of nuisance plants from their boating equipment before entering or leaving a lake.

- Avoid products containing phosphates.
- Avoid perfumed detergents and fabric softeners.
- Use citrus-based cleansers for surfaces and bilges.
- There are biodegradable products (that work) for every application. Use them in preference to even the best non-degradable products.

If the above admonitions have not convinced you to change your habits, consider that the concert of fumes, perfumes, toxins and vapors that fill your boat may contribute to the discomfort and wooziness associated with sea-sickness.

Aerosols and refrigerants

By now everyone has heard that chlorofluorocarbons (CFC's) are thinning the ozone layer. One chlorine atom from a CFC can destroy 100,000 ozone molecules. These materials are still found in spray cans, especially if they have been knocking about in the boat for a couple of years, and in refrigerant recharge products.

- Avoid aerosols altogether, because some of the propellants that are replacing CFC's are HCFC's, which still cause damage, although less of it, to the ozone layer. Use pump containers if the product must be sprayed, or apply in liquid form.
- Do not attempt to service the refrigerant systems of your own refrigerators, freezers, or air-conditioners. It is unlikely that you possess the necessary expertise or equipment to successfully capture old CFC's for return to the manufacturer.

Halon and fire extinguishing

The Halon fire extinguisher is the most effective and safest equipment of its type, and is most appropriate in the confined spaces of a boat, where outside air is limited and when fire does break out the occupants cannot simply leave the building. However, because of its bromine-based chemistry Halon is 10 times worse for the ozone layer than CFC's. According to a 1987 international treaty to eliminate ozone-destroying chemicals, the use of Halon will be banned in developed countries by the year 2000.

The manufacturers of Halon argue that it is only expelled into the atmosphere when absolutely necessary, that it serves a vital safety function and is not a frivolous consumer product, and that recharging and inspection equipment is 99.9 percent effective in capturing the material for reuse.

- Always have your Halon extinguishers inspected by a certified professional who will state in writing that his recovery meets industry standards.
- Have equipment tested annually to avoid leaky canisters.
- Substitute other equipment for non-critical spaces.

Mechanical fluids

Oil, fuel, transmission fluid, grease and antifreeze must be handled with caution to absolutely avoid spillage, and waste material should be retained in tightly reclosable containers for recycling. Most marinas, gas stations and oil-change shops will take these materials at no cost.

PRESERVING OUR WILDLIFE

Congress passed the Endangered Species Act in 1973 in recognition that species of animals and plants "are of esthetic, ecological, educational, recreational, and scientific value to the Nation and its people." Although some of these benefits are priceless, others, discussed below, carry a measurable value.

■ **For medicinal purposes.** Forty percent of prescriptions written today are based on, or synthesized from, natural compounds from different species. While helping to save lives, these species also contribute to a pharmaceutical industry worth over $40 billion annually. Only 5 percent of known plant species have been screened for their medicinal values, and we continue to lose up to 100 species daily.

■ **For agricultural purposes.** Of the estimated 80,000 edible plants in the world, we depend upon only 20 species to provide 90 percent of the world's food.

■ **For commercial purposes.** Some wild species are harvested commercially, thus contributing directly to local and regional economies.

■ **For ecological purposes.** Species also make up the fabric of healthy ecosystems, such as coastal estuaries, prairie grasslands and ancient forests. We depend on balanced ecosystems for pure air, clean water, as well as for our food supply. The United States Fish and Wildlife Services estimates that losing one plant species can trigger the loss of up to 30 other insect, plant and higher animal species.

The snowy egret, which has long nested undisturbed in island bays and lagoons, is now threatened by intrusion. Remember that exploring secluded islands may unwittingly upset the nesting habits of the local feathered inhabitants.

One example of recent concern is the coral reefs along the Florida Keys. The habitat for hundreds of species of fish, these reefs are dying as a result of pollution off the coast of Florida. Consequently, catches of commercial fish species have begun to decline, and the multi-million dollar tourism industry, which depends on the quality of the environment, is threatened.

■ **For esthetic and recreational purposes.** Species and their ecosystems form the basis of a huge tourism industry, which not only benefits the economy, but also supplies essential recreational and quality-of-life values to boaters and the population at large.

What boaters can do

Many boaters consider wildlife sightings one of the most memorable parts of a day on the water. Responsible skippers keep in mind the following guidelines:

■ Slow to idle speeds in the proximity of wildlife and alert passengers to maintain a sharp lookout. Although collision with wildlife may seem an unlikely occurrence, about 400 turtles are killed by boat collisions each year along the Gulf and Atlantic coasts of the U.S. outside of coastal beaches, and most manatees in Florida bear scars or deformities from being run over by boats and cut by boat propellers.

■ Avoid throwing anything overboard. Each year, numerous cases of wildlife entanglement are reported—resulting from discarded fishing line, plastic six-pack rings and plastic bags.

Loss of habitat has contributed to dramatic population declines among many shorebirds, including the greater yellowlegs. Boaters can help by reducing oil pollution through responsible maintenance, and by eliminating litter.

MAINTENANCE AND MARINAS

Anyone who has worked in a boatyard or maintained their own boat knows how dangerous most marine coatings, solvents and adhesives are, and how wide the toxic mess spreads during a painting or grinding operation. Application and handling of some materials, particularly isocyanate coatings, becomes a tug of war between doing a good job and living long enough to tell about it.

Boat owners who do their own maintenance and repair work must be aware of the environmental consequences, and must learn the basic steps they can take to protect the environment, remembering that they themselves are part of what they will be protecting. If they prefer to use professional maintenance, they should apply the same basic principles to the yard that is doing the work.

■ Wear suitable protective clothing. Wear vinyl or rubber gloves when painting, gluing, sealing or handling solvents. When wearing coveralls tape the sleeves and cuffs tight. Use eye protection and ear protection (sounds as common as city streets and diesel engines will cause hearing loss with time). And, perhaps, most important, use some sort of respiratory protection. Fiberglass dust has many of the characteristics of asbestos when it gets in the lungs. Its post-product configuration tends to be larger and more easily expelled than the pre-production material, but it is still highly undesirable.
■ The fumes from most adhesives, such as polyesters and epoxies, are toxic. They can be avoided by breathing through a charcoal-activated filter mask, and minimized by providing good ventilation.

TEN WAYS TO KEEP BOATING WATERS CLEAN AND BRING BACK MISSING FISH

Most boaters are concerned about the environment, and particularly the world's waters and the species of fish and other animals that have been disappearing from those waters at an alarming rate. One by one, our collective actions in the ways suggested below can have a significant positive effect. The following guidelines were originally published in *Motor Boating and Sailing* magazine:

1 The best rule of thumb to save our waters is to never throw anything into the water that didn't come out of it. Stash all your trash—even food waste—on board and bring it back to recycle or throw away on shore. Federal law requires that boats 26 feet or longer display a garbage disposal placard on board (available from BOAT/U.S., 800-937-BOAT). Meet or exceed its requirements.

2 Fish with the future in mind. Release everything you're not going to eat. Tag and release all billfish. (The Billfish Foundation, 305-649-8930, sells tags). Bring spent fishing line back to recycle at your tackle shop. Join the fight to keep commercial fisheries from wiping out the planet's fish stocks and harming other native life through wasteful fishing practices such as bottom trawls and longlining. (Call the International Game Fish Association, 305-941-FISH, for details.)

3 Respect marine wildlife. Don't feed or harass dolphins and other mammals. Reduce speed and give a wide berth to whales and manatees. (For more information, contact the Save the Manatee Club, 800-432-JOIN.)

4 Tread carefully. Wake can cause shoreline erosion; throttle back in narrow waterways. Use moorings rather than anchoring in environmentally delicate areas such as coral reef. When snorkeling or diving, never touch any live coral. (Call Reef Relief, 305-294-3100, for details.)

5 Install a Coast Guard-approved marine sanitation device on your boat, preferably with a holding tank, and meet or exceed all legal regulations concerning disposal. Consult up-to-date cruising guides for the locations of pump-out facilities. If you can't find one in your area, organize boat owners to convince your local marina to install one.

6 Stay in tune. A tuned engine improves fuel economy and also burns fuel more efficiently, causing fewer emissions. Don't let any fuel or oil leak into the water. Be cautious when topping off your fuel tanks, as it can lead to spillage. Use a "pillow" to soak up spills in your bilge.

7 Practice "green" maintenance. Recycle spent antifreeze, oil, fuel and oil filters, and batteries. Don't use that old illegal, toxic TBT anti-fouling paint. When cleaning, plug your scuppers and wipe up all spills. (For information on how to identify and dispose of hazardous waste, call your state Environmental Protection Agency.)

8 Shop 'til you drop. As the EPA tightens air and water regulations, more and more "green" items are appearing on the market. Comb chandleries and supermarkets for environmentally friendly marine products.

9 Be a watchdog. If you're out on the water and see an oil or chemical spill or other pollution, call the Coast Guard's National Response Center hotline (800-424-8802).

10 Get involved. You can make an even greater impact by donating money and/or your time to environmental action groups, from national organizations like the Center for Marine Conservation (202-429-5609) to regional groups such as the Chesapeake Bay Foundation (410-268-8816). Help protect your local boating waters.

■ Grinding, stripping and chipping operations produce large quantities of dust and detritus which must be kept out of the water, off the ground, and must be disposed of properly. Such material is, technically, hazardous waste, and cannot be simply thrown into a dumpster or taken to the landfill. If the boat is afloat, hang a tarp between the boat and the dock to catch paint splatters and dust. If the boat is hauled, keep a tarp under all work being done, collect the waste material, and dispose of waste properly.

■ Bottom paints are especially toxic, and all power washes, strippings, cleanings, sandings and recoatings must be done over a specially prepared apron in the yard or, if the waste is dry, over carefully arranged tarps.

■ Spray painting releases huge quantities of volatile organic compounds (VOC's) into the atmosphere, and is now tightly controlled by law in the workplace. Charcoal-activated fume scrubbers and filter air recirculators must be used in enclosed spaces. It is not enough to simply vent the toxic fumes outdoors into someone else's face. Many plants blow fumes and dust through burners that incinerate the material before venting it outside. Do not spray anything unless you are satisfied that the above conditions are being met. Many professionals now prefer using sponge rollers and a light "tipping" with dry brush bristles, and claim that their results are almost as good.

■ Do *not* pour spent solvents onto the open ground. They can be reclaimed in a tightly closed slops container to let solids settle out, then reused two or three times before they are fully contaminated; then they must be disposed of properly. Most marinas and factories have made arrangements with a company that takes spent solvents for industrial fuel, a dubious but convenient solution with the full blessings of the EPA. Other companies install distillation equipment that fully recyles solvents and concentrates the residue into small cakes, which are much easier to dispose of.

■ Water-based coatings are the wave of the future, and should be investigated by any concerned boater. These are not the latex products that have been with us for so long, but an entirely new molecular concept using water as the delivery medium and producing very low VOC emissions. These coatings are fully suitable for all interior applications today; there are also waterborne bottom paints on the market. In addition, waterborne exterior varnishes are available, which may be suitable for marine applications; high gloss topcoats which may be suitable as well.

■ Substitutes for familiar but highly toxic solvents are now becoming available. They feature low toxicity, low VOC emissions, and biodegradability, while claiming comparable performance. Do not use any more acetone, methylene chloride, toluene, lacquer thinner, mineral spirits and alcohol unless there are no options whatsoever.

■ Never wash your hands in solvents. Their tiny molecules slip right through your skin into your tissues and bloodstream. Today's citrus-based hand cleaners outperform petroleum-based cleaners anyway.

ZEBRA MUSSEL ALERT

Zebra mussels were accidentally introduced to this continent in 1986, and have already spread throughout the Great Lakes and into the Hudson and Mississippi rivers. They are also found in Chesapeake Bay.

They breed in fresh and slightly brackish water, in such profusion that they form dense colonies on every firm object in a body of water. Their populations are so enormous that as they filter water for food they are numerically capable of consuming every last microorganism from the host water, leaving none for the rest of the food chain, with obvious—and disastrous—consequences. Boaters must take the following precautions to help slow the spread of the zebra mussel:

■ Clean and scrape boat hulls and trailers meticulously before transporting them to another body of water. Mussel larvae will attach to every nook and crevice.

■ Drain bilges and live wells, and clean them thoroughly. Do not dump them into another body of water.

■ Flush motors with clean water. Zebra mussels will colonize all plumbing they can gain access to, and can seriously impair engine cooling.

■ Educate others about zebra mussels.

Prodigious breeders in moderate climes, zebra mussels became an overnight menace when they arrived recently in North America. Because they can survive several days out of water, these mollusks hitchhike easily on boat hulls or, in the larvae or postlarvae stages, in bilges and bait wells—even in engine plumbing.

PILOTING AND NAVIGATION

17 THE MARINER'S COMPASS

The marine compass is the most important navigational tool on any vessel, and a remarkable instrument. It requires no power source; it guides you on all oceans and waterways, in fair weather or foul. Beyond the sight of land or navigation aids, or when caught sailing in a pea-soup fog, your compass is at times your only means of keeping on course.

This chapter will show you how the compass works, as well as how to purchase, install and use a compass. With this information, and the navigation and piloting skills you will acquire in Section 5, "Piloting and Navigation," you will be able to rely on your compass as a simple, trouble-free reference for direction under virtually any circumstance.

HOW A COMPASS WORKS

Responding to the earth's magnetic field, the compass works according to the basic law of magnetism: Opposites attract; likes repel. A north pole is attracted to a south pole, but repels another north. Imagine the earth's magnetic field as a powerful bar magnet located near the earth's center, but not aligned with its geographic axis.

The magnetic north pole is in fact located several hundred miles from "true north," and the same applies to the south magnetic pole with respect to "true south." For navigation purposes, the difference between the magnetic and geographic poles is termed variation, and is discussed on page 376. Errors caused by magnetic influences that are close to the compass are called deviation. When both deviation and variation errors are taken into account, compass readings will be accurate, consistent and reliable.

Basic compass construction

The fundamental principle of a magnetic compass is simple; its construction is illustrated on page 368. A magnetized needle or magnetic bar freely suspended in the earth's magnetic field will align itself parallel to the lines of force of that field, and establish a direction. The end of a magnet that points generally north is termed "north-seeking" pole; the other end is its south pole.

In a compass used on boats and ships, the magnetized bar is attached to a pivoted dial—called a rose or card—that is allowed to rotate. The dial is marked "North," as indicated by the end of the magnetic bar that is north-seeking, with the

other points of the compass added. When mounted in a vessel, the magnetized dial constantly points toward magnetic North and the boat will, in effect, rotate around the dial as it changes direction on the water's surface, as shown below. This simplified illustration ignores deviation to make an important point for the novice helmsman: When you change a boat's direction, it's not the compass card that moves—it's the boat that moves around the compass card.

Compass cards are usually divided into degrees that increase in numerical value moving clockwise. Most small boat compasses display 5-degree increments. Space limitations permitting, the larger the compass the better. Larger compasses mean better visibility and better compass card stability. Regardless of the size or type of compass, it will have to be housed properly and shielded from the sun. At the exact center of the card there is often a short vertical stick called the pivot post, which is used to take bearings and to help align the compass during installation. On a ring around the card, but not touching it, are other posts called lub-

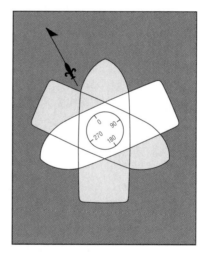

The spin of a turning boat has little effect on a magnetic compass dial, which points consistently toward magnetic north.

ber's lines. The number depends on the compass, but there is always one lubber's line at the forward side of the compass and there are usually two others at the left and right sides. The boat's heading is read as the number on the card next to the forward lubber's line.

Pivoted rings called gimbals isolate the compass from the boat, helping the compass remain level as the boat rolls, pitches or heels. A set of gimbals is like a universal joint on a car's drive shaft, allowing independent movement through two axes. (Incidentally, some compasses with external gimbals can be flipped accidentally so that they face backwards.) To dampen the motion of the gimbals, the compass dome is filled with a liquid such as mineral oil or some other nonfreezing solution. Rapid changes in temperature or air pressure will cause the liquid to expand or contract, sometimes leaving an air bubble under the compass dome that greatly obstructs visibility. For this reason good compasses are built with expansion chambers in their bases.

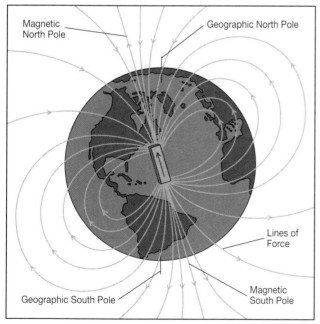

The earth's magnetic field, which is commonly conceptualized as innumerable lines of force, has two regions of magnetism—magnetic north and magnetic south. The actual "magnetic location" of these poles changes over long periods of time, while the geographic poles remain constant.

Inside the compass, a set of magnets is fixed under the card, surrounding the jeweled pivot that supports the center of the card. There usually are four carefully placed, sliver-shaped magnets whose combined force has a north-seeking component and a south-seeking component. These line up with the earth's magnetic field.

The compass card

Since World War II, many navigators have become accustomed to naming directions in degrees, from 000° (or 360°) at North, through 090° at East, 180° at South and 270° at West. The larger the compass card, the more finely marked are the degrees, with most small-craft compasses marking each 5-degree increment. On some compass cards, the width of the major degree markings and the width of the lubber's line are also significant. If the lubber's line is one degree in width, for example, that width can be used to estimate degrees that are intermediate between markings on the compass card, as illustrated opposite at bottom.

Some very small compasses mark larger increments. Also, front-reading, rather than top-reading, compasses show West to the right of North with the lubber's line at the back, rather than the front. Whenever you find yourself at the helm of an unfamiliar boat, take a few moments to study the compass and understand how to read it.

Piloting arithmetic is simplified by the use of 360 degrees rather than points (table, page 370), but note the following caution: Subdivisions of degrees are minutes—a minute rep-

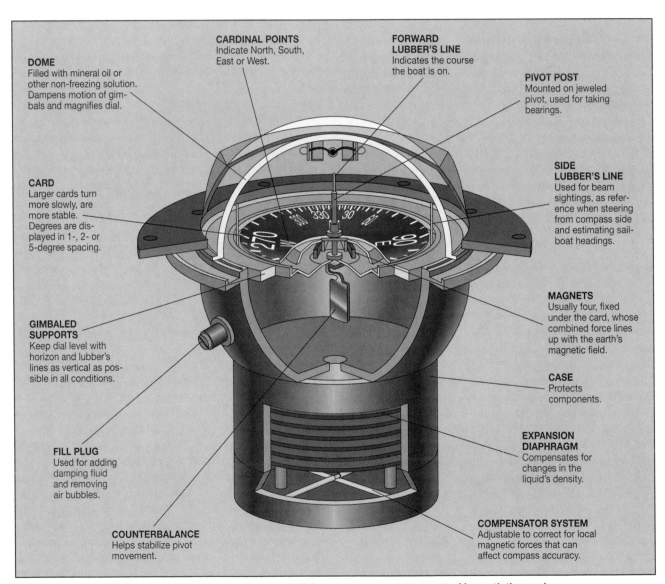

DOME
Filled with mineral oil or other non-freezing solution. Dampens motion of gimbals and magnifies dial.

CARDINAL POINTS
Indicate North, South, East or West.

FORWARD LUBBER'S LINE
Indicates the course the boat is on.

PIVOT POST
Mounted on jeweled pivot, used for taking bearings.

CARD
Larger cards turn more slowly, are more stable. Degrees are displayed in 1-, 2- or 5-degree spacing.

SIDE LUBBER'S LINE
Used for beam sightings, as reference when steering from compass side and estimating sailboat headings.

GIMBALED SUPPORTS
Keep dial level with horizon and lubber's lines as vertical as possible in all conditions.

MAGNETS
Usually four, fixed under the card, whose combined force lines up with the earth's magnetic field.

CASE
Protects components.

FILL PLUG
Used for adding damping fluid and removing air bubbles.

EXPANSION DIAPHRAGM
Compensates for changes in the liquid's density.

COUNTERBALANCE
Helps stabilize pivot movement.

COMPENSATOR SYSTEM
Adjustable to correct for local magnetic forces that can affect compass accuracy.

This cross section of a typical marine compass shows parallel permanent magnets mounted beneath the card. The magnets and card are attached to a light frame, which is supported by a pivot. An expansion bellows for the liquid in the compass is housed inside the case. Other available features, not shown here, include a protective compass hood, which may be fitted over the dome, and a night light, which is usually red.

Compass cards are graduated in various manners—most at 5-degree intervals, as shown at near right, with heavier 10-degree marks. Numbers usually are at 30-degree intervals, and cardinal headings may be shown as letters rather than numbers. However, compasses for larger vessels sometimes have graduations down to one degree with cardinal and intercardinal points as, shown at far right.

resents $1/60$ of a degree. What this means is that using a calculator to add and subtract compass directions might require the conversion of a degree to a decimal fraction, though such small divisions are seldom of practical value aboard a small boat.

Spherical compasses

A hemispherical dome magnifies the compass card; this makes it much easier to read at a distance. Further, if the compass card has a concave or dishlike shape (as opposed to a flat shape), it is not necessary to stand more or less directly over the compass in order to read it. A compass with such a card of 5-inch "apparent diameter" can be read from a distance of 10 feet or more.

If the compass as a whole is spherical, bowl as well as dome, there is a considerable gain in the stability of the card. The effect of a whole sphere is to permit the fluid inside to remain relatively undisturbed by roll, pitch or yaw; the result is superior performance in rough seas.

Some compasses have special features for use aboard sailboats. These include more extensive gimbaling so as to permit free movement of the card at considerable angles of heel, and additional lubber's lines 45 degrees and 90 degrees to either side of the one aligned with the craft's keel as an aid in determining when to tack. These additional lubber's lines are also useful when the helmsman sits to one side, as when sailing upwind. They can also be used to sight horizontal angles to determine distance off.

Binnacles

Compasses are usually mounted on a horizontal surface, but on large boats they may be mounted in a case called a binnacle, shown on page 375. The binnacle protects the compass from deterioration, especially from sunlight, and also shields it so that the card is easier to read. While binnacles are often chrome-plated, many skippers prefer a black finish to avoid reflecting sunlight into the helmsman's eyes.

Lighting for the compass should be red and of the correct intensity to avoid impairment of the helmsman's night vision. In better installations, the light intensity can be varied to suit the conditions and avoid eye strain.

The binnacle itself must be non-magnetic to avoid influencing the compass. If the binnacle is mounted on a steering pedestal, as is often the case on sailboats, the pedestal and steering gear must be checked for their influence on the compass. Sometimes a link in a stainless steel steering chain will have a ferrous attraction to the compass.

Magnetic influence is rarely absent and may be produced by permanent iron and steel objects near the compass or from electrical wiring, such as the power source for the night light. Whatever the cause, the compass must be compensated (adjusted). This is accomplished with additional small magnets called compensators sometimes placed in the binnacle. Refer to page 385 for more information on local magnetic influences and how to deal with them.

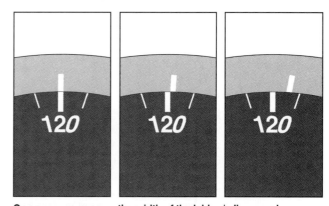

On some compasses, the width of the lubber's line equals one degree on the card. The center drawing shows how this can be used to read one degree to either side of a main graduation. As shown at right, a reading slightly more or less than half-way between marks would indicate two degrees more or less than the nearest mark.

CONVERSION OF POINTS AND DEGREES		
Direction	*Points*	*Degrees*
North to East	N	0°00'
	N by E	11°15'
	NNE	22°30'
	NE by N	33°45'
	NE	45°00'
	NE by E	56°15'
	ENE	67°30'
	E by N	78°45'
East to South	E	90°00'
	E by S	101°15'
	ESE	112°30'
	SE by E	123°45'
	SE	135°00'
	SE by S	146°15'
	SSE	157°30'
	S by E	168°45'
South to West	S	180°00'
	S by W	191°15'
	SSW	202°30'
	SW by S	213°45'
	SW	225°00'
	SW by W	236°15'
	WSW	247°30'
	W by S	258°45'
West to North	W	270°00'
	W by N	281°15'
	WNW	292°30'
	NW by W	303°45'
	NW	315°00'
	NW by N	326°15'
	NNW	337°30'
	N by W	348°45'
	N	360°00'

The system in common use before World War II was the point system. Though few boaters will learn to "box the compass" through all of its 128 points, the major points are still familiar and very useful. In descending order, the points are known as the cardinal (North, East, South and West), the intercardinal points, the combination points and the bypoints.

Compass maintenance

The chief enemy of the compass is sunlight, so the compass should be covered when not in use. In winter climates care should be taken that metal elements on the boat have not acquired a magnetic field over the winter storage period; a magnetized object could, of course, confuse the compass. In other areas, where winter is not a factor, metal can become magnetized from welding onboard or a lightning strike. As a general rule, the compass should be kept free from other magnetic influences such as a metal tool left near the binnacle. Other maintenance consists in monitoring the compass and making sure that the pivot bearing is still moving freely and that the liquid has not leaked.

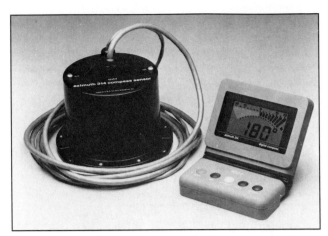

Fluxgate electronic compasses react to the same magnetic field of the earth as do traditional compasses, but there are no moving parts. The output is an electronic signal that can be displayed for steering or used as an input to radionavigation systems and dead-reckoning plotters.

Fluxgate compasses

Without moving parts, a fluxgate compass gives a digital read-out, which can be accurate as long as the compass is level. The local magnetic influences that produce deviation errors in a conventional compass affect fluxgate compasses in roughly the same way as they affect magnetic compasses, but the fluxgate has a substantial advantage: Its sensing unit can be placed almost anywhere in the boat—far away from disturbing magnetic influence. (One common location is under a forward berth.)

A fluxgate can be used in much the same way as a card compass, except that there can be more than one indicator and the indicator itself can present the course information more clearly than a compass card. Aboard boats with electronic navigation systems, the fluxgate can present information directly to the navigator's computer, and can be used to guide integral autopilots. Variation can be input by the user so that readings are given as true directions. In addition, most fluxgates are continuously self-compensating so that deviation calculations are unnecessary.

Since the fluxgate uses solid state electronics to amplify signals from the earth's magnetic field, it has few opportunities to fail mechanically. However, it does require a constant source of electricity. On a small boat, this can be a problem and on a larger craft, the buyer must consider the possibility of electrical failure and the consequences to navigation.

Other compass types

Larger ships and aircraft are normally fitted with a gyrocompass—an expensive and complex instrument that senses changes in the vessel's direction. If you are familiar with the gyroscope as a toy, remember how it resists turning forces when it is spinning. That same principle is applied to one type of gyrocompass which, because it is independent of the magnetic field, reads directions in true. Another type of gyro-compass orients itself according to the earth's rotation. However, even gyrocompasses are not perfect and adjustments must be made—for changes in latitude, for example.

A hand bearing compass is used to sight bearings. Most models are inexpensive and can be worn around the navigator's neck and held up to eye level for reading, as shown at right. Such bearings are taken mainly for position finding *(Chapter 20)* but are also used by racing sailors to determine the relative position of rival boats.

Hand bearing compasses have also been incorporated into binoculars. This is particularly useful because an object can be sighted more easily, especially at night when the binocular is able to gather more light than the eye.

At least one manufacturer has gone a step further and has combined the function of hand bearing compass, range finder, chronometer and monocular into one instrument. With this device, an object onshore or offshore can be sighted and identified. When the object's height is known and a bearing can be taken with an exact time reference, you can establish your position.

A compass located belowdecks, above the skipper's berth or at the navigation station, is called a telltale compass. Usually these are designed to be read from the bottom. This type is useful to indicate wind or current shifts when a boat is anchored, and to provide a check on the helm.

A pelorus is a sighting device used mainly for compass adjustment. Two sighting vanes are rotated around a compass card that can be fixed on any bearing.

A sun compass is a shadow pin mounted on a compass card and used to read the sun's bearing. If the sun compass is properly oriented to the boat and well-gimbaled, it shows true course—but accuracy depends on knowledge of the sun's true bearing. That, of course, requires complex calculations and precise information regarding latitude, date and time. It's also important to choose a time when the sun's relative motion is as slow as possible.

In the hands of an experienced navigator, a sun compass is useful for checking compass error. Some dome-type compasses have a shadow pin mounted on the card at the center. This is also useful for taking relative bearings.

The accuracy of a fluxgate compass, such as the hand bearing model shown above, depends on the compass being level to the horizon.

Compasses offer a variety of features and mounting possibilities. The bulkhead-mounted sailboat compass at left indicates angle of heel on the scale below the bowl. The light-shielding hood at center cuts off excessive sunlight to aid in reading the compass. Most of today's compasses have two sets of internal compensating magnets, usually in the base of the binnacle. The East-West adjusting screw can be seen at the front of this unit.

SELECTING A COMPASS

Although a compass is a simple instrument it is the most important navigational tool aboard your boat. Select it carefully. This is not the time for a hasty decision or for saving a few dollars; sooner or later, your safety will depend on it.

Almost any new compass may look fine in the store, but its behavior underway—when the sea makes up and the craft pitches, rolls and yaws—is what is important. Will the card stick at an angle of heel? Will its motion be jerky, making it hard to read? Are the card markings legible and easily distinguishable? Is it protected against temperature changes?

Examine a number of compasses by comparing their motions when they are tilted and turned. Do the cards have a smooth, stable motion coming to rest, without swinging back and forth past the lubber's line? Does the compass have internal compensating magnets, and have they been "zeroed in"? (Zeroing in is discussed opposite, but most high-quality compasses will already have been properly set.)

Choosing the compass size and card

A small boat may well need a larger compass simply because its motion is more pronounced. In rough weather on a small boat, it may also be harder to read a small compass. Choose a compass suitable for your boat and your budget.

Cards vary in their legibility and the fineness of their markings. More markings, showing gradations of fewer degrees, are not always better. While a larger vessel may be held to a steady course and make good use of one-degree markings, experience has shown that divisions smaller than 5 degrees may not be desirable.

Cards should be simple enough to be easily read for long periods in adverse conditions. Consider, for example, a sailboat with an open cockpit in rough weather. Small, uniform markings will be easily mistaken, especially when the compass is covered in spray or rain. Remember that the helmsman can lose sight of a point on the card, steering 065° instead of 055°, and never be sure how long the boat was off course. Large markings and contrasting colors are a great help in guiding the skipper's eye to the correct course.

Testing the compass

Price is often a good indicator of quality. There are also two tests that can identify a poor choice; make these tests on a comparative basis on several brands and models:

■ In order to avoid magnetic interference, make sure that the compass you are testing is at least 4 feet away from other compasses. Test for a sticky pivot by turning the case until a card marking is exactly aligned with the lubber's line. Then by placing a small piece of metal, a magnet (or another compass) near the card, deflect the card 2 to 5 degrees to one side. Remove the object abruptly and watch the card. The card should return to its exact former position. Also try deflecting to the other side. Do not purchase a compass that does not pass this simple test.

■ Now test for proper damping. Repeat the deflection, but this time, draw the card to each side by about 20 or 30 degrees. Watch the amount of over-swing as the card returns back to and past its original setting. Choose the compass with the least over-swing and minimum oscillation.

SELECTION CRITERIA

When shopping for a compass, choose a quality instrument. Consider the points listed below, and remember that your compass is the most important navigational tool aboard your boat. This is no place to cut corners.

✓ Can the compass be mounted in a location on your boat that allows comfortable viewing for long periods of time?

✓ Is the card easily read and appropriately marked?

✓ Does the card remain level? It should not stick through reasonable angles of pitch and roll.

✓ Does the card move uniformly through any course change (simulated by turning slowly through 90 degrees or more)?

✓ Is the card "dead-beat"—that is, does it swing only once to a steady position?

✓ Are there built-in compensating magnets?

✓ Is there provision for night lighting, preferably with an adjustment for intensity?

✓ Is the dome hemispherically shaped rather than flat (with the exception of some sailboat tactical compasses that must be mounted in vulnerable situations)?

✓ Are the card and lubber's line fully gimbaled? Internal gimbals are best.

✓ Is there a metal or rubber expansion chamber to allow for temperature changes?

✓ Can the compass be mounted vertically in the position you have chosen? Is adjustment possible?

✓ Is there any significant parallax error when the compass is viewed from the side as compared to the back?

✓ Is the compass second hand? If so, be especially cautious.

COMPASS INSTALLATION

Whether you buy a fluxgate or a standard compass, both require the same precision in positioning, installing and maintaining. Installing your compass is a complex and time-consuming operation—certainly no Friday evening job. If your most important navigation instrument is going to be useful and reliable, you will have to set aside some time for installation and give it some thought. Even if your compass is already installed, don't hesitate to take it through the same checks that are described here for a new installation. Many factory- and owner-installed compasses are inaccurate.

On a small boat there is rarely an ideal location for the compass. Its placement is usually a compromise between different steering positions and various magnetic influences. On a larger craft, where the helmsman is more likely to be standing or sitting in the same place, the compass can be located more easily. Ideally, it should be between 22 and 30 inches from the helmsman's eyes and not more than 20 degrees from the horizontal line of vision.

Compasses are often located off the center line of the boat, and special care must be taken to ensure that they are properly aligned. The center line of the hull must be parallel with a line running through the lubber's line and the center of the compass card.

Sometimes a compass mounting requires the helmsman to view the card from the side. In this case, there may be parallax error. The error may be significant, so check the view from behind and see whether any error is introduced.

On many boats that are either wide or always steered from one side or the other—such as catamarans, racing sailboats or even workboats, for example—additional compasses can be located at the side in order to make viewing more direct and accurate.

Make sure the compass is zeroed in

Although good quality compasses are normally zeroed in at the factory, you should know how to do it yourself. In addition to assuring yourself that the process has been properly carried out, you can also be sure that the compensator screws have not been "un-adjusted" accidentally.

Well away from the boat and any magnetic influences, mount your compass temporarily on a board, with the center line roughly aligned with one edge. Remove any magnetic influences from the area—your wristwatch and belt buckle, for example, and use a non-magnetic screwdriver to make the adjustments. Non-magnetic screwdrivers are often made of bronze, but you can easily make one of your own. (Buy ¼-inch brass rod in a hardware store, and grind it to fit the compensator slots like a screwdriver.)

Turn the compass until the lubber's line points to North. Place a reference edge, such as a book or straight-edged board, against the mounting board. Holding the reference edge, move the compass board away, turn it 180 degrees and slide it back against the reference. The lubber's line should be at South.

Boats smaller than this one nearly always present problems in locating a compass due to limited space and a poor magnetic environment. Finding a suitable location takes ingenuity and patience.

If not, use your non-magnetic screwdriver to adjust either the N-S or the E-W compensator, whichever of the two has the larger effect. Remove half of the error. Then realign the compass with the lubber's line at South, and slide the reference edge back into place. Reverse the compass board and, again, remove half of the error. Repeat these steps until all of the error is removed, then complete the same operation on the East-West axis.

If you are not able to remove all of the error, the compass is defective or there is a magnetic object nearby.

Check for magnetic influence

With a properly zeroed-in compass, go back aboard and look for magnetic influences. Ideally the mounting location should be at least two feet from instruments, gauges and radios. Fortunately, magnetic effects vary as the inverse square: If you double the distance you have reduced the influence to a quarter. Stainless steel is almost always non-magnetic, but there are many alloys. Check by bringing the compass close to each item and circling around it while maintaining the compass's north-south orientation.

There is an important difference between an object that is magnetized and one that is made of magnetic material. Try to

On vessels with steel hulls, it normally is necessary to mount two quadrantial spheres of soft iron on the binnacle, and adjust them as part of the compensation process.

bring the north compass pole near the object first, then the south pole. If the object attracts one pole and repels the other, it is magnetized.

While it is best to remove the object, that is not always possible. However, a magnetized object can be demagnetized with equipment that is available in electronic repair shops—degaussing coils used for television repair or a bulk magnetic tape eraser, for example. If this operation has to be performed on the magnetized object in place on the boat, take care to remove the compass and any other instruments that might be properly magnetic, including all radio speakers and electrical instruments.

Any movable metal objects should be moved to check their influence on each of the four cardinal headings. Turn the helm lock to lock, open the windshield, move the throttle and gear shift and swing the helm seat.

Steel boats

Installing a compass aboard a steel-hulled craft requires expertise beyond the scope of this book. However, as an owner of a steel boat, you should be aware that your compass may require quadrantial spheres of soft iron, the use of a soft iron bar called a flinders bar and possibly heeling magnets that are designed to eliminate only the deviation induced by sailboat heeling. All this is for the professional adjuster, or for the skipper who has achieved professional competence. Further, iron and steel vessels are subject to changes in deviation upon large changes in latitude. This may be a consideration when cruising.

Electrical influences

Current flowing through electrical wires may also influence the compass. Switch all electrical loads such as the radio, bilge pump, depth sounder, lights and windshield wipers on and off. Start the engine. Try each item, one at a time, on both north and south headings.

Two wires on the same circuit can be twisted together to avoid the creation of a magnetic field. Make sure that the wiring for the compass light is twisted. Wiring beneath the compass should not be neat and tidy—a "bird's nest" is more likely to eliminate magnetic field creation.

In an ideal world, these influences would be eliminated. In actual practice, however, you may have to settle for two deviation cards, one for each condition—wipers on and wipers off, for example.

Vibration

Pivot wear will be accelerated by vibration, but there is also another concern. Certain frequencies can actually force the card to spin. Check for vibration by running the engines over a full range of rpm. Avoid vibration by mounting the compass on a structural member and by padding the mount with foam rubber. Boats with a slow-turning diesel may need a special vibration-damping binnacle.

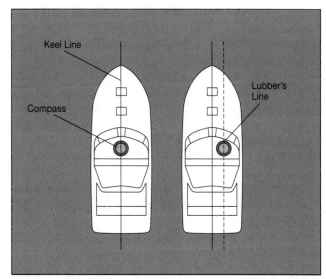

If the compass is not mounted directly over the keel line, take care to make sure that a line through the center of the card and the lubber's line is directly parallel to the center line of the boat.

Mounting

While the ideal compass mount is amidships, over the center line of the boat, this is rarely possible. However, the compass must be aligned with the center line; keep the following guidelines in mind:

- There must be no iron or steel nearby, including tools, knives, keys, pens, and even soft drink cans.
- The compass must be at least 3 feet away from any magnetic influence, including instruments, gauges and radio speakers. (If you must install a radio or speaker close by, try mounting it well above or below the compass. This type of equipment affects compass accuracy most when installed level with the compass.)

Establishing a line parallel to the boat's center line is simple, but takes some time. Find the center of your transom with a measuring tape and mark it with a line on a piece of masking tape. Find and mark a second center point forward of the compass location—this might be the mainsail track on a sailboat. Stretch a length of twine between the two marks.

Measure an offset to your compass location and establish a new line at that distance from the center line. Mark another piece of masking tape at that new position on the transom and at the forward position. Stretch the twine between these new endpoints. If the twine is above the compass, use a plumb bob to bring the position down to the mounting surface (make sure the boat is on an even keel before you do this). Once the line is established, you may want to mark it permanently. Line up the compass lubber's line, or the marks on the compass housing.

Every compass is designed for a specific type of installation. If you have a slanted bulkhead on your boat and buy a compass designed for vertical installation, you must provide a shim for it. Otherwise, it will not behave properly in a seaway: The gimbals will bottom when the boat rides down a wave, which will eventually damage the pivot. A more difficult (and fairly common) problem is a bulkhead that is not perpendicular to the keel line, for example a rear bulkhead of a cabin on a smaller boat, or a surface ahead of the helm that is not horizontal. Very often, after trying to compensate the compass in this type of mounting, you will have a steady error that you find impossible to correct. You must then insert a wedge on either side of the compass to correct the error. Experiment with the wedge; use a temporary wedge until you find the right thickness, then fashion one that will contour the compass base.

Finally, make sure that electrical wires, especially the wires for the compass light, are twisted together. Always leave enough play in the wiring of the compass to allow removal for storage or for bulb replacement.

Fastening the compass

Drill one mounting hole only so that the compass can be slightly turned after its compensation checks. After compensation, the job can be completed. Use non-magnetic fasteners and, if possible, non-magnetic tools. An alignment check should be repeated when the mounting is complete.

A compass bracket that has only two holes for mounting demands precise alignment and leaves very little room for further adjustment. Often circular compass mounts have slots built in for fastening, and fasteners are tightened when alignment is complete. If these slots are not present, try using either masking tape or duct tape to hold the compass temporarily in place.

Compass maintenance

Today's compasses are made from many materials, ranging from traditional brass to space-age plastics. However, every compass still requires a certain amount of maintenance.

The life of a compass can be significantly lengthened by keeping it protected from the sun and salt spray. The sun tends to "cook" plastic components and render them brittle; it will also fade the painted parts such as the card and can have a harmful effect on the compass fluid. As well, the sea

In a binnacle mount, the compass housing often has slots for mounting screws that allow for adjustment.

spray can scratch the compass surface and dull the glass. Remember that although a black compass is attractive, if it is left unprotected in the sun, its components can be stressed when they reach high temperatures. You can protect your compass by following the guidelines below:

■ Clean regularly with fresh water and mild detergent, such as dishwashing soap.
■ Polish with soft wax.
■ Keep covered when not in use.
■ Protect from bumps and knocks.
■ Avoid using the following substances: abrasive cleaners or waxes, glass cleaners that contain ammonia or solvents.

Checking a compass underway

Keep in tune with your compass by comparing your headings with a chart on a frequent basis. Line up with a channel that has a magnetic heading indicated, for example; check to make sure that your compass heading matches, or is confirmed by the boat's deviation card. You should also make note of compass readings on frequently run courses and be alert to any changes in the reading.

In addition, keep in mind that passengers aren't navigators. They often walk around on deck with portable radios or flashlights; their children play with magnetized toys, and leave them in inconspicuous places. Remember that these elements can seriously affect a nearby compass.

COMPASS ERRORS

Before a compass can be used for accurate navigation, you first must understand compass errors—the natural differences between compass readings and true directions measured from geographic north. Normally, when working with your charts, you record and plot courses and bearings with respect to true north, although many boaters work in terms of magnetic directions.

Variation

The first and most basic compass error is variation (V or Var). For any given location on land or sea, variation is the angle between the magnetic meridian and the geographic meridian, and is illustrated below. In other words, it is the angle between true north and north, as indicated by a compass, which is free from any nearby influences. Variation is designated as east or west in accordance with the way the compass needle is deflected. Any statement of variation, except zero, must have one of these labels: E or W. A navigator can do nothing about variation except recognize it and make allowances. Aviators have a more complex problem in dealing with variation because of the way lines of equal variation bend downward near the poles, but aboard a boat, only two aspects of variation will affect your navigation:

■ **General variation**. The earth's magnetic field is not uniform, and because the magnetic poles are not at the geographic poles, variation changes with location. The illustration at top right, shows the result of failure to apply different variation as a vessel moves from one location to another.

At any given place, the amount of variation is essentially constant. There is usually a small annual change, but if you are using a chart not more than two or three years old, this quite small amount of change can be ignored. The amount of variation, and its annual rate of change, is found within each com-

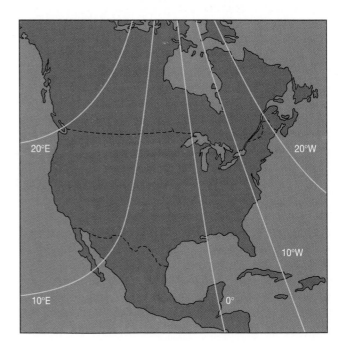

Do not overlook the change in variation with the change in location. In the example above, the true and magnetic courses from X to Y are both 039° initially, but magnetic soon changes while the true course remains constant. Staying on a magnetic heading, an aviator would be at Z, 150 miles west, but the skipper of a boat would run aground on the Rhode Island coast.

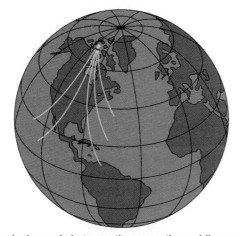

Variation is the angle between the magnetic meridian and the true meridian. Variation depends upon geographic location, and in any part of the globe *(above)* it is the same for all vessels in any given vicinity regardless of heading. In North America *(right)*, variation is generally easterly on the Pacific and Gulf coasts, and westerly on the Atlantic Coast.

pass rose on the chart, as shown below. These are circular figures a couple of inches in diameter with three concentric circular scales. (If you have to fold your charts, try to use a "navigator's fold"—one with a compass rose on each panel.)

On most types of government charts there will be several compass roses suitably placed for convenient plotting. The outer scale is graduated in degrees, and it is oriented so that its zero point points to true (geographic) north. The inner pair of scales is graduated in degrees and in the point system down to quarter-points. The zero point of these scales shows the direction of magnetic north at that place. On some charts, the innermost scale in points is omitted.

The angle at the center of a compass rose between the star and arrow symbols is the variation in that vicinity for

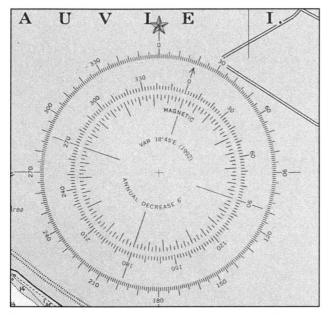

Most charts have several compass roses which show the variation graphically and descriptively. These are located so as to be convenient for plotting. On any chart, especially on small-scale charts of large areas, always use the compass rose nearest the vicinity concerned.

the year stated. This information is printed at the center of the rose to the nearest 15 minutes; for example, "Var 18° 45'E (1992)," as shown above. The annual rate of change is noted to the nearest 1 minute, and whether the variation is increasing or decreasing; for example, "Annual decrease 6'" or "No Annual Change." Round off the variation shown on a compass rose to the nearest whole degree; fractions of a degree are not practical for small craft.

■ **Local attraction.** In addition to the general overall magnetic variation, the navigator may also encounter "local attraction." (Here "local" means a limited geographic vicinity, as opposed to magnetic influences on board the boat.) In a few localities, the compass is subject to irregular magnetic disturbances in the earth's field over relatively small areas. A

striking example is found at Kingston, on the Canadian side of Lake Ontario. There, variation may change as much as 45 degrees in a distance of a mile and a half (2.4 km).

Charts of areas subject to such local attraction will bear warnings to this effect. Other means of navigation are needed when within range of such disturbances.

Deviation

A boat's compass rarely exists in an environment that is completely free of nearby magnetic materials or influences. Normally it is subject to magnetic forces in addition to those of the earth's field. Material already magnetized, or even capable of being magnetized by the magnets of the compass, will cause the compass needle to deviate from its proper alignment with the magnetic meridian. Currents flowing in improperly installed electrical wiring can have the same effect.

The deflection of the compass from its proper orientation is called "deviation" (D or Dev). It is the angle between the magnetic meridian and a line from the pivot through the north point of the compass card; the angle between the direction the compass would point if there were no deviating influences and the direction in which it actually does point. Theoretically, it can range from 000° to 180°, but in practice large values cannot be tolerated. Just as for variation, deviation can be east or west depending on whether compass north lies to the east or west of magnetic north *(below)*. Deviation must carry one of these labels, unless it is zero.

While variation changes with geographic location, deviation changes with the craft's heading and does not change noticeably in any given geographic area. (Causes for this effect are explained on page 382.) To cope with these changes a vessel needs a deviation table—a compilation of deviations, usually for each 15 degrees of heading by the compass—as shown on page 384.

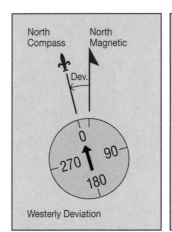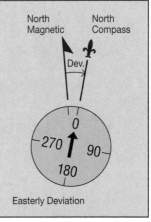

Deviation is the difference between north, as indicated by the compass, and magnetic north. It can be easterly or westerly, and depends on the magnetic conditions on a vessel. It changes with the boat's heading, but is not noticeably affected by changes in position within a geographic location.

COMPASS CALCULATION

A boat's heading is the angle that the center line of the boat makes with some other line of reference. (If the boat is "on course," this is also the vessel's course.) Any one of three lines of reference is commonly used; the direction to true north, the direction to magnetic north and the direction pointed to by north on the compass. Consequently, there are three ways to name a course—true course, magnetic course and compass course. These three qualifiers, shown in the illustration at right, also apply to bearings.

Compass error

Compass error (CE) is sometimes used in compass calculations as a specific term. It is the algebraic sum of the variation and deviation. Don't let the term "algebraic" bother you. Here it means only that either quantity might have to be added or subtracted. Variation depends on where a craft is—some places have more than others, and in some places variation is east while in others it's west. Therefore, variation will be added in some cases and subtracted in others.

Deviation depends on the individual boat and on what direction the boat is heading at the moment. It also changes according to the boat's various operating conditions—for

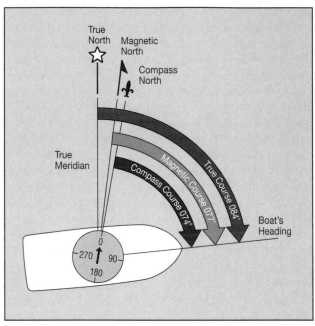

A course, heading or bearing can be named in any one of three systems based on the reference direction used.

example, whether it is at present heeling or level. Like variation, deviation is sometimes added and sometimes subtracted. Boaters customarily express direction only to the nearest whole degree.

Compass error is a convenient term, but the compass is not actually in error—it is simply responding to the magnetic forces that control its behavior. Nevertheless, we use the term error to describe the angular difference between compass north and true north.

Since both variation and deviation can be east or west depending on geographic location, there are four ways in which they can combine, as shown at left.

Applying variation and deviation

To use your compass well you must learn to convert directions of any one type to any other type, and you must be able to do so quickly and accurately. These conversions have to be performed on headings, on courses and on bearings. Normally you record true bearings on your chart and in your log, but magnetic directions, the intermediate step between true and compass, are also directly useful.

To simplify the procedure, let's consider a single step first. As a means of remembering whether deviation and variation are to be added or subtracted to the direction to be converted, we assume a hierarchy: first, true directions; second, magnetic directions; third, compass directions. True directions are considered to be more "correct" than magnetic, and magnetic more "correct" than compass directions.

Think of true as having no "errors," while magnetic has the one "error" (variation) and compass has two "errors" (variation and deviation).

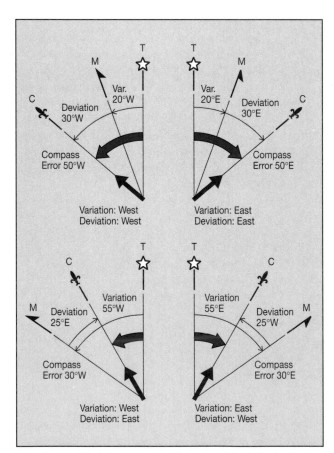

Variation and deviation are sometimes combined algebraically into a single value, termed "compass error (CE)." These intentionally exaggerated drawings show the four possible combinations of easterly and westerly deviation and variation.

If true is more correct, then getting from compass to magnetic is properly thought of as "correcting" and likewise, getting from magnetic to true is also "correcting." The converse, going from true to magnetic, or from magnetic to compass, is "uncorrecting."

Now we can establish the basic rule: When correcting, add easterly errors. That can be shortened to correcting, add east, or even CAE.

Note that to use this phrase in remembering whether to add or subtract, you can change words in the phrase to their opposites, but you must change two of them—never only one and never three. For example, you could say "uncorrecting add west" because you've changed two words, but you could not say "uncorrecting add east" because that changes only one word. Look at each of the following examples to get a feel for how the phrase can be applied.

EXAMPLE 1

Given: The magnetic course is 061°; the variation for the area we are navigating in is 11°E according to our chart. Deviation is zero.
Required: The true course (TC).
Answer: The conversion is a correcting conversion because we are going from magnetic to true. The variation is east, so we add it.
061° + 11° = 072°. The true direction (TC) is 072°.
The basic rule is easily restated for other conversions; correcting, subtract west.

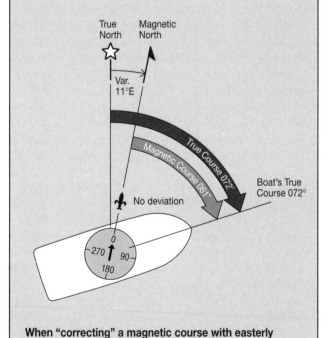

When "correcting" a magnetic course with easterly variation to a true course, add the variation.

EXAMPLE 2

Given: The magnetic course is 068°; the variation here is 14°W. Deviation is zero.
Required: The true course (TC).
Answer: We are, once again, correcting rather than uncorrecting because in this case we are going from magnetic direction to true direction. But this time our variation is west. So we have to subtract.

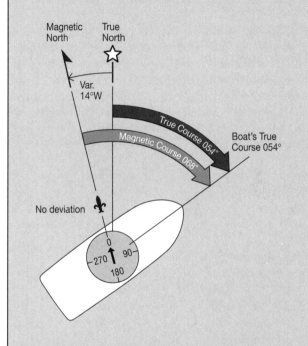

When "correcting" a magnetic course with westerly variation to a true course, subtract the variation.

EXAMPLE 3

Given: The boat's course according to our compass is 212°; the deviation for that heading, according to our deviation table, is 5°E.
Required: The magnetic course, or MC.
Answer: The conversion is still a correcting conversion and, since the deviation is east, we add it.
212° + 5° = 217°. MC 217°.

Now consider the process of uncorrecting. Again we can change two words in the basic rule: Uncorrecting, add west. But only two words. "Add west" inverts to become "subtract east," resulting in "uncorrecting, subtract east." Keep the basic rule for correcting, add east in your mind and make sure that if you change the rule, you change two words.

EXAMPLE 4

Given: The true course is 351° and the variation is 12°W.
Required: The magnetic course (MC).
Answer: This time we are going from true to magnetic so we are uncorrecting and the variation is west. The way to state the rule is uncorrecting, add west.
351° + 12° = 363°. But, the compass has only 360 degrees, so the answer is really MC 003°.

Taking two steps at a time

The same rules apply when two-step conversions are made either from true to compass, or from compass to true. It is important to remember that the proper rule must be applied for each step separately. In any case, it will always be either correcting or uncorrecting, but as to whether we add or subtract, that factor will be determined by the east or west nature of the variation and deviation.

EXAMPLE 5

Given: The true course is 88°, the variation is 18°W and the deviation is 12°W.
Required: The compass course (CC).
Answer: This time both conversions are uncorrecting (going toward the compass course) and both errors are westerly. The appropriate statement of the rule is uncorrecting, add west.
088° + 18° + 12° = 118° . Or CC 118°

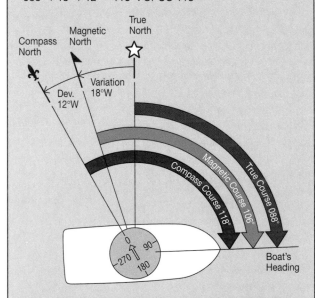

In the example above, a true course is "uncorrected" to a compass course, with the error of variation and deviation both westerly.

EXAMPLE 6

Given: The compass bearing is 107°, the variation is 6°E and the deviation for the heading the boat is on is 2°W.
Required: A true bearing (TB).
Answer: Note that the boat in this case is not on a course of 107°. It's the bearing we are interested in: a sighting across the compass rose to a distant object. But we need the deviation for the boat's heading because that deviation is changing the reading for our bearing.

Both conversions are correcting. However, the variation is easterly and the deviation westerly. Two statements of the rule are required. Correcting, subtract west. Correcting, add east.
107° - 2° + 6° = 111°. The true bearing is 111°, usually written as, TB 111°.

Other memory aids

Correcting, add east is only one of several memory aids. You should choose your favorite and apply it consistently and repeatedly until you find that the conversion process has become automatic.

Try this one: "Compass least, error east; compass best, error west." This can be used for conversions shown in the accompanying examples (try it on a few); however, it's also particularly valuable when the difference between compass and magnetic is known numerically but you must decide whether the deviation is east or west.

EXAMPLE 7

Given: The magnetic course is known to be 192°, but the compass reads 190°.
Required: The deviation.
Answer: The numerical difference is 2° and the compass is "least" (190° is less than 192°). If compass least, error east. The deviation must be 2°E.

EXAMPLE 8

Given: The magnetic course is 192°, but the compass reads 195°.
Required: The deviation.
Answer: Here the compass is "best," the error is west. The deviation is 3°W.

Now try the same rhyme for variation instead of deviation. Magnetic least, error east; magnetic best, error west.

Many boaters find another memory aid more helpful because it can easily be arranged in the form of a picture.

Place these letters vertically, as illustrated in the diagram below, to remind yourself of the three ways of naming a direction—either true, magnetic or compass—with the respective errors, variation and deviation, inserted between them. The resulting sequence of letters is T V M D C (true variation magnetic deviation compass).

Many people apply one of two mnemonic devices to remember that sequence: "True Virtue Makes Dull Company" and, in reverse, "Can Dead Men Vote Twice?"

With those phrases in mind, arrange the two series vertically as illustrated in the diagram.

On the left side a down arrow indicates conversion from true to compass (uncorrecting), while an up arrow on the right indicates conversion from compass to true (correcting). Now sketch in the appropriate arithmetical operations. Correcting, add east, so on the up arrow, add east and subtract west; conversely, on the down arrow, the procedure is to subtract east and add west, as shown.

Let's try it out.

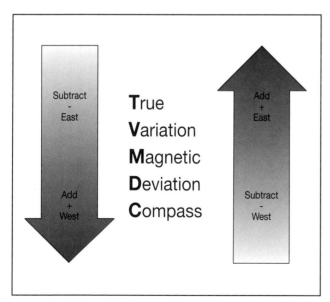

A pictorial "TVMDC" diagram can be an aid in remembering the rules for converting between true, magnetic and compass directions. The basic rule is "Down Add West," but the other rules can be derived from this by changing two, but only two, of these three words.

The two conversions above, examples 10 and 11, could be done in one single step.

COMPASS COMPENSATION

Before your compass can be used its deviation has to be measured. Much of this deviation can be removed by compensation, but some deviation may remain. This has to be measured and recorded so that compass directions can be corrected to magnetic directions, and magnetic directions to compass directions.

If your boat were completely non-magnetic, there would be no deviation on any course. The lubber's line would always indicate magnetic north, regardless of the boat's heading. However, even aboard small boats we are likely to find metallic objects with magnetic properties, for example, anchor and chain, motor, fuel and water tanks. Other items such as radios, depth sounders, electronic instruments and tools are likely to be placed close enough to a compass to produce deviation. Even flashlights will cause deviation if placed close to a compass. The boat acquires a unique magnetic character, one that may change. In addition to the permanent magnetism of some objects, there are unmagnetized masses that can affect the compass by acquiring induced magnetism. Each effect is different and must be considered separately.

Effects of permanent magnetism

On a typical wood or fiberglass boat, the effect of permanent magnetism is far greater than that of induced magnetism. To visualize this, assume that the net effect is exerted by a single permanent bar magnet located aft of the compass and slightly askew of the boat's center line.

Two forces now affect the compass—the magnetic field of the earth and of the imaginary magnet. Now, in addition to the effect of the earth's magnetic poles, the compass will

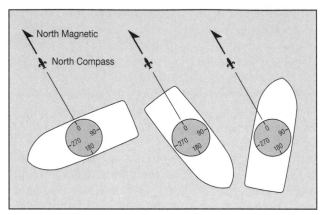

If there are no magnetic influences aboard a boat to disturb its compass—which is rarely the case—there is no deviation on any heading.

be affected by the N (north-seeking) and S (south-seeking) poles of the imaginary magnet. The result is an easterly deviation on some headings and a westerly deviation on others. On some headings, where the effects are balanced between east and west, there will be zero deviation.

Consider a typical case in the diagram below. The boat is heading north (MC 000°). The S pole of the compass, 180° on the card, is repelled by the N pole of the imaginary magnet and is deflected so that the compass reading is 006°. There is a westerly deviation of 6°, written as 6°W.

However, when the boat heads south (MC 180°), the N pole of the compass card is closer to the imaginary magnet, but, instead of being repelled, is attracted to it. The card is

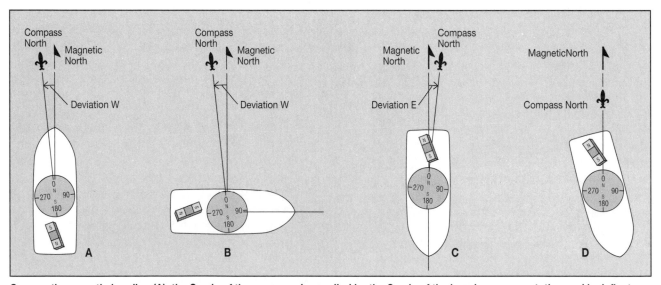

On a north magnetic heading (A), the S pole of the compass is repelled by the S pole of the imaginary magnet; the card is deflected counterclockwise; there is westerly deviation. On an east magnetic heading (B), the N pole of the compass is nearer the S pole of the imaginary magnet, and is attracted to it. The deflection is still counterclockwise, the deviation is still westerly. On a south magnetic heading (C), the N pole of the compass is nearest the S pole of the imaginary magnet and is attracted to it. The card is deflected clockwise, and there is easterly deviation. On this heading (D), the N pole of the compass is attracted to the S pole of the imaginary magnet, but it is already as close as it can get; hence there is no deflection and no deviation on this heading.

deflected and the compass reading is decreased to 174°. The deviation is now 6°E.

If the boat heads east (MC 090°), the N pole of the compass is nearer the S pole of the imaginary magnet, and is attracted. This results in a westerly deviation.

With westerly deviation on some headings, but easterly on others, there must be headings on which the deviation is 000°. Situation (D) in the diagram (*opposite page, lower left*) shows this situation. There is still attraction of the N pole of the compass to the S pole of the imaginary magnet, but the two are as close as they can get. The result is zero deviation.

It is usually the case that deviation resulting from permanent magnetism will swing through a cycle of west to east and back to west, with two zero deviation headings in between. Remember that the imaginary magnet shown in these examples is only for illustration of the principle. Every boat will have a unique magnetic environment.

Induced magnetism

The effect of induced magnetism can be visualized in a series of examples much like the ones above with an imaginary mass of magnetizable material. In this case, the disturbing pole would be the one induced in the mass and its sign would change as determined by the changing sign of the nearest pole of the inducing magnet. The deviation would change from westerly to easterly four times in a complete rotation, 360°, with four headings having zero deviation. When the effects of both induced and permanent magnetism are combined, the deviation pattern is complex. Fortunately, this is rarely the case on a small boat.

Effects of geographic position

On page 374, we mentioned that deviation aboard a steel-hulled craft can change in different latitudes. This seems to run contrary to the rule that deviation changes with heading, while only variation changes with geographic location.

However, deviation can change with changes in "magnetic latitude" of the craft. Aboard a boat, we are almost always concerned exclusively with the horizontal component of the earth's magnetic field. But this horizontal component diminishes in relative strength in higher latitudes. Imagine that the "lines" of magnetism begin to curve downward into the magnetic poles. In this area, the vertical component of the field begins to have an effect on deviation.

Swinging ship

Deviation can be measured by steering the boat on one or more known headings toward charted visual targets and noting the difference between the magnetic course according to a chart and the course according to the compass. This process is called "swinging ship." The target might consist of two charted objects that can be visually aligned with each other to produce a range, or it might be a course between two charted objects such as an aid to navigation and a land-

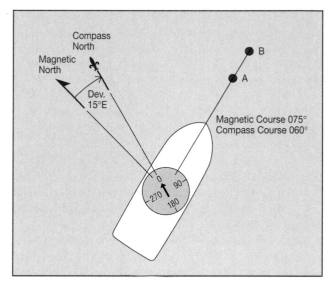

The simplest way to determine deviation on any heading is to locate two objects to use as a range whose magnetic direction can be established from the chart. Head the boat toward this range and read the compass; the difference, if any, is the deviation on that heading.

mark, provided the course passes close aboard the aid and the landmark is far enough away that the slight offset of the boat's actual course is unimportant.

The best ranges are those in the *Light List* because their true directions are accurately recorded. These true directions can be easily uncorrected to magnetic using the techniques on page 379.

However, large harbors or groups of islands offer a number of natural ranges. The edge of a pier and the side of a large building, for example, are useful if their direction can be read from the chart. Remember that the position of an anchored buoy on a chart is actually the position of the buoy's anchor. Fixed aids are preferable because wind and current may alter the buoy's position and/or the anchor may have been dragged in a collision.

Select two points ashore that are accurately charted and easily visible. From the chart, measure the magnetic direction from the nearer to the farthermost point. The boat is run along the range on a steady, accurate course—both points of the range are kept constantly in exact alignment. The compass direction is read and recorded.

In the example above, the range direction is MC 075°, and the compass direction is CC 060°. The deviation amount is 15°, but is it east or west? Using the memory aid discussed on page 380—"Compass least, error east; compass best, error west"—the deviation in this case is east, written as 15°E.

When swinging ship, headings are checked at frequent and regular intervals, traditionally every 15°. It may not be possible to find convenient ranges at those intervals. In that case, an alternative is to use a single observed object sighted through a pelorus.

A pelorus has two sighting vanes that rotate above a compass rose. The compass course is lined up with a mark that is on the lubber's line (so that the compass course can be "pointed at the bow"). The vanes are pivoted to line up with a sighted object of a known (that is, charted) position. The bearing is then read from the base. This means that, while underway, you can take bearings on objects without swinging the vessel to face them. Inexpensive plastic peloruses are available at chandleries.

When swinging ship using a distant range and a pelorus, preparation is the key to simplicity. Choose a calm day. A firm mounting position for the pelorus, one that allows sightings in all directions, is best. If some sight-lines are blocked, these bearings will have to be interpolated.

Note that a single charted object can be used in place of a range (two objects), but in either case, keep all sighted objects at least half a mile from your vessel.

If possible, it is helpful to have three crew aboard—one for steering a straight course, one for taking the pelorus sights on the range and a third for entering the values called out by the pelorus reader.

Before going out, make up a deviation in values table like the one that is shown at right. Enter the values in the first column, entitled "Compass Heading (boat)." You know before you begin that you will be steering courses at 15° intervals. (The illustrated table is simplified for the sake of clarity.

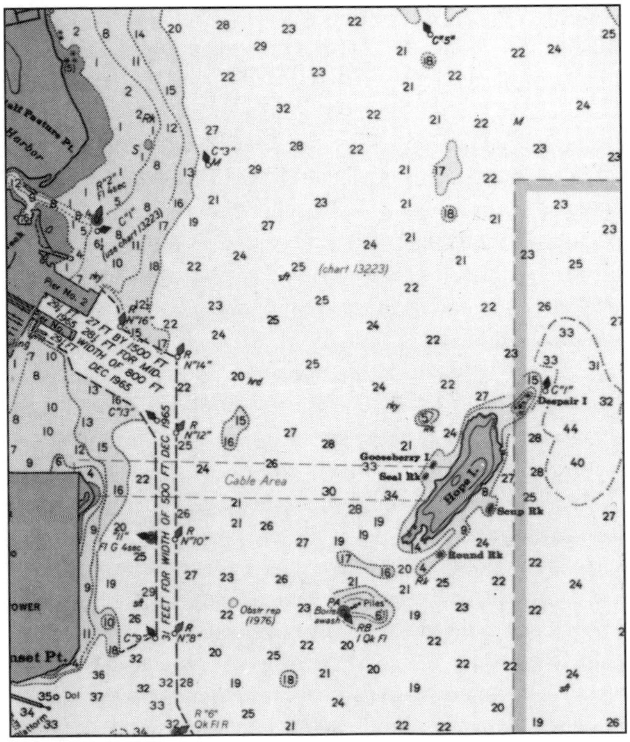

COMPASS HEADING (boat)	COMPASS BEARING (range)	MEAN MAGNETIC (range)	DEVIATION
000°			
015°			
030°			
045°			
060°			
075°			
190°			
105°			
120°			
135°			
150°			
165°			
180°			
195°			
210°			
225°			
240°			
255°			
270°			
285°			
300°			
315°			
330°			
345°			

1 When preparing deviation values, the first step is to construct a table like the one that is shown above. You already know that you will be reading range bearings at every 15° of compass heading, so list the compass headings in the first column of the table.

Carefully run courses between two charted positions can be used to determine deviation on a number of headings. Deviation will not be the same for reciprocal courses, and each direction must be run individually.

The vessel is steered across the range on a series of courses that are successively 15° apart. The compass heading is called out to the pelorus reader, who in turns dials the reading into the pelorus base and then sights the range or object in question. His reading from the sighting vanes is next recorded in column two.

Column three lists the average of all of the sightings in column two. In this case, since 95° will be used in a subtraction for each line, it is listed for each reading. Column four is the difference between compass bearing (column two) and average magnetic bearing (95° in column three). If magnetic is larger, the deviation is west. (In the first line of the table, the values for 000° are 095° for compass, and 093° for magnetic, so the deviation is 2°W.) If the magnetic is smaller, the deviation is east.

COMPASS HEADING (boat)	COMPASS BEARING (range)	MEAN MAGNETIC (range)	DEVIATION
000°	095°		
015°	095°		
030°	096°		
045°	097°		
060°	098°		
075°	098°		
190°	099°		
105°	098°		
120°	097°		
135°	096°		
150°	091°		
165°	090°		
180°	090°		
195°	092°		
210°	093°		
225°	094°		
240°	095°		
255°	095°		
270°	096°		
285°	095°		
300°	094°		
315°	094°		
330°	095°		
345°	095°		
	2,278		
	$\frac{2,278}{24}=94.91$ (95°)		

COMPASS HEADING (boat)	COMPASS BEARING (range)	MEAN MAGNETIC (range)	DEVIATION
000°	095°	095°	0°
015°	095°	095°	0°
030°	096°	095°	1° W
045°	097°	095°	2° W
060°	098°	095°	3° W
075°	098°	095°	3° W
190°	099°	095°	4° W
105°	098°	095°	3° W
120°	097°	095°	2° W
135°	096°	095°	1° W
150°	091°	095°	4° E
165°	090°	095°	5° E
180°	090°	095°	5° E
195°	092°	095°	3° E
210°	093°	095°	2° E
225°	094°	095°	1° E
240°	095°	095°	0°
255°	095°	095°	0°
270°	096°	095°	1° W
285°	095°	095°	0°
300°	094°	095°	1° E
315°	094°	095°	1° E
330°	095°	095°	0°
345°	095°	095°	0°
	2,278		
	$\frac{2,278}{24}=94.91$ (95°)		

2 For the second step, use a pelorus to collect range bearings for every compass heading on your table, and record them in column two. Then, find the mean of your range bearings. This mean is what the range bearing would have been if the compass had no deviation. To find it, sum your bearings and divide by the number of readings.

3 The third step is to subtract the range bearings from the mean magnetic range to find the deviation value for each compass heading. If the compass bearing is larger than the mean magnetic, then the deviation is west, and vice versa.

Up to 2° or 3° of deviation is quite tolerable, but 5° or 6° is usually considered excessive. However, remember that, at this point, the compass has yet to be compensated (as explained below).

Compensating for deviation

Deviation much over 6° can present serious problems in rough weather, even when deviation is carefully recorded for each heading. It is much better to compensate the compass so that the deviation is as small as possible (sometimes zero) on most headings.

Compensation can be made with either internal or external magnets. Most compasses sold today have internal compensator magnets installed at right angles to each other and adjusted by a slot-head screw, one marked N-S and the other E-W. If internal magnets are not available, external magnets can be attached to the surface on which the compass binnacle is mounted.

The effect of the compensator magnets is to create a countervailing magnetic field capable of overcoming the boat's deviating field. The compensators must be zeroed-in (page 373) before compensation begins. This is usually done by the manufacturer, but in any case it would be worthwhile if you checked it yourself. This is also a good time to check the alignment of the lubber's line with the centerline of your boat (page 374). You can check this alignment by sighting an object at a distance of at least half a mile. With your boat motionless, sight down the boat's center line, then try sighting over the compass. In both cases the bearings should be the same; if they differ, the lubber's line is out of alignment.

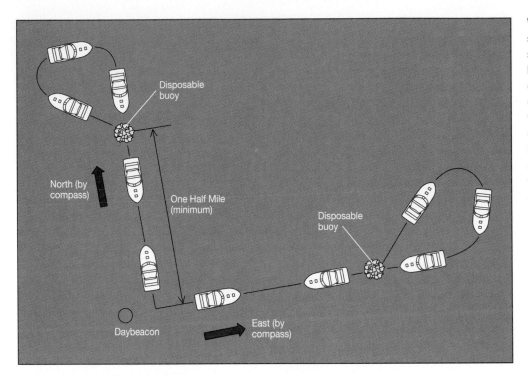

With a little practice, a skipper can learn to make smooth Williamson, or button-hook, turns of 180 degrees and come back directly over the spot where the turn was started. Swing out far enough initially on the opposite side to the main turn so that the reciprocal course can be picked up without overshooting it.

Running reciprocal courses

Putting the boat on a course over the bottom and being able to reverse that course exactly is known as running reciprocal courses. This is not as difficult as it sounds.

Picking a range and running it in both directions is not difficult either, but ranges are seldom available on the cardinal points necessary for compensating the compass. (In some harbors, there are marks made specifically for this purpose.)

On a quiet day, when there is no risk of wind or current skewing the results, begin your compensating run by departing from a fixed mark. A daybeacon or light is best. Run a steady course on a cardinal direction as indicated by your compass until you are ready to reverse course. Drop a dis-

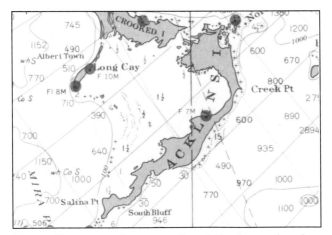

Charts of large areas show magnetic variation by a series of lines for each degree of variation. Each such isogonic line is labelled with its variation.

posable buoy to create the desired range. (This disposable buoy might be wadded-up newspaper with a half-filled plastic bottle attached to make retrieval easier.) Execute a button hook turn (sometimes called a Williamson turn), illustrated on this page. This turn will have to be tight and quick so that your buoy doesn't have time to drift. Choose either a right or a left turn depending on your boat's turning characteristics. Swing away from your course before you begin the turn back toward it so that you end up approaching the disposable buoy smoothly without a lot of over-shoot or correction. (The Williamson turn is worth learning as a rescue technique too, as described in Chapter 4.)

Having completed the turn, line up the disposable buoy with the fixed object that marked your starting point. Steady the boat on this range visually and ignore the compass. Head for the initial point. Run right over the disposable buoy (or very close to it) and continue toward the initial point.

Provided that no wind or current has set the boat to either side of its heading on the outward run from the initial point, this adjustment maneuver will have put the boat on an accurate reciprocal course.

Making the adjustment

The adjustments to the compensating magnets must be made with a non-magnetic screwdriver. This could be a bronze screwdriver, a dime or a piece of heavy sheet copper or brass, or even a brass rod with one end filed to a screwdriver shape. Store every article of the boat's gear in its usual place. Decide whether you're going to need to re-run the whole procedure for a different set of magnetic circumstances such as wipers on and wipers off. Keep your steel eyeglass frames, steel partial dentures or even the steel grommet in your cap away from the compass while you are working on it.

Your first run and reciprocal course should be either 090° or 270° by compass. Plan to run for at least half a mile, but a mile would be better. Make the turn and run the reciprocal course, not by compass, but by steering to the starting point. Read the compass and record the reading.

If the reading is not 180° from the outbound run, use your non-magnetic screwdriver to turn the E-W adjusting screw so as to remove half the difference between the observed reading and the correct reading. Let's assume that you have made the outbound run on 090°: Your compass should be reading 270°.

We assume that the deviation on the reciprocal course is equal and opposite— although not necessarily so, this is a good place to start.

In this case, we would be using the E-W screw, which is the aluminum rod holding the magnets and running through the compass in a fore-and-aft direction. The N-S compensators are mounted on a rod running athwartships.

Since there is no way to know which way to turn the screw, you will have to experiment with it. If the difference between the reading and the actual reciprocal course is 20°, remove only 10°.

Return to the starting mark and head out again on the same compass course that you used the first time. Note that your course over the bottom is different. Drop another buoy, make the turn and head back. Your compass reading should be closer. Again, remove half of the difference. Repeat these east-west runs until the deviation is reduced to the smallest

possible amount. (None is best.) Then do not touch the E-W adjusting screw again.

Follow the same procedure on a north-south run and reduce the deviation with the N-S adjusting screw to the minimum. This process should not change the E-W setting, but remember, it won't hurt to check. Your deviation on the cardinal headings should now be zero or as close as possible to zero. The adjusting screws should not be changed.

Compensating with external magnets

Even without internal compensating magnets, a compass can still be compensated. External magnets can be placed near the compass, then screwed into place. You will need two magnets, each an encased permanent magnet with two holes for non-magnetic screws. The ends of the magnets will either be marked N and S, or colored red for north and blue for south. Use masking tape during the compensation process to place the magnets temporarily.

Carefully mark the longitudinal center of each magnet, then mark two lines in chalk running through the center of the compass, one fore-and-aft and the other athwartships, as shown below.

The procedure recalls the reciprocal course process for compensation with internal magnets. (Keep external magnets far from the compass until they are being placed.)

Assuming that you begin with east-west runs, and the compass reads 290° on the reciprocal of 90°, the compensation is made by placing the magnet in a fore-and-aft position on the athwartship chalked line. Make sure that the magnet is centered on this line and at right angles to it. It can be placed

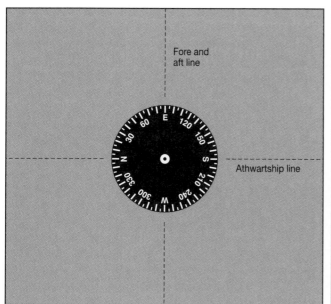

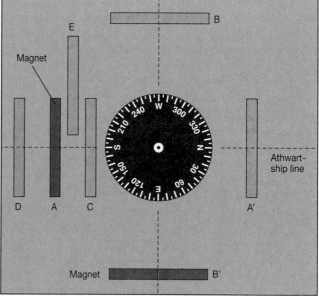

Before installing external compensating magnets, chalk in two lines *(above, left)* through the center of the compass mounting location. The magnets must always be placed so their centers are on one of these lines. Magnets are placed forward or aft of the compass and on one side *(above, right)*. When final placement is determined they are fastened with non-magnetic tacks or screws.

on either side of the compass at positions A or A'. Should the compass reading then be more than 290°, for example, the magnet is increasing, not decreasing, the deviation. Reverse it, or move it to the other side of the compass without reversing it—but choose only one option.

Should the card stop moving before you reach the desired 280° (which is to remove half of the error), shift the compensator magnet closer to the compass along the athwartship line, or vice versa. When the desired reading is obtained, tape the magnet in place. Do not let it get off the center line (as in position E in the diagram).

Repeat the whole procedure making the north-south runs and reciprocals. When the deviation has been reduced to the minimum, fasten the compensator magnets in place with non-magnetic screws. Make one last check on the east-west course.

Compensation by shadow pin

A method of sailing reciprocal courses without setting up temporary ranges with disposable buoys uses a vertical shadow pin in the center of a horizontal disc graduated similar to a compass card; the disc should be gimbal mounted.

Consider the following example: On a sunny day, the craft heads east by the compass. The azimuth disc is rotated by hand so that the shadow of the pin falls on the 090° mark. The turn is made and the boat is steadied on the reciprocal course by steering so that the shadow now falls on the mark 180° from the original—in this case, 270°. Now the compass is read. If it shows 270°, then there is no need to compensate. If there is deviation, the same "reduce by half" method is used to compensate. The same technique is used for the north-south headings.

The shadow pin procedure has the following advantages: The boat need not run far on any one heading; no departure point is needed; no disposable buoys need be thrown overboard and, finally, wind and current have no effect. However, the sun is always on the move, and time thus becomes a serious factor. Each set of outbound and reciprocal runs and adjustments must therefore be completed before the sun moves far enough to upset the adjustments. The earlier or later in the day, the better. (Keep in mind that the sun makes its most rapid moves near noon.)

Heeling magnets

Sailing craft frequently require heeling magnets below the compass. Owners might be able to make a rough adjustment but this is a challenge. An exact adjustment should be made by a professional compass adjuster.

First, place the sailboat on a north-south heading (using the same outbound and reciprocal procedure described on page 386) and then heel the boat slightly. Then, position the compensating magnet vertically under the compass so as to eliminate only the deviation induced by the heeling. Reverse the ends of the magnet if necessary. Even if you are unable to compensate with heeling magnets, you should record as pre-

cisely as possible the deviation that results from heeling on both tacks. Note that this method works only when the vessel is on a north or south heading.

Residual headings

You can determine any deviation remaining on the intercardinal headings—NE, SE, SW and NW—by the method discussed on page 383, or by continuing to make outbound runs on these courses and dropping a disposable buoy for a reciprocal run. But remember that you are no longer compensating the compass; you are merely recording its deviation. Do not touch the adjusting screws.

If deviation is unacceptably high, check the area around the compass for magnetic influences that can be demagnetized *(page 373)*. Prime suspects are tachometer cables and the steering mechanism, especially the steering arms. Test these and other key parts with a thin piece of steel; a 0.05 to 0.10 mm machinist's thickness gauge is ideal. To avoid distorting your findings, make sure that the steel itself is not magnetic. Touch one end to the part being tested. Does it stick? Open up the wheel housing and test each part thoroughly, using a small magnet to detect a part that could either be steel or contain iron—for example, a chain link made of steel, or a cotter pin or shackle on a cable system. A wooden box can serve as a pedestal to distance the compass from the magnetic culprit.

THE UNCOMPENSATED COMPASS

A compass that has not been compensated and for which deviation tables have not been prepared should never be relied upon to show actual magnetic directions. But it may be useful nevertheless. After all, navigators successfully used the compass in a very crude form for hundreds of years with good results.

Your uncompensated compass will measure direction in a repeatable way if local conditions on the boat are unchanged. For example, you could proceed from one point to another and record the direction your compass shows (though it is probably incorrect). On another day you can repeat the run by using the same (incorrect) compass heading even if there is no visibility, provided you have not changed anything that may alter the compass's magnetic environment. In this way, even an incorrect reading is useful if it is consistent.

However, you cannot extrapolate your recorded heading and expect to be able to follow the reverse direction just by subtracting 180°, because your uncompensated compass will be subject to a different deviation value at that heading and possibly at every other heading too.

Keeping a record of headings for runs you make frequently is a good practice particularly if it provides a way home in reduced visibility.

RECORDING DEVIATION

Even after compensation, most compasses retain some deviation. While variation is different in different locations, deviation is the same wherever the boat goes (with the exception of steel-hulled craft on which deviation can change with large changes in latitude).

However, deviation does change as the heading changes. To cope with deviation, a navigator needs a current record from which the amount of deviation for every heading can be read or interpolated. Some boats might even carry deviation records for different circumstances to account for the magnetic influence of movable objects near the compass.

Usually, deviation records take the form of a table listing two columns of values. One column lists the boat's magnetic heading every 15° and the other lists the amount of deviation as a value in degrees and a direction, for example 7°E.

The information can also be presented as a graph plotting magnetic heading against deviation. On such a graph, 0° can be placed through the middle horizontally with deviation west on the bottom half and deviation east on the top.

Some navigators prefer to show deviation as a compass rose within a compass rose. This deviation rose can be made by gluing one rose within another. (A reducing photocopier might be helpful.) The inner rose can represent heading not corrected for deviation, and the outer rose the corrected headings. Arrows connect the inner rose headings with the appropriate positions on the outer rose.

Any deviation record is valid only for the boat for which it was prepared and only for the magnetic condition prevailing at that time. If magnetic materials within 3 to 5 feet are moved, a new deviation record must be prepared.

CRITICAL VALUES TABLE

Magnetic Course (in degrees)		Deviation	Compass Course (in degrees)		Magnetic Course (in degrees)		Deviation	Compass Course (in degrees)	
064-071	072-086	19°W	082-090	091-105	016-018	183-187	0°	016-018	183-187
059-063	087-094	18°W	076-081	106-112	014-015	188-192	1°E	011-015	188-191
055-058	095-103	17°W	071-075	113-120	012-013	193-197	2°E	009-010	192-195
053-054	104-108	16°W	067-070	121-125	010-011	198-204	3°E	006-008	196-201
049-052	109-114	15°W	063-066	126-129	008-009	205-210	4°E	003-005	202-205
047-048	115-121	14°W	061-062	130-135	006-007	211-215	5°E	000-002	206-210
044-046	122-125	13°W	058-060	136-138	004-005	216-222	6°E	356-359	211-216
042-043	126-131	12°W	051-057	139-143	360-003	223-229	7°E	351-355	217-222
040-041	132-135	11°W	048-050	144-146	357-359	230-233	8°E	347-350	223-224
038-039	136-139	10°W	043-047	147-150	355-356	234-240	9°E	345-348	255-230
036-037	140-142	9°W	041-042	151-152	350-354	241-246	10°E	338-344	231-236
034-035	143-147	8°W	037-040	153-156	346-349	247-251	11°E	333-337	237-240
031-033	148-153	7°W	033-036	157-160	343-345	252-257	12°E	330-332	241-246
029-030	154-159	6°W	031-032	161-165	339-342	258-266	13°E	324-329	247-250
027-028	160-162	5°W	029-030	166-167	335-338	263-269	14°E	318-323	251-255
025-026	163-166	4°W	027-028	168-171	331-334	270-275	15°E	315-317	256-261
023-024	167-173	3°W	025-026	172-176	326-330	276-281	16°E	308-314	262-265
021-022	174-178	2°W	022-024	177-180	316-325	282-287	17°E	300-307	266-270
019-020	179-182°	1°W	019-021	181-182	305-315	288-304	18°E	288-299	271-298

A table of critical values allows conversion from magnetic to compass, or from compass to magnetic. For example, if given a magnetic course of 336, you would find it on the line that shows values for 14 degrees of easterly deviation. You would subtract 14 from 336 to arrive at a compass course of 322. Note that these values have been interpreted from the curves on the Napier diagrams on page 391. The deviation values used here have been exaggerated for clarity.

The deviation record

You may need more than one deviation record in order to account for varying magnetic environments. As mentioned earlier, the magnetic effect of windshield wipers may differ depending whether they are on or off; also consider the case of a sailboat heeling. You may want to prepare a compass record on both a port and starboard tack heel or on an even keel. (The installation of heeling magnets may be necessary to provide extra compensation.)

Begin with a simple graph of table values. Make a horizontal base line for compass headings from 0° to 360° and plot easterly deviation vertically above the base and westerly deviation below. When all values are in place, draw a smooth curve through the points, measuring to the nearest whole degree. Verify any value that appears erratic. If the curve is smooth but its horizontal axis lies above or below the zero line, it is likely that the lubber's line may not be aligned with the boat's center line.

The final deviation table can be prepared as a direct reading table of critical values. It can be used with confidence if care is taken to see that the magnetic environment is not altered. Be sure to check the table each year.

Critical values table

Since a navigator needs deviation values in terms of both compass headings and magnetic headings, a simple tool that combines both is a table of critical values. Each line marks one degree of deviation. To one side is the range of magnetic headings corresponding to that deviation. Refer to page 389.

Napier diagram

A Napier diagram *(opposite)* plots deviation values. It permits interpolation of intermediate values and conversion between compass and magnetic directions. The vertical base line (usually in two sections) extends through all 360° with some overlap at the top and bottom. A grid of lines crosses the base line and each other at 60° angles, and at intervals of 15 compass degrees. Lines sloping up to the right are solid; those sloping up to the left are dotted. Deviation values are plotted on the dotted lines, easterly to the right and westerly to the left; then a curve is drawn through the points.

To convert from magnetic to compass, find the value of the magnetic heading on the center line, then move along, or parallel to, a solid cross line (sloping up to the right, or down to the left) until the curve. Next, move back to the center line, this time on a new line along, or parallel to, the dotted lines (sloping down to the right or up to the left). The compass heading is the value of the point where you reach the base line. To convert compass to magnetic, reverse the procedure.

A Napier diagram is most useful when deviations are large and changing rapidly. If deviation values are small, it may serve best as a first step toward a critical values table.

THE DEVIATION ROSE

Another graphical method of recording deviation is the deviation rose. Some find this representation more intuitive and, like the deviation curve on the opposite page, the rose doesn't require any calculation.

However, it does require some "eyeball" interpretation.

The illustration shown here records the same, exaggerated deviation values as are recorded by the graph, the Napier diagram and the table of critical values. A real compass would never be used with such large deviation values.

The deviation rose is made by placing one rose inside another. (You might use a high-quality reducing photocopier.) The degree marks are arranged to coincide—000° on both scales at the top and lined up.

Deviation values are indicated by drawing a line from the magnetic courses on the inside rose to their corresponding compass courses on the outside rose, forming a pattern like skewed wagon-wheel spokes.

Before making a final deviation table or table of critical values, make a simple plot of the values to spot any that are not consistent with the others. This graph can also be used in lieu of a deviation table. Note that the values are exaggerated for clarity.

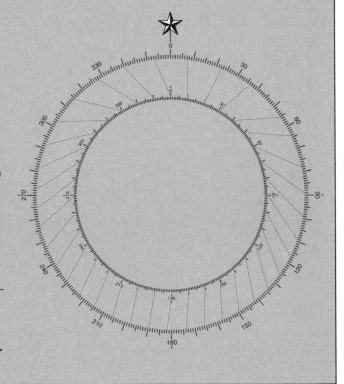

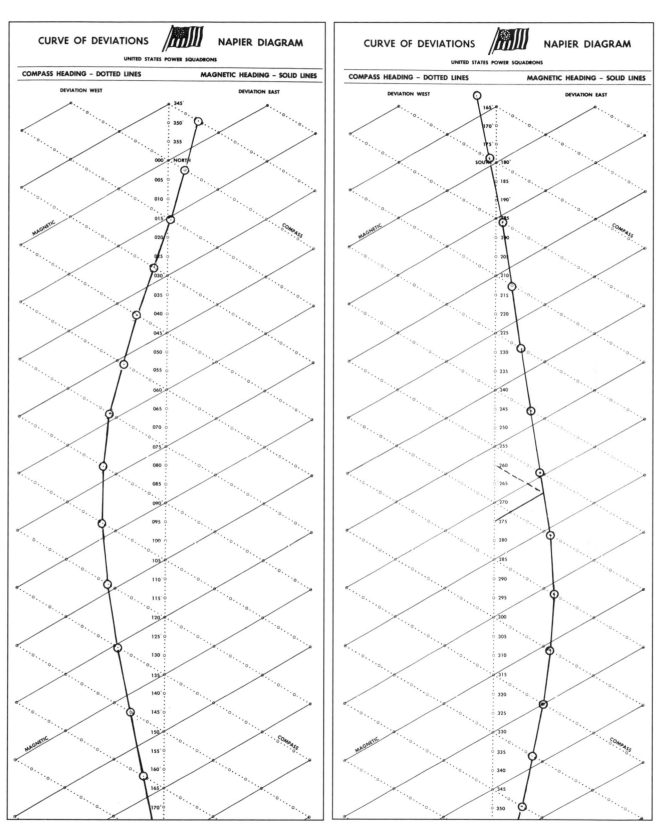

A Napier diagram, with its plot of deviation values, provides a means of converting between magnetic and compass courses without separate tables for each conversion. It is of particular value when the deviations are large and changing rapidly. If the deviations are small, the Napier diagram is less useful, except in the construction of a critical values table.

18 THE NAUTICAL CHART

Safe navigation requires knowledge of water depths, shoals and channels. It requires knowing the exact location of landmarks and aids to navigation, as well as of ports and harbors. A skipper must be able to determine all of these for the present position and for future positions along the intended course.

At any given position, it is generally possible to measure the depth, and to see some landmarks, For true safety, however, the skipper has to know the depth ahead, the actual location of the aids to navigation within sight, and where more aids lie on his or her course. It is essential to know the dangers along the way.

Nautical charts are the best source of this information, and this chapter will help you develop the skills you need to use them wisely.

BASIC CHART CONCEPTS

Nautical charts differ from maps because they emphasize information on water areas—land features are recorded only for their interest to the navigator. Also, rather than simply representing a portion of the earth's surface, they convey information specifically to assist navigation.

A chart contains information about water depth, obstructions and other dangers to navigation, and the locations and types of navigation aids. Charts are printed on durable paper so that they can be used as work sheets for plotting and annotating courses and determining positions. Charts for small-craft skippers even include information on marinas and are often bound into convenient books for particular waterways.

A chart's basic purpose is to give the navigator enough information to make the right decision to avoid danger. Charts must be extremely accurate (far more accurate than the average road map) because even a very small error in the charted position of a submerged obstruction is hazardous.

Various "cruising guides" for important boating areas may contain useful information as part of their text, tables, sketches and even aerial photos. But none of this information is a safe substitute for the information contained in government charts and the corresponding *Notice to Mariners*. Do not rely on cruising guides for navigation.

Geographic coordinates

Charts show a grid of intersecting lines to aid in describing any position. These lines are representations of a system of geographic coordinates used to locate positions anywhere on the earth's surface.

Geographic coordinates are based on a series of circles—great circles and small circles. Great circles are the largest circles that can be drawn on the surface of a sphere. Imagine a sphere cut through its center by a plane (like an orange cut through the core); the resulting edge is a great circle. A small circle would result from a cut by any plane that did not pass through the sphere's center.

The great circles that pass through the north and south geographic poles are called meridians of longitude. The plane that cuts through the earth at Greenwich, England, is known as the prime meridian, or 0 degrees of longitude. Each of the other meridians of longitude is named according to the number of degrees of angle east or degrees of angle west between its plane and the plane of the prime meridian. Since one degree is $\frac{1}{360}$ of a circle, the longitude of any point on the earth can be expressed as degrees east or degrees west up to a maximum of 180° (half of the circle). This means that the designation of "E" or "W" is an essential part of any statement of

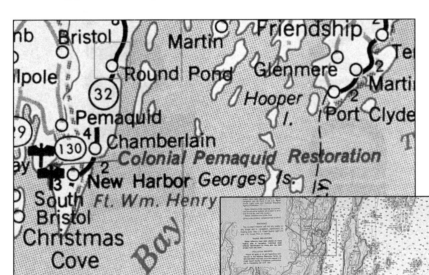

A *map* is designed to emphasize information about land features, such as the roads indicated on this map of the Muscongus Bay area of Maine. Underwater and coastal features are almost ignored.

A *chart* of Muscongus Bay is far more accurate than the road map above, and is almost exclusively concerned with navigation. Note the amount of data that is conveyed by each square inch of the chart—all without compromising its clarity.

longitude; "144°," for example, is not very useful. "Longitude" can be abbreviated as "Long."or "Lo", or as "λ" (the Greek letter lambda).

Parallels of latitude are a series of small circles drawn perpendicular to the earth's geographic polar axis. These parallels are named according to the number of degrees, north or south, in a vertical angle—the angle that would be formed if you were to draw a straight line from any point along the parallel to the center of the earth, and another line from the center of the earth out to any point on the equator. The equator itself is a great circle. Latitude is expressed as degrees north or degrees south; "N" and "S" are essential. "Latitude" can be abbreviated as "Lat." or "La."

Usually, full degrees do not offer sufficient precision, so degrees are subdivided into 60 minutes, and minutes are further subdivided into 60 seconds. (Minutes are sometimes divided fractionally and expressed as decimal numbers.)

Meridians of longitude converge, beginning with their widest separation at the equator and meeting at the poles. Distance between meridians varies with latitude. On the other hand, the distance between parallels of latitude is (for practical purposes) 60 nautical miles; *the arc of one minute of latitude is one nautical mile in length*—a relationship we will put to use in later chapters.

Before we can begin to talk about direction, distance and scale as they are represented on charts, there are two matters that have to be mentioned. The first, and least important to boaters, is that the earth is not a sphere. It's actually somewhat flattened at the poles. This makes the cartographer's task more challenging but need not concern the chart user.

The second matter is more apparent and more complex—how can the spherical earth be represented on a flat chart without serious distortions?

Although there will always be distortions, we can choose which distortion will be least troublesome for the scale of the chart we are using, the use we want to make of it, and the part of the earth we're interested in. Of course, as the area covered by the chart decreases, the importance of the distortion is diminished.

Flat representations of the earth are accomplished with mathematical constructs, which cartographers call chart projections. The two most commonly used projections for nautical charts are the Mercator, used for oceans and coastal areas, and the polyconic, which is used for National Ocean Service (NOS) charts of inland bodies. NOS charts of the Great Lakes, for example, are polyconic projections. The Canadian Hydrographic Service (CHS) uses Mercator projections for everything south of 75°N. There is more information on projections at the end of this chapter.

Direction

In chartwork, direction is measured by the angle between two lines. The first line connects two points of particular interest (your beginning point and destination, for example),

while the second line is a reference line (a meridian). The angle is measured in degrees clockwise from the reference line. A course that happened to point toward geographic north would be 000°.

The meridian being used as a reference line may be either a meridian of longitude or a magnetic meridian—a line that passes through the north magnetic pole. If the reference line is a meridian of longitude, then the direction is described as so many degrees true (T). Otherwise, it is so many degrees magnetic (M). The difference between the true and magnetic is variation. Refer to Chapter 17 for a discussion of magnetic poles and variation.

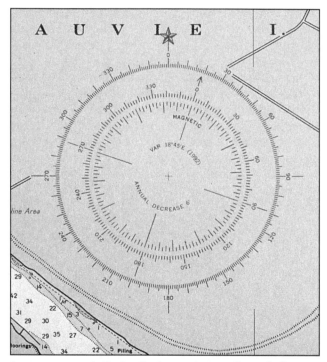

A compass rose indicates the true and magnetic north directions. The outer circle is in degrees with zero at true north; the inner circles are in degrees and "points" with their zero at magnetic north. The innermost circle may be omitted on some small-craft charts.

The compass rose

Direction measurement is simplified by the use of a compass rose printed on the chart. A compass rose is two or three concentric circles a couple of inches in diameter. Each circle is marked in degrees. The outer circle is aligned with 0° at true north and is usually subdivided in intervals of one degree. The next circle has 0° aligned with local magnetic north and is also subdivided—but usually in a different interval (because the circle is smaller). The third circle (if it exists) is also aligned with magnetic north, but it is marked in points and fractions *(Chapter 17)*.

The difference between the orientation of the true circle and the magnetic circle is the variation at the place where the rose is situated on the chart. If there is more than one compass rose on the chart, variation may be different for each one. When working in magnetic, you should always refer your course to the nearest compass rose for a more accurate measure of its direction.

The amount of variation (easterly or westerly) is stated (in words and figures) in the middle of the rose, along with the year that such variation existed and the annual rate of change. If you are using an old variation statement, you may need to apply the rate of change, but such rates are often so small that you can safely ignore them.

Distances

There are four measures of distance in common use on charts:
- Nautical miles ($\frac{1}{60}$ of a degree of latitude) are used on ocean and coastal waters.
- Statute miles (land miles) are used for inland areas—the Great Lakes, Intracoastal Waterway, etc.
- Yards are often used to define distances of a mile or less.
- Meters will see increasing use on U.S. charts, and are already well established on Canadian and other charts.

Conversion factors and rules of thumb are shown on page 396, and a more complete conversion table is found in the Appendices in Section 8.

Conversions are also made graphically. Charts are printed with graphic bar scales in more than one unit of measure. Chapter 19 explains this technique in detail, but, briefly, a length of distance is taken off the course with dividers and the tips of the dividers are set down on whichever graphic bar scale is printed in the appropriate units on the chart. The process is reversible—a unit of distance can be set on the dividers from the bar scale and the course distance "walked-off." The bar scale shows its basic unit to the left of 0 where it is subdivided into fractions for convenient measure of fractional distances.

Chart scales

The amount by which actual distances are reduced for representation on the chart is known as the scale of the chart. Scales can be expressed as a ratio such as 1:80,000. This means that one unit on the chart represents 80,000 of the

One of the cartographer's objectives is clarity; he avoids encumbering the chart with detail that is not essential to its navigational purpose.

same units on the earth. The same ratio might also be expressed as $\frac{1}{80,000}$. Whichever way it is expressed, this is called the natural scale.

The same scale could be expressed as a numerical or equivalent scale when two different units are compared; 1 inch = 1.1 miles. This is a style more common to maps, but you may also come across it in cruising guides.

The terms "large-scale" and "small-scale" are often confusing. Since it's the denominator that changes, a large denominator means a small fraction: 1:80,000 is smaller than 1:40,000, so a chart drawn to a scale of 1:80,000 is a small-scale chart relative to the larger scale 1:40,000 chart.

Scales as large as 1:5,000 may be used for harbor charts, while scales as small as one to several million may be used for large areas of the world.

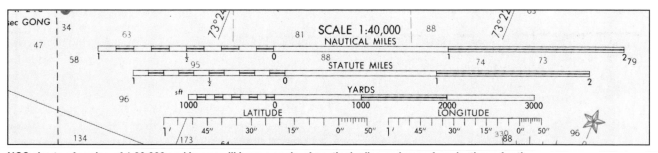

NOS charts of scales of 1:80,000 and larger will have a scale of nautical miles and one of yards; those for the Great Lakes, inland rivers and the Intracoastal Waterway will also carry a scale of statute miles. This small-craft chart, at 1:40,000, also has latitude and longitude scales showing subdivisions of one degree.

A Mercator projection chart offers an advantage with respect to distance measurement: One minute of latitude on the scale at each side of the chart (not along the top or bottom) is equal to one nautical mile. In fact, on charts that cover a large area, distance will have to be measured at that scale. Usually, such charts do not have bar scales, as such scales would have to vary with latitude. The reason for this change of scale with latitude is explained in the section on Chart Projections later in this chapter.

As well as those mentioned so far, there is one more important scale—the logarithmic speed scale. This graphic scale is printed on U.S. charts of 1:40,000 or larger, and on Canadian Hydrographic Service (CHS) charts intended for small-craft navigation. It is useful for solving time, speed and distance problems. The technique is covered in Chapter 19.

Chart sources

U.S. charts are published by three agencies of the United States Federal Government. The Defense Mapping Agency Hydrographic/Topographic Center (DMAHTC) is responsible for charts of the high seas and foreign waters. These are based on surveys conducted by the DMAHTC and other nations. The Bahamas, for example, are covered by DMAHTC charts.

The National Oceanic and Atmospheric Administration (NOAA), part of the Department of Commerce, includes the National Ocean Service (NOS). Within the NOS, the Coast and Geodetic Survey is responsible for charts of the coastal waters of the United States, possessions such as Puerto Rico and the Virgin Islands, and rivers extending inland to the head of tidal action. These are referred to as NOS charts.

Charts of some rivers, lakes and canal systems are published by the U.S. Army Corps of Engineers. Travelers on the Mississippi, for example, would rely on these charts.

All Canadian waters are charted by the CHS, part of the Department of Fisheries and Oceans.

Charts may be purchased directly from the issuing agency (addresses are listed in the Appendices), or from dealers in boating centers, both domestic and foreign. Catalogs of NOS charts, lists of sales agents and foreign sales agents are available free of charge.

The cost of charts has risen significantly, to the point where a full set for a boating region may represent a major expense. However, government charts are still a bargain considering the extent, accuracy and importance of the information they provide. You should keep a set aboard and replace them as they become outdated by newer editions or wear out from use.

Less expensive reproductions of some charts are available from commercial publishers. These are sold as sheets and as bound volumes.

UNIT CONVERSION

On salt water, distances are measured in nautical miles, while the statute mile is used on shore, in fresh-water bodies and along the Intracoastal Waterways. Depths, meanwhile, are usually measured in feet while boating inshore; offshore, the unit of depth measurement is the fathom. Increasingly, metric units are coming into use for both distance and depth.

While it is easy to make conversions graphically by using the various unit scales presented, you may also need to make conversions by using numeric conversion factors given below, or a quick rules of thumb, as shown at bottom.

- nautical miles x .87 = statute miles

- statute miles x 1.15 = nautical miles

- nautical miles x 1,852 = meters

- meters x .00054 = nautical miles

- nautical miles x 2,026 = yards

- yards x .00049 = nautical miles

- statute miles x 1,609 = meters

- meters x .00062 = statute miles

- statute miles x 1,760 = yards

- yards x .00057 = statute miles

- yards x .9144 = meters

- meters x 1.094 = yards

- fathoms x 6 = feet

- feet x .16667 = fathoms

- fathoms x 1.828 = meters

- meters x .5468 = fathoms

Rules of thumb

Roughly 7 nautical miles equals 8 statute miles, so you can convert nautical to statute by multiplying nautical miles by 8 and dividing the product by seven. To reverse the conversion: statute miles times 7, then divide by 8. A nautical mile has about 2,000 yards—close enough for quick calculations.

HOW TO READ A CHART

Clearing the kitchen table and spreading out charts of your favorite cruising area can be a rare pleasure on a winter's evening. It's also the most sensible way to improve your navigation. Most of the vast amount of information contained in a chart should be learned and understood long before it becomes crucial to a difficult or dangerous situation on the water. You might begin your study with Chart No. 1210Tr, a training chart published for just this purpose, and then go on to charts of your home waters. While there is no Canadian equivalent to Chart 1210Tr, the CHS does publish training charts for the use of the Canadian Power and Sail Squadrons. At the very least, charts for a voyage should be examined, and courses laid out, *before* your boat leaves the dock.

Make sure you know when each chart was published, what the source of the information is, and whose interpretation you are accepting. On charts, those questions are answered in the general information block. Here the chart is titled by reference to the waters it covers, the projection type is stated, and the scale is specified. Units of depth measurement are stated as either fathoms, feet or meters, along with the datum planes (the water level that serves as a beginning point for all measurements of depth and another for measurements of height). The chart's number will be printed at several places around the margins.

Other information that cannot be graphically presented will be contained in notes at various places on the chart, usually over land masses. Commonly used abbreviations are defined, such as units of measure for heights above water, notes and cautions regarding dangers, tidal information, references to anchorage areas, etc. One of the most important notes on NOS charts will specify the volume of the *Coast Pilot* (*page 420*) that corresponds to the area covered by the chart. All of the notes should be read at least once, and those applicable to small-craft navigation should be read more often.

Use the latest edition

When hydrographic surveys have been completed, cartographers are presented with vast amounts of information—so much information that, if they were to print it all, charts would be a useless mass of black and colored ink. The cartographer's task is to edit the survey information, to make decisions about what to leave out and what to summarize. Even so, such a large amount of data remains that every element of the printed chart must be made to carry meaning. To learn to read a chart you have to begin to recognize that nothing has been placed there without significance.

Every chart includes an edition number and date of revision. Using the latest chart is extremely important. The revision system used varies significantly between the National Ocean Service and the Canadian Hydrographic Service.

On NOS charts the lower left corner shows the edition number, date and date of revision. Many charts are revised every year or two, while in less active areas revisions may occur as infrequently as every 4 to 12 years.

The title block shows the official name of the chart, the type of projection, scale, plus datum and unit of measurement for depths. Printed nearby is much valuable information, so be sure to read all notes before using any chart.

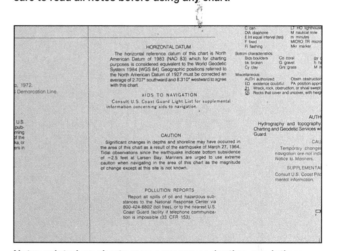

Notes printed on charts may concern navigation regulations, hazardous conditions at inlets, information on controlling depth that cannot be printed conveniently alongside a channel, or other matters that concern navigation.

NOS revisions include all changes that have been published in *Notice to Mariners* and *Local Notice to Mariners* since the last revised printing. They also include corrections that are not published in the *Notices*, but which are, nevertheless, considered to be essential to safe navigation. In addition to revisions, there may also be an unscheduled new edition if significant new information is revealed by surveys.

Assure yourself that you have the latest edition by consulting the NOS booklet *Dates of Latest Editions.* It's issued quarterly and you can find one where you buy charts.

Charts that are in stock and awaiting sale are not corrected by the NOS or local sales agent. That means, when you buy a new chart, you must check all the *Notices* subsequent to the printed edition date and make the applicable corrections. Correct your current charts according to new information published in the *Notices.* Chart changes are also available by modem from USCG computer update systems.

The edition number and date of each NOS chart are printed in the margin, at the lower left corner along with the chart number. Between editions, charts may be revised; the date of revision also will be shown in the margin.

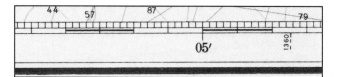

On charts of scales of 1:40,000 or larger, latitude and longitude scales are subdivided into minutes and seconds of arc. This extract from a harbor chart shows meridians at 5-minute intervals, tick marks at 1-minute intervals, and one 1-minute interval subdivided into 5-second units. Note the ten 1-second longitude units at the right of the 03-minute figure.

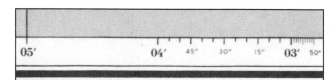

On charts of relatively small scale, the latitude and longitude border markings are in minutes and fractions of minutes of arc. On this 1:80,000 chart, meridians are drawn at 10-minute intervals; subdivisions are in minutes and tenths of minutes. On smaller-scale charts, the smallest subdivisions might be fifths, halves or whole minutes of arc.

In contrast with the NOS system, CHS charts are corrected while they are in stock, before they reach chart dealers or mariners. As they leave the CHS warehouse, they are stamped with the date to which *Notices* have been incorporated. Small-craft charts are not hand-corrected, but changes to these are advertised in the *Notices*. Canadian chart users can assure themselves that they are purchasing the current editions by referring to quarterly listings of the "current chart dates" usually in *Notices*' weekly editions 13, 26, 39 and 52 of each year.

In the CHS system, there are three categories of chart—new charts, new editions and reprints.

A new chart covers any area not previously charted (or not previously charted at particular limits or scale).

A new edition of an existing chart incorporates the changes that have been advertised in the CHS *Notice to Mariners* as well as other unadvertised changes that were not important

enough to warrant a *Notice*. Note that a new edition cancels previous editions of that chart, and mariners can no longer legally use that previous edition.

A reprint incorporates only changes that have been advertised in *Notice to Mariners* and other minor changes such as standardizing notes. A reprint does not cancel previous printings of the chart, and mariners can continue to update their old chart from their *Notice to Mariners*.

Latitude and longitude scales

Conventional charts show north toward the top of the sheet, (unlike some small-craft charts and chart books that may follow the layout of a river or coast without respect to direction). These conventional sheet charts have latitude scales at each side and longitude scales at the top and bottom. Meridians are drawn top to bottom and parallels from side to side in fine black lines. Depending on the scale of the chart, these are drawn at intervals or 2, 5 or 10 minutes.

On NOS charts with a scale of 1:50,000 or larger, such as harbor charts, the subdivisions are in terms of minutes and seconds of latitude and longitude. On smaller-scale charts the subdivisions are in terms of minutes and tenths of minutes on newer charts (minutes and seconds on older charts). Charts at a scale of 1:80,000, such as the training chart 1210Tr, use minutes and tenths, while charts at still smaller scales use minutes and fifths or halves.

Chart books that may not place north at the top indicate subdivisions of latitude and longitude along parallels and meridians in several convenient places, or separately near the graphic scales.

Chart colors

The use of color varies slightly between NOS and CHS charts. In general, water areas are not colored—they retain the white color of the paper itself. However, on NOS charts, shallow areas are shown in light blue; light green indicates shallows that are uncovered at some stages of the tide and covered during others. There are also areas that have been swept to an indicated depth by wire drags (to ensure the absence of isolated rocks or coral heads): These are also indicated in light green on NOS charts.

On CHS charts, blue is also used; the shallowest areas are in darkest blue, with deeper areas in lighter blue. The deepest areas are shown in white.

Charts are often consulted at night under red light (red light does not impair night vision as much as white light), so cartographers have chosen magenta-colored ink for small indications that, even in good lighting, might be hard to see. (Magenta, a pink-purple, is the color of one of the four basic inks used in almost all color printing.)

On NOS charts, buoys and dayboards that are actually red are indicated in magenta. Lighted buoys, regardless of their color, are shown on the charts with a magenta disc over the small circle portion of their chart symbol.

A magenta flare symbol (like an exclamation mark) extends from the position dot that represents lights, lighted ranges, etc. Caution and danger symbols and notes are magenta. Recommended courses and usually compass roses are also magenta. Otherwise, black ink is used for symbols, contour lines, man-made features, text information, etc., and gold or tan ink indicates land areas.

A notable exception to this general color scheme is the DMAHTC pattern which uses gray to indicate land.

Lettering styles

Charts must carry so much information in such a compact format that every possible element is assigned a meaning. Even styles of lettering are significant.

On NOS charts, upright letters (for example: "CANTILEVER BRIDGE") are used for features that are dry at high water and are unaffected by water movement. (Their height-above-water indication will, of course, be affected.)

Letters that lean (for example: *"OUTER BRIDGE REACH"*) are used for water, underwater or floating features with the exception of numbers indicating depth. The size of the lettering denotes the relative importance of the named feature.

Very often, crucial information must be learned from the lettering style because it can't be made obvious any other way. For example, at high tide there is a very important difference between an islet, which is always dry, and a reef, which is often submerged. The only way you will know the difference at a glance is if you recognize that "WRECK ROCK" is in "dry" lettering, and is therefore visible, while *"WRECK ROCK"* is in "wet" lettering and is invisible much of the time.

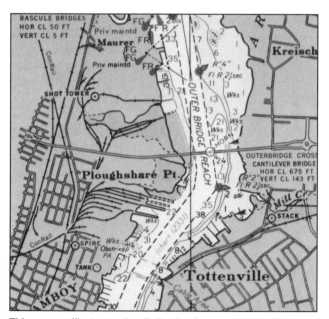

This excerpt illustrates the distinction between vertical lettering for features that are above the water—such as "TANK" and "SPIRE"—in contrast to leaning letters for underwater features like *"Wks"* for wrecks.

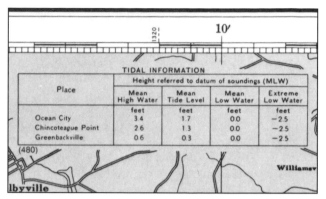

Coast and harbor charts often carry information on the normal range of tides, and the extreme variations from charted depths that may be expected. Check all newly purchased charts for this important information.

Water features

The principal water feature is depth. To indicate depth, we need a value and a reference. This reference is best imagined as a plane, and its vertical position is known as the chart datum. Each chart indicates its datum so that depth measurements, known as soundings, can be interpreted, hour by hour according to tide tables, or adjusted for seasonal variations on lakes and rivers.

The choice of the datum plane is a fairly technical matter, but the primary consideration is to choose one that is very close to normal low water.

However, there are exceptional conditions in which actual water depth can be much less than the depth that is indicated on the chart.

For example, datum has been set at mean lower low water (MLLW) for NOS charts of the Pacific, Atlantic and Gulf of Mexico: Each day has two low waters, different from each other, and the lower water of each day is averaged over a number of years (usually 19 years). On some days, the lower low tide will be below datum because it is below the average. Actual depths will be shallower than charted depths. For this reason, many charts carry additional information about extreme variations in a small, boxed table.

Persistent winds and unusual barometric pressure (or lack of it) may also change the actual water depth, making the water shallower.

Where tides are not a factor, as is the case on the Great Lakes, the datum is usually established at or near long-term average lows.

Heights are also indicated with implicit reference to the stated chart datum. On NOS charts of coastal areas, this is the mean high water (MHW).

The practice on CHS charts is different with respect to choosing chart datum—and it is also much simpler than the system used on NOS charts. On both coasts, lowest low water (the lowest it gets) is chosen as chart datum. Depths are, therefore, never less than indicated.

How depths are shown

Depths are indicated by many small numbers. You must be certain whether these numbers show feet, fathoms or meters. Meters have been in use for many years on non-U.S. charts, and are now being used on newer U.S. charts. Often, a metric depth will be shown as a decimal number, but with the decimal as a subscript to avoid confusion with other dots.

A skipper can learn not only the depth at the point where the number is printed, but also the general characteristic of the bottom. The density of numbers also has significance because the cartographer has chosen only significant depths from the many thousands of sounding points in the raw data. Where depth numbers are widely spaced, the bottom shape is likely to be smooth, regular and gradual. Wherever depths vary irregularly and abruptly, the numbers become denser.

Depth curves

Points of equal depth are often connected by a contour called a depth curve. The choice of depths used to indicate curves is made according to the scale of the chart, the relative ranges of depths, and the type of vessel that is expected to make most use of the chart. Typical depth curves on NOS charts not metrically converted are at 6, 12, 18, 30, 60 feet and multiples of 60 feet. Reading the depth curve is often easier if you note the depth numbers on either side of the line, rather than looking for the indication that is at some point on the line.

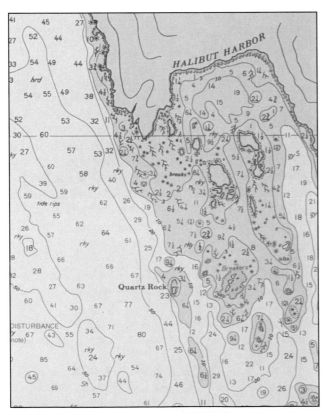

This chart shows depth curves at 10, 20 and 50 fathoms. The blue shade indicates the 10-fathom line and dangerous waters.

On some charts, a depth is chosen that is assumed to be dangerous for the majority of vessels using the chart. A light blue shade is printed over areas that are shallower than this chosen depth. The small-craft chart danger curve is usually set at 6 feet, while 12- and 18-foot curves are used on harbor charts, and 30-foot curves on both coastal and general charts. On some of the latter charts, an area beyond the 18-foot curve may be printed in a lighter shade of blue than the shade used for shallower areas. The meaning of the shades can vary from one chart to another so it must always be checked carefully. While most of the blue shading follows the coastline, isolated, offshore areas that fall within the chosen depth will also be shaded on the chart.

Surveyed soundings may sometimes be too scarce for the proper establishment of a true depth curve. These charts should therefore always be used with great caution. You should also avoid isolated soundings that are shallower than their surroundings, particularly those with solid or dotted curves around them, because it may be doubtful that the shallowest sounding has been found.

Dredged channels

Two dashed lines represent the side limits of dredged channels. The channel depth and the date on which that depth was established are often shown within or near the lines. The limits of a dredged basin are shown in a similar way. While the depth shown is the controlling depth, there may be shallower areas within the dashed lines—the controlling depth might be "on centerline" for example. Often, a width is also indicated, such as "8 feet for widths of 100 feet."

Silting and dredging subsequent to the date may have changed the actual depth. A table near the channel may also show more detail, and this is also the kind of information that should be checked in your copy of *Notice to Mariners* or *Local Notice to Mariners*.

Nature of the bottom and shoreline

Knowing what the bottom is like is extremely useful when anchoring. The chart will often indicate this with an abbreviation for sandy, rocky, muddy, hard or soft. If the abbreviation seems ambiguous, you can check its meaning in the chart's identification block.

The shoreline shown is the shoreline at mean high water (high water in lakes and rivers). The CHS uses higher high water in tidal waters and chart datum in non-tidal waters. This merely underlines the fact that careful pilots always refer to the chart notes. Marsh or mangrove areas are delimited by the outer edge of their vegetation, shown by a fine line. Natural shoreline is distinguished from man-made by the use of a heavier line. If the shoreline is unsurveyed, or if adjoining surveys show any disagreement, a dashed line is shown. The low water line is shown by a dotted line and the intervening region is usually shaded green. The words "grass," "mud" and "sand" may also be noted along the shoreline.

Land area features

Features or land areas are shown only if they are useful for the navigator. The topography is indicated by contours, form lines or hachures ("shading" lines) and specific heights (usually in feet, but often in meters) are printed at suitable points. Unlike depth contours, height contours are not drawn to any standard interval.

Hachures show the approximate location of steep slopes, their length indicating height. A band of hachures would show a cliff, more as an elevation (a side view) than a plan (top view). Heights are merely relative.

Spot heights are given for summits or the tops of man-made features, and are measured from either datum or from

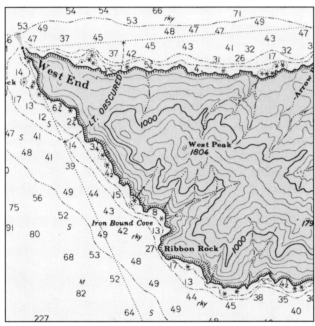

Tops of conspicuous landmarks are often printed on nautical charts. Heights are usually measured from mean high water in feet. Metric system is used on some charts.

mean high water. (This inconsistency is due to the fact that cartographers may have information from topographic sources rather than charting surveys.)

If information on vegetation or ground type is useful, it will be indicated with symbols and sometimes words.

Man-made features

When man-made features directly relate to navigation, they are prominently indicated. These features are as diverse as piers, bridges, overhead power cables, breakwaters, etc. Other features that relate indirectly—roads, buildings, airports, etc., are shown depending on the scale of the chart. However, public buildings such as the customs house and post office are often individually identified.

Locations of prominent features such as tanks or spires are shown accurately because they are useful for bearings.

Descriptions of these features follow a standard terminology and set of standard logos described in Chart No. 1, described on pages 402 to 409.

Bridges over navigable waters are shown and identified as to their type and the clearances they allow—both horizontal and vertical. Usually the vertical clearance is measured with reference to mean high water (on NOS charts) or high high water (on CHS charts), but in some cases other levels may be indicated as well.

When two similar objects are so closely placed that the chart cannot resolve their separation, the word "twin" is added to their description. Occasionally groups of objects are represented as only one charted object but in such a case this one will be distinguished with a qualifying description in parentheses, such as "tallest of three."

Since AM radio antennae are useful for both visual and radio bearing, their locations are marked on both NOS and CHS charts, and their call letters and frequency are often printed next to the tower symbol.

Stacks, radio towers and other very tall, isolated structures are required to have lighting for aircraft. As these lights are often useful for marine navigation, they appear on charts as "FR," "Oc R," or "FlR" (these abbreviations, and others, are defined in the section at the end of the chapter). Also noted on charts are "strobe" lights that show very short, intense flashes both day and night.

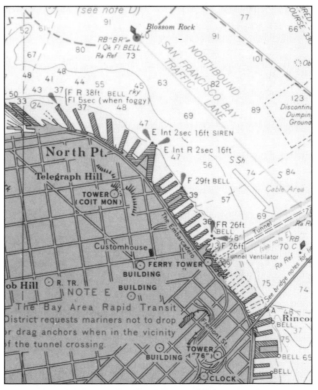

On large-scale charts, detailed information may be shown, including the streets and buildings of a city or town, particularly near the waterfront.

CHART NO. 1: SYMBOLS AND ABBREVIATIONS

Cartographers make extensive use of symbols as a way to compress information. Obviously, these could become confusing unless very careful standards were adhered to. In fact, there is an international convention regarding symbology, administered by the International Hydrographic Organization. The symbols used on NOS charts are collected into a book called Chart No. 1.

On the next seven pages, excerpts of Chart No. 1 have been reproduced. A summary of important symbols is also published on the reverse side of Chart 1210Tr, the Training Chart.

Buoys

Buoys (with the exception of mooring buoys) are shown on NOS charts by a diamond and a small open circle. The circle, unlike the earlier dot, correctly implies that the position is approximate, since the buoy swings on its anchor chain.

A buoy symbol with a line across the short axis shows a horizontally banded buoy. A junction buoy will have both colors indicated and abbreviated with the color of the upper band as it actually appears on the buoy. Colors of vertically banded buoys are not shown on charts, but do have appropriate abbreviations, "RW," for red and white, printed nearby. Special purpose buoys have no color but carry the abbreviation "Y," for yellow.

Unlighted can buoys are shown with a "C," while nuns (cans with a conical top) are shown with an "N."

Superbuoys used for data collection and tanker loading, and large navigation buoys, are given their own set of symbols.

A lighted buoy uses the same symbol as an unlighted one, but with the addition of a magenta disc centered on the small circle. The buoy's colors as well as the colors and rhythm of the light are shown by nearby abbreviations.

The Canadian practice is to show starboard-hand buoys in magenta and port-hand buoys in black (though they are actually green in the water). Cardinal buoys, as well as fairway, isolated danger and bifurcation buoys, are charted as a black outline. All buoys are lettered to indicate color except on some small-craft charts. All lighted buoys have a magenta flash and all buoys, lighted or not, are normally numbered—starboard-hand buoys taking even numbers and port-hand buoys taking odd numbers.

Other aspects of the Canadian buoyage system are explained in the Canadian Coast Guard publication *The Canadian Aids to Navigation System (Appendices)*.

Daybeacons

The symbols for daybeacons may be either triangles or squares, indicating the shape of the dayboard and its color.

The square symbol, colored green and with the letter "G" nearby, is used for daybeacons that have a solid green daymark of this type. The triangle symbol, colored magenta and with the letter "R" nearby, is used for daybeacons with solid red daymarks of this shape.

If the daybeacon has a red-over-green, triangular dayboard, it is shown with an uncolored triangle and the letters "RG." A green-over-red is shown with an open square and the letters "GR." Articulated daybeacons (which pivot above their sinker) are shown with the usual shape and color indicators as well as a circle and the abbreviation "ART." All octagonal, diamond, round or rectangular dayboards are shown with an open square and color abbreviations.

CHS charts show beacons in a color scheme similar to the one used for buoys.

Lights of all types

From the simplest light on a single pile to massive primary seacoast lights, all have the same symbol—a black position dot with a magenta "flare" like a large exclamation mark. Information such as height and observable range (with allowances for earth curvature) are often given.

Identification numbers

Buoys and lights are usually numbered (or less frequently designated with letters or letter-and-number combinations). These numbers are printed nearby and enclosed in quotes to distinguish them from other data that might be adjacent. Primary and some secondary lights are also named.

Ranges

Two symbols are needed to indicate a range—the front and rear lights or daybeacons. A line joining them is solid in the portion that is intended for navigation, and dashed in the non-navigable portion.

Radiobeacons

Radiobeacons are usually associated with other basic aids to navigation. The abbreviation "R Bn" accompanies the other symbol along with a magenta circle around the dot. The abbreviation "AERO" indicates an aeronautical beacon that may be useful to mariners. The frequency is given in kilohertz along with the identifying signal in Morse Code.

CHART NO. 1
UNITED STATES OF AMERICA
NAUTICAL CHART
Symbols Abbreviations and Terms

NINTH EDITION   JANUARY 1990

Chart No. 1 is not really a "chart" at all. It is a most useful booklet showing all chart symbols used on U.S. and foreign charts.

ANATOMY OF A CHART

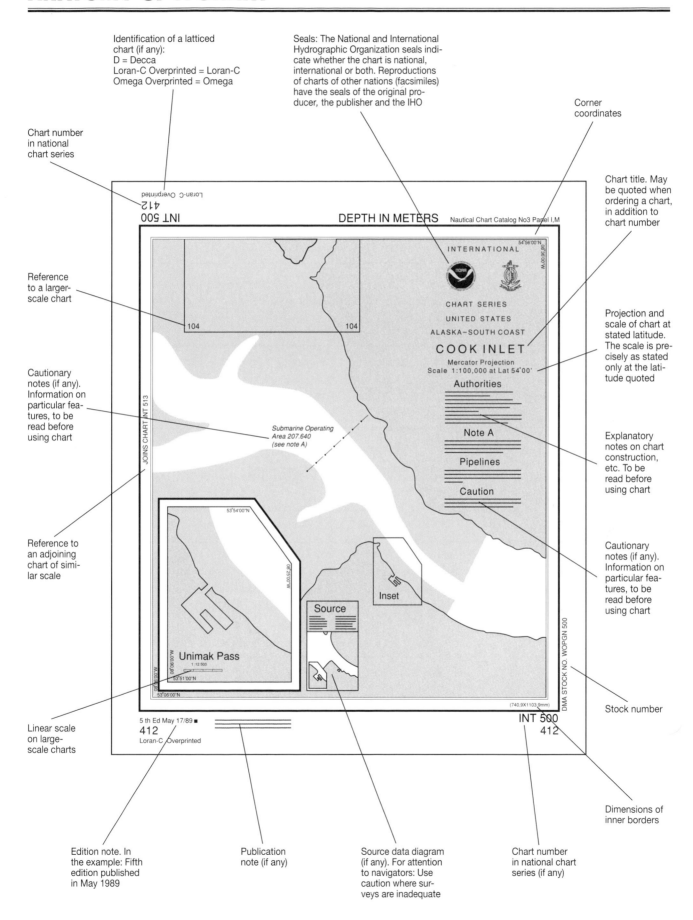

Identification of a latticed chart (if any):
D = Decca
Loran-C Overprinted = Loran-C
Omega Overprinted = Omega

Seals: The National and International Hydrographic Organization seals indicate whether the chart is national, international or both. Reproductions of charts of other nations (facsimiles) have the seals of the original producer, the publisher and the IHO

Corner coordinates

Chart number in national chart series

Chart title. May be quoted when ordering a chart, in addition to chart number

Reference to a larger-scale chart

Projection and scale of chart at stated latitude. The scale is precisely as stated only at the latitude quoted

Cautionary notes (if any). Information on particular features, to be read before using chart

Explanatory notes on chart construction, etc. To be read before using chart

Reference to an adjoining chart of similar scale

Cautionary notes (if any). Information on particular features, to be read before using chart

Linear scale on large-scale charts

Stock number

Edition note. In the example: Fifth edition published in May 1989

Publication note (if any)

Source data diagram (if any). For attention to navigators: Use caution where surveys are inadequate

Chart number in national chart series (if any)

Dimensions of inner borders

Within the chart illustration:

Loran-C Overprinted
INT 500
412

DEPTH IN METERS   Nautical Chart Catalog No3 Panel I,M

INTERNATIONAL

CHART SERIES
UNITED STATES
ALASKA–SOUTH COAST

COOK INLET
Mercator Projection
Scale 1:100,000 at Lat 54°00'

Authorities

Note A

Pipelines

Caution

104   104

JOINS CHART INT 513

Submarine Operating Area 207.640 (see note A)

53°54'00"N

Unimak Pass
1 12 500

Source

Inset

53°51'00"N
53°06'00"N

54°56'00"N

DMA STOCK NO. WOPGN 500

INT 500
412

5 th Ed May 17/89 ■
412
Loran-C Overprinted

(740,9X1103,9mm)

EXCERPTS FROM CHART NO. 1: NATURAL FEATURES

Relief

Supplementary national symbols: f

	Plane of Reference for Heights → H		
10	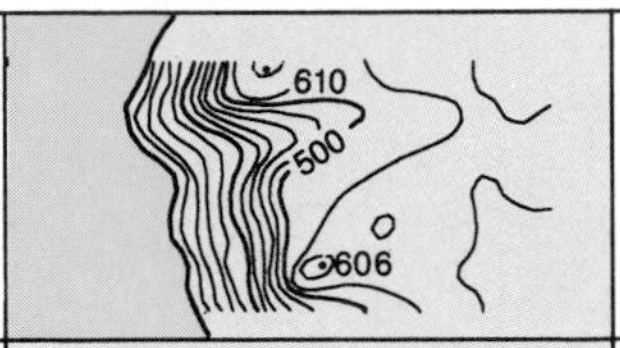	Contour lines with spot height	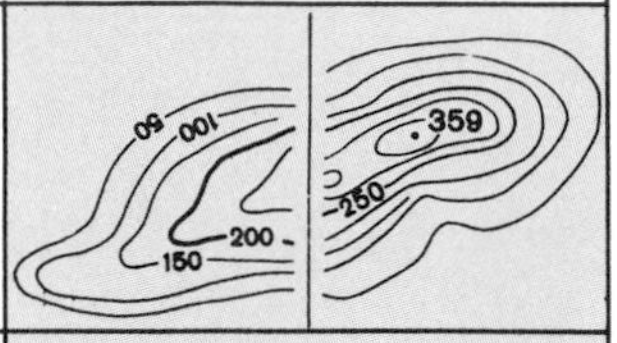
11	256	Spot heights	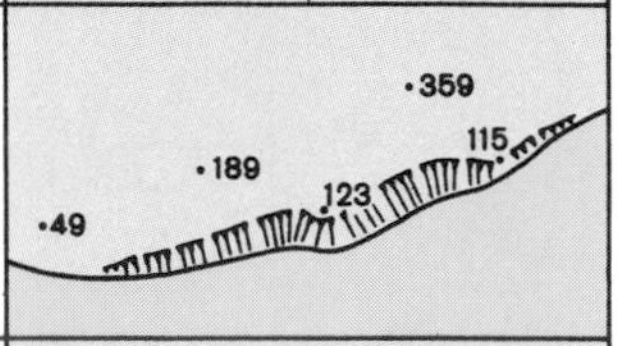
12	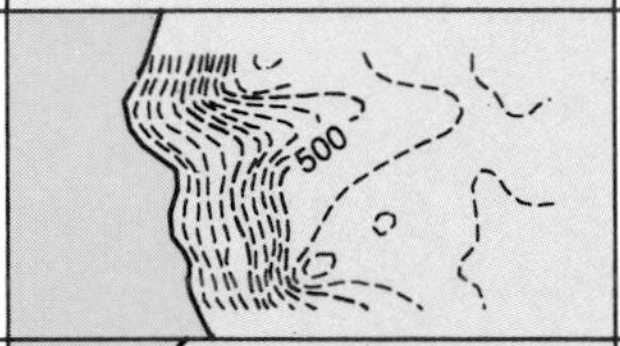	Approximate contour lines with approximate height	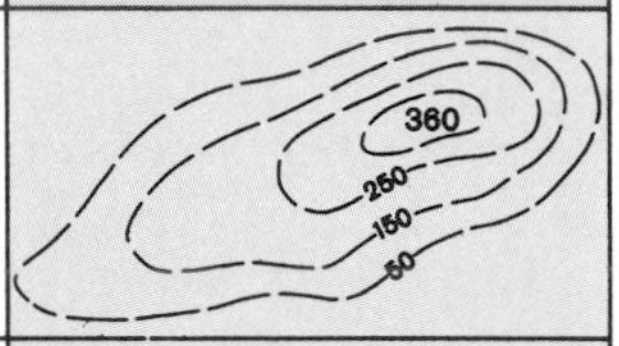
13	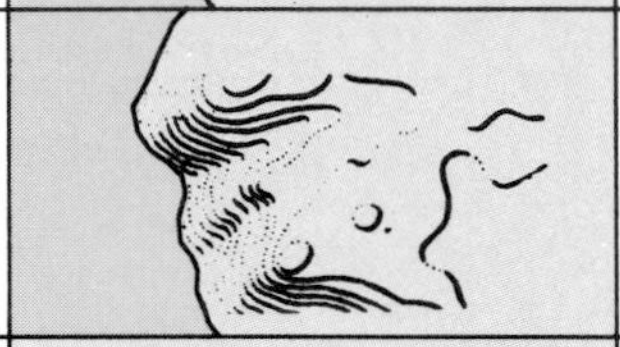	Form lines with spot height	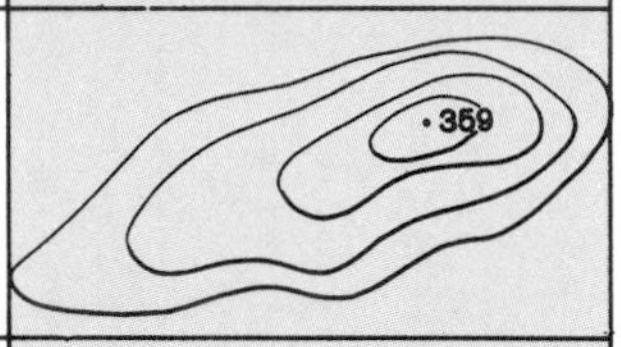
14	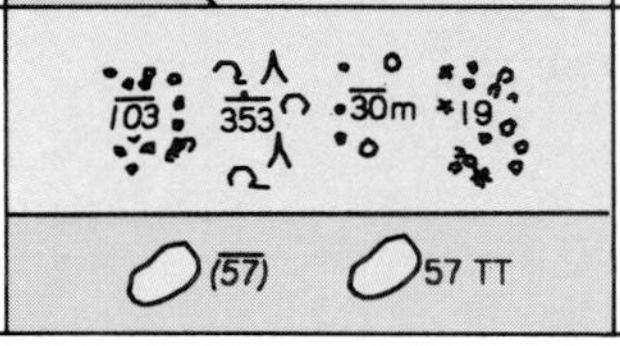	Approximate height of top of trees (above height datum)	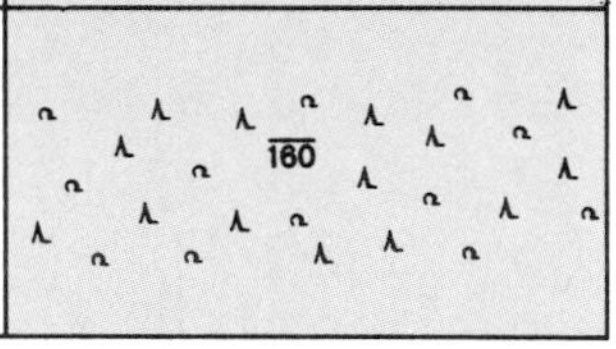

Water Features, Lava

Supplementary national symbols: g, h

20	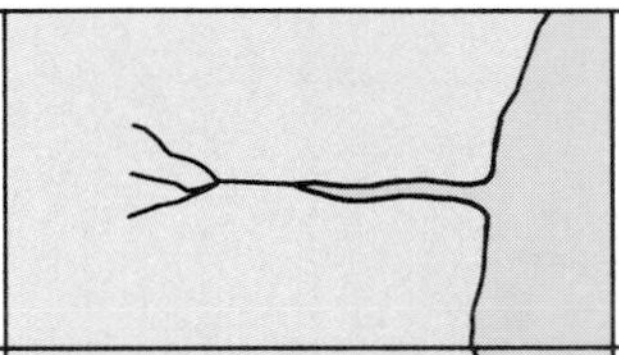	River, Stream	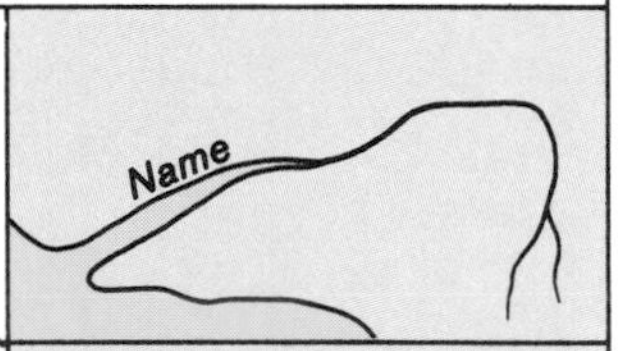
21	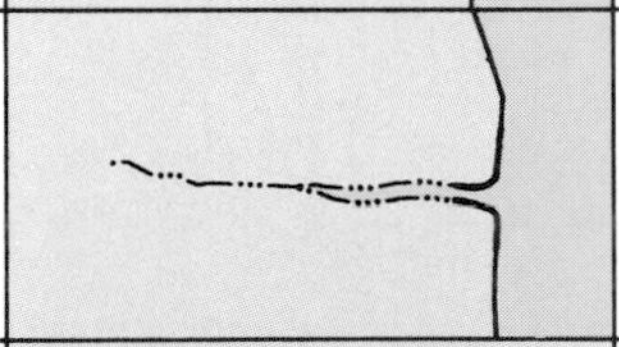	Intermittent·river	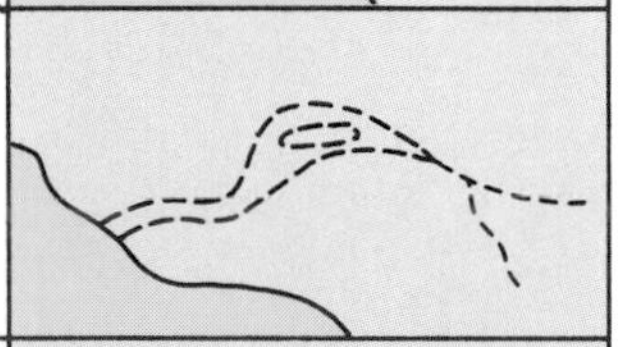
22	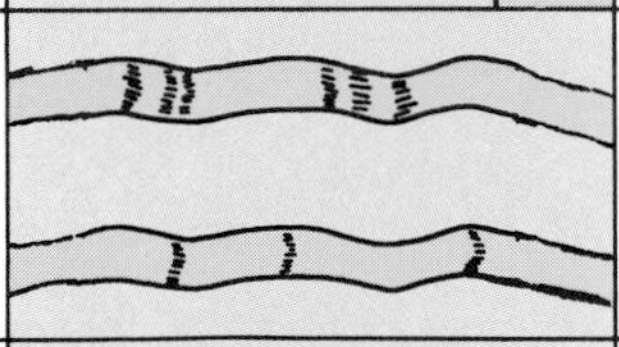	Rapids, Waterfalls	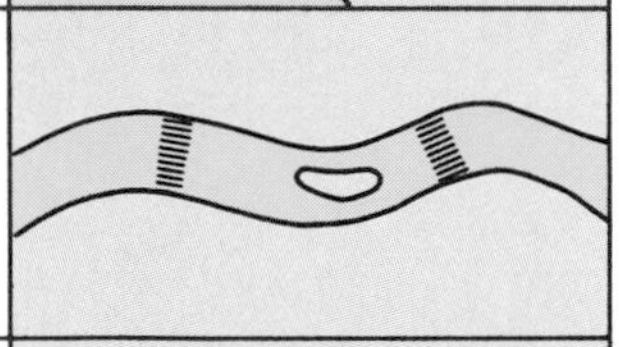
23	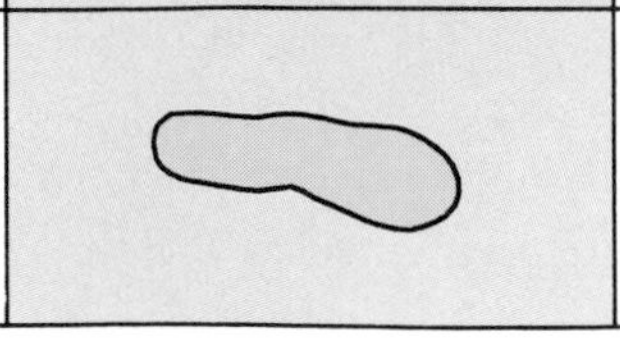	Lakes	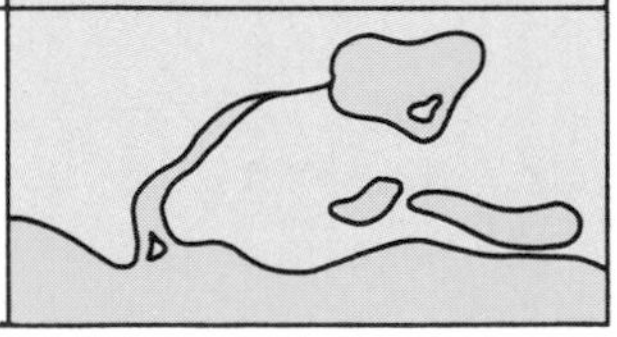

CULTURAL FEATURES

15		Embankment	
16		Tunnel	
17		Airport, Airfield	

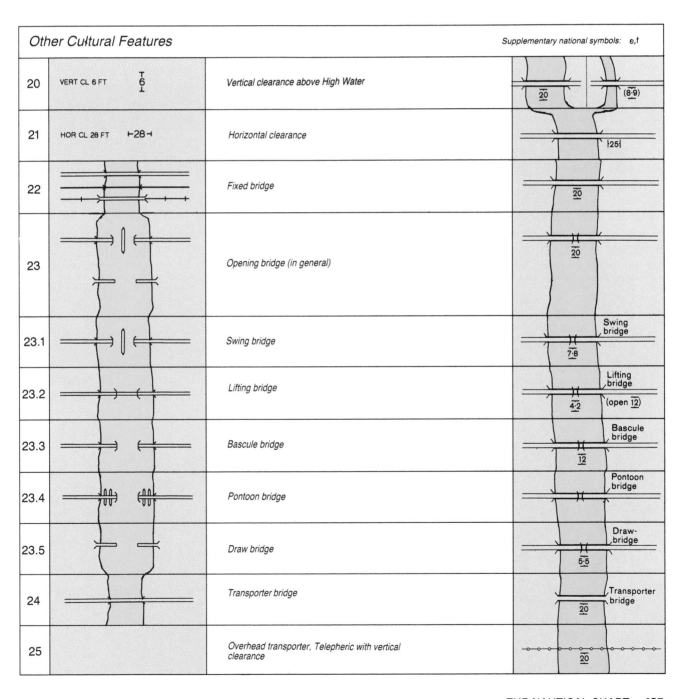

Other Cultural Features			Supplementary national symbols: e,f
20	VERT CL 6 FT	Vertical clearance above High Water	
21	HOR CL 28 FT	Horizontal clearance	
22		Fixed bridge	
23		Opening bridge (in general)	
23.1		Swing bridge	
23.2		Lifting bridge	
23.3		Bascule bridge	
23.4		Pontoon bridge	
23.5		Draw bridge	
24		Transporter bridge	
25		Overhead transporter, Telepheric with vertical clearance	

PORTS

29.1		Floating oil barrier	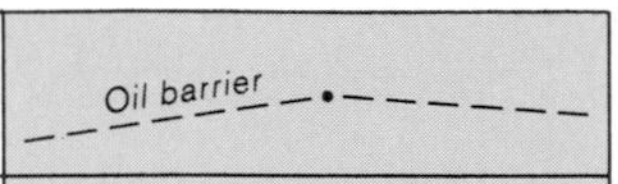 Oil barrier
29.2		Oil retention (high pressure pipe)	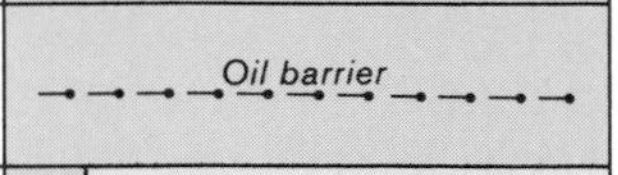 Oil barrier
30		Works on land, with year date	 Dock under construction (1987)
31	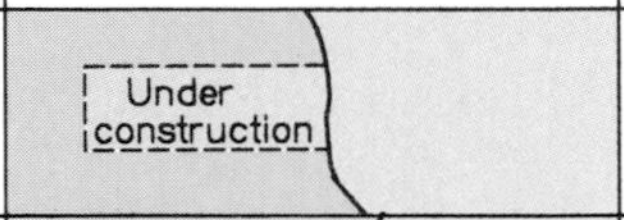 Under construction	Works at sea, Area under reclamation, with year date	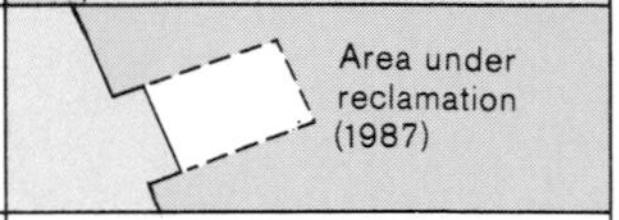 Area under reclamation (1987)
32	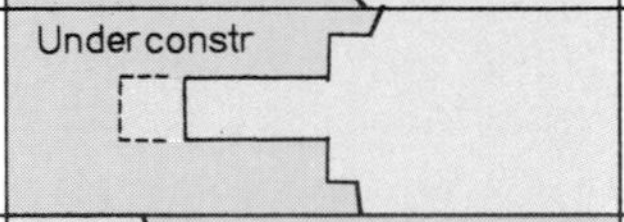 Under constr	Works under construction, with year date	Under construction (1987) Works in progress (1987)
33.1	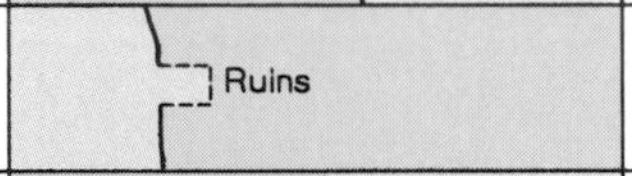 Ruins	Ruins	 Ru
33.2	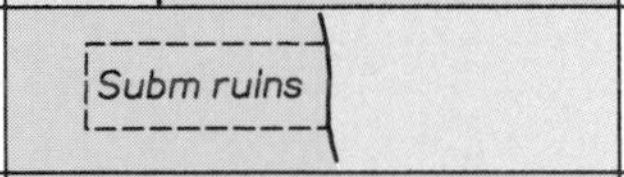 Subm ruins	Ruined pier, partly submerged at high water. Submerged ruins	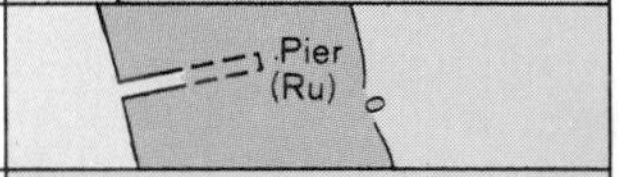 Pier (Ru)
34	 Hk	Hulk (actual shape on large scale charts)	 Hulk

Canals, Barrages

Clearances → D   Signal Stations → T

40	 Canal / Ditch	Canal	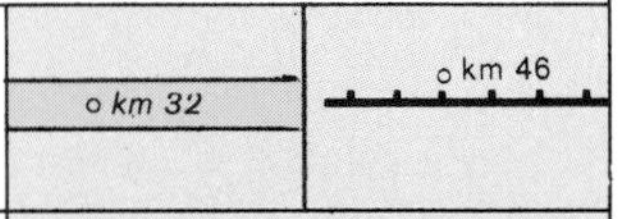 o km 32 o km 46
41.1	 Lock 6 10 6 8 SPIRE	Lock (on large-scale charts)	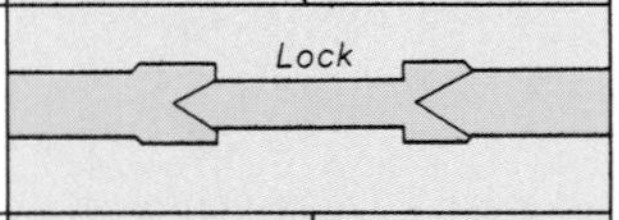 Lock
41.2	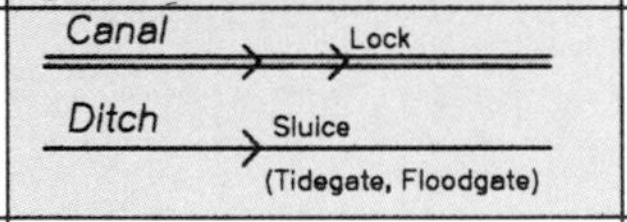 Canal Lock / Ditch Sluice (Tidegate, Floodgate)	Lock (on smaller-scale charts)	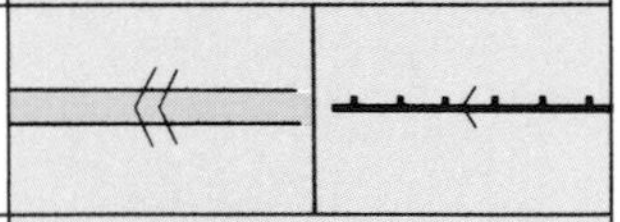
42		Caisson	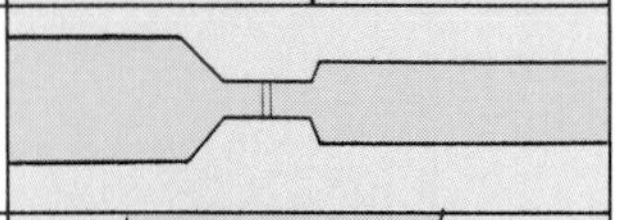
43		Flood barrage	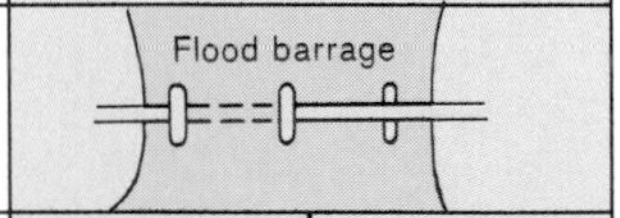 Flood barrage
44	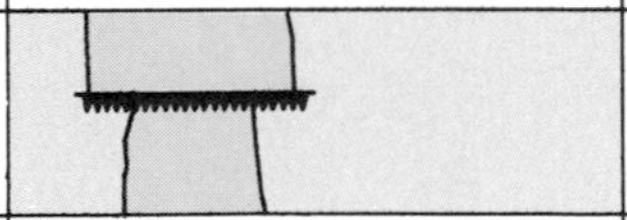	Dam	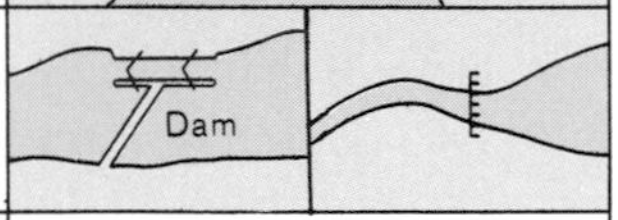 Dam

TIDES, CURRENTS

Tidal Levels and charted Data

Tide gauge → T

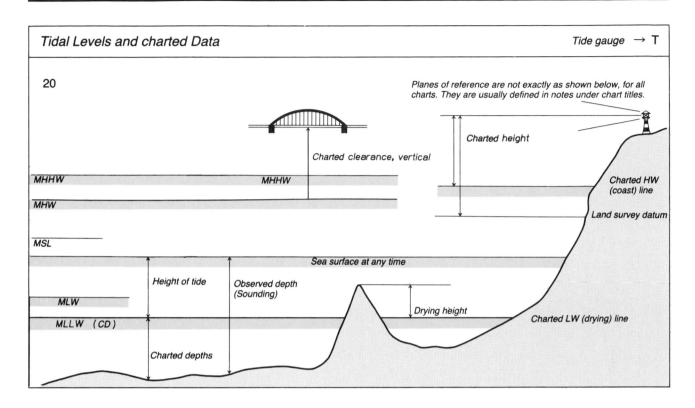

20

Planes of reference are not exactly as shown below, for all charts. They are usually defined in notes under chart titles.

Charted clearance, vertical

Charted height

MHHW   MHHW

Charted HW (coast) line

MHW

Land survey datum

MSL

Sea surface at any time

Height of tide   Observed depth (Sounding)

Drying height

MLW

MLLW (CD)

Charted LW (drying) line

Charted depths

Tidal Streams and Currents

Supplementary national symbols: m – t

Breakers → K

Tide Gauge → T

40	2 kn →	Flood stream (current) with rate	2,5 kn →
41	2 kn →	Ebb stream (current) with rate	2,5 kn →
42		Current in restricted waters	»»»» →
43		Ocean current with rates and seasons	2,5–4,5 kn Jan–Mar (see Note)
44	Tide rips — Symbol used only in small areas	Overfalls, tide rips, races	
45	Eddies — Symbol used only in small areas	Eddies	
46	Ⓐ Ⓑ	Position of tabulated tidal data with designation	◈Ⓐ

Depth Contours

	Feet	Fm/Meters
	0	0
	6	1
	12	2
	18	3
	24	4
	30	5
	36	6
	60	10
	120	20
	180	30
	240	40
	300	50
	600	100
	1,200	200
	1,800	300
	2,400	400
	3,000	500
	6,000	1,000

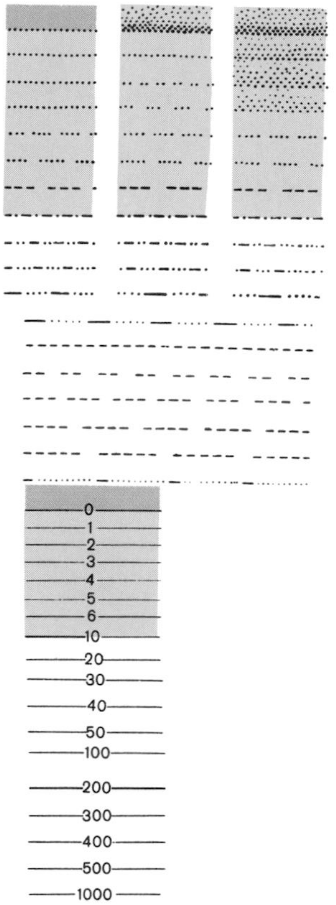

30

0
1
2
3
4
5
6
10
20
30
40
50
100
200
300
400
500
1000

Low water line

One or two lighter blue tints may be used instead of the 'ribbons' of tint at 10 or 20 m

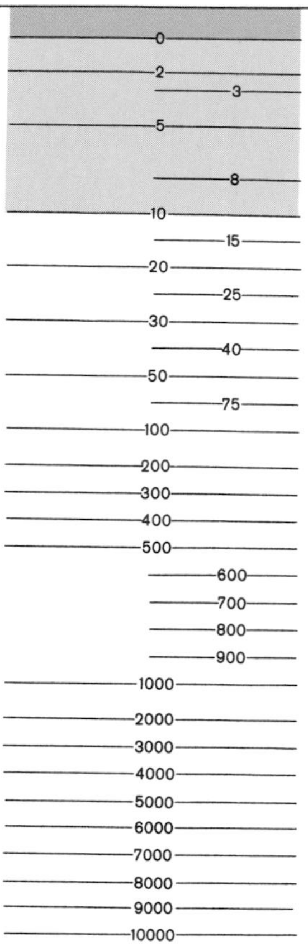

0
2
3
5
8
10
15
20
25
30
40
50
75
100
200
300
400
500
600
700
800
900
1000
2000
3000
4000
5000
6000
7000
8000
9000
10000

31	Approximate depth contour		Approximate depth contours	20
	Continuous lines, with values	*s* (blue or black) 100		50

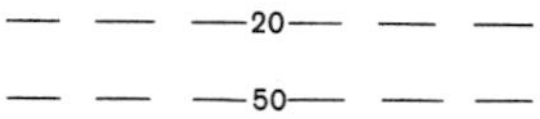

Note: The extent of the blue tint varies with the scale and purpose of the chart, or its sources. On some charts, contours and figures are printed in blue.

Types of Seabed, Intertidal Areas

20.1	 *Gravel*	Area with stones, gravel or shingle	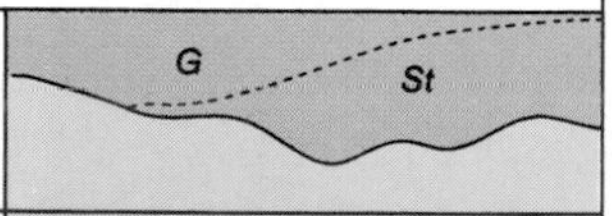 G St
20.2		Small area with stones or gravel	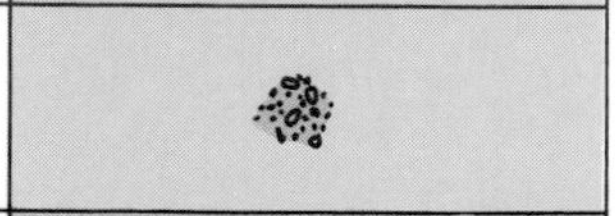
21	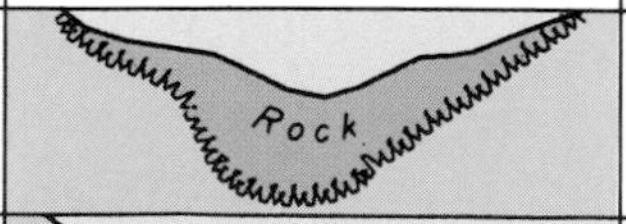 *Rock*	Rocky area, which covers and uncovers	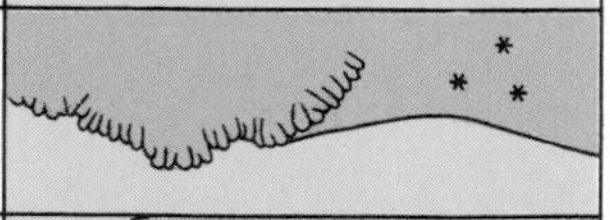
22	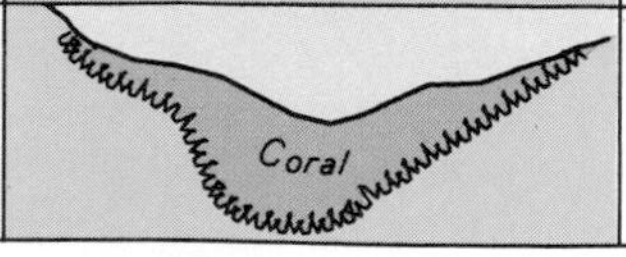 *Coral*	Coral reef, which covers and uncovers	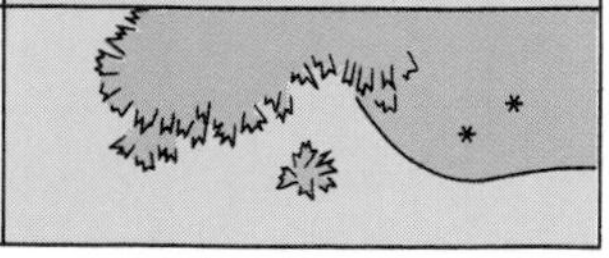

ROCKS, WRECKS, OBSTRUCTIONS

| 31 | *Foul* / *Wks* / # | *Foul* / *Wks* / *Wreckage* | Remains of a wreck or other foul area, non-dangerous to navigation but to be avoided by vessels anchoring, trawling etc. | # | $\fbox{F o u l}$ (dashed) | $\#$ (dashed box with slash) ⅌B |
| | | | | | | |

Obstructions

Plane of Reference for Depths → H   *Kelp, Sea-Weed* → J

40	⁖ Obstn	◌ Obstn	Obstruction, depth unknown	◌ Obstn	Obstn	#
41	(5₂) Obstn	(5₂) Obstn	Obstruction, least depth known	(4₆) Obstn	(16₈) Obstn	
42	(21) Obstn / (5) Obstn	(21) Obstn / (5) Obstn	Obstruction, least depth known, swept by wire drag or diver	(4₆) Obstn	(16₈) Obstn	
43.1	Subm piles / Stakes, Perches	∘∘ Subm piles / Subm piling	Stumps of posts or piles, wholly submerged	◌ Obstn τ τ τ		⊤ (Ⲧ) Subm piles
43.2	∘∘ Snags	∘∘ Stumps	Submerged pile, stake, snag, well or stump (with exact position)	⌁		⌁ ⊤ (T T)
44.1	⊔⊔⊔⊔⊔⊔⊔ Fsh stks		Fishing stakes	⊔⊔⊔⊔ ⊔⊔⊔⊔		
4.2	⬚—		Fish trap, fish weirs, tunny nets	⬚┐		
45	— — —		Fish trap area, tunny nets area	⌐ Fish traps ¬ ⌐ Tunny nets ¬		
46.1	Obstruction (fish haven) / (actual shape)	Obstruction (fish haven)	Fish haven (artificial fishing reef)	⬮ ◇		
46.2	Obstn / Fish haven (Auth min 42 ft)		Fish haven with minimum depth	⬮ (2₄) ◇ 2₄		
47	(Oys)		Shellfish cultivation (stakes visible)	⌐ Shellfish ¬		

THE CHART NUMBERING SYSTEM

All NOS and DMAHTC charts are numbered in a common system, dividing the world into regions and subregions. Boaters will generally be interested only in charts with five-digit numbers (such charts have scales of 1:2,000,000 and larger). The first and second digits refer to a region and subregion of the world; the third digit designates a general area within the subregion, while the final two are assigned roughly sequentially within that area. Many final three-digit combinations are left unassigned to allow for future charts.

The United States and Canada are Region 1; Region 2 covers Central and South America, Mexico, the Bahamas and the West Indies. The subdivisions of Region 1 are shown in the chart on this page.

The CHS numbering system deals only with Canada and follows a simple scheme in which large groups of numbers are reserved for each major region. Boundaries are not always distinct, but sequential numbers are usually used within the same series of charts. For example, the general chart of Lake Huron is 2200, of Georgian Bay is 2201, etc., while detailed charts of the area fall in the range of 2202 to 2299.

The NOS series

The NOS has classified charts into five series:

1. Sailing Charts—the smallest-scale charts, covering long stretches of coastline such as Cape Sable, Newfoundland, to Cape Hatteras, NC. These are published at scales of 1:600,000 or smaller. These charts are used for sailing between distant ports and for approaching the coast from the open ocean. Sailing charts show offshore soundings, principal lights and outer buoys, and landmarks visible from great distances.

2. General Charts—scales in the range of 1:150,000 to 1:600,000. Typical examples cover areas such as Cape May, NJ, to Cape Hatteras, NC. These are intended for navigation generally within sight of land and when positions can be fixed with lights, landmarks, buoys and soundings.

3. Coast Charts—for close-in coastwise navigation, entering and leaving ports and for large, inland bodies of water. The scales range from 1:50,000 to 1:150,000 with most at 1:80,000. Typical examples are the widely used Training Chart 1210Tr and such charts as the series of five that cover Chesapeake Bay, or 18746 that takes a California skipper from Long Beach or Newport to Santa Catalina.

4. Harbor Charts—the largest scale and most detailed. Scales range from 1:50,000 and larger with an occasional inset of even larger scale.

5. Small-Craft Charts—convenient, folded charts designed for use in a confined space. One of the formats is designed to cover long, narrow waterways. This series includes information on marine facilities, tide tables, weather information sources and similar data.

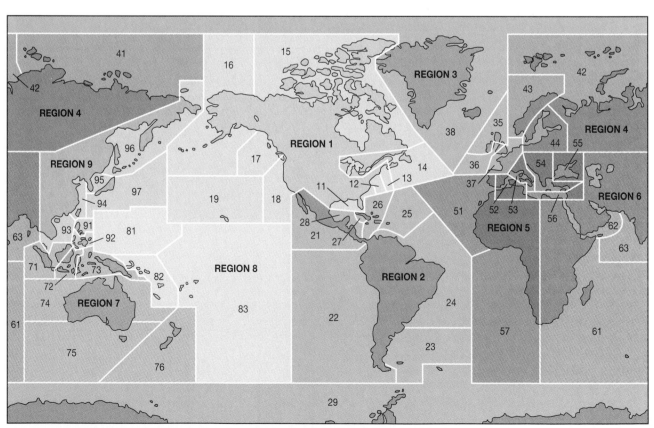

This diagram shows chart regions and subregions. Region 1 covers Canada and the United States. The number of the subregion forms the first two digits of a five-digit chart number.

Chart 12200: Cape May to Cape Hatteras; scale 1:400,000. It covers 130 miles from the coast and shows very little detail, and concentrates on the approaches to Delaware and Chesapeake Bays. On this chart, one inch equals 6 miles.

Chart 12214: Cape May to Fenwick Island; scale 1:80,000. It covers 60 miles from the coast, shows details of the coast up to inlets and shows shipping lanes to Delaware Bay. On this chart, one inch equals 1 mile.

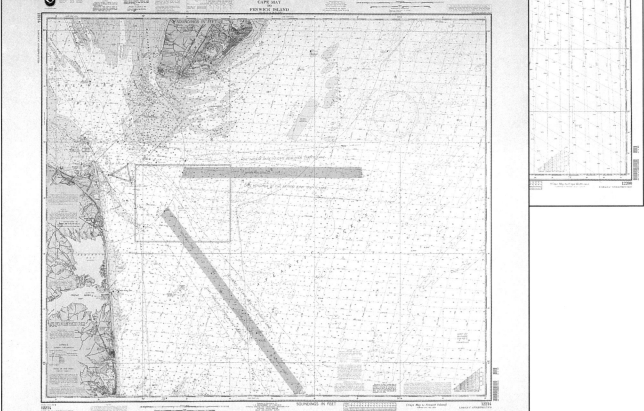

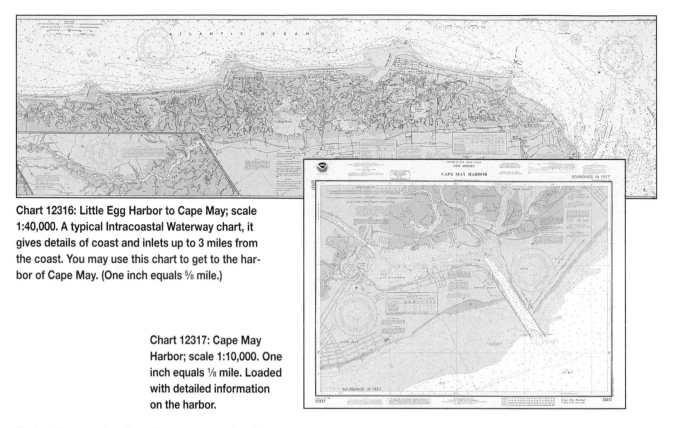

Chart 12316: Little Egg Harbor to Cape May; scale 1:40,000. A typical Intracoastal Waterway chart, it gives details of coast and inlets up to 3 miles from the coast. You may use this chart to get to the harbor of Cape May. (One inch equals ⅝ mile.)

Chart 12317: Cape May Harbor; scale 1:10,000. One inch equals ⅛ mile. Loaded with detailed information on the harbor.

Selecting and using the proper chart

Charts are printed with highly accurate methods on durable paper. They range in size from 19-by-26 inches to 36-by-54 inches with the exception of small-craft charts. Ideally conventional sheet charts should be stored flat or rolled in a dry place. Avoid folding them, but, if you must, fold them so that a compass rose appears on each panel.

Most boating areas will appear on at least two charts from different series and will be covered at different scales. In general, the closer you are to shoal waters and other dangers the larger you will want your chart scale to be.

NOS charts follow a fairly rigid division into categories of scale (see the example above). Coast charts show the major hazards and aids to navigation and give general information on depths. Some charts in this series omit all details in certain areas that are covered by larger-scale charts. For example, Narragansett Bay appears on Chart 13218, but the only detail is a note "(Chart 13221)." Similarly, other charts include parts of the Intracoastal Waterway, but the user is referred to ICW route charts for all detailed information. Many coast charts include an outline of areas that are also covered by larger-scale charts.

What harbor charts show

Harbor charts show more soundings and all aids to navigation, and permit the most accurate position fix from plotted bearings. "Why," you might ask, "select any but the largest-scale charts?" The answer is that you could not cover a large area

completely (there would be gaps in the coverage), or conveniently (a long course would be difficult to lay out).

Carrying the proper charts will usually mean having a mix of both coast and harbor charts. For some areas you will find it useful to have one or more general charts in addition to the coast and harbor charts. For example, the best overall route up Chesapeake Bay is more easily plotted on just the two general charts 12220 and 12260, than on a series of five coastal charts, 12221 to 12273. However, the coast charts will prove useful when used in conjunction with some harbor charts.

In the margin of many charts you will find helpful information indicating which would be the best chart to use next in a particular direction.

Small-craft charts

The charts in the first four series discussed above are referred to as conventional charts and are intended for flat or rolled storage. The fifth series, Small-Craft Charts, is quite different, designed for more convenient use in the limited space available on boats and for folded storage.

NOS charts intended for use on small boats are printed in three formats—folio, route and area.

Folio charts are printed front and back, folded accordion-style and bound in a title cover. Route charts consist of a single sheet printed front and back and accordion folded, some slipped into a title jacket.

Area charts usually consist of a conventional chart printed on both sides of a sheet of paper, then accordion folded.

Both route and area charts are being redesigned into a 5-by-10-inch "pocket fold" format.

Small-craft charts have a great deal of related data printed on the jacket or in the chart margin. Repair yards and marinas are clearly marked on the chart, and the services and supplies are tabulated. A tide table for the year, marine weather information, Rules of the Road, whistle signals and warning notes are all included for ready reference.

Numerous insets show such features as small creeks and harbors in great detail and larger scale.

Many folio and route charts indicate a recommended track. The longer stretches of these tracks are marked to show the true course and distances in miles and tenths. Route charts of the ICW also number each stretch of five statute miles, indicating accumulated distances southward from Norfolk, Virginia, to Florida, and eastward and westward from Harvey Lock, Louisiana. Facilities en route are designated with a numbering system starting with "1" on each chart of the series.

Small-craft chart revisions

NOS small-craft charts are revised and reissued annually or biannually, usually to coincide with the start of the boating season in each locality. These charts are not hand-corrected by the NOS after they are printed and placed in stock. Keep your chart up to date by applying all critical changes as published in *Notice to Mariners* and *Local Notice to Mariners*.

The Canadian Hydrographic Service will send out corrections to small-craft charts upon request. (Refer to the Appendices for the correct address.)

DMAHTC charts

Skippers making long ocean voyages or visiting foreign waters (except Canada) will use DMAHTC charts. These do not differ very much in coloring and symbology from NOS charts, except that land areas are gray and lighted buoys and those with radar reflectors are differently marked. Meters are also in more common use.

The DMAHTC has published special editions for some of the major sailing races. These are standard charts with overprintings for rhumb lines, typical sailing tracks for seasonal winds, additional current data and other useful items. These charts are listed in the section on Miscellaneous Charts and Publications in the DMA Chart Catalog *(Appendices).* Many DMAHTC charts are based on surveys conducted by foreign governments, so the authority for the chart is always given along with the date of the survey.

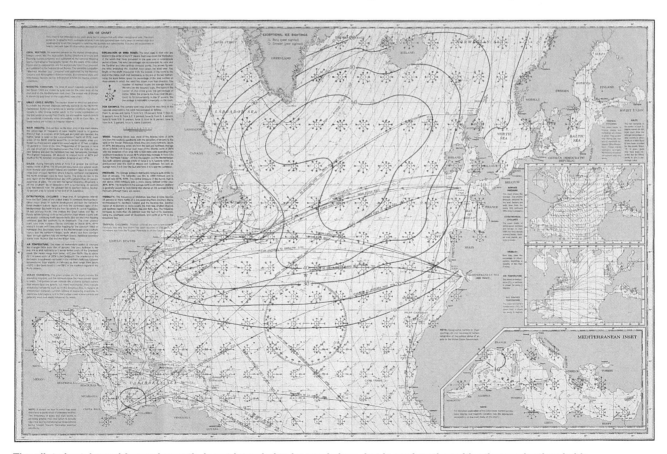

The pilot chart, issued for each month, is not intended to be used alone, but in conjunction with other navigational aids. The chart provides general information based on averages of many years on magnetic variation, great-circle routes, wave heights, gales, cyclones, temperature, ocean currents, prevailing winds, wind strengths, pressure and visibility.

Great Lakes charts

Polyconic charts are used for most of the NOS charts of the Great Lakes. (There are some exceptions: Mercator projections are used for a few smaller-scale charts and for all of those published in metric editions.) Runs between important points on the Great Lakes are frequently shown in statute miles, reflecting the fact that shipping charges for Great Lakes freight used to be set in statute miles.

Special editions of Small-Craft Charts of the Great Lakes and their connecting waters are also available. These editions are bound into convenient chart books.

River charts

River charts for the United States differ in many respects. Unlike conventional charts, they are usually issued in books, each page of which covers a successive stretch of river. Pages of the books may be oriented along the route rather than north-south and some symbols are apt to vary from those on conventional charts. Distances are often indicated as statute miles upriver from a starting point.

The other difference is the lack of sounding data and the substitution of a recommended track. Refer to Chapter 21 for more information on river charts and on piloting on rivers and other inland waters.

Pilot charts

A unique and valuable special chart is issued quarterly by the DMAHTC—the pilot chart. These present, in graphic form, information on ocean currents and weather probabilities for each month. Pilot charts are published in an "atlas" format in which there is a standing pilot chart for each month of the year. A 10-year cycle has been established for updating each atlas. These publications will also contain articles of general navigational interest.

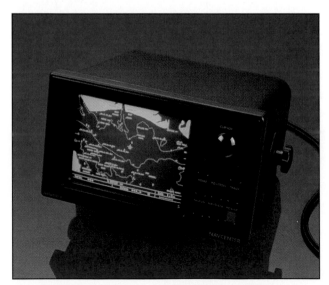

The video chart is simply an electronic representation of a standard chart.

Electronic charts

The increasing use of electronic computing equipment and large viewing screens aboard boats has made it possible to present navigation charts electronically. For the most part, these are paper charts that have been scanned and converted to digital bit maps for storage on magnetic media, including plug-in cartridge and CD-ROM.

Such charts are also available on disk formats compatible with non-specialized small computers.

Having chart information represented by an electronic bit map makes it easy to add other graphic and text information over the chart image on the viewing screen, and to select particular aspects (depth data, for example) while other "layers" of information are suppressed for clarity.

Data collected in real time from the vessel's navigational receivers—Loran, GPS, compass and log—can be displayed automatically along with the chart. Keyboards, mouse pointers and other electronic gadgets such as track balls are used to accept instruction from the navigator. Screens are available in both monochrome and color.

The use of bit-mapped or "raster" graphics, in which every graphic element is stored as a unique series of single points, means that digitizing is inexpensive and screen presentation is relatively undemanding of the computer. However, the resolution of the chart deteriorates quickly as the image is enlarged beyond its original scale.

Some systems, including those used in chart production, make use of "vector" graphics, a method that allows high resolution portrayal of data at any scale.

The United States and Canada are both involved in electronic chart test-bed projects to define just what an "electronic chart" is, to determine the databases needed to support producing and maintaining electronic charts, to develop and test delivery mechanisms and, most importantly, to explore, along with the chart users, the potential that is offered by the technology.

Caution regarding use

The U.S. Atlantic Coast exceeds 24,500 nautical miles; the Gulf Coast 15,000 miles; the Pacific Coast 7,000 miles and the Alaskan and Hawaiian coasts total more than 30,000 miles. Not surprisingly, the NOS publishes almost 1,000 charts that, combined, cover more than 3.6 million square miles—and both figures increase annually. The DMAHTC publishes charts numbered in the thousands and the Army Corps of Engineers also publishes a very large number.

Keeping these documents and all of their supporting data accurate and up to date is a task of staggering magnitude that involves huge archives and necessitates a complex, computerized storage and retrieval system.

Surveys are constantly being made in new areas and rechecked in old areas. In addition, the NOS has a program to make use of reporting by chart users. Formal programs are established with the U.S. Power Squadrons and the U.S. Coast

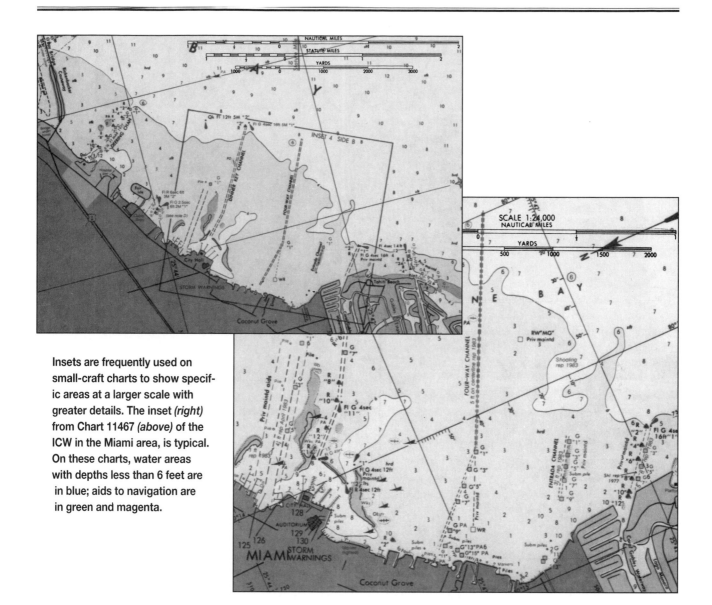

Insets are frequently used on small-craft charts to show specific areas at a larger scale with greater details. The inset *(right)* from Chart 11467 *(above)* of the ICW in the Miami area, is typical. On these charts, water areas with depths less than 6 feet are in blue; aids to navigation are in green and magenta.

Guard Auxiliary, but all individuals are encouraged to report corrections, additions and comments. Comments on other publications such as the *Coast Pilot* are also welcomed. All boaters are urged to help government agencies by reporting any damage to aids, malfunctioning of lights, shifting of shoals and channels or new hazards. These concerns, or any other matters affecting charts or publications of the NOS should be addressed to the Director, National Ocean Service, Rockville, MD 20852.

The CHS, meanwhile, has a similar program with the Canadian Power and Sail Squadrons, known by the acronym MAREP. In addition, a Marine Information Report and Suggestion Sheet is also included in the publication *Notice to Mariners*. This Suggestion Sheet should be used by boaters to report all errors or discrepancies they discover. Forward the form to: Dominion Hydrographer, Canadian Hydrographic Service, Department of Fisheries and Oceans, 615 Booth Street, Ottawa, Ontario K1A 0E6.

While efforts are made to keep all nautical data accurate and up to date, major natural disturbances such as hurricanes and earthquakes are capable of causing sudden and extensive changes in hydrography and have been known to destroy or shift aids to navigation.

Be alert to the possibility of changes. Most charts cite the authority for the information presented and, frequently, the date. Use additional caution when the survey is old—some surveys on which DMAHTC charts are based are more than a century old.

CHS charts also carry a source classification diagram in which both the date and the line-spacing of the sounding data are recorded. For example, the classification diagram might specify that a vessel surveyed a water body at 100-meter or 1,000-meter intervals. This valuable source information can allow a mariner to draw important conclusions about the degree of possibility of a hazard being left undetected between the lines of a sounding profile.

CHART PROJECTIONS

You can navigate your boat quite safely without having any detailed knowledge of the chart projection you are using, but it is always more interesting to know. As in any field, greater knowledge assists in the overall understanding and use of nautical charts.

As mentioned earlier, projections are actually mathematical constructs, though they will be presented below as if they were optical rather than graphical projections.

The Mercator projection

The Mercator projection is often illustrated as a projection of the spherical earth onto the interior surface of a cylinder. In fact, the mathematical construct takes account of the earth's slightly non-spherical shape. Meridians appear on a Mercator projection as straight, vertical lines, as shown at right—an obvious distortion, because meridians drawn on a sphere would converge. Land masses are enlarged in an east-west direction, to an increasing degree, as they near the pole. But shape is an important element to retain so, to minimize the distortion of shape, parallels of latitude are spaced farther and farther apart as they approach the poles.

However, parallels conveniently intersect meridians at right angles and the grid contains only straight lines. A large-scale chart of a harbor would not show this varied parallel spacing, but a chart of the world reveals it.

The Mercator projection is conformal, meaning that directions can always be measured correctly and distances mea-

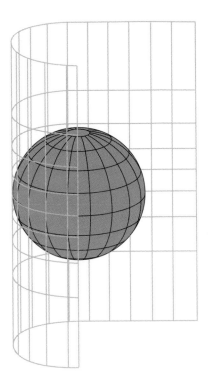

A Mercator projection *(above and below)* can be visualized as the placement of a cylinder around the earth, parallel to the polar axis, and touching the earth at the equator. It shows considerable distortion in near-polar latitudes.

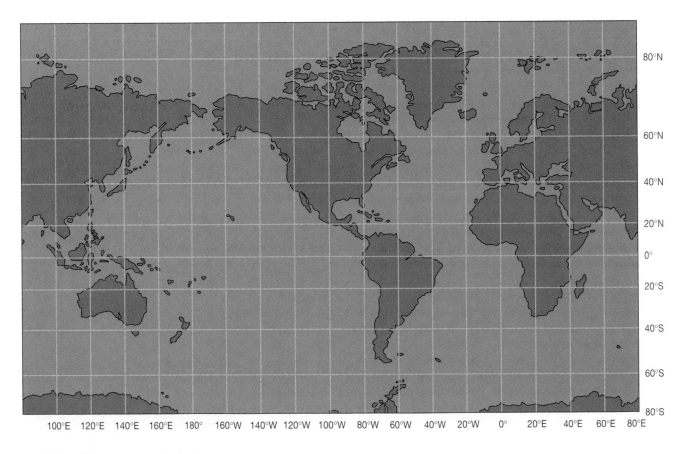

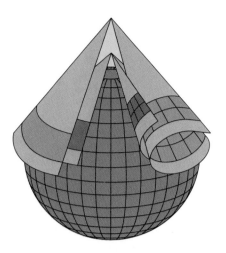

Polyconic projections *(above)* are developed into a series of cones, each cone tangent to a different parallel of latitude. This drawing shows two cones tangent at 20 and 30 degrees north latitude. For clarity, the projection of the earth's surface onto the cones is not shown. The polyconic projection of a large area *(right)* emphasizes the curved characteristics of the parallels and meridians of this type of chart. On charts of small areas, this curvature exists, but it is very slight.

sured to the same scale in all directions. However, because of distortion, and counter-distortion, land areas near the poles are greatly exaggerated—Greenland is not really the same size as South America.

The great advantage of the Mercator projection is that meridians and parallels form a right-angle grid, and directions can always be referred to any meridian or parallel, or to any compass rose. The geographic coordinates of a position can easily be read from the scales along the four borders of the chart. Also, we can draw a straight line between two points on a Mercator chart and actually run a course by determining the compass direction between them—the course has the same heading all along the line. Such a line is called a rhumb line.

However, the shortest distance between two points on the earth—a great circle—shows on a Mercator chart as a curved line. This is more difficult to calculate and plot. For moderate runs, the extra distance of a rhumb line is insignificant, so a rhumb track is used. But radio waves follow great circles and radio bearings on stations that are more than about 50 miles distant will require correction before they can be plotted on a Mercator chart.

The scale of a Mercator chart varies with the distance away from the mid-latitude on which the chart is constructed as a result of the North-South expansion. On harbor charts, this is unimportant, and the graphic scale may be used to measure distance anywhere on the chart.

However, the change in scale becomes significant on charts of larger areas, such as general, coastal and sailing charts. An accurate measure of distance on such charts requires that

you use the latitude scale on each chart directly opposite the region of the chart being used. *Never use the longitude scale at the top and bottom of the chart to measure distance.*

Polyconic projection

The polyconic method is based on the projection of the earth's surface onto a series of cones. A different cone is used for each parallel of latitude. The vertex of the cone coincides with the point where a tangent to the earth at the particular latitude intersects with an extension of the earth's axis.

The polyconic projection results in little distortion in shape. Another advantage to this method is that relative sizes are better preserved than in the much more common Mercator projection. The scale is correct along any parallel and also along the central meridian of the projection. Along other meridians, however, the scale increases with increased differences in longitude from the central meridian.

Parallels appear as non-concentric arcs of circles, while meridians appear as curved lines converging toward the poles and curving inward as a concave toward the central meridian. On the large-scale charts typically used by boaters, these curvatures are not particularly noticeable. Still, these characteristics contrast with the right-angle grid of the Mercator chart and are the reason why the polyconic is not so widely used in marine navigation. Directions from any point should in theory be measured relative to the meridian passing through that point, but in practice, the nearest compass rose is used. NOS Great Lakes charts include a graphic plotting interpolator to facilitate precise measurements of latitude and longitude.

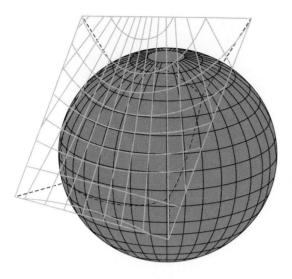

A gnomonic projection *(above)* is made by placing a plane surface tangent to the earth at any location. Points on the earth's surface are then projected onto the plane. A chart made on the gnomonic projection *(right)* shows meridians as straight lines converging toward the nearer pole. Parallels, other than the equator, appear as curved lines.

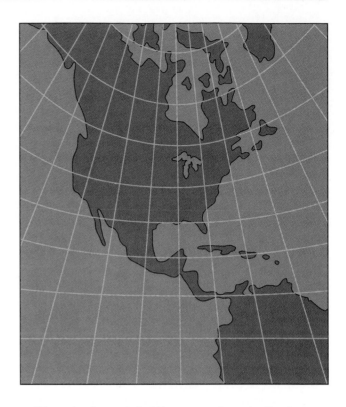

A variation of the polyconic is the "Lambert conformal projection," based on cones that intersect the earth's surface at two parallels. Aviators use the Lambert conformal because a straight line nearly approximates a great circle, and radio bearings can be plotted without the correction needed on Mercator charts.

Gnomonic projection

When meridians and parallels of latitude are projected onto a plane surface tangent to a point on the earth's surface, a gnomonic projection results. Meridians appear as straight lines converging toward the nearer pole, while parallels of latitude, except for the equator, appear as curves.

Distortion is great, but the gnomonic projection has one unique advantage—great circles appear as straight lines. Probably the easiest way to obtain a great-circle plot is to draw a straight line on a gnomonic chart, then transfer points along the line to another chart, such as a Mercator, using the geographic coordinates at each point. Connecting these transferred points with short rhumb lines yields a useful approximation of a great-circle path.

A special case of gnomonic projection occurs when a geographic pole is chosen as the point of tangency. In this case, all meridians appear as straight lines, and the parallels as concentric circles. This is a useful chart for polar regions where Mercator charts cannot be used.

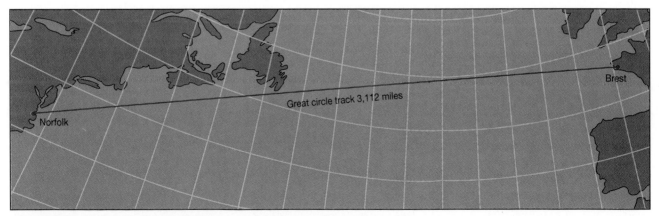

A great circle provides the shortest distance between any two points on the earth's surface, and can be plotted as a straight line *(above)*, on a gnomonic chart.

PILOTING PUBLICATIONS

We think first of charts when we consider government publications designed to make piloting easier and boating safer. It is certainly true that charts are the predominant form of government piloting information, but we can't overlook the dozens of other publications that make piloting easier and more accurate. Generally, these are available from the same agencies that issue charts, as listed below.

Publishing agencies in the United States

Agencies of the U.S. Federal Government that issue publications valuable to the boater include:

- National Ocean Service (NOS), National Oceanic and Atmospheric Administration (NOAA), Dept. of Commerce.
- U.S. Coast Guard, part of the Dept. of Transportation.
- The Defense Mapping Agency Hydrographic/Topographic Center (DMAHTC).
- The U.S. Naval Observatory.
- U.S. Army Corps of Engineers (District Offices).
- National Weather Service, also a part of NOAA.
- Government Printing Office.

The Government Printing Office, an independent agency, does much of the actual printing of federal publications dealing with piloting. The Office of the Superintendent of Documents sells most of the publications, but there seems to be no rule about whether a publication is sold by the GPO or by the government agency that prepared it.

Publications sold by the GPO can be bought by mail from: Superintendent of Documents, Government Printing Office, Washington, DC 20402. You can also buy them at a retail bookstore in the GPO building, North Capital and H Streets in Washington, DC, and by mail or in person from GPO Regional Bookstores in many major cities. Make your checks payable to the "Superintendent of Documents," or charge to your VISA or MasterCard account.

State agencies

State agencies also produce publications of interest to boaters, but there are too many of them to list here. Many are listed in the Appendices, but you should also check with authorities in your own state, and write ahead to other states when you expect to cruise in new waters. Refer to the Appendices for the name and address in each state. Be as specific as possible in requests for information and literature. Information may be obtained that will add to safety and convenience, possibly avoiding legal embarrassment as well. Remember, "Ignorance is no excuse" applies afloat as well as on shore.

Sales agents

Government agencies have designated certain boating supply stores and marinas as official sales agents for their publications. Authorized sales agents may carry publications of the National Ocean Service, the Defense Mapping Agency Hydrographic/Topographic Center, the Coast Guard or a combination of these. It does not hold true that because an establishment is an agent for one source of publications it will necessarily supply the others.

Tide Tables

The National Ocean Service is charged with the survey of the coast, harbors and tidal estuaries of the United States and its insular possessions. It issues the following publications relating to these waters as guides to navigation: Charts, *Coast Pilots*, *Tide Tables*, *Tidal Current Tables*, *Tidal Current Diagrams*, *Tidal Current Charts* and *Chart Catalogs*.

Tide Tables (below) are of great value in determining the predicted height of the water at almost any place at any time. The tables are calculated in advance and are published annually in four volumes, one of which covers the East Coast of North and South America and another the West Coast of these

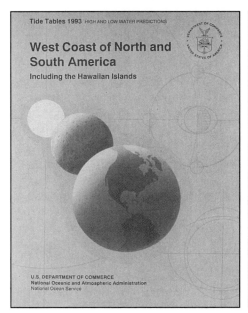

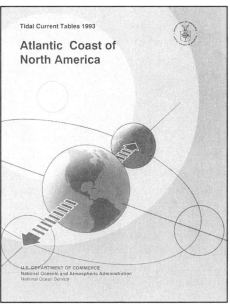

Tide Tables and *Tidal Current Tables,* similar in format for either coast, provide predicted heights of tide for one and strengths and slacks of the current for the other, for virtually any location on the coast.

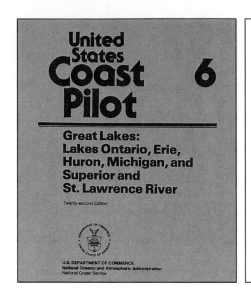

continents with an Alaskan supplement. The other volumes are for Asian and European coasts.

The *Tide Tables* give the predicted times and heights of high and low waters for each day of the year at a number of important points known as "reference stations." Additional data show the differences in times and heights between these reference stations and thousands of other points, termed "subordinate stations." The NOS also publishes a *Regional Tide & Tidal Current Table* for New York to Chesapeake Bay. The tables and their use in piloting are discussed at length in Chapter 15.

Tidal Current Tables

The *Tidal Current Tables* have much the same format of reference and subordinate stations as the *Tide Tables*. However, instead of indicating the times of high and low waters, these tables give the times and directions of maximum currents (ebb and flood), and the times of minimum currents. These times do not correspond to times of high and low tides, and the *Tide Tables* cannot be used for current predictions. Strength of the current is given in knots and direction in degrees true.

Tidal Current Tables is published in two volumes: Atlantic Coast of North America, and Pacific Coast of North America and Asia. Each volume includes tables for calculating current velocity at any intermediate time, and the duration of slack water or weak currents.

Tidal Current Tables and their use in piloting are covered in detail in Chapter 15.

Tidal Current Charts

Tidal Current Charts each consist of a series of 11 reproductions of the chart of the area, with the direction and velocity of tidal currents (shown graphically) for a specific hour with respect to the tide or current prediction for a major reference station. By following through the sequence of charts, hourly changes in velocity and direction are easily seen. These charts make it possible to visualize how tidal currents act at various points throughout every part of the entire 12-hour-plus cycle.

Where currents run at considerable velocity, and especially where tidal currents are complex, often flowing in opposite directions at the same stage of tide, you can gain a real advantage by consulting one of these charts. A few minutes' study may show you how to follow a favorable current through an entire passage, instead of needlessly bucking an opposing flow.

Tidal Current Charts may be used any year. The Narragansett Bay chart is used in conjunction with annual tide tables. All other *Tidal Current Charts* are used with the annual *Tidal Current Tables* for their respective areas.

The *Tidal Current Diagrams* is a series of 12 monthly diagrams to be used with *Tidal Current Charts*.

Coast Pilots

Information on nautical charts is limited by space and by the system of symbols used. You will often need additional information for safe and convenient navigation. The National Ocean Service publishes such information in the *Coast Pilot*, covering the United States coastlines and the Great Lakes in nine separate volumes.

Each *Coast Pilot* contains sailing directions between ports in its respective area, including recommended courses and distances. It describes channels with their controlling depths and all dangers and obstructions. It lists harbors and anchorages with information on boat supplies and marine repairs. It gives valuable information regarding canals, bridges and the Intracoastal Waterways where applicable.

The *Coast Pilot* volumes cover the following areas:

Atlantic Coast:

- No. 1 East Port to Cape Cod
- No. 2 Cape Cod to Sandy Hook
- No. 3 Sandy Hook to Cape Henry

- No. 4 Cape Henry to Key West
- No. 5 Gulf of Mexico, Puerto Rico and Virgin Islands

Great Lakes:
- No. 6 Great Lakes and connecting waterways

Pacific Coast:
- No. 7 California, Oregon, Washington and Hawaii

Alaska:
- No. 8 Dixon Entrance to Cape Spencer
- No. 9 Cape Spencer to Beaufort Sea

All *Coast Pilot*s are published annually, except *Coast Pilots 8* and *9*, which are issued every two years. They are all corrected through the dates of *Notice to Mariners* shown on the title page, so do not use them without checking the *Notice to Mariners* issued after publication of the *Coast Pilot*. Changes to *Coast Pilot*s that affect the safety of navigation and have been reported to NOS in the interim period between new editions are published in the *Local Notice to Mariners*, except those for *Coast Pilot 6*, which are published only in *Local Notice to Mariners*.

Catalogs

The National Ocean Service publishes five free *Chart Catalogs*. There is a catalog for the Atlantic and Gulf coasts, including Puerto Rico and the Virgin Islands; one for the Pacific Coast, including Hawaii and the other U.S. Pacific islands; and one for Alaska, including the Aleutian Islands. A fourth catalog covers the Great Lakes and adjacent waterways.

These are actually small-scale outline charts with diagrams delineating the areas covered by each NOS chart. The catalogs are also sources of additional information regarding other NOS publications and charts, as well as publications of other agencies; they also contain a listing, organized according to state, of the names and addresses of local sales agents for nautical charts and other publications.

A somewhat different catalog is the NOS *Map and Chart Catalog 5: Bathymetric Maps and Special Purpose Charts*. This publication indexes such items as *Topographic-*

A catalog of nautical charts includes listings of other useful NOS publications and other agencies. It shows the area covered by each chart, the scale and the price.

Bathymetric Maps, Bathymetric Maps, Bathymetric Fishing Maps, Geographic Maps, Regional Maps, and *IHB-GEBCO Plotting Sheets. Catalog 6* is a guide to NOAA nautical products and services. The index charts included in this publication show Fishery Conservation Zone boundaries 200 miles offshore, Continental Shelf limits (200-meter depth curve), and the outer edge of the Continental Slope (2500-meter depth curve).

NOS offices

Nautical charts, *Tide* and *Tidal Current Tables, Tidal Current Diagrams, Coast Pilot*s, and other publications of the National Ocean Service can be purchased at the offices of the Distribution Division, 6501 Lafayette Avenue, Riverdale, MD 20737. (Both Rockville and Riverdale are suburbs of Washington, DC.) Publications can be ordered by mail from Riverdale if payment is sent with the order, or by credit card, over the telephone at (301) 436-6990.

For information about NOS charts, publications and activities, write to the National Ocean Service, Rockville, MD 20852. Regional Marine Centers are located at Norfolk, Virginia, and Seattle, Washington.

Light Lists

The Coast Guard produces a series of publications for the coastal and inland waters known as the *Light Lists*. These books provide more complete information concerning aids to navigation than can be shown on charts but they should not be used for navigation in place of *Coast Pilot*s and charts. *Volumes I-IV* and *VI-VII* of the *Light List*s are published annually, *Volume V* every two years.

The *Light List*s describe the lights (all classes), buoys, daybeacons, radiobeacons and racons maintained in all navigable waters of the United States by the Coast Guard and various private agencies. (In this usage, the Navy and all other non-USCG governmental organizations are considered to be "private agencies.") The data shown in the *List*s include a reference number, the official name of the aid, its position, light characteristics (if any), height, range and structure (as applicable), and remarks. The *Light List*s are published in seven volumes as follows:
- *Volume I* Atlantic Coast from St. Croix River, Maine to Ocean City Inlet, Maryland
- *Volume II* Atlantic Coast, from Ocean City Inlet, Maryland, to Little River Inlet, South Carolina
- *Volume III* Atlantic Coast, from Little River Inlet, South Carolina, to Econfina River, Florida, and the Greater Antilles
- *Volume IV* Gulf of Mexico, from Econfina River, Florida, to Rio Grande, Texas
- *Volume V* Mississippi River System
- *Volume VI* Pacific Coast and Pacific Islands
- *Volume VII* Great Lakes

Within each volume, aids to navigation are listed by Coast Guard Districts in the following order: seacoast, major channels, minor channels and Intracoastal Waterway (if applicable).

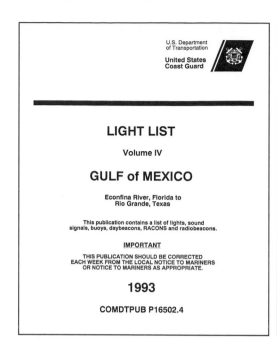

LIGHT LIST

Volume IV

GULF of MEXICO

Econfina River, Florida to
Rio Grande, Texas

This publication contains a list of lights, sound
signals, buoys, daybeacons, RACONS and radiobeacons.

IMPORTANT

THIS PUBLICATION SHOULD BE CORRECTED
EACH WEEK FROM THE LOCAL NOTICE TO MARINERS
OR NOTICE TO MARINERS AS APPROPRIATE.

1993

COMDTPUB P16502.4

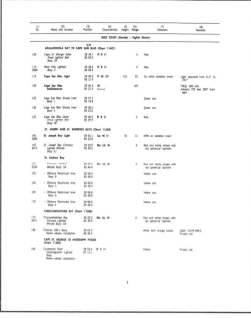

Light Lists, published by the U.S. Coast Guard, provide more detailed information on all types of aids to navigation than can be shown conveniently on charts.

Lighted and unlighted aids appear together in their geographic order, with amplifying data on the same page.

Seacoast aids are listed in sequence from north to south along the Atlantic Coast, from south to north and east to west along the Gulf Coast, and from south to north along the Pacific Coast. Great Lakes aids are listed in a generally westerly direction. On the Atlantic and Gulf coasts, aids along the Intracoastal Waterway are listed in the same sequence. For rivers and estuaries, the aids to navigation are shown from seaward to the head of navigation. Where an aid serves both a channel leading in from sea and the ICW, it will be listed separately in both sequences.

All volumes of the USCG *Light List* are for sale by the Superintendent of Documents, Government Printing Office; the volume for a particular area is sold by authorized chart and publication sales agents within that area. Often, the *Light Lists* for other areas also will be available.

Navigation Rules

The Coast Guard has prepared an excellent booklet on the two sets of Rules of the Road. This is *Navigation Rules, International-Inland* officially designated as Commandant Instruction M16672.2B. This edition contains all changes for both sets of rules as of its publication date of August 17, 1990.

This booklet presents the various Rules and Annexes on facing pages—International on the left, Inland on the right. Illustrations for specific rules appear near the applicable text. There are many illustrations of lights and shapes, each adjacent to the applicable rule.

The demarcation lines separating U.S. Inland Rules waters from International Rules waters are described in detail. The booklet also describes penalties for violations of rules or regulations; it outlines regulations relating to regattas and marine parades, and provides useful information on Vessel Traffic Services and Vessel Separation Schemes at many major ports and harbor entrances.

Copies of *Navigation Rules, International-Inland* may be ordered from the Superintendent of Documents, Government Printing Office or Regional GPO Bookstores; or purchased from local sales agents for charts and nautical publications.

Other USCG publications

The Coast Guard also issues publications about the safety of navigation and covering such topics as aids to navigation, applicable rules and regulations and general safety matters. Refer to the Appendices for a more complete listing. Some of these are free, others are available for a nominal charge.

Federal Requirements for Recreational Boats is a small pamphlet that will be very useful to all skippers. Topics include laws and regulations, numbering and documentation, reporting accidents and approved equipment.

This publication and others can be obtained by writing USCG Headquarters (G-NAB), Washington, DC 20593. Copies may also be available at Coast Guard District offices and some local USCG stations.

DMAHTC publications

The Defense Mapping Agency Hydrographic/Topographic Center has several publications of interest to boaters. Charts, publications and other products of DMAHTC are identified with a prefix to the individual chart or publication number.

The nautical chart identification system uses a numeral of one to five digits, without prefix, as determined by the scale and assigned to regions and subregions. Publications and some other items will retain an "H.O." (Hydrographic Office) prefix until reprinted with a DMAHTC number.

Oceanographic products, primarily publications related to the dynamic nature of the oceans or the scientific aspects of oceanography, are printed by the Naval Oceanographic Office and carry numbers with prefixes that reflect the nature of the particular publication.

Bowditch (Publication No. 9)

The *American Practical Navigator* (known as *Bowditch*), originally written by Nathaniel Bowditch in 1799, is an extensive treatise on piloting, celestial navigation and other nautical matters. It is Publication No. 9 of DMAHTC.

Bowditch has long been accepted as an authority on piloting and other forms of navigation. The current edition consists of two volumes. The 1981 Volume II, which will meet the needs of most boaters, contains tables, data, equations and instructions needed to perform navigational calculations. The 1984 Volume I contains basic reference material.

Other DMAHTC publications

Other Hydrographic/Topographic Center publications that may be useful to a boater include Pub. 117, *Radio Navigational Aids*, and Pub. 102, *International Code of Signals*.

The Hydrographic/Topographic Center publishes a series of *Sailing Directions* that provides supplementary information for foreign coasts and ports in a manner generally similar to the *Coast Pilot*s for U.S. waters.

The *Lists of Lights* published by this agency likewise cover foreign waters and does not duplicate the Coast Guard *Light List*s. These are DMAHTC Pubs. No. 110 through 116.

DMAHTC charts and publications are listed in the *DMA Catalog of Maps, Charts and Related Products, Part 2—Hydrographic Products, Volume I—Nautical Charts and Publications*. The contents are grouped into nine regions that correspond to the chart numbering system, plus a section for Miscellaneous Charts and Publications.

DMAHTC publications include a number of tables for the reduction of celestial observations, and tables and charts for plotting lines of position from Loran-C measurements. These are of interest only to those yacht skippers making extensive voyages on the high seas.

The Appendices list other DMAHTC publications.

Obtaining DMAHTC publications

The distribution function of public sale of Defense Mapping Agency (DMA) nautical charts and publications was transferred to the National Oceanic and Atmospheric Administration (NOAA) in 1992. Along with the transfer, there were some changes, most notably to the *DMA catalog, Part 2, Volume I—Nautical Charts and Publications*. The catalog is now available as nine individual catalogs, each covering a different region. Each catalog contains general, ordering and nautical products information, lists of charts available in the region, graphics displaying chart location, and a miscellaneous charts and publications section.

The catalogs are free of charge and available from your local NOAA chart sales agent or may be ordered from the NOAA Distribution Branch. The stock numbers of catalogs for the nine regions are listed below:

DMANC1 United States, Canada
DMANC2 Central and South America, Antarctica
DMANC3 Western Europe, Iceland, Greenland, the Arctic
DMANC4 Scandinavia, Baltic, the Former Soviet Union
DMANC5 Western Africa, the Mediterranean
DMANC6 Indian Ocean
DMANC7 Australia, Indonesia, New Zealand
DMANC8 Oceania
DMANC9 East Asia

Naval Observatory publications

The Naval Observatory participates and assists in publishing the *Nautical Almanac* annually and the *Air Almanac* biannually. There is also the annual *Almanac for Computers*, useful for programmable calculators and microcomputers; complete almanac and other data are now available on a single floppy disk. These books contain astronomical data that is helpful for celestial navigation.

The Naval Observatory also participates in and assists the publication of other navigational documents such as the *Tide Tables* and celestial sight reduction tables, but it is not the agency directly responsible for them.

Army Corps of Engineers publications

The Corps of Engineers of the United States Army has the responsibility for navigational and informational publications on major inland (non-tidal) rivers such as the Tennessee, Ohio and Mississippi, and many lakes and reservoirs behind large dams.

Intracoastal Waterway booklets

The Army Engineers has prepared two paperbound booklets on the Intracoastal Waterway, which comes under its jurisdiction. These booklets contain descriptive material, photographs, small-scale charts and tabulated data.

Unfortunately, these publications are not periodically updated and they are of far less value than the corresponding volumes of the NOS *Coast Pilot*s with their annual editions and frequent changes in *Notice to Mariners*.

Bulletins on the Intracoastal Waterways are issued periodically by the Engineers District Offices. Addresses of these offices are given in the Appendices.

Rivers and lakes information

Regulations relating to the use of many rivers and lakes (reservoirs), *Navigational Bulletins* and *Notices to Navigation Interests* are issued by various offices of the Corps of Engineers, as listed in the Appendices. Other government publications relating to inland river and lake boating are also listed on that page, together with information on their availability.

National Weather Service publications

The National Weather Service, a part of NOAA, Department of Commerce, prepares weather maps that appear in many newspapers, but boaters generally make greater use of radio and television broadcasts for weather and sea conditions.

To assist mariners and boaters in knowing when and where to listen for radio and TV weather broadcasts in or near the continental United States, NWS publishes a series of *Marine Weather Services Charts* available in annual editions.

Boaters who cruise far offshore and in foreign waters should use the NWS publication *Worldwide Marine Weather Broadcast*, which contains information on frequencies and schedules of stations transmitting in radiotelephone, radiotelegraph and radioteletype modes.

Keeping publications up to date

You should be sure to keep charts and certain other navigational publications fully up to date. Outdated information can be more harmful than no information at all.

Coast Pilots and *Light Lists* are the primary publications that need continual correction. Fortunately, the government has provided a convenient means for executing this important function. The time and effort required are not great, provided a skipper keeps at it regularly and does not permit the work to build up a backlog.

Notice to Mariners

The Defense Mapping Agency Hydrographic/Topographic Center publishes a *Notice to Mariners (opposite),* which is prepared jointly with the National Ocean Service and the Coast Guard. These pamphlets advise mariners of important matters affecting navigational safety, including new hydrographic discoveries, changes in channels and navigation aids, etc. Besides keeping mariners informed generally, the *Notice to Mariners* also provides information specifically useful for updating the latest-edition nautical charts and publications.

Each issue contains instructions on how it is to be used to correct charts and other publications. Supplementary information is published in *Notice* No. 1 of each year; lists of charts affected are included quarterly.

DMAHTC also publishes a semiannual *Summary of Corrections* in regional volumes. Each issue contains the full text of all accumulated corrections from *Notice to Mariners*, except for *Light Lists* and certain other navigational publications. It is easier to use than a file of *Notices* for bringing up to date a chart that has not been kept corrected. The *Summary* does, however, require a paid subscription.

Local Notice to Mariners

The Commander of each Coast Guard District issues *Local Notice to Mariners (opposite).* These are reproduced and mailed from the respective District offices, bringing information to users several weeks in advance of the weekly *Notices* that are printed in Washington, and mailed from there.

Local Notices are of particular interest to small-craft skippers, as the *Notices* from Washington do not carry information regarding inland and other waters not used by large ocean-going vessels.

How to obtain copies

Boaters can get on the mailing list for *Local Notice to Mariners* by sending a written request to the Commander (oan), of the applicable Coast Guard District. See Chapter 27 for district boundaries; you can obtain the District office mailing address from various Coast Guard publications, or your local Coast Guard or Coast Guard Auxiliary unit.

Getting on the distribution list for the weekly *Notice to Mariners* mailed from Washington, DC, is more difficult, and is rarely necessary. Application, with adequate justification, is made to Office of Distribution Services (IMA), Defense Mapping Agency, Washington, DC 20315.

Even if you don't succeed in getting on the mailing list, the information contained in *Notice* and *Local Notice* is nonetheless readily available. Local sales agents receive copies and maintain files that anyone may read. Many yacht clubs and marinas also receive and post copies of *Local Notice.*

Automated *Notice to Mariners* system

Because of the time required for preparation, printing and distribution from Washington, DC, the information in any *Notice to Mariners* is several weeks old by the time it reaches the user. This lag is unavoidable, but there is a way to get information "right up to the minute." *Notice* publications are prepared from a computerized database, and this can be directly accessed by any boater who has a personal computer and modem.

The "Navigation Information Network" is the means of reaching the Defense Mapping Agency computer. Specific information can be requested in terms of blocks of numbers of aids to navigation in volumes of the *Light List* or *List of Lights*, chart numbers or port areas. The caller need simply tell the DMA computer the number of the last printed *Notice to Mariners* on hand, and the computer responds by advising of any subsequent changes that may have occurred.

The system is menu-driven and easy to use. Several phone lines are available for 300, 1,200 and 2,400 bits per second communications speeds. Users can also send information to DMAHTC via this link. There is no charge for accessing the DMA database, but the caller must pay normal telephone long-distance charges; the system operates continuously, and calls can be placed when the rates are lowest. Write to DMA Hydrographic/Topographic Center (Code MCN), Washington, DC 20315-0030 for the necessary password and a system manual; these are also free.

GPS information

The USCG operates a GPS information center, with a Master Control Station in Colorado Springs, Colorado.

Report all useful information

All boaters are urged to help governmental agencies maintain the buoyage system by reporting any damage to aids, malfunctioning of lights, shifting of shoals and channels, or new hazards. Use a radio if the matter is urgent; otherwise, suggestions for the improvement of aids to navigation should be sent to the Commander (oan), of the applicable Coast Guard district.

Data concerning dangers to navigation, changes in shoals and channels, and similar information affecting charts or publications of the NOS should be sent to the Director, National Ocean Service, Rockville, MD 20852.

Quasi-governmental publications

In addition to the governmental agencies and their publications noted above, several activities best described as "quasi-governmental" produce publications of interest to boaters. Two of these are discussed below.

RTCM

The Radio Technical Commission for Maritime Services, better known by its initials, RTCM, includes individuals from governmental agencies such as the FCC, the Coast Guard, NOAA, Maritime Administration and others—user organizations such as ocean steamship operating groups, Great Lakes shipping interests, and the United States Power Squadrons; equipment manufacturers; labor organizations; and communication companies such as the Bell System. The RTCM does not have authority to make binding decisions, but it wields considerable influence through its function as a meeting place for and resolution of conflicting views and interests.

The RTCM publishes the *Marine Radio Users Handbook*, an authoritative pamphlet on the FCC Rules and Regulations that also offers useful information on the selection, installation and proper use of radios on boats. This useful booklet can be ordered by contacting the Radio Technical Commission for Maritime Services, P.O. Box 19087, Washington, DC 20036. A fee is required.

Naval Institute publications

The United States Naval Institute, it should be noted, is not a governmental agency; rather it is a private association dedicated to "the advancement of professional, literary and scientific knowledge in the Navy." As a means toward this goal, one of the Institute's principal activities is the publication of books dealing with naval and maritime matters.

The Naval Institute publishes a number of excellent books on the Navigation Rules, as well as the familiar text *Dutton's Navigation and Piloting*. Like the classic *Bowditch,* this volume has come to be recognized as an all-round authority on matters of piloting and navigation. The current volume is an outgrowth of years of development and expansion from an early work; the book on which it is based was initially known as *Navigation and Nautical Astronomy* by Benjamin Dutton. This useful book—now in its 14th edition—can be purchased in boating supply and book stores.

Publications available in Canada

Numerous Canadian Aids to Navigation (primarily seacoast aids) are listed in *Light Lists Volume I, VI and VII.* These are most useful when they appear visually and/or electronically to mariners transmitting in United States waters adjacent to Canadian waters. The listing of Canadian Aids to Navigation in the U.S. Coast Guard *Light List* is not intended to be a substitute for the equivalent official Canadian publication, which is called *List of Lights.*

Notice to Mariners occurs in two versions: 1) A weekly volume, published by the DMAHTC, covers the entire world except inland waters not used by ocean shipping. 2) A local volume is published monthly, with weekly updates, by the local Coast Guard.

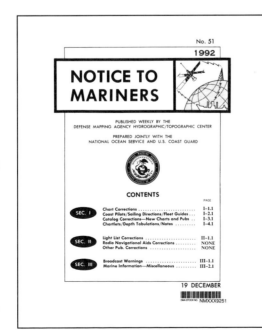

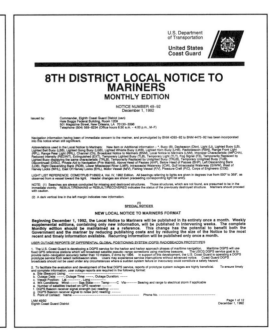

19 BASIC PILOTING

Because conducting a vessel safely and efficiently within coastal areas requires constant attention to position and course, measurement and charting skills are essential. Interpreting observed information takes both time and practice, but analyzing and recording your progress is a matter of simple procedures that are easy to learn.

This chapter covers the dimensions and tools of piloting and their use in dead reckoning, as well as establishing a speed curve for your boat. If piloting is relatively new to you, consider it best to practice your piloting skills in fair weather by "overnavigating." When fog, rain and darkness close in you will be confident and secure.

THE DIMENSIONS OF PILOTING

Piloting is the use of landmarks, aids to navigation and soundings to conduct a vessel safely through channels and harbors, and along coasts where depths of water and dangers to navigation require constant attention to the boat's position and course.

Piloting is one of the principal subdivisions of navigation—the science and art of directing the movements of a vessel from one position to another in a safe and efficient manner. It is a science because it uses principles and procedures based on centuries of observation, analysis and study; it is an art because interpretations of observations and other information require individual judgment and skill.

An adjunct to piloting is dead reckoning, a procedure whereby a boat's approximate location is determined at any time by its movements since the last accurate determination of position. The term may have evolved from *deduced* reckoning, which was abbreviated to "de'ed."

Other types of navigation include celestial and electronic. Electronic navigation is covered in Chapter 25. Celestial navigation is covered in more advanced texts, such as *Dutton's Navigation and Piloting*, for example.

Pilot waters

The navigator of a boat of any size must be constantly alert in pilot waters such as rivers, bays, lakes, sounds and close along the ocean shore. An error of only a few yards can result in running aground. The presence of other vessels demands that the navigator know not only where dangers lie along the intended course, but also where the boat can be steered safely if the sudden threat of a collision is to be avoided.

Direction, distance and time are the basic dimensions of piloting. Other quantities that must be measured, calculated or used include speed, position, and depths and heights. To pilot well you must understand units of measure, calculation and chart plotting, and you must practice regularly, taking advantage of good weather to prepare for bad.

We will look at each of these dimensions and elements with particular respect to units of measure and standard methods of recording them.

Bear in mind that the use of electronic navigation instruments *(Chapter 25)* does not make basic piloting and chartwork obsolete, as many owners of Loran-C and GPS receivers seem to believe. Nor is it simply a question of providing a backup against the possible failure of your electronic navigation system, though this in itself would be sufficient reason to learn and practice piloting.

The reason that piloting and chartwork are still an integral part of electronic navigation is that, without a graphic representation of your pilot waters, you cannot know what lies along the course. Without a chart and without plotting your electronically determined position on a chart, you cannot know whether or not you are headed for danger.

In the near future, all charts may be electronic too, but that in itself will not preclude the need for a basic understanding of piloting. Just as an accountant who uses computers must, nevertheless, understand accounting, a pilot with an integrated electronic navigation system must still understand what his or her system does. Ultimately, good pilots will retain their skills because piloting a boat with pencil and a chart is a pleasure.

Direction

The position of one point in relation to another, without respect to the distance that separates them, is direction. Navigators use a system of angular measurement that may already be familiar to you from Chapter 18—the 360 degrees of a circle are subdivided into minutes (there are 60 minutes in a degree), or into common decimal fractions.

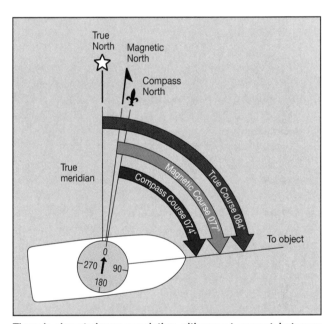

There is almost always a variation, either east or west, between true and magnetic North. Magnetic and compass directions usually disagree too. Directions must always be specified as true, magnetic or compass.

Directions are normally referenced to a base line that runs from the origin point toward the geographic North Pole. Such directions can be measured on a chart with reference to the meridians of longitude and are called true directions. Measurements made with respect to the direction of the earth's magnetic field, at that particular point, are called magnetic directions. Those measured with reference to the magnetic conditions on board, as indicated by the boat's compass, are designated compass directions.

To ensure accuracy, it is essential that the boater always designate the directional reference that has been used, either as true (T), magnetic (M) or compass (C). In addition, directions should always be expressed in a three-digit format. For example, you would not write 89° if you meant a course of just north of east; you would write 089°. In a similar way, North is

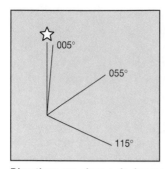

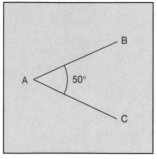

Directions are always designated by a three-digit number; add zeros before a single- or double-digit number *(left)*. An angle between two directions *(right)*, as distinguished from the directions themselves, is not expressed as a three-digit number.

000°, not just 0°. This three-digit format is invariably used, because it easily distinguishes directions from angles that are not directions.

For any given direction there is its reciprocal direction; this is its direct opposite, differing by 180 degrees. Thus, the reciprocal of 030° is 210°; the reciprocal of 300° is 120°. To determine the reciprocal of any direction, add 180 if the given direction is less than 180°; or subtract 180 if the direction is more than 180°.

Distance

Distance is the length of the shortest line that can be drawn on the earth's surface between two points. The basic unit, in the U.S., is the mile, but remember, you may encounter two types of mile. The familiar statute mile is used on inland waters such as the Mississippi River, the Great Lakes, and the Atlantic and Gulf Intracoastal Waterways. At 5,280 feet, the statute mile is shorter than the nautical mile (used on the high seas and tidal waters), which is 6,076.1 feet. There is nothing accidental about this—the "salt-water" mile is equal to one minute of latitude, making it very useful in navigation. A nautical mile is exactly 1,852 meters.

To convert from statute to nautical miles, use a factor of 1.15; roughly 7 nautical miles equals 8 statute miles. Note that you may cruise from an area charted in nautical miles to one charted in statute miles. Be sure you recognize the correct choice. Feet are usually used for depths and heights, but are seldom used for distances.

Charts published by other countries use the nautical mile and the metric system for measures such as distance, depth and height. Eventually, all U.S. charts will be converted to the metric system, but the process will extend over many years. A discussion of conversion factors is found in the Appendices at the end of the book.

Time

While celestial navigators require an exact time of day (the invention of accurate mobile timekeeping was, in fact, motivated by the needs of celestial navigators), the pilot does not need to be so concerned about the exact time.

However, the pilot does have to accurately measure elapsed time at least to large fractions of a minute. A pilot in a race or in a piloting contest (called a "predicted log" contest) will need seconds and fractions of seconds, but otherwise, such small units will only occur in calculations.

The 24-hour clock

In navigation, the time of day is expressed in terms of the 24-hour cycle. "A.m." and "p.m." have no place in navigation. Written time uses four digits: two for the hour (09—not just 9), and two for the minute (01—not just 1). The format helps eliminate confusion about the meaning of a number notation.

The day begins at 0000 and the time one minute later is recorded as 0001, or 12:01 a.m.; 0100 would be "1:00 a.m." if you were ashore. The second half of the day continues in the same pattern; 1700 is unambiguous, unlike "five o'clock." Midnight is 2400, the same as 0000 for the next day.

Spoken time is just as concise: "zero seven hundred" or "fifteen forty." The word "hours" is *not* used. For the sake of consistency, at 1000 and 2000 you would say "ten hundred" and "twenty hundred" rather than "one or two thousand."

While it may seem almost trivial to point it out, you must remember that when you add and subtract times, you borrow or carry based on the 60 units of an hour, not the 100 units more familiar in base-10 arithmetic. Miscalculations resulting from this simple error are all too common.

Time zones

A navigator in pilot waters must also be alert to time zones. Even in coastal or inland waters, you can cruise from one zone to another, necessitating the resetting of clocks.

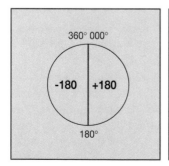

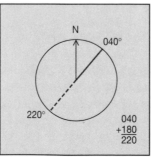

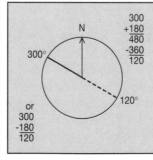

The reciprocal of a given direction can be found by adding 180 degrees to it. To simplify the arithmetic, subtract 180 to find the reciprocal of any directions greater than 180 degrees.

A further complication in time is the prevalence of daylight time during the summer. Government publications are in standard time; local sources of information such as newspapers and radio use daylight time if it is in effect. Daylight time is one hour later than standard time. When converting from standard time to daylight, add one hour; from daylight to standard, subtract one hour.

Speed

Speed is an essential element of piloting and the basic unit of measure is the mile per hour. This might refer to statute miles per hour, or nautical miles per hour, depending on the waters in question. However, nautical miles per hour are correctly expressed as "knots," abbreviated as "kn," or "kt." Since a knot is a nautical mile per hour, the phrase "knots per hour" is a mistake. The conversion between knots and statute miles per hour uses the same factor as for distance—1.15, and for the purposes of rough calculation, 7 knots is very close to 8 miles per hour.

Position

Describing your position accurately to other vessels, the Coast Guard and other professionals is essential. The hesitant and inaccurate descriptions commonly heard on the VHF during a summer weekend are irritating to trained pilots, and potentially expensive and dangerous to the parties directly involved in the communication.

There are two ways to describe position. Something can be located a distance and direction from an identifiable object of known location. This is known as a relative position. Precision depends on the accuracy of the data on which you base the position—you might say, "I am about two miles southwest of Ambrose Light" or, if you had more precise data, "I am 2.2 miles, 230° true from Ambrose Light." The direction reference given here means that if someone were standing at Ambrose Light and measured 230° true, that line would intersect your position. It does not mean that Ambrose Light is 230° from you. These examples have used readily identifiable (and charted) objects.

You might also describe your position as a geographic position, that is, with reference to your latitude and longitude. This would require that you use the scales on either side and at the top or bottom of your chart. The units of measure are degrees and minutes, but these are not the same as degrees of direction or minutes of time. For really precise position you would use seconds, or fractions of minutes of latitude or longitude, as determined by the units shown on your chart.

A statement of geographic position first of all gives the latitude as "north" or "south," then the longitude as "east" or "west." Of course, there's not very much room for misunderstanding in U.S. waters—here, latitude is always north and longitude is always west, but the directions should be stated nevertheless.

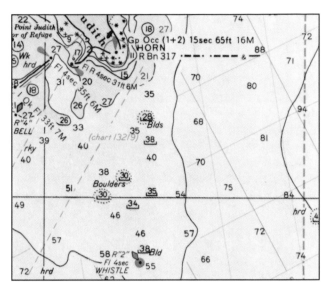

A boat's position may be described in "relative" terms, such as at a certain distance and direction from an identifiable object, for example, "1.8 miles, 120° true, from Point Judith Light."

Skippers of boats with Loran-C receivers can also describe their position in terms of "time difference" readings, but this is seldom done as all such sets now provide a direct readout of geographic position.

Depths and heights

Information on water depth is obviously important to avoid running aground, but less apparent is its value in determining position. With electronic sounders, depths can be measured continuously or occasionally. In pilot waters, depths are measured in feet (or, on metric charts, in meters). In the open ocean, fathoms are used for depth—a fathom is 6 feet.

Remember that before you can make sure of a particular depth, you must note the datum of the chart you are using. (The datum is the horizontal plane of reference of vertical measurements, and is described in Chapter 15.) Depths are referenced to mean low water (Chapter 18) or a specified level on the Great Lakes and other landlocked bodies of water.

Information on heights is also used by pilots. The height of a landmark or an aid to navigation may determine its range of visibility. This is especially important at night when identifying lights. Even more important are the heights of bridges. Bridge clearances are measured in feet (or meters) from the surface of the water.

The usual datum for heights is not the same as for depths. In tidal waters, the datum is mean high water, while for depths it is mean low water as mentioned above; on inland waters, the datum will be some specified level. (The interval is the mean tidal range, as discussed in Chapter 15.)

With reference to depths and heights, note that "mean" means "average." In some instances depths are shallower, or vertical clearances less, than the figure shown. Always interpret the information with reference to tidal data.

PILOTING INSTRUMENTS

Although piloting a boat does not require elaborate and expensive instruments, keep in mind that the instruments you choose will serve you best if they are of good quality and treated with care and respect.

Tools that measure direction

Many instruments are used for measuring direction—both from observation and from the chart. The basic one is the compass. In fact, it's so basic that it has a chapter all on its own—Chapter 17. The directions shown by a compass are compass directions—not magnetic and not true. Usually, before a direction such as 092° (C) can be plotted, it must be corrected for both deviation and variation, as explained in Chapter 17.

While the compass is used primarily to determine the direction in which the boat is headed, it can also be used to determine the direction of other objects from your boat. To find such a direction, you would put your eye on a level just above the compass and sight across it toward the other object. Of course, most steering compasses are mounted in such a way that they are much less useful for taking bearings than they are for steering. In fact, only on larger powerboats does the steering compass have a high and unobstructed view of most of the horizon.

Hand bearing compass

It is more likely that a bearing to another object would be taken with a hand bearing compass. This type of compass comes in many styles—you can even find it integrated into a binocular so that the compass reading appears with a magnified image of the objects viewed. Whatever the style, the hand bearing compass must allow you to look simultaneously at the object and at the compass scale—whether with vertical sights or a prism.

On sailboats, compasses are often mounted in a pedestal binnacle just forward of the wheel in the cockpit. Refer to Chapter 17 for mounting information.

Typically, you would find a clear space to stand and brace yourself (note that you will be concentrating on the sighting and not keeping a weather eye for the next large wave), then raise the hand bearing compass to your eye and take the reading. In most situations, the compass is well clear of the various magnetic influences that cause deviation, but you should be alert to the possibility that you are standing too close to a mass of magnetic material.

To find a sighting position on deck that you can be sure is free of magnetic influences, take bearings on a distant charted landmark with your boat in a known position. Compare your hand bearing readings taken from various locations on deck with the magnetic bearing from the chart. Put the boat on several different headings as you do this in case the orientation of its magnetic influences has an important effect on the hand bearing compass. When taking the bearing make sure that your eyeglasses or a spare battery in your shirt pocket are not causing deviation.

Hand bearing compasses are also very useful in determining whether a nearby vessel is changing position with respect to your boat. Are you on a collision course? Are you winning or losing ground in a race? A hand bearing compass can help you answer these important questions—though not always definitively—while there is still time to do something about it.

A hand bearing compass can be used from almost any spot on a boat, but be careful to keep it away from large masses of magnetic material that could introduce deviation errors.

Pelorus

Directions from the boat can also be measured with a pelorus. Though fairly uncommon, peloruses are simple, inexpensive and useful—particularly for making up deviation tables for a steering compass as described in Chapter 17. A pelorus consists of two vertical sighting vanes that rotate over a card that looks the same as a compass rose. There are no magnets on the pelorus, which explains why it is known as a "dumb compass." The pelorus is often temporarily mounted in such a way that its horizon is unobstructed and its circular scale can be accurately aligned with a line that is parallel to the boat's centerline.

The circular scale can be rotated and clamped in position. When the scale is set so that 000° is dead ahead, an object can be lined up in the sights and the reading from the card will represent a relative bearing. These relative bearings can be converted to compass directions or compass bearings by adding them to the boat's heading as read from the steering compass *at the same moment during which the pelorus sighting was made.*

In practice, the crew reading the pelorus calls "mark" as the bearing is aligned in the sights, and the helmsman reads the compass at that moment. An alternative is to have the helmsman call "mark" each time the boat's actual heading passes through the prescribed heading so that the pelorus reader can make the alignment at that moment.

Since the pelorus scale can be rotated, it is also possible to match the compass heading being steered. Readings taken from the pelorus scale are then direct compass bearings without any need for conversion. However, two cautions are needed: First, the boat must be exactly on course at the moment of the pelorus observation. Second, corrections for deviation must be made according to the heading of the boat, not the direction of the object as read from the pelorus.

Plotting directions on a chart

Once you have determined a direction by observation with a hand bearing compass or a pelorus (or even sighting over the steering compass), you will want to refer the information to a chart. There are several plotting instruments that allow you to easily and accurately transfer a bearing to a chart, or to read a direction from the chart. The most familiar and oldest of these is a set of parallel rulers, but several variations of course plotters are available that make the task easier and more accurate.

In addition to individual tools such as course plotters, there are several more comprehensive and flexible chart-working systems available. These typically offer a means of mounting and protecting a chart, and also provide a set of several specialized plotting devices that can make chartwork much easier to execute and much more accurate in practice. While the principles are the same (and must still be thoroughly understood), such chartwork systems are especially attractive for small boat owners who may often have to do

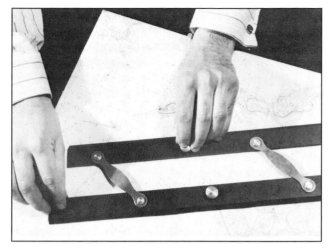

Parallel rulers are a traditional charting instrument. The two straightedges are kept in parallel alignment by the connecting links, and directions are transferred from one place to another by "walking" the rulers from course line to compass rose, or vice versa.

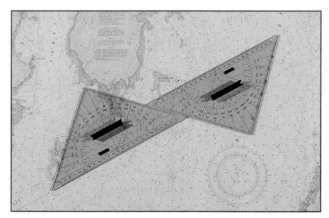

A pair of ordinary drawing triangles can be used for easily transferring a direction from one part of a chart to another, but not for great distances.

their plotting in cramped, uncomfortable and/or wet circumstances. Because each of these systems has its own operating method, no attempt will be made to describe them here. In the section below, we will look at the basic tools with which every pilot should be familiar.

Parallel rulers

The two rulers of a set of parallel rulers are connected by a linkage that allows them to be separated from each other but keeps them strictly parallel. The rulers themselves can be made of black or clear plastic and, like ordinary drawing rulers, have beveled edges that are convenient for drawing a pencil line. There are usually two small knobs that the user grips when "side-stepping" the parallel rulers from one area to another on the chart. One ruler (which we'll call A) is held firmly in place on the chart while the other (which we'll call

B) is moved away toward a compass rose or other goal. Then A is moved up to close the gap. This action can be repeated until B reaches the desired position.

When the direction of a line is to be measured, the ruler is placed along it (or intersecting two objects), and the ruler is stepped to the center of the nearest compass rose. The direction can be read off the true or magnetic circle of the compass rose.

The process can be reversed, taking a direction (magnetic or true) from the compass rose and stepping the rulers until one edge intersects the origin point (a charted landmark, or the starting point of a course, for example). Then a line is drawn along that edge.

Course plotters

Course plotters are usually rectangles of clear plastic with semicircular degree scales and parallel lines printed on them. Usually there are two semicircular scales—protractor scales, one marked from 0° to 180° and the other from 180° to 360°. (These do not follow the three-digit convention because they are not, themselves, directional notations, but merely angular measurements.) There may also be a smaller angular scale offset by 90° from the other scales.

You will read about other applications for course plotters and their various linear scales in the next chapter, but here we will describe the basic operations for measuring direction.

Here is how you would use a plotter to transfer an observed direction to the chart: A line of direction from a given point is measured by placing the plotter on the chart so that one of its longer sides is along your course or bearing line, sliding the plotter lengthwise until the center, or bull's-eye, of the protractor scales is over a meridian (a north-south line), and finally reading the direction from the point on the protractor scale where it intersects the meridian. For an easterly direction line you would use the 0° to 180° scale and for a westerly one, the 180° to 360° scale. Note that this is a true direction because the meridian you have used as a reference is a line that runs through the geographic North Pole, not the magnetic North.

Although you don't actually have to draw in a direction line from the given point, usually this is easier and safer to do. Any of the parallel lines printed on the plotter that happen to be conveniently placed for reading can substitute for the plotter's edge.

When the direction you are measuring is within about 20° of true north or south, it may be difficult to place the bull's-eye accurately on a meridian. That is the purpose of the smaller offset scale. Place the bull's-eye on a parallel of latitude (an east-west line) and read the true course from the intersection of this line with the offset scale.

On the other hand, you may want to plot a specified direction line from a given point on the chart. For example, you may want to plot a 095° direction line from a particular point on the chart. You will have to place the plotter in such a way that three conditions are met: The bull's-eye is on a meridian, the same meridian intersects the 95° mark on the circular scale, and the edge of the plotter intersects your given point.

In practice, you can align the plotter's 95° mark and bull's-eye on the meridian, then slide the plotter carefully up or down the meridian until one edge intersects your given point.

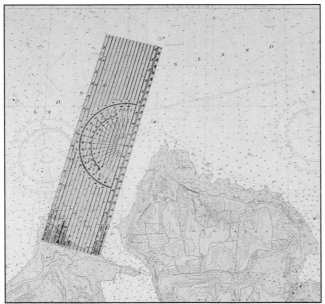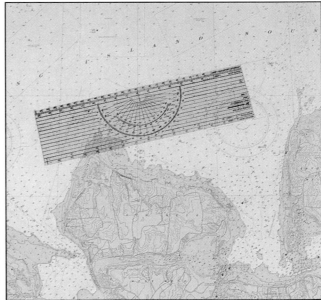

The course plotter is lined up with the course line along one of the longer sides, as shown at left, and then is moved until a meridian cuts through the "bull's-eye." Direction can then be read from the appropriate main scale. In the case of courses within a few degrees of North or South, use the auxiliary inner scales and a parallel of latitude, as shown at right.

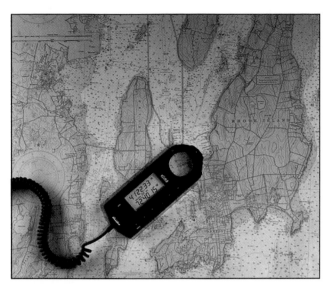

Plotting systems can simplify and speed up many procedures. Some compute position electronically and accept input from other instruments.

Course protractors

A course protractor is a slightly more complex plotting tool that takes a little more practice to use well. Protractors typically consist of a small, clear plastic square marked with a 360° compass scale and a grid of fine lines. Riveted on the bull's-eye is a clear plastic ruler arm that revolves like the hand of a clock—but a very long arm because it extends about a foot beyond the circle of the compass scale. The principle is to duplicate the orientation of the compass rose (particularly the magnetic circle) and transfer it to the point of interest on the chart.

For example, assume you have chosen a given point on the chart and would like to measure the direction of a line from that point. Place the bull's-eye of the course protractor on your given point and swing the arm until its upper edge intersects the center of the chart's nearest compass rose. Holding it firmly in place, read the direction on the rose that the edge of the ruler lies across, and turn the protractor's compass scale until the same reading is aligned with the ruler's edge.

Alternatively, place your (sharp) pencil on the given point and skew the plotter against it until you have all three intersections (95° mark, bull's-eye and plotter's edge) in place.

Now draw the line along the plotter's edge. Again, directions that are nearly north or south can be measured with the offset scale and a parallel of latitude instead of a meridian.

Sometimes the plotter's edge is not long enough to reach the chart position on which you are working. You can use the points of a pair of dividers as a guide. (Dividers are covered in detail on page 434.) Place the divider points on the direction line and slide the plotter's edge against them until you can make your reading or extend your pencil line.

Drawing new lines parallel to existing lines is quite easy. Place the plotter so that one of the parallel lines printed on it is along the existing line and draw the new line against the plotter's edge.

A more elaborate course plotter, called a Quik-Course, is handled in a slightly different manner. The Quik-Course is a larger clear plotter printed with a circular compass scale and a grid. But the compass scale is projected right out to the (straight) edges of the plotter.

By placing the bull's-eye of the Quik-Course on any point along a direction line and orienting the whole plotter with the vertical meridians and horizontal parallels of latitude, you can read true directions from the plotter's compass scale.

Bearings can also be plotted with a Quik-Course after correcting from compass to true. (Chapter 17 discusses how to correct.) Place the bull's-eye of the plotter on the sighted object, align the plotter with the meridians and parallels, find the bearing along an edge of the plotter and pencil-mark it. After you remove the Quik-Course from the chart, you can draw in the line from your pencil mark back to the point of the sighted object.

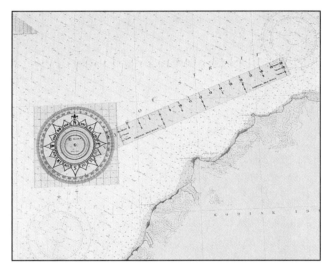

Some navigators prefer to use a course protractor for plotting. The long arm can be moved with respect to the square grid.

Now you have the protractor's compass scale set with the same orientation as the chart's compass rose. Swing the ruler arm until it lies along the direction line that you would like to measure, then read from the point on the protractor compass scale that is aligned with the ruler's edge. That reading is your direction.

If you are working in true, you might also use the grid that is printed on the protractor to align the compass scale against a meridian or a parallel of latitude. Note, however, that only on a Mercator chart can you rely on this grid alignment.

Naturally, if you are laying down a particular direction, rather than measuring the direction of an existing line, you would align the protractor in the same way, then swing the arm to the particular direction and pencil the line against the ruler.

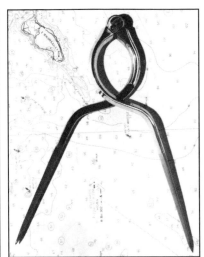

The three styles of dividers are shown at left. When using the type at far left, friction at the pivot holds the arms to the desired opening. Another type *(center)* uses an adjustable center cross-arm to maintain the separation. When using traditional "one-hand" dividers *(near left)*, squeeze the lower part to close, the upper part to open.

Using drafting triangles

Before leaving the subject of direction measurement, mention should be made of the simplest and most readily available plotting tools—a pair of plastic triangles known as draftsman's triangles, usually one 45°- 45° and the other 30°- 60°.

You can move parallel lines around the chart with two triangles. Lay them both on your chart with their long edges (their hypotenuse edges) meeting, and slide them around together until the long side of one of them lies on your direction line; hold one square firm and slide the other against it. Although it takes some practice to do this well, the method works. To move your parallel line any great distance across the chart, you might have to lift one triangle and reposition it above or below the other. Match the longer of the two sides

that meet in a right angle rather than the hypotenuse, hold it firmly and flip the other one to a new position, then continue your slide and shuffle.

Measuring distance on a chart

Although distance to an object can be measured directly by radar, and distance traveled can be measured directly by a summing log or knotmeter, many recreational boats have neither of these items of equipment.

A hand-held optical rangefinder can be used to measure distance to an object up to a thousand yards or so. Most often in piloting, however, distances are measured by taking them from a chart.

Distance is measured on a chart with a pair of dividers. There are three kinds of dividers. The most common is two straight legs with pins at the feet and a friction fit at the hips. The second looks more like a draftsman's compass—it has a threaded rod across the legs, like the bar on the letter "A," so that the distance between the pins can be set and held. This is useful for setting a standard unit, such as a mile, on a particular chart's graphic distance scale, or latitude scale, and holding onto that setting reliably.

The third is the more elegant navigator's dividers with their curved and crossed legs arranged so that you can open and close the distance between the pins with one hand by squeezing either at the top or the bottom.

The points between which you want to measure a distance may lie on your chart within the span of your dividers. If that is the case, place one divider pin on each point, then move the dividers, maintaining the spread, to the graphic distance scale on your chart.

Although your inclination might be to put one pin on the zero position of the scale and then see where the other pin falls to read a distance, a more accurate method exists as follows: Choose a point on the scale that marks a whole number of units and allows the span of the dividers to fall within the part of the graphic scale to the left of zero. You will note that

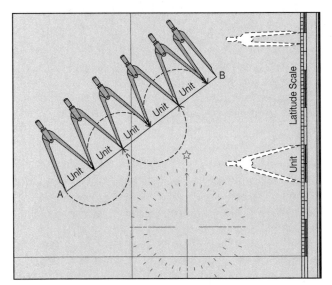

When a chart distance is too great to be measured with a single setting of the dividers, open the points to a convenient whole number of units. Step these along the chart for the required number of times and then measure any small leftover distance in the usual manner.

the left-of-zero part of the scale is marked with subdivisions of the basic scale unit—these subdivisions may be tenths of a mile, hundreds of yards or meters. Your distance is the sum of the whole units to the right of zero and the fractional units to the left.

It is more often the case, however, that the two points on the chart do not fall within the span of the dividers. (About 60 degrees is the widest practical opening.) In this case, set the dividers to an opening that spans a convenient number of whole units on the chart's graphic scale or the latitude scale at the side margin. Step the dividers along the line whose distance you are measuring by swinging one leg past the other as you set the pins alternately on the line. Although you have probably penciled the line first, it is also possible to step the dividers along a straightedge. Count the steps. Then pick up the remainder of the distance by adjusting the dividers to that span and comparing it with the graphic distance scale or the latitude scale.

An important caution is needed here: When you use the latitude scale on a Mercator chart for measuring distances, always use the part that is on the same horizontal plane as the area of the chart on which you are measuring. As you will recall from Chapter 18, parallels of latitude on a Mercator projection are spaced more widely as they approach the poles. Although the effect of this variation may be negligible in most plotting situations, it is a good piloting habit to keep it in mind when doing chartwork.

NOS and DMAHTC charts drawn at a scale smaller than 1:50,000 may not have a graphic scale—distances are always measured from the latitude scales.

A close relation to dividers is the drawing compass. This has the same configuration as dividers with a crosspiece, but one of the pins is replaced with a small pencil. A drawing compass is used to draw circles or arcs in order, for example, to mark a known distance from a given point.

Measuring distances on a chart is also possible with a small metering clock. A tiny wheel is rolled along a line and the meter, with a clocklike face, shows the distance. Accuracy is reduced, even when the wheel is rolled very carefully, but such a chart measurer has distinct advantages when measuring distances along irregular lines such as the course along a river or waterway. Of course, the chart measurer has to be chosen to match the unit desired (statute or nautical miles), and must provide for a range of typical scales. If such a chart measurer does not have a scale to match your chart, use it as described above, then roll it *backwards* along a graphic scale until the indication is zero again, measuring the distance on the graphic scale.

Time

Every pilot on every boat—no matter how small the boat—should know what time it is to within a few minutes. When piloting, it will also be necessary to measure elapsed time to the nearest second.

A stopwatch is useful for measuring elapsed times; it eliminates mistakes that might be made in subtracting clock times.

Electronic digital wristwatches have made this aspect of piloting easy and inexpensive. If you use one, choose a model with a countdown timer and beeper alarm. This will make it much easier to time a planned course change or an anticipated sighting.

A stopwatch or a stopwatch function on your digital wristwatch, as shown above, will help you avoid having to add and subtract times—always a potential source of errors.

If you use a clock, make sure it is easily read from the chart table. A simple kitchen timer is also quite useful for countdown timing.

Speed

Speed used to be calculated by timing the period taken for a floating log (a "chip log") to be passed by the vessel. Once time and distance (the length of the vessel) were known,

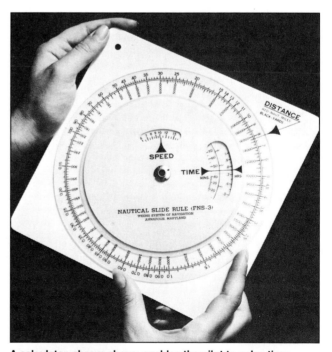

A calculator, shown above, enables the pilot to solve time, speed and distance problems, as well as other conversions or measurements. There are special aids on it for sailors, and a plotting board on the reverse side.

Shown are basic tools for piloting: a high quality, waterproof binocular, hand bearing compass, powerful searchlight, flashlight with magnifying glass, pencil and eraser.

speed could be worked out. Antique stores sometimes display taffrail (or patent) logs, which once measured distance traveled by spinning an impeller in the ship's wake at the end of a line and recording revolutions on a meter. Now, on low-speed boats, an impeller reports its revolutions to an electronic counter, and we read speed directly from a dial or digital display. High-speed boats use a pitot tube in which flow pressure varies with speed.

All of these methods give a more or less accurate reading for speed through the water—which often is much different from speed over the bottom, or "speed made good."

Speed made good (SMG) is calculated using the distance between two points and the time that the boat takes to travel from one to the other.

The arithmetic, which is covered later in this chapter, is simple, but many pilots prefer to make their speed calculations by means of a slide rule. A calculator is especially handy for solving speed-time-distance problems when you need to convert from one unit system to another at the same time. Some calculators are linear, like logarithmic slide rules, and others are circular, such as the one shown on page 435.

Depth measuring tools

Depth can be measured manually or electronically. A lead line (pronounced "led line") consists of a shaped weight on the end of a marked line. It is simple, accurate and reliable, but awkward to use and inconvenient. A lead line can produce only a couple of readings each minute and it is of use only if the boat is traveling very slowly, or if depths are being checked around an anchored boat.

Electronic depth sounders are very common even on small boats. They are convenient, accurate and produce such frequent soundings that they can easily generate a continuous bottom curve.

Pencils

The most important plotting tool is the pencil (with a good eraser). Choose a lead that is hard enough not to smudge, but soft enough to avoid scoring the chart paper. The HB grade, or Number 2, is a good choice. Sharpen several pencils at once and keep them handy. A mechanical pencil is also ideal—use one with a 0.5 mm lead. Your eraser should be the kind used in drafting; an art gum eraser works well for general chart cleaning.

Choosing a binocular

A good quality binocular is essential for piloting. Remember that boating binoculars have to strike a compromise between magnification power and the field of vision. A large field of vision makes it easier to find an object while the boat is in violent motion—just the time when you are most anxious to find that object.

Binoculars are described by two numbers: The first indicates the power of magnification and the second is the diameter of the front lens in millimeters—a 7 x 50 binocular enlarges image size seven times and has a 50 mm front lens. The size of the front lens is an important consideration because a large lens gathers more light and is the main factor in determining how well the optics will brighten your night vision. Most experienced boaters find that a 7 x 50 binocular is the best choice.

Binoculars may be individually focused (IF) for each eye, or centrally focused (CF) for both eyes, with a minor adjustment on one eyepiece to balance any difference between a person's two eyes. Both types are fine for marine use; choice is based on personal preference.

As pointed out above, some binoculars have an integrated compass to be used in place of a hand bearing compass and others have both a compass and an optical device for measuring heights.

Keep your binocular in its case when it is not in use and make sure the strap is around your neck when you are using it. Avoid allowing the binocular to slide off a surface and drop—even one armed with a rubber housing can still be seriously harmed by a hard jolt.

Flashlights

Keep several flashlights (as well as extra batteries) handy in different locations aboard your boat. At least one flashlight should have a red filter on the lens so that it can be used for reading charts at night (red illumination preserves night vision). There are also hand-held chart magnifiers available with internal red lights; these are excellent for picking up chart detail quickly and easily.

Every pilot has a favorite set of plotting tools; no doubt you will develop your own kit of essential items. Don't be concerned with choosing the "right" or the "best" tool—choose the tools with which you feel confident and learn to use them intuitively.

PRECISION AND ACCURACY

In considering the measurement of various quantities in piloting and the calculations within which they are used, you must also consider the appropriate standards of accuracy and precision. In everyday language these terms are often used as if they meant the same thing; however, they don't. In piloting you must make very specific use of each term and understand the difference between them.

The term "precision" describes the degree of fineness of a measurement. It helps answer the question, how small are the units we are going to use? Accuracy, on the other hand, describes the amount of difference we are willing to accept between the quantity with which we work and the quantity that we accept as being true. It answers the question, how close is good enough?

Remember that a measurement can be precise (expressed with a fine standard of precision), but it can also be inaccurate. Take a simple statement of distance as an example. A notation of a distance as "32 miles" has a very different meaning from the notation "32.0 miles." The first statement means that the distance is not 31 miles, nor is it 33 miles. The second statement means that the distance is neither 31.9 nor 32.1 miles. If you write 32.0 miles, you should make sure that the measurement, however accurate it may be, was made to that particular standard of precision.

■ **Direction.** A small boat is seldom steered closer than 2 or 3 degrees to its intended course, so it is unnecessary to measure or calculate directions to a degree of precision finer than a whole degree. Direction in small-craft piloting (and navigation generally) is stated to the nearest whole degree.

■ **Distance.** A tenth of a nautical mile is about 200 yards, and that is close enough for most piloting. Distances are normally expressed to the nearest tenth of a mile.

■ **Time.** Normally, the nearest minute is precise enough for measures of time. The exception would be piloting contests where fractions of a minute are significant and time is usually expressed in decimal fractions.

■ **Speed.** Speed is seldom measurable to units as fine as tenths of a knot or tenths of a mile per hour. But calculation to the nearest tenth is consistent with measures of distance. Current velocity is also expressed to the nearest tenth of either a knot or a mile per hour.

■ **Position.** Geographic coordinates are expressed to the nearest tenth of a minute of latitude and longitude, or to the nearest second, as determined by the scale of the chart. As explained in Chapter 18, latitude and longitude markings are subdivided into minutes and seconds on the larger-scale charts (1:49,000 and larger) and in fractions of minutes on smaller-scale charts (1:50,000 and smaller).

Don't be misled by the displays of Loran and GPS receivers; most models display latitude and longitude to a finer degree of precision than is warranted by the radionavigation system that is being used.

■ **Depths and heights of tides.** Tidal variations in the depth of water are normally tabulated to the nearest tenth of a foot (or meter); calculations are carried out to the same degree of precision. However, you should remember that the unpredictability of the effects of winds and atmospheric pressure make this degree of precision unwarranted.

ROUNDING NUMBERS

In this chapter, the phrase "to the nearest..." appears frequently. Rounding is often used to reduce various quantities to such limitations. For example, if you were to make a distance calculation with a speed of 13 knots and a time of 5 minutes, you would get 1.08333 miles on most calculators. However, since distance is normally stated to the nearest tenth of a mile, the proper expression for your distance would be 1.1 miles, which is arrived at by using the process of "rounding off" described in detail below.

Any mathematical expression of quantity has a certain number of "significant figures." The quantity 4 has one significant figure, while 4.2 and 14 each have two significant figures; 5.12, 43.8 and 609 each have three significant figures.

The process of reducing the number of significant figures is called rounding. If uniform results are to be had, rounding must follow the set of rules below:

1 If the digit you wish to round off is 4 or less than 4, simply discard it or change it to 0. To round 8.23, you would simply change it to 8.2; 432 would be 430.

2 If the digit to be rounded is 6 or more than 6, the preceding digit is raised to the next higher value and the rounded digit is dropped or changed to zero. To round 8.27 you would change it to 8.3; 439 would become 440.

3 If the digit to be rounded is 5, round up or down, but round to the nearest even value. To round 8.25, for example, change it to 8.2; 435 should be 440. This last rule may seem inaccurate, but it provides uniform results. When figures rounded in this way are added together and divided by two for averaging, the result will not require more rounding. However, you will note that slightly different figures will result if you use a calculator. When a calculator is set to display a fixed number of decimal places, a 5 will be rounded off to the next higher value—whether that value is odd or even.

4 Rounding is often applied to more than one final digit, but it must be applied all in one step. For example, do not round 6148 to 6150 and then round 6150 to 6200—instead, round 6148 in one step to 6100.

DEAD RECKONING

You should always have at least a rough idea of your boat's location on the chart. The set of skills used in arriving at this position is dead reckoning, abbreviated as DR.

Dead reckoning is the advancement of the boat's position on the chart from its last accurately determined location, using the course steered, the speed through the water and the elapsed time. Note that no allowances are made for the effects on the boat's position of wind, current, waves or steering error, even when we know that such factors are present and substantial. This may seem strange, but the reason will become apparent in Chapter 20.

Even though much piloting is now done entirely with electronics, dead reckoning is not some relic of nautical folklore—it is an essential part of the navigation of any vessel.

Dead reckoning follows some important conventions for recording information on the chart. The DR track or DR track line is the path that the boat would be expected to follow, or is believed to be following, without any adjustment except for the offsetting influences mentioned above. The DR track line is drawn from the last known position using courses and distances through the water.

"Course," abbreviated C, is the intended direction in which the boat is steered—in other words, the direction of travel through the water. Courses should be plotted as true directions; remember to use leading zeros as necessary to make a three-digit value, and to add a "T" following it.

"Heading" is different from course; heading is the direction in which the boat is actually pointing and is not necessarily the direction in which it is traveling through the water. For example, a sailboat sailing upwind will typically have a heading that varies from its course by an angle of 2 or 3 degrees. Heading is often given in terms of magnetic or compass direction, and the values are not usually part of the plot.

"Speed," abbreviated S, is the rate of travel through the water. This DR track speed is used, along with elapsed time, to determine the DR position along the track line.

Finally, "distance," abbreviated D, may be used with a DR plot to indicate future intended track.

Basic principles

There are three principles of dead reckoning that will keep you out of trouble.

1. A DR track is always started from a known position.
2. Only true courses steered are used for a DR track.
3. Only the speed through the water is used for determining distance traveled and the DR position along the track. (The reason why speed over the bottom is not used is discussed in Chapter 20.)

Why keep a DR track?

A DR track should be kept whenever position fixes are not possible, and especially when aids to navigation and landmarks are not available, or when visibility is poor. You should also keep a DR track whenever there is any possibility of an emergency, and it might suddenly be crucial to report your position to the Coast Guard or another source of assistance. In other words, keeping a DR track is part of safe boating and is almost always important.

The DR track is the primary data on your boat's path, even though it does not actually show your boat's path. Rather, it is the base to which other factors, such as current and steering error, for example, are applied when information from other sources is available.

Plotting standards

Plotting is fundamental to dead reckoning, and standard symbols and labels are fundamental to plotting. Your chartwork should be instantly clear to you and to anyone else who may

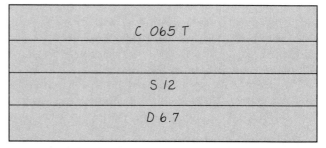

The course is labeled above the line as shown here, with direction as a three-digit number (add zeros as necessary), followed by T, M or C for true, magnetic or compass. Speed is labeled below the line, with the letter S in front of it. Alternatively, distance may be shown below the course line, with the designator D. Note the space between the numbers and the letters.

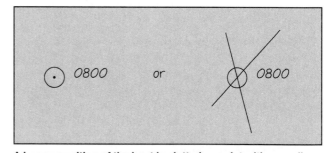

A known position of the boat is plotted as a dot with a small circle around it. If it is at the intersection of two lines, the dot need not be used. Label the position with the time as a four-digit number in the 24-hour system, written horizontally.

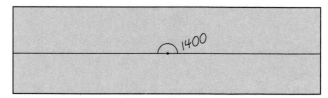

A DR position along a track is plotted as a half-circle around the point on the line. Add the time in the same manner as for a known position, except that it is not written horizontally.

need to refer to the chart. In order to meet that requirement you must be accurate, neat and complete, and you must consistently follow the same style of notation. Your careful observations and readings, made from the wet cockpit of a small bouncing boat, may be worth very little if the notations are not legible. This is more demanding than it first appears, but gets easier with practice.

Avoid crowding your charts with any extra notes or by drawing more lines than are absolutely necessary. When time permits, check your calculations and measurements a second time before finally recording them on the chart. The goal is always to ensure that, if you need to refer to the information many hours later in what might be a difficult situation or adverse conditions, you can arrive confidently and quickly at the right conclusion.

Standard labeling

Draw your plot lines lightly, and no longer than necessary. Offset your straightedge from the intended line just enough to account for the width of the pencil point—your pencil may be quite fine, but such small errors can accumulate and throw off your DR position considerably.

Immediately after placing any line, or any point, on a chart, label it according to the following rules:

■ The label for any line is placed along that line.

■ The label for any point should not be along any line—it should make an angle with the line so that it is clearly referring to the point.

■ The direction label is placed above the track line and has three parts: the letter C for "course," a three-digit direction, and the letter T or M or C, for true, magnetic or compass respectively. Note that the degree symbol (°) and period are not needed.

■ Speed along the DR track is indicated with a label placed under the track line, usually immediately below the direction. Use the letter S along with a number. Units, knots or miles per hour are omitted.

■ A known position at the beginning of the DR track, which is called a fix, is shown simply as a dot with a circle around it. A fix can also be marked with a circle around the point of intersect of two or more bearings or lines of position. This circle (and dot) symbol is labeled with the exact time, placed horizontally next to it.

■ A DR position, calculated as a distance along the track at the set speed through the water, is shown as a half-circle (with a dot) along the track line. It is labeled with the time placed at an angle to the course line, not horizontally. This particular convention distinguishes the DR label both from a fix label and from a line label.

■ When plotting a planned run from a known position to another, speed may not be known in advance, as it is often affected by sea conditions. In this case, distance (D) may be labeled below the track line in lieu of speed. Units of distance are not shown.

There are other symbol and labeling conventions that will be covered as the need arises in later chapters.

Lines on your chart should be erased when they are no longer needed, but erase lightly and carefully to preserve the surface of the chart paper. On the other hand, chart notations made in previous years can sometimes remain useful—an additional reason why they should be clearly notated.

D, T and S calculations

As mentioned earlier, calculations involving distance (D), time (T) and speed (S) are often made using a small calculator, but you should also be able to make your calculations accurately and quickly without relying on one, using only a simple set of equations and ordinary arithmetic. The three basic equations are:

$$D = ST \qquad S = \frac{D}{T} \qquad T = \frac{D}{S}$$

Where D is distance in miles, T is time in hours, and S is speed in knots or miles per hour as determined by the type of mile being used. Note carefully that T is in hours in these basic equations. To use time in minutes, as is more normally the case, the equations are modified to read:

$$D = \frac{ST}{60} \qquad S = \frac{60D}{T} \qquad T = \frac{60D}{S}$$

Examples of the use of these practical equations may serve to make them clearer:

1. You are cruising at 14 knots; how far will you travel in the next 40 minutes?

$$D = \frac{ST}{60} \qquad D = \frac{14 \times 40}{60} = 9.3 \text{ miles}$$

Note that the calculated answer of 9.33 is rounded to the nearest tenth according to the rule for the degree of precision to be used in stating distance.

2. On one of the Great Lakes it took you 40 minutes to travel 11 miles; what is your speed?

$$S = \frac{60D}{T} \qquad S = \frac{60 \times 11}{40} = 16.5 \text{ mph}$$

3. You have 9½ miles to go to reach your destination; on a broad reach you are sailing at 6.5 knots; how long will it take you to get there?

$$T = \frac{60D}{S} \qquad T = \frac{60 \times 9.5}{6.5} = 88 \text{ minutes}$$

Note again the rounding of results; the calculated answer of 87.6 minutes is used as 88 minutes. In powerboat piloting contests it would probably be used as 87 minutes 36 seconds.

The equations are also usable with kilometers and km per hour. Memorize the three equations for distance, speed and time. Practice using them until you are thoroughly familiar with them, and can get correct answers quickly.

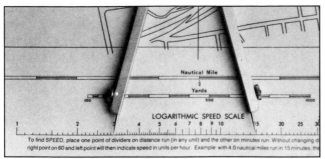
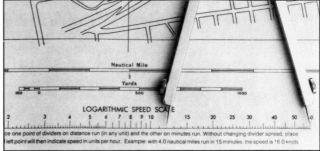

To use a logarithmic speed scale, set one point of the dividers on the scale division indicating miles traveled, and the other on the number corresponding to the time, in minutes. With the dividers maintaining the same spread, transfer them so the right point is on the "60" of the scale; the left point then indicates boat speed in knots or mph.

For short distances, the "Three-Minute Rule" provides a handy calculation of distance. Two zeros added to the speed that you are making in knots gives the distance, in yards, that you will travel in three minutes, to an approximation close enough for practical navigation. For example, if you are traveling at a speed of 10 knots, in 10 minutes you will have covered 1,000 yards, or about half a mile.

Use of logarithmic scale on charts

Charts of the National Ocean Service (NOS) at scales of 1:40,000 and larger have a logarithmic speed scale printed on them. To find speed, place one point of your dividers on the mark on the scale indicating the distance in nautical miles, and the other point on the number corresponding to the time in minutes, as shown above. Without changing the spread between the divider arms, place the right point on the "60" at the right end of the scale; the left point will then indicate on the scale the speed in knots.

The same logarithmic scale can be used to determine the time required to cover a given distance at a specified speed (for situations not exceeding one hour). Set the two divider points on the scale marks representing speed in knots and distance in miles. Move the dividers, without changing the spread, until the right point is at "60" on the scale; the other point will indicate the time in minutes.

Likewise, distance can be determined from this logarithmic scale using knowledge of time and speed. Set the right point of the dividers on "60" and the left point at the mark on the scale corresponding to the speed in knots. Then, without changing the spread, move the right point to the mark on the scale representing the time in minutes; the left point indicates the distance in nautical miles.

The logarithmic scale can be used in exactly the same manner to determine speeds in mph when distances are measured in statute miles.

NOS charts have instructions for determining speed printed beneath the logarithmic scale, but do not explain the procedures for determining distance or time. However, as long as you know two of the time, speed and distance values, you can determine the third.

Use of S-D-T calculators

It is not possible here to give detailed instructions for operating all models of speed-distance-time calculators. In general, they will have two or more scales, each logarithmically subdivided. The calculator will be set using two of the factors and the answer, the third factor, will be read off at an index mark. Refer to page 435.

If you have a calculator for S-D-T problems, read the instructions carefully and practice with it sufficiently, using simple, self-evident problems, to be sure you can get reliable results later, even in emergency situations.

Speed curves

Although some boats now have marine speedometers, the more common method for determining the speed of powerboats involves the use of engine speed as measured by the tachometer in revolutions per minute (rpm). A speed curve can then be prepared as a plot on cross-section (graph) paper, giving the boat's speed, either in knots or mph, for various engine speeds in rpm.

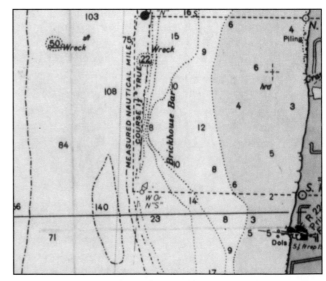

Measured miles are often indicated on charts for the purpose of measuring boat speed.

Factors affecting speed curves

The boat's speed at a specified engine setting may be affected by several factors. The extent of each effect will vary with the size of the boat, type of hull and other characteristics.

Load is a primary factor influencing a boat's speed. The number of people aboard, the amount of fuel and water in the tanks, and the amount and location of other weights on board will affect the depth to which the hull sinks in the water and the angular trim. Both displacement and trim may be expected to have an effect on speed.

Another major factor affecting speed is the underwater hull condition. Fouling growth such as barnacles or moss increases the drag (the resistance to movement through the water), and slows the boat at any speed. Fouling on the propeller itself will drastically affect performance.

Whenever preparing speed data on a boat, note the loading and underwater hull conditions as well as the figures for rpm and speed. If you make a speed curve at the start of the season, when the bottom is clean, check it later in the season if your boat is used in waters where fouling is a problem.

You may need a new speed curve, or you may be able to determine a small correction that can give you a more accurate measure of speed. You should also know what speed differences to expect from tanks that are full to half to nearly empty; the differences can be surprising.

Obtaining speed curves

Speed curves are obtained by making repeated runs over a known distance using different throttle settings and timing each run accurately. You can use any reasonable distance, but it should not be less than a half-mile so that small timing errors will not excessively influence the results; to avoid excessive time and fuel requirements for the trials, it need not be more than a mile.

The run need not be an even half-mile or mile if the distance between the two points is accurately known. Do not depend upon floating aids to navigation—they may be slightly off station and, in any event, they have some scope on their anchor chains and will swing about under the effects of wind and current. Many areas will have measured miles (or half

During the speed trials for *Trident*, described on page 442, the results were tabulated as shown at top. Runs were made in each direction to account for the effect of current. Entries in the boat's log showed its bottom condition, and fuel and water loads aboard. The speed curve at bottom, plotted from this data, is accurate only for load and hull conditions similar to those during the speed trials.

RPM	NORTH – SOUTH		SOUTH – NORTH		AVERAGE	CURRENT
	TIME	SPEED	TIME	SPEED	SPEED	
900	7M 54S	7.60	11M 2.5S	5.26	6.43	1.17
1100	6M 53S	8.72	9M 14.2S	6.50	7.16	1.11
1300	6M 08.8S	9.76	7M 38.6S	7.88	8.82	.94
1500	5M 35.8S	10.72	6M 40.4S	9.86	9.00	.86
1700	5M 10.8S	11.59	5M 54.2S	10.17	10.88	.71
1900	4M 38S	12.96	5M 06.4S	11.76	12.36	.60
2150	3M 48.6S	15.65	4M 05.6S	14.73	15.24	.51

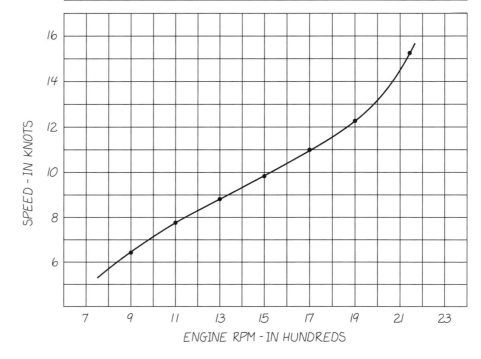

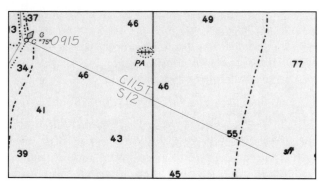

A dead reckoning plot is started when leaving a known position. This is plotted as a fix, with the time; course and speed are labeled along the DR track.

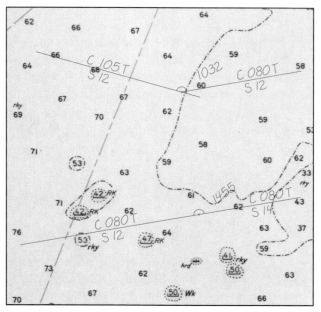

Whenever a change in course is made, a DR position is plotted for that time; the new course and speed are labeled along the new DR track. If a variation is made in speed without a change in direction, a DR position is plotted for the time of the change, and new course and speed labels are entered following it.

miles), as shown on the chart on page 440. These are accurately surveyed distances with each end marked by ranges. Use these courses whenever possible; they are accurate, and calculations are made considerably easier with the even-mile distance. But do not let the absence of a measured mile keep you from making a speed curve. Wharves, fixed aids to navigation or points of land will also give you the accurate distance you require. You need only to measure the distance on the chart between two such points.

In most speed trials you will need to run the known distance twice, once in each direction, in order to allow for the effects of current. Even in waters not affected by currents, you should make round-trip runs for each throttle setting to allow for wind effects.

For each one-way run, measure the time, and steer your boat carefully to make the most direct run. Compute the speed for each run using the equations on page 439, or use purchased tables that give speeds for various elapsed times over a measured mile. If the measured distance is an exact half-mile, just divide the tabulated speeds by two. Then average the speeds of each pair of runs at a given rpm for the true speed of the boat through the water.

The strength of the current is one-half the difference between the speed in the two directions of any pair of runs. Caution: Do not average the times of a pair of runs to get a single time for use in the calculations; this will not produce the correct value for speed through the water.

If time is measured with a regular clock or watch, be careful in making the subtractions to get elapsed time. Remember that there are 60 seconds in each minute, not 100, and likewise 60 minutes in one hour. Most people are so used to decimal calculations that they make errors when "borrowing" in the subtraction of clock times.

If you are willing to use a slightly more complex equation, the boat's speed through the water (or the strength of the current) can be found from a single calculation using the times of the two runs of each pair.

In preparing a speed curve for a boat, make enough pairs of runs to provide points for a plot of speed versus rpm; six or eight points will usually be enough for a satisfactory curve. With some types of hulls, there will be a break in the curve at a critical speed when the hull changes from displacement action to semi-planing action. At this portion of the curve you may need additional, more closely spaced measurements, so it is a good idea to calculate speeds during runs, making a rough plot as you go along.

You may also want to calculate the current's strength for each pair of runs. The current values will probably vary during the speed trials, but the variations should be small and in a consistent direction, either steadily increasing or decreasing, or going through a slack period. You will get the best results by running your trials at a time of minimum current.

Example of a speed curve

A set of speed trials was run for the motor yacht *Trident* over the measured mile off Kent Island in Chesapeake Bay. This is an excellent course as it is marked by buoys offshore as well as by ranges on land. The presence of the buoys aids in steering a straight run from one end of the course to the other; the ranges are used for accuracy in timing.

On this particular day, it was not convenient to wait for slack water, but a time was selected that would result in something less than maximum ebbing current. A table was set up in the log, and runs were made in each direction at practical increments from 900 rpm to 2150 rpm, the maximum for this diesel model.

The results of the runs are shown on page 441. An entry was also made in the log that these trials were made with fuel tanks 0.4 full, the water tanks approximately one-third full, and with a clean bottom. The column of the table marked "Current" is not necessary, but serves as a flag to quickly expose any inconsistent data. Note that on these trials the current is decreasing at a reasonably consistent rate.

After the runs had been completed, a plot was made on graph paper showing the boat's speed as a function of engine rpm. The result is the speed curve shown on page 441.

Dead reckoning plots

With knowledge of dead reckoning terms and principles, the rules for labeling points and lines, and the procedures for making calculations involving distance, time and speed, you can now consider the use of DR plots.

There are several specific rules to keep in mind when making and using DR plots, as listed below.

■ A DR plot should be started when leaving a known position, as shown top left, page 442.

■ A DR position should be indicated whenever a change is made in course, or simply in speed, as shown bottom left, page 442.

■ A DR position should be plotted each hour on the hour (more frequently under conditions of reduced visibility), as shown below.

■ A new DR track should be started each time the boat's position is fixed. The old DR position for the same time as the fix should also be shown at the end of the old DR track, as shown below, lower right.

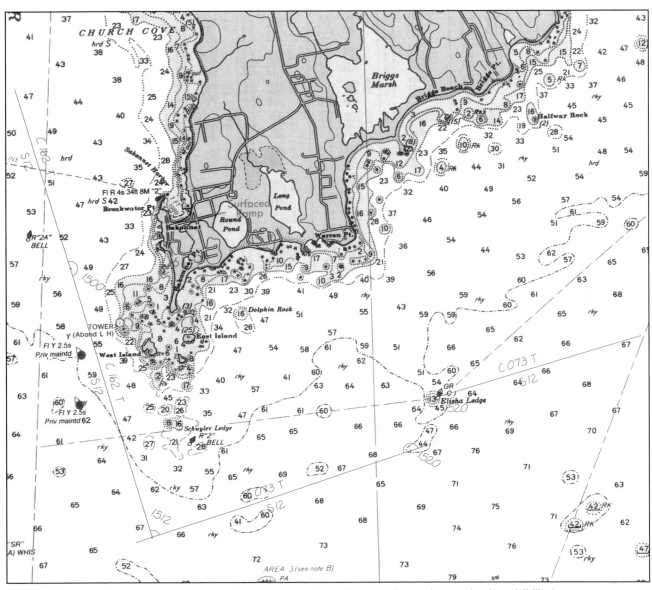

A DR position should be plotted every hour on the hour in normal conditions, and more frequently when visibility is reduced. Start a new DR track whenever the boat's position is fixed. In this example, a fix is obtained when the boat passes alongside a known marker. Label the old DR position for the same time as the fix.

20 POSITION DETERMINATION

Underway on a body of water of any size where the safety of your crew and boat is at stake, it's not "where you ought to be," or "where you think you are," but your knowledge of "where you are for sure" that counts.

The art of piloting reaches its ultimate purpose when you know your exact position. This chapter helps you develop an ability to determine your position quickly and accurately under a wide range of conditions—one of the most essential skills in safe boating.

LINES OF POSITION

It is your duty as skipper to make a careful judgment as to the precision and frequency with which your vessel's position should be fixed, and then to see that these fixes are carefully made and recorded. This is true whether you are doing the piloting or someone else is—you can delegate the function, but not the responsibility.

The actual procedures in position determination may vary widely in practice. When you are proceeding down a narrow channel, positioning is informal and a chart plot may not be maintained. In this case, position determination is not being omitted, rather it is being done continuously by visual reference to the aids to navigation. On the other hand, during an open ocean passage, a dead reckoning plot will be determined only three or four times each day, or even only once a day by noon sights.

Between these two extremes are the normal cruising situations in pilot waters. Cruising just offshore or in larger inland water, a skipper will usually maintain a DR plot of his track with periodic fixes, perhaps every 15 or 20 minutes, perhaps at hourly intervals.

Your ability to determine your position—to fix your position—with appropriate accuracy under any conditions of visibility or sea is essential. Your limitations in these skills must restrict the extent of your boating activities, setting the boundaries of the waters and weather conditions that you will enter deliberately to avoid embarrassing and hazardous situations.

Remember that knowledge of where you are, extended from a recent position determination, is essential if you must call for help. If another boat is in trouble, you can set a direct course to render assistance *only* if you are both certain of each boat's location.

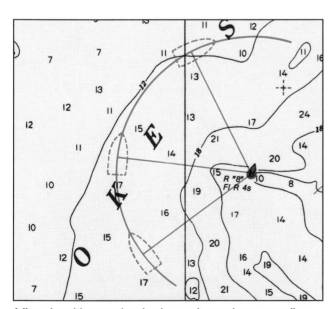

A line of position may be circular, as shown above, as well as straight. A circular LOP results from a measurement of distance from an identified object. Usually it is plotted as an arc through the most likely area of position.

Definitions of terms

■ A line of position (LOP) is a line along which an observer can be presumed to be located. The observer, in the absence of other information, might be anywhere along the LOP. An LOP may result from an observation or measurement—from visual, electronic or celestial sources. It may be straight, or curved. A circular LOP is sometimes called a circle of position. An LOP, in a running fix (defined below), may be "advanced" to a later time according to the movement of the vessel; or, in a rare case, it may be "retired" to a previous time "as needed."

■ A bearing is the direction of an object from the observer. Bearings are expressed in degrees as three-digit numbers—005°, 056°, 157°, etc. A true bearing is a bearing measured with reference to true north. A magnetic bearing is one mea-

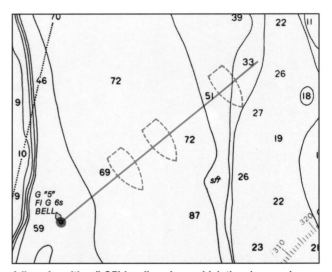

A line of position (LOP) is a line along which the observer is located. Although a single LOP does not determine position, it does tell the observer where the boat is *not* located, and such information can be useful in itself in many situations.

sured with reference to local magnetic north, and a compass bearing is one taken over a compass and affected by the compass deviation at the time it was taken. (Refer to Chapter 17 for a discussion of true, magnetic and compass direction.)

■ A relative bearing is one measured with reference to the vessel's heading. It is measured clockwise from the fore-and-aft line, with 000° as dead ahead, 090° as broad on the starboard beam, and 180° as dead astern, etc.

■ A range consists of two objects that can be observed in line with each other and the observer—all three are on the same straight line.

■ A fix is an accurately located position determined without reference to any assumption of estimation of prior position.

■ A running fix may also be derived from two LOPs, one of which has been advanced (or retarded) from a different time—thus introducing an element of estimation.

■ An estimated position (EP) is the best position obtainable

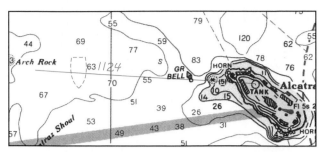

When two objects can be observed in line, the special LOP that results is called a range. It will be labeled only with the time of the observation. Some range objects will have been set up specifically for that purpose, but any identifiable charted objects or features can provide a range.

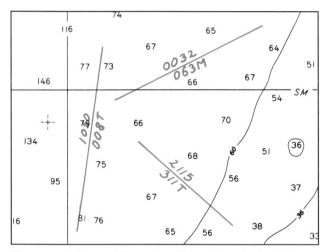

The correct labeling of lines of position is important; unlabeled or mislabeled lines cause confusion. Time is shown above the line in the 24-hour clock system, and direction as a three-digit number below the line.

short of a fix (or running fix). It is the most probable position, determined from incomplete or questionable data relating to course run, speed and drift, etc.

Lines of position

Lines of position are the basic element of position determination. An observer lies somewhere along the length of a line of position. If two lines of position intersect, the observer must be at the intersection—the only place where he can be on both lines at once. A fix is usually determined by crossing two lines of position.

Since LOPs are drawn on charts they should be clearly and consistently labeled as they are drawn. Their labels should identify them completely; extra information can be confusing on a much-used chart. The label must specify the time the LOP was observed or measured and its basic dimension such as direction toward or distance from the reference object.

A bearing is a line of position that has both time and direction. Time is always shown above the line of the bearing and direction below it. Remember to write time as a four-digit figure in the 24-hour system. Specify direction as true (T) or magnetic (M) and write it as a three-digit group with leading zeros as necessary. Take note that the degree symbol (°) is omitted because all three-digit numbers in labels are obviously directions.

A circle of position has dimensions of time and of distance and may be plotted as a complete circle or as an arc. Time is written above the line, and distance (and units of distance) written below.

A range is an LOP whose direction is self-evident from the two points that lie along it. In this case, the label need show only time, which is written above the range line. The line need not be plotted completely through both objects of the range—

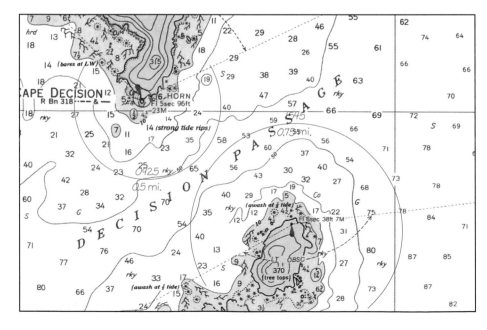

Circles of position are labeled in the same way as lines of position, with time above and distance below. Time may be inside or outside the circle as determined by the curvature of the arc.

draw it only long enough to make clear which two objects define it. This will minimize the need to erase lines drawn over important chart symbols.

An LOP that has been advanced from an older line is labeled with both times above it—the original time first and the time to which it has been advanced, separated by a dash.

Remember to always label your LOPs immediately to avoid mistakes. Unlabeled lines on a chart are a dangerous source of confusion.

Fixes

A fix is an accurately located position. On many occasions in small-craft piloting, position will be determined by passing close by an identifiable object, often an aid to navigation. When such a fix is established, the skipper should note the time on the chart.

A fix that is obtained from lines of position will be the intersection of two or more such lines. Note that the angle of intersection of two LOPs affects the accuracy of the position determination. When two lines cross at right angles (90°), an error of a couple of degrees in one or the other LOP will have only a small effect.

Where LOPs cross at small angles, however, an error in one or both observations or measurements will have far more serious implications.

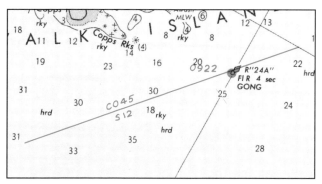

An excellent, yet simple, determination of position occurs when a boat passes close to an aid to navigation or other identifiable point. Note the time on the chart.

Two lines of position should intersect as nearly as possible at right angles and the angle should never be less than 60 degrees if possible.

A fix resulting from LOPs intersecting at angles smaller than 60 degrees may not be a fix at all and should be regarded with doubt.

Even lines that intersect at large angles will cover what are known as areas of uncertainty. While we label our lines with specific directions, we know that there may be an uncertainty in each line of 2 or 3 degrees. If the uncertainty is potentially dangerous, it should be represented graphically by adding two dashed lines on either side of the LOP that define the limits of the inaccuracy. LOPs from various sources will

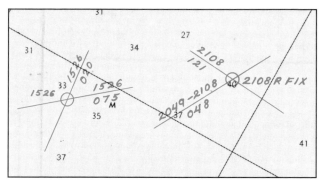

A fix is labeled with the time, but the word "fix" is not used. For a running fix, however, the label "R FIX" is added along with time of the second observation.

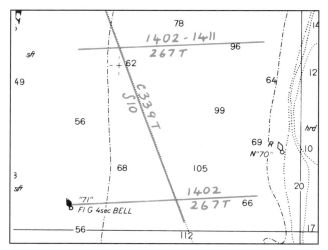

An advanced LOP is labeled with the original time and with the time for which it was replotted. The direction remains the same.

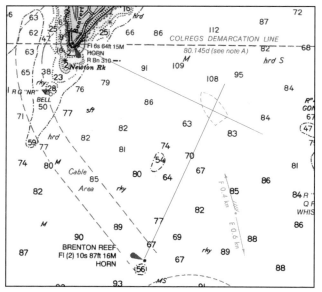

A fix is an accurately determined position for the observer and his or her boat, determined from currently observed lines of position, or other data obtained.

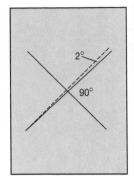
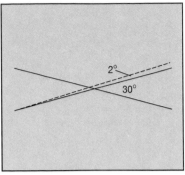

Note the difference a change of two degrees in one LOP makes in the intersection point when the lines cross at 90° *(left)* or at 30° *(right)*.

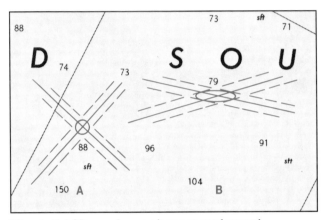

When both LOPs may have an inaccuracy of several degrees, there is a large area of uncertainty around the intersecting point (A). This area grows as the intersection angle narrows. Be very cautious with intersecting angles of 30° or less (B).

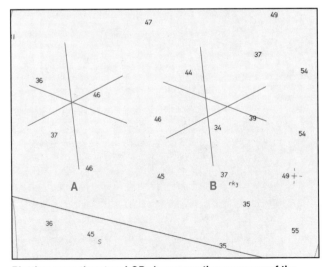

Plotting more than two LOPs increases the accuracy of the resulting fix. If they were perfectly accurate (A), all three would intersect at the same point. However, they will almost always form a small triangle (B).

have different levels of inaccuracy—only an experienced pilot can judge these levels.

If both questionable LOPs are drawn with their dashed lines at the maximum and minimum possible values, the dashed lines will enclose an "area of uncertainty" at their intersection. The area of uncertainty is not the quadrilateral enclosed by the lines, but an elliptical area. (It is circular only if the two LOPs cross at exactly 90 degrees.)

More than two LOPs

Whenever possible, a third line of position should be drawn to reduce the uncertainty. Of course, a fourth and fifth LOP might also be available, but this is seldom the case and almost always unnecessary.

If the observer is on all three lines of position at the same time, then they should all intersect. The more common result is that they nearly intersect and instead of defining a point, they form a small triangle. (Theoretically the three bearings should be taken simultaneously, but in practice they can be taken in sequence as the distance traveled by the boat in this short interval is too small to show up on the chart plot.)

The best result is obtained when all three lines form 60 degree angles. If this is the case, their inherent inaccuracy will have the least effect.

In practice two bearings should be taken promptly, one after the other, spaced as closely as possible to 90 degrees, and a third chosen to split them as evenly as possible.

The triangle that almost always results when three LOPs are plotted is known as the triangle of position. A large triangle suggests a serious inaccuracy in at least one of the LOPs and check should be made on the observation for reading error, deviation, calculation or plotting error.

A small triangle (how small is a relative judgment depending on the proximity of danger) can be "eyeballed" to find its center, and this center used as the fix.

Labeling the fix

A fix is plotted on the chart as a small circle with a dot in its center; the dot should be omitted at the intersection of two LOPs. The word "fix" is not needed, but the circle and dot must have a label, written horizontally, that records the time of the fix. A running fix is shown with the same circle-and-dot symbol, but the label should contain "R Fix" in addition to the time *(page 457).*

When the fix is obtained by passing close by an aid to navigation, the dot may take the place of the dot-and-circle. The usual distance off (50 to 100 yards or meters) is insignificant at most chart scales.

The value of a single LOP

While a fix is typically made with two or more LOPs, don't underestimate the value of a single LOP. Of course, a single LOP cannot tell the skipper where the boat is at the moment, but it can tell him (within its limits of accuracy) where the

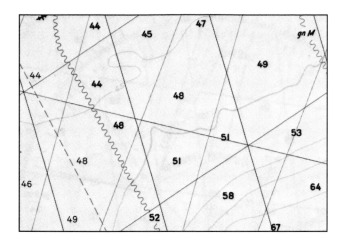

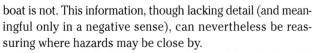

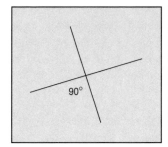
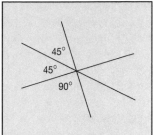

An optimum set of three LOPs cross at 60° *(left)*, but this is seldom possible. Alternatively, you might choose objects whose LOPs will cross at 90° (or as near as possible to 90°), ensuring a good fix, and add a third LOP at about 45° as insurance if there is time and a suitable object for the third observation.

boat is not. This information, though lacking detail (and meaningful only in a negative sense), can nevertheless be reassuring where hazards may be close by.

Further, a single LOP can often be combined with a DR position to obtain a useful EP (estimated position). This EP is the position along the LOP that is closest to the DR position for the same time that the LOP was observed. To obtain such an EP, draw a line from the DR position, perpendicular to the LOP until the lines intersect. An EP is marked with a square. A square is used exclusively for EPs, so the label does not have to say "EP." Time may also be omitted because it is the same as the time that appears on the LOP or at the DR position.

It is also possible to obtain an "EP with current." This requires an estimate of the set and drift of the current, either from predictions or from accurate measurements of the effects of the current on the boat's course and speed made good.

From the DR position for the specified time, an EP with current would be obtained as follows: A line is drawn representing the effect of the current during the time period since the DR track was started from the last fix. The line is drawn in the direction of the set of the current and to a length equal to the total drift. (The length of the line would be drift multiplied by the elapsed time since the last fix.) This total drift line is labeled, and from its end another line is drawn to intersect the LOP at a right angle (just as in a regular EP plot). The intersection obtained is your EP with current.

Running fixes, and the use of a single LOP with depth measurements, will be discussed later in this chapter.

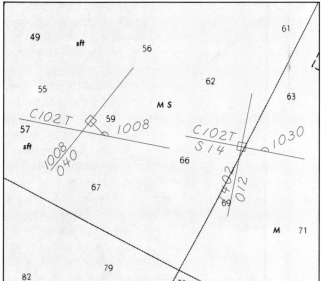
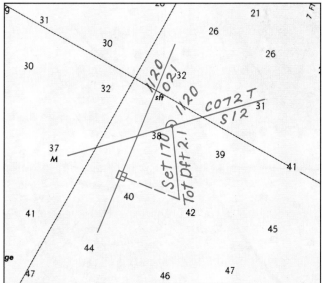

An estimated position *(left)* can be obtained from a single LOP. It is the point on the LOP closest to the DR position for that time; see A. If a beam bearing is used, as at B, the EP will fall along the DR track. If information about the current is available, an improved "estimated position with current" can be plotted *(right)*. The offsetting effect of the current since the start of the DR track is calculated and plotted; the nearest point on the LOP from this current-influenced point is the EP.

VISUAL OBSERVATIONS

In typical small-craft navigation, the primary source of lines of position will be visual observation. Observations will include bearings, ranges and even horizontal and vertical angle measurements. Correct identification is essential. Although other methods and other equipment such as radio direction finders, radar electronics bearing lines and depth measurements may also provide LOPs, these will normally be secondary to your visual observation.

The aids to navigation depicted on charts comprise a system consisting of fixed and floating objects with varying degrees of reliability. A prudent boater, therefore, will not rely on any *single* aid to navigation, especially a floating aid, to fix his position.

If the pilot has a choice of objects to sight for bearings, he should select the nearer ones provided they will make good intersection angles on the plot. The reason is that a measured angular inaccuracy, if one exists, will be the same whether the object is near or far. However, the linear inaccuracy will be amplified as the LOP is extended over a greater distance. For example, an angular error of one degree extended to one mile will result in an error of about 100 feet. At two miles, the error will double. In a case where a light is being

observed at night over a distance of a dozen miles, a one-degree error is potentially quite serious.

Perhaps the simplest and most accurate visual observation is a bearing taken dead ahead and read from the vessel's steering compass. The movement needed to swing the boat off course to line it up on an object is rarely important to the DR track since the boat is held on the heading just long enough for the boat to be lined up and for the compass to settle down and be read—perhaps only 20 or 30 seconds. Of course, this is somewhat more difficult on a sailboat because the dead-ahead alignment from the helm is more likely to be obscured by rigging.

The skipper must be sure of his general location and of surrounding traffic so that the off-course swing can be made

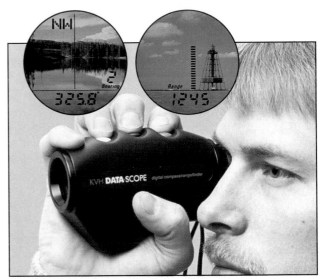

Today's range finders include the model shown above, which displays bearing *(inset, left)*, range *(inset, right)* and time information in your field of view.

safely. This is a quick, accurate and simple way to get a bearing, and has the additional advantage that it can be accomplished by the helmsman alone.

If the observed object on which the bearing is to be taken is on the beam, a swing off course to line it up with the bow may not be feasible. Perhaps the limited width of the channel, or other vessels, restrict such a deviation from the DR track. In this case, choose some part of the boat that will give you an accurate right angle from the centerline. This might be the line of bulkhead, a point on the cabin top lined up with the top of a stanchion, etc. While the helmsman maintains course on the DR track, wait until the object comes into view along this line. Such sights will determine when the object is dead abeam—either 090 or 270.

If waiting until the object comes abeam is not feasible or desirable, then the heading of the craft can sometimes be temporarily altered slightly to bring the sighted object on the beam more quickly. Should such a temporary change of head-

A rough bearing can be taken from the boat's steering compass. The observer would place his eye near the level of the compass and sight across the card, lining up the object with the lubber's line and the pivot post.

ing be made, be sure that the 90 degrees is added to or subtracted from the compass reading at the moment the sighted object is abeam; do not use the normal base course.

It is extremely important to note that any of these bearings taken from the steering compass is a compass bearing and, as such, is subject to both deviation and variation. If you are to plot them as true bearings, you will have to correct for both (*Chapter 17*).

In the case of the 90-degree adjustment for sightings abeam remember that 90 degrees must be added or subtracted after the compass reading has been corrected for deviation (and for variation) because, while variation will be the same on any heading, deviation will differ from one heading to another. The deviation is found on the deviation table opposite the boat's heading (because deviation varies with heading), not opposite the direction for the bearing.

Plotting bearings

The direction measured for a bearing is from the boat toward the object. When the plot is being done, the position of the boat is not yet known, but it is still possible to draw the bearing line of position so that it will have the correct direction and will lead to or through the point on the chart that locates the object.

It is also possible to plot a line outwards from the position of the sighted object toward the observer's position by using a reciprocal of the corrected bearing. If this method is being used, be sure to correct the bearing for deviation (as well as for variation, just to be consistent) before converting it to a reciprocal by adding or subtracting 180 degrees.

Avoid magnetic plotting

It is also possible to convert bearings to magnetic and to plot them as magnetic directions using the magnetic circle of the compass rose on the chart. However, this conversion is not recommended because it requires that all directions be plotted as magnetic—courses, ranges and currents. A less confusing plot will result if you become accustomed to plotting in true directions.

Bearings without changing heading

Getting a bearing, either dead ahead or abeam, may not always be safe or convenient, especially under sail. Of course, bearings can also be taken without changing the boat's heading. Such bearings may involve the boat's steering compass, a hand bearing compass or a pelorus.

On many boats, it may be possible to take a bearing in most directions by sighting over the steering compass. Sometimes the accuracy of such a bearing is increased by the use of sighting vanes placed over the compass, but usually the sighting can be taken across the card itself. Once again, be sure that you correct for deviation and variation, and that you use the deviation value appropriate to the boat's heading, not the direction of the bearing.

Using a hand bearing compass

Very often, visual bearings are made with a hand bearing compass. While such a compass is also vulnerable to deviation, the usual practice is to choose a location on board that is sufficiently distant from magnetic influences that a deviation correction is not needed. Some practice might be required to find a spot that is clear of obstruction, provides a secure platform and is free from magnetic influence. (Remember, the metal frame of your glasses, the grommet in your cap and the batteries in the flashlight you may be using to illuminate the card can affect the compass.) Once you have avoided magnetic influences you need only correct the hand bearing reading for variation to obtain a true bearing for plotting.

Using a pelorus

A pelorus is also used to obtain bearings, usually as relative bearings. A pelorus can be used anywhere that the object is clearly in view and where the pelorus card can be accurately aligned with the boat's fore-and-aft axis. In practice this might mean predetermining two or three convenient positions on deck.

Although the pelorus card can be adjusted (after fore-and-aft alignment) to the boat's compass heading, and sights made directly as compass bearings, this is less desirable than using the pelorus to read relative bearings, as described next. In all cases, the compass bearings must be converted to true bearings before plotting.

Relative bearings

To take a relative bearing with a pelorus, the pelorus scale is set with 0° dead ahead. The helmsman is alerted and requested to steer a steady course, reading the compass continuously. Before the pelorus observation is made the reader calls "Stand by," and as it is made, the reader calls "Mark."

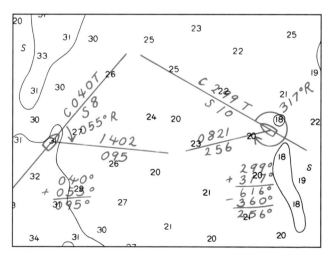

Relative bearings must be converted to true bearings before they are plotted. The relative bearing is added to the boat's true heading at the instant of the observation. If the sum exceeds 360 degrees, subtract 360.

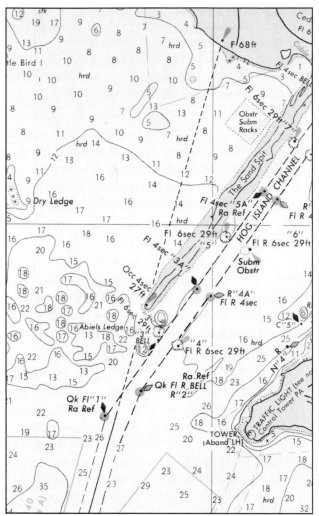

Caution must be exercised when following a range because there is always a limit to the extent of safe water. The range line on the chart will be solid where it lies within the channel, and dashed when it lies outside the channel. Sometimes buoys mark the beginning and end of a range-marked channel.

At his call, the helmsman notes the reading on the steering compass and calls it out to the recorder. If the steering compass reading has not been accurate, the pelorus reading must be discarded. If it is very difficult to steer a steady course, the helmsman can call "Mark" each time he is confident of an accurate reading. The pelorus reader makes his observation at each "Mark."

The relative bearing that is obtained by either pelorus technique, or by simply sighting along a 90-degree line must be corrected to true for plotting. First the compass reading is corrected for deviation and variation, then the pelorus (or sighted) reading is added. (If the result exceeds 360, then 360 is subtracted.)

Once again, avoid a common error: Always be sure to use the deviation value appropriate to the boat's heading—not the bearing direction.

Let's look at a couple of examples, shown on page 450: In the first case, an observer is on a boat which is heading 040T and takes a relative bearing on a buoy at 055°. To determine the true bearing of this buoy, simply add the two numbers, 40 + 55 = 95, so the bearing is 095 T.

Here's a more complicated example: A boat is heading 303 C when a relative bearing of 317° is measured. The variation for this location is 6°W and the deviation for this particular compass at 303° is 2°E. Convert the boat's heading to true this way: 303 – 6 + 2 = 299°. The sum of the relative bearing and the true heading is 317 + 299 = 616. Subtract 360 and the true bearing is 256°.

Ranges

Lines of position from ranges are of exceptional value in position determination. They are free from all of the magnetic effects that might cause errors in bearings taken with reference to a compass (whether sighted on the bow or across the boat, or taken with a pelorus).

LOPs from ranges are also much more easily obtained than bearings. No matter how small the boat, or how rough the weather, if you can see both objects, you can line them up with absolute accuracy. The accuracy of your LOP then depends only on the accuracy of the range locations on the chart. You now have half of a very accurate fix.

Ranges fall into two groups. First, there are those that consist of two aids to navigation constructed specifically to serve as a range and are charted with special symbols. The direc-

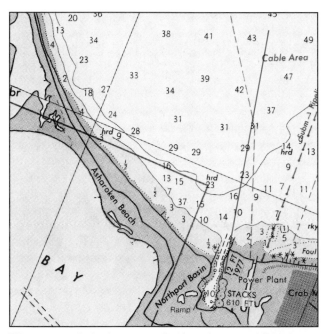

Pilots are not limited to ranges that have been established specifically as aids to navigation—many natural and man-made features are excellent incidental ranges. For example, these four stacks at Northport, Long Island, provide a range that is within a degree of magnetic south.

tion of such a range can be measured from the chart, but is better determined from information in the *Light List*. However, any two objects can be identified and located on the chart such as ordinary aids to navigation, spires, towers, radio towers, stacks, the center of bridges and even clearly demarcated edges of natural features. Be careful using natural features because shoreline edges may change with changes in water level and exact points may be hard to determine.

Taking an LOP from a range requires no more than the observation of the time when your boat comes into alignment with the two objects. The LOP is plotted by lining up the symbols with a straight edge and drawing a light, solid line over the portion of the chart where your DR track or other LOP is likely to cross. The actual direction will not ordinarily be noted, but it should be labeled with the time as soon as it is drawn. The range LOP can be crossed with another range or an LOP from any other source. If none is available at the time of alignment, the range line of position can be advanced at a later time and used as part of a running fix. In this case, the direction should be noted so that the advanced line can be related to the original and easily labeled.

The United States Coast Guard, and other authorities, often establish ranges to indicate the center of a hazardous narrows, dredged channel or simply an important waterway, especially if there are strong currents to contend with. Such a range line is printed on the chart, and it is often used for direct steering rather than as an LOP. However, two cautions are needed: First, a vessel traveling in the opposite direction on the range will be on a collision course. Second, a range can be followed for too great a distance into dangerous waters. Buoys will often mark the limits of such a range, but study your chart carefully to determine when to turn off a range in order to avoid danger.

Horizontal angles

Another way to obtain good LOPs without having to correct for compass error is to measure two horizontal angles. Often these two angles can be taken from three objects identifiable on the chart. A sextant, normally used to measure vertical angle in celestial navigation, can easily be read sideways to a very high degree of accuracy.

Horizontal angles can be plotted with a three-arm protractor. The two measured angles are set on the outer arms in relation to the center arm. The protractor is moved about on the chart, several positions being tried, until one allows all three arms to intersect the locations of the sighted objects, the edge of each arm representing a line of position. The center of the protractor (the apex of both angles) is the position of the observer. You plot it by placing a pencil point through a hole.

The same plot can be accomplished very easily with tracing paper. After drawing the angles on the tracing paper, they are moved around in the same way until all three are intersecting the locations of their respective objects.

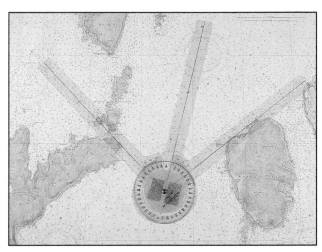

A three-arm protractor is a special plotting instrument for finding a position with horizontal angles. The angles are carefully set on the protractor, then it is moved around on the chart until the arms lie over their respective objects.

Be careful when selecting the three objects to be observed; if they and the boat all lie on the circumference of a circle, no fix can be obtained. When you study the diagram on page 454, you will see three sighted objects—X, Y and Z—and an observer at both A and at B. Both observations will give the same angle values, and will do the same almost anywhere between X and Z.

This situation, known as a "revolver," can occur if the center object sighted is farther away from the observer than the other two. By selecting three objects so that they are essentially in line, or that the center one is closer to the observer, you can avoid an indeterminate situation.

A revolver should be avoided, but if one does develop it can be made determinate by the addition of another LOP, such as a single bearing on one of the three objects, or on any other point.

The geographic coordinates of a position can be calculated from the known latitude and longitude of the three objects and the measured angles between them, but the complexity of the mathematics makes the use of a calculator or microcomputer program necessary.

Using horizontal angle with a radius

A fix can also be determined from lines of position derived from two horizontal angles that may or may not share a common point. Each angle can be used to establish a circle of position.

Consider one angle at a time. There is a circle which contains both of the objects sighted upon (in measuring the horizontal angle) as well as the observer. The radius of this circle can be calculated using the distance between the sighted objects.

Here's how to proceed. First, measure the distance between the two sighted objects on the chart. Find the sine of the measured horizontal angle using your calculator or a trigonometric table from *Bowditch*. Next, multiply the sine by two and use that product to divide the distance between the objects. This is the radius of the circle on which your boat and all the sighted objects lie. (It's easy enough to find with a calculator.)

The next step is graphical. Set a pair of dividers (or a drafting compass) to that radius (on the chart scale), and scribe two intersecting arcs, one centered on one object and one on the other. That intersection is the center of the circle along which your boat and the two sighted objects lie, so put the compass point there and scribe as much of the circular LOP as you think you need.

Do the same procedure on your second set of objects. You now have two circular LOPs and you are at their intersection. (Actually, if you were to draw very long circular LOPs, there would be two intersections, but common sense or a third LOP will tell you which one is your position.)

While this procedure sounds complex, it is actually quite useful, especially aboard a boat in circumstances where the compass bearing is very hard to read because of rough weather. A simple plastic sextant and an appropriate calculator are quite inexpensive. You may also find this an interesting sampling of the sextant in more advanced navigating techniques.

Vertical angles

All of the points (in a plane) that are a particular distance from an object lie in a circle—the distance is the radius of a circle. Such distances are often found by measuring the vertical angle from the bottom to the top of a known height, then using a simple trigonometric formula. For this reason, the

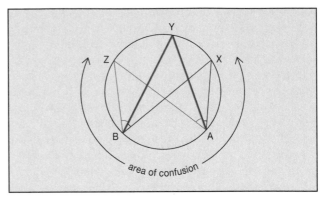

In a revolver situation, regardless of your position between **X** and **Z**, you will read the same angles if you happen to be on the circumference along with the sighted objects, **X, Y and Z.**

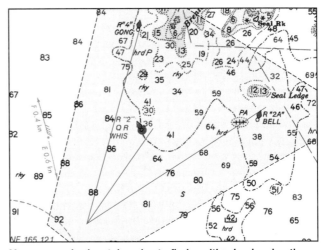

You can use horizontal angles to find position by drawing them on tracing paper. Move the paper around on the chart until the lines intersect the objects that were sighted. The apex is the position at the time the measurements were made.

heights of many man-made and natural features are carefully measured and recorded on your chart.

Such features include towers, lighthouses (usually measured to the light, not the top of the tower so as to be useful at night), radio towers and bridges.

Before you use such a recorded height, determine whether it has been measured from the base of the object or from some standard datum plane such as mean high water. Frequently, a correction will be required depending on the tidal level at the time of the observation *(Chapter 15)*.

Using a sextant, or some other device for measuring sighted angles, get an accurate measure of the angle from bottom (water level or base) to top. Call this angle "A" and the known height "h." The distance "d" can be calculated as: $d = h / \tan A$.

Again, use *Bowditch* or a calculator to find the tangent.

There are also specialized optical range finders, like the one shown on page 450, that are adjusted to provide a reading from a scale.

A sextant, such as the one shown above, is usually used for measuring vertical angles in celestial navigation, but it can also be used in piloting for measuring horizontal or vertical angles to calculate distance off.

Danger bearings and angles

Safety can often be ensured without a complete fix. As noted opposite, a single LOP has value—it can tell you where you are not. In many situations, a line of position can be chosen that will keep a boat in safe waters without defining its position.

A bearing line can be chosen that will divide a safe area from an unsafe area. If you stay on the correct side of such a line, your vessel will be safe, while crossing such a line will invite danger. Take the example shown at right: A shoal is indicated on the chart, but not marked by any aid to navigation. A lighthouse can be observed on shore and can be identified on the chart just beyond the shoal. The danger bearing is indicated, therefore, by a line that extends from the lighthouse toward your vessel tangent to the shoal. This line is drawn on the chart and its direction is measured. The line is labeled with the direction preceded by the letters "NMT" for "not more than," or "NLT" for "not less than." Time is not included in the label because this is not an observed line. You might add hachures or use a red pencil to emphasize the line's importance.

As the vessel approaches the area, a series of observations is made on the lighthouse (or whatever object was chosen). It should be beyond the danger area and on the same side of the boat. If the shoal lies to port, then any bearing greater than the danger bearing indicates trouble. If the hazard were to starboard, the opposite would apply.

Danger bearings are not always possible. They require a prominent object (which could be natural) that can be identified on the chart.

Horizontal danger angles

A horizontal angle measured between two objects (identifiable on the chart) defines a circle of position, or circular LOP. In the diagram at right, an observer at either X or Y would measure the same angle between point A and point B. He would also measure the same angle at any point along that segment of the circular arc. If the observer were on the other side of the center of the circle, at X' or Y', or at other points along that segment, a constant (but different) angle would be observed. Note that the angle will be greater than 90 degrees in the first case (observer and objects on the same side of the circle), and less than 90 degrees in the second case.

Such a circle becomes very useful as a vessel approaches a hazard. It can establish a boundary between positions of safety and danger. When such a circular LOP is established, based on a horizontal angle, it is known as a horizontal danger angle. A single horizontal danger angle is used to avoid an unmarked shoal.

The problem is how to stay far enough offshore to avoid the shoal. Find two prominent, identifiable objects that lie on the other side of the shoal from the area of safety. There's no need to actually draw the circle. Measure the angle on the chart from the most seaward point of the shoal to the chosen

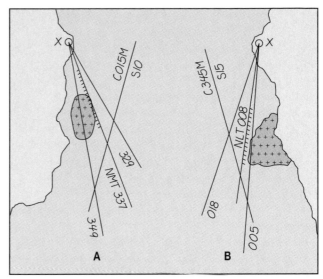

A danger bearing can be used to avoid an unmarked hazardous area. In A (above) any bearing on object X that is more than 337° indicates danger. In B, the reverse is true—a bearing less than 008° indicates danger.

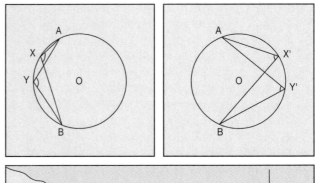

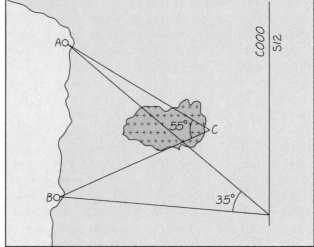

The points at which there is a constant angle between the lines of sight to two objects form a circle *(top, left and right)*. The angle between the lines to A and B is the same at X and Y, as well as at points X' and Y'. Horizontal angles between A and B *(above)* are measured as the boat approaches the hazardous area. Any angle *less* than 55° means the boat is in safe waters.

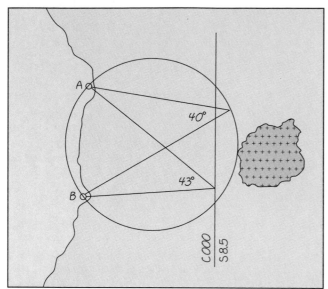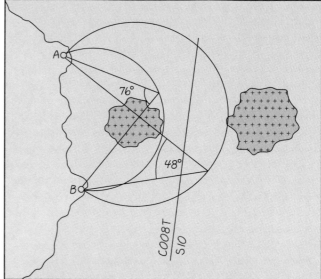

Here are two more situations that call for horizontal danger angles. In the figure at left, the problem is to pass safely inshore of a hazard, so the angle observed from your boat must be greater than the danger angle. In the figure at right, you must steer a course that results in horizontal angles that are between a maximum and a minimum.

objects. This is the horizontal danger angle, shown above. As you approach the shoal, frequent measurements of the horizontal angle between the two objects will reveal whether or not you are standing outside the danger area. Angles less than the danger angle indicate that you are on a circular arc of a radius that is greater than the radius of the arc on which the danger lies. In other words, you're farther offshore than the tip of the shoal—and you are safe.

On the other hand, if the measured horizontal angle becomes greater than the danger angle, you are closer inshore than the tip of the shoal and may be in danger.

It is preferable to measure the angles with a sextant because you will have to take frequent and very accurate measurements, but they can also be determined by taking either relative or compass bearings on the objects.

The same technique can be used to pass inshore of a danger area—just make sure that your angles remain greater than the angle of the threatening extent of the shoal.

Double horizontal danger angles

The technique described above can be used to establish two horizontal danger angles where the problem is to pass safely between two offshore hazards. The principle is the same, as you will note from the diagram above, right. The safe angle lies between the upper and lower danger limits.

Vertical danger angles

Where only a single object is available, it may be possible to use a vertical angle to establish a boundary between safe and hazardous waters. Using the vertical angle technique, a circle is drawn that has the identifiable object of known height at its center and encloses all of the hazards. The radius is mea-

sured from the chart and used in a formula d x h = tan A where "d" is distance, "h" is height, and tan A is the tangent of the angle. The angle itself can be found with a calculator or looked up in *Bowditch*, which also provides a table to substitute for the whole calculation (Volume II, Table 9). The danger circle is labeled with the vertical danger angle.

On approach, a series of vertical angle measurements is taken and as these values approach the danger angle, course is altered to maintain or decrease the measured values. If the angle were maintained, the course would describe a circular arc around the sighted object (outside the area of hazard). A decreasing angle would mean that the boat was getting farther away from the sighted object and also from the hazardous area.

Vertical angles are also used in pairs in a manner similar to that described for horizontal angles. Two vertical angles can be used to define a safe passage between two hazards, one indicating the inshore limit and the other indicating the offshore limit. Range finders can also be used in this situation.

Using range finders

Range finders, generally designed to be used at distances less than a mile, are available in two types. One, called coincident, matches split images like a camera lens; the distance is read on a scale. Accuracy decreases with distance. The other type of range finder uses a reticle graduation technique, like the periscope of a submarine. Its accuracy is relative to the height of the target in the viewer, distance and ability to match the target with the grid. For a 5 x 30 lens, the accuracy for a target 20 feet high will be, at 300 feet, ± 6% and at ¼ mile ± 25% (since the vertical height in the viewer is half of the first one).

POSITIONING PROCEDURE

A basic fix is obtained by crossing two lines of position, and a third LOP is desirable. Such a fix assumes that the observations or measurements for these LOPs are made simultaneously, but the usual situation on a small boat is that there is only one bearing-taker. Observations are taken sequentially rather than simultaneously, but if they are taken quickly, the distance traveled between them is negligible and too small to be plotted on a chart. Adherence to the procedures that are described here will minimize the error from sequential observations.

As the boat moves along its course, a bearing angle will change. Those on the beam will change more rapidly than those on the bow or stern; bearings of closer objects will change more rapidly than those of distant objects. To obtain the most accurate fix from two LOPs, deal first with the object whose bearing will change slowly—the one that is farthest forward or aft. Then take a sight on the second, faster-changing object and finally, do a check on the first. You now have three bearings on two objects. Plot them by using the average of the two bearings on the slowly changing object and the single bearing on the faster-changing object. If circumstances permit only two sightings, take the slowly changing one first.

If you are able to sight three objects, take them in order of rate of change—the slower-changing ones first, and consider using the averaging technique if you are able.

The time of the fix should be the approximate middle of the sequence. At typical cruising speeds and chart scales, a difference of a minute or two will not be significant. At 12 knots, for example, a boat will travel 0.2 miles in one minute; on a 1:80,000 scale chart, that's a distance of less than ³⁄₁₆ of an inch.

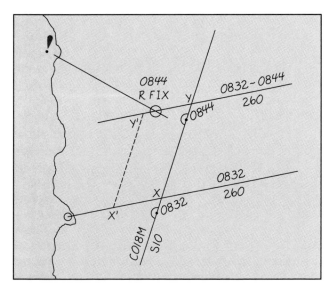

A line of position is advanced by moving forward any point on it an amount equal to the boat's motion during the time interval, and redrawing the line through the advanced point. The intersection of this LOP and the other LOP is a running fix.

As described in Chapter 19, there are generally accepted standards of precision for the description of position. If geographic coordinates are used, latitude and longitude (in that sequence) are stated to the nearest tenth of a minute on charts with scales of 1:50,000 or smaller, and to the nearest second on charts of larger scale.

If the position is stated with respect to some aid to navigation or landmark, direction from that point is given to the nearest degree (true) and distance to the nearest tenth of a mile.

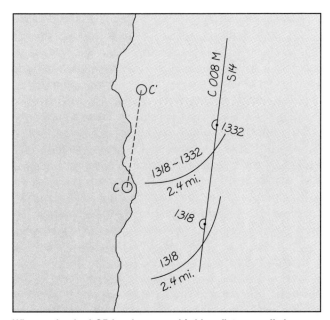

When a circular LOP has been used (with a distance-off observation) it can be advanced by moving its center by the same distance and in the same direction as the movement of the boat according to the DR track. The line C—C' is equal and parallel to the line segment between the two DR positions 1318 and 1332.

The running fix

In some cases it is possible to get a good sighting on one object, but no second object is available. In this situation a standard two-LOP fix is impossible, but a running fix (R Fix) can be used instead. A running fix is usually not as reliable because it incorporates an element of dead reckoning rather than simple observation.

The technique is to observe and plot the single LOP that is available. Some time later, after the vessel has traveled a known distance, that plotted LOP will be advanced (or retired) to a new position on the chart. Think of the LOP sweeping along across the water, without changing its angle, as your boat moves forward. To complete the running fix at a later time, a second LOP is plotted from a sighting on the same object or a new object and the "old" LOP is advanced to a new position—the position it would have reached in the period between the time it was sighted and the time the second LOP was sighted according to the speed and direction of the boat. You will note the dependence on an accurate measure of the speed and direction of the vessel in the intervening time.

Here is how the technique is actually accomplished. The first LOP is observed and plotted, its time and direction carefully noted. A DR track is maintained. At a later time, a second sighting on the same object or some other object is made and plotted, time and direction recorded.

The "old" LOP must be advanced to a new position according to the DR track, so a point is selected somewhere on the older LOP and moved forward in the direction of the boat's travel for a distance representing the distance covered since the first sighting was observed. A new line is drawn through that advanced point—parallel to the old LOP. This new, advanced LOP is labeled as soon as it is drawn with the original time followed by the new time, and the original direction. The point where the advanced LOP crosses the LOP of the second observation is the position of the boat at the time of the second observation—the running fix.

Sometimes, the LOP is an arc of a circle, as when a vertical angle is used to establish distance away from an observed object. In that case, the point chosen to advance the old LOP to the new position is the center of the circular arc. The advanced LOP is scribed with the same radius as the old, but on an advanced center point.

If the track of the boat in the interval between sightings is a straight line of constant speed, the DR is simple. However, the boat may vary both direction and speed between observations. This complicates the DR track, of course, but it does not change the principle of advancing an LOP. Typically, the DR plot would be maintained through these variations of speed and direction. When it is time to advance the point on the LOP, it is advanced along a line parallel to and equal in length to a line drawn between the original DR position and the DR position at the time of the running fix.

Current may also play a role in the advancement of the LOP. If current is predictable, the advanced point is moved according to the DR track, and then offset by the appropriate direction and distance according to the estimated drift and set of the current—both calculations using the elapsed time between the two observations.

In all cases, a fix that is obtained from two simultaneous observations is preferable to a running fix because the accuracy of the original fix can only be decreased by errors and uncertainties in the DR data for the boat's speed and direction during the interval between first and second observation. When current is also a factor, this data becomes less and less certain.

Obviously, increasing the length of the time between observations decreases accuracy. Yet, enough time must be allowed to pass in order to pick up a second object, or to achieve a substantial angular change for the second observation of the same object.

In piloting, this interval is rarely more than 30 minutes, while in celestial navigation on the high seas, the interval might be as much as several hours since inaccuracy is less dangerous in those circumstances.

It is a matter of judgment whether a DR track should be interrupted and restarted on the basis of a running fix.

Observations on a single object

The running fix can be one form of observation on a single object (a running fix can also use two objects at different times), but there are other techniques for dealing with one available object. Successive observations of one object can use the bow-and-beam bearings, doubling the angle on the bow, two bearings and run between, and two relative bearings. Each of these different techniques is described in detail in this section.

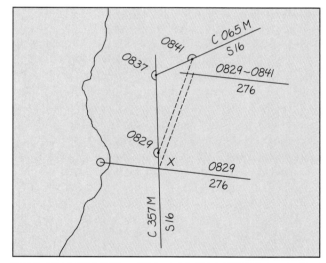

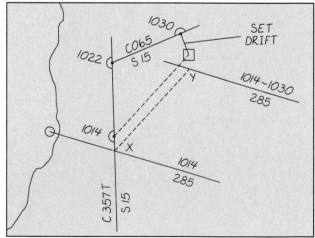

To advance an LOP (*above, top*) you must take into account all changes of course and speed during the time interval. The net effect is determined by drawing a light line between the two DR positions for the times concerned. You then advance the LOP. Current drift must be taken into account (*above*), then the LOP advanced to second DR position.

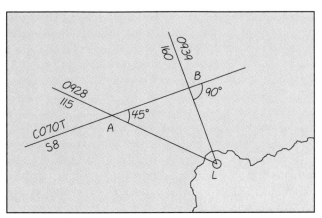

This is really just a more general application of the 45°-90° technique: If the second bearing is double the first, the distance to the sighted object is equal to the distance made good between bearings. The boat has traveled one side of an isosceles triangle and the distance to the object is the other side.

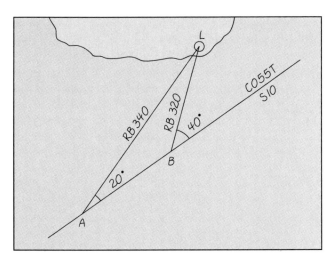

If two observations are made so that the second relative bearing is twice that of the first, as measured from the bow to either starboard or port, the distance to the sighted object at the time of the second bearing is the same as the distance made good between the sightings: L-B = A-B.

Bow-and-beam bearings

This technique uses two sightings that are easy to make with good accuracy, even if no special tool is available—a 45-degree sighting off the bow and a 90-degree beam sighting off the same side. Both can be made with crude tools, even a 45-degree triangular drafting square, or no tools at all—just objects on deck that define a 45-degree and a 90-degree angle with the centerline. For this reason, bow-and-beam bearings can often be made by the helmsman single-handedly.

As the object comes into view, the observer waits for it to reach the 45-degree alignment. As usual, the time is recorded. Course and speed are maintained. The same object is observed when it reaches the 90-degree alignment and the time is then recorded.

Picture a 45-degree drafting square—the long edge corresponds to the LOP of the first (45-degree) observation. The other two edges are the same length. One of these edges is the LOP of the second observation and the other is the DR track of the boat between observations.

You recorded the time of the first observation and of the second, so you know how far the boat traveled in the interval. That traveled distance equals the distance from the sighted object. You have a distance and an LOP, so you can plot a fix.

Doubling the angle on the bow

Doubling the angle on the bow makes use of a similar principle as the bow-and-beam method, but it requires that relative angles be accurately measured, which means that two people are usually required.

As the boat approaches an observed object a relative bearing is taken. Let's assume that the bearing is 20 degrees to port. The boat continues along a DR track until the observed object bears 40 degrees to port. The time interval and the distance traveled are calculated. Again, as is the case with the bow-and-beam method, the distance traveled between observations is equal to the distance from the object at the time of the second observation.

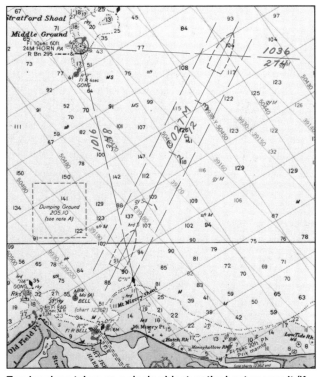

Two bearings taken on a single object as the boat passes it (if distance and direction between them is known) can be plotted on the chart as a fix. There are only two points on the LOPs that will fit a line representing the distance traveled at an angle representing the direction. The second point is the boat's position at the time of the second observation.

There's an advantage with this method in that the boat's position can be fixed before the object is abeam. A hazard that may be present can more easily be avoided because the boat's course can be projected forward from the early known position. Typically, a headland can be sighted and given a wide berth well in advance.

Two relative bearings

A more generalized solution from two relative bearings can be used if a copy of *Bowditch*, Volume II, is on board. Table 7 of that book uses two items of information—the angle between the course and the first bearing (the first relative bearing) and the difference between the course and the second bearing (the second relative bearing). Columns of the table are in terms of the first item and lines are in terms of the second item above; the interval between tabular entries is 2 degrees in both cases.

For any combination of the two relative bearings within the limits of Table 7, two factors will be found. The first number is a factor by which the distance run between the bearings is multiplied to obtain the distance away from the sighted object at the time of the second bearing. The second factor of the same entry in Table 7 is the multiplier to be used to determine the distance off when the object is abeam, assuming, of course, that the same course and speed are maintained. (Refer to the illustrations below and at right.)

Two-bearings-and-run-between

Yet another method is available when only a single object can be observed. In this procedure, a bearing is taken on the object as before. The boat proceeds along its course. A second bearing is taken after the angle has changed by at least 30 degrees. The second bearing may be taken either before or after the object has passed abeam. A distance run between observations is calculated from the boat's DR track.

Both LOPs are plotted along with the course of the boat. A pair of dividers is opened to a span representing the distance run between observations. Then the dividers are placed in such a way as to have a point touching each LOP and have the line between them parallel to the boat's course. In other words, the boat's course is moved "sideways" until the distance traveled exactly spans the decreasing distance between the two LOPs. The divider points now indicate the boat's position at the time of each observation.

Note that the distance run must be the distance over the bottom—suitable corrections having been made already for current. Accuracy depends on the usual factors, but it also depends on the accuracy of the course steered in the time interval between the observations. The net effect is to make this procedure somewhat less desirable than those described earlier.

TABLE 7 Distance of an Object by Two Bearings														
Difference between the course and second bearing	Difference between the course and first bearing													
°	34°		36°		38°		40°		42°		44°		46°	
44	3.22	2.24												
46	2.69	1.93	3.39	2.43										
48	2.31	1.72	2.83	2.10	3.55	2.63								
50	2.03	1.55	2.43	1.86	2.96	2.27	3.70	2.84						
52	1.81	1.43	2.13	1.68	2.54	2.01	3.09	2.44	3.85	3.04				
54	1.63	1.32	1.90	1.54	2.23	1.81	2.66	2.15	3.22	2.60	4.00	3.24		
56	1.49	1.24	1.72	1.42	1.99	1.65	2.33	1.93	2.77	2.29	3.34	2.77	4.14	3.43
58	1.37	1.17	1.57	1.33	1.80	1.53	2.08	1.76	2.43	2.06	2.87	2.44	3.46	2.93
60	1.28	1.10	1.45	1.25	1.64	1.42	1.88	1.63	2.17	1.88	2.52	2.18	2.97	2.57
62	1.19	1.05	1.34	1.18	1.51	1.34	1.72	1.52	1.96	1.73	2.25	1.98	2.61	2.30
64	1.12	1.01	1.25	1.13	1.40	1.26	1.58	1.42	1.79	1.61	2.03	1.83	2.31	2.09
66	1.06	0.96	1.16	1.07	1.31	1.20	1.47	1.34	1.65	1.51	1.85	1.69	2.10	1.92
68	1.00	0.93	1.11	1.03	1.23	1.14	1.37	1.27	1.53	1.42	1.71	1.58	1.92	1.78
70	0.95	0.89	1.05	0.99	1.16	1.09	1.29	1.21	1.43	1.34	1.58	1.49	1.77	1.66
72	0.91	0.86	1.00	0.95	1.10	1.05	1.21	1.15	1.34	1.27	1.48	1.41	1.64	1.56
74	0.87	0.84	0.95	0.92	1.05	1.01	1.15	1.10	1.26	1.21	1.39	1.34	1.53	1.47
76	0.84	0.81	0.91	0.89	1.00	0.97	1.09	1.06	1.20	1.16	1.31	1.27	1.44	1.40
78	0.80	0.79	0.88	0.86	0.96	0.94	1.04	1.02	1.14	1.11	1.24	1.22	1.36	1.33
80	0.78	0.77	0.85	0.83	0.92	0.91	1.00	0.98	1.09	1.07	1.18	1.16	1.28	1.27
82	0.75	0.75	0.82	0.81	0.89	0.88	0.96	0.95	1.04	1.03	1.13	1.12	1.22	1.21
84	0.73	0.73	0.79	0.79	0.86	0.85	0.93	0.92	1.00	0.99	1.08	1.07	1.17	1.16
86	0.71	0.71	0.77	0.77	0.83	0.83	0.89	0.89	0.96	0.96	1.04	1.04	1.12	1.12
88	0.69	0.69	0.75	0.75	0.80	0.80	0.86	0.86	0.93	0.93	1.00	1.00	1.08	1.07
90	0.67	0.67	0.73	0.73	0.78	0.78	0.84	0.84	0.90	0.90	0.97	0.97	1.04	1.04
92	0.66	0.66	0.71	0.71	0.76	0.76	0.82	0.82	0.87	0.87	0.93	0.93	1.00	1.00
94	0.65	0.64	0.69	0.69	0.74	0.74	0.79	0.79	0.85	0.85	0.91	0.90	0.97	0.97
96	0.63	0.63	0.68	0.67	0.73	0.72	0.78	0.77	0.83	0.82	0.88	0.88	0.94	0.93
98	0.62	0.62	0.67	0.66	0.71	0.70	0.76	0.75	0.81	0.80	0.86	0.85	0.91	0.90
100	0.61	0.60	0.65	0.64	0.70	0.69	0.74	0.73	0.79	0.78	0.84	0.83	0.89	0.88
102	0.60	0.59	0.64	0.63	0.68	0.67	0.73	0.71	0.77	0.76	0.82	0.80	0.87	0.85
104	0.60	0.58	0.63	0.61	0.67	0.65	0.72	0.69	0.76	0.74	0.80	0.78	0.85	0.82
106	0.59	0.57	0.63	0.60	0.66	0.64	0.70	0.68	0.74	0.72	0.79	0.76	0.83	0.80
108	0.58	0.55	0.62	0.59	0.66	0.62	0.69	0.66	0.73	0.70	0.77	0.74	0.81	0.77
110	0.58	0.54	0.61	0.57	0.65	0.61	0.68	0.64	0.72	0.68	0.76	0.71	0.80	0.75
112	0.57	0.53	0.61	0.56	0.64	0.59	0.68	0.63	0.71	0.66	0.75	0.69	0.79	0.73
114	0.57	0.52	0.60	0.55	0.63	0.58	0.67	0.61	0.70	0.64	0.74	0.68	0.78	0.71
116	0.56	0.51	0.60	0.54	0.63	0.57	0.66	0.60	0.70	0.63	0.73	0.66	0.77	0.69
118	0.56	0.50	0.59	0.52	0.63	0.55	0.66	0.58	0.69	0.61	0.72	0.64	0.76	0.67
120	0.56	0.49	0.59	0.51	0.62	0.54	0.65	0.57	0.68	0.59	0.72	0.62	0.75	0.65
122	0.56	0.47	0.59	0.50	0.62	0.53	0.65	0.55	0.68	0.58	0.71	0.60	0.74	0.63
124	0.56	0.46	0.59	0.49	0.62	0.51	0.65	0.54	0.68	0.56	0.71	0.58	0.74	0.61
126	0.56	0.45	0.59	0.48	0.62	0.50	0.64	0.52	0.67	0.54	0.70	0.57	0.73	0.59
128	0.56	0.44	0.59	0.46	0.62	0.49	0.64	0.51	0.67	0.53	0.70	0.55	0.73	0.57
130	0.56	0.43	0.59	0.45	0.62	0.47	0.64	0.49	0.67	0.51	0.70	0.53	0.72	0.55
132	0.56	0.42	0.59	0.44	0.62	0.46	0.64	0.48	0.67	0.50	0.70	0.52	0.72	0.54
134	0.57	0.41	0.59	0.43	0.62	0.45	0.64	0.46	0.67	0.48	0.69	0.50	0.72	0.52
136	0.57	0.40	0.60	0.41	0.62	0.43	0.65	0.45	0.67	0.47	0.70	0.48	0.72	0.50
138	0.58	0.39	0.60	0.40	0.63	0.42	0.65	0.43	0.67	0.45	0.70	0.47	0.72	0.48
140	0.58	0.37	0.61	0.39	0.63	0.40	0.65	0.42	0.68	0.43	0.70	0.45	0.72	0.46
142	0.59	0.36	0.61	0.38	0.63	0.39	0.66	0.41	0.68	0.42	0.70	0.43	0.72	0.45
144	0.60	0.35	0.62	0.36	0.64	0.38	0.66	0.39	0.68	0.40	0.71	0.41	0.73	0.43
146	0.60	0.34	0.63	0.35	0.65	0.36	0.67	0.37	0.69	0.39	0.71	0.40	0.73	0.41
148	0.61	0.32	0.63	0.34	0.66	0.35	0.68	0.36	0.70	0.37	0.72	0.38	0.74	0.39
150	0.62	0.31	0.64	0.32	0.66	0.33	0.68	0.34	0.70	0.35	0.72	0.36	0.74	0.37
152	0.63	0.30	0.65	0.31	0.67	0.32	0.69	0.33	0.71	0.33	0.73	0.34	0.75	0.35
154	0.65	0.28	0.67	0.29	0.68	0.30	0.70	0.31	0.72	0.32	0.74	0.32	0.76	0.33
156	0.66	0.27	0.68	0.28	0.70	0.28	0.72	0.29	0.73	0.30	0.75	0.30	0.77	0.31
158	0.67	0.25	0.69	0.26	0.71	0.27	0.73	0.27	0.74	0.28	0.76	0.28	0.78	0.29
160	0.69	0.24	0.71	0.24	0.73	0.25	0.74	0.25	0.76	0.26	0.77	0.26	0.79	0.27

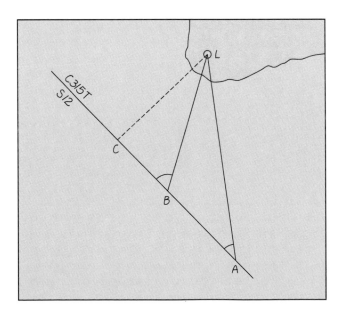

Left: Distance off at the time of second bearing L-B and distance off when abeam, L-C, can be found by applying multiplying factors to the distance run, A-B. These factors for various pairs of angles are given in *Bowditch*, Table 7. A sample of this table is shown above.

RADIO AND RADAR NAVIGATION

The subject of electronic navigation is covered in Chapter 25, but there are two electronic techniques that are common and directly comparable to visual techniques. These are radio bearings and radar bearings.

With relatively simple equipment, bearings can be taken on radio stations even though they may lie far beyond visual range. The suitability of radio signal sources follows in this rough order:

- The United States Coast Guard operates radiobeacons as aids to navigation.
- Other beacons used primarily for aeronautical navigation can be used by boaters too.
- Standard AM broadcasting stations can be used.
- Note that single side-band (SSB) signals are *not* suited for direction finding.

Radio bearings can be taken in any condition of visibility and at distances up to about 100 miles or more with decreasing accuracy. Radio bearings are also possible with VHF signals but at lesser range.

A radio direction finder, discussed in Chapter 25, is usually referred to as an RDF if it is manually operated, and an ADF if it is automatic.

Radio bearings are plotted in the same manner as visual bearings but some additional cautions regarding accuracy are required. Radio bearings are not as sharp as visual bearings; an error of at least 2 to 3 degrees should be assumed even with an experienced operator. For that reason, three LOPs are even more desirable than in the case of visual bearings.

It is important to obtain accurate identification of the station being received. The exact location of the transmitting antenna must be plotted on your chart if it is not already shown there.

Radiobeacons, both marine and aeronautical, are normally indicated on the chart, although you may be able to transcribe some additional aeronautical radiobeacons from aviation charts. Standard AM broadcast radio stations are identified on the chart along with their call letters and their frequency, and other AM stations can be added.

Radio waves follow a great circle path just like light waves. But since radio sources are at much greater distances than visually observed objects, attention must be given to the representation of a great circle on a Mercator chart when radio bearings are being used. In general a range of greater than 50 miles can be considered to require correction, and this can be found in *Bowditch*, Volume II, Table 1.

Just as is the case with visual bearings, two or three radio bearings can be taken in quick sequence and boat movement largely ignored when these are plotted. The time of the resulting fix should be the median time between first and last bearings. RDF LOPs can also be advanced or retired like LOPs from visual sources.

A compass rose placed on each radio source on the chart often can be very helpful; in fact some commercial charts

with this feature are published. Alternatively, a skipper can place his or her own transparent, plastic compass rose in position on a regular chart.

Radio bearings are referenced to the boat's heading, which must be corrected for deviation and variation in the usual way. Of course, the steering must be steady and accurate while the bearings are taken.

In addition to the correction for Mercator charts, radio bearings also have their own radio deviation; but unlike compass deviation, radio deviation does not vary with heading; it varies with relative bearing.

Since radio fixes are less accurate, they should be recorded on the plot with a label that calls attention to them, such

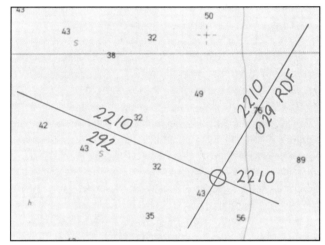

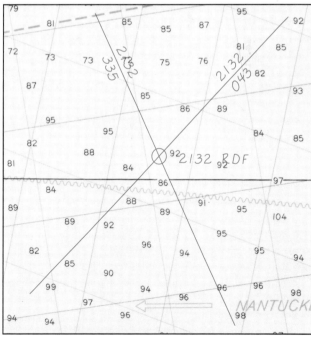

Bearings obtained from a radio direction finder are typically less accurate than sighted bearings. They should be labeled "RDF," as shown at top. When RDF bearings are intersected for a fix, the fix should also be labeled "RDF," as shown at bottom.

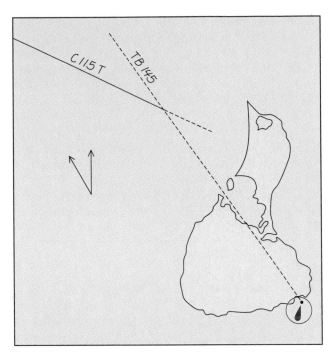

From his or her chart, a skipper notes that a bearing of 145° on Southeast Point, Block Island, will bring him safely to Great Salt Pond. He holds his 115° heading, taking frequent radio bearings. When they increase to 145° he changes course and homes in on the signal.

as "RDF" after the time notation. When radio LOPs are mixed with visuals (which is often a necessity and a useful technique), they should also be labeled as such.

When navigating in hazardous waters with radio bearings, the extra caution of plotting the minimal and maximal error limits on either side of the basic LOP should be followed. This will indicate an area of uncertainty that is a truer indication of possible position.

A single radio source can also be used in the same manner as a single visual object to take a fix with two bearings. The first radio bearing is taken and the LOP plotted, then sufficient time is allowed to pass so that the bearing will change significantly. At this point, the second LOP is plotted. The first LOP can be advanced and an RDF running fix is then established.

Radio direction finding can also help the skipper who is not equipped with an RDF. An RDF-equipped rescue craft or shore station can take bearings on his signal, then calculate his position in order to guide him home or to render assistance. There are limitations on this procedure, however—VHF has a small range and the single-sideband signals do not serve this purpose well.

Radar navigation

While the subject of radar is covered in greater detail in Chapter 25, some mention of it in this section is appropriate. Radar has a unique advantage in navigation in that a single instrument can measure both direction and distance to both moving and still targets—and can do so under any condition of visibility. Excellent detailed information on radar can be found in the DMA Publication No. 1310, *Radar Navigation Manual (Appendices)*.

Radar measurements of direction are not as accurate as those made visually, but radar can almost always make a measurement despite fog, light rain and darkness. Heavy rain will often decrease radar's accuracy.

On the other hand, measurements of distance are quite accurate—much more so than vertical sextant measurements or optical range-finder readings.

Direction and distance fixes determined with radar are used in much the same manner as LOPs from visual sources.

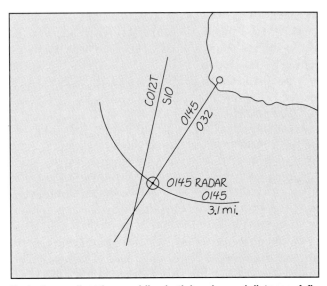

Radar is excellent for providing both bearing and distance. A fix obtained from a radar observation should be plotted with a line and an arc, and labeled with the time and the word "RADAR."

Fixes are obtained with two directional LOPs, a direction with a distance, but best of all—given radar's distance accuracy—distance measurements on two objects. A radar fix is labeled with time and "RADAR."

When the opportunity exists, an excellent combination is a visual direction LOP and a radar distance to the same object. Of course, radar distances can be used in the manner described for vertical angles in order to avoid unmarked hazardous areas.

Radar observations of isolated objects such as buoys, offshore lighthouses, etc. are usually unambiguous. When the radar target is onshore, however, some identification problems may arise.

Radar, even more than other piloting methods, requires a good deal of practice and accumulation of experience. Work out your radar exercises during clement weather and controlled conditions so that they are readily available in difficult circumstances.

USING DEPTH INFORMATION

The depth of water under the vessel is valuable piloting information. A single depth reading cannot tell a boater where he is, but it can tell him where he is not. If an accurate depth reading is 26 feet, you may be at any number of places that have a 26-foot depth, but you are not at a place that has significantly greater or less depth. When sufficient depth data have been obtained and corrected for height of tide, they can be used for positive position determination in combination with an LOP from another source, or on its own.

Remember, a depth sounder can be adjusted to display water depth either from the bottom to the surface or from the bottom to the transducer, which is usually several feet below the water line. Be sure you know how the sounder is calibrated. Also remember that depth figures on charts are those at low tide.

Depth information and a single LOP

Given a bottom with relatively uniform slope, it may be possible to get position information with depth and a single LOP. Typically this would be a beam bearing and a single depth reading. The LOP is plotted, then a point along the line is found that matches the depth indication on the chart, corrected for tidal stage. Such a position should be regarded as an estimated position and marked "EP." If there are several such points on the LOP, you will not be able to estimate your position.

In some instances a rough estimate of the boat's position can be obtained by matching a series of depth readings, tide-corrected, against a series of depth figures on the chart. Choose a distance interval to take depth readings—one that corresponds to the density of depth figures on the chart in question. Mark your depth readings on tracing paper at the appropriate distance intervals, then move the paper around on the chart, keeping the line of soundings parallel to a line representing the direction of your course steered while the soundings were made. Look for the best match between your series, corrected for tidal stage, and a series on the chart. Don't expect to get an exact concurrence.

Shorelines foul with offshore rocks or areas of irregular depth are not suited to this technique, nor are areas of uniform depth. Confirmation of position cannot be positive but certain denial can be very useful.

Fathom curve piloting

When cruising over a bottom with a uniform slope, piloting can be simplified by choosing a depth curve that follows a safe path. The boat is steered so as to cross this depth, then is steered along it with gentle course alteration to stay within a few feet of the chosen curve.

Don't use this method where there is any chance of meeting hazards by covering more ground than anticipated or by distorting the curve at sudden, sharp changes in direction.

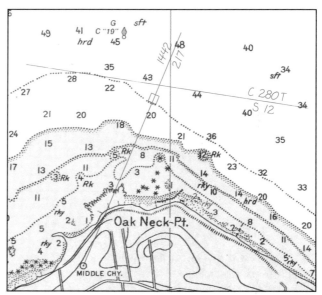

A single LOP can often be combined with depth information to provide an estimated position (EP). The LOP shown above is a beam bearing. A depth reading of 21 feet has indicated that the estimate should be further inshore than the DR track indicates.

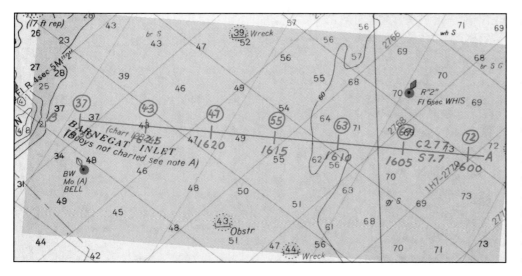

A series of soundings can be plotted on a piece of tracing paper, each depth noted with its time, then used to estimate position. The tracing paper is moved about on the chart until a good match is found between the measurements from your depth sounder and the depths shown by the chart. Of course, readings must be corrected for the state of the tide.

CURRENTS AND PILOTING

One of the more interesting problems in small-boat piloting is the matter of currents, their effect upon boat speed, the determination of courses which must be steered to make good a desired track, and the time required to reach a destination. This is known as current sailing.

As a boat is propelled and steered through the water, it moves with respect to it. At the same time the water may be moving with respect to the bottom and the shore because of current. The resultant motion of the boat is the net effect of these two motions combined, with regard to both speed and direction. As a consequence, the actual course made good over the bottom will not be the same as the DR track, in terms of either course or speed.

Leeway, the leeward (away from the wind) motion of a vessel due to the wind, affects sailboats and, to a lesser extent, larger motorboats. However, the wind's effect need not be

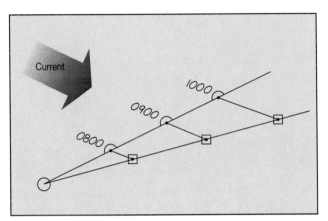

If the current is known, or can be estimated, a DR plot (the half-circles) can be modified to show a series of estimated positions (EPs, plotted as squares).

considered separately from current—the two may be lumped together along with such factors as wave action on the boat. The total offsetting influence of all of these factors collectively is termed "current."

A prediction of current effect can be added to a plot of a DR track to obtain an estimated position (EP), plotted as a small square with a dot in the center.

Among all of these possible influences acting on a vessel, tidal current is by far the most important and it should never be underestimated. Unexpected current is always a threat to the skipper because it can quickly carry his boat off course, and possibly into dangerous water. Note that the overall risk is greater with slower boat speeds and under conditions of reduced visibility.

Definition of current sailing terms

The terms "course" and "speed" are used in DR plots for the motion of the boat through the water without regard to current. Before we introduce the influence of current, there are a few more terms to learn.

- The "intended track" is the expected path of the boat, as plotted on a chart, after consideration has been given to the effect of current.
- "Track," abbreviated as TR, is the direction (true) of the intended track line.
- "Speed of advance," SOA, is the intended rate of travel along the intended track line.

Note that the intended track will not always be the actual track, and so two more terms are needed:
- "Course over the ground," COG, is the direction of the actual path of the boat, the track made good; sometimes termed "Course made good" (CMG).
- "Speed over the ground," abbreviated as SOG, is the actual rate of travel along this track; it is sometimes termed "Speed made good" (SMG).
- "Set" and "drift" are discussed in Chapter 15.

Current situations

A study of the effects of current resolves itself into two basic situations. The first situation occurs when the set of the current is in the same direction as the boat's motion, or is in exactly the opposite direction. In the second situation, the direction of the current is at an angle to the boat's course, either a right or an oblique angle.

The first situation is the simplest to solve. The speed of the current—the drift—is added to or subtracted from the speed through the water to obtain the speed over the ground. The course over the ground (or intended track) is the same as the DR course—COG equals C, as does TR.

Current diagrams

When the boat's motion and the set of the current form an angle with each other, the solution for the resultant course and speed is more complex, but still not difficult. Several methods may be used, but a graphic solution using a current diagram is usually the easiest to understand.

The accuracy with which the resultant course and speed can be determined depends largely on the accuracy with which the current has been determined. Values of the current usually must be taken from tidal current tables or charts, or estimated by the skipper from visual observations.

Basically, a current diagram represents the two component motions separately, as if they occurred independently and sequentially—which, of course, they do not. These diagrams can be drawn in terms of velocities or distances. "Velocity" has a more detailed meaning than speed, since it is speed in a given linear direction, at a timed rate and within a frame of reference. The diagrams in this text will graph motions in terms of their velocities.

Such diagrams may also be called "vector triangles of velocity." The term "vector" in mathematics means quantity that has both magnitude and direction—directed quantities. In current sailing, the directed quantities are the motions of the boat and the water (the current).

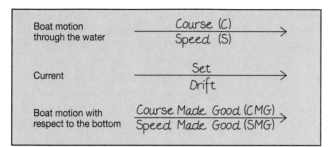

Boat motion through the water	Course (C) / Speed (S) →
Current	Set / Drift →
Boat motion with respect to the bottom	Course Made Good (CMG) / Speed Made Good (SMG) →

Just like lines plotted on a chart, the current diagram line must always be carefully labeled. Direction is shown above the line and speed shown below.

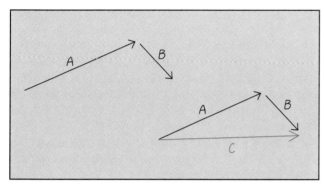

Vectors may be combined (or "added") graphically. In this diagram, vectors A and B are added—the sum is vector C. The sum vector can be measured both for magnitude (length of line) and direction in the same way that you would measure a line plotted on a chart.

Vectors

A vector may be represented graphically by an arrow, a segment of a straight line with an arrowhead indicating the direction, and the length of the line scaled to the speed (*right*). If we specify that a certain unit of line length is equal to a certain unit of speed—that one inch equals one knot, for example—then two such vectors can graphically represent two different velocities. Any speed scale may be used, the larger the better for accuracy. However, the size of the available paper and working space will normally control the scale.

Current diagrams may be drawn on a chart either as part of the plot or separately. If drawn on plain paper it is wise to draw in a north line as the reference for measuring directions. However, the easiest way to manipulate current diagrams is with a maneuvering board as explained later in this chapter.

Since boats are subject to two distinct motions—the boat through the water, and the water with respect to the bottom—we will now consider how the resultant motion, or vector sum, is obtained by current diagrams.

Vector triangles

When the two motions are not in line with each other, they form two sides of a triangle, as shown in the lower illustration above. Completing the triangle gives the third side, which

will be a vector representing the resultant motion or velocity. Consequently, when any two velocity vectors are drawn to the same scale and form the sides of a velocity triangle, the third side will be the resultant velocity vector (the vector sum of the other two), and its direction and magnitude may be measured from the diagram.

It may be easier to visualize the component motions if a time period of one hour is used and the points that are the corners of the triangle are considered as positions of the boat before and after certain motions, as follows:

- "O"—the origin
- "DR"— the DR position of the boat as a result solely of its motion through the water.
- "W"—the position of the boat solely as a result of the motion of the water.
- "P"—the position (intended or actual) of the boat as a result of the combined action of the component motions.

It should be noted that, although in some cases, two of the above letters are applicable to a position, it is customary to use only one.

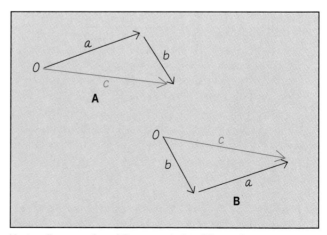

A vector has direction (shown by the arrowhead) and magnitude (shown by the length of the line). Both are referenced to a convenient scale.

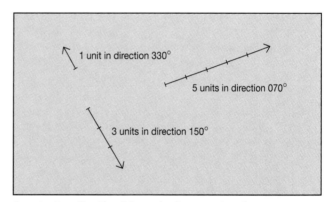

Vector diagrams A and B appear to be different because vectors a and b have been drawn in reverse order. But the sum (c) is the same in both cases.

"Tail-to-head" relationships

Note carefully how the vectors, one representing current and the other representing the boat's motion through the water are drawn "tail-to-head." (This rule applies only when one of the vectors is current, not when they both represent the boat's motion.)

If boat motion through both the water and current are known, either may be drawn first from the origin. In the diagram on page 465 (*right, bottom*), drawing A and drawing B both yield the same result for vector c.

The four "cases" of current problems

There are four typical current problems—Cases 1, 2, 3 and 4.
- Case 1: What is the effect of a known current if no allowance is made for it while running the DR course?
- Case 2: What is the nature of an unknown current from observation of its effect?
- Case 3: What is the corrected course to be steered, without regard for the effect of speed or estimated time of arrival?
- Case 4: What is the course and the speed to arrive at a specified time? This is the "rendezvous" or "contest" case.

CASE 1: FINDING THE EFFECT OF CURRENT ON A BOAT'S COURSE AND SPEED

If the set of the current is as shown in the diagram, then the boat will be set off to the right of the direction in which it is being steered.

We will use a current diagram (*shown at right*) to determine the exact extent of this effect; we will also determine the path that the boat can be expected to follow, as well as its speed along that path (in other words, the intended track and speed of advance).

We first draw in a north line as a reference for measuring directions in the diagram, and then the vector for the boat's speed through the water, O-DR, a line drawn from the origin in the direction 070° for a length of 10 units. Next we add the vector for current, DR-W, three units in the direction 130°. Note that we have observed the "tail-to-head" relationship rule. (Either of these two vectors could have been drawn first; the triangle would appear differently, but the result will be the same.)

Because these vectors form two sides of a triangle of velocities, the third side, O-W, is the resultant velocity at which the boat moves with respect to the bottom under the combined influences of its propulsion and the current. The point W can now be relabeled "P." The intended (or expected) track (TR) and the speed of advance (SOA) can be measured from the O-P line.

In this example, the results indicate that the boat can be expected to sail a course over the ground of 083° and to have a speed of advance of 11.8 knots. Bear in mind that the directions of these vectors are plotted as true directions.

Summarizing briefly, we have drawn vectors to indicate independently the motion of the boat from two different influences—that of its own propulsion and that of the current. Actually, of course, the boat will not go first from O to DR and then on to P. All the time, it will travel directly along the intended track O-P. The boat is steered on course C, the direction of O-DR, but due to the effect of current, it is expected to travel along the intended track O-P. This is the intended route that must be considered for shoals and other hazards to navigation.

The reference north line is drawn first, but is not needed if the diagram is plotted directly on a chart. This shows the vector line for the course and speed.

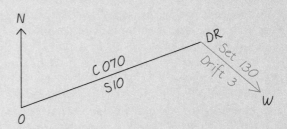

The vector for current set and drift is added.

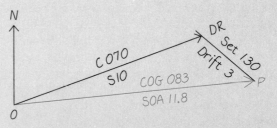

The connecting vector from O to P shows the resultant motion and speed of the boat over the bottom.

CASE 2: DETERMINING CURRENT SET AND DRIFT

This is a situation in which you know the course you have steered and the speed through the water from either the speed curve of your boat or a marine speedometer. It is also obvious to you that you did not arrive at your DR position. From your chart plot, you have been able to determine the course and speed over the ground. Current has acted to set you off your course—you desire to know its set and drift.

After again drawing a north reference line, plot vectors for your motion through the water—C 255°, S 12 knots, and your motion with respect to the bottom—COG 245°, SOG 13.4 knots. These vectors are both drawn outward from the origin, O, to points DR and P respectively. The "tail-to-head" rule is not applicable as neither of these vectors represents current.

The action of the current has been to offset your boat from DR to P (which is also point W in this case), thus the set is the direction from DR toward P, and the drift is the length of this line in scale units.

In the diagram, the current is found to be setting 192° with a drift of 2.6 knots. This is the average current for the time period

and location of the run from O to P for which the calculations were made; it is not the current at P. For the next leg of your cruise, these current values can be used as is, or modified as required by the passage of time and/or the continuing change in position of the boat.

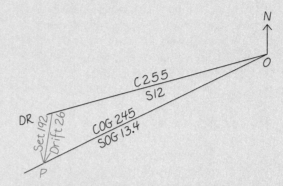

The prevailing current (actually the net effect of all offsetting influences) can be found graphically by plotting vectors for the DR track of the boat and its actual course and speed for a given time, then adding the vector from DT to P.

CASE 3: A TYPICAL CRUISING SITUATION

Here you know the track you desire to make good (TR 080°), you have decided to run at your normal cruising speed through the water (S 10 knots), and you have calculated (or estimated) the current's set (140°) and drift (4 knots). What you desire to know is the course to be steered (C) and the speed of advance (SOA), which can be used to figure your estimated time of arrival (ETA).

Draw in a north line and measure direction from it (see the diagram at right). Plot the current vector O-W, at the specified direction and length, and a line (not a vector yet) in the direction of the intended track—this line should be an indefinite length at this time. From point W, swing an arc, with dividers or drawing compass, equal in length to the speed through the water in scale units. The point at which this arc intersects the intended track line is point P and the vector triangle has been completed.

The direction of W-P is the course to be steered (C 060°); the length of the vector O-P is the speed over the ground (SOA 11.4) and from this the ETA can be calculated.

Let us look at the reasoning behind this graphic solution of Case 3. Again considering the component motions separately for the sake of simplicity, the boat is moved by current from O to W. It is to move from W at the specified speed though the water, but must get back on the intended track line—the problem is to find the point P on the track which is "S" units from point W. The solution is found by swinging an arc as described above.

Remember that all vectors are plotted as true directions, including C, the course to be steered in the preceding solution.

This must be changed to a compass direction (course) for actual use at the helm.

In accordance with the principles of dead reckoning, it is desirable to plot the DR track even though a current is known to exist. This line, drawn from point O in the direction C and with a length of S scale units, forms a basis for consideration of possible hazards if the current is not as calculated or estimated.

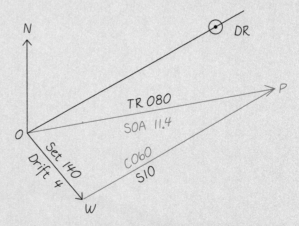

If you know your desired track, and your speed through the water, a graphic solution can be used to determine the course to be steered and the speed of advance. For safety, a DR plot is added.

CASE 4: RENDEZVOUS

This is a variation of Case 3, in which you want to arrive at a specified point at a given time. It may be that you are competing in a predicted log contest, or merely that you have agreed to meet friends at that time and place. In addition to the data on current that you have, you have decided upon your track and your speed of advance.

In the diagram at right, let us assume that the current sets 205° at 3 knots. You need to make good a track of 320°, and a quick distance-time-speed calculation sets your required speed of advance at 11.5 knots.

From the north reference line, draw the current vector O-W and the intended track vector O-P. Complete the triangle with the vector W-P, which will give you the course to be steered (C 332 True) and the speed to run through the water (S 13.0) to arrive at the destination at the desired time. Line O-DR should be drawn in from the origin as a dead-reckoning track for the sake of safety.

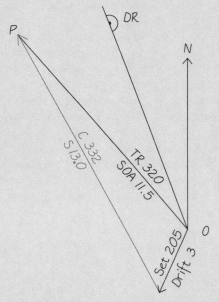

This problem concerns the course to be steered and the speed at which to run in order to arrive at a specified destination at a predetermined time. This could be used in establishing a rendezvous with another boat, or in predicted log contests.

Motoring toward a rendezvous point, a skipper compensates for currents on his piloting, and this way can have a realistic estimated time of arrival (ETA).

PILOTING WITH A CALCULATOR

Among calculators there is a wide range of features and prices. Even the simplest and least expensive can be very useful for solving piloting problems. But those that include trigonometric functions or storable programs as well, are particularly useful. (The use of personal computers is a much more general subject, and is covered in Chapter 25.)

The first and most important point to note about the use of calculators and programs is that the problem to be solved must be understood by the operator. You must still know the procedure and know what data to use, even if the calculator makes the work easier.

Even the simplest calculator will be sufficient for problems of distance, time and speed. The usual equations are:

$$D = S \times T \text{ where } T \text{ is hours}$$

$$D = \frac{S \times T}{60} \text{ where } T \text{ is minutes}$$

These equations can be algebraically transposed depending on which factors are known and which required.

Remember that when doing arithmetic with numbers representing time, there are 60 minutes in an hour, not 100.

The trigonometric functions—sine, cosine and tangent and their inverse functions, arc sin, etc.—can greatly reduce the work involved in current problems.

Height of tide

Calculating the height of tide at a time intermediate between high and low water can be done much more easily with a calculator. The equation is based on the variation of the height of tide from low to high, or high to low, following a cosine curve. This is the procedure used by the National Ocean Service in the preparation of their Table 3, but remember that, due to short-term, local conditions, actual conditions of time and height will not always match predictions. The predicted height of tide at any desired time is the low water predicted height plus a correction:

$$Ht_D = Ht_{LW} + Corr$$

The correction is equal to the product of a factor (F) which varies with time, and the range of the tide.

$$Corr = F (Ht_{HW} - Ht_{LW})$$

The correction factor is determined by use of a haversine relationship:

$$F = \frac{1 - \cos \left(\frac{T_{LW} \sim T_D}{T_{HW} \sim T_{LW}} \times 180° \right)}{2}$$

T_{LW} is the time of low water,
T_{HW} is the time of high water,
T_D is desired time.

The symbol ~ means absolute difference, the lesser quantity subtracted from the larger. It is used in order to avoid negative numbers.

It is important to be aware of the following caution: Although times may be expressed in terms of hours and minutes for subtraction, they must be expressed as decimal numbers for division.

Thus, the equation for the height of tide at a desired time is as follows:

$$Ht_D = Ht_{LW} + (Ht_{HW} - Ht_{LW}) \left[1 - \cos \left(\frac{\frac{T_{LW} \sim T_D}{T_{HW} \sim T_{LW}} \times 180°}{2} \right) \right]$$

While the mathematics may appear formidable in these examples, in practice they are much simpler since all that is required is that you punch a few buttons on your calculator. Although your results may vary by a small amount from those obtained in Table 3, they are actually more precise because the table values are not interpolated.

Calculations may be similarly made for a subordinate tide station after applying time differences and height differences or ratios.

To help understand this, refer to the calculation that is shown in detail below:

$$Ht_D = -1.1 + [10.5 - (-1.1)]$$

$$\left[\frac{1 - \cos \left(\frac{2223 - 1700}{2223 - 1505} \times 180° \right)}{2} \right]$$

$$= -1.1 + 11.6 \left[\frac{1 - \cos \left(\frac{5.38}{7.30} \times 180° \right)}{2} \right]$$

$$= -1.1 + 11.6 \left[\frac{1 - \cos 132.7°}{2} \right]$$

$$= -1.1 + 11.6 \left[\frac{1 - (-0.685)}{2} \right]$$

$$= -1.1 + (11.6 \times 0.842)$$

$$= -1.1 + 9.77$$

$$= 8.67 = 8.7 \text{ ft}$$

Strength of current

A generally similar method is used for determining the strength of current at a desired time. However, in this instance the time interval is between a maximum current and slack water rather than between one maximum and the opposite maximum. The equation to use is as follows:

$$S_D = S_M \times \cos\left[90° - \left(\frac{T_D \sim T_S}{T_M \sim T_S} \times 90°\right)\right]$$

T_D is the desired time
T_S is the time of slack water
T_M is time of maximum current, ebb or flood
S_M is strength of maximum current, ebb or flood
S_D is strength of current at the desired time

The direction of the current is the same as the maximum used, ebb or flood; ignore any negative signs appearing in the answer. The equation is to be used only with the normal reversing type of tidal current found in bays, sounds and rivers. It is not for use with hydraulic currents that exist in connecting waterways, such as Hell's Gate in New York, or the Cape Cod Canal.

To help understand this, refer to the calculation example shown at top right.

$$S_D = 1.2 \cos\left[90° - \left(\frac{1811 - 1520}{1811 - 1456} \times 90°\right)\right]$$

$$= 1.2 \cos\left[90° - \left(\frac{2.85}{3.25} \times 90°\right)\right]$$

$$= 1.2 \cos (90° - 78.92°)$$

$$= 1.2 \cos 11.08° = 1.2 \times 0.981 = 1.18$$

$$= 1.2 \text{ knots}$$

Current sailing

Rather than using the graphic techniques for solving current sailing problems, you can use a calculator. The general procedure is the resolution of two vectors into their north-south and east-west components, the addition (or subtraction) of

CASE 1: ADDING TWO VECTORS:

Path over ground = Path thru water + Current

$$\text{COG} = \tan^{-1}\left(\frac{S \sin C + \text{Drift} \sin \text{Set}}{S \cos C + \text{Drift} \cos \text{Set}}\right)$$

$$= \tan^{-1}\left(\frac{10 \sin 70° + 3 \sin 130°}{10 \cos 70° + 3 \cos 130°}\right)$$

$$= \tan^{-1}\left(\frac{9.40 + 2.30}{3.42\,(-1.93)}\right)$$

$$= \tan^{-1}\left(\frac{11.70}{1.49}\right) = 82.74°$$

$$= 083°$$

$$\text{SOG} = \frac{S \sin C + \text{Drift} \sin \text{Set}}{\sin \text{COG}}$$

$$= \frac{9.40 + 2.30}{0.99} = 11.82$$

$$= 11.8 \text{ knots}$$

In the above calculations and all other examples, do not be misled by the long results which are produced by the calculator. The value for sin 70° may be shown as 0.9396926208, and this will be used in the machines' internal operations. Although the result may be 11.78982612 knots, this is really 11.8, or 12 knots.

These equations will work when the times involved straddle a midnight and fall into two days, but be careful. The simplest method is to add 24 hours to the times of the second day so that they are numerically larger than those of the first day. For example, a low water time of 2254 and a desired time of 0115 the following day is best handled as 2515 – 2254 = 2:21.

(It is desirable to actually write down the later time with 24 hours added rather than trying to accomplish the addition then subtraction mentally.)

Some calculators have a key for changing angles in degrees, minutes and seconds (D.MS) to degrees and decimal fractions (DD.d). This function works equally well for converting hours, minutes and seconds (H.MS) to hours and decimal fractions (HH.h).

The conversion process is usable in either direction and is very helpful in equations such as those used here where times must be both subtracted and divided.

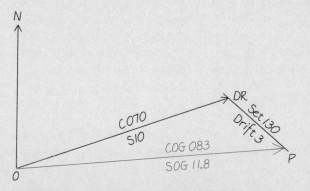

The black lines represent the known data: boat speed and course through the water, plus current set and drift. The blue line shows the course and speed over the ground as determined by use of the hand calculator. Although the formula looks quite complex, its application is very quick and simple.

CASE 2: SUBTRACTING TWO VECTORS

Again, if two vectors are known, subtraction will yield the other vector:

$$\overrightarrow{\text{Current}} = \overrightarrow{\text{Path over ground}} - \overrightarrow{\text{Path thru water}}$$

$$\text{Set} = \tan^{-1}\left(\frac{\text{SOG sin COG} - \text{S sin C}}{\text{SOG cos COG} - \text{S cos C}}\right)$$

$$= \tan^{-1}\left(\frac{13.4 \sin 245° - 12.0 \sin 255°}{13.4 \cos 245° - 12.0 \cos 255°}\right)$$

$$= \tan^{-1}\left(\frac{-0.55}{-2.56}\right)$$

$$= \tan^{-1} 0.216 = 12°*$$

$$= 192°$$

$$\text{Dft} = \left(\frac{\text{SOG sin COG} - \text{S sin C}}{\sin \text{Set}}\right)$$

$$= \left(\frac{13.4 \sin 245° - 12 \sin 255°}{\sin 192°}\right)$$

$$= 2.617 = 2.6 \text{ knots}$$

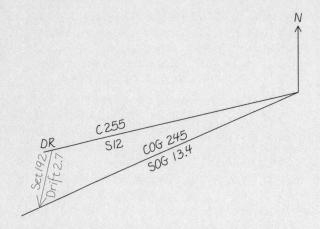

The known values are boat course and speed through the water, plus the course and speed made good over the bottom. The blue line indicates the calculator solution to the set and drift of the current, which is actually the sum of all offsetting influences.

*As the calculator result will be an angle between 0° and 90°, this answer is "angle in quadrant." From inspection of a rough sketch of the vectors, it will be seen that the set of the current is 180° + 12°, or 192°.

CASE 3: FINDING THE COURSE TO STEER

In this instance, one vector is known; this is the set and drift of the current. Boat speed through the water is also known, as well as the intended track. To find the course to be steered and speed of advance, a different type of solution is required:

$$C = \text{TR} - \sin^{-1}\left[\left(\frac{\text{Drift}}{\text{S}}\right)\sin(\text{Set} - \text{TR})\right]$$

$$= 080° - \sin^{-1}\left[\left(\frac{4}{10}\right)\sin(140 - 80°)\right]$$

$$= 080° - \sin^{-1}(.346)$$

$$= 080° - 20.3° = 59.7 = 060°$$

$$\text{SOA} = [\text{S cos(C} - \text{TR})] + [\text{Drift cos(Set} - \text{TR})]$$

$$= [10 \cos(060 - 080)] + [4 \cos(140 - 080)]$$

$$= (10 \cos - 20°) + (4 \cos 60°)$$

$$= (9.40) + (2.00)$$

$$= 11.4 \text{ knots}$$

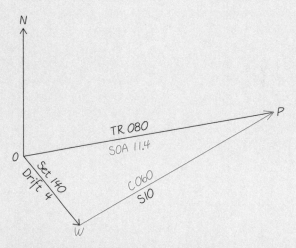

Here the known values are set and drift of the current, the boat's speed through the water, and the direction of the track along which it is desired to run. The calculator easily and quickly solves the vector triangle for the course to be steered, and the speed of advance along the intended track.

CASE 4: SUBTRACTING KNOWN VECTORS

This is, again, the subtraction of one known vector from another to obtain the third, unknown vector:

Path thru water = Path over ground – Current

$$C = \tan^{-1}\left[\frac{\text{SOA sin TR} - \text{Drift sin Set}}{\text{SOA cos TR} - \text{Drift cos Set}}\right]$$

$$= \tan^{-1}\left[\frac{11.5 \sin 320° - 3 \sin 205°}{11.5 \cos 320° - 3 \cos 205°}\right]$$

$$= \tan^{-1}\left[\frac{-7.39 - (-1.27)}{8.81 - (-2.72)}\right]$$

$$= \tan^{-1}\left[\frac{-6.12}{11.53}\right] = 28.0°$$

Again this is an angle in quadrant; C = 360° – 28.0° = 332°.

$$S = \frac{\text{SOA sin TR} - \text{Drift sin Set}}{\sin C}$$

$$= \frac{-6.12}{\sin 332°} = 13.05$$

$$= 13.0 \text{ knots}$$

Some calculators have a key for conversion from rectangular to polar coordinates. This simplifies the task of resolving a vector into its N-S and E-W components, which are then added to or subtracted from the components of another vector. After the net components are determined, the inverse procedure is used to obtain the resultant vector.

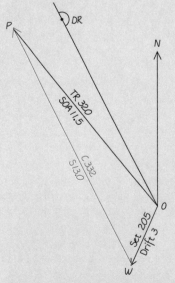

The vector triangle is solved here for the course to be steered and speed to be run through the water in order to reach a specified destination at a predetermined time. This problem is typical of predicted log contests, and it is useful when a rendezvous with another boat has been set.

these components, and the establishment of that third vector from these net values.

For comparative purposes, the examples below correspond to the graphic solutions on pages 466-468.

Bearings and distances

As you have read earlier in this chapter, a fix can be obtained from two successive bearings on a single object. In some instances it may not be convenient or prudent to wait until special pairs of easily handled angles can be used and a more general solution is required. *Bowditch*, Volume II, Table 7, supplies a solution for many sets of bearings, but a calculator can provide more generalized results.

In the following calculation, a critical input element is the distance traveled in the interval between bearings. The boat's course must be compared with estimated current to obtain course over ground (COG) and speed over ground (SOG)—this latter figure being combined with time to obtain the distance traveled. Note that all of these calculations can be made with a calculator.

For further clarification, refer to the example shown on page 460. The first bearing is the angle at A, the second is the angle at B, the distance traveled is AB, and the distance off when abeam is LC.

Although the distance LA could be calculated, this cannot be done until the boat has reached B, where the second bearing is taken—hence, it is of little interest and the position at B is the one normally determined. Quite often, the point of nearest approach to L is of interest, the distance off when abeam L. It, too, can be easily calculated, and in advance of reaching point C.

$$LB = \frac{D \sin B_1}{\sin(B_2 - B_1)}$$

$$LC = Lb \sin B_2$$

where D is distance run between the two bearings
B_1 is the first bearing (at A)
B_2 is the second bearing (at B)

Note carefully that B_1 and B_2 are angles to the course over ground (COG); relative bearings must be corrected for any difference between COG and C, the course being steered.

Example: (Table, page 460): First bearing 37°, second bearing 61°. Distance run between bearings is 2.3 miles.

$$LB = \frac{2.3 \sin 37°}{\sin(61 - 37°)}$$

$$= \frac{2.3 \times 0.602}{0.407} = 3.40$$

$$= 3.4 \text{ miles}$$

$$LC = 3.40 \times \sin 61° = 3.40 \times 0.874$$

$$= 3.0 \text{ miles}$$

Distance to horizon

The distance to the horizon for a given height of eye can be determined easily by using any calculator that has a square root function:

$$D = 1.17\sqrt{h}$$

where D is in nautical miles and h is in feet, or

$$D = 2.12\sqrt{h}$$

where D is in nautical miles and h is in meters.

If the distance is required in statute miles, multiply D by 1.15; if required in kilometers, multiply D by 1.852.

Traverse sailing

When a boat is running a course with several legs of different directions and lengths, the net change of position can be calculated by means of a traverse table. This situation arises in some navigational contests, when sailing, or when a boat is trolling for fish out of sight of land or aids to navigation. Again, solution is possible using *Bowditch,* Volume II, Table 3 in this instance. With or without a copy of *Bowditch,* the problem is easily solved by calculator and the simplest trigonometric equations.

The various legs of the DR track are broken down into north-south and east-west components, the components are summed up taking care that southerly and westerly components are given a negative sign, and the resultant single course and direction determined from the net N-S and E-W components. This is simply vector addition of as many legs as have been run.

Other applications

A skipper can develop many specialized applications to meet his own piloting needs once he has gained some experience and developed a moderate level of skill with his calculator. Typical of these uses are: position determination by two non-simultaneous bearings with a run between them (on separate objects rather than on a single object as described before, determining course over ground from three bearings on a single object (without knowledge of distance run between times of each bearing), compass deviation table preparations, true and apparent wind, and many others that are limited only by the skipper's needs, imagination and his ability with a calculator.

A calculator can also be put to good use for general arithmetic problems including speed over a measured distance and fuel consumption and cost.

Piloting under sail

The principles of piloting a small sailboat are no different from piloting a powerboat. However, much of successful piloting is not principle, but practice, and the practice aboard a sailboat may differ in several respects.

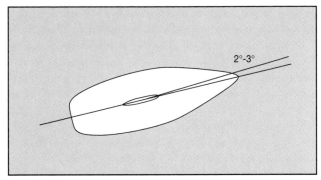

Sailboat keels (much like airplane wings) operate with a slight angle of attack. This means that there may be a difference of two or three degrees between the centerline of the hull and the actual course over the bottom—in perfect conditions. In rough conditions and with less than optimal keels, leeway will be much greater.

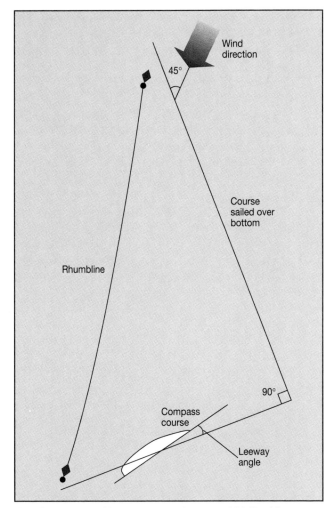

The direct course (the one a powerboat would follow) is known as the rhumb line. The actual course that a sailboat might follow, both upwind and down, is considerably longer and more difficult to reckon. The values shown above are typical of a well-trimmed, deep-keel boat.

Most important is the fact that sailboat speeds are much more difficult to predict. While a powerboat pilot might establish a timetable for a particular set of legs of his trip (refer to "Using a predicted timetable" in this chapter, page 480), a sailboat skipper would be much less likely to be able to predict the boat's speed several hours in advance along a particular leg of the trip.

In addition to the built-in complexity of a particular track, a sailboat navigator also makes extra calculations and plots to account for the fact that his boat will tack upwind and often downwind too.

For a powerboater, this leg may be a simple straight line with an easy-to-predict speed and direction. But for a sailor it becomes a series of doglegs, each with its own requirements for compass deviation calculations, speed measurements (or estimates) and other variables to do with steering the fastest possible course following a shifting wind, rather than a straight line.

This makes it far more important for a sailboat navigator to keep track of his DR track at every tack and jibe, and to make an estimate of position just before the course is changed.

It may be possible to sail equal times of each tack to simplify the calculation, but this is useful only when the destination is directly upwind, or down.

Since sailboats generally travel upwind with a "leeway angle" *(Chapter 10)*, allowances must be made for the difference between the compass orientation to the centerline of the hull and the hull's actual direction of travel through the water. It might vary by 2 or 3 degrees—much smaller than a typical steering error, but of potential significance as an additional factor over a very long leg.

All of these variations mean that a sailboat skipper must become adept at the calculations, described in this chapter, designed to resolve trigonometric problems.

A rule of thumb for sailing a tacking leg when the wind is not directly from or to your destination is to sail the longest leg first, except when the shorter leg may provide an opportunity for a fix that would be missing on the longer leg.

Finally, the actual chartwork aboard a sailboat can be more difficult due to a number of factors. The navigator may be working at an extreme angle of heel, for example, and is much more likely to be soaking wet.

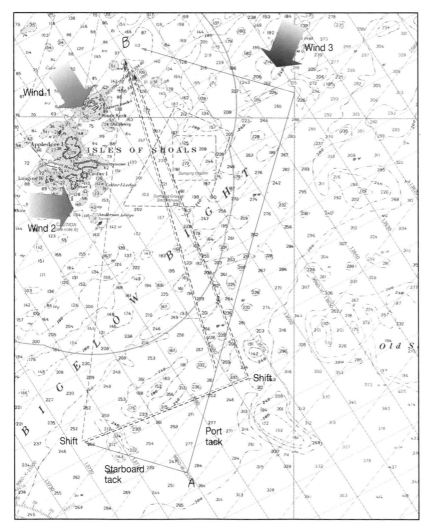

When a windward course requires two legs of unequal length, the longer one is usually sailed first. If the wind shifts, you will be in a better position to take advantage of the new angle—either by heading closer to the mark (and sailing a shorter course) on a counterclockwise shift, or tacking (and sailing a shorter course) on a clockwise shift. This illustration shows different possibilities and possible wind shifts.

SPECIALIZED TECHNIQUES

Beyond the basic techniques described in the preceding pages there are many other specialized techniques that are useful in specific situations. These techniques should not be regarded as shortcuts. Their use requires a thorough understanding of the principles, and they should not be approached until the basics have been covered.

Although the bow-and-beam technique has already been covered earlier in this chapter, you should know that there are other pairs of bearings that are not as easily obtained, but are easily used to plot a fix.

Special pairs of bearings
The following sets of bearings have a relationship to each other such that the run between the first bearing and the second will nearly equal the distance away from the sighted object when it is passed abeam:

20°-30°	21°-32°	22°-34°
23°-36°	24°-39°	25°-41°
27°-46°	29°-51°	30°-54°
31°-56°	32°-59°	34°-64°
35°-67°	36°-69°	37°-71°
38°-74°	39°-77°	40°-79°
41°-81°	43°-86°	44°-88°

Note that these are pairs of relative bearings to port as well as to starboard. In the table above, "20°-30°" can be either relative bearings 020° and 030°, or 340° and 330°; "31°-56°" can be either RB 031° and 056°, or RB 329° and 304°, etc.

The seven-eighths rule
If observations are made when the relative bearings are 30° and 60° on either bow, simple calculations will give two useful items of information. The distance run between the observations is equal to the distance to the object at the time of the second bearing (remember doubling the angle on the bow). Also, this same distance multiplied by ⅞ is the distance that the boat will be off from the sighted object when it is broad on the beam, provided that the vessel's course has not changed.

The seven-tenths rule
A comparable situation to the seven-eighths rule above is one in which the relative bearings are 22.5° and 45° to port or starboard. In this case, as before, the distance away from the sighted object is equal to the distance run between bearings, but the multiplier to determine distance off when the object is abeam is ⁷⁄₁₀.

Three-bearings-and-run-between
In all of the exercises involving two bearings, the run between must be carefully measured for course over ground. Current along a strange coast or heavy headwinds may make this measurement difficult.

By taking a third bearing and timing a second run (between the second and third bearings), enough information can be obtained to find the direction made good. Even without the speed and actual position, this direction made good may be quite useful in staying out of danger on a strange coast.

As soon as you spot the identifiable object onshore, take a bearing on it and note the time; record both items on the chart. Plot the bearing's LOP on your chart. In the example shown on page 476, top, that first LOP is XA. Next, when the object is exactly broad on the beam, note the time. Plot this second LOP and XB. Later, when the bearing on X has changed enough to give a good angle of intersection, take the third bearing, note the time carefully and plot it as XC in the diagram.

Since you have recorded the time of each bearing, you can determine the two elapsed times and compute the ratio of the first time interval to the second. For example, if you ran for 32.5 minutes between the first and second bearings, and then for 22.5 minutes more to the third bearing, the ratio would be 32.5/22.5, which can be reduced to 6.5/4.5.

Through a convenient point B, on the beam bearing LOP, draw a light "construction" line in the direction of your course

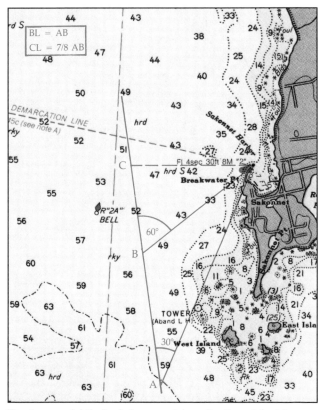

The "seven-eighths" rule is a special application of doubling the angle on the bow. If 30° and 60° are chosen as the first and second relative bearings, we know two things—the distance off at the second bearing is equal to the distance made good since the first bearing, and the distance off when we draw abeam of the object will be seven-eighths of the distance between the first and second bearing.

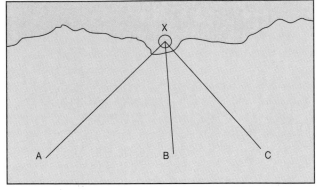

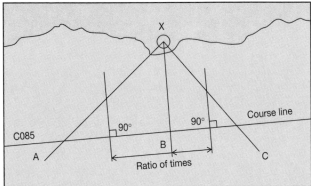

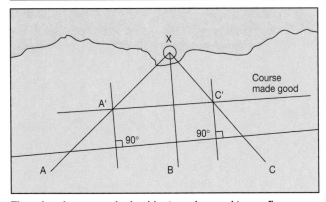

Three bearings on a single object can be used to confirm direction made good. The technique is to use the ratio of the distance traveled between the bearings, projected to the LOPs, to determine an actual course.

(C) as steered. Using point B as the reference or zero point, measure off to each side, along the construction line, distances proportional to the ratio of the time intervals, using any convenient scale.

Draw lines perpendicular to the construction line at the points determined by these proportional distances. These perpendiculars intersect the LOPs XA and XC at points A' and C'.

Connect points A' and C', and you have your answer. The direction of line A'C' is the course you are making good and includes the effects of currents, wind and errors in steering. Its direction may be taken from the chart and compared with the intended course. *It must be noted that this is not the actual track*—the selection of scale to represent the two time inter-

One of the easiest ways to acquire what is often referred to as a "sailor's eye" is to learn the simple but important principle of relative motion. For example, you find that your boat is converging on another boat that has the right of way. If you hold your course and speed, will you clear? What if your sailboat is on port tack and must offer right of way to a starboard tack boat? Do you hold and clear ahead, or duck under its stern? You have laid a course for a buoy, making allowances for current: Have you made the right allowance?

Relative motion is simply the motion of two boats in relation to each other. A boat approaching you on an opposite parallel course at 5 knots while you are making 4 knots has a relative motion of 9 knots. When meeting, if the skipper of the other boat turns to run alongside your boat to chat, your relative motion will be 1 knot, you will see his boat going slightly faster than yours.

The relative bearing of an object can be estimated within 5 or 10 degrees, with practice. When the direction of your own boat changes, the relative bearing also changes, though its true bearing remains the same. For example, if you are on a course of 050° true and sight an object bearing 090° relative, the true bearing of the object will be 140° (50 + 90). If you change your course by coming left to a course of 020°, the relative bearing of the object will now be 120°. But the true bearing remains the same at 140° (20 + 120).

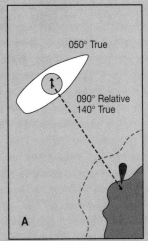
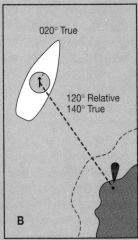

If a boat's heading changes, the relative bearing of an object is changed by the same amount. From the situation at A to that at B, the true heading of the boat has changed from 050° to 020°. The relative bearing has changed by the same amount, from 090° to 120°. Note that the sum of the heading and relative bearing remains constant.

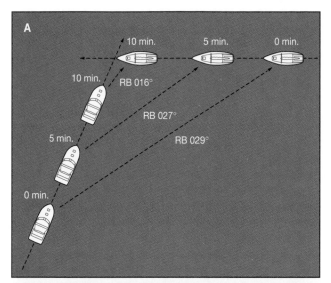

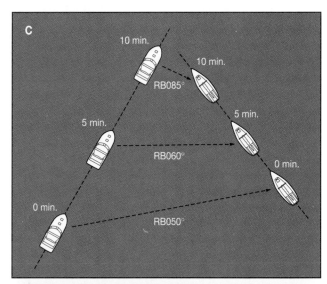

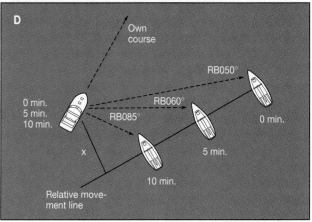

true) bearings, or to maintain a steady course. In practice, it is easier to maintain a steady course and observe the change in relative bearings. The actual relative bearing is far less important than the direction and rate of change.

What we want to know in any crossing situation is: Will we cross ahead, or astern, or will we collide? Because we are interested in relative and not absolute motions, it is convenient to think of our own boat as being stationary.

We have three basic situations:

1. The relative bearing of the other boat moves ahead (or toward our bow).

2. The relative bearing of the other boat moves aft.

3. The relative bearing of the other boat does not move at all.

The illustration at left shows the first situation: the other boat passing ahead. The successive positions of the two boats show a steadily decreasing relative bearing. Part A shows the

Here are two views of the same crossing situation. An observer in a balloon might see version A, while version B suggests the view from our own boat—the one that appears to be stationary. Crossing situations are much easier to predict if we imagine our own boat to be stationary and the other boat to be moving relative to our own.

vals would determine the location of points A' and C', and hence the line's position, though not its direction.

It is because ratios are used, and not actual speeds, that an accurate speed over the bottom is not needed here as it was in the case of the technique of two-bearings-and-run-between. Although it does not allow the navigator to determine his position or his speed over the bottom, this technique does show plainly whether he is making good his intended course, and helps determine whether the actual track parallels or converges with the shoreline.

To cross or not to cross

When determining the relative motion of another boat, it is necessary either to convert relative bearings to compass (or

The crossing pictured at the top, left of the page (*A and B*) had the other boat passing ahead of ours. We could make this prediction because its relative bearing moved toward our bow. In the situation above, the other boat's relative bearing moves aft. We know it will pass astern. In both cases, the separation at the point of closest approach is the distance x.

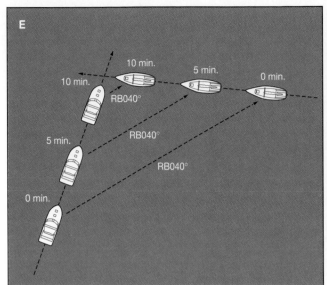

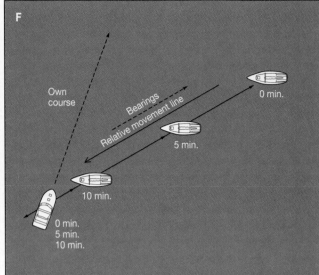

In this crossing the relative bearing remains constant—unless someone alters course or speed, they will collide. The line of relative motion passes through our boat and x is the separation at point of closest approach.

boats are in absolute motion and part B shows how it looks from our own boat if we imagined it to be stationary.

The line connecting the two boats in part B is the line of relative movement, the course and distance traveled by the other boat in relation to our own. Provided both boats maintain course and speed, it is a straight line. In this situation, when the line of relative motion is extended, it passes the bow of our "stationary" boat; therefore, the other boat following that line will cross ahead. The distance X, is the minimum distance that will separate the two boats in this case. It is known as the closest point of approach (CPA).

The second case, page 477, illustration C and D, is when the relative bearing moves aft. The line of relative movement passes aft, and so will the other boat.

If the relative bearing does not change, the line of relative motion will pass through our boat's position. You might say that the CPA is zero, but you would be more likely to say "He's going to hit us!"

It is important to note that these illustrations are not actual chart plots of the boats. The position of the other boat cannot be plotted unless distance and bearing information were available, and this is unlikely unless you are using radar.

The significance here is that bearing information only, which is available to any skipper, will indicate how the two boats will converge and whether they will collide. The CPA cannot actually be known unless a plot is made, but this is not significant.

Crossing situations

The rules developed from the observations covered above are as follows:
- Maintain a reasonably steady course and speed.
- Observe the relative bearing of the other boat only when

you are on your specified compass course. You must be on the same course each time you take a relative bearing.
- Watch the other boat for changes in course or speed which would obviously change the relative motion.
- If the relative bearing moves ahead, the other boat will pass ahead. If the relative bearing moves aft, the boat will pass astern. If the relative bearing is steady, there is a very real danger of collision.

Offsetting effects of current or wind

Relative bearings can also be taken to help in compensating for the effects of offsetting currents or wind. In the illustrations on page 479, the skipper has put his boat on a course that he believes will put a buoy close aboard and avoid a shoal. At the time of the first bearing ("0 minutes") the buoy bears 340° relative. Five minutes later, the relative bearing is 350°. It is clear that the boat is being set down more than expected and that the line of relative movement of the buoy will pass ahead of the boat (the boat will pass on the shoal side). If the bearing on the buoy remained steady, the boat would pass close to it, and if the bearing shifted gradually away from the bow, the skipper would know that he would clear the shoal safely. In the illustration, part G shows the problem in terms of the boat moving relative to the buoy, while in part H, the boat is considered to be stationary and the relative motion shown is that of the buoy. Note that the lines of relative movement in each case are parallel to each other, equal in length and opposite in direction.

Deliberate course offsets

A very useful technique in making a landfall confidently is to use a deliberate course offset—in fact, by deliberately missing your target. When you lay your course you set it decidedly

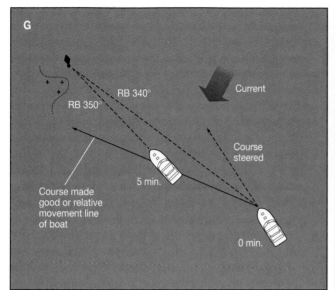

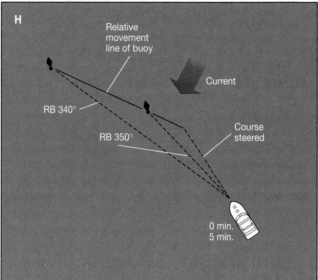

A graph of relative motion is also useful when the other object really is stationary. In this situation, we can use the graph to determine whether we will leave the buoy to port or to starboard. In G, our motion is relative to the buoy. In H, its "motion" is relative to us.

to one side of your objective. The advantage of this procedure lies in the fact that when you do not arrive at your destination, you know which way to turn. If you had aimed directly and, through unpredicted current or steering errors, had not arrived at your destination, you would not be sure whether it lay on your port or starboard bow. With the deliberate offset, you can make a confident alteration of course, usually parallel to the shoreline.

For example: You've been fishing somewhere between Block Island and Martha's Vineyard. After several hours of trolling, drifting and circling around your position is uncertain. Just as you decide that your fishing luck has run out and it's time to head back to Block Island, the fog closes in. Your best position estimate is that you are east of the bell buoy "1,"

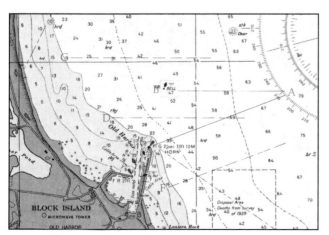

If you fail to make your predicted landfall, which way should you turn? The answer is to make a large, deliberate "error" to one side or the other—then the choice is clear.

marked as point B in the example below, left. You believe that you are somewhere near point A on the chart.

The solution to your problem is a deliberate offset. It's a good plan to lay your course for the off-lying bell buoy, but even if there were no buoy there is still merit in laying the course decidedly off to one side of the ultimate objective—Block Island Harbor.

Suppose you lay your course AB to the bell buoy and miss it by ⅛ mile to the north. When you pick up the 3-fathom (18-foot) curve at C, you know you are north of the harbor—because you would have picked it up much sooner if you were south of the harbor entrance.

Had you missed it by ⅛ mile to the south and picked up the 3-fathom curve at D, you would still be able to follow the curve southeastward to buoy "3." Even if your position were ¼ mile south of A when you laid your course westward, you would still pick up the 3-fathom curve at the entrance to the harbor.

You find added assurance of your general position north of the harbor when you find depths holding generally at 3 fathoms on your course southeastward. If your calculations were completely wrong and you ran southeastward from any point below the harbor, depths would increase.

Let us consider what would have happened if you had laid a course directly for buoy "3" and had missed your objective, E, by ¼ mile to the south. Picking up the 3-fathom curve at F, you could not be sure whether you were north or south of the entrance.

Your first conclusion might be that, since you have run a few minutes overtime before reaching the 3-fathom curve, you are north of the harbor. But don't forget that you didn't accurately know your starting point. Suppose you had been several minutes eastward of where you thought you were when the fog set in. In this event, the additional few minutes' running time before reaching the 3-fathom curve is reasonable.

On the assumption that you are indeed somewhat north of the harbor, you turn south, proceeding slowly and carefully. A few minutes pass, but still no buoy or harbor entrance. How far to continue? That buoy may be just ahead, obscured by the fog. On the other hand, doubt creeps in. You couldn't have been that far off in your reckoning—or could you? So you're in the fog—literally and figuratively.

In the first example, where you laid a deliberate offset, the intended track was about ⅜ mile to the north of the objective. How much deliberate offset should be made is a matter of judgment. On a long run in toward a long beach that runs for miles in either direction with few identifying marks, even if visibility is good, you may prefer to make allowances of a mile or more. But don't use this technique blindly. Study the chart carefully for possible dangers that may lie along the beach.

The same procedure may be used in crossing the Gulf Stream. Rather than attempting to make an exact allowance for the distance that the stream will set northward, make a somewhat over-generous allowance. If you don't pick up your target landfall after the allotted passage time, you can turn northward with confidence, rather than facing a 50-50 chance of being wrong.

Using a predicted timetable

If you are anticipating fog, you can take most of the worry out of the process by planning and plotting your run in advance. This same "timetable" technique can make a night run a pleasure instead of a trial.

Don't wait until you are underway to lay out your course, distances, running times, etc. Go over the entire trip in advance and acquaint yourself with each leg of the cruise, the aids to navigation that you will pass, the characteristics of lights, etc.

If you are piloting a powerboat and you can predict your speed with precision, set up a timetable. Set your time of departure as 0000 and note, in orderly fashion, the predicted time of arrival abeam of every light and buoy on both sides of your intended track. Alongside each entry show the characteristics of the navigational aid and the compass course at the time. You can also enter into your timetable the approximate times that major lights can be expected to become visible.

Use a watch or luminous clock with an alarm and set it at 0000 (12 o'clock). The elapsed time of each event along the track will provide a quick aid to identification for each light or sound signal along the way.

By using elapsed time rather than actual time, you build some flexibility into your plan. A late or early departure will not upset your entire timetable. Any discrepancies that creep in can be compensated for by a reset of the clock.

Coastwise piloting at night

The lights of towns along shore can be used to estimate distance offshore. An experienced boater may be able to judge his distance by whether or not he can see the glow from the street and sign lights, or whether he sees the lighting directly. This might be a useful technique on a long, straight shoreline of consistent elevation. Of course the height at which the lights might be seen directly will vary with the observer's height of eye and should be tested by observing the shoreline at known distances.

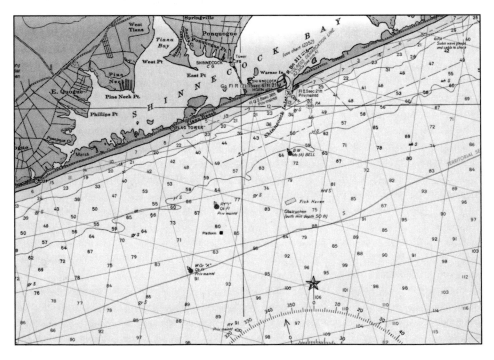

Many coastal areas with regular slopes offer depth information that can determine distance off. A rough, but useful, measure of distance off can also be made by using height of eye for your boat and observing the buildings onshore.

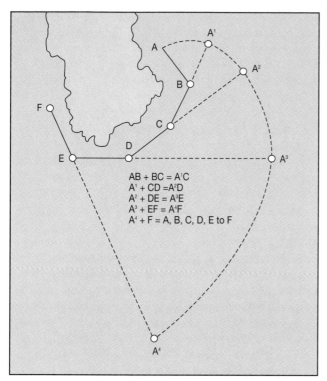

$$AB + BC = A^1C$$
$$A^1 + CD = A^2D$$
$$A^2 + DE = A^3E$$
$$A^3 + EF = A^4F$$
$$A^4 + F = A, B, C, D, E \text{ to } F$$

A pair of dividers can make quick work of adding the length of several straight segments of a curved course. Span the first segment, swing the A point to A1 and plant it. Move the B point to C, swing the A1 point to A2, etc. Lay the total span against your distance scale.

You may also be able to follow a shoreline (without the help of a depth sounder) by noting the point at which the beach, or shoreline disappears from view. This requires straight shoreline of consistent elevation as well as some experience, but it can be quite a useful check.

Let's say you wish to parallel the New Jersey or Long Island beaches. From the deck of a typical small boat, at about 4.5 miles offshore, the beach will be under your horizon. If you can just see the beach, you are about 4 miles off. Fog and haze will make this observation unreliable and the height of your eye on your particular boat will also vary this distance. Experiment when you have other means to calculate your actual distance offshore.

You can also use your view of buildings on shore to estimate distance. For example, if you can make out individual windows on houses, you are probably about 2 miles offshore. With this rule of thumb check, you could confidently stay from 2 to 4 miles off a long beach with no other reference.

Echo piloting

An interesting variation on the technique for estimating distance off a beach is one used in Alaska and British Columbia, where the problem is often to maintain a distance off a rocky cliff face. It consists of sounding a short blast on the whistle or horn and timing the return of the echo.

The interval in seconds (preferably measured on a stopwatch) is divided by two because the sound wave goes to the cliff face and back. Multiply that figure by 1,100, which is a rough value for the speed of sound in air in feet per second. (Multiply by 340 for the distance in meters.)

For example, you sound a blast and the interval is 5 seconds. Multiply 2.5 seconds (the one-way trip) by 1,100 and you have 2,650 feet, or a distance off of slightly less than ½ nautical mile.

In some cases a pilot might use an echo from both shores to stay in the middle of a passage simply by determining which one returns first, then altering course away from it.

The rule-of-sixty

This is another instance in which a convenient mental calculation can be made to reach a safe approximation. While it should never act as a substitute for position determination, this kind of calculation can be useful in making a decision while cruising shorthanded.

The rule-of-sixty provides a simple way of determining a new course to clear an off-lying danger area by the desired amount. You need to know your present course, your present distance off and the distance by which you would like to clear the danger area.

Let's assume that you are in the position shown on the chart below. You have come out of Portsmouth Harbor and are running a southerly course down the coast to Cape Ann. Somewhere off Newburyport you pick up the light on

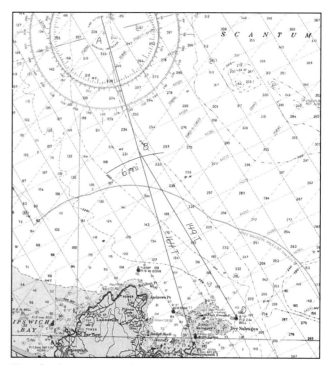

The rule-of-sixty can provide a shortcut for calculating the change in course required to clear an obstacle. It can be applied without making a chart plot.

Straitsmouth Island (marked C in the diagram), dead ahead. Your course made good along the line AC has been 164° true. A bell buoy has been placed 1.5 miles eastward of the light, marking a number of rock ledges. You want to make a course change to clear the shoals. By how many degrees should you change course?

You could get out the chart and plot your position—which, if you are able, you should do. But you can also apply the rule-of-sixty and determine your new course in your head.

You know that the light you are seeing on the horizon is visible for 8 miles. (We'll assume that it is a clear night; if it isn't, you will have to establish distance by some other means). The procedure is to divide 60 (the rule) by 8 (the distance,) to get 7.5. Since you want to clear the light by 1.5 miles, multiply 7.5 by 1.5 and get 11.25. Round this to 11—the number of degrees by which you will have to change course. Thus your new course is 164° – 11° = 153° true. Long before you need to be concerned about the rock ledges, you will pick up the bell buoy north of Flat Ground.

The rule-of-sixty is never a substitute for proper plotting, but in rough weather or other difficult circumstances, it can be a reassuring guide.

Distance along an irregular course

A pilot is often required to measure a total distance along a course that consists of several short, irregular legs. Of course, each leg can be measured and added, but there's a much easier, graphic method.

In the illustration on page 481 at top, the boat is at A. You need to know the total run to F, along the track B, C, D, E, F. The figure shows guide lines which extend each leg outwards, but after you become familiar with the procedure you can use your eye to make the same extensions.

Place your divider points on A and B. Swing the A point from A to A¹ (which lies along an extension of the next leg). Plant the divider point at A¹ and stretch the other leg to C. Again, swing the A¹ point to A² (the extension of the next leg.) Plant the point at A² and stretch the dividers to D. Repeat in this pattern until you have the dividers planted at A⁴ and stretched to F.

Now you can lay that divider span along the graphic scale or the latitude scale at either side of the chart. You can make the measurement quickly and more accurately this way than by measuring and adding each leg.

Practice—and more practice

Position determination cannot be learned totally "from the book." Study is essential, but you must put into practice the various procedures and techniques that you have studied. Remember, just as important as knowing the rules is knowing how to apply them. It's a good practice and good entertainment to "over-navigate" during daylight and in good weather so that you will be experienced, capable and confident when the sun sets and the weather closes in.

THE MANEUVERING BOARD

The Defense Mapping Agency Hydrographic/Topographic Center publishes a plotting sheet known as the Maneuvering Board. These forms are used by ships at sea for the solution of relative motion problems. Complicated movements of large task forces, as well as the tracking of a single ship, are plotted on maneuvering boards in order to facilitate the solution of problems of interception and the determination of the course and speed of radar contacts. For use in recreational boating, refer to *Bowditch*, *Dutton's* and DMA Publication No. 217, *Maneuvering Board Manual*.

Description of the sheet
To observe the physical appearance of a maneuvering board, refer to the illustration at right, which shows one reduced to about 40 percent of its original size of approximately 12 inches square. On it is printed, in green, a large circle with bearing lines radiating outward from the center every 10 degrees, and 10 concentric circles a half-inch apart to indicate speed or distance. At the right and left sides are lines of scale with numbered marks spaced equal to the distance between the concentric circles.

Thus, a speed line drawn out to the fifth circle could indicate 5, 10, 15, 20 or 25 knots as determined by your choice of scale. At the bottom of the sheet are three lines divided into logarithmic scales for use in solving time, distance and speed problems. If two of these quantities are known, the third may be found by drawing a line between the known values on the appropriate scales, and finding the answer at the intersection of this line with the third scale.

The bearing lines and circles of distance facilitate the plotting of positions of other boats or objects relative to yours. These radial lines and concentric circles can also be used for vector diagrams with lines drawn to represent actual and relative motion. Each vector, according to its length and direction, depicts a statement of fact in the problem.

A vector line indicates graphically the direction and velocity of an element of the problem, such as the course and speed of your boat, another boat, the wind or the current. In some instances, the vector will not be drawn from the center of the sheet, but its direction is always measured with reference to the center point and the outer circular scale.

Points on diagrams of position are labeled with upper-case (capital) letters; points on vector diagrams are labeled with lower-case letters.

Maneuvering board sheets are printed on both sides, and the paper is sufficiently heavy that both sides may be used. The cover sheets of both the 5090 and the 5091 pads include instructions for their use in various problems. The 5090 or 5091 sheets are particularly useful on board radar-equipped vessels where distance as well as bearing can be measured.

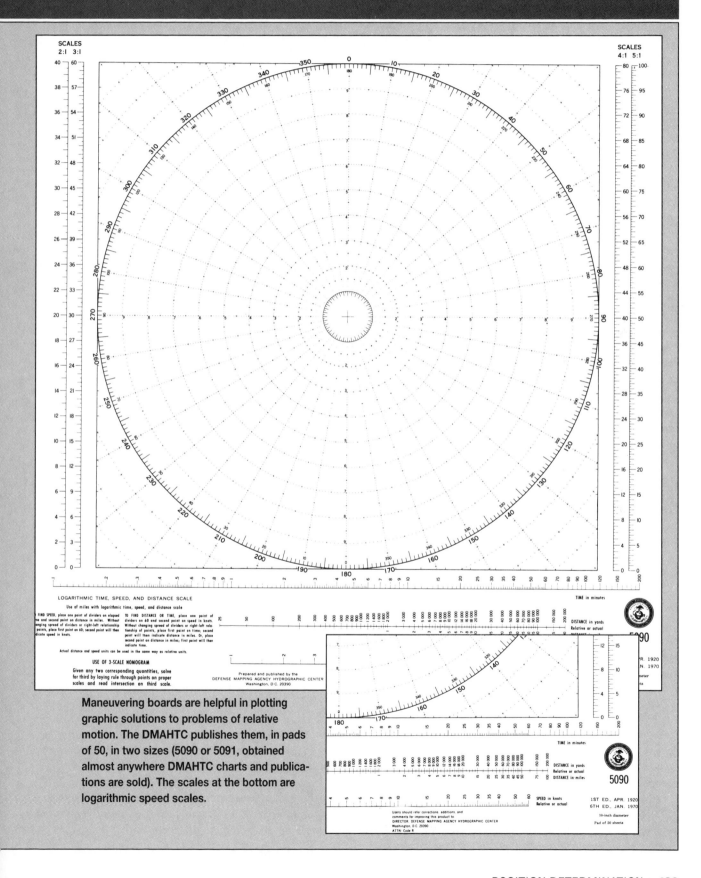

Maneuvering boards are helpful in plotting graphic solutions to problems of relative motion. The DMAHTC publishes them, in pads of 50, in two sizes (5090 or 5091, obtained almost anywhere DMAHTC charts and publications are sold). The scales at the bottom are logarithmic speed scales.

21 INLAND PILOTING

Some of the finest cruising is found on inland rivers and lakes. This waterway network gives access to areas far removed from tidal waters. Throughout the U.S. there are more than 30,000 miles (48,000 km) of waterways navigable by small boats. Using the Mississippi, the Great Lakes, the N.Y. State Barge Canal, and other waterways linking these with the Atlantic and Gulf Intracoastal Waterways, a boater can navigate the entire eastern portion of the U.S.—a cruise of more than 5,000 miles (8,000 km).

Boating on inland lakes, rivers and canals is different from boating on coastal rivers, bays and sounds, and along saltwater shores. This chapter explains these differences and the importance of knowing how to apply them.

RIVER PILOTING

While rivers seldom offer vast open expanses where you will need the usual techniques of coastline piloting, they do require special piloting skills. Local lore often outweighs certain piloting principles that are the coastal skipper's law, because a river's ever-changing conditions put a premium on local knowledge. Consequently, river navigation is often more an art than it is a science.

The fundamental difference between river piloting and coastal piloting is the closeness of the shore, usually with easily identifiable landmarks or aids to navigation. Knowing where you are is therefore not a problem. The skill of river piloting lies in directing your boat to avoid hazards—on many rivers, this is no simple matter.

Water level changes

Inland waters are non-tidal, but that doesn't mean that they have no water level fluctuation. The variations in level are apt to be seasonal in nature as spring freshets, loaded with debris, flood down from the headwaters, overflow banks and course rapidly on down to the sea. The annual changes in level can be astounding. At St. Louis, for example, the seasonal fluctuations in river level from winter-spring flood conditions to low levels in summer and fall may be as much as 50 feet (15 m). In some smaller navigable streams, sudden hard rains may raise the water level several feet (a meter or two) in a matter of hours.

Aids to navigation and piloting directives

The larger inland rivers, those that are navigable from the sea, have aids to navigation maintained by the U.S. Coast Guard. These aids to navigation follow the basic U.S. system of buoyage. Many of their lights, buoys and dayboards are like those discussed in Chapter 22, but a few are specially designed for their "inland" purpose. Some rivers follow the Western Rivers System of buoyage, and many other rivers under state jurisdiction have aids to navigation conforming to the Uniform State Waterway Marking System (USWMS), also discussed in Chapter 22. In the Western Rivers System only, river piloting directives refer to the "right" and "left" banks. For example, the right bank is the one on your right when traveling with the flow of the river (seaward). With the basic U.S. system, right and left banks are not identified as such. This means that the right side of the river will be to your starboard as you go upstream (from seaward).

However, on the New York State Canal System, where regulations refer to the "starboard" side of the canal, they mean the right side when entering from Waterford (near Albany). That means the starboard side of the Champlain Canal is the east side, and on the adjacent Erie Barge Canal, the starboard side is the north side. Check your charts carefully.

A "mile" on an inland waterway is assumed to be a statute (land) mile, not a nautical mile. Aids to navigation along many waterways are conspicuously marked with mileages showing the distance from a designated reference point. It is always easy to get a fix on a river because you can easily relate the mileage figure on the dayboard or light structure with the mileage figures on your chart. In the Western System, these take the place of the odd and even numbers used on navigation aids in coastal waters, and are helpful in computing distance and speed.

Lights

Most lights on major rivers, such as the Mississippi, show through 360 degrees—they are visible all around the horizon. However, a beam may occasionally be projected in one direction only, or the intensity of the beam may be increased by a line in a particular direction. A beam's width provides information; a narrower beam marks a more critical channel.

According to the IALA-B system, described in Chapter 22, lights on a river will show a single green flash for the right bank and a double red flash for the left bank. You may still encounter the odd white flashing light where it has not yet been changed to the new system.

Each waterway system has at least a few of its own variations on the basic U.S. Inland System. Careful reading of chart notes, *Light Lists* and *Notices to Mariners* are just as important for inland pilots as for coastal pilots, and visiting skippers should make a practice of seeking out local knowledge.

WATERWAYS INFORMATION

Three federal agencies have jurisdiction over U.S. waterways. In Canada, navigable waterways are charted by the Canadian Hydrographic Service.

The overall source for U.S. waterway information is the U.S. Army Corps of Engineers, whose map *Major Waterways and Ports of the United States* presents the whole picture. Color maps of smaller river regions show details of interest to boaters—marinas, ramps, sanitary facilities, camping and picnic sites, as well as dams and locks. Their series of *Lakeside Recreation* maps for each region of the U.S. is particularly useful. These are available from every Corps office and from the U.S. Army Corps of Engineers (*Appendices*), Publications Department .

In addition, each local office of the Corps publishes its own series of maps. An example is the Mississippi River: The Chicago District covers the middle and upper region, and the Vicksburg, Mississippi District covers the lower Mississippi. Refer to the "Chart and Cruising Information Sources" (*Appendices*) for Corps offices of interest to boaters.

The U.S. Geological Survey (USGS) publishes a series of brochures, *River Basins of the United States*. These include general maps of major rivers, along with information of historical, hydrographic and geological interest.

Another service, the Tennessee Valley Authority's Mapping Services Branch (*Appendices*), publishes navigational charts of the waters under its jurisdiction.

In Canada, all but the smallest lakes and rivers are charted by the Canadian Hydrographic Service; the exceptions are covered by other agencies. The Canada Map Office publishes topographic maps showing water areas, but without depth information. The Ontario Ministry of Natural Resources publishes provincial Fishing Maps, which show water depths as well as other fishing-related detail. Canada's major sub-arctic lakes and rivers are charted by the Saskatchewan Property Management Corporation at a scale of 1:50,000 as well as by the Canadian Hydrographic Service. Maps Alberta supplies charts of that province's lakes and rivers.

A further source of information on U.S. lakes and rivers, particularly the "Wild and Scenic River System," is the National Park Service of the United States Department of the Interior in Washington, DC.

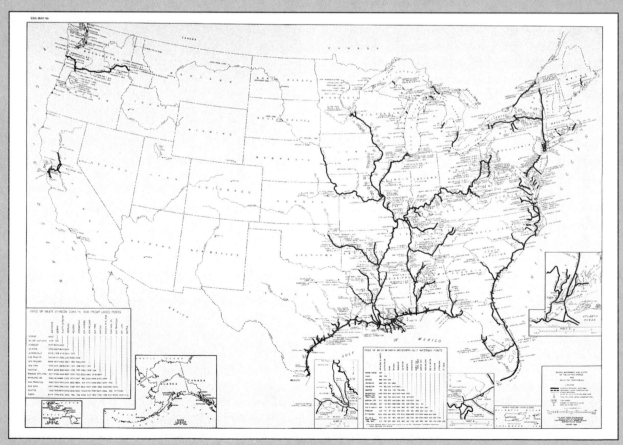

The U.S. Army Corps of Engineers publishes *Major Waterways and Ports of the United States*, an overview of the waterways under their jurisdiction.

Dayboards and buoys

The basic U.S. system of buoyage *(Chapter 22)* is the standard. It covers all rivers and lakes except where the Western Rivers and the Uniform State Waterway Marking systems are used. They are a compatible variation.

The basic U.S. system shows "passing dayboards" of either square green with green reflective borders to your port, or to your starboard as you are going upstream, red triangles with red reflective borders.

In addition, the Mississippi—part of the Western Rivers System—uses "crossing dayboards" that are diamond-shaped, green or red. These indicate that the channel is crossing from one bank to the other. If lighted, these dayboards are green with a white light (single flash) and red with a white light (double flash), with their respective reflective borders.

Buoys will be either red with red light (double flash) or green with green light (single flash). The Uniform State Waterway Marking System (USWMS) uses a red buoy with red light and a black buoy with a green light. The USWMS makes use of the white light for mooring and cardinal markers.

Buoys marking wrecks are lateral buoys showing a quick-flashing light of the appropriate color. The USWMS uses cardinal buoys with a white light, when used.

Isolated danger buoys will be red and black horizontal bands and, if lighted, will have a group (2) flashing white light (not used on the Western Rivers System).

Preferred-channel buoys will be red-over-green or green-over-red horizontal bands and, if lighted, a composite group (2-1) light of the appropriate color will be used.

Particular attention must be paid to the notion of "right" and "left." The choice is not always intuitive, but is fundamental to the coloring of buoys.

Ranges

On a number of major rivers, such as the Hudson and the Connecticut, where channels through flats are stabilized and maintained by dredging, ranges with conspicuous markers on shore help you stay within narrow channel limits. If you align the front and rear markers properly, you will be able to hold your course safely in mid-channel despite off-setting currents or crosswinds.

Refer to Chapter 22 for markings used by the Western Rivers System, as well as the Uniform State buoyage system.

River charts

River charts are often issued in the form of books, with each page covering a successive, short stretch of river and oriented to make best use of the page size rather than to maintain North at the top of the page.

Beacons, unlike buoys, are fixed to the river bottom. They may have triangular daymarks to make them readily visible.

A good example is the New York State Canal book, NOS Chart 14786. Charts on it resemble the coastal charts described in Chapter 18. Land areas are in a gold tint; channels 12 feet (3.7 m) deep or more are white, with lesser depths light blue and depth contour lines at 6 and 12 feet (1.8 and 3.7 m). Black lines delineate the banks. Buoy symbols have magenta discs if they are lighted. Aids to navigation are numbered, and scattered depth figures give the skipper a good idea as to whether it is wise to venture out of the channel to seek an anchorage or for any other reason. Rocks and wrecks are indicated with standard symbols from Chart No. 1 *(Chapter 18)*. Arrows indicating current flow direction, used on many other inland charts, do not appear on those of New York inland waterways.

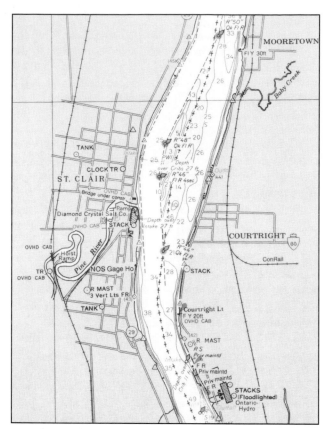

A section of NOS Chart 14852 shows the boundary between Canada (on the right) and the United States. Depths are referenced to the Great Lakes datum. Two channels are marked—upbound and downbound.

Missing from typical river charts is the compass rose. Instead, they generally carry an arrow indicating true north.

Statute mileages are given every five miles, with small red circles at one-mile intervals. A detailed, alphabetical table lists all towns, cities, bridges, mouths of tributaries and other important features along the main channel, with their distances and the number of the chart on which they appear.

River chart variations

River charts from different sources, such as the Corps of Engineers, do not all use the same symbol and coloring scheme. Before you use one of these charts, study it very carefully—particularly its legend. In addition to the usual content of the legend (navigation symbols, abbreviations, topographic and hydrographic information), characteristics peculiar to that chart are often described.

An example is the bound volume published annually by the Mississippi River Commission, Vicksburg, Mississippi, to cover the Mississippi from Cairo, Illinois, to the Gulf of Mexico. With a few exceptions, depth information is omitted, as is information on the shoals and ledges that would be shown on a coastal chart. The course of the river is traced in a blue tint between heavy black lines delineating the banks. A broken red line indicates the center of the navigable channel. Navigation lights are shown by a diamond and dot symbol with the name of the lights and a number indicating their distance upstream from a reference point—in this case, "AHP," meaning "Above the Head of Passes." (The Head of Passes is the point where the river divides into separate channels leading through the delta into the Gulf of Mexico.)

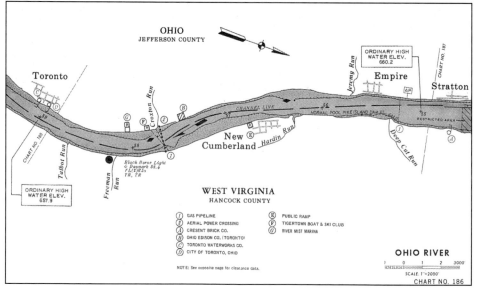

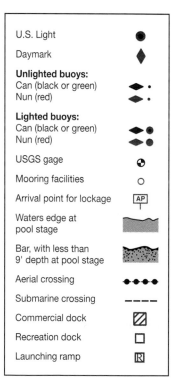

On this chart for the Ohio River, the arrow at the top indicates true north, which is seldom at the top of the chart. Locations of bulletin boards that show river stages are also on the chart, along with the reference point for gage readings. Symbols for nun and can buoys differ from those on National Ocean Service charts; these and other river chart symbols are shown in the legend at right, excerpted from the chart.

ILLINOIS WATERWAY - Illinois River					
Name of aid	Number of miles from Grafton	Bank or side of channel	Daymark		Remarks
Character and period of light			Up	Down	
BEDFORD, ILL.	48.5	Right ...	...	...	
Pilot Peak Bend Light .... Gp. Fl. W., 5 sec., 2 flashes.	47.8	Left	TR	TR	Visible 360° with higher intensity beam oriented downstream.
BUCKHORN ISLAND DAYMARK	46.1	Right ...	SG	SW	
Van Geson Island Light .... Gp. Fl. W., 5 sec., 2 flashes.	44.9	Left	TR	TR	
Grand Pass Bridge Upper Light .... Fl. W., 4 sec.	44.1	Right ...	SW	CW	Visible 360° with higher intensity beam oriented upstream.

Charts for the Mississippi River System should be supplemented by United States Coast Guard *Light List*, *Volume V*, which provides more details on aids than can be shown on the charts.

The book of Illinois Waterway charts shows the main channel in white with shoal areas tinted blue and land areas colored yellow.

Navigation "tools" and local knowledge

On most rivers, as opposed to other waters, you will place much less reliance on a compass. Generally you will use a binocular more, to sight from one navigational aid to the next. In fog, recreational boat traffic can come to a virtual standstill, although large commercial vessels normally carry on with radar. This does not mean you can dispense with a compass on all rivers—some are wide enough that, even in fog, you can continue with conventional piloting using a speed curve, stopwatch and caution. Also, some rivers feed into large lakes.

Not even the best charts and publications can tell you everything about a particular stretch of river. Remember that rivers are particularly prone to seasonal and irregular changes; take every opportunity to speak to experienced local people about hazards or recent changes.

Currents

Broadly speaking, river currents, although they fluctuate in velocity, will always trend in one direction—from the headwaters to the mouth. Tidal rivers may nevertheless have strong tidal conditions at the mouth, which back the water up so that you can take advantage of a favorable current going upstream. On the Hudson, for example, an economy-minded skipper electing to run at 9 to 10 knots can time a trip to carry a favorable tidal current all the way from New York to Albany, a distance of 150 miles (241 km) inland. Tides at Albany, even so far from the sea, may range in excess of 6 feet (1.8 m), although at other points downstream, the range will be much less.

The strength of current usually varies widely from season to season. Speeds on some sections of the Mississippi range from 1 to 6 miles per hour (1.6 and 9.7 km per hour) under average conditions. At extreme high water stages, current strengths may be much greater—9 mph (14.5 km per hour) or more in narrow and constricted areas. Sometimes, moving upstream is not feasible at all.

Pilots of deep-draft, mainly commercial, vessels can cut their time and operating costs substantially by finding the more favorable or weaker current as they move upstream. This search will often take them very close to the river bank and even into small coves, since friction along the bottom slows the current. The smaller, shallower-draft vessel may be affected by a different current altogether.

A boat that cruises at 12 mph in a 4-mph current will make either 8 mph or 16 mph—an important difference even where fuel costs are not crucial to the success of the trip. Even for a 20-mph craft, the difference between 16- and 24-mph speeds is 50 percent.

Channels at river bends

As a river flows around a bend, it tends to carve out the outside curve and slow down around the inside, depositing silt, forming shoals and, ultimately, bars. Man-made structures and unusual bottom contours may alter this pattern, but generally, river channels going around bends will shoal on one side and deepen on the other over time.

With this river flow characteristic in mind, you will be less likely to cut corners by running a straight course from one buoy to the next. You will be more inclined to look for the deeper water on the outside of the curve and to follow the bend, especially as most river charts do not indicate depth. The rule of thumb is to stay about one-quarter of the river's width off the outside bank.

Study the topographic contours of the river banks for clues about the contour of the river bottom. Contour lines crowded together near shore indicate a bluff rising steeply from the bank that may imply good depth close by. The bluff may also serve as a landmark to steer by.

By staying in mid-channel, this small boat avoids the shoals that build up along the inside of river bends. A deep-draft vessel may need to follow the outside edge of the bend in order to make sure there is sufficient depth.

Shoals and dredging

Most river channels require dredging to remove silt carried downstream by faster currents that scrub away the upstream river banks. In some rivers dredging goes on year-round.

In the Mississippi River sedimentary deposits also take the form of "flocculation"—a jellied mass of ooze sometimes reaching a height of 10 to 15 feet (3.0 to 4.6 m) above the bottom each year. Deep-draft vessels usually plow through it.

Shoals that build up at the mouth of a river or at the confluence of two rivers can cause other problems. Strong outflowing currents, opposed by crosswinds, can build up difficult wave patterns and rough seas.

An experienced river pilot will have an intuitive sense of where to find deep water, and will also know which way to turn when the water suddenly shoals.

Eyeball piloting

Much of a river pilot's success depends on his acquired skill of interpreting what he sees. The surface condition of the river presents clues as to depth and current, but the interpretation is not easy. On one hand, where there is chop in the channel, there may be smooth water over bars—but it may be due to weeds. On the other hand, the wind may create ripples over a bar that are not evident in the channel.

In some narrow channels, with wind against current, a small sea builds up in which the larger waves indicate the

As a rule, the outside edge of a river bend provides the deepest water. The contour of the river bank is also an indication of the underwater contour, but experience and judgment are required for correct interpretation. Local knowledge is a valuable commodity for the visitor.

The Guntersville Yacht Club in Alabama uses floating piers to accommodate the seasonal fluctuation in water level.

deeper water and grow smaller at the channel's edge. Only a knowledgeable and experienced pilot will know how to interpret different wave patterns.

Your wake can also provide clues as to depth. As it rolls away from your stern into shallow water, the wake's smooth curves may give way to a sharper formation, or may crest and break on flats. If your wake crowds in toward you and appears short and peaked, sheer off, and fast, away from that side of the channel into deeper water.

River safety

River boaters are subject to many of the general requirements for safety and good seamanship covered in other chapters, and must also be prepared for the special hazards of river cruising. For example, boat handling near piers and slips may be complicated by swift river currents. Grounding on river shoals may be more troublesome than it is in tidal areas because you can't expect to float off on a rising tide.

While you can usually find shelter from a blow close at hand, you will also find situations where a sizable chop is generated by current and opposing wind. You may also need to seek protection from the wakes of passing river traffic.

Many rivers now provide safety harbors (areas where the banks have been cleared of stumps, boulders, snags or other underwater hazards) and landings for use in bad weather and other emergencies. These are shown on the chart. Direction boards on shore mark the entrances, and cross boards mark the upper and lower limits.

In some barge canals, protective terminals are available for recreational boaters, although they are sometimes in use by commercial vessels. You should be equipped with plenty of large fenders to avoid damage by the rough concrete sides.

On some rivers, marinas are built on floating piers to allow for seasonal changes in water level. However, this means a long climb up at low water.

RIVER PILOT PUBLICATIONS

Army Corps of Engineers publications
The Army Engineers at Vicksburg, Mississippi, publish a pamphlet called *Mississippi River Navigation*, which contains information compiled "for part-time pilots" as well as interesting background information on the river.

Army Engineers District and Divisional offices issue several regular publications about current conditions. These are variously termed *Divisional Bulletins*, *Navigational Bulletins*, *Navigational Notices*, *Notices to Navigational Interests* (weekly) and *Special Notices to Navigation Interests* (as required). These publications show river conditions such as channel depths and widths, current velocity estimates, controlling bridge clearances, construction projects and other hazards. They also locate and describe marine facilities such as railways and lifts.

Coast Guard *Notices*
The Second Coast Guard District, headquartered in St. Louis, issues *Local Notices to Mariners* covering changes to aids to navigation, hazards, etc., for the Mississippi River System. The USCG also issues *Channel Reports*, noting the least depths found by Coast Guard cutters and buoy tenders on their river patrols.

Light List
One of the most helpful documents is the Coast Guard's *Light List*, *Volume V*, covering all of the Mississippi River System. It tabulates lights, buoys and other aids to navigation and gives mileages from specified points. Aids are described in greater detail than can be supplied by chart symbols and abbreviations.

Under no circumstances should boaters compromise the maneuvering room available to river tows (a series of linked barges propelled by a powerful, deep-draft tug). Avoid passing them in river bends.

Anchoring

A widening of the river may provide an opportunity to anchor out of the main traffic. The configuration of a bank or bar may offer a harbor with complete protection. Islands in midstream often leave a channel for small boats opposite the side used by deeper-draft commercial vessels. When a river cuts a channel behind a section of bank, a "towhead" is formed. Sometimes these are filled in or dammed across the upper end by river deposits, forming a harbor that can be entered by the lower end.

When entering between islands or between an island and the bank, beware of submerged wing dams at the upstream end. To be safe, enter and leave from the downstream end.

When anchoring on a larger river near a sandbar or island, or when beaching a small boat, pick the downstream rather

This typical Mississippi River bank is riprapped with concrete to protect it against erosion. Use care near such banks to avoid damage to your boat's bottom.

than the upstream end. If your anchor were to drag, the current at the upstream end would push you harder ashore. Current at the downstream end may be quieter, and the eddies that usually form there may help to free you.

Be cautious when going ashore or camping on sandbars exposed at low water. They may be very unstable.

The character of river bottoms varies widely, but in their lower reaches, they are often soft mud. At least one broad-fluked anchor should be inboard—one that will dig down until it reaches a good holding. A grapnel anchor, with its spidery arms, will be of little use in mud, but may be the best choice over hard or rocky bottoms.

When anchoring in areas full of snags and roots, it is wise to rig a trip line to the anchor's crown. Make fast a small float to the end—an empty plastic bottle will do—so that you can raise the anchor by its crown.

Leave an anchor light burning all night if there is any chance of other vessels being underway nearby.

Making fast to the bank

Riverbanks must often be approached with caution. Of course, you should check that the depth is adequate (a lead line is very handy here) and free of obstacles. Be aware of submerged tree stumps that might prove dangerous when a large wash from a passing vessel comes ashore. Avoid vertical banks that show signs of active erosion—exposed tree roots, for example. Banks are often protected from wash by rocky "riprap," which can be very hard on a boat's bottom.

Even on non-tidal rivers there may be good reason to allow plenty of mooring line slack for water level fluctuations and for heavy wash from passing traffic, especially large tugs. Always observe and imitate the local practice.

THE CHALLENGES OF RIVER CRUISING

River conditions can change drastically from one season to the next. On one cruise you may encounter high water and floating debris, and run across shoals in the same area only a few weeks later. In some conditions you may be wise to seek out an experienced local pilot.

Eddies and whirlpools

On the Mississippi, "sand boils" may be caused by sand welling up from the river bottom. Sometimes, in flood, these can throw a boat out of control.

Debris

Floating and partially submerged debris such as tree trunks can be a hazard to small boats. Keep a sharp lookout. Debris is usually worst in the spring when flood waters sweep away fallen tree trunks from above the normal high-water line.

Submerged buoys

River currents can occasionally flow so fast that buoys are towed under and completely submerged. In that case only a "V" on the surface marks their position. Sometimes such a buoy will be visible to upbound traffic or will pop out in the wake of a passing vessel.

Stationary surface disturbances

Avoid any fixed surface disturbance: There is likely a submerged obstacle lurking beneath. The exception may be the "V" created by the convergence of two currents—such a "V" always points downstream, never up.

Misplaced buoys

Keep in mind that river buoys can easily be carried away by strong current and floating debris.

Large, exposed areas

Many rivers, especially the Mississippi, can open out into wide, shallow lakes with hazardous bottoms. Lake Peppin is a typical example. Long fetches of shallow water often produce short, high waves that, when combined with the wash from other traffic, may present a serious hazard to a small boat.

Construction and dredging equipment

Hydraulic pipeline dredges with long lengths of floating pipe, barges carrying bank-protection equipment that extend hundreds of feet out from the shore, and other construction equipment often work along rivers. Keep well clear, and be especially cautious when approaching such equipment from upstream— avoid being swept into, or even under, cranes and similar structures. Using your VHF radio, contact working vessels and barges for advice and permission to pass.

Confusing lights

Obviously, special caution is required when running even well-lit rivers at night. The searchlights of commercial traffic may blind you, and shore lights, with their reflections, may add to the confusion. Floating debris often cannot be seen at all.

Commercial traffic

You must know how to handle your boat to avoid hindering commercial traffic. In a narrow channel, a tug or barge may require most of the available water. Most tugs actually push, rather than tow, the barges and this allows better control. Nevertheless, passing on a bend can be very dangerous. There may be ample room to pass at the beginning of the barge's swing, but this space may close up very quickly, leaving no room for a boat to maneuver. If you must pass, it's usually better to do so on the inside of the curve.

Jumbo tows

Big barge rafts (tows) on the Mississippi may cover acres of water, and you should never jeopardize their activities, regardless of right-of-way. Integrated tows may consist of a bow piece, a group of square-ended barges and a tug pushing at the stern, all lashed together in one unit 1,000 feet (305 m) or more in length. At night, the lights of the tugboat may be more conspicuous than the side lights on the barges far out ahead. Inland Rules require that barges pushed ahead must show a quick-flashing yellow light all the way forward on the centerline.

Stay away from the front of tows. Even modest ones may need a half-mile to come to a full stop.

Small-boat whistle signals are usually inaudible at the helm of a tug, so use the VHF on channels 13 and 16 to communicate your whistle signals. (On the Mississippi below Baton Rouge, Channel 67 is required in addition to 13.) Skippers often send their signals verbally, saying "one-whistle" or "two whistles" as they approach, rather than sounding blasts on their horns.

Approach locks with care

Locks are often paired with river dams. As you approach from upstream, it may be very difficult to see the edge of a dam where water pours over a sill, especially at night. Study the chart well before your approach so that you can correctly interpret aids to navigation, lock signals and the orientation of the lock entrance.

Spillways below locks and dams can change from tranquil to treacherous without any warning as flood valves are opened.

Watch your wake

Your wake can do serious damage to the fragile river banks of many waterways, especially when they are narrow, and can also threaten smaller boats. Regulate your speed so as to pro-

CANAL BOATING

Before the construction of dams and locks, many of our rivers were unnavigable. Water coursed down valleys at the land's natural gradient, dropping hundreds of feet in not many miles, running too fast and encountering too many obstacles for safe navigation. To overcome such obstacles, engineers dam natural waterways to create a series of pools or levels—"locks"—that may be compared to a stairway. In many waterways, locks in a series actually follow one after another like stairs going up or down as needed.

Water levels

For the river pilot, the term "poolstage" indicates the height of water in a pool at any given time with reference to the datum for that pool. On many rivers, poolstages are posted on conspicuous bulletin boards along river banks so as to be easily read from passing vessels. Charts state the locations of these bulletin boards.

On the Ohio River, gauges at the locks of each dam show the depth of the pool impounded by the next dam downstream. For example, if the chart indicates a 12-foot (3.7 m) gauge reading for a normal pool, a reading of 11.7 feet (3.6 m) indicates that the next pool is 0.3 feet (0.1 m) below normal elevation.

Much of our waterway system is man-made, and requires ongoing maintenance. Speeds are stringently regulated.

Locks and dams

Without locks, dams on our inland waterways would restrict river cruising to the individual pools, and would prevent through navigation except for boats light enough to be portaged. But locks permit boats to move from one level to another. Since almost all locks were designed to handle commercial traffic, lock sizes seldom restrict recreational boats. Most locks can accommodate many vessels at a time.

Locks are watertight chambers with gates at each end and, usually, underwater valves to admit and release the natural flow of the waterway. Before a boat is to be locked upstream the gates are first closed and valves on the lock's downstream side are opened to let the water run out to the lower level. Then the downstream gates are opened so that the vessel can enter the lock. The downstream gates are then closed and water flows into the lock from upstream, through another set of valves until the chamber is filled to the level of the upper pool. The upstream gates are opened and the vessel exits the lock on its way upstream. Locking a vessel down is the reverse process.

The fact that locks use the natural flow of the current and not pumped water explains why some locks are restricted in the number of openings during droughts or dry seasons.

Small locks may not use independent valves, but may, instead, simply open each gate slightly to allow water into or out of the chamber.

On Canada's Trent-Severn Waterway, the famous lock at Peterborough, Ontario, is actually a hydraulic elevator in which two large tanks, containing the boats, counterbalance as they rise and fall to the upper and lower water levels. The same waterway in another section uses an ingenious marine railway with a unique cradling device to carry boats up and down a steep grade and deposit them at the end.

Locking signals

Whistle signals are prescribed for vessels approaching a lock, to be answered by the lockmaster. The signals vary from one waterway to another and, in many places, VHF radio is used for communications with the lockmaster. On the Ohio River, vessels sound a long and a short blast on the whistle from a distance of not more than one mile from the lock. Approaching boats must wait for the lockmaster's signal before entering. Where locks are in pairs (designated as "landward" and "riverward"), the lockmaster on the Ohio may also use an air horn to give directions, as follows: one long, enter landward lock; two longs, enter riverward lock; one short, leave landward lock; two shorts, leave riverward lock.

On the Mississippi, signs on the face of the guidewall warn small boats not to pass a certain point until signaled by the lockmaster. Boaters use a signal cord near the sign if their own horns are not loud enough to attract the lockmaster's attention. Similar arrangements are found on the Columbia River running between Oregon and Washington, on the Okeechobee Waterway in Florida, and elsewhere.

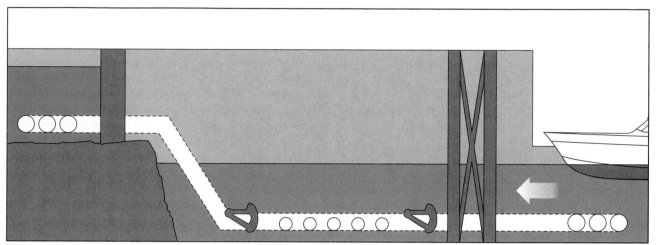

1 After the water has run out of the lower level lock, the downstream gates are opened so that the approaching vessel can enter the lock.

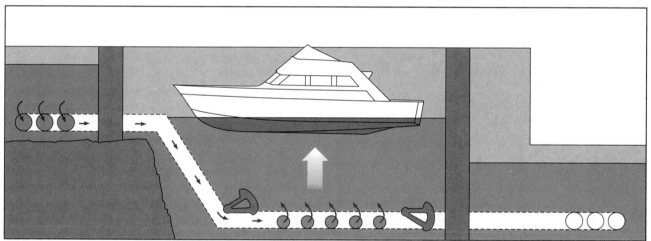

2 The downstream gates are then closed, and water flows into the lock from upstream, through another set of valves, until the chamber is filled to the level of the upper pool.

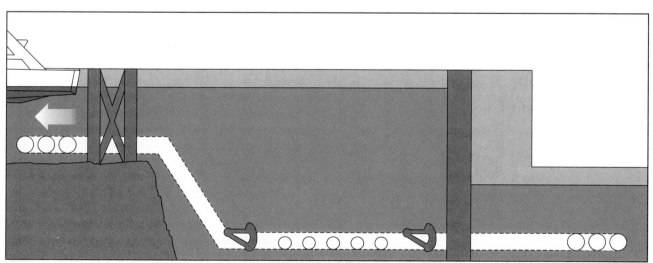

3 The upstream gates are opened, and the vessel exits the lock on its way upstream. When a craft is headed downstream, the process is reversed.

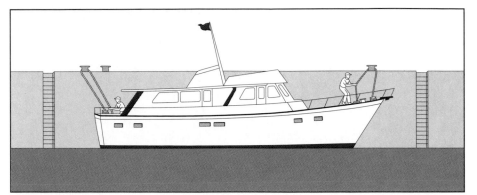

Two mooring lines should be used, led from bow and stern, to the bollards on the pier and back to the deck. While they can be snubbed against a cleat, they should never be cleated on the way down. Some skippers like to lead their lines to the side opposite the wall when the lock is very deep.

Signal lights

Traffic signal lights on the Ohio locks resemble those you see on city streets. Flashing red warns "do not enter, stand clear"; flashing amber (or yellow) signals mean "approach, but under full control"; flashing green is the "go-ahead." Simpler traffic signals are used on the New York State canals: fixed green to enter, and fixed red to wait.

Lockmasters often arbitrate among the interests of different vessels that are moving in different directions. The Secretary of the Army, the ultimate authority over U.S. locks controlled by the Army Engineers, established the order of priority as follows: U.S. military vessels, mail boats, commercial passenger boats, commercial tows, commercial fishing craft and non-commercial boats.

Recreational boaters often lock through with commercial vessels, even on large systems like the St. Lawrence Seaway, jointly administered by the United States and Canada. Some restrictions may be applied, especially when petroleum and other hazardous substances are being carried.

Locking techniques

The concrete or stone walls of locks are often rough and dirty; ordinary cylindrical fenders simply roll, picking up dirt and smearing it on your topsides. Instead of ordinary fenders, you should equip your boat with fender boards consisting of a construction-grade plank suspended horizontally, with the fenders arranged between the board and your topsides. These work best, and are needed most, amidships on the boat (or where a boat's sides are reasonably straight).

Bags of hay have also been used, but these also tend to roll, except on heavily flared bows. Tires wrapped in burlap would be ideal, but their use is prohibited since a tire lost in the canal or lock would sink and probably foul the lock valves and gates. You can never be sure which side of the lock you may have to take, so it is wise to have fender boards and fenders for both sides.

Entering and leaving

Since moving quickly around the deck while watching upward is an easy way to miss your footing, make sure that all your deck crew are wearing PFDs before entering the lock.

It is imperative to approach with enough speed to maintain good steerage, since there may be some turbulence from the valves or from commercial vessels, but not so much speed that you cannot stop short. Small boats are often arranged in rafts—this is practical as long as all skippers are cooperative and cautious. It is usually good strategy for smaller boats to enter the lock last, and raft alongside larger boats.

The lockmaster will control the rate of flow in the lock to minimize turbulence. However, in a light boat, use extra caution when locked in with a larger vessel. A tug, for example, will kick out a heavy wash as it prepares to leave the lock.

Be especially cautious when approaching a lock and dam from upstream—follow the marked channel carefully. There are stories on every waterway of boats missing the upstream lock entrance and heading over the adjacent dam. Don't forget that, from the upstream side, especially at night, the water spilling over the sill of a dam may not be conspicuous at all. Pay close attention to the chart, the buoys and the general configuration of the lock profile.

On the Ohio River, there are cases where it is actually correct to go over the dam. In several places there are lock chambers on one side and "bear traps" on the other. Between them is a series of movable wickets that can be held in an upright position during low water stages, and lowered at high water. When the wickets are up, vessels use the lock. With the wickets down at high water, vessels run through the navigable pass, right over the (submerged) dam. By day, bulletin boards have to be consulted for the right choice. At night, control lights are shown at the guidewalls. When the navigable pass is being used, a gauge reading on the powerhouse board shows the depths of water over the dam sill—the figures are in red on a white background, preceded by the word "Pass."

Tending lines

Locking requires plenty of line. Even in locks where mooring bollards are attached to steel cylinders that float up and down inside recessed channels with the water level, you should be prepared with enough line to double the depth of the deepest lock at both the bow and stern. Since the line is roughly treated over concrete edges and gets dirty very quickly, it's best to use less expensive manila. Half-inch manila is often used for boats of 35 to 50 feet (10.7 to 15.2 m), and three-eighths-inch for smaller craft.

In general, you should moor to the lock wall by passing your line around the bollard and back on board, then tending it by hand. Cleating the mooring line can have very serious consequences on the way down if it is not released and the boat becomes hung up. Even where floating bollards are used, there is a possibility of a float jamming in its track. However, it is good practice to snub the dock lines against a cleat to take most of the load off your arms. Many experienced river boaters recommend snubbing the line to the side of the boat away from the wall so that, as the line angles upward to the top of the lock, it tends to pull the boat into the wall.

Ladders set into the lock walls may allow a small boat crew to "hand-over-hand" the boat up and down the wall, but this is sometimes prohibited because the ladders are rescue devices and must be kept clear.

Many locks provide mooring bollards mounted on floating chambers that are trapped in a vertical track on the lock wall. This makes mooring much easier, but a careful watch on the lines is still needed.

If fender boards are not available, large fenders will handle best the rough treatment most small boats are given in large locks.

The watchword in locks is safety. Whether the water level is rising or falling, tend your lock lines carefully at all times. You will need one crew forward and another crew, often the helmsman, aft. In some locks special caution is required if the topsides rise above the top of the pier—they may not be adequately fendered as the gunwale clears the wall.

Information on locking is available from the Army Engineers in a booklet entitled *Locking Through*. Similar material is published by Canadian authorities.

Spillways

Boaters must keep clear of the spillway area below dams. Though the fishing may be attractive there, the hazards are too great. Spillway areas are subject to sudden and violent changes as the dam's gates and valves open and close—placid waters become turbulent with no warning at all as heavy streams of water boil up unexpectedly from beneath. Heed the warning signs and stay out of the spillway.

Artificial canals

Many canals are actually completely artificial trenches dug through the landscape. Lake Champlain, for example, is accessible from the upper reaches of the Hudson River only because of a narrow, 24-mile (38.6 km) ditch cut in the land.

Narrow canals such as this pose special problems. A dredged canal may have a surface width of 125 feet (38 m), but a bottom width of only 75 feet (23 m) with a depth of 12 feet (3.66 m). Normal cruising speeds would quickly wash the canal banks down into the channel. In artificial waterways, speed limits are rigidly enforced. In New York State canals, the limit is 6 mph (9.7 km per hour) in land cuts and 10 mph (16.1 km per hour) in the system's river and lake sections. Lockmasters inform each other by phone of approaching vessels, so speeders are easily caught. Many sets of locks operate on time schedules, so it serves no purpose to go too fast.

In other land cuts, erosion may not be a serious problem, but the combined wakes of several boats may reinforce each other sympathetically, building up a wave large enough to threaten smaller boats. A small boat thrown against a rough rock wall can suffer serious damage. Speed limits are posted for very specific reasons, and must be obeyed.

Regulations

On many waterway systems, special regulations may apply. You should read these carefully from the literature supplied by the lock authorities.

LAKE BOATING

The term "lake boating" has extreme limits. The waters designated as lakes range from the smallest of natural or artificial lakes and reservoirs to the Great Lakes, which are more accurately regarded as a group of inland seas.

While most lakes are "protected waters" at all times, the Great Lakes can produce waves hazardous even to very large ships. While waves on these lakes are seldom high, even in a blow, they are usually very steep and often require more caution than ocean waves in similar wind conditions.

An inland boater can cruise hundreds of miles and never be far from shelter in case of bad weather. Nonetheless, the larger lakes must be treated with respect.

Lake Superior, for example, is the largest body of fresh water in the world. Deep, with rock-lined coasts and subject to storms and fog as well, it can present a challenge to even the saltiest skipper.

On Lake Erie, smaller and comparatively shallow, seas in a gale cannot shape up in the normal pattern of open ocean waves. Instead they are short and steep, frequently breaking in heavy squalls. Even Oneida Lake, in mid-state New York on the Barge Canal route, can build up seas that are challenging to an offshore boat.

Water levels

Lake levels vary from year to year and show a seasonal rise and fall as well—low in the winter and high in the summer. Monthly bulletins published during the navigation season show current and projected levels of the Great Lakes as well as average and record levels. More current information is contained in weekly reports released to newspapers and to radio and television stations.

In larger lakes, a steady strong wind will pile up water at the leeward end of the lake and lower levels at the windward end. Barometric pressure changes can also affect lake levels, sometimes causing a sudden and temporary, but drastic, change in water level on any portion of a lake—a phenomenon known as a "seiche."

Lake charts

Many smaller lakes do not require piloting and are not charted except on topographical maps. On medium-sized lakes, piloting is usually required, especially in changeable weather. On the largest lakes, piloting is carried out in a conventional manner with the exception that tide calculations are not required.

Many lakes provide a surprisingly large cruising range and enough depth for larger yachts. However, trailerable boats are the best choice for the boater who wants to explore more inaccessible areas.

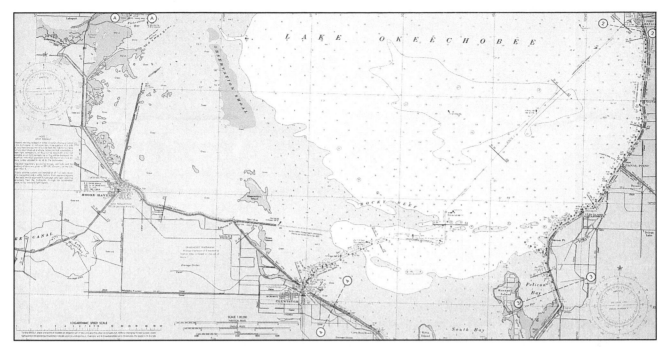

On larger lakes, you need to plot your course using a compass and standard time-speed-distance calculations. Lake charts often show principal routes between major ports, giving the course in degrees (true) and the distance in statute miles.

For the Great Lakes, charts published by the National Ocean Service (NOS) and the Canadian Hydrographic Service (CHS) are excellent. The U.S. charts have historically been polyconic projections but are gradually being reissued in Mercator, while the Canadian charts have been Mercator for some time. Scales vary from as large as 1:2,500 to 1:20,000 for harbor charts, to 1:400,000 or 1:500,000 for general charts of individual lakes.

Great Lakes charts have a compass rose showing both true and magnetic, with variation stated in the usual way. However, variation is often much greater than a coastal pilot might encounter. In parts of the Great Lakes the variation is zero, but in other locations great deposits of iron ore in the earth produce strong local effects. This is most pronounced along the north shore of Lake Superior, where changes in variation have been observed from 27 to 7 degrees within a distance of only 650 feet (200 m).

Many lake charts show principal routes between major ports, giving course in degrees (true) and distance in statute miles. Comparative elevations are referred to mean tide as calculated at New York City. Local depths and heights are measured from an established datum for each lake.

To supplement the information on Great Lakes charts, the NOS publishes *Coast Pilot 6*. This very useful annual volume provides full descriptions of the waters charted; laws and regulations governing navigation, bridge clearances, signals for locks and bridges; dimensions and capacities for marine railways and weather information. The Ninth Coast Guard District in Cleveland, Ohio, issues updates to *Coast Pilot 6* in its *Local Notices to Mariners*.

Similar pilots to the Great Lakes are published by the Canadian Hydrographic Service *(Appendices)*. In addition, the USCG publishes the *Light List, Volume VII*, covering the Great Lakes. This *Light List* identifies Canadian buoys and lights by the letter "C"; except for minor differences in design, the buoyage systems used in Canada and the U.S. are the same. The main difference is the use of cardinal buoys.

Rules and regulations

Many smaller lakes do not fall under federal jurisdiction in the United States, but are regulated by states or agencies. You should always be aware of the regulatory situation on each lake and waterway you cruise. The Appendices contain information sources for major U.S. lake and river authorities.

Rules of the Road conform to U.S. Inland Rules in U.S. waters and to Canadian rules in Canadian waters. Both are similar to the International Rules of the Road *(Chapter 6)*.

Pollution controls

Water pollution is a very serious concern on all lakes, and many complex regulations apply. Overboard discharge regulations are very strictly enforced and particularly important for boaters crossing state or international boundaries. Refer to Chapter 16 for more information on environmental issues. Some states are known for their zealous application of the environmental laws, especially regarding pleasure boating. When visiting from out of the area, be sure to check with the local authorities. The best way to avoid spoiling your pleasure while traveling is to be zealous in the care of your immediate surroundings.

Aids to navigation are the road signs of the water. Interpreting them with confidence requires experience and practice because variations frequently occur where buoy systems overlap.

This chapter describes all of the buoyage systems used in the United States. It also describes the buoys, lights, daymarks and other aids that you will encounter, and how to correlate what you see on the water to what is marked on your chart. Once you develop the skill of effectively using navigation aids, they will serve you well. They are there simply to assist you on your way—in making landfalls, spotting isolated dangers, following channels and recording a chain of charted marks for precise piloting in coastal waters.

BUOYAGE SYSTEMS

Just like the roads and highways on which we drive, the waterways have road signs that tell us our location, the route or distance to a destination, or of hazards along the way. These are called aids to navigation, a term that encompasses all those man-made objects used by mariners to determine their position or their safest course. Though this chapter deals with physical aids such as buoys, daybeacons, lights and ranges, Chapter 25 explains electronic aids such as Loran, GPS and radar beacons.

All aids to navigation are shown on charts, but not on all charts—only where the scale is appropriate. Good piloting starts with the ability to correlate what appears on the charts with what you actually see on the water.

Wherever you are traveling in the navigable waters of the United States, Canada, and other countries of the Western Hemisphere, the basic system is invariably the same; you needn't learn a new system each time you navigate in new waters. However, variations will be found in rivers and lakes, especially those under state jurisdiction.

Aids established by the federal government are placed only where the amount of traffic justifies their cost and upkeep. Within bounds of necessity and cost, each aid is designed to be seen or heard over the greatest possible area.

Operating agencies

The United States Coast Guard is the agency responsible for maintaining aids to navigation (ATON) on U.S. waters that are under federal jurisdiction or that serve the needs of the U.S. armed forces. Each Coast Guard District has supply and buoy depots, and special vessels for maintaining the aids.

State-maintained aids

On bodies of water wholly within the boundaries of a single state, and not navigable to the sea, the state is responsible for establishing and maintaining aids to navigation. Although each state keeps authority over its waters, a uniform system of aids and regulatory markers has been agreed to by all states *(page 508)*.

"Private" aids to navigation

With prior approval, aids to navigation may be established in federal waters by individuals or agencies other than the Coast Guard. Commercial, naval, scientific, sporting and other private interests may set aids to navigation for their own specific purposes. These might consist of such diverse aids as buoys at loading docks, data-gathering devices for oceanographers or racing marks for regattas. See any Coast Guard District office for information and procedures. These private aids must be patterned after federal aids, and any fixed structure planned for navigable waters requires a permit from the Army Corps of Engineers.

All such aids to navigation—whether established by an individual, a corporation, a state or local government, or even a federal agency other than the Coast Guard (the Navy, for example)—are private aids. They have the same appearance as Coast Guard-maintained aids, but are specially designated in the *Light List* publications *(Chapter 18)*.

Protection by law

Whether or not established by the Coast Guard, all aids to navigation are protected by law. It is a criminal offense to cause any damage or hindrance to the proper operation of any aid. Do not deface, alter, move or destroy any aid to navigation. Never tie your boat to a buoy, daybeacon or light structure. Avoid anchoring so close to a buoy that you obscure the aid from the sight of passing vessels.

If you should unintentionally or unavoidably collide with, or damage, an aid to navigation, report the fact to the near-

Buoys, minor lights and daybeacons are consistent and generalized, while primary lights (lighthouses like the one in the background) are more distinctive and diverse.

est Coast Guard unit without delay. For your own safety and that of others, report any missing or malfunctioning aid immediately after returning to port. In any case when you believe the safety of navigation is threatened seriously, it's best to make your report by radio.

Should you have any suggestions for improvements to aids to navigation, the standard procedure is to submit them by mail to Commander (oan)—meaning "office of aids to navigation"—of the Coast Guard District concerned.

Lateral and cardinal systems

There are two main principles used in buoyage systems—the lateral and the cardinal.

Each mark in a lateral system indicates a point along the edge of an area of safe water. The safe area might, for example, be a narrow channel with both of its edges, left and right, marked by a series of lateral buoys. Lateral buoys might also mark the edge of an extremity of the shoreline where unsafe areas border on safe areas. Although buoys are either right or left in the lateral system, in order to verify whether an individual or isolated buoy might be left or right, there must be an agreement about the direction of travel. In the lateral system, "right" is understood to signify the right-hand side when proceeding "from seaward."

Usually "from seaward" is obvious, but there are many cases in which a channel winds back on itself, resulting in ambiguity. In these circumstances, it's possible to be following a course that points toward the sea, yet the vessel is, nevertheless, traveling "from seaward." This sounds more difficult and confusing than it is in actual practice. In general, such a situation only presents a potential problem if you are navigating out of an unfamiliar port (especially if you didn't navigate into it), and have not studied the chart.

Along the coastline, an arbitrary choice has been made to set red buoys closer to the shore. Therefore, on the continental shelf, the notion of direction is that boats are traveling "from seaward" as they travel around the edge of the continent in a clockwise direction.

The cardinal system depends on relative direction. If there is a hazard to be avoided, a cardinal mark placed north of it would be marked to show that it is a "north" buoy—one placed west of the hazard would be marked differently as a "west" buoy. The navigator reading these markings would know that he must pass north and west, not south or east of such marks. Cardinal marks take their name from the four cardinal directions of the compass.

Both lateral and cardinal buoys are used in the U.S. and Canada, but lateral buoys are far more common in the U.S.

The IALA

The International Association of Lighthouse Authorities has established two uniform systems of colors and shapes. These systems are refered to as IALA-A and IALA-B, and together they regulate navigational markings throughout most of the world. System A is used in England and France, west to Ireland, north to Norway and Sweden, then east to Poland and Russia; it is also used in Australia and parts of Asia. System B, meanwhile, is used in North America, South America, Japan, Korea and the Philippines.

A pilot familiar with one system would not necessarily feel at home with the other because there is an essential contrast between the two: The IALA-B (mainly U.S.) system is the red-to-starboard system (the mnemonic device used by many is "red, right, returning") while the IALA-A system (mainly northwestern Europe) is a red-to-port system. There are other important differences between the two systems that are beyond the scope of this book. In this chapter we will concern ourselves with IALA-B—the North American system—along with its U.S. variations listed below.

■ **The Intracoastal Waterway.** It is actually a code of additional information overlaid on the same system.

■ **The Western Rivers System.** Another variation of the IALA-B system, it is employed on the Mississipi River and its tributaries above Baton Rouge, Louisiana, and on certain other rivers which flow toward the Gulf of Mexico.

■ **The Uniform State Waterway Marking System.** This system was developed in 1966 to provide an easily understood system for operators of small boats on small rivers and lakes that would not otherwise be on a nautical chart.

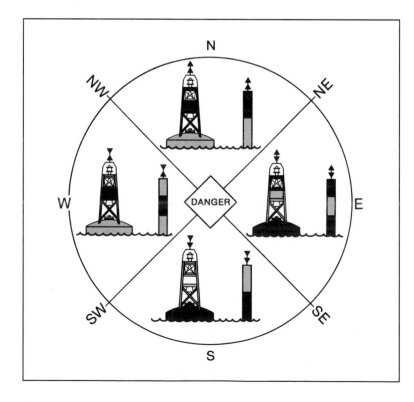

Cardinal buoys indicate the location of the safest or deepest water by reference to the cardinal points of the compass. White lights are used.

BUOYS, DAYBEACONS AND MINOR LIGHTS

Buoys are anchored to the bottom at specific locations, and are shown on charts by special symbols and lettering that indicate their shape, color and visual and/or sound signals. They vary widely in size. Buoys are secured to the bottom, with chain attached to heavy concrete "sinkers" weighing as much as 6 tons. Although the length of the chain will vary with the location, it may be as much as three times the depth of the water.

The buoyage system adopted for U.S. waters consists of several different types of buoys, each kind designed to serve under definite conditions. Broadly speaking, all buoys serve as daytime aids, but many have lights and/or sound signals so they may be useful at night and also during periods of poor visibility.

A buoy's size is usually determined by the importance of the waterway, the sizes of vessels using it and the distance at which the buoy must be seen. The USCG maintains about 20,000 unlighted and 4,100 lighted and combination buoys in waters under its jurisdiction. Additional buoys are maintained by state and private agencies in non-federal waters.

Can buoys are flat on top and are painted green. They carry odd numbers and are placed on the left side of the channel when entering from seaward.

Buoy shapes

The majority of unlighted buoys may be classified according to their shape as either "can" or "nun." Can buoys are characterized by a cylindrical above-water appearance, quite like a can or drum floating with its long axis vertical and flat end upward. Two lifting lugs may project slightly above the flat top of a can buoy, but they do not significantly alter the appearance of the aid.

Nun buoys have an above-water appearance like that of a cylinder topped with an upward-pointing cone. The cone may come to a point or may be slightly rounded. Smaller nun buoys have a single lifting ring at the top; larger buoys have several lugs around the sides.

Unlighted buoys come in standardized sizes; a nun's above-water portion may vary from 30 inches to 14 feet, while can buoys range from roughly 18 inches to nearly 10 feet above the waterline. Boaters should remember that a considerable portion of a buoy is under water, so that it is much larger and heavier than first appears. Some smaller buoys are now made of plastic materials.

In addition to the more common can and nun buoys there are also spherical buoys. Their uses in the revised U.S. lateral system and in the Uniform State Waterway System are discussed later in this chapter.

Other buoys of special shapes sometimes will be found in use as markers, but these are not regular aids to navigation.

Nun buoys are conical in shape, painted red and have even numbers. Nuns are on the right-hand side of the channel when entering from seaward.

This green buoy can be heard and seen. Its radar image is enhanced by the angled vertical plates on top.

The clappers on a bell buoy are outside the bell so that they produce a sound even in very small waves.

The U.S. Coast Guard has now eliminated the use of spar buoys, but they are still used in Canada and in private systems. They are usually large logs, trimmed, shaped and appropriately painted, and anchored at one end by a chain.

Lighted, sound and combination buoys are described by their visual and/or audible signals rather than by their shape, as discussed below.

Sound buoys

A separate category of unlighted buoys includes those with a characteristic sound signal to aid in their location in fog or other reduced visibility. Different sound signals are used to distinguish between different aids that are within audible range of each other.

■ **Bell buoys**, such as the one shown above, are steel floats surmounted by short skeleton towers in which a bell is mounted. They are effective day and night, and especially in fog, and are much used because of their moderate maintenance costs. Bell buoys are operated by the motion of the sea using four clappers, loosely hung externally around the bell. When the buoy rolls in waves, wakes or ground swells, a single note is heard at irregular intervals. Since bell buoys require some sea motion, they are not normally used in sheltered waters; a horn buoy is used there instead if a fog signal is needed.

■ **Gong buoys** are similar in construction to bell buoys, except they have gongs instead of a bell. They have four gongs of different tones, with one clapper for each gong. As the sea rocks the buoy, the clappers strike against their gongs, sounding four different notes in an irregular sequence.

■ **Whistle buoys** have a whistle sounded by compressed air that is produced by sea motion. These are used principally in open and exposed locations where a ground swell normally exists (*below*).

■ **Horn buoys** are rather infrequently used. They differ from whistle buoys in that they are electrically powered. They are placed where a sound signal is needed and sea motion cannot be depended upon.

Lighted buoys

Buoys may be equipped with lights of various colors, intensities and flashing characteristics (called "rhythms"). Colors and characteristics of the light convey specific information to the mariner. Intensity depends upon the distance at which the aid must be detected, as influenced by such factors as background lighting and normal atmospheric clarity.

Both whistle and light are visible on this even-numbered buoy.

Lighted buoys are metal floats that are equipped with a battery-powered light and mounted atop a short skeleton tower (*above*). Lighted buoys can operate for many months without servicing, and have daylight controls that automatically turn the light on and off as darkness falls and lifts. Power is taken from storage batteries that are kept charged by panels of solar cells on top of the buoy. Lights on buoys may be red, green, white or yellow according to the specific function of the buoy; the significance of these colors will be discussed later in this chapter.

Buoys with both a light and sound signal are designated "combination buoys." Typical of these are "lighted bell buoys," and "lighted gong buoys."

Exposed location buoys (ELBs) are usually equipped with RACON (radar beacon), lights, sound signal, meteorological equipment and self-sufficient power sources, both solar and wave-activated.

Large navigational buoys

Called "super buoys," these aids were developed to replace lightships, and placed at points where it was impractical to build lighthouses. Because of their immense size, 40 feet in diameter with light towers about 40 feet in height, and the expense of their maintenance, they are now being replaced with exposed location buoys (ELB). These ELBs are still fairly large (9 feet in diameter) and are equipped with lights, sound signal, weather and electronic navigational equipment, and power generator.

Buoy color

Buoys may be of one solid color, or they may have a combination of two colors in horizontal bands or vertical stripes. The colors used in the IALA system are red, green, yellow, white and black. The specific application of colors is discussed later in this chapter in connection with the uses of various buoys.

Almost all unlighted buoys are fitted with areas of reflective material, to help boaters find them at night with searchlights. The material may be red, green, white or yellow, in banding or patches. The colors have the same significance

as lights of the same colors. This material can also be placed on the numbers or letters of either lighted or unlighted buoys of all types.

Radar and optical reflectors

Many buoys have radar reflectors—vertical metal plates set at right angles to each other so as to greatly increase the echo returned to a radar receiver on a ship or boat. The plates are shaped and mounted to preserve the overall characteristic shape of an unlighted buoy or the general appearance of a lighted buoy.

Light rhythms

The lights on lighted buoys will generally flash in one of several specific rhythms. Flashing conserves the buoy's energy source, and allows easier detection against a background of other lights. Flashing patterns can also signal specific information during hours of darkness—for example, the need for special caution at a certain point in a channel—and can differ from each other to distinguish clearly between buoys of similar functions that are within visible range of each other. Various light rhythms are shown diagrammatically below.

■ **Flashing lights** are those that come on for a single brief flash at regular intervals—the time of light is always less than the time of darkness. Coast Guard-maintained flashing buoys will flash their lights not more than 30 times per minute. "Slow flashing" is the more generally used term, but the official and correct description is simply "flashing."

■ **Quick flashing lights** will flash not fewer than 60 times per minute. They are used for situations requiring quick sighting and where particular attention to piloting is required.

■ **Composite group flashing (2 + 1)** lights show two brief flashes, a brief interval, a single brief flash, and then an interval of darkness of several seconds' duration.

■ **Morse code "A"** flashing lights have a cycle of a short flash and a brief dark interval, then a longer flash and a longer dark interval, repeated every 8 seconds. This is the "dot-dash" of the letter "A" in Morse code.

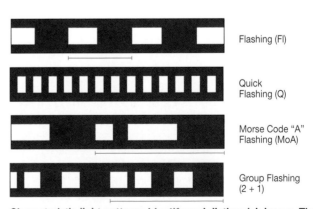

Flashing (Fl)

Quick Flashing (Q)

Morse Code "A" Flashing (MoA)

Group Flashing (2 + 1)

Characteristic light patterns identify and distinguish buoys. The patterns are named (as indicated in these schematic patterns) and identified on charts. ⊢——⊣ indicates one cycle.

Daybeacons have unlit boards, called dayboards, in either triangular shape (corresponding to nun buoys), or square shape.

The period of a light is the time it takes to complete one full cycle of flash and dark interval, or flashes and dark intervals. A light described as "Flashing 4 seconds" has a period of 4 seconds. One flash and one dark interval lasts just that long before the cycle is repeated. Three standard periods are used—flashing at intervals of 2.5, 4 and 6 seconds.

The term "characteristics" as applied to a lighted aid to navigation includes the color as well as the rhythm, and may also cover physical features such as nominal range.

Cautions in using buoys

Do not count on floating aids always maintaining their precise charted positions, or unerringly displaying their characteristics. Although the Coast Guard works constantly to keep aids on station and functioning properly, obstacles to perfect performance are so great that complete reliability is impossible. In any case, it is important to remember that a buoy does not maintain its position directly over its sinker, as it must have some scope on its anchor chain.

Buoys are heavily anchored, but may shift, be carried away, or sunk by storms or ships. Heavy storms may also cause shoals to shift relative to their buoys.

Under the influences of current and wind, a buoy swings in small circles around the sinker, which is the charted location. (Refer to Chapter 18 for information on chart symbols.) Swinging is unpredictable, and a boat attempting to pass too close risks collision with a yawing buoy. In extremely strong current a buoy may be pulled beneath the water surface.

Lighted buoys may malfunction and show no light, or show improper light characteristics. Audible signals on buoys are operated by action of the sea, and may be silent in calm water or may fail to sound because of a broken mechanism.

Buoys may also be temporarily removed for dredging operations, and in northern waters they may be discontinued for the winter or changed to prevent damage or loss from ice floes. The *Light List* volumes show dates for changes or for seasonal buoys, but these are only approximate and may be changed by weather or other conditions.

Temporary or permanent changes in buoys may be made between editions of charts. Keep informed of existing conditions through reading *Notices to Mariners* or *Local Notices to Mariners—(Appendices)*.

All buoys, especially those in exposed positions, should be regarded as warnings or guides, and not as infallible navigation marks. Whenever possible, navigate with bearings or angles on fixed aids or objects on shore as well as by soundings rather than by total reliance on buoys.

Daybeacons

Rather than floating like buoys, daybeacons are unlighted aids that are fixed structures. They may be either on shore or in waters up to about 15 feet deep.

Daybeacons vary greatly in design and construction, depending upon their location and the distance from which they must be seen. Daybeacons in United States waters, and their chart symbols, are illustrated later in this chapter.

The simplest daybeacon is a single pile with signboards, called dayboards (or sometimes called daymarks), at or near its top, usually two facing in opposite directions. The pile may be wood, concrete or metal.

A larger, more visible and sturdier daybeacon is the "three-pile dolphin" type—three piles a few feet apart at their lower ends, all bound tightly together with wire cable at their tops. There are also some five-pile dolphins (four piles around one central pile.) The Coast Guard maintains approximately 10,000 daybeacons.

A dayboard usually bears identification in the form of a number or, occasionally, a letter or a number plus a letter. Dayboards are normally either square or triangular, corresponding to can and nun buoys. Square dayboards are green with green reflective border. Triangular dayboards are red with red reflective border. The number or letters will also be of reflective material. In special applications, a dayboard may also be octagonal or diamond-shaped, carrying a brief warning or notice.

For reasons that are probably obvious, the use of daybeacons is restricted to relatively shallow waters. Within this limitation, however, a daybeacon is often more desirable than a buoy because it is firmly fixed in position and taller than a buoy, and therefore easier to see and identify, and also easier to maintain.

Daybeacons are used primarily for channel-marking, and they serve in basically the same manner as do buoys in the buoyage systems that will be described in some detail later in this chapter.

Minor lights

Just as daybeacons are something substituted for unlighted buoys, lighted buoys may, in similar fashion, be replaced with "minor lights." These are fixed structures having the same overall physical features as daybeacons, but equipped with a light generally similar in characteristics to those found on buoys. Most minor lights are part of a series marking a channel, river or harbor.

The term "minor light" does not include the more important lights marking harbors, peninsulas, major shoals, etc. These "secondary" or "primary seacoast" lights are discussed in detail later in this chapter.

Minor lights are placed on single piles, on multiple-pile dolphins, or on other structures either in the water or on shore. They carry dayboards for identification and reflective material for nighttime safety in case, for whatever reason, the light is extinguished.

Light and sound characteristics

A minor light normally has the same color and flashes with the same phase characteristics as a lighted buoy. Intensity will generally approximate that of a lighted buoy, but visibility may be increased by its greater height above water and its more stable platform.

In some locations, minor lights may be equipped with an audible fog signal—an electrically operated horn or siren. In some cases the signal operates continuously for months when fog is expected.

Articulated lights

A more recent type of aid to navigation is the articulated light; this is something of a cross between a minor light and a lighted buoy. A sealed hollow metal cylinder a foot or so in diameter and up to 50 or more feet in length is attached at one end by a swivel to a normal buoy "sinker." Because the cylinder is buoyant, it floats in an essentially vertical position (in some locations, an additional buoyancy collar may be attached to the cylinder just below the surface). Because no scope of chain is used, the aid is always very close to the established position with a negligible swinging circle. The length of the cylinder is selected to be the normal depth of the water, plus tidal range, plus 10 to 15 feet above the surface. At the top is mounted a typical light and dayboards in a manner similar to a minor light. (Without a light, the aid is an articulated daybeacon.)

Articulated lights will be used where a position must be marked more precisely than is possible with a buoy, yet the depth of water, up to 40 feet, is too great for a normal pile or dolphin structure.

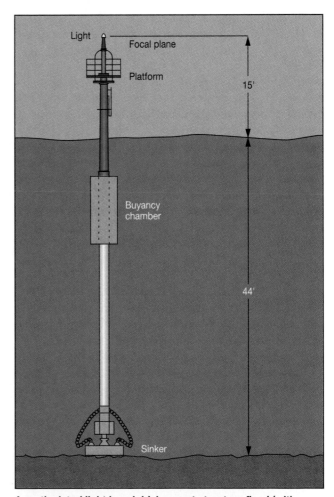

An articulated light is a rigid, buoyant structure fixed (with an articulated couple) to the seabed. It provides more precise position information than an anchored buoy.

THE BASIC U.S. SYSTEM

The U.S. Aids to Navigation system of buoyage is uniformly used in all federal-jurisdiction areas and on many other bodies of water where it can be applied. In this lateral system, the shape, coloring, numbering and light characteristics of buoys are determined by their position with respect to the navigable channel, natural or dredged, as such channels are entered and followed from seaward toward the head of navigation. They follow the traditional three-R rule of "red, right, returning." Returning from seaward and proceeding toward the head of navigation is generally considered as moving southerly along the Atlantic Coast, westerly along the Gulf Coast and northerly along the Pacific Coast. In the Great Lakes, the conventional direction of buoyage is generally considered westerly and northerly, except on Lake Michigan, where southerly movement is considered as returning from sea.

Shape and colors

All buoys are painted distinctive colors and have distinctive shapes to indicate the side on which to pass them or to show their special purpose. Distinguishing shapes are particularly valuable when you first sight a buoy in line with the sun and can see only its silhouette, rather than its color. In the lateral system the significance of shapes and colors is as follows:
- **Can buoys, painted green,** mark the channel on your port side when entering from seaward, or a wreck or other obstruction that must be passed by keeping the buoy to port.
- **Nun buoys, painted red,** mark the channel on your starboard side when entering from seaward, or a hazard that you must pass by keeping the buoy to your starboard. The traditional mnemonic phrase "red, right, returning" applies here.
- **Red-and-green horizontally banded buoys** mark a preferred channel. If the topmost band is green and the buoy is can-shaped, the preferred channel is with the buoy to port of your boat. If the topmost band is red and the buoy is nun-

shaped, the preferred channel is with the buoy to starboard. (Note: When heading for the sea, it may be impossible to pass such buoys safely on either side—particularly if you are following one channel downstream and another channel joins in from the side, as shown opposite. In this case, the buoy will be spotted; always consult the chart for the area.)
- **Buoys painted with red-and-black bands** are "isolated danger marks"; normally anchored above the danger, they have two black spherical topmarks arranged vertically. If lighted, they will show group flashing (2) white.
- **Spherical buoys painted with red-and-white vertical stripes** are "safe water marks"—they are used as an offshore approach point (often called "sea buoys") and to mark fairways, or midchannels. If lighted, there will be a red spherical "topmark" above the light that is roughly one-fifth the diameter of the buoy. If unlighted, these may be spherical or similar in construction to sound buoys and will have the topmark. Note that areas of color running horizontally are "bands"; arranged vertically they are "stripes." These terms are used in other color combinations in the case of special-purpose buoys.

Sound, light and combination buoys

No special significance is to be attached to the shape of sound, light or combination buoys. The purpose of these is indicated by their coloring, number or the rhythm of the light. Special caution must be exercised when a buoy is first sighted under conditions in which its color cannot be determined, such as when proceeding in a direction toward a sun low in the sky.

Numbering

Most buoys have "numbers" that actually may be numbers, letters or a number-letter combination, to help you find and identify them on charts. In the lateral system, numbers indicate on which side the buoy should be passed, as follows:

IALA-B LATERAL SYSTEM OF BUOYAGE						
				Lights or Lighted Buoys		
Returning from sea *	**Color**	**Number**	**Unlighted Buoy Shape**	**Light color**	**Light Rhythm**	**Daymark Shape**
To your starboard	Red	Even	Nun	Red	Flashing or quick flashing	Triangular
To your portside	Green	Odd	Can	Green	Flashing or quick flashing	Square
Preferred channel	Red-and-green horizontally banded **	Not numbered; may be lettered	Nun or can **	Red or green **	Group flashing (2 + 1)	Triangular or square **
Midchannel or fairway	Red-and-white vertically striped	Not numbered; may be lettered	Spherical	White	Morse code "A" flashing	Octagonal

or entering a harbor from a larger body of water, such as a lake.
** Preferred channel is indicated by color of uppermost band, shape of unlighted buoy and color of light, if any.*

Shown above are the characteristics of buoys in U.S. waters after conversion to IALA-B system.

- **Odd-numbered buoys** mark the port (left-hand) side of a channel leading in from seaward. In accordance with the rules, these will be green buoys, cans if they are unlighted.
- **Even-numbered buoys** mark the starboard (right-hand) side of channels—these will be red buoys, nuns if unlighted.

Numbers increase from seaward and are kept in approximate sequence on the two sides of a channel by omitting numbers as appropriate if buoys are not uniformly placed in pairs. Occasionally, numbers will be omitted on longer stretches without buoys, to allow for possible later additions. Numbers followed by letters, such as 24A and 24B, are buoys added to a channel with the series not yet renumbered.

A buoy marking a wreck will often carry a number derived from the number of the buoy next downstream from it, preceded by the letters "WR." Thus, a buoy marking a wreck on a channel's left-hand side between buoys 17 and 19 would be "WR17A." A wreck buoy not related to a channel may be designated by one or two letters relating to the name of the wrecked vessel or a geographic location.

Letters without numbers are sometimes used for red-and-white vertically striped buoys marking fairways, and for green-and-red horizontally banded buoys.

Numbers followed by letters may be used on buoys marking offshore dangers. For the buoy marked "2TL," for instance, the number has the usual sequential significance and the letters "TL" indicate a shoal known as "Turner's Lump."

Color of lights

For all lighted buoys in the lateral system, the following system of colors is used:
- **Green lights,** either on green odd-numbered buoys or green-and-red horizontally banded buoys with the green band uppermost, indicate the left-hand side of a channel from seaward.
- **Red lights,** either on red even-numbered buoys or red-and-green horizontally banded buoys with the red band uppermost, mark the right-hand side of a channel from seaward.
- **White lights** in the IALA-B system are used only on safe-water marks with the Morse letter "A" rhythm, and on isolated danger marks with a group flashing (2) rhythm.

Light rhythms

- **Flashing lights** are placed only on green or red buoys.
- **Quick flashing lights** are placed only on channel-edge-marking green and red buoys—these are used to indicate that special caution in piloting is required, as at sharp turns or changes in the width of the waterway, or to mark hazards that must be passed on only one side.
- **Group flashing (2) lights** are used on isolated danger marks.
- **Composite group flashing (2+1) lights** are used only on buoys with red-and-green horizontal bands, at channel junctions and at wrecks; they can be passed on either side.
- **Morse code "A" flashing lights (white)** are placed only on red-and-white vertically striped buoys marking a fairway or midchannel; they are passed close to on either side.

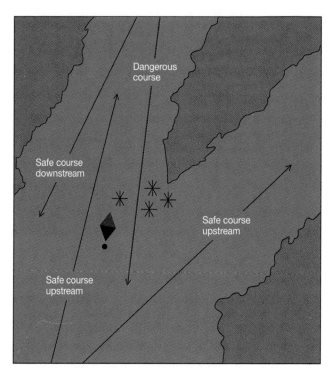

A preferred channel buoy, painted with horizontal red-and-green bands, must be treated differently depending on whether you are proceeding up or downstream. Upstream, either course is safe; downstream, one course is dangerous.

Daybeacons and minor lights

The lateral system of buoyage has been described in terms of unlighted and lighted buoys, and the same descriptions apply fully to comparable daybeacons and minor lights.

Daybeacons with red triangular dayboards may be substituted for nun buoys, or ones with green square daymarks may replace can buoys. Minor lights may be used in place of lighted or combination buoys. Structures subject to being repeatedly struck by vessels may be set back from the channel edge, as noted in the *Light List* publications.

If a daybeacon is used to indicate a channel junction or obstruction, the dayboard will be red-and-green horizontally banded, with the color of the uppermost band indicating the main or preferred channel. The dayboard shape will be either square or triangular as determined by the color of the top band, as with a can or nun buoy used for this purpose.

Daybeacons marking fairways or the midchannel have an octagonal-shaped dayboard, painted red and white, divided in half vertically down the middle.

A diamond-shaped dayboard has no significance in the lateral system, though a typical application might be to increase the daytime detectability of a minor light that is not part of a channel or waterway series. These are often used to mark a shoal, rock, submerged object or other hazard; they may also mark prohibited areas where boats must not enter.

Minor lights, and the lights on buoys, are equipped with electronic daylight controls that automatically turn the lights on during periods of darkness and off during daylight. These controls are not of equal sensitivity; therefore all lights do not go on and off at the same time. Take care to identify aids correctly during twilight periods when some may be on and others are not.

Wreck buoys

Buoys that mark dangerous wrecks are generally lighted, and placed on the seaward or channel side of the obstruction and as near to it as possible. Wreck buoys are solid red or green if they can be safely passed on only one side—if lighted, they will be quick flashing and numbered as previously discussed. Be careful around wreck buoys, because sea action may have shifted the wreck since the last Coast Guard check.

Isolated danger marks

Introduced in 1991, these marks are erected on, or moored above or near, an isolated danger surrounded by navigable water. These marks should not be approached closely without special caution. They are colored with red and black horizontal bands and, if lighted, display a group flashing (2) white light. A topmark consisting of two black spheres, one above the other, is fitted for both lighted and unlighted marks.

Seasonal buoys

In some areas subject to severe icing during winters, the normal buoys are removed to prevent damage or loss. These are temporarily replaced with ice buoys, lighted or unlighted buoys of special sturdy construction. The placement and removal of such buoys are announced in *Local Notices to Mariners*. In some instances, lights on shore may be activated to guide vessels in the absence of buoys.

RACONs

Some major aids to navigation are equipped with RACONs. These are radar beacons which, when triggered by pulses from a vessel's radar, transmit a reply that results in a better defined display on that vessel's radarscope than would result from mere reflection, thus increasing the accuracy of range and bearing measurements.

The reply may be coded to facilitate identification, in which case it will consist of a series of dots and dashes (short and/or long intensifications of the radar blips beginning at and extending beyond the RACON's position on the radar screen). The range is the measurement on the radarscope to the first dot or dash nearest its center. If the RACON is not coded, the beacon's signal will appear as a radial line extending from just beyond the reflected echo of the aid, or from just beyond where the echo would be seen if detected. Details of RACON coding will be found in the *Light List* publications. The coded response of a RACON may not be received if the radar set is adjusted to remove interference or sea return from the scope; interference controls should be turned off when reception of a RACON signal is desired.

Reporting discrepancies

All boaters should realize that the Coast Guard cannot keep the many thousands of aids to navigation under constant observation, and for that reason, it is impossible to maintain every light, buoy, daybeacon and fog signal operating properly and on its charted position at all times. Remember that the safety of all who use the waters will be enhanced if every person who discovers an aid missing, off station or operating improperly will notify the nearest Coast Guard unit of the situation that has been observed.

Special marks

Special marks are not intended to assist in navigation, but rather to alert the mariner to a special feature or area. The feature should be described in a nautical document such as a chart, *Light List*, *Coast Pilot* or *Notice to Mariners*. Some areas which may be marked by these aids to navigation are spoil areas, pipelines, traffic separation schemes, jetties or military exercise areas. Special marks are yellow in color and, if lighted, display a yellow light.

Information and regulatory marks

Information and regulatory marks are used to alert the mariner to various warnings or regulatory matters. These marks have orange geometric shapes against a white background. The meanings associated with the orange shapes are as follows:
1. An open-faced diamond signifies danger.
2. A diamond shape having a cross centered within indicates that vessels are excluded from the marked area.
3. A circular shape indicates that certain operating restrictions are in effect within the marked area.
4. A square or rectangular shape will contain directions or instructions lettered within the shape.

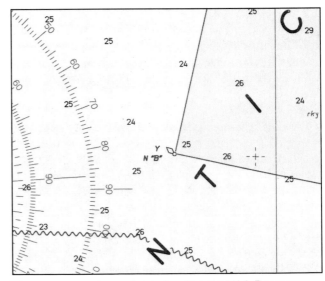

There are some circumstances in which the IALA-B system uses yellow buoys that have no lateral significance. Generally these mark area limits for dredging, anchoring or fishing.

U.S. AIDS TO NAVIGATION SYSTEM
on navigable waters except Western Rivers

LATERAL SYSTEM AS SEEN ENTERING FROM SEAWARD

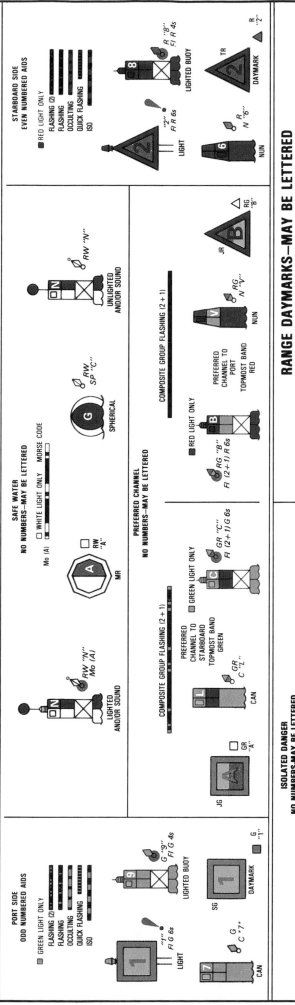

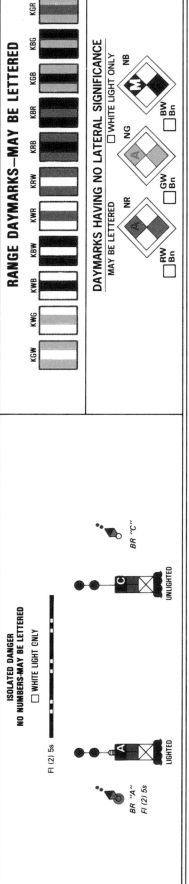

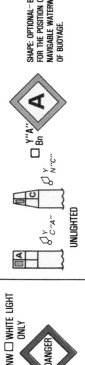

RANGE DAYMARKS—MAY BE LETTERED

KGW | KWG | KWB | KBW | KRW | KWR | KRB | KBR | KGB | KBG | KGR | KRG

DAYMARKS HAVING NO LATERAL SIGNIFICANCE
MAY BE LETTERED ☐ WHITE LIGHT ONLY

NR — RW Bn | NG — GW Bn | NB — BW Bn

SPECIAL MARKS—MAY BE LETTERED

Y "A" Bn | Y "C" / Y N"C" unlighted

SHAPE: OPTIONAL—BUT SELECTED TO BE APPROPRIATE FOR THE POSITION OF THE MARK IN RELATION TO THE NAVIGABLE WATERWAY AND THE DIRECTION OF BUOYAGE.

☐ YELLOW LIGHT ONLY
FIXED / FLASHING

Y "B" Fl — LIGHTED

TYPICAL INFORMATION AND REGULATORY MARKERS

NW ☐ WHITE LIGHT ONLY | W ☐ Bn

DANGER

INFORMATION AND REGULATORY MARKERS
WHEN LIGHTED, INFORMATION AND REGULATORY MARKS MAY DISPLAY ANY LIGHT RHYTHM EXCEPT QUICK FLASHING AND FLASHING (2).

DANGER | RESTRICTED OPERATIONS | EXCLUSION AREA

Aids to navigation marking the Intracoastal Waterway (ICW) display unique yellow symbols to distinguish them from aids marking other waters. Yellow triangles △ indicate aids should be passed by keeping them on the starboard (right) hand of the vessel. Yellow squares ☐ indicate aids should be passed by keeping them on the port (left) hand of the vessel. A yellow horizontal band provides no lateral information, but simply identifies aids as marking the ICW.

Plate 1

VARIATIONS IN THE U.S. SYSTEM

Intracoastal Waterway Aids to Navigation

The Intracoastal Waterway (ICW) runs parallel to the Atlantic and Gulf coasts from Manasquan Inlet on the New Jersey shore to the Mexican border. Aids to navigation marking these waterways have some portion of them marked with yellow. Otherwise, the coloring and numbering of buoys and daymarks follow the same system as that observed in all other U.S. waterways.

In order that vessels may readily follow the Intracoastal Waterway route where it coincides with another marked waterway, such as an important river, special markings are employed. These special markings are applied to the buoys or other aids to navigation which already mark the river or waterway for other traffic. These aids to navigation are referred to as "dual-purpose" aids to navigation. The marks consist of a yellow square, indicating that the aid to navigation on which it is placed should be kept on the port-hand side when following the Intracoastal Waterway down the coast. Aids to navigation that should be kept on the starboard hand-side have a yellow triangle affixed to them. The yellow squares have the same meaning as can buoys and the yellow triangles have the same meaning as nun buoys. A yellow horizontal band provides no lateral information but simply identifies aids as marking the ICW.

The conventional direction of buoyage in the Intracoastal Waterway is generally south along the Atlantic Coast and generally west along the Gulf Coast.

The Western Rivers System

This system is employed on the Mississippi River and its tributaries above Baton Rouge, LA, and on certain other rivers which flow toward the Gulf of Mexico. It differs from the U.S. basic system as follows:

■ Aids to navigation are not numbered.
■ Numbers on aids to navigation do not have lateral significance but, rather, indicate mileage from a fixed point (normally the river mouth).
■ Diamond-shaped crossing dayboards, red or green as appropriate, are used to indicate where the river channel crosses from one bank to the other.
■ Lights on green aids to navigation show a single-flash characteristic which may be green or white.
■ Lights on red aids to navigation show a group-flash characteristic which may be red or white.
■ Isolated danger marks are not used.

In an effort to eliminate white light from lateral buoyage (green or red), the U.S. Coast Guard is trying to restrict its use only to crossing daymarks.

Uniform State Waterway Marking System

While designed for use on lakes and other inland waterways that are not portrayed on nautical charts, the Uniform State Waterway Marking System (USWMS) was authorized for use on other waters as well. It supplements the existing federal marking system and is generally compatible with it. The conventional direction of buoyage is considered upstream or toward the head of navigation.

The USWMS varies from the standard U.S. system as follows: The color black is used instead of green.

It is important to be familiar with three aids to navigation that reflect cardinal significance:

■ A white buoy with red top represents an obstruction, and the buoy should be passed to the south or west.
■ A white buoy with black top represents an obstruction, and the buoy should be passed to the north or east.
■ A red and white vertically striped buoy indicates that an obstruction exists between that buoy and the nearest shore.

Mooring buoys are white buoys with a horizontal blue band midway between the waterline and the top of the buoy. This buoy may be lighted and will generally show a slow flashing white light.

Bridge markings

Bridges across navigable waters are generally marked with red, green and/or white lights for nighttime navigation. Red lights mark piers and other parts of the bridge. Red lights are also used on drawbridges to indicate when they are in the closed position.

Green lights are used on drawbridges to show when they are in the open position. The location of these lights will vary according to the bridge structure. Green lights are also used to mark the center line of navigable channels through fixed bridges. If there are two or more channels through the bridge, the preferred channel is also marked by three white lights in a vertical line above the green light.

Red and green retro-reflective panels may be used to mark bridge piers and may also be used on bridges not required to display lights.

Main channels through bridges may be marked by lateral red and green lights and dayboards. Adjacent piers should be marked with fixed yellow lights when the main channel is marked with lateral aids to navigation.

Center lines of channels through fixed bridges may be marked with a safe-water mark and an occulting white light when lateral marks are used to mark main channels. The center line of the navigable channel through the draw span of floating bridges may be marked with a special mark. The mark will be a yellow diamond with yellow retro-reflective panels; while not obligatory, it may exhibit a yellow light that displays a Morse code "B."

Clearance gauges may be installed in order to enhance navigation safety. The gauges are located on the right channel pier or on any pier-protective structure facing approaching vessels. They indicate the vertical clearance available under the span.

Drawbridges equipped with radiotelephones display a blue and white sign that indicates which VHF radiotelephone channels should be used to request bridge openings.

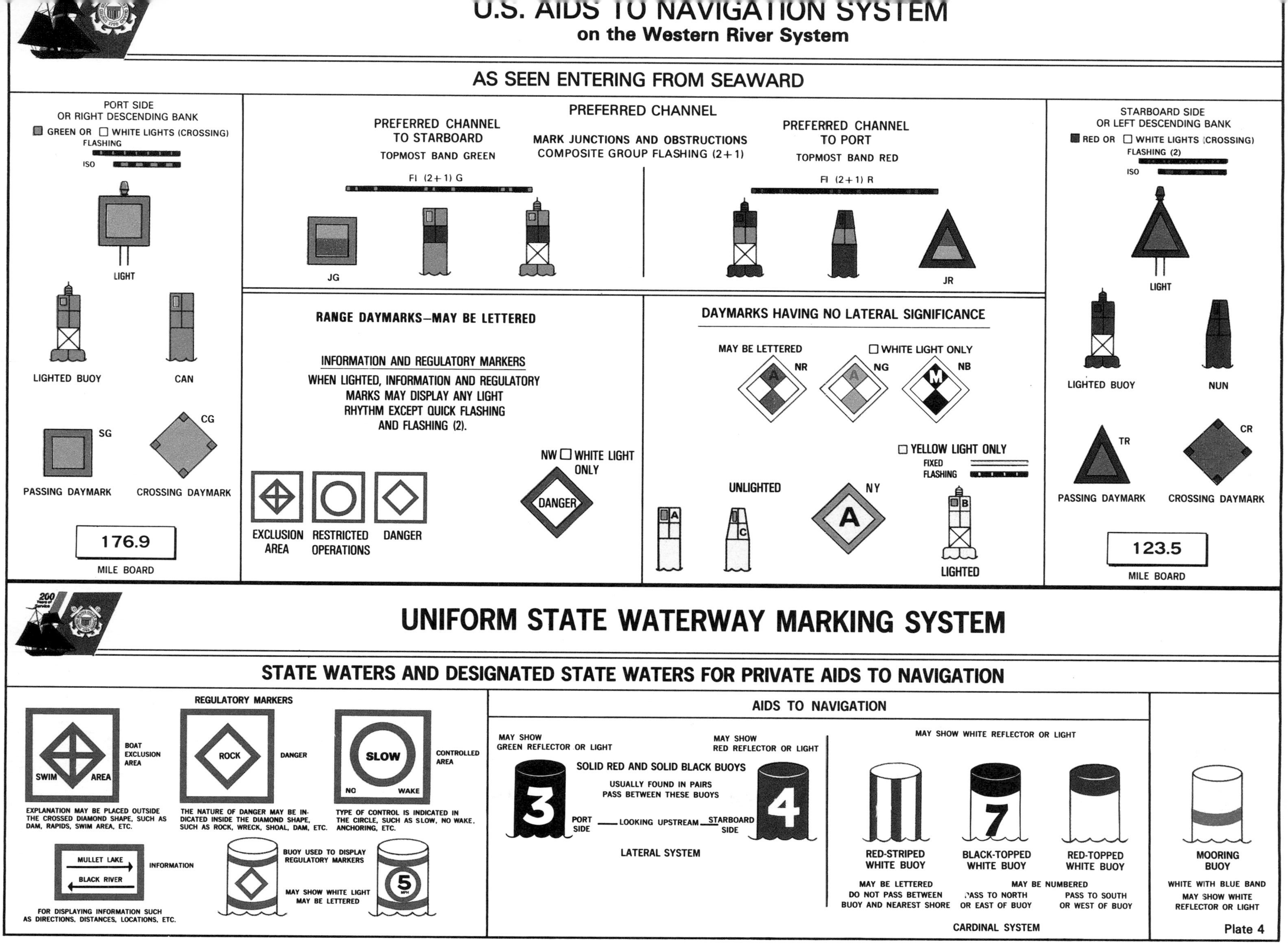

U.S. AIDS TO NAVIGATION SYSTEM
on the Western River System
AS SEEN ENTERING FROM SEAWARD
PORT SIDE
OR RIGHT DESCENDING BANK
GREEN OR WHITE LIGHTS (CROSSING)
FLASHING
ISO
LIGHT
LIGHTED BUOY
CAN
SG
CG
PASSING DAYMARK
CROSSING DAYMARK
176.9
MILE BOARD
PREFERRED CHANNEL
PREFERRED CHANNEL TO STARBOARD
TOPMOST BAND GREEN
Fl (2+1) G
JG
MARK JUNCTIONS AND OBSTRUCTIONS
COMPOSITE GROUP FLASHING (2+1)
PREFERRED CHANNEL TO PORT
TOPMOST BAND RED
Fl (2+1) R
JR
STARBOARD SIDE
OR LEFT DESCENDING BANK
RED OR WHITE LIGHTS (CROSSING)
FLASHING (2)
ISO
LIGHT
LIGHTED BUOY
NUN
TR
CR
PASSING DAYMARK
CROSSING DAYMARK
123.5
MILE BOARD
RANGE DAYMARKS—MAY BE LETTERED
INFORMATION AND REGULATORY MARKERS
WHEN LIGHTED, INFORMATION AND REGULATORY MARKS MAY DISPLAY ANY LIGHT RHYTHM EXCEPT QUICK FLASHING AND FLASHING (2).
NW WHITE LIGHT ONLY
DANGER
EXCLUSION AREA
RESTRICTED OPERATIONS
DANGER
DAYMARKS HAVING NO LATERAL SIGNIFICANCE
MAY BE LETTERED
WHITE LIGHT ONLY
NR
NG
NB
A
A
M
YELLOW LIGHT ONLY
FIXED
FLASHING
UNLIGHTED
NY
A
A
C
B
LIGHTED
UNIFORM STATE WATERWAY MARKING SYSTEM
STATE WATERS AND DESIGNATED STATE WATERS FOR PRIVATE AIDS TO NAVIGATION
REGULATORY MARKERS
SWIM AREA
BOAT EXCLUSION AREA
EXPLANATION MAY BE PLACED OUTSIDE THE CROSSED DIAMOND SHAPE, SUCH AS DAM, RAPIDS, SWIM AREA, ETC.
ROCK
DANGER
THE NATURE OF DANGER MAY BE INDICATED INSIDE THE DIAMOND SHAPE, SUCH AS ROCK, WRECK, SHOAL, DAM, ETC.
SLOW
NO WAKE
CONTROLLED AREA
TYPE OF CONTROL IS INDICATED IN THE CIRCLE, SUCH AS SLOW, NO WAKE, ANCHORING, ETC.
MULLET LAKE
BLACK RIVER
INFORMATION
FOR DISPLAYING INFORMATION SUCH AS DIRECTIONS, DISTANCES, LOCATIONS, ETC.
BUOY USED TO DISPLAY REGULATORY MARKERS
MAY SHOW WHITE LIGHT
MAY BE LETTERED
5
AIDS TO NAVIGATION
MAY SHOW GREEN REFLECTOR OR LIGHT
MAY SHOW RED REFLECTOR OR LIGHT
SOLID RED AND SOLID BLACK BUOYS
USUALLY FOUND IN PAIRS
PASS BETWEEN THESE BUOYS
3
4
PORT SIDE
LOOKING UPSTREAM
STARBOARD SIDE
LATERAL SYSTEM
MAY SHOW WHITE REFLECTOR OR LIGHT
7
RED-STRIPED WHITE BUOY
BLACK-TOPPED WHITE BUOY
RED-TOPPED WHITE BUOY
MAY BE LETTERED
DO NOT PASS BETWEEN BUOY AND NEAREST SHORE
MAY BE NUMBERED
PASS TO NORTH OR EAST OF BUOY
PASS TO SOUTH OR WEST OF BUOY
CARDINAL SYSTEM
MOORING BUOY
WHITE WITH BLUE BAND
MAY SHOW WHITE REFLECTOR OR LIGHT
Plate 4

PRIMARY SEACOAST AND SECONDARY LIGHTS

Lighthouses, the most familiar aid to navigation, are properly known as "primary seacoast and secondary lights." They are so designated because of their greater importance as aids to navigation, physical size, intensity of light and complexity of light characteristics. These lights are more diverse than minor lights and buoys, and only broad, general statements can be made about them as a group.

Primary seacoast lights warn the high-seas navigator of the proximity of land. They are the first aids seen when making a landfall (except where there may be a light tower, or large navigational buoy). A coastwise pilot can use these lights to keep farther offshore at night than by using other visual aids.

Primary seacoast lights may be located on the mainland or offshore on islands and shoals. Offshore, they may mark a

New London Ledge Light, Connecticut.

specific hazard or they may serve merely as a marker for ships approaching a major harbor.

Many primary seacoast lights are classified as such because of the importance of their location, the intensity of the light and the prominence of the structure. Other aids are classed as secondary lights because of their lesser qualities in one or more of these characteristics. The dividing line is not clear, however, and lights that might seem to fall more properly in one category may be classified in the other group in the *Light List* publications.

Structures

The physical structure of a primary seacoast light and of many a secondary light is generally termed a lighthouse although this is not an official designation used in the *Light List* publications. The structure's principal purpose, of course, is to support a light source and lens at a considerable height above water, but the same structure may also house a fog signal, radarbeacon, other equipment and quarters for the operating personnel. Auxiliary equipment and personnel are sometimes housed instead in a group of nearby buildings referred to as a light station.

Lighthouses vary greatly in their outward appearance, depending on where they are, whether they are in the water or on shore, the importance of the light, the ground they stand on, and the prevalence of violent storms.

Lighthouse structures also vary with the range of visibility they need—a great range requires a tall tower or a high point of land, with a light of high candlepower. However, at points intermediate to principal lights, and where ship traffic is lesser, long range is not so necessary and a simpler structure can be used.

Characteristics

Lighthouses and other light structures are marked with colors, bands, stripes and other patterns to distinguish them against their backgrounds and assist in their identification.

Primary seacoast and secondary lights have distinctive light characteristics—lights of different colors and lights that show continuously while others show in patterns. Their three standard colors are white, red and green.

Varying the intervals of light and darkness in both simple and complex ways yields many different rhythms for major lights. The term "flashing" has already been defined as a light

Greens Ledge Light, Connecticut.

Thomas Point Light, Maryland.

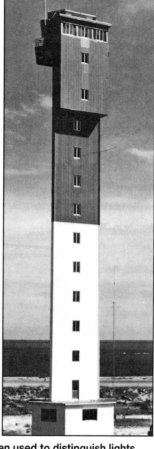

Bands or stripes of color are often used to distinguish lights from their backgrounds, and as an aid to their identification.

that is on less than it is off in a regular sequence of single flashes occurring less than 30 times each minute. Some primary seacoast and secondary lights will flash in accordance with the definition, although their characteristics will have no relation to the flashes of buoys and minor lights. In general, a flashing major light will have a longer period (time of one complete cycle of the characteristic) and may have a longer flash—for example, Cape Hatteras Light flashes once every 15 seconds with a 3-second flash.

In most instances, however, the actual light source is constant, and the "flashes" are produced by a rotating set of optical lenses so that, at close range, a weak steady light may be seen. Although a few major lights have a "fixed" characteristic (a continuous light without change of intensity or color), the light phase characteristics of primary seacoast or secondary lights are generally more complex. These lights are described in the table on page 516 and described below with current abbreviations.

Complex characteristics

Light phase characteristics may be combined. Examples might include "Group flashing white, alternating flashing red" (Fl W (3), Fl R)—Gay Head Light—with three white and one red flash

in each 40-second period, or "Fl W (1+4+3)"—Minots Ledge light, where 1½-second intervals in groups of one, four and three separated by 5-second intervals and followed by a 15½-second longer interval to indicate the proper starting point of the 45-second period, or others of a generally similar nature.

Sectors

Many lights will have sectors—portions of their all-around arc of visibility in which the normally white light is seen as red. These sectors mark shoals or other hazards, or warn of land nearby. Lights so equipped show one color from most directions, but a different color or colors over definite arcs of the horizon, as indicated on charts and in the *Light List* publications. A sector changes the color of a light when it is viewed from certain directions, yet it does not alter the flashing or occulting characteristic. For example, a fixed white light with a red sector, when viewed from within the sector, will appear as fixed red.

Sectors may be a few degrees in width, as when marking a shoal or rock, or wide enough to extend from the direction of deep water to the shore. Bearings referring to sectors are expressed in degrees as they are observed from a vessel toward the light.

You should almost always avoid water areas covered by red sectors, but you should also check your chart to learn the extent of the hazard. Although some lights are basically red (for danger) with one or more white sectors indicating the direction of safe passage, a narrow white sector in another may simply mark a turning point in a channel.

Lights may also have sectors in which the lights are obscured and cannot be seen. These will be shown graphically on charts and described in the *Light List* publications.

The visibility of lights

A light's theoretical visibility in clear weather depends on two factors: its intensity and its height above water. Its intensity fixes its nominal range, which is defined in the *Light List* as "the maximum distance at which the light may be seen in clear weather (meteorological visibility of 10 nautical miles)."

Height is important because of the earth's curvature. Height determines the geographic range at which the light can be seen. It is not affected by the intensity (provided that the light is bright enough to be seen out to the full distance of the geographic range).

The nominal range of a major light is generally greater than the geographic, and the distance from which such an aid can be seen is limited only by the earth's curvature. Such a light is often termed "strong," while a light limited by its luminous range is a "weak light."

The glare, or "loom," of strong lights is often seen far beyond the normal geographic range and under rare atmospheric conditions the light itself may be visible at unusual distances. The range of visibility is obviously also lessened by rain, fog, snow or haze.

CHARACTERISTICS OF LIGHTS

Flasing pattern and cycle (⊢——⊣)	Type	Description	Abbreviation
	Fixed	A light showing continuously and steadily.	F
	Fixed and flashing	A light in which a fixed light is combined with a flashing light of higher luminous intensity.	F Fl
	Single flashing	A flashing light in which a flash is regularly repeated (frequency not exceeding 30 flashes per minute).	Fl
	Group flashing	A flashing light in which a group of flashes, specified in number, is regularly repeated.	Fl (2)
	Composite group flashing	A light similar to a group flashing light except that successive groups in the period have different numbers of flashes.	Fl (2+1)
	Isophase	A light in which all durations of light and darkness are equal.	Iso
	Single occulting	An occulting light in which an eclipse, of shorter duration than the light, is regularly repeated.	Oc
	Group occulting	An occulting light in which a group of eclipses, specified in numbers, is regularly repeated.	Oc (2)
	Composite group occulting	A light, similar to a group-occulting light, except that successive groups in a period have different numbers of eclipses.	Oc (2+1)
	Continuous quick	A quick light in which a flash is regularly repeated at a rate of 60 flashes per minute.	Q
	Interrupted quick	A quick light in which the sequence of flashes is interrupted by regularly repeated eclipses of constant and long duration.	IQ
	Morse code	A light in which lights of two clearly different durations (dots and dashes) are grouped to represent a character or characters in the Morse code.	Mo (A)
	Alternating	A light showing different colors alternately.	Al; Alt
	Long flashing	A flashing light in which the flash is 2 seconds or longer.	L Fl
	Group quick	A group of 2 or more quick flashes, specified in number, which are regularly repeated.	Q (2)

Light phase characteristics of primary and secondary lights permit rapid and positive identification at night. One full cycle of changes is the light's period. Light phase characteristics may be combined—fixed and flashing for example.

Light List publications show the nominal range for all lighted aids except navigation ranges and directional lights, and show how to convert nominal range to "luminous range" (the maximum distance at which a light may be seen in existing visibility). Both nominal and luminous ranges take no account of elevation, observer's height of eye, or the curvature of the earth. For lights of complex characteristics, nominal ranges are given for each color and intensity.

The geographic range of a light is not given in the *Light List*, but can be determined from the given height of the light source. The distance to the horizon may be taken from a table in the front pages of each *Light List* volume, or calculated using the equation $D = 1.17(H)$, where H is the height in feet and the distance is in nautical miles, or $D = 2.12 (H)$, where H is in meters and distance is still in nautical miles. For distances in statute miles, the factors are 1.35 and 2.44.

The light's range will be the distance from the light to the horizon plus the distance from the height of your eye to the horizon. Determine each distance separately, then add. Skippers should know their height of eye when at the controls or any other point that can be climbed to see farther. Lights on inland waters are frequently "weak" lights whose intensity need not reach the full limit of their geographic range.

Identification of lights

Charts describe the characteristics of a primary seacoast or secondary light using abbreviations and a notation of the total period of the light cycle. Consult the *Light List* to be sure.

Cautions in using lights

Complex lights with several luminous ranges may appear differently at extreme distances where, for example, a white fixed (or flashing) light could be seen, but a red flash of the same light was not yet within luminous range. Examination of a *Light List* will show that usually the nominal range of a red or green light is 15 to 30 percent less than that of the white light from the same aid. Be cautious when identifying lights such as these.

The effect of fog, rain, snow and haze on the visibility of lights is obvious. Colored lights are more quickly lost to sight in poor weather than are white lights. On the other hand, refraction may also cause a light to be visible from a greater distance than normal.

Be cautious also when using light sectors in your navigation. Light sectors shade gradually from one color into the other. Note too that the brilliant shore lights used for advertising, illuminating bridges and other purposes may cause marine navigational lights, particularly those in densely populated areas, to be outshone and difficult to distinguish from the background lighting.

A light can also be out for some reason. Unattended lights that are broken may not be immediately detected and corrected. If you do not see a light reasonably soon after your course and speed suggest that you should, examine the situation carefully. Do not rely on any one light, except perhaps if you are making a landfall. For positive identification, use several lights together as a system, checking each individual light against the others.

At some locations, there is a high intensity light with a greater intensity than the main light normally operated from that location. This is operated only in reduced visibility.

Emergency lights of reduced nominal range are displayed from many light stations when the main light is inoperative. These standby lights may or may not have the same characteristics as the main light. The existence of the standby light (if any) and its characteristics (if different) are noted in the *Light List* publications.

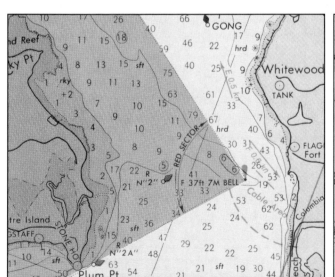

A hazardous area is often covered by a red sector on a light, and this red sector is indicated on the chart. Aside from being red, this sector shares characteristics with the normal white sector of the light. A light may also be obscured in a particular sector. (The colors used here for clarity do not actually appear on the chart.)

RANGES AND DIRECTIONAL LIGHTS

Ranges and directional lights serve to indicate the center line of a channel and therefore aid in the safe piloting of a vessel. Although they are used in connection with channels and other restricted waterways, and shown on all the appropriate charts, they are not a part of the lateral system of buoyage. A range consists of two fixed aids to navigation positioned with respect to each other so that, when seen in line, they indicate that the observer's craft may be in safe waters. Ranges may be lighted or unlighted.

It is important to note that even when the range is aligned the vessel may not be in safe waters. A range is "safe" only within specific limits of distance from the front marker—a vessel too close or too far away may be in a dangerous area. Check your chart to determine the usable portion of the range.

Ranges are described in the *Light List* publications by first giving the position of the front marker, usually in terms of geographic coordinates—latitude and longitude—and then stating the location of the rear marker in terms of direction and distance from the front marker. This direction, given in degrees and minutes (true) need not be used in ordinary navigation, but is useful in making checks of compass deviation. The rear dayboard (and light, if used) is always higher than the one on the front aid.

Ranges are among the best aids to navigation because of their fixed nature and the accuracy with which they can help position a vessel.

Unlighted ranges

Although any two objects may be used as a range, the term is properly applied only to those pairs of structures built specifically for that purpose. Special shapes and markings are used for the front and rear aids of a range for easier identification and more accurate alignment. Differing designs have been used in the past, but the U.S. Coast Guard has now standardized the use of rectangular dayboards, longer dimension vertical, painted in vertical stripes of contrasting colors. The design of specific range daymarks will normally be found in the *Light List* volumes.

In Canada, ranges are designed as two triangles. The rear marker is inverted so that, when aligned, the triangles touch point-to-point.

Lighted ranges

Because of their importance and high accuracy in piloting, most range markers are equipped with lights, in addition to the usual dayboards, to extend their usefulness through the hours of darkness. Entrance channels are frequently marked with range lights—the Delaware River on the Atlantic Coast and the Columbia River on the Pacific Coast are examples.

Range lights may be of any color used with aids to navigation—white, red or green—and may show any of several characteristics. The principal requirement is that they be easily distinguished from shore backgrounds and from other lights. However, front and rear lights will normally be of the same color with different rhythms. (White is frequently used because of its greater visibility range.) Since both lights must be observed together for the proper steering of the craft, range lights often have a greater "on" interval than other lights do. Range rear lights are normally on more than their front counterparts; many ranges now show an isophase (equal interval) rear light and a quick-flashing front light.

Many range lights are fitted with special lenses that give a much greater intensity on the range center line than off it. The lights rapidly decrease in brilliance when observed from only a few degrees to either side. In some cases, the light will be visible only from, on or very near to, the range line. In other cases, a separate, lower light of lesser intensity may be seen all around the horizon—this can be either from the main light source or from a small auxiliary "passing" light. Light is shown around the horizon when the front aid also serves to mark the side of a channel at a turn of direction.

Some range lights will be of such high intensity that they can be seen and used for piloting in the daytime, being of more value than the painted daymarks.

Using a range

Imagine the range markers as the back and front of a wedge (like a door-stop) that should point right at you. If you were off to one side or the other, you would see the wedge partially "from the side." When you are underway, and when the rear marker appears exactly above the front marker, you are on a straight line that runs from the near marker, through the front marker and through your position.

It is important to note that simply aligning the range is not enough. You must also know whether you are on the line segment that lies within safe water. This segment, specified on the chart and in the *Light List* publications, usually runs down the middle of a channel or between two headlands.

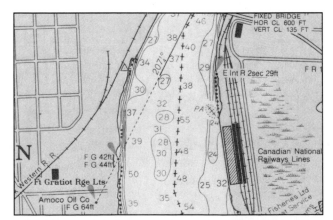

Lighted ranges are often used to mark channels in rivers. This range is in the St. Clair River on a true bearing of 207° (shown above the solid segment of the range line). Note that the front range light is at 44 feet with an all-around passing light at 42 feet. The cross-dashed line is the international border.

Ranges are just as useful outbound as they are inbound. Make sure that you do not meet head-on with a vessel using the range line as a course that is reciprocal to your own.

Directional lights

The establishment of a range requires suitable locations for two aids, separated adequately both horizontally and vertically. In some areas, this may not be possible and a single light of special characteristics will be employed.

A directional light is a single light source fitted with a special lens so as to show a white light in a narrow beam along a desired direction, with red and green showing to either side. Width of the sectors will depend upon the local situation, but red will be seen if the pilot is to the right of the center line as he approaches the aid from seaward, and green if he is to the left of the desired track. A typical directional light, at Deer Island, Massachusetts, shows white for a sector of 2°24' with red and green showing for 8°30' to either side. Another directional light, in Delaware Bay, has a white beam width of 1°50' with red and green sectors of 6°30' to either side. Directional lights will normally have an occulting or isophase characteristic, so that they are easily followed.

A skipper should take care not to rely too strongly on the various colors of a directional light for safe positional information. As with light sectors, the boundaries between colors typically are not sharp and clear. The light shades imperceptibly from one color to the other along the stated, and charted, dividing lines.

New lights on the horizon

Recent technological advances, notably in laser technology, promise to boost the effectiveness and reliability of short-range aids to navigation. Prototype range light systems in particular show great potential for improving safety at sea.

Three concepts are crucial: cloud-cutting laser beams, easy-to-distinguish harbor lights and daytime visibility.

Laser light produces a beam that is visible in all weather. A solid bar the diameter of a dinner plate, the beam is aimed horizontally, 80 feet (24.3 meters) overtop the water.

The extended-light is useful in big city harbors, where a preponderance of lights dazzles the eye. Changing the shape of conventional points of light to vertical bars or lines, similar to laser lines, better enables mariners to detect one light among many, and thus to locate the center of the channel.

The third concept boosts the visibility of daytime-range systems. Using low-pressure sodium lamps, a prototype has achieved a daytime visual reach of 16 miles; by comparison, the largest conventional system reaches only 5 miles.

A skipper can keep within a narrow channel by following a range. At A, front and rear markers are in line with a higher rear mark directly above the lower front mark; he is "on range." If he gets "off range," the markers will not be aligned, as in B. Ranges may fail to reach the front marker, as seen in C.

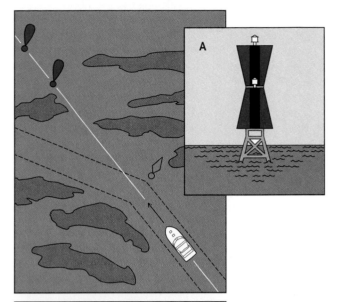

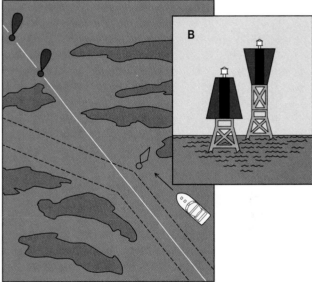

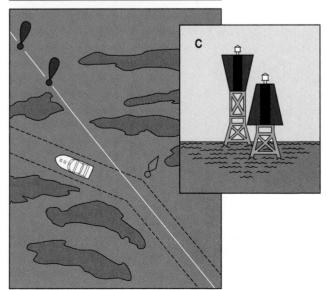

ELECTRONIC EQUIPMENT

23 ELECTRICAL SYSTEMS

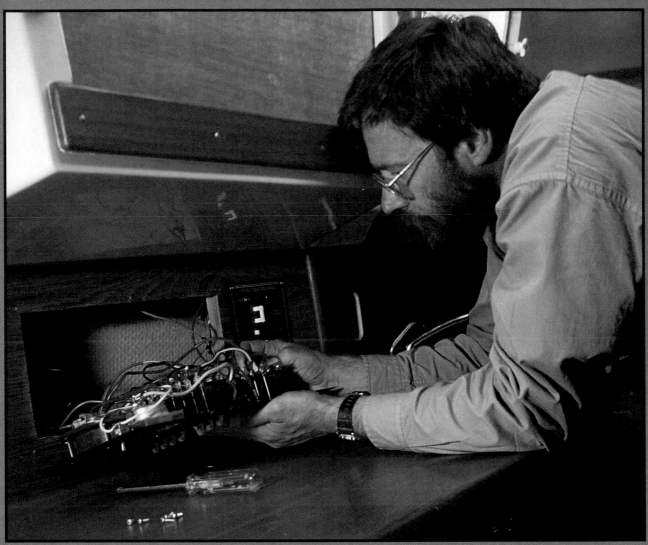

The importance of electrical power aboard boats has increased enormously. Nowadays we take for granted many electrical appliances that, formerly, would never have been afloat.

More importantly, we place a greater reliance on electronic navigation and communication devices that must be reliably and constantly supplied with electrical power as a matter of safety rather than convenience.

Acquiring and delivering this power has become a complex issue, necessitating a knowledge of required standards and an ongoing awareness that the boat's batteries are under constant demand. This chapter will give you the basics.

GENERATING AND STORING ELECTRICAL POWER

Electricity has become an essential ingredient in boating. Originally used for engine starting and lighting only, electrical power is now used for a multitude of tasks—for heating and cooking, for running electronic navigation and communications equipment, and for such labor-intensive chores as raising the anchor and lifting the tender aboard.

The on-board supply of electrical power divides into three broad categories:

- Power stored in batteries.
- Power brought aboard a vessel from land lines via a "shore-power" connection.
- Power generated on board as needed and used.

Associated with each of these categories are one or more distinct, identifiable supply sub-systems. For instance, electrical power that is created on board a boat as needed may be produced by alternators that are belt-driven by the vessel's main propulsion engine or engines. Often it may also be produced by an auxiliary generating plant driven by its own separate engine.

Supply sub-systems feed power to the vessel's electrical delivery system, which consists of a network of distribution panels, bus bars, circuit breakers, switches, wiring, outlets and the like. There is little need for the boater to delve deeply into the physics of electrical power—after all, most of us deal with electricity perfectly well at home without first undertaking a course in electromotive forces. Nevertheless, some fundamental background is helpful: with the convenience of electrical power aboard boats, come certain potential hazards and maintenance problems.

Measuring electrical needs

Conceptually, the behavior of electricity flowing in wires can be likened to that of water flowing in pipes. The units of electrical measurement are likewise analogous: Voltage is analogous to pressure in a water pipe. An ampere (amp) measures the amount of current that is flowing, which is somewhat like the volume of water moving through a pipe. And ohms measure resistance, which can be visualized as corresponding to the friction that is generated when water flows through pipes.

There is a simple equation that explains the relationship between voltage (E), current (I) and resistance (R):

$$E = I \times R$$

By inverting the equation, we see that

$$I = \frac{E}{R}$$

Current flow is therefore directly proportional to voltage and inversely proportional to the resistance in the circuit. In other words, the voltage *drop* in a circuit (in volts) equals the current flow in that circuit (in amperes, usually called "amps," abbreviated "A") times the resistance of that circuit (in ohms).

Watts and kilowatts (1 kW = 1,000 watts) are measures of power. The wattage rating on an item of on-board equipment provides the boater with a measure of the maximum amount of power that the electrical item will require when operated. By adding together the maximum wattage requirements of all electrical equipment that will be operated simultaneously, a vessel's maximum requirements for electrical power can be determined. (But note that this is not a measure of the energy consumed over a period of time.) Wattage ratings also provide important information about the required sizes for wiring, and the required ratings for protective circuit breakers and/or fuses.

A simple equation expresses the relationship between watts, volts and amps: Watts = Volts x Amps.

For example, using the above equation, we can tell that a 12-volt appliance requiring 120 watts of power will draw 10 amps of current. Notice, by the way, that a 120-volt appliance requiring the same 120 watts of power will draw only 1 amp. This comparison is discussed later in the chapter.

If your boat's maximum electrical load at any one time will consist of, say, six 40-watt interior lights, four 25-watt navigation lights, one 60-watt pressure fresh-water system pump, and one VHF radio drawing 80 watts of DC input power, then strictly speaking the total maximum wattage for which you need to provide is 480. However, in practice, it would be prudent to provide for at least 700 watts—in case, unexpectedly, you need to run another appliance, such as a bilge pump, while all of these other items are switched on.

However, you should understand that the equations given are accurate only for appliances that produce resistive loads—incandescent lamps, electric ranges and heaters, for example. Some electric appliances, such as fluorescent lamps and tools with induction-type motors, actually draw significantly more current (amperage) than their nominal wattage ratings indicate, and this must be taken into account when calculating maximum power loads.

If you'll be running electrical equipment with power from your batteries at times when your engines are shut down, then you need to ensure the batteries have ample capacity. If the total wattage of all the equipment likely to be switched on at one time is 480 watts (using our previous example), then assuming the equipment runs on 12-volt current, and using the equation given earlier, the load will draw 40 amps of current. If the maximum expected duration of that load will be 4 hours, then the vessel's batteries must be able to supply 160 amp-hours of power (40 amps x 4 hours), while retaining sufficient charge to start the vessel's propulsion engines and/or auxiliary generating plant so that recharging can be accomplished. Batteries are discussed in detail later in this chapter.

The right size and type of wiring

The higher the current (amperage) draw of an appliance, the heavier the wire that carries the current has to be. Insufficient wire size (diameter) means increased resistance. Excessively

---

ELECTRICAL STANDARDS ON BOARD

When it comes to understanding and following various standards of construction and recommended practices, there is no more important area for standards than that of the vessel's electrical systems. If improperly installed or poorly maintained, these systems can pose not only fire and explosion hazards (corrosion), but also the potential for electrocution.

The United States Coast Guard (USCG) has certain basic electrical standards, which are applicable to gasoline-powered vessels, and that speak primarily of ignition protection (reduction of explosion hazard) and overcurrent protection (to avoid overheating and fires). A review of these standards will show that they are very basic and provide little "practical" information on vessel wiring other than for these two purposes.

The National Fire Protection Association (NFPA) publishes *Standard No. 302 for Recreational and Commercial Motor Craft*. This covers a good range of various topics with respect to fire protection, especially in the areas of electrical circuits and lightning protection.

However, by far the most comprehensive standards available today are those published by the American Boat and Yacht Council *(Appendices)*. In covering almost every major system on a vessel, the ABYC Standards go into great detail on the subjects of DC and AC electrical systems, battery chargers and inverters, lightning protection, cathodic protection and others. The ABYC Standards also have been used for the development of various international standards being adopted in Europe.

In addition to these various standards, the National Marine Manufacturers Association (NMMA) also operates a certification program for the manufacturers of vessels; this program is based on the standards written by the ABYC.

---

higher resistance results in greater voltage drop (less voltage at the appliance). This in turn results, at best, in a loss of efficiency (with power being lost in the conversion of electrical energy to heat), and at worst, in damage to electric motors and other appliances—even, in extreme cases, fire. Any wire, when subjected to excessive current, may overheat to the point of igniting adjacent combustible materials. It is for this reason that circuit breakers or fuses are utilized to limit the amount of current that a wire can safely carry.

Many potential problems can be avoided by ensuring that all wiring is adequate in size for the amperage involved. It is often the case that wiring installed by the builder was adequate for the equipment on board the boat when it was delivered. However, subsequent additions may have overloaded the system. Electrical problems encountered with newly installed items may be traceable to the inadequacy of the original wiring.

In this respect, it's important to keep in mind that wire sizes in North America are generally specified according to American Wire Gauge (AWG) standards, under which a lower number designates a larger diameter (for example, #10 AWG wire is heavier than #16 AWG). The system is established so that a change of three numbers, either up or down, changes the cross-sectioned area of the wire by a factor of two; this doubles, or halves, the resistance of the wire (but odd numbers are generally not used in small gauges). A change of six numbers changes the area, and resistance, by a factor of four.

When it comes to electrical wiring in a marine environment, size is not the only consideration—wire type is also very important.

Wire with solid conductor or less than sixteen strands should not be used on a boat because it is prone to fracture due to vibration, especially where the conductor may have been nicked when stripping the insulation for connection during installation. Instead, flexible, multi-strand wire should be chosen for all systems aboard.

It is recommended to use pre-tinned copper conductor in boat wiring, even though it is expensive. Conductor strands that are coated with tin resist corrosion much better than bare copper ones. That's important not only at terminal fittings, where the copper is stripped for insertion into crimp-type or other terminal fittings, but all along the conductor. The type of corrosion to which copper is subject in a salt-damp environment tends to "creep" along bare copper wires, up under its protective insulation; and so plain copper conductor is potentially subject to severe and hidden corrosion when used in the marine environment.

Recommended wire gauges

In DC systems, typically 12-, 24- or 32-volt, the voltage "drop" that occurs due to the resistance of the wire becomes a critical consideration for certain types of equipment. The ABYC recommends that "non-critical" applications (for example, where the voltage drop does not seriously compromise the function of equipment such as motors, cabin lights, etc.) be limited to 10 percent. "Critical" devices such as navigation lights, bilge blowers and most electronics equipment should be more than 3 percent. The ABYC Standards provide details and tables for these calculations.

A simple check of equipment "as installed" can be made by using a DC voltmeter; first read the voltage at the fuse or breaker panel, then at the equipment itself. This must be done with all "normal" loads turned on and the DC charging source (engine or battery charger) operating. Additionally the equipment under test must be running, in other words, pumping water with the bilge pump or transmitting on the radio. If 13.2 volts were available at the fuse panel, then 12.8 volts (13.2 minus 13.2 x 3%) should be the reading at the equipment for no more than a 3 percent drop.

Direct and alternating current

Most boaters, especially those with cruising vessels, have to deal with two different kinds of electrical current—direct current (DC), the kind your car uses, and alternating current (AC), the kind you use at home.

Direct current in a circuit flows in one direction. In contrast, alternating current flows through a circuit first in one direction, then a small fraction of a second later in the other direction. The frequency of this change of direction has an effect on some electrical appliances, notably those with motors. Alternating current is, therefore, regulated—in North America it is 60 cycles per second (60 Hertz); in Europe and some other parts of the world it is 50 cycles per second (50 Hertz). A motor that is designed to run on 60 Hertz AC will run slower when powered with 50 Hertz AC. In some cases that slowdown can cause operating problems, if not damage.

Shorepower is always alternating current, as is that produced by an auxiliary generating plant or DC to AC inverter. Power supplied by storage batteries is always direct current. However, it should not be assumed that, although a vessel's AC and DC systems are isolated from one another, there is never an interchange of power between them. Quite to the contrary, the AC brought aboard from a shorepower connection, and that produced by an on-board auxiliary generating plant, can be rectified by a battery charger into DC and used to recharge a vessel's storage batteries. DC drawn from the ship's storage batteries can be changed into AC by an inverter and used to power the vessel's AC distribution system, but only for relatively low-power loads.

Not only does electrical current differ in terms of being direct or alternating; it differs in terms of voltage. Appliances designed for one voltage must not be used on systems having other voltages. (Most modern electrical equipment is designed to cope with a modest range of voltage; but it is always important to check and comply with the manufacturer's specifications for that range. Otherwise irreversible damage to the equipment involved may occur.)

ELECTRICAL WIRE GAUGE SELECTION: 12-VOLT WIRING FOR ELECTRONIC LOADS

Current (Amps.)	Wire length (feet): source to load, plus return to source					
	10 (or less)	15	20	30	40	50
5	16	16	16	14	14	12
10	16	14	14	12	10	10
15	14	14	12	10	8	8
20	14	12	10	8	8	8
25	12	10	10	8	6	6

The American Boat and Yacht Council (ABYC) standards for electronic purposes, such as radios and navigation equipment. The ratio of wire gauge in relation to conductor length ensures a voltage drop of not more than 3 percent.

ELECTRICAL WIRE GAUGE SELECTION: NON-CRITICAL 12-VOLT LOADS

Current (Amps.)	Wire length (feet): source to load, plus return to source					
	10 (or less)	15	20	30	40	50
5	14	12	10	10	8	6
10	10	10	8	6	6	4
15	10	8	6	6	4	2
20	8	6	6	4	2	2
25	6	6	4	2	2	1

ABYC standards for wire gauges for non-critical purposes, such as lights and pumps. A 10 percent voltage drop can be tolerated by common electrical loads. All wires should be stranded to reduce mechanical fatigue.

As noted above, a system using a higher voltage has the advantage that, for a given wattage demand, it does not require as heavy wiring as at a lower voltage. Moreover, higher voltages are better at overcoming localized resistances, for example, minor build-ups of corrosion at connecting terminals.

When high wattages are involved, the reduced wire gauges that are practical with higher voltages are advantageous in terms of cost, weight and the physical difficulties of installation. (Smaller-diameter wires are lighter and more flexible, making them easier to snake through the constricted passages available on boats.) This is why, for instance, high-demand electric cooking ranges and household dryers are most often designed to operate on 240-volt AC, rather than the 120-volt electricity used for light bulbs, stereos, TVs and the like.

In marine applications, winding the bared, twisted end of a conductor around the terminal screw on an appliance, breaker or bus bar just won't do. In fact, this practice is prohibited by industry standards. Such a connection is simply too prone to corrosion and to loosening due to vibration. Instead, some form of terminal fitting should be employed, one which provides a fork or even better a closed loop end that makes for a secure mechanical connection.

At one time, terminal fittings were soldered to the wire conductor; but that procedure is both time-consuming and expensive, and over the past twenty or so years crimp fittings have gained almost universal acceptance. Crimp fittings are tinned copper fittings consisting of a tubular shank with a plastic sheathing, at one end of which is a fork or loop. The sheathing extends up over the wire insulation. The best quality sheathing is nylon. Unlike the cheaper PVC, nylon will not crack or punch through when crimped, and resists the corrosive effects of UV, oil and diesel.

The stripped end of the wire is inserted into the tubular shank of the crimp fitting, and a special tool is used to squeeze the shank tightly around the conductor. If properly done, the connection, although mechanical, is excellent and long-lasting. And if pre-tinned copper wire is used, and the terminals are tinned, the potential for corrosion between the wire and the crimped shank of the fitting is minimal.

It is possible to solder a crimped fitting after it has been crimped. But this is not preferred practice, as the heat will usually destroy the vinyl insulation that protects the shank on the crimp fitting. Additionally, the solder will "wick" part of the way up the wire past the crimped fitting and, effectively, destroy the flexibility of the stranded wire, tending to make it brittle and prone to breakage from the vibration that exists on all boats. And where enhanced resistance to corrosion is desired, it is better either to coat the terminal with one of the liquid vinyl compounds available for that purpose, or to employ modern vinyl heat-shrunk tubing.

Shrink tubing is applied by sliding a piece of appropriately sized material over the wire before crimping the terminal on. After crimping, the tubing is slipped into position so that it covers the shank of the crimp fitting and overlaps onto the wiring insulation. The assembly is then heated with a heat gun or a portable hair-dryer, whereupon the tubing shrinks tightly to the contours of the wire and fitting, at the same time exuding a sealant/adhesive that seals the underlying connection from moisture intrusion. A more recent (and convenient) variation of this approach is a combination crimp and heat-shrink terminal fitting, which is first crimped in the normal manner, then heated. Both standard crimp fittings and these combination crimp/heat-shrink fittings are available as well in configurations for joining two wire ends.

1 Strip the wire of its insulation, and slip it into the crimp fitting—a loop or a fork. Then squeeze the crimp with a special tool until exactly the right dimension is maintained.

2 Slide a length of heat-shrink tubing (available in several sizes) over the crimp.

3 Shrink the protective tubing with gentle heating. A hair-dryer is also effective.

At dockside in North America, you'll find one or both of 120-volt AC and 240-volt AC power. In Europe and many other parts of the world, shorepower is 220-volt AC. Actually, these voltage designations are nominal—the designed voltages of shorepower will vary from 110 to 120 AC, and 220 to 240 AC, respectively. Moreover, in practice, shorepower voltage may drop well below these lower range limits.

Many items of equipment used on boats, such as battery chargers, microwaves, televisions, stereos and fluorescent lights, contain transformers for the purpose of changing the voltage within the equipment. When operating on "foreign" power (such as 50 Hertz), it is imperative that this equipment be "compatible" with the 50 Hertz shorepower source. This may be ascertained by looking at the nameplate on the equipment and verifying that it says "50/60 Hz." If this type of equipment is not installed on your boat, you have two choices: Either order special equipment to be compatible or, when in "foreign" ports, operate this equipment only from the vessel's auxiliary generating plant in order to obtain the requisite 60 Hertz power.

There are transformers that can step shorepower AC voltages up or down to match the voltage requirements of a vessel's AC equipment *(page 533)*. However, none of these changes the frequency of the shorepower alternating current; so care must be taken when hooking up to foreign shorepower sources, even when you have managed to adapt to non-compatible outlet configurations. If a shoreline transformer is installed on board the boat, it must be compatible with 50 Hertz use if operation in "foreign" ports is anticipated where this frequency is to be encountered.

Battery voltage

Today, direct current for shipboard use is generally either 12, 24 or 32 volts DC. These voltage choices evolve from the fact that most batteries are made up of a number of individual nominal 2-volt cells, connected in a voltage-additive series, and the fact that manufactured batteries use certain common multiples of cells: 3 cells (a 6-volt battery), 4 cells (an 8-volt battery) and 6 cells (a 12-volt battery). The fully charged nominal 2-volt cell will, in reality, produce a voltage of approximately 2.13 volts. Using this information, it is readily apparent that a 12-volt battery (6 cells) will have a fully charged voltage of approximately 12.8 volts, a 24-volt battery (12 cells) will produce roughly 25.6 volts, and a 32-volt battery (16 cells) will have a fully charged voltage of 34.1 volts. This becomes an important consideration when calculating voltage drop as discussed previously.

For 12-volt systems, a 12-volt battery can be used. Alternatively, two 6-volt batteries can be hooked together in series (with the positive post on one connected to the negative post on the other). Where the use of higher-voltage DC current is indicated, two 12-volt or three 8-volt batteries can be wired in series (for 24 volts), or four 8-volt batteries can be wired in series (for 32 volts).

Batteries must be installed so that they are secure and rigidly held in place. Ventilation is needed to prevent the build-up of gases, particularly explosive hydrogen (which rises). Lids are essential to prevent the terminals from accidentally shorting should a conductive object like a wrench fall on them.

Years ago 6-volt electrical systems were fairly common in both automobiles and boats, but DC electrical systems are now almost universally 12-volt or higher. And although by far the greatest number of DC appliances are manufactured for 12-volt current, an increasing proportion of marine-related equipment is being built for 24- or 32-volt applications.

We've already touched briefly on the reasons for this: For a given power need (wattage) and a particular length of run (distance from the power source to the appliance and back again), higher voltage allows the use of lighter wiring. Conversely, for the longer runs present in larger yachts, higher voltages keep the required size of wiring within acceptable limits for cost and installation.

Storage batteries

A boat's batteries store and later release, upon demand, electrical energy. They accomplish this by means of a natural galvanic (electro-chemical) reaction between two molecularly dissimilar metals that are connected together and immersed in a current-carrying liquid.

The metals involved have differing natural electrical potentials (voltages). The one with the higher natural voltage is called the anode, while the one with the lower natural voltage is known as the cathode. The current-carrying liquid, meanwhile, is the electrolyte.

The battery most commonly found in marine (and automotive) applications is the wet-cell lead-acid type. This form of battery utilizes lead-antimony and pure sponge-lead plates immersed in a water-diluted solution of sulfuric acid.

When a circuit is closed between a charged lead-acid battery and an electrical appliance (load), the lead-dioxide and the sponge-lead react chemically to form lead-sulfate. In the process, electrons flow from the sponge-lead to the lead-dioxide via the part of the circuit that is external to the battery,

This charger was designed to charge batteries fast and full, but above all to protect by sensing continually to protect the batteries being charged.

namely, the circuit leg running from the positive battery post through the electrical appliance involved to the negative battery post; and that flow of electrons drives the appliance. As the chemical reaction exhausts the available lead-dioxide and sponge-lead in the plates, the voltage of the battery drops, until it reaches a point where it is too low to be useful, at which point the battery must be recharged. (In actual practice, it should be recharged well before this point is reached.)

When a lead-acid battery is recharged, electrical energy from an external source—an engine-driven alternator, or AC-energized battery-charger—drives the above-described chemical reaction in reverse. In the process, lead-sulfate is broken down, and the battery is restored to a "charged" condition.

In more recent years, a newer form of storage battery, the gel-cell, has been gaining in popularity. These essentially maintenance-free batteries employ significantly different technology than the wet-cell lead-acid battery. In this newer type, the electrolyte is a gel composed either of sulfuric acid or a

CARING FOR LEAD-ACID STORAGE BATTERIES

There are five essential components in the proper maintenance of wet-cell lead-acid batteries:

■ Minimize or eliminate deep-discharge cycles.
Each time a storage battery is cycled (discharged, and then recharged), some of its useful life is lost. This is because the galvanic reaction that produces the discharge causes the plates to gradually deteriorate, and because most of the time some amount of lead-sulfate by-product remains unreconverted after recharging. Eventually, either the accumulation of unreconverted lead-sulfate or the degeneration of the cell plates, or both, is great enough to disrupt the battery's ability to function. At this point, replacement of the battery becomes necessary.

■ Utilize properly controlled charging procedures.
Wet-cell lead-acid batteries are subject to other problems. If the recharging current is too high to be completely absorbed by the battery's chemical reaction, that current breaks down the water in the battery's electrolyte into components of hydrogen and oxygen gas. These gasses then escape, causing the electrolyte level to drop, at times to the point of drying out and, consequently, damaging irreversibly part or all of the battery plates.

■ Maintain the correct electrolyte level.
Unless you are dealing with sealed, so-called "no-maintenance" batteries, you must check electrolyte levels regularly and replace any lost electrolyte by refilling the battery with distilled water according to the manufacturer's specifications. (By using distilled water you will avoid the introduction of foreign chemicals and minerals into the electrolyte.)

■ Keep the battery clean and its terminal connections corrosion free and tight.
Regularly clean the tops of your batteries with a cloth dampened in a baking soda solution (the baking soda neutralizes any acid that has escaped via the cell vent caps). Be careful not to drip any baking soda solution into the battery's interior, as that will degrade the electrolyte.

Using a wire brush, keep the terminals and cable connectors clean and shiny; make certain the connections are tight. After cleaning and reinstalling the cable connections, coat the terminals with an appropriate battery terminal compound to retard corrosion. Do not use petroleum jelly, which tends to liquefy and seep into the connection, causing more harm than good.

■ Provide good ventilation.
Lead-acid batteries produce explosive hydrogen gas during recharging. And although hydrogen gas is lighter than air and quickly dissipates, it does represent a danger that should not be ignored. Batteries can explode, so the prudent skipper is especially careful when working around them. When dealing with terminal connections, take care to ventilate the battery space well, make certain that the batteries are not being charged at the time, and take care not to create sparks. Moreover, it is always a good idea to wear splash-proof safety goggles when you are dealing with batteries.

Caution: If you accidentally come in contact with battery acid, wash it off immediately to avoid severe burns to your skin. If battery acid contacts your eyes, flush them immediately with cool water, and seek medical attention. Also, remember that battery acid will eat holes in most fabrics.

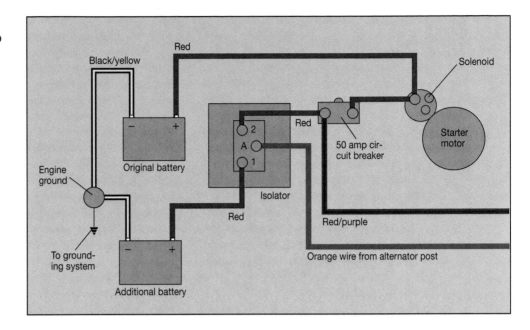

Shown is a wiring diagram of a battery isolator for two battery banks charged by a single engine alternator.

combination of sulfuric and phosphoric acids. And lead-calcium/copper alloy plates are employed.

The "black box" with a post at each end that we generally think of as a battery is really just an arbitrary module composed of a number of individual galvanic cells connected in a voltage-additive series. A single galvanic cell in a lead-acid or gelled electrolyte battery produces a nominal 2-volt current. Thus, what we commonly know as a 12-volt lead-acid battery is really six cells connected internally in series.

Choosing battery size and type

It's extremely important to have the appropriate type and size of battery for the job at hand. Each battery must be installed in its own individual container. Each discharge-charge cycle in a storage battery results in a degree of irreversible chemical degradation of its plates. The "deeper" the cycle—that is, the more the battery is discharged before being recharged—the greater the resultant chemical degradation. For that reason, deep-cycling is one of the major factors in, if not the primary cause of, premature battery failure. Using a battery with a capacity two times (or more) greater than any anticipated total current draw is the best way to ensure maximum battery life.

However, capacity alone is not the sole consideration in choosing battery size and type. Even if two batteries have the same nominal capacity, a starting battery needs to be different from a ship's service battery. Starting batteries are called upon to supply large amounts of current for very short periods of time, after which they are recharged quickly by an alternator driven by the vessel's propulsion engine. Starting batteries are, therefore, built with a large number of thin plates which, for given external dimensions and a given overall weight, maximizes plate surface area, thereby facilitating the necessary chemical reactions.

Unfortunately, the numerous, thin plates of starting batteries do not provide the reserve capacity and resistance to sulfation required for the deeper cycling to which ship's service batteries are often subjected. And therefore, ship's service batteries should be of the "deep-cycle" variety, constructed with relatively fewer and far thicker plates. Of course, you can use a starting battery for ship's service and vice versa, but if you do so, don't expect to get maximum performance or longevity per unit size.

Some so-called deep-cycle batteries are little more than relabeled starting batteries. So when purchasing batteries, check the specifications of similarly sized starting and deep-cycle batteries. For a given overall external size and weight, the deep-cycle battery will have fewer, and therefore significantly thicker, plates.

ABYC Standard E-9 *Direct Current Electrical Systems* provides a great deal of additional information on the sizing of batteries for the anticipated load on board the boat. ABYC Standard E-10 *Storage Batteries* contains information about the location, ventilation and mounting of batteries in order to be in compliance with both USCG regulations and voluntary industry standards.

Battery testing and charging

After initial selection, the second most important factor in battery performance and longevity is proper control of discharge/recharge cycles. Draining a battery below about half its full charge before recharging greatly accelerates the deterioration of its plates. So does leaving a battery in a partial or fully discharged state for long periods of time.

The most common method of recharging shipboard storage batteries is by means of an alternator that is belt-driven by the vessel's propulsion engine. When charging a gel-cell battery, considerations are different; refer to page 530.

Maintenance-free gel-cell batteries are becoming more common. They offer some advantages. For instance, their semi-solid electrolyte cannot spill out and so they can be installed in any position.

Gel-cell batteries do, however, require somewhat different handling when it comes to charging, as they can be ruined quickly (gassed and dried out) by charging at too high a voltage. Of course, so can a wet-cell battery; but in the case of such an open-cell battery (with removable vent caps), you will be likely to notice the drop in liquid electrolyte. Then you can add water, and (hopefully) correct the problem before any permanent damage to the battery occurs.

In contrast, there is no easy visual way to measure deterioration of the semi-solid electrolyte in a gel-cell battery, so such batteries usually require re-regulation of the vessel's charging systems to a maximum 14.1 volts. For dockside charging, it is also best to employ one of the newer type chargers on the market, those that have alternate programmed charging cycles available for gel-cells. Moreover, since the gel-cell suffers quickly when left in a partially (50 percent or more) discharged state for extended periods of time, it's critical to ensure that such batteries are "topped up" before shutting down and leaving your boat. Beyond that, what's good for the life of a common wet-cell lead-acid battery is good for a gel-cell.

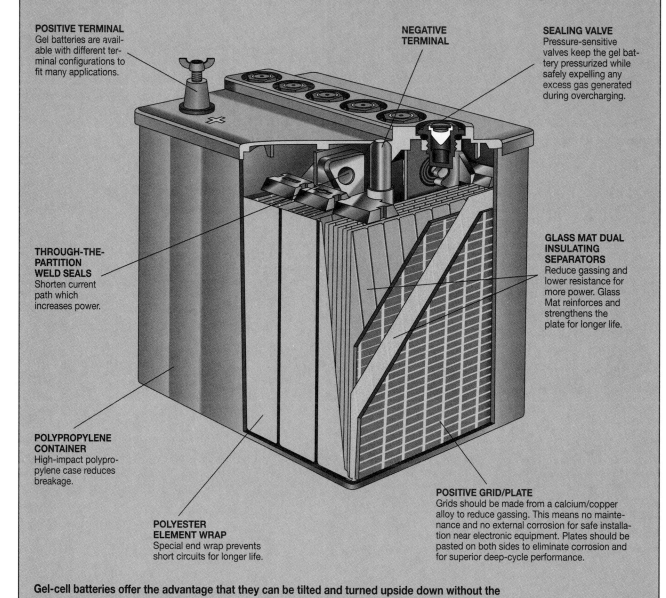

POSITIVE TERMINAL
Gel batteries are available with different terminal configurations to fit many applications.

NEGATIVE TERMINAL

SEALING VALVE
Pressure-sensitive valves keep the gel battery pressurized while safely expelling any excess gas generated during overcharging.

THROUGH-THE-PARTITION WELD SEALS
Shorten current path which increases power.

GLASS MAT DUAL INSULATING SEPARATORS
Reduce gassing and lower resistance for more power. Glass Mat reinforces and strengthens the plate for longer life.

POLYPROPYLENE CONTAINER
High-impact polypropylene case reduces breakage.

POLYESTER ELEMENT WRAP
Special end wrap prevents short circuits for longer life.

POSITIVE GRID/PLATE
Grids should be made from a calcium/copper alloy to reduce gassing. This means no maintenance and no external corrosion for safe installation near electronic equipment. Plates should be pasted on both sides to eliminate corrosion and for superior deep-cycle performance.

Gel-cell batteries offer the advantage that they can be tilted and turned upside down without the risk of spilling electrolyte. This is an advantage for any boat, but particularly for sailboats.

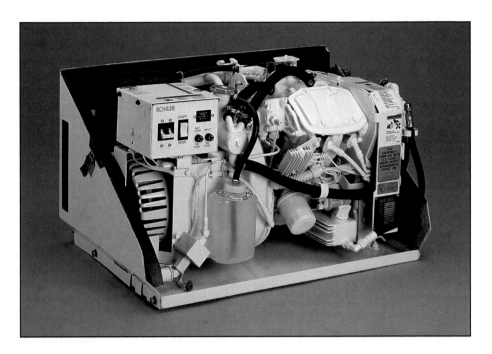

Larger yachts, with a greater demand for power, are usually fitted with a gas- or diesel-powered generator so that AC power is available whether or not the propulsion engine is in operation. This one is enclosed in a noise-insulating box.

It is wise to regularly check and pay close attention to the readings on your battery-condition gauges. At one time, the only battery-related gauges found aboard boats were ammeters, which measured either the current (amps) being drawn from the battery, or the current being pumped back in by the boat's charging system. On most recently built boats, ammeters are supplemented with, and sometimes replaced by, voltmeters, which are often given special dial faces and called battery-condition meters.

For each battery, there is a maximum voltage point at which the battery is considered fully charged and a minimum voltage point at which it is effectively discharged.

There are slight differences between individual batteries, but most 12-volt units are considered fully charged at 12.8 volts and discharged at 11.7 volts. In between those levels, the battery's state of charge can be measured as a percentage of fully charged voltage. This is what the voltage gauges, with so-called "battery-condition" dial faces, actually do.

Such battery-condition gauges are inexpensive compared with the cost of good quality batteries and they significantly aid in avoiding deep-cycling. They can also help ensure that your batteries are being fully recharged, a factor that is critical in a battery's longevity. There are also rather expensive digital meters that indicate the count-down of stored ampere-hours as the battery is used, and the count back up of ampere-hours during recharging.

The specific gravity of the electrolyte in a lead-acid battery varies with the battery's state of charge. It is thus possible to measure state of charge with a hydrometer—in fact, for many years, this was standard practice. (Using a hydrometer is still an easy way to identify a failing cell within a battery that is, otherwise, in good condition.) However, it is far more practical to use a voltmeter.

Your battery-condition meters may reveal that your batteries are not being fully charged when you run your engine. Or they may indicate that, while your starting battery comes to full charge, your ship's service battery, which has been drained overnight by your lights, refrigerator, radio, etc., does not. Such a situation is common and is one of the leading causes of accelerated battery deterioration.

Such deterioration occurs because the standard charging regulators fitted to most propulsion engine charging systems are designed only for recharging starting batteries. Starting batteries, on the other hand, are called upon to provide heavy current for a very, very brief period of time. Consequently, they can be recharged with a relatively large amount of current over a short period of time.

As a battery is recharged, its voltage rises. Standard regulators sense this voltage rise and taper off the charging current until it is too low to fully charge a ship's service battery within a reasonable time period. This causes problems when you are away from dockside hook-ups, and can also lead to accelerated deterioration due to failure to achieve a full recharge before you start the discharge period again.

Maintaining a proper charge in ship's service batteries sometimes requires a special charging regulator. These bypass or replace the pre-programmed cycle of the standard charging regulator and ensure that the ship's service battery receives the large amounts of current necessary for a full recharge. With such a device, it is also possible, from time to time, to intentionally "overcharge" the batteries slightly—a procedure called "equalization," which, in a lead-acid battery, drives excess unreconverted lead sulfate back into solution.

This equalization reverses some otherwise permanent plate deterioration. However, it is critical to monitor very carefully battery temperature and peak voltage in accord with the manufacturer's recommendations as excess heat can build up and "gas out" electrolyte or damage the battery's plates. In extreme cases, it can even melt down the battery case and cause a fire.

These special regulators for ship's service batteries are currently available in both manual and automatic types. The automatic units, though generally more expensive, guard against inadvertent damage to the batteries due to forgetting to cut back charging current as they reach full charge.

Multiple charging sources and battery isolators

On boats with multiple batteries and one or more sources of DC charging power (alternators and battery chargers), it is often desirable to be able to use one of the charging sources to serve at least two battery banks. An example of this is where one alternator would be used to charge both the cranking battery and the "house battery." In order to accomplish this, battery isolators are available from a number of sources. These are devices containing diodes which permit the flow of current in one direction only so that the output of the alternator or battery charger can be directed to both batteries simultaneously. The isolator prevents one battery from being charged or discharged by the other battery. It is important to note, however, that the use of isolators introduces a slight voltage drop in the charging circuit and, unless the charging device's output is adjusted higher, a little less than full charging will occur to the batteries.

Auxiliary generator sets

In addition to alternators that are belt driven by a propulsion engine for the production of DC power, a vessel may have one or more auxiliary generator sets. These supply AC in either nominal 120- or 240-volt power for distribution to the vessel's wiring system.

Generator sets are not connected to the vessel's drive train, but comprise a large alternator that is close-coupled to a dedicated engine, which may be either a gasoline or diesel unit. Of course, the generator should use the same type of fuel as the propulsion engines. They also incorporate an engine speed governing system, regulating circuitry, and sometimes special load-sensing circuitry that automatically starts (and stops) the unit according to demand.

The advantage of a generator set is that it can supply power for large, house-type electrical loads, while at the same time allowing a vessel to be independent of shorepower connections. The capacities of most manufacturers' lines of generator sets generally start at about 2.5 kW (2,500 watts) and extend up to 15 kW and higher.

Although the AC produced by a generator set cannot be used directly to charge a vessel's storage batteries, it is possible to wire the generator set so that it powers the same battery charger which would otherwise be driven by shorepower. In this way, any generator set capacity in excess of the vessel's immediate needs can be used to recharge its batteries at times when its propulsion engines are not being run.

Solar power

Sunlight can be converted into direct electricity by photovoltaic cells. The low voltage produced can be used to operate small electrical appliances—for instance, calculators and small ventilator fans. And a number of photovoltaic cells can be connected together in cased arrays called "solar panels" to charge, albeit in a limited way, a vessel's storage batteries.

In order to charge storage batteries, the charging power must be at a higher voltage than the battery, whose voltage may be 12, 24 or 32 volts. In solar panels an appropriate number of individual photovoltaic cells are, therefore, first connected in voltage-additive series. Then a number of these cell groups may be arrayed in current-additive parallel to provide greater amounts of power (amperage). The result is a quiet, non-polluting on-board source of electrical power.

Unfortunately, it's difficult to find enough deck space for enough panels to provide sufficient current for most shipboard appliances. And most appliances whose current demands could be so satisfied directly, do not find their major use at times when there is sunlight to be converted. For example, a solar panel of practical size for, say, a 35-footer, could run an electric lamp. But the lamp would be needed most at times when there is no sunlight available to power the solar panel. For that reason, and because solar panels are still relatively expensive when measured against unit output, the practical on-board application of solar power is limited and usually relegated to supplementary charging of storage batteries.

Wind generators

In recent years, significant strides have been made in the manufacture of wind-driven generators for boats. Strong, ultra-light composite materials have become available for rotor blades and other structural parts; and compact, efficient alternators have been developed. As a result, wind-driven generators are available in sizes and weights that make them practical for installation aboard yachts and other small craft.

As an on-board source of electrical power, wind-driven generators offer some important advantages over solar panels: They produce significantly greater amounts of current (for the amount of room they take up), and they work at night and on cloudy or rainy days.

However, they have their disadvantages as well: They're still relatively expensive for the amount of electrical power they develop; and they tend to be somewhat awkward looking, unless their installation is quite carefully designed and executed. As well, they're most useful at anchor, when a vessel is away from shorepower, lacks a generator set, and is not running its propulsion engine(s). Consequently, they're usually found on sailing craft, for if properly installed, they can be used underway when under sail alone. After all, there would be little point in utilizing a wind-driven generator on a power-boat underway, as the propulsion engine(s)-driven alternator(s) would provide many more times the amount of current, at very little, if any additional cost in fuel or engine wear.

REGULATING AND TRANSFORMING POWER

Electrical appliances have fairly specific power requirements. For instance, a 24-volt DC electric motor will not run properly on 12-volt DC current, but instead will run too slowly, overheat, and possibly even burn up. Similarly, 24 or 40 volts fed in to charge a 12-volt battery will overcharge and destroy it. And alternating current appliances will not operate on DC, and vice versa.

It's true that some DC electronic equipment and other appliances are equipped with internal power circuitry that tolerates input voltages from, say, 10 to 32 volts; but this kind of tolerance does not generally extend to AC/DC appliances, except in today's on-board refrigeration systems and some other units that have the capacity to choose a higher voltage if both voltages are available (a refrigerator will choose 120 AC over 12 DC). And therefore, at times when the frequency and voltage characteristics of source currents do not match requirements of the equipment to be powered, it is necessary to employ either a regulated power supply (DC), an inverter (DC to AC) or a transformer (AC).

DC-DC converters

DC-DC converters are devices that take a higher DC voltage such as 24 volts, and reduce it to a lower DC voltage, such as 12 volts. These are especially useful in powering certain items of electronic equipment which are generally available only in 12 volts when on-board vessels with either 24- or 32-volt DC electrical systems. The DC-DC converter is preferable to a simple "dropping" resistor in that its output voltage is maintained at a constant level regardless of the connected load current.

Transformers

When transformers are used simply to step up or step down the voltage of an AC system, without providing isolation from the shorepower system, they are properly known as polarization transformers. If the transformer is connected so as to provide complete galvanic isolation from the shorepower system, then it is known as an isolation transformer. ABYC Standard E-8 contains a great deal of additional information on the subject of both of these types of transformers.

Transformers are most frequently used to step the voltage of AC systems either up or down, but in some circumstances they are used without voltage change in order to isolate a vessel's on-board power system from a shorepower system. They can be so used because transformers magnetically couple their input and output circuits, creating current in the latter by induction, rather than by means of a direct conductive connection.

Inverters

If a vessel is wired for 120-volt AC or higher voltage, it will likely have on-board appliances that are designed specifically for these voltages, which the crew will undoubtedly want to continue to use when away from a shorepower hook-up. If

An inverter can power 110-volt AC appliances without having to run an auxiliary generator.

the vessel has an auxiliary generating plant of sufficient capacity, then the necessary supply of 120- or 240-volt power is no problem. However, there are cases in which the boat is too small to accommodate a generator set comfortably; and there may be times when the crew wants 120-volt AC without the additional noise and vibration of a running generator set—which is always present to some extent, however well-silenced and resiliently mounted the unit is. And in such instances, an inverter really shows to advantage.

Years ago, most inverters consisted of a DC motor driving an AC generator. But the modern yacht inverter is most often a stationary, solid-state device that electronically steps up and changes 12-volt (or 24- or 32-volt) DC power to 120-volt AC power.

Such inverters are available in very small output capacities on up to capacities large enough to run small motor-operated equipment such as low-capacity air conditioners and undercounter refrigerators, whose compressor motors require moderately high starting currents. (But keep in mind that the energy required by such appliances would be impractically large for most battery installations.) Size, weight and cost are pretty much directly proportional to output capacity.

Beyond output capacity rating, some inverters are better than others at producing current whose wave pattern is closer or identical to the "sine wave" characteristics of shorepower. The least expensive inverters produce what is known as "square wave" current. These are fine for running lights and other resistive appliances, as well as some appliances with small motors, such as coffee grinders, kitchen mixers and blenders, and some (but only some) small electric tools. However, square wave inverters may not be able to start some induction-type motors even if the nominal wattage rating of the motor is well within the inverter's capacity; and they may cause speed-sensitive equipment such as tape decks and VCRs to run erratically.

The best all-around performance is secured with an inverter that produces either pure sine wave current, or at least "modified sine wave" current that is guaranteed by the manufacturer to operate all motors whose power draws are within the output capacities of the inverter. (In that respect, keep in mind that certain appliances, such as refrigerator and air conditioner compressor motors, may draw as much as three times their rated running current when they first start up.)

Today, there are some very advanced solid-state inverters on the market which incorporate highly sophisticated sensing circuitry, as well as sophisticated integral three-stage battery chargers. These units are wired to the storage batteries and into the vessel's 120-volt distribution system. When there is 120-volt input from either a shorepower connection or a generator set, the inverter automatically charges the storage batteries; and when that input ceases, such units automatically switch to inverter mode to supply current in response to a sensed demand on their output circuit.

Provided that the inverter is of sufficient capacity, it is possible to run all manner of "household style" devices on board, from fans to electric tools to kitchen appliances, without relying on either a shorepower connection or a shipboard generator set. However, it's also necessary to have sufficient storage battery capacity, or you will run your batteries flat in no time at all. Keep in mind that a 100-watt lamp draws only .83 amps at 120 volts, but that, even neglecting inherent power losses (to heat) during current conversion, the inverter powering that lamp will be drawing 8.3 amps, or 10 times as much current. And if your ship's service battery is of average size for a small boat—say, 90 amp-hour capacity—and you allow for a 50 percent discharge, that 100-watt lamp will use the available stored power in less than 6 hours. So, if you want to use an inverter for more than, for example, running an electric drill for a few minutes at a time, you need to ensure that your ship's service storage batteries are of much greater capacity than normal.

The addition of a DC to AC inverter on board the boat will be a complex installation at best to ensure the following: that batteries are properly sized, that DC wiring is of adequate capacity, that the device automatically switches itself off when shorepower is available and that it is properly integrated into the vessel's electrical system so that it does not attempt to power all AC loads simultaneously. When making such an installation, it is wise to employ a competent marine electrician; consult ABYC Standard E-8 *AC Electrical Systems* to ensure compliance with all necessary recommendations.

Connecting to shorepower

The shorepower connection is sometimes sarcastically referred to as the boat's "umbilical cord." This is because some boaters (basically, those without generator sets or inverters) are loath to break the shorepower connection and give up the conve-

ADAPTER SELECTION GUIDE

Male end		Female end			
15A 125V	20A 125V	30A 125V	20A 125V	20A 125V	15A 125V
20A 125V		20A 125V	15A 125V		
30A 125V		50A 125V	20A 125V	20A 125V	15A 125V
50A 125V		30A 125V	20A 125V	15A 125V	
50A 125/250V		50A 125/250V			

A wide selection of adapters is available on the market, off the shelf, to make cable configurations to dockside outlets.

nience of "house-type" alternating current. But the very nature of this disparagement indicates just how integrated the shore-to-ship power connection has become in boating today.

In North America, the voltage of shorepower current is usually nominal 120, but may in some cases be nominal 240, so diligent care needs to be taken at all times in hooking up and using such power. Shorepower connections should be made only to properly wired and protected dock outlets.

Further, the vessel should be equipped with proper shore-power cords (with lock-type fittings and water-shedding boots and collars), appropriate inlet fittings, and a correctly fused and switched main distribution panel. The configurations of proper cords and inlet fittings ensure that neither skipper nor crew will ever handle a "live" cord with exposed (male end) prongs—as that is a certain invitation to potentially fatal electric shock.

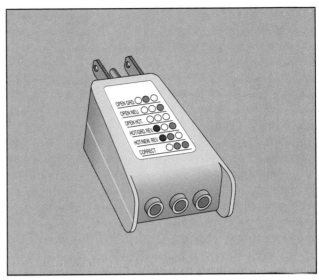

The circuit tester shown above is one of many available that can quickly diagnose a faulty wiring situation.

CHECKLIST FOR USING ADAPTERS

Whenever using adapters, the following three points must always be considered:

✓ Outlet and equipment always must be of the same voltage rating.

✓ Total amperage drawn should never be allowed to exceed the amperage rating of the lowest-rated component of the adapter.

✓ Polarity and grounding continuity must be maintained.

As well, it is advantageous if the vessel's distribution panel incorporates both a voltmeter and an ammeter to measure the characteristics of the incoming power and avoid overloading of the shorepower cord and connections, and the dock circuit.

Properly wired dock outlets are found in a wide variety of configurations, each associated with particular combinations of voltage and current. For example, the size and pattern of 120-volt outlets with 15-, 30- and 50-amp current capacity respectively differ from one another. And they all have configurations different from those of 240-volt outlets.

Moreover, because wiring codes are not consistent across the country, and certainly not across international borders, the outlets at a strange dock may not match the end on your shorepower cord. Therefore, if you travel far afield and wish to connect to shorepower, it may be necessary to have aboard a variety of adapters that will allow connection of your shorepower cord to different types of dock outlets.

Regardless of what adapters you must use in order to accommodate the dock outlets, always ensure that the grounding conductor (green wire) is connected to an outlet

or metallic device that truly provides an effective ground. All too often one sees adapters where the grounding (green wire) "pigtail" is connected via its clip to a piece of plastic conduit or water pipe, or just left "dangling" in the air. The grounding conductor is essential for the safety of persons on board the boat and those in the water surrounding the vessel whenever it is connected to shorepower; *never sacrifice its integrity*.

There are also adapters available (or which can be made up using proprietary, off-the-shelf parts) that can be used to split or merge current. For instance, if your boat has two 30-amp inlets, but the dock outlet is a single 50-amp unit, a properly wired adapter can likely be used to split the 50-amp outlet into connections for two 30-amp cords. In reverse manner, if your boat has a single 50-amp inlet, and the dock two 30-amp outlets, the right adapter can be used to merge the two 30-amp outlets into a single 50-amp cord. And there are adapters available that will match a 50-amp dock outlet to a 30-amp boat inlet, a 30-amp dock outlet to a 50-amp boat inlet, and a 15-amp dock outlet to a 30-amp boat inlet—though in the last two cases, it's important to remember that there may not be sufficient current available in such a hook-up to run high-demand appliances that may be aboard.

Another way of protecting yourself and your boat's electrical system is to verify the electrical connections at the dock before hooking up. This is done with an outlet circuit tester. Selling for just a few dollars, the instrument employs a combination of neon lights to indicate the following situations: correct wiring, reversed polarity, open ground wire, open neutral wire, open hot wire, hot and ground reversed and hot wire on neutral terminal, and hot terminal unwired. An outlet circuit tester is also a practical tool for testing extension cords or for verifying any electrical work that has been done on the boat.

It is pretty obvious that electrical power generated, stored or brought aboard via a shorepower connection is of little value unless it can be distributed properly to various on-board appliances. Yet, while much time, attention and money is frequently spent on the source of on-board electricity, the distribution side of the system is almost as often given short shrift. And that's a shame, because relatively modest efforts and expenditures in this area can go a long way in ensuring the reliable and safe utilization of on-board electrical power.

Caution: Whenever 120-volt or 240-volt AC electrical systems are installed on board vessels, there is the possibility that, due to the failure of equipment or insulation somewhere in the future, AC voltage can inadvertently be applied to the vessel's DC electrical system. When and if this occurs, portions of the DC electrical system, especially the engine and its propulsion system (which is connected via the battery negative), can now be energized at a potential of 120 volts AC above "ground." This poses an imminent danger, not only to persons on board the vessel who may inadvertently contact such equipment, but also to swimmers in the water, especially in freshwater areas, as they may be in the potential gradient or "field" created around the vessel.

In order to guard against this occurrence, the ABYC and NFPA Standards require the connection of the AC system grounding wire (green) to the DC system negative (ground) on board the vessel. This connection must be made on all vessels equipped with shorepower, other than those utilizing isolation transformers. The location of this connection should be ascertained, and its integrity checked on a regular basis. In years past, there have been articles written about disconnecting this circuit or "cutting" the green wire to shore to reduce the incidence of galvanic corrosion on board the boat. This is not only improper, but dangerous. There are other ways to combat galvanic corrosion when using shorepower; these will be covered later in this chapter.

Main switches

The 12- (or 24- or 32-) volt DC and the 120-volt AC (or 240-volt AC, if applicable) sub-systems should each be controlled by its own main switch that will cut power off entirely. This is an important protection, both for someone working on the system and in the event of an electrical or other fire, when it can be vitally important to be able to power down quickly and positively.

The one exception to this rule is the automatic bilge pump circuit. This circuit should be wired so as to remain active even if the main switches are turned off—especially if it's your practice, as it is with many boaters, to turn off the mains whenever the boat is left unattended. That way, the protection of automatic bilge pumping will not be lost.

According to ABYC, E-8.14.3, 1992, conductors shall be identified to indicate circuit polarity according to the table shown at right.

The main switch for the higher voltage sub-systems (120 and 240 volts) will customarily be incorporated in the main distribution/circuit-breaker panel. However, since the lower voltage sub-systems (12-, 24- and 32-volt varieties) supply current to the engine starter(s), the main switch for these circuits necessarily has to carry very high currents (often 300 amps or more); consequently, it is imperative that the switch be of robust construction. The low-voltage main switch is, therefore, usually separated from the main distribution/circuit-breaker panel.

Low-voltage main switches are often constructed to control two separate battery banks. These switches can be iden-

RECOMMENDED MARINE WIRING COLOR CODE		
Color	**Item**	**Use**
DC systems		
Green (G) or green w/yellow stripe(s) (GY)		DC grounding conductors
Black (Bl) or yellow (Y)*		DC negative conductors
Red (R)		DC positive conductors
Brown/yellow stripe (BY) or yellow (Y)**	Bilge blowers	Fuse or switch to blowers
Dark gray (Gy)	Navigation lights	Fuse or switch to lights
Brown (Br)	Pumps	Fuse or switch to pumps
Orange (O)	Accessory feeds	Distribution panel to accessory switch
Purple (Pu)	Instrument feed	Distribution panel to electric instruments
Dark blue (BL)	Cabin and instrument lights	Fuse or switch to lights
AC systems		
Black (B)		Ungrounded conductor
White (W)		Grounded neutral conductor
Green (G)		Grounding conductor
Red, orange, blue		Additional ungrounded conductors
Black w/red stripe, black w/blue stripe or black w/orange stripe		Additional colors for ungrounded conductors (black)

As of 1990, white foreground in the low voltage (DC) has been changed to yellow with the intention of recommending the use of black and white as high voltage (AC system) colors only.
**If yellow is used for DC negative, blower must be brown with a yellow stripe.*
Note: These colors are associated with the boat, not the engine(s).

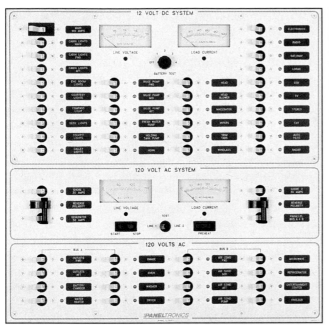

An example of a main switch breaker and meter panel, front and back view for both high and low voltage for a medium-size boat.

tified by their labeling, which will show positions for bank 1, bank 2, all (or both) and off. The all (or both) position puts the two battery banks in parallel, thereby doubling the batteries' available capacity, while keeping voltage at the same level. This is handy at times for engine-starting under cold or otherwise difficult conditions. (Note that if this type of switch is to be used for battery paralleling, it must be rated by its manufacturer for that type of service, and selected according to the amount of cranking current that the starter on the engine will draw.)

The low-voltage main switches are often also wired to control the propulsion engine charging circuit, that is, starting current runs from the storage batteries to the starter(s) according to the setting of the switch, and charging current from the engine alternator(s) runs back to the battery or batteries according to the switch settings. Such an arrangement affords the advantage of being able to direct charging current to one of bank 1 or 2, or to both.

A battery switch provides positive battery disconnect, isolates all circuits and also protects against the hazards of electrical fire and explosion.

However, when the main switch is used in this way in order to control the charging circuit, the boater must always take care that the main switch is of the make-before-break type, and also that it incorporates an alternator field disconnect circuit. (Note that with certain types of alternators, the field circuit is integral to the regulator built into the alternator and, therefore, it is impossible to utilize the field disconnect circuit provided on some battery switches. If this is the case, it is important always to ascertain that the alternator and its regulator are immune from damage that would otherwise result from disconnecting the alternator from the battery while it is operating.) The reason for this precaution is that serious damage can occur to the alternator's rectifying and blocking diodes if ever the charging circuit is left without a battery connected to it while the engine is running—even momentarily. Thus, when you switch, say, from bank 1 to bank 2 with the engine running, the make-before-break type switch automatically connects bank 2 before disconnecting bank 1. Also, the alternator field disconnect circuit shuts down current to the alternator's field coil, thereby putting the alternator into "idle" or non-current-producing mode, if you should happen to turn the switch to the "off" position while the engine is running.

If the propulsion engine charging circuit is wired in such a way that it bypasses the main switch and goes directly to the storage batteries, the above precautions may not be necessary. But even if that is the case, it is usually necessary to incorporate a battery isolator, as previously discussed, to prevent inadvertent crosscurrents between the vessel's starting and service battery banks, currents that can leave you with a flat starting battery.

The distribution/circuit-breaker panel

All circuits should be protected from overload and dangerous short circuits, which can cause fire, by fuses or circuit breakers that sense excessive current loads and shut off power to the circuit.

Fuses accomplish this by means of a one-time destruction of an internal metal strip that melts when a predetermined amount of current is drawn through it. Circuit breakers, on the other hand, perform the same function, but are resettable after the problem in the circuit has been corrected. Except in the smallest, least expensive boats, circuit breakers are today almost universally used in preference to fuses, at least when it comes to main distribution panels and when currents of 5 amps or greater are involved. (Occasionally an individual piece of sensitive electronic equipment will be additionally protected with an in-line fuse rated at 3 amps or less; and the manufacturer's installation manual should always be followed in this respect. Electronic components of some modern diesel engines are also protected in this manner.)

Fuses of the correct size offer safe on-board circuit protection. However, fuses have several disadvantages as compared to circuit breakers:

- When a fuse blows, it is more difficult to replace it than simply to reset a circuit breaker.
- It is dangerously easy to replace a blown fuse with an improper one of excess current-carrying capacity.
- If a fuse blows and no replacement is handy, there is the temptation to shunt it with a length of wire, a practice which leads to fire.
- In damp corrosive atmospheres, fuse clips tend to corrode, offering a high-resistance connection which results in voltage drop.

The main distribution panel is used to distribute current to various on-board circuits. To both the DC and AC panels, heavy conductors are brought to a heavy bus bar on the panel. Branch (or sub-) circuits are then wired on the panel from the bus bar through an appropriately rated circuit breaker, which is often also used as a switch for that branch circuit. In this way, circuit faults usually result in the "tripping" of a breaker on the labeled main distribution panel, and are therefore easier to trace and correct. The use of a main distribution panel also facilitates checking the on/off condition of various circuits. Trip-free circuit breakers are a recommended protective component for on-board application. These are designed so that the reset handle cannot be manually held to override the current interrupting mechanism. This makes "cheating" on the breaker impossible.

An important caution: When the low-voltage and higher-voltage distribution panels are combined into a single unit (usually side-by-side), it is critical to make sure that no inadvertent cross-connections are made. Any such cross-connections would result in feeding 120- or 240-volt current into the vessel's 12-, 24- or 32-volt system. This in turn could cause at least the destruction of low-voltage equipment. In the worst-case scenario, it could cause the electrocution of a crew member or a swimmer.

The wiring system

The correct type and gauge of wiring should always be used in order that the system may carry its electrical loads efficiently and safely. Proper color coding of wiring insulators should be observed without fail in order to facilitate the identification of circuits and the tracking of wires during troubleshooting procedures.

Identification should also be ensured with a complete wiring diagram that can be understood by a non-expert. Enclose it in plastic and post it near the main switch panel. Keep it up to date as additions and changes are made. Proper terminal connections, bundling and support of the wire runs should always be provided for, in order to minimize the potential for failures due to corrosion (connections lying loose in wet bilges) and failures due to mechanical problems (connections pulling loose under the substantial weight of wiring or due to vibration).

Wiring and the compass

Wiring that supplies DC current to the compass's night-light and other DC wiring in proximity to a vessel's compass or auto pilot is a potential cause of serious magnetic deviation. When carrying current, such wiring can be the source of magnetic fields that will interfere with the proper functioning of the compass.

Even worse, because electrical circuits are sometimes on and sometimes off, and because the magnetic fields they generate change with variations in current, the magnetic interference they produce is sporadic and variable. Therefore, this form of magnetic deviation cannot generally be eliminated by compensating the compass, and so it becomes necessary to take a preventive, rather than a corrective approach to the problem.

The primary preventive measure is to keep all DC wiring at least 3 feet—and preferably 6 feet—away from the vessel's magnetic compass (and the sensing unit of an autopilot). Obviously, that is not always possible, particularly in the case of wiring that runs to the compass's own night lighting. Wiring that cannot be routed well away from the compass should be run in twisted pairs, that is, each DC feed wire should be paired with a DC return wire and the two tightly (not loosely) twisted round and round together. This procedure will cause the magnetic field of one wire to be "canceled" by the field of the other.

The wiring installation should always be checked as a safety measure. You can do this by observing the compass while you switch the involved circuit first on, then off. If the wires have been properly twisted, the compass card will not react. However, if the wires have not been properly paired and twisted, the card will shift quite rapidly to a new heading each time the circuit is switched.

ELECTRICAL APPLIANCES AND EQUIPMENT

Clearly, electrical appliances are a boon for today's boater. Indeed, the convenience they afford is one of the two major reasons for having electrical power on board—the other being the use of modern sophisticated electronic navigation and communications equipment. Electrical appliances can, however, also be a bane; for unless properly chosen and installed, they will deteriorate and break down quickly, as well as cause problems for critical electronics. The prudent skipper will, therefore, refer to the installation standards promulgated by such organizations as ABYC and NFPA and, in all cases, pay strict attention to the recommendations of the manufacturers of the equipment in question.

Just as for applications ashore, choose electrical equipment that bears the listing mark of Underwriters' Laboratories (UL) whenever possible. Underwriters' Laboratories "Marine" lists certain devices intended specifically for installation on board vessels, especially AC and DC electrical equipment. These listed devices should be used whenever there is a choice of equipment.

Choosing and installing microwaves

For on-board use, microwave ovens offer some significant advantages over conventional electric ovens and ranges because they reduce cooking time, hence power consumption. They also reduce the amount of heat released into the surrounding cabin, which improves the comfort of the crew and, if the boat is simultaneously being air conditioned, further reduces overall power consumption.

Microwave ovens are available in different sizes and wattage ratings. The larger ovens are usually more powerful (faster cooking) and require more current, but not in all cases; so it is important to check wattage ratings carefully when comparing units of the same physical size. Beyond that, the choice of preferred size and wattage is determined basically by the same cooking considerations pertinent in shoreside

A microwave drastically reduces cooking time, and a judiciously installed unit can greatly enhance life afloat.

applications; although final selection is limited by a number of other considerations relating specifically to on-board use.

First, on all but the largest yachts, galley space is relatively limited in comparison to on-shore applications—so it may not be possible to fit in a full- or apartment-size microwave.

Second, unless the craft is fitted with an auxiliary generating set, supplying AC for the microwave can be a problem when shorepower is not available—for example, at anchor. Yet, such times are precisely when microwave cooking affords the greatest advantages. Consequently, it may be important to ensure that the unit can be powered by an existing inverter, and that there is sufficient storage battery capacity to supply current. For example, a 1,000-watt unit set on high power will draw about 8.33 amps at 120 volts. Assuming that the inverter has an efficiency of 85 percent (with 15 percent of the input current lost to heat), the current draw on a 12-volt battery will be about 93 amps—a pretty heavy load that would deeply discharge the average group 27 size (deep-cycle) battery in less than half an hour.

In contrast, if the microwave were a 500-watt unit used for appropriately light duty, the battery draw would be about 47 amps; and since microwave cooking is, happily, fast, the 10 or so minutes needed would probably only discharge the vessel's batteries by about 7 to 8 amp-hours. And naturally, if the unit were in use on a powerboat underway, that amount of power would easily be supplied by the propulsion engine alternator(s), without a drain on the storage batteries.

Microwave ovens are relatively heavy and need to be securely mounted. It's also critical to make sure that they have sufficient ventilation, as lack of cooling ventilation is probably one of the most frequent causes of failure in on-board use. Therefore, if the unit is being built in or enclosed in a locker, ventilation holes of adequate size should be cut in its enclosure.

There is at least one "marine-grade" microwave oven on the market specifically built for boating applications. These units reportedly utilize more corrosion-resistant materials and are specially built to resist vibration damage and avoid interference with on-board electronics, all important considerations in a boating environment. The retail cost of such units, however, is more than double that of many household types of equivalent power; and it has to be noted that the vast majority of production boat builders currently install household-type units in their craft with no greater incidence of warranty claims than for most other on-board equipment. Thus, whether the additional money spent on a special marine microwave oven is cost-effective is a matter of personal judgment.

But, if a household-type microwave is chosen, albeit a unit of the lower-wattage "mini" variety, it's worth paying a bit extra for a model with splash-resistant touch-pad controls, rather than knobs. Touch-pad controls are much more resistant to moisture intrusion than knobs mounted on shafts, and therefore less likely to cause problems on board a boat, especially in a salt atmosphere.

Refrigeration and air conditioning

Refrigeration and air conditioning units that use sealed, electrically driven compressors are probably among the most, if not the most, reliable pieces of equipment to be found aboard a yacht.

One reason for this is that they incorporate shore-based technology—albeit adapted to the use of corrosion resistant materials—that has reached a high level of refinement. In these units, the compressor motor is sealed inside the condenser casing with the compressor itself, and so is protected from the ravages of the marine environment. The evaporator units have no moving parts. And the refrigerant tubing that runs between the two is sealed (or should be if properly installed). Thus, if a fresh desiccant cartridge is soldered

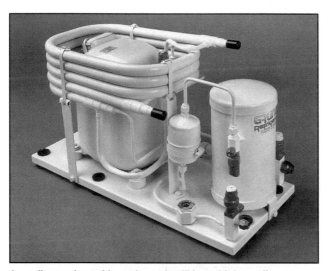

A quality marine refrigeration unit will have high-quality, long-lasting parts. They will be well mounted, secured against vibration and shocks, and protected against the harshness of the salt-water environment.

into the refrigerant circuit when it's first charged, and the system remains sealed, the basic unit will last for years without the need of attention, even if run continuously.

Of course, this is not necessarily true of certain peripheral components, such as the evaporator fans and the electric pumps which supply cooling water to the condenser unit in water-cooled systems. But again, in the better systems, even these components are rated for years of operational life, even under continuous use.

The important thing to remember about refrigeration and air conditioning units is that their compressor motors draw starting current (amperage) that is at least twice, and can be as much as three times, their rated current draw when running. This means, for example, that a 6,000 Btu AC system which is rated at 7.5 amps at 120 volts can actually be drawing 15 or more amps each time the compressor starts up. And it's critical to take this into account when matching generator sets, inverters, wiring and fusing to such systems.

Ground fault circuit interrupters

There are occasions when, due to faulty wiring, terminals or other defects in a circuit, current will escape its normal (safe) path and head directly to ground via some other conductor. The condition is called a "ground fault" in an AC circuit. If the external conductor happens to be your body, you can be in big trouble, especially if heavy current manages to pass through your heart. A ground fault circuit interrupter, or "GFCI" as it has come to be known, senses such a ground fault before any potentially injurious amount of current can be conducted, and in a fraction of a second breaks (interrupts) the power to the faulty circuit.

GFCIs are available in different sizes and capacities, some portable and some designed to be wired into the electrical distribution system. Some are even integrated into the distribution outlets themselves (you've no doubt noticed these in the bathrooms and kitchens of recently wired houses, and probably on many newer boats as well). No vessel with 120 or higher voltage on board should be without appropriate GFCIs in its distribution system. And portable GFCIs should be employed as necessary on deck and on the dock—indeed, anywhere near the water or where one might be showered upon—whenever electrical tools are employed. This caution simply cannot be overstated: Numerous fatalities have resulted from the failure to take these precautions, and when electrical tools have dropped in the water or developed wiring faults while the operator was standing in a puddle or was otherwise well-grounded.

GFCIs are not listed as "ignition protected" devices and, in order to avoid an explosion hazard, should not be installed in the engine room or fuel tank areas of gasoline-powered vessels. Additional information about the use and installation of GFCIs is covered in ABYC Standard E-8 *AC Electrical Systems.*

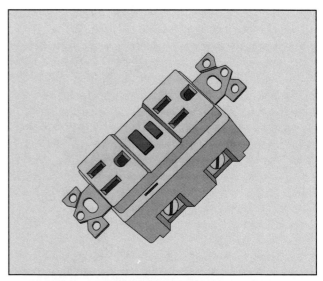

A ground fault circuit interrupter is designed to protect people from line-to-ground electrical shock hazards which may develop from faulty appliances, tools or cords.

PROTECTING YOUR BOAT AND EQUIPMENT

Properly directed and controlled, electrical power can be a tremendous asset in the safe operation of a vessel. But stray or uncontrolled currents can be destructive to both hull and gear, as well as potentially very dangerous to the crew and those who may be in proximity to the boat, whether in the water or out.

Ignition protection

By their very nature, many electrical devices spark or "arc" in their normal operation; items such as switches, relays, engine starters, many DC motors and alternators are all examples of such devices. In the presence of gasoline or propane vapors, this "arc" can produce sufficient energy to ignite the vapors and produce a violent explosion.

In order to prevent this, the USCG, the ABYC and the NFPA all require that electrical devices be "ignition protected" if they are to be installed in engine compartments or fuel tank compartments on gasoline-powered vessels. In addition, NFPA and ABYC have extended these ignition protection requirements to boats equipped with propane under certain conditions. There are various equipment test standards for ignition protection, including the Society of Automotive Engineers Standard SAE J1171 and Underwriters' Laboratories Standard UL 1500. When installing or replacing any electrical component in compartments where vapors may be present, it is imperative that the component has been tested under one of these standards and the product itself is marked "ignition protected," or bears one of these two standard numbers.

Safe battery installation

Storage batteries must be installed in a ventilated area so that gases generated during charging will be dissipated safely. They should also be protected from extreme heat and cold, and from spray. Starting batteries must be close to the engines in order to have short starter cables, to reduce any voltage drop in the cables. Gasoline fumes are explosive and any spark from a battery connection is dangerous. Gasoline fumes should be kept away from the battery installation.

Batteries must be secure against shifting as well as against vertical motion that would allow them to pound. They should be chocked on all sides and supported by a non-absorbent material that will not be affected by contact with electrolyte. Air should circulate all around the battery. A tray of fiberglass or other electrolyte-proof material must protect aluminum and steel surfaces of the boat.

Batteries should be accessible to inspection, cleaning, testing and watering. They should also be covered with a non-conductive material, with sufficient small holes to allow the escape of any gases from charging.

Avoiding galvanic and electrolytic corrosion

When two metals with widely differing electrical potential (voltage) are connected electrically and immersed in an electrolyte—that is, a current-carrying liquid such as salt water—a natural battery is formed. When that happens, direct current flows in the circuit comprised of the metal parts, the electrical connection (say, a bonding wire or a metal hull skin) and the electrolyte.

The direction of this current has important implications for the longevity of a vessel's underwater and bilge-mounted metal parts, including the hull (if it is metal). In the segment of the circuit that is formed by the electrolyte, current flows from the anode, the metal with the higher voltage, to the cathode, the metal with the lower voltage. This causes the anode to progressively disintegrate in a process known as "galvanic corrosion."

If the natural current in the circuit is supplemented by the introduction of current from an external source—for example, from an electrical wire that is shorting directly to ground—the rate of the anode's deterioration will be greatly accelerated in a process popularly called "electrolysis"—an especially virulent sub-case of galvanic corrosion.

The terms "anode" and "cathode" are relative. In any galvanic couple, the metal with the higher electrical potential behaves as the anode, while the metal with the lower potential acts as the cathode. Aluminum hull plating, for instance, will act as an anode relative to a copper radio grounding plate, which will be the cathode in this couple. However, a bar of pure zinc would be an anode relative to both the aluminum housing and the copper grounding plate. For this reason, the traditional method for protecting critical underwater parts is to bond them all together in a single circuit that includes special sacrificial zinc anodes. For when a piece of zinc of sufficient volume and exposed surface is introduced into a galvanic circuit, the higher voltage of the zinc overcomes the tendency of current to flow away from other metal parts in the circuit. Instead, current flows from the zinc to those parts, which are in the process thus protected, although intentionally at the cost of the zinc.

Since zincs are cheaper and easier to replace than critical metal parts such as hull plating, propellers and the like, this preventative for galvanic corrosion has, through the years, been almost universally used. Unfortunately, the use of static sacrificial zinc anodes doesn't always work as well as intended. (Occasionally the term "passive" is used in regard to zinc anodes, but that tends to confuse matters, as in any galvanic circuit the zincs are usually the most "active" metal.) The size and wetted surface of the zinc or zincs is critical: If too small, the desired effect of reversing destructive current flow will not be achieved.

Placement is also critical. If the zincs are too distant from the part or parts that require protection, the voltage of the zinc will not be able to overcome the resistance of the current path through the electrolyte; and therefore, the zinc(s) will fail to reverse potentially destructive galvanic currents.

For both of these reasons, systems that provide more "active" corrosion protection have been developed in the last few years. These are systems that sense and work actively to overcome potentially destructive voltage differentials. These systems divide into the two types described below: anodic and cathodic.

Anodic systems

Anodic systems overcome the problems of size and anode-to-cathode distance, which are endemic to a traditional arrangement of "static" sacrificial zincs. These anodic systems incorporate an electronic controller that senses voltage and/or current flow in a galvanic circuit. The controller then works to ensure that sufficiently high voltage is present in the system's sacrificial anode or anodes by supplying current from an external source (a battery) to the anode or anodes. And this in turn ensures that critical underwater metal parts are at all times in a cathodic (non-corroding) condition.

Cathodic systems

Cathodic systems also incorporate an electronic controller, which senses the voltages and/or currents present in any galvanic couples. However, in cathodic systems, the controller uses external power to boost the voltage of a dedicated cathode to the point where that voltage is equal to the voltage of the anodes in the circuit. Then, since all metal parts in the galvanic circuit are at the same electrical potential, there is no current flow. Cathodic systems thus block the passage of destructive galvanic and electrolytic currents.

Mercury Marine's Quicksilver MerCathode system, for example, electronically measures the voltage of a boat's submerged critical metal parts, in particular, the aluminum stern-drive housing found on many smaller boats. Then, utilizing current from the boat's battery, it raises the voltage of a permanent, submerged titanium electrode (the cathode) so that it equals the voltage of the endangered part or parts (the natural anodes). With the titanium electrode and the otherwise endangered metal parts at the same electrical potential, there is no current flow, and thus no galvanic corrosion.

But whether a traditional system of sacrificial zincs is employed, or a more modern impressed-current system, the sensible boater still avoids mixing galvanically incompatible metals. Bronze through-hulls, for example, are not used in direct contact with aluminum or steel hull plating. Instead, type 316 stainless steel is often used, as it is much closer to aluminum and steel on the galvanic scale (that is, there is less natural voltage differential between the two). Even better, non-conductive fiber-reinforced plastic fittings are sometimes used in smaller metal boats to completely eliminate the danger—though such plastic fittings are not as yet generally available in sizes suitable for very large yachts.

If galvanic corrosion is an illness, electrolytic corrosion is a plague. The most common offenders are improperly wired shoreside electrical hook-ups and items of on-board equipment that are leaking current directly to ground (the water) or to the yacht's bonding system through shorted or defectively insulated internal components and/or bad wiring.

Correct polarity

Many shorepower-related electrolytic problems can be avoided by making certain that there is correct "polarity" when plugging in—that is, that the black wire is hot, the white neutral, and the green connected to ground. Your boat's 120- or 240-volt main distribution panel may incorporate a reverse-polarity indicator, but such a unit provides less information and, ultimately, less protection than a simple and inexpensive hand-held indicator, of the type used by electricians.) What you really need to watch out for is a case in which improper shorepower wiring ends up with the current running to ground through the green wire, rather than through the white neutral wire.

Using an isolation transformer

Additional protection can be had by incorporating, whenever possible, some form of "isolator" in any ship-to-shore electrical connection. In this respect, the best solution is an isolation transformer that will eliminate any direct conductive connection between the shorepower source and a vessel's electrical system. As previously mentioned on page 533, such transformers do not step the voltage up or down. Instead, they produce current for the boat's distribution system via a magnetic connection (induction) with the shorepower input. Unfortunately, isolation transformers are relatively large and heavy. They are also expensive. For these practical reasons, therefore, they are used for the most part only on larger yachts.

Where an isolation transformer is not practical for reasons of space or cost, one useful alternative is to install a "galvanic isolator" in the shorepower connection ground (green) line. These relatively inexpensive units work to isolate the boat's grounding system from the shorepower ground and, therefore, they help alleviate the potential for electrolytic corrosion. Since the galvanic isolator is connected in series with the AC system grounding conductor (green wire) to shore, it is imperative that the isolator meet certain minimum standards; otherwise the integrity of the grounding conductor will be compromised, if not lost completely. These requirements are reflected in ABYC Standard E-8 *AC Electrical Systems*. The only way you can be sure that you are complying with these standards is by using only galvanic isolators that bear the Underwriters' Laboratories Marine listing mark.

Beyond some form of shorepower isolation, the prudent skipper will also check for any current flow where it shouldn't be, for instance, between a refrigeration compressor unit casing and the vessel's bonding system.

A word to the wise: Some inland boaters believe that galvanic isolation and electrolytic corrosion is of no concern to them. Their argument is that they keep their boats in fresh water, which is not an electrolyte. But they are in error, for much inland fresh water is now so polluted that it functions as a weak electrolyte.

Lightning protection

Although the incidence of vessels being damaged by lightning strikes is relatively low, when it does happen serious, even fatal, consequences can ensue. The voltages involved in lightning are massive, so that materials normally considered non-conductive become conductors, and that includes the human body. The voltages are so high that, if they start to travel through a boat's structure—say, through its mast—then meet with high resistance (for instance, the hull skin) the current discharge, in its drive to reach ground, may simply blow a hole in the non-conductive barrier. The prudent skipper must ensure that his vessel is appropriately protected. Reference should be made in detail to the standards for lightning protection promulgated by ABYC and NFPA.

Faraday's cage

The theory in any shipboard lightning protection system is to create what is known as a "Faraday's cage," after the nineteenth-century scientist Michael Faraday. The principle of a Faraday's cage is to provide a surrounding, well-grounded metal structure, all of whose parts are bonded together and at the same electrical potential. Such a "cage" attracts and carries any lightning strike to ground, thereby protecting life and limb within. (The effectiveness of this approach was established by Faraday in experiments, during which he risked his own life to prove the theory.) It also has the tendency to bleed off charge build-up in its general vicinity, possibly averting a lightning strike in the first place.

In a boat, the "cage" is formed by bonding together, with heavy conductors, the vessel's mast and all other major metal masses—for example, engines, stoves, air conditioning compressors, railings, arches and the like—and providing a direct, low-resistance conductive path to ground (the water) usually via the engine and propeller shaft, or keel bolts, or, better still, a separate external ground plate, at least 1 ft² (0.093 m²). Of course, it's necessary to ensure that crew fall within the protection of the confines of the "cage," something that is not always feasible when the vessel is not built of steel or aluminum. And in this respect, on a fiberglass or wooden boat, it's advantageous to have a mast or other conductive metal protrusion extending well above the vessel, creating what is known as a "cone" or zone of protection.

It's generally accepted that this zone of protection extends 45 degrees from the vertical from all around the tip of such a metal protrusion. Thus, if the aluminum mast of the average sailing vessel is properly bonded to the vessel's other major metal masses, and given a direct, low-resistance conductive path to ground, the entire boat should fall within the protected zone, that is, inside the "cage." If a sailing vessel has a wooden or plastic composite mast, the same effect can be achieved by installing a 6- to 12-inch metal spike at the truck and running a sufficiently heavy conductor from it down the mast and as directly as possible to ground, usually through the engine and propeller shaft.

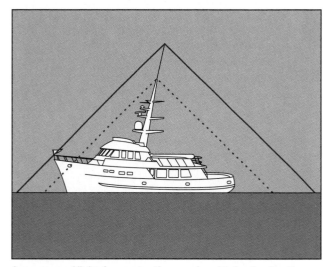

A measure of lightning protection can be obtained using the principle of the "Faraday cage." A high, pointed conductor, heavily wired to all of the conductive parts of the boat, seems to cast a cone-shaped umbrella in which lightning does not strike. Instead, the voltage is conducted safely to "ground" in the water via submerged metal parts such as the rudder, sailboat keel or propeller.

Protection overhead

Although it is not directly related to electrical systems, it should be mentioned here that sailboats face a serious danger from contact with overhead power lines—both underway and, more often, as they are prepared for trailering or launching. Sailors must always be aware of power lines and be sure of their clearances. *Caution: A lightning protection system offers no protection when the boat is out of the water, nor is it intended to afford protection if any part of the boat comes in contact with power lines while afloat or ashore.*

In the case of powerboats, ensuring sufficient mast height is quite often difficult; and it may not be possible, given the limitations, to ensure that a person standing on deck always falls within the zone of protection. Keep in mind that you cannot rely on fiberglass radio antennas for this purpose, as they do not afford a sufficiently low-resistance path, and possibly, because of their construction, no path at all. (The most common antennas, those used for VHF, CB or SSB radio, offer no conductive path.) The best advice in such cases is to work with an expert in the field, if you're considering the possibility of using an antenna as a lightning mast.

It is possible in a powerboat to install a separate lightning mast. But if the mast is hinged for getting under bridges, the details of keeping resistance low at the joint are again best worked out by a qualified expert. In all cases on powerboats, it will generally be necessary to pay close attention to keeping crew within the zone of protection and isolated from contact with any metal objects during a lightning storm.

Additional information on lightning protection will be found in ABYC Standard E-4.

24 COMMUNICATIONS

Today's electronic equipment has become so small and compact, and its drain on a boat's electrical system so reduced, that few craft are too small to carry one or more electronic items.

From a safety viewpoint, the priority of purchase and installation in most cases will be a VHF radiotelephone for communication. This chapter discusses the particulars of selecting, licensing and operating a VHF radiotelephone, as well as the other options available to you—communicating via other electronic equipment or visual signals. Keep in mind that perhaps the most important function of any type of communication is signalling distress. Make sure you know the format for Mayday and other distress signals, discussed in Chapter 4.

VOICE RADIO COMMUNICATIONS

In the very early days of electronic ship-to-shore and ship-to-ship communications, the use of Morse code predominated. This continued to be the case in military and commercial contexts for quite some time (and in some cases still is). Today, however, the vast majority of marine electronic communications, especially for recreational boats, are effected through voice transmission.

Marine voice transmissions proceed, for the most part, much like conversations between two parties over shoreside telephones. However, there are at least two major differences between ordinary telephone conversations and marine communications.

There are very specific licensing requirements and more stringent procedural regulations for marine communications. Most marine communications are "simplex," that is, the person on the receiving end cannot interrupt and communicate to the person currently transmitting, until the latter stops transmitting and provides the opportunity. This technique is sometimes difficult for a beginner to grasp in practice—but this is the reason why you must pause and release the microphone key. In fact, this is the only way you will hear the reply from the party at the other end.

In case it is not obvious, it should be noted that communications regulations and certain procedures vary from one country to the next. Unless otherwise stated, then, the material in this chapter should be understood as pertaining exclusively to the United States.

Safety and operational communications

Perhaps the most important point for skippers of recreational craft to understand is that, by law, the primary function of regulated electronic communication at sea is *safety,* and that radio communications related to safety have absolute priority over all other communications. Other uses of marine radio are allowed; but the overriding rule is if you're talking to another vessel or to a shore station about matters other than safety—for example, weather, or whether a destination marina has a slip available for your arrival—you *must* without exception cease transmitting if there is a safety-related communication competing for the airways. In fact, even among safety-related communications there is a specific hierarchy of priority that must, again under law, be observed. These points will be discussed later in this chapter.

In addition to safety, electronic voice communication is also allowed for "operational" purposes which, strictly speaking, are those having to do with the navigation, movement and management of vessels at sea. In the recreational sector, these categories of operational uses are, for the most part, interpreted liberally. For example, ship-to-ship communications between two yachts about where to stay for the night would be considered as having to do with "movement." And ship-to-shore communications between a yacht skipper and the attendant at a fuel dock would be considered as having to do with "management."

Personal and social communications

Nevertheless, it's important to keep in mind that, however liberally the concepts of "safety" and "operational" are interpreted, the laws governing marine communications strictly prohibit superfluous personal or social chit-chat between boats on most channels (frequencies). Communications of a strictly personal or social nature are allowed, but only in certain contexts and on certain channels specifically designated for that purpose.

These circumstances and channels have primarily to do with ship-to-shore communications, in which a radio connection is made with a land-based telephone system via a designated communications controller known as the "Marine Operator." In such cases, the boat's radiotelephone becomes part of the land-based telephone system; calls may be placed to, or received from, any shoreside home or business telephone, and for any purpose allowed under the laws governing land-based telecommunications. Keep in mind, however, that calls placed through the Marine Operator are subject to "linkage" and other charges. The procedures for placing and receiving calls through the Marine Operator will be discussed in detail later in this chapter.

Marine radio basics

Unless you are interested in obtaining an advanced (marine or general) radiotelephone operator's license, it's not necessary to delve deeply into the physics of radio transmission or, even more daunting, the esoterics of wave versus particle theory. For most boat owners, it's sufficient simply to understand a few very basic principles and distinctions, and to treat the rest in "black box" fashion—that is, to interface with marine radio as an intelligent user who is conversant with correct operating procedures, and without significant reference to what actually transpires inside the equipment.

Suffice it then to say that radio energy is generated or transmitted as waves with specific physical characteristics. For our purposes, the two most important of these are amplitude (the height of the wave from trough to crest) and frequency (the rapidity with which the crests of the waves arrive at a given point). Frequency is today universally expressed in kilohertz (kHz) and megahertz (MHz), where 1 MHz = 1,000 kHz.

A radio transmitter is "tuned" to generate radio waves at a particular frequency. In order for those waves to be received and demodulated, a receiver must be "tuned" to the same frequency. Radio waves transmitted at significantly different frequencies do not, for the most part, interfere with one another, which is why frequency selection and control makes possible unimpeded simultaneous communication between numbers of sending and receiving stations.

Only certain radio waves—those with medium, high and very-high frequencies—are used for voice communications. Low and very-low frequencies are used for navigational radio, and super-high frequencies are used for radio detection and ranging (RADAR) *(Chapter 25).*

FREQUENCY SPECTRUM

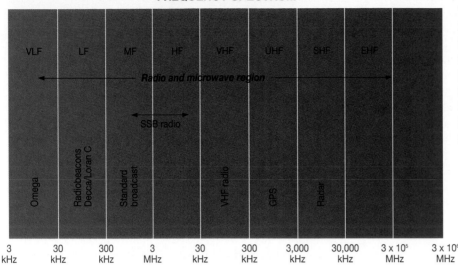

The radio frequency spectrum is divided into broad "bands" from very-low frequency (VLF) to extremely high frequency (EHF). In boating, all bands from VLF (Omega navigation) to SHF (radar) may be used. Radio communications are in the MF, HF and VHF bands.

Different bands (or ranges) of frequencies are, by international treaty and domestic law, assigned to different uses. More specifically, marine communications are assigned a segment of the very-high frequency (VHF) band from 156 to 163 MHz, a segment of the medium frequency (MF) band from 2 to 3 MHz, and a number of relatively narrow segments of the high frequency (HF) band respectively near 4, 6, 8, 12, 16, 22 and 25 MHz.

In order to be useful for communications, radio waves generated at a given frequency must be further modulated. It is this modulation of the signal that ultimately produces audible voice emulation at the receiving end. Some radio units encode their transmitted signals by means of frequency modulation (FM) and some by amplitude modulation (AM).

Amplitude modulation, in double sideband (DSB) form, employs a carrier wave plus two sidebands, one either side of the carrier. AM also is used by regular broadcast stations in the 550 to 1600 kHz band. For many years, DSB AM was also used in marine radiotelephone communications, but has been replaced by single sideband (SSB) AM, which employs a reduced or suppressed carrier wave and only one sideband, for long-range communications. VHF marine radiotelephones employ frequency modulation. FM does not employ a "carrier" wave or sidebands, but rather encodes its signal by varying the frequency.

FM radio signals have the advantage that they are not significantly affected by atmospheric noise (static) or noise from shipboard electrical equipment. They also exhibit what is known as "capture effect": When AM signals from two different stations are transmitted simultaneously on the same frequency, they interfere with one another and often render both unreadable. However, when FM signals from two transmitting stations are competing for the same channel, the stronger signal "captures" the receiver and is clearly read, to the exclusion of the other, weaker signal. This, by the way, is why signal output wattage is important; higher wattage may not signifi-

cantly increase range, but it will help to get your signal through when a frequency is crowded with traffic.

FM radio waves have the disadvantage that, in virtue of their forced variance either side of their nominal frequency, they take up more space on the radio wave spectrum. Consequently, FM transmission is used only in the VHF and higher frequencies, where adequate radio spectrum "space" is still available.

Radio waves are generated in all directions at once. Some are simply absorbed by the earth, while others escape unreceived into space, where their energy eventually dissipates. Of the useful waves generated during radio transmission, some travel pretty much in a straight line from transmitter to the horizon. These are known as "ground waves." Others travel toward space, but are reflected back by the earth's ionosphere. These are known as "sky waves." The range of ground waves is, therefore, relatively small, while the distance that sky waves travel can be very great, especially if they are of sufficient strength to "bounce" more than once. But if the frequency of the sky waves is too high, such as marine VHF and higher, the signals penetrate the ionosphere and are not reflected back.

Radiotelephones

Radio receivers—like the AM/FM stereos most of us have at home—capture radio waves, a form of energy, and convert them to audible sound. Conversely, radio transmitters capture audible sound, convert it to radio energy, and transmit that energy in the form of "waves." Most of the electronic voice communications equipment found on small craft combines both functions in a single unit, known as a transceiver.

The radio communication equipment authorized for use on boats, and by persons holding no personal license or the very rudimentary, easy-to-obtain Restricted Radiotelephone Operators Permit, is specially constructed to ensure that only certain designated frequencies are used, and that it is impossible to transmit inadvertently on non-authorized frequencies.

This is accomplished by eliminating the need for operator tuning, and instead incorporating "switch-selectable" channels. And because the simplified operation of such units, and their primary devotion to voice communication, are reminiscent of shoreside telecommunications, the units have come to be known as radiotelephones.

In many contexts, the terms "(marine) transceiver" and "radiotelephone" are used interchangeably. For the purpose of clarity, however, we will refer to voice communication units that incorporate a limited number of discrete, switch-selectable channels as "radiotelephones." And we'll reserve the more general term "transceiver" for equipment with the capability of being operator-tuned to a continuum of frequencies whose assignments include the transmission of telegraphic and other non-voice transmissions.

Licensing

All transmitting shipboard radio equipment must be licensed. That includes not only VHF-FM and SSB (single-sideband "high seas") radiotelephones, but radars and EPIRBs (Emergency Position Indicating Radiobeacons, discussed on page 558) as well. The license must be posted on board.

With over 660,000 marine radio stations on the air, the need for licensing and regulations can easily be seen. The FCC issues its Rules and Regulations in various parts, of which "Part 80—Stations in the Maritime Services" applies to recreational boats.

The FCC uses a system of licenses controlling the use of radio stations to hold down interference and permit emergency and essential communications. Recognizing that harmful interference could result from either malfunctioning equipment or from misuse of a properly operating set, licenses are required for both the station and the person operating it (with exceptions to be noted later). Although it is termed a station license, FCC authorization relates to the transmitting component only. The set owner need not be concerned with the many technical requirements for equipment, provided that he has a set that is "type accepted."

Applying for a station license

A station license may be issued to a U.S. citizen, corporation, or an alien individual, but not to the government of a foreign nation or its representative. This license can be applied for by mail using FCC Form 506—provided you have your state registration numbers or a Coast Guard documentation number. Form 506 is a multipart form; detailed instructions for completion of the application appear on the first two pages. Read and heed these carefully to avoid having your application returned for correction or additional information. The next two pages are the actual application that will be mailed to the FCC. Be sure that you ask for all frequency bands that you know you will need, or which you can anticipate needing in the future. These include frequencies for VHF, SSB, radars and EPIRB. A fee of $35 must accompany the application; the Fee Type Code, to be completed on this form is "PAS." These

papers are mailed to the Federal Communications Commission, Marine Ship Service, P.O. Box 358275, Pittsburgh, PA 15251-5275. If the application is returned as defective, a second fee payment may not be required; the returned papers will indicate this.

If you need immediate use of the radio, the final two-page sheet of paper becomes Form 506A, a temporary license valid for 90 days, within which time you should receive the formal papers. It provides information on generating a temporary call sign (based on your registration or documentation numbers) that can be used for interim operation. The use of such a temporary call sign must cease as soon as you receive the regular license and call sign, even though the 90-day period has not expired.

Radio station licenses in the U.S. are issued in the name of the owner and the vessel. A station license is not automatically transferred to another person upon sale of the boat, nor may a license be moved with the radio set to a new boat owned by the same person; the license must be modified using Form 506 (plus a fee of $35). A simple change in the name of the boat or licensee (but not a change in ownership) or a change in the licensee's address does not require license modification. Just send a letter (or Form 405A) to the FCC advising of the change; a copy of this form or letter must be posted on board along with the license. A simple change in equipment requires no action at all.

FCC regulations require that a station license be conspicuously posted aboard the vessel. You must apply for renewal before expiration of its five-year term, using Form 506 as was used for the original license. This, with the fee of $35, is sent to the same address in Pittsburgh given above. If you did make timely application for renewal, operation may continue even if you have not received the renewed license before the expiration date. If the use of the radio station is ever permanently discontinued, you must return the license to the FCC at P.O. Box 1040, Gettysburg, PA 17325, for cancellation.

Applying for an operator's permit

A personal license, a radio operator permit, is not required for the operation of a VHF set on a "voluntarily equipped" U.S. vessel—a recreational boat, or one carrying six or less passengers for hire—"on a domestic voyage." (An offshore fishing trip can be considered a domestic voyage despite going beyond the limit of territorial waters—12 miles—if the waters of another country are not entered.) For other operation of such craft, or operation of a single-sideband (SSB) radio (page 555), the lowest grade of radio operator license, a Restricted Radiotelephone Operator Permit, is adequate.

For vessels carrying more than six passengers for hire, and for vessels over 65 feet in length on the Great Lakes, whether commercial or non-commercial, the operator must have a Marine (formerly "Third Class") Radio Operator Permit. At least a Restricted Permit is required on board vessels that must comply with the Bridge-to-Bridge Radiotelephone Act—

vessels over 65 feet in length, tugs over 26 feet and dredges in channels. A higher class license is available for trained individuals making tuning adjustments and repairs. In situations where a licensed operator is required, an unlicensed person may talk into the microphone, but a licensed operator must be present and responsible for the proper use of the station.

An applicant for any grade of U.S. operator's license must be a U.S. citizen or a foreign national eligible for work in the U.S. (there are some exceptions for special cases). For a Restricted Radiotelephone Operator Permit, you do not have to appear in person at any FCC office. It is obtained by filling out FCC Form 753 and mailing it to the Federal Communications Commission, Restricted Permit, P.O. Box 358295, Pittsburgh, PA 15251-5295. The permit is issued, without test or examination, by declaration. The applicant must "certify" that he can speak and hear, keep at least a rough written log, and is familiar with the treaties, laws and regulations governing the station that he will operate. He must also certify that he has need for a permit because he intends to engage in international voyages and is eligible for employment in the United States. The Restricted Permit is valid for the lifetime of the person to whom it is issued, unless it is suspended or revoked. Follow the instructions carefully to avoid having the application returned to you for correction. The fee is $35. A portion of Form 753 may be retained as a temporary operator permit, valid for 60 days; this allows you to get on the air immediately if your operations require a permit.

For the Marine Radio Operator Permit, an examination is required, requiring a visit to an FCC office. This test is non-technical, in a multiple-choice format, covering only operating rules and procedures. You will find the examination not at all difficult if you prepare for it properly. A free Study Guide is available from FCC offices. Application is on Form 756. The permit is valid for five years and must be renewed using the same forms and paying the same fee. For skippers of recreational boats the privileges of this higher class license are no greater than those of a Restricted Permit, but for many it is a matter of pride to qualify and post it aboard their craft.

If your radio operator permit is lost or becomes illegible, apply immediately for a duplicate. Use the same form as for an original and submit the same fee as before. State the circumstances fully and, if the license has been lost, you must certify that a reasonable search has been made. Continued operation is authorized if a signed copy of the application for a duplicate is posted. If a lost license is found later, send either that license or the duplicate to the FCC for cancellation.

■ **Canadian licensing.** Canadian yachts are subject to parallel installation and operator licensing requirements, the only significant difference being that the Canadian restricted operator's permit requires the completion of a brief exam on correct operating procedures. Application for current licensing information and the appropriate forms can be made to Communications Canada, Ottawa, Ontario. The exam for the restricted operator's license may be taken at a local office.

LICENSES, APPLICATION FORMS AND FEES

The Private Radio Bureau Licensing Division of the Federal Communications Commission can be contacted by writing to Gettysburg, PA 17325-7245 or by calling 1-717-337-1212.

Each application for a U.S. license or permit should be accompanied by a check or money order payable to the Federal Communications Commission, addressed to the appropriate department, as listed below.

Ship Station License
■ **New, modification and/or renewal**
FCC Form 506 $35
Federal Communications Commission
Marine Ship Service
P.O. Box 358275
Pittsburgh, PA 15251-5275

■ **Renewal of license only**
FCC Form 405B $35
Federal Communications Commission
405B Station Renewal
P.O. Box 358290
Pittsburgh, PA 15251-5290

Restricted Radiotelephone Operator Permit
FCC Form 753 $35
Federal Communications Commission
Restricted Permit
P.O. Box 358295
Pittsburgh, PA 15251-5295

Commercial Radio Operator License
FCC Form 756 $35
Federal Communications Commission
P.O. Box 358105
Pittsburgh, PA 15251-5105

Canadian permits
A Restricted Operator Certificate (available free of charge) must be obtained before applying for a Non-compulsory License ($46 per year). Both are available from the following Canadian governmental department:
Communications Canada
473 Albert Street, 4th Floor
Ottawa, Ontario K1R 5B4
(613) 998-3693

VHF-FM RADIOTELEPHONES

Most marine electronic voice communications, especially in the recreational sector, use a VHF-FM radiotelephone. In fact, by law a VHF-FM radio must be licensed and installed aboard as a precondition to the licensing and installation of any other form of marine radiotelephone. The reason for this is that VHF-FM is, by domestic law and international treaty, the prescribed vehicle for local communications, both ship-to-ship and ship-to-shore.

VHF-FM transmissions are basically line-of-sight, that is, these signals are *not* reflected by the ionosphere. Consequently, VHF-FM transmission is fairly well restricted to a limited geographical area, on average 10 to 15 nautical miles in ship-to-ship situations, and 25 to 30 miles ship-to-shore, depending on the heights of both the transmitting and receiving antennas. That means a boat transmitting in, say, Jacksonville, Florida, on 156.3 MHz will not interfere with one transmitting on the same frequency at the exact same time in St. Augustine, Florida, 45 miles away. And the potential for interference is further decreased in VHF-FM radiotelephones by the legal limitation of their maximum output power to 25 watts, the requirement for a switch-selectable one-watt output for close-in communications, and by the capture effect previously mentioned.

Equipment selection

Remember that VHF-FM radiotelephones are limited by law to 25 watts output power, and are required to have a 1-watt switchable low-power setting. Output power does not bear directly on operating range, which can be considered as line-of-sight between the transmitting and receiving antennas, regardless of transmitting or radiating power. However, output power does have a bearing on capture effect, namely, the ability of the signal to be received clearly in spite of potential interference from simultaneous signals from other transmitters. As a practical matter, every VHF-FM set manufactured today, except hand-held models, is built with the maximum allowable 25 watts output power.

By law, every VHF-FM radiotelephone is required to have at least the following channels:
- Channel 16 (156.8 MHz), the International Distress, Safety and Calling frequency.
- Channel 6 (156.3 MHz), the Intership Safety frequency.
- One additional "working" channel.

All contemporary sets, including hand-helds, incorporate many more channels than this, often 54 to 90 or more.

At one time, frequency control was provided by crystals that were individually tuned for a single specific frequency. Today's VHF-FM radiotelephones almost universally employ frequency synthesizers—digital electronic circuits that control frequency without relying on a corresponding array of crystals—and most major-brand sets, even the less expensive ones, come with more channel capability than most recreational skippers will ever need. The only exception is for vessels cruising internationally, in which case it is wise to

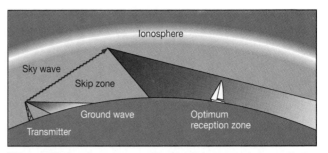

MF and HF signals are transmitted both by ground waves that extend out along the earth for a few hundred miles, and by sky waves that are reflected by the ionosphere and return to earth farther out. Between the reception zones for ground and sky waves is the "skip zone," an area of no signals.

make sure that a prospective purchase has the correct channel capability for the destination country or countries. In this last respect, it is also important to ensure that the unit chosen has the correct weather-broadcasting channels for one's intended area(s) of operation.

Following—or perhaps coordinate with—channel capability, the two most important factors in equipment selection are sensitivity and selectivity (adjacent channel rejection). Sensitivity is usually expressed as the number of microvolts required to produce 20 decibel (dB) "quieting." (When comparing nominal specifications, it's important to confirm that the 20 dB standard is being used.) This rating effectively measures the minimum signal strength that will trigger a set's receiver capability. And in this case, the lower the microvolt number, the higher the radiotelephone's sensitivity, and, consequently, the better its ability to receive transmissions that are weak or distant.

Selectivity is usually expressed as a negative dB number (for example, "-65 dB") and measures a set's ability to screen out interfering signals on channels or frequencies close to the one being used. The higher the absolute dB number, the better the set's selectivity (-70 dB is better than -60 dB) and the better the set will be at rejecting potential interference from simultaneous transmissions on other frequencies.

VHF transmitters, like the one shown here, should use low power wherever it is sufficient, especially for short distances. It must be used on Channel 13.

SELECTED MARINE CHANNELS AND THEIR USES

Channel Number	Frequency (MHz) Transmit	Frequency (MHz) Receive	Communications Purpose
06	156.300	156.300	Intership safety communications (mandatory).
09	156.450	156.450	Commercial and non-commercial intership and coast-to-coast (commercial docks, marinas and some clubs); also used by recreational boaters as alternate calling channel. This is also used at some locks and bridges.
12	156.600	156.600	Port Operations—traffic advisory—still used as channel to work USCG shore stations.
13	156.650	156.650	Navigational—ship's bridge to ship's bridge (1 watt only). Available to all vessels and is required on passenger and commercial vessels (including many tugs), as well as power-driven vessels more than 20 meters in length.
14	156.700	156.700	Port Operations (intership and ship-to-coast).
16	156.800	156.800	Distress Safety and Calling (mandatory). All distress calls should be made on Channel 16. Recreational boats may monitor Channel 09 as well as Channel 16.
22A	157.100	157.100	Coast Guard Liaison and Maritime Safety Information Broadcasts; used for communications with USCG ship, coast and aircraft stations after first establishing communications on Channel 16.
25	157.250	161.850	Public telephone (ship-to-coast); includes Channels 24, 27, 84, 85, 86, 87, 88.
26	157.300	161.900	Public telephone (first priority).
28	157.400	162.000	Public telephone (first priority).
65A	156.275	156.275	Port Operations (intership and ship-to-coast); same as Channel 12.
66A	156.325	156.325	Port Operations (intership and ship-to-coast); same as Channel 12.
67	156.375	156.375	Commercial intership all areas, plus non-commercial intership (Puget Sound and Strait of Juan de Fuca). In the Lower Mississippi River, use limited to navigational bridge-to-bridge navigational purposes (1 watt).
68	156.425	156.425	Non-commercial intership and ship-to-coast (marinas, yacht clubs, etc.).
69	156.475	156.475	Non-commercial intership and ship-to-coast.
70	156.525	156.525	Distress and safety calling, and general purpose calling; may *only* be used by vessels equipped with Digital Selective Calling (DSC).
71	156.575	156.575	Non-commercial intership and ship-to-coast.
72	156.625	156.625	Non-commercial intership only.
73	156.675	156.675	Port Operations intership and ship-to-coast.
74	156.725	156.725	Port Operations intership and ship-to-coast.
78A	156.925	156.925	Non-commercial intership and ship-to-coast.
79A	156.975	156.975	Commercial intership and ship-to-coast. Non-commercial intership on Great Lakes only.
80A	157.025	157.025	Commercial intership and ship-to-coast. Non-commercial intership on Great Lakes only.
WX1		162.550	Weather broadcast (receive only).
WX2		162.400	Weather (receive only).
WX3		162.475	Weather (receive only).

This table lists the required, and some recommended, VHF channels for recreational (non-commercial) boats. Select the one or ones needed for your cruising area. If your radio has only one weather channel, consider use of a separate weather receiver for the second and third channels. In some areas, the Coast Guard Auxiliary may use Channel 83A (157.175 MHz) for official activities.

Beyond channel capability, sensitivity and selectivity, there is a plethora of other features of potential interest, the inclusion of which directly affects the price of a unit. One factor to look at is the water-resistance of the unit. Some units, for example, are more splash-proof than others, hence more suitable for mounting in exposed locations, and some are even rated as waterproof.

Some units incorporate an automatic "dual watch" and/or scanning feature that allows you to monitor (as you must under law when the radio is on) Channel 16 plus one or more other channels on which you might be expecting to receive a call. Some incorporate a weather alert system that sounds a warning tone to advise of a special hazardous weather broadcast on the local VHF weather channel. Others include a special distress alarm generator that broadcasts a two-tone signal to attract attention to a subsequent Mayday signal.

Some very new radiotelephones are available with the new Digital Selective Calling (DSC) system that allows a DSC-equipped vessel or shore station to call using a "data stream" on Channel 70. With such units, a connection can be made and the set switched to a working channel without first trans-

Small hand-held VHF transceivers now have the same features as full-size sets, including coverage of all channels, memory and scanning.

mitting the call on Channel 16. A ringer alerts an operator to an incoming call—bringing radiotelephone communication ever closer to the ease and convenience of shoreside telephone use. In any event, a wise skipper will compare the latest specifications and features of a number of units in a given price range before making a final selection of VHF-FM radiotelephone equipment.

Hand-held units

Over the last few years, small portable (as opposed to installed) VHF-FM radiotelephones have gained significantly in popularity. Generally referred to as hand-held units, this type is fitted with an integral microphone, speaker and antenna, as well as a rechargeable battery. These units often incorporate jacks for a speaker and/or microphone; the normal attached antenna can be replaced by a cable leading to an

external antenna, usually larger and mounted higher. A hand-held unit can be valuable as follows:

- As a back-up for the regular radiotelephone.
- On larger vessels where it is sometimes useful to have radio access when away from the regular radiotelephone.
- For communication between a dinghy or tender and the vessel that it accompanies.
- For two-way emergency communications in the event of having to abandon ship.

Keep in mind, however, that it is *not* legal to use a hand-held radio to communicate with the vessel's main radio from a position on board that vessel. In other words, you cannot legally use a hand-held unit for intercom purposes.

Hand-helds also have other significant limitations. First, they have limited output power. Second, their integral antennas are, naturally, situated no higher than the hand that holds the unit. These factors combine to make hand-helds unsuitable for anything more than relatively close-in communications. And so, while they definitely have their place, they are rarely, if ever an adequate substitute for full-power, fully featured installed sets.

There is an additional point regarding hand-helds, which is often overlooked in practice, and worth considering: Contrary to uninformed belief and all-too-common practice, hand-held VHF-FM marine radiotelephones are not authorized as walkaround, portable units. Except for licensed stationary shore stations, mobile marine radio is authorized only for shipboard use (which includes yachts and tenders). Using a hand-held from a shoreside location—for example, to call your vessel from a shoreside shop—is a violation of the marine radiotelephone regulations.

Installation and maintenance

Most of today's VHF-FM radiotelephones come from the factory fully tested and ready to operate, requiring only connection to a power source and an appropriate antenna. Installation does not necessarily require the services of a trained technician.

If you choose to install one of these units yourself, it's important to keep a few points in mind: When hooking the radio up to the vessel's DC electrical system, be certain that correct polarity is observed, and that an appropriate in-line fuse is used. (Refer to Chapter 23 and the radiotelephone manufacturer's installation instructions.) Mount the unit in as protected a location as possible, consistent with convenient use for both receiving and transmitting. As some heat is generated from the operation of the set, allow for adequate ventilation around the case. When mounting the unit, remember that it's necessary to run not only power to it, but the antenna cable as well. Never attempt to splice coaxial cable, but instead employ, when necessary, appropriate cable couplers. And avoid sharp bends in the antenna cable by employing, if necessary, a right-angle cable connector of the kind available at any marine electronics dealer.

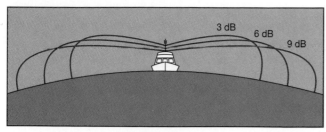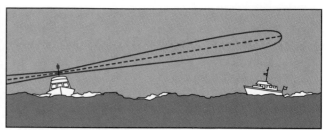

Higher-gain antennas achieve greater range by "squeezing down" the radiation pattern *(left)*, increasing signals at lower, desirable angles and decreasing the power that is wasted in upward, unproductive angles. An antenna with too much gain—too flat a radiation pattern—may be disadvantageous in rough water. As the boat rolls and pitches *(right)*, the radiated signal may go above the receiving boat or down into the water. Either will cause fading and intermittent reception.

Make sure that all coaxial cable connections are correctly made; use properly soldered connectors, which are much more reliable in a marine environment than so-called solderless connectors. Finally, be sure to ground the radio case according to manufacturer's recommendations. Although grounding is not necessary for the operation of a VHF-FM radiotelephone, it helps eliminate interference from adjacent electronic equipment.

Once a VHF-FM radiotelephone is installed, there is actually very little maintenance that can be performed by the operator who is not also a trained radio technician. It's wise to inspect the antenna and power line connections periodically for signs of resistance-inducing corrosion. And the same is true for the ferrules of in-line fuses. Any corrosion should be removed, and any soldered connections re-done if broken or deteriorated.

It's good practice to operate the radiotelephone frequently, at the very least in receiving mode. When turned on, a unit's internal circuitry produces dehumidifying heat that helps forestall internal condensation and consequent corrosion. It's also good practice to work all of the unit's switches and buttons periodically, as many of these have self-cleaning contacts that, when operated, remove any build-up of corrosion—something they do better if the corrosion is not allowed to build up from non-use over a period of time.

Beyond that, dust, dirt and salt spray residue should be removed regularly from the unit's case with a soft rag dampened (not flooded) with fresh water and a mild detergent used to remove greasy fingerprints.

Antennas and cables

A VHF-FM radiotelephone is virtually useless without an appropriate antenna. It can sometimes receive signals, but only relatively strong ones; and it cannot transmit. (Indeed, a radiotelephone's circuitry can be damaged if the transmitter is triggered without an antenna being attached.)

Virtually all VHF-FM radiotelephone antennas today are of the "whip" variety—that is, they're supported at their bottom end only. In shorter lengths (30 to about 42 inches) the whips are sometimes made of a self-supporting stainless steel rod; but in longer lengths, they are almost always construct-

ed of a thin wire surrounded and supported by a flexible, wrapped fiberglass-reinforced plastic casing, the casing being "transparent" to radio waves.

At 156 to 163 MHz, a simple 36-inch piece of wire suffices as a basic "half-wavelength" antenna. Lengthening and other modifications of such a basic antenna can result in significant increases in effective radiating power. These increases are known as "gain."

Gain is designated in decibels, with every 3 dB representing a doubling of effective radiated power. For example, the effective radiated power of a given radiotelephone with a 3 dB gain antenna is double that of the same unit with a 0 dB gain antenna. With a 6 dB gain antenna the effective radiated power of the same unit is double that with the 3 dB gain antenna, or four times that with the 0 dB gain antenna. And with a 9 dB gain antenna, the radiated power is eight times what it would be if the unit were attached to a 0 dB gain antenna. It is clear that the use of a gain antenna significantly enhances transmitted signal strength.

However, the proper course of action is *not* to install the highest-gain antenna possible, for two reasons. First, increased gain usually requires increased length; and physical limitations may prevent installation of a very high-gain antenna. In addition, as previously noted, radiated power does not have a major effect on range; only antenna height does. Therefore, it is sometimes more effective to use a lower gain antenna mounted high up, for instance, at the truck of a sailboat mast or on a powerboat antenna extension mast.

Secondly, gain antennas work by concentrating the radiated signal: They squeeze the normally more vertical limits of the wave pattern into a more horizontal configuration and, in doing so, lose less energy to useless skyward radiation. (Remember VHF signals are not, to any useful extent, reflected back to earth by the ionosphere.)

That vertically concentrated pattern is an advantage only as long as the transmitting vessel remains relatively level. However, if the transmitting vessel heels or rolls to any great extent (for example, a sailboat under a press of sail, or a powerboat running in a heavy beam sea), this vertically concentrated pattern results in the transmitted waves being, at one moment, directed toward the sea (leeward heeled side) and, at the next moment, beamed uselessly skyward (windward heeled side). For that reason, it is usual practice *not* to choose an antenna gain greater than 3 dB for sailing vessels, and to limit gain to 6 to 9 dB on powerboats, depending on their size and stability.

Effective radiated power can often be improved significantly *without* resort to an antenna with higher gain. Too many and/or poor coaxial connections in the cable run between the transceiver and its antenna can result in significant loss in signal strength (due to increased resistance). The same is true, more or less, of antenna cable that is too light or insufficiently shielded for the length of run involved. Consequently, in most cases, it's advantageous to minimize the number of coaxial connectors in the line, and to employ heavier RG8 or a high-performance equivalent cable in preference to the lighter, more commonly supplied type RG58.

If a vessel operates in open waters in rough conditions (when distress calling is most likely needed), there is always the risk of losing or seriously damaging a vessel's whip antenna. The prudent skipper carries either a spare or an emergency antenna. The best spare or emergency antenna is one that can be readily mounted on deck and that is fitted with a cable of sufficient length and the correct coaxial connector for attachment to the vessel's VHF-FM radiotelephone. (This is true for sailboats, as well as powerboats, since the situation in which a sailboat is most likely to have lost its mast-mounted antenna is during a partial or complete dismasting.)

Operating rules

A "voluntarily equipped" ship (in the FCC Rules, the term "ship" includes a boat of any size) is not required to have its VHF radiotelephone on; but when it does, it is required by law to monitor Channel 16 when not actively listening to, or engaged on, another channel. A non-commercial vessel, such as a recreational boat, may alternatively maintain a watch on Channel 09.

Calls not related to distress or safety may be initiated on Channel 16, but such transmissions must be limited to establishing contact and determining a working frequency to be used. Any single calling transmission must not exceed 30 seconds duration, and if no reply is received, a two-minute pause must be observed before repeating the call. A maximum of three call attempts, separated by two-minute silences, may be made before a 15-minute silence must be observed (this silence may be reduced to three minutes if the call transmissions will not interfere with traffic from other stations). No transmissions on Channel 16 may exceed one minute. These limitations do not apply to emergency situations. Non-emergency transmissions on Channel 16 are absolutely limited to reaching agreement on the working channel to be used; not even the briefest messages are to be transmitted.

In order to lessen the congestion on Channel 16, which has been steadily increasing, the FCC has authorized the voluntary use of Channel 09 by non-commercial vessels for call-

ing. It has achieved this goal, but you are cautioned that maintaining a watch for calls on Channel 09 may result in their missing warnings and announcements from Coast Guard stations, calls from Marine Operators, and other important transmissions, as well as calls for your boat from others who are not aware of your Channel 09 watch. Remember, Channel 16 is the only channel to be used for distress calls and messages. If you have a set with the dual-watch feature, it would be an excellent practice to monitor Channels 16 and 09, and to try Channel 09 first for calling other recreational boats.

Once contact is made on an appropriate working channel, the ensuing exchange of transmissions must be:
- Of a legally permissible nature.
- Of the minimum possible duration.

The phonetic alphabet should be used to spell call signs, names, places, etc., *only* when absolutely necessary to ensure clarity. In most circumstance, when reception is clear, use of phonetics, while it sounds "professional" to some, only prolongs exchanges unnecessarily.

As well in this regard, superfluous words and phrases, such as "Do you read me?" and "Come in, *Bluejay*" should be avoided as much as possible in order to shorten transmission times. And to avoid unnecessary interference with other transmissions on the same frequency, the minimum practical transmitting power setting must by law be used— one watt for close-in communications.

Transmitting stations are required to identify themselves with their official call sign at the beginning and end of an exchange of transmissions; it is not necessary to use the call sign after shifting to a working channel. It is normal procedure for a transmitting ship station to include the name of the vessel, but this is not a legal requirement.

The Communications Act of 1934 and the radio operating rules set down by the FCC forbid any person from divulging, except to the intended addressee or his authorized agent, any information gained from receiving or intercepting any radio transmissions not addressed to him, *and from using to his own benefit any such information.* This does not apply to distress communications or to public broadcasts, but it does apply to all other conversations.

The distress, safety and calling channel

The most important frequency on the VHF radiotelephone band is Channel 16 (156.8 MHz), the international distress, safety and calling frequency. It is on Channel 16 that all "Mayday," "Pan-Pan" (pronounced "pahn, pahn") and "Securite" (pronounced "saycuritay") calls are made.

Mayday calls are absolute first-priority distress calls involving imminent danger of loss of life or vessel. Refer to Chapter 4 for Mayday call format. Pan-Pan calls, also covered in Chapter 4, are second-priority urgent communications concerning the safety of a ship, aircraft, other vessel or person in sight or on board. Securite calls are third-priority safety messages concerning navigation or weather. When a transmission is preceded by one of these priority call identifiers, other operators must stay clear of the channel (even if that means cutting short a transmission in progress) until it is clear that the priority call has been concluded.

It's important to understand and use these priority signal identifiers correctly, as misuse, especially of the Mayday signal, can cause dangerous confusion and expensive false alarms. For example, while running aground on a falling tide in a calm sea a couple of hundred yards from shore may be inconvenient, it does *not* generally warrant a Mayday call. If, in such a case, your stranded vessel would be a hazard to navigation, say, in a heavy fog, such a situation might warrant a Securite call, but probably a normal call to advise the

Coast Guard of your situation and location, and to ask them to switch to their working channel would be more in order. The same is true if you have simply run out of fuel, or if your engine has died or won't start.

Channel 16 is also the international channel on which initial brief contact with another ship or shore station may be made for the purpose of switching to an appropriate working channel. This type of traffic is allowed on Channel 16 in order to ensure that a great many stations will be listening on the channel at any one time, thereby improving the chances that an urgent or distress signal, even a weak one, will be heard. Hailing calls in the U.S., however, have undermined the distress purpose of the channel to such an extent that in many Coast Guard districts, Channel 9 is is now the hailing frequency, leaving Channel 16 available for distress traffic only.

OPERATING PROCEDURES

Ship-to-ship communications are usually initiated on Channel 16; recreational craft are encouraged to use Channel 09. Immediately after contact is established, the communicating stations are required to shift to an appropriate "working" channel. A typical contact and shift would proceed roughly as follows:

"*Bluejay...Bluejay*, this is *Desolate*, WA2345, over." (Boat names can be repeated up to three times each, but this is not normally necessary, and is undesirable.)

"*Desolate*" (repeated only if necessary because of poor conditions) "this is *Bluejay*, WA7865."

"*Bluejay*, this is *Desolate*. Switch six-eight."

"Roger, *Desolate*. This is *Bluejay*. Roger six-eight." (It is desirable to acknowledge the number of the working channel to avoid loss of contact when switching.)

(Both stations retune to Channel 68.)

"*Bluejay*, this is *Desolate*, over."

"*Desolate*, this is *Bluejay*..."

(And at the end of the call:)

"*Desolate*, WA2345, out."

"*Bluejay*, WA7865, out."

Non-commercial craft are required to keep to their specifically designated working channels, except when communicating with a commercial vessel, in which case Channel 09 may be used.

Ship-to-shore communications are sometimes initiated on Channel 16, but where possible should be made directly on an appropriate working channel when it is known that the shore station being called—for example, a marina dockmaster's office or a bridgetender—monitors that channel.

Calls to the Marine Operator are normally initiated directly on the working channel. And even if a call is initiated by the Marine Operator on Channel 16, a ship station should respond only on the appropriate working channel, as the Marine Operator may not be listening on 16.

Mayday calls

Transmit a Mayday call *(Chapter 4)*, repeating at intervals until an answer is received. If you fail to receive an answer on Channel 16 after a number of attempts, repeat the message on another available channel where it is most likely to draw attention.

If your Mayday is received by the Coast Guard, you may be asked to perform a "long count" or other suitable extended signal transmission to permit radio direction finding stations to determine your position. Always end your transmissions with the name of your vessel and your ship station call sign.

If you must abandon ship, consider taping down your VHF radiotelephone microphone button; this will provide a continuing signal on which rescue vessels may home. (This is best done by arrangement with any rescue vessel, with your set tuned to a channel other than 16, as locking onto Channel 16 will interfere with ongoing rescue-related communications.)

Radio information services

In the U.S., marine weather information and forecasts are broadcast continuously from many locations by the National Weather Service. In Canada and many other countries, similar continuous weather broadcasts are made by equivalent government agencies.

Virtually every VHF marine radiotelephone is today equipped with switch-selectable capability for receiving such broadcasts. There are seven U.S. continuous weather broadcast channels, but nearly all stations use one of the first three. The Canadian weather service employs two other frequencies. And there is an additional frequency assigned to continuous weather broadcasting, but unused in North America, for a total of nine channels, usually designated WX-1 through WX-9. Commercial broadcast stations and the various Marine Operators also transmit weather information, though this is of varying timeliness and accuracy.

At any time, the Coast Guard may broadcast special safety information, including weather summaries and forecasts, on Channel 22A, the Coast Guard's assigned working channel. Such special broadcasts are preceded by an alerting announcement (and possible warning tone) transmitted on Channel 16. Alpha "A" symbols are assigned to those channels used within the U.S., where the frequencies are different from those same channels used in the International Service. Remember "A" for U.S.A.

Single-sideband (SSB) radio

VHF radio is intended mainly for short-range communications. Reliable direct voice communication over distances exceeding about 25 miles (depending on antenna heights) requires the use either of medium frequency (MF) and/or high frequency (HF) radiotelephones, or equipment that sends signals to relaying communications satellites. Satellite communications are discussed in a later section.

Marine radiotelephone equipment that operates in the MF and HF bands is today universally, and by international treaty, of the single-sideband (SSB) variety. SSB is amplitude modulated, though it utilizes only a single sideband adjacent to, rather than double sidebands on either side of, a carrier wave. MF and HF marine radio is sometimes referred to as AM radio, but this is a holdover from the days when marine MF and HF sets were of the double sideband (DSB) type; and it's currently more accurate and usual to use the term "SSB" when referring to them.

Licensing SSB radio

A vessel cannot be licensed for SSB radiotelephone unless it is already licensed for, and equipped with, a VHF-FM set. Moreover, to help ease the crowding on the MF and HF bands, an SSB operator is required by law to attempt communication on VHF *before* using the 2-3 MHz band or higher frequencies, unless the transmitting station is clearly beyond normal VHF range. (MF and HF transmissions carry very far distances because of signal "bounce," and SSB signals tend to interfere with one another.)

In most cases, the Restricted Radiotelephone Operator permit is sufficient licensing for SSB operation. That permit is good for equipment up to and including 100 watts carrier wave power or 400 watts peak envelope power (PEP). Naturally, higher-level licenses, such as the Marine Radio Operator permit and various commercial radio operator licenses, are valid for SSB operation.

Selection and installation of SSB

SSB radiotelephones are commonly available with output power from 50 to 150 watts. Unlike the range of VHF transmissions, which is essentially line-of-sight and remains relatively unaffected by output power, the range of SSB transmissions is affected by, among other things, the strength of the radiated signal.

By regulation, all marine SSB radiotelephone stations in the 2-3 MHz band must be able to operate on 2182 kHz, the international distress and calling frequency. They must also be able to operate on at least two other frequencies. However, in order to achieve maximum utility from an SSB installation, the savvy skipper will usually pick a set with a much wider frequency capability, as frequency selection affects range. Most sets will have the desirable feature of one-button selection of the 2182 kHz distress frequency, and some systems will also automatically generate the radiotelephone alarm signal on this channel.

The maximum reliable range of SSB transmission in the 2-3 MHz (MF) band during the day is 50 to 150 miles. Transmission in the HF bands can reach for thousands of miles, depending on a number of factors such as the frequency used, atmospheric noise and other interference, the time of day, even the level of sunspot activity.

For example, transmissions in the 4 MHz band carry to only about 100 miles at noon local time, while they reach to about 300 miles just before sunset and to 600 miles or more after dark. Transmissions in the 8 MHz band will usually carry nearly 500 miles at noon local time, but may reach several thousands of miles at night. And transmissions on still higher frequencies can reach 10,000 miles or more under the right conditions.

Digital Selective Calling (DSC) is also now available on some SSB sets. DSC-equipped SSB radiotelephones can automatically alert an operator to a call incoming on any of a number of bands, without the need to maintain an audio watch. This is especially useful with SSB equipment because the spectrum of available frequencies is so broad.

Installation of SSB equipment usually requires the services of a trained and licensed technician. Most SSB sets today come pre-tested and adjusted. But unlike VHF-FM radio, SSB requires a large "ground plane" in order to radiate its signals—which, except on metal hulls needs to be installed in the form of a large copper mesh panel (sometimes built into the fiberglass hull). As well, SSB is much more subject to interference from shipboard electrical equipment, and so often requires the installation of special isolators and noise-suppression filters in the vessel's electrical system.

With SSB, antenna selection and installation is also more complicated, since SSB generally requires a physically much longer antenna than VHF, and different antenna "tuning" for different bands. Antennas are employed in both "long wire" and whip form; and most SSB systems currently incorporate automatic antenna-tuning couplers. The final choice of one or more antennas should be made in consultation with a qualified technician and in view of the physical limitations imposed by one's vessel and rigging.

Skippers who plan to cruise to areas where VHF and MF radio does not afford adequate communications capability should consider SSB sets that can transmit and receive on the frequencies assigned to the Coast Guard's Contact And Long Range Liaison (CALL) system, which is also used for high seas emergency, voice-weather, navigation information and medical communications.

OTHER TYPES OF RADIO COMMUNICATIONS EQUIPMENT

Other forms of "two-way" radio found aboard recreational vessels include Citizens Band (CB) radio, amateur radio ("ham"), cellular telephone and various forms of satellite systems. With the exception of satellite systems, these "alternate" forms of radio communication can sometimes be less expensive to buy and install than marine radio with equivalent range capability. However, none can be considered a substitute for true marine radio, since only the designated marine frequencies are monitored continuously for distress calls by the U.S. Coast Guard and the search and rescue bodies of other countries.

Citizens Band radio

As its name implies, Citizens Band radio is intended to afford the general public with economical access to two-way radio communications. CB is allocated 40 specific frequencies between 26.965 and 27.405 MHz, commonly referred to as channels 1 through 40. Any channel may be used with either single or double sideband amplitude modulation (although the older 23-channel sets are compatible with the newer 0-channel sets only on channels 1 through 23). With the exception of Channel 9, which is reserved for "emergency communications involving the immediate safety of life or the immediate protection of property, or for traveler assistance," no channel is assigned to any particular use or user group.

CB stations are limited to 4 watts carrier wave output power on DSB AM, and 12 watts PEP on SSB AM. The usual reliable range of CB is 5 miles, but may, in favorable conditions, extend to 15 or more. These are the ranges for ground waves; sky waves can sometimes reach and be received thousands of miles away. For this reason, external power amplifiers are strictly prohibited by regulation—although more than a few CB outlaws illegally boost the output power of their sets many times over. The problem with such illegal power amplification is that it crowds the airwaves and interferes with the intended purpose as a medium for local communications. FCC rules strictly prohibit CB communication between stations more than 155.3 miles (250 km) apart.

CB radio operation does not require a license, and there are no specific operating procedures. However, the FCC requires the following:

■ That all communications be restricted to the minimum practical transmission time.

■ That exchanges between stations be limited to a maximum five minute duration.

■ That when exchanges have reached the five-minute limit, both stations remain off the air for a minimum of one minute.

These rules do not apply in any case involving emergency communications.

CB communications may be in any language, but use of any code other than the "ten code" is prohibited. And station identification is encouraged, though not required; and the form of station identification is only "suggested." Common practice is to use a CB "handle" or nickname, though the FCC encourages this only in conjunction with a call sign composed of the letter 'K' followed by the operator's initials and residence ZIP code, or an organization name and unit number. "Handles" alone are preferred by many operators because they are untraceable.

If you want to install a CB set on your boat, be sure that the unit chosen is designed or adapted for conditions at sea. And be certain to use an antenna specifically intended for marine applications, as the standard automotive-type antenna will not function satisfactorily.

Amateur radio

Ham radio is used worldwide, with capabilities for both short- and long-range communications. It is authorized for personal, but not business, communications, and is useful to boaters who cruise to faraway ports, and who want to communicate economically over very long distances.

Ham radio is assigned a multiplicity of frequency bands from 1.8 to 24,000 MHz, in fact more frequencies than either marine VHF-FM or SSB. Within this spread, there is a suitable frequency for communication at about any distance around the world. One of the major workhorse ham frequencies is 14.313 MHz, which is where the members of relay "nets" meet to handle permissible traffic and arrange land-line telephone patches for mobile marine stations.

Radiotelegraph (Morse code), radiotelephone (AM or FM), radioteletype, and television signals are also transmitted by properly licensed ham operators on specified sub-bands. Indeed, some hams even "moon-bounce" signals.

The rules governing ham operations do not provide for a specific emergency channel, but several frequencies—for instance, 7,268 kHz and 14,313 kHz—have historically been used as distress channels and are regularly monitored by hams around the world. In addition, hams frequently associate themselves in relay "nets" and will often establish a land-line link-up for a fellow operator. And because of this network, ham radio is frequently useful for communicating across great distances with people who may or may not have access to radiotelephone equipment.

Amateur radio operation requires both a station and an operator license. Ham operator's licenses are issued in different grades—in ascending order, Novice, Technician, General, Advanced and Extra. Each grade up grants the operator wider access to the assigned bands and different modes. Even though only voice communication may be desired, a demonstrated knowledge of, and ability to send and receive, Morse code is required for all grades, except Technician. Sending and receiving Morse code at five words per minute is the minimum for the Novice grade, with higher rates required for advanced licenses. But attainment of the Novice grade is not prerequisite to attainment of Technician grade. However, a "no-code" Technician license restricts operation to frequencies above 30 MHz, which are generally suitable only for shorter-range communications.

Cellular telephones

The increasingly popular cellular telephone systems employ a large number of transceiving antennas/stations, placed around the country, and soon, around the world. Each of these serves a limited geographic area, called a "cell," and is linked together through relay and controlling stations into a network. That network is further patched into the land-based telephone system. Although the range of both a cellular telephone and a cell antenna/station is relatively short, the ultimate calling range of the system is very great because of the relays and the land-line patches accomplished by the cellular telephone network.

Each cellular telephone, actually a radiotelephone set, has its own identifier code. When a call is placed to a cellular number from a land-based telephone or another cellular telephone, the network attempts to contact the called cellular telephone by broadcasting its code. If it succeeds, the called cellular telephone "rings" and is answered much like a land-based telephone. A call is placed from a cellular telephone in the same way as from a land-based telephone.

The major advantages of the system are:
- Users interface with it in much the same way as they do with the standard telephone network, and so operator licensing is not required.
- It affords mobile users full access to land-based telephone systems, and vice versa.
- It employs relatively short-range radio technology (that avoids over-congestion of the airwaves), while overall affording users the capabilities for long-range communications.

The maximum range of a cellular telephone to and from a cell antenna/station varies, but is basically line-of-sight. In some circumstances, broadcast range can be as little as a few miles; in others, it can approach equivalency with VHF radio. Range is further complicated by the fact that the majority of cell antenna/stations are placed with land-based use in mind, so the distance offshore that a vessel can remain in contact with a cell antenna/station is frequently short. Consequently, it is wise to purchase a unit having the maximum allowable output power. This will usually be either an installed-mobile or transportable type, rather than a hand-held portable or "pocket" model. It is also wise to employ one of the antennas intended for marine applications, instead of a standard portable or automotive type, and to mount it as high on the vessel as is practical.

A cellular telephone can be useful and extremely convenient, but is no substitute for proper marine radiotelephony when it comes to safety. (Although if within range you can place a call to the local Coast Guard station, in some areas by merely dialing "*CG.") Moreover, while the cost of cellular equipment and installation is currently minimal—provided you are willing to sign an "activation" contract for one or more years at the time of equipment purchase—the cost of operation can be unexpectedly high: In addition to standard telephone system toll charges when applicable, the cellular user is charged per minute for air time—whether placing or receiving a call. That means that you pay for air time even when someone calls you. There is also a significant fixed monthly charge for the service and, of course, any long-distance charges. The cost of cellular use must be balanced against the relative cost and inconvenience of placing a call to a land-based telephone via the Marine Operator.

The introduction of Integrated Digital Switching has greatly improved the ability of cellular telephone networks to forward calls in search of a given cellular telephone, and to "hand off" from cell station to cell station as a mobile unit moves geographically while engaged in a conversation. And "cell sectorization" technology, in which three 120-degree directional cell antennas replace a single omnidirectional antenna, reduces crowding and interference, and improves cellular performance. Boaters should seek the latest available information from both equipment manufacturers and network service providers before making decisions regarding equipment selection or the purchase of cellular telephone service.

Satellite communications

Satellite communications systems (SATCOM) beam signals around the world via a chain of earth-based and orbiting space relay stations. SATCOM affords users full access to voice, telex, facsimile and data networks. Originally suited for use aboard very large yachts, improvements to the necessary equipment make SATCOM practical for vessels down to 40 feet in length.

Ship-to-shore, ship-to-ship and shore-to-ship communications are established via Coast Earth Stations (CES), which constitute the links into the space segment of the network for shoreside subscribers. In the U.S., the Coast Earth Stations are operated by the Communications Satellite Corporation (COMSAT), which provides access to the worldwide satellite communications space segments that are supplied by the International Maritime Satellite Organization (INMARSAT).

The procedures for placing and receiving calls via the INMARSAT system are highly automated. However, at each CES there are Maritime Services operators who provide directory and calling assistance, as well as other communications-related services, on a 24-hour, 7-day-per-week basis. These operators also provide distress assistance in concert with the system's Rescue Co-ordination Centers.

The shipboard unit used for linking into the INMARSAT system is designated a Ship Earth Station (SES). There are a number of distinct types of SES, each providing a different array of access capabilities to the INMARSAT satellites and thereby to worldwide public telex and telephone networks. INMARSAT-A supports both telex and high-quality telephone voice communications, as well as high-speed data and facsimile transmissions on its voice-quality channels. The INMARSAT-A shipboard terminal, however, employs a relatively large stabilized tracking dish antenna that is suitable for installation on larger vessels only.

EMERGENCY POSITION INDICATING RADIO BEACON (EPIRB)

Every boat that goes offshore beyond reliable VHF radio range, roughly 20 miles, should carry a Class A or Class B Emergency Position Indicating Radiobeacon (EPIRB), or one of the newer generation, described at right. A Class A or B model transmits a distinctive tone signal on two aircraft frequencies—121.5 MHz, the emergency channel of civil aviation, and 243.0 MHz, the "guard" channel for military aircraft. This signal alerts passing aircraft that an emergency exists and guides searchers to the scene of distress. The transmitter is not powerful—one watt or less—but its signals can often be heard out to as far as 200 miles by high-flying aircraft. By law, Class A EPIRBs must be carried on certain types of vessels. A Class A EPIRB must be capable of floating free and activating automatically, including extending its antenna. The less-expensive Class B units are for voluntary carriage by other vessels such as recreational boats. This simpler design need not be capable of floating by itself, but a flotation collar is usually added if the unit is not buoyant; this type of EPIRB can be activated either manually or automatically upon floating in the water.

EPIRBs have a test switch for checking readiness for use. This must be done for *one second only* during the first five minutes of every hour. Avoid "false alarms." Once an EPIRB is turned on in an emergency situation, *it must be left on.* Turning it off for various periods "to save the battery" destroys its effectiveness for homing on the signals by air and surface rescue craft.

There is no assurance that an EPIRB signal will be picked up and the authorities notified; many aircraft monitor 121.5 or 243.0 MHz, but this is not required by law or regulation. As these devices send out radio waves, they must be licensed; this is easily done by modification of the radio station license (if no other radio is licensed on the boat, a separate EPIRB license

must be obtained). A Class S EPIRB is similar to a Class B unit, except that it floats, or is an integral part of a survival craft.

The new generation
The latest EPIRB models operate on a new frequency, 406.025 MHz, communicating solely with passing satellites. These new units have much advanced electronics, permitting the unit to identify itself, its position, and perhaps the nature of the distress. Satellites no longer have to be within sight of a ground station; they can store the EPIRB's message and transmit it later as they pass within range of an earth terminal. (The new model also transmits a "homing" signal on 121.5 MHz so that it can be located.) Categories I and II of the 406 MHz EPIRBs correspond to Classes A and B of the earlier designs.

Class A and B EPIRBs are battery-powered, and are required by the FCC to operate continuously with rated power for at least 48 hours (many will operate for as long as a week); the battery must be marked with dates of manufacture and proper replacement (50 percent of life remaining). The transmitter is completely transistorized and suitable for storage in a marine environment over a long period of time.

INMARSAT-C utilizes a more compact omnidirectional antenna that can be fitted conveniently to smaller vessels. INMARSAT-C supports data transmissions at up to 600 bps, but does not support voice communications.

The INMARSAT-B and INMARSAT-M have recently been introduced. INMARSAT-B is a digital version of INMARSAT-A; and INMARSAT-M is a small digital voice terminal that employs a smaller, simplified tracking dish antenna suitable for installation on smaller vessels. A receive-only version of the INMARSAT-C SES is available for automatic reception of maritime safety broadcasts in offshore and other areas not reached by coastal NAVTEX service.

NAVTEX
The international NAVTEX system automatically distributes offshore weather forecasts and advisories (but not coastal weather information), navigational warnings, ice warnings,

Gulf Stream location, radionavigational information and rescue messages via self-contained printing radio receivers.

The shipboard NAVTEX unit is a receiver only. It is compact, relatively low in cost and smart: A NAVTEX receiver can be programmed to check every incoming message to see whether it has been previously received, and whether it falls into a category of designated interest to the receiving station. If the message has been previously received, or does not fall into a category of designated interest, it is ignored. If the incoming message is a new one, and fits one of the receiver's programmed categories of interest, it is saved to be later printed, called up on a display and/or printed out.

The advantages of NAVTEX are that it operates unattended, messages are not missed because the crew are engaged with other duties and pertinent messages are saved for convenient review by the skipper. There are a large number of NAVTEX transmitting stations, all operating on 518 kHz.

MORSE CODE AND VISUAL SIGNALS

Contrary to what many contemporary skippers believe, Morse code and other forms of signaling have not been totally replaced by electronic voice and data communications. Although radiotelephony and radiotext transmissions predominate, especially in the recreational sector, there remains a place for radio communications (other than in ham radio) that employ Morse code, and for visual forms of signaling, such as the use of hoisted flags.

The international Morse code

The use of Morse code offers a number of significant advantages in radio communications. Because a keyed continuous wave (CW) signal does not require microphone or modulation circuits, the equipment necessary for successfully sending Morse code messages is simple, low-cost, and easy to build and maintain. Moreover, exceptionally low output power—as little as 2 or 3 watts—is often sufficient to transmit CW signals across open ocean to a range in the thousands of miles. And because an experienced radio operator can usually distinguish even a weak Morse code CW signal amid static and interfering transmissions, these signals can often get through in circumstances where both VHF-FM and SSB would likely fail.

Memorizing the Morse code characters, shown at right, takes time, but it can be done by anyone. Once learned, and occasionally used, they will not be forgotten.

Flag signals

There is an established International Code of flag signals. One or more flags are hoisted aloft on a halyard where they can be seen by another vessel. The set of code flags—shown on page 560—consists of 26 alphabet flags, 10 numeral pennants, 3 substitutes (or repeaters) and an answering pennant. The substitutes are used when a given flag or pennant has already been used once in a hoist; and flags and pennants are mixed in a hoist as required.

An internationally established two-letter code facilitates speedier communications. For example, hoisting the alphabet flags 'N' and 'F' means, "You are running into danger."

Today, few yachts carry a full set of international code flags, but many carry one or more that have special uses, for instance, the yellow 'Q' flag that must be hoisted when entering, and requesting permission to use, a foreign port. Racing sailboats (and judging committee boats), however, regularly have recourse to flag signaling; and the sailing skipper who engages in racing needs to be fully familiar with the specialized signals involved.

Flashing light signals

Signaling by short and long flashes of light is much faster than flag signaling. Moreover, because light signals can be narrowly aimed, they are less likely to be intercepted by other than the communicating vessels. Consequently, light signals are still widely used by naval vessels.

Aboard ships, light signaling is often accomplished by means of an Aldis light, a very bright, highly aimable light with a convenient trigger switch. However, light signaling can be accomplished with any form of light that is readily turned on and off, even a flashlight. If it is not feasible to turn the light off and on fast enough for signaling, a shutter can be operated close in front of the light to form short and long flashes. Therefore, there are circumstances in which light signaling can be advantageous to a small craft skipper.

Unfortunately, light signaling requires the ability to send and read Morse code—a rarity among recreational boaters. So it is unlikely to have application for most boat operators—unless perhaps one night he or she is aground, with a general failure of electrical power for radio communication and an urgent need to communicate with a Coast Guard rescue vessel or helicopter, in which case the ability to send light signals with a battery-powered flashlight could prove critical.

THE INTERNATIONAL MORSE CODE ALPHABET

A • —	M — —	Y — • — —
B — • • •	N — •	Z — — • •
C — • — •	O — — —	1 • — — — —
D — • •	P • — — •	2 • • — — —
E •	Q — — • —	3 • • • — —
F • • — •	R • — •	4 • • • • —
G — — •	S • • •	5 • • • • •
H • • • •	T —	6 — • • • •
I • •	U • • —	7 — — • • •
J • — — —	V • • • —	8 — — — • •
K — • —	W • — —	9 — — — — •
L • — • •	X — • • —	0 — — — — —

Procedural signals

Period • — • — • —
Comma — — • • — —
Interrogative • — • • — • (RQ)
Distress call • • • — — — • • • (SOS)
From — • • • (DE)
Invitation to transmit (go ahead) — • — (K)
Wait • — • • • ($\overline{AS}$)
Error • • • • • • • • (EEEE etc.)
Received • — • (R)
End of each message • — • — • ($\overline{AR}$)

Equivalents

A dash is equal to three dots.
The space between parts of the same letter is equal to one dot.
The space between two letters is equal to three dots.
The space between two words is equal to five dots.

INTERNATIONAL FLAGS AND PENNANTS

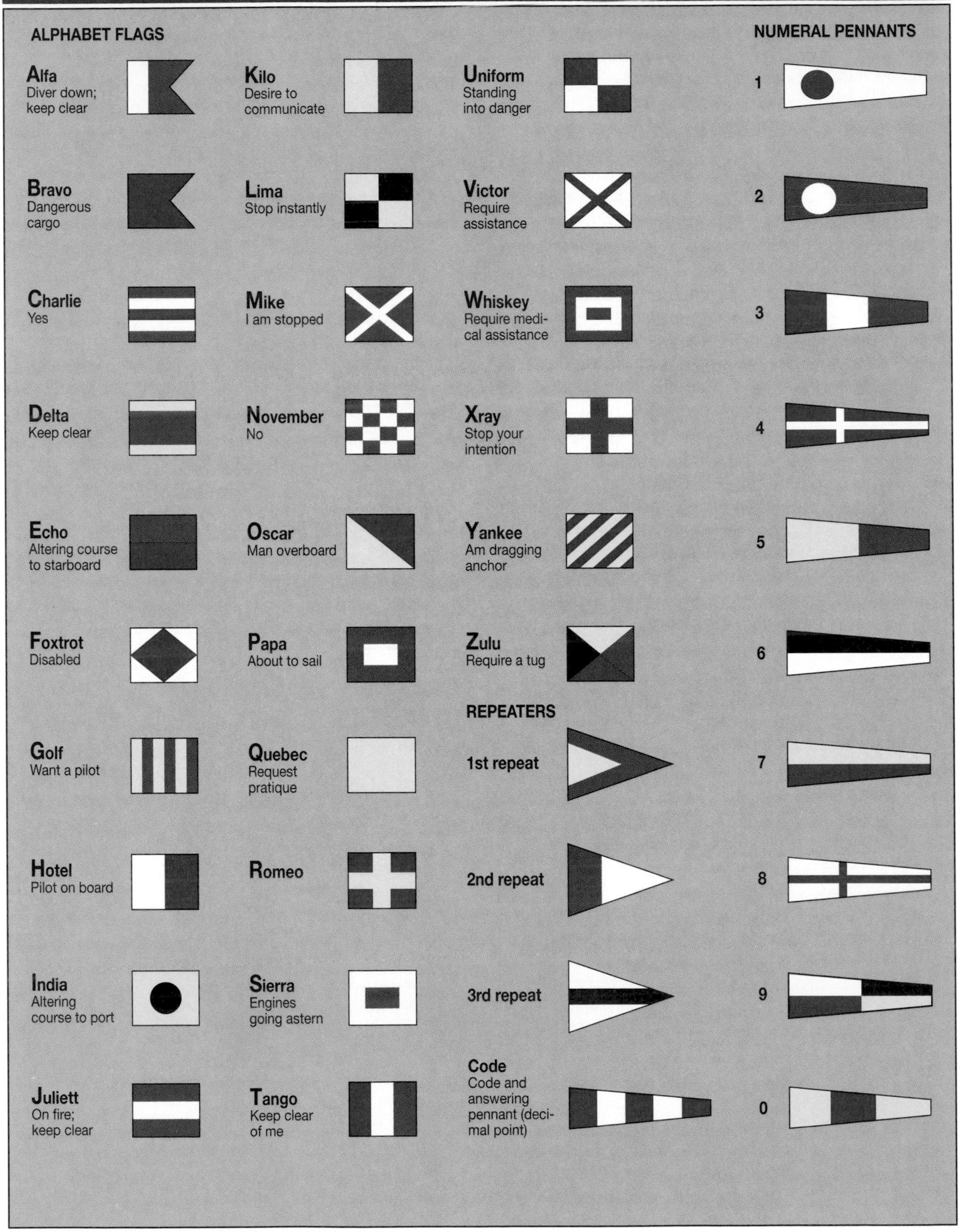

ALPHABET FLAGS

Alfa
Diver down; keep clear

Bravo
Dangerous cargo

Charlie
Yes

Delta
Keep clear

Echo
Altering course to starboard

Foxtrot
Disabled

Golf
Want a pilot

Hotel
Pilot on board

India
Altering course to port

Juliett
On fire; keep clear

Kilo
Desire to communicate

Lima
Stop instantly

Mike
I am stopped

November
No

Oscar
Man overboard

Papa
About to sail

Quebec
Request pratique

Romeo

Sierra
Engines going astern

Tango
Keep clear of me

Uniform
Standing into danger

Victor
Require assistance

Whiskey
Require medical assistance

Xray
Stop your intention

Yankee
Am dragging anchor

Zulu
Require a tug

REPEATERS

1st repeat

2nd repeat

3rd repeat

Code
Code and answering pennant (decimal point)

NUMERAL PENNANTS

1

2

3

4

5

6

7

8

9

0

SIGNALING USING FLAGS

1-,2- AND 3-CHARACTER SIGNALS

Single letter

B

B—I am taking on, or discharging, or carrying dangerous goods. Very urgent, important or commonly-used signals.

Two letters

K

N

KN—I cannot take you in tow.

General messages.

Two letters and numeral

K

N

1

KN1—I cannot take you in tow but I will report you and ask for immediate assistance. Numeral added to general message to provide variation in meaning, to ask or answer a question, or to supplement the basic message.

REPEATERS (SUBSTITUTES)

B

First repeater
Repeats uppermost flag.

C

Second repeater
Repeats second flag from top.

BBCB

T

1

3

Second Repeater

0

T1330

A repeater (substitute) repeats the class of flags that it immediately follows—in the case above right, a numeral pennant.

ANSWERING PENNANT

At the dip
Hoisted by receiving vessel as each hoist of transmitting ship is seen.

Close up
Receiving vessel indicates it understands the hoist. At end of signal, indicates message is complete.

PLAIN LANGUAGE MESSAGE, SPELLED OUT

The words that follow are in plain language. Use is optional; may be omitted if spelling in plain language is obvious.

R

E

Y

Z

A

D

M

O

T

O

R

Second Repeater

B

O

A

T

I

N

G

Special signals are no longer used to indicate separation between spelled words or the end of spelling. Words should be selected and/or divided so that the meaning of the hoist is clear.

RACE SIGNALS OF THE UNITED STATES YACT RACING UNION

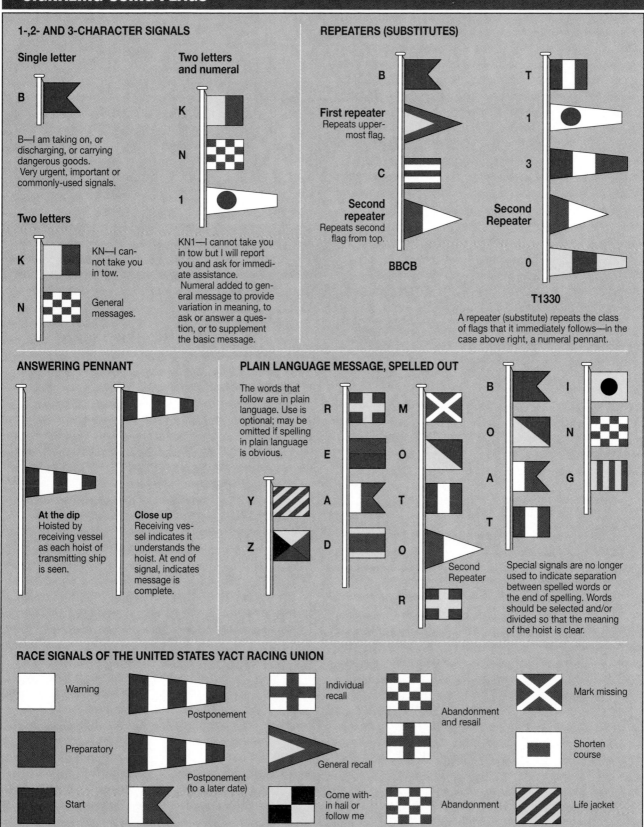

Warning

Preparatory

Start

Postponement

Postponement (to a later date)

Individual recall

General recall

Come within hail or follow me

Abandonment and resail

Abandonment

Mark missing

Shorten course

Life jacket

25 ELECTRONIC NAVIGATION

It was in the early 1900s that Guglielmo Marconi first transmitted radio waves through the atmosphere and received them at distant locations, creating the basis of much of today's maritime communications and electronic navigation. It was the early 1920s when Reginald A. Fessenden created the first electronic depth sounder and Elmer Sperry developed the first gyroscopically controlled automatic steering gear for ships. British and American technicians did not develop radar until 1934.

Only since the advent of the space age in the late 1950s has it become possible to navigate the waters of the world using radio signals transmitted from satellites circling the earth. This chapter describes the technology that is such an integral element of boating today.

DEPTH SOUNDERS

Depth sounders are today's replacement for the handheld lead lines used for centuries to determine the depth of water beneath a ship. Modern electronic devices furnish a vastly greater amount of information, and do it with far greater ease, especially in nasty weather. A depth sounder provides both safety and convenience, so it is doubly advantageous to have on board.

How depth is measured and displayed

Depth sounders determine depth by measuring the round-trip time required for pulses of ultrasonic energy to travel from the boat to the bottom of the water and then to be reflected back to the vessel. A transmitter sends out the pulses from a transducer, and the same device picks up the returning echoes, interprets them, and sends information to some type of display such as one or more flashing lights on a circular calibrated dial, a digital readout or a video picture. Most sounders use a liquid crystal display (LCD) that is easily read in daylight and does not require a light shield in bright-light conditions such as in an open boat or on a flying bridge; it can also be backlighted for night use. Depth information generally is available in feet, fathoms or meters.

The video display sounder presents a visual "elevation" picture of the bottom, plus underwater objects such as large fish or schools of fish. The display changes constantly as the boat moves along its course, but you can "freeze" it for a more detailed study.

Some sounder models display the information received on a cathode-ray tube (CRT) in various shades of green or amber; others have a display in different colors based on the strength of the various echoes.

Correction to "zero" depth

A depth sounder's transducer generally is mounted on the hull several feet below the water surface, but some distance up from the lowest point of the keel. As depths are measured from the transducer, the readings will be *neither* the actual depth of the water nor the clearance between the keel and the bottom. On some models, the zero reading can be offset plus or minus a few feet so that the depth indications will be either the true water depth or the clearance under the boat, without adding or subtracting a fixed amount from each.

Although actual water depth readings are advantageous for navigation, some skippers feel better with a direct reading of clearance under the keel.

Interpreting displays

An analog or digital display sounder shows an average depth and does not identify the bottom by type. The flashing-light sounder indicates the nature of the bottom by the sharpness of its light flashes. The LCD sounder display uses two shades to differentiate between a soft and hard bottom and can also identify weeds and fish. The amber video display adds definition with up to four tones of the same color. The

color video display may have from 8 to 16 colors, which provide the most accurate rendition of the nature of the bottom and any fish detected.

Depth alarms

Most depth sounders have at least a shallow-water alarm, and some have multiple depth alarms. The latter are useful when the boat is anchored. With one alarm set just below the present depth and the other set just above it, with allowance made for tidal changes, the unit sounds if the boat drags anchor toward either shallower or deeper water.

Another recent development is the so-called "forward-looking" depth sounder. Actually, sounders of this type measure depth only directly downward, but a microprocessor evaluates the trend of soundings and predicts the depth for brief intervals—typically 10 or 20 seconds—and sounds an alarm if appropriate. Obviously, such models are of most value over a gently sloping bottom and would give *no warning* of an isolated rock, coral head or similar underwater obstruction.

"Scanning sonar" units are also available. These can direct a beam of ultrasonic sound up to 360 degrees around a vessel or to any desired sector. The beam can be directed from minus 3 degrees to plus 80 degrees in elevation to greatly expand the volume of water that is being checked. Though they sound like the ideal device to warn of underwater obstructions, their manufacturers do not recommend they be used for that purpose; in shallow water where they could be most useful, sonar echoes become so chaotic that they cannot be correctly interpreted by the untrained eye.

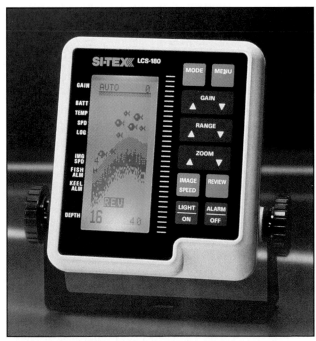

Depth sounders that use a liquid crystal display (LCD) provide water depth information, and can also identify schools of fish and underwater structures.

RADIO DIRECTION FINDERS

Although old-fashioned when compared with modern electronic marvels, the radio direction systems in North America remain useful for mariners. On the seacoast, the Great Lakes or the Gulf of Mexico, a radio direction finder (RDF) can be used to determine your position or home in on a beacon.

A radio direction finding system needs the following elements: an RDF set on the boat, up-to-date charts covering the locations both of transmitters and the boat, and someone who knows how to operate the system. Competence and confidence are important: An incorrect radio bearing can lead to disaster; a correct bearing that is ignored because of mistrust can be equally disastrous.

Basically, an RDF is a receiver with a directional antenna and a "visual null indicator." The directional antenna rotates mechanically or electronically through 360 degrees showing two positions of maximum strength and two positions of minimal strength, called nulls. The maximums are broad and poorly defined, while the nulls are marked and relatively precise. It is the nulls that are used for direction finding. The visual null indicator consists of a small meter that will show a maximum or minimum deflection with its needle in accordance to the set's instructions. Some modern units will do this automatically, and may display the digital frequency.

An RDF may cover any one of three frequency bands—a low frequency (LF) beacon band, the standard AM broadcast band (MF) and the VHF band. Many of these units double up as AM-FM-shortwave radios.

The locations of beacons operated by the U.S. Coast Guard are shown on standard charts and in the *Light List*. Note that land-based Coast Guard VHF transmitters may not be at the site of the named Coast Guard station. Charts show the location of radiobeacons and major broadcast station antennas, together with call letters and frequencies.

Marine radiobeacons

Radiobeacons are rated in terms of "service range," from 200 miles to only 10 miles (for beacons of limited local interest). Radiobeacons are identified by one, two or sometimes three letters sent in Morse code. You don't need to know the code; the dots and dashes are printed on the chart. Often the letters relate to the location they identify, such as AC for Atlantic City—but sometimes they do not, such as U for Miami.

Positioning with an RDF

Radio bearings are plotted in much the same manner as visual bearings, but two cautions must be observed: The RDF must have been calibrated for radio deviation (refer to the manufacturer's manual), and bearings are less precise—roughly 2 to 4 degrees in width. Take three cross bearings, if possible, and use the strongest signals available.

Homing with an RDF

When the directional antenna is set on 000 degrees relative, a craft may be directed toward a radio station or another vessel by steering to keep the signal strength at the deepest point of the null. One RDF model has a direct-reading meter that shows the helmsman whether he or she is to the right or left of the course. This homing procedure provides a simple navigational technique for getting into port in poor visibility or when other navigational aids are not available—but be sure the direct course doesn't lead into shoal waters or other dangerous areas. A few harbor entrances have low-power radiobeacons, usually at the outer end of a jetty, if one exists.

Homing also makes possible the steering of a boat on the most direct course to the scene of a distress situation. Such action is normally only possible on VHF channels with RDFs for such frequencies or a transceiver having a DF capability. Single-sideband transmissions on MF and HF frequencies are poor sources of signals for direction finding.

Be sure not to run directly into the source of the signals. (Although this may seem like rather obvious advice, it has happened many times.)

VHF radio direction finding

Direction finders for VHF are of the automatic (ADF) type. All VHF direction finders require a special separate antenna, and all are more expensive than LF-MF models. Many USCG vessels now have VHF homing devices on board for rescue work.

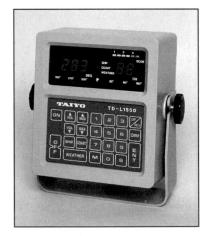

This automatic direction finder for marine VHF channels enables the user to take bearings on shore stations at known locations, such as NOAA weather broadcasts, or to steer directly toward other vessels using a homing indicator.

The Coast Guard does not operate any radiobeacons on the VHF band, but the continuous transmissions of the NOAA weather stations provide a good signal for determination of a line of position (LOP); the range would be the same as in regular reception of weather information. You must know the location of the transmitting antenna and have that plotted on the chart you are using. This will normally provide only one LOP, but in limited areas it may be possible to receive two weather stations and, therefore, to obtain a fix. Coast Guard stations and Marine Operators normally have multiple antenna sites, and it is not possible to use their signals for taking bearings. The usual applications, however, of a VHF direction finder will be for homing or for taking bearings on other boats and ships.

RADAR

Radar is an acronym for RAdio Detection And Ranging. The basic technology that radar employs has been around since before World War II, but the advent in recent years of digital signal processing and integrated circuitry have allowed a number of improvements in its ability to define (clearly outline) targets, as well as in how its information is displayed. A good radar set is an extremely valuable piece of equipment because of its ability to detect the presence, range and bearing of distant objects in any weather.

Radar equipment

A radar's components consist of a transmitter that generates the radio waves and includes a modulator that causes the radio waves to be generated in brief pulses; an antenna that radiates the radio waves and collects the returning echoes; a receiver that detects the returned reflections and amplifies them to usable strength; and a display that presents the pattern of received echoes on a cathode-ray tube (CRT) or liquid crystal display (LCD) and includes rotary knobs, buttons and/or a joystick or trackball for certain operator-controlled functions.

The radars used on small craft normally group these components in two units: The antenna, the transmitter and a portion of the receiver are housed in one unit, mounted as high on the vessel as practical; the remainders of the receiver and the display are housed in a second unit, normally installed near the vessel's helm. Some manufacturers also offer a remote display that allows a second presentation of the picture on the master display at a second steering station such as on a powerboat's flying bridge.

Transmitters for use on recreational vessels are rated by their peak pulse power output and range from 1 kW to about 10 kW; the power taken from the boat's electrical system is much less, from 100 watts to about 300 watts

Small-craft radar antennas range in length from about 17 inches to 6.5 feet. Antennas under about 2 feet in length in some cases are enclosed in a radome, a fiberglass housing most often used to prevent a sailboat's sails from becoming entangled in the rotating antenna. A radome does not affect the quality of an antenna's radio wave transmission.

The longer an antenna, the narrower the horizontal width of the beam of radio waves it transmits. A 17-inch radome antenna, for example, would typically transmit a 5.7-degree horizontal beam; a 3.5-foot open array antenna might transmit a 2.4-degree beam; and a 6.5-foot antenna might transmit a 1.23-degree beam. The narrower a radar's beam width, the greater will be its ability to define targets; this is called bearing discrimination.

The maximum range scales for radars found on board recreational boats generally vary from about 16 miles to 72 miles, but these figures can be misleading. The maximum range at which an object can be detected is most limited by the height of the antenna. Output power levels and size of the antenna are a lesser factor in the performance of the set.

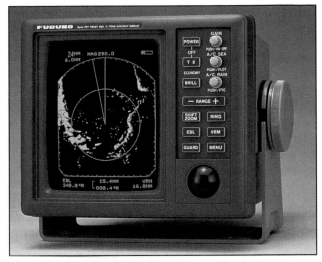

A standard radar display presents the vessel's position at the center of its screen and the vessel's heading as the 12 o'clock position. With each sweep of the antenna, reflected radio waves reveal the objects they detect.

Longer ranges provide coverage of greater areas, but at a cost of less detail and poorer target definition.

Radar displays using CRTs "paint" a presentation of reflected radio waves on phosphor screens with each sweep of the antenna. Because the signal display of conventional radars has to be relatively weak to keep from burning an image into the phosphor, it fades rapidly. Newer "raster scan" radars digitally process signals to keep them from fading before the next antenna sweep. Digitally processed signals can be "frozen" to allow a more precise range or bearing to be taken on a detected object.

Most radars found on recreational vessels have a monochrome display in either green or amber. More expensive radars offer varying levels of "quantization," which means they present the strongest echoes they receive in the darkest green or amber, and the weakest echoes received in the lightest green or amber. Some radars offer a display that presents echoes of different strengths in different colors: Red for the strongest, yellow for those of medium strength, and blue or green for the weakest.

Radar capabilities

Radar displays normally allow an operator to select from a variety of scales ranging from ⅛ mile up to the unit's maximum range. Most use concentric circles of light to divide the selected range into a number of equal units to allow rapid estimates of the distance to any object that is reflecting the antenna's transmitted radio waves. Most also offer at least one variable range marker (VRM), a movable concentric circle that the operator can place directly over the image of a detected object with a knob, push-button, joystick or trackball. The display will then read out digitally the range to the object. Another common feature is an electronic bearing line

(EBL), a movable straight line that pivots around the center point of the screen, which the operator can place over the image of a detected object. The display will then digitally read out the relative bearing from the vessel to the object. More expensive radars offer multiple VRMs and EBLs.

Some radars allow the operator to zoom in on a portion of the display to present that segment in greater detail. While most radars display the vessel's position at the center of the screen, some radars allow the operator to "off-center" the display to provide greater coverage to one particular portion of the display.

The standard orientation of a radar display is "heads up"—the vessel's heading is always toward the 12 o'clock position on the radar screen. The display of radars that are interfaced with an electronic compass can present a "north-up" display in which compass north is in the 12 o'clock position on the screen. Some electronic compasses can be programmed to automatically compute variation and present true north in the 12 o'clock position on the screen of an interfaced radar.

More sophisticated radars also offer such features as echo tracking, which graphically presents the track of other vessels on the display screen. Some radar manufacturers also offer optional target plotter adapters, which allow selected models of their radars to track up to 10 targets simultaneously; display their range, bearing and closest point of approach (CPA); and sound an alarm if a target violates pre-set CPA limits. If these radars are also interfaced with an appro-

HOW RADAR DETECTS OBJECTS

Radar works by transmitting a tightly focused beam of super high frequency radio waves from a rotating antenna mounted as high as practical on a vessel, then measuring the time it takes those radio waves to be reflected off distant objects and return to the antenna. By multiplying that time interval by the speed of radio waves (186,000 miles per second), the system can determine the distance between the antenna and objects that reflect radio waves back to it.

The bearing to an object is determined by the direction in which the antenna is pointing when it transmits its radio wave beam and receives a reflection (sometimes called an echo). The antenna's rotation is not a factor in determining the bearing of an object because it makes only one revolution every 2 to 4 seconds but transmits pulses of radio waves at the rate of 400 to 6,000 per second. Since it takes the radio waves only a fraction over 12 microseconds (millionths of a second) per nautical mile of range to make their round trip, the antenna can send and receive up to 30 pulses in the time it takes to rotate just one degree, which means that, electronically speaking, it is standing still.

Because the radio waves a radar transmits bend slightly to follow the earth's curvature, its horizon at any particular mount-ing height is about 7 percent farther away than the horizon of the human eye at that same height. The maximum range at which a particular radar can detect an object and the clarity with which it can define targets depend on four factors—the strength of the radio wave signal it transmits, the sensitivity with which it can detect and interpret reflected radio waves, the length of its antenna and the height at which the antenna is mounted on the vessel, and the height of the object itself (see illustration below).

As the reflected radio waves are received, they are displayed on a screen normally mounted adjacent to a vessel's helm. The pattern of all the reflected radio waves that are received on a single sweep of the antenna clearly reveals the existence of the objects they detect.

This does not necessarily mean that the image displayed on the radar screen will match exactly what is seen with the human eye or on a navigation chart. Low-lying targets such as a beach along a coast will not show up as well as tall buildings several hundred yards inland. Radar cannot "see" through a mountain to reveal the harbor entrance beyond, and the reflection from a large object such as a commercial ship can mask the reflection of a smaller vessel behind it.

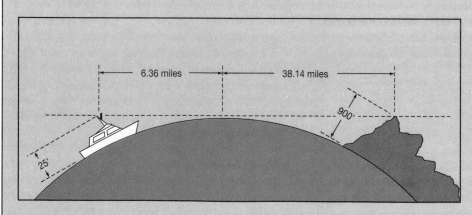

A radar's range depends on the mounting height of its antenna and on the height of the objects that reflect the radio waves it transmits.

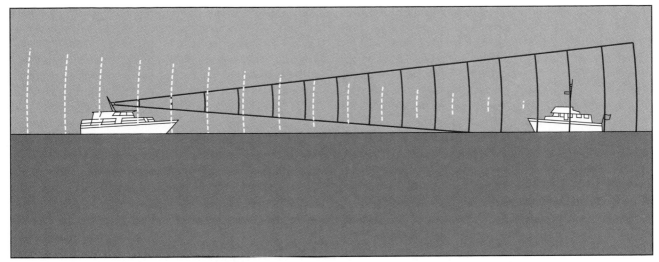

A marine radar set operates by sending brief pulses of super high frequency radio waves, which are reflected back by other vessels, navigational aids, land masses or other targets. The speed is so great that the echo is received before the next pulse is transmitted.

priate navigation sensor such as a GPS or Loran receiver, they can also display target courses in relative or true degrees and present the time to the closest point of approach (TCPA).

More sophisticated radars can be interfaced with navigation sensors such as GPS or Loran receivers to digitally display vessel course and speed on the radar screens. Some can utilize Read Only Memory (ROM) cards to display computerized chart representations on their screens and, if they are interfaced to appropriate navigation sensors, can graphically plot the vessel's track on either their radar picture or the chart representation.

Most radars allow a guard zone to be drawn around the vessel on which they are installed, and sound an alarm if that zone is violated. This feature can be valuable as an anti-collision device when underway, and also as an anchor watch. Many radars also can indicate if they detect radar operating on another vessel in their vicinity.

Radar navigation

Radar offers an excellent means of extending the coverage provided by a visual lookout, especially at night and in reduced visibility. This greater range of detection affords more time for a vessel to maneuver in order to avoid another craft or a detected obstacle. With a radar plot, an early determination can be made of another vessel's course and speed. Radar also helps when making a landfall from offshore; running a coast and picking up landmarks for fixes; or traveling in confined waters, entering an inlet, and the like. Radar has real advantages, even in the daytime, and of course becomes particularly helpful at night or in conditions of reduced visibility.

Radar's ability to measure distance is also helpful in establishing fixes. A visual bearing on a single object whose position is known will produce only a line of position along which your vessel lies. Combining that with radar's ability to deter-mine your distance from that same object allows you to determine a fix. Using radar to establish your distance from two or more objects whose location is known can also produce a fix. As range discrimination is usually better than bearing discrimination, a fix from two measurements of distance is to be preferred over one using two bearings.

Passive radar reflectors

The strength of radar echoes is based on the reflectivity of objects that return a minute portion of the outgoing radio energy from the radar set. Such common boat-building materials as wood and fiberglass have less reflectivity than steel and thus are relatively poor radio wave reflectors.

A boat owner who does not have radar equipment aboard his vessel can still use radar to increase safety by installing a passive radar reflector as a highly desirable "defensive" device to alert radar-equipped vessels in his vicinity as to his presence and position. Even radar-equipped craft should have a passive reflector. Having an operating radar aboard does not increase the likelihood of its being detected by other vessels unless those vessels themselves have operative equipment aboard that detects the presence and source of radar emissions.

Most passive radar reflectors consist of thin metal sheets or fine-mesh screening arranged in mutually perpendicular planes. These may fold for storage, but must be flat and rigid with respect to each other when open for use. A reflector with each surface only about 2 feet (60 cm) square can provide a strong return signal if properly used. For maximum effectiveness, a reflector should be hoisted up from three corners so that one of the eight "pockets" is straight up; this is sometimes termed the "rain catching" position. In certain cases, the reflector planes are held in their optimum configuration within a fiberglass shell.

LORAN

Though the term Loran is an acronym for LOng RAnge Navigation, it is actually a medium-range navigation system for both marine vessels and aircraft. Unlike Global Positioning System *(pages 571 to 575)*, Loran covers only the U.S. and Canadian coasts and the Great Lakes, plus limited other areas of the world, as discussed on page 570. Despite the system's limited coverage, within the areas where its signals can be received, a good Loran receiver is a versatile and valuable navigation instrument. Because Loran receivers are less expensive than GPS receivers, they often are the primary electronic navigation choice for recreational boaters who do not venture outside the system's coverage area.

Today's Loran system (technically called Loran-C) was deployed during the late 1970s and is based on the earlier Loran-A system which was developed during World War II for use by the U.S. military. This association with the military helps explain Loran's somewhat spotty coverage pattern as its areas of coverage were initially designed to benefit the military forces of the U.S. and its allies.

With the advent of the Global Positioning System, many feared that United States government support of the Loran system would be withdrawn. While the U.S. has announced that it will terminate its support of overseas Loran systems by 1994, it is committed to maintaining and in fact expanding the Loran system covering the contiguous 48 American states and southeast and southern Alaska, and has informally indicated it intends to maintain that service until at least 2015.

The operation and maintenance of overseas Loran systems originally installed and operated by the United States are now being taken over by the governments in the areas that they serve, as shown on page 570. Canada, for instance, now has full responsibility for the Loran systems covering its own coastal waters; the Republic of Korea now operates the East Asian (formerly called the Commando Lion) system; Japan now operates the Loran-A system covering the Northwest Pacific; several northern European governments have assumed responsibility for the system covering the Norwegian Sea; and Spain, Italy and Turkey have announced their intention to continue operation of the system covering the Mediterranean Sea. Russia and the United States jointly operate the Russian-American system which covers the area between western Alaska and eastern Russia, and Russia operates two Loran systems independently. Saudi Arabia operates three Loran systems covering its coastal waters, and China and India are actively developing new Loran systems for their own use.

Loran utilizes a network of shore-based radio transmitters that are grouped in "chains." Loran chains are designed to provide accurate navigational fixes within 50 nautical miles from shore or out to the 100-fathom curve, whichever is greater. (In practice, usable Loran signals can be received at much greater distances.)

A Loran chain consists of one master transmitter (designated M) and two, three or four secondary transmitters (designated W, X, Y and Z), each of which sends out pulsed radio signals, on 100 kHz, which travel through the atmosphere at 186,000 miles per second. In order to enable Loran receivers to identify the source of these signals, the transmitters send out their pulses in sequence at precise intervals of an assigned number of microseconds (millionths of a second). The interval between transmissions from the master transmitter is referred to as the Group Repetition Interval (GRI), and each chain is assigned a distinctive GRI.

Assuming all transmitters in a chain are transmitting properly, fixes can be obtained from the system continuously. A typical Loran receiver updates its position approximately once every second.

Loran accuracy

Loran ground wave transmissions have a maximum range of 1,000 to 1,200 miles from their transmitters. Within the ground wave coverage area, the absolute accuracy of initial fixes normally is within 0.1 to 0.25 nautical miles.

The reason Loran is not totally accurate is that its functioning is based on the assumption that radio waves travel at a constant speed. That is true if they are passing over seawater, but where they must pass over land they can be distorted by soil conductivity and terrain features that are referred to as Additional Secondary Factors (ASF). The LOP overlays on the first generation of Loran charts were printed with no allowance for ASF. When field observation indicated the LOPs on some charts were off by as much as 2 miles, those charts were reissued to reflect the theoretical effects of ASF. In recent years, the Coast Guard has initiated a Chart Verification Program to correct Loran LOPs on the basis of observed rather than theoretical data, and the latest National Oceanic Survey (NOS) charts contain a notice to that effect. The Defense Mapping Agency Hydrographic/ Topographic Center (DMAHTC) publishes a series of Loran-C Correction Tables based on actual field observations which also can be used to offset some of the effects of time difference (TD) "warping," and thus improve accuracy.

The accuracy of Loran's repeatability—its ability to reestablish a position it has fixed earlier—is even greater than the absolute accuracy of initial fixes. In ideal situations it can be on the order of 50 feet. The reason is that because the ASF in a particular area are more or less constant, the error rate is approximately the same when an earlier Loran fix is used to reestablish the same location.

Loran sky waves can be received at ranges up to 3,000 miles, but the margin of error for fixes based on sky waves can be up to eight times greater than that of ground wave signals. This makes them virtually useless to yacht skippers unless they can be verified by another position-fixing system. Charts published by DMAHTC include sky wave correction factors, but even using these factors in plotting, the prudent mariner will still verify his position by some other means of navigation.

Loran should be used only with up-to-date nautical charts labeled as being based on the NAD-83 (North American Datum, 1983) or WGS-84 (World Geodetic System, 1984) datum systems. If used with older charts based on the NAD-27 datum, position errors of up to 160 meters will result.

If a Loran transmitter malfunctions, an element is incorporated into its signal that causes the display on receivers within its coverage area to blink, thereby alerting users that its signal should not be used for navigation.

On-board Loran equipment

Loran receivers for recreational marine use come in both handheld and installed models.

Some portable Loran receivers are designed only to be handheld and to operate off their integral antenna. Others can be either handheld and operated off an internal antenna or mounted in a holder at a vessel's navigation station or helm and connected to an external antenna. A handheld Loran receiver that is not connected to an external antenna lacks the ground required for optimum signal reception and therefore is significantly less accurate than a receiver that is connected to an external antenna.

Some installed Loran receivers include their signal acquisition and navigation computing equipment, along with their displays, in a single unit that is mounted at a vessel's navigation station or helm. Other installed receivers have their signal acquisition and computing equipment in one "black box," which can be mounted in an out-of-the-way location, and a separate display that is mounted at the navigation station or helm. The two components must be connected by cables. For vessels that have more than one helm, these units can power multiple displays from a single "black box."

A typical external Loran antenna is an 8-foot metal whip encased in fiberglass and connected to a coupler that adds about 1 to 1½ feet to its height. The antenna should be mounted as far as possible from metal objects such as masts and rigging. The receiver should be well rounded.

Loran receiver capabilities

While Loran receivers find position by TDs and can display position in that format, all Loran receivers also are able to convert TDs to latitude and longitude and express position in that format as well.

Most Loran receivers also have the ability to display course headings in either true or magnetic degrees and can allow for magnetic variation. More sophisticated Loran receivers have ASF correction built into their circuitry. In boundary areas where the coverage of two Loran chains

HOW A LORAN WORKS

Once a Loran receiver captures the radio signals from the master transmitter and one secondary transmitter in a chain whose geographical positions have been programmed into its memory, it measures the difference in time it took the two signals to reach it. Since speed, time and distance are interrelated, that time difference (TD) locates the receiver on a hyperbolic line-of-position (LOP). The receiver then repeats the process with signals from the master and a different secondary to establish a second line of position. Using the two TDs, that position can be plotted on a chart overprinted with a grid of Loran LOPs.

It is important to remember that, unlike the Global Positioning System (GPS), a Loran-C receiver is not concerned with its absolute distance from any transmitter, only with its relative distances from the master transmitter and the secondary transmitters in a given Loran chain.

Hyperbolic line of position

Assume that each ring represents not distance, but one second of time. If there is no time delay in the Loran signals received from both transmitters M and X, the vessel must lie along line A-A (not shown). If there is a two second time delay in the signal received from transmitter X, relative to the signals received from transmitter M, the receiver must lie along line B-B (not shown), which is a hyperbola (a curve generated by a point so moving that the difference of the distances from two fixed points is a constant).

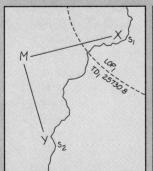
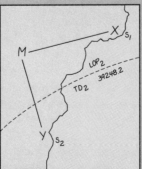
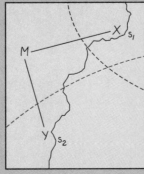

At far left, an LOP is set from TD1. At middle, another LOP is set from TD2. Position is the point where the LOPs cross, shown at near left.

overlap, more sophisticated Loran receivers will automatically select signals from the secondary transmitters providing the strongest signals, and if the vessel on which they are carried voyages from the coverage area of one Loran chain into the coverage area of another chain, will automatically switch to the new chain's GRI.

Like GPS receivers *(page 572 to 574)*, a full-function Loran receiver can tell a mariner a great deal more than his or her vessel's geographical position with a usable degree of accuracy. It can display elapsed time and distance from given points astern, and provide the vessel's cross-track error, with optional audible alarm. It can also calculate and display vessel course-over-ground and speed-of-advance, displaying the course required to reach points ahead ("waypoints") and how far away they are, and to indicate which way the helmsman should steer to stay on course. It can display how long it will take to reach a certain point and the vessel's ETA. It can also be interfaced with an autopilot to steer the vessel to waypoints in a route, and can sound an alarm as the vessel draws close to a particular location. Most Loran receivers can be programmed with a hundred or more waypoints in each of 10 or more routes.

Some Loran receivers also can be interfaced with a radar or video depth sounder to superimpose a digital display of vessel position, course and speed on the radar or video depth sounder screen. Some Loran receivers can be interfaced with electronic chart plotters to superimpose a graphic/digital display of position, course and speed on a monochrome or multicolored representation of a chart or a full-color digitized chart on the plotter's screen. Fully integrated Loran receivers incorporate Read Only Memory (ROM) cards for purposes of storing and displaying monochrome representations of navigation charts on their own screens, on which they can graphically/digitally superimpose the position, course and speed.

The Loran system discussed above is properly called Loran-C; Loran-A is now used only in Japanese waters.

LORAN CHAINS

Chain name	Group repetition interval
UNITED STATES	
Northeast U.S.	9960
Southeast U.S.	7980
North Central U.S.	8290
South Central U.S.	9610
Great Lakes	8970
U.S. West Coast	9940
Gulf of Alaska	7960
CANADA	
Canadian East Coast	5930
Canadian West Coast	5990
NORTH ATLANTIC	
Labrador Sea	7930
Norwegian Sea	7970
Icelandic	9980
PACIFIC OCEAN	
North Pacific	9990
Northwest Pacific	9970
East Asian (formerly Commando Lion)	5970
MEDITERRANEAN SEA	
Mediterranean Sea	7990
SAUDI ARABIA	
South Saudi Arabia	7170
North Saudi Arabia	8990
RUSSIA	
Eastern Russia	7950
Western Russia	8000
CHINA	
Chinese	6930

Both the operation and maintenance of overseas Loran systems is now being taken over by the governments in the areas that they serve.

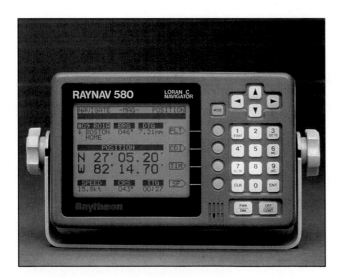

The Loran-C receiver shown at left incorporates a track plotter that can store up to 200 waypoints.

GLOBAL POSITIONING SYSTEM

The Global Positioning System (GPS) is an advanced, worldwide radionavigation system designed and operated by the U.S. Department of Defense (DOD) as the principal electronic navigation system for the military forces of the U.S. and its allies. The system is also available to civilian users at a level of accuracy somewhat less than that available to the military. The DOD began designing the system in 1973, and started launching initial test satellites in 1977. By 1991, enough satellites were in place to allow mariners to reliably determine latitude and longitude virtually anywhere in the world.

GPS is based on a constellation of 21 active and three fully functional but "spare" satellites which operate in six orbital planes at an altitude of 10,900 nautical miles (20,200 km) and at an inclination angle to the equator of 55 degrees. Each satellite takes approximately 12 hours to complete a single orbit and follows the same ground pattern on each orbit, but is observable from a fixed position on earth approximately four minutes earlier each 24 hours due to the difference between its orbital speed and the speed of the earth's rotation.

The satellites' orbits are subject to small, gradual changes. Since the entire system is based on the satellites being able to transmit their precise location in space to GPS receivers, their orbit information must be periodically updated. Satellite orbits are tracked by five monitoring stations, which feed data on changes to the system's Master Control Station at Colorado Springs, Colorado. The Master Control Station recomputes that information and feeds updated navigation messages back to the satellites through a network of five ground antennas.

Because of the altitude of the satellites and their orbital patterns, at least five satellites are observable by a ground-based GPS receiver at all times. This means fixes can be obtained from the system continuously. Signals from any three satellites are sufficient to fix latitude and longitude. Reception of signals from a fourth satellite is necessary only to determine altitude, which is not a requirement for recreational marine applications.

GPS accuracy

The Global Positioning System produces two levels of fix accuracy. One, the Standard Positioning Service (SPS), is available to all users and is stated by the DOD to produce fixes accurate to 100 meters (2 dRMS) 95 percent of the time. (The 2 dRMS qualification means that 95 percent of all fixes that can be obtained with the system at any one place will fall within the 100-meter accuracy level). A second, the Precision Positioning Service (PPS), is available only to the military forces of the U.S. and its allies and a very limited number of non-military users. Its guaranteed accuracy rate is 17.8 meters (2 dRMS) 95 percent of the time.

In practice, marine users of the Standard Positioning Service routinely obtain fixes accurate to within 25 to 30 meters and in some extreme cases to within less than 10 meters. These "excursions" into instances of greater accuracy, however, tend to be short-lived, and over a 24-hour period at a given loca-

tion the system will not perform at that level. Mariners should not assume a GPS fix is accurate to within less than 100 meters unless they can verify a closer accuracy rate by some other position-fixing means.

Discrimination between the two levels of accuracy are achieved by having each satellite transmit signals on two frequencies—L_1 at 1575.42 Mhz, and L_2 at 1227.6 Mhz. Non-military users are able to receive only the L_1 signal, which carries a Course/Acquisition code (C/A code).

The 100-meter guaranteed accuracy of fixes based on the C/A code could be approximately 30 meters except for the fact that, in the interest of national security, the DOD imposes on its transmission a technique called Selective Availability (S/A) which deliberately degrades its accuracy by introducing errors into the satellite clock and navigation message. Civilian users have brought significant pressure to bear on the DOD not to impose Selective Availability during periods of political stability and low levels of hostile threat, but so far the DOD has refused to alter its policy.

GPS should be used only with up-to-date nautical charts labeled as being based on the NAD-83 (North American Datum, 1983) or WGS-84 (World Geodetic System, 1984) datum systems. If used with older charts based on the NAD-27 datum, position errors of up to 160 meters may result.

GPS integrity

GPS has no inherent way to alert users if one or more satellites have malfunctioned and are transmitting incorrect data. This normally is not a problem for mariners because with five satellites in view at all times, their receivers can calculate a fix from three healthy satellites; it is a much greater problem for aviation users. This lack of integrity information in GPS, however, again points up the maxim that the prudent navigator will never rely on a single source for determining position but will always verify his position by at least one other navigational means. Differential GPS *(page 574)* incorporates an element that alerts users if a GPS satellite is malfunctioning.

Sequential vs. continuous tracking

The channels in a GPS receiver that receive the satellite signals must perform three tasks—acquire the satellites from which they will read messages, make pseudorange measurements to the satellites they are reading, and read the satellites' navigation messages to determine their orbital position from which vessel position is calculated. The strength of the satellites' signals required for a receiver to acquire (or re-acquire) them is about five times greater than the signal strength required for a receiver to track satellites and read their messages. The signals from satellites at a low elevation relative to a receiver are weakened as they must pass through more of the earth's atmosphere. A receiver's tracking of a satellite's signal can be broken if the satellite is momentarily shaded from the receiver's antenna by a vessel's mast or rigging or other structures.

In essence, what a marine GPS receiver does is to measure the distance between itself and three satellites in space, use those distances as the radii of three spheres, each having one of the satellites as its center, then with spherical geometry determine its position as the intersection of those three spheres.

Here's how it does that: The signal transmitted by each GPS satellite has two parts. One is a digital code, unique to that particular satellite, which identifies it. Superimposed over that code is a navigation message that contains updated information about that satellite's orbit (technically referred to as "ephemeris data"); what time it is as far as the satellite is concerned (GPS time); almanac data for all the satellites in the constellation; and coefficients the receiver can then plug into a computer model stored in its memory to calculate how the atmosphere is affecting the signal's transmission through the ionosphere. (This is known as its "propagation.")

The satellite tells the receiver the instant in GPS time that it transmitted its signal, and the receiver synchronizes itself (approximately) to GPS time. Since time, speed and distance are interrelated, by multiplying the difference between the time the satellite transmitted the signal and the time it reached the receiver by the signal's speed (186,000 statute miles per second), the receiver calculates its approximate distance (called a pseudorange) from the satellite. The receiver's computation of this distance could be absolutely accurate if it contained an atomic clock, but that would make the receiver prohibitively expensive. Instead, a GPS receiver uses for a time reference an affordable crystal oscillator that synchronizes it and the satellite with nearly but not total accuracy.

If the receiver could determine distance with absolute accuracy, signals from two satellites would be sufficient to fix latitude and longitude. Since it cannot determine distance with absolute accuracy, it acquires the pseudorange from a third satellite and adjusts the three pseudoranges in equal amounts until the three LOPs converge to determine the clock error in all three signals and eliminate it.

The receiver uses the pseudoranges it has computed from the satellites it is observing to solve three simultaneous equations (one for each satellite), with three unknowns (latitude, longitude and clock error), and produces an estimate of its position.

It next must account for its own velocity during the process of acquiring and processing the satellite signals. It does this by comparing the frequencies of the satellite signals against that of a reference signal the receiver generates internally. From the Doppler effect (the effect you note in the sound-wave frequency of a train's whistle as it approaches you, passes you, then recedes into the distance) the receiver computes its velocity relative to each of the satellites it is observing. It then recalculates the earlier three equations using velocity rather than pseudoranges. After using the solution to those three equations to allow for its own velocity in the earlier estimated position, the receiver produces a fix.

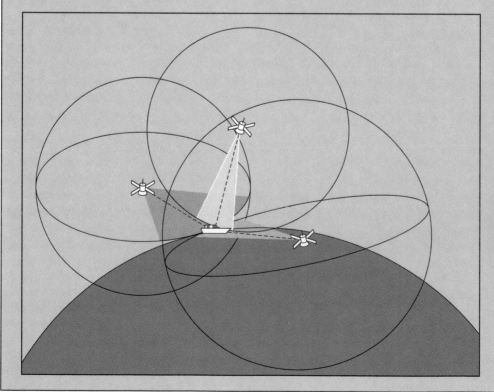

As shown in this illustration, a GPS receiver determines vessel position by taking virtually instantaneous readings from at least three satellites, each of whose position becomes the radius of a sphere. The receiver calculates the vessel's position as the point at which the three spheres intersect.

GPS receivers for recreational marine use have two basic types of channel configurations: Single-channel multiplexing units read the signals from one satellite at a time on one, two or three channels; multi-channel units read the signals simultaneously from three to six satellites.

A multiplexed GPS receiver is a sequential unit which uses one or more channels and switches up to 50 times per second to read the digital codes from the satellites it is observing; it reads the navigation message from all observable satellites continuously. This allows a multiplexed GPS receiver to compute and update fixes more rapidly than non-multiplexed sequential receivers, but since it still must re-acquire each satellite before reading its navigation message, it is less effective than more sophisticated receivers where satellite signal strength is weak.

A multi-channel continuous GPS receiver for boats employs from four to six channels to read the digital codes and navigation messages from satellites simultaneously, which allows it to compute and update fixes more rapidly than a single-channel multiplexing receiver. Since this type of receiver remains locked on a satellite and does not have to continually reacquire it to read its navigation message, it is far more effective than a single-channel (multiplexed) receiver in conditions where satellite signal strength is weak.

Portable vs. installed GPS receivers

GPS receivers are available in both portable and installed versions. Some portable GPS receivers are designed only to be handheld and operate off an integral antenna. Others can be handheld and operated off an integral antenna, or mounted in a holder at a vessel's navigation station or helm, using an externally mounted antenna and drawing power from the boat's electrical system.

Some installed GPS receivers include their signal acquisition and navigation computing equipment along with their display in a single unit that is mounted at a vessel's navigation station or helm. Other installed receivers have their signal acquisition and computing equipment in one "black box" that can be mounted in an out-of-the-way location and a separate display mounted at the navigation station or helm. The two components must be connected by cables. For vessels that have more than one helm, these units can operate multiple displays from a single "black box."

GPS antennas

External GPS antennas are small. Some are 1 to 2 inches in diameter and 12 to 15 inches high; others measure 6 inches in diameter but only 4 inches high. All must be mounted on a vessel's exterior with a 360-degree view of the horizon.

GPS receiver capabilities

A full-function GPS receiver can do a great deal more than simply tell a mariner his or her vessel's geographical position with a usable degree of accuracy. Because of its ability to

The advantage of a portable GPS receiver is that it is powered from internal batteries and can be taken from one boat to another. With the addition of an external antenna, its performance is fully as good as an installed unit, and it can be powered from the boat's electrical system.

"remember" previous locations and the time the vessel was at those locations, it can display elapsed time and distance from given points astern, and provide the vessel's cross-track error. It can also calculate and display vessel speed-of-advance and course-over-ground, display the course required to reach one or more "waypoints" entered by the skipper and how far away they are, and indicate which way the helmsman should steer to stay on course. Combining its knowledge of speed, time and distance, it can display how long it will take to reach a certain point and an estimated time of arrival (ETA). Most GPS receivers allow an operator to save vessel position at any time at the push of a button. This feature could be extremely valuable in a crew overboard situation.

Some GPS receivers can also be interfaced with an autopilot to steer a vessel to a waypoint or along a series of points (called a route), and can even sound an alarm as the vessel draws close to a particular location. Most GPS receivers can be programmed with as many as 100 or more waypoints in each of 9 or more routes, and can automatically sequence from one waypoint to the next in order. Some can automatically sequence from one route to the next.

Most GPS receivers can be interfaced with an automatic pilot so that the cross-track error information is used to steer the boat back onto course and reduce the error to zero. (But don't forget always to keep a sharp lookout for other vessels and navigational hazards.)

Some GPS receivers also can be interfaced with a radar or video depth sounder to superimpose a digital display of vessel position, course and speed on the radar or video depth sounder screen. Some GPS receivers can be interfaced with electronic chart plotters to superimpose a graphic/digital display of vessel position, course and speed on a monochrome representation of a chart or a full-color digitized chart on the plotter's screen.

Fully integrated GPS receivers incorporate Read Only Memory (ROM) cards for storing and displaying monochrome or multicolored chart representations on their own screens. These can also graphically or digitally superimpose on the chart representations of vessel position, course and speed.

Some GPS receivers can also be programmed to stand an anchor watch by describing a small circle around a vessel's anchored position and having the receiver sound an alarm if the vessel drifts outside that circle.

Differential GPS

In addition to Selective Availability, the accuracy of fixes obtained from GPS by civilian users of the system is further degraded by the fact that the C/A code contains only a predicted model of how the atmosphere is delaying GPS signals' propagation, not how it is affecting the signals in real time. Both of these sources of error, however, can be offset by a refinement of GPS called Differential GPS (DGPS).

DGPS is being developed by the U.S. Coast Guard to provide the 8- to 20-meter acccuracy required for harbor and

This six-channel continuous satellite tracking GPS receiver updates vessel position approximately every second. The instrument can store up to 20 different routes, with as many as 20 different waypoints in each route.

COMPUTERS ON BOARD

Computers—in the form of microchips—are now at the heart of virtually every piece of marine electronic equipment. Increasingly, boaters are installing on-board computer systems to assist them in the operation of their vessels.

With the advent of solid-state technology, which packages more and more power and versatility in smaller and smaller components, using a sophisticated personal computer with a rechargeable power supply aboard a recreational vessel is not difficult or complicated.

Typical desktop personal computers require 120-volt AC power input, but that's because they are designed primarily for use on land where that is the power normally available. In fact, the computer circuits themselves run on less than 6 volts of DC electrical current, which is provided by the computer's "power supply" (a step-down rectifying transformer that converts 120-volt AC power to multiple DC voltage such as 12, 5 or 3.3). The easiest way to install a personal computer aboard a boat with 12-volt battery power is to use an inverter that changes the battery's 12-volt DC power to 120-volt AC power, which the computer's power supply will then step down and rectify to the required voltages. The computer's power supply should be via a dedicated circuit with its own breaker on the main distribution panel to protect it from sudden voltage drops as other equipment comes on and off line. The computer should then be connected to the inverter through a surge protector to guard against sudden voltage spikes.

At 120-volt input, the current draw of a personal computer is on the order of 2 amps (200 watts). If the AC power is being produced by an inverter, that equates to approximately a 23-amp DC draw on a 12-volt system, after allowing for the inverter's 15 percent efficiency loss. While this is an easily manageable power level aboard a boat equipped with an AC generator, it would be too great for a vessel that relies strictly on an engine alternator to recharge its batteries.

On board smaller boats without AC generators, "laptop" and "notebook" computers can be operated for several hours on the power of their internal batteries. With some portable computers it is possible to recharge the battery externally by using a small solid-state DC voltage converter to change the boat's electrical power, actually about 13.2 volts, to an appropriate voltage for the battery concerned; great care should be taken to avoid damage to the computer battery as a result of charging too rapidly or for too long a period of time. This should *not* be attempted with the battery installed in the computer unless this is specifically approved by the manufacturer. The drain from the boat's power system is so small—less than one amp—that it should present no problem. Some newer models of these computers have inputs for external full-sized keyboards and monitors, making them, in effect, compact, lightweight central processing units.

Precautions

There are certain cautions to keep in mind regarding computer installation on board a boat:

■ Computer equipment must be carefully protected from rain and spray, and should be run frequently to dry its internal parts.

■ Disk and CD-ROM drives and printers have moving parts that can be damaged by vibration and shock. They must be mounted securely and cushioned as much as possible. Laptop and notebook computers that are designed to travel are more resistant to shock and vibration, but even they should be cushioned when underway.

■ Computer circuits often generate radio interference and should be mounted well away from sensitive navigation and communications electronics.

harbor approach navigation that cannot be provided by the Standard Positioning Service of GPS alone, whether or not Selective Availability is activated.

The system employs a series of fixed reference stations, whose precise geographical coordinates are known. As these reference stations receive signals from Global Positioning System satellites, they compare their position as indicated by the satellite signals with their known position, and compute the difference, generating a compensating correction for each. These reference stations then broadcast corrected pseudorange data which specially designed GPS receivers within their broadcast range can use to improve their fix computations; these have an additional radio receiver and a data processing unit.

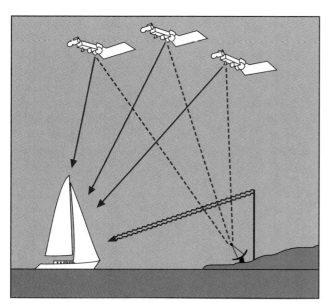

Differential GPS employs land-based sites, in addition to satellites, to accurately determine position.

The broadcasts are made over frequencies already approved by international treaties for maritime radionavigation beacons. Though DGPS is initially planned as a harbor and harbor approach system, the overlapping coverage of its transmitters ultimately will provide DGPS for all the coastal waters of the contiguous United States, including the Great Lakes, Alaska, Hawaii and Puerto Rico and out to about 200 to 250 nautical miles offshore.

In DGPS, a separate, independent integrity monitor is associated with each reference station; this can alert users if a satellite is transmitting an unreliable signal.

On-board DGPS equipment

To utilize the pseudorange corrections transmitted by DGPS, a GPS receiver must be capable of utilizing the SC104 Version 2.0 data format in which they are broadcast, and must have circuitry to receive the radiobeacon signals either through an add-on device or as part of their internal mechanism.

Many small items of electronic equipment can be installed on a boat for the greater safety and convenience of those aboard. Remember that each extra item will add to the load on the battery and electrical wiring. Although they are not all directly related to navigation purposes, they are nonetheless considered important by many boaters.

■ **Emergency position indicating radiobeacon (EPIRB).** Refer to Chapter 24.

■ **Fuel vapor detectors** provide a visual, and in most units an audible, warning of the buildup of any dangerous concentration of fuel vapors in the bilges. It is important to remember that these units are not an absolutely positive means of warning of a hazardous condition; they are not as infallible as the human nose. If in doubt, open the hatches and use your nose—it is the best "bilge sniffer."

■ **Rudder position indicators.** A small unit is installed at the rudder post and wires are run forward to a meter located within easy view of the helmsman. This meter is calibrated in degrees of right or left rudder. A quick glance will tell the exact position of the rudder at that moment.

■ **Engine synchronization indicators.** Twin-engine boats, whether inboard or outboard, gasoline or diesel, operate most smoothly when the two engines are "in synch"—turning at the same rpm. A skipper can tell if the engines are synchronized by their sound, but an even better job can be done by this small electronic device. Some models use a panel meter with a needle that swings to one side or the other, indicating the engine that is turning more slowly; other models use a flashing light or a series of LEDs to indicate synchronization conditions. This concept can be carried one step further to a device that actually synchronizes the speed of the two engines—the throttle of one is "slaved" to the other.

■ **Carbon monoxide detectors.** Carbon monoxide poisoning, described in Chapter 9, is more hazardous on gasoline-powered boats than on those with diesel engines. It is most likely to be a problem with blunt-stern craft; the more blunt the stern, the more likely the exhaust gases will be drawn into the hull and occupied spaces.

■ **Wind instruments** are used on sailboats to measure wind speed and direction at the masthead; display is at the helm. Displays can be combined or separate, digital or analog. Wind direction is measured as relative; an input of the boat's heading can change this to true wind.

THE BOATING COMMUNITY

26 BOATING CUSTOMS

Boating is an informal kind of recreation, no longer bound to the ceremony of "yachting etiquette." However, there are many occasions when proper observances are expected, even if only as common courtesy to your boating neighbors.

You need not belong to a yacht club, but it helps to understand club practices that you encounter. You should be able to recognize a race in progress, for example, and take steps to avoid it. Likewise, you should be able to drop your hook in an anchorage, make fast at a marina or raft up with other boats without causing friction. You should also know the proper procedures for displaying flags.

This chapter covers the customs and traditions that remain a part of recreational boating today. They simply represent good sense and good manners afloat.

COURTESY AFLOAT

Except when cruising the high seas, or some remote inland waters, you will generally be boating within sight of other boats. Often you will be close enough that any maneuvers you make, even activities on board your boat, will have an impact on others. Some actions are beyond those required by the Navigation Rules, which apply only when a danger of collision exists. The situations suggested below are a matter of good manners, of causing the least interference to the vessel with the most limited maneuverability.

When underway

A faster boat overtaking close to a slower one in open waters should slow down sufficiently to cause no damage or discomfort. Often overlooked is the fact that it may be necessary for the slower boat itself to reduce speed. For example, if the slower boat is making 8 knots, the faster boat can slow only to about 10 knots in order to have enough speed differential left to get past. But at that speed the passing boat may make a wave that is uncomfortable to the other craft. The overtaken boat should slow to about 4 knots to allow the other boat to pass at 6 or 7 knots with little wake.

If adequate depth of water extends outward on one or both sides of the course, it is courteous for the passing boat to swing well out to the safe side in order to minimize the discomfort to the overtaken boat. A powerboat, of course, should pass a sailboat well to leeward, or astern of it in a crossing situation.

Near regattas and other events

A fleet of sailboats all headed in the same general direction is a sure indication of a race in progress. While it might be possible to pass through such a fleet "legally," observing the proper Navigation Rules, this action might interfere with the courses and tactics of the racing skippers. Stay well clear so that neither your wake nor your "wind shadow" will have any effect on the race boats.

Although cruising-type sailboats engaged in a long-distance race may not be easy to identify as competitors in an event, whether such a boat is racing or just cruising, it is best to take no action which would interfere with its progress.

Marine parades, powerboat races and other such events may be held—with a regatta permit from the USCG—in waters otherwise subject to normal marine traffic. The Coast Guard, Coast Guard Auxiliary or the organization sponsoring the event may provide patrol boats to keep non-participating craft clear of the event. You must obey instructions given from any such patrol boat. In addition to the danger of blundering out into the path of speeding race boats, it is discourteous to interfere with the performance of any regatta.

Anchorages, moorings and marinas

Be a good boating neighbor when you drop the hook in an anchorage, lie at a mooring, or make fast at a yacht club or marina pier. Enter an anchorage dead slow; a wake that upsets

TIPS FOR GUESTS ON BOARD

Whether you plan to invite guests along on a cruise for a day, a weekend or a more extended period, let them know in advance what is expected of them, particularly if they are without previous cruising experience.

Tell them to bring a minimum of clothes appropriate for the season and the destination—including swimsuits, and even shorewear if you will be stopping at yacht clubs or sightseeing. Explain the limited storage space aboard, and be sure to suggest that they pack all gear in duffle bags or other collapsible containers. Assign each guest a locker, which you have cleared, for the clothing brought aboard; let guests know they are not to leave clothes or gear scattered about as it may interfere with the operation of your boat.

When you give a sailing time, explain that this is based on tide, currents, normal weather patterns and length of the planned trip—or whatever might be the case—and that guests should be on board and ready to leave well before this sailing time.

Explain also that rising and bedtimes are a matter of convenience to everyone on board, due to the limited washing and toilet facilities. As skipper, you should be the first to rise in the morning. Hearing you up and about will signal to others that it is time to get up. Likewise, let it be known in the evening when you announce that it's time to retire, everyone is obliged to do so.

Give guests precise instructions for use of the manual or electric head. Point out the importance of applying sunscreen; in order to avoid grease on fiberglass or teak decking, explain that hands must be washed or wiped with a towel after applying sunscreen.

Acquaint guests with all safety and emergency procedures covered in Chapters 3 and 4. Explain why they must stop smoking when fuel is taken on, for example, and why care must be taken even when smoking is permitted. A carelessly slipped cigarette ash or butt can start a fire in a berth, awning or compartment. Let cigar- or pipe-smoking guests know they can enjoy their smokes in the open air (when smoking is permitted on your boat), but that in confined spaces of cabins these may be offensive to others.

Point out that small particles of anything (such as pipe tobacco and ashes, peanut shells, bits of potato chips or crumbs) have a way of getting into cracks and corners, beyond the reach of ordinary cleaning facilities that are found on a boat.

Note that there is some controversy about your guests sharing in the expenses of a cruise. This could be viewed by the USCG as a partial charter and commercial operation, as explained in Chapter 2.

someone's dinner or drink will not win friends among the other boaters. In addition, refrain from the unnecessary use of spotlights. Avoid anchoring too close to other boats: Keep in mind that a wind shift changes a boat's position; anchor rodes can foul in a matter of minutes, and hulls can be damaged if they bang together. Remember the first boat to anchor has a right to appropriate swinging radius. Also consider the state of the tide and the effect of its range on your swinging radius. If a guest mooring is free, use it only after you have obtained permission; it may be reserved for another boat, or it may be unsuitable for your vessel. As for fuel piers, make fast to them only briefly. When others are waiting, never use fueling time as an opportunity to make a trip to the store. Likewise, when boating in some salt-water areas, avoid using a marina's limited fresh-water reserves to wash your boat; ask first for permission.

In the evening hours, take care not to disturb people on other boats in the area. Sound travels exceptionally well across water, and many cruising boat crews turn in early for dawn departures. You should resist the temptation to visit among the other boats with a dinghy and outboard motor. The quiet of using oars will be appreciated by others. Make sure that those aboard your boat keep their voices down and play music only at low levels. Remember that any comments you make about other boats will carry as well. If you are one of the early departees, leave the mooring with an absolute minimum of noise.

When rafting, the boat that will be last to leave is the one to take the mooring, lie alongside the pier or wharf or drop the anchor (provided ground tackle is adequate). The others should lash up in order of departure, so that the first to leave will be farthest outboard.

Whether on the water for the day, or departing for an extended cruise, taking the family pet along includes extra responsibilities. Fair weather or foul, you must be prepared to take a dog ashore periodically—and to pick up after it.

Don't throw trash and garbage overboard; even if it is biodegradable, it is unsightly and illegal. Secure any flapping halyards; they can be a most annoying source of noise (and can chafe the surface of the mast). When coming into or leaving an anchorage or boat basin, do so at dead slow speed to keep your wake at an absolute minimum. Remember that you are responsible for any damage caused by your wake. Pets should be well trained to avoid barking in an anchorage. Exercise them ashore in authorized areas, or well away from normal traffic areas; make sure you pick up after your pet. When you go ashore, for whatever reason, leave the area as you found it—or even cleaner. Observe all signs and regulations, extinguish fires and dispose of refuse if permitted.

When two or more boats are rafted, the boat at anchor (according to plan, the last one to leave) must have adequate ground tackle. All rafted boats should be well protected by fenders.

Cruising in company

When in a group cruise, maintain speed and keep a constant distance from the other boats, according to a pre-arranged plan. Agree in advance about places to stop for fuel, supplies, sightseeing or other reasons. Do not use VHF-FM marine radio for social communication between boats: This equipment is for safety and operational traffic only. CB radio, however, is suitable for social use.

If you are rafted, avoid crossing from one boat to another unnecessarily and, unless you are on informal terms with your neighbors, ask permission before you do so. Be sure to supply your share of fenders, fenderboards and lines—as well as ingredients for parties and meals that are planned.

At an anchorage or marina, turn down radios or similar equipment and keep other noise levels low. Many boating crews turn in early after a day's cruise.

Clubs and organizations

If you are a member of a recognized yacht club, it is customary for other yacht clubs to extend you courtesies—the use of guest slips, moorings and clubhouse facilities, for example. Remember, though, that proper procedure requires asking permission to use such facilities, even if you wish to make fast briefly at the club dock to pick up a member who is planning to join you.

When visiting a yacht club of which you are not a member, take the time to inform yourself about the actions and routines of the local owner-members and club officers. This can be especially important in respect to evening "colors," or flags: Remember that not all clubs strictly calculate the daily time of sunset, and some sunset signals for colors may be earlier than you would normally expect.

Yacht clubs and organizations such as the United States Power Squadrons generally have by-laws or handbooks that spell out requirements for ceremonial procedures, such as the exchange of salutes, daily color ceremonies, salutes between vessels, precedence in boarding or leaving launches, and flag courtesies.

In many cases an 0800 gun is sounded as a signal to raise colors and a sunset gun for lowering colors. If you expect to be away from your boat at the time of sunset, take in your flag before you leave the boat.

If hired personnel are not on hand when a boat is coming in to make fast near your position, it is good manners to offer to help with the docking lines. (In fact, many a long-lasting friendship has begun this way.) Always ask permission before boarding another boat. As for approaching an anchored or moored boat in your dinghy or tender, traditional naval practice suggests pulling up alongside that boat's starboard side.

CHRISTENING A BOAT

There are three ceremonies that can be celebrated during the construction, naming and commissioning of a vessel—those that observe the keel laying, christening and launching of the ship or boat. Although all three began with strict protocol, recent practice has dispensed with much of the pomp and has introduced lots of variation in the ceremony.

Among recreational boaters, a combined naming and launching ceremony is the most common celebration—a good occasion for a social get-together, which may be combined with a short cruise. Although tradition dictates that the "sponsor" of the ship (usually a woman, often the owner's wife) names the ship and breaks a bottle of champagne against the bow, these days, the woman involved is probably the co-owner. Mothers, sisters, daughters and nieces also qualify, and many owners choose their children to perform the naming and bottle breaking.

While you may design the spiritual and social side of this occasion according to your own tastes and beliefs (blessing the boat, toasting the voyage, etc.), you should be much stricter about the practical side of breaking a champagne bottle on your boat. Following a "tradition" that some say originated in Polynesia, some boat owners choose a gentler approach to christening with champagne by simply pouring it over the bow, as pictured on page 578. If you do decide on the more dramatic breaking-the-bottle approach, however, first take some time to score the surface of the bottle with a glass cutter or a file. (Champagne bottles are surprisingly robust.) Guard against flying glass by applying tape around the bottle. Have the sponsor practice a few swings before the ceremony, and provide instructions about what to hit—she should probably aim for the metal stemhead, though most fiberglass hulls won't flinch.

The usual form of the naming is "I hereby christen you ...," and then the vessel is lowered into the water, or slipped down the ways. You and the builder will have to decide, in advance, who will buy lunch.

Flags are flown aboard boats and on shore to convey a variety of information to the boating community. An ensign—the national flag—identifies the country of registration. A burgee indicates a yacht club or boating organization of which the boat owner is a member. Other flags give information about the owner—office held in a club or organization, for example. A pennant, such as some of those shown on pages 588 and 589, is generally a signal flag. The flags shown below include flags commonly seen on boats in North America.

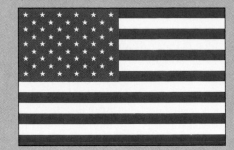

U.S. NATIONAL ENSIGN AND MERCHANT FLAG
Is flown from the stern staff of all boats at anchor and underway according to the circumstances (page 583).

U.S. YACHT ENSIGN
Is the proper flag to display except in international or foreign waters.

U.S. CUSTOMS FLAG
Flies at every U.S. Customs Service office.

U.S. COAST GUARD ENSIGN
Is flown day and night on active USCG units afloat or ashore.

MEXICAN NATIONAL ENSIGN
Identifies Mexican vessels.

CANADIAN NATIONAL ENSIGN
Identifies Canadian vessels—naval, mercantile or pleasure—and Canadian Customs offices.

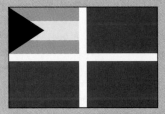

BAHAMAS CIVIL ENSIGN
Flown by ships and boats of all sizes; different from flag flown ashore.

YACHT CLUB BURGEE
May be triangular (typical of many designs) or swallow-tailed.

YACHT CLUB COMMODORE FLAG
Identifies the Commodore's boat.

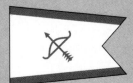

YACHT PRIVATE SIGNAL
Individual yacht owners may have their own flags; the one above is typical.

YACHT PROTEST
Also International Code flag "B," is seen at sailing races and other events.

TRANSPORTATION OR TENDER FLAG
Is used on launch service boats and as International Code flag "T."

DIVER'S FLAG,
Generally flown on a small float near a diver, warns other craft to "stay clear."

RIGID REPLICA OF INTERNATIONAL CODE FLAG "A"
Signals underwater operations as specified in the Navigational Rules, 27(e).

REQUIRED MEDICAL ASSISTANCE
Also International Code "W." Refer to Chapter 24 for significance of International flags.

THE ETIQUETTE OF FLAGS

There is no legislation governing the flying of any flag on numbered, undocumented or unlicensed vessels. However, through the years, customs have been established for the types of flags that may be flown, and when and where they are to be displayed. In recent years new procedures have evolved, such as flying the national ensign from the stern staff of a sailboat underway.

The term *colors* actually applies only to the flag at the stern of a vessel to denote the boat's nationality. In practice, however, it has come to be used for all flags flown, and will be used in that context in this chapter.

In general, it is not considered proper practice to fly more than one flag on a single hoist. There are a few exceptions, however. Many vessels, because of their size or construction, cannot accommodate single hoisting; these may multiple hoist where necessary, with proper order of precedence observed.

U.S. Power Squadrons guidelines for flag display are given in the chart on page 584. Pages 588-589 show the flags, pennants and burgees that may be flown from American-owned recreational boats, and the proper methods for their display.

Flying various flags

■ **The United States ensign.** The U.S. ensign is proper for all U.S. craft without reservation. This is "Old Glory," with 50 stars and 13 stripes. It is flown from the stern staff of powerboats underway on inland waters. On the high seas it need be flown only when meeting or passing other vessels. If the powerboat has a mast and gaff, the proper display is at the gaff. On a sportfisherman, where a stern staff would be in the way of the action, the practice is to fly the ensign from a halyard rigged just behind the tuna tower.

On Marconi-rigged sailboats under sail alone, the practice for many years had been to fly the ensign from the leech of the aftermost sail, approximately two-thirds the length of the leech above the clew. This puts it in about the same position it would occupy if the boat were gaff-rigged, and on gaff-rigged sailboats it is still proper to fly the ensign from the peak of the aftermost gaff.

The advent of the modern high-aspect-ratio rig, with the boom end well inboard of the stern, has made it possible to fly the ensign from the stern staff of a sailboat underway, and this is now accepted practice. However, the ensign should never be displayed while the boat is racing. Under power alone, or at anchor or made fast, the ensign should be flown from the stern staff of all sailboats. If an overhanging boom requires that the staff be off-center, it should be on the starboard side.

■ **The United States yacht ensign.** This is the 13-star "Betsy Ross" flag, with a fouled anchor in the union. Originally restricted to documented vessels of a specific classification, it is now flown on recreational boats of all types and sizes instead of the National Flag. Many yacht clubs now follow bylaws requiring that the U.S. yacht ensign be flown regardless of boat size or documentation status. Whenever a boat is tak-en into international or foreign waters, however, the 50-star U.S. ensign is the proper flag to display.

■ **The United States Power Squadrons ensign.** The USPS ensign is flown as a signal that the boat is commanded by a USPS member in good standing. The USPS, described in Chapter 27, is a national fraternity of boaters dedicated to better and safer boating through education and civic service.

The preferred location for flying the USPS ensign is the starboard yardarm or spreader, underway or at anchor, or made fast to shore, on motor and sailing craft. It may be flown from the stern staff in place of the U.S. or yacht ensign, but this is usually done only on smaller boats that lack a mast. On sailboats underway, it may be flown from the aftermost peak or leech in place of other ensigns.

The USPS ensign may be flown at its proper location on boats displaying the USCG Auxiliary ensign to indicate that the owner is a member of both organizations; however, it cannot be flown if the craft is under U.S. Coast Guard orders.

■ **The U.S. Coast Guard Auxiliary ensign.** Known as the "blue ensign," the USCG Auxiliary ensign is flown on a boat that has been approved as a "Facility" by the organization for the current year, as described in Chapter 27. This flag is flown both day and night.

On a vessel without a mast, the blue ensign is flown at the bow staff; if there is one mast, it is flown at the masthead. On a vessel with two or more masts, the USCG Auxiliary ensign is displayed at the main masthead. It is never flown in place of the national ensign.

When this ensign is displayed, it is improper to hoist a guest, owner absent, meal, cocktail or other novelty flag.

■ **The United States Coast Guard Auxiliary operational ensign.** The boat of a member of the USCG Auxiliary that meets a particularly high standard of equipment and availability is called an "Operational Facility," and can be called on for use under Coast Guard orders in assistance and patrol missions. When operating under USCG orders, these boats fly the U.S. Coast Guard Auxiliary operational ensign—white with the Coast Guard's "racing stripes" of red and blue—in place of the "blue ensign."

■ **The yacht club burgee.** Generally triangular in shape, although sometimes swallow-tailed, the yacht club burgee may be flown by day only, or by day and night, as defined by the individual yacht club. It is flown from the bow staff of mastless and single-masted powerboats, at the foremost masthead of vessels with two or more masts, and the main masthead of ketches or yawls. The burgee may be flown while underway (but not racing) and at anchor. You may substitute the owner's private signal for the burgee on single-masted yachts without bow staff, when the boat is underway.

■ **The Squadron pennant.** A distinguishing USPS squadron pennant which has been authorized by the U.S. Power Squadrons may be flown in lieu of a club burgee and from the same positions. This pennant may be flown by day only, or both day and night.

USPS GUIDE TO ON-BOARD FLAG DISPLAY

Flag	When Flown	Power Yacht Without Mast	Power Yacht With Signal Mast	Sailing Yacht With One Mast	Power Or Sail Yacht With Two Masts
U.S. Ensign, U.S. Yacht Ensign	0800 to sunset	Flag staff	Flag staff	Flag staff. Optional when underway: peak of gaff if so rigged or ⅔ up leech of mainsail	Flag staff. Optional when underway: peak of aftermost gaff if so rigged or ⅔ up leech of aftermost sail
Foreign Ensign	According to local custom when in foreign waters	Bow staff	Starboard spreader (outboard halyard)	Starboard spreader (outboard halyard)	Starboard spreader (outboard halyard) of foremost mast
	When foreign dignitary on board	Bow staff	Bow staff	Forestay	Bow staff or forestay
USPS Ensign	Day and night except 0800 to sunset when flown in lieu of U.S. ensign*. Only when in commission and under command of USPS member	Antenna amidships or, if no suitable antenna, from bow staff*	Starboard spreader. If foreign ensign flown: Inboard starboard spreader halyard, if equipped, or port spreader*	As for power yacht with signal mast*	Foremost starboard spreader*
Officer (Incumbent or past)	Day and night when in commission	Radio antenna (beneath USPS ensign); bow staff	Masthead	Masthead	Aftermost masthead
Private Signal (House Flag)	Day and night when in commission	Bow staff	Masthead	Masthead	Aftermost masthead
Squadron Burgee, Yacht Club Burgee	Day and night when in commission	Bow staff	Bow staff	Masthead (or bow staff if so equipped)	Foremost masthead (or bow staff if so equipped)
Union Jack	0800 to sunset when not underway on Sundays or holidays or when dressing ship	(Not flown)	(Not flown)	(Not flown)	Jack staff
Officer-in-Charge	Day and night during activity of which in charge	Above officer flag	Above officer flag	Above officer flag	Above officer flag
Cruise Pennant	Day and night during organized water activity	Radio antenna (above USPS ensign)	Where best seen	Where best seen	Where best seen
Owner Absent	Day and night when owner not on board	(Not flown)	Starboard spreader but inboard of foreign or USPS ensign if flown (or at port spreader if necessary)	As for power yacht with signal mast	Foremost starboard spreader as for power yacht with signal mast
Guest	Day and night when owner absent and guests in charge	(Not flown)	As for Owner Absent	As for Owner Absent	As for Owner Absent

*In U.S. waters the USPS ensign may be flown in lieu of (and at the same times and locations as) the U.S. ensign.

The United States Power Squadrons fulfills its mandate to provide information to the boating community at large by designing education aids, including the chart above. This quick-reference guide identifies flags, pennants and burgees that may be flown from U.S.-owned recreational boats, and the proper methods for their display.

■ **Owner's private signal.** This is generally swallow-tailed in shape, but it may be rectangular or pennant-shaped. It is flown from the masthead of a single-masted motorboat or sailboat, or from the aftermost mast of a power or sailing vessel with two or more masts. It may be flown by day only, or day and night.

A mastless motorboat may fly this signal from the bow staff in place of a club burgee.

■ **Officer flags.** Flags designating yacht club or USPS officers are rectangular in shape, blue (with white design) for senior officers; red for next lower in rank; and white (with blue design) for lower ranks. Other officers' flags (except fleet captain and fleet surgeon) may be swallow-tailed or triangular in shape, as provided in the regulations of those organizations making provisions for such flags.

An officer flag is flown in place of the owner's private signal on all rigs of motor and sailing vessels except single-masted sailboats, when it is flown in place of the club burgee at the masthead. On smaller motorboats without a signal mast, a USPS officer flag may be flown from a radio antenna either singly or beneath the USPS ensign.

■ **USCG Auxiliary officer flags.** The flag of a USCG Auxiliary officer flies day and night when the officer is on board. On a vessel without a mast, it is flown at the bow staff in place of the Auxiliary ensign; on a vessel with a mast, it is flown at the starboard spreader. Past officers' burgees are displayed in the same manner.

Only one officer's pennant may be flown at a time, and an incumbent officer's pennant invariably takes precedence. When the USCG Auxiliary ensign is displayed, it is considered improper to hoist a guest, owner absent, meal, cocktail or other novelty flag.

Size of flags

Although flags come in a fixed, standardized series of sizes, there are guidelines that will help in selecting the proper size for your boat.

Keeping in mind that flags are more often too small than too large, use the rules given below, and round upward to the nearest larger standard size:

The flag at the stern of your boat—U.S. ensign, yacht ensign or USPS ensign—should be one inch on the fly for each foot of overall length. The hoist will normally be two-thirds of the fly, but some flags such as the USCG Auxiliary ensign have different proportions.

Other flags such as club burgees, officers' flags, and private signals for use on sailboats should be approximately ½ inch on the fly for each foot of the highest mast above the water. For flying on powerboats, these flags should be roughly ⅝ inch on the fly for each foot of overall length. The shape and proportions of pennants and burgees will be prescribed by the appropriate organization to which they relate. A Union Jack should be the same size as the corresponding portion of the National Ensign.

GUIDE TO MISCELLANEOUS FLAGS

■ **Diver down**
There are two flags flown in connection with diving operations, a red flag with a single diagonal stripe of white, and a rigid replica of the International Code flag "A." It is not proper for them to be flown on shore.

■ **Race committee or regatta committee flag**
This is a blue rectangular flag with a single vertical fouled anchor in white with the letters "R" and "C" alongside the anchor in white or red. This flag is frequently large, and may be flown at any position for greatest visibility. Often other flags are taken down to avoid confusion.

■ **Transportation or tender flag**
This flag is used in many harbors where boats lie at moorings, and where yacht clubs or commercial operators provide launch (water taxi) service to and from the shore. This is the International Code flag "T"; it is normally used with a sound signal.

■ **Quarantine flag**
International Code letter "Q" is flown when entering a foreign port (except Canada and a few others), or returning to a U.S. port from a foreign cruise. It signals that the vessel is "healthy" and requests clearance into the port; it is taken down after customs and immigration formalities have been completed.

■ **Protest flag**
International Code flag "B" is seen at sailing or other contests. It signals that the vessel flying it will file a protest on another vessel (or vessels) at the event's conclusion.

■ **Man overboard**
The generally recognized signal is the International Code flag for the letter "O"; this flag is often fixed to a staff, which in turn is attached to a life ring.

■ **Union Jack**
A rectangular blue flag with 50 stars—the upper quadrant of the national ensign nearest the hoist. It may be flown only at the jack staff on sailing yachts or the jack staff of motor yachts with more than one mast only during the day, and only while not underway on Sundays and national holidays, or when "dressing ship." On modern craft, the normal bow staff is used as the "jack staff."

Raising and lowering flags

"Colors are made" each morning at 0800; as mentioned, at yacht club and similar organization docks or anchorages, this may be signaled by a morning gun. The national ensign or yacht ensign is hoisted at the stern (or set in place on its staff). This is followed by the USPS ensign at the starboard spreader (if not already flying on a day-and-night basis), provided the skipper is a USPS member. Then comes the club burgee or Squadron pennant at the bow, and the private signal at the masthead. (An officer's flag, if flown in place of a private signal, would be flown continuously.)

If the boat bears a valid USCG Auxiliary Facility decal, it would be flying the Auxiliary ensign at the masthead, day and night. The USCG Auxiliary officer's pennant or burgee may be flown, day and night, at the starboard spreader. On smaller craft, the same sequence should be followed, with the flags on their staffs being set in the appropriate locations as illustrated on pages 588-589.

At sunset, colors not properly flown on a day-and-night basis should be lowered in reverse sequence, the ensign at the stern always being the last to be secured. A cannon report also may be used as a sunset signal.

Dressing ship

On national holidays, at regattas and on other special occasions, yachts often "dress ship" with International Code signal flags. Officers' flags, club burgees and national flags are not used. A ship is dressed at 0800, and remains so dressed until evening colors (while at anchor only, except for a vessel's maiden and final voyages, and participation in a marine parade or other unique situation).

In dressing ship, the yacht ensign is hoisted at the stern staff, and the Union Jack may be displayed at the jack (bow) staff. A rainbow of flags of the International Code is arranged, reaching from the water line forward to the water line aft, by way of the bowsprit end (or stem if no bowsprit exists) and the masthead(s). Flags and pennants are bent on alternately, rather than in an indiscriminate manner. Since there are twice as many letter flags as numeral pennants, it is good practice, as in the Navy, to follow a sequence of two flags, one pennant, two flags, one pennant, throughout. The sequence recommended here provides a harmonious color pattern throughout: Starting from forward: AB2, UJ1, KE3, GH6, IV5, FL4, DM7, PO Third Repeater, RN First Repeater, ST Zero, CX9, WQ8, ZY Second Repeater.

Honoring other national flags

As a matter of courtesy, it is proper to fly the flag of a foreign nation on your boat when you enter and operate on its waters. There are only a limited number of positions from which flags may be displayed; consequently, when a flag of another nation is flown, it usually must displace one of the flags commonly displayed in home waters. It is not hoisted until clearance has been completed and the yellow "Q" flag has been removed.

The following are general guidelines to follow regarding courtesy flags:

■ On a mastless powerboat, the courtesy flag of another nation replaces any flag that is normally flown at the bow of the boat.

■ When a motorboat has a mast with spreaders, the courtesy flag is flown at the starboard spreader.

■ On a two-masted motorboat, the courtesy flag displaces any flag normally flown at the forward starboard spreader.

■ On a sailboat, the courtesy flag is flown at the boat's starboard spreader, whether the United States ensign is at the stern staff, or flown from the leech. If there is more than one mast, the courtesy flag is flown from the starboard spreader of the forward mast.

Although these points serve as protocol in most waters, keep in mind that customs observed in various foreign waters differ from one another; in case of doubt, inquire locally or observe other craft from your country.

As noted previously, it is preferable for U.S. vessels while in international or foreign waters to fly the U.S. ensign (50-star flag) at the stern or gaff or leech, rather than the USPS ensign or the yacht ensign. When the starboard spreader is used for the "courtesy ensign" of the foreign country, the USPS ensign or similar flag may be flown from the port spreader; if the vessel has multiple flag halyards on the starboard spreader, the USPS ensign is flown there, inboard from the courtesy ensign.

The U.S. ensign, club burgee, officer's flag and private signal are flown as in home waters.

Do not fly a foreign courtesy ensign after you have returned to U.S. waters. Although this may show that you've "been there," it is not proper flag etiquette.

Display of state flags

Any citizen of any state may fly the flag of that state unless doing so is specifically prohibited by law. On a vessel with one or more masts, the state flag is flown at the main masthead in place of the private signal, officer's flag, or USCG Auxiliary ensign (and in this case an Auxiliary officer cannot fly the officer's pennant from the starboard spreader). When the state flag displaces a yacht club or USPS officer's flag, the officer's flag cannot be flown from any other hoist. On a mastless boat, the state flag can be flown at the bow staff in lieu of a club burgee, or it may replace any flag flown from a suitable radio antenna.

The flying of a state flag at the stern of a boat is not proper; nor is it proper to fly from this place of honor any Confederate, "pirate" or other "gag" flag and certainly not the flag of a foreign country of one's heritage.

Flag display ashore

The flagpole or mast of a yacht club is considered to represent the mast of a vessel, and the peak of the gaff, if one is used, is the place of honor from which the U.S. ensign is flown, just

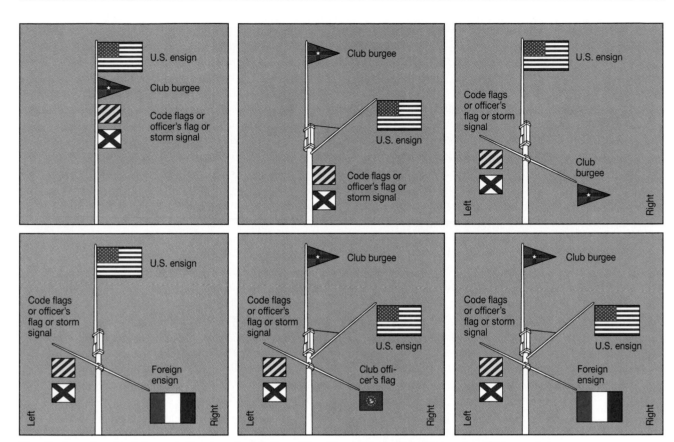

Flag displays at yacht clubs or similar shore installations: The officer's flag is that of the senior officer present on the grounds, or aboard his boat in the club anchorage. Storm signals may be substituted for the International Code Flags, which are displayed on national holidays or other days of special yachting significance.

as it would be on a gaff-rigged boat. The flag should be hoisted briskly, but lowered slowly and ceremoniously.

There has been some confusion because proper flag etiquette requires no other flag to be flown above the U.S. ensign, and obviously another flag, such as a yacht club burgee at the masthead, will be higher than the U.S. flag when the latter is at the gaff. This is entirely proper because "above," in flag etiquette, means "directly on top of." The illustrations above show the standard mast and pole displays as if you were ashore, facing seaward.

Note that signal flags should be flown from a conspicuous hoist; that on national holidays and days of special yachting significance you may fly the flags of the International Code; and that flags flown ashore at private homes may follow the code used for yacht clubs and similar organizations.

Half-masting flags

A flag is flown at half-mast (or half-staff) in respect for a deceased person. Although there are no laws governing the half-masting of flags on private vessels, or at private homes and clubs, most citizens follow the flag display customs that are used on U.S. government buildings and ships.

The only authorities who can direct that the U.S. ensign be flown at half-mast are the President and the governor of a state, territory or possession. The duration varies from a few days to 30 days, determined by the deceased person's position. It is not correct for a yacht club commodore, or official of a similar organization, to order the U.S. ensign to be flown at half-mast to honor a deceased member—only the burgee or organization flag may be half-masted. On Memorial Day, the U.S. flag is flown at half-mast until 1220, the time of the final gun of the traditional 21-gun salute commencing at noon.

On a simple flagstaff—as at the stern of a vessel or a flagpole ashore—the "half-mast" position is approximately three-fourths the way up to the top. If the flagpole has a yardarm, or yardarm and gaff, the half-mast position is that which is level with the yardarm.

When the U.S. flag is displayed at half-mast on a vessel, other flags remain at their normal position. When it is half-masted ashore, fly only a private signal or club burgee at the masthead of a gaff-rigged mast with it. When the U.S. ensign is flown at half-mast, it should be hoisted fully and smartly, then lowered ceremoniously to half-mast position. Before lowering, it is again raised to full height and lowered from there. Some yacht clubs follow the practice of flying their burgee at half-mast for a period of mourning on the death of a club member. A private signal may be flown at half-mast on the death of the owner of that vessel.

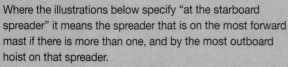

Where the illustrations below specify "at the starboard spreader" it means the spreader that is on the most forward mast if there is more than one, and by the most outboard hoist on that spreader.

When referring to the illustration captions, note that conventions for a vessel "at anchor" also apply to other non-underway statuses—at a mooring or made fast to the shore.

On a typical small cruiser with radio antenna, a USPS officer's flag or past officer's signal, or a USCG Auxiliary ensign may be flown from the antenna at the same height as if on a signal mast. Flags at bow and stern are the same on a cruiser with signal mast with spreader.

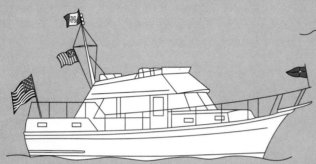

On a cruiser with signal mast with spreaders, the U.S. or yacht ensign is flown from the stern staff, and the squadron pennant or club burgee is at the bow staff. The officer's flag, private signal or USCG Auxiliary ensign is at the mast-head. An owner absent or guest flag, or the USPS ensign (if not flown astern), is displayed at the starboard spreader.

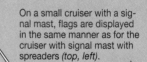

On a small cruiser with a signal mast, flags are displayed in the same manner as for the cruiser with signal mast with spreaders (top, left).

When a gaff is added to the signal mast, it is the place for the U.S. or yacht ensign while underway. At anchor, these are flown at the stern.

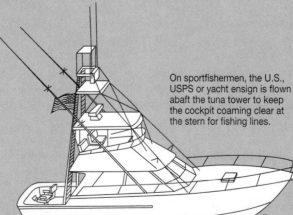

On sportfishermen, the U.S., USPS or yacht ensign is flown abaft the tuna tower to keep the cockpit coaming clear at the stern for fishing lines.

On a mastless motorboat the U.S. ensign (or if not in foreign waters, the USPS or yacht ensign) is flown from a stern staff and the club burgee, USPS Squadron pennant, USCG Auxiliary ensign or private signal is flown from the bow staff.

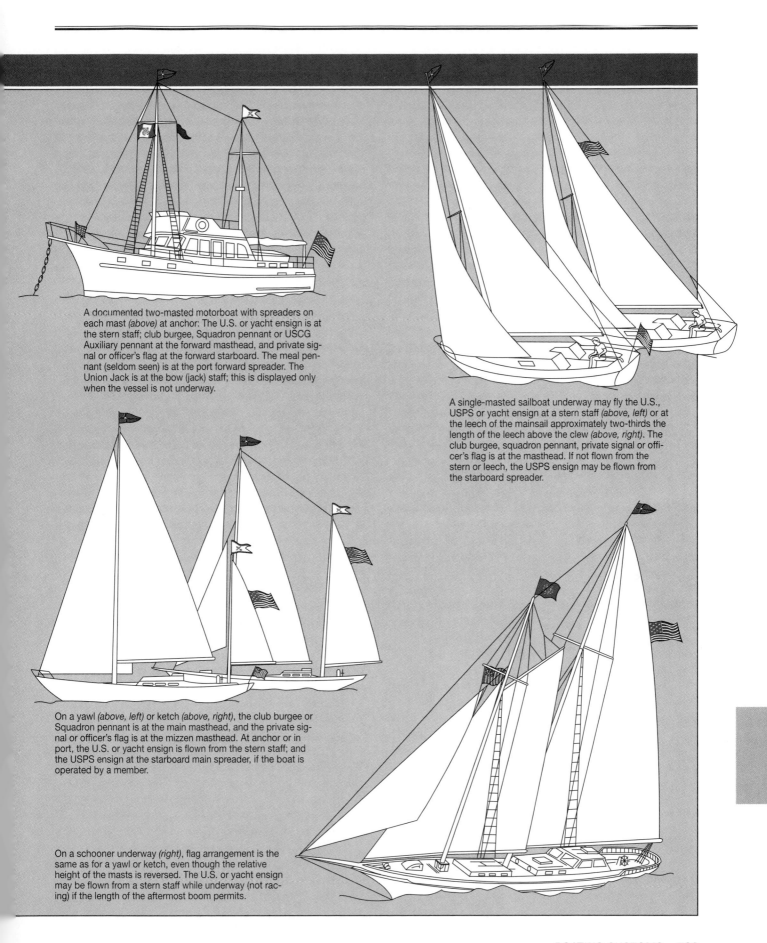

A documented two-masted motorboat with spreaders on each mast *(above)* at anchor: The U.S. or yacht ensign is at the stern staff; club burgee, Squadron pennant or USCG Auxiliary pennant at the forward masthead, and private signal or officer's flag at the forward starboard. The meal pennant (seldom seen) is at the port forward spreader. The Union Jack is at the bow (jack) staff; this is displayed only when the vessel is not underway.

A single-masted sailboat underway may fly the U.S., USPS or yacht ensign at a stern staff *(above, left)* or at the leech of the mainsail approximately two-thirds the length of the leech above the clew *(above, right)*. The club burgee, squadron pennant, private signal or officer's flag is at the masthead. If not flown from the stern or leech, the USPS ensign may be flown from the starboard spreader.

On a yawl *(above, left)* or ketch *(above, right)*, the club burgee or Squadron pennant is at the main masthead, and the private signal or officer's flag is at the mizzen masthead. At anchor or in port, the U.S. or yacht ensign is flown from the stern staff; and the USPS ensign at the starboard main spreader, if the boat is operated by a member.

On a schooner underway *(right)*, flag arrangement is the same as for a yawl or ketch, even though the relative height of the masts is reversed. The U.S. or yacht ensign may be flown from a stern staff while underway (not racing) if the length of the aftermost boom permits.

27 BOATING ORGANIZATIONS

In addition to private and commercial yacht clubs and boating schools, boaters in the U.S. and Canada have access to education and other boating-related support from government and other non-profit organizations. The never-ending work of the USCG, for example, with assistance from the civilian-supported Coast Guard Auxiliary, touches the vast majority of U.S. boaters. In the private sector, the United States Power Squadrons and the Canadian Power and Sail Squadrons fill an important role as well. This chapter tells you what these organizations can do for you.

THE UNITED STATES COAST GUARD

The United States Coast Guard (USCG) is a military service and a branch of the Armed Forces. It is not, as many people think, normally a part of the Department of Defense. In peacetime, the USCG functions as an agency of the Department of Transportation, with duties that include assisting and protecting the boating public. In time of war or national emergency, however, the Coast Guard, or units thereof, may be transferred to the Navy.

The flag of the United States Coast Guard, its distinctive ensign, is closely connected with the organization's history. The ensign bears 16 red-and-white vertical stripes, which represent the number of states in the Union when the flag was first authorized in 1799.

The Coast Guard Ensign, illustrated on page 601, has the unusual feature in that it is flown day and night on active USCG units afloat as well as ashore—a constant reminder that the Coast Guard is always on duty to render assistance.

Coast Guard cutters, ships, boats, aircraft and vehicles, such as the three shown on this page, are easily identified by the distinctive red-and-blue slanted stripes, with the USCG emblem on the red.

Functions relating to boating

Boaters generally come into contact with the Coast Guard for two reasons: law enforcement and safety. The following aspects of U.S. Coast Guard operations directly affect recreational boating.

■ **Boating regulations**. Many of the federal laws relating to boating are implemented by regulations issued by the Commandant of the Coast Guard. The Federal Boat Safety Act of 1971 is an important legislation, and serves as the basis for the registration and numbering of motorboats. The

United States Coast Guard operations use helicopters and other specialty craft.

Small Coast Guard vessels are equipped to handle many types of emergencies as well as search and rescue operations.

Coast Guard performs this task itself only in Alaska; the boat registration systems of the other states carry out this function for boaters in their respective states, and must be approved by the Commandant. Coast Guard patrol vessels, however, have the authority to check the registration papers of boats on all U.S. waters.

As discussed in Chapter 2, boats of more than a specified minimum size may be "documented" rather than registered and numbered. In all states and U.S. territories, this function is performed by officials of the Coast Guard.

As discussed in Chapter 3, Coast Guard regulations also spell out the details of the safety equipment required by the various federal laws. USCG personnel are authorized to make inspections of boats to determine the adequacy of such equipment. Boardings may be made at any time without a search warrant to check for illegal activities.

■ **Safety activities**. Coast Guard vessels make frequent patrols to keep a watchful eye for any reckless operation of boats and all hazards to navigation. Many races, regattas and other marine events are patrolled to ensure the safety of both participants and spectators.

Medium-size Coast Guard cutters such as this 110-footer fill the gaps between the smaller craft that operate near shore and the ocean-going vessels of several hundred feet in length.

In addition, the Coast Guard often has booths and exhibits at boat shows and other marine events. These provide boaters with information, advice and assistance on problems relating to safety on the water. According to Coast Guard philosophy, the organization would much rather prevent an accident than rescue victims.

■ **Aids to navigation.** From unlighted buoys and daybeacons to large lighthouses, the Coast Guard is responsible for operating thousands of aids to navigation. It also operates hundreds of radiobeacons and many stations of the Loran and Omega electronic navigation systems.

This is a quiet and unspectacular, but most necessary, service to all who travel on the water. The installation and maintenance of lighted and unlighted aids to navigation is a major function of the Coast Guard, and one that affects boaters every time they leave their moorings.

■ **Search and rescue.** Many boaters venture out on the waters, offshore or inland, with a greater sense of security knowing that the Coast Guard is standing by to help, living up to its motto "Semper Paratus"—"Always Ready." The rescue of mariners in distress is probably the most dramatic activity of the Coast Guard, the one that makes the headlines—when a ship goes down in a storm, for example. Less publicized, but equally important, are the many instances when the USCG comes to the aid of the skipper who has lost his way at sea, gone aground, suffered dismasting or engine failure, or merely run out of fuel. Requests for assistance in non-life-threatening situations, such as mechanical or fuel problems in stable weather conditions, are referred by the Coast Guard to commercial operations.

Coast Guard search and rescue surface units include ships known as "cutters" and small craft of many sizes. Fixed-wing aircraft and helicopters extend the search capabilities of surface vessels, and in many cases, are used to perform rescue missions when wind and sea conditions permit.

Organization and personnel

The Commandant of the Coast Guard, an Admiral, and his staff are located at USCG Headquarters in Washington, DC. Operational activities are grouped geographically into

There are eight Coast Guard Districts in the continental United States, with Hawaii as the 14th District and Alaska as the 17th. Note that there are no districts 3, 4, 6, 10, 12 or 15.

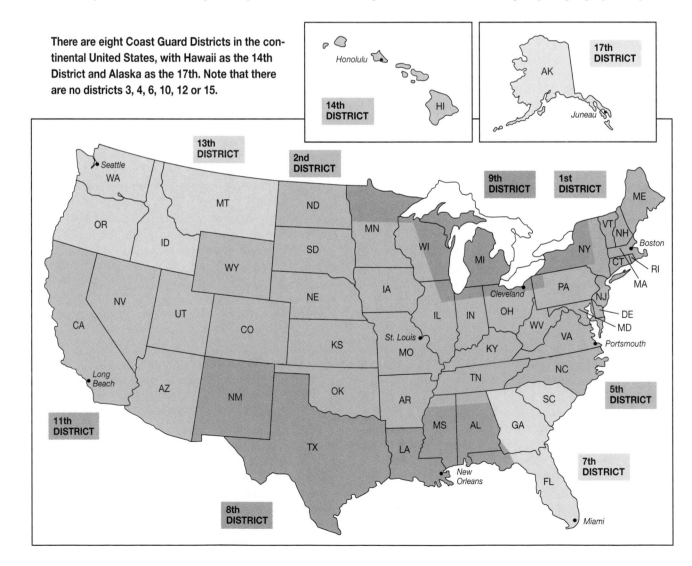

The Canadian Coast Guard (CCG) is part of the federal Department of Transport. Its mandate is to ensure a safe and efficient marine transportation system and to protect the marine environment in waters under the jurisdiction of the Government of Canada. The organization operates under the CCG flag—the Canadian national ensign, shown in Chapter 26.

Coast Guard vessels place and remove buoys, deliver supplies to lightstations, service radio and radar beacons and provide ice-breaking and pollution clean-up support. Radio operators keep around-the-clock watch on the international distress and calling frequencies, ready to assist the mariner in trouble. As well, weather reports and important navigational information is broadcast continuously, helping mariners to navigate safely.

These services encourage not only efficiency, but are important elements of the Coast Guard's "safety net"—whose components work together to prevent marine incidents from occurring. In the event that a vessel falls through the safety net, Coast Guard Search and Rescue (SAR) authorities stand at the ready to respond to mariners in distress.

Search and Rescue

The Coast Guard delivers its SAR services within the framework of the Canadian federal government's SAR program. The National SAR program is a coordinated effort involving a number of organizations that include not only the Canadian Coast Guard, but also the Department of National Defence, the Department of Fisheries and Oceans and the Royal Canadian Mounted Police. Of the many organizations that play a part in SAR in Canada, it is the Canadian Coast Guard that has primary responsibility for the provision of marine SAR services and prevention programs within the Canadian area of responsibility. This responsibility is defined under the International Maritime Organization (IMO) agreements.

The Coast Guard units that provide primary SAR response capability vary from small inshore rescue crafts to large ocean-going ships and high-speed hovercrafts. The Department of National Defence provides the primary airborne response to air and marine SAR incidents.

For operational purposes, the CCG delivers its services through six regions across Canada: the Western, Central, Laurentian, Maritimes, Newfoundland and Northern regions. Each region is responsible for its assigned geographical area.

Canadian Coast Guard headquarters in Ottawa is responsible for formulating policies, procedures and systems affecting delivery of marine SAR services in Canada.

Safety of ships at sea

Marine surveyors, under the authority of a number of statutes and regulations, carry out surveys of vessels under construction, inspection and certification of vessels in service, cargo surveys, examination and certification of officers and crew, and accident and pollution investigation.

Overall, the Canadian Coast Guard is the watchdog of marine traffic on Canada's vast network of waterways. The challenge of the future of the Coast Guard is defined by the organization itself: "to maintain this high level of service within an environment of fiscal restraint, not losing sight of the needs of clients, and the importance of a strong transportation infrastructure in guaranteeing Canada's continued growth as a nation."

Districts, as shown opposite. Each District has a Commander, who is a Rear Admiral. For operational matters, the Districts of the Atlantic/Gulf of Mexico and Pacific coasts have been placed under the Atlantic Area and the Pacific Area commands, respectively.

The operating units of the Coast Guard—individual bases, stations, cutters, boats, aircraft units, etc.—may be under the direct control of a District, or these may be under an intermediate level, called a "Group."

Personnel of the Coast Guard include commissioned officers, warrant officers and enlisted men and women, and their ranks are the same as in the U.S. Navy. Uniforms are single-breasted, the same for officers and enlisted personnel, and are of a distinctive lighter shade of "Coast Guard blue" cloth. The distinguishing United States Coast Guard device is a small shield that is worn above an officer's stripes on both uniform jacket sleeves and on the lower right sleeve of an enlisted man or enlisted woman's uniform jacket. There is a United States Coast Guard Reserve to support the regular establishment.

Functions of the United States Coast Guard not directly related to boating include the Merchant Marine Inspection Program that sets and enforces safety standards for vessels and crews, and pollution control for spills of oil and toxic chemicals. Icebreakers and cutters of reinforced construction keep harbors open for commercial navigation in winter, and each spring cutters and aircraft work with the International Ice Patrol tracking icebergs in the North Atlantic shipping lanes.

In 1977 the Coast Guard became responsible for enforcement of offshore fishery laws out to 200 miles (370 km). In recent years, the interdiction of drug smugglers and illegal aliens has become a primary task of the organization in certain coastal areas.

The final major function of the Coast Guard is to maintain at all times a high state of readiness to function as a specialized service in the Navy in time of war. Under those circumstances, the U.S. Coast Guard operates under the Department of the Navy.

THE U.S. COAST GUARD AUXILIARY

The Auxiliary members and flag

The Coast Guard Auxiliary is an active civilian organization functioning under the direction of the Commandant of the U.S. Coast Guard. It is composed of people interested in the Coast Guard and its principals—people who are dedicated to the interests of their country, and concerned about the safety and welfare of their fellow men and women. Despite its uniforms and insignia, the Auxiliary is a non-military body.

Eligibility for the Auxiliary extends to men and women who are U.S. citizens, at least 17 years old, and who own at least 25 percent of a boat, aircraft, or land-fixed or mobile radio station (or who have some other needed special qualification). Auxiliarists donate their time and abilities to the cause of safety on the water. The only compensation for services rendered is personal satisfaction, and only minor reimbursement of expenses for some official activities.

To become a Basically Qualified (BQ) Member, one must meet the eligibility requirements and pass the BQ examination. Members are encouraged to take advanced training toward the higher status of AUXOP member and/or "Auxiliary Coxswain." The boat, aircraft or radio station is termed a "Facility."

A boat that has qualified as a Facility may fly the Coast Guard Auxiliary Ensign. This rectangular blue flag with a white diagonal slash on which the USCG Auxiliary emblem appears is shown on page 595. Like the USCG Ensign, the Auxiliary Ensign may be flown from boats day and night.

The Coast Guard Auxiliary Operational Ensign is white with the Coast Guard red-and-blue slanted stripes; the Auxiliary emblem is on the red stripe. This is flown in place of the blue-and-white flag when a Facility is operating under USCG orders.

Purposes

The U.S. Coast Guard Auxiliary has several fundamental purposes that are stated as follows in the Act of Congress that established the organization:

- To promote safety and effect rescues on and over the high seas and on the navigable waters.
- To promote efficiency in the operation of both motorboats and yachts.
- To foster a wider knowledge of, and better compliance with, the laws, rules and regulations governing the operation of motorboats and yachts.
- To facilitate other operations of the Coast Guard.

Activities

In carrying out its stated purposes, the Auxiliary has three basic program areas—Public Education, Vessel Examinations and Operations. Described below, these are focused on the objective of greater safety for small-craft boaters.

- **Public Education.** The Auxiliary offers several courses to the boating public. These courses are tailored to meet the needs of various types of boating—power or sail, large or small. Courses consist of from one to 13 lessons, with class-es held in the evenings or on weekends. Constant attention is given to the improvement of these courses and the development of new lessons or courses as required.

Auxiliary members are actively encouraged to take "specialty" courses to improve their knowledge and increase their value to the organization. Possible subjects of study would include communications, search and rescue, patrol procedures and weather.

- **Vessel Examinations.** Many members of the Coast Guard Auxiliary are active in the Vessel Examination program. As discussed more fully in Chapter 3, boat owners are urged each year to request a "Courtesy Marine Examination (CME)." This purely voluntary action ensures that a thorough check is made of all safety-related equipment. Boats that pass the examination are awarded the CME sticker for the current calendar year. Boats that do not pass are not reported to any authority; the owner is simply advised of the deficiencies and is encouraged to resubmit the boat for another check when those deficiencies have been corrected.

Auxiliarists are also busy each year inspecting the boats of other members to determine their fitness for continued

Boats that are owned by members of the USCG Auxiliary and have met the higher inspection standards of a "Facility" may fly the blue-and-white Auxiliary flag; an elected or appointed officer also flies the pennant of his or her office.

United States Coast Guard Auxiliary flags include those shown at right, as well as 13 other officers' flags, ranging from National Vice Commodore to Flotilla Staff Officer.

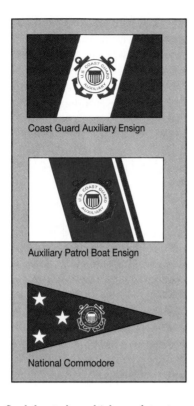

Coast Guard Auxiliary Ensign

Auxiliary Patrol Boat Ensign

National Commodore

designation as Facilities. Such boats have higher safety standards and equipment requirements, because they will be allowed to fly the Auxiliary flag. The highest standards are required for a craft that is designated an "Operational Facility," because it will be used in operational programs under Coast Guard orders.

■ **Operational Programs.** Personnel and vessels of the Auxiliary are used to perform various missions in fields where the resources of the regular Coast Guard are not sufficient to meet the demands placed upon them—regatta patrols and search and rescue missions, for example. This often occurs on weekends and during holiday periods. For such duties, orders are issued by a designated Coast Guard officer.

To improve operational efficiency, the USCG Auxiliary conducts an extensive Boat Crew Qualification Program for those of its members engaged in such work. This leads progressively to designation as "Crewman," "Vessel Operator" and "Auxiliary Coxswain."

Auxiliary members have no law enforcement powers. When a Coast Guard officer or petty officer is embarked in the Auxiliary vessel, however, the boat may fly the regular Coast Guard Ensign.

Auxiliary vessels also conduct safety patrols as well as patrols to check on aids to navigation and to report errors and needed changes on charts—a part of the Chart Updating Program of the National Ocean Service.

Auxiliary aircraft may be used to supplement regular Coast Guard units in search and rescue operations and administrative support missions. In some areas Auxiliary aircraft even make "twilight patrols" at the end of days of heavy boat-

ing activity to spot any boat that may need aid in reaching port safely.

■ **Fellowship Activities.** Units of the Auxiliary work hard at their basic responsibilities, but not to the complete exclusion of social activities. Rendezvous, parties, dances and other Auxiliary events promote goodwill and fellowship.

Organization

The basic unit of the Coast Guard Auxiliary is the "Flotilla." This is a local group of members and their facilities who work together in the various programs. Depending on the group, the membership may include dozens, or even hundreds, of members. Flotillas are grouped geographically into "Divisions"; this is the normal intermediate level between the local flotilla and the "District." In some cases, however, a District is divided into two or more "Regions" for better control.

Auxiliary units are headed by their own elected officers—Flotilla Commander, Division Captain or District Commodore. These are assisted by other elected and appointed officers. The USCG Auxiliary as a whole is headed by a National Commodore, with a National Vice Commodore and three National Rear Commodores. At all levels, there are appointed staff officers for the various Auxiliary operational and administrative functions.

Uniforms and insignia

Auxiliary uniforms have evolved through several distinct phases, and are now more "military" than "yachting" although the organization remains basically civilian in nature.

The USCG Auxiliary has "dinner dress," "service dress" and "working uniforms," plus "tropical blue" and "tropical white" outfits. Members need not own all of these, only those appropriate to their area and normal activities. Uniform jackets and raincoats are also available. Uniforms are required for certain activities, such as official patrols and participation in Courtesy Marine Examinations; instructors normally wear uniforms. The purchase and maintenance of uniforms is at the individual Auxiliarist's expense.

The office held by members is indicated by sleeve lace, shoulder boards and pin-on insignia, all patterned after those worn by regular Coast Guard officers, but with differences that distinguish the Auxiliarist.

Lace on sleeves and shoulder boards is of silver rather than gold, and is worn in stripes, half-stripes, and broad stripes in a series comparable to those worn by Ensigns to Vice Admirals in the Coast Guard and Navy. The Auxiliary, however, does not use rank titles like those of the regular and reserve services; insignia are prescribed for the offices held rather than for rank titles.

Shoulder boards, worn on many uniforms, carry a varying number of stripes. Shoulder boards of the most senior Auxiliary officers are of solid silver braid with one, two or three stars as appropriate to the office held. The Auxiliary shield is placed above the stripes or stars of shoulder boards.

Coast Guard Auxiliarists donate many hours of their time to take part in safety patrols, and assist in search and rescue operations along with the regular Coast Guard.

Collar insignia consist of the same series of designs used for officers of the U.S. Armed Forces, but with a letter "A" superimposed in blue or red. Similar insignia, in larger sizes, are worn on uniform jackets (windbreakers) and raincoats.

Officers and members of the Auxiliary wear frame caps similar to those used by regular officers. Chin straps of members' frame caps are black; those of officers are silver. Visor ornamentation in silver is worn on the caps of senior officers. A "working cap" of boating style is authorized in Coast Guard Blue. The fore-and-aft "garrison cap" may be worn with service dress or working uniforms when more convenient than the frame cap.

How to join the USCG Auxiliary

If you are an eligible boater, why not join the Auxiliary? The rewards include learning a great deal about boating safety and enjoyment. In addition, there is nothing finer than the sense of satisfaction that comes from helping others. Ask any local Coast Guard unit or Auxiliarist where you can "sign up."

THE CANADIAN MARINE RESCUE AUXILIARY

The Canadian Marine Rescue Auxiliary (CMRA) was created in 1978 in an effort to supplement the Canadian Coast Guard's Search and Rescue (SAR) resources. With a clear statement of purpose, the CMRA organization was designed for volunteers who wanted to "sign up" their boats and their efforts to support the common objective of "the prevention of loss of life and/or injury, including (where possible and directly related thereto) reasonable efforts to minimize damage to or loss of property." This is carried out through two primary areas of activity: SAR response and SAR prevention.

The CMRA, like the Canadian Coast Guard, is organized on a regional basis. Each regional CMRA Association is registered as a non-profit corporation that has a president and board of directors elected by the membership at an annual general meeting held for that purpose. The board of directors, under the leadership of the president, manages the activities of the organization in consultation with the Canadian Coast Guard. With some 3,600 members and 1,400 vessels nationally, the CMRA responds to over 20 percent of all SAR incidents reported each year. The Coast Guard provides training to these dedicated volunteers and covers the out-of-pocket expenses they incur while participating in SAR operations.

Upon joining the organization, CMRA members agree to serve the SAR system in the following ways:

■ Make available fully seaworthy and crewed vessels meeting all safety equipment and capability standards established by the CMRA and CCG, and to have the vessel inspected prior to enrollment. The CMRA and CCG may allow a person without a vessel, but who can contribute a particular skill to join.

CMRA members fly the CMRA pennant.

■ Follow the CMRA Association By-laws and Guidelines established by the CMRA in conjunction with the CCG.

■ Undertake training prescribed by the CMRA and CCG necessary for the safe *and* effective conduct of SAR activities.

■ Undertake only those activities which can be done without causing undue risk to themselves, their vessels, other persons and other vessels, and to take all reasonable precautions that may be prudent under the circumstances.

■ Conduct themselves professionally, so as not to bring disrepute to the CMRA, the CCG or the Government of Canada.

Complementing the Coast Guard's operational response capability is a prevention program, which seeks to reduce marine SAR incidents through education. From producing instructional videos to promoting new safety-related technology through advertising, the Coast Guard expends considerable effort in making mariners safety conscious, thus reducing the likelihood they will have to call upon the Coast Guard and/or the CMRA for assistance. A toll-free information line is available for boating safety information at 1-800-267-6687.

THE UNITED STATES POWER SQUADRONS

How the USPS began

In 1912, the motorboat was beginning to challenge the sailboat for a place in the field of recreational boating. A group in the Boston Yacht Club felt that there was a serious lack of knowledge on the part of some who were adopting this new form of boating. They decided to improve the situation by conducting classes. This program led to the formation of the "Power Squadron of the Boston Yacht Club," and set the educational basis for the United States Power Squadrons (USPS).

On 2 February 1914, with Charles F. Chapman in attendance, a meeting held at the New York Yacht Club resulted in the formation of the "United States Power Squadrons." Following World War I, the programs of the USPS were reorganized into a new format that emphasized instruction as a service to boaters and boating in general. Growth was rapid and steady, with local Squadrons being organized in numerous coastal and inland boating areas.

With the end of World War II, recreational boating boomed, and with it new U.S. Power Squadrons were formed in areas around the world, including Japan and Okinawa, as well as Hawaii, Alaska, Puerto Rico and the Canal Zone, although not all are still active.

The USPS today

The United States Power Squadrons today is a non-governmental, private membership organization, self-supporting in its efforts to enhance boating safety through education. In 1992, the U.S. Power Squadrons comprised more than 65,000 members in more than 440 Squadrons assigned to 33 Districts across the United States.

The purposes of the USPS may be described by quoting the "Objects" of the organization as stated in its constitution:

"To selectively associate congenial citizens of the United States of America of good character having a common love and appreciation of yachting as a nation-wide fraternity of boatmen.

"To encourage and promote yachting, power and sail, and to provide through local Squadrons and otherwise a practical means to foster fraternal and social relationships among citizens of the United States of America interested in yachting.

"To encourage and promote a high amateur standard of skill in the handling and navigation of yachts, power and sail; to encourage and promote the study of the science and art of navigation, seamanship, and small boat handling; to develop and promote instructional programs for the benefit of members; and to stimulate members to increase their knowledge of and skill in yachting, through instruction, self-education, and participation in marine sports events and competitions.

"To encourage its members to abide by recognized yachting traditions, customs, and etiquette.

"To encourage its members to render such altruistic, patriotic, or other civil service as it may from time to time determine to elect."

The USPS Ensign

The USPS Ensign, pictured on page 600, consists of seven blue and six white vertical stripes with a union of red, on which is the same white fouled anchor and circle of stars as on the yacht ensign.

The Ensign of the United States Power Squadrons may be flown on boats only when they are skippered by members of the organization. Rules for where and when it can be flown are given in Chapter 26.

In the form of decals and stickers, automobile emblems, boating cap insignia, etc., the USPS design can be worn or displayed only by Power Squadrons members in good standing. Those members also receive *The Ensign*, the USPS monthly publication.

Membership

The USPS is a private organization and membership is by invitation. Members must be male or female U.S. citizens over 18 years of age who have met entrance qualifications set by the national organization and who have been selected by the local unit. Because the USPS is a volunteer organization dependent upon its membership for support, an important aspect of prospective members' qualifications is their willingness to "give" of their time and talents as well as to "take" the knowledge and improved skills that USPS offers.

Family membership is available. There must be at least one "Active Member" (either husband or wife). Others between the ages of 12 and 25, male or female, living at home or full-time students living at school with residence listed at the family address, may join as "family members." These members may take courses, teach and/or serve on educational and social committees; however, they may not vote, hold office or wear uniforms, except for the USPS blazer. Alternatively, there may be more than one Active Member in a family group; for example, both husband and wife may have that status.

There are also provisions for invitation to Apprentice status for youths of U.S. citizenship who are at least 12 years of age. This status may be retained until that Apprentice member's 18th birthday. Apprentices may enroll in the USPS Advanced Grades and Elective Courses, but they have no membership rights.

Organization

The basic unit of the USPS is the local Squadron. These have names of geographic significance, and may have as few as 20 members or as many as 500 or more.

Squadrons are grouped into Districts which are numbered; this is the intermediate level between the local unit and the National organization.

All levels of organization are led by elected officers. Squadrons and Districts have a Commander plus several Lieutenant Commanders and Lieutenants. The USPS as a whole is directed by a Chief Commander and five depart-

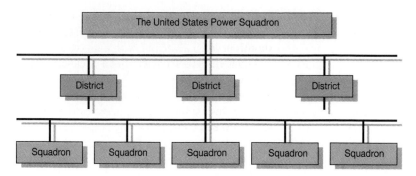

The United States Power Squadron

District   District   District

Squadron   Squadron   Squadron   Squadron   Squadron

Simplified USPS organizational diagram: There are 33 Districts and more than 440 Squadrons. The number of Squadrons in a District varies from five to more than 30, and each echelon is led by elected officers.

ment heads with the rank of Vice Commander. National Committee Chairmen and other national staff officers hold the rank of Rear Commander or Staff Commander. All officers are unpaid volunteers; there is a paid office staff at the National Headquarters at Raleigh, NC. Although the United States Power Squadrons is not a military organization, it has winter and summer, formal and informal uniforms for men and women. Members are not required to purchase these uniforms, and many do not. Most officers, however, do wear uniforms for meetings, rendezvous ceremonies and other special occasions. Uniforms may or may not be worn to various USPS educational classes.

An officer's rank in the United States Power Squadrons is indicated on the uniform coat by sleeve braid and embroidered insignia (pages 600 to 602). A varying number of dark blue stripes is used with three different widths of braid that are used in combination. White shirts have shoulder board insignia but not the braid.

The uniform cap is worn with all the various USPS uniforms. The rank of various Squadron, District and National officers is also indicated on the cap. A USPS cap ornament may be worn on non-uniform boating caps, but in such cases no insignia of rank is shown.

Further details of the Power Squadrons uniforms and insignia of rank are spelled out in the organization's Operations Manual. An illustrated table of information on officers' sleeve braid and insignia, cap insignia and flags is found on pages 600 to 602.

Educational programs

The educational programs of the USPS are a major activity. There are three major areas of educational effort. One of these is for the general public. The other programs are for members only, and include courses for further personal study and the internal training of the membership to improve their teaching abilities. A general description of courses offered is given below.

The USPS Boating Course

Each local Squadron is encouraged to give each year at least one series of classes of the USPS Boating Course for the general public. Many Squadrons give the classes two or more times each year, varying the place and/or night of the week in order to reach the greatest number of boaters as well as their families.

The USPS Boating Course covers basic topics, including the following:

- Boat handling and elementary seamanship.
- Registration, equipment, regulations and safe operation.
- Marlinespike.
- Charts and aids to navigation.
- Navigation rules.
- Marine radiotelephone.
- Sailing, weather and trailer boating.

The course material is prepared and distributed on a national basis, as is the end-of-course examination. Instruction is by local USPS members, supplemented in some instances by outside experts. The instruction is given free of charge by the local Squadron, although students will usually find it desirable to purchase course material, a recommended textbook (Chapman), notebook binder, plotting instruments, etc., if they do not already have them. In some areas, the course is presented as a part of the adult education program of a local school system, and a small registration fee may be charged by that organization.

Family groups are encouraged to take the USPS Boating Course together; the minimum age for registration is 12 years.

Boating Safely

Boating Safely is a four-lesson course presented by either the USPS or the U.S. Coast Guard Auxiliary, or by a joint effort of both organizations. It is intended to teach safe boating to teenagers and non-traditional boaters such as those engaged in hunting and fishing. The course is basic and covers the essentials needed by anyone using a boat. It is designed so that it may satisfy the educational requirements that some States have for mandatory operator education. Boating Safely is particularly appropriate as a preliminary to the USPS Boating Course or the Coast Guard Auxiliary's Boating Skills and Seamanship Course.

The Advanced Grades Program

In keeping with its stated purpose of encouraging the study of the science of navigation, the USPS offers all of its members a progressive series of five courses. These courses are described opposite.

■ **Seamanship (S)**. Building on the basics taught in the USPS Boating Course, Seamanship is the recommended first course for new members, powerboaters and sailors alike. The student learns practical marlinespike, navigation rules, hull design and performance, responsibilities of the skipper, boat care, operating a boat under normal and abnormal conditions, what to do in various emergencies and weather conditions, nautical customs and common courtesy on the water. This course provides an introduction to the USPS educational program and a strong foundation for other Advanced Grades courses and Cruise Planning and/or Sail.

■ **Piloting (P)**. Piloting is the first of a two-part program of study of inland and coastal navigation. Focus is on the fundamentals of basic piloting—keeping track of your movements on the water, determining where you are at any given moment, and laying out a course to your planned destination. Included are a thorough study of charts and their use, aids to navigation, mariner's compass, variation and deviation, bearings, dead reckoning, and developing skill at plotting and labeling.

■ **Advanced Piloting (AP)**. The second part of the study of inland and coastal navigation, with strong emphasis on the latter, is Advanced Piloting. The student learns many more advanced positioning techniques and is introduced to the phenomena of tides and tidal currents and their impact on piloting. Also covered are the simple use of the marine sextant as well as various modern electronic navigation systems for positioning and course planning.

■ **Junior Navigation (JN)**. Junior Navigation is the first of a two-part course in offshore (open ocean) navigation. Designed as a practical, "how to" course, it leaves the theoretical and more advanced techniques for the Navigation course. The subject matter includes: the basic concepts of celestial navigation; using the mariner's sextant to take sights of the sun, moon, planets and stars; the importance and techniques of accurate time determination; use of the nautical almanac; how to "reduce" sights to establish lines of position (LOPs); the use of special charts, plotting sheets, and other navigational data for offshore positioning and passage planning.

■ **Navigation (N)**. This is the second part of the study of offshore navigation. It further develops the student's understanding of celestial navigation theory, essential to shortcut emergency methods. The student is introduced to additional sight reduction techniques and develops greater skill and precision in sight taking, positioning, and the orderly methods of carrying on the day's work of a navigator at sea. Of particular interest and importance is the study of offshore navigation using minimal data and/or equipment—skills needed such as when on a disabled vessel or lifeboat.

The Elective Courses Program

The USPS also offers to its members six elective courses in specialty subjects; these do not constitute a series and may be taken in any sequence.

■ **Cruise Planning (CP)**. This course provides essential information for planning a cruise, whether the cruise is for a day, a week, a month or longer. Whether you are going to cruise rivers, lakes, along the coasts or across the oceans, valuable information is provided by experienced boaters who have already been there. Some of the topics discussed in the course include: planning the voyage, financing the voyage, equipping the boat, crew selection, provisioning, voyage management, navigation planning, weather, communications, entering and clearing foreign and domestic ports, anchors and anchoring, emergencies afloat, medical emergencies and security.

■ **Engine Maintenance (EM)**. This course covers the general construction, operating principles, maintenance and repair of marine gasoline and diesel engines, as well as cooling, electrical, fuel and lubricating systems and associated propulsion components—clutches, shafting and propellers. Since one of the major objectives of this course is to help the student become more self-reliant afloat, trouble diagnosis and temporary remedies are emphasized along with safety measures. The course is not intended to produce trained mechanics but rather more intelligent and more resourceful boat engine operators.

■ **Marine Electronics (ME)**. Essential information about your boat's electrical and electronic systems is studied in this course. Proper wiring, grounding, electrolysis control, and batteries and their maintenance are included. Depth finders, marine radiotelephones, radar, Loran, Omega and advanced systems for electronic navigation are also studied. Information is provided on FCC requirements for station licensing and operator permits for radiotelephone. Note that this is not a technical course, and is well within the capabilities of the average USPS member.

■ **Sail (Sa)**. This course provides a thorough study of the terminology of sailing; types of hulls, rigs and sail plans; running and standing rigging and their adjustment and tuning; and sailboat marlinespike. The dynamics of sailing are also covered, including: hull and water forces caused by wind and waves, forces versus balance, techniques of sailing, points of sail, sail handling, sailing under various wind conditions from light air to storm survival, boat operation and emergency techniques unique to sailboats.

■ **Weather (W)**. Awareness of weather phenomena, how to read the weather map and the sky, and understand and anticipate weather developments for more pleasurable boating are the objectives of this course. Subjects studied include: the characteristics and structure of the atmosphere, what weather is and its basic causes, normal development and movement of weather over the earth, as well as the factors that must be considered in weather forecasting. Observations that the skipper can make afloat include both instrumental and visual, including cloud sequences and the weather they predict; air masses, fronts, storms and fog, as well as the use of radio and television weather broadcasts. Throughout the course the student is encouraged to make observations and

UNITED STATES POWER SQUADRONS FLAGS and INSIGNIA

USPS ENSIGN

The Ensign of United States Power Squadrons may be displayed only by enrolled members of USPS. It is an outward and visible sign that the vessel displaying it is under the charge of a person who has made a study of piloting and small boat handling, and will recognize the rights of others and the traditions of the sea. The Squadrons' Ensign also marks a craft as being under the command of a man who has met certain minimum requirements and is so honored for meeting them.

NATIONAL OFFICERS

OFFICE	INSIGNIA	FLAG	SLEEVE
CHIEF COMMANDER			
VICE COMMANDERS			
REAR COMMANDERS			
STAFF COMMANDERS			
NATIONAL FLAG LIEUTENANT			
AIDES TO C/C CHAPLAIN			

DISTRICT OFFICERS

OFFICE	INSIGNIA	FLAG	SLEEVE
DISTRICT COMMANDER			
DISTRICT LIEUTENANT COMMANDERS			
DISTRICT 1st LIEUTENANTS			
DISTRICT LIEUTENANTS			
DISTRICT FLAG LIEUTENANT			
DISTRICT AIDES CHAPLAIN			

EDUCATIONAL INSIGNIA

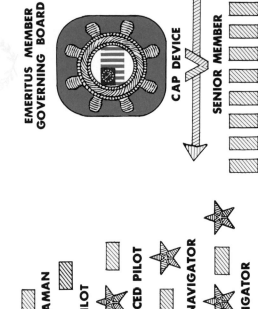
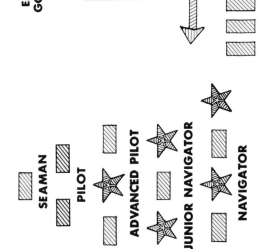
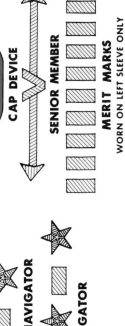
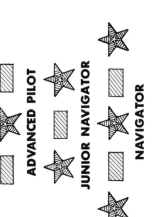

NATIONAL COMMITTEES		LOCAL BOARDS	
MEMBERS		MEMBERS	CHAIRMAN
RULES		ADVANCED GRADES	
ELECTIVE COURSES		ELECTIVE COURSES	
GOVERNING BOARD GENERAL MEMBERS			

CRUISE PENNANT

Authorized to be flown by vessels commanded by USPS members during organized "on-the-water" activities when directed by a Squadron or District Commander, or the Chief Commander.

EMERITUS MEMBER GOVERNING BOARD

CAP DEVICE

SENIOR MEMBER

MERIT MARKS
WORN ON LEFT SLEEVE ONLY

SEAMAN

PILOT

ADVANCED PILOT

JUNIOR NAVIGATOR

NAVIGATOR

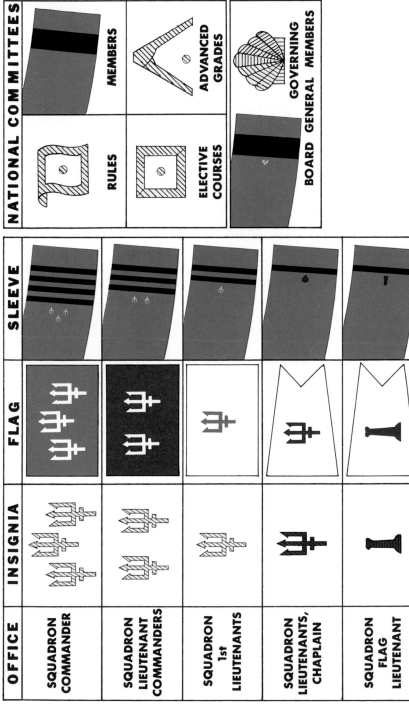

OFFICE	INSIGNIA	FLAG	SLEEVE
SQUADRON COMMANDER			
SQUADRON LIEUTENANT COMMANDERS			
SQUADRON 1st LIEUTENANTS			
SQUADRON LIEUTENANTS, CHAPLAIN			
SQUADRON FLAG LIEUTENANT			

PAST OFFICERS' SIGNALS

PAST CHIEF COMMANDERS

PAST VICE COMMANDERS

PAST REAR COMMANDERS

PAST STAFF COMMANDERS

PAST DISTRICT COMMANDERS

PAST SQUADRON COMMANDERS

predictions in order that he or she may gain experience in applying the principles taught and develop greater insight into weather phenomena.

■ **Supplemental Programs**. To provide further educational "packages" for members who have completed their basic boating education, the USPS has designed a series of Supplemental Programs. These generally are shorter and below the level of USPS courses.

Topics covered include diverse subjects ranging from the use and care of hand tools, predicted log racing and the magnetic compass to boat insurance and the use of calculators for navigation purposes.

■ **Instructor Qualification (IQ)**. The development of practical skills and methods in preparing for both classroom and meeting presentations are the objectives of this unique course. The course includes practice assignments in preparation and delivery of presentations in the classroom, including the use of visual and other aids. All types of aids that can enhance a presentation are studied, and students are afforded the opportunity to become familiar with their best use. Attendance at the majority of the class sessions is mandatory before taking the examination. USCG Auxiliary members, as well as other governmental authorities that are involved with boating activities, may also take the IQ course.

Other USPS activities

■ **Cooperative Charting Program**. The USPS participates in a Cooperative Charting Program with the National Ocean Service. In this effort, the boating activities of thousands of USPS members are coordinated toward the reporting of changes to nautical and geodetic charts. The limited field facilities of NOS are thus much strengthened and expanded, resulting in more accurate charts.

Many Squadrons also participate in events and services of a local nature such as boat shows and the annual observance of National Safe Boating Week.

■ **Social activities**. At the USPS, it's not "all work and no play." Squadrons hold a wide variety of social activities both afloat and ashore. Each District has a fall and a spring conference. Although these are working sessions, they are usually preceded or followed by evening social gatherings. The national level Annual Meeting in January, and the Spring and Fall Governing Board Meetings, combine both intense official events with those of a much lighter nature.

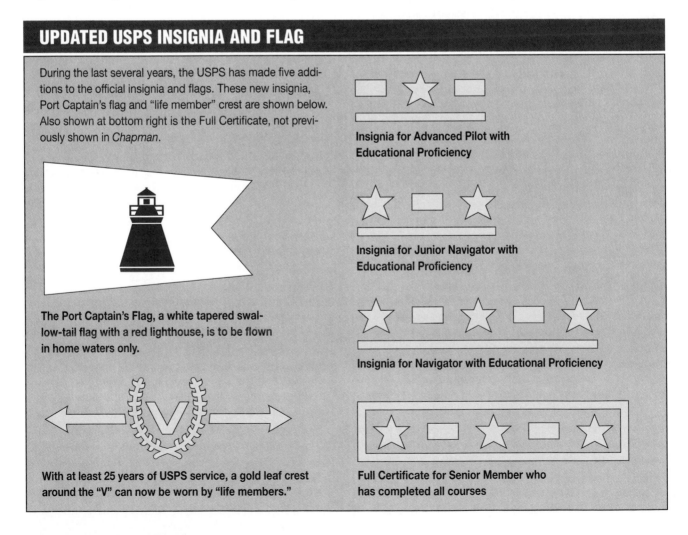

UPDATED USPS INSIGNIA AND FLAG

During the last several years, the USPS has made five additions to the official insignia and flags. These new insignia, Port Captain's flag and "life member" crest are shown below. Also shown at bottom right is the Full Certificate, not previously shown in *Chapman*.

The Port Captain's Flag, a white tapered swallow-tail flag with a red lighthouse, is to be flown in home waters only.

With at least 25 years of USPS service, a gold leaf crest around the "V" can now be worn by "life members."

Insignia for Advanced Pilot with Educational Proficiency

Insignia for Junior Navigator with Educational Proficiency

Insignia for Navigator with Educational Proficiency

Full Certificate for Senior Member who has completed all courses

CANADIAN POWER AND SAIL SQUADRONS

Organization

Founded in 1938, the Canadian Power Squadrons became Canadian Power and Sail Squadrons (CPS) in 1985. In French, the organization is called *les Escadrilles canadiennes de plaisance (page 605)*. Like its counterpart across the border, CPS is dedicated to improving boating safety through education. This is accomplished with a variety of courses available to the general public, as well as a number of advanced and elective courses for CPS members. CPS is a non-profit organization, incorporated under the Companies Act of Canada, and all administrative and instructional work is carried out by members on a volunteer basis.

The basic unit of CPS is the Squadron. There are 176 such Squadrons across Canada, offering both English and French

The Canadian Power and Sail Squadrons (CPS)— *les Escadrilles canadiennes de plaisance* (ECP) in French—fly this flag.

courses to the boating community at large, as well as some advanced and elective courses that are available to Squadron members only.

A number of Squadrons in a given area are sometimes grouped together to form a District. There are presently 17 Districts in Canada, which are generally given the name of the areas they serve—for example, Atlantic, Georgian-Trent, and Vancouver Island.

In addition to training recreational boaters on the principles of safe boating, many local law enforcement agencies and municipal authorities regularly request courses from CPS. Training has been given to such organizations as the Royal Canadian Mounted Police, firefighters' groups, Boy Scouts, Sea Cadets and other organizations in various communities across the country.

The Canadian Power and Sail Squadrons head office, which is staffed by 10 employees, is located at 26 Golden Gate Court, Scarborough, Ontario M1P 3A5. The office can be reached by telephone at (416) 293-2438 or toll-free by calling (800) 268-3579.

Public courses

■ **The Boating Course** is open to the Canadian boating public and may be taken in the classroom or by correspondence course. Subjects covered include boat handling under normal conditions, boat handling under adverse conditions, seamanship and common emergencies, aids to navigation, government regulations and equipment requirements, rules of the road, compass and chart familiarization, and introduction to piloting. Successful completion of the Boating Exam qualifies a person for membership in CPS.

■ **Boatwise** is designed for children from 8 to 12 years of age. Among other things, youngsters learn to identify various vessels and parts of a boat, the use of safety equipment, the rules of the road, the importance of lifejackets, an understanding of aids to navigation and the importance of watching the weather.

■ **The Safe Boating Seminar** provides the new boater with a basic start-up knowledge of safe-boating rules and practices. The course content is a condensed version of the Boating Course.

■ **Skipper Saver** is intended to prepare any spouse, crew or passenger, in the event that the skipper is incapacitated, by teaching the rudiments of chart reading, methods of signalling for help, first aid and the proper use of the radiotelephone (VHF).

■ **The Maritime Radiotelephone Course (VHF)** teaches students the phonetic alphabet, as well as correct radiotelephone operating procedures. Also, this course prepares the student to undertake the Department of Communications' Restricted Radiotelephone Operator's Certificate Examination, which is normally given at the conclusion of each teaching session.

The Canadian Power and Sail Squadrons is accepted as the foremost educational boating authority in Canada, and offers a wide variety of courses coast to coast. Boating course subjects, for example, range from boat handling and common emergencies to using nautical charts, anchors and lines.

Squadrons across Canada offer advanced and elective boating courses in English and/or French.

Advanced courses

■ **Seamanship** expands piloting knowledge to include relative bearings and running fixes, effects of current and leeway and new skills in coastal navigation.

■ **Advanced Piloting** covers the basic navigation principles, such as how to determine a course, and how to fix a position by using landmarks, buoys and other aids to navigation, allowing for current, leeway and the prediction of tides and tidal currents.

■ **Junior Navigator** includes extensive use of the sextant. The student will also learn celestial observation; time diagram; Nautical Almanac; sight reduction by Ageton-Bayless and calculator; plotting sights, Pilot, Great Circle and Mercator Charts and the Sailing Triangle.

■ **Navigator** develops the various systems of coordinates by celestial bodies, their identification and their use for navigation. Sight reduction is accomplished by Compact Tables and formula, as well as the use of PUB 229 and 249. Traverse, Mercator and Great Circle sailing are also detailed.

Elective courses

■ **Seamanship Power** contains information on power trains, engine controls and instruments; buoyancy and stability; handling and cruising under power; mooring and anchoring; the skipper's legal responsibilities; engine and trouble diagnosis; fuels and fuel systems; electrical systems; cooling and lubrication; maintenance and fire safety.

■ **Seamanship Sail** teaches some of the basic techniques for safe operation under various conditions. Among the topics covered are spars and rigging; sails and theory of sail action; buoyancy and stability; balance under sail; sailboat handling; weather, wind and wave action; adverse conditions; marlinespike; piloting under sail and cruising under sail.

■ **Weather** course content consists of atmosphere, clouds, pressure, wind, temperature and moisture, stability and instability, air masses, frontal weather, precipitation and fog, general circulation, tropical hurricanes, wave theory and forecasting the weather.

■ **Marine Maintenance** covers seasonal maintenance and repairs to wooden, fiberglass and metal hulls. Sections are devoted to maintenance of marine engines; electrical and mechanical systems; spars, rigging and ground tackle; fire and safety protection; moorings and berths; trailers; tools and fittings.

■ **Marine Electronics** covers electronic communications and position-finding systems, such as radio direction finders, radar, Loran and GPS. Other electronic devices used on the boat—such as depth sounders, rudder position indicators, vapor detectors and autopilots—are also studied.

Other activities

■ **Port captains** assist the boating traveller by providing a contact and a source of information about local conditions and facilities such as location of marinas, yacht clubs, repair facilities, marine supplies, fuel, pumpouts, charts and publications, restaurants, grocery stores, places of interest and any relevant local conditions.

■ **Marep (marine report) hydrographic programmes** allow CPS to assist the Hydrographic Service in keeping nautical

In addition to administrative and instructional work, the CPS schedules a number of social events each year, such as this cruise to Desolation Sound, approximately 100 miles north of Vancouver, British Columbia.

charts and publications up to date by reporting any observed changes detected by CPS members. Items reported include obstructions in or out of the water, new or changed marine facilities, new construction and landmarks that could be useful for navigation.

■ **Weather observation** by CPS is intended to assist the Atmospheric Environment Service (AES) in providing updated weather information to mariners. Data is relayed to AES via VHF radio.

Social activities

Many Squadrons arrange one or more events during the summer months—for example, a cruise, predicted log race, sail past, picnic or other rendezvous. As well, in winter, it is common practice to organize monthly social evenings, which may include special guest speakers, wine and cheese nights, student nights and parties of various kinds.

What makes the CPS successful?

The dedication of CPS members has provided an unequalled community service to boaters and would-be boaters.

The organization thrives on the knowledge and experience of members, who without remuneration, and frequently without formal recognition, donate their time and energy to something in which they believe—safe, proficient and fun-filled boating in Canada.

For information on CPS courses, boaters are encouraged to call toll-free in Canada: 1-800-268-3579.

LES ESCADRILLES CANADIENNES DE PLAISANCE

La plus importante association nationale d'adeptes de la plaisance au Canada offre de la formation couvrant tous les aspects de la plaisance. C'est un organisme de bienfaisance non-gouvernemental et non-militaire, constitué de 25 000 membres. Plus de 3 000 bénévoles répartis dans des escadrilles à travers le Canada offrent de la formation en plaisance sécuritaire tant à voile qu'à moteur. Nous faisons partie d'un mouvement nord-américain originaire des Etats-Unis, les "US Power Squadrons."

La formation en plaisance comme service au public
Depuis 50 ans, les Escadrilles canadiennes de plaisance (ECP) offrent leur cours de navigation de plaisance au public. La plupart des escadrilles offrent ce cours deux fois l'an: au printemps et à l'automne. L'heure, les dates et le lieu sont annoncés dans les journaux et autres médias locaux. Des cours-ateliers permettent aussi de maintenir chez les plaisanciers le souci constant de la sécurité.

Participer, c'est apprendre et partager
Les escadrilles locales sont impliquées dans une vaste gamme d'activités nautiques et sociales. On incite les membres des ECP à élargir leurs connaissances en s'inscrivant aux cours avancés comme le matelotage, le pilotage avancé et la navigation astronomique. La réussite de l'examen conduit à l'obtention du grade correspondant et confère aux membres qui le désirent le droit de porter l'insigne de leur grade.

Collaboration avec les organismes gouvernementaux
Les ECP ont conclu des accords de coopération avec le Service hydrographique du Canada—signaler des corrections et des ajouts aux cartes marines—et avec le Service de l'environnement atmosphérique—signaler des corrections, des avertissements ou des renseignements supplémentaires concernant la météo.

Les ECP sont un des groupes choisis par le ministère des Communications pour administrer l'atelier et l'examen d'obtention du certificat restreint de radiotéléphoniste.

Le programme d'attribution des trophées Mustang en plaisance sécuritaire est coordonné par les ECP. Les trophées sont décernés pour un acte exceptionnel relié à la sécurité sur l'eau: sauver une vie, prévenir une tragédie, effectuer un sauvetage ou apporter une contribution exceptionnelle à l'enseignement de la plaisance sécuritaire.

Les ECP sont reconnues, respectées et souvent consultées par les gouvernements fédéral, provinciaux et municipaux, les agences de sûreté, la Garde côtière canadienne, la Croix Rouge, l'Association canadienne du yachting, plusieurs autres clubs de yachting et de plaisance, la Ligue navale, et par les comités de régie interne de nombreuses sociétés.

Le volet social mène à des amitiés durables
Partagez la camaraderie qui prévaut parmi les adeptes de la navigation de plaisance: activités nautiques, croisières, rendez-vous, concours de navigation, respect d'un itinéraire préétabli; divertissement à terre: pique-niques, barbecues, diners-conférences, repas dansants, etc.

Participation à la promotion de la plaisance sécuritaire
Comme dans tout club social ayant un volet social et un volet yachting, des membres doivent voir aux fonctions d'administration et de formation ce qui leur permet de transmettre à d'autres ce qu'ils ont reçu de l'organisation. Comme d'autres clubs, les ECP ont des tenues, un cérémonial, des rituels, des pavillons et des grades—traditions destinées à favoriser la fierté et l'appartenance à une organisation.

Voilà votre chance de participer à la promotion de la plaisance sécuritaire comme service à la population et de partager l'amitié et les plaisirs des autres plaisanciers.

A Toronto: 283-2436; partout ailleurs 1-800-268-3579.

APPENDICES

CHART, CRUISING AND SAFETY INFORMATION SOURCES

Charts of Various Waterways

■ **U.S. Coastal Waters and Great Lakes.** Atlantic, Pacific and Gulf Coasts; the Atlantic and Gulf Intracoastal Waterways; the Hudson River north to Troy, New York; the Great Lakes and connecting rivers; Lake Champlain; New York State Canals; and the Minnesota-Ontario Border Lakes; National Ocean Service, Distribution Division (N/CG33), Riverdale, MD 20737, or local sales agents listed in chart catalogs.

■ **New York State Canals.** Bound booklet of charts of the Champlain, Erie, Oswego and Cayuga-Seneca canals: National Ocean Service Distribution Division, (N/CG33) Riverdale, MD 20737 or local sales agents.

■ **Mississippi River and Tributaries.** Middle & Upper Mississippi, Cairo, Illinois, to Minneapolis, Minnesota; Middle Mississippi River from Cairo, Illinois, to Grafton, Illinois; Mississippi River from Cairo, Illinois, to Gulf of Mexico; Small Boat Chart, Alton, Illinois to Clarksville on the Mississippi River and Grafton, Illinois, to LaGrange, Illinois, on the Illinois River; Illinois Waterways from Grafton, Illinois, to Lake Michigan at Chicago and Calumet Harbor: published by U.S. Army Corps of Engineers and available from Jefferson National Expansion Historical Association (Gift Shop), Old Courthouse, 11 North 4th Street, St. Louis, MO 63012. Tel: (314) 231-5474 or 1-800-537-7962.

■ **Mississippi River and Tributaries, Below Ohio River.** Mississippi River Commission, P.O. Box 80, Vicksburg, MS 39180-0080. This office also has a free booklet, *Mississippi River Navigation*, which discusses its history, development and navigation.

■ **Mississippi River and Connecting Waterways, North of the Ohio River.** U.S. Army Engineer Division, North Central, 111 N. Canal Street, Room 1216, Chicago, IL 60606-7206.

■ **Ohio River and Tributaries; Pittsburgh, Pennsylvania, to the Mississippi River** as well as **Tennessee and Cumberland Rivers.** U.S. Army Engineer Division, P.O. Box 1159, (550 Main St.) Cincinnati, OH 45201-1159.

■ **Missouri River and Tributaries.** U.S. Army Engineers, Missouri River Division, P.O. Box 103 Downtown Station, Omaha, NE 68101-0103.

■ **Tennessee Valley Authority,** Maps & Surveys, 200 Haney Building, 1101 Market Street, Chatanooga, TN 37402-2801

■ **U.S. Army Corps of Engineers,** Publications Depot, 2803 52nd Ave., Hyattsville, MD 20781-1102.
Tel: (301) 436-2064.

■ **Canadian Waters.** Chart Distribution Office, Department of the Environment, P.O. Box 8080, 1675 Russell Road, Ottawa, Ontario KIG 3H6. Charts include coastal waters; Canadian sections of the Great Lakes including Georgian Bay; the St. Lawrence River; Richelieu River; Ottawa River; the Rideau Waterway; and other Canadian lakes and waterways. Indexes of charts for any area are free, and chart prices and details are given in a Coastal and Inland Waters catalog.

■ **Waters of Other Nations.** Defense Mapping Agency, NOAA Distribution Branch (N/CG33), National Ocean Service, Riverdale, MD 20737-1199; Tel. (301) 436-6990; Fax: (301) 436-6829; or authorized sales agents. Nine regional catalogs are available (free).

Notices to Mariners

■ **Notice to Mariners.** Weekly publication of the Defense Mapping Agency Hydrographic Topographic Center. Available (free) from the Director, DMA Combat Support Center, Attn: PDO, Stop D-18, 6001 MacArthur Blvd., Bethesda, MD 20816-5001; Fax: (301) 227-3365.

In Canada, **Notices to Mariners** are available from Marine Navigation Services Director, Canadian Coast Guard, Transport Canada, Ottawa, Ontario KJA 0N7.

■ **Local Notice to Mariners.** Issued as necessary by the Commanders of Coast Guard Districts, and available from District offices.

Coast Pilots

■ **U.S. Waters.** Atlantic, Gulf and Pacific Coasts; Atlantic and Gulf Intracoastal Waterways; the Great Lakes; Distribution Branch N/CG33, National Ocean Service, 6501 Lafayette Ave., Riverdale, MD 20737, its distribution offices, or sales agents as listed semi-annually in *Notice to Mariners*.

■ **Canadian Waters.** Chart Distribution Office, Department of the Environment, P.O. Box 8080, 1675 Russell Road, Ottawa, Ontario KIG 3H6. Coastal and Inland Waters Catalog gives details.

Light Lists

■ **Light Lists.** Published by the U.S. Coast Guard; Superintendent of Documents, Washington, DC 20402, or many of the sales agents listed in NOS Chart Catalogs.

Tide and Current Tables

■ **Tide Tables, Current Tables, Tidal Current Charts, Tidal Current Diagrams.** Distribution Branch N/CG33, National Ocean Service, 6501 Lafayette Ave., Riverdale, MD 20737, its distribution offices, or many of the sales agents listed in NOS Chart Catalogs.

Rules of the Road

- **Navigation Rules, International-Inland**. The latest edition of the Navigation Rules was published in August 1990. This book contains the International Regulations for Preventing Collisions at Sea, commonly called the 72 COLREGS, and the Inland Navigation rules which supersede the old Inland Rules, Western Rivers rules, Great Lakes Rules and other Pilot rules. The book also includes sections on COLREGS demarcation lines, penalty provisions, alternative compliance, and the Vessel Bridge-to-Bridge Radiotelephone Regulations. Available from the Government Printing Office for $8.00, or from the Superintendent of Documents, U.S. Government Printing Office, Washington, DC 20402.

Cruising Guides

- **Waterway Guide.** Four regional editions provide annually updated information on the Intracoastal Waterway and adjacent waters. Northern: Maine to New Jersey; Middle Atlantic: Cape May to the Georgia/Florida border; Southern: all of Florida, the Bahamas, and the Gulf Coast from Alabama to Mexico; Great Lakes: all the Great Lakes (except Superior) and their connecting canals and rivers. Also available: Waterway Guide Chart Books—reproductions of government charts in spiral-bound books covering seven regions from Maine to the Florida Keys to New Orleans. Waterway Guide, 6151 Powers Ferry Road, NW, Atlanta, GA 30339.

- **Guide to the Virgin Islands**. Annually updated guide to the U.S. and British Virgin Islands. Tropic Isle Publishers, Inc., P.O. Box 610938, N. Miami, FL 33261-0938

- **Yachtsman's Guide to the Bahamas.** Annually updated guide to the Bahamas. Tropic Isle Publishers, Inc., P.O. Box 610938, N. Miami, FL 33261-0938.

- **Cruising Charts, Guides and Booklets for State of Texas**. Available from local Convention & Visitors Bureaus or toll free 800-88 88 TEX.

- **Quimby's Cruising Guide**. Covers all navigable inland waterways with details of harbors, services, cities, towns, transportation, tourist interests, some history, locks and dams, sources of navigation charts and books, hazards. Waterway Journal, 319 N. 4th, Suite 650, St. Louis, MO 63102.

- **Guide for Cruising Maryland Waters**. Prepared by Maryland Dept. of Natural Resources. Twenty full-color charts, with more than 200 courses and distances plotted; marina and facility information reference listing. Department of Natural Resources, Tawes State Office Bldg., Annapolis, MD 21401. A Maryland Basic Boating Course is available from the same address.

- **Ports Cruising Guides**. Three separate guides covering: Lake Ontario/Thousand Islands; Georgian Bay/North Channel; Trent-Severn Waterway/Lake Simcoe. Ports Cruising Guides, 94 Wheeler Avenue, Toronto, ON M4L 3V2.

U.S. Coast Guard Publications

- **This Is the Seal of Safety...Get a Free Motorboat Examination**. Flyer explains the Auxiliary Courtesy Marine Examination and the standards that must be met to be awarded a CME decal. Commandant (G-NAB) U.S. Coast Guard, Washington, DC 20593-0001.

- **Federal Requirements and Safety Tips for Recreational Boats.** A booklet for the boat operator that contains information about U.S. laws, equipment requirements and safety recommendations for recreational vessels. There are other equipment and considerations that are recommended for boat operator and passenger safety. Available at all Coast Guard offices.

- **Visual Distress Signals**. Illustrated booklet provides description and guidance for use of distress signals suitable for boats. Free from U.S. Coast Guard District offices, or Headquarters, U.S. Coast Guard, Washington, DC 20593.

Publications of the Defense Mapping Agency

DMA Publications are available from the NOAA Distribution Service (N/CG33), National Ocean Service, Riverdale, MD 20737-1199; Tel. (301) 436-6990; Fax (301) 436-6829.

Each regional NOAA/NOS Catalog of DMA products lists some of the more popular index charts, world charts, general nautical charts, magnetic charts, oceanographic and bottom sediment charts, aeronautical charts, Loran charts published by the agency.

Public sales of DMA charts and publications are available through a network of NOAA chart sales agents. Your local agent may place an order for you, or you may order directly from NOAA at the following address: NOAA Distribution Branch, N/CG33; National Ocean Service; Riverdale, Maryland 20737-1199. Telephone and Fax orders are also accepted by the NOAA Distribution Branch: General information and one-time orders only 301-436-6990. Chart agent orders and information 301-436-8726. Fax orders 301-436-6829.

- **Sailing Directions.** Books supplementing DMAHTC charts contain descriptions of coastlines, harbors, dangers, aids, port facilities and other data that cannot be shown conveniently on charts.

- **Pilot charts**
PUB105. Atlas of Pilot Charts-South Atlantic Ocean, 1981.
PUB106. Atlas of Pilot Charts-Central American Waters, 1982.
PUB107. Atlas of Pilot Charts-South Pacific Ocean, 1981.

PUB108. Atlas of Pilot Charts-North Atlantic, 1983.
PUB109. Atlas of Pilot Charts-Indian Ocean, 1989.

■ List of Lights, Radio Aids and Fog Signals

PUB110. Greenland, the East Coasts of North and South America, (excluding Continental U.S.A., except the East Coast of Florida) and the West Indies.
PUB111. The West Coasts of North and South America, (excluding Continental U.S.A. and Hawaii), Australia, Tasmania, New Zealand, and the Islands of the North and South Pacific Oceans.
PUB112. Western Pacific and Indian Oceans including the Persian Gulf and Red Sea.
PUB113. The West Coasts of Europe and Africa, the Mediterranean Sea, Black Sea and Azovskoye More (Sea of Azov).
PUB114. British Isles, English Channel, and North Sea.
PUB115. Norway, Iceland and Arctic Ocean.
PUB116. Baltic Sea with Kattegat, Belts and Sound, and Gulf of Bosnia.

■ Miscellaneous DMA Publications

PUB9. American Practical Navigator, originally by Nathaniel Bowditch. Volume I (1984); Volume II (1981).
PUB102. International Code of Signals.
PUB117. Radio Navigation Aids, Marine Direction-Finding Stations, Radio Beacons, Time Signals, Navigational Warnings, Distress Signals, Medical Advice and Quarantine Stations, Loran and Regulations Covering the Use of Radio in Territorial Waters.
PUB150. World Port Index.
PUB217. Maneuvering Board Manual.
PUB226. Handbook of Magnetic Compass Adjustment and Compensation.
PUB1310. Radar Navigation Manual.

Weather Publications

■ **Marine Weather Service Charts.** A series of 15 charts containing broadcast schedules of radio stations, National Weather Service telephone numbers and locations of warning display stations. Charts cover the Atlantic, Gulf and Pacific coasts and waters adjacent to Hawaii, Puerto Rico, the Virgin Islands and Alaska. Distribution Division (N/CG33), National Ocean Service, 6501 Lafayette Ave., Riverdale, MD 20737.

■ **Worldwide Marine Weather Broadcasts.** Broadcast schedules of marine weather information from all areas of the world where such service is available. Superintendent of Documents, U.S. Government Printing Office, Washington, DC 20402.

■ **Daily Weather Maps Weekly Series.** This publication is available as a yearly subscription through the National Weather Service, Analysis and Information Branch Room 805, 5200 Auth Road, Camp Springs, MD 20746 (301) 763-8071.

Miscellaneous Publications

■ **The American Nautical Almanac.** Compact publication from the United States Naval Observatory contains all ephemeris material essential to the solution of problems of navigational position; star chart is included. Superintendent of Documents, Washington, DC 20402, or sales agents.

■ **Dutton's Navigation and Piloting** by Elbert S. Maloney; 14th Edition, 1985. U.S. Naval Institute, Annapolis, MD 21402.

■ **A Mariner's Guide to Rules of the Road** by William H. Tate. A concise and comprehensive presentation of the 1972 International Rules of the Road and current U.S. Inland Rules; extensively illustrated. U.S. Naval Institute, Annapolis, MD 21402.

Canadian Addresses

■ **Canadian Coast Guard**, Navigation Safety, 344 Slater Street, 12th Floor; Ottawa, ON KIA ON7. Tel. (613) 991-3137. **Transport Canada**, Public Affairs, Place de Ville, Tower C, 21st Floor; Ottawa, ON KIA ON5. **Hydrographic Chart Distribution Office,** Fisheries and Oceans Canada, P.O. Box 8080, 1675 Russell Road, Ottawa, ON K1G 3H6. **Environment Canada**, Main Floor, 351 St. Joseph Blvd., Hull, QC KIA 0H3.

Safety Publications

■ **Safety Standards for Small Craft** available from the ABYC, Suite 3, 405 Headquarters Drive, Millersville, MD 21108.

■ **Fire Protection Standard No.302 for Motor Craft (Pleasure and Commercial)**, available from NFPA, 470 Atlantic Ave., Boston, MA 02110.

ASSOCIATIONS AND ORGANIZATIONS

United States Sailing Association (USSA)
Box 2090
Newport RI 02840-0209
(401) 849-5200
(401) 849-5208 (Fax)

Yacht Architects & Brokers Association
584 Bellerive Drive, Suite 3D
Annapolis, MD 21401
(410) 974-4472
(410) 757-3809 Fax

BOAT U.S. Foundation
880 South Pickett Street
Alexandria, VA 22304-4606
(703) 823-9550
(703) 461-2847 Fax

American Power Boat Association (APBA)
17640 E. Nine Mile Road
P.O. Box 377
Eastpointe, MI 48021
(313) 773-9700
(313) 773-6490

BUC Information Services
1314 N.E. 17th Court
Fort Lauderdale, FL 33305
(800) 327-6929
In Florida (305) 565-6715
Fax (305) 561-3095

The American Boat & Yacht Council Inc.
3069 Solomon's Island Road
Edgewater, MD 21037-1416
(410) 974-8112
(410) 956-2737 Fax

Marine Department of Underwriters Laboratories (UL)
12 Laboratory Drive
P.O. Box 13995,
Research Triangle Park, NC 27709-3995
(919) 549-1400
(919) 549-1842 Fax

National Fire Protection Association (NFPA)
1 Battery March Park
Quincy, MA 02269
(617) 770-4543
(617) 770-0700 Fax

National Marine Manufacturers Association (NMMA)
401 N. Michigan Ave.,
Chicago, IL 60611
(312) 836-4747
(312) 329-9815 Fax

The American Bureau of Shipping (ABS)
1 World Trade Center, 106th Floor
New York, NY 10048-0203
(212) 839-5000
(212) 839-5130 Fax

Lloyds of London
1 Lime Street,
London, EC3M 7HA,
England

Canadian Yachting Association
1600 James Naismith Drive
Gloucester, ON K1B 5N4
(613) 748-5687

British Meteorological Office
London Road
Bracknell, Berkshire RG12 2SZ
England

United Safe Boating Institute
1504 Blue Ridge Road,
Raleigh, NC 27622
(919) 821-0281
(919) 836-0813 Fax
For information on boating courses,
call 1-800-336-BOAT.

STATE NUMBERING CERTIFICATES

All undocumented vessels equipped with propulsion machinery must be registered in the state of principal use. A certificate of number will be issued upon registering the vessel. These numbers must be displayed on your vessel. The owner/operator of a vessel must carry a valid certificate of number whenever the vessel is in use. When moved to a new state of principal use, the certificate is valid for 60 days. Check with your state numbering authority for numbering requirements. Some states require all vessels to be numbered. The U.S. Coast Guard issues the certificate of number in Alaska; all others are issued by the states or U.S. territories. In Alaska, application forms for Coast Guard registration numbers may be obtained through local post offices or any Coast Guard facility. The following is a list of vessel numbering issuing authorities:

Boat Registration Supervisor
Marine Police Division
Dept. of Conservation and
Natural Resources
64 North Union Street, Room 756
Montgomery, AL 36130

Watercraft Registration Supervisor
Arizona Game and Fish Department
222 West Greenway Road
Phoenix, AZ 85023

Manager, Registration
Department of Finance
and Administration
P.O. Box 1272 - Revenue Division
Little Rock, AR 72203

Department of Motor Vehicles
2415 First Avenue
Sacramento, CA 95814-7291

Division of Parks and Outdoor
Recreation
13787 South Highway 85
Littleton, CO 80125

Department of Motor Vehicles
Marine Vessel Section
60 State Street
Wethersfield, CT 06109

Boat Registrations
Department of Natural Resources
& Environmental Control
Division of Fish and Wildlife
P.O. Box 1401
Dover, DE 19903

Metropolitan Police Department
Harbor Section
550 Water Street, S.W.
Washington, DC 20024

Department of Natural Resources
Division of Law Enforcement
3900 Commonwealth Blvd.,
Mail Sta. 660
Tallahassee, FL 32399-3000

Boating Registration Unit
2189 Northlake Parkway
Suite 108, Building 10
Tucker, GA 30084

Department of Transportation
Harbors Division
79 South Nimitz Highway
Honolulu, HI 96813

Licensing Section
Department of Parks & Recreation
Statehouse Mail
Boise, ID 83720

Department of Conservation
Division of Law Enforcement
524 South Second Street
Springfield, IL 62701-1787

Bureau of Motor Vehicles
Department of Natural Resources
IGCN, Room 409
100 North Senate Ave.
Indianapolis, IN 46204

Licensing Bureau
Department of Natural Resources
Fish and Wildlife Division
Wallace State Office Building
E. Ninth & Grand Avenue
Des Moines, IA 50319-0034

Licensing Division
Department of Wildlife and Parks
RR2, Box 54A
Pratt, KS 67124

Title Branch, Natural Resources
& Environmental Cabinet
Kentucky Water Patrol
107 Mero Street
Frankfort, KY 40601

Motorboat Registration
Department of Wildlife and Fisheries
P.O. Box 14796
Baton Rouge, LA 70898-4796

Director of Licensing
and Registration
Department of Inland
Fisheries & Wildlife
284 State Street
Augusta, ME 04333

Licensing & Watercraft
Registration Services
Tawes State Office Building, B-1
580 Taylor Avenue
Annapolis, MD 21401

Department of Fisheries, Wildlife
& Environmental Law Enforcement
Division of Law Enforcement
100 Nashua Street
Boston, MA 02114

Secretary of State
Information Services Division
7064 Crowner Drive
Lansing, MI 48918

License Bureau
Department of Natural Resources
500 Lafayette Road
St. Paul, MN 55155

Department of Wildlife,
Fisheries & Parks
P.O. Box 451
Jackson, MS 39205

Motor Vehicle Bureau
Department of Revenue
P.O. Box 200
Jefferson City, MO 65105

Registrar's Bureau
Department of Justice
925 Main Street
Deer Lodge, MT 59722

Registration Supervisor
Nebraska Game & Parks Commission
P.O. Box 30370
Lincoln, NE 68503-0370

New Hampshire Department of
Safety, Division of Motor Vehicles
10 Hazen Drive
Concord, NH 03305

Division of Motor Vehicles
Marine Law Enforcement Bureau
N.J. State Police, P.O. Box 7068
West Trenton, NJ 08628-0068

Motor Vehicles Department
P.O. Box 1028
Santa Fe, NM 87504-1028

Department of Motor Vehicles
Empire State Plaza
Swan Street Building
Albany, NY 12228

North Carolina Wildlife
Resources Commission
322 Chapanoke Road
Raleigh, NC 27603

Licensing Supervisor
State Game & Fish Department
100 North Bismarck Expressway
Bismarck, ND 58501-5095

Registration and Titling Div. of
Watercraft
Ohio Dept of Natural Resources
1952 Belcher Drive - C2
Columbus, OH 43224-1386

Oklahoma Tax Commission
409 N.E. 28th
Oklahoma City, OK 73105

Registration Manager
State Marine Board
435 Commercial Street, N.E.
Salem, OR 97310

Boat Registration Division
P.O. Box 1852
Harrisburg, PA 17105-1852

Licensing Unit, Division of
Business Affairs, Department
of Environmental Management
83 Park Street
Providence, RI 02903

Titling & Registration
Wildlife & Marine Resources Dept.
P.O. Box 167
Columbia, SC 29202

Department of Motor Vehicles
Public Safety Building
118 W. Capitol Avenue
Pierre, SD 57501-2017

Boat Registration
Tennessee Wildlife Resource
Agency
P.O. Box 40747
Nashville, TN 37204

Texas Parks & Wildlife Department
4200 Smith School Road
Austin, TX 78744

Tax Commission
Motor Vehicle Division
1095 Motor Avenue
Salt Lake City, UT 84116

Department of Motor Vehicles
Vermont State Police Marine
Division
103 South Main Street
Waterbury, VT 05676

Boating Law Administrator
Dept. of Game and Inland Fisheries
P.O. Box 11104
4010 W. Broad Street
Richmond, VA 23230-1104

Titling and Registration Services
Department of Licensing
Highway Licenses Building PB-01
Olympia, WA 98504

Division of Motor Vehicles
Department of Natural Resources
State Office Building
1800 East Washington Street
Charleston, WV 25305

Department of Natural Resources
P.O. Box 7924
125 S. Webster Street
Madison, WI 53707

Boating Law Administrator
Wyoming Game and Fish Department
5400 Bishop Boulevard
Cheyenne, WY 82006

Director, Numbering & Registration
Department of Natural Resources
P.O. Box 5887
Puerta de Tierra, PR 00906

Guam Boating Law Administrator
Harbor Unit, Guam Police Dept.
287 West O'Brien Drive
Agana, Guam 96910

Boating Law Administrator, Dept.
of Planning & National Resources
231 Nisky Center
St. Thomas, U.S. Virgin Islands 00802

Department of Public Safety
Pago Pago, AS 96799

Department of Public Safety
Civic Center
Saipan, CNMI 96950

CAPTAINS OF THE PORT/MARINE SAFETY OFFICES

Commanding Officer
U.S. Coast Guard,
Marine Safety Office
Ryan Wash Bldg., 2nd Floor
Mobile, AL 36652-2924
(205) 690-2202

Commanding Officer
U.S. Coast Guard, Marine Safety Office
Federal Bldg. & U.S. Courthouse
222 W 7th MC #17
Anchorage, AK 99513-7565
(907) 271-5137

Commanding Officer
U.S. Coast Guard, Marine Safety Office
2760 Sherwood Lane, Suite 2A
Juneau, AK 99801-8545
(907) 586-7344

Commanding Officer
U.S. Coast Guard, Marine Safety Office
P.O. Box 486
Valdez, AK 99686-0486
(907) 950-3861

Commanding Officer
U.S. Coast Guard, Marine Safety Office
Coast Guard Island, Bldg. 14
Alameda, CA 94501-5100
(415) 437-3135

Commanding Officer
U.S. Coast Guard, Marine Safety Office
165 N. Pico Ave.
Long Beach, CA 90802-1096
(213) 499-5500

Commanding Officer
U.S. Coast Guard, Marine Safety Office
2710 North Harbor Drive
San Diego, CA 92101-1046
(619) 557-5860

Captain of the Port
Long Island
c/o USCG Group
120 Woodward Avenue
New Haven, CT 06512-3698
(203) 773-2450

Commanding Officer
U.S. Coast Guard, Marine Safety Office
Room 2131
2831 Talleyrand Avenue
Jacksonville, FL 32206-3497
(904) 791-2640

Commanding Officer
U.S. Coast Guard, Marine Safety Office
155 South Miami Avenue
Miami, FL 33130-1609
(305) 536-5691

Commanding Officer
U.S. Coast Guard, Marine Safety Office
155 Columbia Drive
Tampa, FL 33606-3598
(813) 228-2191

Commanding Officer
U.S. Coast Guard, Marine Safety Office
P.O. Box 8191
Savannah, GA 31412-8191
(912) 944-4371

Commanding Officer
U.S. Coast Guard, Marine Safety Office
1026 Cabras Hwy, Suite 102
Piti, Guam 96925-4610
(671) 477-3340

Commanding Officer
U.S. Coast Guard, Marine Safety Office
433 Ala Moana Blvd., Room 1
Honolulu, HI 96813-4909
(808) 541-2061

Commanding Officer
U.S. Coast Guard, Marine Safety Office
610 South Canal Street
Chicago, IL 60607-4573
(708) 789-5830

Commanding Officer
U.S. Coast Guard, Marine Safety Office
P.O. Box 7509
Paduca, KY 42002-7509
(502) 442-1621

Commanding Officer
U.S. Coast Guard, Marine Safety Office
600 Federal Place, Room 360
Louisville, KY 40202-2230
(502) 582-5194

Commanding Officer
U.S. Coast Guard, Marine Safety Office
800 David Dr., Room 232
Morgan City, LA 70380-0800
(504) 384-2406

Commanding Officer
U.S. Coast Guard, Marine Safety Office
Tidewater Bldg., 1440 Canal Street
New Orleans, LA 70130-3476
(504) 589-6196

Commanding Officer
U.S. Coast Guard, Marine Safety Office
P.O. Box 108, 76 Pearl Street
Portland, ME 04112-1096
(207) 780-3251

Commanding Officer
U.S. Coast Guard, Marine Safety Office
Customhouse, 40 S. Gay Street
Baltimore, MD 21202-4022
(301) 962-5121

Commanding Officer
U.S. Coast Guard, Marine Safety Office
447 Commercial Street
Boston, MA 02109-1096
(617) 223-8480

Commanding Officer
U.S. Coast Guard, Marine Safety Office
Foot of Mt. Elliott Avenue
Detroit, MI 48207-4380
(313) 568-9580

Captain of the Port
c/o USCG Group Grand Haven
650 Harbor Avenue
Grand Haven, MI 49417
(616) 847-4502

Captain of the Port
c/o USCG Group
Sault St. Marie
Sault St. Marie, MI 49783-9501
(906) 635-3210

Commanding Officer
U.S. Coast Guard, Marine Safety Office
Canal Park
Duluth, MN 55802-3252
(218) 720-5286

Commanding Officer
U.S. Coast Guard, Marine Safety Office
P.O. Box D-17
St. Louis, MO 63188-0017
(314) 539-2655

Captain of the Port
c/o USCG Group New York
Governors Island
New York, NY 10004-5098
(212) 668-7917

Commanding Officer
U.S. Coast Guard, Marine Safety Office
Room 1111, 111 W. Huron St.
Buffalo, NY 14202-2395
(716) 846-4168

Commanding Officer
U.S. Coast Guard, Marine Safety Office
272 North Front St.
Suite 500
Wilmington, NC 28401-3907
(919) 343-4882

Commanding Officer
U.S. Coast Guard, Marine Safety Office
1055 East Ninth Street
Cleveland, OH 44414-1092
(216) 522-4405

Commanding Officer
U.S. Coast Guard, Marine Safety Office
234 Summit Street, Rm 101
Toledo, OH 43604-1590
(419) 259-6372

Commanding Officer
U.S. Coast Guard, Marine Safety Office
6767 N. Basin Avenue
Portland, OR 97217-3929
(503) 240-0305

Commanding Officer
U.S. Coast Guard, Marine Safety Office
1 Washington Avenue
Philadelphia, PA 19147-4395
(215) 271-4803

Commanding Officer
U.S. Coast Guard, Marine Safety Office
Suite 700, Kossman Bldg.
Forbes Ave. & Stanwix St.
Pittsburgh, PA 15222-1371
(412) 644-5808

Commanding Officer
U.S. Coast Guard, Marine Safety Office
P.O. Box S-3666
San Juan, PR 00904-3666
(809) 722-2697

Commanding Officer
U.S. Coast Guard, Marine Safety Office
John O'Pastore Federal Bldg.
Providence, RI 02903-1790
(401) 528-5335

Commanding Officer
U.S. Coast Guard, Marine Safety Office
196 Tradd Street
Charleston, SC 29401-1899
(803) 724-7683

Commanding Officer
U.S. Coast Guard, Marine Safety Office
200 Jefferson Ave., Suite 1301
Memphis, TN 38103-2300
(901) 521-3941

Commanding Officer
U.S. Coast Guard, Marine Safety Office
P.O. Box 1621
Corpus Christi, TX 78403-1621
(512) 888-3192

Commanding Officer
U.S. Coast Guard, Marine Safety Office
P.O. Box 446
Galena Park, TX 77547-0446
(713) 672-6639

Commanding Officer
U.S. Coast Guard, Marine Safety Office
601 Rosenberg
Galveston, TX 77550-1705
(409) 766-3655

Commanding Officer
U.S. Coast Guard, Marine Safety Office
Federal Bldg.
2875 75th Street & Hwy 69
Port Arthur, TX 77640-2099
(205) 690-4344

Commanding Officer
U.S. Coast Guard, Marine Safety Office
200 Granby Street Mall
Norfolk, VA 23510-1888
(804) 441-3302

Commanding Officer
U.S. Coast Guard, Marine Safety Office
1519 Alaskan Way S.
Bldg. 1, Pier 36
Seattle, WA 98134-1192
(206) 286-5550

Commanding Officer
U.S. Coast Guard, Marine Safety Office
P.O. Box 2412, 1415 6th Ave.
Huntington, WV 25725-2412
(304) 529-5524

Commanding Officer
U.S. Coast Guard, Marine Safety Office
2420 S. Lincoln Memorial Drive
Milwaukee, WI 53207-1997
(414) 362-3788

THE METRIC SYSTEM

The Metric Conversion Act of 1975 (as amended in 1988) declares, as the policy of the United States, that the metric system of measurement is the preferred system of weights and measures for U.S. trade and commerce.

The terms 'metric system,' 'SI,' 'SI metric,' and 'SI units' refer to units belonging to the International System of Units (abbreviated SI from the French *Le Système International d'Unités*). They include the SI units (together with their multiples and submultiples); three other metric units—the liter, hectare, and metric ton—that are accepted for use with the SI units because of their practical importance; and a small number of other metric units that are accepted because of their use in specialized fields. SI provides a logical and interrelated framework for measurements in science, industry, commerce and other forms of human endeavor.

The modern metric system is based upon a foundation of base units, with multiples and submultiples expressed in a decimal system using various prefixes.

The SI units

The base units of most interest to boaters are length, weight and temperature. These units and their symbols are:

Length	meter (m)
Mass (weight)	kilogram (kg)
Temperature	degree Celsius (°C)

Note that 'degree Celsius' was formerly known as 'centigrade.' Also, the SI unit for time is the second. The minute, hour and day are units that are accepted for use with SI.

The symbols, shown in parentheses, are *not* abbreviations. They are written in lower case letters except for those units (such as degree Celsius) named after a person. Periods are not used with any symbols.

Derived units

Other units in the metric system are derived from the base units. Typical of those expressed in combinations of base units and of interest to boaters are:

Area	square meter (m^2)
Volume	cubic meter (m^3)
	liter (L)
Speed, velocity	meter per second (m/s)
	kilometer per hour (km/h)

Multiples and submultiples

Units larger and smaller than the base units are formed by adding prefixes to make multiples and submultiples. The prefix symbol is added to the symbol for the base unit. Prefixes that are multiples or submultiples of 1,000 (kilo, centi, milli) are generally preferred as follows:

1000	10^3	kilo	k
100	10^2	hecto	h
10	10^1	deka	da
0.1	10^{-1}	deci	d
0.01	10^{-2}	centi	c
0.001	10^{-3}	milli	m

Retained inch-pound units

Certain units that are not metric units are so widely used that they are accepted for use with the metric system. Of interest to boaters are degrees, minutes and seconds as measurements of arc. (The radian is the metric measurement of arc, but its use has been limited to scientific applications.)

Other inch-pound units, which are continued for a limited time subject to future review, include the nautical mile and knot as measurements of distance and speed.

Conversion

The following conversion factors are rounded for general use and in most cases will yield practical results.

Customary units to metric

Known value		Multiply by	To find	
in	inches	25.4	millimeters	mm
ft	feet	0.3048	meters	m
yd	yards	0.9144	meters	m
s mi	statute miles	1.609	kilometers	km
n mi	nautical miles	1.852	kilometers	km
oz	ounces (weight)	28.35	grams	g
lb	pounds	0.4536	kilograms	kg
oz	ounces (liquid)	29.57	milliliters	mL
qt	quarts	0.9464	liters	L
gal	gallons	3.785	liters	L
°F	Fahrenheit (temperature)	5/9 after subtracting 32	Celsius (temperature)	°C

Metric units to customary

Known value		Multiply by	To find	
cm	centimeters	0.3937	inches	in
m	meters	3.281	feet	ft
m	meters	1.094	yards	yd
km	kilometers	0.6214	stat. miles	s mi
km	kilometers	0.5400	naut. miles	n mi
g	grams	0.03527	ounces (weight)	oz
kg	kilograms	2.205	pounds	lb
mL	milliliters	0.03381	ounces (liquid)	oz
L	liters	1.057	quarts	qt
L	liters	0.2642	gallons	gal
°C	Celsius (temperature)	9/5 then add 32	Fahrenheit (temperature)	°F

ABBREVIATIONS & ACRONYMS

ABYC American Boat and Yacht Council. (*See also Glossary*).

AC Alternating Current.

ADF Automatic Direction Finder, an advanced variation of a radio direction finder, RDF.

AM Amplitude Modulation, one form of broadcast radio transmission, modulating the carrier wave in accordance with the strength of the audio signal.

AP Advanced Piloting, a course and a grade in the U.S. Power Squadrons.

ATON Coast Guard acronym for Aids to Navigation.

C Course, used in marking charts while plotting; Celsius, the metric temperature scale.

CE Center of Effort

CB Citizens' Band, a short wave radio frequency service; compass bearing.

CME Courtesy Motorboat Examination.

CMG Course Made Good.

CNG Compressed Natural Gas, a fuel used for cooking and heating.

CO Carbon monoxide, a poisonous gas.

CO^2 Carbon dioxide; a type of fire extinguishing agent.

COLREGS U.S. Coast Guard acronym for International Regulations for the Prevention of Collisions at Sea. (*See also Glossary*).

CPS Canadian Power and Sail Squadrons.

CQR A brand of plow anchor.

D Direction, used in marking data on a chart plot; also distance, used in marking data on a chart plot.

DC Direct Current.

DF Direction Finder; Direction Finding.

DMA Defense Mapping Agency.

DMAHTC DMA Hydrographic/Topographic Agency.

DR Dead Reckoning; label for a DR position on a chart plot.

E East, cardinal compass point.

EP Estimated Position.

EPIRB Emergency Position Indicating Radiobeacon. (*See also Glossary*).

ETA Estimated Time of Arrival.

ETD Estimated Time of Departure.

F Fahrenheit, usually shown as °F.

FBSA Federal Boat Safety Act (U.S.).

FCC Federal Communications Commission, the U.S. regulator and licensor of radio transmission facilities.

FM Frequency Modulation, a communications technology that changes the frequency of the transmitting radio in accordance with the sound.

FRP Fiberglass reinforced plastics.

GMT Greenwich Mean Time; essentially the same as Coordinated Universal Time (UTC).

GPO Government Printing Office, a source of charts and documents (U.S.).

H Hertz, a unit of frequency measurement, equivalent to cycles per second.

HF High Frequency (radio).

HIN Hull Identification Number.

hp Horsepower, a unit of power, equal to 746 watts in the U.S.

ICW Intracoastal Waterway.

IntRR International Rules of the Road.

JN Junior Navigator, a course and a grade in the U.S. Power Squadrons.

kHz Kilohertz, unit of radio frequency, one thousand Hertz.

km Kilometer, one thousand meters, .62 of a statute mile, .54 nautical mile.

kn Knot, speed measurement, one nautical mile per hour (sometimes abbreviated "kt").

lat. Latitude.

LF Low Frequency (Loran-C).

LNM Local Notice to Mariners.

LOA Length overall. (*See also Glossary*).

long. Longitude.

LOP Line of Position.

LORAN-C Long Range Navigation system using several timed signals from different locations.

LPG Liquified Petroleum Gas, a fuel.

LWL Length on the waterline or load waterline. (*See also Glossary*).

m Meter, unit of linear measurement.

MF Medium Frequency.

MHW Mean High Water, a tidal datum for heights.

MHz Megahertz, unit of radio frequency, one thousand kHz, or one million Hertz.

MLLW Mean lower low water, a tidal datum for depths.

MLW Mean low water, a tidal datum for depths.

MSD Marine Sanitation Device.

N North, cardinal compass point; also Navigator, a course and highest educational grade in the U.S. Power Squadrons.

NavLights Navigation lights.

NE Northeast, intercardinal compass point.

NFPA National Fire Protection Association.

NM Notice to Mariners.

NMMA National Marine Manufacturers Association.

NOAA National Oceanic and Atmospheric Administration.

NOS National Ocean Service.

NW Northwest, intercardinal point on compass.

NWS National Weather Service.

P Piloting, a course and a grade in the U.S. Power Squadrons.

PFD Personal Flotation Device.

PPI Plan Position Indicator, a type of radar display.

Q flag Yellow Quarantine flag, so-called; the International Signal Code is "My vessel is healthy and I request free practique."

RACON A radar beacon which, when triggered by pulses from a vessel's radar, transmits a reply.

RDF Radio Direction Finder. (*See also Glossary*).

rpm revolutions per minute.

S South, cardinal compass point; Seamanship, a course and grade in the U.S. Power Squadrons.

SAR Search and Rescue, Coast Guard and CG Auxiliary term.

SE Southeast, intercardinal compass point.

SHF Super High Frequency (radar).

SOLAS Safety of Life at Sea Convention.

SOS Morse code signal of distress.

SSB Single Side Band, radio term for a short wave communications technique.

SW Southwest, intercardinal compass point.

T flag Transportation flag, signal flag hoisted as a signal requesting a tender or launch service.

UHF Ultra High Frequency (radio).

UL Underwriters Laboratories, a safety organization that conducts product tests.

USCG United States Coast Guard.

USCG Aux United States Coast Guard Auxiliary.

USN United States Navy.

USPS United States Power Squadrons. (*See also Glossary*).

USWMS Uniform State Waterway Marking System.

UTC Universal Coordinated Time.

VHF Very High Frequency (radio).

VLF Very Low Frequency (Omega).

W West, cardinal compass direction.

WWV Continuous broadcast time signal station, based in Colorado.

WWVH Hawaii-based 24-hour radio time signal station.

GLOSSARY OF SELECTED TERMS

A

- **abaft** Behind, toward the stern.
- **abeam** To one side of a vessel, at a right angle to the fore-and-aft line.
- **abreast** Even with, by the side of, side by side.
- **ABYC** American Boat and Yacht Council, Inc., the organization that sets voluntary safety and construction standards for small craft in the U.S.A.
- **admeasure** To measure a vessel for the purpose of documentation.
- **adrift** Floating free without propulsion; not moored, aground, nor fastened to the shore.
- **admiralty law** Law of the sea; a term for maritime law derived from the British Admiralty department, which administers naval affairs.
- **aft, after** Near or at the stern.
- **after bow spring line** A mooring line running aft from a point at or near the bow to shore to control forward and backward motion of a vessel in its berth.
- **agonic line** An imaginary line on the earth's surface, along which there is no magnetic variation.
- **aground** With the keel or bottom fast on the sea bottom.
- **aids to navigation** Markers on land or sea that are established to enable navigators to avoid danger and fix their position; buoys, lights, beacons, radiobeacons, daybeacons with known charted positions.
- **aloft** Above the deck, usually in the rigging.
- **amidships** In the center, the center portion of a vessel.
- **anchor** A heavy metal device, fastened to chain or line, to hold a vessel in position, partly because of its weight, but chiefly because the designed shape digs into the bottom.
- **anchorage** A customary, suitable and (usually) designated harbor area in which vessels may anchor.
- **anchor bend** A specific knot, generally used to fasten an anchor line to an anchor.
- **anchor light** An all-round white light required by the Navigation Rules when a vessel is at anchor or moored; also called a riding light.
- **anchor rode** A line, chain or steel cable used to hold a vessel fast to the anchor.
- **anchor watch** Person or persons kept alert on deck while the vessel is at anchor or moored in order to cope with unexpected situations.
- **anemometer** An instrument that measures wind velocity.
- **aneroid barometer** A device to measure and indicate air pressure for meteorology, using a mechanical means, rather than a liquid such as mercury. The pressure is generally indicated as the equivalent of so many millibars, formerly millimeters, or as inches of mercury.
- **anti-fouling** A type of paint, used on the bottoms of boats, that repels barnacles, marine grass and many other undesirable adhesions.
- **apparent wind** The direction and force of the wind relative to a moving vessel, differing from true wind. The motion of a sailboat or powerboat under way makes the effective wind, acting on sails or hull, vary from the actual wind. Apparent wind can be indicated by a telltale or instruments.
- **astern** The direction toward the stern of a vessel, or beyond the stern.
- **athwart** At right angles to the center line.
- **autopilot** An automatic steering device. The heading of the boat is sensed by a compass and the craft is steered to maintain a preset course by a combination of electronic and mechanical/hydraulic devices; on sailboats a similar system is used to steer a course based on the apparent wind.
- **auxiliary** A sailboat that has an engine.
- **aweigh** Off the bottom, said of an anchor.

B

- **backing (wind)** Wind changing its direction, counter-clockwise in the northern hemisphere, clockwise in the southern hemisphere; opposite of veering.
- **backsplice** A splice in which the strands are reversed and interwoven, to make a rope end.
- **backstay** A stay supporting the mast, running from the masthead to the stern.
- **ballast** Additional weight placed low in the hull to improve stability; ballast may be either internal or external.
- **bar** A sand, mud or debris shoal, as across the mouth of a river or harbor.
- **barograph** A weather instrument that continuously records atmospheric (barometric) pressure.
- **barometer** An instrument that measures and displays atmospheric pressure, showing it in millibars (or in inches or in millimeters of mercury) usually on a dial with an indicating needle.
- **batten down** To close all openings, such as hatches, and fasten all loose gear, in heavy weather; wooden hatches used to be covered with a tarpaulin, and then fastened with battens and wedges.
- **battens** Thin flexible strips of wood or plastic, used in batten pockets of a sail to support (stiffen to keep flat) the roach; battens are also used in awnings.
- **beam** One of the principal dimensions of a boat, the width; also, the direction at right angles to the center line of a vessel, as "the lighthouse is broad on the beam."
- **beam reach** A point of sailing with the apparent wind blowing at right angles to the boat's fore-and-aft line.
- **bearing** The direction of an object (vessel, buoy, etc.) from an observer; bearings can be visual, or by radio or radar.
- **bear off** To turn away from the wind, to turn leeward, also "to bear away."
- **beating** Sailing against the wind, in alternate tacks.
- **Beaufort wind scale** A scale indicating the force of the wind, invented by Admiral Beaufort in 1808; the original scale indicated the effect on a full-rigged frigate under sail; it has been extended to cover effects on shore as well as at sea, plus criteria that can now be measured, such as speed of the

wind; the scale usually shows wind forces, 0 through 12, but it has been expanded to 17. Each increase of force (number) means a doubling of the pressure (not velocity) of the wind.

■ **becket** A loop or eye made in the end of rope or wire; a rope handle.

■ **bedding compound** Caulking material used for mating two surfaces, rendering them watertight.

■ **bend** One of several types of knots, a combination of turns and tucks, used to fasten a line to a spar or another line; to fasten by means of a bend or knot.

■ **bend on** To prepare a sail for hoisting; to rig.

■ **berth** A position, as a place to sleep or in which a vessel may be made fast; a margin of safety, as a "wide berth."

■ **bight** The middle part of a slack rope; a loop; an indentation in a shoreline.

■ **bilge** The lowest point of a vessel's interior hull; also the part of the exterior between the bottom and the topsides, the "turn of the bilge."

■ **binnacle** A compass box or case, or a stand, usually illuminated at night.

■ **binocular** A telescopic instrument for the use of both eyes at once, having two tubes, each furnished with lenses. It uses prisms as well as lenses to keep the size down.

■ **bitt** A strong post of wood or iron, similar to a samson-post, on deck in the bow or the stern, to which anchor, mooring and towing lines may be fastened.

■ **bitter end** Inboard end of an anchor rode, the extreme end of any line.

■ **block** Complete assembly of sheaves or pulleys and shells (plates) on which ropes run; can be wooden, plastic or metal.

■ **block-and-tackle** Any of several arrangements of blocks (pulleys) and line to gain a mechanical advantage.

■ **boarding ladder** A temporary set of steps lowered over a vessel's side.

■ **boat** A small vessel, propelled by oars, sail or power; a vessel that can be carried aboard a ship.

■ **boathook** A hook on a pole, used for retrieving or picking up objects and for fending off.

■ **bollard** A strong vertical fitting, usually iron, on deck or on a pier or wharf, to which mooring lines may be fastened.

■ **boom** A spar used to extend the foot of a sail.

■ **boomvang** A system of fittings to hold the boom down under some sailing conditions.

■ **boot-top** A painted stripe at the waterline.

■ **bosun** A boatswain, a petty officer in charge of hull, rigging and sail maintenance as well as deck operations; other phonetic spellings are bos'n, bo's'n, bo'sun.

■ **bosun's chair** A seat, sometimes a rigid plank, sometimes made of canvas, used to hoist a person aloft to repair rigging; pockets for tools are often included.

■ **bosun's locker** A shipboard storage area for deck supplies, paint, rigging fittings and tools.

■ **bow** The forward part of a boat.

■ **bow & beam bearings** A set of bearings on an object ashore or an aid to navigation whose position is known, used to determine distance off.

■ **Bowditch** A standard reference work on navigation, containing useful tables and instructional text; it is named after Nathaniel Bowditch, the nineteenth-century author of the first "Bowditch."

■ **bowline** The "king of knots," used to make a loop in a line; this knot is simple, strong, virtually slip-proof and is very easily untied.

■ **bowsprit** A fixed spar, projecting from the bow, to which forestays and/or the headstay are fastened; also useful for anchor handling.

■ **braided line** A modern configuration of rope (usually called the line aboard a boat or ship); it may be a single braid or double braid, one braid (core) inside another.

■ **breakers** Waves cresting as they reach shallow water, as at or on a beach.

■ **breakwater** A structure, usually stone or concrete, built to create a harbor or improve an existing one.

■ **breast line** Mooring or dock line, extending laterally from the vessel to a pier or float, as distinguished from a spring line, which controls fore and aft movement of the vessel.

■ **bridge** The control station of a vessel; the persons in charge of a vessel, or (by extension) of an organization, such as the U.S. Power Squadrons; a structure over water to carry pedestrian, vehicular or railroad traffic.

■ **brightwork** Polished brass, bronze or stainless steel aboard a vessel; also, varnished wood as trim.

■ **Bristol fashion** Shipshape; clean, neat, orderly and conforming to high standards of seamanship.

■ **broach to, broaching** The sudden, unplanned and uncontrolled turning of a vessel so that the hull is broadside to the seas or to the wind.

■ **broad on the beam** At a right angle to a vessel.

■ **broad reach** A point of sailing with the apparent wind broad on the beam.

■ **bulkhead** A transverse wall in the hull; the interior compartmentalization of a vessel is created by bulkheads; in some cases bulkheads are watertight, adding to the safety in case of damage to the hull.

■ **buntline hitch** A simple, useful hitch for attaching a halyard to a shackle; strong, secure, easily undone.

■ **buoy** A floating aid to navigation showing channels or otherwise indicating location, rocks and other obstructions, and prohibited areas on the water; turning points in races; to buoy an anchor is to temporarily fasten the anchor line to a float, so that the anchor need not be raised when a vessel is leaving its anchorage.

■ **burdened vessel** The vessel which must "give way" to another vessel in a crossing or overtaking situation, following the *Navigation Rules*.

■ **burgee** A special flag flown on a vessel or on a flagstaff of a shore installation, indicating either the ownership of the vessel or the identity of a yacht club or similar organization.

C

- **camber** Curvature of either sail or keel; the curve of the deck, usually being higher in the center so that the water can run off.
- **can** A cylindrical buoy, generally green.
- **Canadian Power & Sail Squadrons** A private membership organization that specializes in boating education and safe boating practices.
- **canvas** Firm, closely woven cloth (originally hemp, linen or cotton) used for sails and awnings; a set of sails; today the word "sailcloth" is generally used for modern sailmaking fabrics such as polyester (Dacron) and nylon.
- **capsize** To turn over; to turn bottom side up.
- **capstan** A vertical winch on deck, used for hauling, such as the anchor line.
- **carbon fiber** Modern fiber used with epoxies in order to stiffen a component.
- **cardinal points** The four principal compass points: North, East, South and West.
- **carlins** Fore and aft members of the deck frame; they support the coamings of the cockpit, the cabin trunk sides and the hatch coamings.
- **carrick bend** A useful knot for fastening two lines together; a number of variations exist, but these are of little or no value.
- **carry away** To break loose, said of gear that is stressed beyond the strength of its fastenings.
- **carvel** Smooth skin planking.
- **cast off** To loose, unfasten; to undo all mooring lines in preparation for departure.
- **catalyst** Chemical used to activate polyester resins and other polymers.
- **catamaran** A twin-hulled vessel, sail or power.
- **catboat** A simple rig for a sailboat, with one mast and one sail, which may be either Marconi or with a gaff.
- **catenary** In a rope or chain run between two points, the sag from a straight line due to the effect of gravity.
- **cavitate, cavitation** Turbulence in the water caused by rotation of a propeller; causes wear on the propeller and a reduction in propeller efficiency.
- **ceiling** The inside lining of the hull.
- **celestial navigation** Position determination (and the total process of navigation based on it) by reference to sun, stars and moon. Usually a sextant measures the altitude of the observed heavenly body, a highly accurate source of time information is used to determine the time of the sight, and tables and/or a navigational electronic calculator are used to determine a position line; the place where two position lines cross is a fix.
- **centerboard** A board or metal plate, moving vertically or pivoting up and down in a slot in the keel, which adds lateral resistance to the hull form of a sailboat; in effect the boat's sideways motion through the water is thus controlled by increasing the area of the keel.

- **certificate** A government paper, such as a boat's license, or a seaman's or master's license allowing the operation of a commercial vessel.
- **chafe** Abrasion, wear.
- **chafing gear** Cloth, tape or other material fastened around a line or other rigging to prevent wear.
- **chain** Interlocking steel or iron links, used for anchor rodes and, on larger vessels, certain rigging parts.
- **chain locker** Stowage space for anchor chain.
- **chainplates** Fittings on the sides of the hull or the outer edges of the deck of a sailboat, to which the port and starboard rigging, called shrouds, are fastened.
- **chandlery** Items of nautical gear or the shop where these are sold.
- **channel** The navigable portion of a waterway; the marked and designated area where there is a known depth of water; boats may not normally anchor in a channel.
- **Charlie Noble** A stovepipe fitting in a cabin top or deck, through which the metal "chimney" of a boat's cooking or heating stove passes; usually equipped with a cooling rim of water and a partial cap, to exclude rain and control smoke.
- **charts** Seagoing maps; most charts are issued by governmental sources, and their data is based on surveys of the land and underwater areas, showing depths as well as buoys and other aids to navigation; they are updated periodically.
- **chart table** Also called navigation table, where charts are handled for the purpose of navigating.
- **chine** The intersection between the topsides and bottom.
- **chock** A rigging fitting, essentially shaped like a U or an O, normally mounted on deck or in the toe rail, to control a rigging or mooring line.
- **chockablock** Full up, tight, drawn up as far as possible, as when two blocks in a tackle are closed up and no more movement of the line is possible.
- **chop** Short, steep waves.
- **clamp** The inner longitudinal timber or plank in the construction of a wooden vessel that acts as the bearer for beams or joints.
- **classes** Organized groups of boats (essentially for racing), with either identical measurements and specifications, or variable measurements to fit a formula, designed to equalize boat performance to some degree and thus put a premium on skill and tactics.
- **cleat** A rigging fitting to which mooring lines, sail control lines such as sheets and halyards, and miscellaneous lines are temporarily attached.
- **cleat hitch** The distinctive criss-cross or figure-eight hitch used to fasten (belay) a line to cleat.
- **clevis pin** A large pin that secures one fitting to another.
- **clew** The lower, after corner of a sail, to which the sheet is attached.
- **close-hauled** Hard on the wind, a point of sailing in which the sheets are hauled tight, enabling the boat to sail "against the wind."

- **clove hitch** A double-loop hitch, generally used around a piling or bollard; easily adjusted, but it can work loose.
- **club- footed** Foot of sail, such as a jib or foresail, supported by a small boom.
- **coaming** A raised edge, as around part or all of a cockpit, that prevents the seawater from entering the boat.
- **Coast Pilots** Reference books, issued by the U.S. National Ocean Service, listing navigation aids and other information useful in coastal piloting; the nine books (covering East, Gulf and West coasts, Hawaii and Alaska) include sailing directions, recommended courses, distances between ports, channels, harbors and anchorages.
- **cockpit** A space for the crew, lower than the deck and often watertight or self- draining.
- **cockpit sole** The actual floor of a cockpit.
- **code** In signaling, any of several systems used to transmit messages visually, by sound or electronically; alphabet code flags and dot-dash (Morse) systems are most often used; in addition to spelling out words, code flags are used in combinations to transmit brief phrases or to describe marine situations such as emergency conditions.
- **cold front** A term used in weather reporting/forecasting to describe the forward edge of a mass of cold air meeting warmer air; as the warmer air is forced upward, heavy clouds are formed, often bringing rain and strong winds.
- **cold molding** Process of bending multiple thin layers of wood in sequence with glue to achieve a total desired thickness as opposed to forming by steam bending or sawing.
- **colors** The national ensign; the act or ceremony of raising the colors, including other flags.
- **COLREGS** U.S. Coast Guard term for International Regulations for Preventing Collisions at Sea, also known as the Navigation Rules of the Road.
- **come about** To tack, to change direction relative to the wind.
- **companionway** A hatch or entrance, from deck to cabin.
- **compass** Navigation instrument, either magnetic needles or bars attached, which floats or pivots in a bowl; older compasses used a system of graduated points while most modern ones use the 0-360 degree system; a plotting tool used to draw circles or circular arcs.
- **composite construction** Made with more than one component and of different nature, e.g. plywood and fiberglass.
- **cordage** A term that includes all rope and small line, whether made of natural or of synthetic fibers.
- **cored construction** The use of a core material sandwiched between an outer layer and inner layer, e.g. deck made of fiberglass inner and outer layers and balsa core.
- **Corinthian** An amateur yachtsman.
- **cotter pin** A small pin used to secure a clevis pin and to keep turnbuckles from unwinding; a small pin used to keep any nut from backing off.
- **counter** The portion of the hull, at the stern, above the waterline and extending aft.

- **course** The direction in which a vessel is to be steered; in racing, the preset course or series of courses, often triangular, to be followed.
- **cowls** (scoops) Direct the flow of air and vapors in or out of ducts.
- **cradle** A frame used to support a vessel on land.
- **crest** Top of a wave.
- **cringle** A rope loop or circular eye, made on a metal or plastic thimble, used for fastening on the corner of a sail, awning or other canvas item.
- **crossing situation** When two vessels meet, not head on or nearly head on, but with each having the other forward of a direction 22½ degrees aft the beam; the vessel having the other on its starboard side is the give-way vessel and must keep clear.
- **cunningham** A line controlling tension along a sail's luff, invented by Briggs Cunningham.
- **current** Horizontal movement of water, as from the normal flow of a river or when caused by the rise and fall of tides.

D

- **DRS** Sail known as a drifter/reacher/spinnaker.
- **Dacron** Trademark name for a type of polyester.
- **daggerboard** A centerboard that is retracted vertically rather than hinged.
- **danger angle** A piloting angle, in which on both chart and the water a measured angle between the directions to two points—such as buoys, landmarks or rocks— indicates to the mariner an unsafe limit for his/her vessel.
- **davit** A swing-out device, a crane, used to joist; a pair of davits, at the stern or at the side of the vessel, handles a dinghy or other small boat; a single davit at the bow is often used to handle a heavy anchor.
- **dayboard** A large geometric shape atop a pile to mark one side of a channel or an obstruction such as a submerged jetty; the combination of the dayboard and pile or dolphin if unlighted is a daybeacon, if lighted it is termed a "light."
- **daysailer** A boat without a cabin that is used for short sails or racing.
- **dayshape** A special geometrical marker, such as a black ball, cone or cylinder hung aloft to indicate a vessel's type, occupation or state; one black ball means "at anchor," three means "aground."
- **dead ahead, dead astern** Directions exactly ahead of or behind a vessel.
- **deadlight** A fixed skylight, comparatively small, in a deck or cabin top, admitting light to the space below; a non-opening port.
- **dead reckoning** The navigation means used to determine position, calculated from the course steered and the speed through the water, without obtaining a fix; a dead reckoning position is indicated on a chart by marking a half circle with a dot on the track line; the time is placed at an angle to the horizontal and to the track line.

deadrise Height between the bottom of a vessel and its widest beam, also expressed as an angle.

departure, point of The last fix obtained by an outward bound vessel; it is marked on the chart as the beginning of the track until the next fix or estimated position.

depth sounder An electronic depth-finding instrument, measuring the time a sound wave takes to go from the vessel to the bottom and return, then displaying the result in feet, fathoms or meters.

deviation The amount by which a ship's magnetic compass needle points to one side or the other of magnetic north; iron, steel, magnets and DC currents in wires, cause the compass to vary by different amounts on different headings.

dinghy A small boat used as a tender; the term is also used for a small racing sailboat.

displacement The weight of the water displaced by a floating hull; the volume of water will vary depending on whether it is fresh water or seawater.

displacement hull A boat supported by its own buoyancy while in motion; see planing hull.

distress signals Standardized or improvised signals, which may be visual, audible or electronic, that are used on board a boat to indicate distress and seek assistance; various signals are listed in the *Navigation Rules*.

ditty bag A small bag for tools and personal items.

dock An enclosed or nearly enclosed water area; all the port installations; a place where vessels can make fast, as at a pier, wharf or floating dock.

documentation A special federal license or registration for a vessel.

dolphin A small group of piles, in the water, tied together into a single structure, generally used for mooring or as a channel marker.

Dorade vent Designed deck box ventilation to keep water out with a baffle while letting air in below decks.

double-braid Rope made with a braided core and a braided cover, usually of synthetic fibers.

double-ender A design of boat with a sharp stern, resembling the bow in configuration.

douse To drop or lower a sail quickly; to put out a lamp or a fire.

downhaul A rigging line used to haul down, or to hold down, a spar or sail.

downwind A direction to leeward, with the wind.

draft The vertical distance from the waterline to the lowest point of the hull or attachments such as propellers and rudders, thus the minimum depth of water in which a vessel will float; a vessel is said to "draw" a certain amount of water; the curvature built into a sail.

drift A current's velocity.

drogue An open-ended cone, usually canvas, serving to slow a boat in heavy weather.

drydock An enclosed dock from which the water can be pumped out, so a ship can be repaired or cleaned.

dry rot Decay of wood timbers, as in a boat, actually occurring in moist conditions.

drysail Drying out the boat after each sail outing.

dry storage Storing on land, out of the water.

ducts Channel movement of air for the actual displacement of fumes from the space being ventilated.

E

ease To let out a line under full control, gradually as with a sheet or a docking line.

ebb A tidal current flowing toward the sea.

electronic navigation Piloting by manual or automatic electronic devices: echo sounders, electronic compass, radio direction finder, radar and various position-finding systems such as Loran-C, Omega, Decca, VHF Omnirange (VOR) and satellite systems.

ensign The national flag, or that of an organization such as the Coast Guard Auxiliary or the U.S. Power Squadrons.

entry Forward-designed section of hull in the water; qualifies the type of hull in terms of efficiency and behavior in relation to wave action (for example, a sharper entry means faster hull speed for a racing hull).

EPIRB Emergency Position Indicating Radio Beacon, a small continuously operating transmitter, using a standard distress frequency to alert authorities to the existence of a distress situation and to lead rescuers to the scene.

estimated position (EP) A navigational point (less precise than a fix) based on course run, speed and estimates of such factors as drift caused by wind or currents.

eye splice A fixed loop in the end of a line, made by intertwining strands of rope or by tucking an outer core of double-braid rope back into itself.

F

fairlead A rigging fitting designed to change the direction of a line, control the line and minimize friction.

fastening Any of several methods of holding planks in a wooden boat to the frames: screws, nails, rivets; a screw or bolt used to fasten rigging and plumbing fixtures.

fathom A nautical linear measurement, 6 feet, used primarily to measure depth and anchor rodes.

Fathometer The trademark name for one brand (Raytheon) of electronic instrument for measuring depth of water.

FCC Rules Regulations of the Federal Communications Commission in the U.S. that govern radio equipment and radio operations.

fender A cushioning device hung between the boat and a float or pier.

fetch (1) To sail a course that will clear a buoy or shoal, also "lay"; (2) the distance across water over which the wind is or has been blowing.

fiberglass Fiber-reinforced plastic; glass in fibrous form, usually reinforced with synthetic resin such as polyester; may be woven or mat form.

- **fid** A tapered, pointed tool used to separate strands of rope, as in splicing.
- **figure-eight** A knot, usually in the end of a line as a stopper, to prevent the end of the line from passing through a block or fairlead.
- **fin keel** Keel shaped like the fin of a fish, shorter and deeper than a full- length keel.
- **finger pier** A narrow pier projecting from the shore or at right angles from a larger pier.
- **fix** The position of a vessel, determined by bearings, either visual or electronic, or by any other means believed to be acceptably accurate.
- **flame arrester** A safety device, such as a metal mesh protector to prevent an exhaust backfire from causing an explosion; operates by absorbing heat.
- **flare** A pyrotechnic signal that can indicate distress; the outward curvature of the topsides.
- **flashing** A light that is on less than it is off in a regular sequence of single flashes, occurring less than 30 times in each minute.
- **flemish** To coil a line spirally, laid flat on deck, either for appearance or to make a mat.
- **flinders bar** A soft iron bar, in or on the binnacle, to compensate for compass error from vertical magnetism in a vessel with a steel hull.
- **flood** The rising, incoming tide.
- **floor** Structural members in the bottom of a boat, running athwartships from bilge to bilge.
- **flotsam** Wreckage debris floating on the water.
- **fluke** The flat palm-shaped or shovel-shaped part of an anchor (on the end of each arm) that digs in to the bottom to prevent dragging.
- **flush deck** Deck without any superstructure.
- **flying bridge** A high steering position, usually above the normal wheelhouse of a power cruiser; also called **flybridge.**
- **following sea** Waves from astern.
- **foot** The bottom edge of a sail; also, to steer slightly lower than close- hauled in order to increase boat speed.
- **fore** Located at the front, as of a vessel.
- **fore-and-aft** From stem to stern, from front to back, oriented parallel to the keel.
- **forecabin** Forward cabin of a boat as opposed to aft cabin.
- **forecast** Formalized weather prediction.
- **forecastle** The forward portion, below decks, of a vessel; the place where the crew is quartered. Pronounced and often spelled fo'c'sle.
- **foredeck** The forward part of the main deck of a vessel.
- **forepeak** The extreme forward compartment of a vessel, usually used for stowage.
- **forestay** A stay, from high on the mast to the foredeck; the headstay runs from the top of the mast to the bow and is the outermost stay.
- **forestaysail** A sail attached to the forestay, similar to a jib, which is on the headstay.

- **foretriangle** The area bounded by the mast, foredeck and headstay.
- **forward** On board a vessel, the direction to the front, toward the bow.
- **forward quarter spring line** A mooring line running forward from the quarter to control the forward and backward motion of a vessel in its berth.
- **founder** To sink.
- **fractional rig** A rig in which the jib of a sloop does not reach to the top of the mast, a three-quarter rig is an example of this rig.
- **frames** Ribs; transverse structural members of a vessel.
- **freeboard** The vertical distance between the waterline and the top of the deck.
- **fronts** Boundaries between air masses that have different temperatures.
- **fully battened** Sail with batten running full length of the sail horizontally.
- **furling** Folding, rolling or gathering a sail on its boom when it is not in use.

G

- **gaff** A spar holding the upper side (head) of a four-sided sail; a device used to boat a large fish.
- **galley** The kitchen on a boat or ship.
- **garboard strake** The strake (plank) next to the keel.
- **gel coat** Standard finish of a fiberglass boat.
- **genoa** An overlapping jib.
- **geographic position** Charted position.
- **gimbals** Pivoted rings holding a compass or other device so that it can tip in any direction or remain level when the support tips.
- **give-way vessel** The vessel that does not have the right of way in a crossing or overtaking situation; the vessel that is burdened.
- **Global Positioning System** A worldwide radionavigation system of high accuracy using orbiting satellites.
- **grab rail** A convenient grip, on a cabin top or along a companion ladder.
- **granny knot** A faulty knot, often tied in error; it is not sure to hold, nor is it always easy to unfasten; neophytes confuse it with a square knot.
- **great circle** A circle formed on a sphere, such as the earth, by the intersection of a plane passing through the center of the sphere; an arc of a great circle is the shortest distance between two points, hence a great circle route is the shortest route between the points.
- **grommet** A ring or eyelet, as in a sail; a rope grommet is a circle made by unlaying the rope, then using one strand spirally, twisting onto itself, replacing the original strands.
- **gross tonnage** The total interior space of a ship, including non-cargo space, computed at 40 cubic feet equals one ton; **net tonnage** is found by subtracting engine rooms, crew's quarters, stores and navigation space; **displacement tonnage**

is the weight of the vessel, which is the same as the weight of the water displaced.

- **ground swells** Swells that become shorter and steeper as they near the shore, because of the shoaling water.
- **ground tackle** Anchor, anchor rode (line or chain) and all the shackles and other gear used for attachment.
- **gunwale** The upper edge of the side of a boat, usually a small projection above the deck; toe rail.
- **guy** A rigging line for control, attached to the end of a movable spar.
- **gyres** Giant, circular oceanic current.

H

- **hail** A call to a ship or boat.
- **half-hitch** The simplest knot, usually part of another knot, as two half hitches or a fisherman's bend.
- **halyard** A line used to hoist a spar or sail aloft.
- **hand bearing compass** A portable compass, used primarily for sighting or taking bearings.
- **hand lead** A weight, attached to a line, lowered into the water to find out the depth.
- **handsomely** Slowly and carefully, as to "ease a line handsomely," in a proper manner.
- **handy-billy** Block and tackle (movable).
- **hanging locker** A storage place for clothing.
- **hank** Small snap hook securing the jib luff to the headstay.
- **harbor** A safe anchorage, protected from most storms; may be natural or man-made, with breakwaters and jetties; a place for docking and loading.
- **harbormaster** The person in charge of anchorages, dock spaces, refuse collection and similar matters.
- **hard-chined** Hull shaped with flat panels joined at an angle.
- **hard over** All the way in one direction, as a tiller or wheel can be "hard over" to make an abrupt turn.
- **hatch** A deck opening providing access to the space below; normally a hatch cover, hinged or sliding, is fitted.
- **hauling** Hauling out is removing a boat from the water; pulling on an anchor line, halyard, or a rope or line is simply called hauling.
- **hauling part** The part of a fall or tackle to which power is applied.
- **hawse hole** An opening in the hull, through which mooring lines are run.
- **hawsepipes** Fittings in the hawse holes through which dock or anchor lines may be run, and, in larger vessels, in which the upper part of the anchor may be stowed.
- **hawser** A large diameter rope, generally 4½ inches or larger, used for towing and dock lines on larger vessels.
- **head** The bow or forward part of a vessel; the upper end of the vertical part, such as rudder head; the upper corner of a triangular sail; the upper edge of a four-sided sail; the toilet aboard ship (fixture only or entire compartment).
- **heading** The direction in which a vessel is pointed at any given moment.

- **headsail** Any of several sails set forward of the mast, or in the foretriangle.
- **head seas** Waves coming from the direction in which a vessel is heading.
- **headstay** A stay from the bow to a point high on the mast; the foremost stay.
- **headway** Forward motion of a vessel through the water.
- **heave** To pull strongly on a line; to throw a line.
- **heaving line** A light line, coiled and thrown from vessel to vessel or between vessel and shore, to be used for pulling a larger line, such as a dock line.
- **heaving to** Setting the sails so that a boat makes little headway, usually in a storm or a waiting situation; in power-driven vessels, heading into the seas, or nearly so, and reducing speed to the minimum necessary to maintain control.
- **heavy weather** Stormy, windy weather, usually connoting rough or high seas and danger or discomfort.
- **heel, heeling** To tip, to lean to one side; heeling may result from uneven distribution of weight or the force of the wind; a **list** is a continuous condition; a **roll** is a repeated inclination, from side to side.
- **heeling error** The additional or changing deviation in a compass caused by heeling, when the relative position of heavy iron (keel, engine) is changed so that the magnetic force varies.
- **helm** The tiller, wheel, and other steering gear; a boat is said to have a weather helm if it tends to turn its bow to windward, lee helm if it tends to fall away to leeward.
- **helmsman** The person (man or woman) who is steering.
- **high** An area of high atmospheric pressure in a weather system.
- **high tide** High water, the highest level reached.
- **hitch** A knot attaching a line to an object, such as a cleat, ring, spar.
- **holding tank** Storage tank for sewage, so that it will not be pumped overboard into the water.
- **homing** Steering directly toward a radiobeacon or other source of radio signals, using a direction finder.
- **horizontal angle** An angle, usually measured with a sextant, between two landmarks, providing a line of position (the arc of a circle).
- **horseshoe buoy** A lifebuoy or Personal Flotation Device, used in rescues, shaped like an inverted U and mounted in a bracket at the rail; used for crew-overboard situations.
- **hull** The structural body of a vessel, not including superstructure, masts or rigging.
- **hurricane** A tropical revolving storm of high intensity (Force 12 in the Beaufort scale); this term is used in the North Atlantic and the Caribbean; the same kind of storm in the Pacific is called a typhoon; inland it is a cyclone.
- **hydrofoil** A type of boat with underwater foils on which the boat rides (planes) when high speeds are reached.
- **hydrography** The science of surveying the waters of the earth.

I-J-K

■ **inboard** More toward the center of a vessel; inside; a motor fitted inside the boat.

■ **inboard cruiser** Powerboat with an inboard engine.

■ **inflatable** Craft that has an inflatable structure.

■ **Inland Rules** Rules of the road that apply to vessel operations in harbors as well as certain rivers, lakes and inland waterways.

■ **inlet** A bay or recess in the shore of a sea, lake or river.

■ **Intracoastal Waterways** ICW: bays, rivers and canals along the coasts (such as the Atlantic and Gulf of Mexico coasts), connected so that vessels may travel without going into the open sea.

■ **irons, in** Up in the wind and unable to pay off on either tack. A sailboat that loses headway (and therefore steerageway) when attempting to **come about** is said to be "in irons" or "in stays."

■ **isobars** On a weather map, lines drawn connecting places of equal atmospheric pressure; isobars close together indicate a steeper gradient of pressure and stronger winds.

■ **isogonic lines** Lines, on a chart, connecting points of equal magnetic variation.

■ **Jacobs ladder** A rope ladder, lowered from the deck, as when pilots or passengers come aboard.

■ **jetty** A structure, usually masonry, projecting out from the shore; a jetty may protect a harbor entrance.

■ **jib** A triangular sail, set on the headstay.

■ **jibe** To change direction, when sailing with the wind aft, so that the wind comes on a different quarter and the boom swings over to the opposite side; an accidental jibe can be dangerous.

■ **jiffy reefing** A reef that is tied in.

■ **keel** The main structural member of a vessel, the backbone; the lateral area beneath the hull to provide steering stability and reduce leeway.

■ **ketch** A two-masted sailing rig; the after (mizzen) mast is shorter than the forward (main) mast and stepped forward of the rudder post, so the mizzen sail on a ketch is relatively larger than it might be on a yawl.

■ **king plank** The center plank on a laid deck.

■ **king spoke** The topmost spoke of a steering wheel when the rudder is in a centered position.

■ **knees** Structural members connecting (and reinforcing) two parts that meet, as the sternpost to the keel.

■ **knot** (1) Unit of speed, one nautical mile per hour; (2) a general term for a hitch or bend.

L

■ **laid up** In dry storage.

■ **lapstrake** A type of hull construction in which each strake (plank) overlies the next one below, also called clinker- built.

■ **latitude** Geographic distance north or south of the equator, measured in degrees and minutes, and seconds or fractions of a minute.

■ **launch** (1) To move a boat into the water from land; (2) a powerboat used as a ferry between land and a moored boat; also "shore boat."

■ **lay** The twist of a stranded rope, usually to the right.

■ **lazarette** A small storage compartment at the stern.

■ **lead** A shaped weight on a marked line, used to measure water depth and to pick up bottom samples (mud, clay, sand).

■ **lead line, hand lead** A weight, attached to a line, lowered into the water to find out the depth.

■ **lee** The direction toward which the wind blows; an object sheltered from the wind is "in the lee." A lee shore is the coast lying in the direction toward which the wind is blowing.

■ **leeboards** Anti-drift boards attached to the gunwale.

■ **leech** Trailing edge of a sail.

■ **lee helm** The tendency of a sailboat to turn the bow to leeward, compared to weather helm, unless corrective rudder action is taken.

■ **leeward** Toward the lee.

■ **leeway** Sideways drift of a boat, primarily caused by the wind or a current.

■ **left-hand lay** Stranded rope made with the twist to the left; also called S-twist; most rope is right-hand lay, or Z-twist.

■ **length overall (LOA)** The distance between the tip of the bow and the end of the stern.

■ **lifelines** Lines, usually of wire rope, often covered with plastic, at the sides of a boat's deck to keep persons from falling overboard.

■ **life preserver** A flotation coat, vest, ring or cushion; called Personal Flotation Device (PFD) in the U.S.

■ **life raft** A small survival craft, usually inflatable.

■ **lights** Lighthouses or beacons; fixed aids to navigation equipped with light sources having prescribed characteristics.

■ **limber holes** Drainage holes in the bilge timbers of a vessel, allowing water to run to a low point for pumping out.

■ **line** A rope in use aboard a vessel; laid line is formed by twisting three (sometimes four) strands; braided line may be single or braid over a core.

■ **linestoppers** Also called jamcleats. Designed to use more than one line with a winch; they will keep the tension on the line while stopped or jammed.

■ **list** (1) A continuous leaning to one side, often caused by an imbalance in stowage or a leak into one compartment; (2) a light list is a printed listing of aids to navigation, in geographical order.

■ **LOA** Length over all; the maximum length of a vessel's hull, excluding projecting spars or rudder.

■ **load waterline** LWL; the planned waterline of a boat, to which it is expected to float when fully loaded and equipped.

■ **locker** A storage place, a closet.

■ **log** (1) A device for measuring distance run through the water; (2) a written record, usually in a book, of a vessel's course, speed, weather encountered, radio transmissions and receptions, as well as other details of navigational and maintenance.

- **longitude** Geographic distance east or west of the prime meridian (0°) which runs through Greenwich, England.
- **long splice** A splice joining two rope ends, made by untwisting strands, thinning and removing the ends, so that the final splice is no thicker than the original line; a long splice will thus go through a block without jamming, but it is not as strong as a short splice.
- **lubber's line** The index mark, usually inside the compass, by which the course is read and the vessel is steered.
- **luff** The forward part or leading edge of a sail.
- **LWL** Length on the waterline; the length of a vessel—including rudder post— when measured at the line of flotation.

M

- **magnetic course** Course of a vessel in relation to magnetic north.
- **magneticmeridian** A line of force along which the needle of a magnetic compass settles.
- **magnetic north** The direction a compass needle points when there are no local disturbing influences (deviation).
- **mainsail** The sail hoisted on the after side of the mainmast, pronounced "mains'l."
- **make fast** Action of attaching a line.
- **manila** Natural fiber rope, largely supplanted by synthetics.
- **marina** A place, essentially a dock area, where small recreational craft are kept; usually floats or piers, as well as service facilities, are available.
- **marine railway** Railway used to haul out boats in a marina or boat yard.
- **marline** Light two-stranded line, formerly made from hemp, tarred or untarred, used for lacings, whippings, seizings and servings.
- **marlinespike** A pointed steel tool for splicing line.
- **mast** A vertical spar, the main support of the sailing rig in sailboats and used for radio antennas and signal flags in both sail and power boats.
- **masthead light** A white light, at or near the masthead, used underway by a vessel under power at night; the range of visibility required varies with the size of the vessel; the arc of visibility is from dead ahead to 22.5 degrees abaft the beam, on both sides, depending somewhat on the applicable rules.
- **MAYDAY** A radio distress call, from the French *m'aidez* (help me); SOS in Morse code.
- **meridian** A line passing through both poles and intersecting the equator at right angles, known as longitude. The prime meridian is that of Greenwich (0 degrees).
- **messenger** A light line used to carry another line such as a halyard or a large hawser from a ship to the shore or to another vessel; see **heaving line.**
- **midships** Location near the center of a vessel measured either from side to side or fore-and-aft.
- **mile** The statute mile on land is 5280 feet (1852 meters); the nautical mile is 6076.12 feet; a knot, a measurement of speed, is one nautical mile per hour.

- **mizzen mast** In a ketch or yawl, the aftermost mast; the mizzen sail is set on this mast.
- **monkey fist** A special and fancy knot, used to weight the end of a heaving line.
- **moored** Anchored, made fast to a pier, wharf, etc.
- **mooring** Permanent ground tackle; a place where vessels are kept at anchor.
- **Morse code** A communication code invented by Samuel Morse, originally for the land telegraph; the code, modified for radio use, uses dots and dashes for letters, numerals and a few special signs.
- **motorboat** A boat propelled by an internal combustion engine; the United States Motor Boat Act divides motorboats into four classes.
- **motor sailers** An auxiliary sailboat with an especially large engine and spacious accommodations.
- **mouse, mousing** Turns of twine, taken across a hook, to prevent accidental unhooking.
- **multihull** Any of several boat designs with more than one hull, as a catamaran or trimaran.
- **mushroom anchor** Generally a mooring type of anchor, desirable because it will not snag an anchor line or chain; small mushrooms are also used for fishing anchors or for prams and dinghies.

N

- **Napier diagram** A graphic plot of compass deviation values.
- **Nautical Almanac** An annual publication, issued jointly by the U.S. Naval Observatory and H.M. Nautical Almanac Office at Greenwich, England, containing tables of the positions and movements of celestial bodies.
- **nautical mile** 6076.12 feet, or 1852 meters, an international standard.
- **naval architects** Architects specializing in marine design.
- **navigation** The art/science of guiding a vessel from one place to another safely and efficiently; coastal navigation, using visual (surface) reference points, is more usually called piloting; celestial navigation uses observations of heavenly bodies (usually with instruments) and tables or calculators; radionavigation is the technical term when electronic devices and systems are used.
- **navigation lights** Lights shown by a vessel that indicate course, position and status such as fishing or towing.
- **Navigation Rules** The Rules of the Road in the U.S., governing navigation lights, rules for vessels meeting or passing, sound signals, and distress signals; the rules for International and U.S. waters differ in only a few small details.
- **neap tides** Those occurring when the sun and moon are furthest from being in line (quarter and three-quarter moons); neap tides have the least range (rise and fall). See **spring tide.**
- **net tonnage** The capacity of a vessel, determined by measuring the hull interior and subtracting the volume of engines and other equipment. See **gross tonnage.**
- **non- slip** Anti-skid.

- **Notices to Mariners** Official advices from the U.S. Coast Guard and the Defense Mapping Agency Hydrographic Center, concerning navigational safety items such as changes in channels and navigation aids; this information is useful for updating charts and technical publications; various notices are both national and local in scope.
- **numbering** The federally mandated "licensing" of boats in the U.S., usually by the states, except in Alaska, where the Coast Guard registers boats.
- **nun** A type of cylindrical buoy, tapering toward the top, used in the American system of aids to navigation; typically nun buoys are red and are identified with an even number.
- **nylon** A polyamide synthetic material with a long-chain molecule; nylon fibers are used for rope and some sailcloth, when elasticity is desirable; hard nylon is used for some rigging parts, such as sheaves.
- **oarlock** A U-shaped or sometimes O-shaped pivoting device in which oars are set when rowing.
- **offshore** (1) Out of sight of land; (2) from the land; toward the water.

O-P

- **Omega navigation system** A global radionavigation system.
- **outboard** (1) A propulsion unit for boats, attached at the transom; includes motor, driveshaft and propeller; fuel tank and battery may be integral or could be installed separately in the boat; (2) outside or away from a vessel's hull; opposite of inboard.
- **outdrive** A propulsion system for boats, with an inboard motor operating an exterior drive, with driveshaft, gears and propeller; also called stern drive and inboard/outboard.
- **outhaul** A line, tackle or geared mechanism used to tighten or adjust the foot of a sail on a boom.
- **overall length** The extreme length of a vessel, excluding spars or rigging fittings. See **LOA.**
- **painter** A towline or tie-up line for a dinghy or other small boat.
- **palm** The broad tip of an anchor fluke; a device, usually leather, worn on the hand and used somewhat like a thimble for sewing on canvas and for whipping lines.
- **parallax error** The error in reading an instrument such as a compass or gauge resulting from the distance between the needle or pointer and the numerical scale.
- **parallel rulers** A navigation device, used in chartwork, that enables a person plotting a course to work from a plotted line on a chart to a compass rose, and vice versa, to determine the direction of the line, plot a bearing, etc. It consists of two rulers of equal length, connected by crosspieces of equal length, movable about the joints so as to keep the rulers parallel to each other even when moved across a chart.
- **parcel** To wrap tape or other small stuff around a wire or fiber rope, to prevent chafe; usually used with "worming" that fills in the spaces between the twisted strands of rope.
- **passage** One leg of a voyage; a journey.

- **patent log** A device, including rotor on a towline and counter, for measuring distance and run and speed.
- **pay out** To release line in a controlled manner, as with an anchor rode.
- **pedestal** Base upon which is mounted the wheel or helm.
- **pelorus** A sighting device, without a compass, used to determine relative bearings.
- **pennant** (1) A small flag, typically a signal flag; (2) a short length of line or cable between a mooring chain and the boat, sometimes called a pendant.
- **personal flotation device** A **PFD** is any of several articles, such as buoyant cushions and vests or coats, "horseshoes" or life preserver rings.
- **PFD** U.S. official terminology for life preserver; personal flotation device.
- **pier** A structure, usually wood or masonry, extending into the water, used as a landing place for boats and ships.
- **pile, piling** A vertical wooden, concrete or metal pole, driven into the bottom; may be a support for a pier or floats; also used for mooring.
- **piloting** Navigation using visual reference points (aids to navigation, landmarks, etc.) and water depths.
- **pitch** (1) The alternative rise and fall of the bow of a vessel proceeding through waves; (2) the theoretical distance advanced by a propeller in one revolution; (3) tar and resin used for caulking between the planks of a wooden vessel.
- **planing hull** A hull designed so that forward speed creates water lift, reducing friction and increasing speed.
- **planking** Lengths of wood used for the external skin or the deck of a vessel.
- **Pleasure Vessel License** A form of USCG documentation that does not allow commercial use.
- **plumbbow** Hull with vertical bow shape.
- **polyester** Synthetic material (one trade name, Dacron) used for fibers for rope and sailcloth; polyester is stronger and has less elasticity than nylon.
- **polypropylene** Lightweight synthetic material used for cordage fibers, for ski tow ropes, dinghy painters and other uses where flotation is desirable; not as strong as other synthetics, the fibers are sometimes combined with others for special purposes.
- **port** (1) Left, as the port side of a boat, or a direction, as "to turn to port"; (2) an opening, for light and/or ventilation, in the side of a vessel; (3) general area of a shore establishment having facilities for landing and maintaining vessels.
- **port tack** A sailing vessel with the wind coming from the left, or port, side is said to be on the port tack; such a vessel normally does not have the right of way when meeting a vessel on the starboard tack.
- **position finding** The navigation process of determining the position of a vessel on a chart or in the water.
- **pram** A small boat used as a tender; a dinghy in the U.S., usually with a squared-off bow.
- **prevailing winds** Average direction of wind.

- **prime meridian** The meridian of longitude through Greenwich, 0°.
- **privileged vessel** One having the right of way, as to both course and speed, when meeting another vessel.
- **propeller** A rotating device, with two or more blades, that acts as a screw in propelling a vessel.
- **protractor** Navigation device used in chartwork to measure and lay down angles.
- **psychrometer** A weather instrument, usually two hygrometers, one dry and one with a wet bulb, to measure the moisture in the air.
- **pulpit** The forward railing structure at the bow of a boat.
- **pump out** Action of pumping out waste tank.
- **purchase** A mechanical device for lifting or pulling; on shipboard the term is used specifically for a block and tackle.

Q-R

- **quarter** The side of a vessel, from amidships to the stern; the term is used to identify dock lines as in "fasten the quarter spring."
- **quartering sea** Seas coming from the quarter.
- **quay** A masonry structure at the water's edge, where vessels can tie up, load and unload cargo.
- **radar** An electronic system using super high-frequency radio waves; when reflected they show on a screen the position, size and distance of an object; radar is used at night and in bad visibility for both collision avoidance and navigation.
- **radar arch** Supporting structure for radar that is shaped as an arch.
- **radiobeacon** A transmitter, at a fixed and known location, used by vessels with appropriate electronic equipment to determine their position (see **radio direction finder**).
- **radio bearing** A direction determined by radio.
- **radio direction finder** A radio receiver with special antenna and circuitry used to determine the direction to a source of radio waves.
- **radionavigation** Electronic piloting; the determination of a vessel's position, course and speed by various electronic devices and systems.
- **rafting, rafted** The mooring procedure for two or more vessels, tied up side-by-side at a dock or on an anchor.
- **rail** A protective edge on deck; also a solid bar on supports, similar to a lifeline.
- **raised deck** Deck level arranged to be higher than the actual gunwale.
- **rake** (1) The slant of a ship's funnels, bow or stern; (2) the slant, fore and aft, of a mast.
- **RDF** Radio direction finder, an electronic device used in conjunction with transmitters, in order to determine a vessel's position.
- **reach (reaching)** (1) To sail across the wind; (2) a channel between the mainland and an island.
- **reciprocal** A direction precisely opposite another; differing by 180 degrees.

- **reef** (1) An underwater barrier, such as rock or coral; (2) to shorten sail by reducing the area exposed, by rolling the sail on a boom or tying in reef points.
- **reef knot** The knot used to tie in a reef; a square knot, also useful for tying around an object, but not good for fastening two lines together.
- **reef points** Tie lines, placed at intervals horizontally on a sail, used to reduce sail area when they are tied around the foot of the sail.
- **reeving** Leading a line through a block or fairlead as in setting up a purchase, or rigging a halyard.
- **registration** The numbering or licensing of a boat.
- **relative bearing** A direction in relation to the fore-and-aft line of a vessel, expressed in degrees.
- **rhumb line** A straight line on a Mercator chart; it intersects all meridians at the same angle; for short distances a rhumb line provides an adequate course, but a great circle is actually the shorter distance.
- **reverse sheer** Sheer the reverse of normal. The sheerline rises above the straight line from stem to stern instead of curving below.
- **RIB** See rigid inflatable.
- **ribs** Another term for **frames,** the transverse members of a wooden hull to which the planks are fastened.
- **riding light** The anchor light.
- **rig (rigs)** (1) The spars, standing rigging and sails; (2) to make a boat ready for sailing or to prepare a sail or piece of gear for use.
- **rigging** The wire rope, rods, lines, hardware and other equipment that support and control the spars and sails; standing rigging is semi-permanent once set up; running rigging is continually adjusted as the sails are hoisted, doused, trimmed or reefed.
- **right-hand lay** The twist of stranded rope commonly used, with the strands twisting to the right; Z-twist.
- **right of way** In both normal boat operation and racing, certain boats (privileged or stand-on vessels) have priority in crossing or overtaking situations, or at turns in races; the other craft (burdened or give-way vessel) must yield to the boat that has the right of way in a particular situation; the boat on starboard tack, or the vessel coming from the right in the case of power boats, will have the right of way under most conditions.
- **rigid inflatable** Inflatable boat with a rigid bottom.
- **rode** The anchor line, which may be line (fiber rope), chain or wire rope.
- **roll** The alternating motion of a boat, leaning alternately to port and starboard; the motion of a boat about its fore-and-aft axis.
- **roller furling** The method of furling a sail by winding it on a stay, most used for jibs but used for mainsails on some cruising boats.
- **roller reefing** Reduction of sail area by winding the sail on a rotating boom.

- **rolling hitch** A knot useful for attaching a line to another line or to a spar.
- **rope** Cordage, lines made of fiber or steel; rope may be braided or formed with twisted strands; when in use aboard ship it is generally called line.
- **round turn** A turn, of line, around an object or a line; part of a knot.
- **rowlock** See **oarlock**.
- **rub rail, strake or guard** An outer member on the side of a vessel's hull, designed to absorb friction and pounding from contact with pilings, docks, etc.
- **rudder** The control surface, usually aft, by which a boat is steered.
- **rudder post** The shaft that carries the rudder and to which the tiller or wheel is connected.
- **rules of the road** A general term for the regulations governing vessels, used to prevent collisions; in the U.S. the technical name is now Navigation Rules; the rules vary slightly inland and in international waters, but are generally similar.
- **running fix** A navigation fix obtained by using a line of position taken at or near the current time together with another earlier LOP that has been advanced for the movement of the vessel between these two times.
- **running lights** The required lights, called Navigation Lights, that a vessel shows at night or in poor visibility, to indicate position, course and status.
- **running rigging** The adjustable lines (and certain hardware items) used for the control of spars and sails.
- **safety harness** Harness made with webbing to keep crew from falling overboard attached with safety line.
- **samsonpost** In a small vessel, a single bitt forward used to fasten the anchor and dock lines; in larger vessels the term is applied to a small forward derrick mast, used with a cargo boom.

S

- **satellite navigation** A form of position finding using radio transmissions from satellites with sophisticated on-board automatic equipment.
- **schooner** A fore-and-aft rigged sailing vessel with two to six masts, with the foremast shorter than the mainmast.
- **scope** Technically, the ratio of length of anchor rode in use to the vertical distance from the bow of the vessel to the bottom of the water; generally, the amount of anchor cable in use; a minimum scope of three to one is used for anchors such as the Yachtsman; six or seven to one is used for lightweight anchors, with more scope in storm conditions.
- **screw** A propeller; sometimes called a wheel.
- **scudding** Running before the wind in a gale.
- **scuppers** Drain holes on deck, in the toe rail, or in bulwarks or (with drain pipes) in the deck itself.
- **scuttlebutt** Gossip, rumors, so called because sailors used to gather around the scuttle butt, a cask for drinking water.
- **sea anchor** Canvas shaped like a parachute to keep the bow of a boat to the seas in open water and reduce drift to a minimum. It is not a means of anchoring.
- **sea cock** A through-hull valve, a shut-off on a plumbing or drain pipe between the vessel's interior and the sea.
- **seakindly** Comfortable in rough seas, moving through the water without undue motion or strain; said of a vessel's hull design.
- **seamanship** All the arts and skills of boat handling, ranging from maintenance and repairs to piloting, sail handling, marlinespike work and rigging.
- **seiche** An oscillation of the surface of a lake or landlocked sea that varies in period from a few minutes to several hours.
- **seizing** Binding two lines together, or a rope to a spar and so on, using light line.
- **self- draining** Drains automatically.
- **sentinel** Weight suspended from the rode to help keep the pull on the anchor as horizontal as possible to prevent dragging in rough weather.
- **serving** Covering and protecting a portion of a line, to prevent wear; a serving may be as simple as a whipping (small stuff wrapped around) or more elaborate, with worming, parceling and the addition of waterproofing.
- **set (e.g. sails are set out)** (1) To raise a sail; (2) the direction of a current.
- **sextant** A precision navigating instrument, used for measuring angles, as in celestial navigation when the altitudes of heavenly bodies are taken, or in piloting, when the known heights of objects ashore or the known distance of two objects from each other can be used to find distance.
- **shackle** A metal link fitting with a pin across the throat, used to connect lines to an anchor, fasten blocks to a spar in rigging, or a line to a sail.
- **shear pin** A safety device, used to fasten a propeller to its shaft; it breaks when the propeller hits a solid object, thus preventing further damage.
- **sheave** A grooved wheel or pulley over which rope or rigging wire runs, used to change the direction of force; often sheaves are parts of blocks.
- **sheer** (1) The curvature of the deck, fore and aft, as seen from the side; (2) a turn off course, from poor helmsmanship or difficult steering, or a swing, as on a moored boat.
- **sheerstrake** The topmost plank on the side of a wooden planked boat; the one that shows the sheer of the deck.
- **sheet** A line used to control a sail's lateral movement, either directly or by limiting the movement of a boom or other spar.
- **sheet bend** A knot useful for **bending** a line to an eye or to join two lines of different sizes.
- **ship** (1) A large seagoing vessel; (2) a three-masted sailing vessel with square sails, called "full-rigged," on each mast; (3) to take something aboard, as water in rough seas; (4) to place gear in place, as to ship a rudder or to ship oars, to bring them inboard when not in use.
- **shipshape** In good order, in good condition, properly rigged and ready.

■ **shock cord** An elastic "rope," originally developed for aviation, useful in limited rigging or stowage situations.

■ **short splice** A quick splice, as the end of two lines together, that is moderately strong but will not always run through a block or fairlead, because of its bulk. (See **long splice**).

■ **shrouds** Fixed rigging on either side of the mast.

■ **sidelights** Red and green navigation lights, visible from forward or on the beam. See **running lights.**

■ **signal halyard** Halyard for hoisting the signal flags and pennants.

■ **slack** (1) Not moving; (2) loose; (3) to ease.

■ **slack water** The period of little or no water movement between flood and ebb tidal currents.

■ **sliding hatch** Hatch mounted on slides.

■ **slip** (1) A berth for a boat between two piers or floats or piles; (2) the percentage difference between the theoretical and the actual distance that a propeller advances when turning in water under load.

■ **small stuff** Cordage such as marline, spun yarn, sail twine, primarily used for whippings and servings.

■ **snub a line** To check a running rope quickly, usually by tension around a bitt or cleat.

■ **sole** The cabin or cockpit floor.

■ **soundings** Measurements of the depth of water as shown on a chart; a vessel is "off sounds" if it is in water too deep to use a long (deep sea) lead line; inside the 100 fathom line is usually "on soundings."

■ **spars** Masts, booms, gaffs and poles used in sailboat rigging; today spars are made of wood, aluminum extrusions, and composites of synthetics.

■ **spinnaker** A three-cornered sail of light, stretchy cloth, usually nylon, used in downwind sailing.

■ **splice** To join two lines, or make an eye, by tucking strands or otherwise interweaving parts of rope; braided rope that has a core and a cover is usually spliced by tucking one inside the other.

■ **spoon bow** A full round bow that is shaped like the bowl of a spoon.

■ **spring line** One of the standard dock lines, used to control fore and aft motion of a boat made fast to a pier or float.

■ **spring tide** One that occurs when there is a new moon, with the sun and moon in conjunction, or when there is a full moon, the moon and sun being in opposition; at such times, high tides are higher than normal, and low tides are lower; the tidal range is greater. See **neap tide.**

■ **squall** A sudden and violent windstorm often accompanied by rain; a line squall or line of squalls quite often accompanies an advancing cold front.

■ **square knot** Another name for the reef knot, useful for tying two ends of a line together, as around an object; not a good knot to use when fastening two lines where the strain will be intermittent.

■ **square rigged** Vessel rigged with sails that are hung laterally and of square shape.

■ **stanchion** A metal post, used to hold lifelines along a deck.

■ **stand** Period of time when vertical rise or fall of the tide has stopped.

■ **standing part** The portion of a line not used in making a knot, or the part of the line around which the knot may be tied; in a block and tackle, the part of the purchase that does not move when power is applied to the hauling part.

■ **standing rigging** The permanent stays and shrouds, as well as some other rigging parts, used mainly to hold up the mast and take the strain of the sails; although necessarily somewhat adjustable the standing rigging is not continually changed as is the running rigging.

■ **stand-on vessel** The boat that has the right of way in a crossing or overtaking situation; the privileged vessel. See **give-way vessel.**

■ **starboard tack** A vessel sailing with the wind coming over the starboard side is on the starboard tack and generally has the right of way over a boat on the port tack.

■ **stateroom** Sleeping quarters for guests or captain.

■ **statute mile** A unit of measurement on land, 5280 feet; see **nautical mile.**

■ **stays** Rigging, generally wire or rods, used to support the masts in a fore- and-aft direction and to carry certain sails.

■ **staysail** An additional foresail that is set between the mast and the jib.

■ **steadying sail** Sail hoisted more for steadying effect of the wind on it than for propulsion.

■ **steerageway** Sufficient motion through the water to enable a vessel to respond to its rudder.

■ **stem** The forward member of the hull, or the corresponding portion of the hull in composite construction.

■ **step** At the base of the mast, the special part of the boat in which the heel of the mast is set; to raise the mast and put it in place.

■ **stepped** Referring to the mast, keel stepped or deck stepped.

■ **stern** The after portion of the boat.

■ **stern drive** An inboard/outboard engine system, with the motor inside the hull; steering is done by turning the outboard (propeller) unit.

■ **stern line** The dock or mooring line that runs from the stern to the pier, float or pile.

■ **sternway** Opposite of headway; having a reverse motion through the water.

■ **stores** Supplies.

■ **storm jib** A small, strong, triangular headsail that is used in heavy winds.

■ **stow** To put in the proper place

■ **strakes** Lines of planking, as from stem to stern. See **sheer strake** and **garboard strake**.

■ **stuffing box** A through-hull fitting for the drive shaft or rudder post, also called a gland.

■ **suit of sails** The full complement of a boat's sails.

■ **superstructure** Cabins and other structures above deck.

- **surf** Waves breaking on a shore, reef or bar.
- **survey** Inspection for purposes of purchase or insurance by a marine surveyor.
- **surveyor** A professional who surveys (examines boats and ships) for insurance purposes or prior to a purchase.
- **swamp** To fill with water, not from a leak but from water coming over the deck and gunwales.
- **swell** A long, large wave that does not crest; swells come from such a distance that the wind causing them is not apparent locally.
- **swim platform** Platform installed at the transom for ease of boarding.

T

- **tachometer** An instrument that indicates an engine's revolutions per minute.
- **tack** The forward bottom corner of a sail, or either bottom corner of a square sail; each leg of a zigzag course sailed to windward or downwind.
- **tacking** The sailing maneuver in which the direction of the boat is changed, often with rigging adjustments, so that the wind is coming from the other side of the vessel.
- **tackle** A purchase, a block and tackle, a combination rig of one or more blocks with lines to obtain mechanical advantage.
- **tack rag** A slightly sticky cloth used to pick up dust and dirt from brightwork before varnishing.
- **telltale** A wind-direction indicator, mounted on the rigging, sail or mast.
- **tender** A small boat accompanying a yacht or other pleasure vessel, used to transport persons, gear and supplies; a dinghy; a vessel is said to be tender if it is relatively unstable.
- **tensile strength** The load, in pounds of "pull," at which a rope, chain or other item would break.
- **thimble** Metal fitting used in rigging, forming a reinforced place of attachment.
- **throat** The forward upper corner of a four-sided fore-and-aft sail, the point where the throat halyard attaches.
- **thwart** A crossways seat, usually contributing to structural strength in a rowboat or other small open boat.
- **tidal current** Regular current caused by the rise and fall of the tides. See **current**.
- **tides** The vertical rise and fall of ocean water, and waters affected by the ocean, caused by the gravitational forces of the moon and the sun.
- **tide tables** A set of data giving the times and heights of high and low tides for one or more locations.
- **tiller** An arm or lever attached to the top of a rudder post for the purpose of controlling the position of the rudder and so steering the craft.
- **toe rail** The low bulwark on a small decked boat.
- **tonnage** A measure of the capacity or displacement of a vessel. See **gross tonnage, net tonnage.**
- **topping lift** A running rigging line to control a spar; typically an adjustable topping lift would run over a sheave or through a block at the top of the mast down to the end of a boom or spinnaker pole.
- **topsides** (1) The sides of a vessel above the waterline; (2) on deck as opposed to below deck.
- **towing** Pulling a vessel through the water, as a tow boat pulls a barge or a yacht club tender pulls one or more racing sailboats; an assistance or rescue maneuver.
- **track** (1) Metal or plastic rigging fitting, used to control spars, blocks and other rigging parts; (2) the path, normally shown on a chart, between one position and another, as a dead reckoning track.
- **traffic separation scheme** A plan, generally internationally agreed on, by which vessels in congested areas use one-way lanes to lessen the danger of collisions.
- **transom** The transverse part of the stern.
- **trim, trimmed** (1) The way in which a vessel floats, on an even keel, or trimmed by the head (bow) or stern, for example; adjustable by shifting ballast; (2) to set sails, to adjust by means of sheets and certain other rigging lines.
- **trimaran** A boat with three hulls.
- **trip line** A line fast to the crown of an anchor by means of which it can be hauled out when dug too deeply or fouled; a similar line used on a sea anchor to bring it aboard.
- **trough** Depression between two waves. See **crest**.
- **true course** A course corrected for variation and deviation; one that is referenced to geographic north.
- **true north** Geographic north.
- **true wind** The actual direction and force of the wind, as distinct from apparent wind, which varies with the speed and direction of the vessel.
- **tumblehome** The inward curving of the topsides, above the waterline.
- **tune** To adjust the rigging and sails for maximum efficiency; the term is also used for engine adjustments.
- **tunnel hull** Hull with tunnels shaped for the propeller to reduce draft.
- **turnbuckle** A threaded, adjustable rigging fitting, used for stays, lifelines and sometimes other rigging.
- **turning circle** The course followed by a boat when it is turning; the smallest possible circle when the rudder is hard over.
- **twine** Small stuff, light line used for whippings or servings; sail twine is used for sewing.
- **two-blocked** Fully closed up, raised as far as the gear permits, as when both blocks in a purchase are drawn completely together.
- **two half-hitches** A useful knot, in which the hitches are made upon the standing part of the line and then drawn up (tightened).

U-V

- **underway** In motion, en route, not at anchor or aground or made fast to the shore.
- **Underwriters Laboratories** One of the chief testing orga-

nizations that helps to set the safety standards used in the United States.

- **upwind** To the windward of.
- **USCG** United States Coast Guard. The federal marine law enforcement and rescue agency in the U.S.
- **USPS** United States Power Squadrons, a private membership organization that specializes in boating education and good boating practices.
- **V-hull** Hull shaped in a V.
- **V-drive** Mechanism used with an engine installation that has the normally aft-facing end of the engine facing forward.
- **variation** A compass "error" resulting from the fact that at most points on the earth's surface the direction of the magnetic lines of force is not toward the geographic North Pole or South Pole.
- **vector** A line drawn to represent magnitude and direction, such as leeway a boat makes in a given time period as a result of wind or water current.
- **veer** To change direction, to swerve; to veer out is to let out rope, as an anchor line; when the wind veers it changes direction clockwise, as opposed to **backing** (counterclockwise).
- **vent** An opening in a boat's ventilation system.
- **ventilators** Openings that are fitted with **cowls (scoops)** to direct the flow of air and vapors in or out of ducts.
- **vessel** A boat, ship or other moving and floating craft; a barge is a vessel, a float at a dock is not a vessel.
- **VHF radio** A Very High Frequency electronic communications and direction finding system.
- **voyage** A complete trip, as distinguished from a **passage**.

W-X-Y

- **wake** The track in the water of a moving vessel; commonly used for the disturbance of the water (waves) resulting from the passage of the vessel's hull.
- **wash** The loose or broken water left behind a vessel as it moves along; the surging action of waves.
- **water ballast** Ballast in the form of water in tanks.
- **waterline** The intersection of a vessel's hull and the water's surface; the line separating bottom paint and topsides.
- **waves** Undulations of the sea; the height of a wave is measured from trough to crest; the length is the distance between crests; the period is the time between two successive crests.
- **weather helm** The tendency of a vessel to turn to windward, requiring a slight amount of helm to keep it on course; normally this is considered a sailboat safety element.
- **weather shore** The coast lying in the direction from which the wind is blowing, as opposed to a lee shore. See **lee**.
- **weather side** Side of a boat upon which the wind is blowing.
- **weigh** To raise the anchor, to depart.
- **well-found** With adequate equipment and stores, well supplied and fitted out.
- **wetted surface** The area of the wetted part of a hull (including rudder) in the water, affecting speed.

- **wharf** A structure, parallel to the shore, for docking vessels.
- **wheel** (1) The steering wheel; (2) the propeller.
- **whipping** Twine wound around a line, as on the end or at an eye splice, to add strength and prevent fraying or abrasion.
- **whistle signal** A standard communication signal between boats, to indicate change of course, danger or other situations.
- **winch** A device, on deck, on a spar or otherwise mounted, which is used to haul on a line; if geared or used with a handle (lever) it provides a mechanical advantage.
- **windage** Wind resistance.
- **windlass** A special form of winch, a rotating drum device for hauling a line or chain.
- **windward** The direction from which the wind is blowing.
- **workboat** A small vessel or boat used for such chores as ferrying stores or putting down moorings.
- **working sails** The sails used in normal winds, as distinguished from light weather sails or storm sails.
- **worm** To fill in the spaces in laid rope, as part of the procedure known as worm-and-parcel.
- **yacht** A pleasure vessel, a pleasure boat; in American usage the idea of size and luxury is conveyed, either sail or power.
- **yard** (1) A spar, crossing the mast, on which square sails are fitted; (2) a place where boats are stored, constructed, or repaired.
- **yaw** To swing or steer off course, as when running with a quartering sea.
- **yawl** A rig for two-masted sailboats, in which there is a mainmast and a smaller mizzen mast, stepped aft of the rudder post.

Note: More specialized terms are defined in appropriate chapters throughout Chapman. Refer to the index for further information.

INDEX

Atmospheric pressure, 318, 325, 498
barometer readings, 308, 309-310
weather maps, 322
Automated Mutual-Assistance
Vessel Rescue (AMVER) system, 102
Auxiliaries, 17, 32, 183
Aweigh, 31
AWG (American Wire Gauge), 524

B

Backdrafting, 209
Backfire flame arresters. *See*
Flame arresters
Backing plates, 32
Backing up, backing down, 177, 197, 198, 208
outdrives, 189, 190
single-screw boats, 191-192, 193
twin-screw boats, 194-195
Back splices, 289, 291
Backstays, 37
Baggywrinkles, 33
Bailers, 70, 75, 243
Ballast, 27
Ballasted hulls, 27
Ball mounts, 166, 170
Balsawood cores, 30
Bareboat charters, 54
Barges, 18, 142, 492, 493
Barometers, 40, 322
changes, 309-310, 314, 325, 333, 498
local weather signs, reading, 325
types, 308
wind velocity and wind shifts, 310
See also High barometric pressure;
Low barometric pressure
Bars (in rivers), 43, 489, 490
Battens, batten down, 38
Batteries, gel-cell, 528-530
Batteries, starting, 529, 531-532, 537
Batteries, storage, 83, 170, 242, 525
capacity, 523, 529
charging, 527, 528, 529, 531-532
fuel efficiency, 353-354
installing, 527, 541
inverters, 534, 539
isolators, 529, 532, 537
testing, 353, 354, 529, 531-532
wet-cell, lead-acid, 527-530, 531
Battery-condition meters, 531
Beams, 19
Bearing Buddies, 166, 170
Bearings, 19, 448
bow-and-beam technique, 459-460
calculating, 470-471
danger bearings and angles, 455
labeling, 461-462
magnetic bearings, 41, 445
plotting techniques, 475-477
positioning procedure, 457-460

radio and radar navigation, 461-462
relative bearings, 31, 41, 445, 451-452, 456, 460-461, 476-478
true bearings, 41, 445, 451-452
two-bearings-and-run-between
technique, 460
visual observations, 450-456
See also Compasses, magnetic;
Position determination
Beaufort Scale of Wind Force, 306, 307
Beaufort, Sir Francis, 306
Becket hitches, 283, 285
Bedding compound, 30
Bell buoys, 504
Bends (knots), 281, 283-287
Bends, river, 129, 489-490
Bernoulli, Daniel, 212
Berths, 20, 43, 48
boat handling, 196-209
clearing, 207-209
leaving, 129
Bights, 281
Bilges, 23, 24, 26, 80, 242
discharge, 355-356
flooding control, 70, 90-91
pumps, 70, 75, 83, 536
safety and fumes in, 69, 87, 88
Biminis, 21, 24
Binding (rope), 281
Binnacles, 22, 369, 374, 375
Binoculars, 40, 371, 430, 436, 489
Bitter ends (rope), 260, 264, 272, 281
Blocks, 32, 36, 95
basic principles, 292-293
line sizes, 280, 290
Bloopers, 38
Bluff bows, 25
Boarding, 69
Board of Steamship Inspection
(Transport Canada), 72
Boat handling, 177
adverse conditions, 241-247
assisting and getting assistance, 131, 248-251
boat terms and principles, 183-184
clearing berths, 207-209
dock lines, 200-203
landing, 204-206
maneuvering with directed
thrust, 188-190
propellers, 185-187
rudders, 185-187
seamanship training, 598-599, 604
single-screw inboard
maneuvering, 191-193
stranding, 248-251
tight quarters, 196-209
towing, 249-251
twin-screw craft maneuvering, 194-195
See also Sailboat handling

Boathooks, 70, 248
Boats, 25, 51, 153
boating environment, 42-43
buoyancy, 97, 153
categories, 17-19
covers, 20, 159, 169, 171, 173
fuel efficiency, 351-354
shows, 45-46, 48, 50
types, 20-24
See also individual types
Boatwrights, 28
Bolt rope, 277
Booms, 30, 37, 61
Boomvangs, 37
Bottoms, for anchoring, 257, 331
characteristics, 263, 268, 272
on charts, 400
types of anchors for, 253-257
Bow-and-beam bearings technique, 459-460
Bow chocks, 254
*Bowditch (American Practical
Navigator)*, 423, 425
position determination, 453-454, 456, 460, 461
Table 1, 461
Table 3, 473
Table 7, 460, 471-472
Table 9, 456
Bowditch, Nathaniel, 423
Bowline knots, 283, 284, 285
Bow lines. *See* Dock lines
Bow pulpits, 33
Bowriders, 20
Bows, 19, 25
Bowsprits, 39
Braided lines, 178, 258, 277
dipping, 291
splicing tools, 278, 287
strength, 279
taping, 291
textures, 280
whipping, 291
See also Double-braid lines
Brakes, 166, 167-168
Breaking out the anchor, 33, 254
Breakwater, 43
Breast hooks, 29
Breast lines. *See* Dock lines
Bridges, 21, 142, 429
clearances, 130, 330, 335
drawbridges, 129-130
Bridge-to-Bridge Radiotelephone
Act, 127, 547-548
Bridles, towing, 249, 250, 251
Brightwork, 28
British Board of Trade, 72
British Meteorological Office, 306, 307
Broaching, 31, 177, 243-244, 246
Broad on the bow, 31
Broad on the quarter, 31

Double-braid lines
    anchor rode, 257, 258, 260
    care of, 289, 290
    towing, 250
    See also Braided lines
Double cabins, 21
Double ended hulls, 25
Double tackle, 293
DR. *See* Dead reckoning (DR)
Draft (amount of water), 26, 151, 184, 249
Draft (distance), 19, 25-26, 37
Drag of sails, 35-36
Drawing compasses, 435
Dredging, 43, 141, 142, 490, 493
Dressing ship, 585, 586
Drift of currents, 43, 341, 464, 466-468
Drifter/reacher/spinnaker (DRS), 38
Drive types, 35
Drogues, 31, 243, 244, 246-247
DRS (Drifter/reacher/spinnaker), 38
DR tracks, 438, 439, 442, 443, 460
    and current effect, 464
    and depth information, 463
    periodic fixes, 445
    positioning procedure, 457
    and visual observations, 450
Drugs
    smugglers, 593
    testing, 53-54
Drysailed boats, 43
DSC (Digital Selective Calling) system, 551, 555
Dutton, Benjamin, 425
Dutton's Navigation and Piloting (Naval Institute), 425

E

Earth
    atmosphere, 297, 308
    centrifugal force, 329-332
    currents and effects of, 329-332, 333-334
    gravity, 329-332
    magnetic field, 367, 370, 376, 382-383, 427
    rotation, 305, 308, 341
    tides and effects of, 329-332
    weather and atmosphere of, 297, 308
Earth lightning conductor, 87
Ebbing tides, 43, 246, 341-344
Echo piloting, 481
ELBs (Exposed Location Buoys), 505
Electrical systems
    delivering power, 536-538
    engine starting, 156, 159
    fuel efficiency, 354
    generating and storing power, 523-532
    maintaining, 81
    protecting boats and equipment, 541-543

radiotelephones, 551
regulating and transforming power, 531, 533-535
safety, 87, 89
standards, 524
training, 599
See also Appliances, electrical
Electrical wiring
    alternating and direct current, 524, 525, 527, 532-543
    CME requirements, 76
    color code, 536
    and compasses, 538
    distribution/circuit-breaker panel, 536, 538
    gauges, 524-525
    installing, 538
    leak control, 90-91
    magnetic influcnce, 369, 374, 375, 538
    main switches, 536-537
    measuring needs of, 523-524
    regulations and codes, 535
    size and types, 524
    terminal fittings, 526, 527, 528
    trailer vehicles, 166, 167, 170
Electrolysis, 81, 541
Electronic equipment, 23, 24, 70, 414
    See also individual devices
Electronic navigation, 370, 523
    computers, 326, 414, 453, 574
    depth sounders, 31, 70, 159, 429, 436, 463, 562, 563
    GPS, 41, 70, 427, 571-574
    Loran, 70, 354, 427, 429, 437, 566-567, 568-570
    radar, 70, 565-567
    RDFs, 70, 564
    training, 599, 604
    See also specific device
Electronic voice communications. *See* Communications
Emergency position-indication radio beacons. *See* EPIRBs
Emergency procedures
    abandoning ship, 83, 99, 554
    COB accidents, 83, 92-95
    collisions, 83, 96
    controlling leaks, 90-91
    deadheads, 96
    dismasting, 96-97
    EPIRBs, 70, 98, 99, 130, 547, 558
    fire and explosions, 83, 87-89
    grounding, 83, 97
    heavy weather, 97
    helicopter rescue, 98, 591, 592
    preparation and statistics, 83
    summoning assistance, 84-86
    swamping, foundering and capsizing, 83, 97
    See also Safety guidelines

Engines, 17, 30
    and alternators, 523-524, 539
    boat handling in thick weather, 245
    CO poisoning, 209
    corrosion rate, 48
    direction and naming of, 35
    distribution of electrical power, 536-537
    drag types, 35
    fires, 89
    fuel efficiency, 352-353
    and generators, 532, 540
    maintenance training, 599
    recharging batteries, 529, 531-532
    and trailerboating, 154-158, 169
    See also individual types; Propulsion
Ensigns, 582
    See also Flags
Entering (customs), 54
Environment, 55
    bilge discharge, 355-356
    boat maintenance principles, 362-363
    dingies vs. rowboats, 356
    fuel efficiency, 351-354
    litter, solid waste and recycling, 357-359
    potable water, 355
    recycling, 354, 357-359, 362
    toxic substances, 360, 362-363
    waste systems, 355
    wildlife preservation, 352, 356, 361, 362, 363
    See also Pollution
EPIRBs, 70, 130
    FCC regulations, 558
    licensing, 547
    on liferafts, 98, 99
Epoxy, 30
Equilization (batteries), 531
Equipment
    electrical appliances, 523-525, 527, 534, 539-543, 546
    trailerboating, 159
    See also Instruments
Equivalent scale, 395
Erosion, 43, 492, 497
Escadrilles canadiennes de plaisance (ECP), Les, 603, 605
    See also Canadian Power and Sail Squadrons
Estimated positions (EPs), 445-446, 449, 463, 464
Evaporation, 302, 303
Expansion chambers, 367-368
Explosions. *See* Fire extinguishing systems; Fires and explosions
Exposed Location Buoys (ELBs), 505
Express cruisers, 21
Eye splices, 201, 282, 285
    maintenance, 272, 273
    making, 288-289

relative position, 121
visibility, 122
Radiation (ground) fog, 203, 303
Radio, 21, 98, 159, 318
   antennas, 401, 543
   basic principles, 545-546
   bearings by, 461-462
   capture effect, 546
   CE requirements, 76
   distress and urgency calls, 84-86, 88, 89
   electrical standards, 525
   equipment arrangement, 23, 24
   great circles and radio waves, 417, 461
   operator's permit, 546, 547-548
   radiofacsimile, 326
   triangulating geostationary satellites, 41
   See also Communications; Radio channels
Radio beacons, 402, 461-462, 564, 575
Radio channels, 70, 461, 493
   Channel 06, 550
   Channel 09, 553, 554, 556
   Channel 12, 130
   Channel 13, 122, 127, 129, 130, 493
   Channel 16, 98, 102, 122, 127, 129, 130, 245, 321, 493, 549, 550, 551, 553, 554, 555
   Channel 21, 98, 317
   Channel 22A, 99, 321, 554-555
   Channel 67, 127, 493
   Channel 70, 551
   Channel 83, 550
   distress calls, 99, 554
   ham radio, 556
   ITU, 99
   weather, 309, 317, 324-327, 554-555
   See also Communications
Radio direction finders (RDFs), 461-462, 564
Radio Navigator Aids (DMAHTC), 423
Radio Technical Commission for Maritime Services (RTCM), 425
Radiotelephones, 556, 603
   antennas and cables, 552-553
   Digital Selective Calling (DSC) system, 551
   distress, safety and calling channels, 553-554
   equipment selection, 549, 551
   hand-held units, 551
   installation and maintenance, 551-552
   licensing, 545, 546, 547, 548, 549
   operating rules and procedures, 553, 554
   radio energy principles, 546-547
   radio information services, 554-555
   SSB radio, 555
Rafting (anchoring), 33, 270, 271

Rails, 32-33
Rain fog, 303
Raised decks, 32
Raked bows, 25
Ramps, 174-176
Range finders, 434, 450, 456, 462
Range lights, 145
Ranges (aids to navigation), 402, 487, 518-519
Ranges (in positioning), 445, 446-447
   anchorage, 264
   LOPs, 452-453
Ranges (tides), 330, 332
   prediction, 343
   Tide Tables, 334-335
   variation, 331
RDFs. *See* Radio direction finders (RDFs)
Reaching sailing technique, 230
Receiver hitches, 166
Reciprocal courses, running, 385-387, 388
Recycling, 354, 357-359, 362
Red Cross. *See* American Red Cross
Reduction gear, 34
Reefing, 38, 71, 243
Reef knots, 283, 284, 286, 291
Reeving (blocks), 292-293
Refrigeration, 24, 534, 540
   fuel efficiency, 354
   safety, 73
   toxic substances, 360
   voltage toleration, 533
Regattas, 52, 56, 57, 579, 591-592
Regional Tide & Tidal Current Table (NOS), 420
Registration, 49, 50, 169, 171
   CE requirements, 76
   CME requirements, 76
   numbers, 51-52
   See also Licensing Regulations
   chartering, 54
   commercial vessels, 53-55
   customs, 54-55
   environment, 55
   lake boating, 499
   locks and canal boating, 497
   regattas, 52
   trailerboating, 169, 171
   USCG, 52, 118, 119, 591
Regulations (Army Corps of Engineers), 423
Relative bearings, 31, 41
   defined, 445
   estimation of, 476, 477-478
   radio deviation, 461
   true bearing conversion, 451-452
   use of sextant for, 456
   using *Bowditch* tables for, 460
   using the pelorus for, 451-452
   See also Bearings
Relative motion, 476, 477
Relative positions, 121, 135, 429

Rescue breathing, 102-103, 105
   See also First aid
Rescue crafts
   helicopters, 98, 591, 592
   inflatables as, 18-19
   teams, 57
   See also Search and rescue operations
Resistance (electricity), 523-543
Restricted Radio Operator's Certificate, 76
Restricted Radiotelephone Operator Permit, 546, 547, 548
Restricted visibility, 119, 131-133
Retrieving (boats), 176
Reverse sheer, 25
Reverse surgeon's knots, 286
Reverse transoms, 25
Revolver situations, 453, 454
Rhumb lines, 417, 473, 474
RIBs (Rigid inflatable boats), 19, 178
Riding lights, 135
Rigging, 19, 33
   running, 222-224
   standing, 220-221
Right bank, 485, 487
Right of way, 121, 122-124
Righting moment, 216
Rigid inflatable boats (RIBs), 19, 178
Rigid wing sails, 237-238
Rip currents, 42
Riprap, 43, 492
River Basins of the United States (USGS), 486
River charts, 414, 487-489, 494
River piloting
   aids to navigation, 485, 487, 489, 507
   anchoring and making fast, 492
   bars, 43, 489, 490
   channels, 489-490
   cruising, 493
   currents, 42, 340, 342, 489, 490
   dayboards and buoys, 485, 487
   erosion, 43, 492
   eyeball piloting, 120, 490-491
   lights, 485
   local knowledge, 485, 489, 490, 492
   publications, 491
   ranges, 487
   regulations, 118
   river charts, 414, 487-489, 494
   safety, 131, 491, 493
   sand boils, 493
   shoals and dredging, 490
   water level changes, 485
   waterways information, 486
   See also Aids to navigation
Roadsteads, 43
Rod-Stop rescue method, 94
Roll clouds, 316-317
Roller reefing system, 71

Twine, 281, 289
Twin engine installations, 156, 157, 160
Twin-screw boats
    basic helmsmanship, 183
    heaving-to, 246
    maneuvering, 194-199
    turning, 187, 243
Twin-screw installation, 34-35
Two-blocked, 293
Two-cycle, water-cooled (TC-W)
    specifications, 162
Two-fold tackle, 293
Two half-hitches, 283, 284, 285, 286
Typhoons, 319

U

UL. *See* Underwriters Laboratories (UL)
Undertow, 42
Underway, 31, 119, 196, 267-268
Underwriters Laboratories (UL)
    marine lists, 77, 539, 542
    standards, 70, 539, 541
Underwriters Laboratories (UL) of
    Canada, 72
Uniform State Waterway Marking
    System (USWMS), 485, 512, 513
    aids to navigation, 502
    buoys, 487, 503
Uninspected Passenger Vessel
    license, 53
U.S. Aids to Navigation, 508-513
    See also Aids to navigation
U.S. Animal and Plant Quarantine, 54
U.S. Army Corps of Engineers, 419
    charts, 396, 414, 488
    locks, 496, 497
    private aids to navigation, 501
    publications, 423, 486, 491, 497
    waterway information, 486, 497
U.S. Coast Guard (USCG), 419
    accidents, 52, 83, 86, 93, 117
    aids to navigation, 461, 501, 503, 506,
        507, 510, 592
    AMVER system, 102
    boating regulations, 118, 119, 591
    bridge openings, 130
    capacity plates, 68, 153
    Channel 22A, 554-555
    classes, 45
    computer chart update system, 397
    contacting, in rough weather, 246
    Contact and Long Range Liaison
        system, 99, 555
    drug testing, 53-54
    electrical standards, 524, 529, 541
    emergency pumps carried by, 91
    fire extinguishers, 87, 88, 89
    flags, 582, 591
    Flotation Standard, 68
    functions, 591-592, 593

garbage disposal regulations, 358-359
guests on board, 579
helicopter rescue, 98, 591, 592
licenses, 53
Marine Assistance Request
    Broadcast, 86
organization and personnel, 592-593
personal watercraft, 179
publications, 424, 425, 491
range establishment, 453
regatta regulations, 52, 591-592
Reserve, 593
river aids to navigation, 485, 489, 491
RTCM, 425
rules on lights, 62, 135, 142, 143, 144,
    145
Safe Powering Standard, 68
safety regulations, 61, 62, 66, 70-71,
    72-73, 153
search and rescue operations, 57, 84,
    85, 591, 592
towing, 251
Ventilation Standard, 78-81
weather forecasts on radio, 321
U.S. Coast Guard (USCG) Auxiliary
    aids to navigation, 595
    Channel 83, 550
    classes, 53, 77, 594-595
    CME, 75-76, 594-595
    flags, 582, 583, 585, 594, 595
    members, 594, 595, 596
    non-distress calls, 86
    Operational Facility, 76, 583, 594-595
    purposes and activities, 594-595
    regattas and events, 579
    reporting by chart users, 414-415
    safety requirements, 75-76
    search and rescue teams, 57, 595, 596
    uniforms and insignia, 595-596
U.S. Customs Service, 54-55
U.S. Department of Commerce, 317, 396,
    419
U.S. Department of the Interior, 486
U.S. Department of Transport (DOT), 63,
    419, 591
U.S. Environmental Protection Agency
    (EPA), 351
U.S. Food and Drug Administration
    (FDA), 108
U.S. Geological Survey (USGS), 486
U.S. Immigration, 54
U.S. Inland Navigation Rules. *See* Inland
    Rules
U.S. National Weather Service.
    See National Weather Service (NWS)
U.S. Navy, 142, 591, 593
    Naval Institute, 425
    Naval Observatory, 419, 423
U.S. Power Squadrons (USPS), 56
    background and purposes, 597
    flags, 583, 584, 597, 600-602

insignia, 600-602
membership and organization, 597-
    598
reporting by chart users, 414-415
RTCM, 425
training programs, 45, 53, 77, 584, 598-
    600
U.S. Public Health Service, 54
U.S. Sailing Association, 56
Upslope fog, 303
Upwind sailing technique, 228, 230, 232
Urgency calls, 84-86, 88, 89
    See also Pan-Pan urgency calls
USCG. *See* U.S. Coast Guard (USCG)
USGS (U.S. Geological Survey), 486
USPS. *See* U.S. Power Squadrons
    (USPS)
USWMS. *See* Uniform State Waterway
    Marking System (USWMS)
Utility boats, 18, 153, 260

V

Variation, 367, 370
    applying deviation and, 378-382, 451
    bearings, 41
    compass rose, 376-377, 394-395
    general variation, 376-377
    local attraction, 377
V-berths, 20
V-drives, 35
Vectors
    in current calculations, 470-472
    in current diagrams, 464-468
    in maneuvering boards, 482-483
Veering (anchors), 265
Velocity (currents), 341, 342, 343, 464
Velocity (wind), 212-214
Ventilation, 33
    batteries, 527, 528
    CME requirements, 75, 76
    CO poisoning, 209
    electrical appliances, 539
    fueling, 67-68, 78-81, 162
    propellers, 186
    radiotelephones, 551
    rope lockers, 261
    rough weather preparation, 242
    safety, 62, 78-81, 87
Ventilation (propeller spin), 160
Ventilation Standard, 78-81
Veritas, 77
Vertical angles (in positioning), 454, 456,
    458
Vertical load (anchors), 254
Vessels, 17, 51, 118, 119
Vessel traffic service (VTS), 122
VHF-FM radiotelephones. *See*
    Radiotelephones
V-hulls, 25, 26-27, 178
Vibration, 374

PICTURE CREDITS

ACKNOWLEDGMENTS

ACIF Inc., Montreal, QC, Canada
Brian Aitken, Toronto, ON, Canada
American Red Cross, Washington, DC
Applied Biochemists, Mequon, WI
Arizona Office of Tourism, Phoenix, AZ
Astro Pure Water Purifiers, Margate, FL
Curtis Baer, Baltimore, MD
Kelley Birtz, Rouses Point, NY
Jon Blair, Port Sandfield, ON, Canada
John Bleasby, Toronto, ON, Canada
Boathouse, Dorval, QC, Canada
Bombardier Corp., Sea-Doo Division,
    Palm Bay, FL
Huguette Brazeau, Dollard-des-Ormeaux,
    QC, Canada
Bristol Flare Corporation, Bristol, PA
Frances Brochu, Montreal, QC, Canada
Elizabeth Cameron, Westmount,
    QC, Canada
Canadian Coast Guard, Ottawa, ON, Canada
Canadian Department of
    Transportation, Ottawa, ON, Canada
Canadian Hydrographic Service, Dept. of
    Fisheries & Oceans, Ottawa, ON, Canada
Canadian Power & Sail Squadrons/
    Escadrilles canadiennes de plaisance,
    Scarborough, ON, Canada
Canadian Red Cross, Ottawa, ON, Canada
Chesapeake Bay Foundation, MD
Eric Cassini-Brochu, Montreal, QC, Canada
Center for Marine Conservation,
    Washington, DC
Clayton Antique Boat Museum, Clayton, NY
Cordage Institute, Hingham, MA
D.B.H. Cordage Products Inc., Dorval,
    QC, Canada
Pierce Crosbie, Toronto, ON, Canada
Steve Davis, Port Townsend, WA
Dale Dawson, Vermont Ware, VT
Lorraine Doré, Montreal, QC, Canada
Donna Duseigne, Outremont, QC, Canada
East Penn Manufacturing Co., Inc., Lyon
    Station, PA
Andrea Elvidge, Toronto, ON, Canada
Federal Communications Commission,
    Washington, DC
Mike Fitzsimmons, Alexandria Bay, NY
Foster & Associates, Hingham, MA
Friends of the Earth, Ottawa, ON, Canada
Melanie Gagnon, Montreal, QC, Canada
E. Charles Game, P.E., Consulting Engineer,
    Asheboro, NC 27203
General Ecology of New England,
    Trumbull, CT
André Giasson, Montreal, QC, Canada
Glendinning Marine Products, Inc.,
    Conway, SC
Grand Banks Yacht, Greenwich, CT
Eric Gravel, Outremont, QC

Derek Griffiths, Toronto, ON, Canada
The Guest Company, Inc., Meridien, CT
Haft/SL Marine Products, Bradenton, FL
Harken, Pewaukee, WI
Dave Harris, Toronto, ON, Canada
Hathaway, Reiser & Raymond, Inc.,
    Stamford, CT
Frederick Hayes (Lifesling), Bellevue, WA
High Seas Technology, Inc. Fort
    Lauderdale, FL
Henry R. Hinckley & Co., Southwest
    Harbor, ME
Ariel Home-Douglas, Montreal,
    QC, Canada
Marty Hornstein, St. Jerôme, QC, Canada
Marsh Howard, Dorval, QC, Canada
Paul Howard, Toronto, ON, Canada
Robert Hudson, Toronto, ON, Canada
Sonya Hudson, Toronto, ON, Canada
Steve Killing, Port McNicholl, ON, Canada
Brenda Kokiv, Montreal, QC, Canada
Jacques Lacasse, St. Bruno, QC, Canada
Land and Sea, Grand Rapids, MI
Les Expertises Marine Nord-Sud Inc.,
    Ile Perrot, QC, Canada
Aben MacKenzie, Ste Anne de Bellevue,
    QC, Canada
Freya MacKenzie, Ste Anne de Bellevue,
    QC, Canada
Jan MacNeill, Ottawa, ON, Canada
The Mailing Co. Hubbell, West Haven, CT
David Manley, San Juan Bautista, CA
Nicholas Manley, San Juan Bautista, CA
Marina Bo-Bi-No, Laval, QC, Canada
Marina Jean Beaudoin Inc., Montreal,
    QC, Canada
Marine Patrol, Clinton County Sheriff's
    Department, Plattsburgh, NY
McGarr Marine, Longueuil, QC, Canada
McGill Maritime Services, Montreal,
    QC, Canada
Mercury Marine, Fond du Lac, WI
Midwest Industries, Idagrove, IA
Alex Milne Associates, Toronto, ON,
    Canada
Alf Mortimer, Port Sandfield, ON, Canada
Motor Boating and Sailing, New York, NY
Mystic Seaport Museum Library, Mystic, CT
National Safe Boating Council, Inc.,
    Washington, DC
National Oceanic & Atmospheric
    Administration (NOAA), Rockville, MD
National Ocean Service (NOAA)
National Weather Service (NOAA)
National Wildlife Federation,
    Washington, DC
Ian Nener, Montreal, QC, Canada
Paul Oler, Baltimore, MD
Steve Olver, Toronto, ON, Canada

PMI Technologies, Newport News, VA
Paneltronics, Hialeah Gardens, FL
Para-Tech Engineering, Santee, CA
Charles-Guy Paré, Pompano Beach, FL
Brian Parsons, Montreal, QC, Canada
Petrokem, Patterson, NJ
Jean Poliquin, Montreal, QC, Canada
Deborah Pollard, Rouses Point, NY
Denis Poupart, Lachine, QC, Canada
RGM Industries Inc., Titusville, FL
Revenue Canada, Public Relations,
    Montreal, QC, Canada
Donald Richardson, Ottawa, ON, Canada
Ritchie Navigation Instruments,
    Pembroke, MA
St. John Ambulance, Montreal,
    QC, Canada
Odette Sévigny, Montreal, QC, Canada
Shewmon, Inc, Safety Harbor, FL
Kathy Simo, Toronto, ON, Canada
Si-Tex Marine Electronic Inc., Clearwater, FL
State of Vermont, Agency of Natural
    Resources, Waterbury, VT
Dr. Charles J. Stine, Ellicott City, MD
Jodie Stine, Baltimore, MD
Story Litchfield, Bangor, ME
Catherine Szabo, Rouses Point, NY
Debbie Thomas, Toronto, ON, Canada
Margie Troy, Baltimore, MD
Elissa Turnbull, Toronto, ON, Canada
Joyce H. Turnbull, Toronto, ON, Canada
Simon Turnbull, Toronto, ON, Canada
Twin Disc Inc., Racine, WI
U.S. Marine Corporation, Arlington, WA
United States Coast Guard Auxiliary,
    Washington, DC
United States Army Corps of Engineers,
    Washington, DC
United States Coast Guard Headquarters,
    Washington, DC
United States Power Squadrons, Raleigh, NC
United States Sailing Association.,
    Newport, RI
VA Sea Grant, University of North Carolina,
    Charlottesville, VA
Jan VanderKap, Toronto, ON, Canada
Voiles Windyne Sails, Dorval, QC, Canada
Jocelyn Wakefield, Montreal, QC, Canada
West Products, Watsonville, CA
John Whiting, Block Island, RI
Sara Wood, Toronto, ON, Canada
Zodiac of North America, Inc.,
    Stevensville, MD